W9-CDY-784

GOLOMBEK'S ENCYCLOPEDIA OF CHESS

EDITORS AND CONTRIBUTORS

Editor-in-chief

Harry Golombek O.B.E., international master and chess judge, who has officiated at six World Championship matches. Three times British champion, he has represented his country many times in Olympiads, international matches etc. Founding member of the FIDE Commission on the Rules, Golombek is president of Zone 1 of FIDE. He is author of thirty-seven books on the game and is the *Times* Chess Correspondent.

Andrew Soltis is an international master and the leading writer on chess among the modern American school. His work in this encyclopedia has concentrated on American chess, about which he has recently written a book.

Associate Editors

Professor Divinsky has been a leading Canadian player and has represented that country in the Olympiads. He has a special interest in the great players of the late nineteenth and early twentieth centuries, and has written authoritative works in that field.

William R. Hartston, an international master who has played with great distinction for Britain in the Olympiads, the Clare Benedict team tournaments etc. Twice British champion, with a profound knowledge of the game in all its aspects, he has written a number of successful books on chess and his mathematical abilities make him eminently fitted to deal with the question of chess and computers.

Wolfgang Heidenfeld, many times champion of South Africa and Ireland, is a master with a keen eye for a combination. This has made him a specialist in middle-game tactics and a writer of books relating to that field of chess.

Raymond Keene, international grandmaster and former British champion, has written a number of books with an emphasis on two different fields, opening strategy and biography. He has united these two interests in a remarkable work on Nimzowitsch.

Kevin O'Connell, one of the world's most promising younger chess-writers, and noted both for his wide knowledge and meticulous accuracy. He is the editor of the *Batsford Year Books* and also assistant editor of the *British Chess Magazine*.

Contributors

David Hooper, a former British championship contender, has in the past twenty years developed into an outstanding authority on the endings.

Stewart Reuben, as International Judge and the expert controller of many Swiss System tournaments, has a considerable knowledge of the workings of this system and its most complicated ramification, the accelerated Swiss.

John M. Rice, international master for chess composition and for many years editor of the Problem Section of the *British Chess Magazine*, has proved his mastery of the field of chess problems with many a fine composition. He has also written a standard work on the subject.

John Rogers, for many years editor of *Correspondence Chess*, the quarterly magazine of the British Correspondence Chess Association. Rogers has a considerable knowledge of all forms of correspondence chess.

Arthur Roycroft is an International Judge for chess composition, and the creator of a number of fine endgame-studies. Roycroft edits the only magazine solely devoted to the endgame study and has also written a comprehensive work on the subject.

Jonathan Webber, whose work on post-graduate studies of linguistic philosophy at Oxford, united with a passion for chess, has led him to discover a marked influence that the game has had on modern philosophy.

GOLOMBEK'S ENCYCLOPEDIA OF CHESS

Edited by
HARRY GOLOMBEK

CROWN PUBLISHERS, INC., NEW YORK

Published in the USA in 1977 by Crown Publishers, Inc.,
New York

Library of Congress Catalog Card Number: 77–7635

First published in Great Britain in 1977 by Batsford

Created, designed and produced by
Trewin Copplestone Publishing Ltd, London

ISBN: 0–517–53146–1

Library of Congress Cataloging in Publication Data

Golombek, Harry, 1911–
Golombek's Encyclopedia of chess.
Bibliography: p. 354
Includes index.
1. Chess – Dictionaries. 1. Title. 11. Title:
Encyclopedia of chess.
GV1314.5.G64 1977 794.1′03 77–7635
ISBN 0–517–53146–1

Filmset by Oliver Burridge Filmsetting Ltd
Printed in Great Britain
by Chapel River Press, Andover

Cover

The *cover photograph* was taken by Aubrey Dewar, of a chess set supplied by The Chess Centre, 3 Harcourt Street, London W1.

INTRODUCTION

When I was first approached on the subject of an encyclopedia of chess, I protested that there were already on the market a Russian, an English and an American encyclopedia. 'Precisely,' was the reply, 'that's why we want you to write one.'

I looked into the subject and soon realized what was meant by a *cri de coeur*. The Russian one was a *slova*, a dictionary, and whilst quite good as such contained too many vast tracts that could only appeal to a palsied party member. The English encyclopedia did not have the right balance and, in some places, was inaccurate or out-of-date. The American editor, whilst well meaning, had two basic weaknesses – ignorance and a strange conception as to what constituted the rules of chess.

There was no escaping my task. I set to it and within six months had worked out my plan and chosen my fellow-workers with the care that is given to the choice of a doctor or a wife or husband.

Meanwhile a French encyclopedia had been published which was interesting to read but which was insular and inadequate. Later there appeared an Italian publication which suffered from too much weighting towards problems.

In this encyclopedia, I and my associates have endeavoured to avoid the Scylla of insufficiency and the Charybdis of subjectivity. We have tried to bear in mind that chess is an international game and that we are catering for the whole world of chess. We have realized the vast nature of the game and have flung our nets as wide as possible. We know that to be inaccurate is a betrayal of the reader's trust, and we are aware that if we fail to be interesting we shall suffer the ignominy of being unreadable.

Here it might perhaps be asked – what sort of reader have you in mind, for whom are you writing and, in any case, is an encyclopedia of chess necessary in this day and age?

After all, the chess presses are groaning with books of reference; books on all aspects of the game pour out with almost bewildering profusion, and never has the chess-player or the chess-book reader been offered such a rich and wide choice of literature.

Apropos this, it must be pointed out that all these works are almost solely designed to increase the playing strength of the constant player. They seek only to instruct and not necessarily to inform. We, in this encyclopedia, have precisely the reverse aim. Our prime duty is to inform; whilst there is also a great deal of instruction to be found in the pages that follow, it is almost incidental to our main purpose of providing information on every aspect of the game of chess.

We should perhaps mention here that the type of chess with which we are concerned is the European form, and we are not talking about such games as Chinese chess (the so-called River-Game), or Japanese chess (Shogi) or Go etc. All these are so far removed from our game that they hardly deserve the appellation of chess.

Then, as far as the necessity of this work is concerned, it must be pointed out that, with the vast increase in popularity of the game over the last six years, there is a new thirst for chess knowledge among hundreds of thousands, possibly millions, of people who know the moves and not a great deal more. For them the books of reference, the chess magazines and the year-books are worse than useless. They merely serve to muddle and confuse the minds of those who have only recently taken up the game.

Then too, the game has proliferated so widely that even those who do know a fair amount about chess will have to confess that there is a great deal more about the game of which they are ignorant. It is to these as well as to the beginner that our encyclopedia is offered as a source of information.

For the purpose of compiling this work we have spent what was, on the whole, an agreeable if arduous and lengthy period of time in perusing whole libraries of reference books, year-books, histories, magazines and text-books. We have gone through the whole range from the manuscript of Alfonso the Wise, through the works of Ruy Lopez and Lucena, on to Philidor and Staunton, to Steinitz and Tarrasch, to the great hypermoderns (Nimzowitsch, Réti and Tartakower) and to the present day with names too numerous to mention.

The task has been an onerous one, but well worth doing if we have to any extent filled the gap and supplied knowledge and information to those who ask for it.

How we have succeeded I must leave the reader to judge. But before quitting my personal stand I take the opportunity of thanking my fellow-workers for the unremitting labour they have put into the enterprise.

The encyclopedia is dedicated to my friends and fellow-members of the St Antony's College Chess Club, Oxford, in the hope and certain expectation that when we next meet they will be even more knowledgeable than before.

Harry Golombek, December 1976

HOW TO USE THIS BOOK

The information in this encyclopedia is arranged in alphabetical order. Under the heading **ENDGAME** and **PROBLEM** the material is long and detailed enough to require individual alphabetical treatment (and these sections contain entries for Composers, and Problemists).

Match results
Results are given in the order: wins (+), losses (—), draws (=).

Moves and games
The descriptive notation is used: N = Knight, (Q) = Queens, + = check, and the identifying square is shown in brackets (except under PROBLEM and for some VARIETIES OF CHESS where the notation is algebraic and the usual convention of S = Knight is followed).

Personal dates
These are based on Gaige's *Catalog* and on personal enquiry; unavoidable gaps remain.

Titles
Titles to be understood as FIDE awarded unless otherwise stated, e.g. for awards in the USSR where Soviet Master is distinguished from Soviet international master. A capital 'C' indicates a World Championship event.

Literature
The best literature by or on the subject of an entry usually follows that entry. Other works are given in the 'Select Bibliography' (page 354). Where possible details of an edition in English are given, based on Betts' *Chess: an annotated bibliography*, Boston 1974, or *The Van de Linde-Niemeijariana Catalogue*, The Hague 1955, failing the author's own copy of a work.

General Index
The index (p. 356) will help readers to a full coverage of a topic where cross references each time would have been confusing. It will also locate terms described in the text but not found alphabetically in the text.

AARON, Manuel *(b. 30 December 1935)*
India's first international master, obtaining the title in 1961. Champion of India on seven occasions since 1959 and five times in succession from 1969 to 1975, though tied for first place he was placed second on tie break; all this in a total of fourteen Indian Championships. Qualified for the Stockholm 1962 Interzonal and defeated Portisch and Uhlmann in that tournament, although finishing in last place. *(R.D.K.)*

ABN EZRA *(1088–1167)*
Born in Toledo, Abn Ezra (Abraham ben Ezra) was a celebrated Spanish rabbi who wrote a Hebrew poem of seventy-six lines describing the game of chess and giving the pieces the moves of the ancient Muslim school. Presumably he was a little out of date since the only respect in which the moves of the pieces vary from the older Muslim form is that the Queen may make a leap. *(H.G.)*

ABRAHAMS, Gerald *(b. 15 April 1907)*

Gerald Abrahams watching the opening at the Hastings Chess Congress 1947

Brilliant British amateur who in the 1930s was playing master-chess. In that period he was the most dangerous attacking player in England.

He was in the prize-list (i.e. in the first four) in the British championship on three occasions, 1933, 1946 and 1954. His best international performance was in the Major Open at Nottingham in 1936 where he came =3rd with Opocensky. Another fine result was his score of $1\frac{1}{2}$–$\frac{1}{2}$ against the Soviet grandmaster, Ragozin, in the 1946 Anglo-Soviet radio match.

He is the inventor of the Abrahams variation in the Semi-Slav Defence to the Queen's Gambit: 1. P–Q4, P–Q4; 2. P–QB4, P–QB3; 3. N–QB3, P–K3; 4. N–B3, P×P; 5. P–QR4, B–N5; 6. P–K3, P–QN4; 7. B–Q2, P–QR4; 8. P×P, B×N; 9. B×B, P×P; 10. P–QN3, B–N2.

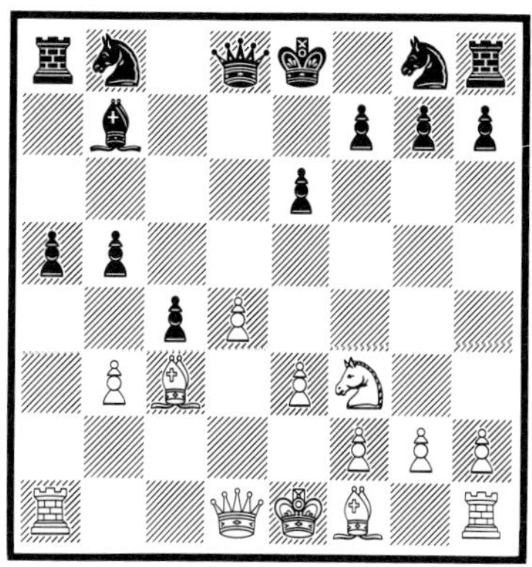

This is sometimes known as the Noteboom variation after the Dutch master who played it in the 1930s, but Abrahams was playing it in 1925 long before Noteboom.

He is a witty and prolific writer on many subjects: on law (he is a barrister by profession), philosophy, and chess; he also writes fiction. His main chess works are: *The Chess Mind*, London 1951 and 1960; *Not Only Chess*, London 1974. *(H.G.)*

'ABSOLUTE' 7th RANK
'Absolute' 7th rank is a term coined by Nimzowitsch to describe the control of the 7th rank by a Rook (or Rooks) in such a way as to keep the hostile King permanently confined to the back rank. He postulated that, other things being equal, the 'absolute' 7th rank combined with a passed pawn always wins, and proved that the same configuration justifies considerable sacrifices in material.

Nimzowitsch–Bernstein, Vilna 1912. In an attempt to reduce the material still further, Black played 1.., R–KB1, and there followed 2. R×NP, P–B3; 3. B–B5, R–B1 *(if 3.., R–B2; 4. R–N7, R×R; 5. P×R+, K×P; 6. P×P)*; 4. P×P, R×B; 5. P–B7, R–B1; 6. R–N7, B–Q6; 7. R–K7, B–N4; 8. K–B4, R–R1; 9. P–KR7, B–R5; 10. K–K5, B–N4; 11. K–B6, P–K4; 12. K–N7, resigns. *(W.H.)*

ADJOURNMENT
In tournament and match play, a game unfinished at the conclusion of the playing session is adjourned and resumed at a later time. Hours or days may elapse before the continuation and both players are free to analyse in depth during this interval. In order to avoid giving one player the advantage of being able to consider a position in which it is his turn to move, the universal practice (first introduced at the Paris 1878 tournament) is to 'seal' the last move before adjournment: the player on move decides upon his next move, but instead of playing it on the board he writes it on a sheet

of paper and encloses it in an envelope, which is then entrusted to the care of the tournament arbiter.

The player sealing a move must not stop his clock until the envelope has been closed. The sealed move envelope should also contain a copy of each player's scoresheet (in case of dispute) and the position and clock times elapsed should be noted on the outside. Upon resumption the envelope is opened, the move is played on the board, clocks are started and play continues as usual. If an ambiguous or illegal move has been sealed the offender loses the game.

Some special rules exist to cover situations in which one of the two antagonists is late for resumption. Suppose A plays B and A has sealed a move. If A is present and B is absent at the agreed starting time, B's clock is started but the sealed move envelope is not opened until B actually arrives at the board. If B is present and A is absent, the envelope is opened and the move is played normally. If A has still not arrived by the time B has decided on his reply, B has the option (rarely exercised in practice) of sealing this reply. *(R.D.K.)*

ADORJÁN, Andras *(b. 31 March 1950)*
One of Hungary's most talented young grandmasters. Adorján secured the title in 1973, having gained that of international master in 1970 and having won the European Junior championship. Has had a number of good results in international tournaments including first places at Varna 1972, Luhacovice 1973, Olot 1974 and Lanzarote 1975. Played in Junior tournaments under the name Jocha. *(W.R.H.)*

AHUES, Carl Oscar *(26 December 1883–31 December 1968)*
A German international master, prominent in Berlin, Königsberg and in the last decades of his life Hamburg. His greatest success was the sixth place in the extremely strong tournament at San Remo 1930, where he shared the brilliancy prize with Monticelli for their games against Bogoljubow. Prize-winner at Berlin 1926, Kecskemet 1927, Liège 1930, Bad Nauheim 1936, he played 1st board for Germany at the International Team tournament Hamburg 1930, and 2nd board at Prague 1931 and Munich 1936. Won the championship of Germany at Duisburg 1929.

Ahues retained his playing strength to a very advanced age; in 1946, at the age of sixty-three, he finished first or second in five German master tournaments; in his eighties he still won the lightning championship of Hamburg. *(W.H.)*

A.I.P.E.
L'Association Internationale de la Presse Echiquéenne (the International Association of the Chess Press) was founded in 1968. Its aim is to spread important chess news throughout the world and, above all, to popularize the game. The organization's major success to date has been the establishment of the world chess Oscar – the brainchild of Jordi Puig, the founding father of A.I.P.E. The first chess Oscar was awarded in 1967 to Bent Larsen. In subsequent years the award of the Oscar has been combined with the selection of the ten outstanding players of the year. The results have been:
1968: 1 Spassky, 2 Korchnoi, 3 Larsen, 4 Petrosian, 5 Fischer, 6 Tal, 7 Portisch, 8 Smyslov, 9 Keres, 10 Bronstein.
1969: 1 Spassky, 2 Korchnoi, 3 Petrosian, 4 Larsen, 5 Polugayevsky, 6 Hort, 7 Portisch, 8 Smyslov, 9 Geller, 10 Gligorić.
1970: 1 Fischer, 2 Spassky, 3 Larsen, 4 Taimanov, 5 Geller, 6 Polugayevsky, 7 Portisch, 8 Keres, 9 Hort, 10 Korchnoi.
1971: 1 Fischer, 2 Petrosian, 3 Korchnoi, 4 Smyslov, 5 Hort, 6 Spassky, 7 Savon, 8 Tal, 9 Polugayevsky, 10 Stein.
1972: 1. Fischer, 2 Spassky, 3 Portisch, 4 Karpov, 5 Korchnoi, 6 Hübner, 7 Petrosian, 8 Ljubojević, 9 Larsen, 10 Polugayevsky.
1973: 1 Karpov, 2 Spassky, 3 Portisch, 4 Korchnoi, 5 Tal, 6 Petrosian, 7 Mecking, 8 Larsen, 9 R. Byrne, 10 Polugayevsky.
1974: 1 Karpov, 2 Korchnoi, 3 Tal, 4 Petrosian, 5 Ljubojević, 6 Spassky, 7 Polugayevsky, 8 Vasiukov, 9 Browne, 10 Larsen.
1975: 1 Karpov, 2 Ljubojević, 3 Geller, 4 Polugayevsky, 5 Portisch, 6 Keres, 7 Hort, 8 Petrosian, 9 Spassky, 10 Browne.
1976: 1 Karpov, 2 Larsen, 3 Mecking, 4 Hort, 5 Petrosian, 6 Polugayevsky, 7 Portisch, 8 Korchnoi, 9 Tal, 10 Tseshkovsky.

The Secretary of A.I.P.E. is Lars Grahn, Smedjegaten 1, 21421 Malmö, Sweden. *(K.J.O'C.)*

AITKEN, Dr James Macrae *(b. 27 October 1908)*
Talented Scottish amateur who won the Scottish championship ten times, Dr Aitken's chief international activity was representing Scotland in the Olympiads.

At Stockholm 1937 he scored 32.4% on top board but had the distinction of beating the Swedish grandmaster Ståhlberg. At Munich 1958 he scored 67.6% on 2nd board; at Tel Aviv 1964, 28.1% on 2nd board; at Skopje 1972, 38.9% on 6th board. *(H.G.)*

AJEEB
The second notable addition to chess automata. Designed and built by Charles Alfred Hooper, a cabinet maker, the device, containing a hidden operator, was first exhibited at the Royal Polytechnical Institute and subsequently went on display at the Crystal Palace. In 1886 Ajeeb, like the Turk to which it was also similar in appearance, went to the United States. It was while being exhibited in the Eden Musée in New York that the cabinet met its great claim to fame – Harry Pillsbury who worked for some time as its concealed operator. It is fitting that Ajeeb did not play any chess after Pillsbury's death, only draughts.

See also under AUTOMATONS. *(K.J.O'C.)*

AKHMILOVSKAYA, Elena
Qualified for the 1976 Women's Interzonals by finishing fourth in the 1975 USSR Women's championship which was also a Zonal tournament. In the Interzonal at Roosendaal, Netherlands she finished =1st with Kushnir, thus obtaining the newly created title of international woman grandmaster and qualifying for the 1977 Women's Candidates. *(K.J.O'C.)*

ALA'ADDIN AS TABRIZI [**Ali Shatranji**] *(Fifteenth century)*
Aladdin, to give him the name he is usually known by in the West,

was a lawyer at the court of Timur (the Mogul emperor who died in 1405).

So successful was he as a chess-player, in particular as an odds-giver, that he became known as Ali Shatranji (Ali *the* chess-player).

Some of his life story is to be found in the preface to a fifteenth-century manuscript containing a collection of problems by him, composed according to the rules of Shatranji, i.e. in accordance with the original rules of the game, that is to be found in the library of the Royal Asiatic Society in London.

There he says 'I have passed my life since the age of fifteen among all the masters of chess of my time, and since that period till now, when I have arrived at middle age, I have travelled through Iraq, Khurasan, and Transoxiana, and I have met there with many a master of this art, and I have played with all of them, and . . . I have come off victorious.'

That he was also a fine blindfold player is shown by a later passage: 'I have carried on four different games with as many adversaries without seeing the board, while I conversed freely with my friends all along, and through the Divine favour I conquered them all.' *(H.G.)*

AL-ADLI *(Ninth century AD)*

The first great Arabic chess-player and writer. He was the acknowledged champion during the reign of the Caliph Mutawakkil in the latter half of the ninth century.

But it was as a writer that he was the more important for he produced a work on the game in which he formulated the ideas of his contemporary and preceding grandmasters. In his work is to be found the celebrated *Dilaram mansuba* (problem). *(H.G.)*

ALAPIN, Semyon Zinovievich *(7 November 1856–15 July 1923)*

One of the strongest Russian masters at the turn of the century. Alapin shared first place with Chigorin at St Petersburg 1878–9, and drew a match with Schlechter in 1899, but never looked a likely contender for a place among those fighting for the World Championship. Made a number of theoretical contributions, largely in obscure variations, such as those bearing his name: Alapin's Opening, 1. P–K4, P–K4; 2. N–K2, and Alapin's Defence to the Ruy Lopez, 3. . , B–N5. *(W.R.H.)*

ALATORTSEV, Vladimir Alexeyevich *(b. 1909)*

One of the older school of Soviet masters, Alatortsev came to the forefront of Soviet chess in the early 1930s. He had consistently good results in the Leningrad championship, finishing 3rd in 1931, 2nd in 1932 and equal 1st in 1933. Alatortsev also shared first place in the Moscow championship of 1936 and 1937. His best result was perhaps 2nd behind Botvinnik in the 1933 USSR championship.

Alatortsev never made any great impression in international competition, but was appointed as one of a small group who worked on theoretical investigations designed to improve the results of Soviet players. For many years he was chess editor of the newspaper *Vechernaya Moskva.* *(W.R.H.)*

ALBANIA

Chess in Albania has had a short and murky career. Albania first competed in Olympiads in 1960, where they finished 28th out of 40 teams, came 26th out of 37 in 1962, then withdrew from international competition until 1970. In that year's Olympiad they already introduced some problems of a political nature into the game by refusing to meet South Africa. On that occasion they finished 38th out of 60 teams.

The next Olympiad, at Skopje 1972, was the last seen of Albania in FIDE competitions. Their team had clearly improved in strength and had qualified for the B final, where unfortunately they had to play matches with Israel and Greece, both of which were deemed politically unacceptable. The Albanian team did not appear for the Israel match and was defaulted. An appeal by nine team captains led to the match being rescheduled owing to the Albanian captain's plea of mechanical failure to explain his team's non-arrival. On their refusal to play the match on the newly-arranged date, the Albanians were expelled from the competition and from FIDE until such time as they agreed to abide by the rule banning political motives from chess events.

Chess in Albania is organized by Commission Centrale des Echecs de la Rép. Populaire d'Albanie, Rruga Kongresi Permetit 41, Tirana. *(W.R.H.)*

ALBIN, Adolf *(14 September 1848–1 February 1920)*

An Austrian master of Romanian birth, who was regarded as a promising player when, after a *succès d'estime* at Dresden 1892, he finished 2nd to Lasker in New York 1893 and to Steinitz in New York 1894. However, in the great events of the subsequent decade (Hastings 1895, Nuremberg and Budapest 1896, Berlin 1897, Cologne 1898, Monte Carlo 1902 and 1903) he was uniformly unsuccessful. Albin wrote *Schach-Aphorismen und Reminiszenzen*; Hanover 1899, and a primer in Romanian. His chief contribution to chess was the Albin Counter-gambit: 1. P–Q4, P–Q4; 2. P–QB4, P–K4. *(W.H.)*

ALBURT, Lev Osipovich *(b. 21 August 1946)*

Soviet international master (1976). A teacher in Odessa. His best tournament results: 1st Ukraine championship 1974, =5th USSR championship 1974 and =2nd Odessa 1976. *(K.J.O'C.)*

ALEKHINE, Alexander *(18 October 1892–23 March 1946)*

World Champion 1927–35 and 1937–46, Alekhine was born in Moscow in 1892 of parentage that was noble on his father's side and rich on his mother's. It was his mother who taught him the game and he soon developed a passion for it that was to be all-absorbing all his life. Like Keres after him, he played much correspondence chess when a boy and he started playing in tournaments when in his middle teens. At that time and ever since then, the great master Chigorin was a dominating influence in Russian chess and Alekhine, for some time, tried to play like him, even choosing the openings in which Chigorin had specialized.

In 1908 he became a law student in the Imperial High School at Moscow. It is interesting to note that, many years later, when he had left Russia for France, it was to the study of law that he turned again, since he obtained a doctorate in law at the Sorbonne in Paris in 1925.

His first steps in the international field were good, but not sensationally so. An equal 7th at Hamburg 1910 was followed by an equal 8th at Carlsbad 1911.

The break-through came at Stockholm 1912 where he won first prize. He was again 1st at Scheveningen 1913 and in 1914 he came equal 1st with Nimzowitsch in a very strong All-Russian championship at St Petersburg.

This gave them both the right to take part in the celebrated Grandmaster Tournament at St Petersburg later that year. He qualified to play in the finals of that tournament but was outclassed by both Em. Lasker and Capablanca, coming 3 points below the Cuban who scored $2\frac{1}{2}-\frac{1}{2}$ against him in their individual encounters.

When the First World War interrupted and stopped the Mannheim international tournament he was leading with $9\frac{1}{2}$ points above Vidmar $8\frac{1}{2}$. Along with his fellow Russians he was interned but through the influence of his family was released and when he went back to Russia served on the Austrian front, in the Red Cross, where he was wounded. It was in hospital during that time that he is supposed to have played his famous Queen sacrifice game against Feld.

Alekhine stayed on in Russia after the Revolution and is supposed at one time to have been arrested and sentenced to death, but rescued from both sentence and prison by his first wife, Anneliese Ruegg. He is said too to have adopted all sorts of shifts to make a living, including acting in films.

What is certain is that he won the first Soviet championship in Moscow 1920 and that in the following year he managed to emigrate to Switzerland since his wife was a Swiss nurse who had come with the Red Cross to Russia. It is also true that once he was safely in Switzerland he deserted his wife and went to live in Paris where he became a French citizen in 1925. This ruthless behaviour was characteristic of Alekhine the supreme amoralist. Those who knew him at all well realized that he had two great passions, Alekhine and Chess.

But now indeed he had a magnificent run of tournament successes, achieving firsts in the following international tournaments: Triberg, Budapest, The Hague 1921; Hastings 1922; Carlsbad 1923; Baden-Baden 1925 and Kecskemet 1927. In 1926 he had won a hard-fought match against Euwe by +3−2=5. By 1927 he felt that he was ready to challenge Capablanca for the world title. He himself said that only when he mastered the phase in the game that concerns the transition from the middle-game to the ending did he regard himself as sufficiently mature for the match.

Since he came second to Capablanca at New York 1927 he was confirmed in his position as Capablanca's nearest rival, but he was also deemed certain to lose the match. However, in a long trench-warfare type of match he gained the upper hand and won by +6−3=25.

As Champion he studiously avoided playing Capablanca but defeated Bogoljubow in two matches, in 1929 and 1934. In the interim he scored two terrific tournament successes at San Remo 1930 and Bled 1931. Always a hard drinker, he drank more and more heavily and this was the cause of his losing the title to Euwe in a match in 1935 by +8−9=13. The shock was salutary. He disciplined himself to avoid excessive drinking and won the return match in 1937 by +10−4=11.

Alexander Alekhine, Margate 1938

The Second World War saw him in two roles, that of a fervent patriot whilst France was still undefeated and that of a collaborator when Germany was triumphant. As positive evidence of the latter was a series of anti-Semitic articles published in Germany under his name during the war. After the war Alekhine firmly denied that they were his but when, many years later, his third wife died in Paris, amongst the papers in her possession was discovered the manuscripts of the articles in Alekhine's handwriting.

The last two years of his life were passed in Spain and Portugal and he was endeavouring to get the British Chess Federation to organize a match between him and BOTVINNIK when he died at Estoril in 1946.

His play was in many respects the most attractive of all the World Champions, cultured and lively, brilliant where brilliance was necessary and positional where there was no need for dashing tactics. With the possible exception of Keres, no one has left such a legacy of beautiful games.

His important works include: *New York 1924*, London 1925; *My Best Games of Chess 1908–23*, London 1927; *My Best Games of Chess 1924–37*, London 1939.

The following game, played at Margate 1938, contains one of the finest intuitive sacrifices ever played.

White: Alekhine; *Black:* Böök
Queen's Gambit Accepted
1. P–Q4, P–Q4; 2. P–QB4, P×P; 3. N–KB3, N–KB3; 4. P–K3,

P–K3; 5. B × P, P–B4; 6. O–O, N–B3; 7. Q–K2, P–QR3; 8. N–B3, P–QN4; 9. B–N3, P–N5; 10. P–Q5, N–QR4; 11. B–R4+, B–Q2; 12. P × P, P × P;

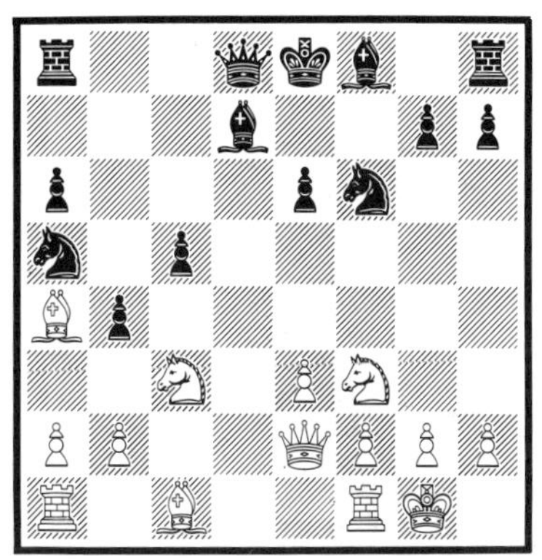

13. R–Q1, P × N; 14. R × B, N × R; 15. N–K5, R–R2; 16. P × P, K–K2; 17. P–K4, N–B3; 18. B–KN5, Q–B2; 19. B–B4, Q–N3; 20. R–Q1, P–N3; 21. B–KN5, B–N2; 22. N–Q7, R × N; 23. R × R+, K–B1; 24. B × N, B × B; 25. P–K5, resigns. *(H.G.)*

ALEKHINE'S DEFENCE

The defence 1. P–K4, N–KB3 is known as Alekhine's Defence, because Alekhine introduced it into modern master-play at Budapest 1921. As usual with such startling introductions it was essentially the employment of an old move with a modern meaning. The move is mentioned and analysed in Allgaier's *Lehrbuch* in 1811 and the Russians at one time called it Chaikin's Defence after an amateur who played it in the nineteenth century.

The idea as introduced by Alekhine is purely hypermodern and is a plan to lure White's centre pawns on to destruction.

At one time the main line was the Four Pawns Attack: 2. P–K5, N–Q4; 3. P–QB4, N–N3; 4. P–Q4, P–Q3; 5. P–B4, but this is now rarely seen and the modern and quieter line is 3. P–Q4, P–Q3; 4. N–KB3,

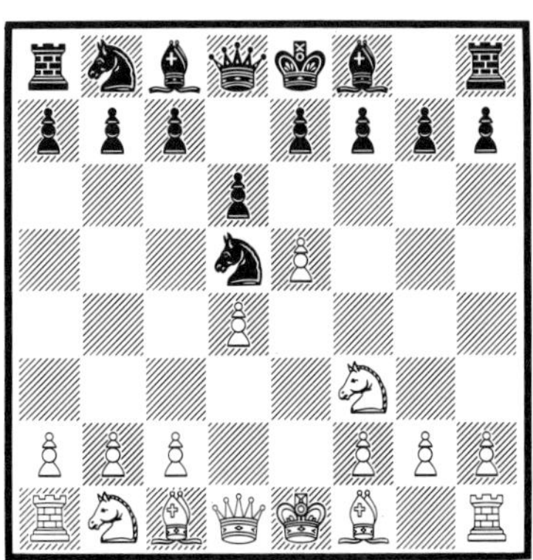

and now Black can choose between 4.., B–N5 and 4.., P–KN3 (an idea introduced by Golombek in Amsterdam 1960).

Other lines occasionally used by White are 2. P–K5, N–Q4; 3. P–QB4, N–N3; 4. P–B5, and, in this line, 3. N–QB3, N × N; 4. QP × N. *(H.G.)*

ALEKHINE MEMORIAL TOURNAMENT

The first tournament organized by the USSR Chess Federation to honour the memory of Alexander Alekhine was held in Moscow in 1956. The list of invited participants was intended to include most of the world's greatest masters and in this aim it was totally successful. World Champion Botvinnik and his recent challengers, Bronstein and Smyslov, headed the list of dignitaries, with Taimanov and Keres completing the Soviet contingent. Eleven grandmasters and masters from other countries made up the list to form one of the strongest tournaments of that era. First place was shared by Botvinnik and Smyslov with 11, half a point ahead of Taimanov with 10½ and with Gligorić 10.

Another decade passed before the Soviet Federation decided again to hold a tournament to commemorate their greatest player. The second Alekhine Memorial was held in Moscow 1967, again with an impressive array of grandmasters, but this time the World Champion and his most recent challenger were not able to repeat the success of their predecessors. Champion Petrosian could, in fact, only manage to score fifty percent, while Spassky could manage only a little better to share sixth prize. The honours at this event were taken by Leonid Stein, who finished with 11 points from 17, a full point ahead of Gipslis, Bobotsov, Smyslov and Tal who shared second place. Other scores: Portisch, Bronstein and Spassky 9½, Geller, Keres, Petrosian and Najdorf 8½, Gheorghiu 8, Gligorić 7½, Bilek, Filip, Pachman and Uhlmann 6.

The third Alekhine Memorial tournament did not have to wait so long, and the list of participants for the 1971 event was fully as impressive as either of the two previous. With five past, present or future World Champions playing the competition was fierce. Again Stein excelled to take first place, but this time he was not alone, for the tournament marked the first outstanding success of the young Anatoly Karpov. Both the winners were undefeated with a score of 11, with Smyslov 10½, Tukmakov and Petrosian 10.

The fourth Alekhine Memorial was again held in Moscow (though originally scheduled for Alma-Ata) in 1975. Though perhaps not quite the strength of the previous events, this tournament contained all the leading Soviet players, with the exception of the World Champion, Karpov, and a good selection of foreign competitors. Results were as follows: Geller 10½, Spassky 10, Kholmov, Korchnoi and Vaganian 9½, Hort and Petrosian 9, Belyavsky and Tal 8½, Forintos 7, R. Byrne 6, S. Garcia and Lengyel 5½, Planinc 5, Stean 4, Bohm 3. *(W.R.H.)*

ALEXANDER, Conel Hugh O'Donel
(19 April 1909–15 February 1974)

British international master and twice British champion, Alexander was one of the finest players Britain has ever produced. He was born in Cork in Ireland, his father having been professor at the university there. But the family soon moved to Birmingham and the early years of his chess career are associated with the Midlands town.

He played much chess at King Edward's School and this school developed a great tradition for producing notable chess-players; Britain's first official grandmaster, Tony Miles, attended it nearly fifty years later. It was as a representative of that school that he went to play in the British Boys championship in 1926 and duly won the title.

In the next few years, while still at school, he competed regularly in events in the Hastings Christmas Congress. The progression was an orderly one of success: 2nd in the First Class Section A 1926/7; 1st in the Major Reserves 1927/8 and 1st in Major B in 1928/9.

Then he went up to King's College, Cambridge as a mathematics scholar and by 1931 was playing with great success on top board for his university. In 1932 he tied for second place with Van den Bosch in the Cambridge Easter International Tournament, below Sultan Khan, and he was second again to Sultan Khan in the British championship at London that year.

C. H. O'D. Alexander in play against Sultan Khan, Hastings 1933/4

Leaving the university to become mathematics master at Winchester, he now had more time for competing in international events and the next six years saw his steady rise in the B.C.F. team in the International Team Tournaments. In Folkestone 1933 he made the best score of the team, albeit on bottom board. At the Warsaw Olympiad of 1935 he had 50% on third board and at Stockholm 1937 he again scored highest with 11 out of 17 on second board. He played on first board at the 1939 Buenos Aires Olympiad.

Meanwhile he had been playing regularly in the Hastings Premier tournaments and in 1937/8 he had one of his best tournament results ever when he came equal 2nd with Keres, below Reshevsky but above Fine and Flohr. In 1938 too he won the British championship at Brighton.

With the coming of the Second World War he took no more part in chess competitions and was engaged in directing the breaking of German naval codes at Bletchley Park, a work which he performed with much zest and success. He was awarded the O.B.E. for his services at the Park and after the war continued with his work at the Foreign Office, receiving the C.B.E. during his employment there and the C.M.G. on his retirement.

He managed to get in quite a lot of fine chess in the half-dozen years following the end of the war. A score of 1–1 against Botvinnik in the 1946 Anglo-Soviet radio match created a sensation and he easily won first prize in the 1946/7 Hastings Premier. In 1947 he had a good fifth place in the Hilversum Zonal tournament and then, though continuing to play, found the demands of his profession too exacting.

Still, in the 1951 Staunton Memorial Tournament he had an excellent fifth place and at Hastings 1953 he shared first prize with Bronstein, beating both him and the other Soviet grandmaster, Tolush. He scored 50% on top board at the 1954 Olympiad in Amsterdam, and won the British championship again at Blackpool two years later.

Now came a slow decline due to advancing years and the heavier weight of responsibilities at his work. He still obtained fine results from time to time – 50% on top board at the 1958 Munich Olympiad and 2nd prize in the 1960 British championship, showing that he was still a great force. But in the early 1960s he decided to abandon over-the-board play in favour of correspondence chess.

He became an excellent non-playing captain and concentrated more on writing about the game. He was chess correspondent for the *Sunday Times*, the *Financial Times*, the *Evening News* and the *Spectator* and he wrote some fine books on the game.

A severe illness in 1972 left him much weakened physically but mentally as alert and keen as ever. When he died in 1974 he was in the midst of writing a book on twentieth-century British chess.

The fact that in chess he was an amateur all his life, while giving him an added zest for the game, meant that he lacked the consistency of a professional. Had he been a professional then he might well have aspired to World Champion status. As it was, he played like a grandmaster and was recognized as such by the other great players in the world.

His principal works were: *Alekhine's Best Games of Chess 1938–45*, London 1949; *Fischer v. Spassky, Reykjavik 1972*, London 1972; *A Book of Chess*, London 1973; *Chess*, London (1974 edition). *(H.G.)*

ALEXANDER MEMORIAL 1975
International tournament, honouring the memory of C. H. O'D. Alexander, held in Middlesbrough, England, in September 1975. This was one of a series of great chess events held in the Teesside and the County of Cleveland in the 1970s and it was won convincingly by Geller 9½/14 ahead of Smyslov 8½; Bronstein, Hort and Hübner 8; Sax and Timman 7½; Kavalek and Olafsson 7; Miles 6½; Gheorghiu, Lombardy and Stean 6; Keene 5½; Hartston 4. Hübner defaulted his final game against Miles after a dispute over the starting time of the last round. *(R.D.K.)*

ALEXANDRIA, Nana *(b. 13 December 1949)*

Soviet international woman master. Winner of 1971 Women's Interzonal Tournament and participant in the Candidates cycles of 1971 and 1974. In the latter Alexandria defeated Levitina in the final to earn a match for the World Championship, which she lost to Gaprindashvili. *(W.R.H.)*

ALFONSO THE WISE [El Sabio]

Alfonso the Wise was King of Castile from 1251–84. It was by his orders that the monks of the Escorial completed a work on chess and kindred games in 1283. This is generally known as the Alfonso manuscript and is the earliest complete European work on chess that has come down to us.

Manufacturing gaming tables, from the 'Book of Games' 1232, illuminated at the court of Alfonso the Wise

Bound in sheepskin, it has written on the back *Juegos de axedrez, dados y tablas* ('Games of chess, dice and boards') and on the fly-leaf there is *Juegos diversos de axedrez, dados, y tablas con sus explicationes, ordenados por mandado del rey don Alfonso el sabio* ('Various games of chess, dice and boards with their explanations arranged according to the instructions of the King Don Alfonso the Wise').

The importance of the work is that the section on chess shows the game basically in its older form, but with some variations (e.g. promoted Queens can leap three squares) that foreshadow the change to the modern game. *(H.G.)*

ALGERIA

Algeria is still very much a chess developing nation. A team entered the 1974 Nice Olympiad and finished =70th. In 1976, in the 'Against Chess Olympiad' at Tripoli, Algeria finished =13th.

The address of the national chess federation is: Federation Algérienne des Jeux d'Echecs, 7 bis rue Elisée Reclus, Alger. *(K.J.O'C.)*

ALLGAIER, Johann Baptist *(19 June 1763–2 January 1823)*

Originally a student of theology, Allgaier became one of the most famous Austrian players and theoreticians of the pre-tournament era. His work *Neue theoretisch-praktische Anweisung zum Schachspiel*, published in Vienna, 1795, was re-issued seven times up to 1843. His name is commemorated in the Allgaier Gambit (see King's Gambit), a line originally mentioned by Ponziani. *(W.H.)*

AMBUSH

A defence established from behind the threatening enemy piece so that the defender is so to speak pulled along by the attacker. Marshall–Duz-Khotimirsky, Carlsbad 1911:

White has to defend Black's threatened mates on KR7 and KN7. He plays Q × N, removing the Queen's support for the mate on KR7 and establishing an ambush to guard the other mate. *(W.H.)*

AMERICA

See under UNITED STATES CHESS FEDERATION and USA.

'AMERICAN CHESS BULLETIN'

A bi-monthly magazine that was founded by Hermann Helms in 1904. It was published in New York City and bore the imprint of its owner and editor, 'the dean of American Chess', in that it united solid worth with as much instruction as possible. Sixty volumes were produced between 1904 and 1963. Helms was editor until 1956 when Edgar Holladay took over. The magazine ceased publication in February 1963, one month after Helms' death.

The atmosphere of the magazine and its contributors was expressed by its sub-title: 'A Magazine Devoted to the Interests of all Branches of the Royal Game, Home and Abroad.' *(H.G.)*

ANDERSEN, Borge *(b. 19 March 1934)*

Danish international master (awarded title 1965). Danish champion 1967, 1968. Played in the Olympiads of 1954, 1958, 1964, 1966, 1974. *(R.D.K.)*

ANDERSON, Frank Rose *(b. 3 January 1928)*

Born in Toronto, Anderson learnt chess in 1944 when confined to bed with arthritis. In 1948 he tied for first in the US Junior. In 1953 Anderson tied for first in the Canadian championship and won the title outright in 1955. In 1954 he won the prize for second board with 82% at the Amsterdam Olympiad. He drew a match with Vranesic and beat Fuster $5\frac{1}{2}$–$4\frac{1}{2}$. Anderson is especially expert in opening theory. *(N.D.)*

ANDERSSEN, Adolf *(6 August 1818–9 March 1878)*

Adolf Anderssen (who was born and lived all his life in Breslau), for many years the champion of German chess, was one of the most brilliant combinational players and one of the most successful tournament contestants of all times.

He won the first truly international tournament (London 1851); won two more first prizes at Manchester 1862 and Baden-Baden 1870, and third prize at Vienna 1873, while coming 6th at PARIS 1878, at the age of sixty. In local events he won first prizes at the London Club 1851, and German master tournaments at Hamburg 1869, Barmen 1869, Leipzig 1871, Altona 1872, Leipzig 1876, and second prizes at Aachen 1868, Krefeld 1871 and Leipzig 1877.

Anderssen may be regarded as the first great tournament specialist, but in match-play his record is far less impressive. In 1845 he lost to Bledow by −5=0; in 1858 to Morphy by +2−7 =2; in 1866 to Steinitz by +6−8=0; in 1871 to Zukertort by +2−5=0; in 1876 to L. Paulsen by +4−5=1, and in 1877 to the same opponent by +3−5=1, while he drew matches against Harrwitz in 1848, Kolisch in 1860, and L. Paulsen in 1862. As against that, he won matches against Löwenthal, Harrwitz, Mayet, Suhle, Dufresne, Carstanjen, Hirschfeld, Kolisch, Minckwitz, and Zukertort, but except for Harrwitz and Zukertort these could hardly be considered in Anderssen's class. A professor of mathematics who led a quiet bourgeois life, Anderssen really let himself go at the chess board – the Evergreen Game and the Immortal Game are the outstanding examples of his style of play. Yet he was far from being the cut-and-thrust hero as whom he was depicted (and revered!) during his lifetime and many decades after. As Reinfeld has shown in *The Human Side of Chess*, Anderssen had a fine understanding of positional principles and a positive flair for the treatment of close and semi-close positions. Anderssen also was a problemist of note and in 1842 published a book, *Aufgaben für Schachspieler*. Biographical game collections of Anderssen have been made by Von Gottschall and Maróczy.

His combinative power is to be seen in the following game from the Baden-Baden 1870 tournament.

White: Steinitz; *Black:* Anderssen
Vienna Game
1. P–K4, P–K4; 2. N–QB3, B–B4; 3. P–B4, P–Q3; 4. N–B3, N–KB3; 5. B–B4, P–B3; 6. P×P, P×P; 7. Q–K2, QN–Q2; 8. P–Q3, P–QN4; 9. B–N3, P–QR4; 10. P–QR3, Q–N3; 11. N–Q1, P–R5; 12. B–R2, O–O; 13. N–K3, B–R3; 14. N–B5, P–N5; 15. P×P, Q×P+; 16. P–B3, Q–R4; 17. N–N5, QR–Q1; 18. Q–B3, Q–N3; 19. B–N1, P–R6; 20. P–QN4, B×NP; 21. P×B, Q×P+; 22. K–K2, P–R7; 23. B–Q2, Q–N4; 24. R×P, N–B4; 25. R×B, Q×R; 26. B–N4, R–N1; 27. B×N, R–N7+; 28. K–K3, Q–R4; 29. R–Q1, Q×B+; 30. P–Q4, P×P+; 31. K–B4, P–R3; 32. N–R3, R–K1; 33. Q–Q3, P–N4+; 34. K–B3, P–N5+; 35. K–N3, R×P; 36. Q–B1, Q–K4+; 37. K–R4, P×N+; 38. K×P, R–N6+; 39. P–N3, R–B5; 40. N×P+, K–B1; 41. Q–B4, R–R5+;

42. K–N2, R×RP+; 43. K×R, Q×P+; 44. K–R1, Q–R6+; 45. K–N1, R–N6+; White resigns as he is mated in three moves. *(W.H.)*

ANDERSSEN'S OPENING

1. P–QR3; a move which, in effect, gives Black White's normal right to the opening initiative. It was employed by Anderssen in his match with Morphy (Paris 1858) but otherwise has minimal claim to any theoretical significance. *(R.D.K.)*

ANDERSSON, Ulf *(b. 27 June 1951)*

Swedish grandmaster, and one of the world's leading players in the 1970s. Swedish national champion in 1969, Andersson became an international master in 1970 and obtained the grandmaster title in 1972. Principal tournament successes include: =2nd Raach (Zonal) 1969, 1st Wijk-aan-Zee Masters 1970, =1st Göteborg 1971, =1st Dortmund 1973, 1st in the 11th Capablanca Memorial, Cienfuegos 1974, again 1st in the 12th Capablanca Memorial, Cienfuegos 1975 and 1st in Santiago de Cuba 1976. He has represented his country on top board in the Olympiads of 1970, 1972, 1974 and 1976.

Reykjavik 1972
White: Andersson; *Black:* Stein
Sicilian Defence
1. P–K4, P–QB4; 2. N–KB3, N–QB3; 3. P–Q4, P×P; 4. N×P, N–B3; 5. N–QB3, P–Q3; 6. B–QB4, Q–N3; 7. N–N3, P–K3; 8. O–O, P–QR3; 9. B–K3, Q–B2; 10. B–Q3, B–K2; 11. P–B4, P–QN4; 12. P–QR4, P–N5; 13. N–N1, P–QR4; 14. N(1)–Q2, O–O;

15. Q–K2, P–K4; 16. P–B5, P–Q4; 17. P–N4, P×P; 18. N×KP, N–Q4; 19. P–B6, P×P; 20. B–KR6, R–Q1; 21. R–B3, N–B5;

22. R×N, R×B; 23. P×R, B–K3; 24. N×P+, B×N; 25. R×B, B×N; 26. R–QB1, B–Q4; 27. Q–KB2, R–K1; 28. R–QB5, B–K3; 29. Q–R4, K–R1; 30. R–KB2, resigns.
(R.D.K.)

ANDORRA

Despite the smallness of its population Andorra's tradition of chess goes back almost to the introduction of the game into Europe.

The country competed in the Olympiads of 1968 (53rd out of 53), 1970 (56th/60), 1972 (58th/63) and 1974 (72nd/74).

Chess in Andorra is regulated by the Federacio d'Escacs, Valls d'Andorra, Avda Co-princep Degaulle No. 8, ler, Les Escaldes/Pté. d'Andorre. *(R.D.K.)*

ANGLO-SOVIET RADIO MATCH 1946

In June 1946 a double round match between teams representing the USSR and Britain was played by radio. The British team assembled in London and played the match in the Gambit Chess Rooms with a running commentary being transmitted on the match by the BBC. The Soviet team played the match in Moscow.

The match, which lasted from 19–22 June, took, or seemed to take, an inordinately long time in playing. The delay seemed to lie in the process by which the moves were transmitted by tellers, who were not always conscientious in their work.

This apart, the match took place without any untoward incident and proved to be a much closer affair than had been anticipated. The previous year the Soviet team had beaten the USA by $15\frac{1}{2}$–$4\frac{1}{2}$ in a match on ten boards and it was rightly supposed that the British team was weaker than the American, since it possessed no grandmasters of the calibre of Reshevsky or Fine. Moreover youth was on the side of the Soviet players since, at thirty-five, Golombek was the youngest of the British team, whereas only a couple of the Soviet players, Flohr and Ragozin, were older than Golombek.

Nevertheless, there was a resilience about the British side which was lacking in the American. On top board Alexander made a level score against the future World Champion Botvinnik, beating him in a famous game in the second round. On fourth Golombek held Boleslavsky to two draws, Winter won one and lost one to Bronstein on seventh board and Abrahams actually had a plus score of $1\frac{1}{2}$–$\frac{1}{2}$ against that fine player Ragozin.

So the loss by 6–14 compared most favourably with the American's $4\frac{1}{2}$–$15\frac{1}{2}$. It is true that both British women lost their games but since the Americans fielded no women players comparison was impossible.

Britain		*USSR*	
1. C. H. O'D. Alexander	0 1	M. Botvinnik	1 0
2. E. Klein	½ 0	P. Keres	½ 1
3. I. König	0 0	V. Smyslov	1 1
4. H. Golombek	½ ½	I. Boleslavsky	½ ½
5. W. A. Fairhurst	0 ½	S. Flohr	1 ½
6. P. M. List	0 0	A. Kotov	1 1
7. W. Winter	1 0	D. Bronstein	0 1
8. J. M. Aitken	0 0	I. Bondarevsky	1 1
9. B. H. Wood	0 ½	A. Lilienthal	1 ½
10. G. Abrahams	½ 1	V. Ragozin	½ 0
	6		14
Women			
1. E. Tranmer	0 0	V. Byelova	1 1
2. R. M. Bruce	0 0	L. Rudenko	1 1
	0		4

The game played in the second round with which Alexander created a sensation by demolishing Botvinnik's favourite French Defence.

White: Alexander; *Black:* Botvinnik
French Defence
1. P–K4, P–K3; 2. P–Q4, P–Q4; 3. N–QB3, B–N5; 4. P–K5, P–QB4; 5. P–QR3, B×N+; 6. P×B, N–K2; 7. Q–N4, P×P; 8. Q×NP, R–N1; 9. Q×RP, Q–R4; 10. R–N1, Q×P+; 11. B–Q2,

Q–B2; 12. P–KB4, QN–B3; 13. N–B3, B–Q2; 14. N–N5, R×N; 15. P×R, O–O–O; 16. Q×P, Q×P+; 17. K–Q1, N–B4; 18. P–N6, N–K6+; 19. K–B1, Q–K5; 20. B–Q3, Q×P(N7); 21. R–K1, N–K4; 22. Q–B4, N–B6; 23. R–K2, Q–R6; 24. B×N, P–K4; 25. Q–B7, P×B; 26. P–N7, Q–N5; 27. P–R3, Q–N8+; 28. K–N2, Q–N6;

29. B–N6, N–Q5; 30. P–N8=Q, R×Q; 31. Q×R+, K–B2; 32. Q–R7, K–Q3; 33. B–Q3, P–K5; 34. Q–R6+, K–B2; 35. R×P, Q–K4; 36. K–R2, N–B4; 37. Q–N5, B–K3; 38. B–K2, P–Q5+; 39. R(K3)–N3, P–N4; 40. Q–Q2, P–Q6; 41. B–N4, resigns. *(H.G.)*

ANTOSHIN, Vladimir Sergeyevich *(b. 14 May 1929)*
USSR Correspondence champion 1960 and international grandmaster over-the-board since 1964. Member of the successful USSR Student Olympiad teams of 1954–6, but never outstanding in international tournaments except for his first place at Zinnowitz in 1966. *(W.R.H.)*

APHORISMS, Chess
Chess, though a silent game, has been a favourite field for verbal wisecracks – aphorisms, *aperçus*, paradoxes etc. These either deal with chess as a phenomenon – game, art, science, struggle – or with details of the conduct of the game, opening play, endgame precepts, tactics, strategy.

In the first category we have: 'Chess is a lake in which a gnat may bathe and an elephant may drown' (Indian proverb). – 'You cannot play at chess if you are kindhearted' (French proverb); in R. J. Fischer's updated version this becomes 'There are tough players and nice guys, and I'm a tough player'. – 'All chess is one long regret' (Stephen Leacock). – 'Chess is like a drug – beneficial in rare doses, fatal in frequent ones' (Prof. Landau).

'Not only does chess admit of two points of view – without two points of view there would be no chess' (Heidenfeld). – 'Chess has this in common with making poetry, that the desire for it comes upon the amateur in gusts' (A. A. Milne). – 'The game has three phases: the first when one hopes one has an advantage; the second when one believes one has an advantage; and the third when one knows one is going to lose' (Tartakower). – This 'Tartakowerism' offers an easy transition to the second type of aphorism: nobody, in fact, has done more to interpret the rules in his own witty way than the late grandmaster: 'Gambit is the catch-as-catch-can style of chess.' – 'Castling is the first step towards a well-ordered life.' – 'The blunders are all there on the board waiting to be made.' – 'The great master places a Knight at K5; checkmate follows by itself.' – 'A passed QRP looks more dangerous on the second rank than on the seventh.' – 'Tempi are not meant to be counted but weighed.'

While Tartakower may well claim the title of the Chesterton of chess, many other masters have contributed their darts to the verbal armoury of chess. 'In a gambit you give up a pawn for the sake of getting a lost game' (Boden). – 'From Anderssen I learnt how to make combinations; from Tarrasch I learned how to avoid making them' (Spielmann). – 'Pawn endings are to chess what putting is to golf' (Purdy). – 'Black pawns run faster than white ones' (Folklore). – 'Never miss a check, it might be mate' (Proverbial, generally ascribed to Blackburne). – 'Whereas the tactician knows what to do when there is something to do, it requires the strategist to know what to do when there is nothing to do' (Abrahams). – 'Kiebitzers are known to be right only when they are wrong' (Kmoch). – 'He is a player who can be relied upon to snatch defeat from the jaws of victory' (J. J. Walsh). – 'Place the contents of the chessbox in your hat, shake them up vigorously, pour them on to the board at a height of two feet, and you get the style of Steinitz' (Bird).

'Rubinstein is not one of those players who try to cash in on the cunningly subtle difference between variations AI6 and CII7(a) and, while firing blanks from toy pistols, are under the impression they are discharging heavy artillery' (Brinckmann). – 'Your moves are every bit as good as mine – only you don't make them at the right time' (Blackburne, to an opponent in a simultaneous display). – 'This move poor Lipschütz had not expected' (Bogoljubow, commenting on a surprise move). – 'Never move a pawn and you will never lose a game' (Tarrasch). – 'Exchanging is the soul of chess' (Kieninger).

The last word should come from the wisdom of Dr Emanuel Lasker, and it contains a good deal of his chess philosophy: 'He who sees much can endure much'. *(W.H.)*

APSCHENEEK, Fritzis [Franz] *(7 April 1894–25 April 1941)*
One of Latvia's strongest players in the period between the wars. Took second place in the 'World Amateur Championship' at Paris 1924. *(W.R.H.)*

ARAIZA, José Joaquin *(23 March 1900–27 September 1971)*
Mexican chess-master and that country's leading player till the arrival of C. Torre.

The high point of his career came in Mexico in 1932 with 3rd prize, scoring 6/9 in a tournament, below Alekhine and Kashdan with 8½, but ahead of Asiain, Vasquez, Medina etc. *(R.D.K.)*

ARBITERS, International
The title of International Arbiter (or International Judge) was created by FIDE in 1951 and is awarded by their qualification committee.

Candidates for the title are nominated by their federations and must have the following credentials: a perfect knowledge of the rules of play and all FIDE regulations; objectivity in tournament direction; a working knowledge of two of the official FIDE languages (English, French, German, Spanish and Russian); experience of controlling at least four important chess events of which at least two were international.

To date the title has been awarded to more than two hundred arbiters. Among the holders are Dr Euwe, Harry Golombek, I. Kashdan and Dr Dorazil. *(W.R.H.)*

ARGENTINA

Argentina's first chess club was founded in about 1860. Though the leading South American chess nation up to the present day, it was only the third to establish a chess magazine, though the two forerunners were short-lived. The *Revista del Club Argentino de ajedrez* (still the most important club) commenced publication in 1905 and, though it died in 1926, the country has never since been without one or more magazines.

The national championship was instituted in 1921/2 and D. M. Reca was the first champion of Argentina. The national champions since 1960 have been:

1960	M. Najdorf	1968	R. Sanguineti
1961	H. Rossetto	1969	C. E. Juarez
1962	R. Sanguineti	1971	J. Rubinetti
1963	R. Garcia	1972	H. Rossetto
1964	M. Najdorf	1973	R. Sanguineti
1965	R. Sanguineti	1974	R. Sanguineti
1966	M. A. Quinteros	1975	M. Najdorf, O. Panno
1967	M. Najdorf	1976	J. Szmetan

The world's second-longest established series of regular tournaments commenced at Mar del Plata in 1928, the year after an Argentinian team had become the first South American side, and one of the first sixteen in the world, to compete in an Olympiad.

Argentina has competed in 19 of the 22 Olympiads, missing only the three from 1930 to 1933. Their results have been as follows: 12th in 1927, 8th in 1928 and 1935, 4th in 1937, 5th in 1939 (in Buenos Aires), 2nd in 1950, 1952 and 1954, 4th in 1956, 3rd in 1958, 7th in 1960, 3rd in 1962, 9th in 1964, 5th in 1966, 7th in 1968, 8th in 1970, 14th in 1972 and 1974, and 4th in 1976.

Apart from the 1939 Olympiad in Buenos Aires, the most important events staged in the country have been the 1939 Women's World Championship, held concurrently with the Olympiad, the 1927 World Championship match between Capablanca and Alekhine, and the final of the 1971 Candidates series between Fischer and Petrosian.

The address of the national federation is: Federacion Argentina de Ajedrez, Carlos Pellegrini 1362, Buenos Aires. *(K.J.O'C.)*

ARONIN, Lev Solomonovich *(b. 20 July 1920)*

Soviet international master since 1950, when he made his career best result to share second place in the USSR championship. *(W.R.H.)*

ASHTĀPADA

The Sanskrit name for the board on which *chaturanga* (the earliest form of chess) was played in north-west India from the sixth century AD onwards. It was borrowed from a much older game, a type of backgammon played with dice and pieces, and, as time passed, *ashtāpada* came to indicate the game as well as the board. This was unchequered and the sixty-four squares were merely outlined. *(H.G.)*

AṢ-ṢŪLĪ *(Tenth century)*

Descended from a Turkish prince named Sul-takin, Abū-Bakr Muḥammad ben Yaḥyā aṣ-Ṣūli was the most outstanding Arabic chess author and also the best chess-player of his time. In his writings, he improved on his great predecessor al-Adli, and his fame lasted for more than six hundred years. *(H.G.)*

ASZTALOS, Dr Lajos *(29 July 1889–31 October 1956)*

Hungarian-Yugoslav international master and International Judge who became a considerable organizer and teacher of chess.

He was born in Hungary and was Hungarian for the first thirty years of his life. Second place at Temesvar 1912, a point below Breyer, secured for him the Hungarian national master title and he was 1st in a small tournament at Debrecen 1913 ahead of Réti and Breyer. In a much stronger tournament at Budapest that year he came =8th with Vidmar and in the celebrated tournament in memory of Charousek that was held at Kassa (Kaschau) in 1918 he was 5th, below Réti, Vidmar, Breyer and Schlechter, but above Grünfeld, Mieses, Balogh and Havasi etc.

After the First World War he left Hungary for Yugoslavia, remaining there till 1942. He played for Yugoslavia in two Olympiads, London 1927 and Prague 1931 and also in the so-called Olympiad in Munich 1936, obtaining excellent scores in all three events.

He also played in some strong international tournaments in this period, his best results being a 3rd at Györ 1924 above, amongst others, Maróczy and the Steiner brothers; 3rd at Bartfeld (Bardiov) 1926, below Mattison and Tartakower but ahead of Colle, Kostić and Kmoch; an excellent 4th at Kecskemet 1927, below Alekhine, Nimzowitsch and L. Steiner but ahead of many famous names, was probably the peak point in his career. He came next to bottom in Bled 1931 but put up a determined resistance to all the great masters who played there. Thereafter his =5th in Ljubljana 1938 showed some decline and he stopped playing for some time.

In 1942 he returned to Hungary and had some small successes in tournaments there: 3rd at Diosgyör 1943 and 4th at Kolozsvar 1943 and =3rd at Debrecen 1948, this being his last tournament. Then he played no more and confined himself to organizational work. A cultured and kindly man, he was a vice-president of the Hungarian Chess Federation and a bridge between the communist and western countries of Europe. *(H.G.)*

ATKINS, Henry Ernest *(20 August 1872–31 January 1955)*

British international master and regarded by many as Britain's most talented player in the history of the game. Born in Leicester and never very fond of leaving England, Atkins was a schoolmaster and devoted relatively little time to chess, yet he became one of the strongest amateurs ever known to chess. He was known on the Continent as 'the little Steinitz'.

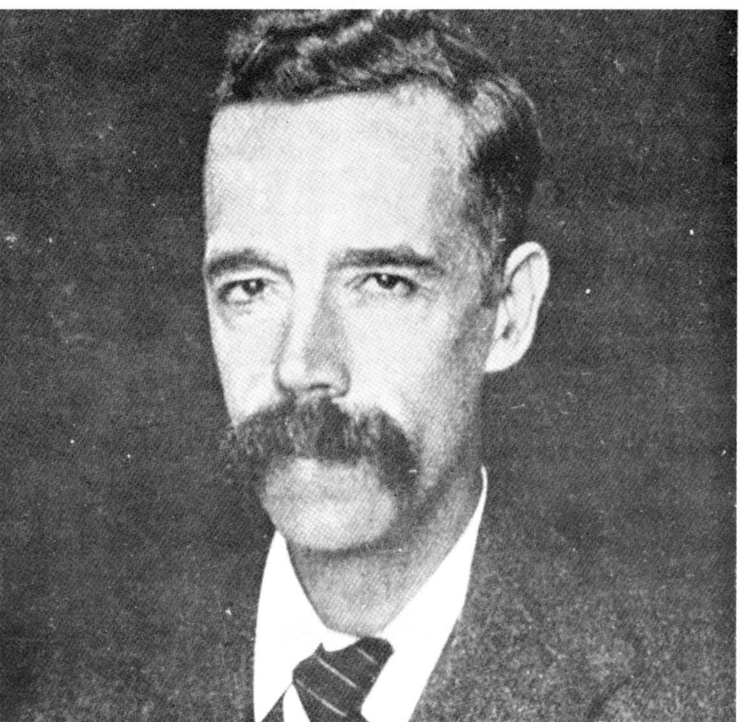

Henry Atkins

His record in the British championship is unique; out of eleven appearances he won the event nine times: 1905, 1906, 1907, 1908, 1909, 1910, 1911, 1924 and 1925. It should be added that in 1904 (his first attempt) he finished =1st and only lost to Napier after a play-off and in 1937 (his last championship) he finished =3rd at the age of 65!

His international career comprises only six events. In 1895 Atkins was placed =2nd behind Maróczy in the Hastings Minor Tournament and in 1899 he won the Amsterdam tournament, leading the field by 4 points. At Hanover 1902 he scored his most notable result: 3rd prize behind Janowski and Pillsbury but ahead of Chigorin and Marshall among others. At London 1922 he finished only 10th of 16, but still claimed Rubinstein and Tartakower among his victims. He represented the B.C.F. in the Olympiads of 1927 and 1935.

Atkins was retrospectively awarded the title of international master in 1950 on his pre-war record. *(R.D.K.)*

AUSTRALIA

Considering the initial disadvantages with which chess commenced in Australia, it is indeed amazing to see what strides the game made in the sub-continent. The strength attained in the 1960s and 1970s which enabled Australia to compete on equal terms in the Olympiads with many a country where chess has been much longer established is astonishing.

To mention the disadvantages first: chess is not indigenous in Australia. That is to say, since chess was not introduced till the middle of the nineteenth century, there could be no tradition of early chess as there was in European countries. An even bigger handicap was the vast spaces and the spare nature of the population which rendered matches between, for example, neighbouring states, either impossible or exceedingly difficult and costly.

The way all this was surmounted was in the first place through the energetic enthusiasm of a few bright and great spirits, and secondly by a constant flow that became almost a flood during the European troubles caused by the rise of the Nazis in Europe in the 1930s and also by the imperialist designs and actions of the USSR from Stalin's time onwards. Australia was one country that benefitted from the incursion of politics into the lives of chess-players.

The history of chess in Australia really starts with the rise of such almost legendary figures as F. K. Esling, W. Crane, A. E. N. Wallace and H. Charlick in the latter half of the nineteenth century. Charlick is also noted for being what one might call the half-holder of the record for the Longest Game.

W. S. Viner and Spencer Crakanthorp were the chief players and moving spirits of the early 1900s but the first real stir that created strong chess in Australia was made by the two founding fathers of modern chess in that country, C. J. S. Purdy and G. Koshnitsky, both of whom have been rightly awarded the honour of M.B.E. for their great services to chess. Purdy was particularly active as a writer and his witty pen was most effective in the *Australian Chess Review*, whilst Koshnitsky excelled as player and organizer.

These two were joined in the 1930s by one of England's most noted opening theorists, M. E. Goldstein and, after the Second World War, by Lajos Steiner, one of Hungary's and therefore one of Europe's strongest players. Together with other additions, mainly from the Baltic republics taken over by the Soviet Union, they provided a firm basis for an Australian national team and, as time went on, indigenous players of master strength (Max Fuller, D. G. Hamilton and international master Jamieson) built up the team to its present excellent standard.

Each state has its own organization and the overall command of these is in the hands of the Australian Chess Federation which was founded in 1922. The A.C.F. organizes biennial national championships and is also responsible for international matches and all international affairs. It sends a team to the Olympiads and also representatives to FIDE Zonal tournaments and the other FIDE championships (Junior, Students, etc.).

The record of the Australian team at the Olympiads is quite extraordinary. They first competed at Tel Aviv 1964, where they came 43rd and won their final group D. Quite a leap of an increase occurred on their next venture, at Lugano 1968, when they came 29th and won final group C.

In the next two Olympiads they had the powerful aid of Walter Browne on top board.

Their best result was at Siegen 1970 when they came 15th and were 3rd in final group B. They were 32nd at Spokje 1972, winning group C in the finals and 33rd at Nice 1974 when they again won group C. At Haifa in 1976 they came 17th and this was an event played entirely on the Swiss System.

There is clearly a bright future for chess and chess-players in Australia and their best players have a habit of traversing the world almost like the old Vikings so that more can be hoped from them individually as well. The national champions:

1885	F. K. Esling	1945	L. Steiner
1887	H. Charlick	1948	C. J. S. Purdy
1888	W. Crane	1953	L. Steiner
1893	A. E. N. Wallace	1955	J. Purdy
1897	W. Crane	1957	K. Ozols, S. Lazare
1897	J. L. Jacobsen	1959	L. Steiner
1899–1906	Title vacant	1960	L. Endzelins
1906	W. S. Viner	1963	J. Purdy
1922	C. G. Watson	1965	D. Hamilton
1924	W. S. Viner	1969	W. S. Browne
1926	S. Crakanthorp	1970	A. Flatow
1931	C. G. Watson	1972	M. Fuller, T. Hay
1933	G. Koshnitsky	1974	R. M. Jamieson
1935	C. J. S. Purdy	1976	S. Rubinraut
1939	G. Koshnitsky		

The address of the national federation is Australian Chess Federation, c/o G. H. Hartland, 661 George Street, Sydney, NSW 2000. Its official publication is *Chess in Australia*, c/o B. H. Johnson, 9 Robert Street, Belmore, NSW 2199.

(H.G. & K.J.O'C.)

AUSTRIA

Chess in Austria may be said to have begun with Allgaier. He was not only the sole Austrian player of note in the early years of the nineteenth century, but also the teacher of a whole generation of Austrian players through his *Neue theoretisch-praktische Anweisung zum Schachspiel*, Vienna 1795, a handbook that went into seven editions (three of them posthumously). Allgaier was followed by Witthalm, Hamppe, Jenay, Matschecko and others, but the most famous mid-nineteenth-century player was Falkbeer. Unlike their British and German contemporaries, and the representatives of the Vienna *remis-monde* which followed them thirty or forty years later, most of the Austrian players of that period were brilliant and inventive. The most famous representative of this school was the young Steinitz before he became the founder of modern positional chess (it was in those days that he acquired the nickname of the 'Austrian Morphy'). Austrian, or perhaps better Hapsburg, chess reached the period of its full flowering between 1882, the year of the great Vienna tournament, and 1914. This period witnessed a number of great tournaments, especially the 38-round Emperor Franz Joseph Jubilee tournament of 1898, and the Carlsbad events of 1907 and 1911. But these events, important though they may have been, were really of less significance than the general chess atmosphere, especially of Vienna, the home of coffee-house chess on the Continent. The Viennese did not need tournaments specially designed to be international. All local tournaments were international because of the cosmopolitan character of the Hapsburg Empire and especially its capital, Vienna, which in those days was at once the cultural and chess centre of Europe. The leading masters who had made Vienna their home came from all over Central Europe: Albin and Marco from Romania, Perlis from Poland, Halprin from Russia, Vidmar from Yugoslavia, Spielmann from Moravia, Heinrich Wolf from Silesia, Tartakower from the Ukraine, Réti from what was then Hungary and is now Czechoslovakia, Martinolich from Trieste, the aptly-named veterans, Schwarz and Weiss from Hungary, and Schlechter, Englisch, Berger, Fähndrich, Krejcik, Zinkl and others from Austria itself. The social centres of this cosmopolitan chess life were the *Wiener Schachklub* and the *Café Central*, the literary centre the *Wiener Schachzeitung* under the editorship of Georg Marco, and the central competitive events, from 1907 onwards, were the annual Trebitsch tournaments. The First World War smashed many of the institutions (e.g. the Hapsburg Empire) though others, such as the Trebitsch tournaments, survived. Yet the successful rebuilding of Austrian chess resulted in a lower-key chess life. It was still international, with many survivors from the 'Golden Age' and a new master generation with Vuković and König from Yugoslavia, Takács from Hungary, and such as Grünfeld, Becker, Kmoch, Lokvenc, Müller, Hönlinger and finally Eliskases representing the home country. Again, there were great international events, like Vienna 1922, and Semmering 1926 and 1937, but the wonderful tournaments of Carlsbad 1923 and 1929 could no longer be classified as Austrian. Another institution that survived was the *remis-monde*: Grünfeld, Becker, Lokvenc and even Eliskases played a modernized but essentially the same careful scientific style that always aimed at keeping the draw in hand, as Schlechter, Englisch, Marco and Berger had done before them. But the sparkle and the flamboyance had gone out of Austrian chess long before the Nazis took over and killed whatever had survived the First World War. The second re-building, after the trauma of the Second World War, was even more modest than the first had been. Before 1939 it would have been unthinkable for an Austrian team in the Olympiads not to finish in the upper half (their best were fourth places in The Hague 1928 and Hamburg 1930); now creditable performances such as 13th/34 at Moscow 1956, 12th/36 at Munich 1958, and 12th/37 at Varna 1962 mingled with such poor results as 17th/25 at Helsinki 1952 and 15th/26 at Amsterdam 1954, and since Tel Aviv 1964 Austria has never risen higher than the B finals. Though there have been many smallish international tournaments, no great individual event was organized in the country since the Second World War – the greatest organizational feat was the holding of the European Team championship finals in Vienna in 1957. Similarly, despite the present-day grandmaster inflation, Austria has only one grandmaster, Robatsch, and no Austrian master has won an international tournament of any importance. The one great triumph for Austrian chess came when, at the Olympiad of Leipzig 1960, Robatsch won the gold medal for the best individual performance at board 1 (84.4%). In Robatsch, Dückstein, Beni, Prameshuber etc. Austria has a solid array of meritorious players, but it is a long way from the great period of the Viennese School.

The name and address of the Austrian Chess Federation is: Österreichischer Schachbund, Brockmanngasse 18, A 8010, Graz.

(W.H.)

AUTOMATONS

The Automaton Chess Player – Kempelen's Turk

The history of chess automatons (or automata) began with the appearance of Kempelen's Turk in 1769. This was the first step on the road to chess-playing robots. The Turk contained a concealed operator, as did its imitative successor Ajeeb. The next step was taken in 1878 when Gumpel's Mephisto made its appearance; though still controlled by a human operator, the player could now, thanks to electricity, operate the mechanism at a distance. An enormous leap forward came in 1890 with the first genuine attempt to design a chess-playing automaton by the Spanish scientist Torres y Quevedo, who built a machine that played the ending of King and Rook against King. An excellent account, by Henri Vigneron, of Torres y Quevedo's device can be found in Levy's *Chess and Computers*, London 1976. Subsequently there was no significant development until 1949 and the publication of 'Programming a Computer for Playing Chess' (*Philosophical Magazine*, volume 41) by Claude E. Shannon. For developments in the field of chess automata since 1949 see under COMPUTERS. *(K.J.O'C.)*

AVERBAKH, Yuri *(b. 8 February 1922)*

Soviet grandmaster who was one of his country's leading players in the 1950s without ever quite reaching World Championship calibre. Perhaps his best result came in the Interzonal tournament in 1952 in which he shared 5th place, thereby qualifying for the Candidates. Shared first place in the 1956 Soviet championship with Taimanov and Spassky, but only managed second place in the play-off.

Contributed important additions to chess literature in his three-volume work on the endgame. Five volumes of the eight volume English edition have now appeared.

Recently Averbakh has given most of his attention to chess organization in the USSR. Besides being the main editor of *Chess in the USSR*, he has, since 1971, been president of the Soviet Chess Federation. *(W.R.H.)*

A.V.R.O. 1938

A double-round tournament held in November 1938 under the sponsorship of the Dutch wireless company, Algemene Verenigde Radio Omroep. The participants – Alekhine, Botvinnik, Capablanca, Euwe, Fine, Flohr, Keres and Reshevsky – included the reigning World Champion and all his potential challengers. The sponsors intended the event to be regarded as an unofficial Candidates tournament, and the winner (or the runner-up in the case of a victory by Alekhine) was promised financial backing for a World Championship title match.

For a tournament of such importance, the playing conditions were appalling. The players travelled through Holland – ten venues in different towns were used – and on playing days the competitors were often forced to miss dinner. These circumstances naturally favoured the younger grandmasters at the expense of Alekhine and Capablanca.

The final scores were: Keres and Fine $8\frac{1}{2}$/14; Botvinnik $7\frac{1}{2}$; Alekhine, Reshevsky, and Euwe 7; Capablanca 6; Flohr $4\frac{1}{2}$. The tie for 1st place was broken in favour of Keres, who had the superior Sonneborn–Berger rating.

The projected match between Alekhine and Keres did not take place, since Alekhine had already contracted to defend his title first against Flohr, who was the official FIDE World Championship challenger. Alekhine did promise to play a subsequent match against Keres if he retained his title, but the start of the Second World War terminated all negotiations.

One of the best, possibly the best of the tournament, was Botvinnik's game v. Capablanca, 1938.

White: Botvinnik; *Black:* Capablanca
Nimzo-Indian Defence
1. P–Q4, N–KB3; 2. P–QB4, P–K3; 3. N–QB3, B–N5; 4. P–K3, P–Q4; 5. P–QR3, B×N+; 6. P×B, P–B4; 7. BP×P, KP×P; 8. B–Q3, O–O; 9. N–K2, P–QN3; 10. O–O, B–R3; 11. B×B, N×B; 12. B–N2, Q–Q2; 13. P–QR4, KR–K1; 14. Q–Q3, P–B5; 15. Q–B2, N–N1; 16. QR–K1, N–B3; 17. N–N3, N–QR4; 18. P–B3, N–N6; 19. P–K4, Q×P; 20. P–K5, N–Q2; 21. Q–B2, P–N3; 22. P–B4, P–B4; 23. P×P e.p., N×BP; 24. P–B5, R×R; 25. R×R, R–K1; 26. R–K6!, R×R; 27. P×R, K–N2; 28. Q–B4, Q–K1; 29. Q–K5, Q–K2;

30. B–R3!!, Q×B; 31. N–R5+!, P×N; 32. Q–N5+, K–B1; 33. Q×N+, K–N1; 34. P–K7, Q–B8+; 35. K–B2, Q–B7+; 36. K–N3, Q–Q6+; 37. K–R4, Q K5+; 38. K×P, Q–K7+; 39. K–R4, Q–K5+; 40. P–N4, Q–K8+; 41. K–R5, resigns. *(R.D.K.)*

B

BACHMANN, Ludwig *(11 August 1856–22 June 1937)*
A German chess historian, Bachmann was the biographer of Anderssen, Charousek, Pillsbury and Steinitz; he also wrote *Aus Vergangenen Zeiten* (2 volumes, Berlin 1920) and *Das Schachspiel und seine historische Entwicklung* (Leipzig-Berlin 1920). But perhaps his most famous contribution to chess literature was the compilation of chess annuals (*Schachjahrbücher*) from 1897 to 1930. *(W.H.)*

BACK RANK
The back rank, or bottom rank, is the rank on which each side has its pieces placed in the initial position. Its significance comes to light in the *back rank mate*, a frequent combinational motif based on the inability of the King to step back off the rank or to step forward when no loophole has been opened. Perhaps the most famous combination utilizing this motif is shown in the diagram.

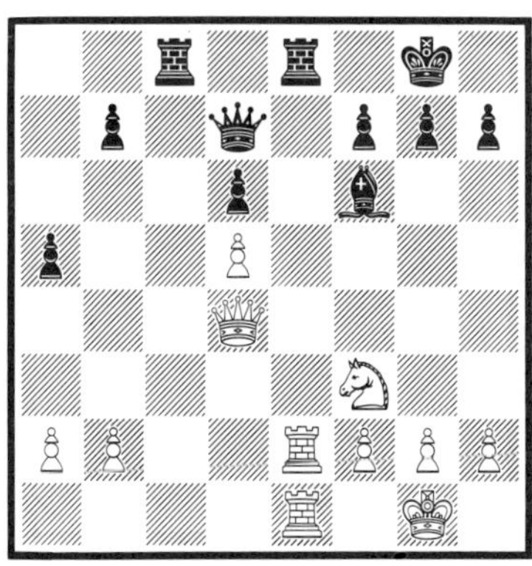

White continued 1. Q–KN4, Q–N4; 2. Q–QB4, Q–Q2; 3. Q–B7, Q–N4; 4. P–QR4, Q×RP; 5. R–K4, Q–N4; 6. Q×NP, resigns; he can no longer stop the back rank mate without heavy material loss.

The extraordinary aspect of this beautiful combination is that it was an American amateur, E. B. Adams, who pulled it off against the Mexican grandmaster, Carlos Torre. *(W.H.)*

BACKWARD PAWN

Of all the occupational diseases the average pawn is prone to, backwardness is the worst. Hanging pawns, doubled pawns, isolated pawns all have some redeeming features; the backward pawn – i.e. a pawn that has one or several neighbours on adjacent files but has been left behind and can no longer be protected by any of them – has none, and its only hope is that its backwardness may be eliminated in the course of the game. This elimination process is, in fact, the theme of some modern opening variations in which one side voluntarily saddles itself with a backward pawn for compensation *elsewhere* on the board and a high degree of probability of eliminating the backwardness of the pawn, as e.g. in the Boleslavsky Variation of the Sicilian Defence: 1. P–K4, P–QB4; 2. N–KB3, N–QB3; 3. P–Q4, P×P; 4. N×P, N–B3; 5. N–QB3, P–Q3; 6. B–K2, P–K4 rendering the Black QP backward. *(W.H.)*

BAD BISHOP
A Bishop hemmed in by pawns of its own side on squares of its own colour. In the middle-game such a Bishop can serve only defensive functions; in the ending he is inferior to the good Bishop and usually loses to a Knight. See also under ENDGAME. *(W.H.)*

BADEN-BADEN 1870
The first international tournament to be held in Germany, this was the last great tournament Anderssen was to win. In it he demonstrated that, though he had lost a match to Steinitz four years earlier, he was still his superior in tournament chess and he won a famous game with a beautiful finish against his rival in this event. (The game appears in the entry on ANDERSSEN.)

There was a time limit of 20 moves per hour and this was controlled by a type of clock known as the Schwarzwald (Black Forest).

The Franco-Prussian war broke out during the tournament and this affected the French-based players, Stern withdrawing shortly after the tournament began and Rosenthal forfeiting his games against De Vere and Minckwitz.

The tournament also signalled the rise of the English grandmaster Blackburne in the international field. Leading scores: Anderssen 13, Steinitz 12½, Blackburne and Neumann 12. *(W.H.)*

BADEN-BADEN 1925
'Capablanca *is* World Champion, Dr Lasker *was* World Champion, but Dr Alekhine plays as a World Champion ought to play', was the comment by one of his colleagues on Alekhine's perform-

ance at Baden-Baden (April–May 1925). Winning twelve and drawing eight of his games, he completely dominated a field of strong Central European internationals reinforced by Marshall and Torre from the Americas and the Soviet master, Rabinovich. Rubinstein confirmed his standing among the leading masters, while Bogoljubow (with five losses) and even more so Nimzowitsch and Réti must have been disappointed with their showing. The surprise of the tournament was Sämisch, who was never to equal this performance in any event of similar strength. Leading scores: Alekhine 16, Rubinstein 14½, Sämisch 13½, Bogoljubow 13. The following game was later described by the winner as one of the two most brilliant he had ever played:

White: Réti; *Black:* Alekhine
King's Fianchetto Opening
1. P–KN3, P–K4; 2. N–KB3, P–K5; 3. N–Q4, P–Q4; 4. P–Q3, P×P; 5. Q×P, N–KB3; 6. B–N2, B–N5+; 7. B–Q2, B×B+; 8. N×B, O–O; 9. P–QB4, N–R3; 10. P×P, N–QN5; 11. Q–B4, QN×QP; 12. QN–N3, P–B3; 13. O–O, R–K1; 14. KR–Q1, B–N5; 15. R–Q2, Q–B1; 16. N–QB5, B–R6; 17. B–B3, B–N5; 18. B–N2, B–R6; 19. B–B3, B–N5; 20. B–R1, P–KR4; 21. P–N4, P–R3; 22. R–QB1, P–R5; 23. P–R4, P×P; 24. RP×P, Q–B2; 25. P–N5, RP×P; 26. P×P,

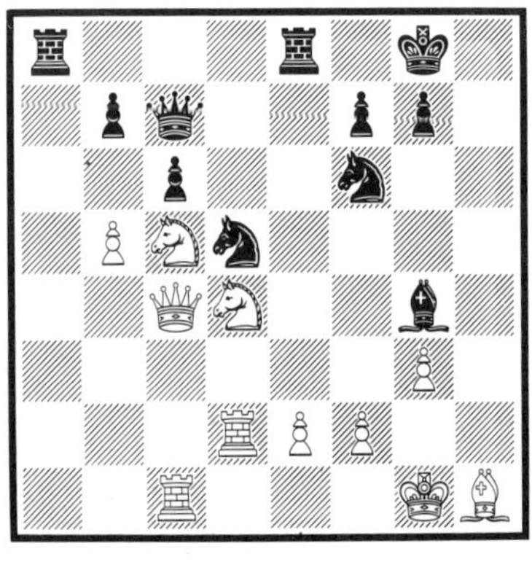

26.., R–K6; 27. N–B3, P×P; 28. Q×P, N–B6; 29. Q×P, Q×Q; 30. N×Q, N×P+; 31. K–R2, N–K5; 32. R–B4, N×BP; 33. B–N2, B–K3; 34. R(4)–B2, N–N5+; 35. K–R3, N–K4+; 36. K–R2, R×N; 37. R×N, N–N5+; 38. K–R3, N–K6+; 39. K–R2, N×R; 40. B×R, N–Q5; White resigns (for if now 41. R–K3 (or B2), N×B+; 42. R×N, B–Q4). *(W.H.)*

BAD KISSINGEN 1928

A compact single-round tournament of only twelve players (only one of whom would not be designated as an international grandmaster in present-day terminology), this event in August 1928 was Capablanca's first appearance after the loss of his title. He had clearly not overcome the shock of this defeat: not only was he once again headed by Bogoljubow, who thus confirmed his status as the most highly qualified challenger for Alekhine's title, but many of his games (e.g. against Spielmann, Nimzowitsch, Tartakower) did not suggest the 'chess machine' of his heyday. The tournament did not only bring to light a future challenger, but also a future champion: Euwe's joint third place was his first success in a major tournament.

Leading scores: Bogoljubow 8, Capablanca 7, Euwe and Rubinstein 6½. *(W.H.)*

BAGIROV, Vladimir Konstantinovich *(b. 1936)*

Soviet international master since 1963. Shared fourth place in the 1959 USSR championship, but his best result has been to share first place in the Tbilisi international tournament in 1971. *(W.R.H.)*

BAHAMAS

The Bahamas emerged in the chess world at the 1974 Nice Olympiad where they finished 72nd. Early in 1976 they lost a match against Cuba by 11–1.

The organizing body is the Bahamas Chess Federation, P.O. Box 6154, Nassau N.P. *(K.J.O'C.)*

BALASHOV, Yuri *(b. 12 March 1949)*

Yuri Balashov in play at the Alekhine Memorial Tournament, Moscow 1971

One of the group of leading young Soviet grandmasters, Balashov was awarded the title after he took second place, behind Tal, at the Wijk-aan-Zee tournament in 1973. Has played many times in the USSR championship and was a frequent member of the national team in Student Olympiads.

After some fine performances in 1972–3 his results were uninspiring until he again ran into form in 1975. His best results since then have been =2nd in the 1975 Capablanca Memorial, =1st in the 1975 Vilnius Zonal, =6th in the 1975 USSR championship and, in 1976, 1st at Halle and 2nd, behind Karpov but ahead of three ex-World Champions, in the USSR championship. *(W.R.H.)*

BALINAS, Rosendo Carrean Jr. *(b. 10 September 1941)*

Philippine international grandmaster and a lawyer by profession, Balinas was born in Manila and learnt chess at the age of seven, but did not really start playing till he was fifteen.

Second in the Philippine Junior championship in 1960, he won the Philippine Open championship and proceeded to win it five more times.

In 1968 he tied with Gligorić for first place in the Philippine Open tournament at Manila.

Balinas played for the Philippines on a high board at the Olympiads of 1964, 1966 (scoring 77.5% on 3rd board) and 1968. Then from 1970 to the end of 1973 he stopped playing and completed his law studies.

In 1974 he played in the Olympiad again and in the following year he gained the international master title by coming =3rd in a Zonal tournament at Melbourne. In October 1975 he played in a very strong tournament in Manila, the 4th Marlboro Grandmaster Chess Classic, and came =6th with Gligorić, a result that gave him his first grandmaster norm.

It was in 1976 that he enjoyed most success. In May he came =4th with the Polish international master Sydor at Dortmund. Then, in a strong international tournament at Odessa, he became the first foreign master to win an international tournament in the USSR since Capablanca in 1936, scoring 10 points and beating such grandmasters as Savon and Lutikov. This was his second grandmaster norm and gave him the title of international grandmaster.

A busy year ended for him when he played in the Haifa Olympiad in November, scoring 50% on 2nd board. *(H.G.)*

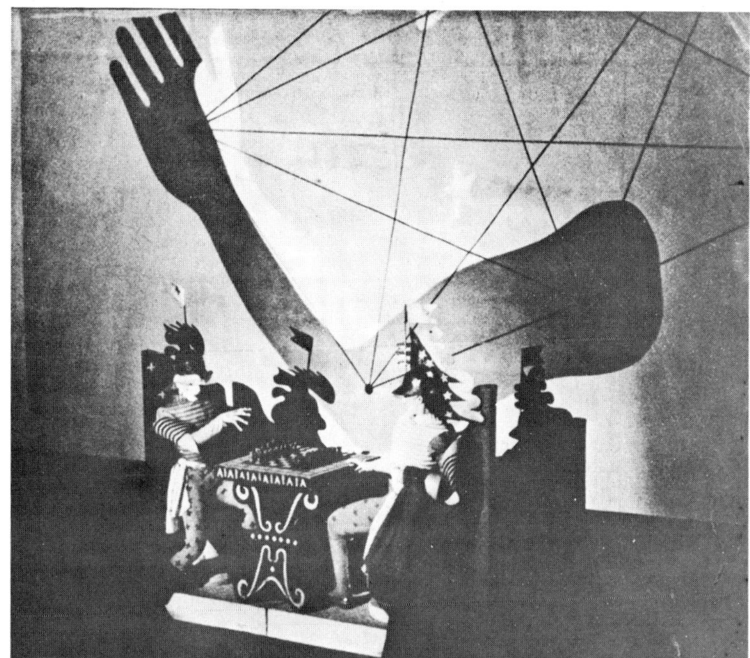

First night of the ballet 'Checkmate' at Sadler's Wells, 1937

BALLET, Chess in the

Chess in the ballet is almost as old as the ballet itself since the chessboard and the pieces with their stylized moves provide both the decor and the steps for dancing.

Thus, for example, a 'Ballet des Echecs' was performed in Paris before Louis XIV, but this, like masques in seventeenth-century England, merely portrayed gorgeously dressed personages who made stately progressions on a chessboard in steps that resembled the moves of the chess-pieces. Such action as there was showed the killing (i.e. capture) of enemy pieces who were identified with enemies of state.

The first ballet which genuinely utilized the game of chess for dramatic symbolism was 'Checkmate' which had its première on 1 June 1937, in the Théâtre des Champs-Elysées as part of the Paris World Exhibition. The choreography was by Ninette de Valois, the costumes and settings were by E. McKnight Kauffer and the book and music were by Arthur Bliss. The Vic-Wells Ballet performed 'Checkmate' as it also did at the English première on 5 October 1937.

Unfortunately, the original settings and costumes were lost when the Vic-Wells Company was touring in the Netherlands during the German invasion in the Second World War in 1940. The ballet was revived with success in 1947, but the new decor and costumes were not so effective as those of the earlier production.

The ballet is a successful one, despite suffering from the usual Ninette de Valois defect of laying too much emphasis on scene and spectacle. It owes much to the powerful dramatic quality of Bliss's music. Bliss was himself a keen chess-player (he opened the 1962 Hastings Chess Congress and made Smyslov's first move for him on that occasion) and the story he composed evolved naturally out of the game itself.

The ballet starts with a Prologue in which two chess-players, personifying Love and Death, are seen playing a game. Love makes a move. Death replies and Love, starting from his seat, falls dead – it is checkmate.

The war dance of the Black Queen

The story that then unfolds itself is principally an attack by the Black Queen on the Red King. On the way the Queen is opposed by the Red Knight and the struggle between these two is one of the most striking parts of the ballet. Eventually the Black Queen triumphs but she disdains to kill the enemy King. Surrounded by enemy pawns, the latter collapses lifeless – this too is checkmate.

At the première June Brae made a most striking Black Queen and Harold Turner a brilliant Red Knight. Robert Helpmann was a fine Black King and Frederick Ashton took the part of one of the chess-players.

Other ballets with chess as a theme have been composed since 'Checkmate' but none have been so successful. *(H.G.)*

BĀNA

A Sanskrit historian of the early seventh century who, in his account of the rule of north-west Indian kings, the *Harshachārita*, gives the second earliest known allusion to chess and supports the evidence of the *Vāsavadattā* as to the origin of chess in the sixth century. *(H.G.)*

BARCZA, Gideon *(b. 21 August 1911)*

Gideon Barcza (left) in play against Bent Larsen, Hastings 1972/3. Standing l. to r. Hort, P. Clarke, Balashov, Wade, Uhlmann.

Hungarian grandmaster and first mathematics teacher and then a director of scholastic studies in Budapest, Barcza was for many years during the late forties and the fifties second only to Laszlo Szabo in Hungary.

His first international performance was a score of 10½/16 (+7−2=7) on sixth board (ten boards were played) at the 1936 Munich Olympiad.

Second in a small tournament at Gablonz in 1938, he played in a number of Hungarian tournaments during the Second World War with good results and was 6th in the Munich so-called European championship of 1942.

After the war he won the Hungarian championship in 1947 and was to win the title five more times, with intervals, from 1949 to 1957.

He also represented Hungary in seven international team tournaments (or Olympiads), 1952, 1954, 1956, 1958, 1960, 1962 and 1968. In this last one he scored 75% on fifth board.

He twice qualified for the Interzonal, at Mariánské Lázně in 1951 where he came =3rd and again at Budapest 1960 where he was 1st. He had little success in the Interzonal tournaments, coming 15th/21 at the Saltsjöbaden Interzonal of 1952 and 14th/23 at the Stockholm Interzonal of 1962.

His best international performances in individual tournaments have been: 2nd at Karlovy Vary and Mariánské Lázně 1948 and likewise 2nd at Venice that year; =4th with Foltys, Gligorić and Golombek at Venice 1949, =2nd at Sczawno Zdroj 1950, =3rd at Moscow in 1962, =3rd at Sombor 1966, =3rd with Taimanov at Leningrad 1967.

He played more rarely and his results noticeably worsened in the 1970s. In 1975 he was 7th/16 at Decin and in that year he was 12th/16 at Brno in the international Czech championship.

Possessor of a dry, almost arid style he was once heard to remark, apropos a dead-drawn looking position: 'My King is better than his'.

He has written a number of books on the game, mostly in collaboration with other authors; his best is probably, written in conjunction with Alfoldy and Kapu, *Die Weltmeister des Schachspiels* (The World Chess Champions), 2 vols., Hamburg 1975, also published in Hungarian in Budapest, 1959. *(H.G.)*

BARCZAY, Laszlo *(b. 21 February 1936)*

Hungarian grandmaster who is variable in his play and his results. His first appearance on the international scene was in 1964 when he came =5th/16 at the Asztalos Memorial tournament at Pecs. In the same year he was =6th at Varna, and he was 7th/12 at Reggio Emilia in 1964/5.

The years in which he broke through to master and grandmastership were 1966 and 1967. At the Havana Olympiad of 1966 he had the remarkable score of 11/12 on bottom board (+10=2) and he gained the international master title the same year. He also came =3rd at Sombor 1966.

It was in 1967 that he became a grandmaster. He came =1st at the Asztalos Memorial tournament at Salgotarjan and was 3rd at the Vrnjačka Banja Zonal tournament of 1967, thereby qualifying for the Interzonal tournament at Sousse. There he did little, coming 17th/22.

He had a number of steadily good performances the next year: =4th at Berlin, 5th at Sarajevo and =4th at Kecskemet tieing with, amongst others, Barcza on that occasion.

In 1969 he was 1st at Polanica Zdroj and 3rd at Lublin. But most of his later results were not of this quality. Again at Polanica Zdroj, in 1974, he was =6th/16. In 1975 at Kecskemet in the 5th Laszlo Toth Memorial tournament he was =7th/14 and in the same year he was =6th/18 in the Hungarian championship. Also in 1975 he came 2nd at Lublin. *(H.G.)*

BARDA, Olaf *(17 August 1909–2 May 1971)*

Norwegian international master and six times Norwegian champion in the period 1930–57. Best known for his postal play in which he attained the rank of grandmaster. He came 4th in the First World Correspondence championship. He played in the Norwegian team at the 1956 Moscow Olympiad. *(R.D.K.)*

BARDELEBEN, Kurt von *(4 March 1861–31 January 1924)*

A German master and theorist. After winning the Vizayanagaram ('Challengers') tournament at the London 1887 congress, he scored no further outright tournament win in a career spanning thirty-five years, but shared first place with Riemann at Leipzig 1888, with Walbrodt at Kiel 1893, and with Schlechter and Swiderski at

Coburg 1904. In the great Hastings 1895 tournament, where he lost one of the most famous games in chess history to Steinitz, he finished equal 7th. In matches he beat Teichmann and Von Gottschall, drew with Blackburne, Caro, and Von Scheve, and lost to Lasker, Walbrodt, Teichmann and Bogoljubow. He wrote various monographs on the openings and collaborated with Mieses on a *Lehrbuch des Schachspiels*. *(W.H.)*

BARDEN, Leonard William *(b. 20 August 1929)*
British master and joint British champion 1954, Barden was born in Croydon and learned to play chess at his school, Whitgift, which became quite a frequent producer of fine players.

In 1946 he tied for first place in the London Boys championship and in the following year he tied with Jonathan Penrose for first place in the British Boys championship, but lost the play-off.

In 1952 he came first at Paignton ahead of the Canadian grandmaster Yanofsky and he reached his peak in 1954 when, after tieing for first place with the Belgian grandmaster O'Kelly de Galway at Bognor, he tied for first place in the British championship at Nottingham with A. Phillips. The play-off was drawn and so the players became joint champions.

He played for the B.C.F. in four Olympiads from 1952 to 1962 and then abandoned competitive chess, applying all his energies to writing (he is chess correspondent of the *Guardian*, the *Financial Times*, the *Evening Standard* and the *Field*, and has written many books on the game).

He also developed two special interests, in junior chess and in grading, working with the utmost persistence and energy in both of these fields.

Amongst his best works are: *A Guide to Chess Openings*, London 1957; *The Ruy Lopez*, Oxford 1963; *The King's Indian Defence*, London 1968. *(H.G.)*

BARENDREGT, Dr Johan *(b. 16 February 1924)*
Dutch international master since 1962. Participated in Dutch championship four times and represented The Netherlands in 1952 Olympiad. Finished 3rd behind Parma and Scafarelli at Hoogoven 1961. Since 1962 Barendregt has lectured in clinical psychology at the University of Amsterdam. *(R.D.K.)*

BARMEN 1905
This German town was the scene in 1905 of a chess festival on a grand scale. Not only were two great tournaments played but there were also a number of festivities with a 'Singspiel', a musical comedy with a chess theme as the *pièce de résistance*.

The tournaments were divided into two categories, the 'A' being reserved for the experienced grandmasters and masters and the 'B' for the promising young players who had not yet won tournaments.

The A tournament was exceedingly strong, containing as it did a number of grandmasters who were either prospective World Championship challengers or players (like Janowski, Marshall, Schlechter and Chigorin) who were of undoubted World Championship standard and had already competed for the title. The tie for first place between the dashing Janowski and the massively sound Maróczy was most fitting. Chigorin was clearly declining and in fact died just over two years later. Mieses did badly but in recompense won the first brilliancy prize. Leading scores: Janowski and Maróczy 10½, Marshall 10, Bernstein and Schlechter 9.

The B tournament witnessed the early appearance of the great gambit player Rudolf Spielmann, and the standard-bearer of the hypermoderns, Aron Nimzowitsch. Neither of these was as yet mature enough to win a major prize. But it was Fleischmann, a Hungarian otherwise known as Forgacs, who carried off the first prize with some ease. Leading scores: Fleischmann 13, Swiderski 12, W. Cohn 11½.

The sparkling violence that earned Mieses the first brilliancy prize was much admired at the time.

White: Mieses; *Black:* Von Bardeleben
French Defence
1. P–K4, P–K3; 2. P–Q4, P–Q4; 3. N–QB3, N–KB3; 4. B–N5, B–K2; 5. B×N, B×B; 6. N–B3, O–O; 7. B–Q3, P–B4; 8. P–K5, P×P; 9. P×B, P×N; 10. BP×P, K×P; 11. P×P, N–B3; 12. N–Q4, P–K4; 13. Q–R5, P×N; 14. Q×RP+, K–B3; 15. Q–R6+, K–K2; 16. O–O, B–K3; 17. QR–N1, R–QN1; 18. P×P, R–KR1; 19. Q–K3, K–Q2; 20. P–KB4, P–B4; 21. KR–Q1, Q–R5; 22. P–KR3, KR–N1; 23. B–K2, R–N6; 24. B–B3, Q×RP; 25. R–K1, B–B2; 26. P–B4, K–B2; 27. P×P, QR–N1;

28. R×P+, K×R;
29. P×N+, K–R1;
30. P–B7+, R×B;
31. Q–K8+, R×Q;
32. R×R+, resigns. *(H.G.)*

BASMAN, Michael *(b. 16 March 1946)*
British National master and the player of whom Botvinnik said, on the occasion of the 1966/7 Hastings, that he was one of the most unusually gifted of all British players and that he reminded him very much of Simagin.

He made a strong impression on British chess by winning a number of junior events. Winner of the 1963 under-21 championship in 1963, he followed this up by scoring 8½/12 on second board in the Sinai Student Olympiad.

He came =3rd at Hastings 1965/6. Playing on top board in 1966/7 at Harrachov, he was part of a team that came 3rd in the World Student competition. By 1970 he had gone to live in Erevan, having dual nationality, and he won the Erevan championship there. In 1973 he was equal first with Hartston in the British championship but lost the play-off. He had another creditable result at Hastings in 1973/4 where he came 10th with 7/15.

He is a pioneer in the production of audio chess tapes. *(H.G.)*

BECKER, Albert *(b. 5 September 1896)*
Becker was a successful Austrian master between the wars (2nd at Vienna 1927, =2nd with Lichtenstein, Spielmann and Tartakower at Vienna 1928, 1st at Vienna 1931, 1932 and 1935, =1st with Eliskases at Linz 1934). He rarely played in great international events, but finished joint 5th with Euwe and Vidmar at Carlsbad 1929. Since the team Olympiad in Buenos Aires 1939 he has lived in the Argentine.

An excellent theoretician and voluminous writer, he has contributed a great deal to the literature of the openings; his collaboration with Grünfeld on the annotations in the famous tournament book of Teplitz–Schönau 1922 has greatly helped to make this volume outstanding. *(W.H.)*

BEDNARSKI, Boguslav Jacek *(b. 12 March 1939)*
Polish international master since 1964 and Polish champion in 1963. Bednarski played for Poland in all Olympiads from 1964 to 1972. Tournament results include: =2nd Zinnowitz 1964, 1st Lublin 1972, =2nd Oslo 1973, 1st Eksjö 1976. *(R.D.K.)*

BELAVIENETZ, Sergei Vsevolodovich *(1910–1941)*
Talented Soviet master and theoretician who was twice champion of Moscow, in 1937 and 1938. His best result was, however, to finish third in the 1939 USSR championship. Belavienetz was killed in battle during the Second World War. *(W.R.H.)*

BELGIUM
Though chess is and always has been popular here, Belgium has produced few great players, a circumstance reflected in the Olympic performance of the country: apart from a sixth place at Dubrovnik 1950, the Belgian team has always finished low down in the list.

The strongest Belgian player was probably Colle, who had good international results in the 1920s. He was assisted and then succeeded by Koltanowski, and when Koltanowski emigrated to the USA O'Kelly de Galway was very much the leading figure and is so to this day.

The golden period for Belgium as far as international tournaments are concerned was in the early 1900s when the series of great Ostend tournaments took place. After these the only international tournament of real importance was Liège 1930, won by Tartakower.

The Royal Belgian Chess Federation was founded in 1920. Its address is Fédération Royale des Echecs de Belgique, c/o Paul Mauquoy, Martelaarslan 447, 9000-Ghent. *(H.G.)*

BELYAVSKY, Alexander Gennrikhovich *(b. 13 April 1951)*
One of the youngest of the Soviet Union's grandmasters, Belyavsky secured the title while still only twenty-one in 1973. He had previously earned the international master title by winning the World Junior Championship at Teesside in 1973. His best results have

been 1st at Sombor 1972, =2nd at Las Palmas 1974 and =1st with Tal in the 1974 USSR championship (having finished bottom the previous year). *(W.R.H. & K.J.O'C.)*

BENI, Alfred *(b. 3 June 1923)*
Austrian international master. Joint Austrian champion in 1947 and many times a member of the Austrian international team at the Olympiads, his best international result was second place at Vienna 1950, behind Paoli. *(W.H.)*

BENKO, Pal *(b. 15 July 1928)*
US international master who is known chiefly for his two performances in Candidates tournaments and for popularizing the 'Benko Gambit' (1. P–Q4, N–KB3; 2. P–QB4, P–B4; 3. P–Q5, P–QN4). He is also an accomplished problem composer and one of the most successful competitors in US Swiss System events.

Although born in Amiens, France, Benko grew up in Hungary where he became one of the best junior players in Eastern Europe after the war. In 1948 he won the Hungarian championship and came =2nd at Bad Gastein. Results of 1st at Lodz and 2nd at Bucharest the following year gave Benko the international master title.

After the Hungarian uprising in 1956 Benko left the country and eventually settled in America. His =3rd at Portorož 1958 made him a grandmaster. In two Candidates tournaments he came 8th in 1959 and 6th in 1962. In the latter event Benko defeated Fischer and Tal in the first week of play with 1. P–KN3, which became known as 'Benko's Opening'.

Benko won invitations to two further Interzonals but came 16th at Amsterdam 1964 and gave up his place to Fischer in 1970, thus paving the way for Bobby's rise to the World Championship. In American events Benko won the US Open in 1961, 1964–7, 1969 and 1974 but his best result in a US Closed championship was =2nd in 1974.

Other results include =4th at Caracas 1970, 2nd at Vršac 1969 and 2nd at Orense 1974. He is the author of *The Benko Gambit*, New York 1974, London 1975. *(A.S.)*

BENKO GAMBIT
1. P–Q4, N–KB3; 2. P–QB4, P–B4; 3. P–Q5, P–QN4!?; 4. P×P, P–QR3; 5. P×P, B×P. A modern counter-gambit introduced by the American grandmaster Pal Benko. Black intends to undermine White's advanced pawn centre and create open files on the Q-side for his major pieces. The absence of immediate tactical threats allows White a certain latitude, but there is no known refutation, and the gambit is probably sound enough to secure Black equality. A typical continuation is: 6. N–QB3, P–KN3; 7. P–K4, B×B; 8. K×B, P–Q3; 9. P–KN3, B–N2; 10. K–N2, O–O when Black has considerable pressure on the Q-side to compensate for the sacrificed pawn.

Black can vary with an early . . , P–K3 (e.g. on move 5 or 6) to produce the Volga Gambit, an inferior system closely related to the Blumenfeld Counter-gambit. *(R.D.K.)*

BENONI DEFENCE
The defence 1. P–Q4, N–KB3; 2. P–QB4, P–B4 first analysed in 1825 by Aaron Reinganum, who coined the name *Ben-Oni* ('Son of Sadness') for it since he used his analytical labours as a refuge from melancholy. The opening was little used in the nineteenth century – two games won by Staunton as White against Saint-Amant are among the few recorded instances – and it was not until the 1930s that it became respectable, largely through the efforts of Alekhine, Spielmann and Tartakower. In its modern form the Benoni is considered a sharp counter-attacking weapon which offers good practical chances.

After White's natural 3. P–Q5 the second player has a choice between 3. . , P–K4 (the Old Benoni – variation A) and 3. . , P–K3 (the Modern Benoni – variation B):

A (1) 3. . , P–K4; 4. N–QB3, P–Q3; 5. P–K4, B–K2; 6. N–B3, O–O; 7. B–K2, N–K1; 8. O–O, N–Q2.

B (2) 3. . , P–K3; 4. N–QB3, P×P; 5. P×P, P–Q3; this is the basic Modern Benoni position. White now has several alternatives, including:

(a) the K-side fianchetto 6. P–KN3, P–KN3; 7. B–N2, B–N2; 8. N–B3, O–O; 9. O–O, Q–K2;

(b) the pawn storm 6. P–K4, P–KN3; 7. P–B4, B–N2; 8. P–K5, KN–Q2;

(c) natural development with 6. P–K4, P–KN3; 7. N–B3, B–N2; 8. B–K2, O–O; 9. O–O, R–K1.

The Modern Benoni abounds in combinative traps and tactical chances and is ideal for those who enjoy complications. *(R.D.K.)*

BERGER, Johann Nepomuk *(11 April 1845–17 October 1933)*
A true polyhistorian of chess, Professor Berger, who was born at Graz, won first prize at the 1870 tournament in his home town, but had only modest international successes in his later tournament career of almost forty years (4th at Nuremberg 1883, joint 5th at Frankfurt 1887, 6th at Barmen 1905). Berger was a great problemist, endgame composer, writer and polemicist. His most famous works are *Theorie und Praxis der Endspiele*, Leipzig 1890 (a revised edition appeared in 1922 and an appendix in 1933) – a classic volume later superseded by the works of Fine and Chéron; *Katechismus des Schachspiels*, Leipzig 1891, and preceding these, *Das Schachproblem und dessen kunstgerechte Darstellung*, Leipzig 1884. It was in the problem field that he fought pitched literary battles with Kohtz. *(W.H.)*

BERLIN ('Berliner Tageblatt') 1928
The grandmaster event organized by the *Berliner Tageblatt* (October 1928) has the unique distinction of being controversial and boring at the same time. Boring because Capablanca was so superior to the tail-enders that he was able to afford a whole string of meaningless draws higher up – and duly availed himself of the opportunity (his four games against Nimzowitsch and Tartakower between them ran to 66 moves!). The tournament was controversial because after Tarrasch dropped out (following defeats by Capablanca, Rubinstein and Tartakower in the first three rounds) the host country was not represented at all. (Leading scores: Capablanca 8½, Nimzowitsch 7, Spielmann 6½, Tartakower 5½.) There was so much ill-feeling that Berlin chess circles almost simultaneously organized a weaker but more interesting rival tournament (with Bogoljubow, Sämisch, Grünfeld, Kostić, P. Johner and the leading Berlin masters), won by Bogoljubow, who a few months earlier had beaten the elite at Bad Kissingen. *(W.H.)*

BERLIN PLEIADES
The name given to a circle of strong Berlin players and analysts meeting in the years between 1836 and 1845. The group comprised Von Bilguer, Bledow, Hanstein, Horwitz, Von der Lasa, Mayet and Schorn. Both the *Handbuch* and the *Deutsche Schachzeitung* owe their existence to the labours of the Berlin Pleiades. *(W.H.)*

BERMUDA
The chess federation of Bermuda is one of FIDE's three youngest members, having joined in 1976 at Haifa where the national team finished 41st in its Olympic debut. Chess is organized by the Bermuda Chess Federation, P.O. Box 1632, Hamilton 5. *(K.J.O'C.)*

BERNSTEIN, Dr Ossip Samoilovich
(2 October 1882–30 November 1962)
Franco-Russian grandmaster and financial lawyer by profession, Bernstein was not, strictly speaking, of Russian origin, since he was born at Zhitomir in the Ukraine, but it was not long before Moscow became his home and remained his base till the Revolution.

Bernstein was remarkable for being able to unite great virtuosity on the chessboard with an equal skill in his legal profession. He faced the frequent turns of fortune that affected him during two World Wars with a calm equanimity and a masterly strength of will that compelled admiration.

He first made his mark in chess by coming 2nd to Chigorin in the All-Russian tournament of 1903 and during the next decade he demonstrated by a consistently fine record that he belonged amongst the upper reaches of the world's grandmasters. An =4th with Marco at Coburg 1904 was followed by an =4th with Schlechter in the great Barmen tournament of 1905.

In 1906 he obtained a doctorate in law at Heidelberg University and in that year he came =1st with Schlechter at Stockholm and 5th in a very strong final Ostend tournament, this tournament having been conducted on a very complicated qualifying group principle.

In 1907 he came =1st with Rubinstein at Ostend but this was the master tournament, not the grandmaster event which was won by Dr Tarrasch who thereby received the title of world tournament champion.

Now, under the pressure of professional work, his tournaments became less frequent. A good 5th at St Petersburg 1909 was followed by a disappointing =8th with Spielmann at San Sebastian 1911. In that year he scored a narrow victory in a match at Warsaw with the Polish grandmaster Winawer by +3−2=1.

In 1912 he came 2nd to Rubinstein at Wilno (now Vilnius), above some names that were to become famous (Alekhine and Nimzowitsch) and in 1914 he came =5th with Rubinstein in the preliminaries of the great St Petersburg tournament of 1914. This meant he failed to qualify for the final but he did beat the World Champion, Dr Em. Lasker.

With the First World War and the Revolution he left Russia for Paris in 1920 where he became a French citizen.

There came a long pause while he occupied himself with professional matters; but in 1932 he made a solid comeback with an =5th with Bogoljubow at Berne. In 1933 he drew a training match with Alekhine in Paris by +1−1=2. In the following year he came =6th with Nimzowitsch at Zürich.

Dr Ossip Bernstein v. Arturo Pomar

Then came a long interval and he resumed playing at the age of sixty-four when he came 2nd in the A section (the stronger section) at the London international tournament of 1946. In that year too he came =15th out of 20 with Guimard at Groningen.

With increasing years his tournament participation became rarer. But he could still play fine chess as he showed by winning a small international tournament at the Mandrake Club in London in 1949. In 1954 at Montevideo, to the whole chess-world's delight, he came =2nd with Najdorf below Letelier, and won a brilliancy against Najdorf. In the same year he scored 50% on top board for France in the Amsterdam Olympiad.

A decline now set in. He came 5th out of 8 in a small international tournament at Ostend in 1956, and though in that year he went to Moscow with the intention of playing for France in the Olympiad, he fell ill before he could play a game. He played unsuccessfully in the I.B.M. tournament at Amsterdam 1961, and died the following year in a sanatorium in the French Pyrenees.

Bernstein's style was both massive and sparkling. Had he been a professional chess-master he might have hoped for world honours. As it was, he remained recognized as one of the strongest amateurs in the history of the game.

A pretty game from his earliest period, played at Vienna in 1904:

White: A. Albin; *Black:* O. Bernstein
Giuoco Pianissimo
1. P–K4, P–K4; 2. N–KB3, N–QB3; 3. B–B4, B–B4; 4. N–B3, P–Q3; 5. P–Q3, N–B3; 6. B–KN5, B–K3; 7. N–Q5, B×N; 8. B×B, P–KR3; 9. B×N+, P×B; 10. B×N, Q×B; 11. P–B3, R–QN1; 12. P–QN4, B–N3; 13. Q–R4, P–Q4; 14. P×P, P–K5;

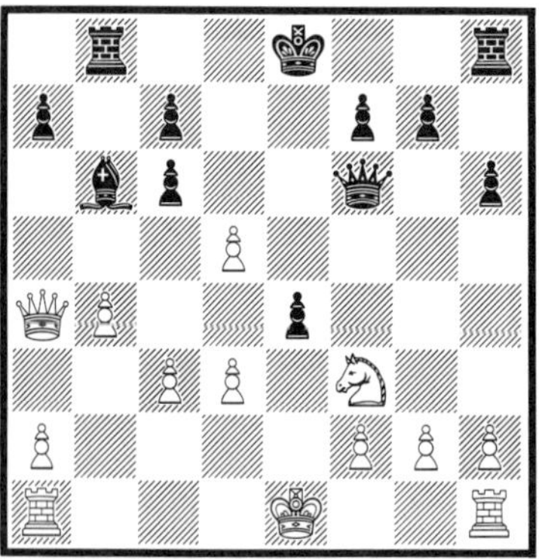

15. P×KP, Q×P+; 16. K–K2, Q–B5+; 17. K–K1, Q×KP+; 18. K–B1, O–O; 19. Q×BP, KR–K1; 20. K–N1, R–K3; 21. Q–Q7, R–Q3; 22. Q–R4, Q–K7; 23. R–KB1, Q×N; 24. P×Q, R–N3 mate. *(H.G.)*

BERTOK, Mario *(b. 2 September 1929)*
Yugoslav international master, chess journalist by profession. He has competed no less than fifteen times in the Yugoslav championship. Bertok won the international master title in 1957 and represented Yugoslavia in the 1960 Olympiad. He also took part in the 1962 Interzonal tournament.

His best tournament result is =9th with Uhlmann and Kovačević at Rovinj-Zagreb 1970, ahead of Walter Browne. *(R.D.K.)*

BEVERWIJK
See under HOOGOVEN CHESS TOURNAMENT.

BHEND, Edwin *(b. 9 September 1931)*
Swiss international master since 1960. Champion of Switzerland in 1966 and a frequent member of the national team in Olympiads and international matches. Author of a book on the King's Gambit. *(W.R.H.)*

BIELICKI, Carlos *(b. 5 May 1940)*
Argentine international master who won the World Junior Championship in 1959, thus gaining the master's title. In recent years

he has withdrawn from active chess, though his appearance in the 1976 Argentinian Metropolitan championship may herald a come-back. *(R.D.K.)*

BILEK, Istvan *(b. 11 August 1932)*

Istvan Bilek in play, Moscow 1967

Hungarian grandmaster since 1962; champion of Hungary in 1963, 1965 and 1970. He qualified for the Interzonal tournaments of 1962 and 1964, but did not perform well on either occasion. He has had a busy international career including shared first places at Balatonfüred 1960, Salgotarjan 1967 and Debrecen 1970. *(W.R.H.)*

BILGUER, Paul Rudolf von
(21 September 1815–16 September 1840)
One of the Berlin Pleiades, Bilguer was a strong player, both over-the-board and blindfold, and an excellent analyst. Originator of the famous *Handbuch* (referred to in Germany as 'der Bilguer') he died in Berlin at the early age of 25 before its publication in 1843. This first edition, as well as the four following, was edited by Bilguer's friend Von der Lasa. *(W.H.)*

BIRD, Henry Edward *(14 July 1830–11 April 1908)*
British amateur but of grandmaster strength. He was born in Portsea, Hampshire and learned to play chess when he was fourteen. Within two years he was a regular patron of Simpson's Divan, an establishment which he continued to frequent until its closure in 1903. By 1850 he was ranked as one of the strongest London amateurs and participated in the London 1851 tournament, losing in the first round to Horwitz. His tournament career continued until 1900 and included firsts in the *New York Clipper* tournament of 1876, Gouda 1879, and the B.C.A. tournament of 1889. In major international competitions he was less successful, although he was among the prize-winners at Vienna 1873, Paris 1878, Nuremberg 1882 and Manchester 1890. In 1866 Bird narrowly lost (+6−7=7) a 20-game match against Steinitz, then fresh from his victory over Anderssen.

Bird was an accountant by profession and the author of a book on railway finance as well as numerous chess writings, including *Chess Masterpieces*, London 1875, *Chess Openings Practically Considered*, London 1877, and *Chess Novelties*, London, New York 1895.

Bird's style was original and combinative. The opening 1. P–KB4 bears his name. He had a fondness for Knights, as the following game well illustrates:

5th Match Game 1866
White: Bird; *Black:* Steinitz
Ruy Lopez
1. P–K4, P–K4; 2. N–KB3, N–QB3; 3. B–N5, N–B3; 4. O–O, N×P; 5. R–K1, N–Q3; 6. B×N, QP×B; 7. P–Q4, P–K5; 8. N–B3, P–KB4; 9. N–K5, B–K3; 10. P–Q5, P×P; 11. N×QP, N–B2; 12. N–KB4, Q–B3; 13. N–B3, B–K2; 14. N–R5, Q–N3; 15. N–Q4, B–Q2; 16. P–QB4, O–O–O; 17. N–B4, Q–Q3; 18. N–Q5, N–K4; 19. Q–N3, KR–K1; 20. B–B4, P–KN4; 21. P–B5, Q–QR3; 22. B×N, B–R5;

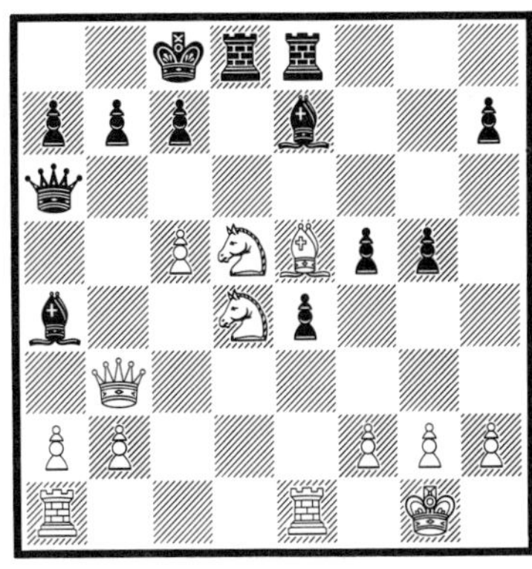

23. N×QBP, B×Q; 24. N×Q, B–B5; 25. N–B7, R–N1; 26. N×P, B–B1; 27. N–Q6+, resigns. *(R.D.K.)*

BIRD'S OPENING

During the latter half of the nineteenth century 1. P–KB4 was popularized by the English master Bird. Its main point is the control of White's K5 and other important central dark squares, but it has some drawbacks. The position after 1. P–KB4, P–Q4; 2. P–K3, N–KB3; 3. N–KB3, B–N5; 4. B–K2, B×N; 5. B×B, QN–Q2; 6. P–B4, P–K3; 7. P×P, P×P; 8. N–B3, P–B3; 9. O–O, B–K2 is even. Black can also essay the From Gambit 1. P–KB4, P–K4; 2. P×P, P–Q3; 3. P×P, P×P with a dangerous initiative for the sacrificed pawn. *(R.D.K.)*

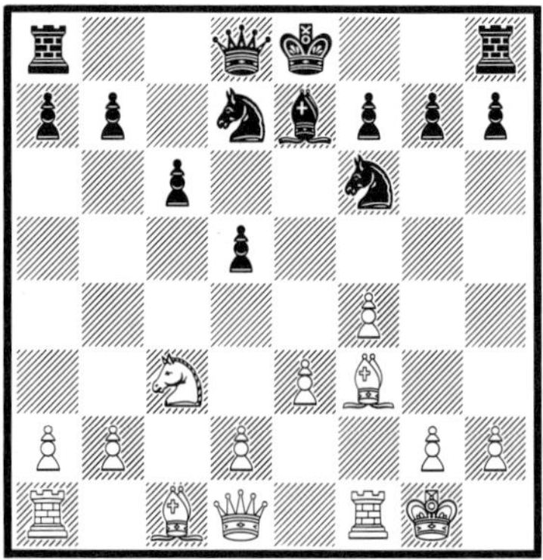

BISGUIER, Arthur B. *(b. 8 October 1929)*

US grandmaster and US champion from 1954–7, Bisguier has been a frequent participant in international events from the early 1950s onwards.

Born in New York, Bisguier was considered the most talented of the young post-Second World War masters who included Evans and the Byrne brothers. In 1948 he won the US Junior championship and came =7th in his first international event held in New York. Two years later at Southsea, England, he took first prize and obtained the international master title.

During the 1950s Bisguier won the US Open three times and won the US Closed championship in 1954. In the 1962/3 Closed tournament Bisguier led most of the way but was edged out by Fischer in a last-round game. Bisguier played in two Interzonals, coming =17th at Göteborg 1955 and 16th at Stockholm 1962.

Bisguier's best results include =2nd at San Juan 1969 and 1st at Lone Pine 1973. He is co-author of *American Chess Masters – from Morphy to Fischer*, New York 1974. *(A.S.)*

BISHOP

In the original game, *chaturanga*, the pieces were the four arms of war and one of them, the elephant, was the predecessor of our modern Bishop. The piece remained an elephant when the game went to Persia when it was called *Pil* and on Caliph Omar defeating the Sassanid ruler of Persia, the piece was called *Fil* or *Al-fil*, meaning 'the elephant'.

In all these cases the elephant had a much more restricted scope than our Bishop and could move only diagonally, leaping across one square.

So it remained when the game came to Europe. Its limited powers too were unaltered but its name and even its character and appearance changed according to which country the game visited.

The Spaniards, who were under the direct influence of the Moors (i.e. the Arabs), retained the word Alfil. The Italians changed it to *Alfiere* meaning 'standard-bearer', and the French changed it to *Aufin*. With the French the change in character was even more startling. Mistaking the dip in the elephant's forehead for a fool's cap they portrayed it as a jester and so to this day it is known as the *Fou* which means 'the fool' in the sense of jester.

In Germanic circles, Germany and the Netherlands, the piece became a 'runner' (*Läufer* in German, *Looper* in Dutch). In countries where the Viking influence was strong the piece had its modern sense of Bishop. The reasons are variously given as the head looking rather like a bishop's mitre, and (perhaps more reasonably) since the piece was on the right hand of the King, as its being a dignitary of the church, i.e. one of the King's principal advisers.

The Bishop still had this limited leaping move of two squares until the end of the fifteenth century when it changed to its present shape and function, travelling diagonally as far as the diagonals stretched and were vacant, but losing the power of leaping.

For present-day rules see LAWS OF CHESS, Articles 3 and 6. *(H.G.)*

BISHOP'S OPENING

Held in high esteem by Philidor and Staunton, the opening 1. P–K4, P–K4; 2. B–B4 nevertheless failed to gain much popularity. In recent times Larsen has had some success, utilizing its surprise value, though theory still considers its [illegible]ategy of a direct attack on the KBP as too naive to give mo[illegible]an equality. *(W.R.H.)*

BIYIASIS, Peter *(b. 19 November 1950)*

Canadian international master; he received the title in 1972 after winning the Toronto Zonal which was also that year's Canadian championship. In 1975 he again won the Canadian championship and Calgary Zonal. He has not made any impact in the two Interzonals in which he has competed, coming 15th at Petropolis 1973 and 17th at Manila 1976. However, he seems certain to become Canada's third grandmaster; he achieved his first grandmaster norm at the 1976 Haifa Olympiad. *(K.J.O'C.)*

BLACKBURNE, Joseph Henry

(10 December 1841–1 September 1924)

British grandmaster and highly successful tournament player who was one of the most prominent masters of the nineteenth century. He did not learn to play chess until the age of nineteen, but his natural gifts soon brought him into the front rank of British players, and in 1868 he abandoned his business interests and adopted chess as a profession.

Blackburne's international tournament career spans an impressive fifty-two years from London 1862 to St Petersburg 1914 – a total of 53 events in which he played 814 games, scoring over 62%. Although he rarely won international events, he generally finished in the top half of the table and his fierce competitive

spirit coupled with his great combinative ability earned him the pleasant nickname of 'the Black Death'. His most notable successes were =1st with Steinitz at Vienna 1873 (Blackburne lost the play-off match), 1st at Berlin 1881 ahead of Paulsen, Schallopp, Chigorin, Winawer and Zukertort, and 2nd to Tarrasch at Manchester 1890.

Blackburne won the B.C.A. championship (see BRITAIN) in 1868 and for many years was ranked as Britain's foremost player. In 1914 – at the age of 72 – he shared first prize at the B.C.F. congress in Chester.

In match play his success was mixed. He defeated Bird in 1888 (+4−1) and Gunsberg in 1881 (+7−4=3) but lost a second match to Gunsberg in 1886 (+2−5=6). He lost to Lasker (+0−6=4) in 1892 and was defeated heavily twice by Steinitz: in 1862/3 (+1−7=2) and in 1876 (+0−7=0), the latter of these matches being for the World Championship.

Blackburne excelled at blindfold play and in simultaneous exhibitions, which provided a major portion of his income. He died in Lewisham, a much respected veteran of eighty-three.

Berlin 1881
White: Blackburne; *Black:* Schwarz
French Defence
1. P–K4, P–K3; 2. P–Q4, P–Q4; 3. N–QB3, N–KB3; 4. P×P, P×P; 5. N–B3, B–Q3; 6. B–Q3, P–B3; 7. O–O, O–O; 8. N–K2, B–KN5; 9. N–N3, Q–B2; 10. B–K3, QN–Q2; 11. Q–Q2, KR–K1; 12. QR–K1, N–K5; 13. Q–B1, QB×N; 14. P×B, N×N; 15. RP×N, B×P; 16. K–N2, B–Q3; 17. R–R1, N–B1; 18. R–R3, P–KN3; 19. QR–R1, QR–Q1; 20. B–KN5, R–Q2; 21. P–QB4, P×P; 22. B×BP, P–KR4; 23. R–R4, P–N4; 24. B–N3, N–K3; 25. B–B6, N–B5+; 26. Q×N, B×Q;

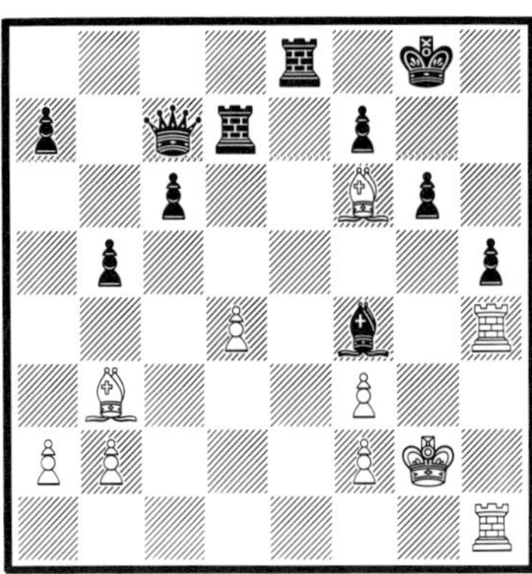

27. R×P, P×R; 28. R×P, resigns. *(R.D.K.)*

BLACKMAR GAMBIT
1. P–Q4, N–KB3; 2. P–KB3, P–Q4; 3. P–K4, P×P; 4. N–B3. This vehement, but not particularly sound gambit, is sometimes known as the Diemer gambit after the German player who has played and analysed it. Black can now either capture the pawn with 4. . , P×P or else develop with 4. . , B–B4. *(H.G.)*

BLAKE, Joseph Henry *(3 February 1859–11 December 1951)*
A leading British player in the 1890s and for many years editor of the Games Section of the British Chess Magazine between the two World Wars. Blake's best tournament performance came at the age of sixty-three when, at Weston-super-Mare in 1922, he came 1st ahead of Maróczy, Kostić, Sir George Thomas and Yates.

The remarkable feature about Blake's chess career is that he retained his skill and his comprehension of the game for a much longer period than most chess-players. This extended from 1887 when he was 1st at the Counties Chess Association tournament at Stamford ahead of Bird and Pollock, a performance he was to repeat in 1891 at Oxford, to 1909 when he tied with H. E. Atkins for first place in the British championship, to 1923 when he won the Weston-super-Mare tournament, right into the 1930s when he was principal annotator for the British Chess Magazine. *(H.G.)*

BLAU, Max *(b. 19 December 1918)*
Swiss international master who gained the title in 1953. He was Swiss champion in 1953, 1955, 1956, 1957 and played in all the Olympiads from 1952 to 1968. Blau's best tournament result was first prize at Lucerne 1949. *(R.D.K.)*

BLED 1931
The longest tournament of the between-the-wars period, Bled (August–September) was at once one of the strongest and best-planned of events. Ten great masters representing the establishment were to meet four of the most promising young players born in the first decade of the century: of the latter only Euwe was absent, of the former Capablanca and Rubinstein. Unlike at San Remo there were no weaker brethren, and even the tail-ender virtually scored what Dr Tarrasch used to call his *Meisterdrittel* (his 'Master Third', i.e. a score of $33\frac{1}{3}\%$). The result was another overwhelming victory for Alekhine, who went through the 26 games without a loss and only allowed Kashdan, Spielmann and (somewhat surprisingly) Asztalos to share the points. Three of the four newcomers succeeded in sharing fourth to seventh prizes with Vidmar. Alekhine's domination was now such that Nimzowitsch complained: 'He is playing with us as though with children' – a complaint readily understandable in view of the following game:

White: Alekhine; *Black:* Nimzowitsch
French Defence
1. P–K4, P–K3; 2. P–Q4, P–Q4; 3. N–QB3, B–N5; 4. N–K2, P×P; 5. P–QR3, B×N+; 6. N×B, P–KB4; 7. P–B3, P×P; 8. Q×P, Q×P; 9. Q–N3, N–KB3; 10. Q×NP, Q–K4+; 11. B–K2, R–N1; 12. Q–R6, R–N3; 13. Q–R4, B–Q2; 14. B–KN5, B–B3; 15. O–O–O, B×P; 16. KR–K1, B–K5; 17. B–R5, N×B;

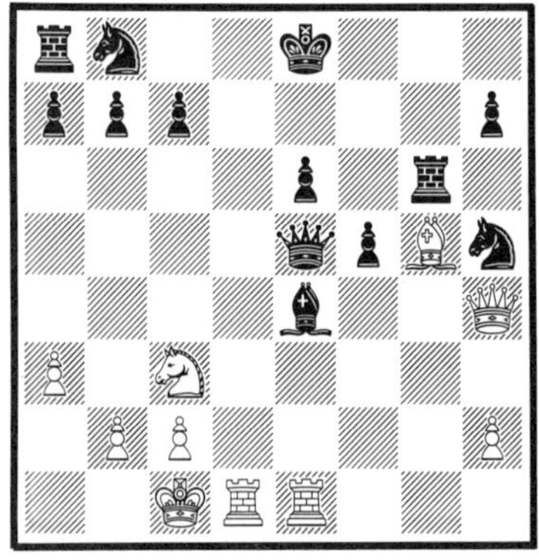

18. R–Q8+, K–B2;
19. Q×N, resigns. *(W.H.)*

BLED 1961
Thirty years after the famous Alekhine victory at Bled (Yugoslavia) a memorial tournament in honour of Alekhine's great victory was held at the same beautiful place by the side of Lake Bled in the Croatian Republic of Yugoslavia. The tournament entry was magnificent, being confined to grandmasters with the exception of some local Croatian players. The USSR sent four of their best players, including Mikhail Tal, newly dispossessed of his world title, and there was much speculation as to how the eighteen-year-old Bobby Fischer would fare against such terrific opposition.

World Championship Candidates tournament Bled, Yugoslavia, 1959

What he intended doing he revealed in the second round when he beat no less a player than Tal himself, and in fact he was to score $3\frac{1}{2}$ points against his four Soviet opponents, of whom only Keres escaped with a draw.

Although he held the lead for the first half of the tournament, he gradually slipped back into second place as Tal, playing like a great World Champion even if one has to add 'ex' to this appellation, won game after game and was especially severe against the weaker players. Though Fischer went through the tournament unbeaten, it was Tal who justly came first, and it was fitting that the World Champion's success in 1931 should be followed by a similar success by the ex-World Champion in 1961. Leading scores: Tal $14\frac{1}{2}$, Fischer $13\frac{1}{2}$, Gligorić, Keres and Petrosian $12\frac{1}{2}$.

Nor should this at all detract from the amazing performance of the eighteen-year-old Fischer. It was after this tournament that Gligorić said 'Bobby is going to be World Champion'. *(H.G.)*

BLEDOW, Ludwig Erdman *(27 July 1795–6 August 1846)*
A professor of mathematics, Bledow was regarded as the strongest Berlin player after the death of Mendheim. He never took part in tournaments but won small matches against Jänisch, Buckle, Aaron Alexandre, Mongredien and Anderssen (+4 −1 =0). He was the guiding spirit of the *Berliner Schachgesellschaft*, as well as the founder of the *Deutsche Schachzeitung*, the first number of which appeared a month before his death. *(W.H.)*

BLIND CHESS OLYMPIADS
See under CHESS OLYMPIADS FOR THE BLIND.

BLINDFOLD CHESS
The practice of playing chess 'blindfold' against one or more opponents is very old, and goes back to the days of Muslim chess in the ninth and tenth centuries, when men spoke in awe of great Arab masters who could play as many as four games blindfold.

Celebrated Chefs Match, at Parsloe's.

Philidor giving a blindfold display

This practice fell into disuse, but was revived by Philidor in the eighteenth century, possibly because he was so far superior to the other players of his time. In 1744, at the age of eighteen, he created a sensation in Paris when he played two players blindfold simultaneously. He continued this practice throughout his career and a letter written by Diderot to him when Philidor was reported to have given a simultaneous blindfold display in London in 1782, warns him against such dangerous experiments.

The practice developed and expanded so that by the late nineteenth century great players were giving displays on as many as twenty boards. Usually players were not blindfolded but sat with their backs to the games and this is the way blindfold displays are conducted nowadays.

Perhaps the best simultaneous blindfold display of all time was given by Pillsbury at Hanover 1902 against twenty-one players of near master strength and another magnificent display was given by Alekhine when he played against twenty-six players at New York in 1924.

A specialist in blindfold play is the American-Belgian master George Koltanowski, who held the record with a display against thirty-four players at Edinburgh in 1937. His talents are such that he has produced many more brilliancies in blindfold play than he has done in sighted play.

Another great blindfold player is the Argentine grandmaster Miguel Najdorf. He established two world records, at Rosario in the Argentine in 1943 against forty players and at Sao Paulo in Brazil in 1947 against forty-five players.

The current world record is held by the Hungarian international master, János Flesch, who, in 1960 at Budapest, played blindfold against fifty-two players with a score of +31−3=18.

A pretty game won by Koltanowski in a blindfold simultaneous display at Antwerp in 1929.

White: Koltanowski; *Black:* Dunkelblum
Max Lange Attack

1. P–K4, P–K4; 2. N–KB3, N–QB3; 3. B–B4, B–B4; 4. O–O, N–B3; 5. P–Q4, P×P; 6. P–K5, P–Q4; 7. P×N, P×B; 8. R–K1+, B–K3; 9. N–N5, Q–Q4; 10. N–QB3, Q–B4; 11. QN–K4, B–QN5; 12. P–QB3, P×P; 13. P×P, B–R4; 14. P–N4, Q–N3; 15. N×B, P×N; 16. P–B7+, K×P; 17. N–N5+, K–N1; 18. R×P, Q–Q6; 19. Q–K1, R–KB1; 20. R–K8, Q–Q2; 21. R×R+, K×R; 22. B–R3+, N–K2; 23. R–Q1, Q×P+; 24. K–B1, Q×N;

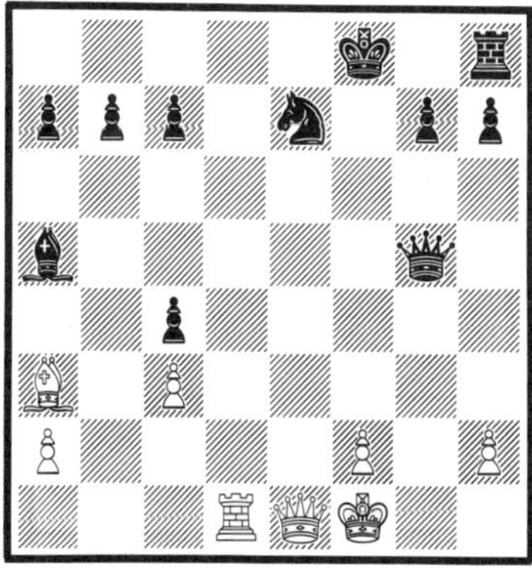

25. R–Q5, Q–R5; 26. R–R5, Q–B3; 27. R–KB5, resigns.

(H.G.)

BLOCKADE

Originally used by Nimzowitsch to designate the mechanical stopping of a hostile pawn by a piece other than a pawn, the term *blockade* to-day has a much wider meaning, referring as it does to the characteristic features of a whole position rather than an individual manoeuvre. A blockade is said to exist where one side is permanently prevented from bringing his pieces into play without loss, regardless of whether the cramping effect is brought about by the opponent's pieces or pawns. In most cases – such as the most economically executed blockade of this game – the two will work together.

Munich Team Tournament 1936
White: Feigin; *Black:* Monticelli
Nimzo-Indian Defence

1. P–Q4, N–KB3; 2. P–QB4, P–K3; 3. N–QB3, B–N5; 4. Q–B2, P–B4; 5. P×P, N–B3; 6. N–B3, B×P; 7. B–N5, N–Q5; 8. N×N, B×N; 9. P–K4, B×N+; 10. Q×B, O–O; 11. P–K5, N-K5; 12. B×Q, N×Q; 13. B–K7, R–K1; 14. B–R3, N–R5; 15. P–QN3, N–N3; 16. B–Q6.

The blockade of Black's game is now complete and White threatens P–QR4–R5.

16.., P–QR4; 17. B–B7, R–R3; 18. P–B5, N–Q4; 19. B×R, N×B; 20. B–B4, P–QN3; 21. P×P, N–R1; 22. O–O–O, N×P; 23. R–Q6, resigns.

(W.H.)

BLUMENFELD, Benjamin Markovich
(24 May 1884–5 March 1947)
One of the best-known Russian opening theorists, Blumenfeld studied law at Berlin and Moscow Universities before turning seriously to chess. Though one of the strongest Moscow players between the wars, he is now best remembered for his theoretical contributions, including the Blumenfeld Counter-gambit. *(W.R.H.)*

BLUMENFELD COUNTER-GAMBIT
After the sequence 1. P–Q4, N–KB3; 2. P–QB4, P–K3; 3. N–KB3, P–B4; 4. P–Q5, 4. . , P–QN4 constitutes the gambit. The intention is to destroy White's centre at the cost of a pawn. The gambit enjoyed a considerable reputation in the 1920s after its celebrated international début, Tarrasch v. Alekhine, Pistyan 1922. However, modern theory considers the line dubious if White declines the offer with 5. B–N5. *(R.D.K.)*

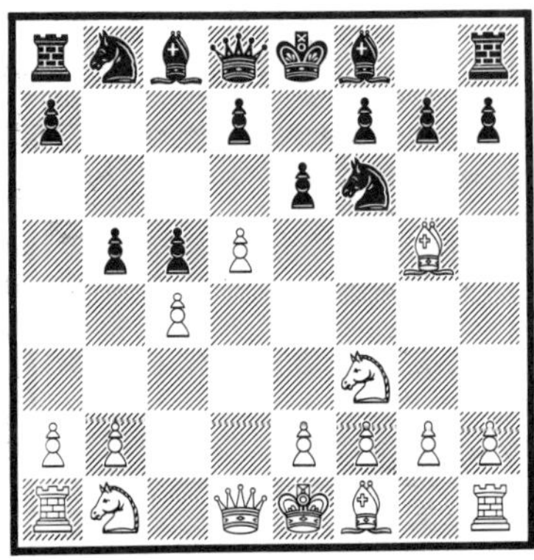

BOBOTSOV, Milko *(b. 30 October 1931)*

Milko Bobotsov in play, Moscow 1967

The first Bulgarian grandmaster, who was awarded the title in 1961. The best result of his career was the sharing of second place in the very strong Alekhine Memorial tournament, Moscow 1967. First places in other events include Varna 1957 and Sarajevo 1971. He suffered a stroke in 1972 since when he has only infrequently competed internationally. Married to woman master Antonia (*née* Ivanova). *(W.R.H.)*

BODEN, Samuel Standidge *(4 April 1826–13 January 1882)*
British master, considered by Morphy to have been the strongest opponent whom he played while in England (Boden's record against Morphy in casual games was +1–6=4). Tournament results include 2nd Manchester 1857 and 2nd Bristol 1861. Chess editor of the *Field* 1858–73. His name is linked with the Boden-Kieseritsky Gambit: 1. P–K4, P–K4; 2. B–B4, N–KB3; 3. N–KB3, N×P; 4. N–B3, N×N; 5. QP×N, P–KB3. *(R.D.K.)*

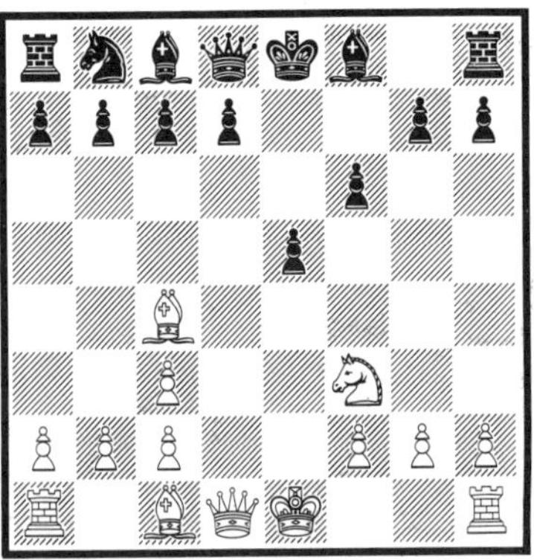

BOGDANOVIĆ, Rajko *(b. 15 November 1931)*
Yugoslav international master (1963). Has competed ten times in Yugoslav championships with mediocre success. For many years the best Bosnian player but internationally relatively unknown. Best result: 8 out of 9 with Bukal, Sarajevo 1970, ahead of Browne and Padevsky. Journalist and radio reporter by profession. *(R.D.K.)*

BOGOLJUBOW DEFENCE
1. P–Q4, N–KB3; 2. P–QB4, P–K3; 3. N–KB3, B–N5+. Otherwise known under the hideous name of Bogo-Indian Defence, this defence often transposes to other openings (Nimzo-Indian, Queen's Indian, Catalan etc.). *(H.G.)*

BOGOLJUBOW, Efim Dmitrievich *(14 April 1889–18 June 1952)*
International grandmaster of Ukrainian birth and, since 1927, German nationality, Bogoljubow was one of the greatest masters of the current century.

After a modest début in the All-Russian championship 1913 and at Mannheim 1914 (8th on both occasions), Bogoljubow, like the other Russian players at Mannheim, was interned at the outbreak of war; he then proceeded to win five of the seven tournaments the interned masters played amongst themselves, and finished second in the other two.

Thus trained, he embarked on his triumphant career of the 1920s, which culminated in his victory at Moscow 1925 where, for the first time, a team of young Soviet masters crossed pawns with an international field comprising Lasker, Capablanca, Marshall, Torre, Tartakower, Réti, Grünfeld, Rubinstein and Spielmann. Other first prizes of major importance were those garnered at Pistyan 1922, Carlsbad 1923 (jointly with Alekhine and Maróczy) and Bad Kissingen 1928. These were supplemented by a string of firsts in less important events: Berlin Four Masters Tournament 1919, Stockholm 1919 and 1920, the Russian championships 1924 and 1925, Breslau 1925, Berlin 1926, Bad Homburg 1927, Berlin

1928. On the strength of this record Bogoljubow challenged Alekhine for the world title in 1929. The match was full of exciting, almost savage chess, but was lost by Bogoljubow +5−11=9. The return match in 1934 differed little in the numerical result (+3−8=15), but showed a distinct falling-off in the ingenuity of Bogoljubow's play.

The two matches between them seem to have sapped Bogoljubow's self-confidence, always his strongest asset. In the years between he scored no significant success, though a number of respectable places in very strong events (4th at San Remo 1930, 2nd at Bled 1931, 4th at Zürich 1934).

After the second Alekhine match, a few first prizes (Bad Nauheim 1935, Stuttgart 1939) alternated with mediocre showings in strong events (6 out of 11 at Zandvoort 1936; 5½ out of 15 at Nottingham 1936, 4½ out of 9 at Noordwijk 1938). In many of the strongest tournaments of this period his name was absent from the lists (Kemeri 1937, Semmering 1937, A.V.R.O. 1938), After the Second World War Bogoljubow no longer belonged to the world élite. Successful in smaller events (Lüneburg 1947, Kassel 1947, Flensburg 1947, the German championship 1949, Oldenburg 1949), he failed to make an impression on the strong fields at such events as Dortmund, Bad Pyrmont and Staunton Memorial 1951 and Belgrade 1952. In matches Bogoljubow beat, among others, Nimzowitsch, Euwe (twice), Ståhlberg, Romanovsky, Rabinovich, Rödv, Kieninger and Grob, but lost – in addition to the two Alekhine matches – to Rubinstein, Spielmann, Euwe, Eliskases and Ahues.

Being primarily interested in the fight over the board, Bogoljubow has left little in the way of a literary legacy: a collection of Chigorin's games, (Leningrad 1925); a poorish book of his own greatest triumph, Moscow 1925; three anthologies of modern games, (Berlin-Leipzig 1926–8); a monograph on the QP opening, (Triberg 1928); and a commentary on the 1934 title match – none of them deep or brilliant. Bogoljubow's wonderful skill in conducting operations on both wings is shown in this game from the 1925 Baden-Baden tournament.

White: Bogoljubow; *Black:* Mieses
Dutch Defence
1. P–Q4, P–KB4; 2. P–KN3, N–KB3; 3. B–N2, P–K3; 4. N–KB3, P–Q4; 5. O–O, B–Q3; 6. P–B4, P–B3; 7. N–B3, QN–Q2; 8. Q–B2, N–K5; 9. K–R1, Q–B3; 10. B–B4, B×B; 11. P×B, Q–R3; 12. P–K3, QN–B3; 13. N–K5, N–Q2; 14. R–KN1, N×KN; 15. QP×N, N×N; 16. P×N, B–Q2; 17. QR–Q1, P–QN4; 18. Q–N2, O–O; 19. Q–R3, KR–Q1; 20. P×NP, P×P; 21. Q–R6, Q–R4;

22. B×P!, P×B; 23. R×P+!, K×R; 24. Q–B6+, K–N1; 25. R–N1+, Q–N5; 26. R×Q+, P×R; 27. P–B5, KR–QB1; 28. P–K6, B–B3; 29. Q–B7+, K–R1; 30. P–B6, R–KN1; 31. Q–B7, QR–QB1; 32. Q–K5, P–Q5+; 33. K–N1, B–Q4; 34. P–B7+, R–N2; 35. Q×B, resigns. *(W.H.)*

BOHATIRCHUK, Feodor *(b. 14 December 1892)*
Born in Kiev and coming to Canada in 1948, Bohatirchuk is a professor of radiological anatomy in Ottawa. Bohatirchuk had a distinguished chess career in Russia and the USSR. He won the Kiev title in 1910 ahead of Bogoljubow. He tied for 3rd in the Russian championships of 1912, 1923 and 1924. Bohatirchuk was 11th at Moscow 1925, ahead of Rubinstein and Spielmann. He came equal first in the USSR championship of 1927 and stood high in those of 1931, 1933 and 1934. In MOSCOW 1935 he was 16th, drawing with Lasker and Capablanca and beating his pupil Botvinnik. Bohatirchuk was 2nd in the 1938 USSR championship. In 144 games in international competitions Bohatirchuk scored +88−18 =38. In 1951 Bohatirchuk came 3rd in the Canadian championship. *(N.D.)*

BOI, Paolo *(1528–98)*
Sixteenth-century Sicilian master, born in Syracuse and hence sometimes known as 'il Siracusano'.

He was a dashing combinative player, known for his quick sight of the board and for his ability to play three blindfold games simultaneously, which astonished his contemporaries.

Itinerant throughout his life, he prospered on the patronage of the nobility. Pope Pius V is said to have offered him a rich benefice if he would consent to taking holy orders. In 1575 Boi visited Spain and defeated the two leading Spanish players, Ruy Lopez and

Ceron, as had his countryman Leonardo da Cutri a few months earlier. For this success, King Philip II rewarded Boi with official appointments in Sicily producing an annual income of 500 crowns and gave him a letter of introduction to his brother, Don John of Austria.

While returning to Italy, Boi was captured by Algerian pirates and sold as a slave, but earned his freedom by making for his master a fortune at chess. His subsequent travels took him to Genoa, Milan, Venice, and even as far as Hungary, where he played games against Turks while mounted on horseback. He died in Naples in 1598 under suspicious circumstances, possibly as a result of poison. *(R.D.K.)*

BOLBOCHAN, Jacobo *(b. 26 December 1906)*
Argentine international master and elder brother of Julio. A strong master who played little abroad, except in Olympiads, and whose results have tended to become confused with those of his brother, partly by reason of their first name commencing with J, and partly because Julio gradually became stronger than Jacobo and therefore was credited with Jacobo's earlier and excellent performances. Most reference books (such as an English and an Italian encyclopedia and a German history of tournaments) have got the two utterly confused.

Jacobo played in three Olympiads, all before the Second World War. At Warsaw 1935 he scored 63.2% on second board; he had a poor result on second board at Stockholm 1937 and on third board at Buenos Aires 1939 he scored 68.4%.

He played in fourteen Mar del Plata tournaments, from 1934 to 1959, with the following results: 1934 =3rd/14; 1936 =7th/16; 1941 13th/18; 1942 4th/18; 1943 9th/14; 1945 8th/16; 1946 =5th/19; 1947 =8th/18; 1948 =10th/18; 1949 =6th/18; 1952 6th/18; 1953 =11th/20; 1956 5th/17; 1959 =11th/15 with Pilnik.

He has made one sortie abroad after the Second World War when he played in a strong international tournament at Tel Aviv 1966 and came =12th out of 16. *(H.G.)*

BOLBOCHAN, Julio *(b. 10 March 1920)*
Argentine international master and younger brother of Jacobo. Practically all his international career stems from the period in the 1940s after the Second World War whereas his elder brother's chess career is nearly all before the war.

Julio played in six Olympiads: at Dubrovnik 1950 he scored 88% on second board, 1952 Helsinki 64.3%; 1954 Amsterdam 76.7%; 1956 Moscow 60% on second board; 1962 Varna 58.8% on second board; in 1966 at Havana he scored 59.4% on third board.

He played in ten Mar del Plata events with increasing success: 1941 9th/18; 1945 =4th/16; 1947 =5th/18 with Euwe; 1950 =4th/18 with Pirc; 1951 =1st with Eliskases, the tournament also being a South American Zonal; 1952 =1st with Rossetto; 1953 3rd; 1956 =1st with Najdorf; 1965 =4th/16; 1966 =5th with Uhlmann.

In his one major international abroad, apart from Interzonals, at Trenčianské Teplice (Czechoslovakia) in 1949, he came =4th with Rossolimo out of 20.

He has had bad luck with his Interzonal tournaments in which ill health has precluded him from demonstrating his great talent. He qualified for three Interzonals. At Saltsjöbaden in 1952 he had to withdraw after playing a few games. Coming second in a South American Zonal tournament in 1961, he did manage to play in the 1962 Interzonal at Stockholm where he came 13th/23. Again he qualified for the Sousse Interzonal in 1967 but here ill health prevented him from playing at all. *(H.G.)*

BOLESLAVSKY, Isaak Yefremovich *(b. 9 June 1919)*
One of the most talented of the Soviet grandmasters, Boleslavsky possesses an understanding of chess strategy admired by many of the world's leading players. Perhaps only a lack of ambition prevented him reaching even higher levels of achievement, though he is still regarded as one of the great chess teachers.

His greatest success was in sharing first place with Bronstein in the Candidates tournament of 1950, but he lost the play-off match thus forfeiting the right to challenge for the World Championship.

Boleslavsky's contributions to opening theory are numerous, the most important being in the development of the King's Indian Defence as a viable system for Black, and the introduction of new ideas in the Sicilian incorporating an early P–K4 for Black.

In recent years Boleslavsky has been playing less, but has written several works on opening theory. As a trainer and analyst he is a frequent companion of Soviet teams competing outside their own country and is also the trainer and second of Tigran Petrosian. It is a commonly-held opinion that Boleslavsky's help in theoretical preparation played a large part in Petrosian's winning the World Championship in 1963.

In his prime, his theoretical knowledge and analytical ability made Boleslavsky a feared opponent; and even in more recent games he has often shown that the ability to attack can survive the passage of years as, for instance, in the following game played in the USSR in 1967.

White: Boleslavsky; *Black:* Dzhindzhihashvili
Queen's Gambit Accepted
1. P–Q4, P–Q4; 2. P–QB4, P×P; 3. N–KB3, N–KB3; 4. P–K3, P–K3; 5. B×P, P–B4; 6. O–O, P–QR3; 7. N–B3, P–QN4; 8. B–N3, B–N2; 9. Q–K2, QN–Q2; 10. R–Q1, Q–N1; 11. P–Q5, P×P; 12. N×QP, N×N; 13. B×N, B×B; 14. R×B, Q–N2; 15. P–K4, B–K2; 16. B–N5, N–N3; 17. QR–Q1, P–R3; 18. B×B, N×R; 19. B×P, N–K2; 20. N–K5, R–QB1; 21. R–Q7, R–B2;

22. R–Q8+!, K×R; 23. N×P+, K–Q2; 24. Q–N4+, K–B3; 25. Q–K6+, resigns. *(W.R.H.)*

BOLIVIA
Though a team representing Bolivia has competed in six Olympiads, no tournament of any significance has been held in this country. Bolivia's Olympiad results have been: 25th in 1939, 36th in 1960, 45th in 1964 and 1966, 46th in 1972 and 40th in 1976. The federation's address is: Federaçion Boliviana de Ajedrez, c/o Carlos L. Merida Bello, Presidente, Casilla 2626, La Paz. *(K.J.O'C)*

BONCH-OSMOLOVSKY, Mikhail Aleksandrovich *(1919–1975)*
Soviet chess-master. Active in Moscow circles in the late 1940s and in the 1950s, Bonch-Osmolovsky had his best results in the Moscow championship tournaments (=5th 1949, =3rd 1960). He obtained the Soviet national master title in 1951, but never succeeded in qualifying for the finals of the USSR championship (best results in qualifying tournaments =7th in the 19th Semi-final and 7th in the 20th Semi-final). As a player he achieved some distinction by his contributions to opening theory but he was better known in organizing circles, being a Soviet chess judge and president of the central chess section of the Burivyestnik Club. *(H.G.)*

BONDAREVSKY, Igor Zakharovich *(b. 12 May 1913)*

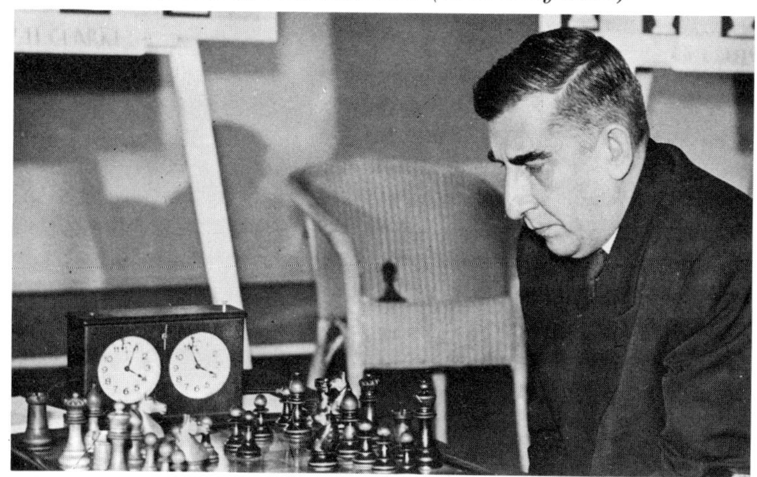

International grandmaster, correspondence chess grandmaster and International Judge, Bondarevsky is clearly a man who believes in spreading his considerable talents. Besides this impressive collection of titles, he was Spassky's trainer at the time the latter won the World Championship, and his wife, Kozlovskaya, is one of the world's leading women players.

His own results include sharing first place in the 1940 USSR championship ahead of Smyslov, Keres and Botvinnik. In 1948 he qualified from the Interzonal tournament for the Candidates of 1950, but illness prevented him from playing in that event.

Bondarevsky contributed significantly to opening theory, particularly in the French Defence and Queen's Gambit Declined. Publications include a monograph on *Combinations in the Middlegame* (1960).

As is true of other players of his generation, Bondarevsky might well have been a serious challenger for the World Championship had not war intervened just as he was reaching his peak. *(W.R.H.)*

BÖÖK, Eero *(b. 9 February 1910)*
Finnish international master and engineer by profession, Böök, though an amateur all his life, was professional in his outlook on the game and was an outstanding opening theorist who represented his country with considerable effect in six Olympiads, from 1935 to 1960.

The real start of his international career was in 1935. In that year he came =1st with Spielmann in a tournament at Helsinki and had an excellent result on top board in the Warsaw Olympiad, scoring 61% and coming third among top boards, below Alekhine and Keres. Two further good results on top board, at Munich 1936 and Stockholm 1937, were followed by an =11th out of 18 at the very strong Kemeri tournament in 1937.

He came =4th at Margate 1938 and enjoyed another success at the powerful Kemeri-Riga tournament of 1939 with a 5th place out of 16 ahead of Bogoljubow and Petrov.

After the Second World War he scored a fine =1st with Stoltz in the North European Zonal tournament at Helsinki, 1947, qualifying for the Interzonal at Saltsjöbaden 1948 where he had a creditable =11th with Gligorić and Pirc out of 20.

He played in the Olympiads at Dubrovnik 1950 and Helsinki 1952, but then the increasing duties of his profession caused him to abandon international chess for some time. He did indeed make a small come-back in the late 1950s, playing in two more Olympiads in 1958 and 1960 and some national and small international events. But the really important stage of his international career was at an end.

He has also written much on chess, mostly in Finnish, publishing a collection of his games in Helsinki in 1945, and, in Swedish, a book on Gösta Stoltz in Stockholm 1947.

Böök first won the Finnish championship in 1930 and then from 1934 to 1936 and in 1946 and 1963. *(H.G.)*

BORISENKO, Georgi Konstantinovich *(b. 1922)*
Soviet master and international correspondence chess grandmaster after taking second place in the 4th World Correspondence championship which finished in 1965. Played frequently in USSR championship but never finished better than 12th.

Married to woman master Valentina Borisenko (*née* Belova). *(W.R.H.)*

BORISENKO, Valentina Mikhailovna *(b. 28 January 1920)*
Born Valentina Belova, Borisenko became one of the strongest women players in the world after the Second World War. Five times USSR Woman champion, her best result was sharing third place in the World Championship tournament of 1949/50. *(W.R.H.)*

BOTTERILL, George Steven *(b. 8 January 1949)*
British national master and British champion 1974, Botterill, who was born in Bradford, learned chess at the age of seven.

He played for Oxford University in the years 1969–72 and by now was becoming one of Britain's leading younger players. In 1971 he came first in the Slater Young Masters tournament at

Hastings and over the turn of the year, at Hastings 1971/2, he came highest of the British competitors with 6/15.

In 1974 he figured in a seven-way tie in the British championship at Clacton and in the play-off at Llanelli in Wales at the end of the year he came first, half a point ahead of and beating Hartston, thereby winning the title.

In that year he took up an appointment as lecturer in philosophy at the University of Wales at Aberystwyth and threw in his lot with Wales from the international point of view. Playing on top board in the Preliminary Group of the European championship he scored $1\frac{1}{2}-\frac{1}{2}$ against the Dutch international grandmaster, Jan Timman, and 1–1 against the English top board, international master Hartston.

As a player he is well equipped in opening theory, has a flair for a fine combination and can always be guaranteed to produce interesting chess.

He has written books on his favourite lines of play and is known in particular for his collaboration with Raymond Keene in the production of *The Modern Defence*, London 1973, and *The Pirc Defence*, London 1974. *(H.G.)*

BOTVINNIK, Mikhail Moiseyevich *(b. 17 August 1911)*

World Champion 1948–57, 1958–60, 1961–3. Born near St Petersburg, Botvinnik became the first Soviet (as distinct from Russian) master to achieve world predominance. In his training methods and general attitude to the game, he epitomized the ideals of the emergent Soviet school.

Botvinnik learned to play chess in 1923 at the age of twelve and within three years had become one of the strongest players in Leningrad. In 1927 he was invited to fill a last-minute vacancy in the 5th USSR championship in Moscow, finishing =5th and gaining the title of master. After studies at the Leningrad Polytechnic Institute Botvinnik graduated in electrical engineering in 1931. In the same year he won the 7th USSR championship, the first of seven victories in the national championship (1931, 1933, 1939, 1941, 1944, 1945 and 1952).

During the next few years the isolationism of Soviet chess gradually diminished: top foreign masters were invited to Soviet tournaments and Soviet players were allowed to compete abroad. Botvinnik was one of the first to benefit and to gain international recognition. He drew a match with Flohr (+2−2=6) in 1933 and in 1934 won a tournament for Leningrad masters in which Euwe and Kmoch also participated. After a relative failure on his first venture abroad – Hastings 1934/5 where he finished only =5th – a string of successes soon established him as a grandmaster of world class: =1st Moscow 1935 (equal with Flohr, ahead of Lasker, Capablanca and Spielmann), 2nd Moscow 1936 (behind Capablanca), =1st Nottingham 1936 (tied with Capablanca, ahead of Euwe, Fine, Reshevsky, Alekhine, Lasker, Flohr, etc.). The Nottingham result made Botvinnik a national hero – in chess at least Soviet revolutionary society had caught up with and surpassed the West! In a curious victory telegram printed in *Pravda* two days after the event ended, Botvinnik cabled his thanks to the whole nation, the party and to Stalin, the 'beloved teacher and leader', for their support.

In the important A.V.R.O. 1938 tournament Botvinnik managed only third prize, a point behind Keres and Fine. Nevertheless, by his victories in individual games over Alekhine and Capablanca, he strengthened his claim to be considered as a World Championship candidate. Botvinnik won the 11th USSR championship in 1939 but in the 12th of 1940 slipped back into shared fifth place equal with Boleslavsky behind Bondarevsky and Lilienthal (=1st), Smyslov and Keres. Instead of the expected play off match between the joint winners, the Chess Committee decided to stage an Absolute Championship between the top six players. Given a second chance, Botvinnik reasserted his supremacy and won by a margin of $1\frac{1}{2}$ points.

During the war years Botvinnik worked as an electrical engineer at power plants in the Urals and in the Molotov High-tension Laboratory. From 1943 onwards he was given some time off to play chess and he won both the wartime national championships, the 13th in 1944 and the 14th in 1945. When peace returned, Botvinnik emerged as victor in the first important post-war tournament, Groningen 1946.

The death of Alekhine left vacant the World Championship, and in 1948 FIDE staged a match-tournament for the title among the five leading contenders: Botvinnik, Smyslov, Keres, Reshevsky and Euwe. (Fine was also invited but did not participate.) Botvinnik finished as a clear winner, 3 points ahead of Smyslov, his nearest rival.

Winning the World Championship seemed temporarily to sate Botvinnik's chess ambitions. He returned to his engineering studies and obtained a doctorate in 1951. He played almost no serious chess until his first defence of the world title in 1951 against Bronstein which ended in a drawn match (+5−5=14), the Champion retaining his title. From 1951–4 he played more regularly, but without the success which normally attends the World Champion. His one notable achievement in this period was victory in the 20th USSR championship 1952 after a play-off match with Taimanov. In the 1954 contest Botvinnik faced Smyslov and history repeated itself – another drawn match (+7—7=10) allowed Botvinnik to keep the title for a further three years.

In 1955 Botvinnik played in his last Soviet championship, the 23rd, finishing =3rd behind Geller and Smyslov. The next year saw him share 1st prize with Smyslov in the powerful Alekhine Memorial tournament. Finally in 1957 he was dethroned, losing the World title to Smyslov +3—6=13. His play may then have been affected by his wife's illness, for in the following year he claimed the ex-Champion's right to a return match and regained the throne by +7—5=11.

A similar experience awaited him in 1960 when he lost the World Championship again, this time to TAL (+2—6=13) only to get it back in 1961 in the return match +10—5=6. Finally in 1963 he surrendered the World title for the third time: to Petrosian +2—5=15. This time the loss was permanent, for by a new FIDE ruling Botvinnik was no longer entitled to a return encounter and he felt disinclined to attempt to qualify through the 1965 Candidates matches. Throughout his tenure of the Championship, Botvinnik was never a truly dominating force – rather he was 'first among equals'. It would be fair to say that the chess-world grew up around him; games became much harder to win as opening theory and positional technique improved and the differences in strength among the leading players (especially in the Soviet Union) became very slight.

With the World Championship a thing of the past, Botvinnik continued to obtain good results in Olympiads, Soviet team events and tournaments, including 1st Hastings 1966/7, =2nd Palma 1967, 2nd Monte Carlo 1968 and =1st Hoogoven 1969. In 1970 he announced his retirement from active play. At present he is part of a team of Soviet scientists working on a computer chess program.

Botvinnik (left) v. Smyslov, Moscow 1954. Behind (left) Chief Arbiter Opocensky and Assistant Golombek

Part of the secret of Botvinnik's genius was his immense capacity for hard work. Every game he played was subjected afterwards to intensive analysis and he proved to be his own most severe critic, without a trace of self-deception. He was the first to suggest that tournament preparation should include physical as well as mental exercises.

He disliked tobacco and, feeling that he was sometimes distracted by opponents who smoked, acquired immunity by requesting his trainer, Ragozin, to smoke constantly during training games!

One of the best games of the great 1954 match (the 12th game):

White: Botvinnik; *Black:* Smyslov
Queen's Gambit Declined, Slav Defence
1. P–Q4, P Q4; 2. P QB4, P–QB3; 3. N–KB3, N–B3; 4. N–B3, P×P; 5. P–QR4, B–B4; 6. P–K3, P–K3; 7. B×P, B–QN5; 8. O–O, QN–Q2; 9. N–R4, O–O; 10. P–B3, B–N3; 11. P–K4, P–K4; 12. N×B, RP×N; 13. B–K3, Q–K2; 14. Q–K2, P×P; 15. B×P, B–B4; 16. B×B, Q×B+; 17. K–R1, P–KN4; 18. P–KN3, QR–Q1; 19. B–R2, KR–K1; 20. QR–Q1, N–B1; 21. R×R, R×R; 22. P–K5, N–Q4; 23. N×N, P×N; 24. Q–Q2, N–K3; 25. P–B4, P×P; 26. P×P, Q–B3; 27. P–B5, N–B4; 28. Q–N5, R–Q2; 29. R–KN1, P–B3; 30. P×P, N–K5; 31. P–B7+, R×P; 32. Q–Q8+, K–R2;

33. B×P, N–B7+; 34. K–N2, Q–B3; 35. Q×Q, R×Q; 36. K×N, R×P+; 37. B–B3, R–B5; 38. R–N4, resigns.
(R.D.K.)

BOUWMEESTER, Hans *(b. 16 September 1929)*
Dutch international master (1954). Best results: 1st (with Pirc) at Beverwijk 1954; =3rd at Beverwijk 1958. In 1957 and 1967 he was 2nd in the Dutch championship. He played in the Olympiads of 1956, 1960, 1962, 1964, 1966, 1968, 1970 and was non-playing captain of the Dutch team in 1972.

Though not very active in tournaments, Bouwmeester plays an important part in Dutch chess life; he was appointed first official coach of the Royal Dutch Chess Federation. He has written a book on efficient chess training.

Editor of *Losbladige Schaakberichten* from 1956 till 1968. His publications include *Mikhail Tal* and various books on chess from the pedagogic point of view. *(R.D.K.)*

BRAZIL
Chess in Brazil has always suffered from the vast distances which have to be covered in that immense country. However, there always has been quite a strong interest in the game there, particularly in Rio de Janeiro. In the 1930s a number of European masters made tours in Brazil, notably Alekhine, Tartakower and Réti.

Brazil has frequently sent teams to play in the Olympiads. Its first was to the 1936 Munich Olympiad (the one that was played without the auspices of FIDE) where it came 16th/21. It had a good result at the 1939 Buenos Aires Olympiad where it qualified for the top final section, coming 4th (below England but above Canada) in its preliminary group. Its final position overall was 14th, the best it has ever done in an Olympiad. On that occasion its players were (in board order): Trompowsky, Silva Rocha, Walter Cruz, Souza Mendes and Oswaldo Cruz.

At Helsinki 1952 it came 19th/25; at Lugano 1968 25th/52 with Mecking scoring 67.6% on top board; at Siegen 1970 27th/60; Skopje 1972 36th/62 and Nice 1974 35th/74.

Brazil's one great player has been Henrique Mecking, who came to the fore in the late 1960s. Appropriately, when an Interzonal tournament was held in Petropolis in Brazil in 1973, Mecking came first.

The organizing body in Brazil is the Confederaçao Brasileira de Xadrez, 101 Avenida Passos, Sala 309, Rio de Janeiro 20.000 and its journal is the *Boletim Informativo da C.B.X.* (*H.G.*)

BREAKTHROUGH

A combination involving multiple pawn sacrifices. It can occur (a) in the middle-game for the purpose of clearing the path for the free interplay of pieces hemmed in by the sacrificed pawns, or (b) in the endgame in order to queen a pawn.

(a): Alekhine–Johner, Zürich 1934. White continued with 1. P–K5, QP × P *(if 1.., BP × P; 2. P–B6+, Q × P; 3. Q × P+, followed by B–K4)*, 2. P–Q6, P–QB4; *(if 2.., P × P, 3. P–B5)* 3. B–K4, Q–Q2; 4. Q–R6, resigns.

(b): Lund–Nimzowitsch, Kristiania 1921. Black played: 1.., P–N5; 2. P × P, R × N; 3. P × R, P–N6; 4. P × P, P–B6+; 5. P × P, P–R6; resigns. (*W.H.*)

'BRENTANO'S CHESS MONTHLY'

An opulently produced magazine published in New York for only sixteen months in 1881–1882. Its predecessor was a column in *Brentano's Monthly*, a literary magazine, the style of which was retained in its chess counterpart. (*K.J.O'C.*)

BREVITY [Miniature]

A short game not exceeding some twenty-odd moves and usually not a draw. The most celebrated is probably the following between the great Paul Morphy and the Duke of Brunswick in consultation with Count Isouard, played in a box at the Paris Opera during a performance of *The Barber of Seville* in 1858.

White: Morphy; *Black*: Allies
Philidor Defence
1. P–K4, P–K4; 2. N–KB3, P–Q3; 3. P–Q4, B–N5; 4. P × P, B × N; 5. Q × B, P × P; 6. B–QB4, N–KB3; 7. Q–QN3, Q–K2; 8. N–B3, P–B3; 9. B–KN5, P–N4; 10. N × P, P × N; 11. B × NP+, QN–Q2; 12. O–O–O, R–Q1; 13. R × N, R × R; 14. R–Q1, Q–K3; 15. B × R+, N × B;

16. Q–N8+, N × Q;
17. R–Q8 mate.

Shorter still is the following brevity played in Paris 1924.

White: Gibaud; *Black*: Lazard
Queen's Pawn Opening
1. P–Q4, N–KB3; 2. N–Q2, P–K4; 3. P × P, N–N5; 4. P–KR3, N–K6!; 5. resigns. (*H.G.*)

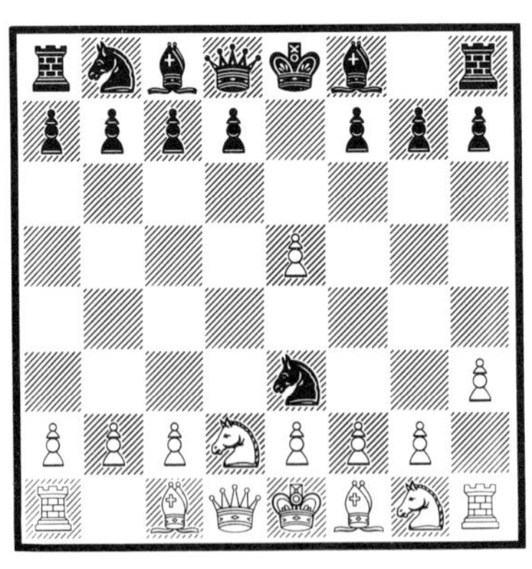

BREYER, Gyula [**Julius**] *(3 April 1894–10 November 1921)* Hungarian master and pioneering leader of the hypermoderns.

It can be said of some chess-masters that their play has left a more lasting impression than their results, and this was the case with Breyer. Born in Budapest, his first foray into international chess came at Cologne 1911, when he took sixth prize (out of sixteen) in a medium-strength event.

Soon after this a marked improvement became apparent when he won outright at Temesvar 1912, ahead of such players as Asztalos, Von Balla, Havasi and Réti. Yet in terms of practical playing strength Breyer never advanced much beyond this stage, normally finishing in the middle of the field in his events over the following eight years. A definite breakthrough seemed imminent when he scored a major success at Berlin 1920. This was a very strong grandmaster tournament which Breyer won in decisive fashion ahead of Bogoljubow, Tartakower, Réti, Maróczy, Mieses, Tarrasch, Sämisch, Leonhardt and Spielmann; yet the fruits of his success were never to materialize, for Breyer died one year later at Bratislava without being able to participate in another event of a similar calibre. Truly a lost talent.

For most of his brief life Breyer was fascinated by intellectual problems of all kinds which possibly explains his interest in chess. It was indeed in the sphere of ideas that Breyer left his greatest mark and he was considered a leading member of the 'Hyper-Modern school' (which included Réti and Nimzowitsch) which challenged the fixed notions of chess strategy advocated by classical masters such as Tarrasch, Teichmann and Rubinstein. Many of Breyer's games leave a mysterious, paradoxical impression – masterpieces imbued with rich and strange hues which make one wonder what he could have achieved had he survived beyond his twenty-seventh year.

Breyer also made important contributions to opening theory. The most popular variation of the modern Ruy Lopez is named after him, although nobody is very sure when or where he advocated Black's paradoxical ninth move: 1. P–K4, P–K4; 2. N–KB3, N–QB3; 3. B–N5, P–QR3; 4. B–R4, N–B3; 5. O–O, P–QN4; 6. B–N3, B–K2; 7. R–K1, P–Q3; 8. P–B3, O–O; 9. P–KR3, N–N1.

The idea of Black's Knight retreat is to redeploy the piece to Q2, bolstering his pawn on K4. For detailed analysis of the line, see *Ruy Lopez: Breyer System* by L. S. Blackstock, London 1976.

A notable example of Breyer's play:

Budapest 1917
White: Breyer; *Black:* Esser
Queen's Gambit Declined, Semi-Slav Defence
1. P–Q4, P–Q4; 2. P–QB4, P–K3; 3. N–QB3, P–QB3; 4. P–K3, N–B3; 5. B–Q3, B–Q3; 6. P–B4, O–O; 7. N–B3, P×P; 8. B–N1, P–QN4; 9. P–K4, B–K2; 10. N–N5, P–KR3; 11. P–KR4, P–N3; 12. P–K5, P×N; 13. RP×P, N–Q4; 14. K–B1, N×N; 15. P×N, B–N2; 16. Q–N4, K–N2;

17. R–R7+, K×R; 18. Q–R5+, K–N2; 19. Q–R6+, K–N1; 20. B×P, P×B; 21. Q×P+, K–R1; 22. Q–R6+, K–N1; 23. P–N6, R–B2; 24. P×R+, K×P; 25. Q–R5+, K–N2; 26. P–B5, P×P; 27. B–R6+, K–R2; 28. B–B4+, K–N2; 29. Q–R6+, K–N1; 30. Q–N6+, K–R1; 31. K–K2, B–R5; 32. R–R1 and wins.

(R.D.K.)

BRILLIANCY PRIZE

A brilliancy or 'beauty' (German: *Schönheitspreis*) prize is a special award for a particularly brilliant (or beautiful) game.

While many tournaments are run without any such awards, others feature a large number (as e.g. TEPLITZ-SCHÖNAU 1922, which had seven brilliancy prizes). These awards have often been the subject of violent controversy. Thus at New York 1927 the winners of the second and third brilliancy prizes both considered they should have been awarded the first (which went to Capablanca for his win against Spielmann). Alekhine commented on his game against Marshall: 'This game was declared by the umpire to be the most beautiful of the tournament, but nevertheless it received only the second special prize because the "quality" of the Capablanca game was supposed to be higher', while Nimzowitsch, commenting on his 23rd move against Marshall in *My System*, said: 'This move contains an original point which the prize judges probably failed to appreciate; otherwise they would have awarded this game the first beauty prize rather than the third'.

Even more cutting was Tarrasch's verdict on the awards at St Petersburg 1914 in the tournament book concerning his game against Nimzowitsch: 'This game was awarded the second brilliancy prize whereas the first went to Capablanca v. Bernstein. I do not permit myself one word of criticism in this book but confine myself to exposing the names of the prize judges to the judgment of the present and future generations: they were Messrs. Burn, Pollner and Znosko-Borovsky'.

Nothing, however, can match Tartakower's sarcasm in the final note on his game against Maróczy (see TEPLITZ-SCHÖNAU 1922) from his volume *My Best Games of Chess 1905–1930*: 'The judges awarded this game the third brilliancy prize, although a majority of them declared in peremptory fashion that such sacrifices are incalculable in advance in all their ramifications and that, in consequence, they deserve no encouragement'. *(W.H.)*

BRINCK-CLAUSSEN, Björn *(b. 1942)*
Danish master, played in the Hastings Premier tournament in 1963/4, having won the Challengers tournament the previous year. Also winner of the Northern Open at Whitby 1965. *(W.R.H.)*

BRINCKMANN, Alfred *(3 January 1891–30 May 1967)*
A German international master and arbiter. With the exception of Berlin 1927, where he finished ahead of Bogoljubow, Nimzowitsch and Sämisch in first place, his tournament results were modest; but he made a name for himself as a chess writer. A brilliant stylist, he introduced important literary and philosophical subjects into his books, such as *Schachmeister*, *Wie Sie Kämpfen Und Siegen* and *Der Angriff in der Schachpartie*, as well as the tournament books of Bad Niendorf 1927, Rogaska Slatina 1929 and Aachen 1934. He also wrote biographical works on Bogoljubow, Richter and Tarrasch, while a selection from his writings, *Streifzüge und Irrtümer auf 64 Feldern*, appeared in the year of his death. *(W.H.)*

BRITAIN
It is usually held that chess came to Britain with the Norman Conquest, but this is, to put it moderately, an over-simplification of what occurred. For one thing it is quite clear that there was trade and cultural intercourse between the continent of Europe (in particular France and what were later known as the Low Countries) and Britain for many years before the Norman Conquest.

Next, and perhaps still more important, the Vikings also came to Britain hundreds of years earlier and they were one of the greatest carriers of the game of chess throughout the world. One has only to think of the Isle of Lewis chessmen, coming in all probability from Iceland in the eleventh century (and therefore from a country that was first populated by the Vikings); and of course King Canute (Knut), who was ruler of both Denmark and England, and is supposed to have learned how to play chess on a pilgrimage to Rome in the year 1027.

It is however true that a vast impetus to the spreading of chess in the country was provided by the Conquest. The Norman Kings all seem to have played the game to varying degrees. King John, for example, in typical fashion, used it as an excuse for failing to relieve the siege of Rouen and Edward I very nearly had his reign cut short by a fall of rock onto the very place he had just left when playing a game of chess.

Chess became popular at court and it was fashionable for courtiers to play it. Monks, too, it seemed, were inclined to play it overmuch for the good of their souls and there came stern pronouncements from the high ecclesiastical authorities that the game should not be indulged in by holy men. But it is very apparent from the writings of the monks that they either ignored such pronouncements or else paid mere lip-service to them.

The title page from a 17th century play by Saul: 'Famous game of chesse-play'

Under the influence of the court, the game then spread to the nobility and to the learned. But no further for hundreds of years. It became more popular in the sixteenth and seventeenth centuries when the middle classes made their appearance. Elizabethan and Jacobean plays are full of references to chess and there was even a play called *Game at Chess* by Thomas Middleton in 1624. The Prologue sets the scene:

'What of the game, call'd Chess-play, can be made
To make a Stage-play, shall this day be plaid.
First, you shall see the men in order set,
States, and their Pawnes, when both the sides are met.'

It was not long after this play was produced that the great Italian master Gioachino Greco visited England in 1622 and played against all the leading players in London. His game collections show that he played against Sir Francis Godolphin and Nicholas Mountstephen who were amongst the best English players. This was part of a grand *tournée* that Greco made and from which he had acquired a small fortune, only to lose it all to English robbers on his travels in England.

By the end of the seventeenth century, when coffee-houses had come into vogue and when in consequence men could get together and play chess, London had become a centre for chess. In the eighteenth century Slaughter's Coffee House became the headquarters of the leading players of the country. In 1735 Captain Bertin's *Noble Game of Chess* was 'sold only at Slaughter's Coffee House' and Stamma came from France to work and play chess in England. It was at Slaughter's that Philidor won his famous match against Stamma in 1747.

British chess was most powerfully influenced by Philidor who was even retained by a London Chess Club at Parsloe's in St James's to come each spring and give lessons and blindfold chess displays there. The later edition of Philidor's *Analysis of Chess* was published in London where edition succeeded edition throughout the century (see under PHILIDOR).

The chief British players and writers in the early part of the nineteenth century were Sarratt and Lewis, but the first great British player to arise in that century was the Irishman Alexander McDonnell who played and lost his famous match against La Bourdonnais in 1834.

He was followed by a still greater player, Howard Staunton, who, in defeating Saint-Amant in 1843, attained the position of the leading player in Europe. Staunton was also a great writer on the game and his works became models for text-books throughout Europe and throughout almost the whole of the century.

It was due to Staunton's initiative too that the first international chess tournament was held in London in 1851. Staunton's defeat there and his occupation in such literary matters as a new edition of Shakespeare caused his interest in actually playing the game to wane. His avoidance of a match with Morphy who came to England purposely to play was another sign of this loss of interest.

After Staunton the next great British player was the Lancastrian, J. H. Blackburne. He was the most successful tournament player this country has ever produced and had he been as formidable in matches might well have hoped for a period of reign as World Champion.

The latter half of the nineteenth century saw a series of great tournaments held in England. The first of these, London 1862, was organized by the British Chess Association, which had come into being in 1857. It was the 1862 event that introduced the idea of every competitor playing all the others. The tournament was won by Anderssen and the last prize was won by Wilhelm Steinitz of Vienna who eventually decided to stay in Britain. This was in fact a period in which a number of Europe's greatest players decided to emigrate to England, Steinitz being followed by Zukertort and he in turn by Em. Lasker, to mention only the three greatest.

It was Steinitz who won the next great tournament, London 1872, and the even greater London 1883 went to Zukertort who won the first prize with three rounds to spare and then collapsed, losing the last three games. The most important tournament of the nineteenth century was held at Hastings in 1895 and though it included the World Champion, Lasker, the former World Champion, Steinitz, and many other great players such as Tarrasch and Chigorin, it was won by the young American Pillsbury.

Chess Masters at Hastings 1895

The Masters tournament, Hereford 1885. Standing l. to r. Gunsberg, Thorold, Bird, Pollock, Smith, Schallop, Rev. Owen, Rev. Skipworth. Seated l. to r. Mason, Blackburne, Anthony, Capt. McKenzie, Rev. Ranken

By this time the British Chess Association had died (about the year 1891) and it was not till 1904 that a new national organization was formed, the British Chess Federation. New British names appeared at the turn of the century, chief of them being H. E. Atkins, a player who was to win the British championship no less than nine times. He played however but little in international events, being a genuine amateur who was devoted to his profession as a schoolmaster.

By the time of the First World War two rivals had appeared, F. D. Yates and Sir George Thomas. Neither was quite as good as Atkins but both had more time for the game and played much more international chess. The war years saw no international chess, but as soon as the war ended a Victory tournament was held at Hastings in 1919 that was won by Capablanca. He too won first prize at the strong London 1922 tournament. Yates and Sir George Thomas were still the leading British masters in the 1920s but were joined by Winter and Buerger. Yates was to win the British championship five times in all and Sir George and Winter twice.

In the late 1920s there arrived in England the Indian phenomenon Mir Sultan Khan, who was to win the British championship three times in six years. In that brief space of time, despite the handicap of having known and played the game originally under the old rules, he showed himself to be an accomplished and formidable grandmaster in the international field. But unfortunately he returned to India and was not heard of again, as far as international chess was concerned.

One event of outstanding importance in international chess was the holding of the first International Team Tournament (later known as Olympiad) under FIDE auspices in London in 1927. The B.C.F. held another such event at Folkestone in 1933.

With the 1930s a fresh generation made its presence felt with the three leading young masters of the country being C. H. O'D. Alexander, P. S. Milner-Barry and H. Golombek. But their careers in the chess world were temporarily stopped owing to the incidence of the Second World War. The war also stopped the British championships and the historic series of annual Christmas Congresses that had commenced at Hastings in 1921.

Fishermen playing chess 1936

The war ended, normal chess life resumed its way. Alexander achieved some notable results in the Hastings tournaments and distinguished himself by beating Botvinnik in an Anglo-Soviet Radio Match. Golombek won the British championship three times and led the B.C.F. team to its best result in International Team tournaments at Moscow in 1956. In this event, however, much the best British result was achieved by Jonathan Penrose on second board. For the next dozen years he was to be the leading British player and to reveal himself as one of the best players this country had ever produced. His results were impressive both internationally and nationally and he obtained the record number of British championships, winning the title no less than ten times.

Britain v. USSR 1954, Golombek, Smyslov, Bronstein, Wheatcroft

By the time that he had accomplished all this and was declining in his powers some hard, persistent and most successful work in junior chess by the B.C.F. and other organizations had produced a wealth of new talent: Hartston, Keene, Stean, Miles, Nunn and Mestel. These players made a considerable impact on the international field, especially in junior chess where Miles won the World Junior Championship in Manila in 1974, going on to achieve grandmaster status in 1976.

With the B.C.F. expanding its activities both nationally and internationally and with the Friends of Chess helping in the international aspect, a large number of important international events were held in Britain in the 1970s.

A grandmaster tournament was held in Teesside in 1972, first prize going to the Danish grandmaster, Bent Larsen. In 1973 there were the finals of the European Team championship at Bath which were won, as expected, by the USSR and in the same year the World Junior Championship was held in Teesside and won by the Soviet player Belyavsky. In 1974 the World Students Team championship was held in the County of Cleveland (formerly Teesside) and won by the USSR; and the Soviet grandmaster, Geller,

Chess in a London Pub

won first prize at the Alexander Memorial tournament, again in Cleveland in 1975.

In the last twenty years there has been a considerable increase in the numbers of those playing chess in Britain and with this has come a corresponding increase in the playing strength. This has already manifested itself by the acquisition of two international grandmaster titles (Tony Miles and Ray Keene), and beyond all doubt there are more to come.

Nor is this merely a titular addition of strength. British teams have penetrated to the European Team championship finals and have taken bronze and silver medals at the 1976 Olympiads and their individual players have won big events.

Clearly, there is still much to be done. But, with youth on their side, Britain's players have good chances of improving still further the status of British play in international circles. *(H.G.)*

BRITAIN v. USSR MATCHES

Two matches between the teams of Great Britain and the USSR have taken place since the Second World War. Both were held in London and both were won very easily by the Soviet team.

The first was played in September 1947 and the venue, the Holborn Town Hall, proved too small for the purpose, thousands of spectators queueing for the event. The British team did surprisingly well to lose the first round by only 4–6, the two top boards Alexander and Golombek holding Keres and Smyslov to draws and the young Gordon Crown even beating Kotov on fourth board. But the home side was heavily defeated by 9–1 in the second round and lost the match overall by 5–15.

Britain		*USSR*	
1. C. H. O'D. Alexander	½ 0	P. Keres	½ 1
2. H. Golombek	½ 0	V. Smyslov	½ 1
3. Sir G. Thomas	0 0	I. Boleslavsky	1 1
4. G. T. Crown	1 0	A. Kotov	0 1
5. W. Winter	0 ½	I. Bondarevsky	1 ½
6. P. S. Milner-Barry	½ 0	A. Lilienthal	½ 1
7. W. A. Fairhurst	½ ½	S. Flohr	½ ½
8. Dr J. M. Aitken	0 0	V. Ragozin	1 1
9. G. Abrahams	0 0	D. Bronstein	1 1
10. R. H. Newman	1 0	A. Tolush	0 1
	4 1		6 9

Seven years passed and the next match was played in July 1954 at the Caxton Hall.

This time the teams each contained eight men and two women and the British team had a most disastrous start, losing all their games in the first round. The second round was only a little better and the loss this time was by 1½–8½ so that the Soviet team emerged victors by 18½–1½, a colossal score by the Soviet side that perhaps was a more just reflection of the comparative strengths of the game than their earlier encounter.

Britain		*USSR*	
1. C. H. O'D. Alexander	0 ½	V. Smyslov	1 ½
2. H. Golombek	0 0	D. Bronstein	1 1
3. R. G. Wade	0 0	P. Keres	1 1
4. J. Penrose	0 0	Y. Averbakh	1 1
5. R. J. Broadbent	0 0	E. Geller	1 1
6. P. S. Milner-Barry	0 0	T. Petrosian	1 1
7. L. W. Barden	0 0	M. Taimanov	1 1
8. W. A. Fairhurst	0 ½	I. Boleslavsky	1 ½
9. Miss E. Tranmer	0 0	Mme. E. Bykova	1 1
10. Miss A. Sunnucks	0 ½	Mme. K. Zvorikina	1 ½
	0 1½		10 8½

One of the most entertaining games was that won by P. Keres in this last match in the second round.

White: Keres; *Black:* Wade
French Defence
1. P–K4, P–K3; 2. P–Q4, P–Q4; 3. N–QB3, N–KB3; 4. B–KN5, B–K2; 5. P–K5, KN–Q2; 6. P–KR4, B×B; 7. P×B, Q×P; 8. N–R3, Q–K2; 9. N–B4, P–QR3; 10. Q–N4, K–B1; 11. Q–B3, K–N1; 12. B–Q3, P–QB4; 13. B×P+, R×B; 14. R×R, K×R; 15. O–O–O, P–B4; 16. R–R1+, K–N1;

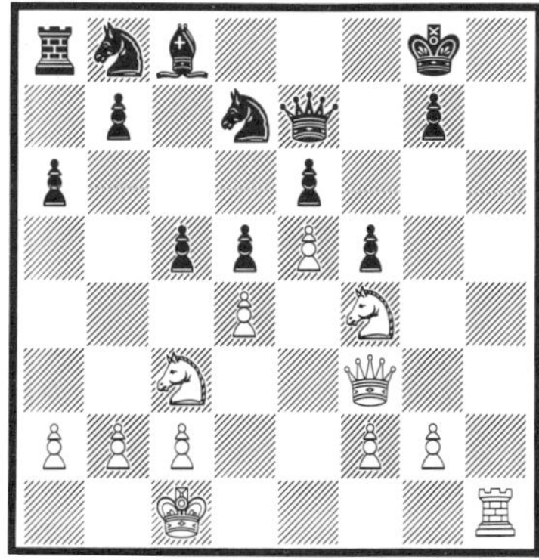

17. R–R8+, resigns. *(H.G.)*

BRITISH BOYS CHAMPIONSHIP

Although there had for some years previously been an annual boys tournament in Hastings, the first British Boys championship organized by the B.C.F. was held there in 1933. The winner on this occasion was A. W. J. Down. With the exception of the war years the event was held annually, and in 1954 became part of the British Chess Federation's yearly Congress. In 1956 the increase in number of entries made it necessary to divide the contestants into two age-groups: under-18 and under-15. A further sub-division took place in 1963 when the under-15 disappeared, to be replaced by under-16 and under-14 sections. The latest innovation is a section for under-11s introduced in 1975. The only British Boys under-18 champions who subsequently won the British championship are to date (years of winning the Boys championship in brackets): J. Penrose (1947), P. N. Lee (1962), and R. D. Keene (shared in 1964). *(W.R.H.)*

BRITISH CHAMPIONSHIP

The first tournament for the British Chess championship was held under the auspices of the British Chess Association in 1866 as part of the London Congress. There were six contestants, each of whom was required to play a match against each of the other five. The winner of each match was the first player to score three victories, and the tournament winner was determined by the total number of games won by each. The first British champion was Cecil de Vere. For the next six years, the championship was held biennially, but between 1872 and 1904 no such tournament was held. On several occasions during this period an 'Amateur championship' was organized, but it was a thoroughly unrepresentative event not on a par with the earlier tournaments.

In 1904 the newly formed British Chess Federation revived the championship and its first president, F. G. Naumann, presented a trophy. (The trophy for the earlier events had been won outright by J. Wisker as a result of his winning the championship two years in succession; Naumann ensured that his trophy would be competed for perpetually by omitting any such clause from the new rules.) The trophy itself is a grandiose silver crown, surmounted by pawns and knights, with two armoured figures attempting to hack each other to pieces in the centre of a large chessboard inside its rim. It is very difficult to keep clean and is at present in a poor state of repair.

From 1904 until 1949 the tournament consisted of twelve players, selected by a Federation committee, who competed in an all-play-all. Dissatisfaction about the methods of selection led, in 1950, to this being replaced by a Swiss System tournament of eleven rounds and between thirty and thirty-eight players. Qualifying tournaments spread over much of the previous year are held throughout the country to determine who shall have the right to enter the championship. The final tournament is held each year in August, at varying venues. There is an entry fee and competitors must pay their own expenses. The first prize is the William Sims bequest, a sum varying between £200 and £400 according to the value of the pound sterling and the state of the stock market. It is the interest on a sum left to the Federation for the purpose of providing a more worthwhile prize than the £35 which had hitherto been offered.

The youngest player ever to win the British championship was Jonathan Mestel at the age of 19 in 1976; the record for the most victories is held by Dr J. Penrose with ten wins in this event, though the most consecutive victories is still held by H. E. Atkins, who won all seven championships between 1905 and 1911.

The rules preclude the possibility of the title being shared by an insistence that the first prize can be paid to one man only. In the event of a tie, a play-off match is arranged to decide the title. Only in 1954 did this not suffice, when Barden and Phillips proved to be each other's match and the Federation conceded that the title could be shared on that occasion only. The biggest tie for first occurred in 1974 when seven players finished equal at the top of the table. In the subsequent play-off tournament the emergence of Botterill as clear winner averted the threat of yet another play-off.

In 1973 William and Jana Hartston won both men's and women's championships, to become the first married couple to hold both national titles simultaneously in this country. The complete list of British champions to date is as follows:

1866	C. de Vere	1947	H. Golombek
1868	J. H. Blackburne	1948	R. J. Broadbent
1870	J. Wisker	1949	H. Golombek
1872	J. Wisker	1950	R. J. Broadbent
1904	W. E. Napier	1951	E. Klein
1905	H. E. Atkins	1952	R. G. Wade
1906	H. E. Atkins	1953	D. A. Yanofsky
1907	H. E. Atkins	1954	L. W. Barden and A. Phillips
1908	H. E. Atkins	1955	H. Golombek
1909	H. E. Atkins	1956	C. H. O'D. Alexander
1910	H. E. Atkins	1957	Dr S. Fazekas
1911	H. E. Atkins	1958	J. Penrose
1912	R. C. Griffith	1959	J. Penrose
1913	F. D. Yates	1960	J. Penrose
1914	F. D. Yates	1961	J. Penrose
1920	R. H. V. Scott	1962	J. Penrose
1921	F. D. Yates	1963	J. Penrose
1923	Sir G. A. Thomas	1964	M. J. Haygarth
1924	H. E. Atkins	1965	P. N. Lee
1925	H. E. Atkins	1966	J. Penrose
1926	F. D. Yates	1967	J. Penrose
1928	F. D. Yates	1968	J. Penrose
1929	Mir Sultan Khan	1969	J. Penrose
1931	F. D. Yates	1970	R. G. Wade
1932	Mir Sultan Khan	1971	R. D. Keene
1933	Mir Sultan Khan	1972	B. R. Eley
1934	Sir G. A. Thomas	1973	W. R. Hartston
1935	W. Winter	1974	G. S. Botterill
1936	W. Winter	1975	W. R. Hartston
1937	W. A. Fairhurst	1976	J. Mestel
1938	C. H. O'D. Alexander		
1946	R. F. Combe		

(W.R.H.)

BRITISH CHESS ASSOCIATION

The British Chess Association, originally known as the Chess Association, was formed in 1861 and did much good work for the organization of chess in the country for thirty years. At its meeting in Bristol in 1861 it planned to hold a great tournament in London the following year, the importance of this being that it was the first event which abandoned the system of small matches and a knock-out tournament. The Bristol Congress also produced a code of the laws of chess but suffered considerable opposition from Staunton in so doing.

For all the remaining years of his life, Staunton was to prove a bitter opponent of the Association and when he died he was followed in the same role by the Rev. A. B. Skipworth. This quarrelsome reverend supported a rival organization, the Counties Chess Association (formed in 1865) and the two organizations were eventually to kill each other.

Nevertheless, both continued to hold congresses and to flourish for some time. The B.C.A. held the first tournament for the British championship at its 1866 London Congress where the title was won by De Vere and it continued to hold the event biennially till 1872.

The highest point in the career of the Association came in 1885 when the Poet Laureate, Alfred Lord Tennyson, became its President and such distinguished figures as John Ruskin, Lord Randolph Churchill and Sir Robert Peel became vice-presidents. The secretary of the B.C.A. was Leopold Hoffer and its auditor was H. E. Bird.

Despite all this magnificence the end of the Association was drawing near. It did hold some important chess congresses and the last it held, at London in 1892, was won by Emanuel Lasker. Thereafter it dwindled away and by the middle of the 1890s was no longer in existence. *(H.G.)*

BRITISH CHESS FEDERATION

The British Chess Federation (usually known as the B.C.F.) is an organization that controls, directs and encourages chess in England. It conducts the British championships, and selects and directs English representation internationally. It was founded in 1904 and as time went on it came to include Wales and Northern Ireland within its region of activities. But now it has reverted to its original domain.

The basic complete unit of the Federation is the club. The clubs in turn make up a bigger unit, the county, and the counties group into the largest units of all, the unions.

There are four unions, the Southern Counties, the Midland Counties, the West of England and the Northern Counties. In addition, and on a par with the unions, there is the London Chess League. The B.C.F. also includes a number of non-territorial constituent units such as the Braille Chess Association, the British Chess Problem Society, the British Correspondence Chess Association, etc.

The affairs of the B.C.F. are run by a system of committees and representative bodies. The chief one is the Council, which might be regarded as the legislative body. It has an Executive Committee consisting of the officers of the Federation, representatives of the unions and elected members.

The officers consist of the President, Deputy President, General Secretary, Hon. Treasurer, FIDE Delegate, Adjudications Secretary, Chief Controller of the B.C.F. Congress, Trustees of the Permanent Invested Fund, the Publicity Officer, the Registration Records Secretary, the Editor of the *Year-Book* and the *News Flash*.

At present these last three functions are filled by the General Secretary who is the only paid and full time officer of the Federation.

The various activities of the B.C.F. are controlled by standing committees consisting of the B.C.F. Congress, Development, Finance, Grading, Home Chess, International, and Junior. Its activities are supported financially partly by its registered players and partly by governmental subsidies.

The name of the General Secretary is Paul Buswell and the address of the B.C.F. office is 4 The Close, Norwich. *(H.G.)*

'BRITISH CHESS MAGAZINE'

The oldest chess magazine that has had a continuous run till now is the *British Chess Magazine* which was founded in 1881 and which, before that, had been the *Huddersfield College Magazine* which began on 1 October 1872.

It was a monthly when it started and has remained so. The organization consists of a general editor together with a select band of specialists for such matters as annotated games, problems and news. This formula has been followed throughout its career to the present day.

It has never been the official organ of the national federation since most editors have been jealously independent.

In the period from 1881 to 1976 there have been only seven general editors, one for every thirteen-odd years, which is, one supposes, a tribute to the longevity of the sort of person capable of editing the B.C.M. They were:

J. Watkinson 1881–1888; R. F. Green 1888–1894; I. M. Brown 1894–1919; R. C. Griffith 1920–1938; H. Golombek 1938–1939; R. C. Griffith 1939–1940; J. du Mont 1940–1949; B. Reilly 1949–. Address: 9 Market Street, St Leonards-on-Sea, Sussex TN38 0DQ. *(H.G.)*

BRITISH JUNIOR CHAMPIONSHIP

This takes place each year during the British Chess Federation Congress. The event is open to any player under the age of twenty-one, and is run on the Swiss System. The winner of the tournament has the right to compete in the following year's British championship. With many of Britain's leading junior players often competing in the British championship itself, the Junior championship is rarely representative and so far no British under-21 champion has proceeded to win the British championship, though the 1971 winner, A. J. Miles, did go on to win the World Junior title.

The championship was first held in 1953, when D. F. Griffiths was the winner. It continued for three years, but was then abandoned until 1961 when the event was re-inaugurated and has been contested every year since. *(W.R.H.)*

BRITISH LADIES CHAMPIONSHIP

The British Chess Federation organizes a Ladies championship at the same time as the men's (though the latter is open to any woman who survives the qualifying rounds). Unlike the men's championship, entry is unrestricted to the final of the Ladies, the numbers of those entering deciding whether the event is run as a Swiss or all-play-all tournament. The trophy, presented by Captain Alexander Beaumont in 1904, is a silver rose bowl.

The record for the most victories in the British Ladies championship is held by Rowena M. Bruce who has won the title on eleven occasions (of which three were shared). Most consecutive victories were scored by Jana Hartston with five wins between 1970 and 1974.

Rowena Bruce (*née* Dew) and Elaine Pritchard (*née* Saunders) are the only players to have both their maiden and married names engraved on the trophy. The full list of winners is as follows:

1904	K. B. Finn	1947	E. Tranmer
1905	K. B. Finn	1948	E. C. Price
1906	F. Herring	1949	E. Tranmer
1907	F. Herring	1950	R. M. Bruce
1908	G. Curling	1951	R. M. Bruce
1909	G. A. Anderson	1953	E. Tranmer
1910	M. M. Houlding	1954	R. M. Bruce
1911	M. M. Houlding	1955	J. Doulton and R. M. Bruce
1912	G. A. Anderson	1956	E. Pritchard
1913	A. Moseley	1957	A. Sunnucks
1914	M. M. Houlding	1958	A. Sunnucks
1919	E. M. Holloway	1959	R. M. Bruce
1920	A. Stevenson	1960	R. M. Bruce
1921	G. A. Anderson	1961	E. Tranmer
1922	E. C. Price	1962	R. M. Bruce
1923	E. C. Price	1963	R. M. Bruce
1924	E. C. Price	1964	A. Sunnucks
1925	A. Stevenson	1965	E. Pritchard
1926	A. Stevenson	1966	M. E. Clarke and G. Moore
1928	E. C. Price	1967	R. M. Bruce and D. Dobson
1929	M. D. Gilchrist	1968	D. Dobson
1930	A. Stevenson	1969	R. M. Bruce and D. Dobson
1931	E. Michell and A. E. Wheelwright	1970	J. Hartston
1932	E. Michell	1971	J. Hartston
1933	Miss Fatima	1972	J. Hartston
1934	M. D. Gilchrist	1973	J. Hartston
1935	E. Michell	1974	J. Hartston
1936	E. M. Holloway	1975	S. Jackson
1937	R. M. Dew	1976	J. Hartston
1938	M. Musgrave		
1939	E. Saunders		
1946	E. Saunders		

The victories of Eileen Tranmer in 1947 and Jana Hartston in 1973 were the only occasions on which the victor registered a 100% score of 11 out of 11. *(W.R.H.)*

BROADBENT, Reginald J. *(b. 3 August 1906)*
British master, and twice British champion. Broadbent was Northern Counties champion from 1934 to 1946 and won the British championship in 1948 and in 1950. A civil servant, Broadbent could not devote much time to chess but he has represented England in numerous international matches, with considerable success, especially against The Netherlands, against whom he enjoyed an unbroken run of victories.

Broadbent possessed a sound strategic style that excelled in the open positions so favoured by the great British masters of the nineteenth century. *(R.D.K.)*

BRONSTEIN, David *(b. 19 February 1924)*

One of the rare chess geniuses of our time, Bronstein shares with Schlechter the unenviable distinction of having come as close as possible to the World Championship without actually winning it.

His debut in the USSR championship at the age of twenty in 1944 was not a success, for he finished third from last in fifteenth place. However, already the following year he registered a distinct improvement in winning third prize behind only Botvinnik and Boleslavsky. Thereafter his results marked him out as one of the world's leading players. In 1948 he shared first place with Kotov in the USSR championship and repeated the feat the following year by sharing with Smyslov.

In 1948 also, his success in winning the Interzonal tournament, without defeat, gained Bronstein the right to compete in the 1950 Candidates. There he was to share first place with Boleslavsky whom he later beat (+3−2=9) to gain a match with Botvinnik. After an intense struggle, Bronstein just failed to capture the title, letting the World Champion equalize the score in the penultimate game and hold on to draw the match.

David Bronstein giving a simultaneous display, London 1952

Since then Bronstein's results have never approached similar heights, though he has remained to the present day one of the most respected grandmasters.

Chief tournament successes include: =1st Liverpool Students 1952; =2nd Candidates 1953; =1st Hastings 1953/4; 1st Belgrade 1954, Göteborg 1955, and Gotha 1957, =1st Moscow 1959, Szombathely 1966, Berlin 1968 and Hastings 1975/6 and 1st Sandomierz 1976.

His developments in chess theory are manifold, and he has always been a highly dangerous opponent in sharp opening variations.

Petropolis Interzonal 1973
White: Bronstein; *Black:* Ljubojević
Alekhine's Defence
1. P–K4, N–KB3; 2. P–K5, N–Q4; 3. P–Q4, P–Q3; 4. P–QB4, N–N3; 5. P–B4, P×P; 6. BP×P, P–QB4; 7. P–Q5, P–K3; 8. N–QB3, P×P; 9. P×P, P–B5; 10. N–B3, B–KN5; 11. Q–Q4, B×N; 12. P×B, B–N5; 13. B×P, O–O; 14. R–KN1, P–N3; 15. B–KN5!, Q–B2; 16. B–N3, B–B4; 17. Q–KB4, B×R;

18. P–Q6!, Q–B1; 19. K–K2, B–B4; 20. N–K4, QN–Q2; 21. R–QB1, Q–B3; 22. R×B, N×R; 23. N–B6+, K–R1; 24. Q–KR4, Q–N4+; 25. K–K3, P–KR4; 26. N×P, Q×B+; 27. P×Q, N–Q4+; 28. K–Q4, N–K3+; 29. K×N, N×B; 30. N–B6+, K–N2; 31. Q×N, KR–Q1; 32. P–K6, P×P+; 33. K×P, R–KB1; 34. P–Q7, P–R4; 35. N–N4, R–R3+; 36. K–K5, R–B4+; 37. Q×R, P×Q; 38. P–Q8(Q), P×N; 39. Q–Q7+, K–R3; 40. Q×QNP, R–KN3; 41. P–B4, resigns. *(W.R.H.)*

BROWNE, Walter Shawn *(b. 21 January 1949)*
US grandmaster and US champion 1974, 1975. He is considered the strongest American player born after the Second World War. Although born in Sydney, Australia, Browne was brought by his parents to the USA at an early age and obtained dual citizenship. He learned chess at the age of eight and joined the Manhattan Chess Club at thirteen. In 1966 he won the US Junior championship.

Browne returned to Australia in 1968 and won the national championship. He obtained the international master title after tieing for first place in the 1969 Asian Zonal and a few months later earned the grandmaster title at San Juan where he finished =2nd behind Spassky.

Browne's best results before returning to the USA in 1973 included =3rd at Malaga 1970, =2nd at Amsterdam 1971, 1st at Venice 1971 and 4th at Wijk-aan-Zee 1972. As first board on the Australian team he scored 73.7% at Siegen 1970 and 79.5% at Skopje 1972.

With the year 1974 it was soon apparent that a new Browne, with a more assured technique and a true grandmaster appreciation of the game, was in action. A period of almost continuous successes set in and his progress in the ensuing two years was to demonstrate that he belonged to the class of the world's top dozen players.

At the strong Wijk-aan-Zee tournament there came his first win of a major international event and in July he won the US championship at Chicago, following this up by winning the first Pan-American championship at Winnipeg in August and September.

In March 1975 he was first in the third International German championship at Mannheim and he again won the US championship at Oberlin in June, this tournament also serving as the US Zonal tournament qualifying him for the Interzonal.

With this improvement in play there also came a marked improvement in tournament etiquette and behaviour. Always noted for his fighting spirit, there had been a number of occasions when his allegedly unsporting behaviour had offended both organizers and players alike. But the new Browne, whilst retaining his competitive and aggressive spirit, was more amenable to tournament discipline and in consequence a more formidable grandmaster.

A professional player since the age of eighteen and a constant and accomplished backgammon and poker player, Browne, with the withdrawal of Bobby Fischer from the fray, looks the USA's likeliest bet for progress in the World Championship cycle.

Played in the 1975 US championship at Oberlin, Ohio:

White: R. Byrne; *Black:* W. Browne
Sicilian Defence
1. P–K4, P–QB4; 2. N–KB3, P–Q3; 3. P–Q4, P×P; 4. N×P, N–KB3; 5. N–QB3, P–QR3; 6. B–K3, P–K3; 7. B–K2, QN–Q2; 8. P–KN4, P–R3; 9. P–B4, P–QN4; 10. P–N5, P×P; 11. P×P, R–R6; 12. B–KB4, P–N5; 13. N–Q5, P×N; 14. P×N, N×P; 15. N–B6, Q–N3; 16. P×P, N–K5; 17. Q–Q4, Q×Q; 18. N×Q,

P–N4; 19. B–QB1, B–KN2; 20. N–B6, N–N6; 21. R–KN1, N×B;

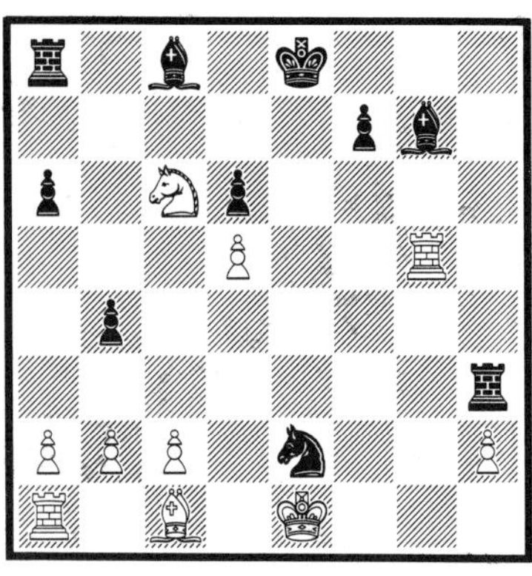

22. R×P, N–Q5; 23. R×B, N×P+; 24. K–Q1, N×R; 25. R–N8+, K–Q2; 26. R–B8, R–Q6+; 27. B–Q2, R×P; 28. N×P, R–KB4; 29. B–B3, P–R4; 30. N–Q3, P–R5; 31. resigns. *(A.S. & H.G.)*

BRUCE, Rowena Mary [née Dew] *(b. 15 May 1919)*
International Woman master and eleven times British Ladies champion or co-champion.

At the age of fifteen in 1935, Miss Dew won the Girls World championship and two years later, still under her maiden name, she won the British Ladies championship at Blackpool. Thereafter she won the championship under her married name in 1950, 1951, 1954, 1955, 1959, 1960, 1962, 1963, 1967 and 1969.

Her best international result was a 2nd in the 1951 Western European Zonal tournament, qualifying for the Women's Candidates tournament in Moscow 1952, where she came 12th/16. She has represented England in a number of team events, has excellent combinative powers, but lacks steadiness in strategy. *(H.G.)*

BUCHHOLTZ SYSTEM
This is a method used in Swiss System tournaments for tie-breaking by reckoning the sum of the opponents' scores. The scores achieved by one's opponents in the tournament are added together. The player with the highest total is adjudged the highest placed competitor. Where opponents have withdrawn or defaulted their games, their score is adjusted upward proportionately.

The illogical nature of this system lies in the fact that a player has no control over his pairings. *(H.G.)*

BUCKLE, Henry Thomas *(11 November 1821–29 May 1862)*
Eminent historian and leading mid-nineteenth-century British amateur, Buckle was born at Lee in Kent. Hampered from childhood by persistent ill-health, he nevertheless became a distinguished scholar who spoke seven and read twelve languages. Buckle won what was perhaps the first of all chess tournaments – the 'Divan' tourney of 1849. In match play he defeated Kieseritsky in 1848 (+3–2=3) and Löwenthal in 1851 (+4–3=1). He also won a match against Staunton in 1843 (+6–1), receiving odds of pawn and move. After 1851 Buckle rarely played in serious competitions, complaining that the game overtaxed his stamina, but remained a devotee of the 'Divan' where he enjoyed casual games at odds. Buckle died prematurely of typhoid fever in Damascus, Syria, and the major part of his greatest historical work, a *History of Civilization*, was published posthumously.

Match, 1851
White: Buckle; *Black:* Löwenthal
Bird's Opening
1. P–KB4, P–KB4; 2. P–QN3, N–KB3; 3. P–KN3, P–K3; 4. B–QN2, B–K2; 5. B–N2, P–B3; 6. N–QB3, N–R3; 7. N–R3, P–Q3; 8. O–O, O–O; 9. P–K3, B–Q2; 10. Q–K2, P–R3; 11. QR–K1, Q–B2; 12. N–B2, P–K4; 13. P×P, P×P; 14. N–Q3, B–Q3; 15. P–K4, P–B5; 16. P×P, B–KN5; 17. Q–B2, Q–Q2; 18. Q–R4, N–R4; 19. P–B5, N–B3; 20. N–K2, B×N; 21. R×B, QR–K1; 22. K–R1, P–QN4; 23. B–KB3, Q–KB2; 24. R–KN1, K–R2; 25. R–N6, R–KN1; 26. R(2)–N2, N–N1; 27. N–B2, N(1)–Q2; 28. P–Q3, K–R1; 29. B–B1, B–K2; 30. B–R5, Q–B1; 31. Q–R3, N×B; 32. Q×N, N–B3; 33. Q–R3, B–R6; 34. B×P, N–R2;

35. B×P+, R×B; 36. R×R, Q×R; 37. R×Q, K×R; 38. N–N4, B–B8; 39. Q–R5, R–K2; 40. Q–N6+, K–B1; 41. P–B6, resigns. *(R.D.K.)*

BUDAPEST 1896
It was in this tournament that the young Charousek was to demonstrate his enormous talent for the game. A few months earlier, at Nuremburg, he could only reach twelfth place. Now he tied with Chigorin for first place but lost the play-off by 1–3. In the tournament, however, he beat his rival with a King's Gambit that was conducted with a brilliant energy typical of his play.

Tarrasch, who otherwise had a poor result, gained a consolation prize for the best performance by a non-prizewinner against the prizewinners. Leading scores: Chigorin and Charouselk $8\frac{1}{2}$, Pillsbury $7\frac{1}{2}$, Janowski and Schlechter 7. *(H.G.)*

BUDAPEST COUNTER-GAMBIT
1. P–Q4, N–KB3; 2. P–QB4, P–K4; 3. P×P, N–N5 (or 3. . , N–K5, the Fajarowicz variation); the gambit announced by Black's second move is generally supposed to have been introduced into master chess by Vidmar (Black) v. Rubinstein in their game from the tournament at Berlin 1918, but it was Breyer who first played it against Esser at Budapest 1916. It is now regarded as unfavourable in view of the tempi Black must expend in order to regain his gambit pawn. *(R.D.K.)*

BUKIĆ, Enver *(b. 2 December 1937)*
Yugoslav grandmaster. He received the title of international master in 1964 and the higher title in 1976. He has produced consistently good results in the Yugoslav championship in the last ten years: =2nd in 1967, =11th in 1968, =4th in 1969, =14th in

1971, =4th in 1972, =2nd in 1974, =5th in 1975, =2nd in 1976. He has rarely managed to reproduce this form in international competitions, though he shared first place at Vršac 1975, Stip and Uljma 1976, all on home territory. *(K.J.O'C.)*

BULGARIA
Chess in Bulgaria was slower to develop than in most other European countries, with the first national championship being contested in 1933. There was almost nothing on an international level until the formation in 1945 of the Bulgarian Republic, when the end of the war was celebrated by a victory tournament in Sofia, the local players being joined by Gligorić (who won the event) and Milić. Since then several international tournaments have been held in Sofia, Plovdiv, Varna and occasionally other towns. The most important event to be organized in Bulgaria was the 1962 Olympiad in Varna. Winners of the championship have been as follows:

1933	G. Gesev	1955	N. Padevsky
1934	G. Gesev	1957	O. Neikirch
1935	G. Gesev	1958	M. Bobotsov
1936	G. Gesev	1959	V. Popov
1937	M. Nantarjiev	1960	Z. Milev
1938	A. Tsvetkov	1961	Z. Milev
1940	A. Tsvetkov	1962	N. Padevsky
1942	Y. Tosev	1963	G. Tringov
1943	O. Neikirch	1964	N. Padevsky
1945	A. Tsvetkov	1965	N. Minev
1946	P. Petrov	1966	N. Minev
1947	Y. Tosev and K. Piskov	1967	P. Peev
1948	A. Tsvetkov and O. Neikirch	1969	N. Spiridonov
		1970	L. Popov
1949	K. Dimitrov	1971	I. Radulov
1950	A. Tsvetkov	1972	S. Bohosian
1951	A. Tsvetkov	1973	Y. Ermenkov
1952	Z. Milev	1974	N. Kirov
1953	N. Minev	1975	I. Radulov
1954	N. Padevsky	1976	Y. Ermenkov

The first Bulgarian grandmaster was Bobotsov, later joined by Padevsky, Radulov and Tringov. The address of the Bulgarian Chess Federation is: Boul. Tolbuchin 18, Sofia. *(W.R.H.)*

BURN, Amos *(31 December 1848–25 December 1925)*
British grandmaster and second only to Blackburne in late nineteenth-century British chess. He was born in Hull and learned to play chess at sixteen, but devoted little time to the game at first, preferring to establish himself in a commercial career.

He returned to chess in his middle thirties, his first major national successes being first prize at Nottingham 1886 and second prize at London 1886. Within three years he had gained an international reputation by winning at Amsterdam 1889, ahead of Lasker, and finishing 2nd to Tarrasch at Breslau 1889. Burn continued to appear in international tournaments until the age of sixty-four, his most notable triumph being first prize at Cologne

Amos Burn (left) and the Rev. J. Owen

1898 in front of Charousek, Steinitz, Chigorin and Schlechter. He was chess editor of the *Field* from 1913 until his death in 1925.

1st Brilliancy Prize (shared), Carlsbad 1911
White: Tartakower; *Black:* Burn
King's Gambit Declined
1. P–K4, P–K4; 2. P–KB4, B–B4; 3. N–KB3, P–Q3; 4. P×P, P×P; 5. P–B3, N–QB3; 6. P–QN4, B–N3; 7. B–N5, N–B3; 8. N×P, O–O; 9. N×N, P×N; 10. B×P, N×P; 11. P–Q4, Q–B3; 12. B×N, Q–R5+; 13. K–Q2, Q×B; 14. Q–B3, Q–R5; 15. P–N3, Q–N4+; 16. Q–K3, Q–Q4; 17. R–K1, B–N5; 18. K–B2, P–QR4; 19. P×P, R×P; 20. B–R3, P–QB4; 21. P×P,

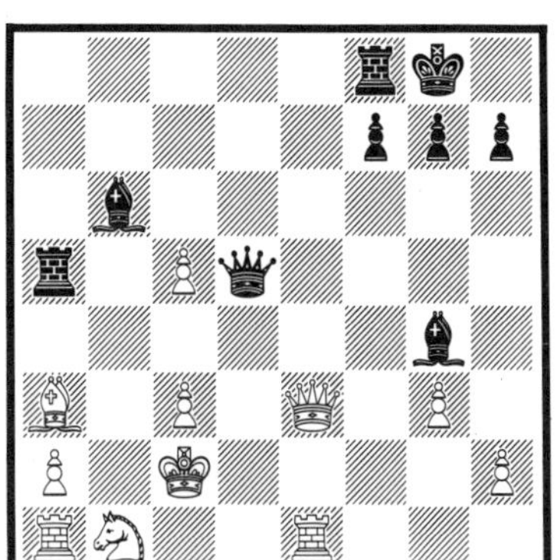

21.., R×B; 22. N×R, B×P; 23. Q–K5, B–B4+; 24. K–N2, Q–N2+; 25. K–B1, B×N+; 26. K–Q2, R–Q1+; 27. K–K3, R–Q6+; 28. K–B2, Q–B6+; 29. K–N1, R–Q7; 30. Q–K8+, B–KB1; 31. resigns. *(R.D.K.)*

BYKOVA, Elizaveta Ivanovna *(b. 4 November 1913)*
Soviet international master and third Woman World Champion. Winner of USSR Women's championship three times: 1947, 1948 and 1950. Won the Women's Candidates tournament at Moscow in 1952 to earn the right to a World Championship match with Rudenko, whom she defeated the following year. Lost the title to Rubtsova in 1956, but regained it in the return match in 1958. Successfully defended against Zvorikina in 1959/60, but was decisively defeated in 1962 by Gaprindashvili. She was awarded the title of international woman grandmaster in 1976. *(W.R.H.)*

BYRNE, Donald *(12 June 1930–8 May 1976)*
US international master (1962).

Many observers considered Donald stronger than his brother Robert until the late 1950s. But he was hampered by ill-health in his quest for the grandmaster title. Like his brother, Donald Byrne chose a career as a college teacher. But he had time to win the US Open championship in 1953 and to tie for 1st place in it four years later.

Byrne's biggest success, however, was a +3−1 score against Averbakh on fourth board in the 1954 US–USSR match in Moscow. Byrne played infrequently in foreign events, his results including =4th at Mar del Plata 1962 and 6th at Vinkovci 1968. *(A.S.)*

BYRNE, Robert *(b. 20 April 1928)*

Robert Byrne (left) in play against Portisch, Hastings 1970/1

American grandmaster and the older brother of D. Byrne. After more than fifteen years as a college teacher, Byrne became a chess professional in the late 1960s and registered his best results.

Byrne grew up in New York where he was a rival of Bisguier and Evans in the late 1940s. His first major success was a series of wins over grandmasters at the 1952 Olympiad at Helsinki. For this Byrne received the international master title. Although he did not advance to grandmaster for twelve years, Byrne scored several good results in the USA. He won the US Open in 1960 and came 2nd in the US championship in 1959/60 and 1961/2. In the US–USSR matches he scored 1½–2½ against Kotov on sixth board in 1954 and ½–3½ against Keres on fifth board the following year. Internationally Byrne took a number of high places including 1st at Santa Fé 1961, 3rd at Buenos Aires 1964 and =5th at Sarajevo 1967. However, after his =8th place result at Moscow 1971, Byrne's results improved markedly. He won the US championship in 1972 after a three-way tie with Reshevsky and Kavalek. This qualified him for the 1973 Leningrad Interzonal where he came 3rd and was seeded into the Candidates matches. In January 1974 Byrne lost the quarter-final match to Spassky in San Juan by −3=3. In 1973 Byrne succeeded Horowitz as chess columnist for the *New York Times*. He wrote *Both Sides of the Chess Board*, New York 1974. Played in the top final section of the Nice Olympiad 1974. He won the international tournament at Turremolinos in 1976.

White: Timman; *Black:* R. Byrne
Queen's Gambit Declined
1. P–QB4, P–K3; 2. N–QB3, P–Q4; 3. P–Q4, N–KB3; 4. B–N5, B–K2; 5. P–K3, QN–Q2; 6. R–B1, O–O; 7. P×P, P×P; 8. B–Q3, R–K1; 9. KN–K2, N–B1; 10. O–O, N–N3; 11. P–QN4, P–QR3; 12. Q–N3, P–B3; 13. B(N5)×N, B×B; 14. P–QR4, B–K3; 15. B×N, RP×B; 16. N–B4, B–B4; 17. N(3)–K2, Q–Q3; 18. R–B3, B–K2; 19. P–N5, RP×P; 20. P×P, P–N4; 21. N–N3, B–R2; 22. N(4)–K2, R(K1)–N1; 23. R(1)–B1, R–R4; 24. P×P, P×P; 25. Q–Q1, R–R3; 26. P–B3?, Q–K3; 27. P–K4, B–N5; 28. R–K3, P–KB4; 29. R–N3, QP×P; 30. P×P, P–B5; 31. Q–Q3, P×N!; 32. R×B, R×R; 33. Q×R, P×P+; 34. K×P, B×P; 35.N–N3,

35.., B×P!; 36. Q–K2, Q–R6+; 37. K–N1, B–Q4; 38. resigns. *(A.S. & H.G.)*

BYZANTIUM
Chess in the form of *chatrang* came to the Byzantine empire from Persia some time in the eighth century AD. It was given the name of *zatrikion*, the Byzantine Greek *zat* being the nearest they could get to the Persian *chat*. It was taken up with much enthusiasm by the Emperor and his court. Nicephorus, Emperor in 802 AD, played it and his courtiers, under which term are comprised the savants and the learned men of the time, followed suit.

The game reached its peak of popularity in the early twelfth century when, according to his daughter Princess Anna Comnena, in her biography of her father (the *Alexiad*), the Emperor Alexis Comnena was a passionate addict of the game.

This, however, aroused the wrath of John Zonares, a former captain of the imperial guard turned monk, who issued a directive from Mount Athos banning chess as a kind of debauchery. This ban, which classed chess as a Persian luxury very much as the Ancient Romans regarded pursuits derived from Persia with the gravest suspicion, did seem to have some limiting effect on the expansion of the game.

But it was still played and no doubt the scholars who came to Italy from Byzantium when that empire collapsed in the fifteenth century had their part in the propagation of chess that was to make Italy a leading chess-playing country in the world.

It is also possible that chess came to Russia very early in the ninth century AD through the route Byzantium–Kiev. (See also HISTORY OF CHESS.) *(H.G.)*

CABLE MATCHES

In 1896 a series of cable matches between Great Britain and the USA commenced. The first match was on eight boards and, after a close struggle, the American team won by $4\frac{1}{2}$–$3\frac{1}{2}$.

Great Britain		*USA*	
1. J. H. Blackburne	1	H. N. Pillsbury	0
2. A. Burn	0	J. W. Showalter	1
3. H. E. Bird	0	C. F. Burille	1
4. S. Tinsley	0	J. F. Barry	1
5. C. D. Locock	$\frac{1}{2}$	E. Hymes	$\frac{1}{2}$
6. D. Y. Mills	$\frac{1}{2}$	A. B. Hodges	$\frac{1}{2}$
7. H. E. Atkins	$\frac{1}{2}$	E. Delmar	$\frac{1}{2}$
8. E. M. Jackson	1	D. G. Baird	0
	$3\frac{1}{2}$		$4\frac{1}{2}$

In 1897 the number of players was increased to ten a side and the match was won by Great Britain $5\frac{1}{2}$–$4\frac{1}{2}$.

Results of ensuing years:

	Great Britain	*USA*
1898	$5\frac{1}{2}$	$4\frac{1}{2}$
1899	4	6
1900	4	6
1901	5	5
1902	$4\frac{1}{2}$	$5\frac{1}{2}$
1903	$4\frac{1}{2}$	$5\frac{1}{2}$

After an interval of four years the matches were resumed with the following results:

1907	$5\frac{1}{2}$	$4\frac{1}{2}$
1908	$3\frac{1}{2}$	$6\frac{1}{2}$
1909	6	4
1910	$6\frac{1}{2}$	$3\frac{1}{2}$
1911	6	4

This was the end of the Newnes Trophy series, known as such since Sir George Newnes presented a trophy to be held by the winning team. The duel between Blackburne and Pillsbury on top board (in the first six matches) was won by Blackburne with a score of $3\frac{1}{2}$–$2\frac{1}{2}$.

Another series of cable matches, the Insull Trophy series, commenced in 1926, but this was not a match between countries but a match in which London was challenged by an American city. In 1926 London beat Chicago by 4–2; in 1927 London beat New York by 4–2. In 1928 London were leading Washington by 3–2, but there was a dispute about the bottom board and on the matter being referred to FIDE the match was annulled. In 1930 London drew with Washington 3–3 and in the last match in 1931 London beat Philadelphia by $3\frac{1}{2}$–$2\frac{1}{2}$.

There was also a series of matches between Oxford and Cambridge Universities and teams representing the American Universities. These ran from 1899 to 1910 and were played on six boards like the Insull Trophy matches. Out of the ten matches the Oxford and Cambridge side emerged victorious by $5\frac{1}{2}$–$4\frac{1}{2}$; but another match, held in 1924 between a team representing English Universities and a team of the American Universities, was won by the American side by $3\frac{1}{2}$–$2\frac{1}{2}$.

In the 1907 match, J. R. Capablanca (Columbia) playing on top board for the American team, drew with H. J. Rose (Balliol).

Another interesting cable match was that played in 1897 between the British House of Commons and the United States House of Representatives. This was drawn $2\frac{1}{2}$–$2\frac{1}{2}$. *(H.G.)*

CAFÉ DE LA RÉGENCE

Paul Morphy playing blindfold in the Café de la Régence

A celebrated resort of chess-players in the eighteenth century situated not far from the present Café de la Régence in Paris. All the great French masters of the eighteenth and nineteenth centuries frequented it, from Légal, Philidor and Stamma to La Bourdonnais, Deschapelles, Saint-Amant, Kieseritsky and Harrwitz etc.

A famous chess-board was preserved on which these great players had played, as well as such celebrated people as the Duc de Richelieu, Marshal Saxe, Diderot (who used the Café de la Régence as the scene of his story *Le Neveu de Rameau*), Voltaire, Jean-

Jacques Rousseau, Grimm, Franklin and Napoleon (who frequented it as a young officer, possibly at the same time as Robespierre). *(H.G.)*

CAISSA

The Muse or Goddess of Chess. Since neither the Ancient Greeks nor the Ancient Romans knew of chess this lady was a late, post-classical invention. In his *Scacchia Ludus*, Vida (1490–1566) describes the game of chess and calls the nymph who was instrumental in bringing chess to mankind Scacchis, but the name did not stick.

'Caissa' was the name of a poem written in 1763 by Sir William Jones (1746–94) and published in his *Poems*, Oxford 1772. The poem, obviously based on Vida's, describes the pieces and their moves and then gives the origin of the game:

'A lovely dryad rang'd the Thracian wild,
Her air enchanting, and her aspect mild:
O'er hills and valleys was her beauty fam'd,
And fair Caissa was the damsel nam'd.'

Mars fell in love with her and a naiad, hearing his love laments, advised:

'Canst thou no play, no soothing game devise,
To make thee lovely in the damsel's eyes?'

Mars accepts the advice and invents chess:

'He taught the rules that guide the pensive game,
And called it Caissa from the dryad's name:
Whence Albion's sons, who most its praise confess
Approv'd the play, and nam'd it thoughtful Chess.'

This last piece of false etymology has been responsible for a number of errors about the history of chess. *(H.G.)*

CALVO, Ricardo *(b. 22 October 1943)*

Spanish international master (1973). A doctor by profession, he has been able to devote only limited time to chess. Played for Spain in the Olympiads of 1966, 1968, 1972 and 1974. His best tournament result was in 1976: =2nd (behind Karpov) at Montilla-Moriles. Here his score was sufficient for the grandmaster norm. *(K.J.O'C.)*

CAMBRIDGE SPRINGS 1904

The first major US tournament since New York 1889 was held in April/May 1904 at the Pennsylvania resort town of Cambridge Springs. Lasker, Schlechter, Janowski and Chigorin accepted invitations but Tarrasch and Maróczy refused. The Americans were led by Marshall and Pillsbury.

This was Pillsbury's last strong event and the first time since Hastings 1895 that he failed to win a prize. But his defeat of Lasker in revenge for their Queen's Gambit Declined at St Petersburg 1895/6 was instrumental in keeping the World Champion from first prize. Marshall's score of eleven wins and four draws at Cambridge Springs was the best of his career. It established him as a World Championship challenger and led to the 1907 match with Lasker. Leading scores: Marshall 13, Janowski, Em. Lasker 11, Marco 9.

Janowski took an early lead after Lasker was defeated by Schlechter and Pillsbury. But Marshall's string of victories in the middle of the tournament gave him a lead of $1\frac{1}{2}$ points before the final round. Lasker defeated Janowski with the black pieces in that round and thereby saved a share of second prize.

The top three prizes were $1000, $600 and $300. The tournament bulletins by Helms were continued as the *American Chess Bulletin* which lasted until Helms' death in 1963. No tournament book was printed until Fred Reinfeld assembled notes from several annotators in 1935. The event is also known for a Queen's Gambit variation often employed during it – 1. P–Q4, P–Q4; 2. P–QB4, P–K3; 3. N–QB3, N–KB3; 4. B–N5, QN–Q2; 5. P–K3, P–B3; 6. N–B3, Q–R4. *(A.S.)*

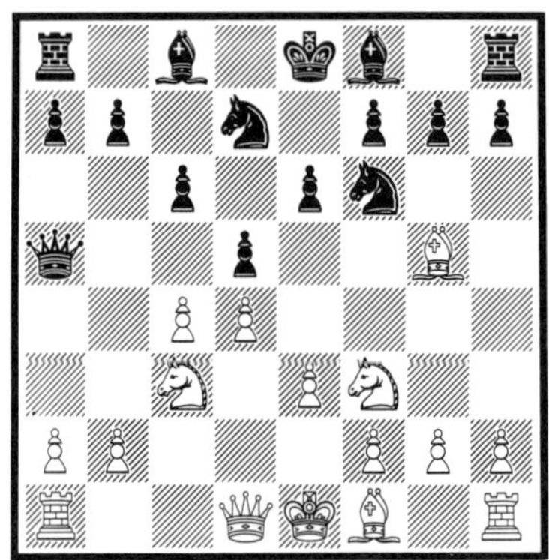

CANADA

Samuel De Champlain (1567–1635), founder of Quebec City, played chess and since then Canadian chess has continued to receive strong stimulus from immigrants to the New World. The Chess Federation of Canada (CFC) was founded in 1872 (it was originally called the Canada Chess Association) and its first president was Professor J. B. Cherriman of Toronto. The CFC sponsors Canadian championships, selects Olympiad teams and organizes matches against the USA and a few international events. Bernard Freedman of Toronto was the first serious national organizer. He discovered and sponsored Canada's first grandmaster, Yanofsky, and he successfully arranged for Canada's first Olympiad team in Buenos Aires 1939. John Prentice of Vancouver has carried on in this tradition and he has seen to it that Canadian teams have been at all Olympiads since Tel Aviv 1964. Prentice has also been very active as Vice-President of FIDE.

The first Canadian championship was held in 1873 and A. Ensor of Montreal won the title. Since then there have been some 58 championships. Canadian Open tournaments began in 1956 and winners have included Spassky and Larsen. Internationally, the last eight games of the 1894 Lasker–Steinitz match were held in

Montreal, the Canadian Centennial grandmaster tournament was held in Winnipeg 1967, and the Fischer–Taimanov match of 1971 in Vancouver.

Some half-dozen players have dominated Canadian chess since the turn of the century.

Magnus Smith, born in Ireland in 1874, won the national title in 1899, 1904 and 1906. He was a modest shoemaker in Winnipeg but a fine analyst and opening theorist. He beat Pillsbury in Winnipeg in 1900 and contributed to *Lasker's Chess Magazine.*

John Stewart Morrison, born in Toronto in 1889, won the national title in 1910, 1913, 1922, 1924 and 1926. He played in New York 1918 (beating Janowski) and in London 1922 (beating Euwe and Maróczy).

Maurice Fox, born in England in 1898, an electrical engineer, came to Canada in 1923 and lives in Montreal. He won the national title eight times: 1927, 1929, 1931, 1932, 1935, 1938, 1940 and 1949, and he came high up in the 1966 Open. Fox played in Bradley Beach 1929 where he came 5th, ahead of Marshall.

From the Second World War onwards a new surge of great players revivified and reinforced Canadian chess.

The first wave was formed by emigrés from Europe: Dr Feodor Bohatirchuk, the Soviet grandmaster who had been a leading player in the USSR in the 1920s and 1930s; Zvonko Vranesić from Yugoslavia and Paul Vaitonis from Lithuania, both of whom were to prove staunch bulwarks of the Canadian Olympic team; and three Hungarian immigrants, Geza Fuster, Laszlo Witt and Professor Elod Macskasy who won the 2nd Canadian Open in 1958.

First coincident with and then subsequent to this wave was an even stronger native element. D. A. Yanofsky, Canada's first grandmaster (technically an immigrant since he was born in Poland, but Canadian from a very early point in his life) was the spearhead of the Canadian advance internationally and he was most ably helped by Frank R. Anderson in several Olympiads.

Finally, Duncan Suttles, who became Canada's second grandmaster in 1973, made a powerful impact on the whole chess world and showed that Canada's best players could compete successfully with the grandmasters of the rest of the world.

Canada's longest running chess magazine, *Canadian Chess Chat*, was founded in 1947 by D. A. MacAdam.

The name and address of the organizing body of chess in Canada is: The Chess Federation of Canada, c/o Canadian Forest Products Ltd., 505 Barrard Street, Vancouver B.C., V9X 1B5. *(N.D.)*

CANAL, Esteban *(b. 19 April 1896)*

Peruvian international master whose best results were in the 1920s and 1930s. Canal was born in Chiclayo, Peru, but went to live in Italy in the early 1920s and has been there ever since.

A second at Trieste in 1923 was followed by an excellent =2nd in the strong Meran tournament of 1926. He played in three important tournaments in 1929: =10th at Budapest, =10th/22 at the great Carlsbad event and =7th at Rohitsch-Sauerbrunn.

A second at Budapest 1932 was followed by =4th at Bad Sliac in the same year. He was first at Budapest 1933; =5th at Mähritsch-Ostrau again in 1933, and first at Reus, Spain 1936.

He played in some Italian and Austrian tournaments after the Second World War; =2nd at Venice 1947, =6th at Bad Gastein 1948, =2nd at Venice 1948, and =12th at Venice 1949.

He made one appearance at an Olympiad, Dubrovnik 1950, where, playing on top board for Peru, he scored 26.7%. *(H.G.)*

CANDIDATES MATCHES

With the abandonment of the old-style Candidates tournament, the first series of Candidates matches was begun in 1965 and proved very successful from the point of view of sporting interest. The eight contestants consisted of the top six from the Interzonal together with the two highest available players from the previous cycle (Botvinnik's decision not to play allowing Geller to take part). In the first round matches, Geller disposed of Smyslov with remarkable ease by the score of 5½–2½, with Tal beating Portisch, and Larsen beating Ivkov by the same margin. In the most exciting match, and the only one to go the full ten games, Spassky beat Keres 6–4.

Many had expressed the opinion that the winner of the Spassky–Keres match would triumph in the whole event, and this indeed proved to be the case. Spassky went on to demolish Geller 5½–2½, while Tal was scoring a very narrow victory 5½–4½ against Larsen. This was perhaps the most exciting match of the whole event with the scores level until the final game, which was won by Tal after a brave Knight sacrifice. In the final match Spassky drew the first, lost the second and won the third games against Tal, before a run of five draws left the situation very tense. Then, however, Tal lost his balance and the next three games to leave Spassky the winner 7–4 with a game to spare.

In the match for third place, important in that it gave the winner a free place in the following Interzonal, Larsen and Geller were equal after the scheduled eight games, but Larsen won the ninth to end the match.

The Seventh Candidates event, and second on the new match system, was held in 1968. Again the quarter-final and semi-final matches were of ten games, with the final of twelve. In the first round matches there were few surprises; Larsen beat Portisch 5½–4½, Spassky beat Geller again by 5½–2½, Tal beat Gligorić 5½–3½ and Korchnoi easily disposed of Reshevsky by 5½–2½.

The semi-finals were more dramatic. Spassky won the first three games against Larsen and finally coasted home by 5½–2½, while Korchnoi overcame Tal in a hard match by 5½–4½. Spassky won his second Candidates series by defeating Korchnoi 6½–3½ in the final. Larsen again won the match for third place, this time by a score of 5½–2½ at Tal's expense.

The 1971 series of matches was dominated by Fischer. His victories in this event were so complete and so astounding that the other matches have almost been forgotten. In the quarter-final, hardly anyone gave much for Taimanov's chances against the American grandmaster, but when he lost by a score of 6–0 it seemed inconceivable. Meanwhile Larsen had beaten Uhlmann 5½–3½, Korchnoi beat Geller 5½–2½, and the Petrosian–Hübner match ended with Hübner retiring when 4–3 down.

Before anyone had recovered from the shock of Taimanov's

debacle, Fischer did it again. This time the score line read Fischer 6 Larsen 0. Admittedly both Taimanov and Larsen made several uncharacteristically bad blunders in these matches, but this hardly detracts from Fischer's achievement. In the other semi-final Petrosian and Korchnoi drew their first eight games, Petrosian won the ninth and drew the tenth, to reach the final by a score of 5½–4½.

Korchnoi triumphs over Petrosian in the 1974 Candidates semi-final. World Champion Fischer looks on.

Fischer won the first game of the final, but lost the second, almost a sensation after his thirteen consecutive victories! The next three were drawn but then Petrosian collapsed to lose four games in a row, making the final score 6½–2½.

The third series of Candidates matches was held in 1974. This time again two places were reserved for contestants from the previous cycle, but the other six qualifiers had arrived by reaching one of the top three places in one of the two parallel Interzonals. The winners of each Interzonal were seeded together with the two survivors from 1971, Spassky and Petrosian, to reach the semi-finals. Three of them justified their seedings, but Mecking fell victim to Korchnoi. The rules for the matches had again been modified, with the winner of each match being the first to reach a specified number of wins, rather than the leader after a fixed number of games. This was intended to encourage positive play, though in each round there was still a maximum number of games specified to avoid too great a burden falling on the organizers. In the quarter-finals three victories were necessary, with a maximum of sixteen games. Spassky beat R. Byrne 3–0 with three draws, Karpov beat Polugayevsky 3–0 with five draws, Korchnoi beat Mecking 3–1 with eight draws, and Petrosian beat Portisch in the most exciting match of the round by 3–2 with eight draws. In this match Petrosian's early lead of two games was slowly overhauled, but just when Portisch had equalized, the Soviet grandmaster scored the valuable third win. In the semi-finals Korchnoi revenged himself for the defeat three years earlier by beating Petrosian 3–1 with one draw; though four wins were nominally necessary for victory, Petrosian conceded the match through ill-health. In the other semi-final Karpov beat Spassky 4–1 with six draws, despite a loss in the first game.

The final was expected by many to be an easy match for Karpov after his secure victory over Spassky. He won the second and sixth games to lead 2–0 but a long series of draws brought no further change in the score. Finally the run was broken when Korchnoi blundered away game 17. With a three-game lead and a mere seven games at most remaining, it seemed all over, but only now did the match come back to life. Wins for Korchnoi in games 19 and

Karpov disposes of Spassky in the 1976 Candidates match. World Champion Fischer rests his sword

21 left the match poised once again, but with both contestants very tired the last three games were fairly incident-free draws leaving Karpov the winner by 3–2; he had not reached the stipulated five victories, but had held his lead until game 24, to earn the right to a match for the World title. *(W.R.H.)*

CANDIDATES TOURNAMENTS

At the end of the Second World War, with Alekhine's death leaving the Champion's throne vacant, the International Chess Federation (FIDE) took the opportunity to introduce some order into the process of determining a challenger to future World Champions to replace the old and unsatisfactory system of arbitrary challenges being issued by any who could put up sufficient stake money.

The new system led, through the regional stages of Zonal and Interzonal tournaments, to the Candidates tournament every three years, the winner of which had the right to a match for the World Championship.

The first Candidates tournament, Budapest 1950, was to consist of five qualifiers from the previous Interzonal, together with the four unsuccessful participants from the World Championship tournament of 1948, and Reuben Fine, who had been unable to compete in that event. Visa difficulties for the Americans and Dr Euwe's withdrawal left numbers short, so FIDE gave numbers 6 to 9 from the Interzonal the right to compete. Finally ten players took part in a double-round all-play-all event with the following results:

Boleslavsky and Bronstein 12, Smyslov 10, Keres 9½, Najdorf 9, Kotov 8½, Ståhlberg 8, Flohr, Lilienthal and Szabo 7.

The rules specified that a match must be played between the winners to determine Botvinnik's challenger. After the scheduled twelve games scores were level; another two games were played and saw Bronstein emerge as the winner by the narrowest of margins, 7½–6½.

The second Candidates tournament was held in Switzerland, at Neuhausen and Zürich, in 1953. Originally there were to be twelve participants with five qualifying from the Interzonal. In the event, fifth place in the Interzonal was shared by four contestants; it was felt invidious to split the tie and all were admitted to the Candidates. This left an enormous tournament of fifteen players and twenty-eight rounds, lasting nearly two months. The tournament was won by a margin of two points by Smyslov. Full scores: Smyslov 18, Bronstein, Keres and Reshevsky 16, Petrosian 15, Geller and Najdorf 14½, Kotov and Taimanov 14, Averbakh and Boleslavsky 13½, Szabo 13, Gligorić 12½, Euwe 11½, Ståhlberg 9.

After this gigantic event, both organizers and players felt the time had come to limit the number of participants; it was too tiring for the players and too expensive for the hosts to stage such long tournaments! After an initial resolution to restrict the number to seven participants, it was finally agreed to let in nine qualifiers from the Interzonal together with Smyslov, as loser of the previous title match.

Thus, the third Candidates tournament, held in Amsterdam 1956, was the same format as the first, but produced the same winner as the second, Smyslov again outshining his rivals to earn another crack at Botvinnik's throne. Full results:

Smyslov 11½, Keres 10, Bronstein, Geller, Petrosian, Spassky and Szabo 9½, Filip and Panno 8, Pilnik 5.

The rules were changed once again for the 1959 Candidates tournament, held in Bled, Zagreb and Belgrade. The number of players was restricted to eight but each met each of the others four times, giving a total of twenty-eight rounds again. This event was of particular importance historically, since it marked the first appearance at this level of an American teenager named Fischer. He was, however, overshadowed by the genius of Mikhail Tal. Full scores:

Tal 20, Keres 18½, Petrosian 15½, Smyslov 15, Fischer and Gligorić 12½, Olafsson 10, Benko 8.

Among other interesting features of this tournament was Tal's victory in the games against Fischer by a score of 4–0.

The fifth Candidates tournament was held under the same system at Curaçao, in the Dutch Antilles. Five players had survived from the previous event and were joined by Geller, Filip and Korchnoi. Unfortunately Tal was in ill-health throughout the event and had to withdraw at the start of the final quarter. This was a much closer tournament than any of the previous ones with three players in contention for first place. Eventually Petrosian emerged a deserving winner without losing a single game. Full scores:

Petrosian 17½, Geller and Keres 17, Fischer 14, Korchnoi 13½, Benko 12, Filip and Tal 7.

It was after this tournament that Fischer published complaints about the system and particularly about the attitude of the Soviet contestants. He complained of their tendency to draw games amongst themselves to save energy for the games against other players. Whatever the merit of his allegations, it was evidently felt that having a large number of players from one country could be an advantage in such an event for the players of that country, and it was decided, partly for this reason and partly for the increased sporting interest, that in future cycles the Candidates tournaments would be replaced by a series of Candidates matches. *(W.R.H.)*

CANDIDATES, Women's

See under WOMEN'S WORLD CHAMPIONSHIP.

CAPABLANCA MEMORIAL TOURNAMENT

Capablanca Memorial Tournament, Havana, 1962: Pomar (left) v. Suetin (watched by Donner)

Twenty years after the death of Capablanca a strong international tournament in his memory was held at Havana, Cuba, from 25 April to 20 May 1962. This, the first Capablanca Memorial tournament, comprised twenty-two players and was won by Najdorf ahead of Spassky and Polugayevsky who shared second place half a point behind him.

From 1962 to 1976 thirteen such tournaments have been held in Cuba and they have always contained very strong contingents from the countries of the Soviet bloc. The 1976 event, for example, contained three Soviet grandmasters, Gulko (who won first prize), Razuvayev and Belyavsky, and players from East Germany, Poland, Bulgaria, Hungary and Czechoslovakia, in addition to Cuban and South American players.

Perhaps the most celebrated in the series was the fourth which was held in Havana in 1965 and won by Smyslov, half a point ahead of Fischer, Geller and Ivkov who tied for second place.

It was a time when relations between the USA and Cuba were strained and the US State Department refused to endorse Fischer's passport as valid for Cuba. So Fischer played his games at the Marshall Chess Club in New York, the moves being transmitted by telex to and from Havana where Fischer's moves were relayed by Capablanca's son, Dr José Raúl Capablanca Jr.

A lively and amusing game that was played in Round Five with

Fischer improving on some book analysis on move 18.

White: Tringov; *Black:* Fischer
Sicilian Defence
1. P–K4, P–QB4; 2. N–KB3, P–Q3; 3. P–Q4, P×P; 4. N×P, N–KB3; 5. N–QB3, P–QR3; 6. B–KN5, P–K3; 7. P–B4, Q–N3; 8. Q–Q2, Q×P; 9. R–QN1, Q–R6; 10. P–K5, P×P; 11. P×P, KN–Q2; 12. B–QB4, B–N5; 13. R–N3, Q–R4; 14. O–O, O–O; 15. N×P, P×N; 16. B×P+, K–R1; 17. R×R+, B×R; 18. Q–B4, N–QB3!; 19. Q–B7, Q–B4+; 20. K–R1, N–B3; 21. B×B, N×P; 22. Q–K6, N(K4)–N5; 23. resigns.

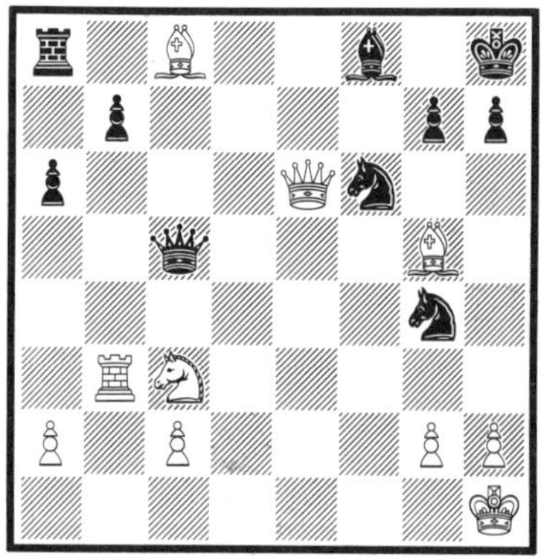

Black not only threatens R×B but also a Philidor mate. *(H.G.)*

José Raúl Capablanca in 1921 when he won the world title

Capablanca at Margate 1935

CAPABLANCA Y GRAUPERA, José Raúl
(19 November 1888–8 March 1942)
World Champion 1921–7.
One of the greatest players (perhaps the greatest *natural* player) the world has ever seen, Capablanca was born in Havana, Cuba, in 1888. He learnt chess at the age of four through watching his father play with a friend. His rapid development as a player is shown by his winning a match against Juan Corzo, champion of the Havana Chess Club, by 7–5 at the age of twelve.

Capablanca then went to the USA and studied at the University of Columbia. In 1909 he beat Frank Marshall +8−1=14. For this performance he was invited to play at San Sebastian 1911 where he caused a sensation by winning first prize. Both Bernstein and Nimzowitsch, who had objected to his participation on the grounds of his not having won first prize in an international tournament, were well and truly beaten by him!

In 1913 Capablanca entered the Cuban Foreign Office as a commercial attaché and this enabled him to travel abroad and to take part in chess events all over the world.

In 1914 he came second to the then World Champion, Emanuel Lasker, at St Petersburg, and before this he played and won exhibition matches against many masters, including the young Alekhine. At the end of the First World War he won at Hastings 1919 and in the same year defeated Boris Kostić by 5–0. The World title became his in 1921 when he beat Emanuel Lasker at Havana +4−0=14.

Capablanca was now approaching the peak of his powers. A 1st at London 1922 was followed by a 2nd to Lasker at New York 1924 and a 3rd to Bogoljubow and Lasker at Moscow 1925. Then came his greatest tournament triumph, a 1st at New York 1927 ahead of Alekhine, Nimzowitsch, etc.

To practically everybody's surprise, he lost the World title to Alekhine at Buenos Aires 1927 by +3−6=25. Capablanca was never to be allowed a return match, though he played in a number of events in a successful attempt to prove himself the natural challenger for the title.

Main results in the later period were: 2nd Bad Kissingen 1928; 2nd Carlsbad, 1st Ramsgate, Barcelona, Budapest 1929. In 1931 Capablanca beat Euwe, +2−0=8. 4th Hastings, Moscow 1935, 1st Moscow 1936, =1st with Botvinnik, Nottingham 1936. He did badly in the A.V.R.O. tournament 1938 but scored +6−0=4 on top board for Cuba in the 1939 Buenos Aires Olympiad.

Capablanca had a heart-attack at the Manhattan Chess Club and died 8 March 1942.

Though he wrote comparatively little, he was a lucid and excellent writer on chess.

Of debonair appearance, intelligent and handsome, he had a sort of magnetic aura that was well expressed by a cartoon in a London evening newspaper during the 1922 tournament there which depicted him with a sort of electric ray about his forehead.

His influence on the chess-world was and is enormous and he has left a great mark on opening theory, notably in the Nimzo-Indian and Queen's Gambit.

Of his games it has been said that 'they breathe a serenity, a lucid crystal clarity, a type of model perfection . . . This simplicity of perfection was the product of supreme art.'

A good example of his lucidly brilliant style:

1st Brilliancy Prize New York 1927
White: Capablanca; *Black:* R. Spielmann
Queen's Gambit Declined
1. P–Q4, P–Q4; 2. N–KB3, P–K3; 3. P–B4, N–Q2; 4. N–B3, KN–B3; 5. B–N5, B–N5; 6. P×P, P×P; 7. Q–R4, B×N+; 8. P×B, O–O; 9. P–K3, P–B4; 10. B–Q3, P–B5; 11. B–B2, Q–K2; 12. O–O, P–QR3; 13. KR–K1, Q–K3; 14. N–Q2, P–N4; 15. Q–R5, N–K5; 16. N×N, P×N; 17. P–QR4, Q–Q4;

18. P×P, Q×B; 19. B×P, R–N1; 20. P×P, R–N4; 21. Q–B7, N–N3; 22. P–R7, B–R6; 23. KR–N1, R×R+; 24. R×R, P–B4; 25. B–B3, P–B5; 26. P×P, resigns.

His most outstanding works were: *My Chess Career*, London, New York 1920; *Chess Fundamentals*, London, New York 1921. *(H.G.)*

CARDOSO, Rodolfo Tan *(b. 25 December 1937)*
Philippine international master (1957). Philippine champion 1958, 1963. Won Asian Zonal 1957–8. In the 1958 Olympiad he won the prize for best score on top board, final group B.

He is noted as the player who defeated Bronstein in the last round of the 1958 Interzonal at Portorož, thereby depriving him of qualification for the Candidates. *(R.D.K.)*

CARLS, Carl *(16 September 1880–11 September 1958)*
German international master, Carls won the German championship in 1934 and had other excellent results in local master tournaments (2nd Oeynhausen 1922; 1st Rostock 1942, ahead of Junge) but his international results were indifferent. He represented Germany in the team Olympiads of 1927 and 1930, as well as the Team tournament Munich 1936. Carls was an inveterate addict of the English (or Bremen) Opening, which gave rise to the famous story of an opponent glueing the QBP to the board. *(W.H.)*

CARLSBAD 1907
The first of the four great Carlsbad tournaments, Carlsbad (August–September 1907) has become famous in chess history as the breakthrough of the 'new generation' – i.e. the plethora of great masters born in the 1880s. At Ostend, three months before, the establishment (in the persons of Schlechter, Marshall, Janowski and Chigorin, in addition to Tarrasch and Burn) was still able to regard the grandmaster event as its own province; here they had to mix, and the young masters observed with considerable satisfaction that except for Maróczy (absent from the Ostend tournament) and Schlechter the establishment did not fare too well, while the upstarts carried off most of the prizes: Rubinstein the first, Leonhardt (whose only great success this was destined to be) the third, Nimzowitsch the fourth in a tie with Schlechter, Vidmar the sixth and Dûras the seventh in a tie with Teichmann. *(W.H.)*

CARLSBAD 1911
A field of twenty-six competed in the second Carlsbad tournament (August–September 1911), the numerically strongest of these four great events. Though Schlechter started with a series of seven wins, he could not keep up the pace, and at the halfway stage after round 13 led Teichmann by a mere half point (10 to 9½), with the young Russian master, Rotlewi, on 8½ and Rubinstein on 8.

From then on these four continued to fight for the lead, but Teichmann, who beat all three of his rivals in their individual encounters, gradually drew ahead and with five rounds to play was two full points ahead of the other three.

This was the only occasion in his long chess career that Teichmann lived up to his enormous potential. Most of his games were full of imaginative ideas, and besides winning first prize he achieved what few great masters ever succeed in doing: he beat his strongest rival in a brilliancy game.

White: Teichmann; *Black:* Schlechter
Ruy Lopez
1. P–K4, P–K4; 2. N–KB3, N–QB3; 3. B–N5, P–QR3; 4. B–R4, N–B3; 5. O–O, B–K2; 6. R–K1, P–QN4; 7. B–N3, P–Q3; 8. P–B3, O–O; 9. P–Q3, N–QR4; 10. B–B2, P–B4; 11. QN–Q2, Q–B2; 12. N–B1, N–B3; 13. N–K3, B–N2; 14. N–B5, KR–K1; 15. B–N5, N–Q2; 16. B–N3, N–B1; 17. B–Q5, N–N3; 18. B×B, N(N)×B;

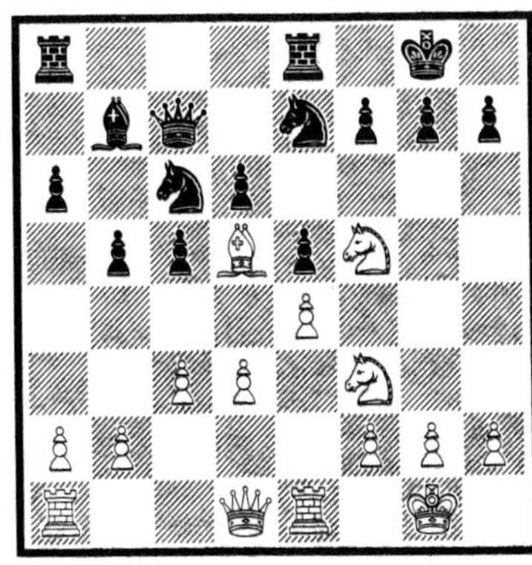

19. B×P+, K×B; 20. N–N5+, K–N1; 21. Q–R5, N×N; 22. Q×P+, K–B1; 23. Q×N+, K–N1; 24. Q–N6, Q–Q2; 25. R–K3, resigns.

CARLSBAD 1923

The third of the great Carlsbad tournaments (April–May 1923) was in many ways the most important as well as most interesting event between the end of the First World War and the great double-round tournament of New York 1924. Though Lasker, Capablanca and Vidmar were missing, the field included all the leading hypermoderns as well as the older masters; among the former Nimzowitsch made his reappearance after a long absence, especially during 1922, from many similar Continental tournaments. Moreover, he and Réti vied with each other in laying out their games in true hypermodern style, and it is hardly an exaggeration to say that Réti, finishing in a tie for fourth and fifth places half a point behind the joint winners, was the moral victor of the event: scoring 9 points against the top twelve, he could only get a miserable 1½ against the last five.

If thus the hypermoderns had their triumphs at Carlsbad, so did the 'old school'. Apart from Dr Lasker's victories, it was to be the only first prize in post-war events that fell, at least partly, to one of the old guard, and it made Maróczy one of the few great masters to succeed in a major event in their fifties. *(W.H.)*

CARLSBAD 1929

On paper the strongest tournament of the 1920s, Carlsbad 1929 (July–August) included all the leading players of the period except Alekhine and the presumably retired Dr Lasker. For a long time it seemed as though Spielmann would repeat his Semmering success, for he established a long lead and after ten rounds, just short of the halfway mark, had scored 9, ahead of Capablanca and Vidmar (7), Bogoljubow and Nimzowitsch (6½). Then his tremendous effort began to tell and he lost twice within the next four rounds (to Rubinstein and Canal) and by round 15 was sharing the lead with Capablanca, ahead of Nimzowitsch, with Rubinstein and Vidmar next. Though he beat his co-leader in round 20, he could not cope with the finishing burst of Nimzowitsch, who thus scored the greatest success of his career.

The tournament book is outstanding in every respect (published by the *Wiener Schachzeitung*), and Kmoch's round-by-round reports are perhaps the wittiest chess reportage ever written. The following game shows the winner at his best:

White: Mattison; *Black:* Nimzowitsch
Nimzo-Indian Defence

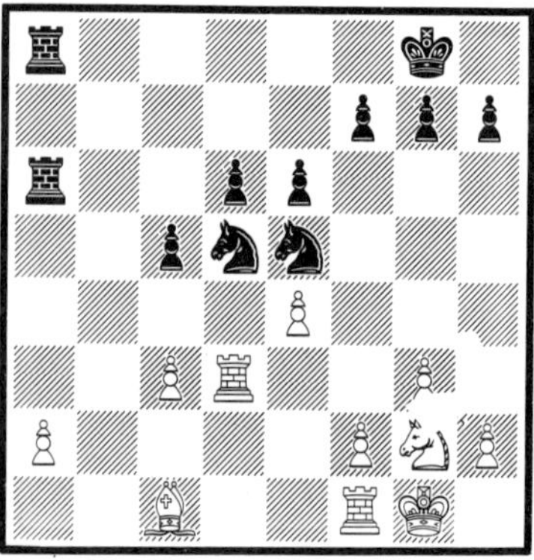

1. P–Q4, N–KB3; 2. P–QB4, P–K3; 3. N–QB3, B–N5; 4. N–B3, B×N+; 5. P×B, P–Q3; 6. Q–B2, Q–K2; 7. B–R3, P–B4; 8. P–N3, P–QN3; 9. B–KN2, B–N2; 10. O–O, O–O; 11. N–R4, B×B; 12. K×B, Q–N2+; 13. K–N1, Q–R3; 14. Q–N3, N–B3; 15. QR–Q1, N–QR4; 16. Q–N5, Q×Q; 17. P×Q, N–B5; 18. B–B1, P–QR3; 19. P×RP, R×P; 20. P×P, NP×P; 21. N–N2, N–Q4; 22. R–Q3, KR–R1; 23. P–K4, N–K4; 24. resigns. *(W.H.)*

CARO, Horatio *(5 July 1862–15 December 1920)*

A minor English master who spent most of his chess life in Berlin. Though he had indifferent tournament and not much better match results (he lost to Mieses and Winawer, drew twice with Von Bardeleben, and beat Lewitt), his name has become immortal through the Caro-Kann Defence, which he expounded in his own journal, *Brüderschaft*, in 1886. *(W.H.)*

CARO-KANN DEFENCE

The invention of the defence 1. P–K4, P–QB3 is attributed to the Viennese player of the last century, M. Kann, though its first analysis was published in German by H. Caro in 1886. Black plans to simplify the central situation after 2. P–Q4, P–Q4 by exchanging his QP for the opponent's KP. There are a number of important variations:

(a) 3. P–K5, the Advance variation, allows Black free development with 3. . , B–B4. Tal secured poor results as White in this line against Botvinnik in their 1961 World Championship match.

(b) 3. P×P, P×P; 4. B–Q3, the Exchange variation, not considered very dangerous, but still causing Black some problems, as Fischer has demonstrated.

(c) 3. P×P, P×P; 4. P–QB4, the Panov Attack, first analysed by Vassily Panov. White tries to exchange the Black QP, leaving himself with an advantage in space and chances of an attack on the King.

(d) 3. N–QB3, P×P; 4. N×P, B–B4 is the Classical System, popularized for Black by Capablanca. The main line continues 5. N–N3, B–N3; 6. P–KR4, P–KR3; 7. N–B3, N–Q2; 8. B–Q3, B×B; 9. Q×B, Q–B2; 10. B–Q2, KN–B3; 11. O–O–O, when Black's solid position makes it difficult for White to utilize his spatial advantage.

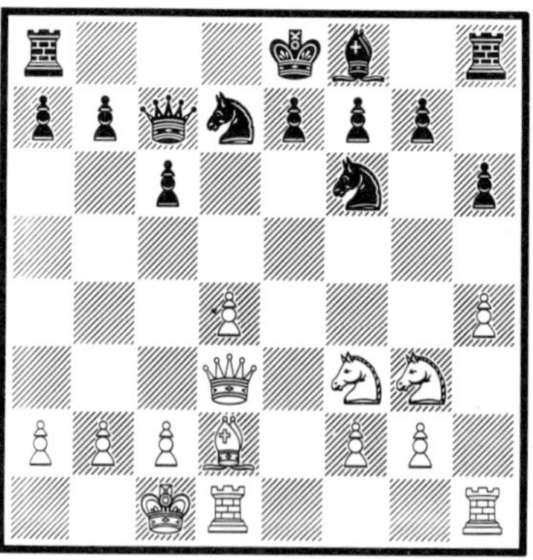

(e) 3. N–QB3, P×P; 4. N×P, N–Q2 is another solid line with which the names of Nimzowitsch, Flohr and Smyslov have been

associated. Black intends 5. . , KN–B3 to challenge the central White Knight.

(f) 3. N–QB3, P×P; 4. N×P, N–B3 is a sharper attempt by Black. After 5. N×N+, either . . , KP×N or . . , NP×N gives Black open lines in compensation for his damaged pawns.

Other possibilities for White include the Two Knights' System: 2. N–QB3, P–Q4; 3. N–B3, and a dubious gambit introduced by the moves 2. P–Q4, P–Q4; 3. P–KB3, while it is also possible to side-step the main lines completely with 2. P–Q3.

The Caro-Kann has enjoyed a sound reputation in recent years since Botvinnik's adoption of this defence in the 1958 World Championship match. *(W.R.H.)*

CARRERA, Pietro *(12 July 1573–18 September 1647)*
Italian player, theorist and writer who was a priest and, for most of his life, chaplain at S. Maria della Stella in Militello where he was born.

In 1617 he published a big treatise on the game, *Il gioco degli scacchi di don Pietro Carrera diviso in otto libri*. This work, not without theoretical importance, is very useful as a source of information on the players of his time.

Transferred first to Messina and then to Catania, he wrote on historical subjects about the localities where he exercised his functions and produced another work on chess which attacked Salvio strongly. *(H.G.)*

CASTALDI, Vincenzo *(15 May 1916–6 January 1970)*
Italian international master and dentist by profession, Castaldi was for many years the leading Italian player but the demands of his profession prevented him from properly utilizing his undoubted gifts for the game.

Italian champion in 1936, he won the title five more times, in 1937, 1947, 1948, 1953 and 1959. He came 9th/14 at the Hilversum Zonal tournament 1947, but his best results came in international team matches. He played on top board for Italy at the Stockholm Olympiad 1937 where he won two famous games against Tartakower and Reshevsky. He also played in the Dubrovnik Olympiad of 1950. *(H.G.)*

CASTLING
A composite move of the King and Rook; see LAWS OF CHESS, Article 6.1.

CASTRO ROJAS, Oscar Humberto *(b. 8 April 1953)*
Colombian international master who caused a sensation by beating the Soviet grandmasters Geller and Petrosian at the 1976 Interzonal tournament at Biel.

He was Colombian junior champion in 1969 and University champion in 1972. In the same year he won the Colombian championship, a success he was to repeat in the following year.

Castro played in the World Junior Championship in Stockholm 1969 and again in Athens in 1971. In 1972 he played in the Students Olympiad at Graz in Austria. He played in the Pan-American tournament at Winnipeg 1974 and in that year represented Colombia in the Nice Olympiad, scoring 47% on top board. At the 1976 Haifa Olympiad he scored 44% on second board.

He became an international master in 1975 when he won the St Domingo Zonal tournament. The following year he played in the Biel Interzonal and scored 6 points, coming 18th/20. Towards the end of the year he had an excellent result at the Costa Brava tournament at Maresme in Spain where he came 2nd to Larsen, ahead of Szabo, Zwaig, Marović etc. *(H.G.)*

CATALAN OPENING
1. P–Q4, N–KB3; 2. P–QB4, P–K3; 3. P–KN3. The idea of this opening is to reinforce the pressure exerted on the white squares by White's central pawns by a fianchetto of the K Bishop. It differs from the Queen's Gambit form of the Catalan in that Black refrains from an early P–Q4. *(H.G.)*

CENTRAL CHESS CLUB, Moscow
The *Tsentralny Shakhmatny Klub* of the USSR was opened on 18 August 1956 and quickly became the centre of chess organization in the Soviet Union. Each year the Central Chess Club holds a small international tournament. The first, in 1959, was the strongest of the series with =1st Bronstein, Smyslov and Spassky.

The club lies near the centre of Moscow, at 14 Gogolyevsky Boulevard, and its director is Viktor Davidovich Baturinsky. Before the Revolution it was the residence of the Civil Governor of Moscow and some of the rooms still are decorated in an early nineteenth-century style strongly resembling that of the English Regency period. As well as spacious premises and a good library, the club possesses an electronic demonstration board which was used for the first time during the 1972 World Championship match. *(W.R.H.)*

CENTRALIZATION
Centralization is the total body of a variety of stratagems with the object of controlling the centre and exerting influence over the board as a result of such control. Among the stratagems to be so exploited are prophylaxis, over-protection of central squares, outposts in a central open file, the 'mysterious rook move', the play against blockading pawn chains, and so on and so forth. In the ending, the main application of the principle of centralization is to secure a centralized position for the King so that it can infiltrate on either wing for either defence or attack; similarly a centralized Knight has greater effect than one on the wing. *(W.H.)*

CENTRE

In the narrow meaning of the term, the area consisting of each side's K4–Q4–Q5–K5 squares. In a wider sense, it is the squares encompassed by each side's 3rd and 6th ranks and the two B-files. The importance of the control of the centre (especially in the narrower sense) came to be realized as soon as chess began to be played according to positional principles. Thereafter, control of the centre was generally equated with the occupation of the centre by pawns; it took the hypermoderns to discover that such an approach was too formalistic and that control of the centre might be exerted by observation rather than occupation and that, if occupation there must be, it was in many cases more effective by pieces than by pawns. *(W.H.)*

CENTRE COUNTER DEFENCE

The opening 1. P–K4, P–Q4 suffered from a poor reputation for many years, since after 2. P×P, Q×P; 3. N–QB3, Black loses time with his Queen. It became fairly popular around 1960 when the move 2. . , N–KB3 was analysed and found to improve Black's prospects, though not, according to latest theory, sufficiently for equality. May transpose to the Caro-Kann after 2. P×P, N–KB3; 3. P–QB4, P–B3; 4. P–Q4, P×P. *(W.R.H.)*

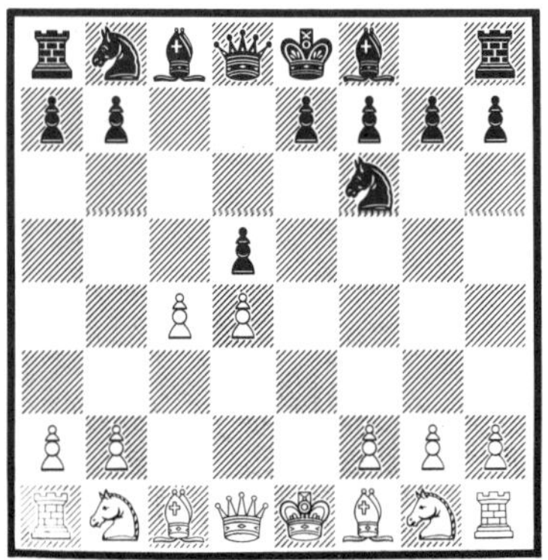

CENTRE GAME

By the moves 1. P–K4, P–K4; 2. P–Q4, P×P; 3. Q×P, White hopes for quick development and attacking chances. Its drawback is the early exposure of White's Queen, allowing Black to gain time with 3. . , N–QB3 and gain easy equality. This opening has virtually disappeared from master practice, having now only surprise value. *(W.R.H.)*

CHAJES, Oscar *(1873–28 February 1928)*

US master who was Austrian-born but emigrated to America before 1914 and became one of the most successful players in US events until the arrival of the generation of Fine and Reshevsky in the 1930s. Chajes settled in New York where he was secretary of the Isaac L. Rice Progressive Chess Club. He played in one major European event, Carlsbad 1911, where he tied for last place with Jaffe in a field of 26. His US accomplishments included winning the Western Open in 1909, the Manhattan Chess Club championship in 1920 and again in 1924, and coming 3rd behind Capablanca and Janowski at New York 1916. Chajes' win over Capablanca in the second round of the finals of the 1916 event was the last loss by the Cuban until 1924. *(A.S.)*

CHAROUSEK, Rudolph *(19 September 1873–18 April 1900)*

Hungarian grandmaster. He learned to play chess as an impoverished student at the Hungarian College at Kashau (Kassa) – it is said that he copied out by hand Bilguer's *Handbuch* since he could not afford to buy it – and soon displayed immense ability. Charousek made his international debut at the strong Nuremberg 1896 tournament, finishing only 12th out of 19, but defeating the winner, World Champion Dr Lasker, in their individual game. A few months later he came =1st with Chigorin at Budapest 1896, losing the play-off match. During the next two years Charousek produced a string of tournament successes, including notably first prize at Berlin 1897 and shared second prize at Cologne 1898. He was widely hailed as a brilliant player and potential World Championship contender, but ill-health had always dogged him and he died tragically, at the age of twenty-seven, of tuberculosis. *(R.D.K.)*

CHATRANG

The name which the Persians gave to chess when the game spread to Persia from north-west India some time in the sixth century AD. This was clearly derived from *chaturanga* and both the rules and the nature of the pieces remained the same.

The Persian romance *Karnamak*, written in the early seventh century, gives the names of the pieces. The *chatrang* equivalents of *chaturanga* were: Chaturanga Raja = *Shah* (modern King); Minister = *Farzin* ('wise man', modern Queen); Elephant = *Pil* (modern Bishop); Horse = *Asp* (modern Knight); Chariot = *Rukh* (modern Rook) and Foot-soldier = *Piyadah* (modern pawn). This is derived from *pai* which is Persian for 'foot'.

It is from the Persian that our modern 'checkmate' is obtained. Persian 'mat' meant 'helpless or defeated', so *shah-mat* eventually became 'checkmate'. *(H.G.)*

CHATURANGA

When the game of chess was invented in north-west India in the sixth century AD it was called *chaturanga* which is Sanskrit for 'four-membered'. Since the Indian armies were then composed of four divisions – infantry (*padati*), cavalry (*ashwa*), chariots (*rat-ha*) and elephants (*hasti* or *gaja*) – this was the equivalent of 'army game'.

The pieces, and the game, were an admirable reflection of contemporary warfare, hence the immediate popularity chess achieved. But the action of the pieces, likewise reflecting military methods of the time, was considerably slower than that of modern chess.

The *raja* (modern King), the *ashwa* or Horse (modern Knight) and the *rat-ha* or Chariot (modern Rook) all moved as their modern equivalents do, but the *mantri*, meaning Minister or Advisor (modern Queen), could move only to one adjacent diagonal square.

The *hasti* or Elephant (modern Bishop) moved diagonally, leaping over the adjacent square to the next. The *padati* or Foot-soldier (modern pawn) moved as the pawn does now; but it could not move two squares initially and when it reached the eighth rank it had to be promoted to a Minister, which did not much increase its strength.

Castling was not known, but the objective of the game was the same as it has always been – to deliver checkmate. Or a player could win by capturing all his opponent's army (with the exception of the *raja*, which, like the modern King, was not to be taken).

The pieces were initially arranged as their modern equivalents on a board of sixty-four squares known as *ashtāpada*. This was, however, unchequered and was borrowed from a much older type of game that was the ancestor of modern backgammon. *(H.G.)*

CHAUDÉ DE SILANS, Chantal *(b. 9 March 1919)*

International Woman master and undoubtedly the strongest woman player France ever produced, Chaudé de Silans represented her country in the (Men's) Olympiad at Dubrovnik in 1950 and later on at the Women's Olympiad of 1957.

In the first Women's World Championship to be held after the Second World War, Moscow 1949–50, she came =5th out of 16.

Thereafter a system of qualifying tournaments (Zonal and Candidates) was organized by FIDE. In the first Candidates tournament, at Moscow 1952, she came 10th out of 16. In the second, likewise at Moscow, in 1955 she was 12th out of 20.

First in a Women's Zonal tournament at Amsterdam 1961, she failed at the Candidates at Vrnačka Banja, Yugoslavia, later that year, coming =13th out of 17.

One of the most charming personalities in the chess-world, she excelled over the board in combinative play but was less at home in positional play. *(H.G.)*

CHECK

See under LAWS OF CHESS, Article 10.

CHECKMATE

See under ENDGAME.

CHÉRON, André *(b. 25 September 1895)*

French endgame theorist and composer of studies and problems whose four-volume *Lehrund Handbuch der Endspiele*, Berlin 1952–58, is his life's work and an important contribution to the art of chess. The latest revisions are Vol. 1 1971, Vol. 2 1969, Vols. 3 and 4 1970. This work is a study of basic endgames (with material drawn from many sources) and a selection of endgame studies.

Chéron is a theorist concerned with detailed proof of his statements about the endgame rather than with the needs of the practical player. It may seem surprising in one who has been three times French champion (1926, 1927 and 1929); that he has lived in retirement in Switzerland for many years. See also ENDGAME, HISTORY OF LITERATURE. *(D.H.)*

'CHESS'

The magazine *Chess* was founded in 1935 by the well-known Birmingham journalist and player B. H. Wood with the design of enlivening the British chess scene by a chattier approach to the game than the more staid *British Chess Magazine* had shown over the years.

This he succeeded in accomplishing and, by a remarkable tour de force, has continued in his post as editor, analyst, newshound and even, of recent years, as printer, without a break for forty-one years. Address: Sutton Coldfield, B73 6AZ. *(H.G.)*

'CHESS AMATEUR'

Published in England, it ran from 1906 to 1930. Fairhurst was a major contributor and, at the time, he gave a good appreciation of Tarrasch's principles. The magazine's problem section has earned it more lasting renown.

A magazine with the same title appeared in Malta in 1890; it ceased publication the same year. *(K.J.O'C.)*

'CHESS INFORMANT'

First published in 1966 in Belgrade when it was known as the *Chess Informator*, this is a twice-yearly publication which is principally concerned with giving the best and most significant games (from the point of view of opening theory) played in tournaments and matches in the preceding year.

To quote the preface to the first volume: 'The publication of *Chess Informator* represents the first attempt to follow and work out world chess trends with methods applied in modern science. All those games that discover chess secrets and its beauty – by their contributions to opening theory or their general contents – should find their place in this periodical.'

A figurine notation (algebraic) is used so as to make the work genuinely international and use is also made of six languages (English, French, German, Russian, Spanish and Serbo Croat) in the accompanying text. The notes are done by a set of symbols that is explained in every issue.

The *Informant* is published under FIDE auspices and devotes some space in each issue to FIDE information such as rating lists etc. Its editor is Aleksandar Matanović. *(H.G.)*

CHESSLET

A word invented by Dr J. Schumer to describe a witty method of annotating a game by the use of apposite quotations from poetry. He published a collection of such annotated games in 1928 (*Chesslets*, by Dr J. Schumer, London). In the following year he published a Chesslet in the London *Evening Standard*, giving the twelfth game of the match Alekhine–Bogoljubow with annotations by Shakespearean quotations. The witty pertinence of the poetic annotations is illustrated by a quotation used to describe White's (Bogoljubow's) 46th move when his King had been driven out into the open on KB4: 'I am desperate of my fortunes if they check me here'.

Chesslets have been largely forgotten, though the American grandmaster Larry Evans did pay Schumer the compliment of using the doctor's quotations at third hand to annotate a game.

Dr Schumer's taste was catholic and he searched far and wide for his quotations among Shakespeare, Scott, *Ingoldsby Legends*, W. S. Gilbert, T. Hood, Pope, nursery rhymes and proverbs.

He was best, however, with Shakespeare as his source of inspiration. As a sample we give Game No. 5 from the collection, just as Schumer portrayed it.

A brilliant game played in the tournament for the title 'Master of Berlin', in 1926. Annotated with Shakespearean quotations.

White: Von Hanning; *Black:* Langer (*Ruy Lopez*)

1. P–K4 P–K4
A stage, where every man must play a part.
2. N–KB3 N–QB3
I see you stand like greyhounds in the slips.
Straining upon the start.
3. B–N5 P–QR3
You two are bookmen . . .
4. B–R4
Wisely, and slow; they stumble that run fast.
N–B3
5. O–O N×P
Smooth runs the water where the brook is deep . . .
6. P–Q4 P×P
. . . some of us will smart for it.
Condemn the fault and not the actor of it.
7. R–K1
Then venom to thy work.
P–Q4
8. P–B4!
First thrush the corn, then after burn the straw . . .
P×P e.p.
9. N×P B–QN5
We have scotched the snake, not killed it . . .
10. B–KN5
Come not within the measure of my wrath.
P–B3
11. N–K5!
Double, double toil and trouble,
Fire burn, and cauldron bubble.

I pause for a reply.
O–O
12. B×N B×N
There is small choice in rotten apples.
13. B×P+
Well roared, Lion!
K–R1
Show me the steep and thorny way to heaven.
14. Q–R5!
Is she not passing fair?

On horror's head horrors accumulate.
B×N
Unquiet meals make ill digestions.
15. B×N
A snapper-up of unconsidered trifles.
P–KN3
When sorrows come, they come not single spies,
But in battalions!
16. B×KNP
This was the most unkindest cut of all.
Q–Q2
A woman moved is like a fountain troubled;
Muddy, ill-seeming, thick, bereft of beauty.
17. R×B!
These violent delights have violent ends.
P×R
18. R–Q1
If you have tears, prepare to shed them now.
Q–N2
She is a woman, therefore may be wooed;
She is a woman, therefore may be won.
19. B–B6!
The end crowns all.
Resigns
Now cracks a noble heart
Good night, sweet prince

The rest is silence. *(H.G.)*

'CHESS LIFE' 1946–1969

The official publication of the United States Chess Federation first appeared in 1946. It appeared monthly and the editors were, in succession, Burt Hochberg, Montgomery Major and J. F. Reinhardt. A copy of the publication was sent to every member of the US Chess Federation. Twenty-four yearly volumes were published until *Chess Life* was amalgamated with the *Chess Review*. *(H.G.)*

'CHESS LIFE AND REVIEW' 1969

In 1969 the United States Chess Federation acquired the rights of the *Chess Review* from Horowitz and united the magazine with *Chess Life* to form a new publication, *Chess Life and Review*, the first number appearing in November 1969.

The new magazine, which became the organ of the US Chess Federation, retained some of the features of *Chess Life* but was much closer to *Chess Review* in content and format. Like *Chess Life* it was sent to every member of the Federation.

Its editor is Burt Hochberg and its associate editor is Jack Straley Battell.

It is published monthly by the USCF, 186 Rt.9W, New Windsor, N.Y. 12550, USA. To non-members the subscription is $13.50 per year, single copy $1.50. *(H.G.)*

'CHESS MONTHLY' (Great Britain)
One of the very finest chess magazines; it began in September 1879 and continued until 1896. The principal editor was Leopold Hoffer, no mean chess journalist. However, it was the co-editorship of Zukertort, until his death in 1888, that gave the magazine its special quality. There were four regular sections each month: news, annotated games, problems and endgames. This was one of the first magazines to use the modern system of properly annotated games which had been partly pioneered by Zukertort in the *Berliner Schachzeitung*. *(K.J.O'C.)*

'CHESS MONTHLY' (USA)
This short-lived magazine was published from 1857 until 1861. Its two principal claims to fame lie in the names of the editors associated with it. The American bibliophile Daniel Willard Fiske (1831–1904) acted as editor throughout. A fine literary stylist, he also had great charm and succeeded in persuading Paul Morphy to act as games editor from 1858 until 1861. Morphy's notes are somewhat disappointing to the contemporary eye, for, though they are good, there are not very many of them. *(K.J.O'C.)*

CHESS OLYMPIADS FOR THE BLIND
Blind Chess Olympiads are genuine Olympiads in that, unlike the sighted variety, they are held once every four years. The organizing body is the International Braille Chess Association and the rules followed are those laid down by the association. Each team has four players and a reserve.

It is interesting to observe that the strength of the blind players is a faithful reflection of the strength of the sighted players in their respective country and, as the event has developed, so the predominance of Soviet and Yugoslav chess has become evident.

The first Olympiad was a modest affair in which only seven countries competed. It was held in 1958 at Meschede in West Germany. Yugoslavia came 1st, West Germany 2nd and Austria 3rd.

After an exceptional interval of 6 years, the second Olympiad took place at Kuhlungsborn in East Germany in 1964 with nine countries competing. Yugoslavia was again 1st, Hungary 2nd and East Germany 3rd.

The big advance came in 1968 when the Olympiad was held at Weymouth in the south of England. This time nineteen countries took part and the method of play was eleven rounds on the Swiss System.

This was the first occasion on which the Soviet Union took part and a struggle between the Soviet side and Yugoslavia was confidently expected. This did indeed take place. They met in the second round and a hard-fought 2–2 draw was the result. However, at first it was the Yugoslavs who took and held the lead. They faltered in the seventh round against Romania and it was not long before the Soviet side overhauled them.

So the USSR came 1st with 35 points. Yugoslavia 2nd with 33 and Romania 3rd with 31½, followed by East Germany 28½, Czechoslovakia 28, Austria 25½, Hungary and West Germany 23½, Spain 23, Eire 22½, United Kingdom 22, Poland 21½, Denmark and USA 21 etc.

Baretić of Yugoslavia, the blind champion who plays without braille

Even more teams, twenty-four, entered for the fourth Olympiad which was held at Pula, Yugoslavia in 1972. But the Swiss System was not used and instead the teams were divided into four preliminary groups of eight out of which two countries per group qualified for the top final section.

From Group A there came the USSR and Spain; from Group B Yugoslavia and England; from Group C Romania and Hungary and from Group D USA and East Germany.

The battle between the USSR and Yugoslavia in the top final group was even closer than before. In the end the USSR just managed to pass their rivals by half a point and so they retained their title with 21 points, followed by Yugoslavia 20½, Romania 15½, East Germany 14½, Spain 11, England 10½, USA and Hungary 9½.

In 1976 the fifth Olympiad was held at Kuortane in Finland. Twenty-one countries competed and this time the organizers reverted to eleven rounds on the Swiss System.

The title-holders sent a team with three new players and this made the rivalry between them and Yugoslavia even closer. Both teams were clearly in a class by themselves and in the end they tied for first place with 34½ points. But the Soviet team remained champions as they had the superior match point count (10½ match wins to Yugoslavia's 9½). Third was East Germany 27½, followed by Romania 27, West Germany 26½, USA 25½, Czechoslovakia 24, England 22½, Hungary 22½, Spain 21, Poland 20½ etc.

The following beautiful game was awarded the prize for the best played game of the third Olympiad at Weymouth in 1968.

White: Sandrin (USA); *Black:* Loftus (Eire)
Queen's Gambit Declined
1. P–Q4, P–Q4; 2. P–QB4, P–K3; 3. N–QB3, N–KB3; 4. B–N5, QN–Q2; 5. P×P, P×P; 6. P–K3, P–B3; 7. B–Q3, B–K2; 8. Q–B2, O–O; 9. N–B3, P–KR3; 10. P–KR4, R–K1; 11. O–O–O, P×B; 12. P×P, N–K5; 13. N×N, P×N;

14. P–N6!, N–B3; 15. P×P+, K×P; 16. N–K5+, K–N1; 17. B×P, N×B; 18. Q×N, B–B3; 19. Q–R7+, K–B1; 20. Q–N6, B–K3; 21. P–K4, Q–B2; 22. R–R5, B×N; 23. P×B, QR–Q1; 24. R×R, Q×R; 25. R–R8+, B–N1; 26. Q–R7, Q–N4+; 27. K–N1, K–B2; 28. P–K6+, K×P; 29. R×B, K–B2; 30. R×R, K×R; 31. Q–R3, Q–Q1; 32. Q–R8+, K–Q2; 33. Q×P+, K–B1; 34. Q–N4+, K–B2; 35. Q–B4+, K–B1; 36. Q–N4+, K–B2; 37. Q–K2, Q–R5; 38. P–R3, Q–R8+; 39. K–R2, Q×P; 40. Q–K3, Q–N3; 41. Q–N3+ and wins. *(H.G.)*

CHESS PIECES AND CHESS SETS

The chess-piece is a symbol of power and, as F. Lanier Graham puts it in his introduction to *Chess Sets,* it is 'a tool . . . used to exert an imaginary force within the world of the game'.

This being so, then, for the player who is merely concerned with the playing of chess, the best pieces are those that convey that symbolism with the most clarity and with the widest general acceptance as to their particular function.

Chessmen and chess sets have varied enormously over the ages, but, except where special works of art have been commissioned or when the creator of the set had some specialized objective other than producing pieces for play, general (indeed world-wide) acceptance has come to regard the Staunton pattern of chessmen, as devised by Nathaniel Cook in 1839 and registered in 1849 for the firm of Jaques which has manufactured them right down to the present day, as the normal set with which to play.

The earliest history of chess-pieces, thinking of them in relation to the years and indeed centuries immediately succeeding the invention of chess, is more than obscure. The oldest-known complete chess set is the Isle of Lewis chessmen dating probably

Russian, 2nd century A.D.

17th century German chessboard with floral marquetry

14th century German King

16th century German Knight

13th century Irish, believed to be a chess piece made of fictile ivory

10th century Byzantine rock crystal thought to be a chess piece

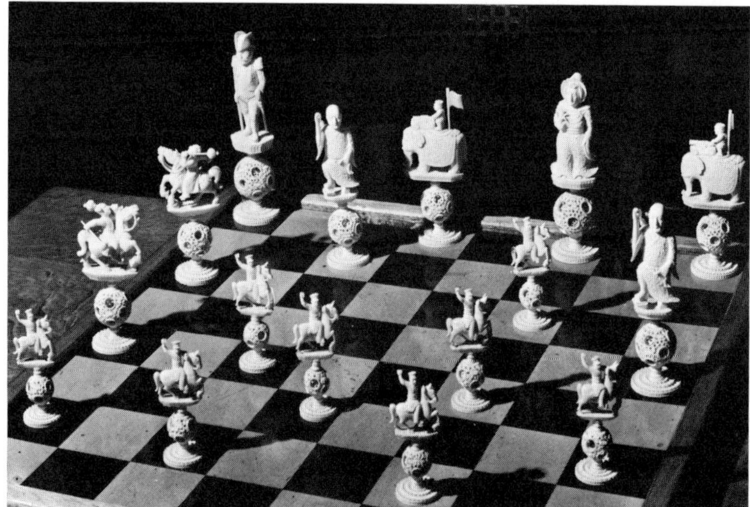

19th century Cantonese ball mounted chess set

18th century rare Chinese chess pieces carved from Indian ivory

Jasper ware pawn, modelled by John Flaxman 1785

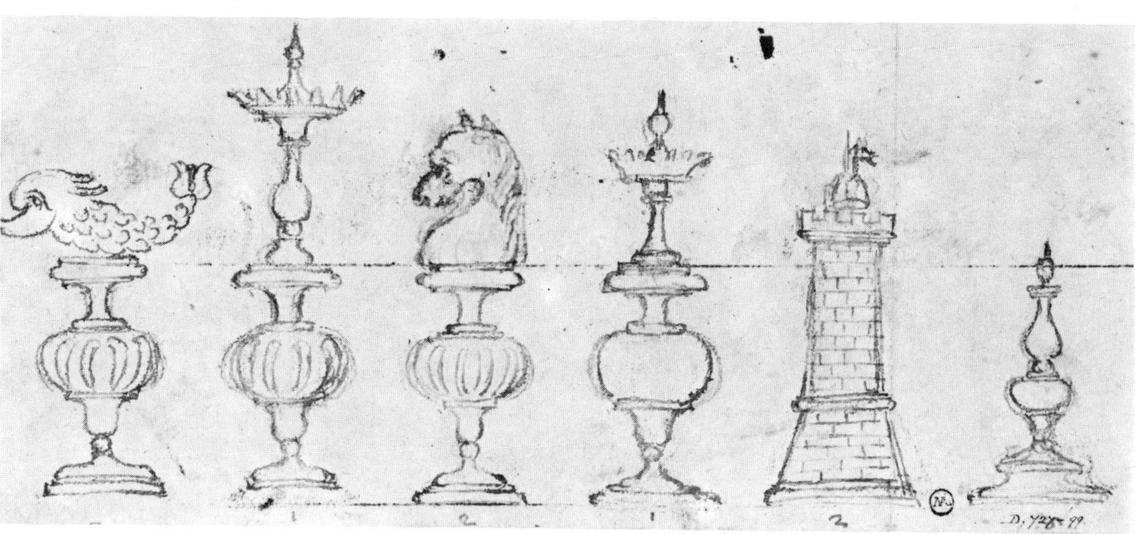

17th century Italian designs for a chess set

19th century Indian chess set in the shape of the British Raj v. Oriental warriors

English 19th century set in dark green and clear, cut glass

Modern chess pieces in the Tajik style

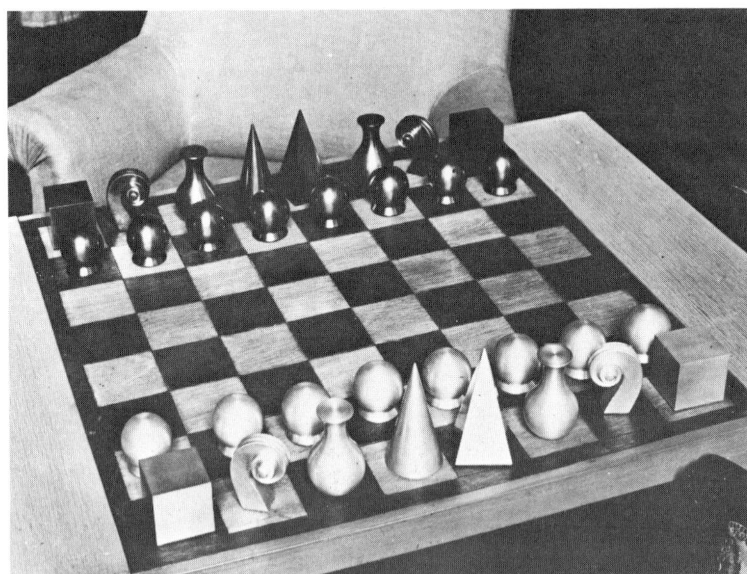

20th century artists have experimented with new shapes in an attempt to reflect the Movements to which they belonged

The 'war game' chess set by the American sculptor Roy Schiffrin

Pieces in the Staunton style

from the eleventh century AD and again probably Viking in origin.

Individual pieces survive from earlier periods and, if the Soviet archaeologists are right in assuming that two small animal figures discovered at the ancient site of Dalverzin-tepe in Uzbekistan in 1972 are in fact chessmen, then these pieces even precede the generally accepted date of the invention of chess by more than three centuries. The two pieces, one an elephant and the other a zebu, are dated second century AD and there is no special reason to assume they are chessmen.

The earliest known piece would seem to be a most beautifully carved ivory King, clearly of an Indian type, but with an Arabic inscription serving to show that it was indeed made by the Arabs in the eighth or ninth century when they had become the chess powers of the world.

Almost as old but much more rudimentary in character are some Arabic bone pieces to be seen in the Germanisches National-museum at Nuremberg and some Persian pieces excavated by Charles K. Wilkinson at Nishapur. The latter are slightly more representational in that an attempt has been made to portray the elephant. Both are dated eighth or ninth century.

Evidence of the part the Vikings played in bringing chess to Europe and in spreading the game there is to be found in the early European chess pieces that have come down to us. We have already mentioned the Lewis set but there were a few pieces that preceded this.

One remarkable evidence of the role the Vikings played in the spreading of chess is to be found in the Musée de Cluny in Paris where there is an ivory Knight of Nordic origin but based on an Arab model. This is dated as ninth to tenth century. The British Museum also has an early Bishop, made from whalebone and dated as tenth century. It is supposed to be Anglo-Saxon but looks just as Nordic as the Cluny Knight. Possibly the first English piece that has come down to us is quite an elaborate King that may be seen in the Salisbury and South Wiltshire Museum. It is dated twelfth century and made of morse ivory (Walrus) like the Isle of Lewis men.

It was rock crystal that was used for the more elaborate chess-pieces on the Continent of Europe at this time. Such a set is mentioned in the will of the Count of Urgel (near the modern Andorra) dated 1008, in which he leaves his chessmen to the convent of St Giles, and the daughter of the Count of Carcassonne left 'to St Giles of Nîmes her crystal chessmen' in her will of 1058. Possibly one or other of these is the source of the Ager chessmen, so-called because they were found in a church at Ager, a village near Urgel, and these pieces are certainly of rock crystal.

Now the chess-pieces, at least those that have come down to us, became more elaborate. At the same time, while still showing signs of the old Arabic rules, they take on a medieval and wholly European air. Two good examples date from the late eleventh and early twelfth century and originate in South Italy. One shows the Queen, which is still however a Vizier or Minister, flanked as it were by two court pageboys. The other is an ivory King with two bodyguards bearing sword and shield.

In the next couple of centuries a sort of heavy and complicated Gothic naturalism characterizes the pieces in keeping with the architecture of the time.

With the Renaissance there comes a fresh simplicity and the pieces begin to bear a distinct resemblance to our modern ones. Chess and chess-pieces are more popular so that by the fifteenth and sixteenth centuries many household inventories mention a chess set. More elaborate sets are mentioned in the inventories of such monarchs as Henry VIII and Queen Elizabeth I of England. But it is significant that even such a magnificent set as the fifteenth-century Burgundian pieces to be seen in the Musée de Cluny in Paris, made as it is of rock crystal, topaz and silver, would already be recognized by a modern chess-player as King, Queen, Bishop and Knight, etc. By the end of the sixteenth century chess-pieces appear that would call for no comment in the nineteenth and twentieth centuries.

As regards the quality and style of the more ceremonial chess sets, it has to be admitted that a general decline occurred in the seventeenth and eighteenth centuries. First, baroque and then rococo applied a much too ornate air to the pieces. By a sort of natural compensation, the Chinese and Indian sets that were produced in profusion in the eighteenth and nineteenth centuries were often of great artistic value and nearly always interesting. They were made principally for export to Europe (in particular this applies to the Chinese who did not play our form of chess) and where they did err in the matter of over-ornateness it was in deference to European bad taste.

The Chinese developed their own special type of chess-piece mounted on most beautifully carved hollow balls of ivory. These were mostly made in Canton and a fine specimen of this type is to be found in the Chess Room of the British House of Commons.

A favourite device was to show the pieces as two rival armies, the one side Chinese and the other some foreign army: Mongol, English or French. With a fine sense of export values, those sets destined for France portrayed the White King and Queen as Napoleon and Josephine, and those for England as King George and his consort.

An interesting and fairly common type of set is known as the Portuguese, from the fact that the pieces were made in the Portuguese colony of Macao. In fact, they were Chinese and all carved by Chinese workmen living in the colony. They were very much for export only and consisted of a representation of human heads mounted on two ivory or coral carved balls. Since they were meant for England, the King and Queen were always English monarchs and the White Rooks carried as their flag the Union Jack.

Indian sets were all made of ivory and many reflect the fact that the real struggle to gain possession of India was between the East India Company and the native rulers, so that we quite often find sets in which the two forces are represented on either side. Certainly the most beautiful Indian sets come from Kashmir and were made at the end of the eighteenth century. The elaborate carvings have a lace-like, ethereal quality.

One striking type of Indian set was made in Delhi and the surrounding districts towards the end of the nineteenth century. These show the busts of celebrated personages mounted on the lower half of a chess-piece. One famous type shows Sir Colin

Campbell and Nana Sahib as opposing Kings and refers to the Indian Mutiny of 1857.

Towards the end of the eighteenth century and certainly in the nineteenth the quality and ingenuity of chess sets in Europe, particularly in France and in England, improved noticeably. In the late eighteenth century Josiah Wedgwood produced wonderful chess sets in pottery at his Etruria works. They were based on the designs of John Flaxman and were the first portrait chess sets to be produced in pottery. The firm is still (1976) producing magnificent chess sets of high artistic merit.

A number of fine attractive sets were made in France, notably in Paris and Dieppe in the early half of the nineteenth century. Many depict variations on the theme of the Napoleonic Wars between France and England with, on the one side, such characters as Napoleon, Ney and Massena and, on the other, Nelson and Wellington.

Ordinary playing sets in England had, as has already been said, fallen into the Staunton pattern by the middle of the nineteenth century and a sign of its enduring popularity appears from the fact that the Icelandic organizers of the match between Spassky and Fischer in Reykjavik in 1972 had to send to England for the Staunton set at the special request of Fischer.

Artists in the twentieth century experimented with new shapes for chess-pieces in the spirit of the various movements of the century. The Dadaists produced sets made out of nuts and bolts; the Surrealists and the Expressionists fanciful sets in their own almost subconscious way; and the Bauhaus with its functional forms designed pieces of a squat ugliness.

Then, in the 1960s, there came a significant return to former artistic values. Artists began to create chess-pieces that were a pleasure to look at and to handle whilst still being recognizable as pieces. The American sculptor Roy Shifrin made a striking set in bronze in which he returned to the original concept of chess as a war game and other artists employed modern materials such as perspex and even the everyday plastic to great and harmonious effect.

Literature:

Chessmen, Donald Macy Liddell, with the collaboration of Gustavus A. Pfeiffer and J. Maunoury, New York, London 1938; *The Book of Chessmen,* Alex Hammond, London, New York 1950; *Chess, the Story of Chesspieces from Antiquity to Modern Times,* Hans and Siegfried Wichmann, London, New York 1964; *Chessmen,* Alfred Ernest James Mackett-Beeson, London 1968; *Chess Sets,* F. Lanier Graham, New York, London 1968. *(H.G.)*

'CHESS PLAYER, THE'

The third periodical to carry this title began publication in 1971. The success of *Chess Informant* and other publications principally devoted to opening theory led its founder, Tony Gillam, to produce an *Informant*-style magazine. For the first three years complete tournaments were included, then a switch was made to giving the material in opening order and then, at the end of 1976, *The Chess Player* approached still closer the style of its rival publication when the magazine form was dropped; it now appears as three bound volumes a year. Address: 12 Burton Avenue, Carlton, Nottingham NC4 1PT. *(K.J.O'C.)*

'CHESS PLAYER'S CHRONICLE'

The first successful English-language magazine devoted exclusively to chess; George Walker's short-lived *Philidorian* had met with very little response in 1837–8. The proprietor and editor from 1841 to 1854 was Howard Staunton. He had always had a wish to earn his living from his (at times vitriolic) pen and the magazine was a successful basis for this.

In 1854 R. B. Brien took over the magazine, but was unable to continue its success and publication ceased in 1856. It reappeared in 1859, edited by Kolisch, Zytogorski and Kling, but survived only until 1862. Thereafter magazines bearing the same, or slightly modified, title appeared from 1863 to 1867, 1868 to 1875 and 1877 to 1902. However, the quality never again compared with that achieved under Staunton's editorship and competition from the *British Chess Magazine,* by the turn of the century a superb magazine, put an end to the title. *(K.J.O'C.)*

'CHESS REVIEW' 1933–1969

Founded in 1933, the *Chess Review,* published monthly in New York, prided itself on being a pictorial magazine. Its first editor was the grandmaster, Isaac Kashdan, who was in charge for only a year.

He was succeeded by Israel Albert Horowitz, usually known as Al, and he remained editor of the magazine till the end of its days in 1969 when it was sold to the US Chess Federation and amalgamated with *Chess Life.* *(H.G.)*

CHESS, Varieties of

See under VARIETIES OF CHESS.

'CHESS WORLD' (Australia)

This Australian magazine, edited by C. J. S. Purdy, ran from 1946 until 1966/7. It followed on from *The Australasian Chess Review* (1929–1944) and *Check!* (1944–1945). *Chess World* set a very high standard of readability and its valuable instructional articles make it still sought after. *(K.J.O'C.)*

'CHESS WORLD' (Belgium)

Subtitled the 'International Chess Review', this magazine, which ran during 1932 and 1933 under the editorship of George Koltanowski, was very much international in outlook. It was the first English-language chess magazine to be published in a non-English-speaking country. *(K.J.O'C.)*

CHIBURDANIDZE, Maia *(b. January 1961)*

The first real prodigy among women players and another product of Georgian women's chess (see also ALEXANDRIA and GAPRINDASHVILI). Her best results in the USSR Girls' championship have been 3rd in 1973 and 1st in 1976. Those results are less remarkable than her performances in the USSR Women's championships: 17th in 1973, =5th in 1974, =7th in 1975 and =9th in 1976.

Maia Chiburdanidze giving a simultaneous display

=5th in 1974, =7th in 1975 and =9th in 1976.

Maia was awarded the title of international woman master in 1974, thus becoming the youngest title holder, of either sex, in the history of the game. Her best results have been 1st at Braşov 1974, =1st at Tbilisi 1975 and, most impressive of all, =2nd in the 1976 Tbilisi Women's Interzonal (missing the grandmaster title by half a point) and thus qualifying for the 1977 Candidates. *(K.J.O'C.)*

CHIGORIN [Tschigorin, Tchigorin], Mikhail Ivanovich
(12 November 1850–25 January 1908)
A Russian player generally accepted as the father of the present Soviet chess school. Chigorin only took up serious chess comparatively late in life, when he was already over twenty, but within a couple of years he was already established as one of the best players of St Petersburg. In the years 1878–80 he played a series of matches with one of the leading players of the country, Emanuel Schiffers. Chigorin won three and lost only one of these matches and subsequent victories against Schmidt (in three matches in 1879) and Alapin (in 1880) established him as Russia's leading player.

His international debut at Berlin 1881 was successful since he shared 3rd prize behind Zukertort and Blackburne. A poor performance at Vienna 1882 was followed by another excellent showing in the strong tournament of London 1883 (4th place behind Steinitz, Zukertort and Blackburne).

Chigorin's first attempt to deprive Steinitz of the World Championship crown in 1889 was unsuccessful, clearly but not disastrously (+6−10=1). The same year Chigorin shared first place (with Weiss) at New York ahead of Gunsberg, Blackburne, Burn and others.

Chigorin then turned his attention more to match-play with some of the world's leading players: 1890 drew with Gunsberg (+9−9=5), 1892 lost again to Steinitz (+8−10=5), 1893 drew with Tarrasch (+9−9=4) and also won some matches against the leading Russian players.

Chigorin resumed his successful tournament career at Hastings 1895 (2nd) and Budapest 1896 (1st), but in the following few years his results deteriorated and he never again made a serious bid for the World Championship.

Chigorin took a very active role in the organization of tournaments in Russia and continued to score good results both in national and international events in his homeland until the year of his death.

His contribution to chess theory cannot be over-estimated. It might even be suggested that Chigorin's competitive results suffered from his intense, even over-riding, desire for victory in his purely polemical dispute with the followers of the dogmatic Tarrasch school.

His defence to the Ruy Lopez survives even today as one of Black's most popular and respected choices; and while the same cannot truthfully be maintained of his defence to the Queen's Gambit, there is no doubt that here, too, the ideas behind it have influenced chess thinking to the present day. His ideas in the Old Indian Defence led to much of the early development of the King's Indian, and contribute much towards Chigorin's reputation as one of the great original chess thinkers.

Chigorin's chess style was at its most effective in positions allowing open piece play.

Budapest 1896
White: Chigorin; *Black:* Charousek
Two Knights Defence
1. P–K4, P–K4; 2. N–KB3, N–QB3; 3. B–B4, N–B3; 4. P–Q4, P×P; 5. O–O, B–B4; 6. P–K5, P–Q4; 7. P×N, P×B; 8. R–K1+, B–K3; 9. N–N5, Q–Q4; 10. N–QB3, Q–B4; 11. N(3)–K4, B–N3; 12. N–N3, Q–N3; 13. N×B, P×N; 14. R×P+, K–Q2; 15. N–R5, KR–K1; 16. N–B4, Q–B2; 17. Q–B3, QR–Q1; 18. B–Q2, P×P; 19. QR–K1, R×R; 20. N×R, R–K1; 21. N–N5, R×R+; 22. B×R, Q–K2; 23. Q–B5+, K–Q1; 24. B–Q2, Q–K7; 25. Q×P+, N–K2; 26. P–KR4, P–Q6; 27. N–B7+, K–B1; 28. Q–R8+, K–Q2; 29. Q–Q8+, K–K3; 30. N–N5+, K–B4; 31. Q–KB8+, resigns.

Chigorin, Steinitz and others at the 1889 match

CHILE

One of the stronger chess nations of South America. The national side has competed in eight Olympiads: 12th in 1939, 8th in 1950, 22nd in 1956 and 1960, 24th in 1964, 38th in 1966 and 1974, and 16th in 1976.

The controlling organization is the Federacion de Ajedrez de Chile, Serrano 14, Of. 102, Santiago. *(K.J.O'C.)*

CHINA

'European' chess seems not to have reached China before the mid-nineteenth century. Although a visit by Alekhine to Shanghai in 1933 aroused some interest, it was not until the mid 1950s that the game became widespread.

China emerged into world chess in 1975 when the Philippines national team toured Peking, Shanghai and Hangchow, playing six matches against the Chinese national side. For a country completely new to international chess competition the Chinese performed creditably, losing only by 25–35.

The official body is the Chess Association of the People's Republic of China, 9 Tiyukuan Road, Peking. *(K.J.O'C.)*

CHRISTIANSEN, Larry Mark *(b. 27 June 1956)*

One of the United States' most promising young players. He won the US Junior championship in successive years from 1973 to 1975, equalling the record set by Rogoff in 1971. Silver medallist in the 1975 World Junior Championship, he has subsequently finished =2nd (after Petrosian) at Lone Pine 1976 and achieved his first grandmaster norm at Torremolinos 1976. *(K.J.O'C.)*

CHURCHILL, Lord Randolph *(13 February 1849–24 January 1895)*

Winston Churchill's father was, to quote from one of his very last letters, 'an ardent chess-player'. He played and followed chess devotedly from his early college days till the time when his political career took up all his energies. He was a vice-president of the British Chess Association and took lessons from both Zukertort and Steinitz. He was often to be seen as a spectator at the great London tournament of 1883. *(H.G.)*

CINEMA, Chess in the

Film makers have made constant use of chess for two particular purposes: one is pictorial in that the game, its board and pieces are photogenic and add much to the handsomeness of a picture. The other is that of intellectual snobbery. The film industry has always been conscious of the necessity for at least appearing to appeal to the intellect and, by invoking chess themes, it hopes to persuade its public that it also concerns itself with intellectual matters.

A common means for demonstrating that the personages of the film world are thinking human beings is the showing of them engaged in playing chess. Thus, for example, in *The Thomas Crown Affair*, an American film of the 1970s, Crown, a highly successful bank-robber, plays chess with equal success against a highly personable female investigator. Similarly, advantage was taken of the fact that Humphrey Bogart was known to be a keen chess-player in real life to show him playing chess with Peter Lorre in the film *Casablanca* made in America in 1943.

On an altogether higher plane was the use made of a chess theme by the great Swedish film director, Ingmar Bergman, in *The Seventh Seal*. In this a game of chess is the central point of the argument which is in the nature of a medieval morality.

Antonius, a Swedish knight returning from the Crusades, finds a Europe beset by the plague and torn by dissension and doubt. A wanderer in a black cloak reveals himself as Death and the two play a game of chess with Antonius pledging his life as the stake and Death promising to reveal the secret of human existence if he loses.

This staking of one's life on a game of chess is also to be found in the French romantic film *L'Atlantide*, based on Pierre Bénoit's romance of the same name. A French soldier, wandering in darkest Africa, comes across a native kingdom ruled by a white princess who is it seems a fine chess-player. His life is spared even though he is brilliantly defeated by the princess in a game that runs a recognizable and credible course.

The film was made twice, once in the 1930s and then again in 1950 with Maria Montez as the Princess Antinea and Jean-Pierre Aumont as the Lieutenant de Saint-Avit. It was from the later version that Ahmed Alkdir made an ingenious reconstruction of the game based on the shots of the chessboard taken by the camera. It was published in the July issue of the 1950 *Ajedrez Español* and ran as follows:

White: Antinea; *Black:* Lt. de Saint-Avit
Centre Gambit
1. P–K4, P–K4; 2. P–Q4, P×P; 3. N–KB3, B–B4; 4. B–Q3, N–K2; 5. O–O, O–O; 6. P–B3, P×P; 7. N×P, P–Q3; 8. B–K3, N–Q2; 9. P–QR4, N–QB3; 10. P–R5, P–QR3; 11. R–R4, P–QN4; 12. P×P e.p., B×P; 13. B×B, P×B; 14. P–K5, N(Q2)×P; 15. N×N, P×N; 16. Q–B3, Q–B2; 17. R–QB4, B–N2; 18. R–B1, P–QN4; 19. N–Q5, Q–R4;

20. B×P+, K×B; 21. Q–R5+, K–N1; 22. N–B6+, P×N; 23. R–N4 mate.

Another romantic film on a chess theme that had some sort of historical basis was *The Chess Player* which was taken from a rather feeble French novel by H. Dupuy-Mazuel. The story concerned Kempelen's chess automaton and had as its high point an encounter with the Russian Empress Catherine the Great. The film, a silent one made in 1926, was of higher quality than the novel, as it was dramatized by Marcel Achard and had as its principal actor

'The Thomas Crown Affair'

'L'Atlantide'

Ingmar Bergman's 'The Seventh Seal'

'The Wooden Horse'

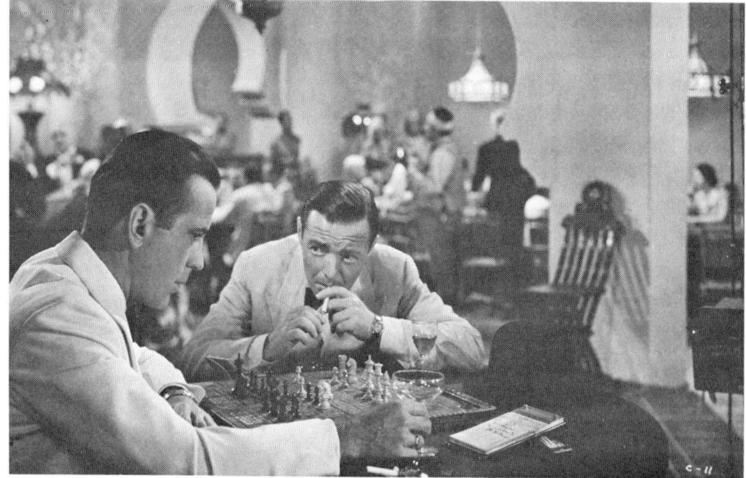

Bogart in 'Casablanca'

Pierre Blanchard. An excellent sound version was made in 1938 by Jean Dréville, with Françoise Rosay as the Empress Catherine and Conrad Veidt as Kempelen.

Remarkably, chess has also been used as the stuff of a film comedy. This was the earliest film of the great Pudovkin and was entitled *Chess Fever*. He took advantage of the fact that the 1925 international tournament was taking place in Moscow to show the excitement and fascination of the game to the general public, utilizing such real personages as Capablanca and Lasker as figures in his short film.

The comic element in the film is supplied by a Russian student so absorbed by chess that he wanders across Moscow's busiest streets with his eyes fixed on a pocket chess set and totally ignoring the traffic. This is bad enough but when his chess fever reaches such a pitch that he forgets and ignores his fiancée, the latter goes to Capablanca for advice. 'Simple', he says, 'all you've got to do is to learn how to play chess yourself'. She takes his advice and the film ends with the two lovers wandering off hand-in-hand and gazing in adoration at a pocket chess set.

The film is extant and occasionally shown in London and New York. Harry Golombek saw it during a visit to Moscow in 1957 when he acted as judge in a World Championship match between Botvinnik and Smyslov. *(H.G.)*

CIOCÂLTEA, Victor [**Ciocîltea**] *(b. 16 January 1932)*
Romanian international master and seven times Romanian champion. International master since 1957. He has had several international tournament successes including first places at Reggio Emilia 1966/7 and 1968/9, Dortmund 1974 and Bucharest 1975.

ČIRIĆ, Dragoljub *(b. 12 November 1935)*
Yugoslav grandmaster. International master title 1961. Awarded grandmaster title for performance at Sochi 1965. Ambitious and hard-working, Čirić rose almost to the top of the Yugoslav chess hierarchy. Best results: =1st with Tal, Sarajevo 1966, =1st with Lein, Sarajevo 1968 and =1st Sant Felin de Guixols 1975. He has represented Yugoslavia in two Olympiads; but in recent years there has been a sudden decline and falling away in his results due to bad health. *(R.D.K.)*

CLARE BENEDICT TEAM TOURNAMENT
Annual international team-of-four tournament for Western European nations, named in honour of the expatriate American authoress Mrs Clare Benedict (*d.* 1962) who first sponsored the competition in 1953. The original Clare Benedict trophy was won outright by West Germany in 1963, when it became the first nation to win the event six times, but a new cup was donated by the President of the West German Chess Federation.

The tournament was not held in 1975 and its future continuation is uncertain, owing to lack of proper financial support. Past results:

Mont Pélérin sur Vevey, Switzerland 1953
1. The Netherlands
2. Austria
3. Switzerland
4. France
5. Italy
6. Belgium

1954 No competition

Mont Pélérin sur Vevey, Switzerland 1955
1. The Netherlands
2. Switzerland
3. Austria
4. Italy
5. England
6. Belgium

Lenzerheide, Switzerland 1956
1. West Germany
2. The Netherlands
3. Italy
4. Switzerland
5. Austria
6. England

Gurten-Kulm, Switzerland 1957
1. West Germany
2. The Netherlands
3. Austria
4. Switzerland
5. Italy
6. France

Chaumont, Switzerland 1958
1. Switzerland
2. Spain
3. West Germany
=4. Austria and
The Netherlands
6. Italy

Lugano, Switzerland 1959
1. West Germany
=2. Spain and Austria
4. Switzerland
5. The Netherlands
6. Italy

Biel, Switzerland 1960
1. West Germany
2. England
3. Switzerland
4. Austria
5. Italy
6. Spain

Neuhausen am Rheinfall, Switzerland 1961
1. Austria
2. West Germany
=3. England and
The Netherlands
5. Switzerland
6. Italy

Gurten-Kulm, Switzerland 1962
1. West Germany
2. Spain
3. England
4. Austria
5. Switzerland
6. The Netherlands

Lucerne, Switzerland 1963
1. West Germany
2. The Netherlands
3. England
4. Austria
5. Spain
6. Switzerland

Lenzerheide, Switzerland 1964
1. West Germany
2. The Netherlands
3. Austria
4. Spain
5. Switzerland
6. Italy

West Berlin, Germany 1965
1. West Germany
2. Spain
3. The Netherlands
4. England
5. Austria
6. Switzerland

Brunnen, Switzerland 1966
1. The Netherlands
2. Spain
3. West Germany
4. Austria
5. England
6. Switzerland

Madrid, Spain 1971
1. The Netherlands
2. England
3. Spain
4. Austria
5. West Germany
6. Switzerland

Leysin, Switzerland 1967
1. West Germany
=2. England and Spain
4. The Netherlands
5. Austria
6. Switzerland

Vienna, Austria 1972
1. West Germany
2. The Netherlands
3. Spain
4. England
5. Switzerland
6. Austria

Bad Aibling, West Germany 1968
1. West Germany
2. The Netherlands
3. England
4. Spain
5. Switzerland
6. Austria

Gstaad, Switzerland 1973
1. West Germany
=2. England and Denmark
4. The Netherlands
5. Spain
6. Austria
7. Switzerland
8. Italy

Adelboden, Switzerland 1969
1. The Netherlands
2. Switzerland
=3. West Germany, England and Spain
6. Austria

Menorca, Spain 1974
1. England
2. West Germany
3. Switzerland
4. Denmark
5. Sweden
6. The Netherlands
7. Spain
8. Austria

Paignton, England 1970
=1. Spain, England and West Germany
4. Switzerland
=5. The Netherlands and Austria

(R.D.K.)

CLARKE, Peter Hugh *(b. 18 March 1933)*
A British master, and chess correspondent of the *Sunday Times*.

Peter Clarke was born in London and his early chess was played in that city.

Possessor of a clear-cut and competent style, he became one of the leading young British players and had excellent results in the British championship tournaments in which, though he never secured the title, he came second on five occasions.

He represented the B.C.F. at the Zonal tournaments of 1957, 1960 and 1964, but his best results were achieved not in individual international tournaments but in team events where his equable temperament and solid worth made him a valuable member of the English team.

He played in the Olympiads of 1954, 1956, 1958, 1960, 1962, 1964, 1966 and 1968. His best performance was at Moscow 1956 where, as number 5 of the team, he obtained 79.2% (+7—0=5). As his career developed, however, he became over-objective in his play and lost his incisiveness. In the 1968 Olympiad at Lugano he failed to win a game, drawing 7 and losing 1.

As his playing career declined so his writing career increased in scope and activity. He has written a number of lucid and competent works on the game, specializing in Russian subjects, since he is a Russian scholar.

His chief works are: *Mikhail Tal's Best Games of Chess,* London 1961; *Petrosian's Best Games of Chess, 1946–1963,* London 1965.

(H.G.)

CLOCKS

Although mechanical clocks have been in existence for some four hundred years, and sand glasses considerably longer, it was not until the latter half of the nineteenth century that either was introduced to chess for the purpose of limiting the amount of time a player might spend on a game.

Although a chronometer was used to record the amount of time taken over each move in most of the games of the Staunton v. Saint-Amant match of 1848, it was not, apparently, until 1861 that any kind of time limit was enforced.

In 1861 the Anderssen-Kolisch match in London saw the innovation of timing by means of an hour glass for each player; the time limit was 24 moves in two hours. It is hard to believe that sand glasses were not used before 1861, but if they were it is not known when or where.

The London tournament of 1862 was the first tournament in which the players had to face a time limit (20 moves in two hours), again regulated by sand glasses.

It was not long before mechanical clocks were introduced. According to Le Lionnais, independent clocks were used in the

Anderssen–Steinitz match of 1866. As with sand glasses, the drawbacks of this system were soon noted.

By the early 1880s the first mechanical 'double' chess clock had been invented. Its designer was Thomas Bright Wilson (1843–1915) of Manchester. The 'chess clock' as such made its debut at the great London tournament of 1883.

FATTORINI & SONS' CHESS TIMING CLOCKS,
Complete 12/6 Net.
Pair of Clocks on Stand, 12/6 Net.
The Clocks are perfection as timekeepers.
Every one guaranteed.
Pair of Clocks on Stand, 12/6 Net.
The Clocks are perfection as timekeepers.
Every one guaranteed.
FATTORINI & SONS
As used at the National Tournament, London, 1887; International Tournament, Bradford, 1888; International Tournament, Amsterdam, 1889; International Tournament, Manchester, 1890; Great Tournament, Vienna, 1890; and all the principal tournaments in Europe during the past five years. In every case giving the greatest satisfaction.

The early chess clocks operated on a pendulum method which can best be understood by consulting the illustration – the clock in mid-air being the one in motion.

The change from the pendulum clock to the modern push-button variety occurred between 1895 and 1900. Another three quarters of a century passed before the next major development – the appearance, in the early 1970s, of electronic digital clocks. *(K.J.O'C.)*

COBO, Eldis [**E. Cobo Arteaga**] *(b. 5 September 1929)*
A post office engineer, he was, during the 1960s, the number two in Cuba behind Jimenez. A regular member of the Cuban Olympiad squad in eight of the ten Olympiads in which they have competed (he missed 1939 and 1974); in the first six of them he registered the best or second best score for his team. In 1976 he tied for first place in one of the master groups of the Capablanca Memorial tournament in Cienfuegos. *(K.J.O'C.)*

COCHRANE, John *(4 February 1798–2 January 1878)*
A barrister of the Middle Temple and a leading London player of the early nineteenth century. In 1821 Cochrane visited France and while there played matches against Deschapelles (at odds of pawn and two moves) and La Bourdonnais (at level terms), losing both. He left England in 1824 to join the Indian Bar and remained in India until his retirement in 1869. During 1841–3 Cochrane returned to London on leave and during this period played over six hundred casual games with Staunton, losing the majority, and a match with Saint-Amant, winning +6–4=1. His style was brilliant but frequently unsound. *(R.D.K.)*

COHN, Erich *(1 March 1884–28 August 1918)*
A talented young German player, Cohn never quite fulfilled his promise, mainly because of his frail constitution. His best results were therefore obtained in very short contests such as the Berlin Four Master tournaments in 1910 (=1st), 1911 (1st), and 1914 (=1st). His only good result in a long event was 3rd at Abbazia 1912 (Spielmann 1st, Důras 2nd). He beat Carls and Post in short matches. He was killed in action towards the end of the First World War. *(W.H.)*

COHN, Wilhelm *(6 February 1859–17 August 1913)*
A German chess professional at the turn of the century. His best performances were a share in second prize (with Charousek and Chigorin, behind Burn) at Cologne 1898, and 3rd at Barmen 1905. In big events, like London 1899 and Ostend 1907, he made negative scores; in match-play he was beaten by Walbrodt (1894) and Post (1910). *(W.R.H.)*

COLLE, Edgar *(18 May 1897–20 April 1932)*
Belgian master and a player of enormous combinational ability, Colle lived most of his short life in ill-health. His photographs show a face pinched with pain but a look in the eyes of pathetic hope.

His tournament results reflected this. But for the operations he had to undergo he would certainly have been a grandmaster with aspirations towards World Championship honours. As it was he showed himself to be the leading player of his country (ahead of another master of undoubted talent, George Koltanowski) and produced a flow of beautiful brilliancies.

Ghent was his home town and he won its championship in 1917, gaining the Belgian championship five years later.

Colle's international career commenced in 1923. Playing in a tournament at Scheveningen where ten foreign masters played against ten Dutchmen headed by Dr Euwe, he scored 8/10 and came =3rd with Maróczy and Réti. An =3rd with Yates at Hastings 1923/4 was followed by a creditable =7th with Opocensky and L. Steiner at Meran 1924 and a good 3rd in the top final section of the Paris Olympiad. In that year, too, he lost an exciting match to Dr Euwe by +3–5=0.

In 1925 he demonstrated his superiority to Koltanowski by winning a match with the score of +4–0=3, but his international results were spoilt by ill-health.

That he was of grandmaster strength, however, he amply showed in 1926. At a small but powerful tournament in Amsterdam he came 1st ahead of Tartakower and Euwe. At Weston-super-Mare he was 2nd to Euwe. A 4th at Bartfeld was followed by an =7th with Réti out of 16 at the first master tournament organized by FIDE at Budapest. Finally there came a 1st at Meran, ahead of such players as Spielmann, Grünfeld and Tartakower – a true grandmaster success.

After Meran he had a number of successes: 2nd at Hastings 1926/7, 3rd at Niendorf 1927, =1st with Marshall and Takacs at Hastings 1928/9, 3rd at Barcelona 1929, 1st at Scarborough 1930 ahead of Maróczy, Rubinstein, Ahues, Sultan Khan and Grünfeld, =3rd with Nimzowitsch and Ahues at Liège 1930. Then, at another small but very strong double-round tournament, at Rotterdam in December 1931, he came 2nd above Tartakower and Rubinstein.

This was his last tournament. More ill-health was followed by an operation for a gastric ulcer and it was after this that he died.

The celebrated Colle System brought him a rich harvest of brilliancies; but most are well known and we prefer to give an earlier but still exciting game with a lovely finish.

Hastings 1923/4
White: Colle; *Black:* Euwe
Queen's Gambit Declined, Slav Defence
1. P–Q4, P–Q4; 2. N–KB3, N–KB3; 3. P–K3, B–B4; 4. P–B4, P–B3; 5. N–B3, P–K3; 6. B–Q3, B × B; 7. Q × B, QN–Q2; 8. O–O, B–Q3; 9. P–K4, P × KP; 10. N × P, N × N; 11. Q × N, O–O; 12. B–N5, B–K2; 13. B–Q2, R–K1; 14. B–B3, Q–B2; 15. QR–B1, QR–Q1; 16. KR–K1, N–B1; 17. P–KR4, B–B3; 18. N–R2, Q–N3; 19. QR–Q1, Q–R3; 20. N–N4, B–K2; 21. P–Q5, BP × P; 22. P × P, P × P; 23. R × P, B–Q3; 24. R–KN5,

24. . , R × Q; 25. N–R6 +, and mates next move. *(H.G.)*

COLLE SYSTEM

The opening moves 1. P–Q4, P–Q4; 2. N–KB3, N–KB3; 3. P–K3, P–B4; 4. QN–Q2 characterize the favourite system of the Belgian master Edgar Colle. White's plans revolve around the eventual central thrust P–K4, increasing the potential of his pieces. After 4. . , QN–Q2, for example: 5. P–B3, P–K3; 6. B–Q3, B–K2; 7. O–O, O–O; 8. P–K4, QP × P; 9. N × P, N × N; 10. B × N, N–B3; 11. B–B2, P–QN3 with equality. *(R.D.K.)*

COLLIJN, Gustaf *(11 November 1880–November 1968)*

A Swedish player and theorist, not so well known or as active as his brother Ludvig Collijn. His only tournament result was a 9th place at Stockholm 1897.

He collaborated with his brother in the production of many tournament books and also on the *Lärobok i Schack.* *(H.G.)*

COLLIJN, Ludvig *(20 November 1878–4 October 1939)*

The Swedish theorist, administrator and player was chiefly celebrated for his famous *Lärobok i Schack,* which he wrote in collaboration with his brother Gustaf Collijn. But he also wrote a number of tournament books with him and, in his own right, a book for beginners.

His best result as a tournament player was his =7th at Stockholm 1897.

He was active as an organizer and directed the 1937 Olympiad at Stockholm. He was a specialist on the games of Adolf Anderssen. His publications were: *Lärobok i Schack* (in collaboration with his brother), 1898; *Lärobok i Schack for ny borjare,* 1906; *Adolf Anderssen,* 1918. (All Stockholm.) *(H.G.)*

COLOMBIA

The Colombian Chess Federation was formed in 1946. Over the following twenty years the government granted it occasional help mainly for participation in Olympiads or tournaments organized by FIDE; but in 1966 the 'Instituto de Deportes' was created, which allowed chess to develop in more favourable circumstances. Via the Institute the government subsidizes the Federation, thus permitting Colombia to participate in Olympiads, Junior and Student championships, etc. Furthermore, the Ladies Olympiad was held in Medellin in September 1974. The number of registered players is approximately ten thousand.

Colombian chess magazines are as follows: *Ajedrez Colombiano,* ed. Juan Minaya, and *Alfil Dama,* ed. Boris de Greiff. Published regularly 4–5 times a year, with a circulation of 3,000 each.

Leading Colombian players: four international masters: Miguel Cuellar; Luis Sanchez (*b.* 1916, master 1952); Boris de Greiff (*b.* 1930, master 1957); and José Gutierrez (*b.* 1943, master 1972). National masters: Carlos Cuartas (*b.* 1941, one international master result in Quito 1973); Oscar Castro (*b.* 1948). Javier Alzate (*b.* 1941) played in Olympiads at Havana 1966 and Siegen 1970; Luis Garcia (*b.* 1948) played in the Students tournaments of Mayaguez and Graz.

Address of the Colombian Chess Federation: Calle 15 No. 13–82, Apartado Aéreo 53.75, Bogotá, Colombia. Chess clubs in Bogotá: Club Fischer, Club Capablanca. Liga de Ajedrez de Bogotá: Avenida Jimenez Carrera 7, (Sotanos), Bogotá. In Medellin: Club Maacaibo, Club Caissa. *(R.D.K.)*

COMBINATION

Whole books have been written on the combination without their authors making an attempt to define the term (e.g. Du Mont's *The Basis of Combination in Chess*). One is reminded of Louis Armstrong's reply to a questioner who wanted a definition of rhythm:

'If you have to ask, you haven't got it'.

However, some thinkers, writers and players have tried to define the elusive term, and we quote the following:

EMANUEL LASKER: 'In the rare instances in which the player can detect a variation, or net of variations, which leads to a desirable issue by force, the totality of these variations and their logical connexions, their structure, are called a combination.'

P. ROMANOVSKY: 'A combination is a variation (or group of variations) in the course of which both sides make forced moves and which ends with an objective advantage for the active side.'

M. BOTVINNIK: 'A combination is a forced variation with sacrifice.'

E. VOELLMY: 'The combination is a transition that differs in its form from a continuation normally to be expected.'

A. BRINCKMANN: 'The combination is a sequence of moves unambiguously determined by thrust and parry which has a limited goal as its objective.'

The Editorial Board of *Shakhmaty*, summarizing an open forum (1952/3) on the meaning of combination: 'A combination is a forced sequence of moves which uses tactical means and exploits specific peculiarities of the position to attain a certain goal.'

(W.H.)

A chessboard with an automatic and synchronous light display of moves in the Central Chess Club Moscow

COMMONS, Kim Steven *(b. 23 July 1951)*

US international master (1976). In the autumn of 1976 he had two 'legs' of his title but needed a third; in the space of two months he obtained a third and fourth 'leg' by winning three international tournaments in Bulgaria: Plovdiv, Primorsko (=1st) and Odessos. *(K.J.O'C.)*

COMPOSITIONS, Chess

A phrase used by FIDE to describe both chess problems and endgame studies. *(H.G.)*

COMPUTERS

The first serious attempt to produce a computer programme designed to play good chess was made by Claude E. Shannon in the 1950s. In 1949 he had outlined the principles on which a chess-playing programme might be constructed. Since chess is a finite game, one might think it possible to determine the best move in any position simply by looking at all of White's moves in turn, examining all Black's replies to each of these, then the possible White responses and so on until mate or a draw is reached. However, as is quickly seen, the numbers quickly become far too great for even the most sophisticated computer to handle; indeed even just looking two moves ahead for each side will, in a complex middle-game position take one million calculations. Shannon's proposition, therefore, was that the computer could be more selective, eliminating obvious bad moves from its consideration and only pursuing the analysis of sensible continuations. His scheme was implemented some years later, but it was still found that the time taken by the computer even to calculate a short distance ahead was prohibitive, and anyway it did not play very well!

The problem thus falls into two broad categories: first, the computer must somehow be given a technique for analysing tactical variations and recognizing when such analysis is necessary; and secondly it needs a method of positional evaluation, both to select strategically correct moves and to assess positions correctly at the end of lines of analysis. Most of the work in chess programming in the last couple of decades has been concerned with the tactical problem. Botvinnik, in his book *Computers, Chess and Long-Range Planning*, London 1970, describes the programme evolved by himself and some Moscow mathematicians. This is essentially tactical in nature and goes a long way towards showing how a computer may solve the complications of a position, so long as those complications may be analysed. It is when the question of positional judgment comes in that Botvinnik's programme, along with most others developed to date, fails to come up to standard.

Perhaps the best computer so far, as regards chess-playing strength, has been the programme of Richard Greenblatt of M.I.T. This programme had a positional judgment better than that of previous attempts and involving the consideration of more sophisticated notions such as inherent weaknesses of pawn-structure as well as the more crude elements like control of space. The computer, known as MacHack VI, entered amateur tournaments in the USA and was the first to win serious games against human opponents, though it never achieved a rating better than that of an average club player.

The latest developments in programming technique include a machine able to take advice from a chess-master, thus incorporating a learning element into the programme (see 'An Advice-taking Chess Computer', *Scientific American*, June 1973); and the first steps towards reducing the complexities of positional play to a mathematical formulation, as exemplified by R. H. Atkin in a paper entitled 'Multi-dimensional Structure in the Game of Chess' (*International Journal of Man-Machine Studies*, 1972).

Present work seems to be continuing less on the lines of Shannon's original ideas and more towards mimicking the chess-master's thought processes regarding selection of moves. One result of this is that some computers are now producing games which no longer look like machine-made concoctions. This is an encouraging sign for the future, but prognostications vary widely from Botvinnik's confident assertion that computers will soon be producing play of World Championship standard, to Euwe's opinion that the machine will not reach beyond master standard.

Apart from MacHack, there have been relatively few instances of computers playing serious games, though such occurrences are increasing rapidly. In 1972 there was played the first US Computer-chess championship in Boston, won by a CDC 6400 machine using a programme known as Chess 3.5. There was also, in 1968, a computer match between the Moscow Technological Institute and an American university, won by the Russians, though it was emphasized that the match was more an exchange of views than a sporting event. It is worth giving here the game that decided the 1972 US Computer championship to enable the reader to judge for himself just how high the standard of play is among the best computers:

White: 'Chess 3.5'; *Black:* 'Tech'
Ruy Lopez
1. P–K4, P–K4; 2. N–KB3, N–QB3; 3. B–N5, N–B3; 4. O–O, B–B4; 5. N–B3, P–Q3; 6. B×N+, P×B; 7. P–Q4, P×P; 8. N×P, O–O; 9. B–N5, B–KN5; 10. Q–Q3, B×N; 11. Q×B, R–N1; 12. B×N, Q×B; 13. Q×Q, P×Q; 14. P–QN3, R–N5; 15. P–KR3, B–K3; 16. P–N4, R–Q5; 17. QR–Q1, R×R; 18. N×R, K–N2; 19. N–K3, K–N3; 20. P–KB4, K–N2; 21. K–N2, R–QN1; 22. K–B3, R–N4; 23. P–B4, R–QR4; 24. P–KB5, B–Q2; 25. R–B2, R–K4; 26. R–Q2, P–QR3; 27. P–KR4, P–B4; 28. N–Q5, B–B3; 29. N×QBP, B×P+; 30. K–B4, P–KR4;

31. P×P, P–R4; 32. R×P, B×P; 33. P–R6+, K–N3; 34. P–R5+, K×P(R4); 35. R×P, R–K7; 36. K×B, and White won.

There has, in the last few years, been an increase of interest among computer programmers in the subject of artificial intelligence in general and chess in particular, and it is generally hoped that we shall have an answer within the next decade or sooner to the question whether the machine can beat man. It is of interest that international master David Levy, a computer programmer as well as chess-player, has wagered £1000 that no computer programme will be able to defeat him in a ten-game match before 1978. At the present rate of progress it should be a closely run contest. *(W.R.H.)*

COMPUTER WORLD CHAMPIONSHIP

See under WORLD CHAMPIONSHIP, COMPUTER

CORRESPONDENCE CHESS

Chess was played at a distance long before fast and reliable postal services existed. The earliest correspondence chess game was reputedly between Henry I of England and Louis VI of France in about 1119. Other unconfirmed famous correspondence players include Catherine the Great of Russia, Frederick the Great of Prussia, and Voltaire. The authenticated history of correspondence chess began in 1804. The main events:

1804 The earliest correspondence chess games for which the moves were recorded, between F. W. de Mauvillon of Breda and an officer at The Hague.
1824–8 In the first recorded match between any two clubs, Edinburgh beat London +2−1=2. The opening known as the Scotch Game was so called after its use by the Edinburgh team in two of the games (see game below).
Nineteenth century correspondence chess steadily increased in popularity as communications improved.
1906 BCCA (British Correspondence Chess Association) formed – the first national correspondence chess organization.
1928 IFSB (Internationaler Fernschach Bund) founded. *Fernschach* published – the first magazine devoted entirely to correspondence chess.
1935 First European Correspondence Chess Olympiad; won by Hungary.
1946 ICCA (International Correspondence Chess Association) founded.
1947 First Individual World Correspondence Chess championship started.
1949 ICCF (International Correspondence Chess Federation) formed from ICCA.
1959 Hans Werner von Massow became President of ICCF, a post he still holds.

Correspondence match 1824–8
White: Edinburgh; *Black:* London
Scotch Game
1. P–K4, P–K4; 2. N–KB3, N–QB3; 3. P–Q4, N×P; 4. N×N, P×N; 5. Q×P, N–K2; 6. B–QB4, N–B3; 7. Q–Q5, Q–B3; 8. N–B3, B–N5; 9. B–Q2, P–Q3; 10. B–QN5, B–Q2; 11. Q–B4, B–QB4; 12. O–O, O–O; 13. Q–Q3, N–K4; 14. Q–N3, B×B; 15. N×B, P–B3; 16. N–B3, N–B5; 17. B–N5, Q–N3; 18. P–N3, P–B3; 19. B–B1, Q×Q; 20. RP×Q, B–Q5; 21. P×N, B×N; 22. R–N1, P–QN3; 23. R–Q1, QR–K1; 24. R–N3, B–R4; 25. P–KB3, P–KB4; 26. P×P, R–K7; 27. P–KN4, R×QBP; 28. B–B4, R×QBP; 29. B×P, R–K1; 30. R–R3, P–KR3; 31. B–B7, R–K2;

32. R–Q8+, K–R2; 33. R–QB8, R–B8+; 34. K–R2, R(2)–K8; 35. K–R3, R–R8+; 36. B–R2, B–B6; 37. P–B4, B–Q7; 38. P–N3, B–R4; 39. R–K3, R–B7; 40. P–N5, R(8)×B+; 41. K–N4, P–R4+; 42. K–B3, R(R7)–B7+; 43. K–K4, P–N3; 44. R–B7+, K–N1; 45. K–K5, R–B4+; 46. K–B6, R×P+; 47. K×P, R–B1; 48. R–N7+, K–R1; 49. K–R6, B–N5; 50. R–K6, R–B4; 51. R–R7+, K–N1; 52. R–N6+, K–B1;

53. R×BP, R–B4; 54. R–B6+, K–K1; 55. P–N6, R–QB6; 56. P–N4, B–B1+; 57. R×B+, K×R; 58. P–N7+, K–B2; 59. R–R8, R–B3+; 60. K–R7, resigns.

Individual World Correspondence Chess championship
1950–3
1st C. J. S. Purdy (Australia) 10½; =2nd H. Malmgren (Sweden), M. Napolitano (Italy) 10.

Dyckhoff Memorial Tourney
1954–6
1st. L. Schmid (W. Germany) 14; 2nd A. O'Kelly de Galway (Belgium) 12.
1956–9
1st V. V. Ragozin (USSR) 11; =2nd L. Endzelins (Australia), L. Schmid (W. Germany) 10½.
1959–62
1st A. O'Kelly de Galway (Belgium) 6½; 2nd P. Dubinin (USSR) 6.
1962–5
1st V. Zagorovsky (USSR) 9½; 2nd G. Borisenko (USSR) 8½.
1965–8
1st H. Berliner (USA) 14; =2nd J. Hybl (Czechoslovakia), K. Husak (Czechoslovakia) 11.
1968–71
1st H. Rittner (E. Germany) 12½; 2nd V. Zagorovsky (USSR) 12.

Women's World Correspondence Chess championship
1965–72 1st Olga Rubtsova (USSR)
1968– Second World championship in progress

World Team Correspondence Chess championship
1952 Hungary
1955 Czechoslovakia
1961 USSR
1964 USSR
1968 Czechoslovakia
1972 USSR

International Correspondence Chess Grandmasters
R. Arlauskas, L. Endzelins, C. J. S. Purdy (Australia); A. O'Kelly de Galway (Belgium); L. Schmid (West Germany); K. Husak, J. Hybl (Czechoslovakia); H. Rittner (East Germany); M. Napolitano (Italy); E. Arnlind, A. Lundquist (Sweden); I. Bondarevsky, G. Borisenko, A. I. Chasin, P. Dubinin, J. Estrin, M. M. Yudovich, V. Zagorovsky (USSR); H. Berliner (USA); K. Richardson (Britain).

British Postal Chess Federation
Founded in 1962, BPCF is responsible for correspondence chess in Britain. President B. H. Wood; Hon. Sec. R. Gillman, 85 Hillyard Rd, London W7 1BJ.

British Correspondence Chess championship
Up to 1942 there were two major championships held annually–the BCF Individual championship and the BCCA championship. There is some doubt as to which constituted the true British championship. Since 1942, BCCA have organized the tourney on behalf of BPCF.

1942–3	R. W. Bonham	1957–8	P. J. Oakley
1943–4	D. V. Hooper	1958–9	S. Milan
1944–5	B. H. Wood	1959–60	B. Cafferty
1945–6	G. Wood	1960–1	Dr C. S. Hunter and S. C. Davey
1946–7	R. W. Bonham and J. Cairncross	1961–2	S. Milan
1947–8	F. Parr and G. Wood	1962–3	S. Milan
1948–9	H. Israel and F. Parr	1963–4	P. B. Dodson
1949–50	F. Parr	1964–5	S. Milan
1950–1	R. W. Bonham and E. Brown	1965–6	S. Milan and A. S. Hollis
1951–2	A. Hallmark	1966–7	A. S. Hollis
1952–3	H. G. Rhodes	1967–8	J. Timperley
1953–4	J. A. Fuller	1968–9	S. Milan
1954–5	J. A. Fuller	1969–70	B. Hopewell
1955–6	F. Parr	1970–1	A. S. Hollis
1956–7	S. C. Davey	1971–2	F. Boyd

Correspondence Chess League of Australia
Founded 1929, affiliated to ICCF since 1946.
President C. J. S. Purdy; Sec. H. W. M. Lunney, Box 2360 GPO, Sydney NSW 2001. 1,750 members.
Individual Australian champions:
1939 and 1950 C. J. S. Purdy; 1952 R. Arlauskas; 1957 M. C. Salm; 1961 K. Ozols and J. V. Kellner (=1st); 1963 J. V. Kellner; 1965 L. S. Fell; 1968 M. C. Salm and A. Miller (=1st); 1971 C. Barnett.

New Zealand Correspondence Chess Association
Founded 1935, affiliated to ICCF since 1963.
Sec. A. L. Fletcher, 39 Denny Ave, Mt Roskill, Auckland 4. 270 members. Individual champions 1971–2 P. A. Garbett; 1972–3 K. W. Lynn.

USA
Greater New York Correspondence Chess League, founded about 1895, spread rapidly throughout the USA and became Correspondence Chess League of America in 1911. CCLA developed a rating system in the 1930s, affiliated to ICCF in 1946 and is still the leading correspondence chess organization in the USA. CCLA Business Manager D. R. Taylor, Box 4157, Cincinnati, Ohio 45204, USA. No official national championship until one began in 1972; the first winner will be determined in 1976. *(D.J.R.)*

CORTLEVER, Nicolaas *(b. 14 June 1915)*
Dutch international chess-master and owner of a business in natural stones, marbles etc. in Amsterdam.

Cortlever first made his mark in the Netherlands by coming second to Euwe in the Dutch championship of 1938, but he has been second in that event a number of times.

He played in the Olympiads of 1939, 1950, 1952, 1954 and 1956. He was also a member of the Dutch team in Anglo-Dutch matches from 1946 to 1960.

In the early part of his chess career he was a good endgame study composer and some of his studies were published in the *Schaakwereld* during the years 1936–41.

In the 1970s he gave up active play and became the captain of the Dutch team in the Olympiads. *(H.G.)*

COSTA RICA
Chess here is only beginning to be developed. However, in the 1976 Olympiad the national team succeeded in capturing 32nd place, a great improvement on their previous appearance: 49th in 1968. The official organization is the Associacion Costarricense de Ajedrez, Casa España, San José. *(K.J.O'C.)*

COUNTER-GAMBIT
A term used to describe the employing of a gambit to meet a gambit. Examples are the Albin Counter-gambit and the Falkbeer Counter-gambit. The first is a counter to the Queen's Gambit (1. P–Q4, P–Q4; 2. P–QB4, P–K4) and the second is a counter to the King's Gambit (1. P–K4, P–K4; 2. P–KB4, P–Q4).

White, having the first move, usually plays the gambit first so that counter-gambits are normally played by Black; but it is not impossible for White to play a counter-gambit if and when Black is the initiator of gambit play.

Despite this, the practice has grown up of calling any gambit by Black a counter-gambit: e.g. the Budapest Counter-gambit and the Queen's Pawn Counter-gambit. This misuse of the term would seem to be too deeply rooted in the past to be eradicated. *(H.G.)*

COUNTERPIN
See UNPINNING.

COZIO, Count Carlo *(eighteenth century)*
Of Count Cozio very little is known beyond the fact that his name is given to a defence of the Ruy Lopez (1. P–K4, P–K4; 2. N–KB3, N–QB3; 3. B–N5, P–KN3) and that he was the author of a substantial work on chess in two volumes.

There is a further mystery about the date of the publication of his book inasmuch as the copies that have come down to us bear the date 1766. Murray writes that his work is the last piece of chess literature to appear in Italy before the centre of European chess shifted to France and England. But in fact Cozio's book was written before those of the Modena school (Ercole del Rio, Lolli and Ponziani). In the possession of the great library of Lothar Schmid there is the original manuscript of the work, containing some 410 pages and dated 1740. It seems that considerable quantities of the first printing were destroyed by a fire at the Royal Press of Turin.

The work is divided into four parts: part 1 dealing with gambits, part 2 with the ordinary game, part 3 with the Calabrian form of the game and part 4 being a collection of games and positions. *(H.G.)*

CROSS CHECK
A checking reply to a check, the cross check has been found to be a valuable *systematic* expedient for winning the ending of Q+P v. Q. Typical is the final position of Botvinnik v. Minev, Amsterdam 1954:

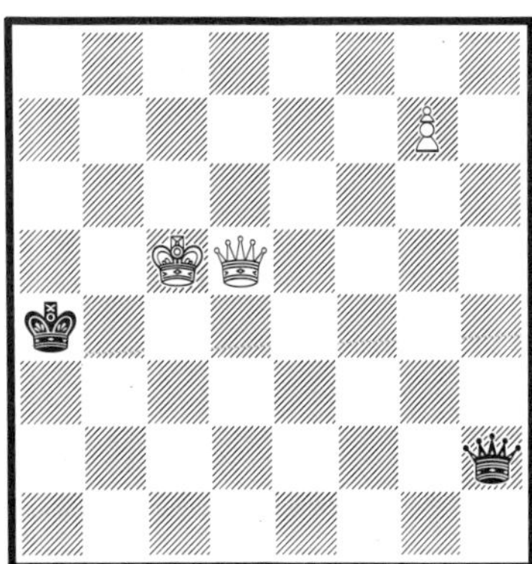

Here Black resigned, for if 1.., Q–B2+; 2. Q–B6+; if 1.., Q–N8 (or KB7)+; 2. Q–Q4+; and if 1.., Q–QB7+; 2. Q–B4+, K–R6; 3. P–N8(Q), but not 3. Q×Q? stalemate. *(W.H.)*

CROWN, Gordon Thomas *(20 June 1929–17 November 1947)*
Gordon Crown is one of the sad might-have-beens of the world of chess. In his short life he had already shown himself to be of master strength and a potentially very great player when suddenly, at the age of eighteen, he died during an operation.

He learnt chess when aged nine and soon became one of the best players, first in Liverpool, his home town, and then in Lancashire, of which county he won the Junior championship three years in succession.

Crown first came into national prominence when he came second in the British Boys championship in 1946. In the Hastings Congress of 1946/7 he won first place in a strong Premier Reserves Section.

The last year of his life even saw him reaching out to international successes. Playing on board 9 for Britain against The Netherlands he scored 1½ out of 2 against L. J. Tummers. Then he won third prize in the British championship at Harrogate. As a result of this success he was promoted to board 4 for Britain against

Australia in a radio match when he beat Dr M. Gellis.

In September 1947 came his last international match when, on board 4 for Britain, he won one game and lost one against the Soviet grandmaster Alexander Kotov.

In November he was hurried to hospital suffering from peritonitis and, being a diabetic, succumbed under the operation.

As a player he excelled in both the opening and endgame phases and possessed a style of play that stamped him as a future grandmaster. As a person he was modest, clever and a very agreeable companion. This was a great loss for British and, almost certainly, world chess. *(H.G.)*

CSOM, Istvan *(b. 2 June 1940)*
Hungarian grandmaster. He obtained the title of international master in 1967. His best performance in the Hungarian championship was his victory in 1972. The following year he was awarded the title of international grandmaster following his sharing first place in the Olot tournament that year. His tournament victories include Hamburg 1974, Cleveland 1975, Olot 1975 and the 1975 Pula Zonal where he qualified for the 1976 Interzonal at Biel, Switzerland, where he came =9th with Geller and Smejkal. He acted as Portisch's second in the 1974 Candidates. *(H.G. & K.J.O'C.)*

CUBA
Before 1959 few Cuban players were known internationally (among the exceptions being Golmayo and of course Capablanca) and the country competed only occasionally in Olympiads (1939 and 1952). Since the 1959 revolution, chess has been given considerable official encouragement and the standard of play has risen greatly. A national team has competed in every Olympiad since 1960, attaining its best performance on home ground in Havana 1966 when the Cubans reached the 'A' finals and finished 14th. Current FIDE title holders are: S. Garcia (grandmaster), Boudy, Cobo, Diaz, Estevez, Fernandez, G. Garcia, Jimenez, Perez, A. Rodriguez and J. Rodriguez – all international masters.

The national champions since 1960 have been:

1960	E. Jimenez	1970	S. Garcia
1963	E. Jimenez	1971	J. Rodriguez
1965	E. Jimenez	1972	J. Rodriguez
1966	R. Ortega	1973	S. Garcia
1967	E. Jimenez	1974	G. Garcia
1968	S. Garcia	1975	G. Estevez
1969	J. Rodriguez	1976	J. Fernandez

Cuban chess is governed by the Federaçion Cuban de Ajedrez, Hotel Havana Libre, Havana 4. A magazine, *Jaque Mate*, is published monthly and an annual international tournament, the Capablanca Memorial, is held in memory of the Cuban World Champion. *(R.D.K.)*

CUELLAR, Miguel *(b. 18 November 1916)*
Colombian international master, who gained the title in 1957. Frequently Colombian champion. Played in Interzonals twice: Stockholm 1962, where he defeated Geller and Korchnoi but placed 22nd out of 23, and Sousse 1967 where he came 19th out of 23. *(R.D.K.)*

CUNNINGHAM, Alexander *(1654–1737)*
Scottish historian and diplomat, British Minister in Venice 1715–20. He popularized the Cunningham Gambit, a defence to the King's Gambit: 1. P–K4, P–K4; 2. P–KB4, P×P; 3. N–KB3, B–K2. *(R.D.K.)*

CYPRUS
After becoming independent in 1960, this small country managed to compete in every Olympiad from 1962 to 1974, finishing respectively: 37th, 50th, 51st, 51st, 57th, 56th and 68th. National championships have also been organized, annually since 1961, by The Cyprus Chess Association, 43 Themest. Dervis St., Nicosia. *(K.J.O'C.)*

CZECHOSLOVAKIA
Czechoslovakia has throughout this century played an important part in European chess, both from the points of view of producing some of the best players and organizing some of the strongest tournaments. Even before the formation of the Czechoslovak Republic after the First World War, some very great tournaments were held in what was then Bohemia. Worth mentioning are Carlsbad 1907 (won by Rubinstein ahead of Maróczy, Leonhardt, Nimzowitsch and Schlechter), Prague 1908 (won by Dûras and Schlechter, ahead of Vidmar, Rubinstein, Teichmann and Maróczy), and Carlsbad 1911 (won by Teichmann ahead of Schlechter, Rubinstein, Rotlewi, Marshall, Nimzowitsch, Vidmar, Alekhine, Dûras, et al.).

After the war, in 1921, two closely linked organizations were formed: the German Chess Association of Czechoslovakia, and the Czechoslovak Chess Association. The former was dedicated to maintaining the links between the German-speaking part of the republic and Germany itself, while the latter represented the whole country, being a federation of the 62 Chess Clubs, numbering 2,200 members in all. The German Association was under the leadership of V. Tietz, who had managed the two previous Carlsbad tournaments.

The years 1922 and 1923 saw the organization of four important and strong tournaments. First came Pistyan 1922, won by Bogoljubow ahead of Alekhine, Spielmann, Grünfeld and Réti (19 players altogether). This was followed by Teplitz–Schönau 1922, won by Réti and Spielmann ahead of Grünfeld, Tartakower and Rubinstein (14 players); Carlsbad 1923, won by Alekhine, Bogoljubow and Maróczy, ahead of Grünfeld and Réti (18 players); and Mährisch-Ostrau 1923, won by Lasker ahead of Réti and Grünfeld (14 players).

After that rush of great events, such tournaments came somewhat less frequently, though subsequent years did see another two comparable events: Marienbad 1925 (won by Nimzowitsch and Rubinstein) and Carlsbad 1929 (won by Nimzowitsch ahead of

Capablanca and Spielmann). There were also two slightly weaker but still important tournaments in 1928: Trenčianské Teplice (won by Kostić) and Brno (won by Réti and Sämisch).

In 1931 Prague hosted the 4th Olympiad. The event was, by all contemporary accounts, splendidly organized, under the personal sponsorship of President Masaryk. The chief arbiter was a judge and his two deputies were an army colonel and a major. There were no disputes concerning their decisions.

Subsequently there was a lull in the organization of important events. Other tournaments worth mentioning include Podebrady 1936 (won by Flohr ahead of Alekhine), Prague 1937 (won by Keres) and Prague 1943 (organized under the German occupation and won by Alekhine). After the war chess activity was soon resumed and Czechoslovakia resumed its place as an important centre of chess. Other important tournaments include: Prague 1946 (won by Najdorf), Trenčianské Teplice 1949 (won by Ståhlberg), Mariánské Lázně 1956 (won by Filip), Mariánské Lázně 1959 (won by Polugayevsky), Mariánské Lázně 1965 (won by Hort and Keres), Luhacovice 1969 (won by Korchnoi ahead of Keres), and Luhacovice 1971 (won by Hort).

There has not been a time this century when Czechoslovakia has not possessed one of the world's strongest masters. In the 1920s and later, Důras and Réti carried the Czech banner, to be followed by Flohr and later Pachman and Hort. Other names deserving mention in this context include Hromadka, Emil Richter, Opocensky, Filip and Smejkal, all of whom made their mark on the international scene. With so many great players, it is hardly surprising that Czechoslovakia has usually occupied a high place in the Olympiads, always finishing in the top ten, and taking third place in 1931 and second in 1933.

Czechoslovakia has four international grandmasters (Hort, Filip, Smejkal, Jansa), though two others (Pachman and Kavalek) gained their titles while still possessing Czech nationality. Their national championship is held biennially since 1968, following a series of unrepresentative events in earlier years. A new system of numbering the national championship was adopted in 1961 (the 'first') since when the winners have been:

1961	L. Pachman	1968	L. Kavalek
1962	L. Kavalek	1970	V. Hort
1963	L. Pachman	1972	V. Hort
1964	V. Jansa	1973	J. Smejkal
1965	J. Augustin	1974	V. Jansa
1966	L. Pachman	1975	V. Hort
1967	J. Kozma	1976	E. Prandstetter

The address of the Czechoslovak Chess Federation is: Ceskoslovensky Sachovy Svaz, Na Porici 12, Prague 1. *(W.R.H.)*

CZERNIAK, Moshe *(b. 3 February 1910)*
Israeli international master and chess journalist by profession, Czerniak was born in Poland, emigrated to Palestine in 1937, was stranded in Argentina during the 1939 Olympiad in Buenos Aires, where he remained till 1952 when he went to Israel.

He played for Palestine in the Olympiads of 1935 and 1939 and then for Israel from 1952 onwards. He has played in a vast number of tournaments and has had many firsts and other prizes, chiefly in small events. Perhaps the most outstanding were firsts at Vienna and Reggio Emilia in 1951.

He is celebrated as part holder of the record for the longest game ever played and is renowned for his persistency in play, having been the last player to finish at two Olympiads, Helsinki 1952 and Varna 1962.

He is the author of many works on the game, perhaps the best being *La Partida Francese,* Buenos Aires 1950, and a work on the endings, *El Final*, Buenos Aires 1951. *(H.G.)*

D

DAKE, Arthur W. *(b. 8 April 1910)*
An American master who, like Fine, enjoyed an impressive but exceptionally brief career before the Second World War. After his début in New York club events in 1930, Dake was considered just as talented as Fine, Denker, Reshevsky or Horowitz, his frequent rivals. Dake played on three winning US teams in the Olympiads. His $15\frac{1}{2}$-$2\frac{1}{2}$ result on fourth board at Warsaw 1935 was the best in the tournament. Individually, Dake was =1st at Antwerp 1931 and =3rd at Pasadena 1932 where he defeated Alekhine in fine style. In US championships Dake never fared better than =6th. In the 1946 match with the USSR, Dake drew two games with Lilienthal. Dake rarely played after that. *(A.S.)*

DAMIANO *(fifteenth–sixteenth century)*
The author of *Questo libro e da imparare giocare a scachi et de li partiti,* the earliest Italian printed work on chess, published in Rome in 1512. Almost nothing is known of Damiano's life except that he was Portuguese by birth, from the town of Odemira, and an apothecary by profession.

His book is a mixture of problems, studies, aphorisms ('When you find a good move, look for a better'), and opening analysis. It enjoyed considerable popularity, running through eight Italian editions in the sixteenth century, and was translated into French, English, and German. It was in this work that Damiano's Defence was first analysed. *(R.D.K.)*

DAMIANO'S DEFENCE

An ancient and inadequate defence characterized by the moves 1. P–K4, P–K4; 2. N–KB3, P–KB3 and virtually refuted by 3. N×P! *(W.R.H.)*

DAMJANOVIĆ, Mato *(b. 23 March 1927)*

Yugoslav grandmaster. Received international master title 1962. Awarded grandmaster title for performance at Sochi 1964. Played in hundreds of tournaments of all kinds – with varied success. Represented Yugoslavia in Olympiad Leipzig 1960. Best result: 1st Zagreb 1969 ahead of Hort and Lombardy. Recent tournament appearances unimpressive apart from =1st Virovitica 1976. *(R.D.K.)*

DANISH GAMBIT

An offshoot of the Centre Game in which White gives up many pawns for swift development. Analysis shows that Black can secure comfortable prospects by returning the pawns; the main line being 1. P–K4, P–K4; 2. P–Q4, P×P; 3. P–QB3, P×P; 4. B–QB4, P×P; 5. QB×P, P–Q4; 6. B×QP, N–KB3; 7. B×P+, K×B; 8. Q×Q, B–N5+; 9. Q–Q2, B×Q+; 10. N×B, P–B4.

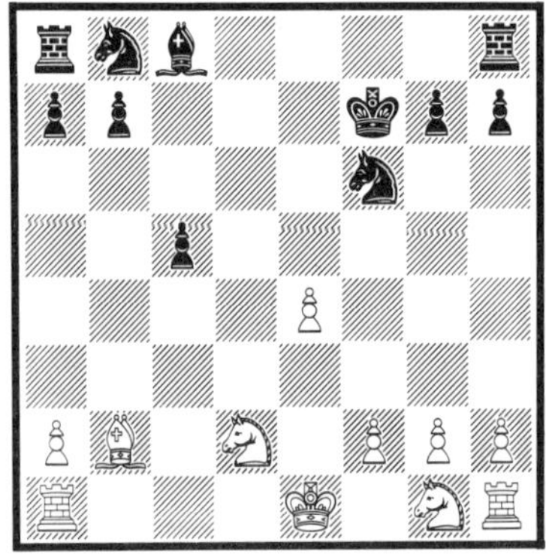

Since the resulting ending is better for Black, the Danish Gambit is rarely seen nowadays. *(W.R.H.)*

DARGA, Klaus *(b. 24 February 1934)*

German grandmaster and twice (1955 and 1961) champion of West Germany. Darga had an almost uninterrupted run of successes between 1955 and 1967 when the pressure of his scientific work forced him into near-retirement. Joint first with Panno (ahead of Ivkov, Olafsson, Penrose, Larsen and others) at the Junior World Championship in Copenhagen 1953, he was 2nd at Hamburg 1955, 2nd at Gijon 1956, 1st at Madrid 1957, 1st at Bognor Regis 1960, 2nd at Graz 1961, =3rd at Sarajevo 1962, =2nd at Enschede 1963 (Zonal tournament), =1st at Palma de Mallorca 1965, and scored his greatest success when he tied with Larsen for first place at Winnipeg 1967, with Spassky and Keres tied for third. In two of the great tournaments he contested, he finished 7th out of 22 at Havana 1963, and 11th out of 24 at Amsterdam 1964 (Interzonal). Darga was a regular member of the West German Olympic team from 1954 to 1972. *(W.H.)*

DECOY SACRIFICE

A sacrifice that lures a hostile piece either to a certain (disadvantageous) square or from an (effective) square or line. The following position, with Black to play (Bogoljubow–Monticelli, San Remo 1930), shows two successive decoy sacrifices:

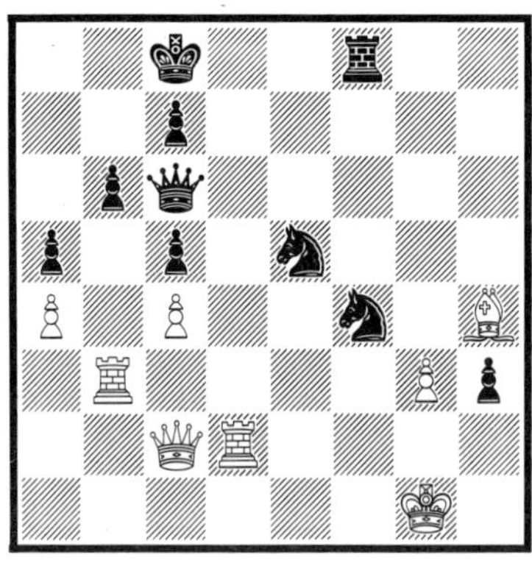

1.., N–K7+ (blocks the White K's access to K2); 2. R×N, R–B8+ (lures the K from N1 where it guards against Q–R8+); 3. K×R, Q–R8+; 4. K–B2, N–N5 mate. *(W.H.)*

'DEFENCE, THE'

A novel by Vladimir Nabokov that originally appeared in Russian in 1935 under the title of *Zaschita Luzhina* ('Luzhin's Defence') by V. Sirin, a pen-name adopted by Nabokov at the time. This was translated into Swedish and, still under Sirin's authorship, was called *Man som spelade schack med livet* ('He who played chess with life') and published by Bonniers, Stockholm 1936.

It is a tale of a chess-master who becomes so obsessed by the game that he loses his reason. The author shows an almost uncanny insight into the mind of the chess enthusiast. *(H.G.)*

DE GREIFF, Boris *(b. 13 January 1930)*

Colombian international master and writer. Editor of *Alfil Dama* since 1969. Chess columnist for *El Tiempo* (Bogotá), leading Colombian paper, since 1956. International master 1957, after winning Zonal tournament in Caracas.

Member of Colombian team Amsterdam 1954, Moscow 1956, Munich 1958, Havana 1966, Siegen 1970, Skopje 1972 and Nice 1974.

Has written an interesting work on the Women's Olympiad at Medellin 1974, published in Caracas 1976. *(R.D.K.)*

DE GROOT, Adriaan *(b. 21 October 1914)*

Dutch chess-master and also professor of psychology. During the 1930s and 1940s he pursued an active chess career, representing his country successfully at the Olympiads of Munich 1936, Stockholm 1937 and Buenos Aires 1939.

In addition he secured a number of good results in individual events, such as 4th out of 12 at Amsterdam 1938 (Netherlands championship), =1st (with Cortlever and Van den Hoek) at Leeuwarden 1942 and a share of fifth prize at Beverwijk (Hoogoven) 1946 and 1947.

In later years he turned increasingly to his profession, in which he has achieved great distinction.

Major chess publication: *Thought and Choice in Chess*, The

Hague, Paris 1965; New York 1966. An important contribution to the analysis of chess-masters' mental processes, based partly on his association and experiments with such prominent players as Alekhine and Fine. *(R.D.K.)*

DELY, Péter *(b. 5 July 1934)*
Hungarian international master since 1962; winner of 1969 Hungarian championship. Took first place at Luxemburg 1961, Reggio Emilia 1960/1, and Luxembourg 1971. *(W.R.H.)*

DENKER, Arnold Sheldon *(b. 20 December 1914)*
US international master and US champion from 1944 to 1946. Denker was a constant rival of Fine and Reshevsky in the 1930s and 1940s. A Manhattan Chess Club regular, Denker slowly moved up in national championships: =11th in 1936, =6th in 1940, =3rd in 1942, and finally first place by one point in 1944. He retained his title in a 1946 match challenge from H. Steiner by 6-4.

Denker's international results include =3rd at Hastings 1945/6, =10th at Groningen 1946 and 0-2 against Botvinnik in the 1945 US–USSR radio match on first board. Denker was awarded the international master title in 1950. *(A.S.)*

DENMARK
The game has always been popular in Denmark, going right back to its first introduction to Northern Europe by the Vikings. Though Denmark had to wait till quite modern times before it produced its great master, Bent Larsen, there has been a steady flow of excellent master players in that country, as evidenced by their gaining second place in the first Olympiad at London 1927.

Since then Denmark has been a constant presence in international chess and has taken part in many Olympiads.

The name and address of its federation: Dansk Skak Union, Byvej 254, 2650 Hvidovre, Denmark.

Its official chess magazine is *Skakbladet,* c/o Hans Rasmussen, Kastanjens Kvarter 19, 2990 Nivaa, Denmark. *(H.G.)*

DESCHAPELLES, Alexandre Louis Honoré Lebreton
(7 March 1780–27 October 1847)
The leading French player after the age of Philidor, Deschapelles was the son of a French marshal and himself served in Napoleon's army, losing his right arm in fighting against the Prussians.

He was a most gifted natural player but paid no attention to the openings and insisted on giving odds to all his opponents. Boastful and vain, he claimed to have learned the game by watching Bernard, the outstanding French player of his day, playing chess one evening and that, by the second day after, he had already attained his full strength as a player. This is a case of *credo quia absurdum est*!

In 1821 Lewis and Cochrane went to Paris with the express intention of playing against Deschapelles and his talented pupil La Bourdonnais. Deschapelles, giving the odds of pawn and move to Lewis, lost one game and drew two. Cochrane lost his games but La Bourdonnais more than held his own against his tutor. An oddity about this set of games is that Cochrane, dissatisfied with their outcome, challenged Deschapelles to a match on level terms and did better than when he received odds.

However, finding that he could no longer give odds to his pupil, Deschapelles withdrew from chess and concentrated on whist, at which he became the most successful player of his time and was reputed to have made between 30,000 and 40,000 francs a year at the game. The famous Deschapelles Coup in whist is named after him and is deemed his invention.

Despite having withdrawn from chess he was still jealous of his reputation as a giver of odds. For, at the end of the La Bourdonnais–McDonnell match in 1836, he challenged any English player to play him at the odds of pawn and two moves. Lewis did indeed accept this challenge but the match never came to pass.

A Bonapartist to the end of his days, Deschapelles was actually imprisoned in 1832 for suspected conspiracy against the Bourbons but was released after one month's custody after he had written a letter to the King, pleading old age, infirmity and innocence of any attempt to conspire against him. *(H.G.)*

DESPERADO
A piece which, either doomed to capture or impeding decisive action elsewhere on the board, clears its square in such a way as to inflict the greatest possible damage on the opponent's forces: it runs amok. Perlis v. Tartakower, Ostend 1907:

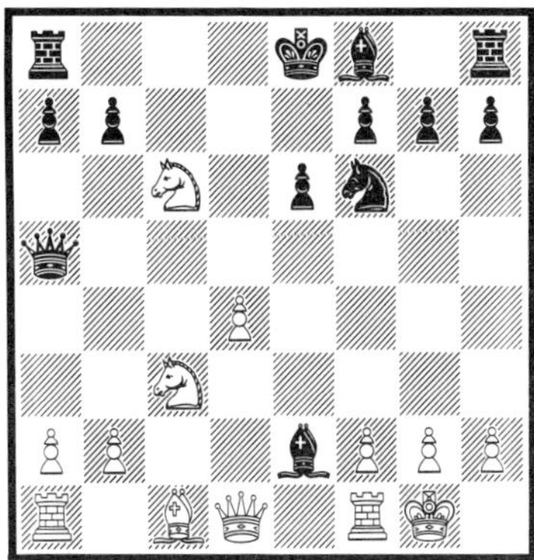

Black to play.
The Q, stopping Black from profitably playing B × Q, has become a desperado and immolates herself by Q × N!, winning a piece in all variations. *(W.H.)*

'DEUTSCHE SCHACHZEITUNG'
Has the distinction of being the oldest chess magazine still in existence. Founded, under the title *Schachzeitung*, by L. E. Bledow in 1846, it assumed its current name in 1872. In 1976 the 126th volume was published, thirty more than its oldest rival (the *British Chess Magazine*) but unlike its British competitor it cannot say 'we never closed' for it suffered a five year break in production at the end of the Second World War. The heyday of the *Deutsche Schachzeitung* was during the first two decades of this century since when it has been in decline. *(K.J.O'C.)*

DE VERE, Cecil *(14 February 1845–9 February 1875)*
The first official British champion and a player of great promise who might well have attained world fame had he not been carried off by that nineteenth-century British scourge, tuberculosis, before he attained the age of thirty.

Most of the details of his life are to be found in the writings of the Rev. G. A. MacDonnell, who met him when De Vere was fourteen and was so struck by his good looks as to refer to him as 'an Adonis'.

His first tournament success came in 1866 at the London Congress organized at the St George's Club in the first few days and then in other venues by the British Chess Association. De Vere played in two events, a Handicap tournament and a Challenge Cup event which was in fact the first British championship tournament.

The Handicap tournament was run on the same lines as London 1851, i.e. it was a knock-out event with matches of three games, draws not counting. De Vere met Steinitz in round 1 and lost by 2-1.

The British championship tournament was an all-play-all event in which the ties were decided by the first player to win three games and in which the championship went to the winner of the biggest number of games. De Vere was an easy winner with 12 wins, followed by MacDonnell and J. I. Minchin 6, H. E. Bird 3 and Sir John Trelawney 0.

Thus De Vere was the first British champion and that at the age of twenty-one. A photograph of him round about this time shows that he bore a remarkable likeness to the international master John Nunn, who won the European Junior championship a hundred years after De Vere's death.

De Vere confirmed his position as a leading British player by coming first in another tournament in 1866 at Redcar in North Yorkshire. This was an event open to all British amateurs and among his opponents were Owen, Thorold and Wisker.

It was in the following year that he commenced his career in international chess. In the important double-round tournament at Paris he occupied an honourable fifth place out of 13 players. At Dundee (the third congress of the British Chess Association) he finished equal 3rd with MacDonnell, below Steinitz but beating him in their individual game and coming ahead of Blackburne.

It was during his visit to Scotland (he went to stay with relatives after the tournament) that he learnt he was afflicted with consumption. This knowledge, together with the death of his mother, drove him to drink which was in fact to accelerate his end.

Inheriting a few hundred pounds, presumably from his mother, he gave up his post at Lloyd's and decided to live on his capital together with such additional sums as he could earn from chess.

In this respect his addiction to drink proved a handicap. For example, he held the post of chess editor of the *Field* in 1872 but lost it after some eighteen months through inattention to work.

Meanwhile he continued to show his great talent for the game. Defending his title of British champion in a very strong field at the next British Chess Association congress (1868/9) he came equal first with Blackburne but lost the play-off at the London Club in March 1869.

In 1870, at the very strong Baden-Baden double-round tournament, he came equal sixth with Winawer but was much outdistanced by Blackburne who came third with $3\frac{1}{2}$ points more than De Vere. But already his illness was taking a strong hold on him. At his next and last appearance in a tournament of note, London 1872, he tied with Zukertort and MacDonnell =3rd out of 8 players. In the play-off for third and fourth prizes he lost to MacDonnell and scratched to Zukertort. Later in the year he did tie for first place with Wisker in a weaker British championship tournament and, with De Vere now clearly ill, Wisker had an easy victory in the play-off.

At his last appearance in a chess event, a match at the City of London Club between that club and Bermondsey, he looked a dying man. A subscription was made to send him to Torquay but it was too late and he died within five days of his thirtieth birthday.

(H.G.)

DIESEN, Mark Carl *(b. 16 September 1957)*
American international master. Strangely, Diesen first made his mark outside the USA; he won the 1973/4 Hastings Challengers, thus qualifying for the 1974/5 Premier. In 1974 he finished =4th in the USA Junior championship, but improved by one place in that year's Junior championship of the Americas. He finished only 15th at Hastings 1974/5 but went on to finish =2nd (after Christiansen) in the 1975 US Junior, an event which he won in 1976. On January 5th 1977 he was crowned World Junior Champion for 1976 and was awarded the title of international master.

(K.J.O'C.)

DIEZ DEL CORRAL, Jesus *(b. 6 April 1933)*
Spanish grandmaster and Spanish champion, 1955, 1965. Del Corral is a genuine amateur (an accountant by profession) whose undoubted talents have been handicapped by his inability to give full time to the game.

He became an international master in 1968 and a grandmaster in 1974, being the second Spanish player to do so (after Pomar). His best results include 2nd/12 Amsterdam Masters 1969, 6th/18 Palma de Mallorca 1969, and =3rd Montilla 1973. *(R.D.K.)*

DISCOVERED CHECK
A check is said to be *discovered* when it is given to the hostile King by a piece, stationary itself, whose line of action is opened by the move of another man (piece or pawn). See also DOUBLE CHECK, PROBLEM: BATTERY and SEE-SAW. *(W.H.)*

DIVAN
See under SIMPSON'S DIVAN.

DIVINSKY, Nathan Joseph Harry, Prof. *(b. 29 October 1925)*

Canadian master and Professor of Mathematics at the University of British Colombia where he is Assistant Dean of Science, Divinsky played an important role in the organization of chess in Canada in the 1950s and 1960s.

His best performance in the Canadian championship was =3rd in 1945 and he represented Canada at the Amsterdam Olympiad 1954 and Havana 1966.

Since 1954 he has been editor of *Canadian Chess Chat.* *(H.G.)*

DJURASEVIĆ, Božidar *(b. 26 April 1933)*
Yugoslav international master, by profession a lawyer. He received the international master title in 1957. Though relatively unknown abroad, he has competed in six Yugoslav championships. Durašević represented Yugoslavia in the 1956 and 1958 Olympiads. Best results: 3rd Belgrade 1961, =2nd Mariánské Lázně 1962. *(R.D.K.)*

DODA, Zbigniew *(b. 22 February 1931)*
Polish international master and Polish champion, 1964 and 1967. Doda gained the international master title in 1964 and his tournament results include: =1st Wijk-aan-Zee (Masters Section) 1968 and =2nd Constanţa 1969. *(R.D.K.)*

DOMINICAN REPUBLIC
This country has competed in six Olympiads, finishing 49th in 1964, 47th in 1968, 48th in 1970, 45th in 1972, 51st in 1974 and 27th in 1976.

The organizing body is the Federacion Dominicana de Ajedrez, Apartado 7, Santo Domingo. *(K.J.O'C.)*

DONNER, Johannes Hendricus [Jan Hein] *(b. 6 July 1927)*
Dutch grandmaster and chess professional. He well remembers the day when he learnt chess. It was 22 August 1941, when he was taught the game by a schoolfellow and, on returning home, he found his mother in tears as she had just been informed that his father, a distinguished member of the judiciary, had been transported as a hostage to Germany.

He played his first tournament in a low section at the Beverwijk Congress 1946. In 1948 and 1949 he won the masters reserves with a 100% score. In 1950 came his first international success when he came first at the Beverwijk top masters section, ahead of Euwe and Rossolimo.

He obtained the international master title by coming second at the 1954 Munich Zonal tournament and thus qualifying for the Interzonal at Göteburg. In that year he won the Dutch championship, being the first person to win it after the long series of championships won by Euwe since 1921. He won the title on two more occasions, ahead of Euwe, in 1956 and 1958.

In 1957 he came =3rd with Larsen in a strong Zonal tournament at Wageningen but lost the play-off for the qualifying place for the Interzonal by $1\frac{1}{2}$–$2\frac{1}{2}$.

He gained the grandmaster title in 1958 and in that year came =1st with Euwe at the twentieth Beverwijk Hoogoven tournament.

Once again he narrowly failed to qualify for an Interzonal tournament by coming =4th in the 1960 Madrid Zonal tournament with Gligorić, Pomar and Portisch but losing the play-off.

One of his best tournament successes was winning the very strong twenty-fifth anniversary Hoogoven tournament ahead of Bronstein, Averbakh, Ståhlberg etc. in 1963 and he scored another fine tournament success by coming first at Venice 1967 ahead of Petrosian.

He has been a most powerful member of the Dutch team at many Olympiads: 1950, 1952, 1954, 1958, 1960, 1962, 1968, 1972, 1974 and 1976. He played on first board in the Olympiads from 1958 to 1972 and at Varna 1962 he beat Bobby Fischer.

He edited the chess column at *De Tijd* from 1956 till its demise in 1974 after which he edited the column in the *Volkskrant.*

Though his style owes much to Euwe's logical and consistent method of play, there is nevertheless an original streak of Donnerian bizarreness in his make-up as a player which one would term Nimzowitschian were it not for the possibility that he would find it insulting.

Away from the chessboard he has been a most colourful part of the Dutch chess scene, a sort of living paradox in that, whilst professing the most reactionary sentiments he has behaved like a rebel against the establishment. However, as, by degrees, he has been overtaken by younger chess-masters, so he has dwindled into a respectable member of Dutch society. *(H.G.)*

DÖRY'S DEFENCE
This occurs after 1. P–Q4, N–KB3; 2. P–QB4, P–K3; 3. N–KB3, when Döry's move is 3. . , N–K5. Although spasmodically patronized by Keres during the 1930s, this defence has now fallen into disuse. Its originator, Baron Döry, was a strong Viennese amateur of the 1930s. *(R.D.K.)*

DOUBLE BISHOP SACRIFICE
A typical combination with the object of smashing the hostile King position. It goes back to Lasker–Bauer, Amsterdam 1889 (see also KING'S FIELD SACRIFICE). A less well-known illustration is the following (Koltanowski–Defosse, Ghent 1936), where from the diagram play continued:

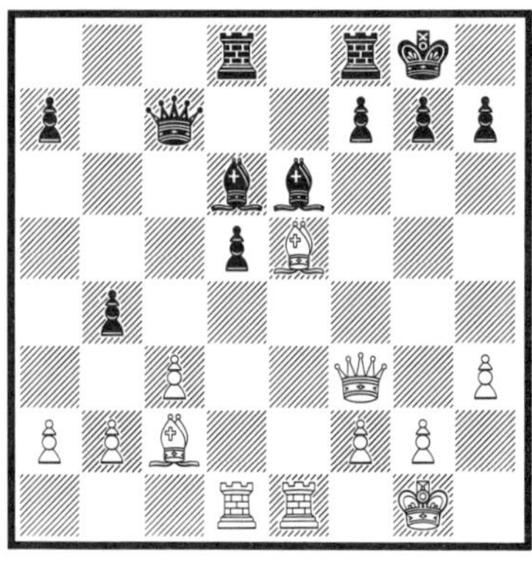

1. B×P+, K×B; 2. Q–R5+, K–N1; 3. B×P, K×B; 4. Q–N5+, K–R1; 5. R–Q4, B–R7+; 6. K–R1, Q–B5; 7. R–Q, B×R; 8. Q×B, R–KN1; 9. R–K5, resigns. *(W.H.)*

DOUBLE CHECK
A discovered check in which both pieces check the hostile King. As a result, both capture and interposition (which could stop only one of the checking pieces) are ruled out as defensive measures, and only the flight of the King remains. A good example is the 22nd move of the Evergreen Game. *(W.H.)*

DOUBLED PAWNS
Two pawns placed on the same file. They are almost invariably a serious positional weakness though in some cases there may be compensating advantages.

Weaknesses are (*a*) the difficulty in providing adequate protection for these pawns since usually there is at most one pawn on the adjacent files for protection; in many cases there is none at all (isolated double pawns); also, the forward pawn cannot be protected by the Rs from behind; (*b*) the danger of allowing the opponent a strong square in front of the doubled pawns when the one neighbouring pawn has been forced to advance, thus making both doubled pawns backward; (*c*) the difficulty in establishing a passed pawn when the doubled pawns are on the majority wing.

Advantages may be (*a*) the opening of the file next to the doubled pawns; (*b*) increased control of central squares in the case of those doubled pawns most frequently arising in various openings, viz. the QB- and KB-pawns; and (*c*) what Nimzowitsch used to call the ability of the doubled pawns to stay put and thus to foil the opponent's attempt to induce the weakness (*b*).

Strictly speaking, it is the central neighbour of the doubled pawns in what is called a doubled pawn complex that is endowed with this ability to stay put exactly because of the existence of the doubled pawns. An excellent illustration of these contexts is shown in the diagram (Nimzowitsch–Rosselli, Baden-Baden 1925):

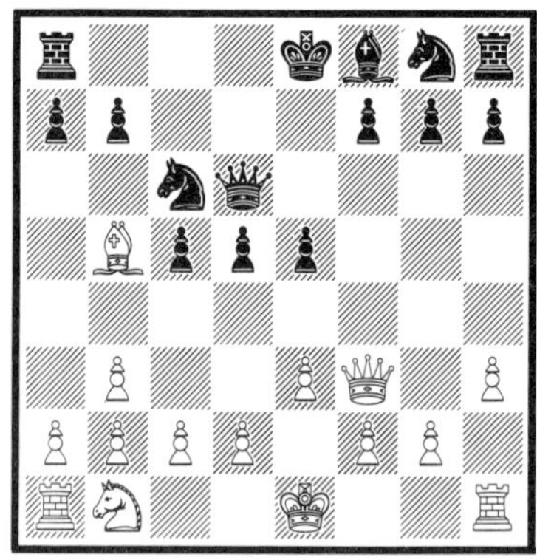

White to move realizes that after 1. B×N+, P×B; 2. P–K4, Black could stay put indefinitely and his Ps on K4, Q4, QB4, QB3 would command the centre; he therefore aims at creating the doubled pawns only *after* the opponent has been made to play P–Q5.

The game continued: 1. P–K4, P–Q5; 2. N–R3, P–B3; 3. N–B4, Q–Q2; 4. Q–R5+, P–N3; 5. Q–B3, Q–QB2; 6. Q–N4, K–B2; 7. P–B4, P–KR4; 8. Q–B3, P×P; 9. B×N – and since 9. . , Q×B would now be answered with 10. Q×P, R–K1; 11. O–O, Q×P; 12. Q–B7+ (or *11. . , R×P; 12. N–K5+*), Black has to play 9. . , P×B and, though temporarily a P up, suffers from a doubled pawn complex in its most disadvantageous form. *(W.H.)*

DOUBLE ROOK SACRIFICE
Unlike the double Bishop sacrifice, this is usually a passive sacrifice, the Rooks being offered to decoy hostile pieces from the main battlefield. For an example see IMMORTAL GAME. *(W.H.)*

DRESDEN 1926
It happens often enough that a great master is revealed to the chess world as the result of his performance in one big tournament (like Pillsbury at Hastings 1895 or Tal in the USSR championship 1957). It is much rarer for a small tournament to make a great master. Dresden 1926 was such a tournament. Not only did Nimzowitsch win it by a score of 8½ out of 9, 1½ points ahead of Alekhine, but all his games (and especially those against Johner, Rubinstein, and Von Holzhausen) were deep and original and showed a mature chess personality of which even his previous successes had given mere glimpses. In theoretical respect Dresden was the birthplace of what Keene has called the 'Dresden Blockade', a very early P–K4 for Black in the Sicilian Defence. *(W.H.)*

DUBININ, Pyotr Vassilievich *(b. 30 June 1909)*
Soviet master since 1938 and international master since 1950, Dubinin has scored his best successes in the field of correspondence chess, taking first place in the 3rd USSR Correspondence championship and being runner-up to O'Kelly de Galway in the third Correspondence World championship. Awarded the title of Correspondence Chess grandmaster in 1962. *(W.R.H.)*

DUBOIS, Serafino *(10 October 1817–15 January 1899)*
Born in Rome, Dubois was Italy's leading player in the nineteenth century and also its foremost opening theorist. The early period of his chess career coincided with a time when the Italian rules of the game still differed from those prevailing elsewhere in Europe. This was evidenced by a series of games he contested against an English player, Sir Brooke Greville, in which alternately the Italian rules and the normal European rules were employed. This was in 1842 and four years later he played a number of games against Marmaduke Wyvill who was then on tour in Italy.

In 1855 he went to Paris and beat de Rivière by +22−8=3.

His chief international performance was fifth prize in the 1862 London tournament ahead of Steinitz, Löwenthal, Blackburne and others. In fact, he tied for fourth place with the Rev. G. A. MacDonnell but the English player won more completed games and so was classed above him. Later on that year he lost a match to Steinitz by +3−5=1.

The latter part of his life was devoted to theoretical studies and writings. Along with Ferrante he was the editor of the first Italian chess column, *L'Album*, in Rome, 1847. His chief work, still concerned with the difference in Italian and French rules, appeared in three volumes, *Le principali apertura del gioco degli scacchi secondo i due diversi sistemi, italiano e francese*, from 1868 to 1873. But he was also the author of a number of pamphlets and articles on the openings.

To him are attributed a variation of the Vienna, 1. P–K4, P–K4; 2. N–QB3, N–QB3; 3. P–B4, P×P; 4. N–B3, P–KN4; 5. B–B4, P–N5; 6. O–O, P×N; 7. Q×P, N–K4; 8. Q×P, Q–B3; and also a defence in the Scotch Game: 1. P–K4, P–K4; 2. N–KB3, N–QB3; 3. P–Q4, P×P; 4. B–QB4, N–B3.

It was he who pointed out the celebrated trap in the Albin Counter-gambit 1. P–Q4, P–Q4; 2. P–QB4, P–K4; 3. QP×P, P–Q5; 4. P–K3, B–N5+; 5. B–Q2, P×P; 6. B×B, P×P+;

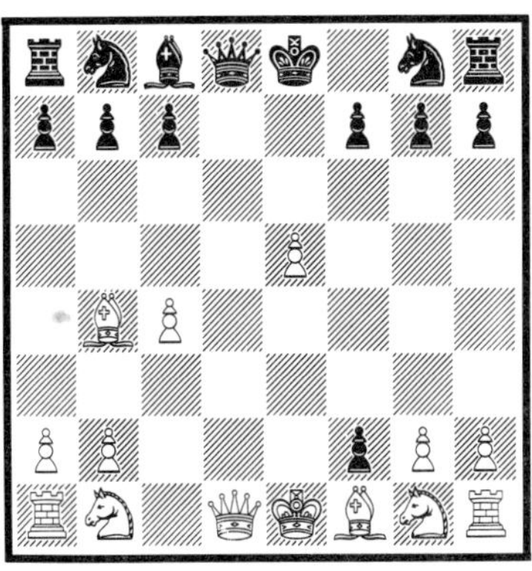

and Black wins, since if 7. K–K2, P×N(N)+. *(H.G.)*

DUCHAMP, Marcel *(28 July 1887–1 October 1968)*
National French master and one of the most important artists of our time, Duchamp was passionately fond of chess all his life. His great importance as an artist is that he was the father of Dadaism and as such also a pioneer of Surrealism. His art and his passion for chess were curiously intermingled. As the *Times* art critic wrote on 14 June 1966: 'Duchamp's lifelong passion for chess may be

'The Chess Players', 1910 by Marcel Duchamp

thought an expression of his dislike for the trappings that cover the purity of thought.'

And then he goes on to quote a remark by Duchamp's friend Man Ray: 'Chess is a game where the most intense activity leaves no trace.'

There exists a most interesting abstract painting by him – 'Portrait of Chess Players', an oil on canvas painted in 1911. This gives a more complete picture of the process of chess-playing than many a stylized representational painting.

He continued to paint in the most original fashion, setting the style for his contemporaries and followers. His last major work, the 'Large Glass', or 'The Bride Stripped Bare by her Bachelors Even' occupied him for the period 1915 to 1923 at the end of which he gave up painting and concentrated on chess. At this he became near-master class, though his one incursion into practical play when he played on fourth board for France in the Hamburg International Team tournament of 1930, was not exactly encouraging. On fourth board he won one, lost eight, and drew six.

He died in New York at the age of 81 shortly after returning from England where he had a retrospective exhibition at the Tate Gallery in London. *(H.G.)*

DÜCKSTEIN, Andreas *(b. 2 August 1927)*
Austrian international master employed in the Finance Department of the Austrian State Electricity Board.

He has been Vienna's strongest player for many years, having won the City championship nine times. He gained the championship of Austria in 1954 and 1956, and from 1956 has represented his country in all the Olympiads except those of 1960 and 1966.

Although handicapped by lack of time (he is a genuine amateur), Dückstein has a mass of solid achievement to his credit in tournaments, e.g. 4th at Vienna 1959, =4th Zürich 1960, =2nd with Teschner in the strong Zonal tournament at Berg en Dal 1960, 2nd

Birseck 1961, 4th Graz 1961, 3rd Enschede 1961, =4th Vienna 1961, 3rd Amsterdam 1964, 6th Copenhagen 1965. *(W.H.)*

DUEBALL, Jürgen *(b. 17 April 1943)*
A German international master, who represented West Germany at the Skopje Olympiad 1972 (+6−1=6) on board 6 and at the Nice Olympiad 1974 (+8−3=5) on board 5. A good result at Raach 1969 (Zonal) was followed by similar successes at Bad Pyrmont 1970, Berlin 1971 and Dortmund 1973 and finally by a joint first prize, with Sax and Popov, at Reggio Emilia 1973/4. *(W.H.)*

DUFRESNE, Jean *(14 February 1829–13 April 1893)*
Dufresne – an anagrammatic pseudonym of E. S. Freund – was a German player and writer. He won a match against Mayet and 1st prize in the tournament of the *Berliner Schachgesellschaft* in 1853, but as a player he is best remembered as the loser of the Evergreen Game. His *Kleines lehrbuch des Schachspiels* (generally known in Germany as *Der Kleine Dufresne*) has acquainted many generations of German players with the first steps on the chequered board. *(W.H.)*

DUNDEE 1867
The active Dundee Chess Club, at that time the strongest chess club in Scotland, invited the British Chess Association to hold its congress in Dundee in 1867. The main event of the congress was an international tournament that not only achieved the distinction of being the first international tournament to be held in Scotland but was also celebrated as the first international tournament at which a draw counted as a half-point.

Although the newly fledged World Champion, Wilhelm Steinitz, was competing, victory went to the German master Gustav Neumann. Steinitz had the consolation of beating Neumann by using, for the first time, his own gambit line in the Vienna. An extraordinary feature of the play was that, with draws counting for the first time, only 3 games out of the 45 were in fact drawn. *(H.G.)*

DUNKELBLUM, Arthur *(b. 23 April 1906)*
Belgian international master and one of Belgium's leading players over a long period extending from the 1930s to the 1960s. He was Belgian champion in 1949 and scored his best international result at Gijon in Spain the following year where he came =2nd with Pomar. He represented Belgium in 11 Olympiads: 1928, 1933, 1937, 1950, 1954, 1956, 1958, 1960, 1962, 1966 and 1968.

Though an amateur, he is renowned for his drawing capacities. *(H.G.)*

DŮRAS, Oldrich *(30 October 1882–5 January 1957)*
Born near Prague in 1882, Důras was the leading player in Czechoslovakia in the early years of this century. A series of excellent tournament results established him as one of the world's best players. These results included second places at Nuremberg 1906, Vienna 1907 and Hamburg 1910; and =1st places at Vienna 1908 and Prague 1908. Důras also won the Czechoslovak championship on three occasions (1905, 1907 and 1909).

In 1914 Důras married a rich wife and withdrew from international competition, his only further contributions to chess being either of a literary nature or in the field of endgame composition at which he also excelled. He published many fine studies in the years between the wars, but never returned to competitive chess. He was, however, present as a spectator at the 1946 Prague International tournament and sat next to the editor of this encyclopedia at the final banquet.

His years as a player characterized him as a clear positional player against whom tactical adventures were always fraught with risk.

Match game 1913
White: Marshall; *Black:* Důras
King's Gambit, Falkbeer Counter-gambit
1. P–K4, P–K4; 2. P–KB4, P–Q4; 3. N–KB3, QP×P; 4. N×P, N–Q2; 5. P–Q4, P×P *e.p.*; 6. B×P, N×N; 7. P×N, B–QB4; 8. B–N5+, B–Q2; 9. B×B+, Q×B; 10. Q×Q+, K×Q; 11. R–B1, P–KB3; 12. P×P, N×P; 13. R–B5, QR–K1+; 14. K–B1, N–N5; 15. B–B4, KR–B1;

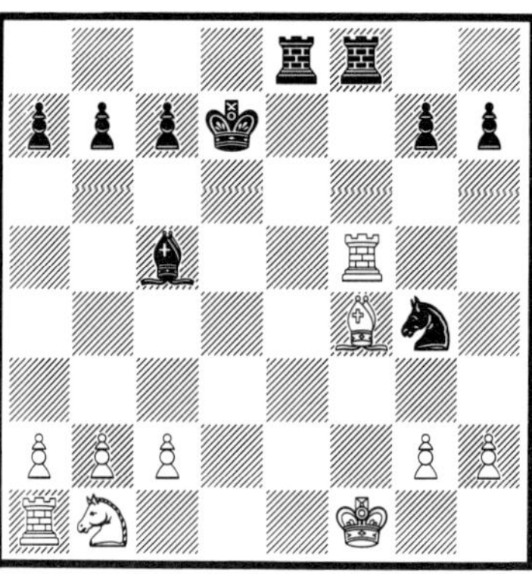

16. R×R, R×R; 17. resigns. *(W.R.H.)*

DUTCH DEFENCE
This aggressive defence was favoured by Morphy but only achieved popularity when adopted by Botvinnik and Alekhine in the 1930s. Black weakens his position but hopes for compensating attacking prospects on the K-side. The chief variations are listed below.

Staunton Gambit: 1. P–Q4, P–KB4; 2. P–K4, P×P; 3. N–QB3. Introduced by Staunton in a match game v. Horwitz, London 1846. White sacrifices a pawn for long-term initiative.

Leningrad System: Black combines . . , P–KB4 with the fianchetto of his KB. This line derives its name from the analyses of Leningrad players during the 1950s.

Stonewall: 1. P–Q4, P–KB4; 2. N–KB3, P–K3; 3. P–KN3, P–Q4. Black furthers his control of the K5 square but the debility of his dark squares is a serious handicap.

Fluid System: (main line) 1. P–Q4, P–KB4; 2. N–KB3, P–K3; 3. P–KN3, N–KB3; 4. B–N2, B–K2; 5. O–O, O–O; 6. P–B4, P–Q3;

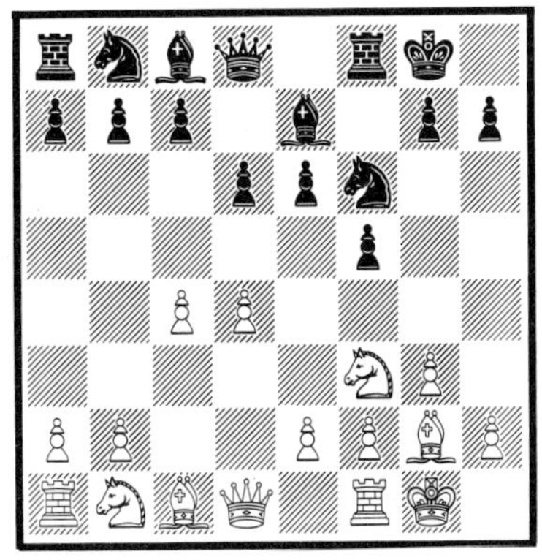

when the success, or otherwise, of Black's strategy depends on White's ability to force through the advance P–K4 under favourable circumstances. *(R.D.K.)*

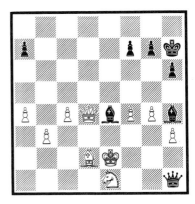

DUZ-KHOTIMIRSKY, Fyodor
(26 September 1879–6 November 1965)
One of the strongest players in Kiev at the turn of the century. He was selected to represent Russia at Carlsbad 1907 where he defeated Nimzowitsch, Janowski, Spielmann and others. Duz-Khotimirsky had a vigorous attacking style which gained him victories against many of the world's strongest players. Won the championship of St Petersburg in 1910 and drew a match 3–3 with Marshall the same year.

Later he became a leading member of the Soviet Chess Federation and had a large part in encouraging the early development of chess in the USSR. Perhaps best known for his victory against Emanuel Lasker at St Petersburg 1909. *(W.R.H.)*

DZHINDZHIHASHVILI [Djindjihashvili], Roman
(b. 5 May 1944)
Israeli international master who was born in Georgia, USSR. An international master since 1970 and one of the strongest players not to have, as yet, attained the grandmaster title. He won the Soviet First League championship in 1973, and in 1976 emigrated to Israel and acquired Israeli citizenship. *(W.R.H.)*

'L'ÉCHIQUIER'
This magazine, published in Belgium from 1927 to 1931 and edited by Edmond Lancel, has a special place in the history of chess as the first publication to introduce figurine algebraic notation whereby the piece is identified by its internationally recognized symbol. Apart from being responsible for a historic innovation, the magazine was notable for the consistently high quality of its content. *(K.J.O'C.)*

ECHO
Essentially a problem theme, the echo is a mating (or winning) line in which two (or more) defences are met with corresponding attacking moves. It rarely occurs in actual play, but see the finish of the game Neumann–Kolisch, Paris 1867. From the diagram play went:

1. . , P–B4 (so that after B × N the Black QB cannot be captured with check); 2. P × P, Q–R7+. If now 3. K–B1, B × N; 4. B × B, Q–N7 mate, while if 3. K–Q1, B × N; 4. B × B, Q–B7 mate – an 'echo' mating position. In the game White played 3. K–Q1, B × N; 4. K × B, Q–R8+; 5. K–K2, Q–B6+; 6. K–K1, B–Q6; 7. resigns. *(W.H.)*

ECUADOR
One of the first South American nations to compete in the Olympiads, finishing 21st in 1939. Subsequent appearances have been rare: 26th in 1964, 39th in 1966 and 47th in 1974.

Though only a 'small-scale' chess country, two international 'Indio Atahualpa' tournaments have been held in Quito: 1975 (won by Rubinetti) and 1976 (won by Panno).

The chess federation's offices are situated at the Federacion Deportiva Nacional del Ecuador, Casilla 3409, Guayaquil. *(K.J.O'C.)*

EDMONDSON, Edmund Broadley Jr. *(b. 1920)*
Edmondson has been considered the most influential man in US chess from the mid 1960s and is credited with playing an essential role in Fischer's rise to the World Championship.

Edmondson was an industrial engineer before entering military service in May 1943 as an aerial navigator. He retired after 23 years from the US Air Force in 1966 with the rank of lieutenant colonel.

During his military career Edmondson played in and helped organize chess events in several cities in the USA and overseas. He was elected a vice-president of the US Chess Federation in 1961 and became president two years later. In 1966 he was appointed executive director of the Federation, its highest-ranking full-time position.

Edmondson became permanent American delegate to FIDE in 1968. He was elected to the FIDE Bureau in 1970 and was re-elected in 1974. During his tenure as executive director of the USCF, membership more than tripled and the federation magazine, *Chess Life*, was merged with *Chess Review*. *(A.S.)*

'E G'
A quarterly magazine devoted to the endgame study, *E G* being the initials of 'endgame'. First issue July 1965. Edited by A. J. Roycroft. Address: 17 New Way Road, London NW9. *(A.J.R.)*

EINSTEIN, Albert *(14 March 1879–18 April 1955)*
The fact that the great physicist was a friend and admirer of Emanuel Lasker has led many people to believe that he was himself a chess-player. Le Lionnais, in his *Dictionnaire des Echecs*, Paris 1967, gives a game he won against Robert Oppenheimer, taking it in turn from Gerhard Henschel's *Freude am Schach*.

However, this game must be apocryphal, since, in a preface Einstein wrote to Hannak's *Emanuel Lasker*, Berlin-Frohnau, 1952, he states categorically 'Ich bin selber kein Schachspieler' (I am myself no chess-player) and goes on to say 'I have to confess that I have always disliked the fierce competitive spirit embodied in that highly intellectual game.' *(H.G.)*

EKSTRÖM, Folke *(b. 12 October 1906)*
Swedish international master and Swedish champion, 1947 and 1948, for a brief period after the Second World War Ekström seemed certain to join the famous Swedish trio, Stoltz, Ståhlberg and Lundin, as a member of Sweden's Olympic team.

At Hastings 1945/6 he came second to Tartakower and was no less than 2 points ahead of Dr Euwe and Denker, both of whom he beat. But then, with his wife objecting to his travelling abroad, he confined his play to Sweden where he showed his strength by winning the championship twice in succession. Even these absences from home being taken amiss, he gave up over-the-board play and took up correspondence play at which he became a master.

His name is attached to a variation of the Open Defence to the Ruy Lopez: 1. P–K4, P–K4; 2. N–KB3, N–QB3; 3. B–N5, P–QR3; 4. B–R4, N–B3; 5. O–O, N×P; 6. P–Q4, P–QN4; 7. B–N3, P–Q4; 8. P×P, B–K3; 9. Q–K2, B–K2; 10. R–Q1, O–O; 11. P–B4, NP×P; 12. B×P, Q–Q2. *(H.G.)*

ELISKASES, Erich *(b. 15 February 1913)*
International grandmaster, first of Austrian, then Brazilian and finally Argentine nationality, Eliskases seemed destined to reach the top of the tree when the Second World War intervened, breaking his career in two.

Austrian champion at sixteen, he succeeded as a very young man in winning four matches against experienced grandmasters: Spielmann in 1932 (+3—2=5), again in 1936 (+2—1=7), and yet again a year later (+2—0=8); and Bogoljubow in 1939 (+6—3 =11). During the same period he won many first prizes in smaller tournaments, such as Budapest 1934, Vienna 1935 (jointly with L. Steiner), Swinemünde 1936, Milan 1938 (jointly with Monticelli), Bad Harzburg 1939, culminating in his success at Noordwijk 1938 (ahead of Keres, Pirc, Euwe, Bogoljubow and five others). For bigger events he was not quite ready, finishing unplaced Moscow 1936 and Semmering 1937; =6th Podebrady 1936.

He represented Austria in the Olympiads of 1930, 1933, 1935 and 1936, and 'Greater Germany' after the *Anschluss* at Buenos Aires 1939, after having won the championship of Germany with record scores in both 1938 and 1939.

Stranded at Buenos Aires, Eliskases embarked on his second career first in Brazil, then Argentina, the principal milestones of which were: first prizes Sao Paulo 1941, and again 1947; Mar del Plata 1948, Punta del Este (Uruguay) 1951; joint first prizes at the South American Zonal 1951, Cordoba 1959; =2nd at Mar del Plata 1949; 3rd prizes at Mar del Plata 1941 and 1947, as well as the double-round event (with Ståhlberg, Najdorf, Euwe and others) at Buenos Aires 1947; =4th in the Capablanca Memorial at Havana 1952.

Eliskases is a careful positional player whose best games are distinguished by a general encroachment of his opponent's position. *(W.H.)*

ELIZABETH I, Queen of England
(7 September 1533–24 March 1603)
Elizabeth I, like all the Tudor monarchs, was a keen chess-player and was taught the game by her tutor, Roger Ascham.

The French ambassador once found the Queen playing chess in her privy chamber and told her that the game was much like human affairs, one lost a pawn and it did not seem to matter, but often this was the equivalent of a loss of the game.

This was at the time when Mary Stuart, Queen of Scots, had married Lord Darnley and the marriage had been regarded as a blow against the Tudor succession to the throne. In fact, it was their son who became James VI, King of Scotland and eventually James I of England. Hence Queen Elizabeth's reply to the ambassador, 'Yes, Darnley is only a pawn, but it may be checkmate if I am not careful.' *(H.G.)*

ELO, Professor Arpad E. *(b. 25 August 1903)*
An American statistician who developed the rating system used by the USCF and FIDE for the grading of tournaments and the award of titles. His name is often used synonymously with the rating list itself. *(W.R.H.)*

EL SALVADOR
No team representing the Federacion Salvadorena de Ajedrez (Comité Olimpico, Coronel Adolfo Arnoldo Majano, Palacio de los Deportes, San Salvador) has ever played in the Olympiads. However, El Salvador did win the 1976 'Against Chess Olympiad' in Libya. *(K.J.O'C.)*

ENDGAME [or Ending]
The phase which follows the middle-game, having somewhat different strategic characteristics. Indexers have sometimes defined the endgame as consisting of positions in which the players have not more than two pieces each besides the Kings and the pawns.

The basic endgame consists of positions in which there is a total of three or fewer pawns on the board. This is the subject of endgame theory, and the strategic characteristics are significantly different. The most distinctive of these are: (*a*) a change in the relative value of the pieces – a piece may be worth no more than a pawn; (*b*) the possibility that having the move may be disadvantageous – such a position is called a *zugzwang*; and (*c*) the defensive resource of stalemate.

The consequence of these factors is that basic endgame positions often do not respond to the common-sense judgments that apply to earlier phases of the game; and talent, even when it amounts to genius, is insufficient without foreknowledge.

Bad Bishop

One obstructed by its own pawns; such a disadvantage is usually permanent, and often fatal.

In position 1 Black has a bad Bishop – it can attack nothing and must defend its pawns; moreover White's King threatens to advance on the dark-coloured squares, none of which Black's pawns control. White to play wins by 'losing the move': 1. B–B1, B–N2; 2. B–K2, B–B1; 3. B–Q3, after which Black must either move his Bishop, losing a pawn, or allow White's King to advance.

In general a bad Bishop is at an even greater disadvantage when opposed by a Knight.

Position 1

Bishop Endings

Endings with Bishops, pawns and Kings. See BAD BISHOP, and BISHOP OF THE WRONG COLOUR.

Bishops of Opposite Colour

A player having only one Bishop which does not move on the same coloured squares as his opponent's single Bishop. Such endings tend to lead to a blockade, and are said to be drawish; in order to win, one needs to have a fairly substantial advantage.

Position 2 is drawn, for White cannot gain control of the relevant dark-coloured squares.

Bishop of the Wrong Colour

King, Bishop and pawn win against the lone King with two exceptions. The first is the notorious and common ending known as Rook's pawn with Bishop of the wrong colour, i.e. the Bishop cannot control the queening square. The defender draws if his King

Position 2

Position 3

can occupy the queening square, as in position 3; Black's King cannot be driven out of the corner, for attempts to do so lead to stalemate.

The other exception: White King at Q6, White Bishop at QR7, White pawn at QN6, and Black King at QN2. This position is drawn for the same reason.

Checkmate

A position in which a player's King is in check and in which he cannot make any legal move to get out of check: the object and the end of the game.

In endings with pieces, but no pawns, the direct objective is checkmate except for a few situations in which one may first trap a stray piece. Results are as follows:

Endings normally won:

K+B+N v. K
K+B+B v. K
K+R v. K
K+Q v. K
K+3 minor pieces v. K+1 minor piece
K+B+B+N v. K+R
K+R+R v. K+2 minor pieces
K+R+2 minor pieces v. K+R
K+Q v. K+1 minor piece
K+Q v. K+R
K+4 minor pieces v. K+Q
K+R+R+1 minor piece v. K+Q

Endings normally drawn:

K+N+N v. K
K+B+N v. K+1 minor piece
K+B+B v. K+B
K+R v. K+1 minor piece
K+R+1 minor piece v. K+R
K+B+N+N v. K+R
K+R+R v. K+3 minor pieces
K+3 minor pieces v. K+Q
K+R+R v. K+Q
K+Q+1 minor piece v. K+Q

K+Q v. K+B+B
K+Q v. K+R+1 minor piece
K+Q+1 minor piece v. K+R+R
K+R+2 minor pieces v. K+Q

Endings with unclear result:
K+B+B v. K+N
K+Q v. K+N+N
K+Q v. K+B+N
K+R+B v. K+N+N

Checkmate with Bishop and Knight
This is the most difficult of the four basic mates. In all of them the idea is the same: the defending King is driven to the edge or to a corner.

Mate with Bishop and Knight can be forced only on or next to a corner square which can be controlled by the Bishop. The defender, when driven, moves his King to the 'wrong' corner, and the checkmate from this position is shown from position 4: 1. N–B7+, K–N1; 2. B–K3 (losing the move), K–B1; 3. B–R7, K–Q1; 4. N–Q5, K–K1 (hoping to escape to the other, 'wrong' corner); 5. K–Q6, K–B2; 6. N–K7, K–N2; 7. B–K3 (White's pieces make a cordon confining Black's King to a few squares around his KR1), K–B3; 8. B–R6, K–B2; 9. B–N5, K–B1; 10. N–N6+, K–B2; 11. N–K5+, K–K1; 12. K–B7, K–B1; 13. K–Q7, K–N2; 14. K–K7, K–N1; 15. B–R6, K–R2; 16. B–B8, K–N1; 17. N–N4, K–R2; 18. K–B7, K–R1; 19. B–N7+, K–R2; 20. N–B6 mate.

From the most unfavourable position this checkmate might take about 34 moves.

Checkmate with Queen
The defender's King must be driven to the edge of the board. From position 5: 1. Q–N6 (the Queen follows the Black King forcing it down the board), K–B5; 2. K–K4, K–B6; 3. Q–N5, K–B7; 4. Q–N4, K–Q8; 5. K–Q3, K–B8; 6. Q–N6 (waiting), K–Q8; 7. Q–N1 mate. The only danger for White is stalemate, if, for instance, he were here to play 6. Q–N3.

The Queen can always mate within 10 moves.

Position 4

Position 5

Position 6

Position 7

Checkmate with Rook
In position 6 Black's King must be driven to the edge and then towards a corner. White first brings his King to the centre: 1. K–N2, K–Q5; 2. K–B2, K–K5; 3. K–B3, K–K4; 4. K–B4, K–K3; 5. K–Q4, K–B4; 6. R–R6 (beginning the drive to the edge), K–B5; 7. R–B6+, K–N4; 8. R–B1, K–N3; 9. K–K5, K–N4; 10. R–N1+, K–R5; 11. K–B4, K–R4; 12. R–N2 (waiting), K–R3; 13. K–B5, K–R2; 14. K–B6, K–R1; 15. K–B7, K–R2; 16. R–R2 mate.

Mate can always be accomplished in 16 or fewer moves.

Checkmate with two Bishops
In position 7 the defending King must be driven to a corner. 1. K–N2, K–K6; 2. B–Q1, K–Q7; 3. B–QB2 (this manoeuvre, repeated on the 8th and 11th moves, forces Black to retreat), K–K6; 4. K–B3, K–B6; 5. K–Q4, K–N5; 6. B–K1, K–B6; 7. B–Q3, K–B5; 8. B–K4, K–N4; 9. K–K5, K–N5; 10. B–KB2, K–N4; 11. B–KB5, K–R3; 12. K–B6, K–R4; 13. B–K6 (waiting), K–R3; 14. B–N4, K–R2; 15. K–B7, K–R3; 16. B–K3+, K–R2; 17. B–B5+, K–R1; 18. B–Q4 mate.

Mate can always be achieved in 18 moves at the most.

Checkmate with two Knights v. Pawn
It is one of the curiosities of chess that although King and two Knights cannot defeat a lone King, they may win if the defender has a pawn which would deprive him of a stalemate defence. In position 8 White to play mates in six: 1. N–B4, P–R6; 2. N–K5, P–R7; 3. N–N6+, K–R2; 4. N–B8+, K–R1; 5. N–R4 (Black is in a 'stalemate' position), P–R8(Q); 6. N(R4)–N6 mate.

This shows the idea: one Knight blocks the pawn whilst the King and the other Knight drives Black's King to a corner. Here Black's King is already cornered, a very favourable situation for White who could mate if instead his blocking Knight were at QN4, QB3, Q3, K2, KB2, KN3 or KR2.

In general, assuming that Black's King is favourably placed and that the blocking Knight is not endangered, White wins against RP or centre P on its 5th rank, BP on its 4th rank, or NP on its 3rd rank; but he draws if the pawn is further forward. The definitive analysis of this endgame was made by Troitzky, and published in book form in the 1930s.

Knight endings

Endings with Kings, Knights and pawns.

King, Knight and pawn normally win against a lone King with two exceptions when the pawn is at R7. The position White King at QB5, White Knight at QN5, White pawn at QR7, and Black King at QR1 is drawn; if White guards the pawn with his King (in order to free the Knight) Black is stalemated.

Position 9 is the other exception. White to move draws. The Knight cannot lose a move: what it can do in 1, 3, or 5 moves it can never do in 2, 4, or 6 moves; and it cannot disturb Black's King which oscillates from QB1 to QB2 keeping White's King in the corner. Black to move loses, for he must at once release the imprisoned King.

In position 10 the Knight wins against a pawn. This is the oldest-known practical endgame, dating from the twelfth century. White to play: 1. K–B1, K–R8; 2. K–B2, K–R7; 3. N–K2, K–R8; 4. N–B1, P–R7; 5. N–N3 mate.

Losing the Move

A manoeuvre peculiar to the endgame. Positions arise in which it is desirable that it should be the opponent's turn to play. In position 1 White loses a move with his Bishop.

In position 11 White to play wins by losing a move with his RP: 1. P–R3, K–R1; 2. P–R4, K–N1; 3. P–R5, K–R1; 4. P–N6, P×P; 5. P×P, K–N1; 6. P–N7. Here 1. P–R4 would draw.

The Rook and the Queen (but not the Knight) can also lose the move. See TRIANGULATION, by means of which the King may lose the move.

Position 8

Position 9

Position 10

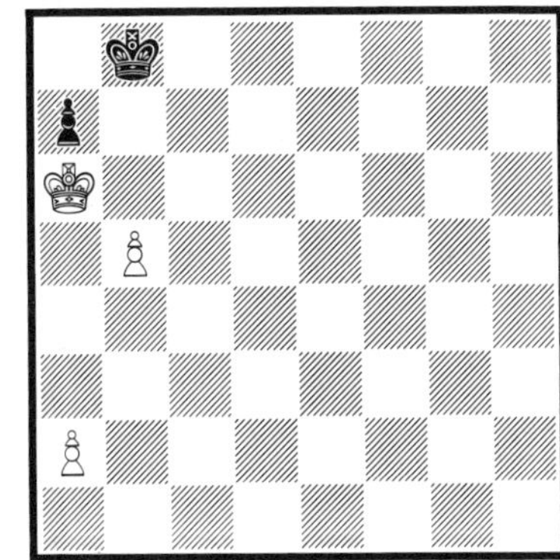

Position 11

Position 12

Position 13

Opposition

A term defining the relationship between the Kings. In position 12 the Kings stand in opposition, more precisely in vertical direct opposition (direct means as near as possible). The player who does not have the move is said 'to have the opposition' – a loose term which is, however, in general use.

Suppose that White has the opposition and he wants to get to the upper ranks on the Queen's side: 1. . , K–B4; 2. K–B3, K–N4; 3. K–N3, K–R4; 4. K–B4 (outflanking), K–N3; 5. K–N4 (re-taking the opposition), K–R3; 6. K–B5, K–N2; 7. K–N5, K–B2; 8. K–R6, etc. Thus the first rule: *the player having the opposition can force his way to any part of the board.*

The use of the opposition is linked with the player's intention. In the above play, after White outflanks, Black could take the opposition, 4. . , K–R5; and he would then have the accruing advantages; but White could move his King to QB8, achieving his objective.

Instead of seeking to advance White might oppose Black's King all along the rank, 1. . , K–B4; 2. K–B3, or 1. . , K–K4; 2. K–K3, etc. This is the defensive opposition, in accordance with the second rule: *the player having the opposition can prevent the advance of his opponent's King.*

If a rectangle were drawn just large enough to contain the two Kings, and if such a rectangle contained an odd number of squares, then the Kings would be standing in opposition. This is so in position 13 (a rectangle of 35 squares). Suppose White has the opposition and he wants to get to the upper ranks on the King's side: 1. . , K–K2; 2. K–B1, K–B2; 3. K–Q1, K–K2; 4. K–K1 (vertical long-distant opposition), K–B2; 5. K–B1, K–N2; 6. K–N1, K–B2; 7. K–R2 (outflanking), K–N3; 8. K–N2 (taking the vertical distant opposition), K–B3; 9. K–R3, K–N4; 10. K–N3, with direct opposition, proceeding as in position 12. Thus the third rule: *all forms of the opposition confer the same advantages or disadvantages.*

Diagram 14 shows the four intertwined oppositional grids. If both Kings were standing on squares having the same letter they would stand in opposition.

In positions 12 and 13 the opposition is really notional, for it is not customary to say that one has the opposition (merely because the Kings stand in a certain relationship) unless the having of it

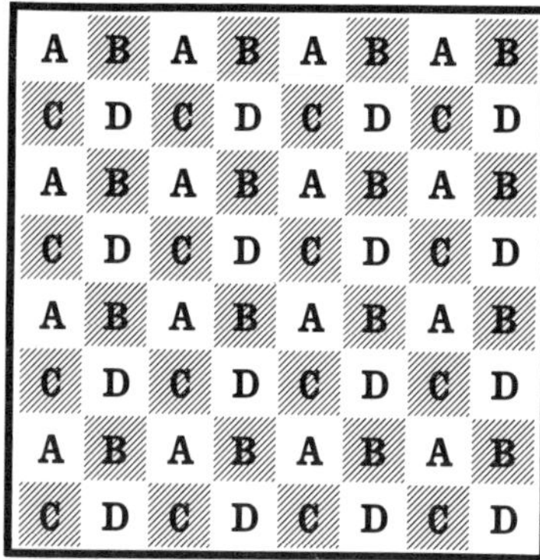

Position 14

Position 15

Position 16

Position 17

confers a decisive advantage. The grids are normally submerged, but here and there in practice (i.e. with other pieces and/or pawns on the board) parts of the grids surface, as it were; and indeed the presence of this extra material may modify the rules.

In position 15 the oppositional grid surfaces along White's 5th rank from KB5 to QR5, and similarly for Black's King on his 2nd rank. If White has the opposition he wins: he can force the advance of his King and thus gain control of the queening square. 1. . , K–K2; 2. K–K5, K–Q2; 3. K–Q5, K–B2; 4. K–B5, K–N2; 5. K–N5 (with his King on the queening file White is ready to outflank), K–B2; 6. K–R6, K–N1; 7. K–N6, K–B1; 8. K–R7, and the pawn promotes. If Black has the opposition he draws by preventing the advance of White's King: 1. K–K5, K–K2; 2. K–Q5, K–Q2; 3. K–B5, K–B2; 4. K–N5, K–N2; 5. K–R5, K R2; etc. (For 6. P–N5, K–N2; 7. P–N6, see PAWN ENDINGS, position 17.)

In the position White King at QB3, White pawn at QB4, Black King at QB8, and Black pawn at QB4, the Kings are in inverted vertical direct opposition. White to play draws: 1. K–Q3, K–N7. Black to play loses: 1. . , K–N8; 2. K–N3, or 1. . , K–Q8; 2. K–Q3, and in either case his pawn is captured.

Here are three instances of horizontal direct opposition; in all cases White to play draws or Black to play loses:

(*i*) White King at QR4, White pawn at QN2, Black King at QB5, and Black pawn at QR4.

(*ii*) White King at QN7, White pawn at QB5, Black King at Q2, and Black pawn at QB2.

(*iii*) White King at QR7, White pawns at QR6 and QB6, and Black King at QB2.

Diagonal opposition is shown in the position White King at QB6, White pawn at QN6, and Black King at QR1. White to play draws: 1. K–B7, stalemate; but Black to play loses: 1. . , K–N1; 2. P–N7, K–R2; 3. K–B7.

Vertical distant opposition is seen in the position White King at Q2, White pawns at QR3 and QN3, Black King at Q3, and Black pawn at QR4. White to play draws, for he cannot get his King to the 4th rank without first moving a pawn. Black to play loses for White's King, having the opposition, can force its way to the 4th rank: 1. . , K–B3; 2. K–K3 (outflanking), K–B4; 3. K–K4, K–B3; 4. K–Q4, K–Q3; and now 5. P–R4, after which the Black pawn falls. See also ZUGZWANG.

Outside Passed Pawn

A lone passed pawn at a distance from the remaining pawns – outside the main battle area, as it were.

In position 16 White has an outside passed pawn (the QRP), and the general idea is that such a pawn will decoy Black's King to one side of the board whilst White gobbles up the pawns on the other side.

White wins after 1. . , P–B5; 2. P–QR4, P–N4; 3. P–R5, K–Q3; 4. K–B4, K–B3; 5. K–Q4, K–N4; 6. K–K4, K × P; 7. K–B5, K–N4; 8. P–R3, K–B4; 9. K–N6.

An outside passed pawn does not necessarily lead to a win.

Pawn endings

Endings with Kings and pawns

For the understanding of the ending K+P v. P, excluding those cases where Black's King cannot get into the 'quadrant', it is necessary to understand the *zugzwang* and the opposition.

Position 17 is a type-position for any pawn on the 6th rank or farther back: Black draws when his King confronts the pawn. Here he withdraws to the queening square, 1. . , K–N1; and now 2. K–R6, K–R1 (taking the opposition); 3. P–N7+, K–N1 and White is in *zugzwang*. If instead Black plays 1. . , K–R1? then the *zugzwangs* favour White: 2. K–R6, K–N1; 3. P–N7, K–B2; 4. K–R7, and the pawn queens.

In general if White wants to win this ending he must get his King in front of the pawn, in order to clear a path, as it were. If White gets his King in front of any pawn (except RP) on the 5th, 6th, or 7th rank he wins. From position 18, White to play, 1. K–R6, K–R1; 2. P–N6, K–N1; 3. P–N7, or Black to play, 1. . , K–R1; 2. K–B7.

When White's pawn (except RP) is on the 4th rank or farther back, however, White needs also to have the opposition, as shown in position 15.

This difference between a pawn on the 5th or farther forward and a pawn on the 4th or farther back is often significant. In position 19 White wins if he has the opposition: 1. . , K–B2; 2. K–K6, K–B1; 3. K–Q6, K–N2; 4. K–Q7, K–N1; 5. K–B6, K–R2; 6. K–B7, K–R1; 7. K × P (position 18). A similar position farther back would be drawn: White King at Q4, White pawn at QN4, Black King at Q3, and Black pawn at QN4; 1. . , K–B2; 2. K–B5, K–N1; 3. K × P, K–N2 and Black has the opposition (position 15).

In the ending K + RP v. K there are no *zugzwangs*. Black draws if his King is anywhere in front of the pawn; if it is advanced to the 7th rank it must be abandoned or Black is stalemated. Black also draws if he can imprison White's King as in position 20, a type-position for RP on any rank; if White frees his King (1. K–R6, K–B3; 2. P–R5, K–B2; 3. K–N5) then Black can get his King in front of the pawn.

In the position White King at Q5, White pawn at QR4, Black King at QB7, and Black pawn at QR4, White to play wins; not 1. K–B5, K–Q6; 2. K–N5, K–Q5; 3. K × P, K–B4 (position 20); but 1. K–B4 (holding off Black's King), K–Q7; 2. K–N5, K–Q6; 3. K × P, K–B5; 4. K–N6.

Position 21 is a type-*zugzwang* for any pawns (except RPs) providing they are not further forward than shown on the diagram. Black to play loses, 1. . , K–N2; 2. K–B5, K–B2; 3. P–N6 +, K–N2; 4. K–N5, K–N1; 5. K–R6, K–R1; 6. P–N7 +, K–N1; and now the tempo-move 7. P–N5 puts Black in *zugzwang*.

King and two pawns normally win against the lone King. The pawns can defend themselves until the King is brought to their aid. In the position White King at QN1, White pawns at QN5 and Q5, and Black King at QB2, if Black plays 1. . , K–Q3 then 2. P–N6, K × P; 3. P–N7, and Black cannot get into the quadrant.

There are two other *zugzwangs*: (*i*) White King at Q6, White pawns at QB7 and QR5, and Black King at QB1. (*ii*) White King at QB1, White pawns at QN3 and Q3, and Black King at QB6. White to play draws: 1. K–N1, K × NP or 1. K–Q1, K × QP. Black to play loses, e.g. 1. . , K × QP; 2. K–N2, K–Q5; 3. K–R3, K–B4; 4. K–R4,

Position 18

Position 19

Position 20

Position 21

Position 22

K–N3; 5. K–N4, and White has the opposition. This *zugzwang* is of practical application: in the position White King at QB1, White Rook at Q1, White pawns at QN3 and QB2, Black King at QB6, and Black Rook at KR6, White wins by, and only by, 1. R–Q3 +.

Position 22 shows the 'Trébuchet', an unusual *zugzwang* in so far as whoever plays loses, a difference of a whole point; a trap to watch for, when attacking a blocked pawn.

In the endgame K + P v. K + P, when the pawns are on adjoining files Black may defend by counter-attack or, on occasion, by sacrificing his pawn. The position White King at Q4, White pawn at QN3, Black King at KB4 and Black pawn at QR3, is a *zugzwang*. White to play draws if: 1. K–B5, Black counter-attacks by 1. . , K–K5; if 1. P–N4, K–K3; 2. K–B5 Black sacrifices, drawing against the RP (2. . , P–R4; 3. P × P, K–Q2 etc.). Black to play loses, for he must give up the option of moving the King either way: 1. . , K–B5; 2. P N4, and 3. K–B5, or 1. . , K–K3; 2. K–B5, winning Black's pawn (2. . , K–K4; 3. P–N4).

When each player has one passed pawn there may be a simple race for Promotion. Sometimes one player may win because he queens with check, or because, with two Queens on the board, he can win the opposing Queen or give checkmate. In the position White King at QN5, White pawn at QB5, Black King at Q4, and Black pawn at QR2 (a *zugzwang*), Black to play loses: 1. . , K–K3; 2. K–B6, P–R4; 3. K–N7, P–R5; 4. P–B6, queening with check; whilst if 1. . , K–K4; 2. K–B6, P–R4; 3. K–N5.

In the position White King at QB5, White pawn at Q6, Black King at QB6, and Black pawn at QR6, White to play wins: 1. P–Q7, P–R7; 2. P–Q8(Q), and if 2. . , P–R8(Q); 3. Q–Q4 +, winning Black's Queen, or if 2. . , K–N7; 3. K–N4, P–R8(Q); 4. Q–Q2 +, K–N8; 5. K–N3, and Black is checkmated.

See also LOSING THE MOVE, OPPOSITION, OUTSIDE PASSED PAWN, QUADRANT, QUEEN'S SIDE MAJORITY, TRIANGULATION, and ZUGZWANG.

Pawn Promotion

When a pawn reaches the 8th rank it must be exchanged for a Queen, a Rook, a Knight, or a Bishop, of the same colour. In practical play the choice is almost always a Queen, although a few cases have occurred in which the pawn becomes a Rook in order to avoid stalemate or a Knight in order to give check as in this well known example from practical play: White King at Q5, White Rook at KR8, Black King at Q6, Black pawn at QB6. White to play: 1. R–R3+, K–Q7; 2. K–Q4, P–B7; 3. R–R2+, K–Q8; 4. K–Q3, and Black draws by 4. . , P–B8(N)+.

Quadrant [Square] of the Pawn

A concept used to describe whether a defending King can hinder the advance of a passed pawn.

Position 23 shows the quadrant, marked by a line, of a pawn at White's QR3. If Black's King cannot get into the quadrant it cannot stop the pawn (with one exception when the pawn is at R7 – see PAWN ENDINGS).

The quadrant is the same for a pawn on the 2nd or 3rd rank, but as the pawn advances to the 4th rank and beyond, the quadrant becomes proportionately smaller. Here White to play wins by 1. P–R4. Black to play draws by 1. . , K–K6 or 1. . , K–B6 entering the quadrant.

Queen against Pawn

The Queen normally wins, with two exceptions when the defender has a BP or a RP on the 7th rank.

Position 24 is drawn. White might play 1. Q–N3+, K–R8; now Black's King is in a stalemate position, and White lacks time to bring up his King. White, to play, could win if his King were nearer, within the area marked by a line. If his King were at K2, for instance, he could play 1. K–Q2, P–R8(Q); 2. Q–B2 mate.

Position 25 is drawn. 1. Q N3+, K–R8; 2. Q×P stalemate. Here too White could win if his King were near enough for a mating attack.

In position 26 White to play wins, for his King is within the marked area (were it outside, he could only draw). 1. K–B3, K–Q7; 2. K–B2, K–Q8; 3. Q–Q4+, K–B8; 4. Q–QN4, K–Q8; 5. Q–K1 mate.

The NP and the centre P offer no stalemate defence; the defender's King is forced to block his pawn, and the attacking King moves nearer step by step.

Queen endings

Endings with Kings, Queens and pawns.

When there are few pawns on the board the defender's chief resource is perpetual check. In position 27 Black to play draws by 1. . , Q–K1+ and (whether or not the pawn queens) White cannot escape perpetual check. White to play might, after due preparation, move out his King, but probably could not avoid perpetual check just the same.

Queen's side Majority

In position 28 White has more Queen's side pawns than Black; White is said to have a Queen's side majority. The general idea is to use this in order to decoy the enemy King: 1. . , K–Q3; 2. P–B4, P×P+; 3. K×P, P–K4; 4. P×P+, K×P; 5. P–QN4, P–B4; 6. P–N5, P×P+; 7. K×P, and White wins as in position 15 (see ENDGAME, OPPOSITION).

A Queen's side majority is not necessarily advantageous. One

Position 23

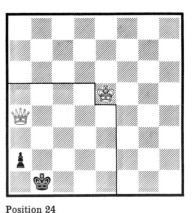

Position 24

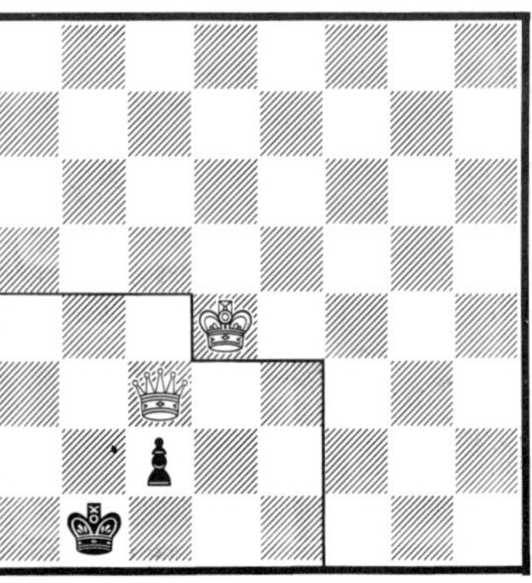

Position 25

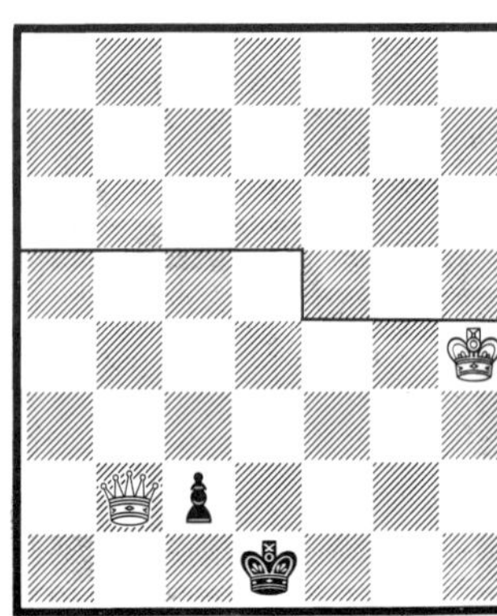

Position 26

Position 27

Position 28

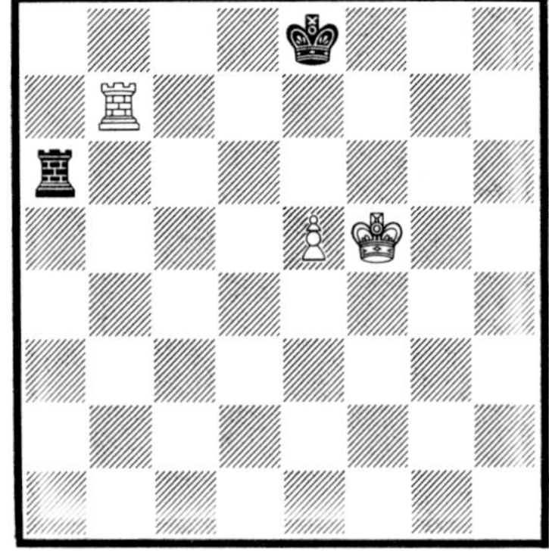

Position 29

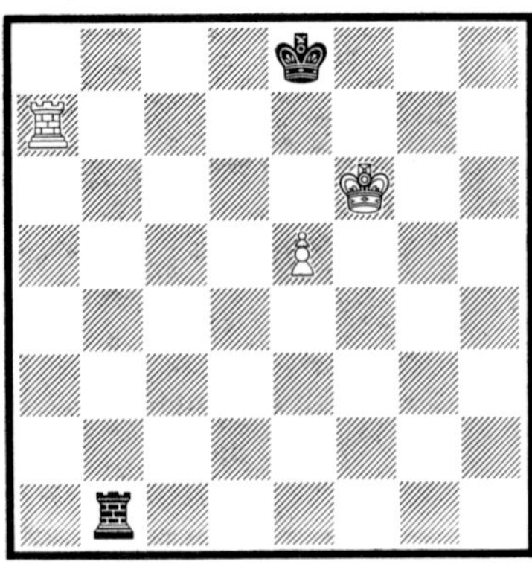

Position 30

reason why it is sometimes more effective than a King's side majority is that players often castle on the King's side, and a remote majority is inherently stronger than a near majority. Even so, a win is unlikely unless one also has other advantages. Here, for instance, Black has advanced and thereby weakened his Queen's side minority.

Pawn majorities, with or without pieces, are the most important single characteristic which can influence end-play; and the principle of decoying the enemy King by such means is probably the most widespread of all strategic endgame ideas.

Queening square
The square on the 8th rank on which a pawn is promoted, or queened, or on which it would be promoted if advanced on the same file without hindrance.

Rook endings
Endings with Kings, Rooks and pawns.

The main characteristics of the ending K+R+P v. K+R are the barriers, used by either player, and the checking sequence used by the defender.

The defender normally draws when his King is in front of the pawn. In position 29 his Rook makes a barrier on the 3rd rank preventing the advance of White's King (which would create mating threats). After 1. P–K6, R–R8; 2. K–B6, R–B8+ Black draws by a checking sequence, driving White's King away from the pawn.

When White's King has advanced unhindered to the 6th rank, Black draws against NP or RP by passive defence. In the position White King at QR6, White Rook at KR7, White pawn at QN6, Black King at QN1 and Black Rook at Q1, Black keeps his Rook on the back rank, and White can make no meaningful threats.

Against BP or centre P Black should defend actively. In position 30, 1. . , R–N1 ? loses because White's Rook can make threats on either side of the pawn: 2. P–K6, R–QB1; 3. R–KR7. Instead Black draws by 1. . , R–K8 attacking the pawn from the rear, so that after 2. R–R8+, K–Q2 or 2. K–K6, K–B1; 3. R–R8+, K–N2; 4. K–Q6, K–B2 the pawn cannot advance. White might try to use his Rook to help the advance of his pawn: 2. K–K6, K–B1; 3. R–R8+, K–N2; 4. R–K8. On his second move Black took care to move his King to the 'short side' of the pawn, so that he could, if necessary, keep the 'long side' clear for a checking sequence on the ranks; accordingly he now plays 4. . , R–QR8 and if White tries to parry the threatened checks by 5. R–Q8, Black simply moves the Rook back to its post at K8.

Position 31 is given by Salvio (1634), who attributes the analysis to Scipione Genovino. This is the famous but mis-named Lucena position. White wins: 1. R–B4, R–R8; 2. R–Q4+, K–K2; 3. K–B7, R–B8+; 4. K–N6, R–N8+; 5. K–R6, R–R8+; 6. K–N5, R–N8+; 7. R–N4, and the sequence of checks is broken. White can win such positions with BP or centre P (but not RP). When Black's King is on the short side, however, a win is less likely. In the position White King at K8, White Rook at KB1, White pawn at K7, Black King at KN2, and Black Rook at QR2, Black to play draws by a checking sequence on the ranks.

Position 31

Position 32

If White has a RP then he cannot win when his King is in front of his pawn unless the defending King is some distance away. In position 32 White to play wins: 1. R–KR2, K–K2; 2. R–R8, K–Q2 or Q3; 3. R–QN8, and the White King escapes; but Black to play draws: 1. . , K–K2; 2. R–KR2, K–Q2; 3. R–R8, K–B2.

The position White King at QB5, White Rook at QR8, White pawn at QR7, Black King at KN2 and Black Rook at QR8 is drawn. Black cannot free his Rook unless his King guards the pawn, but after 1. K–N6 a checking sequence drives the King away.

In position 33 the White Rook makes a barrier on the King's file, cutting off Black's King. White wins: 1. K–N4, R–N1+; 2. K–R5, R–QB1; 3. K–N5, R–N1+; 4. K–R6, R–QB1; 5. R–QB1, K–K2; 6. K–N7, R–B4; 7. K–N6, R–B1; 8. P–B5, K–Q2; 9. R–Q1+, K–K2; 10. P–B6, R–N1+; 11. K–B7, R–N6; 12. K–B8, R–N7; 13. P–B7 (position 31). There are many other positions of this kind in which Black's King is cut off on the file or on the rank, and in some of them the play is very complex indeed.

All the books mentioned under HISTORY OF LITERATURE, and THE MODERN LITERATURE give special attention to Rook endings, which occur more often than any other type. Rook endings are notoriously drawish; the advantage of a pawn up may not be decisive and, in general, one needs to have some added advantage in order to win.

Position 33

Tempo-move

Moving a pawn in order to lose the move; see PAWN ENDINGS, position 21.

There is a limited number of tempo-moves in any given position, and in pawn endings especially it may be important to conserve tempo-moves.

Theory

Theory concerns itself with endgames in which there are not more than two or three pawns on the board. At the turn of the century few of the more difficult endgames had been thoroughly examined in the manner, for instance, of Kling's definitive work on the ending K+R+B v. K+R, published in the 1840s. In this century important analyses have been made by Troitzky (K+N+N v. K+P), Grigoriev (pawn endings and Rook endings), Chéron (Rook endings and K+Q v. K+R+P), Kopayev (Rook endings and Rook against pawns), and Averbakh (minor piece endings and K+Q+P v. K+Q). There are some theoretical gaps to be filled:

(*i*) Endings with no pawns: see CHECKMATE, in which four endings, listed as having an unclear result, have yet to be thoroughly examined. They may seem to be of little practical value; however, the occurrence in a World Championship match (1961) of the ending K+B+B v. K+N shows that such endings can be of importance, and, in time, they will be analysed.

(*ii*) Endings with one pawn: some positions with K+Q v. K+R+P require study. Attention was drawn to the ending K+Q+P v. K+Q by KERES in 1951; it is still under investigation.

(*iii*) Endings with two pawns: a few gaps remain in the endings K+R+P+P v. R, and K+Q+P+P v. Q; the endgame K+Q+KRP+QRP, for instance, has never been studied at all.

Within these groups there are many small areas which have yet to be fully charted in order to complete all basic knowledge. Discoveries are still being made: in 1972 Makhatadze (in the ending K+N+P v. K+N), and Peckover (in the ending K+Q v. K+R+P) showed some new ideas, for instance.

In the immediate future it is probable that endgame books will be increasingly concerned with systematization of available information. This means greater emphasis on type-positions, which will lead to the discovery of many small gaps in theory: these will have to be filled.

Position 34

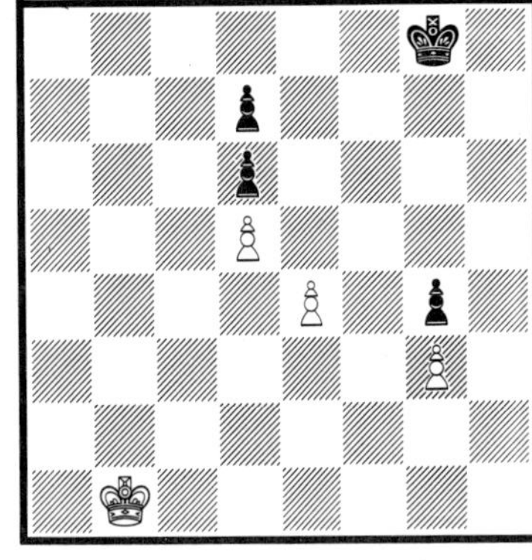

Position 35

When all endgames with two or fewer pawns have been analysed, which will yet take some time, theory will extend its scope to include three-pawn endings, a process which is already taking place and which is far from complete. In time the scope of theory will be extended further still; and the day when it can be said that theory is complete lies in the distant future.

The following endings cannot be won within the terms of the 50-move rule:

(*i*) White King at QB6, White Rook at KN7, White Bishop at QB4, Black King at QR1 and Black Rook at KR8. White to play wins Black's Rook on the 56th move (Crosskill 1856).

(*ii*) White King at KR1, White Rook at KN4, White pawn at QR2, Black King at QB1, Black Bishop at QR8 and Black pawn at QR6. White to play makes his first capture on the 61st move (Chéron 1949).

(*iii*) Many endings with K+N+N v. K+P.

The plea for a special rule has little weight except in the case of (*iii*), for positions (*i*) and (*ii*) are unique, and the chances of their happening in play are infinitesimal. The suggestion that 150 moves should be allowed for the longest-known win (an example of K+N+N v. K+P in which the pawn advances on the 85th move) would unfairly burden the defender.

Trébuchet

The name of a type-*zugzwang* which occurs in the ending K+P v. K+P. See PAWN ENDINGS, position 22.

Triangulation

A manoeuvre by means of which the King can lose the move. In position 34 Black to play loses because he must retreat, and this delays his counter-attack by one, decisive, move: 1. . , K–N3; 2. K–B3, K–R4; 3. K–K2, K–R5; 4. K–Q3, K–N5; 5. K–K3 (*zugzwang*), K–R6; 6. K–Q4, etc.

White to play moves his King around a 'triangle' of squares: 1. K–R3, K–N3; 2. K–N2, K–R4; 3. K–N3, and now it is Black's move.

Zugzwang

A position in which whoever has the move is at a decisive disadvantage. If you are in *zugzwang* (i.e. it is your move) then you will lose half a point, or in the case of the Trébuchet, a full point, simply because it is your turn to play. Sometimes, as in position 1 (see BAD BISHOP), you do not want to have the move but you are able to lose the move. A true *zugzwang*, however, is irreversible: whoever has the move cannot lose it.

The opposition is a kind of *zugzwang* in which the relationship between the Kings assumes a regular pattern as in diagram 14. Position 35 is a *zugzwang* (Locock 1892). Black to play loses: 1. . , K–N2; 2. K–B1 (*zugzwang*), K–N3; 3. K–Q1 (*zugzwang*), K–N4; 4. K–B2 (outflanking), K–R3; 5. K–Q2 (*zugzwang*), K–R4; 6. K–B3 (outflanking), K–N4; 7. K–B4 (losing the move), K–N3; 8. K–Q3 (*zugzwang*), K–B3; 9. K–Q4 (*zugzwang*), and 9. P–K5. Or 1. . , K–R1; 2. K–N2 (*zugzwang*), K–N1; 3. K–N3 (*zugzwang*), K–B2; 4. K–B4 (*zugzwang*), K–N2; 5. K–B3 (*zugzwang*), K–B2;

6. K–Q6 (outflanking), K–B3; 7. K–K2 (losing the move), K–N3; 8. K–Q3 (*zugzwang*). Here the relationship of the Kings to one another takes unusual forms. This is sometimes called the heterodox (as opposed to orthodox) opposition; and such composed positions may be called related square studies. Many have since been composed, following this pioneer example.

There are just sixteen different *zugzwangs*, or *zugzwang* groups, in the endings K+P v. K (4), K+P+P v. K (5), and K+P v. K+P (7). For these see OPPOSITION and PAWN ENDINGS.

There are hundreds of different *zugzwangs* in pawn endings with three or more pawns, and in the ending K+N+N v. P; but in other types of endgame there are comparatively few.

ENDGAME: LITERATURE, History of

A few practical endgames have survived from Arabic manuscripts of the twelfth and thirteenth centuries. There would, however, have been little point for players at that time to have attempted a comprehensive theory, for queening a pawn (the central theme of most endplay today) was not of much significance in the old game.

Evidence from the fifteenth and sixteenth centuries is not extensive, but it would appear that even at that early period the principles of the opposition and of quite a few types of endgame were known. In 1617 Carrera showed that he understood the ideas behind the following endgames: K+P v. K; K+Q v. K+P; K+R v. K+minor piece; K+KRP+KNP v. K+KRP; K+minor piece v. K+P+P; K+minor piece+P v. K+minor piece; K+R+N v. K+R; K+Q v. K+B+B; and K+Q v. K+R+P. He notes that the position Black King at Q1, Black pawn at Q2, and Black Rook at QB3 can be drawn against White K+Q, and that a similar position with BP or NP (but not RP) would be drawn. In this last endgame type, however, many new discoveries were made in the nineteenth and twentieth centuries.

Progress was slow. In 1634 Salvio analysed a key position for Rook endings; in 1766 Cozio gave 127 endgame positions, mostly studies of a simple kind – his work is in no sense a practical handbook. The publication in 1763 of a book by Lolli probably marks the beginning of a period of practical research. He gives 315 pages of his book to examples of endplay which he culled from many sources, and he shows admirable lack of bias in his high praise of Philidor's endgame analyses – for their disagreement about openings theory was notorious.

With the introduction of chess magazines and a spate of chess books, which began in the second quarter of the nineteenth century, many analysts set about the task of finding definitive answers to specific types of endgame, a trend which has continued to the present day.

Three books are worth mention: *Chess Studies* by Kling and Horwitz, 1851; a collection of 210 positions, mostly didactic, with some original research, but the lack of text severely limited the practical value of the book. *Fins de parties d'echecs*, by Durand and Préti, 1871, and *Teoria e pratica del giuoco degli scacchi*, by Salvioli, 1877, both contain extensive sections dealing with practical endplay. The publication of Berger's treatise in 1891 brings us up to modern times. See also THEORY.

Modern Literature

The first comprehensive book in modern times devoted wholly to the practical endgame is *Theorie und Praxis der Endspiele* by J. Berger, published in 1891, revised in 1922, and supplemented in 1933. This was for long the standard work but would not today be regarded as adequate for practical use.

Basic Chess Endings by R. Fine, 1941, is an encyclopedic attempt to collect in one volume all the endgame knowledge then available. The book is mis-named; the analysis of basic endgames is out of date, but his grandmasterly evaluations of many 'non-basic' endgames remain valid. The book is readable, and in spite of its imperfections is still a good book for study.

Lehr- und Handbuch der Endspiele by A. Chéron, a three-volume German translation from the French original (1952), has passed through more than one edition since 1956; a supplement was published in 1970. The volumes contain both extensive analyses of basic endgames and many endgame studies. The book is a major work of its kind, especially for study enthusiasts, but is not designed for the practical player.

Lehrbuch der Endspiele by Y. Averbakh, is a four-volume German translation from the Russian original (1956), revised, shortened, and re-published in two volumes in 1972. There are contributions from I. Maizelis (pawn endings), V. A. Chekhover (Knight endings), W. Chenkin (Queen v. Rook), and N. Kopayev, perhaps the greatest living analyst of Rook endings. This is an accurate and comprehensive book dealing with basic endgames and endgames with more pawns. It may be regarded as the standard work for practical use.

Rook Endings by Smyslov and Levenfish (1971), is an English translation from the Russian (1957). An instructive book which deals, however, with only one kind of endgame.

A Pocket Guide to Chess Endgames, by D. V. Hooper (1970), is intended to show the current state of basic endgame theory. A practical book – the only one to contain no studies – it may be recommended for its systematic presentation of essential information.

See also ENDGAME, HISTORY OF LITERATURE, and ENDGAME, THEORY. *(D.H.)*

ENDGAME STUDY

A composed position where the play shows a forced win or draw in a unique manner has come to be called, over the last century and a half, and for obscure reasons, an endgame study. The position has generally an endgame character, since an artistic principle of economy is applied by the composer, leading to few rather than to many men being present.

At its highest level the study is an art form where strict canons of originality, variety, harmony and beauty may apply. In addition, a study must be *sound*, an obligation which imposes on the composer a discipline akin to that of scientific research. Proof and disproof of soundness has to be via analysis, a task which daunts many would-be enthusiasts. A study is *un*sound in two cases: if there is an unintended solution, or 'cook' (see PROBLEMS); or if the intended solution fails (there is a 'bust'). Great composing skill, equal in degree but differing in nature from that of the over-the-board master, is needed to ensure that White's moves are unique, while at the same time Black must have interesting counterplay and the principle of economy of means has to be observed. The Soviet composer G. M. Kasparian, who is the first holder of the FIDE grandmaster title (for study composition), displays all this skill in the example.

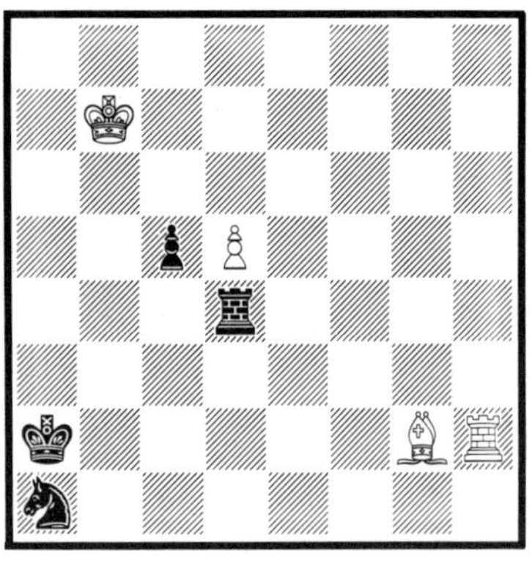

3rd Hon. Mention, Louma Memorial Tourney (Czechoslovakia) 1956
White to move and win 4+4

In a level and open-looking position, one must expect the play to be difficult, as all moves by White in an endgame study must be unique.

1. K–B6 (*a*), R–Q7 (*b*); 2. P–Q6 (*c*), P–B5 (*d*); 3. P–Q7, R×P (*e*); 4. K×R, P–B6; 5. B–Q5+, K–N8 (*f*); 6. K–B6, P–B7; 7. K–N5, P–B8(Q) (*g*); 8. B R2 mate.

(*a*) 1. K–B7?, K–R6; 2. P–Q6, P–B5; 3. P–Q7, P–B6 and White's B–Q5 is not playable, as it is in note (*b*). This is no accident. Such lines must exist, must have been invented by the composer, to refute alternatives and thus ensure that his composition is correct.

(*b*) 1. . , K–R6; 2. P–Q6, N–N6 (*2. . , N–B7: 3. K×P, R–Q7; 4. R–R3+, K–N7; 5. B–Q5 wins*); 3. B–Q5, P–B5; 4. P–Q7, N–R4+; 5. K–B5, R–Q8 (*5. . , N–N6+; 6. K–Q6, N–R4; 7. P–Q8(Q), N–N2+; 8. K–K5 wins*); 6. R–R7 wins.

Or 1. . , N–N6 (*. . , N–B7; 2. B–K4*); 2. P–Q6, N–R4+; 3. K×P, N–N6+; 4. K–B6, R–B5+ (*4. . , N–R4+; 5. K–B7*); 5. K–N5, R–Q5; 6. B–Q5+, K–R6; 7. R–R5 wins.

(*c*) 2. K×P?, N–N6+; 3. K–B4, K–N7; 4. R–R3, N–R4+; 5. K–N5, R×B; 6. K×N, R–N4; 7. R–Q3, K–B7; 8. R–Q4, K–B6. This is the composer's analysis.

(*d*) 2. . , N–N6; 3. P–Q7, N–R4+; 4. K–B7 with a winning position.

(*e*) 3. . , P–B6; 4. B–Q5+ wins.

(*f*) 5. . , K–R6; 6. R–R2+, K–N5; 7. R×N wins.

(*g*) 7. . , K–N7; 8. K–N4 wins easily. Or if 7. . , K–B8; 8. K–B4, K–Q8; 9. K–Q3, P–B8(N)+; 10. K–B3, N–K7+; 11. K–N2, N–B7; 12. B–N3 and wins.

Because they tend towards difficulty, and in addition may demand erudite theoretical endgame knowledge of the solver before their solutions can be fully comprehended, studies are less popular than problems – that is, positions where mate is to be forced in so many moves. But the kinship of the endgame study and the practical game is close enough for every chess-player to derive pleasure from this deep, engrossing and distinctive branch of chess, to which, indeed, many enthusiasts devote themselves to the exclusion of what they consider a 'mere game'.

Test Tube Chess ('A Comprehensive Introduction to the Chess Endgame Study') by A. J. Roycroft, London 1972.

Bent, C. M. *(b. 1919)*
British composer of around five hundred endgame studies.

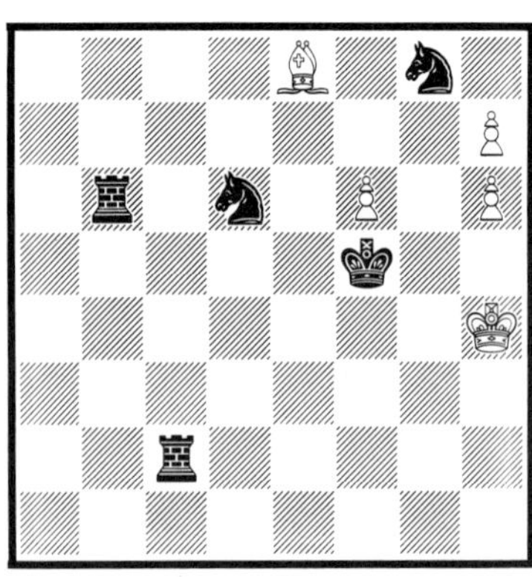

Schakend Nederland, December 1966
White to move and win 5+5

A vigorous study from start to finish, White winning from a poor position against impossible odds.

1. B–N6+ (*a*), K–B5; 2. B×R, N–B4+; 3. B×N (*b*), R×P; 4. P×N(N) (*c*), K×B; 5. P–R7, R–R3+ (*d*); 6. N×R+, K–N3; 7. P–R8(R) wins (*e*).

(*a*) Black was threatening the murderous 1. . , R–N5+. If now 1. . , K×B; 2. P×N(Q)+ wins.

(*b*) 3. K–R3?, R×P; 4. P×N(Q), R×P+; 5. K–N2, R–N3+; 6. Q×R, N–R5+ and 7. . , N×Q.

(*c*) 4. P–R8(Q)?, R×P+ draws at once.

(*d*) A glorious resource, far from easy to see.

(*e*) A Queen would stalemate, while Bishop or Knight would draw only.

Bron, V. A. *(b. 1909)*
Soviet composer of endgame studies and problems.

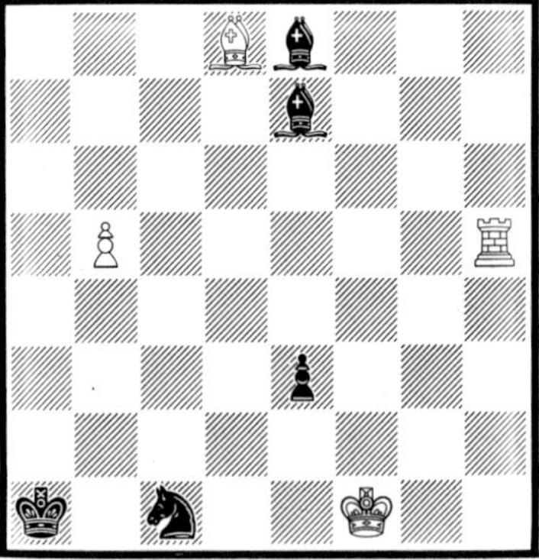

1st Prize, Tourney of the Committee of Physical Culture and Sport of the Armenian Republic, 1955–6
White to move and draw 4+5

1. R–K5, B × P+; 2. R × B, P–K7+ (*a*); 3. K–K1, B × B; 4. K–Q2, B–B2; 5. K–B2, B–B5 (*b*); 6. R–N1+ (*c*), K–R7; 7. R–N4, K–R6; 8. R–K4, B–N4; 9. K–B3, B–R3; 10. K–B2, draws (*d*).

(*a*) 2.., B × B; 3. R–K5, B–N3; 4. R–K6, B–B4; 5. R–K5, B–Q5; 6. R–K4.

(*b*) 5.., P–K8(Q); 6. R–N1+, K–R7; 7. R–R1+, K × R stalemate. The chosen move defends against White's threat of 6. R–N1+, K–R7; 7. R × N.

(*c*) 6. R–N4?, B–K6; 7. R–N8, P–K8(R) wins.

(*d*) Bron demonstrates in the following analysis that White loses if the Rook is played: 10. R–K6?, K–R5; 11. R–K5, B–B5; 12. R–K4+, K–N4; 13. R–K6, K–B4; 14. R–K7, K–Q4; 15. R–K8, B–N4; 16. K–B2, K–Q5 with the winning threat of 17.., B–K6.

V. A. Bron, *Selected Studies and Problems* [in Russian], Moscow 1969.

Grigoriev, N. D. *(1895–1938)*

Soviet composer and endgame analyst, especially of pawn endings and Rook endings.

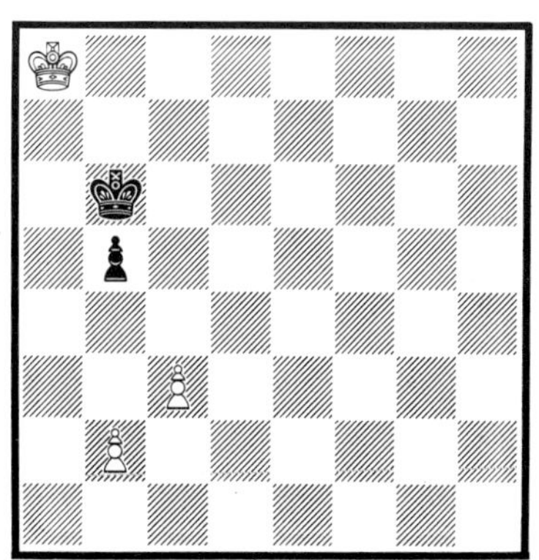

'64', 1930
White to move and win 3+2

1. P–N3 (*a*), K–R4 (*b*); 2. K–N8 (*c*), P–N5 (*d*); 3. P–B4, K–N3; 4. K–B8, K–B3; 5. K–Q8, K–Q3; 6. K–K8, K–K3; 7. K–B8, K–B3; 8. K–N8, K–N3; 9. K–R8!, K–B3; 10. K–R7, K–B2; 11. K–R6, K–B3; 12. K–R5, K–B4; 13. K–R4, K–B5; 14. K–R3!, K–B4; 15. K–N3, K–N4; 16. K–B3, K–B4; 17. K–K3, K–K4; 18. K–Q3 and wins.

(*a*) 1. K–N8?, P–N5 and White would then even lose after 2. P–B4?, P–N6. If 1. P–N4?, K–R3.

(*b*) 1.., K–R3; 2. P–N4, K–N3; 3. K–N8, or 1.., P–N5; 2. P–B4, like the main line.

(*c*) 2. P–N4+?, K–R3 with the opposition. 2. K–N7?, P–N5; 3. P–B4 is stalemate.

(*d*) Again, if 2.., K–N3; 3. P–N4. The remainder of the solution is easily understood, seeing that the Black King must not go outside the square of the passed White pawn. This does not render the long march of the White King any less intriguing.

N. D. Grigorjev (G. Porreca, ed.), *Finali di Scacchi* [in Italian], Milan 1965.

Kasparian, G. M. *(b. 1910)*

Soviet composer of Endgame Studies. First holder (1973) of the FIDE title of Grandmaster of Chess Composition (studies).

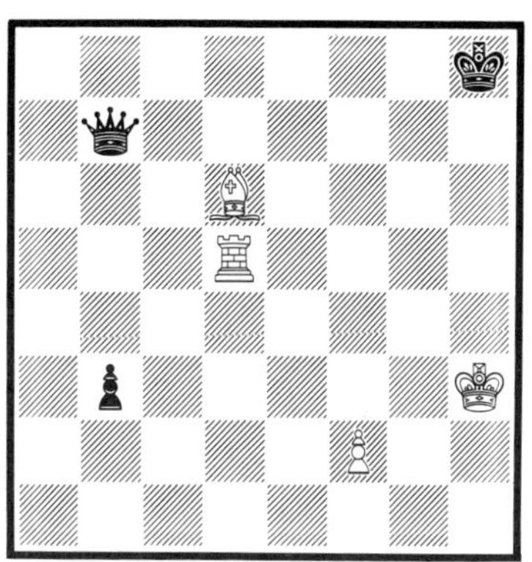

USSR Championship Bulletin 1949
White to move and draw 4+3

Probably only this composer could have so controlled the long-range pieces (Queen, Rook and Bishop) on an open board to create a sound (single solution) study incorporating counterplay, theoretical points and a fantastic terminal position.

1. B–K5+ (*a*), K–N1 (*b*); 2. R–Q8+ (*c*), K–B2; 3. R–Q3, K–K3 (*d*); 4. R–K3, Q–R8+ (*e*); 5. B–R2+ (*f*), K–B4; 6. R × P, Q–B8+; 7. K–N3, Q–B5 (*g*); 8. R–B3+, K–N4; 9. B–N1 (*h*), Q–N5+; 10. K–R2, Q × R stalemate.

(*a*) 1. R–Q3?, Q–R2+. If 1. R–Q2?, Q–B6+; 2. K–R2, Q–R4+; wins, or 2. K–R4, Q–K5+; 3. P–B4, Q–K8+; or if 2. B–N3, K–R2 and the Knight's pawn will cost White the Rook.

(*b*) 1.., K–R2 would occupy the square on which the Black Queen needs to check in order to meet 2. R–Q3.

(*c*) As already indicated, 2. R–Q3?, and 2. R–Q2?, lose to Queen checks. This intermediate check forces Black to block his second rank to eliminate the Black Queen's check from KR2 and allow the White Rook to play to Q3.

(*d*) 3.., Q–R8+; 4. K–N3, K–K3; 5. B–N2, K–B4; 6. R–B3+, K–N3; 7. R × P, Q–N8+; 8. K–R3, Q × P; 9. R–N3+ draws, or here 5.., Q–N8+; 6. K–B3, Q–KB8; 7. K–K3, with 8. R–Q2 and a draw. The next move clears the line to KR2 with tempo to force White's reply.

(*e*) 4.., K–B4; 5. K–R2, Q–R2+; 6. K–N1, Q–N3+; 7. K–B1, Q–R3+; 8. K–N1 drawn, for the advance of Black's pawn is met by its capture, leaving a theoretical draw, the White fortress being impregnable.

(*f*) 5. K–N3?, K–B4; 6. P–B4 (*6. B–N2, Q–N8+; 7. K–R3, Q × P; 8. R × P, Q–B7* wins, as *9. R–N5+, K–K3; 19. R–N4, Q–Q6+; 11. K–R4, Q–K6* soon picks up a piece), Q–N8+; 7. K–B3, P–N7; 8. B × P, Q–B8+; 9. K–N3, Q × P+. Or 5. K–N4?, Q–N7+; 6. B–N3+, K–B3; 7. R–K2, Q–Q4 with the winning threat to capture the Rook and then promote. If in this last line 7. R × P, Q–K5+; 8. K–R3, Q–K3+.

(*g*) Suddenly threatening mate as well as the Rook.

(*h*) 9. K–N2?, Q–K5; 10. B–N1 fails to 10.., K–N5; 11. K–R2, K × R.

G. M. Kasparian, *Studies* [in Russian], Moscow 1972.

Kling, J. *(1811–1876)*
Composer and analyst, co-author with his German compatriot B. Horwitz of *Chess Studies* (London 1851), a landmark in endgame literature.

Korolkov, V. A. *(b. 1907)*
Soviet holder (1975) of the FIDE title of Grandmaster of Composition for endgame studies. The outstanding characteristic of his work is its imaginative content.

6th Place, USSR Team Composing championship, 1957
White to move and win 7+9

1. P–B6+ (*a*), K–R1 (*b*); 2. B×R, P×R; 3. K–N3 (*c*), P–R5+; 4. K–R2, P–N7 (*d*); 5. B×P, B–N6; 6. P–B4 (*e*), B×P; 7. P–K5 (*f*), B×P; 8. P–Q6 (*g*), B×P; 9. P–B7 mate!

(*a*) 1. B×R?, P×R; 2. P–B6+, K–B2.

(*b*) 1.., K–B2; 2. R×P+ wins. Or 1.., K–N1; 2. R–B5, P×R; 3. P–Q6 wins.

(*c*) As will be seen, it is vital to avoid the Black squares, as the Black Bishop would later on gain a vital tempo with a check. If 3. P–B7?, K–N2; 4. P–Q6, P–R7; 5. B–R6+, K–N3; 6. P–B8(Q), P–R8(Q)+ draws.

(*d*) 4.., P–N5; 5. P–B7, K–N2; 6. P–Q6, P–N7; 7. B–R6+, K–N3; 8. P–B8(Q) wins. Or 4.., K–N1; 5. P–Q6, P–N7; 6. B–R6, P–N8(Q); 7. P–B7+. Or 4.., P–R4; 5. B–R6 wins.

(*e*) The quality of the study would suffer if transpositions were possible, here or later. 6. P–K5?, B×P; 7. P–B4, B–Q3; 8. P×P (*8. P–B7, K–N2*), K–N1; 9. B–B3, K–B2; 10. B–R5, B–B5; 11. B×P, B×P draws. Or 6. P–Q6?, B×P; 7. P–K5, B×P; 8. P–B4, B–B2. Or 6. P–B7?, B×P; 7. P–Q6, B×P; 8. P–K5, B–B2; 9. P–B4+, K–N1.

(*f*) 7. P–Q6?, B×P; 8. P–K5, B–B2. Or P–B7?, K–N2.

(*g*) 8. P–B7?, B×P; 9. P–Q6+, K–N1; 10. P×B+, K×P draws; but not here, for Black, 8.., K–N2?; 9. P–Q6+, K–B1; 10. B–R3+.

V. A. Korolkov, *Selected Studies* [in Russian], Moscow 1958.

Kubbel, L. I. [**K. A. L.**] *(1891–1942)*
Soviet composer of endgame studies.

1. N–B6, K×N; 2. B–B6, K–Q4 (*a*); 3. P–Q3, P–R7; 4. P–B4+, K–B4 (*b*); 5. K–N7, P–R8(Q); 6. B–K7 mate.

(*a*) 2.., K–B4; 3. B–K7+ wins.

(*b*) 4.., P×P e.p.; 5. B×P stops the Rook's pawn and retains White's pawn. Black is even worse off if he ever allows his Queen's pawn to be captured.

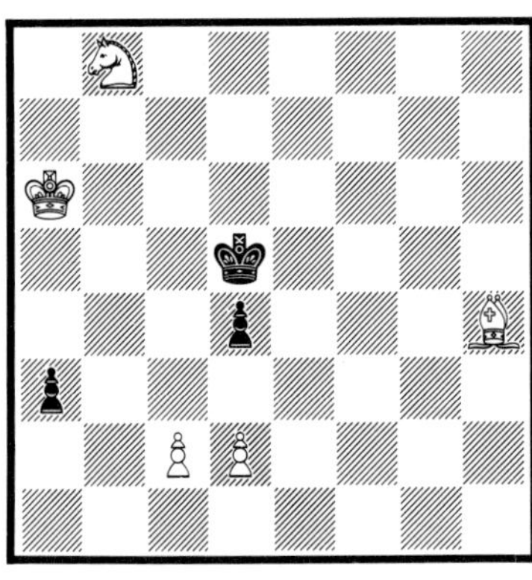

Shakhmatny Listok, 1922
White to move and win 5+3

Liburkin, M. S. *(1910–53)*
Soviet composer of endgame studies of supreme elegance.

4th Prize, *Shakhmaty v SSSR*, 1938 (first half-year)
White to move and win 3+4

1. N–Q4+, K–B6; 2. N–N5+, K–B5 (*a*); 3. N–Q6+, K–B4; 4. N–N7+ (*b*), K–B3; 5. N–Q8+, K–B2; 6. N–K6+, K–Q2 (*c*); 7. N–B8+, K–K2; 8. N–N6+, K–B2; 9. N–R8+, K–N2; 10. R×B, K×N; 11. R–KR1, P–N6; 12. K–K3, K–N2; 13. K–B4, P–N7; 14. R–KN1, N–B8; 15. R×P+, K any; 16. R–KB2 wins.

(*a*) 2.., K–N5; 3. R–N1+ followed by 4. K×B. It will be seen that this supporting motif recurs many times in the solution.

(*b*) But not 4. N–K4+?, K–Q4; 5. N–B6+, K–K4; 6. N–Q7+, K–K3; 7. N–B5+, K–Q4; or 7. N–B8+, K–B2 and White is suddenly no longer able to protect his Knight with gain of time.

(*c*) Here the motif begins to reappear in a horizontal, as distinct from vertical, form, for if 6.., K–Q3; 7. R–R6+ wins. Over forty studies by Liburkin figure in the following anthology of 650 studies by Soviet composers. A. P. Kazantsev et al., *The Soviet Chess Study* [in Russian], Moscow 1955.

Lommer, H. M. *(b. 1904)*
British composer of, and authority on, endgame studies.

Even when White has found a way to meet the threatened promotion, he remains a piece behind, with a Black pawn remaining.

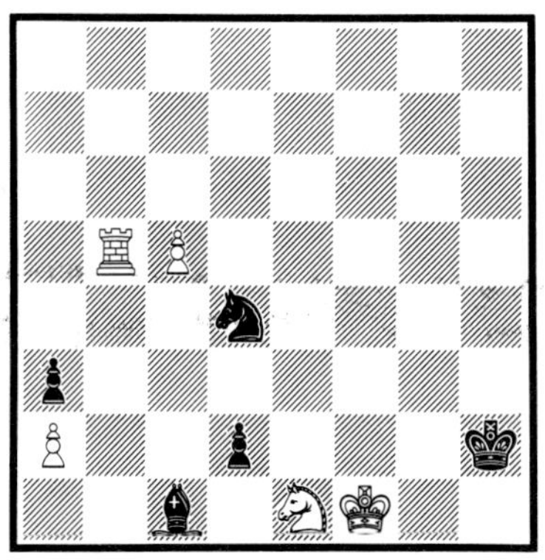

Schweizerische Schachzeitung, 1934
White to move and draw 5+5

1. R–N4, N–B7 (*a*); 2. N–B3+, K–N6; 3. N×P, N×R; 4. N–B4, K–B6; 5. K–K1, K–K5; 6. K–Q1, B–N7 (*b*); 7. P–B6, N×BP; 8. N×B draws (*c*).

(*a*) 1. . , P–Q8(Q); 2. R×N and the Queen is captured 'by domination' after 2. . , Q–R4; 3. R–R4+, or 2. . , B–Q7; 3. R×B+. Or 1. . , P×N(Q)+; 2. K×Q, N–B7+; 3. K–Q1, N×R; 4. K×B also draws.

(*b*) 6. . , K–Q5; 7. K×B may come as a surprise draw too.

(*c*) That 8. K–B2 draws also is a slight flaw in the study, a so-called 'dual' (see PROBLEMS, DUAL), but as the interest lies in the previous play rather than in the final position, the flaw is not serious.

Nadareishvili, G. *(b. 1921)*
Soviet holder of the FIDE title of Master of Composition for endgame studies.

2nd Hon. Mention, *Schakend Nederland*, 1962
White to move and win 4+4

1. P–N7 (*a*), P–N8(Q); 2. R×P+ (*b*), Q×R (*c*); 3. P×N(R)+ (*d*), K–N7; 4. R–N8, Q×R+; 5. K×Q wins.

(*a*) 1. R×P+?, K×R; 2. P–N7, N–N3+; 3. K–B7, P–N8(Q) draws.

(*b*) But not 2. P×N(Q)+?, K×R; or 2. P–N8(Q)?, Q–B4+ in both cases with a draw.

(*c*) 2. . , K×R; 3. P–N8(Q)+, K–B7; 4. Q×Q+, K×Q; 5. K–N7 wins.

(*d*) There is stalemate after 3. P×N(Q)+?, K–N7; 4. Q–N7, K–R8; 5. Q×Q.

G. Nadareishvili, *Selected Studies* [in Russian], Tbilisi 1970.

Perkonoja, P. *(b. 1941)*
Finnish holder of the FIDE title of Master of Composition for endgame studies.

Satakunnen Työ, November 1965
White to move and win 4+3

White's pieces seem very poorly placed for winning purposes. Indeed, most players would be pleased to draw.

1. B–N7 (*a*), R–R7+; 2. K–N6, R–R6; 3. B–B1, R–KN6 (*b*); 4. B–B8, R×P; 5. B×P+, K–R1 (*c*); 6. B–N5 (*d*), R–QB5; 7. B–R6, R–B2; 8. K×R wins.

(*a*) 1. K–N6?, R–KR7; 2. B–B1, R–R8. Or 1. B–R8?, R–KR7. Or 1. B–B6?, R–KR7; 2. B–B1, R–KB7. Or 1. B–Q4?, R–R7+; 2. K–N6, R–R6; 3. B–B1, R–KN6; 4. B–K2, R–N7; 5. B–KB3, R–N6 draws.

(*b*) To obtain a drawing repetitive attack on the White Bishop, as in (*a*), should it defend the pawn.

(*c*) 5. . , K–B1; 6. B–KR3 wins.

(*d*) But not 6. B–R6? at once, because Black will draw by 6. . , R–N2. The Rook is decoyed.

B. Breider, A. Dunder and O. Kaila, *123 Suomalaista Lopputehtävää* [in Finnish], Helsinki 1972.

Platov, M. *(1883–1938)* **and Platov, V.** *(1881–1952)*
Two Latvian composers who were brothers. They composed many endgame studies together.

Düna-Zeitung, January 1904
White to move and win 8+7

1. B–R7+, K×N; 2. K–N7, Q–Q6 (*a*); 3. B×Q, P–K5; 4. B–N5, P×B; 5. K–B6 and wins.

(*a*) 2. . , Q×B+; 3. K×Q, P–K5; 4. K–N8, K–N3; 5. K–B8 wins, capturing the Queen's side pawns.

Prokeš, L. *(1884–1966)*
Czech composer of many hundreds of endgame studies, posthumously awarded the FIDE title of Master of Composition.

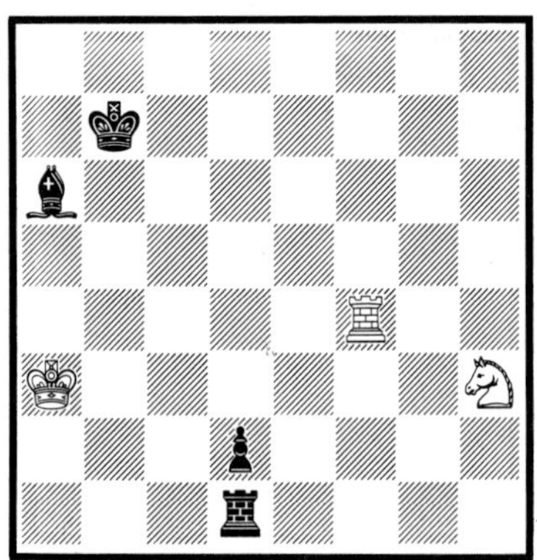

L'Echiquier de Paris, October 1948
White to move and draw 3+4

There is no major surprise in the solution, just a succession of small tactical points.

1. N–B2 (*a*), R–KB8; 2. R–Q4, R×N; 3. K–N4 (*b*), R–N5; 4. K–R5 (*c*), R–B4+; 5. K–N4 (*d*), R–B7; 6. K–B3 draws.

(*a*) 1. R–N4+? or 1. R–B7+? would denude White of his stalemate defence after 1. . , K–B3.

(*b*) 3. K–N3?, B–Q6; 4. R×B, R–B6 wins. Or 3. K–R4?, B–N4+; 4. K×B, R–B4+; 5. K–B4, R–B5.

(*c*) The crucial stalemate defence allows White to repeat moves or approach the pawn.

(*d*) And again, not 5. K–R4?, B–N4+; 6. K–N3, B–Q6; 7. R×B, R–B6 wins.

L. Prokeš, *Kniha Šachovych Studii*, Prague 1951.

Rinck, H. *(1870–1952)*
French composer, very prolific, of endgame studies.

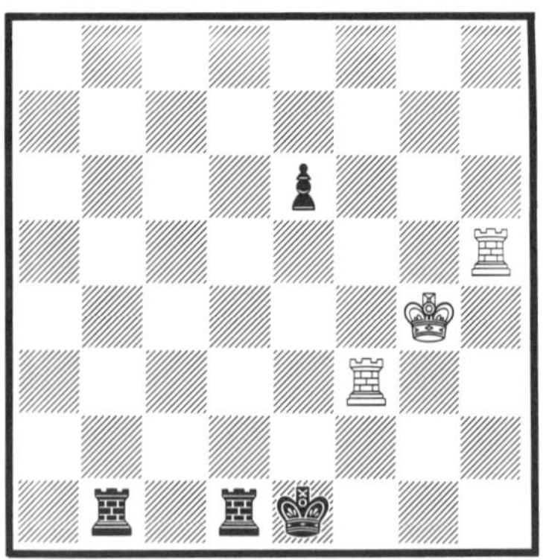

1st Prize, *Chess Amateur*, June 1922
White to move and win 3+4

1. R–R1+ (*a*), K–Q7; 2. R–R2+, K–K8; 3. K–N3, R–Q1; 4. R–R1+, K–K7; 5. R×R, R–N1+; 6. K–B4, with two 'echo' variations: 6. . , R–B1+; 7. K–K4, R×R; 8. R–N2+ wins, or 6. . , P–K4+; 7. K–K4, R–N5+; 8. K–B5, K×R; 9. R–N3+ wins.

(*a*) 1. K–N3?, R–N7; 2. R–R1+, K–Q7; 3. R–B2+, K–K6; 4. R×R(Q1), R×R drawn.

H. Rinck, *1414 Fins de Partie*, Barcelona 1952.

Roycroft, A. J. *(b. 1929)*
British composer, editor of the endgame studies magazine '*E G*'.

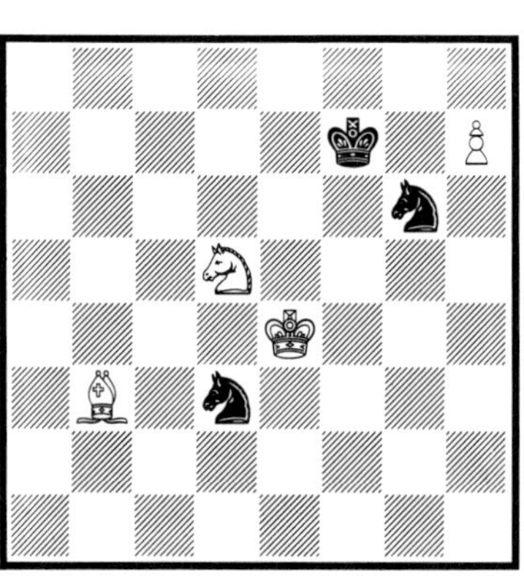

2nd Prize, *New Statesman*, 1954
White to move and win 4+3

1. N–B4+, K–N2; 2. N×N(N6), N–B4+; 3. K–Q5, K×P; 4. B–B2 (*a*), N–N2 (*b*); 5. N–K5 *or* K7+, K–N2; 6. N–B6, K–B2; 7. B–R4 (*c*), K–B1; 8. B–N5, K–K1; 9. N–R5+, and 10. N×N wins.

(*a*) The diagram showed a White Bishop and Knight battery set up against the Black King on a certain diagonal. This move creates a second battery with the same pieces on a parallel diagonal. The idea is repeated yet again in the course of the solution. All the batteries fire. 4. N–B8+?, K–N2 is a draw.

(*b*) 4. . , N–R3; 5. K–Q6 wins, one line being 5. . , N–N5; 6. B–N1, K–N2; 7. N–K5, K–B1; 8. N–Q7+, K–K1; 9. N–B5, K–Q1; 10. B–B5, K–K1; 11. N–K6, K–B2; 12. B–N1, K–B3; 13. N–B7, K any; 14. K–B5 and the Black Knight is dominated.

(*c*) 7. B–B5?, K–K1; 8. B–B8, N–Q1 draws.

Rusinek, J. *(b. 1950)*
Brilliant young contemporary Polish composer of endgame studies.

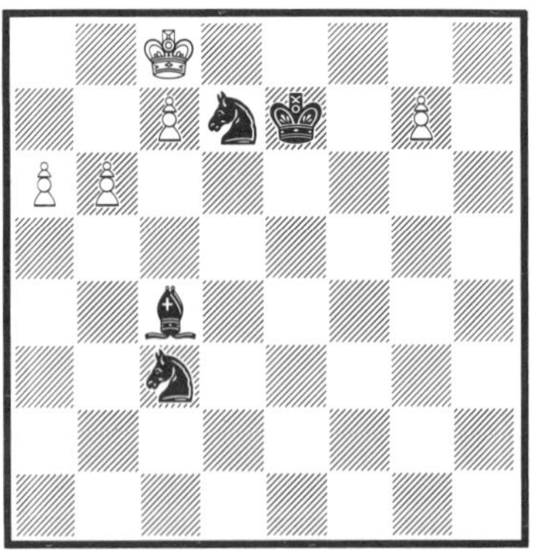

1st Prize, *New Statesman*, 1971
Award: 6 October 1972
White to move and draw 5+4

The position is not too improbable, but the play is, making the study all the more attractive.

1. P–R7 (*a*), B–R3+ (*b*); 2. P–N7, N–K5; 3. P–N8(N)+, K–K1; 4. N–B6+, N(K5)×N; 5. P–R8(B) (*c*), N–K4; 6. K–N8, N–B3+; 7. K–B8, B–B8; 8. P–N8(R) (*d*), B–R3+; 9. R–N7, N–K5 stalemate.

(*a*) 1. P–N8(Q)?, B×Q; 2. P–R7, N–K5; 3. K–N7, B–Q4+; 4. K–R6, N–Q3 wins.

(*b*) 1. . , N×P+; 2. K–N7 draws. Or 1. . , N–K5; 2. K–N7, B–Q4+; 3. K–R6 draws, or in this, 2. . , N–Q3+; 3. K–B6, B–N4+; 4. K–Q5.

(*c*) There has already been a Knight promotion (forced, to give check). Now a second pawn promotes, this time to a Bishop. 5. P–R8(Q)?, N–Q4 leads to mate, but after the promotion to Bishop this results in stalemate.

(*d*) Three of the four White pawns in the diagram have now underpromoted, to different pieces. This composing achievement is enhanced by the study being a draw rather than a win.

Here 8. P–N8(Q)?, B–R3+; 9. Q–N7, N–K5 and 10. . , N–Q3 mate. 8. P–N8(N)? also loses.

Tattersall, C. E. C. *(1877–1957)*
English player, chiefly remembered as the compiler of the first major anthology of endgame studies: *A Thousand End-Games*, published by the British Chess Magazine, Leeds 1910–11 (two volumes).

Troitzky, A. A. *(1866–1942)*
Russian and Soviet composer of endgame studies, probably with the best claim to have been the founder of the modern genre.

3rd Prize, *Shakhmaty v SSSR*, 1935
White to move and draw 3+5

One of scores of discoveries by the Russian composer to have become classics.

1. P–K6 (*a*), R–Q6+ (*b*); 2. K–K5 (*c*), P–K6; 3. R×P, P–K7 (*d*); 4. R×P+, K–B7; 5. R–K4, R–K6; 6. R×R, K×R; 7. P–K7 (*e*), P–K8(Q); 8. K–K6, K–Q5+; 9. K–Q7, or 8. . , K–B5+; 9. K–B7 draws (*f*).

(*a*) 1. R–KN7?, P–K6; 2. R×P+, K–B7 wins.

(*b*) 1. . , P–K6; 2. P–K7, R–Q6+; 3. K–B5.

(*c*) 2. K–B5?, R–Q1; 3. P–K7, R–K1; 4. K×P, P–K6; 5. K–Q3, K–B7; 6. R–B2+, K–B6; 7. R–B7, P–K7; 8. K–Q2, K–B7 wins.

(*d*) 3. . , P–N6; 4. P–K7, P–K7; 5. R–K4.

(*e*) 7. K–B6?, P–K8(Q); 8. P–K7, K–Q5 wins in a standard manner, checks being available.

(*f*) Two variations as similar as these are known as 'echoes'.

V. A. Korolkov and V. A. Chekhover, *Selected Studies of Troitzky* [in Russian], Moscow 1959; A. A. Troitzky, *Chess Studies*, Leeds 1937.

Zakhodyakin, G. N. *(b. 1912)*
Soviet composer of endgame studies.

4th Prize, *Leninsky Put'*, 1967
White to move and draw 3+4

To draw here it is not enough for White to keep his two Bishops – he must succeed in recovering some material.

1. B–Q2 (*a*), R–N3+; 2. K–B2, P–K6+; 3. B×P, N–N5+; 4. K–K2, N×B (*b*); 5. B–K4, R–N6; 6. K–B2, R–R6; 7. B–B3, N–B4; 8. B–N4 and draws.

(*a*) Threatening simply to take the King's pawn and to draw on material. The play develops round Black's strong attempts to win one of the Bishops in exchange for the pawn.

(*b*) With both a White and a Black piece attacked, the normal saving resource, a check, fails. 5. B–R3+?, K any; 6. K×N, R–N6+. And yet the composer's sorcery has unearthed a draw for White, who is a Rook behind. *(A.J.R.)*

'ENDGAME STUDY MAGAZINE'
See under 'EG'.

ENEVOLDSEN, Jens *(b. 23 October 1907)*
Danish international master (1950) and International Judge (1960). Danish champion 1940, 1943, 1947, 1948, 1960. Tournament results include 4th Helsinki Zonal 1947. Noted chess author and theorist. *(R.D.K.)*

ENGELS, Ludwig *(11 December 1905–10 January 1967)*
German international master and one of the leading German players in the 1930s, Engels had a distinctive personal style of play that was incisive and combinational to an outstanding degree.

His first success was an =1st with Koch at a German tournament at Swinemünde 1933. In 1935 he was =2nd with Eliskases at Nauheim and a 2nd to Alekhine at a strong international tournament at Dresden 1936 together with a fine performance on 3rd board at the Munich Team Tournament of that year when he scored 10½/17 really brought him to the notice of the chess world at large.

Another =2nd with Eliskases, at Elster 1938, was followed by a good result at a strong international tournament at Stuttgart (Europa tourney) where he came =3rd with Eliskases, Kieninger and Vidmar.

His European chess career ended in 1939 since he went to Buenos Aires that year and played on 3rd board for the German team in the Olympiad with striking success, obtaining the score of 87.5%. Thereafter he went to live in Brazil and had one good tournament result, a 4th/14 at Sao Paulo 1948. He took little part in further tournaments in South America and confined his chess activities to acting as coach and trainer at the Sao Paulo Chess Club. *(H.G.)*

ENGLAND

See under BRITAIN and BRITISH.

ENGLISCH, Berthold *(9 July 1851–19 October 1897)*

One of the strongest Austrian masters of the late nineteenth century. He won first prize at Leipzig 1879 (the first of the *Deutscher Schachbund* tournaments), and the Vienna quadrangular tournament of 1896 (ahead of Schlechter, Marco and Weiss); was joint 1st with Blackburne and Schwarz at Wiesbaden 1880; joint 5th with Mason and Mackenzie at London 1883, and joint 2nd, with Blackburne, Mason, Tarrasch and Weiss at Hamburg 1885. He lost matches to Lasker and Hruby, but held Pillsbury to a draw (+0—0=5). *(W.H.)*

ENGLISH OPENING

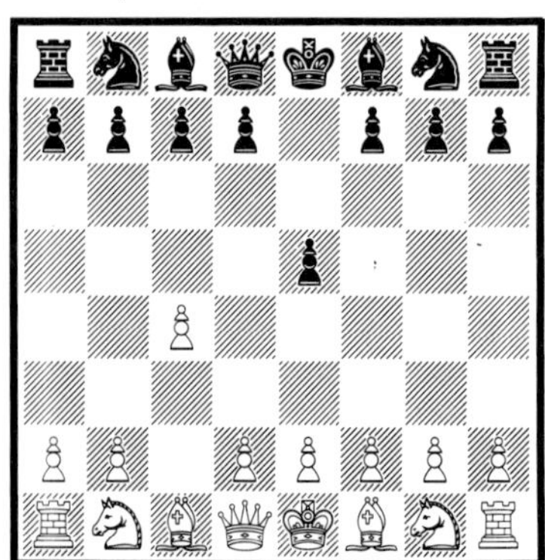

The opening 1. P–QB4, mentioned by Lucena and by Ruy Lopez – the latter adding the comment that the move is so bad that no player of any skill would use it. The modern history of the opening (and its name) derives from its adoption by the English master Staunton in his 1843 match with Saint-Amant. Leading twentieth-century practitioners include former World Champions Smyslov and Botvinnik, and the opening is considered one of White's strongest ways of opening. There are numerous transpositional possibilities into the Réti, Queen's Gambit and various Indian systems. If Black replies with 1.., P–K4 White is effectively playing a Sicilian Defence with colours reversed and an extra move. *(R.D.K.)*

EN PASSANT, capture

The capture by a pawn of an enemy pawn when the latter has advanced two squares initially. This practice was probably the last of the rules introduced in modern chess and appears to have become general by the end of the fifteenth century. It is mentioned by Ruy Lopez in 1561.

In this position if White plays 1. P–K4, Black can, if he likes, reply 1.., P×P *e.p.* See LAWS OF CHESS, Article 6.6(b). *(H.G.)*

EN PRISE

When a player unintentionally places a piece where it may be captured, then he is said to put the piece *en prise*. *(H.G.)*

ERCOLE DEL RIO *(fl. eighteenth century)*

A leading member of the Modena School of theorists in Italy, Ercole del Rio was a lawyer by profession and was the first of his school to publish a work giving the principles and analytical practice of the school.

This was in 1750 and the book bore the title *Sopra il giuoco degli Scacchi, Osservazioni pratiche d'anonimo Autore Modenese* (On the game of chess, practical observations by an anonymous Modenese author).

It was surprisingly advanced for its time and was the first work to give the Scotch Game: 1. P–K4, P–K4; 2. N–KB3, N–QB3; 3. P–Q4, and also the 3. . , P–QR3 defence to the Ruy Lopez. Ercole del Rio's work formed the basis of the more elaborate *Giuoco Di Scacchi* that Lolli was to publish thirteen years later. *(H.G.)*

ESPIG, Lutz *(b. 5 January 1949)*

An international master of East Germany, Espig won his country's championship in 1969 and 1971. His best results in international tournaments have been at Lublin 1970 (1st), Polanica Zdroj (3rd), Lublin 1971 (3rd), Polanica Zdroj 1973 (4th), Varna 1973 (=2nd), Sochi 1974 (=2nd with Suetin) and Varna 1976 (1st). *(W.H.)*

ESTEVEZ, Guillermo *(b. 1947)*

A Cuban international master; he received the title in 1972. He won the 1975 Cuban championship. Two national championships were held in 1976 and his placings were respectively 13th and =2nd. His major international appearance was at the 1973 Leningrad Interzonal, where he came 17th/18. *(K.J.O'C.)*

ESTONIA

Chess in Estonia only began to become popular at the start of the twentieth century, though there had been chess clubs in what are now the towns of Tartu and Tallinn long before this date. The influence of Chigorin had spread from Russia and the start of organized chess competition in Estonia came in 1903 with the founding of a club in Tallinn named after that great master. This club organized championships in 1905 (won by Feinstein), 1906 (Abels), 1909 (Khmelevsky) and 1910 (Feinstein).

After the First World War, chess activity was slow to start up again until about 1930 when Mikenas began to make his name as the strongest Estonian master. Shortly after, Keres emerged as the first and only truly great player the republic had produced.

A number of international tournaments were held in the period between the wars: at Tallinn 1930 (won by Mikenas), Tallinn 1935 (P. Schmidt ahead of Keres), Parnu 1937 (P. Schmidt). During this period Estonia entered teams for the Olympiads, finishing 11th in 1935, 7th in 1937 and 3rd in 1939.

By the end of the war, Estonia had become part of the Soviet Union and ceased to compete separately in international events, though they continued to have their own championship, to produce chess books and magazines in their own language and to enter teams representing the republic in All-Union tournaments. Among notable winners of the Estonian championship after 1945, it is worth mentioning such names as Keres, Nei, Uusi and Arulaid, all of whom held the title on several occasions. International events have been infrequent in Estonia since the war, though 1971 saw something of a resurrection in interest with both Tallinn (won by Keres and Tal) and Parnu (won by Stein) holding strong tournaments. *(W.R.H.)*

ESTRIN, Yakov Borisovich *(b. 1923)*

Soviet master and theoretician, Estrin has had his greatest successes in the field of correspondence chess, finishing third in the 6th and winning the 7th World Correspondence championships. Also winner of the Albena 1973 and Leipzig 1976 international tournaments. Estrin is the co-author (with Kutyanin) of a classic work on the Grünfeld Defence (1959). *(W.R.H.)*

EUROPEAN ECONOMIC COMMUNITY TEAM CHAMPIONSHIP

The first team championship of the EEC was held at Ostend, Belgium, in September 1975. The event commemorated the fiftieth anniversary of the founding of the Ostend Chess Club and the participants were the nine member nations of the EEC: The Netherlands, Denmark, Great Britain, Italy, West Germany, Belgium, France, Ireland and Luxembourg, who finished in that order.

Each team had five players (4 and 1 reserve) and the Netherlands (Sosonko, Ree, Kuijpers, Ligterink and Boersma) revealed their superiority by coming first with 24 points, followed at a respectful distance by Denmark (Fedder, Ost-Hansen, Rath, Jacobsen and Brondum) and Great Britain (Botterill, Pritchett, Stean, Williams and Nunn) with 21½ points each.

It is hoped to hold this event once every two or three years and the venue in 1977 is expected to be Aberystwyth in Wales. *(H.G.)*

EUROPEAN TEAM CHAMPIONSHIP

National team-of-eight championship instituted in 1957 and now played every four years for the Europa Cup trophy.

All European countries are eligible to compete. Entries are grouped geographically into preliminary qualifying sections, with the section winners progressing to an all-play-all final. The winning team from the preceding championship has automatic entry into the final group. The competition has since its inception been dominated by the USSR. The conception of this event was Dr Dorazil's (President of Zone 2 [=Central Europe] of FIDE) and chief arbiter of the first finals at Vienna was Harry Golombek (President of Zone 1 [=Western Europe] of FIDE). Results:

Vienna 1957
1. USSR 41
2. Yugoslavia 34
3. Czechoslovakia 24½
4. West Germany 20½

Oberhausen 1961
1. USSR 74½
2. Yugoslavia 58½
3. Hungary 53
4. Czechoslovakia 41
5. West Germany 37½
6. Spain 35½

Hamburg 1965
1. USSR 66
=2. Yugoslavia 57
  Hungary 57
4. West Germany 45
5. Romania 41½
6. The Netherlands 35½

Kapfenberg 1970
1. USSR 52½
2. Hungary 41
3. East Germany 39½
4. Yugoslavia 37½
5. Czechoslovakia 37
6. Bulgaria 34
7. Spain 20½
8. Denmark 18

Bath 1973
1. USSR 40½
2. Yugoslavia 34
3. Hungary 33
4. Poland 25
=5. West Germany 24
  England 24
7. Romania 23
8. Switzerland 20½

Brilliancy Prize, Bath 1973
White: Botterill (England); *Black:* Tal (USSR)
Sicilian Defence
1. P–K4, P–QB4; 2. N–KB3, P–K3; 3. N–B3, P–QR3; 4. P–Q4, P×P; 5. N×P, Q–B2; 6. B–Q3, N–KB3; 7. O–O, N–B3; 8. N–N3, P–QN4; 9. B–N5, B–K2; 10. Q–K2, B–N2; 11. QR–K1, P–Q3; 12. P–QR3, P–N5; 13. P×P, N×NP; 14. R–R1, O–O; 15. N–R5, B–B1; 16. B–QB4, R–N1; 17. P–B4, P–Q4; 18. P–K5, B–B4+; 19. K–R1, N–Q2; 20. B–Q3, N×B; 21. Q×N, R×P; 22. N–N3, B–N5; 23. N–R2, N–B4; 24. Q–Q4, B–R6; 25. Q–B3, Q–N3; 26. N–Q2, R×N; 27. R×R, B–N5; 28. Q–N2, P–Q5; 29. N–B4, Q–N4; 30. Q×P, B–N2; 31. P–B3, N–N6; 32. Q–Q3, B–B4; 33. R–Q1, P–R3; 34. B–R4, B–R1; 35. P–R3, P–QR4; 36. K–R2, P–R5; 37. Q–K2, B–B3; 38. N–Q6, Q–R4; 39. P–B5, Q×P; 40. B–K7, N–B8; 41. R×N, Q×R; 42. B×R,

42. ., B–K6; 43. K–N3, B–KN4; 44. Q–B4, Q–K6+; 45. K–N4, B–R5; 46. B–K7, B×B; 47. N×P, P–R4+; 48. K×P, B–K1; 49. K–N4, P×P+; 50. K×P, P–N3+; 51. K–N4, B–Q2+; 52. resigns.

(R.D.K.)

'EUROPE-ECHECS'

A monthly French chess magazine, founded in 1959 by Raoul Bertolo who has also directed it ever since. The magazine, which is published in Besançon, is the result of the fusion of two smaller reviews – *L'Echiquier de Paris* and *L'Echiquier de Turenne*.

Its chief editor is Sylvain Zinser who is also largely responsible for the Games Section. The magazine has always laid special emphasis on literary standards and is outstanding in this respect amongst chess magazines. *(H.G.)*

EUWE, Dr Max *(b. 20 May 1901)*

World Champion 1935–7, Dutch grandmaster, born in Watergrafsmeer (Netherlands), Euwe never devoted himself completely to chess and became the only real amateur since Morphy's day to win the World Championship. He holds a doctorate in mathematics and throughout his peak years as a player he lectured in mathematics, mechanics, and astronomy at an Amsterdam lyceum.

Euwe was taught chess at the age of four by his mother and entered his first tournament when he was ten. He became Dutch national champion in 1920 while still at university. His early successes included =2nd at Göteborg 1920 (ahead of Grünfeld and Sämisch) and a drawn match (+2–2=8) with Maróczy in 1921. After he took up his teaching post in 1924 his tournament appearances were largely confined to school holidays, although he continued to achieve creditable results, including notably 3rd at Bad Kissingen 1928 and 1st at Hastings 1930/1 (ahead of Capablanca). In match-play he defeated Colle (+5–0=1 in 1924), Landau (+3–1=2 in 1931), and Noteboom (+3–0=3 in 1931), while losing matches narrowly to Alekhine (+2–3=5 in 1925), Bogoljubow (twice: +2–3=5 in 1927 and +1–2=7 in 1928) and Capablanca (+0–2=8 in 1931).

The period 1932–5 saw the emergence of Euwe as a serious challenger for the World title. Tournament successes included 2nd at Berne 1932, 2nd at Zürich 1934, and 1st at Hastings 1934/5 – all tournaments of the highest quality whose participants included Alekhine, Botvinnik, Capablanca, Bogoljubow, Flohr, Nimzowitsch, and Lasker. In matches he defeated Spielmann twice (+2–0=2 in 1932 and +4–2=2 in 1935) and drew with Flohr (+3–3=10 in 1932). These results led to a match against Alekhine for the World Championship which was played in the Netherlands in 1935. Although Alekhine started as heavy favourite in the eyes of the chess-world, the contest developed into a close-fought marathon with Euwe eventually winning by +9–8=13.

Euwe retained the World title for two years before losing a return match to Alekhine in 1937 by +4–10=11. (After this second match a further five 'exhibition' games were played ending in a score of +2–1=2 to Euwe.)

In the 1938 A.V.R.O. tournament Euwe scored only 50% and at the end of 1939 he lost a close match to Keres, the winner of that event, by +5–6=3. His chess activities were curtailed by the German occupation of the Netherlands, since he would not participate in Nazi-sponsored competitions; but he did play one important match in 1941, defeating Bogoljubow by +5–2=3. After the war his greatest success was 2nd (behind Botvinnik) at Groningen 1946. Euwe finished last in the 1948 Hague–Moscow World Championship tournament, and has since played little serious international chess apart from occasional matches: +5–0=5 against Van Scheltinga in 1949 and +4–0=6 against Donner in 1956.

Dr Max Euwe, Hastings 1949/50

In subsequent years Euwe established himself as a leading expert in the computer-based information sciences. From 1958 to 1964 he was director of the Netherlands Research Centre for Information Sciences, and professor of that subject 1964–71 at the universities of Tilburg and Rotterdam. In September 1970 he became President of FIDE.

He has written extensively on chess and his series of opening monographs, *Theorie der Schaakopeningen*, has been published in Dutch and German. He edited the monthly *Chess Archives* until 1967. Books include: *Judgement and Planning in Chess*, London 1953, New York 1954; *The Development of Chess Style*, London 1968; *The Middle Game* (with Kramer), London 1964, 1965, New York 1965, 1966 and *The Road to Chess Mastery* (with Meiden), New York, London 1968.

26th game of the World Championship match, 1935, known as 'the Pearl of Zandvoort'

White: Euwe; *Black:* Alekhine
Dutch Defence
1. P–Q4, P–K3; 2. P–QB4, P–KB4; 3. P–KN3, B–N5+; 4. B–Q2, B–K2; 5. B–N2, N–KB3; 6. N–QB3, O–O; 7. N–B3, N–K5; 8. O–O, P–QN3; 9. Q–B2, B–N2; 10. N–K5, N×N; 11. B×N, B×B; 12. K×B, Q–B1; 13. P–Q5, P–Q3; 14. N–Q3, P–K4; 15. K–R1, P–B3; 16. Q–N3, K–R1; 17. P–B4, P–K5; 18. N–N4, P–B4; 19. N–B2, N–Q2; 20. N–K3, B–B3; 21. N×P, B×B; 22. N×QP, Q–N1; 23. N×P, B–B3; 24. N–Q2, P–KN4; 25. P–K4, P×P; 26. P×P, B–Q5; 27. P–K5, Q–K1; 28. P–K6, R–KN1; 29. N–B3, Q–N3;

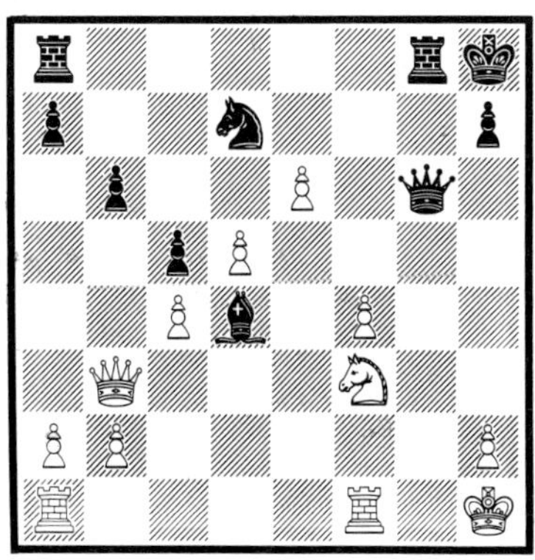

30. R–KN1, B×R; 31. R×B, Q–B3; 32. N–N5, R–N2; 33. P×N, R×P; 34. Q–K3, R–K2; 35. N–K6, R–KB1; 36. Q–K5, Q×Q; 37. P×Q, R–B4; 38. R–K1, P–KR3; 39. N–Q8, R–B7; 40. P–K6, R–Q7; 41. N–B6, R–K1; 42. P–K7, P–N4; 43. N–Q8, K–N2; 44. N–N7, K–B3; 45. R–K6+, K–N4; 46. N–Q6, R×KP; 47. N–K4+, resigns. *(R.D.K.)*

EVANS GAMBIT

Once described as 'a gift of the gods to a languishing chess world', this invention of Captain W. D. Evans did indeed give an infusion of life to the Giuoco Piano. By the moves 1. P–K4, P–K4; 2. N–KB3, N–QB3; 3. B–B4, B–B4; 4. P–QN4, White gives up a pawn to gain time and space with a quick P–QB3 and P–Q4. The Normal variation is 4. . , B×P; 5. P–B3, B–R4; 6. P–Q4, P×P; 7. O–O, B–N3 when White has fair value for the pawn. *(W.R.H.)*

EVANS, Larry *(b. 23 March 1932)*

Grandmaster, chess author and three times US champion. He was the first of the post-war American juniors to mature when he scored 90% on 5th board for the US team at the 1950 Olympiad.

After tieing with Bisguier for the US Junior championship in 1949, Evans made his international debut with 4th place at the 1949/50 Hastings. In the following year at the age of nineteen he became the first player to win a US championship ahead of Reshevsky. He defended his title a year later in a match with H. Steiner, 10–4.

During the early 1950s Evans won the US Open three times and was awarded the international master title in 1952. He became a grandmaster five years later. A landmark in his writing career was *New Ideas in Chess* (London 1958). Evans has written several other books, edited the tenth edition of *Modern Chess Openings* (London 1965), and helped Fischer, a long-time friend, in the preparation of the latter's *My 60 Memorable Games* (New York, London 1969). Beginning journalism in the late 1960s, Evans developed one of the most widely-syndicated American chess columns.

He has played more frequently in US events than in Europe, but his foreign successes include =4th at Buenos Aires 1960, =2nd at Venice 1967, 1st at Portimao (Portugal 1975) and a $2\frac{1}{2}$–$1\frac{1}{2}$ score on last board against Taimanov in the 1954 USA–USSR match. He won the US championship again in 1961/2, and in 1968 when Fischer did not play. In matches he has also defeated Lombardy $5\frac{1}{2}$–$4\frac{1}{2}$ in 1962. *(A.S.)*

EVANS, William Davies, Captain
(27 January 1790–3 August 1872)

The inventor of the famous Evans Gambit was a Welshman and was born at a farm called Musland in the parish of St Dogwell's, North Pembrokeshire. At the age of fourteen he went to sea and for all his working life, until he retired through ill-health and was awarded a pension in 1840, was in the service of the General Postal Department.

It was in 1824, when commanding a postal steam packet plying between Milford in Wales and Dunmore (the port of Waterford) in Ireland, that he invented his gambit. It should be observed that he devised it in a delayed form: 1. P–K4, P–K4; 2. N–KB3, N–QB3; 3. B–B4, B–B4; 4. O–O, P–Q3; 5. P–QN4, whereas what is now known as the Evans Gambit starts with 4. P–QN4, i.e. before castling.

The first occasion on which the gambit was employed seems to have been in the years 1826 or 1827 (the exact date is not known) in a game played in the Subscription Rooms for chess that William Lewis opened in St Martin's Lane, London, in 1825. His opponent was the famous Alexander McDonnell.

We give the game, which demonstrates Captain Evans's skill as a combinative player.

White: Evans; *Black:* McDonnell
1. P–K4, P–K4; 2. N–KB3, N–QB3; 3. B–B4, B–B4; 4. O–O, P–Q3; 5. P–QN4, B×P; 6. P–B3, B–R4; 7. P–Q4, B–KN5; 8. Q–N3, Q–Q2; 9. N–N5, N–Q1; 10. P×P, P×P; 11. B–R3, N–R3; 12. P–B3, B–N3+; 13. K–R1, B–KR4; 14. R–Q1, Q–B1;

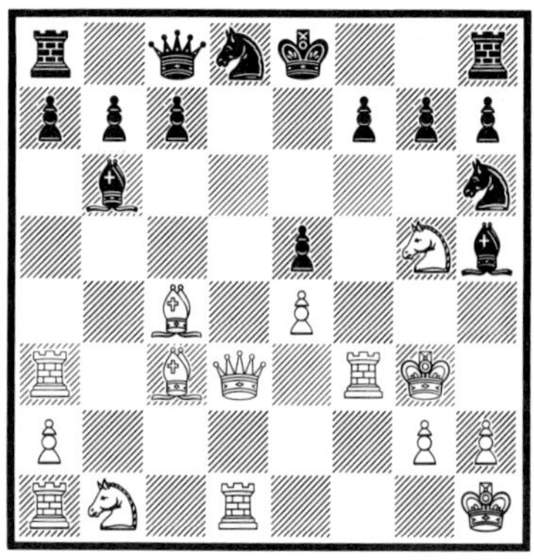

15. R×N+, Q×R; 16. N×BP, Q–R5; 17. Q–N5+, P–B3; 18. Q×KP+, K–Q2; 19. Q–K6+, K–B2; 20. B–Q6 mate.

After his retirement Evans went to live abroad and eventually found a haven in Ostend and there, ill, almost blind and in very straitened circumstances, he dictated a letter on 22 March, 1871, which was published in the *Gentlemen's Journal* Supplement for June, 1872, along with an appeal for him organized by George Walker. The letter gives the authentic facts of his life and is worth quoting in full, if only to refute various unfounded reports about a meeting with the Tsar's brother or, according to that rich source of misinformation, the Rev. G. A. MacDonnell, that the Evans Gambit was discovered off the coast of Africa by a middle-aged lieutenant in the Royal Navy – perhaps the reverend gentleman was confusing Waterford with the Canary Islands.

The letter runs:
'William Davies Evans is a native of Pembrokeshire, South Wales, and was born on 27 January 1790. He commenced a naval career at the age of fourteen. He was about twenty-eight years of age when he first learnt the moves of the game of Chess. Having the advantage of frequent practice with Lieut. H. Wilson, R.N., who was a player of some reputation in his time, beside corresponding on the subject of the game with the late Mr W. Lewis, and also with Mr George Walker, the able Chess Editor of Bell's Life, *he made a rapid progress in the game. Captain Evans received at first the odds of a Rook from Lieut. Wilson. After a continuance of play for some years, the odds were greatly reduced, until ultimately Captain Evans succeeded in defeating his formidable antagonist playing even.*

'About the year 1824, being then in command of a Government Mail Steamer, the passages between Milford Haven and Waterford were favourable to the study of the game of Chess, and at this time he invented the Gambit, which bears his name. The idea occurred to him while studying a narration of the Giuoco Piano in Sarratt's Treatise on Chess.

'Captain Evans was the first who gave to the world a true solution of that very difficult end game, the King and three Pawns unmoved against King and three Pawns also unmoved. This position was handed down to us through a period of some centuries as a drawn game, but Captain Evans proved that the first player can always win. (See Staunton's Handbook, *p. 500.)*

'Captain Evans acquired some celebrity as "Inventor of the System of Tri-coloured Lights for Ships to prevent Collisions at Night", which has been adopted by all nations possessing a marine. For this invention the English Government awarded him the sum of £1,500, and the Czar of Russia a gold pocket chronometer, value £160, together with a donation of £200.'

The subscription that amounted to over £200 was too late. He died in 1872 and was buried in Ostend where his grave bears the inscription:
'To the sacred memory of William Davies Evans, formerly Commander in the Post Office and Peninsular and Oriental Steam Services; Superintendent in the Royal Mail Steam Company, and inventor of the system of tri-coloured light for shipping. Also well known in the Chess World as the author of the Evans Gambit.'

(H.G.)

EVERGREEN GAME

Anderssen's second 'name game', the Evergreen, was played a year after the Immortal Game, in 1852. The name appears to have been coined by Steinitz. Later analysts (Lipke, Em. Lasker) have shown that the brilliant combination beginning with 19. QR–Q1, as a result of which the game was awarded its name, is of dubious merit and should have been replaced by 19. B–K4.

White: Anderssen; *Black:* Dufresne
Evans Gambit
1. P–K4, P–K4; 2. N–KB3, N–QB3; 3. B–B4, B–B4; 4. P–QN4, B×P; 5. P–B3, B–R4; 6. P–Q4, P×P; 7. O–O, P–Q6; 8. Q–N3, Q–B3; 9. P–K5, Q–N3; 10. R–K1, KN–K2; 11. B–R3, P–QN4; 12. Q×P, R–QN1; 13. Q–R4, B–N3; 14. QN–Q2, B–N2; 15. N–K4, Q–B4; 16. B×P, Q–R4; 17. N–B6+, P×N; 18. P×P, R–N1; 19. QR–Q1, Q×N; 20. R×N+, N×R;

21. Q×P+, K×Q; 22. B–B5+, K–K1; 23. B–Q7+, K–B1; 24. B×N mate.

(W.H.)

EXCHANGE
(1) The difference in value between a Rook and a minor piece. See also MINOR EXCHANGE.
(2) A pair of moves by which men of equal value on both sides are removed from the board. See EXCHANGE COMBINATION. *(W.H.)*

EXCHANGE COMBINATION
A combination which, whatever its positional outcome or motivation, materially results in an equal exchange. In its simplest form the exchange combination is seen in many openings: a temporary sacrifice followed by a pawn fork, e.g. after 1. P–K4, P–K4; 2. N–QB3, N–KB3; 3. B–B4, N×P; 4. N×N, P–Q4; 5. B–Q3, P×N; 6. B×P. Another frequent type of exchange combination is based on a pin:

White to move. After the straight exchange, 1. B×B+?, R×B; 2. R×R, K×R; the Black King would be in time to stop the White pawn. By choosing the exchange combination 1. R×B!, R×R; 2. P–N4!, K any; 3. B×R, White gains the decisive tempo. *(W.H.)*

F

FAHRNI, Hans *(1 October 1874–28 May 1939)*
Swiss master (born in Prague). His outstanding result was first place at San Remo 1911, ahead of Levitsky, Przepiórka, Gunsberg, Forgács, Kostić, Réti, etc. Also 1st at Monaco 1909. *(R.D.K.)*

FAIRHURST, William Albert, C.B.E. *(b. 21 August 1903)*
International master, British champion 1937, Fairhurst was born in Alderley Edge in Cheshire and spent his early years there and in Lancashire, playing regularly for the latter in the county championship contests. He soon had established himself as the leading Northern player and one of great promise, his style of play being essentially strategic and influenced by Tarrasch and masters of the Tarrasch school.

His first international success was an =2nd with Yates at Scarborough 1927, beating the first prize winner, the Belgian Edgar Colle, and also Bogoljubow, whom he outdistanced by a full point. This was to be his only important international success since he was a genuine amateur and indeed developed a most distinguished career as a structural engineer, becoming a famous bridge-builder and being awarded the C.B.E. for his services in this respect.

In 1931 he went to live in Scotland and soon became the leading player there, winning the Scottish championship eleven times in all, from 1932 to 1962.

In 1933 he drew a match of six games with the then Austrian master Eliskases, and in 1937 won a strongly-contested British championship at Blackpool.

After the Second World War his results were not so good, partly because of the ever-increasing demands of his profession and partly because his style of play failed to change and develop with the times, so that what had been a scientific and logical approach to the game became too dogmatic.

Nevertheless, he demonstrated that he was still a genuine master-player by his results in representative matches for Great Britain and by playing for Scotland in the Olympiads of 1933, 1956, 1958, 1964, 1966 and 1968, and that not without success.

In the 1970s he left Scotland for New Zealand and played for that country at the Nice Olympiad of 1974. On top board there he scored 40% which must be a record for a player aged seventy. *(H.G.)*

FALKBEER, Ernst Karl *(27 June 1819–14 December 1885)*
An Austrian master, a journalist and contributor to many liberal journals, Falkbeer had to leave Vienna for political reasons in 1848. After sojourning in many German towns, he settled in England in 1855, whence he returned to Vienna in 1864. In his only tournament appearance he tied for first with Löwenthal at Birmingham 1857, but lost the play-off by +1−3=3. In matches he drew with Bird and lost by the extraordinary score of +15−16=0 to Hamppe. His name has become immortalized in the Falkbeer Counter-gambit (see KING'S GAMBIT). *(W.H.)*

FAMILY CHECK
Jocular reference to a multiple Knight fork in which the hostile King is one of the forked units. *(W.H.)*

FARAGO, Ivan *(b. 1 April 1946)*
Hungarian grandmaster who graduated in economics but became a professional player.

At the age of eighteen he was a Hungarian national master. He gained the international master title by his performances at Havana 1973 and Bucharest 1974.

In 1975 he was first in the I.B.M. Master Group at Amsterdam. In the same year he attained his first grandmaster norm by coming =3rd at Leipzig. He completed the requirements for the grandmaster title by coming =4th with Velimirović in the Grandmaster Group of the I.B.M. tournament in 1976. *(H.G.)*

FAROE ISLANDS
With a population of less than 40,000, the smallest country to have competed in the Olympiads: 55th in 1970 and 1972, 58th in 1974 and 44th in 1975. Chess in the islands is organized by the Talvsamband Føroya, c/o H. Petersen, 3860 Vestmanna. *(K.J.O'C.)*

FARRÉ, Mallofré Miguel *(b. 23 February 1936)*
Spanish international master whose chess career was cut short through business occupations. Farré was a most promising junior player and in the 1953 Junior World Championship at Copenhagen he came second in Final Group B. In 1955, at the Junior World Championship in Antwerp he came 3rd in the Final Group A, below Spassky and Mednis but ahead of Portisch and Tringov.

In 1957 he was =2nd in the Spanish championship and =5th in the Madrid International tournament. He was the most successful Spanish player in the 1958 Olympiad at Munich, scoring 66.7% on fourth board. On the same board at the 1960 Olympiad at Varna he scored 56.7% in 1960. He was =4th at Torremolinos in 1961. *(H.G.)*

FATALIBEKOVA, Elena
Young Soviet woman player who has made great strides in the last few years. Soviet Woman champion in 1974, she finished =4th in the Zonal at Frunze in 1975, the year in which she was awarded the international woman master title. In 1976 she won the Women's Interzonal at Tbilisi, earning both a place in the Women's Candidates and the title of international woman grandmaster. *(K.J.O'C.)*

FAZEKAS, Dr Stefan *(23 March 1898–3 May 1967)*
International master and British champion 1957. A dangerous attacking player but weak in positional play, Fazekas was born at Satoraljaujhely on the Hungarian-Czechoslovak border. In the earlier part of his career he was Czechoslovak. This period comprised his international career and he was awarded the title of international master many years later after he had emigrated to England in 1939.

It was his results in 1931 that gained him the title: 2nd at Kosice, 3rd at Prague and 3rd at Brno ahead of Honlinger, Mikenas, Noteboom and Rellstab.

In England he became a much-respected general medical practitioner, and was therefore really an amateur at chess since he devoted himself to his profession. But he played much club and county chess and was eleven times champion of his county, Essex.

In 1957, almost out of the blue, he won the British championship in a strong year that included Penrose and C. H. O'D. Alexander. He played a number of times in the championship after that, but never looked like gaining the title since increasing years took their toll. He was in fact the oldest player ever to have won the British championship.

In 1959 he took up correspondence chess and became an international correspondence chess master. *(H.G.)*

FEIGIN, Movsa *(b. 28 February 1908)*
One of the strongest players in Latvia in the years before the outbreak of the Second World War. Champion of Riga in 1937. Feigin was a member of the Latvian team at Buenos Aires 1939 Olympiad, and remained there when the war began, thus avoiding the fate of his team-mate, V. Petrov, who died in prison after his return home. *(W.R.H.)*

FERS [**fierz**]
The medieval name for the Queen, derived from the Persian vizier.

FIANCHETTO
A term derived from the Italian *fiancata* meaning 'moves played on the side or flank'. Ponziani called any opening entailing the moving of a flank pawn (RP or NP) a fianchetto, but the term now means the placing of a Bishop, when developing it, on QN2 or KN2.

The value of such a development is that the Bishop is placed on the longest diagonal of the board. Its disadvantage lies in the necessity of moving the NP which may make the surrounding squares weak and also demands more time than a normal straightforward development of the Bishop.

In the eighteenth and nineteenth centuries the development was regarded as eccentric; but with the coming of the Hypermoderns in the twentieth century it became recognized as a powerful weapon. It is a basic constituent of the Indian Systems of opening and defence. *(H.G.)*

FICHTL, Jiři *(b. 16 February 1921)*
Czechoslovak international master since 1959. Winner of Czechoslovak championship in 1950 and 1960, beating Ujtelky $2\frac{1}{2}$–$1\frac{1}{2}$ in a play-off on the latter occasion. Winner of Prague 1956 international tournament. *(W.R.H.)*

FIDE
The World Chess Federation, usually known as 'FIDE' after the initials of its French name Fédération Internationale des Échecs, was founded in Paris on 20 July 1924 with the objective of uniting all the chess-playing nations of the world into one main organizing body. In the first instance it was European with the initiative being taken by Pierre Vincent in France and Leonard Rees in England. But gradually the net spread wider and wider to include 97 nations from every quarter of the globe.

The FIDE Statutes, from which we now quote, describe its scope, aims and work.

'FIDE is the international overall organization in the domain of chess. It unites national chess federations and directs the chess world. FIDE has its own flag and its own anthem; its motto is "Gens una sumus" – "We are one family".

'The purpose and aim of FIDE are the diffusion and development of chess among all the nations of the world, as well as the raising of the level of chess culture and knowledge on a scientific, creative and cultural basis.

'FIDE issues the rules of chess and the provisions pertaining to the organization of the World Championships and all other FIDE chess competitions. It awards the international chess titles.

'To facilitate the administrative work in FIDE, zones are created, if possible according to regional points of view. Each member is assigned to a zone.

'The FIDE officials and organizations are: (a) The General Assembly, (b) the Central Committee, (c) the Bureau, (d) the permanent and the temporary commissions, or delegates, (e) the

The FIDE Congress, Moscow 1956, taken outside the Moscow Central Chess Club

President and the three Deputy-Presidents, (f) the Zonal Presidents, (g) the General Secretary, (h) the Treasurer, (i) the Auditor.'

The FIDE presidents have been and are: 1924–49, Alexander Rueb, The Hague; 1949–70, Folke Rogard, Stockholm; 1970–, Max Euwe, Amsterdam.

The three deputy-presidents are: F. Campomanes (the Philippines), B. Kazić (Yugoslavia), J. G. Prentice (Canada).

The General Secretary is Ineke Bakker (Passeerdersgracht 32, Amsterdam C, The Netherlands).

The Treasurer is R. K. Clues (Station Chambers, Aberystwyth, Dyfed, Wales).

The Auditor is Count Gian Carlo Dal Verme (Italy).

The zones and their presidents are as follows:

Zone 1, Western Europe:
Andorra, Belgium, England, France, Guernsey, Ireland, Luxembourg, Monaco, Netherlands, Scotland, Spain and Wales.
(H. Golombek, England)
Zone 2, Central Europe
Austria, Denmark, Faroe Islands, Finland, German Federal Republic, Iceland, Israel, Norway, Rhodesia, South Africa, Sweden and Switzerland.
(Dr W. Dorazil, Austria)
Zone 3, Eastern Europe
Albania, Bulgaria, Czechoslovakia, German Democratic Republic, Hungary, Poland, Romania and Yugoslavia.
(Ing. J. Sajtar, Czechoslovakia)
Zone 4, Soviet
USSR
(Y. Averbakh, USSR)
Zone 5, USA
USA
(Miss Pearl Mann, USA)
Zone 6, Canada
Canada
(J. G. Prentice, Canada)
Zone 7, Central America and Caribbean
Bahamas, Bermuda, British Virgin Islands, Colombia, Costa Rica, Cuba, Dominican Republic, Ecuador, El Salvador, Guatemala, Guyana, Honduras, Jamaica, Mexico, Netherlands Antilles, Nicaragua, Panama, Puerto Rico, Trinidad & Tobago, US Virgin Islands and Venezuela.
(J. Vega Fernandez, Cuba)
Zone 8, South America
Argentina, Bolivia, Brazil, Chile, Paraguay, Peru, Surinam, Uruguay.
(R. Camara, Brazil)
Zone 9, West Asia
India, Iran, Iraq, Jordan, Lebanon, Mongolia, Pakistan, Syria.
(A. Navabi, Iran)
Zone 10, East Asia and Australia
Australia, China, Hong Kong, Indonesia, Japan, Malaysia, New Zealand, Papua New Guinea, Philippines, Singapore and Thailand.
(Dr K. A. Lim, Singapore)
Zone 11, Afro-Mediterranean
Algeria, Cyprus, Ghana, Greece, Italy, Malta, Mauretania, Morocco, Nigeria, Portugal, Tunisia, Turkey, Zaire and Zambia.
(R. Belkadi, Tunis) *(H.G.)*

FILES

According to the Laws of Chess 'the eight rows of squares running from the edge of the chess-board nearest one of the players to that nearest the other are called "files" '. *(H.G.)*

FILIP, Miroslav *(b. 27 October 1928)*
One of Czechoslovakia's leading grandmasters for the last twenty-five years, but never quite established as his country's leading player, having been second board to Pachman in the early years and later overtaken by Hort and Smejkal of the younger generation. Nevertheless Filip did succeed in winning the Czechoslovak championship in 1952 and 1954.

Won first prize in the Steinitz Memorial tournament (held in Prague and Mariánské Lázně) 1956 and shared first in Mariánské Lázně 1960 and Buenos Aires 1961. Qualified for the Candidates tournament of 1956, where he scored 8 out of 18 to share 8th place, possibly his best result considering the opposition. Also qualified for the 1962 Candidates but finished last. *(W.R.H.)*

FINE, Reuben *(b. 11 October 1914)*

Fine had an exceptionally brief but fruitful international career before changing from grandmaster to psychiatrist. Within three years, 1935–8, he developed from an unknown American master into co-winner of A.V.R.O. 1938, one of the highest-rated events ever held. Yet when chess revived after the Second World War Fine was too busy with his studies to accept an invitation to the World Championship tournament of 1948.

Born in New York, Fine learned the moves at the age of ten. He was fond of recalling that he never read a chess book until he was a master. Instead, Fine spent several hours a day for much of his adolescence at the Marshall Chess Club. From speed chess (lightning) games he acquired a sharp tactical skill and gift for counter-attack that characterized his later career.

During the period 1931–2 Fine registered his first significant successes ahead of young rivals such as Reshevsky, H. Steiner, Dake and Horowitz. In his first international event, Pasadena 1932, he was only =7th. But the following year after graduating from college he was a member of the victorious US team at Folkestone in 1933.

Two years later after another good Olympiad performance at Warsaw, Fine came =2nd at Lodz and then 1st at Hastings 1935/6 ahead of Flohr and Tartakower.

There followed a series of improving results: 1st at Zandvoort 1936, =3rd at Nottingham 1936, =1st at Amsterdam 1936, 1st at Stockholm 1937, =1st at Margate and Ostend 1937 and 2nd at Semmering-Baden 1937. In 1937 he defeated Ståhlberg 5–3 in a match and was Euwe's second in his return match with Alekhine.

The high point of Fine's career came at A.V.R.O. 1938 when he began with 5½ points in his first six games. Later losses denied him clear first place. The interference of war and the resumption of Fine's studies kept him from international play for seven years. He finished 2nd at an international event in Hollywood in 1945 and scored ½–1½ against Keres on second board in the 1946 US–USSR match. His last results were 1st at New York 1948, 4th at New York 1951 and a drawn 8-game match with Najdorf in 1949. Curiously, Fine never won a US championship tournament despite several tries.

After A.V.R.O. 1938, Fine concentrated on writing chess books. Altogether he wrote more than a dozen works including *The Easy Way in Chess*, New York 1942, and *Basic Chess Endings*, New York 1941.

'I have often been asked whether I will ever return to chess,' Fine wrote in 1959. 'My ambitions in the game have been satisfied, and there is no incentive for anything other than an actual match for the World Championship.' In his heyday Fine's combinative skill was one of the most dangerous talents in the world.

Match 1934
White: C. Torre; *Black:* Fine
Caro-Kann Defence
1. P–K4, P–QB3; 2. P–Q4, P–Q4; 3. P–KB3, P–K3; 4. N–QB3, N–KB3; 5. B–K3, B–K2; 6. P–K5, KN–Q2; 7. P–B4, P–QB4; 8. N–B3, N–QB3; 9. B–N5, Q–N3; 10. O–O, O–O; 11. K–R1, P–QR3; 12. B×N, P×B; 13. N–QR4, Q–R4; 14. P–B3, P×P; 15. P×P, P–QB4; 16. R–B1, P–B5; 17. P–KN4, P–B3; 18. R–KB2, P×P; 19. BP×P, B–N2; 20. Q–B2, B–QB3; 21. N–B3, N–B4; 22. R(1)–B1, N–Q6; 23. R–N2;

23. . , N×KP; 24. P×N, P–Q5; 25. N–K4, P×B; 26. K–N1, Q–Q4; 27. N–B3, Q–Q6; 28. Q×Q, P×Q; 29. R–N3, P–K7; 30. resigns. *(A.S.)*

FINLAND
Though Finland has never had a great player, chess is popular and widely played in the country and the general standard is high. Finland was one of the founder members of FIDE at Paris in 1924, the Finnish representative on that occasion having been C. Tschepurnoff.

Finland has participated regularly in the Olympiads and always occupied a respectable place. In 1952 the FIDE Olympiad and Congress was held at Helsinki and this was the first time the Soviet

Union participated in an Olympiad. The Finnish team excelled itself by qualifying for the top final section and in coming 9th attained its highest position in such events.

A steady flow of first-rate masters has enabled it to hold its own with its neighbours in international matches and it has done especially well against such countries as Sweden and Estonia. K. Ojanen, many times Finnish champion, has distinguished himself in the match with Estonia by winning brilliantly against Paul Keres.

Other excellent Finnish masters are Eero Böök, Osmo Kaila and Heikki Westerinen. This last is the first Finnish player to gain the international grandmaster title.

The ruling chess body in Finland is the Central Chess Federation and its address is that of its FIDE delegate, Eero Helme, Kulosaaren puistotie 42, as. 37, 00570 Helsinki.

The national chess magazine is *Suomen Shakki* and its address c/o Matti Nukari, Kasavuorentie 12 D 6, 02700 Kauniainen.

(H.G.)

FISCHER, Robert James *(b. 9 March 1943)*
The most widely known, the most controversial and, for many, the greatest player of all time. As with Steinitz, Fischer's genius has often been concealed by controversies away from the board. Like Lasker, Fischer has raised chess to new financial heights despite frequent retreats from serious play. And, like Capablanca, Fischer is recognized by millions of non-players and has won the game many new enthusiasts. Fischer, known by his nickname Bobby, was born in Chicago and spent his first years in several different US cities before settling in Brooklyn, New York. His parents separated early and Fischer's mother, a registered nurse, was the greatest influence on his life until she left the USA when Fischer was seventeen.

After learning the moves with his sister at the age of six, Fischer was introduced to master-play two years later when his mother took him to a simultaneous display given by Max Pavey. Fischer began to play up to six hours a day, usually at the Brooklyn and Manhattan Chess Club. Although influenced most by Capablanca, Fischer concentrated on modern openings and became an expert on the King's Indian Defence and the Najdorf Variation of the Sicilian Defence.

After two years and fifteen tournaments (see GAME OF THE CENTURY), Fischer won his first major title, the US Open championship, in 1957. This was immediately followed by first place in the US Closed championship before his fifteenth birthday. His =5th in the Portorož Interzonal the following year made him the youngest grandmaster in FIDE history.

Unlike two other prodigies, Capablanca and Reshevsky, Fischer dropped out of secondary school at sixteen and became a professional player. Though his victories in the seven US championships in which he competed placed Fischer far above his American rivals, he experienced early setbacks abroad – e.g. =13th at Buenos Aires 1960 and 4th at Curaçao 1962. His victory in the Stockholm Interzonal of 1962 coming on the heels of 2nd behind Tal at Bled 1961 established him as a World title contender.

After his 11–0 score in the 1963/4 US Closed championships, Fischer began one of three extended exiles from competition. He returned to the board to come =2nd at Havana 1965, playing his games by long-distance teletype. He again withdrew from play after scoring 1st at Vinkovci 1968 and did not play until the USSR–World match (see MATCH OF THE CENTURY) in 1970.

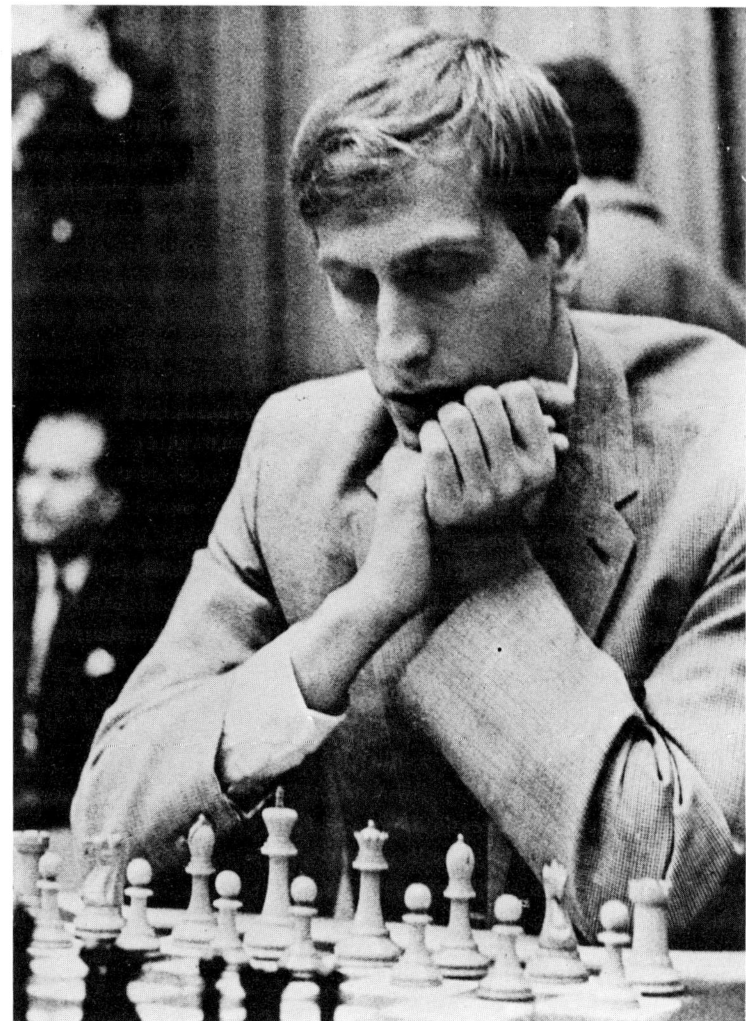

'Match of the Century', Bobby Fischer v. Tigran Petrosian, Belgrade 1970

Fischer boycotted the 1964–5 championship cycle and left the Sousse 1967 Interzonal in disputes with FIDE and tournament officials. His conflict with the US Chess Federation kept him out of the 1969 Zonal, but he was advanced to the 1970 Palma Interzonal when Benko withdrew in his favour. His performance in the Interzonal was sensational. Despite its strength, he made mincemeat of the opposition and finished in first place with $18\frac{1}{2}$ points, no less than $3\frac{1}{2}$ points ahead of his nearest rivals, Geller, Hübner and Larsen.

Even more overwhelming was his progress through the Candidates series of matches in 1971. In the quarter-final he beat the hapless Soviet grandmaster, Mark Taimanov, by 6–0 and repeated this triumph by a victory with the same score over Larsen in the semi-final. The former World Champion, Petrosian, put up a better fight in the final; but he too was soundly beaten by $6\frac{1}{2}$–$2\frac{1}{2}$.

The world awaited with bated breath the clash in 1972 between the World Champion, Boris Spassky, and his challenger, Bobby Fischer. At first it seemed that it would have to wait forever, since not only was Fischer in disagreement with playing the match in Reykjavik but he also objected strongly to the financial conditions. A timely offer of an additional £50,000 towards the prize fund from the British financier Jim Slater caused Fischer to relent and play. Somehow or other the match went on, despite continual protests against the conditions, threats to withdraw and one actual withdrawal. In the end the challenger proved his clear superiority and, by beating Spassky to the tune of $12\frac{1}{2}$–$8\frac{1}{2}$, Robert James Fischer became the first US player to win the World Championship.

In the euphoria of the moment he promised to take part in many chess events. But as time went on he became more and more reluctant to risk his reputation and during the three-year period of his reign as World Champion did not play a single game in a chess competition.

Nor was he satisfied with the regulations for the match between himself and the eventual challenger. It became apparent that he was not prepared to play a match and defend his title unless FIDE agreed with all the changes he demanded. He forfeited the title by refusing to play the challenger, Anatoly Karpov, in 1975 and most regrettably has not, at the time of writing, taken part in any further competition.

Fischer's style is characterized by extensive opening analysis, an intense will to win, and a Capablanca-like mastery of open and semi-open positions.

Curaçao Candidates tournament 1962
White: Fischer; *Black:* Keres
Ruy Lopez
1. P–K4, P–K4; 2. N–KB3, N–QB3; 3. B–N5, P–QR3; 4. B–R4, N–B3; 5. O–O, B–K2; 6. R–K1, P–QN4; 7. B–N3, P–Q3; 8. P–B3, O–O; 9. P–KR3, N–QR4; 10. B–B2, P–B4; 11. P–Q4, N–Q2; 12. P×BP, P×P; 13. QN–Q2, Q–B2; 14. N–B1, N–N3; 15. N–K3, R–Q1; 16. Q–K2, B–K3; 17. N–Q5, N×N; 18. P×N, B×QP; 19. N×P, R–R2; 20. B–B4, Q–N3; 21. QR–Q1, P–N3; 22. N–N4, N–B5; 23. B–R6, B–K3; 24. B–N3, Q–N1; 25. R×R+, B×R; 26. B×N, P×B;

27. Q×P, Q–Q3; 28. Q–R4, Q–K2; 29. N–B6+, K–R1; 30. N–Q5, Q–Q2; 31. Q–K4, Q–Q3; 32. N–B4, R–K2; 33. B–N5, R–K1; 34. B×B, R×B; 35. N×B, Q×N; 36. Q×Q, P×Q; 37. R×P, R–Q8+; 38. K–R2, R–Q7; 39. R–N6, R×BP; 40. R–N7, R–B3; 41. K–N3, resigns.

Writings: *Bobby Fischer's Games of Chess*, New York 1959; *My 60 Memorable Games*, New York and London 1969. *(A.S.)*

FISKE, Daniel Willard *(11 November 1831–17 September 1904)*
American polyglot and Icelandic scholar with life-long interest in chess. Fiske co-edited (with Morphy) the first American magazine *Chess Monthly*. He organized the New York 1857 tournament, and lived later in Iceland where he promoted chess activity and founded the Reykjavik Chess Club in 1900. His publications include *Chess in Iceland and in Icelandic Literature*. The international tournament at Reykjavik 1968 was called the Fiske Memorial in his honour. The Icelandic National Library possesses a Fiske chess collection, donated after his death. *(R.D.K.)*

FLAMBERG, Alexander Davidovich *(1880–24 January 1926)*
Polish master and champion of Warsaw in 1910. Lost matches against Rubinstein and Bogoljubow. Perhaps his greatest success was taking third place, only half a point behind Alekhine and Nimzowitsch, in the All-Russian master tournament of 1913/14. *(W.R.H.)*

FLEISCHMANN [Forgács], Leo *(5 October 1881–17 August 1930)*
A Hungarian Jewish master who had some successes in the first decade of the twentieth century but seems to have abandoned play with the advent of the First World War.

He always played in tournaments under the name of Fleischmann and his first success was a 1st prize at the Barmen 1905 tournament where he easily outdistanced such masters as Spielmann and Nimzowitsch.

An =3rd at the Nuremberg tournament of 1906 was followed by an excellent fifth place at the great tournament at Ostend in 1907.

Other good results were a 3rd at San Remo 1911, again a 3rd, this time at Budapest 1912. His final tournament was a third at Budapest 1913. Thereafter he refrained from taking part in any chess event. *(H.G.)*

FLESCH, János László *(b. 30 September 1933)*
Hungarian international master since 1963. Flesch is best known for his feats in simultaneous blindfold exhibitions, claiming the world record for a display in Budapest 1960 without sight of the boards against 52 opponents. *(W.R.H.)*

FLOHR, Salomon Mikhailovich *(b. 21 November 1908)*
First Czechoslovak, then Soviet grandmaster, Flohr spent most of his early years in Czechoslovakia, though he had been born in Gorodenko in Poland. One of his earliest ventures into international chess was to lead the Czechoslovak team at the 1930 Olympiad. Flohr's score of $14\frac{1}{2}/17$ already established him as one of the world's leading players; only Alekhine and Rubinstein made better results on top board.

From then on, Flohr continued to secure excellent results against the best players of the time. His tournament successes include 1st places at Hastings 1931/2, 1932/3 and 1933/4, Margate 1936, and Podebrady 1936; with shared 1st at Hastings 1934/5, Moscow 1935

Salomon Flohr in play against Alexander Alekhine, Hastings 1934

and Kemeri 1937. Also around that time Flohr proved himself a good match-player with wins against Stoltz in 1931 (+4—1 =3) and Mir Sultan Khan in 1932 (+2—1=3), and draws with Euwe (+3—3=10) in 1932 and Botvinnik (+2—2=8) in 1933.

A match for the World Championship was arranged between Flohr and Alekhine in 1938, but the events in Czechoslovakia prevented this taking place. History must also take the blame for Flohr's disastrous result at the A.V.R.O. tournament in 1938.

During the war Flohr went to live in the USSR, but never again looked a contender for the World title.

His style was always quiet and positional, winning many games on the strength of his magnificent technique particularly in the endgames. Though his later games showed a tendency towards draws, the early part of his career produced a wealth of games very instructive in their clarity.

Kemeri 1937
White: Hasenfuss; *Black:* Flohr
Caro-Kann Defence
1. P–K4, P–QB3; 2. P–Q4, P–Q4; 3. P×P, P×P; 4. P–QB4, N–KB3; 5. N–QB3, N–B3; 6. B–N5, P–K3; 7. N–B3, P×P; 8. B×P, B–K2; 9. O–O, O–O; 10. R–B1, P–QR3; 11. P–QR3, P–N4; 12. B–R2, B–N2; 13. Q–Q3, N–Q4; 14. N–K4, N(3)–N5; 15. Q–N1, N×B; 16. Q×N, B×B; 17. N(4)×B, P–R3; 18. N–K4, N–B5; 19. QR–K1, B–Q4; 20. P–QN3, P–B4; 21. N(4)–Q2, Q–B3; 22. K–R1, QR–B1; 23. Q–N1;

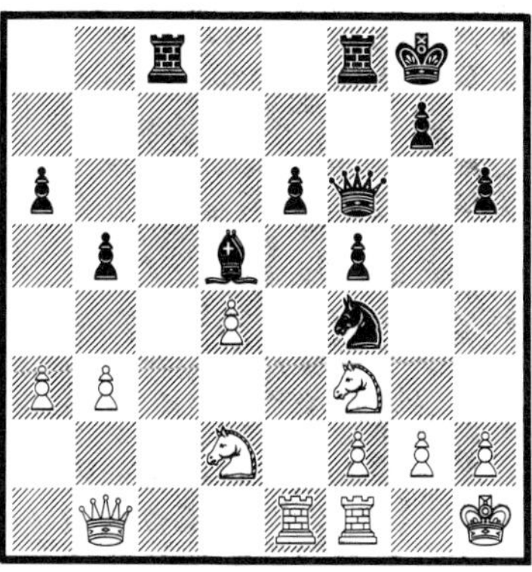

23. . , N×P; 24. K×N, Q–N4+; 25. K–R1, Q×N; 26. R–K3, Q×QP; 27. resigns. *(W.R.H.)*

FLORIAN, Dr Tibor *(b. 2 March 1919)*
Hungarian international master ever since the title was instuted in 1950. Winner of Hungarian championship in 1945 and Belgrade International tournament 1948.

Since 1960 Florian has been very active in chess organization both in Hungary and for FIDE. *(W.R.H.)*

FOLTYS, Jan *(13 October 1908–11 March 1952)*
International master and one of the finest players Czechoslovakia ever produced, Foltys would undoubtedly have become a most formidable grandmaster had not the war years and a premature death after the Second World War intervened.

The first year in which he really made his presence felt in the international world was 1936. In that year he came 3rd at the strong international tournament at Podebrady and scored 12½ on top board in the International Team tournament at Munich.

Fourth in Margate 1937, he came =3rd at Prague that year. Playing on second board below Flohr at the Stockholm Olympiad he obtained 63.9%.

In 1938 he came 3rd at Prague and in the Buenos Aires Olympiad of 1939, playing again on 2nd board, he scored 65.6%.

His best results in the war years were a 3rd at Prague 1942 and an =4th at Prague in 1943.

He achieved his best results almost immediately after the Second World War. An =4th at Prague in 1946 was followed by a 3rd at Budapest and, his best result ever, 1st at Karlovy Vary-Mariánské Lázně, came in a Czechoslovak tournament of 1948.

At Vienna in 1949 he came =1st and at Venice that year he came =4th. He also came 6th at the strong tournament at Trenčianské Teplice that year.

He achieved but little in the Amsterdam tourney of 1950 where he came 13th and also in Salzbrunn of that year where he came 7th.

He qualified for the Interzonal tournament by coming =5th at Mariánské Lázně 1951 but died of leukemia early the following year before he could play in the Interzonal.

His style of play was beautifully clear and aesthetic, and his premature death was a great loss to the chess world. *(H.G.)*

FORGÁCS, Leo
See under FLEISCHMANN.

FORINTOS, Győző *(b. 30 July 1935)*
Hungarian champion in 1968, Forintos gained the international master title in 1963 and the grandmaster title in 1974. Winner of Baja 1971 international tournament. *(W.R.H.)*

FORK
The most frequent tactical device in chess, the fork consists of a double attack on enemy units which is not effected by either skewer or discovery. Forks can be executed by every unit (including the K), but those of most frequent occurrence are N and P forks. Q, N and P forks are part of opening lore in a number of variations. Thus, a Q fork is seen in the Sicilian Defence, after 1. P–K4, P–QB4; 2. P–QB3, P–Q3; 3. P–Q4, N–KB3; 4. P×P, N×P?; 5. Q–R4+; a N fork in the same line after 1. P–K4, P–QB4; 2. P–QB3, N–KB3; 3. P–K5, N–Q4; 4. N–B3, P–Q3; 5. P×P, Q×P; 6. P–Q4, P×P; 7. N×P, P–K4?; 8. N–N5, Q–Q2; 9. Q×N, Q×Q; 10. N–B7+; a P fork in the Vienna Game after 1. P–K4, P–K4; 2. N–QB3, N–KB3; 3. B–B4, N×P; 4. N×N, P–Q4.

The N fork especially lends itself to cumulative effects. Thus a striking example of *successive* N forks is seen in Soultanbeieff v. Dubyna, Liège 1953:

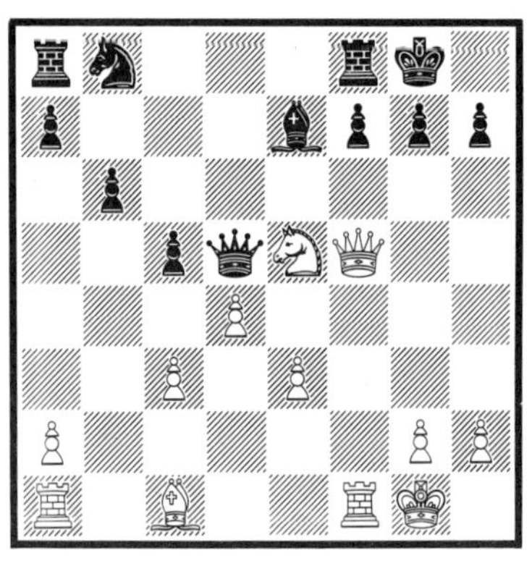

1. N–N6!, Q–N2 (if *1. . , Q×Q; 2. N×B+*. winning a piece); 2. Q–Q5!, N–B3 (or *2. . , Q×Q; 3. N×B+*, as before); 3. Q×N!, and after 3. . , Q×Q the black Q would be forked on a third square. *(W.H.)*

FORSYTH NOTATION

An ingenious but simple method of taking down a position which was invented by David Forsyth of Glasgow who emigrated to New Zealand and died in 1909.

Starting with the top rank of the board the initial letters of the pieces (with the exception of the Knight which is indicated by N) are put down from left to right. The vacant squares are indicated by a figure giving their number and the end of each rank is indicated by a sloping stroke. The White pieces are represented by capitals and the Black by lower case letters.

Thus the diagram below left would be taken down as follows: 6 k 1 / 4 b p 2 / 6 p 1 / 2 p 4 p / b 1 P p P 2 P / 3 Q 1 N P 1 / 1 q 3 P K 1 / 5 B 2. *(H.G.)*

FOUR KNIGHTS GAME
Considered very dull and drawish nowadays, the Four Knights was one of White's most popular openings in the 1920s. After 1. P–K4, P–K4; 2. N–KB3, N–QB3; 3. N–B3, N–B3; 4. B–N5, Black equalizes with 4. . , N–Q5 (the Rubinstein variation). Other lines for White are the Scotch Four Knights introduced by 4. P–Q4, P×P; 5. N×P,

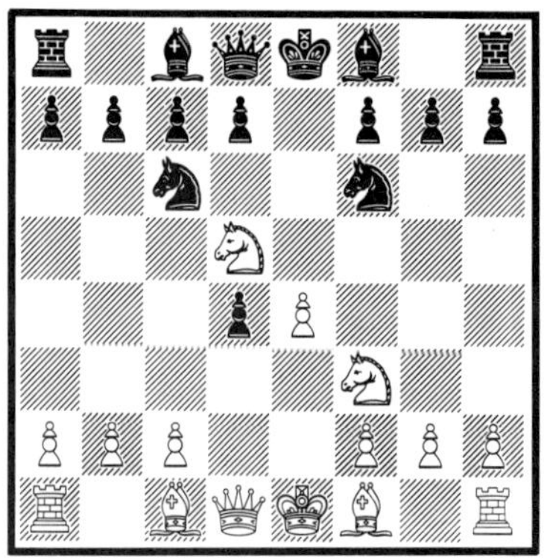

and the Belgrade Gambit, 4. P–Q4, P×P; 5. N–Q5. *(W.R.H.)*

FRANCE
The game first came into France from Spain via the south and retained its Moslem form for some time. By the eleventh and twelfth centuries it was played all over France, and in the Middle Ages chess was popular at court, among the nobility and the lettered classes. How popular it was with this last section of the population is demonstrated by the numerous references to chess in the French romances, many of which were translated into English (notably by William Caxton).

With the advent of the modern game, which came to France almost as speedily as it came to Italy, chess proved more and more popular and by the seventeenth century France had become the centre of chess in Europe. It still remained a court game and was patronized by the French kings. In 1680, for example, a chess academy was conducted at Fontainebleau by a son of the great Condé.

It was in the eighteenth century, when France led the world in civilization, that chess reached its peak there. The first great French player was De Kermur, Sire de Légal and he was followed by the even greater Philidor.

Philidor, by far the greatest player France has ever produced,

André Danican Philidor

Pierre de Saint-Amant

spent most of his later years in England: there now ensued a rivalry between France and England whereby the best player or players of each side contested matches against each other and in which at first France was triumphant.

Philidor was succeeded by the brilliant and highly gifted natural player Deschapelles, and he in turn was followed and even outshone by his pupil La Bourdonnais, who played and won his famous match in 1834 against the Irishman McDonnell.

By now, though, the supremacy of French chess in Europe was rapidly declining. This decline was temporarily checked by Saint-Amant, but when he was beaten in a famous match in Paris by Staunton in 1843 France declined still more rapidly and Saint-Amant was undoubtedly the last great master France produced.

This was all the more paradoxical in that France became a centre of refuge for all the great masters of Europe. This applied in particular to the Polish players in the late nineteenth century, when such grandmasters as Janowski and Taubenhaus were resident in Paris. A fresh influx of refugee grandmasters came as a result of the Russian Revolution in 1917 with such great figures as Tartakower and Alekhine.

'Les jouers d'echecs' by Daumier

But, astonishingly, not a single native grandmaster emerged, nor has there been one till this day.

It was in the field of chess organization that the Gallic genius showed itself. The French Chess Federation was founded by Henri Delaire in 1921 and he was its first President. It was in 1924 that its Secretary-general, Pierre Vincent, played the leading role in the founding of FIDE. Vincent was followed by a series of active presidents, amongst whom Pierre Biscay, Marcel Berman and Raoul Berthelot were the most active.

It was the last-named who organized the Olympiad at Nice in 1974, but a sign that, despite all this intensive organizing activity, French chess was still in the doldrums was that France came as low as 28th at Nice, though this was an advance on its 48th place at Skopje in 1972.

French students take a break from studies

The address of the French Chess Federation: Fédération Française des Echecs, 105 Bvd Sébastopol, 75002 Paris, France.

There are two French chess magazines:

Europe-Echecs, c/o S. Zinser, 47 Av. Kennedy, 68200 Mulhouse.

Mat!, c/o M. Drouilly, 19 Res. l'Arcadie, 1 Grande Rue-Saintry, 91100 Corbeil-Essonnes. *(H.G.)*

FRANCO-INDIAN [Keres] DEFENCE

As its name suggests, this defence combines features of the French and Nimzo-Indian defences. It occurs after 1. P–Q4, P–K3; 2. P–QB4, B–N5+.

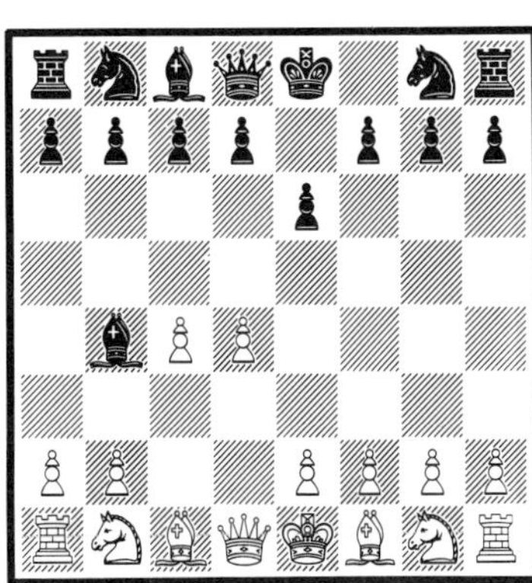

Although barely explored, it probably offers adequate chances to Black. *(R.D.K.)*

FRANKLIN, Benjamin *(17 January 1706–17 April 1790)*
Benjamin Franklin tells in his autobiography how useful the playing of chess was in his life, but his most frequently quoted writings about chess come from a piece entitled *The Morals of Chess*, Philadelphia 1786. In it he likens the game to life itself: 'The game of chess is not merely an idle amusement; several very valuable qualities of the mind, useful in the course of human life, are to be acquired and strengthened by it, so as to become ready on all occasions; for life is a kind of Chess, in which we have often points to gain, and competitors or adversaries to contend with, and in which there is a vast variety of good and ill events that are, in some degree, the effect of prudence, or the want of it. . . .' *(H.G.)*

FRENCH DEFENCE
Characterized by the moves 1. P–K4, P–K3 the French defence is one of Black's most popular responses to 1. P–K4. The most important variations are as follows: 2. P–Q4, P–Q4; and now:

(*a*) 3. P–K5, the Advance variation, favoured by Nimzowitsch, but nowadays relatively unpopular.

(*b*) 3. N–QB3, N–KB3; 4. B–KN5 is the Classical variation, leading to Burn's variation (4. . , P×P); the Chatard-Alekhine Attack (4. . , B–K2; 5. P–K5, KN–Q2; 6. P–KR4); and the MacCutcheon System (4. . , B–N5).

(*c*) 3. P×P, P×P; is the very drawish Exchange variation.

(*d*) 3. N–QB3, N–KB3; 4. P–K5, is the Steinitz variation, originally played with the continuation 4. . , KN–Q2; 5. QN–K2, though nowadays 5. P–B4 is generally preferred.

(*e*) 3. N–Q2 is the Tarrasch variation, usually met by 3. . , P–QB4 or 3. . , N–KB3; though also possible is 3. . , N–QB3 (Guimard's line).

(*f*) 3. N–QB3, B–N5 is the Winawer variation (also known as the Nimzowitsch variation) and forms perhaps the single most important system in this opening today. After 4. P–K5, P–QB4;

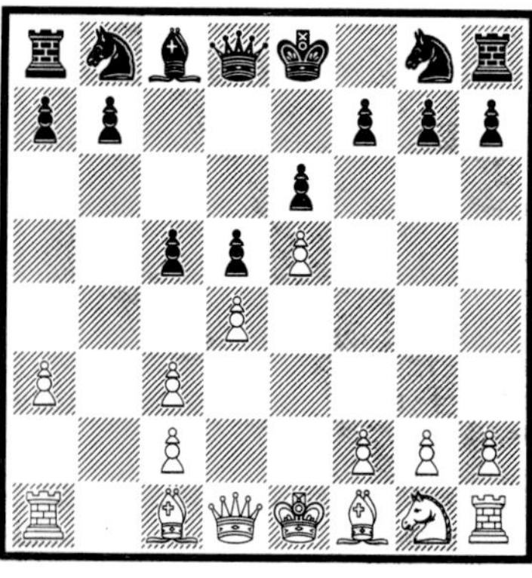

5. P–QR3, B×N+; 6. P×B, Black hopes to take advantage of White's Queen-side weaknesses, while his opponent tries to utilize the Bishop pair and attack the weakened Black squares.

The French was most popular during Botvinnik's reign when the World Champion adopted it with great success; now Uhlmann is probably its chief protagonist. *(W.R.H.)*

FREYMANN, Sergei Nikolayevich *(1882–1946)*
One of the strongest Russian masters around the period of the Revolution. Won a match against Znosko-Borovsky in 1911. Moved to Tashkent on the formation of the USSR, and four times won the championship of Uzbekistan. Took second place in the final of the sixth USSR championship 1929. *(W.R.H.)*

FRIEDGOOD, David *(b. 1944)*
The most talented player to emerge from the Republic of South Africa in recent years, he has nevertheless suffered from the isolated position of South Africa in the world chess fraternity. He was many times winner of the Republic's closed championship and regular top board for South Africa on those occasions when his country's presence in Olympiads was permitted.

His best international results are =7th at the Caorle Zonal tournament of 1972, and =3rd (below Najdorf and Stean) with Keene in the strongest South African Open championship at Cape Town 1976.

His domination of South African internal chess was heavily underlined by his victory in the 'Top Chess' tournament at Durban 1976, ahead of Kroon, De Villiers, Walker, Korostenski and Price. *(R.D.K.)*

FRIENDS OF CHESS
A society founded in 1969 with the express objective of restoring Britain to the leading place it had occupied amongst the world's chess nations in the nineteenth century.

Founding members were: C. H. O'D. Alexander, David Anderson, Sir Richard Clarke, Harry Golombek, Ralph Hopton and Sir Stuart Milner-Barry.

These also constituted the original committee with Clarke as chairman, Anderton secretary and Hopton treasurer. In order to provide funds with which to aid and initiate such chess enterprises as international tournaments, matches, team events etc. and also – perhaps most important of all – to assist British players to take part in such international events, a yearly subscription (for members £8 and for patrons £30) was instituted.

After six years the composition of the committee had changed through the passing of Alexander and Clarke; but both these distinguished members of the society had lived long enough to see some tangible results of the Friends' activities.

Address: The Treasurer, Friends of Chess, Juniper Cottage, South Park Crescent, Gerrards Cross, Bucks SL9 8HJ, England. *(H.G.)*

FROM, Martin *(8 May 1828–6 May 1895)*
Danish master, 12th in the Paris 1867 tournament. The opening 1. P–KB4, P–K4 is called the From Gambit, and dates from his game against Møllerstrøm, 1862. *(R.D.K.)*

FRYDMAN, Paulino *(b. 26 May 1905)*
Polish international master who remained in the Argentine after the outbreak of the Second World War in 1939.

He had a most consistent record in the Olympiads before the

Second World War, playing for his country in all of them with the exception of London 1927. He had some excellent tournament results in the period 1934–41. An =3rd with Flohr at Budapest 1934 was followed by an =3rd with H. Friedmann at Warsaw 1935. In 1936 he came 1st at Helsinki ahead of Keres and Ståhlberg. At the strong tournament of Podebrady that year he came =6th with Eliskases out of 18.

His last good tournament in Europe was at Lodz in 1938 where he came 7th/16.

Left behind at the Buenos Aires Olympiad 1939, he came =4th with Engels at Mar del Plata 1941 and was 3rd at Buenos Aires 1941. Then he gave up chess as far as international tournaments were concerned. *(H.G.)*

FUCHS, Reinhardt *(b. 28 September 1934)*
An East German international master, regular member of the East German team in the decade 1956–66. His most notable international successes were =2nd at Kienbaum 1959, 2nd at Bad Salzungen 1960, =4th at Leipzig 1964, 3rd at Zinnowitz 1966, and 5th at the Zonal tournament of Vrnjačka Banja 1966. *(W.H.)*

FUDERER, Andrija *(b. 13 May 1931)*
Yugoslav international master (1953). Considered for many years even more gifted than Ivkov and Matanovič. In 1955 Fuderer took part in the Göteborg Interzonal, but without distinction. Commanded world attention after his brilliant win 3–1 against World title contender David Bronstein in USSR v. Yugoslavia 1957. Deciding to devote his career to chemical research (he holds a doctorate in chemistry), Fuderer quit chess prematurely, depriving Yugoslavia of a potential World title challenger.

Best result: =2nd Belgrade 1952. Competed six times in Yugoslav championship. Represented Yugoslavia in three Olympiads, Helsinki 1952 (70%), Amsterdam 1954 (71%), Munich 1958 (77%). His style was that of a fighter in the mould of Tal. *(R.D.K.)*

FULLER, John A. *(b 12 May 1928)*
British master and design engineer by profession. British Boy champion in 1946. Fuller was a player of great promise with a fine understanding of the game. But a serious illness disturbed the even flow of his chess career and, though he recovered and made some more appearances in the chess world, he eventually withdrew from chess on an international and national level.

Fuller played twice in the Hastings Premier tournament: =5th 1949/50 and 6th in 1955/6. *(H.G.)*

FULLER, Max(well) Leonard *(b. 28 January 1945)*
Australian master who has spent much of his time in Europe and is a chess professional.

He was New South Wales Under 16 champion in 1960 and New South Wales Junior (Under 18) champion in 1962. In 1963 he won the Australian Junior championship and scored 50% in the World Junior Championship at Vrnjačka Banja in Yugoslavia.

He won the New South Wales championship in 1965 and has been five times Sydney champion (the first time being in 1964). Australian co-champion in 1972, he has won the Australian Open championship in 1973 and 1975.

His record in the British championship is 10th in 1969, =2nd 1970 and again =2nd in 1975.

He made the best score, 6 out of 7, on Board 1 in the Asian Team championship at Penang in 1974.

He has represented Australia in the Olympiads in 1964, 1968, 1970, 1972, 1974 and 1976. *(H.G.)*

FURMAN, Semyon Abramovich *(b. 1 December 1920)*
One of the older generation of Soviet grandmasters, Furman gained the title of international master in 1954 and grandmaster 1966. His best results in the USSR championship were 3rd in 1948 and 5th in 1949. Best result in international competition was undoubtedly his 1st at Harrachov 1966.

Furman is now best known as a theoretician and the chief trainer of Anatoly Karpov. *(W.R.H.)*

GAMBIT
In modern usage, any opening which involves the planned sacrifice of material, usually in the interests of some objective such as central control or rapid development. The word derives originally from the Italian *gamba*, 'a leg'. In the sixteenth century, Italian wrestlers coined the term *gambitare*, meaning roughly 'to set a trap', e.g. by offering the opponent a leg-hold. Ruy Lopez introduced the word into chess vocabulary to describe a variation of Damiano's Defence: 1. P–K4, P–K4; 2. N–KB3, P–KB3; 3. N×P, P×N; 4. Q–R5+, P–N3; 5. Q×KP+, Q–K2; 6. Q×R, N–KB3. *(R.D.K.)*

GAME OF THE CENTURY
The title bestowed by Kmoch on the game won by thirteen-year-old Bobby Fischer against D. Byrne at the Rosenwald tournament, New York 1956. From the accompanying text, however, it is clear that he meant this title to be understood in the context of chess

produced by boy prodigies (*Chess Review*, December 1956). However, the accolade has come to be accepted without any such qualification:

White: D. Byrne; *Black:* Fischer
Grünfeld Defence
1. N–KB3, N–KB3; 2. P–B4, P–KN3; 3. N–B3, B–N2; 4. P–Q4, O–O; 5. B–B4, P–Q4; 6. Q–N3, P×P; 7. Q×BP, P–B3; 8. P–K4, QN–Q2; 9. R–Q1, N–N3; 10. Q–B5, B–N5; 11. B–KN5, N–R5; 12. Q–R3, N×N; 13. P×N, N×P; 14. B×P, Q–N3; 15. B–B4, N×QBP; 16. B–B5, KR–K1+; 17. K–B1;

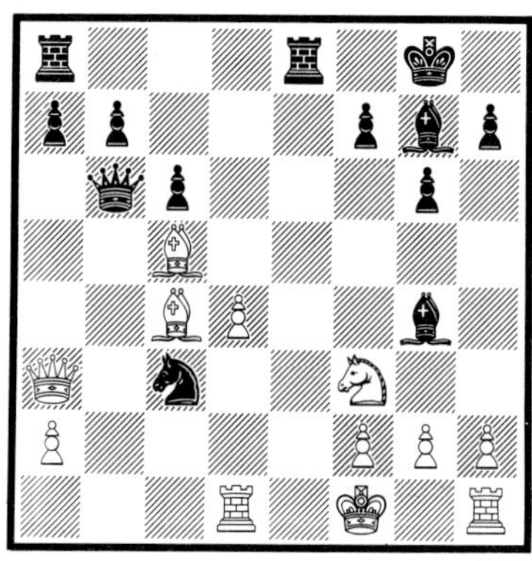

17.., B–K3; 18. B×Q, B×B+; 19. K–N1, N–K7+; 20. K–B1, N×P dis+; 21. K–N1, N–K7+; 22. K–B1, N–B6 dis+; 23. K–N1, P×B; 24. Q–N4, R–R5; 25. Q×P, N×R; 26. P–KR3, R×P; 27. K–R2, N×P; 28. R–K1, R×R; 29. Q–Q8+, B–B1; 30. N×R, B–Q4; 31. N–B3, N–K5; 32. Q–N8, P–QN4; 33. P–R4, P–R4; 34.., N–K5, K–N2; 35. K–N1, B–B4+; 36. K–B1, N–N6+; 37. K–K1, B–N5+; 38. K–Q1, B–N6+; 39. K–B1, N–K7+; 40. K–N1, N–B6+; 41. K–B1, R–B7 mate. *(W.H.)*

GAPRINDASHVILI, Nona *(b. 3 May 1941)*
Born in Tbilisi, Gaprindashvili was to become the most successful woman player of her generation. She won the USSR Women's championship in 1964, when she was already Women's World Champion, having defeated Bykova in the 1962 title match. Subsequently she has successfully defended the title three times against Kushnir and once against Alexandria. She holds the titles of international woman grandmaster (1976) and international master (1962).

Gaprindashvili has also competed with success in men's tournaments, including winning the Hastings Challengers tournament in 1963/4 and finishing 5th in the Premier tournament the following year. In 1976 she played in a strong Swiss System tournament at Sandomierz in Poland and came =2nd with Knaak (East Germany) and Nisman (USSR) with 7 points, below Bronstein 8, but above two grandmasters, Smejkal (Czechoslovakia) and Schmidt (Poland).

The distinctive mark of Gaprindashvili as a player is her power of seizing and retaining the initiative. This is well shown by the following game from her second match with Kushnir in 1969.

White: Kushnir; *Black:* Gaprindashvili
Réti Opening
1. P–QB4, N–KB3; 2. N–KB3, P–B4; 3. P–KN3, P–QN3; 4. B–N2, B–N2; 5. O–O, P–K3; 6. P–N3, B–K2; 7. B–N2, O–O; 8. P–K3, P–Q4; 9. P×P, N×P; 10. P–Q4, P×P; 11. N×P, N–QB3; 12. N×N, B×N; 13. N–B3, N×N; 14. B×N, B×B; 15. K×B, R–B1; 16. B–N2, Q×Q; 17. KR×Q, R–B7; 18. R–Q7, B–N4; 19. B–Q4,

Nona Gaprindashvili wearing the laurel World Champion's wreath, Moscow 1969

19.., P–K4; 20. B×KP, B×P; 21. R×RP, B×P; 22. K–R3, P–R4; 23. B–B4, R–Q1; 24. R–QB1, R–K7; 25. R–B3, B–N8; 26. P–KN4, R–Q5; 27. R–B8+, K–R2; 28. R×P, K–N3; 29. R(B8)–B7, R–Q6+; 30. resigns.

White is mated however she replies. For if 30. K–R4, B–B7+; 31. B–N3, B×B+; 32. P×B, R–R7 mate. *(W.R.H.)*

GARCIA, Guillermo [G. Garcia Gonzales] *(b. 9 August 1953)*
Cuban grandmaster and professional chess-player. He obtained the international master title in 1974 and in that year played with success on top board for Cuba in the World Students Team championship at the Teesside. But his best performance of the year was his =4th with Andersson, Larsen and Polugayevsky with 9½ points at the Las Palmas tournament. This was half a point more than the norm required for the grandmaster title. He failed to repeat this form at the Arrecife de Lanzarote tournament that followed on immediately after the Las Palmas event and came =6th with Martz and Kavalek, achieving an international master result only. He fared even worse on his first appearance at Hastings 1974/5 where he came =12th with Csom. But in 1976 he came =1st with Rogoff and Sigurjonsson at Orense (Spain) and this gave him his second grandmaster norm and the title. He established himself as Cuba's strongest player by winning the Cuban championship in 1974 and 1977. Later in 1975 he won a tournament in Plovdiv and was =1st at Zürich. *(H.G.)*

GARCIA, Raimundo *(b. 27 May 1936)*
Argentine international master (1965). Joint Argentinian champion 1963. =3rd with Mecking in 1969 South American Zonal, he lost the play-off (+0−2=1). *(R.D.K.)*

GARCIA, Silvino [**S. Garcia Martinez**] *(b. 4 August 1944)*
Silvino Garcia Martinez, international master (1970), became the first Cuban to earn the FIDE grandmaster title in 1975. He has won the Cuban national championship three times: 1968, 1970 and 1973. Best results include 1st in Pan-American tournament 1968 and =3rd in Capablanca Memorial, Cienfuegos 1973. Regular member of Cuban Olympic team. *(R.D.K.)*

GELLER, Yefim [**Efim**] **Petrovich** *(b. 8 March 1925)*

One of the most consistent of the post-war grandmasters. However, it was not until the early 1950s that Geller really began to make his mark on the chess-world. In 1951 he shared second place in the nineteenth USSR championship with Petrosian behind Keres, and the following year secured his first good international results with second prize at Budapest and fourth place in the Interzonal tournament. This latter result qualified him for the Candidates tournament and also gained Geller the title of international grandmaster. In the Candidates of 1953 he shared sixth place with Najdorf.

In 1955 Geller won the USSR championship after beating Smyslov in a play-off match. During the next two decades his tournament results continued to be impressive, including first places at Dresden 1959, Göteborg 1967/8, Kislovodsk 1968, Budapest 1973, Middlesbrough (Alexander Memorial tournament) 1975, Moscow 1975 and Las Palmas 1976. His results in the World Championship qualifying competitions have also been remarkably consistent. Geller played in the Candidates stage on six occasions between 1953 and 1971, finishing =6th in 1953, =3rd in 1956 and =2nd with Keres in 1962 (subsequently losing the play-off to decide the runner-up). In the Candidates matches of 1965, Geller scored a surprisingly easy first round win against Smyslov by $5\frac{1}{2}$–$2\frac{1}{2}$, but went out by precisely the same score in the semi-final against Spassky. In the 1968 and 1971 Candidates Geller did not progress beyond the first round, losing $5\frac{1}{2}$–$2\frac{1}{2}$ on both occasions, first to Spassky again and then to Korchnoi.

In recent World Championship contests, Geller has acted as second to Spassky in 1972, and to Karpov throughout the 1975 series. He is noted for his theoretical preparedness and deep understanding of theoretical problems in the openings.

Middlesbrough 1975
White: Geller; *Black:* Stean
Sicilian Defence
1. N–KB3, P–QB4; 2. P–QB4, P–KN3; 3. P–Q4, P×P; 4. N×P, N–QB3; 5. P–K4, N–B3; 6. N–QB3, P–Q3; 7. B–K2, N×N; 8. Q×N, B–N2; 9. B–N5, B–K3; 10. R–QB1, Q–R4; 11. Q–Q2, R–QB1; 12. P–B3!, B×P; 13. N–Q5!, Q×P; 14. O–O!, N×N;

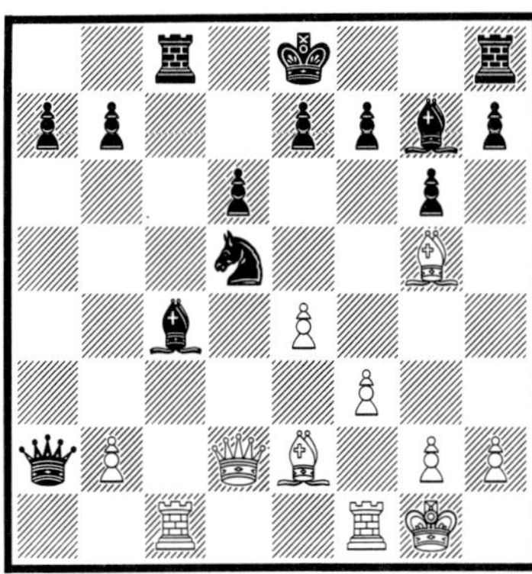

15. R×B!, R×R; 16. Q×N, R–R5; 17. B–N5+, K–B1; 18. R–B1!, resigns. *(W.R.H.)*

GEREBEN, Erno *(b. 18 June 1907)*
Hungarian-Swiss international master who left Hungary for Switzerland in 1956 and made his home there.

Practically all Gereben's successes in the international field have been confined to small tournaments or reserve tournaments (masters as opposed to grandmaster events). In the great Budapest 1952 tournament, for example, he came 15th/18. He represented Hungary in the 1954 Olympiad at Amsterdam and scored 60% on bottom board.

His best results in the Swiss championship are 3rd in 1957, 4th in 1958 and 2nd in 1961.

His tournament successes: 1st at Zoppot 1951; 2nd at S. Benedetto del Tronto 1957; 3rd at Hastings 1958/9 above Darga and Dückstein; =1st at Bognor Regis 1959; =4th with Dückstein at Zürich 1960; =1st with Barcza, Flesch and Teschner at Reggio Emilia 1963/4; 5th in the Masters Section at Beverwijk (Hoogoven) 1965; =2nd in the I.B.M. Amsterdam tournament (Masters group) 1967 and 4th in the Masters group at Monte Carlo 1969. *(H.G.)*

GERMAN, Eugenio *(b. 24 October 1930)*
Brazilian international master since 1952 and Brazilian national champion in 1951. Has represented his country twice in Olympiads (1952, 1968) and qualified for the Stockholm 1962 Interzonal, finishing =19th out of 23. *(R.D.K.)*

GERMAN FOUR MASTERS TOURNAMENT 1937

The Four Masters tournament at Bad Nauheim, Stuttgart and Garmisch-Partenkirchen (July 1937), a small double-round event, was the only tournament of importance Euwe won outright in his whole career. Alekhine set off in the lead, but lost both his games at Stuttgart, against Euwe and Bogoljubow, the former turning out to be the decisive game of the tournament. Bogoljubow was last at half-way but finished with three wins. Sämisch scored only once, but the game showed him to belong in this company. Scores: Euwe 4, Alekhine, Bogoljubow 3½, Sämisch 1.

White: Sämisch; *Black:* Bogoljubow
Queen's Gambit Declined, Cambridge Springs Defence
1. P–Q4, P–Q4; 2. P–QB4, P–QB3; 3. N–KB3, N–B3; 4. N–B3, P–K3; 5. B–N5, QN–Q2; 6. P–K3, Q–R4; 7. N–Q2, B–N5; 8. Q–B2, O–O; 9. B–K2, P×P; 10. B×N, N×B; 11. N×P, Q–B2; 12. O–O, N–Q4; 13. B–Q3, P–KN3; 14. P–QR3, B–K2; 15. QR–B1, B–Q2; 16. N–K5, B–K1; 17. B–B4, R–Q1; 18. N–Q3, B–Q3; 19. P–KN3, Q–K2; 20. KR–Q1, B–Q2; 21. P–K4, N–N3; 22. P–K5, N×B; 23. N–K4, P–QN4; 24. P–QN3, B×RP; 25. P×N, B×R;

26. N–B6+, K–N2; 27. Q×B, P–KR3; 28. P–B5, B–B1; 29. Q–KB4, P–QR4; 30. P–R4, P–N5; 31. Q–K4, R–Q4; 32. N–B4, KR–Q1; 33. P–R5, R×KP; 34. P×R, R×R+; 35. K–N2, R–Q1; 36. P×P, Q×P; 37. P×P, K–B1; 38. Q–R7, resigns. *(W.H.)*

GERMANY

Prior to the 1830s, chess in Germany was of little account. The standard of play was much lower than in Britain or France, and the literature of the game in no way comparable to the works of Philidor, Allgaier, Sarratt and others.

The only man to have made a name for himself, both as a player and a problemist, was Julius Mendheim, of Berlin (*d.* 1836), who was the teacher of Bledow, the acknowledged leader of the 'Berlin Pleiades' whose theoretical, practical and literary achievements began to change the sorry image of German chess. Death and change of domicile brought the period of the Pleiades to an end in 1846, but Berlin chess continued to flourish with such players as Max Lange, Dufresne, Goltz, Von Oppen, and later Hirschfeld, Neumann, Schallopp, Suhle, etc.

But the cultivation of chess was not confined to Berlin in those years. In Leipzig the famous Augustea Chess Club was founded in 1848, and players like Hirschbach, Count von Vitzthum, and later Max Lange and Minckwitz made the city one of the chess centres of nineteenth-century Germany. In Hamburg there were Popert and, for a while, Horwitz, and in Breslau the man who, above all others, helped German chess to attain fame throughout the world: Anderssen.

In the south and south-west of Germany, however, chess stayed mainly in the coffee houses (though there were a handful of chess clubs as early as the 1840s); and the only player of master strength seems to have been Max Bezzel, of Ansbach (Franconia). Anderssen's victory in the first international tournament of modern times, London 1851, and its subsequent confirmation at London 1862, gave a decisive impetus to German chess: from the 1860s to the outbreak of the First World War Germany became the leading chess nation.

Louis Paulsen

The generation of Anderssen and Paulsen, and of their contemporaries and pupils such as Hirschfeld, Minckwitz, and Riemann, was followed by the era of Lasker and Tarrasch, Mieses and Teichmann. Tarrasch especially, the *Praeceptor Germaniae* through his writings in both books and newspaper columns, exerted

Othon, Marquis of Brandebourg playing chess with his wife. From a 14th century drawing.

an influence on German, and with it European, chess that players growing up in today's quite different circumstances would find difficult to imagine (and, perhaps, to endure). Chess that did not bear the seal of approval from the doctor of Nuremberg was no chess at all. Lasker, whose achievements – based on a chess philosophy both more practical and more profound – might have neutralized this dogmatism, was resident in England and the USA for most of the early years of his World Championship tenure, thus giving Tarrasch a free hand in Germany.

But it was not only the players and writers that made German chess pre-eminent in this period, but also the accomplishments of German chess organization. The German Chess Federation was inaugurated in Leipzig in 1877, on the occasion of an international tournament in Anderssen's honour – the veteran himself finished in a tie for 2nd with Zukertort, half a point behind L. Paulsen.

From 1879 onwards, the new organization arranged strong international congresses virtually every other year, featuring a master tournament and, from 1883 onwards, one of several *Hauptturniere* (major tournaments), the only exception being the tenth congress at Eisenach 1896 where, owing to internal dissension, there was no master tournament; however, a rival congress put on what was possibly the strongest event in German chess history, the great tournament of Nuremberg 1896. Important though these master tournaments were, the event that achieved most for the game was the international *Hauptturnier* A (a Premier Reserves event whose winner acquired the master title). It is no exaggeration to say that virtually all the great international masters-to-be received their baptism of fire in these tournaments. To them must be added that of Barmen 1905, where Bernstein and Rubinstein gained the master title; though run on similar lines, this was not an official German Chess Federation congress.

Details of the nineteen congresses held between 1879 and 1914 will be found at the end of this survey. That the last of them, Mannheim 1914, was disrupted by the outbreak of war (the Russian participants being interned in various places in the state of Baden), proved to be a symbol of what was to come: it deprived Lasker of his pre-eminence as a player, Tarrasch of his as a teacher, and the German Chess Federation of its pre-eminence as an organizer.

The post-war generation of German masters – Sämisch, Ahues, Wagner, Carls, Brinckmann, Helling, Richter, etc. – was no longer able to win important international tournaments, while the important events organized on German soil after the war (such as Baden-Baden 1925, Dresden 1926, Bad Kissingen 1928 as well as the various tournaments at Berlin in 1920, 1926, 1927 and 1928) owed their existence to private sponsors and not to the German Chess Federation.

Worst of all, the schooling of a whole international master generation in the *Hauptturniere* had come to an end, and it is at least partly due to this break with a beneficial tradition that the lead in international chess passed to the USSR and the USA: it was not only German, but Western and Central European chess as a whole that was the sufferer. The only two events that kept German chess in the international running in those days were the recovery of Lasker and the naturalization of Bogoljubow.

Em. Lasker in play against Capablanca, the Dynamo Factory 1925

Under the Nazis little of permanent value was added to chess despite the super-spectacle of the 'Olympiad' of Munich 1936. Their main contribution was *Kampfschach* ('fighting chess'), a concept of the same meaningless absurdity as the 'Russian style of chess' of which so much was heard a little later. The war years, however, saw a number of important tournaments, both in Germany and in the occupied territories (Munich 1941, Cracow/Warsaw 1941, Salzburg 1942, Munich 1942, Warsaw/Lublin/Cracow 1942, Salzburg 1943), and the emergence of Klaus Junge, who at the age of eighteen was virtually the equal of Alekhine. His death, during the last days of the war, deprived Germany of her finest prospect since Lasker.

The immediate post-war period brought an interesting development: politically ostracized, Germany organized her own international tournaments: the 'Displaced Persons' tournaments, mostly in the southern and south-western parts of Germany. Thus in the years 1946 to 1948 a country without any overall chess organization put on a whole string of small but very strong tournaments, in which refugees from the East and other displaced players (mostly from the Baltic countries and the Ukraine), such as Paul Schmidt, Bohatirchuk, Bogenko, Endzelins, Zemgalis, Ozols and Tautvaisas, met the surviving German masters (Bogoljubow, Rellstab, Kieninger, Ahues, etc.) and members of the new generation, e.g. Unzicker, Tröger and Niephaus.

The first 'real' international tournament took place in Heidelberg in 1949, and the first FIDE event entrusted to the new German Chess Federation in Bad Pyrmont 1951.

For the past twenty-five years or so German chess, like Germany itself, has been divided between East and West (the only attempt at an all-German championship at Leipzig 1953 not being repeated). Both Germanies have worked their way up into the top echelons of international chess. While the East German team had a couple of near misses, the West German representatives have always finished in the top section of Olympiads and at Dubrovnik 1950 and Tel Aviv 1964 finished as high as third (on the latter occasion they became one of only two teams ever to have inflicted a defeat on the USSR team in the whole history of the Olympiads).

Both countries have a number of grandmasters (Hübner, Unzicker, L. Schmid, Darga, Pfleger and Hecht in the West;

Uhlmann, Knaak and Pietzsch in the East) and many international masters. Two players, Hübner and Uhlmann, have succeeded in qualifying for the Candidates matches of the World Championship cycles. While both countries have organized many strong international tournaments, none of the outstanding post-war events (except for three Olympiads) have taken place on German territory.

The following is a list of the German Chess Federation congresses between 1879 and 1914;

	Master	*Hauptturnier*
Leipzig 1879	1st Englisch 2nd Paulsen	– –
Berlin 1881	1st Blackburne 2nd Zukertort	– –
Nuremberg 1883	1st Winawer 2nd Zukertort	 Tarrasch
Hamburg 1885	1st Gunsberg =2nd Blackburne, Englisch, Mason, Tarrasch, Weiss	Harmonist
Frankfurt Main 1887	1st Mackenzie =2nd Blackburne, Weiss	Bauer (Vienna)
Breslau 1889	1st Tarrasch 2nd Burn	Em. Lasker
Dresden 1892	1st Tarrasch =2nd Makover, Porges	Lipke
Kiel 1893	=1st Von Bardeleben, Walbrodt	Süchting
Leipzig 1894	1st Tarrasch 2nd Lipke	Van Lennep
Eisenach 1896	–	Barnes W. Cohn
Cologne 1898	1st Burn =2nd Charousek, Chigorin, W. Cohn	Pavelik Löwenthal
Munich 1900	=1st Pillsbury, Schlechter	Loerbroeks, Swiderski
Hanover 1902	1st Janowski 2nd Pillsbury	John Forgács
Coburg 1904	=1st Von Bardeleben, Schlechter, Swiderski	Neumann (Vienna)
Nuremberg 1906	1st Marshall 2nd Dûras	Tartakower
Düsseldorf 1908	1st Marshall 2nd Salwe	Köhnlein Moll
Hamburg 1910	1st Schlechter 2nd Dûras	Rotlewi, Barcza, Johner
Breslau 1912	=1st Dûras, Rubinstein	Gregory Krüger
Mannheim 1914	1st Alekhine 2nd Vidmar	Hallegua, Rabinovich

Winners of the German championships have been as follows:

1877	L. Paulsen	1914	Alekhine
1879	Englisch	1921	Post
1881	Blackburne	1922	Post
1883	Winawer	1923	Grünfeld
1885	Gunsberg	1925	Bogoljubow
1887	Mackenzie	1927	Spielmann
1889	Tarrasch	1929	Ahues
1892	Tarrasch	1931	Bogoljubow
1893	Bardeleben and Walbrodt	1933	Bogoljubow
1894	Tarrasch	1934	Carls
1898	Burn	1935	K. Richter
1900	Pillsbury and Schlechter	1937	Kieninger
1902	Janowski	1938	Eliskases
1904	Bardeleben and Schlechter	1939	Eliskases
1906	Marshall	1940	Kieninger
1908	Marshall	1941	P. Schmidt
1910	Schlechter	1942	Rellstab
1912	Dûras and Rubinstein	1943	Lokvenc

Since the Second World War there have been separate championships for East and West Germany. Winners of the West German championship, which has retained the numbering sequence of the original German championships, are:

1947	Kieninger	1961	Darga
1948	Unzicker	1963	Unzicker
1949	Bogoljubow	1965	Unzicker and Pfleger
1950	Unzicker	1967	Besser and Hübner
1951	Teschner	1969	Christoph
1953	Unzicker	1970	Hecht
1955	Darga	1972	Kestler
1957	Tröger	1974	Ostermeyer
1959	Unzicker	1976	Wockenfuss

The first East German championship was held in 1950. The winners have been:

1950	Elstner	1964	Uhlmann
1951	G. Stein	1965	Zinn
1952	Koch	1967	Pietzsch
1953	Fuchs	1968	Uhlmann
1954	Uhlmann	1969	Espig
1955	Uhlmann	1970	Baumbach
1956	Fuchs	1971	Espig
1957	Malich	1972	Schöneberg
1958	Malich	1973	Malich
1959	Pietzsch	1974	Knaak
1961	Zinn	1975	Uhlmann
1962	Pietzsch	1976	Uhlmann
1963	Möhring		

Chess in West Germany is administered by the Deutscher

Schachbund, Sülzhaynerstrasse 11, 1 Berlin 44; in East Germany by the Deutscher Schachverband, Storkowerstrasse 118, 1055 Berlin. Both countries have chess journals. *(W.H. & K.J.O'C.)*

GERUSEL, Mathias *(b. 5 February 1938)*
A West German international master, Gerusel drew attention to himself by finishing second to Lombardy (to whom he lost a sensational miniature) in the World Junior Championship 1957. His best results in international tournaments have been 3rd prize (behind Larsen and Polugayevsky) at Bussum 1969 and =5th at Solingen 1974. *(W.H.)*

GHANA
Only recently affiliated to FIDE, Ghana has yet to make its début in the international arena. The Ghana Chess Federation's address is P.O. Box 94444, Kotoka Airport, Accra. *(K.J.O'C.)*

GHEORGHIU, Florin *(b. 6 May 1944)*
Romanian grandmaster, Romanian Junior champion 1957 and winner of the Romanian championship eight times since 1960. Became World Junior Champion in 1963 and was awarded the grandmaster title in 1965. Tournament results include: 1st at Bucharest 1967, =1st Hastings 1967/8, =1st Reykjavik 1972, 2nd Helsinki 1972, 1st Orense 1973 and =1st Vratza Zonal 1975. Gheorghiu is a lecturer in languages at Bucharest University. *(R.D.K.)*

GHITESCU, Teodor *(b. 24 January 1934)*
Romanian champion in 1963 and international master since 1961. Frequently represented his country in Olympiads and international tournaments. Probably his best result was his first place in the tournament at Bucharest in 1976. *(W.R.H.)*

GIANUTIO HORATIO DELLA MANTIA *(sixteenth century)*
A player and theorist of the sixteenth century who published in Turin in 1597 a work on the game, *Libro nel quale si tratta della maniera di giuocar à Scacchi* which has become extremely rare, though it was translated into English by J. H. Sarratt in 1817.

Gianutio takes much from Ruy Lopez and Damiano and is a little old-fashioned in his ideas about the rules (he favours free castling with the Rook going to B1 but with the King going where it pleases). He deals with King-side and Queen-side openings, discusses odds (such as Bishop and Knight odds etc.) and also gives some games and problems.

According to Ponziani he was a player of some distinction. *(H.G.)*

GIBAUD, Amedée *(b. 1885)*
French master who was five times French champion: =1st in 1924, and then 1st in 1928, 1930, 1935 and 1940.

His chief claim to fame is having been victim in one of the shortest games ever played, losing a brilliant off-hand game to Lazard in Paris, 1924 (see under BREVITY). *(H.G.)*

GILG, Karl *(b. 20 January 1901)*
A West German international master, of Sudeten descent. He represented his native Czechoslovakia in the Olympiads of 1927, 1928 and 1931, and West Germany in the Europa Cup of 1957. In German championships he was 3rd in 1939, =3rd in 1940 and =4th in 1953.

His greatest international success was to get into the top final at Kecskemet 1927, ahead of several grandmasters. *(W.H.)*

GIPSLIS, Aivar Petrovich *(b. 8 February 1937)*
Soviet international grandmaster since 1967 and many times champion of Latvia. His best result was sharing second place at the Alekhine Memorial tournament in Moscow 1967. Also shared first place at Vrnjačka Banja 1975. Editor of Latvian chess magazine *Sahs.* *(W.R.H.)*

GIUOCO PIANO
Introduced by the moves 1. P–K4, P–K4; 2. N–KB3, N–QB3; 3. B–B4, B–B4 the Giuoco Piano (also known as the Italian Game) is, as its name implies, a quiet way for White to begin the game. The variations with 4. P–Q3 (Giuoco Pianissimo) are simply too quiet to pose Black serious problems, while the sharp lines with 4. P–B3 have been exhaustively analysed and are too well known to be ventured in master chess. A typical continuation is 4. P–B3, N–B3; 5. P–Q4, P×P; 6. P×P, B–N5+; 7. N–B3, N×KP; 8. O–O, B×N; 9. P–Q5 (the Møller Attack), B–B3; 10. R–K1, N–K2; 11. R×N, P–Q3; 12. B–N5, B×B; 13. N×B, O–O; 14. N×RP, K×N; 15. Q–R5+, K–N1; 16. R–R4, P–KB4; 17. Q–R7+, K–B2; 18. R–R6, R–KN1; 19. R–K1, Q–B1; 20. B–N5, R–R1; 21. Q×R, P×R; 22. Q–R7+, K–B3; 23. R×N, Q×R; 24. Q×RP+, with a draw.

Closely related to this opening are the Two Knights Defence and the Evans Gambit, which is probably its most important offshoot. *(W.R.H.)*

GIUSTOLISI, Alberto Mario *(b. 17 March 1928)*
Italian international master and lawyer by profession, Giustolisi is a talented combinative player who has won a number of brilliancy prizes, but whose profession has prevented him from obtaining any outstanding successes in the international field since he has been able to give only a limited time to the game.

He has won the Italian championship four times, in 1952, 1961, 1964 and 1966. He has represented Italy in two Olympiads, in 1950 and 1968.

His best tournament results: =3rd with Christoffel at Lucerne 1950, =6th/18 at the Dublin Zonal tournament 1957 and 1st at Reggio Emilia 1961/2. In 1954 he won a short match against Kottnauer by +2−1=1. *(H.G.)*

GLIGORIĆ, Svetozar *(b. 2 February 1923)*
Yugoslav grandmaster and journalist, Gligorić has been Yugoslavia's most successful player of all time. He learnt chess at an early age but was not a boy prodigy. He first attracted attention in 1939 on his début in the Yugoslav championship when he was

awarded the Yugoslav master title, but his development was interrupted by the outbreak of the Second World War, in which he fought actively for the Yugoslav cause. After the war Gligorić quickly rose to prominence replacing first Pirc and then Trifunović as his country's Number One – a position Gligorić kept for nearly twenty years. He received the international master title in 1950 for his performance in the Mar del Plata tournament of the same year. By 1951 he was already a grandmaster and his tournament results from then on show a consistently upward curve.

Only two years later he took part in the Candidates tournament at Zürich, but without distinction, coming 13th. Years of total dedication to chess brought about a radical change in his style: a predominantly attacking player, he disciplined his temperament and evolved to a curious cross between Rubinstein and Capablanca – a style which has made him world famous.

Svetozar Gligorić at Hastings 1960/1

In 1959 he again qualified for the candidates, coming =5th, thereby gaining recognition as one of the best players in the world outside the USSR. Gligorić has taken part in more tournaments than any other player of comparable stature and boasts an impressive tournament record: 1st in a never-ending stream of tournaments including Mar del Plata 1950, Staunton Memorial 1951, Hastings 1951/2, 1956/7, 1959/60, 1960/1, 1962/3, Dallas 1957, Sarajevo 1961, Tel Aviv 1967, Berlin 1971. Domestically his record is equally impressive. He has competed in eighteen Yugoslav championships, winning eleven times! Gligorić has represented Yugoslavia in all post-war Olympiads, with a best result of 80% on top board at Munich 1958. In matches he beat Ståhlberg in 1949 +2−1=9 and lost to Reshevsky in 1952 +1−2=7.

The secret of Gligorić's success is hard work and dedication. A man of many talents and interests including music and languages, he has always found time for chess and has emerged from any crisis more dedicated than before. He is also well known as a chess author and contributes to many chess magazines. His most outstanding works are *Spassky–Fischer World Championship Match*, New York, London 1972; and (with Sokolov) *Sicilian Defence* [in Serbo-Croat].

A player of near-hero status in Yugoslavia, Gligorić has given a great boost to the popularization of chess in his country. There follows a typical Gligorić game with his favourite defence, to the theory of which he has made a considerable contribution.

Rovinj-Zagreb 1970
White: Petrosian; *Black:* Gligorić
King's Indian Defence
1. P–QB4, P–KN3; 2. N–KB3, B–N2; 3. P–Q4, N–KB3; 4. N–B3, O–O; 5. P–K4, P–Q3; 6. B–K2, P–K4; 7. O–O, N–B3; 8. P–Q5, N–K2; 9. P–QN4, N–R4; 10. N–Q2, N–B5; 11. P–QR4, P–KB4; 12. B–B3, P–KN4; 13. P×P, N×BP; 14. P–N3, N–Q5;

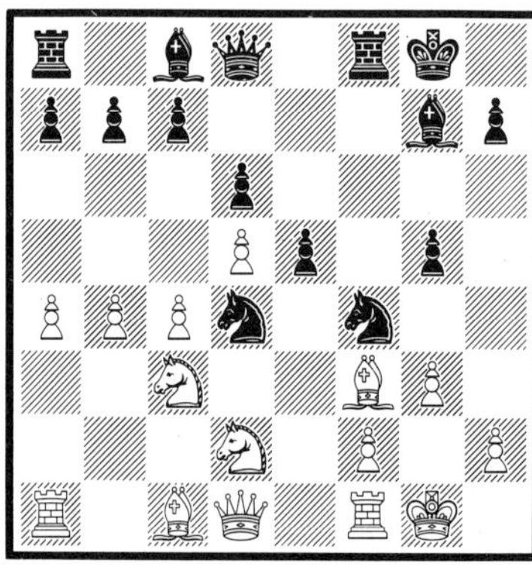

15. P×N, N×B+; 16. Q×N, P–N5; 17. Q–R1, P×P; 18. B–N2, B–B4; 19. KR–K1, P–B6; 20. N(Q2)–K4, Q–R5; 21. P–R3, B–K4; 22. R–K3, P×P; 23. Q×BP, B–N5; 24. Q–R1, P–R7+; 25. K–N2, Q–R4; 26. N–Q2, B–Q5; 27. Q–K1, QR–K1; 28. N(B3)–K4, B×B; 29. R–KN3, B–K4; 30. R(R1)–R3, K–R1; 31. K–R1, R–KN1; 32. Q–KB1, B×R; 33. R×B, R×N; 34. resigns. *(R.D.K.)*

GOGLIDZE, Viktor Arsentyevich

(7 November 1905–15 September 1964)
Soviet international master who was born in Georgia, USSR. He competed three times in Soviet championships, finishing equal fifth in 1937. Given title of international master in 1950. *(W.R.H.)*

GOLMAYO, Celso *(24 April 1820–1 April 1898)*

Born in Logrono, Spain, Golmayo went to Cuba where he practised as a finance lawyer in Havana for many years.

A strong master player, he took part in only one international tournament, the great Paris event of 1867 where he occupied a creditable 7th place.

He specialized in match play and though his start was disastrous when he lost all three games in a small match v. G. R. Neumann in Paris 1867, he returned to the fray sixteen years later and played a match at Havana in 1883 against no less a player than the World Championship, Wilhelm Steinitz, losing by +1−8=2.

All his remaining eight matches were held in Havana, and since his opponents included a selection of the world's best players it is not surprising that he lost nearly all of them. But in many cases he put up a surprisingly good resistance, as the details show.

1887	A. C. Vasquez	+7−0=0
1887	G. H. Mackenzie	+2−5=2
1887	G. H. Mackenzie	+0−5=1
1888	G. H. Mackenzie	+4−7=1
1888	W. Steinitz	+0−5=0
1890	A. C. Vasquez	+7−4=0
1891	J. H. Blackburne	+3−5=2
1893	Em.Lasker	+0−2=1

(H.G.)

GOLOMBEK, Harry *(b. 1 March 1911)*

British international master, three times British champion and the first person to figure in that country's Honours List on account of his services to chess, Golombek was born in London and lived there till the Second World War. Educated at Wilson's Grammar School and the University of London, he became London Boy champion in 1929 and London University champion 1930–3. By this time he was part of a trio of the leading young players in England, the other two being Alexander and Milner-Barry.

His best result in the British championship before the Second World War was =2nd with E. G. Sergeant, ½ a point below Alexander at Brighton 1938. In that year he won first prize in a small international tournament at Antwerp ahead of Koltanowski. In 1938 too he became editor of the *British Chess Magazine* and occupied this post till he entered the army in 1940.

Before the war he had already played in three International Team tournaments (or Olympiads as they subsequently became called) at Warsaw 1935, Stockholm 1937 and Buenos Aires 1939. After the Buenos Aires event he went on to play in an international tournament at Montevideo where he came second to the World Champion, Alexander Alekhine.

In the war he served first in the Royal Artillery, from 1940–1 and then, for the rest of the war, in the Foreign Office at Bletchley Park, employed (like Alexander, Milner-Barry and quite a number of other chess-players) in code-breaking.

After the war he made chess and writing about the game his livelihood, becoming *Times* Chess Correspondent in 1945 and *Observer* Chess Correspondent in 1955. As a player he had a consistently good record in the British championship, coming in the prize list on fourteen out of eighteen occasions he competed in the event. He was British champion at Harrogate 1947, Felixstowe 1949 and Aberystwyth 1955.

He represented England in six more Olympiads, Helsinki 1952, Amsterdam 1954, Moscow 1956, Munich 1958, Leipzig 1960 and Varna, 1962.

His best individual international results were first prizes at small tournaments in Leeuwarden 1947, Baarn 1948 and Paignton 1950 (above Euwe and Donner); =4th with O'Kelly at Beverwijk 1949, =4th with Barcza, Foltys and Gligorić at Venice 1949, and 5th at the European Zonal at Bad Pyrmont 1951, thereby becoming the first British player to have qualified for the Interzonal. He was awarded the O.B.E. in the Queen's Birthday list in 1966.

A founding member of the FIDE Commission for the Rules of Chess, he became a FIDE International Judge and as such officiated at six World Championship matches. He was also chief arbiter at a FIDE Candidates tournament, at an Interzonal and two European team championship finals, etc. When the FIDE President, Dr Euwe, had to return home from Reykjavik before the 1972 Spassky–Fischer match got started, Golombek represented FIDE in Iceland and did much to ensure that the match took place and that it continued to be played.

A prolific writer and translator of books on the game, he has had some thirty-five books published on various aspects of chess. Among them are: *Capablanca's Best Games of Chess*, London, New York 1947; *Réti's Best Games of Chess*, London 1954, New York 1975; *The Game of Chess*, London 1954; *Modern Opening Chess Strategy*, London 1959; *A History of Chess*, London, New York 1976.

(H.G.)

Harry Golombek in play against Borislav Ivkov, Hastings 1955/6

GOLZ, Werner *(8 November 1933–7 October 1974)*
Golz was an East German master, who represented his country in the Olympiads of 1960 and 1964. In East German championships he was 2nd in 1960 and 1964, and 3rd in 1968. He was =1st in the Kurt Richter Memorial tournament in East Berlin 1970. His most important previous success was fifth place in the strong Copenhagen tournament of 1960. After the death of Kurt Richter Golz played an important part on the editorial board of the East German journal *Schach*. *(W.H.)*

GÖTEBORG 1920
Towards the end of and immediately after the First World War, a number of small tournaments were played in territories of the Hapsburg Empire (Kaschau 1918, Budapest 1918) and in Berlin (three Four Masters tournaments in 1918/9), while in the countries on the Allied side there was hardly any international chess.

But the only country with a flourishing chess life in those days was Sweden, where a whole series of tournaments and matches between leading masters were organized. By far the outstanding event was the tournament at Göteborg (August 1920) where, with the exception of Lasker, Alekhine Vidmar and the American grandmasters, all the leading masters of the period competed, while a strong international field of lesser lights did duty in the *Hauptturnier* (major tournaments). In the main event Bogoljubow took an early lead despite his strange third-round loss to Tarrasch, against whom he won a piece on the 10th move. But after scoring 7 out of 9, he lost three games in succession and was passed first by Réti and then by Rubinstein, who fought out a thrilling finish. The disappointments of the tournament were Spielmann and Nimzowitsch. Leading scores: Réti 9½, Rubinstein 9, Bogoljubow 8. *(W.H.)*

GÖTTINGEN MANUSCRIPT
See under LUCENA.

GOTTSCHALL, Hermann von *(16 October 1862–7 March 1933)*
German tournament player, problemist and author. Apart from =2nd (with Mieses, behind Tarrasch) at Nuremberg 1888 and =4th at Kiel 1893, his tournament results were mediocre.

He published two important books: *Adolf Anderssen* (Leipzig 1912), and *Streifzüge durch das Gebiet des Schachproblems* (Berlin-Leipzig 1926). He also edited volumes 4 and 5 of the *Sammlung von Schachaufgaben* founded by Dufresne. *(W.H.)*

GRAF-STEVENSON, Sonja *(15 May 1912–6 March 1965)*
One of the strongest woman players between the wars, Sonja Graf was born in Munich. After local successes she lost to Vera Menchik (+1−3=0) in Amsterdam 1934, and to the German problemist, Heuäcker, by 0–6. Although in Menchik's absence victorious in the Semmering tournament 1936, she was beaten by her at the same venue in 1937 by +2−9=5. After the war she lived in the USA, married to Vernon Stevenson; she was US Woman champion in 1957 and 1964. *(W.H.)*

GRAU, Roberto *(18 March 1910–12 April 1944)*
Argentine master who was the leading player of that country in the period between the First and Second World Wars. A journalist by profession, he devoted most of his time to chess.

He came =4th in the Individual tournament at the Paris Olympiad of 1924 and then played for the Argentine in five Olympiads, 1927, 1928, 1935, 1937 and 1939, mostly on first board.

His best tournament results were both at Mar del Plata; there he was 1st in 1928 and 2nd in 1934. He played three matches, all in Buenos Aires, beating Piazzini in 1935 by +4−2=2 and Jacobo Bolbochan in 1936 by the same score, and losing to Guimard in 1937 by +0−4=4.

He wrote a popular introduction to the game, *Tratado general de Ajedrez*, Buenos Aires 1930. *(H.G.)*

GREAT BRITAIN
See under BRITAIN.

GRECO, Giaochino *(c. 1600–1634)*
The leading seventeenth-century Italian master, Greco travelled widely in Europe playing matches for high stakes. His influence did much to promote interest in chess in those countries which he visited. In 1621 he earned 5,000 crowns by defeating France's three leading players: Arnault le Carabin, Chaumont de la Salle, and the Duc de Nemours. He crossed to England in 1622, where his fortune was stolen en route by brigands. In 1624 he returned to France and spent his last years at the court of Philip IV in Madrid. He died in 1634, while on a trip to the West Indies. Greco published nothing directly, but often sold analyses to wealthy patrons, and some of his manuscripts survive. The Greco Counter-gambit 1. P–K4, P–K4; 2. N–KB3, P–KB4 was not his invention, but he recommended it as sound. *(R.D.K.)*

GRECO COUNTER-GAMBIT
Also known as the Latvian Gambit, this violent attempt by Black to gain the initiative is considered incorrect. After 1. P–K4, P–K4; 2. N–KB3, P–KB4 White has the choice between 3. B–B4, P×P; 4. N×P, Q–N4; 5. P–Q4, leading to complications in his favour; and 3. N×P, Q–B3; 4. N–B4, P×P; 5. N–B3, retaining a positional advantage. *(W.R.H.)*

GREECE
This country's Olympic tradition is reflected in its competition in all the post war Olympiads prior to 1976, results being: 16th in 1950, 20th in 1952, 24th in 1954, 32nd in 1956, 30th in 1958, 35th in 1960, 33rd in 1962, 35th in 1964, 32nd in 1966, 34th in 1968, 31st in 1970, 29th in 1972 and 40th in 1974.

The chronology of the national championships causes considerable confusion because of the habit of holding each tournament in the year after that for which the title is at stake. To avoid, we hope, further confusion, the 24th (1974) championship, played in 1975, was won by Gregoriou and the 25th (1975), played in 1976, was won by Makropoulos. The address of the Greek Chess Federation is Sokratous 79–81, Athens–102. *(K.J.O'C.)*

GREEK GIFT

A term given to the Bishop sacrifice on KR7 with the objective of forcing mate by a concerted action of Queen and Knight. The prerequisite for the Greek gift is that the opponent shall not possess a Knight on either KB3 or KB1; nor should he be in a position to get his Knight to either of these squares in one move after the combination has been executed.

A simple example can be seen in the following position.

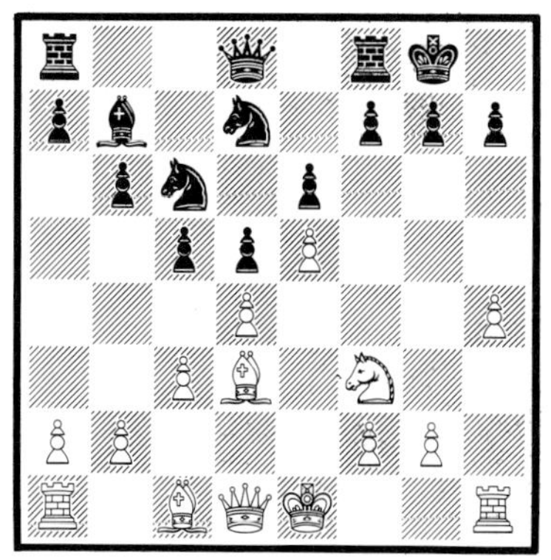

White wins by 1. B × P+, K × B (or *1.., K–R1; 2. N–N5, P–N3; 3. P–R5*); 2. N N5+, and if (*a*) 2.., K–N1; 3. Q–R5, R–K1; 4. Q × P+, K–R1; 5. Q–R5+, K–N1; 6. Q–R7+, K–B1; 7. Q–R8+, K–K2; 8. Q × P mate. Or if (*b*) 2.., K–N3; 3. P–R5+, K–B4; 4. Q–B3 mate, or if (*c*) 2.., K–R3; 3. N × KP+, etc. *(H.G.)*

GREFE, John Alan *(b. 6 September 1947)*

US co-champion in 1973, he became an international master in 1975. He is a devotee of T'ai Chi Chuan and Hatha Yoga. For some years a follower of Guru Maharaj Ji, Grefe's worst results have coincided with newspaper exposées of the Guru's activities. *(K.J.O'C.)*

GRESSER, Gisela *(b. 1910)*

A frequent US Women's champion and representative in women's World Championship qualifying events. She came =12th in the 1949/50 Championship in Moscow. Her best result abroad was =10th in the 1955 women's Candidates event. *(A.S.)*

GROB, Henry *(4 June 1904–8 July 1974)*

A Swiss master, born in Bohemia. International master title 1950. Swiss champion 1939, 1951. The opening 1. P–KN4 is sometimes called Grob's Attack. Best result: =1st with Keres and Fine at Ostend 1937. *(R.D.K.)*

GROB'S ATTACK

1. P–KN4 is a highly irregular opening move which is now seldom played. It does little to further White's development and a lot to weaken his position. After 1. P–KN4, P–Q4; 2. B–N2, P–QB3! Black's position is already preferable. *(R.D.K.)*

GRONINGEN 1946

The 'miracle' tournament of Groningen (August-September 1946) – the miracle being that an event of such magnitude could be organized in war-torn Holland a mere fifteen months after the war – set a new trend in international tournaments. Except for Bogoljubow in the early 1920s and Botvinnik in the 1930s, only two Soviet players had been allowed to play abroad between the wars: Rabinovich at Baden-Baden 1925 and Ragozin at Semmering 1937. Here for the first time a whole team of Soviet masters came to tackle the enemy in his own territory – successfully, as it turned out, for four of the Soviet players occupied first, third, sixth and seventh places and the fifth scored 50%. The tournament thus introduced a period of Soviet domination of international chess which lasted about twenty years till Fischer, Larsen and Portisch succeeded in challenging the might of the USSR.

The contest immediately developed into a duel between Botvinnik and Euwe, the lead changing several times between these two. At half-way (round 10) Botvinnik had scored 9, from Euwe 7½, Denker and Smyslov 7, but five rounds later the score read Euwe 12½, Botvinnik 11½, Smyslov 10½, Szabo 9½. Both leaders were shaky by now, and after Botvinnik had regained the lead both lost in the last round (one of the most sensational on record) – Botvinnik to Najdorf, and Euwe to Kotov.

Leading scores: Botvinnik 14½, Euwe 14, Smyslov 12½, Najdorf, Szabo 11½. *(W.H.)*

GRÜNFELD DEFENCE

1. P–Q4, N–KB3; 2. P–QB4, P–KN3; 3. N–QB3, P–Q4. This defence was introduced by the Austrian grandmaster, Ernst Grünfeld, at the Vienna International tournament of 1922. Its aim is to accentuate pressure on the black squares of the White centre, in particular on White's Q4 and QB3.

The main line used to be 4. P × P, N × P; 5. P–K4, known as the Exchange variation, but this has receded in popularity in favour of quieter treatment such as 4. N–B3, B–N2; 5. P–K3, or 5. Q–N3, P × P; 6. Q × BP, O–O; 7. P–K4, B–N5; 8. B–K3, KN–Q2; (this last move constitutes Smyslov's variation).

It is also possible to play a delayed Grünfeld, otherwise known as the Neo-Grünfeld Defence. This perhaps belongs to the King's Indian Defence but it has much in common with the normal Grünfeld and runs: 1. P–Q4, N–KB3; 2. P–QB4, P–KN3; 3. P–KN3, B–N2; 4. B–N2, P–Q4. *(H.G.)*

GRUNFELD, Ernst F. *(21 November 1893–3 April 1962)*

One of the most successful Austrian grandmasters, especially in the third decade of this century when he played in most of the great international tournaments of the period. In none of these did he come in the bottom half, obtaining high places at Pistyan 1922 (4th), Teplitz-Schönau the same year (3rd), Carlsbad 1923 (=4th), and Mährisch-Ostrau 1923 (3rd). It was, however, in smaller international events that he scored a great number of first prizes, starting with Vienna 1920 (with Tartakower), Margate 1923 (ahead of Alekhine, Bogoljubow and Réti), Merano 1924 (ahead of Spielmann and Rubinstein), Budapest 1926 (with Monticelli), Trebitsch Memorial Vienna 1927, Trebitsch Memorial Vienna 1928 (with Takacs), and Mährisch-Ostrau 1933. A profound theoretician, he originated the Grünfeld Defence to the Queen's Pawn game; he also wrote a volume on the Queen's Pawn openings (1924) and a general opening manual (1953).

Throughout his career Grünfeld was a careful scientific player, who built up his game in accordance with sound principles and shunned incalculable complications. This was both his strength and his limitation; just as he was unable to rise to the occasion of a really big tournament win, so, in the individual game, he was at the wrong end of an unusually large number of brilliancy and other special prizes; so that the games he lost – among others to Maróczy, Vienna 1920; Réti, Pistyan 1922; Alekhine, Carlsbad 1923; Colle, Berlin 1926; Sämisch, Carlsbad 1929; and Eliskases, Mährisch-Ostrau 1933 – belong to the imperishable treasury of chess.

(W.H.)

GUATEMALA

Presided over by the Federacion Nacional de Ajedrez (Palacio Deportes 3er piso, Apartado Postal 1452, Guatemala, C.A.), a team has taken part in two Olympiads, placing 22nd in 1939 and 37th in 1976. *(K.J.O'C.)*

GUERNSEY

Guernsey has competed in every Olympiad since 1970 with the following results: 59th in 1970, 60th in 1972, 63rd in 1974 and 34th in 1976.

An 'Inter Insular' match is played annually against Jersey (not yet affiliated to FIDE). The series, which began in 1931, reached its 39th anniversary in 1976.

The Guernsey Chess Federation is located c/o Mrs W. R. Withers, Grey Lodge, Rohais, St Peter Port. *(K.J.O'C.)*

GUFELD, Eduard Yefimovich *(b. 19 March 1936)*

Soviet international grandmaster. He gained the international master title in 1964 and that of grandmaster in 1967. Winner of international tournaments at Gori 1971, Tbilisi 1971 and 1974. Chess journalist and writer. *(W.R.H)*

GUIMARD, Carlos Enrique *(b. 6 April 1913)*

Argentine grandmaster (1960), international master in 1950. Argentinian champion 1947, 1949, 1953. Best results include: 3rd Mar del Plata 1934, 1st Buenos Aires 1940, 1st Sao Paulo 1941, 2nd Buenos Aires 1945, =5th Mar del Plata 1968. *(R.D.K.)*

GULKO, Boris *(b. 9 February 1947)*

Soviet international grandmaster and psychologist by profession.

Though he learned the game at an early age he did not concentrate on playing it till he had both qualified and established himself as a psychologist. His progress thereafter was astonishingly rapid.

He won the championship of Moscow in 1973 and was first in an international tournament in Moscow University 1973/4.

In 1974 he obtained the first leg of his grandmaster norm by coming =1st with Timman at Sombor. In the same year he came 1st in the 22nd Soviet Championship Qualifying tournament at Daugavpils ahead of Belyavsky and Kupreichik.

In 1975 he was first in the Soviet championship (1st league) at Kishinev. He acquired the international master title that year by coming =1st with Balashov, Savon and Tseshkovsky at Vilnius. In the Soviet championship he came =2nd with Romanovsky, Tal and Vaganian.

In 1976 he obtained the second part of his grandmaster title by coming 2nd at Erevan with 9½ points, a half point above the grandmaster norm. Two months later he won the 13th Capablanca Memorial in Cienfuegos.

A comparative setback followed at the very strong Biel Interzonal that year where he came =13th with Liberzon and Rogoff. This was, however, out of 20 and his 9 point score was almost 50%.

His style of play is original, forceful and that of a true grandmaster. *(H.G.)*

GUMPEL, Charles Godfrey *(d. 1921)*

An English manufacturer of artificial limbs. He was well-known for his inventions, probably the most notable of them being the chess automaton Mephisto. *(K.J.O'C.)*

GUNSBERG, Isidor *(2 November 1854–2 May 1930)*

One of Britain's strongest masters in the late nineteenth century, Gunsberg was of Hungarian Jewish origin, and was born in Budapest. His family emigrated to England in 1863 and he later became a naturalized British subject.

In 1878–9 Gunsberg was employed to work C. G. Gumpel's chess automaton, Mephisto, in which capacity he won the Counties Chess Association Handicap tournament of 1878.

During the 1880s Gunsberg and Blackburne were considered the strongest English players. They contested two matches: the first in 1881 was won by Blackburne (+7−4=2) and the second in 1886 by Gunsberg (+5−2=6). Also in 1886 Gunsberg defeated Bird (+5−1=3). His tournament successes included 1st prizes at Hamburg 1885 and the BCA tournament 1888, and 3rd prize New York 1889. In 1890 he drew a match +9−9=5 against Chigorin and in 1890–1 challenged Steinitz to a match for the World Championship, losing +4−6=9.

After 1893 Gunsberg was troubled by chronic poor health, although he continued to compete in international tournaments until 1914.

New York 1889 (awarded best game prize)
White: Mason; *Black:* Gunsberg
Giuoco Piano
1. P–K4, P–K4; 2. N–KB3, N–QB3; 3. B–B4, B–B4; 4. P–Q3, P–Q3; 5. B–K3, B–N3; 6. P–B3, N–B3; 7. QN–Q2, Q–K2;

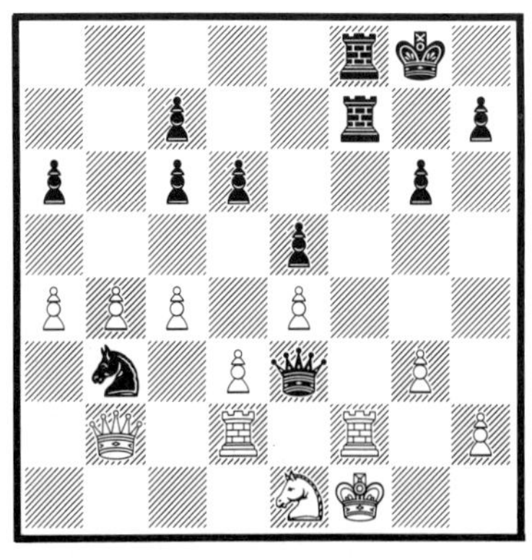

8. P–QR4, B–K3; 9. B–QN5, B×B; 10. P×B, P–QR3; 11. B×N+, P×B; 12. P–QN4, O–O; 13. O–O, N–N5; 14. Q–K2, P–KB4; 15. P×P, B×P; 16. P–K4, B–Q2; 17. N–B4, N–B3; 18. N–K3, P–N3; 19. P–B4, N–R4; 20. P–N3, B–R6; 21. R–B2, N–N2; 22. Q–N2, N–K3; 23. R–K1, R–B2; 24. QR–K2, QR–KB1; 25. N–K1, N–Q5; 26. R–Q2, Q–N4; 27. N(3)–N2, B×N; 28. K×B, Q–K6; 29. K–B1, N–N6; 30. resigns. *(R.D.K.)*

GURGENIDZE, Bukhuti *(b. 13 November 1933)*
Soviet international grandmaster from Georgia. Awarded titles of international master in 1968 and grandmaster in 1970. Shared first place at Tbilisi 1969/70 international tournament and was first outright at Olomouc 1976. Gurgenidze is the trainer of Nana Alexandria. *(W.R.H.)*

GUYANA
The Guyana Chess Association (c/o Miss C. D. Massiah, P.O. Box 1031, Georgetown) has not emerged internationally. However, Guyana has entered the first Telechess Olympiad which is to be played in 1977. *(K.J.O'C.)*

HAÁG, Ervin *(b. 11 January 1933)*
Hungarian international master since 1960. International master at Correspondence Chess since 1961. Shared first place at Debrecen 1961. *(W.R.H.)*

HAMANN, Svend *(b. 8 October 1940)*
Danish international master and in top three of Danish chess in late 1960s and early 1970s. In 1967 he played in a Zonal tournament at Vrnjačka Banja coming =6th with Lengyel, Kostro, Mohrlok and Pachman. The following year he was =4th/14 with Kagan at Natanya. He was second at Amsterdam 1970 half a point behind Adorján. *(H.G.)*

HAMILTON-RUSSELL, the Hon. Frederick George
(12 June 1867–3 September 1941)
One of the great patrons of the game who presented the large gold cup that bears his name to be held by the champion team in the International Team tournament (later known as Olympiad) organized under the auspices of FIDE. This he did for the first event in London 1927 and, as there has been no stipulation that a team winning it a certain number of times retains the trophy it is still the FIDE trophy in the 1970s.

He also donated the founding sum for the Permanent Fund of the World Chess Federation and made many donations to British chess to help finance the Olympiads at London 1927, and at Folkestone in 1933. Every year he gave a liberal donation towards the travelling expenses of British teams abroad, notably at the Olympiads.

When H. E. Dobell gave up the honorary treasurership of the British Chess Federation in 1928, he took it on and continued in that office till 1939, when he succeeded Canon Gordon Ross as President of the British Chess Federation. *(H.G.)*

HAMPPE, Karl *(1814–17 March 1873)*
An Austrian player and theoretician, Hamppe enriched the theory of the King's Gambit and Vienna Game. Brilliant but erratic as a player, he lost a match to Löwenthal (+4−5=0) but beat Falkbeer (+16−15=0). *(W.H.)*

'HANDBUCH'
The *Handbuch* (full title *Handbuch des Schachspiels*) is generally regarded as a book that had a most influential bearing on the development of chess. For players in the late nineteenth and the first two decades of the twentieth century, it was the Bible of Chess. Its light began to fade only after the great hypermodern breakthrough.

Initiated by Bilguer in 1840, it was completed by Von der Lasa and published in Berlin in 1843. The first edition ran to 500 pages, of which 376 were devoted to openings and 124 to endgames. Subsequent editions came out in 1852, 1858, 1864, 1874, 1880, 1891 and 1916–21, the final (8th) edition having an appendix published in 1922–3. By this time the book came to 1040 pp with 52 pp in the appendix. Preceded by a study by J. Kohtz about chess in the Middle Ages, and one by O. Koch about chess in modern times, the first part of the final edition was devoted to opening analysis by Schlechter, Spielmann, Dr Tarrasch and Teichmann; the second part, prepared by Prof. Berger, to endgames. *(W.H.)*

HANGING PAWNS

The term Hanging Pawns stems from Steinitz. It refers to pawns on adjacent files neither of which has additional P support, neither of which is passed and neither of which is opposed by a hostile P on the same file. The strongest position of the hanging pawns is the Phalanx (see diagram). The disadvantage of the hanging pawns is their exposure to attack from all sides, especially by Rooks from the front, without P support to draw on. If such an attack forces one of the hanging pawns to advance from the phalanx position, the other will be backward and can be blocked. The advantage of the hanging pawns is their great mobility with the resultant ability to vacate central squares for attacking pieces; also their power to limit the opponent's mobility in that he has to guard against the advance of one of them with gain of tempo, enabling the other to re-establish the phalanx. Thus, in the diagram, B–Q3 (or B–K3) would be answered with P–K5 (or Q5), with the other P following, threatening to establish a central passed P. As a rule of thumb it can be said that hanging pawns are strong with, weak against superior development. *(W.H.)*

HANSTEIN, Wilhelm *(3 August 1811–14 October 1850)*
A German player of the early nineteenth century, Hanstein was introduced to chess by his cousin Mayet, and like him became one of the Berlin Pleiades. His strength was solid defence, which helped him to beat Jaenisch and Mayet in matches. As a theorist he contributed to the Two Knights Defence, the Philidor Defence, the Centre Counter Defence and other openings. Without Hanstein's efforts the *Berliner Schachzeitung* (later to be renamed *Deutsche Schachzeitung*) could not have survived its teething troubles. *(W.H.)*

HARMONIST, Max *(10 February 1864–16 October 1907)*
The only professional ballet dancer in the annals of chess, Harmonist was a German player who made a name for himself when he won the brilliancy prize against Gunsberg at Frankfurt 1887. His tournament results were moderate, his best achievement being =4th with Louis Paulsen at Nuremberg 1888. *(W.H.)*

HARRWITZ BISHOPS
Two Bishops of the same side controlling neighbouring diagonals are known as Harrwitz Bishops after Harrwitz who was fond of using them in raking formation. They play an important part in many mating positions and also figure in the famous double Bishop sacrifice of the game Lasker–Bauer (see KING'S FIELD SACRIFICE) and its innumerable offspring. Some writers prefer the term 'Parallel Bishops'. *(W.H.)*

HARRWITZ, Daniel *(29 April 1823–9 January 1884)*
Born in Breslau, five years after Anderssen, he made his name as a chess player in London and later at the Café de la Régence in Paris. While resident in London he founded and edited the *British Chess Review* which was published in 1853 and 1854.

Harrwitz's match record reads: 1846 lost to Staunton (−7 on even terms and +3−4 with Staunton giving the odds of pawn and two moves), beat Staunton (+6−1=1, Staunton giving the odds of pawn and two moves), Horwitz (+6−4=1) and Williams (+3=2); 1848 drew with Anderssen (+5−5) and beat Mayet (+5−2=2); 1849 beat Horwitz (+7−6=2); 1852 beat Szén (+3−1=1); 1853 beat Williams (+7−2=3) and Löwenthal (+11−10=10); 1856 beat De Rivière (+5−2) and in 1858 lost to Morphy (+2−5=1).

The second game of the 1858 match was Harrwitz's third successive win against Morphy:

White: Morphy; *Black:* Harrwitz
Philidor's Defence
1. P–K4, P–K4; 2. N–KB3, P–Q3; 3. P–Q4, P×P; 4. Q×P, N–QB3; 5. B–QN5, B–Q2; 6. B×N, B×B; 7. B–N5, N–B3; 8. N–B3, B–K2; 9. O–O–O, O–O; 10. KR–K1, P–KR3; 11. B–R4, N–K1; 12. B×B, Q×B; 13. P–K5, B×N; 14. P×B, Q–N4+; 15. K–N1, P×P; 16. R×P, Q–N7; 17. N–Q5, Q×RP; 18. R(5)–N1, Q–Q3; 19. R–N1, K–R2; 20. Q–K3, P–KB4; 21. N–B4, Q–QN3; 22. Q–K2, R–B2; 23. Q–B4, Q–KB3; 24. N–R5, Q–K2; 25. QR–K1, Q–Q2; 26. P–R3, N–Q3; 27. Q–Q4, R–KN1; 28. R–N2, N–K1; 29. Q–B3, P–B5; 30. R–R1, P–KN3; 31. R(R1)–N1, Q–Q4; 32. Q–K1, Q×N; 33. R–N5, Q×P; 34. Q–K6, R–B3; 35. Q–K7+, R–N2; 36. Q×N, P×R; 37. Q–K1, Q–B3; 36. resigns. *(K.J.O'C.)*

HARSHACHĀRITA
Written in Sanskrit in the early seventh century, this history of Northern Indian kings by Bāna contains one of the earliest (the second) allusions to chess and provides evidence of the origin of chess. In describing the peaceful rule of King Sriharsha he writes: 'Under this monarch only bees quarrel in collecting dews; the only feet cut off are those in metre; only *ashtāpadas* teach the position of the *chaturanga*.'

In fact the last eight words furnish a description of the origin of chess. *Ashtāpadas* are boards on which games are played, and *chaturanga* (meaning the four arms of an army) refers to the game of chess itself. *(H.G.)*

HARTOCH, Robert *(b. 24 March 1947)*
A Dutch master. Received international master title 1971 after his performance at the Wijk-aan-Zee tournament of the same year. Best result: World Junior Championship, Barcelona 1965, second to Kurajica. In matches tied with Timman 1969 +1−1=4. Represented The Netherlands in Olympiads 1970 and 1972. *(R.K.)*

HARTSON, Dr Jana *(b. 9th December 1947)*

Born in Prague, Czechoslovakia, but moved to England in 1970 after her marriage to W. R. Hartston. Czechoslovak Woman champion in 1965 and 1967 (under her maiden name of Malypetrova) and British Ladies champion in the five years 1970 to 1974. International Woman master since 1969. *(W.R.H.)*

HARTSTON, William Roland *(b. 12 August 1947)*

British international master and twice British champion, Hartston was born in London and his early chess was played there, where he became London Boy (Under-16) champion in 1962.

He was educated at the City of London School and Jesus College, Cambridge, where he took a degree in mathematics.

It soon became clear that he was one of the leading young players in England and a rivalry developed between him and Raymond Keene in which first one and then the other obtained the upper hand.

After a number of near misses he won the British championship at Eastbourne in 1973 and again at Morecambe in 1975.

Internationally he has already had a distinguished career and has been especially good and consistent in his representation of England at the Olympiads. At Havana in 1966 he scored 66.7% on board 3 but did not play at Lugano in 1968. Again on board 3 at Siegen in 1970 he obtained the best score on board 3 with 78.1%. At Skopje in 1972 he fulfilled the second norm of the international master title with 12½ points out of 18 on second board. Playing on first board at Nice in 1974 he attained 52.7% and had a most meritorious and well-fought draw with the World Champion, Karpov.

He achieved a breakthrough in the field of international tournament chess when he came third in a strong Premier tournament at Hastings 1972/3 and in 1973 he scored a good first at Alicante. His best tournament result came three years later when he won 1st prize at Sarajevo 1976.

His style of play is sound and competent in all the spheres of the game. That he can be brilliant when necessary he demonstrated in a beautiful brilliancy game against the Finnish grandmaster Westerinen at Alicante in 1973. He has a fine, broad knowledge of the openings and has written a number of articles and books on that theme.

A lucid and entertaining writer, he has also appeared with success in B.B.C. Television chess programmes. Among his chief works are: *The Benoni*, London 1969; *The Grünfeld Defence*, London 1971; *The Best Games of C. H. O'D. Alexander* (with H. Golombek), Oxford 1976. *(H.G.)*

HASTINGS 1895

This has good claims to be considered the strongest tournament ever held in England. The then World Champion, Emanuel Lasker, and the ex-World Champion, Steinitz, were both competing. So too were such world-famous figures as the Russian Chigorin, the German Dr Tarrasch, the Austrian Schlechter and the English Blackburne. And yet, to the chess-world's astonishment, 1st prize was won by the American Harry Nelson Pillsbury on his first participation in an international tournament. Leading scores: Pillsbury 16½, Chigorin 16, Em. Lasker 15½, Tarrasch 14.

First Brilliancy Prize
White: Steinitz; *Black:* Von Bardeleben
Giuoco Piano
1. P-K4, P-K4; 2. N-KB3, N-QB3; 3. B-B4, B-B4; 4. P-B3, N-B3; 5. P-Q4, P×P; 6. P×P, B-N5+; 7. N-B3, P-Q4; 8. P×P, KN×P; 9. O-O, B-K3; 10. B-KN5, B-K2; 11. B×N, QB×B; 12. N×B, Q×N; 13. B×B, N×B; 14. R-K1, P-KB3; 15. Q-K2, Q-Q2; 16. QR-B1, P-B3; 17. P-Q5, P×P; 18. N-Q4, K-B2; 19. N-K6, KR-QB1; 20. Q-N4, P-KN3; 21. N-N5+, K-K1; 22. R×N+, K-B1; 23. R-B7+, K-N1; 24. R-N7+, resigns.

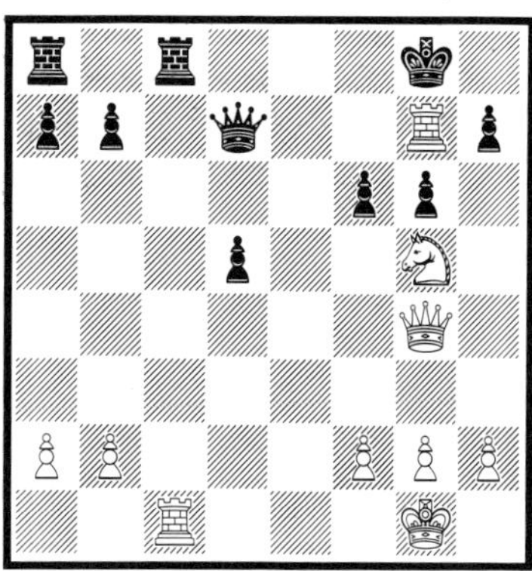

As Steinitz demonstrated immediately afterwards, there is a mate in eleven moves which can only be averted at ruinous cost in material: 24.., K-R1; 25. R×P+, K-N1; 26. R-N7+, K-R1; 27. Q-R4+, K×R; 28. Q-R7+, K-B1; 29. Q-R8+, K-K2; 30. Q-N7+, K-K1; 31. Q-N8+, K-K2; 32. Q-B7+, K-Q1; 33. Q-B8+, Q-K1; 34. N-B7+, K-Q2; 35. Q-Q6 mate. *(H.G.)*

HASTINGS 1919

The first international tournament to be held in allied territory after the First World War took place in Hastings. The entry was largely British but enhanced by the presence of Capablanca who was clearly going to become World Champion. He made short work of the opposition, conceding only one draw to the Yugoslav master Kostić. An aftermath of this tournament was a match between Capablanca and Kostić that the Cuban won without losing a game. Leading scores: Capablanca 10½, Kostić 9½, Sir G. Thomas, Yates 7. *(H.G.)*

A group at the Hastings Victory Tournament, 1919. Left to right: Wahltuch, Capablanca, Burn, Atkins, Sir George Thomas

HASTINGS 1922

The tournament had originally been planned to include both Capablanca and Emanuel Lasker but both the World Champion and the former World Champion proved unable to come. Even so it was a fine event with four of the world's best players, Alekhine, Rubinstein, Bogoljubow and Tarrasch competing in a double round tournament together with two of Britain's leading players in Sir George Thomas and F. D. Yates.

With Bogoljubow losing all games to Alekhine and Rubinstein the real struggle for top place was between these two and it was not decided till the very last round when Rubinstein drew a twelve hour game with Sir George Thomas. Had he won the game he would have tied with Alekhine for first place. But he could only draw and so came second, half a point behind Alekhine but 2½ points ahead of the rest of the field.

One innovation that the organizers made was to lower the time rate of the games to 17 moves an hour. Hitherto, in England at any rate, the speed of play was 20 moves to the hour. Leading scores: Alekhine 7½, Rubinstein 7, Bogoljubow, Sir G. Thomas 4. *(H.G.)*

HASTINGS CHESS CLUB

During the early summer of 1882 two letters appeared in the Hastings and St Leonards *Observer* urging the desirability of starting a chess club in Hastings. The writers were Horace F. Cheshire, the Borough Analyst, and Dr John Colborne, who at that time did not know each other.

At a meeting in June 1882, the club was founded with Dr Colborne as Hon. Secretary and E. Dobell as Hon. Treasurer. E. Dobell's son, H. E. Dobell, joined the club in September 1882 and became secretary, retaining the post for twenty years.

After meeting in two hotels, the Albert and then the Seaside Hotel, the club had a room at the Queen's Hotel, moved away when its membership grew too big for the room and moved back when a room was enlarged specially to contain the club. After the First World War the club purchased the lease of 7 Carlisle Parade and remained there till the end of the Second World War. During this war the club was in the front line as far as bombing was concerned but it remained open every day all the year round. It was in fact bombed towards the end of the war but without loss of life or injury to any of the members.

When the lease expired it purchased the freehold of 2 Cornwallis Terrace and still flourishes in numbers and its activities which include the chess congresses that has made it world famous.

It possesses one of the best chess libraries of any British chess club and also has many photographs and mementoes of the great players from Steinitz to Karpov who have visited Hastings to take part in its international tournaments. For many years it was the scene of the British Boys championship, the first taking place in 1923 when it was won by P. S. Milner-Barry. *(H.G.)*

HASTINGS CHESS CONGRESS

An annual event in the British chess calendar, taking place each year after Christmas. The general congress is open to any who wish to enter and consists of several sections of varying strengths, but the principal event is the Premier tournament, entry by invitation only. The Hastings Premier is the one international tournament held on a regular basis in England, and has maintained its reputation over half a century as an important event in the international calendar.

Until recently the event was financed largely by private donations aided by a grant from the Hastings Corporation, but in later years sponsorship became necessary to support the increasingly expensive Premier tournament. From 1967 to 1969 *The Times* newspaper was joint sponsor with the Hastings and St Leonards Corporation, and in 1975 the event was sponsored by Zetters International Pools, to be followed in 1976 by Ladbroke's. In the intervening years notable benefactors included J. D. Slater, W. R. Morry and the Friends of Chess.

The first Christmas Congress was held in 1920/1, when the principal event was a four-player tournament of British champions, past and present, won by F. D. Yates. The following year the Premier tournament was still almost exclusively British, though the one foreign competitor, B. Kostić, ran away with first prize by winning all seven games. The third Hastings Congress saw the beginning of the long series of genuine international events, with a ten-player tournament including four overseas contestants. This pattern of ten-player events, usually half British, half overseas, continued unbroken except for the war years until 1968 when the number of players was increased to twelve. More recently the pattern has again been improved with the introduction of sixteen-player Premier tournaments, which has been the case since the 1971/2 event.

The list of winners of Hastings Premier tournaments makes impressive reading, containing as it does most of the greatest players of the age. The highest number of victories is that of GLIGORIĆ, who took first place on five occasions. Excluding the all-British Premiers of 1920/1 and 1939/40, the only occasions on which home players have taken first place were 1934/5 when Sir George Thomas shared the honours with Euwe and Flohr, 1946/7 when C. H. O'D. Alexander won outright, 1952/3 when H. Golombek and J. Penrose shared with Medina and Yanofsky, and 1953/4 when Alexander shared with Bronstein.

The main subsidiary event in the Hastings Congress is the Challengers tournament, the winner of which earns the right to an invitation to the following year's Premier. Among those successful in this event was the Woman World Champion Nona Gaprindashvili, in 1963/4. She went on to score 5 points from her nine games in the Premier, including wins against all the English masters. The only other woman to have competed in the Premier was Vera Menchik, who played several times in the 1930s.

Leading scores in the Premier tournaments were as follows:

1920	F. D. Yates 4
1921	B. Kostić 7
1922	Rubinstein 6½, Réti and Siegheim 6
1923	Euwe 7½, Maróczy 7
1924	Maróczy and Tartakower shared first after winning their preliminary section of eight players
1925	Alekhine and Vidmar 8½
1926	Tartakower 7
1927	Tartakower 6½
1928	Colle, Marshall and Takacs 6
1929	Capablanca 6½, Vidmar 5½
1930	Euwe 7, Capablanca 6½, Sultan Khan 6
1931	Flohr 8, Kashdan 7½
1932	Flohr 7
1933	Flohr 7, Alekhine and Lilienthal 6½
1934	Sir G. A. Thomas, Euwe and Flohr 6½
1935	Fine 7½, Flohr 6½
1936	Alekhine 8
1937	Reshevsky 7½, Alexander and Keres 6½
1938	Szabo 7½, Euwe 6½
1939	F. Parr 6
1945	Tartakower 9½
1946	Alexander 7½
1947	Szabo 7½
1948	Rossolimo 6½
1949	Szabo 8
1950	Unzicker 7
1951	Gligorić 7½
1952	Golombek, Medina, Penrose and Yanofsky 5½
1953	Alexander and Bronstein 6½ O'Kelly de Galway 5½
1954	Keres and Smyslov 7
1955	Korchnoi and Olafsson 7, Ivkov 6½
1956	Gilgorić and Larsen 6½
1957	Keres 7½
1958	Uhlmann 8, Portisch 7
1959	Gligorić 7½, Averbakh and Uhlmann 6½
1960	Gligorić 7, Bondarevsky 6
1961	Botvinnik 8, Gligorić 6, Flohr 5½
1962	Gligorić and Kotov 6½, Smyslov 6
1963	Tal 7, Gligorić 6½
1964	Keres 8
1965	Spassky and Uhlmann 7½
1966	Botvinnik 6½, Uhlmann 5½, Basman et al. 5
1967	Hort, Gheorghiu, Stein and Suetin 6
1968	Smyslov 8½, Gligorić 8, Keene 7½
1969	Portisch 7
1970	Portisch 6
1971	Korchnoi and Karpov 11 Mecking and R. Byrne 9½
1972	Larsen 11½, Uhlmann 11, Hartston 9½
1973	Kuzmin, Szabo, Tal and Timman 10
1974	Hort 10½, Sigurjonsson and Vaganian 10
1975	Bronstein, Hort and Uhlmann 10

(W.R.H.)

HAVASI, Kornel *(10 January 1892–30 January 1945)*
Hungarian master who played successfully for Hungary in eight Olympiads, from 1927–1937.

He started his international career by coming 9th/15 at Temesvar 1912. At the Paris Individual Olympics of 1924 he won his preliminary group but came bottom in the top final section. At Gyor the same year he was 10th/15 in a strong event.

In the Budapest Siesta tournament of 1928 he was =7th with Stoner (otherwise known as H. Steiner) and in 1929 at Budapest he did better with an =7th with Colle. Another good result was an =4th with Maróczy at Budapest 1931.

Two more good individual results were a 4th/13 at Sopron 1934 and an =3rd with Castaldi at Milan 1938. *(H.G.)*

HECHT, Hans-Joachim *(b. 29 January 1939)*
Hecht was, at one time, the most frequently employed West German grandmaster. After a long maturing period – he made the German Olympic team as early as 1962 but for some years did not show much improvement – he scored a long run of successes in the early 1970s. After promising results at Büssum 1969 and Raach 1969 (Zonal), he won the German championship at Völklingen 1970 and tied for first with Matanović and Damjanović at Bad Pyrmont the same year; since then he has come first at Olot 1971, Malaga and Montilla-Moriles in 1972, and jointly with Spassky and Andersson at Dortmund 1973. Other good results were 4th at Berlin 1971, 3rd at Forssa-Helsinki (Zonal) 1972, =3rd at Montilla-Moriles 1973, Vršac 1973 and Wijk-aan-Zee 1974, and =3rd at London 1973. *(W.H.)*

HEEMSKERK, Fenny *(b. 3 December 1919)*
Dutch international Woman master (1950) and ten times Netherlands Ladies champion between 1937 and 1961. Tournament results include 2nd in Women's Candidates tournament, Moscow 1952. *(R.D.K.)*

HEIDENFELD, Wolfgang *(b. 29 May 1911)*

Irish chess master, problemist and journalist who was born in Berlin but emigrated to South Africa in 1933. There he had much success in national events and won the South African championship no less than eight times.

In 1957 he went to Ireland and, after a break of four years (1958–62) spent in Germany, he became an Irish citizen and decided to remain in that country.

Six times Irish champion, Heidenfeld represented that country five times in Olympiads, three of these times being on 1st board.

His international record has been sparser than his national career. Possibly this is due to his having been a freelance journalist with little time for playing in long events. It follows that most of his achievements in this field have been in events of short duration. They have been: =1st with Mühring ahead of Euwe, Johannesburg 1955; 2nd at San Benedetto 1956.

His most interesting works: *My Book of Fun and Games*, Johannesburg 1958; *Grosse Remispartien* [in German], Dusseldorf 1968; *Lacking the Master Touch*, Cape Town 1970. *(H.G.)*

HEINICKE, Herbert *(b. 14 March 1905)*
Heinicke is a German international master who was active mainly in the Nazi and immediate post-war periods. He never played in a really important event but had fair results in minor tournaments (2nd Bad Saarow 1935; =6th with Ståhlberg Bad Nauheim 1936; =4th with Eliskases Bad Harzburg 1938; =2nd with Sämisch Bad Harzburg 1946; 2nd Travemünde 1951). He tied for second in the German championship 1953 and represented Germany at the Munich 1936 Team tournament and the Helsinki Olympiad 1952. *(W.H.)*

HELLING, Karl *(10 August 1904–15 August 1937)*
Helling was a prominent Berlin player from about 1926 till his death. Entered the international arena in the first of the three Berlin tournaments of 1928, finishing 5th to Nimzowitsch, Bogoljubow, Tartakower and P. Johner, but ahead of Réti, Ahues, L. Steiner, Sämisch and others. Helling came second to Kashdan at the quadrangular tournament Berlin 1930 and represented Germany on 5th board at the Prague Olympiad 1931, scoring 7/13. *(W.H.)*

HELMS, Hermann *(5 January 1870–6 January 1963)*
A leading American chess journalist. In New York he reported chess news for six newspapers during a career of more than seventy years. Helms published bulletins for Cambridge Springs 1904 that were so popular that he and Hartwig Cassel continued the publication as the *American Chess Bulletin*. Helms edited it until his death. Helms also edited the New York 1924 tournament book. Helms was a talented amateur player who competed mainly in New York events where he scored victories over Marshall and other masters. In 1943 he was named 'Dean of American Chess' by a vote of leading US patrons and players. *(H.G.)*

HENNEBERKE, Franciscus Wilhelmus Johannes *(b. 23 May 1925)*
Dutch international master whose chess career suffered by his being posted as a government official to Indonesia for eleven years.

Second at Baarn 1947 and again in 1949 he came 7th/10 at Beverwijk in 1950. He returned in 1961 and in that year had an international master result in the strong Zevenaar tournament where he came 7th/16 with Johannessen and Milić. *(H.G.)*

HENNINGS, Arthur *(b. 11 July 1940)*
An international master of East Germany, Hennings represented his country in the Olympiads of 1968 and 1970. In the 1970s he achieved excellent results in minor international tournaments (2nd at Kecskemet 1970, =1st at Bucharest 1971, 1st in the master group of Amsterdam 1972, =1st at Lublin 1973). *(H.G.)*

HENRY VIII *(1491–1547)*
Henry VIII, King of England, 1509–47, was a keen chess-player as is evidenced by his Wardrobe Accounts in which there are two inventories of his possessions that relate specifically to chess.

One reads as follows: 'One boxe blacke with chessemen graven in bone. – One paire of tables of brassell. – One bagge of grene velvett with chessemen and tablemen for the same. – A chesse bourde gilte with a case to the same. – A paire of tables of bone clasped with silver with Tablemen and Chestmen. – A case of black leather conteynynge chestmen and table men with a paire of tables. – A paire of tables of bone with tablemen and chestmen. – A chesse bourd with divers kinds of tabulls in yt to playe. – Oon paier of plaieingtables of blacke and white bone with roynt plat and one locke of silver and gilte with a set of chestmen of blacke and white bone to them in a case of blacke leather lined with greane clothe. – A boxe blacke with chessemen graven in bone. – A payre of tables of bone with chestmen belonging to the same. – A payer of chestmen in a case of blacke leather.'

In another inventory of a closet in Greenwich Palace: '2 payre of playing tables of bone. – A payr of chessmen in a case of blacke lether. – A blake satin bag, with chesmen.' *(W.H.)*

HIRSCHFELD, Philipp *(1 October 1840–4 October 1896)*
Probably the strongest player who never won anything. Famous for his brilliant play, he never took part in tournaments, while in match-play he held Anderssen (1861) to a creditable +10−14=5, drew with Kolisch (1864) +4−4=0, lost to Urussoff (1866) by +1−2=2, but was catastrophically defeated by Suhle (1865) +0−7=2. *(W.H.)*

HISTORY OF CHESS
The game of chess was invented in north-west India sometime in the sixth century AD. Its Sanskrit name, *chaturanga*, indicated its origin as a war-game since it means 'four-armed' and thus clearly applies to the four arms of an Indian army: infantry, cavalry, elephants and chariots. According to Murray it was the invention of one man, but this would seem to be the reflection of the writings of previous historians and early chroniclers who gave various mythical explanations of a great philosopher conceiving the whole game at one fell swoop. Of this there is no proof and the likelihood is that it was the derivative from some game played with a board and dice and that changes were passed on by word of mouth long before the two written references, in the *Vāsavadattā* by

Subandhu and the *Harshachārita* by Bāna that appeared in Sanskrit in the late sixth and seventh centuries.

The various mythical ideas of chess having been played by the Ancient Egyptians, the Ancient Greeks or the Ancient Romans have no basis in fact and no written evidence of the game appears earlier than the two Sanskrit romances mentioned here.

Very early on, in the late sixth century, the game spread to Persia and from there to the Byzantine empire. In Persia it was known as *chatrang* and its Byzantine Greek form was *zatrikion*. In both cases it was the same slow game that it had been in origin and its popularity was centred in courts and amongst the learned.

This popularity was given added impetus when the Arabs conquered the Sassanian dynasty in Persia round about the middle of the seventh century. It became a Muslim game under the name of *shatranj*.

The rules were unchanged but the scientific spirit of the Arabs made them study its theory and develop its practice in a way that had hitherto been unknown. The first chess theorists of the game were the Arabs and indeed it was they who introduced the algebraic system of notation.

A game of chess, from the 'Book of Games' 1232, illuminated at the court of Alfonso the Wise

They made no changes in the rules and continued to play it under the old, original rules right down to the seventeenth century. Equally, it was still a game for the courts, in this case for the Caliphs, and the learned men.

Chess came to Europe through four main paths during the ninth and tenth centuries. The first way was that of trade, from regions dominated by the Arabs mostly via the Mediterranean to Europe and from Byzantium to Kiev and other parts of Europe. Another important way was through the Crusades. It is known that Saladin was a keen chess-player and the story (probably mythical) is that he taught Richard Coeur de Lion how to play. A third well-authenticated way was via the Moors in Spain and a fourth recently established way was that the game spread, very early on, from the tribes in Central Asia to Russia.

'The Game of Chess' by Sofonista Anguissola, 1555

By early medieval times the game had come to Western Europe, to Italy, Spain, France and England. The Vikings, in particular, were a strong influence in advancing the game throughout France, England and Iceland. The earliest known chess set, the Isle of Lewis chessmen, is supposed to have been brought there by Vikings from Iceland in the eleventh century.

It was in Spain, under the Moors, that the greatest increase in the popularity of chess came. It was here that the first European work on chess, that of Alfonso the Wise, was written. With the Renaissance, Italy became a centre for the game and by this time it was beginning to assume its modern form. All the slower pieces acquired greater mobility and the power of the Queen became greatly magnified. Castling was gradually evolved and the pawn gained its power of moving two squares initially.

Chess was still a game for courts and the nobility. Elizabeth I of England and Philip II of Spain were both keen players. The latter encouraged and patronized Ruy Lopez and the first real books, by Ruy Lopez, Damiano and Lucena were written.

But it was the Italians, with Leonardo da Cutri and Paolo Boi and later with Greco and Salvio, who dominated the sixteenth and seventeenth centuries.

In the eighteenth century France with the great Philidor led the world. Now the game was passing from the courts and aristocracy to the men of literature and science, in fact to the middle classes, and theory was being rapidly developed on a modern scale.

This in turn meant that England, where the middle classes really first came to some sort of power, was a great centre for chess. Staunton wrested the supremacy from France in a famous match against Saint-Amant, and then, with the remarkable comet-like interval of the great US master Paul Morphy, the chief power in chess came to be Germany.

By the twentieth century chess had spread all over the world and the two chief powers were Europe and America. FIDE, the World Chess Federation, was founded in 1924 and organized team championships of the world were instituted under its auspices. In the 1930s the US team, headed by Fine and Reshevsky, became World Champions but they were overhauled by the Soviet Union which became far and away the dominant chess power.

A sign of the changes in world domination is provided by the list of World Champions from the nineteenth century to the present day. In chronological order: Steinitz (Central Europe), Emanuel Lasker (Germany), Capablanca (Cuba), Alekhine (France but a Russian emigré), Euwe (Netherlands), again Alekhine, Botvinnik (USSR), a succession of other Soviet players (Smyslov, Tal, Petrosian, Spassky), then Bobby Fischer (USA), and – when that remarkable figure, after making chess more popular than it had ever been in its 1,500 years of existence, failed to defend his title – Karpov (USSR). *(H.G.)*

HODGES, Albert Beauregard *(21 July 1861–3 February 1944)*
An American champion (1894–5) whose career was cut short when he gave up chess for business. Hodges was a frequent champion of the Manhattan Chess Club and played in thirteen cable matches with Great Britain at the turn of the century without losing a game. He defeated Showalter for the national title in an 1894 match in New York and then announced his retirement. *(A.S.)*

HOFFER, Leopold *(1842–28 August 1913)*
English chess journalist and player, born in Budapest and originally a Hungarian Jew. Hoffer was born in the same year as Zukertort whose life-long friend and supporter he became.

Hoffer went to Vienna in 1860 and from there to Paris where he was the tournament secretary of the great international tournament of 1867. Throughout his life he was to specialize in the organization of chess events, a rather paradoxical pursuit for one whose temper was so short.

With the advent of the Franco-Prussian War in 1870 he left Paris and came to London, where he settled for good. According to that dubious source, the Rev. G. A. MacDonnell, on his arrival in England he knew no English but, such were his powers of picking up languages, within a few weeks he was speaking excellent English and making jokes in that tongue.

In September 1879 he founded *The Chess Monthly* and remained its editor till it ceased to function in 1896. It was in this magazine that he conducted a fierce and on occasion libellous campaign against his great enemy Steinitz.

When Steinitz went to America in 1882 he succeeded him as chess columnist in the *Field*. Here again he wrote vitriolic pieces against his enemies, though not perhaps quite so bitterly as Steinitz had done.

He was largely instrumental in founding the British Chess Club in London in 1895 and was its first secretary. Hoffer regularly acted as umpire and adjudicator of the Oxford and Cambridge Universities annual chess match. He also continued to control tournaments including the great Ostend Congress of 1907.

Whilst at the British Chess Federation congress at Cheltenham in August 1913 he was taken seriously ill and was rushed to London, where he was sent to a nursing home but died during an operation at the age of seventy.

Hoffer was an excellent writer on the game. His lack of objectivity where his enemies were concerned was compensated for by the vigour and ease of his language. *(H.G.)*

HOLLAND
See under NETHERLANDS, THE.

HOLZHAUSEN, Walter Von *(29 May 1878–9 August 1935)*
A minor German master of the 1920s (3rd at the small international tournament at Hanover 1926 and again at Magdeburg 1927). Important for his work on problems. An excellent composer himself, he published two outstanding books: *Brennpunkt Problem*, 1926, and *Logik und Zweckreinheit in Neudeutschen Schachproblem*, 1928, which established him as the foremost theoretician of the neo-German school. *(W.H.)*

HONDURAS
A newcomer to international chess, the national side took part in an Olympiad for the first time in 1976, finishing 29th. The chess federation's address is Federacion Nacional Deportiva Extra-escolar de Honduras, Apartado Postal 331, Tegucigalpa, D.C. *(K.J.O'C.)*

HONFI, Károly *(b. 25 October 1930)*
Hungarian international master since 1962. Shared first place at Timişoara 1972 international tournament. In 1975 he won the tournament in Kecksmet. In 1976 he won first prize in a strong international tournament at Pecs in South Hungary. *(W.R.H.)*

HONG KONG
Although the first national championship, won by C. M. Sequeira, was held in 1926, it was not until 1961 that the Hong Kong Chess Federation (c/o Mr Ko Chi, No. 6, First floor, Block 2, Government Factory Building, San Po Kong, Kowloon) was formed. The country's first Olympic appearance was made in 1966 since when they have competed regularly, finishing 52nd in 1966, 48th in 1968, 53rd in 1970, 51st in 1972, 59th in 1974 and 39th in 1976. *(K.J.O'C.)*

HÖNLINGER, Baldur *(b. 7 July 1905)*
A regular competitor in the Trebitsch Memorial and other Viennese tournaments. His successes include a 1st at Vienna 1928, ahead of Lokvenc, joint first with Barcza at Szolnok 1930, first at Vienna 1936, ahead of Grünfeld, as well as a 67% score on first board for Austria at The Hague Olympiad. In 1948 he established a world simultaneous record on 213 boards (+187 −13 =13) at Velbert, soon to be surpassed by Koltanowski. *(W.H.)*

HOOGOVEN CHESS TOURNAMENT

The Hoogoven Iron Works in The Netherlands, the biggest works of its kind in Europe, has for many years financed a series of international tournaments, first at Beverwijk and then at Wijk-aan-Zee.

The first congress, in 1938, was on a modest scale with groups of four and was confined to Dutch players. For five years annual tournaments of this kind were held in early January. Then, in 1943 and 1944, the groups were enlarged to eight players.

No tournament was held in 1945 but in 1946 the first international tournament took place. This was still a comparatively short event but an attempt was made to rival Hastings with the main section containing ten players, two coming from abroad – O'Kelly (Belgium) and Stoltz (Sweden) – and the remaining eight being Dutch.

The main tournament continued to comprise ten players until 1953 when the group was enlarged to twelve. In that year, too, an international women's tournament was held.

In 1954 the group reverted to ten players but, with the Hoogoven Works financing the event, the tournaments markedly increased in strength.

In 1963 a great advance took place with the main event comprising no less than eighteen players. Though this number was reduced to sixteen in 1964 the strength of the participants remained such as to make the event the strongest of its type in the world.

In 1968 the event was transferred to the nearby seaside town of Wijk-aan-Zee where it has remained ever since. With the Hoogoven Works being affected by the commercial upsets throughout the world, there was a modification in numbers in 1975 and 1976 so that the main tournament, the so-called Grandmaster Group, contained twelve players.

There follows a list of the winners of the tournaments from 1938 to 1944 and of the main prize-winners from 1946 onwards.

1938	P. Bakker (four players)
1939	Cortlever
1940	Euwe
1941	A. Wijnans
1942	Euwe
1943	Van der Hoek
1944	Van Scheltinga
1946	O'Kelly 7, Stoltz 6½, Kramer 5, Cortlever 4½ (ten players)
1947	Van Scheltinga 7½, Kottnauer 5½, Cortlever 6
1948	Prins 6½, Van Scheltinga 6, Rossolimo and Van Steenis 5
1949	Tartakower 6½, Van Scheltinga and P. Schmidt 6, Golombek and O'Kelly 5½
1950	Donner 7, Euwe and Rossolimo 6, Cortlever 5½
1951	Pilnik 6½, O'Kelly 6, Kieninger and Kramer 5½
1952	Euwe 7½, O'Kelly 5½, Rellstab and Yanofsky 5
1953	Rossolimo 9, O'Kelly 7½, Donner, Euwe, Kramer and Toran 7 (twelve players)
1954	Bouwmeester and Pirc 6, Prins 5½, Van Scheltinga 5 (ten players)
1955	Milić 6½, Bouwmeester and Donner 6, Kramer 5½
1956	Ståhlberg 6½, Pilnik 6, Scafarelli and Toran 5½
1957	Matanović 6½, Ståhlberg 6, Donner 5½, Van Scheltinga 5
1958	Donner and Euwe 5½, Bouwmeester, Matanović and Ståhlberg 5
1959	Olafsson 7½, Eliskases 5½, Donner 5
1960	Larsen and Petrosian 6½, Matanović 5½, Donner and Flohr 5
1961	Ivkov and Larsen 7½, Uhlmann 5½, Olafsson 5
1962	Trifunović 6, Donner and Robatsch 5½, Bisguier and Kottnauer 5
1963	Donner 12, Bronstein 11½, Ivkov, Parma and Pilnik 11 (eighteen players)
1964	Keres and Nei 11½, Portisch 11, Ivkov 10 (sixteen players)
1965	Geller and Portisch 10½, Bobotsov 10, Donner and Ivkov 8½
1966	Polugayevsky 11½, Szabo 11, Bilek 10½, Ivkov 10
1967	Spassky 11, Lutikov 10½, Čirić 9, Larsen 8½
1968	Korchnoi 12, Hort, Portisch and Tal 9
1969	Botvinnik and Geller 10½, Keres and Portisch 10
1970	Taimanov 12, Hort 10½, Ivkov 10, Kavalek 9½
1971	Korchnoi 10, Gligorić, Ivkov, Olafsson and Petrosian 9½
1972	Portisch 10½, Hort and Pomar 10, Browne 8½
1973	Tal 10½, Balashov 10 Vasiukov 9, Hort and Planinc 8½
1974	Browne 11, Donner 8½, Hecht, Matulović and Planinc 9
1975	Portisch 10½, Hort 10, Smyslov 9½, Kavalek 9
1976	Ljubojević and Olafsson 7½, Kurajica and Tal 6½ (twelve players)
1977	Geller and Sosonko 8, Timman 7½, Kurajica 7

(H.G.)

HOOPER, David Vincent *(b. 31 August 1915)*

British amateur (an architect by profession) whose best result was =5th in the British championship at Felixstowe 1949, along with, amongst others, Broadbent and Fairhurst.

Hooper abandoned playing for writing about chess and has become a specialist in two distinct areas. He is an expert on the endings and has a close knowledge of the history of chess in the nineteenth century.

His principal works: *Steinitz* [in German], Hamburg 1968; *A Pocket Guide to Chess Endgames*, London 1970. *(H.G.)*

HOROWITZ, Israel Albert [Al]
(15 November 1907–18 January 1973)
Horowitz was a leading American player and journalist whose *Chess Review* was the only major American chess magazine for nearly thirty years. He was awarded the international master title for an average of 75.5% on four US Olympic teams 1931–50. Although he won or tied for three US Open championships, Horowitz lost a match challenge to Reshevsky for the national title by a 6½–9½ score in 1941. Horowitz wrote the *New York Times* chess column for ten years and was the author of several books. *(A.S.)*

HORT, Vlastimil *(b. 12 January 1944)*
Born in Kladno, Czechoslovakia, Hort was to become his country's leading player. Gained the title of international master in 1962 and grandmaster in 1965. Played in Interzonal tournaments in 1967 (=6th), 1970 (13th) and 1973 (7th) but until his 1976 success (=2nd in Manila), he always missed qualifying for the Candidates. He came near to it in the exceptionally strong Interzonal at Sousse 1967 but was edged out in the subsequent play-off, for one place, with Stein and Reshevsky.

Hort's record in national competitions is impressive: Czechoslovak Junior champion 1960 and 1962 and champion of Czechoslovakia in 1970, 1972 and 1975.

His international record is, if anything, even better than his record in national competitions; his list of tournament successes includes first places at Kecskemet 1965, Mariánské Lázně 1965, Prague 'Socialist Armies Championship' 1966, Hastings 1967/8, Sombor 1968, Venice 1969, Skopje 1969, Havana 1971, Luhačovice 1971, Göteborg 1971, Gloggnitz 1971, Reykjavik 1972, Leipzig 1973, US Open championship 1974, Slanchev Bryag 1974, Hastings 1974/5, Hastings 1975/6, Banja Luka 1976 and Vinkovci 1976. In addition he played on board four for the 'Rest of the World' in the match against the USSR in 1970; he scored 2½–1½ against Polugayevsky.

Chief works: *Na Sedmi Šachovnicich*, Prague 1968 (Prague 1966 tournament book and history of chess in the Czechoslovak army), *O Šachový Trůn*, Prague 1973 ('Match of the Century' 1970, Candidates 1971 and Fischer–Spassky 1972) and, with Jansa, *Zahrajte Si Šachy S Velimistry*, Prague 1975 (a test your chess book). *(K.J.O'C.)*

HORWITZ, Bernhard *(10 May 1807–29 August 1885)*
Horwitz belonged to the Berlin Pleiades before moving to Hamburg in 1839 and to London and Manchester six years later. His chess fame rests largely on the work *Chess Studies*, a collection of endings which he published jointly with the German musician Kling, with whom he also edited the journal *The Chess Player* (1851–3). As a practical player he had indifferent results, losing matches against Staunton, Harrwitz (two), Kieseritsky, Williams and Kolisch, though beating Bird; in his three tournaments (London 1851, Manchester 1857 and Bristol 1861) he played without distinction, being eliminated in the second round in London and in the first round in the other two events. *(W.H.)*

HROMADKA, Karel *(23 April 1887–16 July 1956)*
One of the leading Czechoslovak masters in the period between the wars. Nowadays best remembered for his pioneering work in the opening system 1. P–Q4, N–KB3; 2. P–QB4, P–B4 which is known by his name in Slav circles. *(H.G.)*

HÜBNER, Robert *(b. 6 November 1948)*

International grandmaster and World Championship candidate at his first attempt, West German co-champion 1967, Hübner is the greatest German player since the days of Lasker. In his short international career he won first prizes at Büssum 1968 and Sombor 1970, in addition to small affairs like Castlebar 1969, Houston and Oslo 1974. His two greatest successes so far have been =2nd with Geller and Larsen, behind Fischer, at the Interzonal at Palma de Mallorca, 1970; and the gold medal on first board of the Skopje Olympiad 1972, where he inflicted the first defeat on Petrosian in eight Olympiads. At Beverwijk 1971 he came =6th and at the Interzonal at Leningrad 1973 he finished in a tie for 5th with Larsen. In the Interzonal at Biel in 1976 he again finished in a tie for 5th, this time with Byrne and Smyslov. In matches Hübner lost to Petrosian at Seville 1971 by +0−1=6 in rather unsatisfactory playing conditions, and to Korchnoi at Solingen 1973 by +1−2=5. Hübner is an unusually conscientious player whose tournament career is entirely free of surprise defeats by tail-enders. *(W.H.)*

HUG, Werner *(b. 10 September 1952)*
Swiss international master and World Junior Champion 1971. Hug has become Switzerland's leading player in the 1970s and he has

represented Switzerland in many international competitions.

His first success was the winning of the Swiss Junior championship in 1968. He played in the World Junior Championship in Stockholm in 1969 and very nearly changed the course of chess history, by missing a mate in two against Karpov in a preliminary section and only drawing the game. Had he won, Karpov would not have qualified for the final A section and would not have won the title. As it was, a few months later Karpov secured the grandmaster title at Caracas.

Hug won the World Junior Championship at Athens in 1971, receiving the international master title on that occasion. In the same year he played in the first German international championship and tied with Keene for fifth place.

Has played on top board for his country at the Olympiads of 1972, 1974 and 1976. Has also played on top board in the World Students Olympiad at Graz in 1972 and again at Caracas in 1976. *(H.G.)*

HULAK, Krunoslav *(b. 25 May 1951)*
A Yugoslav whose chess career has made impressive progress during the last three years. He was awarded the international master title in 1974, placing equal first in the tournament at Varna the same year. He won the Yugoslav championship in 1976 and later that year obtained the grandmaster title. *(K.J.O'C.)*

HUNGARIAN DEFENCE
By meeting 1. P–K4, P–K4; 2. N–KB3, N–QB3; 3. B–B4 with 3. . , B–K2 Black avoids the main lines of the Giuoco Piano and Two Knights Defence.

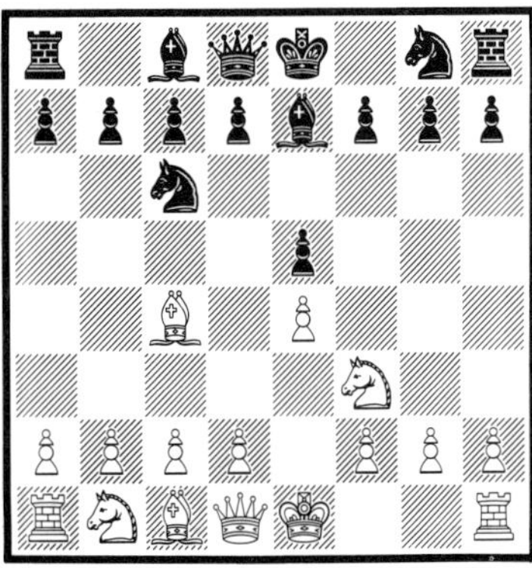

The Hungarian Defence is a passive but playable opening. *(W.R.H.)*

HUNGARY
The first Hungarian Chess Federation was founded in 1911, but survived for only 2½ years through lack of support. Another short-lived attempt was made in 1918, but the foundation of an effective organization to take care of the game nationally only came in 1923. Between the wars Hungary produced several of Europe's greatest masters including Maróczy, Lilienthal (who later went to the USSR) and Szabo. Of the tournaments organized in Hungary during this period perhaps the strongest were Kecskemet 1927, won by Alekhine ahead of Nimzowitsch and L. Steiner; and Budapest 1929, won by Capablanca with Rubinstein second.

In 1949 the Hungarian Chess Federation came under the jurisdiction of the National Sports Federation and began to receive regular support from the state. The game rapidly grew in numbers and strength until the present day when there are more than 2,000 chess clubs in the country.

In recent years the Hungarian team has performed specially well in Olympiads, securing the silver medal position at both the 1970 and 1972 events.

Hungary can boast eleven grandmasters: Adorján, Barcza, Barczay, Bilek, Csom, Forintos, Lengyel, Portisch, Ribli, Sax and Szabo, with first Szabo and then Portisch as the leading player since the end of the Second World War.

The Hungarian championship is an annual event which, despite the fact that several of the leading players are usually absent, nevertheless retains its prestige, and is always strongly contested. National title-holders in the years it has been contested are as follows:

1906	Z. Balla	1952	L. Szabo
1907	L. Forgács	1953	B. Sandor
1911	Z. Balla and Z. Barasz	1954	L. Szabo
1912	G. Breyer	1955	G. Barcza
1913	L. Asztalos	1956	G. Barcza
1922	K. Havasi	1957	L. Portisch
1928	A. Vajda	1958	L. Portisch
1931	L. Steiner	1959	L. Szabo
1932	G. Maróczy	1960	L. Portisch
1933	P. Rethy	1961	L. Portisch
1934	P. Rethy and	1962	I. Bilek
	A. Lilienthal	1963	L. Portisch
1935	L. Szabo	1964	L. Portisch
1936	L. Steiner	1965	L. Portisch
1937	L. Szabo	1966	G. Barcza
1941	G. Füster	1967	L. Szabo
1942	G. Barcza	1968	G. Forintos
1943	G. Barcza	1969	P. Dely
1945	T. Florian	1970	I. Bilek
1946	L. Szabo	1971	L. Portisch
1947	G. Barcza	1972	I. Csom
1948	P. Benko	1973	Z. Ribli
1949	G. Barcza	1974	Z. Ribli
1950	L. Szabo	1975	L. Portisch
1951	G. Barcza	1976	G. Sax

Several international tournaments are held regularly in Hungary with the towns of Balatonfüred, Kecskemet, Debrecen and Budapest frequent hosts. The tournaments of Budapest 1952 and 1973 were two of the strongest events held, with the following results:

Budapest 1952: Keres 12½, Geller 12, Smyslov, Botvinnik and Ståhlberg 11, Szabo 10½, Petrosian and Pilnik 9½, O'Kelly 9, Benko 8½, Barcza and Szily 8, Golombek and Kottnauer 7, Gereben 6, Troianescu 5½, Sliwa 5, Platz 2.

Budapest 1973: Geller 10½, Karpov 9½, Hort, Adorjan, Vaganian and Szabo 8½, Antoshin and Bilek 8, Csom 7½, Ribli 7, Ciocâltea 6½, Velimirović, Sax and Hecht 6, Lengyel and Forintos 5½.

The winners of other notable tournaments held in Hungary include the following: Balatonfüred 1958 (the first Asztalos Memorial tournament): L. Portisch; Kecskemet 1962: R. Kholmov; Zalaegerszeg 1969: M. Taimanov; Budapest 1975: Polugayevsky and Ribli.

Hungary is also very active in the organization of women's chess, and particularly successful in participation. At the present time they possess in M. Ivanka and Z. Veroci two of the leading woman players in the world.

The address of the Hungarian Chess Federation (Magyar Sakkszövetseg) is: Nephadsereg u.10, Budapest-V, Hungary.

The Federation produces a monthly chess magazine, *Magyar Sakkelet*. *(W.R.H.)*

HYPERMODERN SCHOOL

The name given to a number of witty writers and players in the 1920s (Breyer, Grünfeld, Nimzowitsch, Réti and Tartakower), who reacted strongly against the influence of Tarrasch and his severely classical school which they regarded as over-dogmatic and tending to produce routine play.

By the use of paradox and colourful imagery they made a good case that appealed very much to the young. Breyer's famous remark: 'After 1. P–K4, White's game is in the last throes', reveals the chief domain for their activities, the openings.

In this they preferred the half-open defences to the King's pawn (such as Alekhine's Defence, the French, the Sicilian and the Caro-Kann). As Black against 1. P–Q4 they chose and developed to a great degree the Indian Defences and Grünfeld even invented an entirely new defence that was named after him.

They, in particular Réti and Nimzowitsch, brought a new concept to the theory of the centre, preferring always to observe it rather than occupy it.

Réti, Nimzowitsch and Tartakower were the three great writers of the movement, but Tartakower, witty though he was, had nothing like the influence of the other two whose books are still read with attention and belief.

Quite a lot of the theory of the Hypermoderns is still regarded as valid but chiefly as a supplement to Tarrasch's teaching and not as a substitute. *(H.G.)*

I

ICELAND

Iceland is one of those fortunate nations where chess seems to flow naturally in the life-blood of the people and no distinctions of class or culture militate against the universal enjoyment and comprehension of the game. Many devotees of chess have felt the attraction of this chess-playing isle and in the nineteenth century the US professor, Willard Fiske, emigrated to Iceland where his name is still revered. The present popularity of chess is possibly derived from the older board games practised by the people of the country and in Iceland chess-masters are respected to a degree evinced by few other Western lands. In 1931 Alekhine visited Reykjavik to give a simultaneous display, for which great event Parliament was temporarily suspended!

When Fridrik Olafsson acquired the grandmaster title in 1958 he became a national hero and *inter alia* a silver medal was struck in his honour. Even now, when international chess tournaments are held, the portraits of the Icelandic competitors appear on envelopes printed specially for the occasion, while the spectators are more numerous and much better informed than anywhere else outside Eastern Europe.

Considering the size of the Icelandic population (which is not even 300,000), it is astonishing that they have already nurtured two grandmasters in the persons of Fridrik Olafsson and Gudmundur Sigurjonsson. They also have one international master, Ingi R. Johannsson, while Helgi Olafsson has acquired one international master norm at the 1976 Manhattan tournament. In Iceland, players with international titles are automatically offered a pension by the state.

Iceland made a relatively early entry into the Olympiads at Hamburg 1930 with a team of Gilfer, Asgiersson, Thorvaldsson and Gudmundsson, yet their final position was not impressive (=14th out of 18) and it was some time before an improvement became discernible: 14th/15 Folkestone 1933; 16th/19 Stockholm 1937; 16th/26 Buenos Aires 1939; 23rd/25 Helsinki 1952; 12th/26 Amsterdam 1954; 14th/34 Moscow 1956; 22nd/36 Munich 1958; 23rd/40 Leipzig 1960; 23rd/37 Varna 1962; 29th/50 Tel Aviv 1964; 11th/52 Havana 1966 (their best performance; Olafsson made 11½/18 on top board); 22nd/53 Lugano 1968; 27th/60 Siegen 1970; 24th/62 Skopje 1972; 22nd/74 Nice 1974.

Since 1937 the Reykjavik Chess Club has been organizing international tournaments on an increasingly regular basis with the following results: 1937 1st Engels; 1947 1st Yanofsky; 1948 1st Euwe; 1950 Scandinavian Congress 1st Baldur Moller; 1951 1st Rossolimo, =2nd Fridrik Olafsson and Gudjon M. Sigurdsson; 1956 1st Olafsson, =2nd Taimanov and Ilivitsky; 1957 (Swiss System or Monvad as it is known in Iceland) 1st Pilnik, 2nd Ingi R. Johannsson; 1957 (Student Olympiad) 1st USSR with team of Tal, Spassky, Polugayevsky, Gurgenidze and Gipslis; 1957 (international tournament) 1st Olafsson, 2nd Benko (1957 was a rich year, for there was also an international tournament in Hafnarfirdi won by Benko ahead of Olafsson and Pilnik); 1960 1st Ingi R. Johannsson; 1964 1st Tal; 1966 1st Olafsson, 2nd Vasiukov; 1968 =1st Vasiukov and Taimanov, 3rd Olafsson; 1970 1st Sigurjonsson, 2nd Ghitescu; 1971 Nordic Congress 1st Olafsson, 2nd Sejer Holm; 1972 =1st Olafsson, Hort, Gheorghiu; 1972 World Championship, Spassky v. Fischer, Fischer won by 12½–8½; 1974 1st Smyslov, 2nd Forintos; 1975 Zonal 1st Ribli, =2nd Parma and Liberzon; 1976 =1st Olafsson and Timman.

The 1972 Reykjavik match. Left: Spassky's seconds, Geller, Nei, Krogius. Right: Fischer's second, Lombardy; Fischer's spokesman Fred Cramer.

The national magazine *Skak* is published by Johann Jonsson and its address is Posthólf 1179, Reykjavik: *Skak* was also responsible for producing a trilingual de luxe account of the 1972 Fischer–Spassky match. The address of the Central Chess Club is Grensasvegur 46, Reykjavik.

The Icelandic Chess Federation's address is: Skaksamband Islands, P.O. Box 674, Reykjavik. *(R.D.K.)*

IGNATIEVA, Olga Mikhailovna *(b. 16 October 1920)*
International Woman master since 1952 and one of the leading Soviet women players in the early 1950s. Shared second place in the 1952 Women's Candidates tournament. For some years Ignatieva was married to grandmaster Bronstein. *(W.R.H.)*

ILIVITSKY, Georgi Alexeyevich *(b. 30 April 1921)*
One of the strongest Soviet masters in the period immediately after the Second World War. International master since 1955. Perhaps his best tournament result was to share third place in the 1955 USSR championship. Ilivitsky played in the 1955 Interzonal tournament but only finished equal tenth. A successful match player, his victims in short matches include Boleslavsky in 1944, Suetin in 1950 and Pachman in 1956. *(W.R.H.)*

ILYIN-ZHENEVSKY [Iljin-Genevsky], **Alexander** *(1894–1941)*
This Russian's first tournament success was winning the championship of Geneva in 1914! A party official after the revolution, Ilyin-Zhenevsky was a leading force in the spread of chess activity in the USSR besides being a foremost player. Tied for first place in the Leningrad championship of 1925, and made his best tournament result the same year finishing ninth at Moscow. In that event he scored a memorable victory against Capablanca.

His books include: *The Alekhine v. Capablanca Match*, Leningrad 1927 and *International Working-Class Chess Movement*, Moscow-Leningrad 1931. He was killed in Leningrad during the Second World War. *(W.R.H.)*

IMMORTAL DRAW
A name coined by H. Müller because of the sustained inventiveness of both players. The game was played at the international tournament in Vienna 1922.

White: Alekhine; *Black:* Réti
Ruy Lopez
1. P–K4, P–K4; 2. N–KB3, N–QB3; 3. B–N5, P–QR3; 4. B–R4, N–B3; 5. N–B3, P–QN4; 6. B–N3, B–B4; 7. N×P, N×N; 8. P–Q4, B–Q3; 9. P×N, B×P; 10. P–B4, B×N+; 11. P×B, O–O; 12. P–K5, P–B4; 13. B–R3, Q–R4; 14. O–O, Q×B; 15. P×N, P–B5; 16. Q–Q5, Q–R4; 17. P×P, Q–N3+; 18. K–R1, K×P; 19. B×P, B–N2; 20. Q–K5+, Q–B3; 21. B–Q3, KR–K1; 22. Q–R5, P–R3; 23. Q–N4+, K–R1; 24. Q×P, R–K2; 25. Q–Q4, Q×Q; 26. P×Q, QR–Q1; 27. P–B5, P–B3; 28. QR–K1, R–N2; 29. B–K4, R×QP; 30. B×B, R×B; 31. R–K6, K–N2; 32. R×RP, R–QB5; 33. R–B3, R×P; 34. P–KR3, K–B2; 35. R–KN3, R–B7; 36. R–KN6, R×BP; 37. R×P, K–N2; 38. R–KR4, P–N5; 39. R–N4+, K–B2; 40. R–N3, R(B4)–QN4; 41. R–N3, K–N3; 42. K–R2, R–QB4; 43. R–R4, R(B4)–QN4; 44. P–R4, R(N4)–N3; 45. K–R3, R–N1; 46. P–N3, P–B4; 47. R–R5, R–QB1; 48. R–KB3, R–KB3; 49. K–N2, R–B6; 50. R–R8, R×R; 51. K×R, R–B3; 52. R–N8, R–B5; 53. R–N6+, K–N2; 54. P–R5, R–Q5; 55. R–QB6, R–K5; 56. R–N6+, K–B2;

57. P–N4, R×P; 58. R×R, P×R+; 59. K×P, K–N2; drawn. *(W.H.)*

IMMORTAL GAME
The first of the games distinguished by a special name, the Immortal Game was played on the occasion of, but not within, the 1851 London tournament. It is one of the few famous games the actual score of which is in doubt, some sources (such as Von Gottschall's book on Anderssen) rendering Black's 18th move as B×R, with the sequence 19. P–K5, Q×R+; 20. K–K2, leading back to the generally accepted score.

White: Anderssen; *Black:* Kieseritsky
King's Bishop's Gambit
1. P–K4, P–K4; 2. P–KB4, P×P; 3. B–B4, Q–R5+; 4. K–B1, P–QN4; 5. B×P, N–KB3; 6. N–KB3, Q–R3; 7. P–Q3, N–R4; 8. N–R4, Q–N4; 9. N–B5, P–QB3; 10. R–N1, P×B; 11. P–KN4, N–KB3; 12. P–KR4, Q–N3; 13. P–R5, Q–N4; 14. Q–B3, N–N1; 15. B×P, Q–B3; 16. N–B3, B–B4; 17. N–Q5, Q×P;

18. B–Q6, Q×R+; 19. K–K2, B×R; 20. P–K5, N–QR3; 21. N×P+, K–Q1; 22. Q–B6+, N×Q; 23. B–K7 mate.
(W.H.)

IMMORTAL LOSING GAME

The name suggested by Dr W. Lauterbach for a game from the international tournament at Gotha 1957. It refers to the heroic resistance by the loser by means of a series of imaginative mating threats in what seems to be – and is – a hopelessly lost position:

White: Sliwa; *Black:* Bronstein
Dutch Defence
1. P–Q4, P–KB4; 2. P–KN3, N–KB3; 3. B–N2, P–KN3; 4. B–N5, B–N2; 5. N–QB3, N–B3; 6. Q–Q2, P–Q3; 7. P–KR4, P–K3; 8. O–O–O, P–KR3; 9. B–B4, B–Q2; 10. P–K4, P×P; 11. N×P, N–Q4; 12. N–K2, Q–K2; 13. P–B4, N–N3; 14. P–B5, P×P; 15. B×BP, O–O; 16. B–Q6, Q–B2; 17. B×R, R×B; 18. P×P, N–Q4; 19. P–B4, R–Q1; 20. N(K2)–B3, N(Q4)–N5; 21. N–Q6, Q–B1; 22. N×P, N–Q5;

23. N×R, B–N4; 24. N×P, B–Q6; 25. B–Q5, Q–B4; 26. N×N+, Q×B; 27. N–B2, KB×N; 28. P×B, Q×RP; 29. P×N, resigns.
(W.H.)

IMMORTAL ZUGZWANG GAME

Played at the international tournament of Copenhagen 1923, this is a superb example of a war of constriction brought about by a sacrifice. The name however is not technically justified: *zugzwang*, in the proper meaning of the term, does not enter into the game at any stage. In the final position Black threatens R(B4)–B6, against which White has no reply.

White: Sämisch; *Black:* Nimzowitsch
Queen's Indian Defence
1. P–Q4, N–KB3; 2. P–QB4, P–K3; 3. N–KB3, P–QN3; 4. P–KN3, B–N2; 5. B–N2, B–K2; 6. N–B3, O–O; 7. O–O, P–Q4; 8. N–K5, P–B3; 9. P×P, BP×P; 10. B–B4, P–QR3; 11. R–B1, P–QN4; 12. Q–N3, N–B3; 13. N×N, B×N; 14. P–KR3, Q–Q2; 15. K–R2, N–R4; 16. B–Q2, P–B4; 17. Q–Q1, P–N5; 18. N–N1, B–QN4; 19. R–N1, B–Q3; 20. P–K4, BP×P; 21. Q×N, R×P; 22. Q–N5, QR–KB1; 23. K–R1, R(B1)–B4; 24. Q–K3, B–Q6; 25. R(B1)–K1, P–KR3; 26. resigns.
(W.H.)

INDIA

The form of chess played in India was, until the nineteenth and twentieth centuries, the older type of the game and modern chess has only been practised there in the latter half of the twentieth century.

The only FIDE-titled player is international master Manuel Aaron. National teams have competed in the Olympiads of 1956 (finishing 27th out of 34), 1960 (24th/40), 1962 (28th/37) and 1964 (37th/50).

Indian chess is regulated by the All-India Chess Federation, 16 Sri Dhootpapeshwar, Prasad Mangalwadi, Girgaum, Bombay 4.
(R.D.K.)

Chess in India under the Raj, from C. Gold: 'Oriental Drawings' pub. London 1806

INDONESIA
The national team has played in five Olympiads: 26th in 1960, 27th in 1966, 24th in 1970, 26th in 1972 and 39th in 1974.

The Indonesian Chess Federation (Percasi, Senayan Main Stadium, Gate 1, Room 13, Jakarta) has been in the forefront of chess organization in Asia. The 1963 East Asian Zonal was played in Jakarta and a local player, Bachtiar, shared first place. In 1976 Jakarta was also the scene of the Second Asian Masters championship, won by E. Torre; in the first such tournament (Singapore 1975), the Indonesian Suradiradja finished =1st. *(K.J.O'C.)*

'INFORMATOR'
See under CHESS INFORMANT.

'INTERNATIONAL CHESS MAGAZINE'
Founded and edited by Wilhelm Steinitz, this magazine was published in New York from 1885 to 1891. It appeared monthly and seven volumes in all were published. Steinitz wrote most of the copy himself all in that vigorous and uncompromising way that earned him both admirers and enemies throughout the chess world. Most of the theories that are regarded as forming the basis of modern and hypermodern thought are to be found in the pages of the *International Chess Magazine*. *(H.G.)*

INTERNATIONAL JUDGE FOR CHESS COMPOSITIONS
The title of International Arbiter for Compositions was introduced by FIDE in 1956. Among the earliest holders of the title were grandmasters Botvinnik, Smyslov, Keres and Averbakh.

The title has been awarded to more than 250 candidates, of whom more are from the USSR than any other single FIDE member nation. *(W.R.H.)*

INTERPOSITION
Interposition of a unit of smaller value is one method of parrying a hostile attack on a unit of greater value, most frequently the K or Q, but occasionally even a minor piece.

Although the interposition is a basic tactical device, even the greatest masters have been known to overlook it in the heat of battle, as seen from the diagrammed position (Sir George Thomas–Euwe, Nottingham 1936) in which *both* players overlooked a simple interposition.

Black played 1.., N–K3? in belief that 2. R × B, R × R; 3. Q × R, could be answered with 3.., R–Q1; and White, in the same belief, played 2. P–N3?, whereas in the above sequence 4. N–Q7 – the interposition – would have retained the piece (for if 4.., Q × Q; 5. R × Q, N–B1; 6. N–B6+). *(W.H.)*

INTERZONAL TOURNAMENTS
The inauguration of Interzonal tournaments came in 1947 when FIDE took control of the arrangements for the individual World Championship. In order both to establish the man best qualified to challenge for the title and to give all a chance of staking their claims, regional events were held, called Zonal tournaments, from which the top players gained the right to compete in the Interzonal. The eliminating contests then proceeded through stages of Interzonal and Candidates before eventually determining the challenger.

The first Interzonal was held at Saltsjöbaden in Sweden in 1948 with twenty contestants. The conditions under which the event was organized were less rigorous than we expect nowadays, with all the players responsible for providing their own travelling and accommodation expenses; while also it was not made very clear how many players would qualify from this tournament into the subsequent Candidates. The representatives from the United States did not in fact participate owing to the problem of finance.

The results of this first Interzonal were as follows:
Bronstein 13½, Szabo 12½, Boleslavsky 12, Kotov 11½, Lilienthal 11, Bondarevsky, Ståhlberg, Flohr and Najdorf 10½, Trifunović 10, Pirc, Gligorić and Böök 9½, Ragozin and Yanofsky 8½, Tartakower 8, Pachman 7½, Stoltz 6½, L. Steiner 5½, Lundin 4½.

Originally only the first five placed had the right to enter the Candidates, but following the withdrawal of Euwe, Fine and Reshevsky, invitations were extended to all down to Trifunović; the subsequent withdrawal of Bondarevsky led to the exclusion of Trifunović to ensure that there remained an even number of participants.

The second Interzonal was also played in Sweden, half at Saltsjöbaden and half in Stockholm in 1952. The result was a triumph for the Soviet representatives, who filled the top four places. The fifth qualifying place was confused by a quadruple tie, but it was decided to let all concerned compete in an enlarged Candidates.

Results:
Kotov 16½, Petrosian and Taimanov 13½, Geller 13, Averbakh, Gligorić, Ståhlberg and Szabo 12½, Unzicker 11½, Eliskases 10½, Pachman, Pilnik and L. Steiner 10, Matanović 9, Barcza 8, Stoltz 7½, Sanchez 7, Wade 6, Vaitonis 5, Golombek and Prins 4½. In winning the tournament Kotov conceded only seven draws, four of them against the other Soviet players.

The third Interzonal was again played in Sweden, this time at Göteborg 1955. Though the margin of victory was not as great as Kotov's had been in 1952, Bronstein had a comfortable victory. Once more the Soviet players scored heavily, though Panno interrupted their steamroller by taking third place. The young Spassky squeezed into the Candidates by sharing the last qualifying spot.

Results:
Bronstein 15, Keres 13½, Panno 13, Petrosian 12½, Geller and

Szabo 12, Filip, Pilnik and Spassky 11, Ilivitsky and Pachman 10½, Guimard and Najdorf 9½, Fuderer and Rabar 9, Unzicker 8½, Bisguier and Ståhlberg 8, Donner, Medina and Sliwa 5½.

Competitors and chief arbiter at the Interzonal, Portorož, Yugoslavia 1958

The fourth Interzonal in 1958 was moved from Sweden for the first time, being held in Yugoslavia at Portorož. This event marked the coming of age of the new generation of World title contenders, with Tal securing first place, and the fifteen-year-old Fischer astonishing all by qualifying for the Candidates. The Russians did not come up to their own very high standards with both Bronstein and Averbakh edged out of qualifying places.

Results:
Tal 13½, Gligorić 13, Benko and Petrosian 12½, Fischer and Olafsson 12, Averbakh, Bronstein, Matanović, Pachman and Szabo 11½, Filip and Panno 11, Sanguineti 10, Neikirch 9½, Larsen 8½, Sherwin 7½, Rossetto 7, Cardoso 6, de Greiff 4½, Fuster 2.

The fifth Interzonal in 1962 was beset from the start with great difficulties owing to the problems of finding a country in which to hold it. With many governments refusing visas to East Germans, the tournament eventually reverted to Sweden where Uhlmann's participation could be guaranteed. As if to show that all the trouble had not been for nothing, the East German started the tournament very well and looked likely to qualify, but a bad finish robbed him of the fruits of his efforts.

Results:
Fischer 17½, Geller and Petrosian 15, Filip and Korchnoi 14, Benko, Gligorić and Stein 13½, Portisch and Uhlmann 12½, Olafsson and Pomar 12, Julio Bolbochan 11½, Barcza and Bilek 11, Bisguier 9½, Bertok and Yanofsky 7½, German and Schweber 7, Teschner 6½, Cuellar 5½, Aaron 4.

Six players had the right to proceed from this tournament to the Candidates, so a match was arranged among those tieing for sixth place. This ended in favour of Stein who was nevertheless debarred from qualifying owing to the rule prohibiting too many players from one nation in the Candidates. Thus Gligorić, who was second in the play-off, took the final place.

The sixth Interzonal held at Amsterdam in 1964 was the first not to produce an outright winner; in fact, four players shared first prize. The outstanding result was that of Bent Larsen, whose enterprising chess established him as the only non-Soviet player apart from Fischer to be a serious contender for the World title.

Results:
Larsen, Smyslov, Spassky and Tal 17, Stein 16½, Bronstein 16, Ivkov 15, Portisch and Reshevsky 14½, Gligorić 14, Darga 13½, Lengyel 13, Pachman 12½, Evans 10, Tringov 9½, Benko 9, Rossetto, Bilek and Foguelman 8, Quiñones 7, Porath 5½, Perez 5, Berger 4½, Vranesic 4.

Once again Stein was eliminated from the Candidates by the rule limiting the number of players from any one nation. The final Candidates place went to Portisch after his 2½–½ victory in the play-off match with Reshevsky.

The seventh Interzonal: Tunisia's offer to hold this event in Sousse in 1967 made this the first Interzonal outside Europe; it turned out to be the most eventful. The main interest was centred on the actions of Fischer, who twice withdrew during the course of the tournament, returned later on both occasions to resume his participation, then finally left for good when leading the field with a score of 8½ out of 10. The reasons for his behaviour lay mainly in an inability to reach agreement with the controllers on a playing schedule fitting in with his religious holidays. After Fischer's final departure only Larsen seemed able to settle down to serious chess.

Results:
Larsen 15½, Geller, Gligorić and Korchnoi 14, Portisch 13½, Hort, Reshevsky and Stein 13, Matulović 12½, Matanović 12, Ivkov and Mecking 11, Gipslis and Kavalek 10, Suttles 9½, Bilek 9, Barczay 8, R. Byrne 7½, Cuellar and Miagmasuren 6½, Sarapu 4, Bouaziz 3½.

To decide the last qualifying place, a double-round tournament was held among those tieing for sixth place. Hort, Reshevsky and Stein all finished with two points, which gave the verdict to Reshevsky in view of his superior Sonneborn-Berger score in the original tournament.

The eighth Interzonal which took place in 1970 at Palma de Mallorca saw the beginning of Fischer's successful assault on the title. Although he had not participated in the US championship Zonal tournament, and therefore had not won the right to participate in the Interzonal, Fischer was allowed to play in place of Benko who offered to stand down in his favour. A loss to Larsen was the only blot on Fischer's impressive record in this event.

Results:
Fischer 18½, Geller, Hübner and Larsen 15, Taimanov and

Uhlmann 14, Portisch and Smyslov 13½, Gligorić and Polugayevsky 13, Mecking and Panno 12½, Hort 11½, Ivkov 10½, Minić and Suttles 10, Reshevsky 9½, Addison and Matulović 9, Filip, Naranja and Uitumen 8½, Rubinetti 6, Jimenez 5½.

The first six qualified for the Candidates.

The ninth Interzonal: several important changes were made in the system of running the 1973 Interzonals. It was decided to hold two parallel tournaments instead of just one, with the top three qualifying from each. This, of course, allowed a larger number of participants, so apart from the usual qualifiers from Zonal tournaments, there were a number of players given exemption to the Interzonal. These included all six of the previous Candidates who did not reach the final of that event, together with eight nominated players directly chosen by a special FIDE commission. Finally it was agreed to include both winners of the World Junior Championship during the previous three years. The difficult task was to divide the 36 players into two equal groups, and the FIDE committee appointed to perform this duty produced their lists of players amid great criticism from players and public. Larsen delivered a strong complaint that the Leningrad Interzonal was much stronger than that in Petropolis, and many agreed with him. Such arguments however were bound to be encountered in whatever manner the two events were arranged, and no changes were made. It was felt by many that the elimination of Tal, Hübner and Larsen himself was as much the fault of the system as of these players, but eliminated they were.

The results of the Interzonals were as follows:
Leningrad: Karpov and Korchnoi 13½, R. Byrne 12½, Smejkal 11, Hübner and Larsen 10, Kuzmin 9½, Gligorić, Taimanov and Tal 8½, Quinteros and Radulov 7½, Torre and Uhlmann 7, Rukavina 6½, Tukmakov 6, Estevez 4½, Cuellar 1½.
Petropolis: Mecking 12, Geller, Polugayevsky and Portisch 11½, Smyslov 11, Bronstein 10½, Hort 10, Savon 9½, Ivkov and Ljubojević 9, Reshevsky 8½, Keres and Panno 8, Gheorghiu 7½, Biyiasas 6½, Hug, Kagan and Tan 3.

Only two of the runners-up could proceed to the Candidates so a play-off was immediately arranged in Portorož, Yugoslavia, with each of Portisch, Polugayevsky and Geller playing four games against the other two. This resulted in the elimination of Geller who scored 3 points, behind Polugayevsky 3½ and Portisch 5½. These last two named thus joined Mecking, Byrne, Korchnoi and Karpov in the Candidates.

The tenth Interzonal: as in 1973 two parallel tournaments were held. On this occasion the division of the players into two groups was perhaps more successful.

The results of the Interzonals were as follows:
Manila: Mecking 13, Hort and Polugayevsky 12½, Tseshkovsky 12, Ljubojević and Ribli 11½, Balashov, Kavalek and Panno 10½, Gheorghiu, Mariotti, Spassky and Uhlmann 10, Quinteros 9, Browne 8½, Torre 7, Biyiasas 6, Pachmann, L. A. Tan and Harandi 5.
Biel: Larsen 12½, Petrosian, Tal and Portisch 12, Smyslov, Byrne and Hübner 11½, Andersson 10½, Smejkal, Csom and Geller 10, Sosonko 9½, Liberzon, Rogoff and Gulko 9, Sanguineti 8½, Matanović 8, Castro 6, Lombard 5, J. Diaz 2½.

Only two of the runners-up could have a place in the Candidates so, once again, a play-off had to be arranged and this was held two months later in Varese, Italy. Petrosian, Portisch and Tal each played four games against the other two. The result was that Petrosian, with 4½, and Portisch, 4, were successful while Tal, with 3½, was eliminated. Thus Petrosian and Portisch joined the other four qualifiers, Mecking, Hort, Polugayevsky and Larsen, and the pre-qualified Fischer and Korchnoi in the draw for the Candidates quarter-finals. *(W.R.H. & K.J.O'C.)*

INTERZONAL, WOMEN'S

See WOMEN'S WORLD CHAMPIONSHIP.

IRAN

There is an ancient tradition of chess in Iran that goes right back almost to the time when the game was invented (see HISTORY OF CHESS). But in modern times, until the Second World War and its aftermath, the game languished in that country.

There has been a dramatic change in this respect during the last twenty years. Iran is the administrative centre of the West Asian Zone of FIDE. The President of the Iran Chess Federation, A. Navabi, is also president of the West Asian Zone and under his enthusiastic advocacy chess has prospered exceedingly in that area.

Iran possesses two international masters, Hrandi and Sharif, and has competed regularly in FIDE Olympiads since 1958. Its results in the Olympiad have been: 32nd Munich 1958, 29th Varna 1962, 36th Tel Aviv 1964, 32nd Siegen 1970, 35th Skopje 1972, 34th Nice 1974 and 31st Haifa 1976.

The governing body in Iran is the Iranian Chess Federation, 9 Arasteh Avenue, Ramssar St. Shah Reza Street, Teheran. Its official publication is *Ketabe Shahtrandj*, P.O. Vox 14/1706. *(H.G.)*

IRAQ

The Iraqi Chess Federation (P.O. Box 384, Baghdad) has twice sent a team to the Olympiads, obtaining 61st place in 1972 and 66th in 1974. *(K.J.O'C.)*

IRELAND

It is related of King Conchubair that he divided his royal time into three parts: for one-third of the day he watched the sports of the young men; one-third he spent in drinking ale; and one-third playing chess. There are, in fact, many references to chess in medieval Irish poetry and romance.

As for competitive chess, it may be said to have begun with the international congress of Dublin 1865 (won by Steinitz), which gave rise to the foundation of the City and County of Dublin Chess

Club in 1867 – a club still prospering today under the simpler name of Dublin Chess Club.

It was eighty-nine years before another international tournament was played in Ireland, but since the series of Tostal tournaments in Dublin 1954, Cork 1955 and Dublin 1956 (all won by O'Kelly), many small events of a similar nature have taken place: Dublin 1962 (won by Wade), Castlebar 1969 (won by Hübner), the Irish Times Congress 1974 (won by Hecht) – in addition Ireland sponsored a FIDE Zonal in Dublin 1957.

Ireland has been a member of FIDE since its inception in 1924 and has, with few exceptions, played in the Olympiads since Warsaw 1935 (where Reilly created a sensation by beating Fine). For many decades the Irish teams never finished higher than fourth last, but a change began in Tel Aviv 1964, where they had nine teams behind them; steadily moving up the ladder since then, they got out of the lower half for the first time at Nice 1974 (37th of 73).

Individual achievements in the international field are difficult to assess because of the fluidity of the definition of 'Irish'; thus Mason and Alexander (born in Kilkenny and Cork, respectively) were never regarded as representing Ireland; but Pollock and Reilly, both born abroad, are regarded as Irish players.

One international about whom there can be no doubt was J. J. O'Hanlon, for many years the leading figure of Irish chess, who played successfully in many minor tournaments in England and on the Riviera, besides winning the Irish title on nine occasions. In more recent years a number of Irish players have played abroad with varying success; of these E. N. Mulcahy, Dr V. Maher, J. J. Walsh, W. Heidenfeld, M. F. Littleton, E. A. Keogh, M. O'Leary, J. L. Moles, H. McGrillen, N. J. Patterson, P. Henry, D. Cox and B. Kernan deserve special mention.

Partition has never caused any trouble in Irish chess, international team events as well as local tournaments always having been contested by players from both the Republic and Northern Ireland. In recent years the North has come to play an ever-increasing part: of the past ten Irish championships five have been won by Northern players (Moles – twice, Patterson, Henry, McGrillen).

The total list of Irish champions since 1912, the year the title was first contested, is as follows:

1912	J. J. O'Hanlon	1935	J. J. O'Hanlon
1915	J. J. O'Hanlon	1936	J. J. O'Hanlon
1922	T. G. Cranston	1937	T. Cox
1924	P. Baker	1938	T. Cox
1925	J. J. O'Hanlon	1939	B. O'Sullivan
1926	J. J. O'Hanlon	1940	J. J. O'Hanlon
1927	P. Baker	1946	B. O'Sullivan
1928	P. Baker	1947	P. A. Duignan
1929	P. Baker	1948	D. J. O'Sullivan
1930	J. J. O'Hanlon	1949	P. B. Kennedy
1931	T. G. Cranston	1950	V. Maher
1932	J. J. O'Hanlon	1951	A. Bourke
1933	J. Creevey	1952	M. Schuster
1934	J. Creevey	1953	E. N. Mulcahy
1954	T. Kelly	1966	J. L. Moles
1955	V. Maher	1967	W. Heidenfeld
1956	D. J. O'Sullivan	1968	W. Heidenfeld
1957	D. J. O'Sullivan	1969	N. J. Patterson
1958	W. Heidenfeld	1970	P. Henry
1959	B. Reilly	1971	J. L. Moles
1960	B. Reilly	1972	W. Heidenfeld
1961	J. Reid	1973	H. McGrillen
1962	J. Reid and M. F. Littleton	1974	A. Doyle
1963	W. Heidenfeld	1975	E. Keogh and A. Ludgate
1964	W. Heidenfeld	1976	B. Kernan.
1965	M. F. Littleton		

(W.H.)

ISLE OF LEWIS CHESSMEN

A unique collection of carved chessmen, part of a hoard of walrus ivory discovered in 1831 buried in a sandbank on the west coast of the Isle of Lewis, Outer Hebrides. The seventy-eight pieces must have originally belonged to at least seven different sets; they comprise eight Kings, eight Queens, sixteen Bishops, fifteen Knights, twelve Rooks and nineteen pawns. They are of English or Scandinavian origin and date from the eleventh or twelfth centuries.

Sixty-seven of the Lewis pieces are now displayed in the British Museum, London. The remainder can be seen at the Scottish National Museum of Antiquities, Edinburgh. *(R.D.K.)*

ISOLATED PAWN

A pawn that has no neighbours of the same colour on either of the two adjacent files. As a result the isolated pawn is weak for two reasons. In the first place, the square in front of the isolated pawn is a strong point for the hostile forces: not only is a hostile piece on such a square safe from pawn attacks, but the isolated pawn itself would protect it from frontal attack by the Rooks. Secondly, the isolated pawn is weak and easy to capture.

Strangely enough Réti, in his *Masters of the Chess Board*, denies this self-evident truth and maintains there is no reason 'why the opponent should not be able to defend the pawn with as many pieces as are used to attack it'. Naturally this would only be possible when the isolated pawn is at the same time a passed pawn.

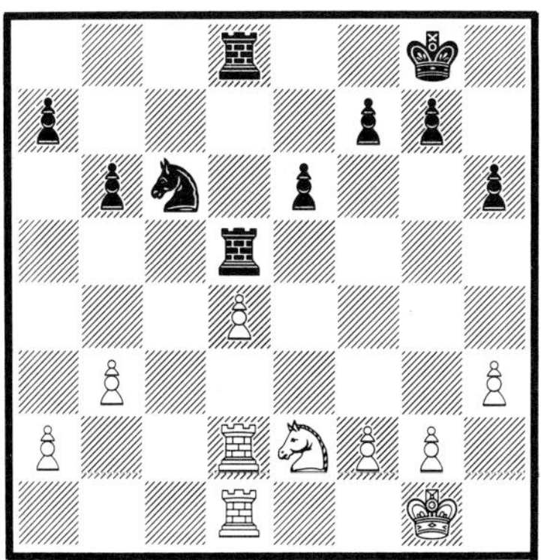

In the diagrammed position the White pawn on Q4 can be attacked more often than defended (by 1. . , P–K4) exactly because it is isolated. If however it were a passed pawn (remove Black's KP and White's KBP) would Réti's dictum be correct. While all the above considerations apply to the isolated pawn in general, the isolated QP specifically has played an important part in opening lore, especially the theoretical discussions at the beginning of the present century. While Tarrasch maintained that the mobility of the isolated QP more than compensated for its defects, the hypermodern school regarded its advantage as transient but its weakness as lasting. Present-day opinion is similar to that regarding the hanging pawns: the isolated QP is strong with, weak against, superior development. *(W.H.)*

ISRAEL

The Palestine Chess Federation joined FIDE in 1934 and competed in two pre-war Olympiads: 15th in 1935 and 9th in 1939. The fine result at Buenos Aires in 1939 ranks, qualitatively, as their best ever Olympic achievement; the team of Czerniak, Foerder (Porath), Winz, Kleinstein and Rauch (the last three comparatively little known) finished ahead of both France and Cuba led, respectively, by Alekhine and Capablanca.

In the post-war Olympiads, under the banner of Israel, their results have been: 11th in 1952, 7th in 1954, 12th in 1956, 17th in 1958, 14th in 1960, 15th in 1962, 14th in 1964 at Tel Aviv, 19th in 1966, 18th in 1968, 13th in 1970, 18th in 1972, 17th in 1974 and 6th in 1976 again on home ground in Haifa.

The Israel Chess Federation's (P.O. Box 21143, Tel Aviv 61–210) achievement of successfully organizing two Olympiads places them in a select band; England, The Netherlands, West Germany and Yugoslavia are the only other countries to have done this.

Until the 1970s the country's best players were mainly home grown but now new arrivals from the Soviet Union are coming to the fore with such players as Liberzon, Shamkovich, Dzhindzhihashvili and Radashkovich among the men, and women such as Kushnir and Podrajanskaya.

The winners of the eighteen national championships held so far have been:

1936	M. Czerniak	1959	J. Porath
1937	J. Porath	1961	I. Aloni
1938	M. Czerniak	1963	J. Porath
1940	J. Porath	1965	I. Aloni
1945	I. Aloni	1967	S. Kagan
1951	M. Oren	1969	S. Kagan
1953	J. Porath	1971/2	U. Geller
1955	M. Czerniak	1973/4	V. Liberzon
1957	J. Porath	1975/6	N. Birnboim

(K.J.O'C.)

ITALY

The Renaissance greatly increased the interest in chess in Italy during the fifteenth century and by the sixteenth century Italy was the country where the modern form of the game was most flourishing with such great figures as Paolo Boi and Leonardo da Cutri playing chess all over Europe with success. This continued on into the seventeenth century and though, in the earlier half of the eighteenth century, the Modena school which then dominated Italy had chosen a by-path in the matter of the rules of the game, there were still players of great renown and capabilities such as Ercole del Rio and Ponziani.

Then a decline seems to have set in. Chess was still popular and great tournaments were organized in Italy right down from the nineteenth century to such modern times and places as Venice 1948, 1949 and 1950 and Milan 1975.

The Italian team has competed regularly in the Olympiads and such fine masters as Monticelli, Castaldi and Tatai have been produced and, most recently, a grandmaster in Mariotti.

The name and address of the Italian Chess Federation: Federazione Scacchistica Italiana, Via Metastasio 3, 20123 Milan and its magazine *L'Italia Scacchistica*, Via Passeroni 6, 20135 Milan. *(H.G.)*

IVÁNKA, Mária *(b. 23 February 1950)*

One of the leading Hungarian woman players, international Woman master since 1968. Qualified for the 1973 Women's Interzonal but was unable to play because she was having a baby at the time. *(W.R.H.)*

IVANOVA, Antonia *(b. 6 June 1931)*

Seven times Bulgarian Women's champion, international Woman master since 1954, and winner of the Leipzig 1954 Women's Zonal tournament. Ivanova is married to grandmaster Bobotsov. *(W.R.H.)*

IVKOV, Borislav *(b. 12 November 1933)*

A Yugoslav grandmaster, he achieved early prominence by winning the World Junior Championship, Birmingham 1951. International master in 1954 following a number of impressive tournament appearances. Only a year later he became a grandmaster for performances in Buenos Aires (=1st) and Mar del Plata (1st). From 1955 to 1965 he took part in numerous tournaments with mixed success; a period in which his style underwent a radical

Borislav Ivkov at Hastings 1955

change from an attacking player to that of a sober positional player, perhaps under the influence of Trifunović.

In 1965 a new Ivkov emerged, instantly commanding world attention: 1st with Uhlmann, Zagreb 1965 ahead of Petrosian, Portisch and Larsen, he came close to winning the great Havana tournament of same year (=2nd) after a lead of two points.

He finally qualified for the Candidates in 1965 but was outclassed by Larsen $2\frac{1}{2}$–$5\frac{1}{2}$. At home he temporarily unseated Gligorić from board 1. All this exhausted Ivkov's creative reserves and he never fully recovered. After his fine achievement in Belgrade 1969 (equal first with Polugayevsky, Gligorić and Matulović, ahead of Geller and Botvinnik) there was a sudden decline in form.

He has represented Yugoslavia in eight Olympiads. Yugoslav champion 1963 and 1972. Played in the USSR v. Rest of the World, Belgrade 1970, where he lost to Keres 1–3.

Bled 1961
White: Ivkov; *Black:* Portisch
French Defence
1. P–K4, P–K3; 2. P–Q4, P–Q4; 3. N–QB3, B–N5; 4. P–K5, P–QB4; 5. P–QR3, B×N+; 6. P×B, Q–B2; 7. Q–N4, P–B4; 8. Q–N3, N–K2; 9. Q×P, R–N1; 10. Q×P, P×P; 11. K–Q1, B–Q2; 12. Q–R5+, K–Q1; 13. N–K2, B–R5; 14. N–B4, Q×KP; 15. Q–B7, B–Q2; 16. B–Q3, Q–Q3; 17. R–K1, P–K4;

18. P–QR4, B–K1; 19. Q–K6, Q×Q; 20. N×Q+, K–Q2; 21. N–B5+, K–B1; 22. R×P, QN–B3; 23. R–K2, R×P; 24. B×P+, K–Q1; 25. N×P+, K–B2; 26. B–B4+, N–K4; 27. R×N, N×B; 28. R–K7+, K–B3; 29. R–B7+, K–N3; 30. R–N1+, K–R3; 31. R–B6+, resigns. *(R.D.K.)*

J

JACOBEAN DRAMA, Chess in

The game of chess is frequently utilized in Jacobean drama either as a political parable in which the dramatist essays to shelter himself from governmental wrath or as a parable on life itself.

The archetype is Thomas Middleton's *Game at Chess*, 1624, the Prologue of which commences:

'What of the game, call'd Chess-play, can be made
To make a Stage-play, shall this day be plaid:
First, you shall see the men in order set,
States, and their Pawnes, when both the sides are met.
The Houses well distinguisht: in the Game
Some Men entrapt, and taken to their shame,
Rewarded by their Play: and in the Close
You shall see Cheque-Mate given to Vertue's Foes:
But the fair'st Jewell, that our hopes can decke,
Is, so to play our Game, T'avoid your Checke.'

The whole play is an attack upon Spain and those who were in favour of a Spanish alliance. But Middleton's attack was too obvious and he was sent to prison for his indiscreet drama.

In *Women Beware Women* the same playwright reveals the plot in a game of chess played between two of the principal characters. Similar use is made of a game of chess in *The Spanish Curate*, 1622, by John Fletcher (probably with the help of Massinger). This was the first time a complete game of chess was shown on the stage.

Bartolus: Bring out the chess-board! Come, let's have a game, wife.
(Enter Egla, with a chess-board, and then exit.)
I'll try your mastery: you say you are cunning.

(H.G.)

JAENISCH, Carl Friedrich Andreyevich
(11 August 1813–17 March 1872)
A Russian master and theorist, Jaenisch was a major in the army until he decided to devote himself entirely to chess.

Not very successful at the game, he lost two matches: one to W. Hanstein in Berlin 1842 by +1−4=1 and another to Staunton in London 1851 by +2−7=1. This second match was played after the great London 1851 event in which Jaenisch had been expected to compete.

His importance in the history of chess is as a theorist. All his works were written in French and they fall into three categories: (1) mathematical – *Découvertes sur le cavalier (aux échecs)* (Discoveries on the Knight in chess), St Petersburg 1837, and three learned volumes, the *Traité des applications de l'analyse mathématique au jeu des échecs* (Treatise on the application of mathematical analysis to the game of chess), St Petersburg 1862–3; (2) on the laws of chess – *Règles du jeu des échecs adoptées par la Societé des amateurs d'échecs de St Petersbourg* (Rules of the game of chess adopted by the Society of chess amateurs of St Petersburg), St Petersburg 1854, and a new recension of the rules published four years later in St Petersburg; (3) openings – *Analyse nouvelle des ouvertures de jeu des échecs*, St Petersburg 1842–3. This contained analysis of the Wing Gambit and Petroff's Defence.

(H.G.)

JAFFE, Charles *(March 1874–12 July 1941)*
One of the strongest players in US events from 1905 to the 1930s. He was born in Dubrovna, Russia and came to America in 1896. Jaffe worked as a silk-mill merchant until 1910 when he became a professional chess player. He finished =3rd at the first National American Chess Tournament, a half-point behind Capablanca. During his career he won two games from Capablanca and registered match victories over Mieses and Chajes.

Jaffe complained bitterly that he was later barred from strong US events because of Capablanca's charges that Jaffe threw his game to Marshall in the 1913 Havana event so that the American would win. Jaffe wrote two books including *Jaffe's Chess Primer*, New York 1937, and edited the short-lived *Jewish Chess Magazine* in 1906.

(A.S.)

JAMAICA
Though two chess magazines (*Chess Bulletin of Jamaica* and *Chess Newsflash*) have been produced in recent years, the Jamaica Chess Federation (43 University Crescent, Kingston 6) has yet to organize the participation of a team in an Olympiad, but a national side did compete in the 1976 Student Olympiad, finishing 20th out of 21.

(K.J.O'C.)

JAMIESON, Robert Murray *(b. 7 July 1952)*
Australian international master and accountant by profession.

Jamieson won the Victorian Junior (U-14 and U-15) championship in 1966 and 1967. He was 4th in the Australian Junior championship in 1970 and in the following year made a 50% score in the World Junior Championship at Athens.

He was runner-up in the Australian Open championship in 1973 and Australian champion in 1974.

He secured the international master title by coming =3rd with Balinas below Torre and Tan at the Melbourne Zonal tournament of 1975.

He has played in the Olympiads of 1974 (with 72% on top board) and of 1976 where he again fulfilled the international master norm.

In 1974 he won the Australian Lightning championship at Comma with 15 points out of 15 and he holds the Australasian record for simultaneous displays – 158 players at Melbourne 1975.

(H.G.)

JANATA, Michael *(b. 27 February 1944)*
Czechoslovak master, shared first place in the 1963 World Junior Championship, drawing all four games of the play-off match with Gheorghiu, but losing the title on tie-split. Employed as foreign correspondent for Czechoslovak news agency.

(W.R.H.)

JANOWSKI, David Markyelovich *(25 May 1868–15 January 1927)*

Franco-Polish grandmaster who apart from Tarrasch was the only player to have defeated the four World Champions, Steinitz, Lasker, Capablanca and Alekhine.

Born at Volkovysk in Poland, he soon left Poland for France, eventually becoming a naturalized French citizen with his base in Paris. His first international tournament was Leipzig 1894 where he came =6th. In the following year he was =12th in the great Hastings tournament and in that year too he drew a match with Mieses in Paris.

A prolific and powerful match-player, he defeated Winawer by +5−2=0 in Vienna in 1896 and drew with Schlechter that year again in Vienna.

His tournament results followed a rising curve, though, being far from consistent, he had his marked ups and downs. He came, for example, 3rd in the great Vienna tournament of 1898 and 9th in the not so great tournament in Cologne that year.

His best tournament period was from 1901 to 1905. In 1901 he was 1st in Monte Carlo and 3rd in Moscow. The fine results continued: 1902, 3rd at Monte Carlo, 1st at Hanover; 1904, =2nd at Cambridge Springs; 1905, =2nd at Ostend, =1st at Barmen.

Then came a decline in his tournament results, and though he sometimes had good results they were never in important events.

He had up-and-down results in match play too, losing to Frank Marshall in 1905 but defeating him in 1908. This last victory made him seek a match for the World Championship with Emanuel Lasker and his patron M. Nardus backed him in such a match in 1909 but Lasker won with great ease by +7−1=2. Lasker won in still more crushing style by +8−0=3 in 1910. During the First World War he went to America and in 1916 lost another match to Marshall (who had beaten him in 1912). But he did come 2nd to Capablanca in a tournament at New York that year.

His post-war results gradually became worse as his health deteriorated but he continued to play till the end, dying on his way to take part in a tournament at Hyères on the French Riviera.

As a player he was a great master of the attack. He always played to win and never to draw, losing many a half-point through a stubborn refusal to accept the draw. He won many brilliancy prizes and was particularly fond of the two Bishops which he used to such effect that the Americans, during his stay in the USA, referred to them as 'the two Jans'. He was celebrated for concentrating the full force of his attack on one particular square in the enemy camp.

Nuremberg 1896
White: Janowski; *Black:* Schallopp
Queen's Gambit Accepted
1. P–Q4, P–Q4; 2. P–QB4, P×P; 3. N–KB3, P–QB4; 4. P–K3, P×P; 5. P×P, B–N5; 6. B×P, P–K3; 7. Q–R4+, N–B3; 8. N–K5, Q×P; 9. N×N, Q–K5+; 10. B–K3, P×N; 11. N–B3, Q×P;

12. B–Q5, P×B; 13. Q×P+, K–Q1; 14. Q×R+, K–Q2; 15. Q–N7+, K–K3; 16. Q–B6+, B–Q3; 17. B–B4, resigns. *(H.G.)*

JANOŠEVIĆ, Dragoljub *(b. 8 July 1923)*
A Yugoslav grandmaster, given the international master title 1964. Grandmaster title 1965 following numerous outstanding performances. Represented Yugoslavia in international matches. A chess columnist by profession. Well-known blindfold simultaneous player. Best tournament result: 1st Vršac 1969 ahead of Benko, Ivkov and Matulović. Famous for having beaten Fischer, Skopje 1967. Very uneven in form, and a passionate poker player. *(R.D.K.)*

JANSA, Vlastimil *(b. 27 November 1942)*
A Czechoslovak grandmaster. Jansa gained the international master in 1965 and the grandmaster title in 1974. Winner of international tournament at Madonna di Campiglio 1973, and shared first at Amsterdam 1974. Czechoslovak champion in 1964 (jointly with Blatny) and 1974. *(W.R.H.)*

JAPAN
Chess in Japan is very much a minority interest. However, following a visit by Dr Euwe in 1975, the Japan Chess Association (Kamata 2-17-7, Tokyo 144) plans to introduce the 'Dan' system, common enough in Judo and Go, to chess and it is hoped that this may lead to more widespread popularity for the game. Japan has competed in four Olympiads, placing 47th in 1970 and 1972, 68th in 1974 and 38th in 1976. *(K.J.O'C.)*

JIMENEZ ZERGUERA, Eleazar *(b. 25 June 1928)*
Cuban international master and Cuba's leading player in the 1960s. He played on 1st board for Cuba in five Olympiads, 1960, 1962, 1964, 1966 and 1968. In 1970 he was on 2nd board, whilst he had descended to 4th board when he played for Cuba in 1974.

In 1963 he came =2nd at the Havana Zonal tournament but failed to qualify for the Interzonal. The same applies also to his 2nd at the Caracas Zonal tournament in 1966. But in coming =1st at Quito in 1969 he did qualify for the Palma de Mallorca Zonal only to come bottom in the Interzonal there. But he did draw with Fischer and should have won. His best result in the Capablanca Memorial tournaments has been 7th/15 in 1968. *(H.G.)*

JOHANNESSEN, Svein *(b. 17 October 1937)*
A Norwegian international master who won the Norwegian championship in 1959 and 1962. He had a long and distinguished record in Olympic chess, playing for Norway on a high board in no less than nine Olympiads. He took part in 1956, 1960, 1962, 1964, 1966, 1968, 1970, 1972 and 1974. He played on top board from 1960 to 1970, scored 64.3% on 3rd board in 1972, and 62.5% on board 2 in 1974. *(H.G.)*

JOHANSSON, Ingi R. *(b. 5 December 1936)*
Icelandic international master who played for Iceland in the Olympiads of 1952, 1954, 1956, 1958, 1966, 1968 and 1974.

He came =7th/20 with Trifunović at the Halle Zonal tournament of 1963, and was =10th with Flesch at the Asztalos Memorial tournament in Salgotarjan in 1967. *(H.G.)*

JOHNER, Hans *(b. 7 January 1889)*
Leading Swiss player, the younger brother of Paul Johner. Eight times Swiss champion (or joint champion) between 1923 and 1938. Tournament results include 1st prize Aarau 1935. Awarded international master title in 1950. *(R.D.K.)*

JOHNER, Paul *(10 September 1887–25 October 1938)*
Noted Swiss player and problemist. Six times Swiss champion (or joint champion) between 1907 and 1932. Tournament successes include: 1st Copenhagen 1916, 1st Trieste 1923, =1st (with Spielmann) Scheveningen 1923, 1st Berlin 1924. Brother of Hans Johner. *(R.D.K.)*

JORDAN
The national team captured 62nd place in the 1974 Olympiad, their first and only appearance so far. In the past few years there has been some government backing for chess, especially in the schools, and R. G. Wade has visited the country as part of a coaching scheme. The Royal Jordanian Chess Federation's address is P.O. Box 2269, Amman. *(K.J.O'C.)*

JOVANOVIĆ, Katrina *(b. 30 November 1943)*
Yugoslav holder of the title international woman master which she received in 1964. Her best tournament results were during the early 1960s, notably her three consecutive victories in the women's tournament at Beverwijk from 1960 to 1962 and her =4th place in the 1964 Women's Candidates tournament. *(K.J.O'C.)*

JUNGE, Klaus *(1 January 1924–27 April 1945)*
Born in Concepcion (Chile), and killed in battle at Welle (Germany) as one of the last victims of the war in 1945, Junge was the most promising German player for many generations. After some local successes he tied for 1st in the German championship 1941 (with Paul Schmidt) at the age of seventeen; the same year he came 4th to Alekhine, Schmidt and Bogoljubow in the second of the tournaments held in occupied Poland. In 1942 at Salzburg he tied for 3rd with Schmidt, behind Alekhine and Keres, but ahead of Bogoljubow and Stoltz; came second to Alekhine in the third of the Polish tournaments; and finally tied for first with the then World Champion at Prague.

Junge was an unusually fine endgame player – a rare accomplishment at the age of eighteen. *(W.H.)*

KAGAN, Bernhard *(13 August 1866–27 November 1932)*
Strong German amateur who lived in Berlin and published tournament books and a chess magazine, *Kagans Neueste Schachnachrichten* in the years 1917–32. Originally the magazine was a hobby but after the German inflation of the early 1920s had reduced his fortunes, the magazine and other publications became his chief livelihood. *(H.G.)*

'KAGANS NEUESTE SCHACHNACHRICHTEN'
A remarkable chess magazine that appeared, first as a quarterly and then monthly in the years 1921–32. It was published in Berlin and its editor Bernhard Kagan, who was also its publisher, used it as a vehicle for giving many master games and articles by such writers as Grünfeld, Tartakower, Tarrasch, Nimzowitsch, Réti and Spielmann. It died when Kagan himself died in 1932.

Many of the great tournaments of the period appeared in supplements to the magazine. *(H.G.)*

KAGAN, Shimon *(b. 6 April 1942)*
Israeli international master and engineer by profession. Israeli champion in 1967, and in 1969 he gained the international master title when he came =1st with Uitumen in the Asian Zonal tournament at Singapore in 1967, confirming this success when he came first in the Asian Zonal tournament at Teheran in 1973.

He has played regularly for Israel in the Olympiads: in 1966, 1968 (when he was awarded the gold medal for the best result on board 4), 1970, 1972, 1974 and 1976. He has also played in a number of World Students Olympiads, his best result having been in 1965 when Israel was second and he had the gold medal for the best result on board 4. He came =1st with Rumens in the Hastings Challengers tournament 1975/6. *(H.G.)*

KAHN, Victor *(1889–1973)*
French master and writer on chess who was born in Moscow of rich Jewish parents. He left Russia in 1912 for Scandinavia, going first to Denmark where he won the Copenhagen championship in 1916 and then to Sweden.

After a stay in the Netherlands he went on to France after the First World War and settled in Nice where he acquired French nationality.

He was champion of France in 1934 but is chiefly known as a witty and entertaining writer on the game who also broke new ground in the method of treating both the opening and the middle-game.

This was done in his pioneering work *L'Ouest Indienne*, Paris 1935 which was revised and published in Monaco 1949 under the title *La Défense du fianchetto de la dame*, in both cases with an instructive introduction by Alekhine.

Two other important works were *La Conduite de la partie d'échecs*, Monaco 1952, and, in collaboration with G. Renaud, *L'Art de faire mat*, Monaco 1947, translated into English as *The Art of Checkmate*, London 1955. *(H.G.)*

KAILA, Osmo Ikmari *(b. 11 April 1916)*
Finnish international master and problemist who had a comparatively brief chess career. Finnish champion in 1939 and 1954 and Nordic champion in 1946, he was a talented combinational player who won a brilliancy prize for his play on 3rd board at the Helsinki Olympiad of 1952.

He was for some time secretary of the Finnish Chess Federation and edited a chess column for many years but as a result of a number of controversies withdrew from his chess activities. *(H.G.)*

KAN, Ilya Abramovich *(b. 4 May 1909)*
One of the strongest Soviet masters before the Second World War. Finished 3rd in the 1929 USSR championship, shared 6th at Moscow 1935 and 7th at Moscow 1936 international tournaments. Given the titles of international master in 1950 and International Judge in 1956. Author of *Chess in the Soviet Army* [in Russian], Moscow 1953. *(W.R.H.)*

KAPENGUT, Albert Zinovievich *(b. 1945)*
Soviet master and theoretician. Was a member of successful Student Olympiad teams in the late 1960s; shared fifteenth place in the 1972 USSR championship final. *(W.R.H.)*

KAPLAN, Julio *(b. 25 July 1950)*
US international master since 1967. Argentinian by birth; Kaplan's family emigrated to Puerto Rico in 1963. Won World Junior Championship in 1967 (ahead of Keene, Timman and Hübner). He came =2nd at Los Angeles 1974. *(R.D.K.)*

KARAKLAJIĆ, Nikola *(b. 24 February 1926)*
Yugoslav international master since 1955. Yugoslav national champion 1955. Tournament results include: 1st Laibach 1955, 1st Wijk-aan-Zee (Masters Section) 1967. Karaklajić works as a disc jockey for the Belgrade radio. *(R.D.K.)*

KARFF, Mona May *(b. 1914)*
Mona Karff was US Women's champion during most of the period 1938–55 and again in 1974. An international Women's master, she was 5th at the 1939 World Championship in Buenos Aires. This is her best result, although she was =6th at Stockholm 1937. *(A.S.)*

KARLOVY VARY and MARIÁNSKÉ LÁZNĚ 1948

Karlovy Vary–Mariánské Lázně Tournament 1948

The great series of Carlsbad tournaments was resumed after the Second World War in 1948 when the Czechs held the first part of an important tournament at Karlovy Vary and its second part at Mariánské Lázně.

At the end of the first half the Australian champion, Lajos Steiner, was sharing the lead with Milan Vidmar junior. But both had a bad finish with Vidmar being particularly unfortunate in that he was attacked by some acute facial inflammation that had to be treated at the local hospital.

The great Czechoslovak player, Jan Foltys, emerged above the field only in the last two rounds but he never lost hold of a leading position and with a strong run in the finish achieved his best tournament result ever.

Play was very hard fought throughout the tournament and much attractive chess was produced. One remarkable point was that in the seventeenth round no less than four players won their opponent's Queen for varying losses of material. Richter won Stoltz's Queen for Rook and minor piece; Golombek did the same to Vidmar; Sajtar 'won' Barcza's Queen for a Rook and two minor pieces and Foltys won Gawlikowski's Queen for Rook and Knight.

The Hungarian, Barcza, also did well and made his best tournament result here. Leading scores: Foltys 13, Barcza 12½, L. Steiner 12, Pirc, Stoltz 11½.

KARPOV, Anatoly Yevgenyevich *(b. 23 May 1951)*
Soviet international grandmaster and World Champion 1975–, Karpov was born in Zlatoust in the Urals. He had to wait four years before he learnt to play chess. Thereafter his progress was extremely rapid, progressing to the (Soviet) level of Candidate Master by the time he was eleven. Karpov gained the international master title in 1969 through his victory in the World Junior Championship and became a grandmaster the following year.

It was already clear that this young player would soon be a leading candidate for the World Championship, but the speed of his further advance was quite remarkable. Qualifying for the series of Candidates matches by sharing first place in the Leningrad Interzonal tournament of 1973, he went on to defeat Polugayevsky and Spassky with apparent ease and then won a narrow match against Korchnoi to secure the right to challenge for the World Championship.

On 24 April 1975 Anatoly Karpov was crowned World Chess

Anatoly Karpov during his match with Boris Spassky, Leningrad 1974

Champion, following Fischer's decision not to defend his title. Karpov thus became the twelfth World Champion in the history of the game, but the first to receive the title by default.

His successes in international tournaments include the following: 1st: Trinec 1966, Groningen Junior 1967, World Junior 1969, Madrid 1973, Llubljana Portorož 1975, Milan 1975, Skopje 1976,

The draw for the final of the Contenders' tournament in the Hall of Trade Unions, Moscow 1974. The match between Karpov and Korchnoi lasted two months

Amsterdam 1976, Montilla-Moriles 1976; 1st equal: Moscow 1971, Hastings 1971/2, San Antonio 1972, Leningrad 1973. At the Olympiad in Nice 1974, Karpov won the gold medal for the best score on top board when representing the USSR. In addition to his numerous other achievements, Karpov has won the Soviet championship, having finished fifth, fourth and second respectively on his three appearances in that event in 1970, 1971 and 1973 and gaining the title on his fourth attempt at Moscow 1976 by a magnificent recovery after a bad start.

Karpov's chess style is calm but determined, rather reminiscent of that of Capablanca. He is especially formidable in his handling of the White pieces; with Black he often seems peacefully inclined. This approach has made him one of the most difficult players to defeat, as witness his record of only sixteen losses in five years of intense competition (from his entry to senior chess to the victory over Korchnoi).

When not playing chess, Karpov is a member of the Economics faculty of Leningrad University. He also collects stamps. He has a slighter physique than most grandmasters, but makes up for this by the power of his attacking play. His first victory in the match against Korchnoi:

White: Karpov; *Black:* Korchnoi
Sicilian Defence
1. P–K4, P–QB4; 2. N–KB3, P–Q3; 3. P–Q4, P×P; 4. N×P, N–KB3; 5. N–QB3, P–KN3; 6. B–K3, B–N2; 7. P–B3, N–B3; 8. Q–Q2, O–O; 9. B–QB4, B–Q2; 10. P–KR4, R–B1; 11. B–N3, N–K4; 12. O–O–O, N–B5; 13. B×N, R×B; 14. P–R5, N×RP; 15. P–KN4, N–B3; 16. N(Q4)–K2, Q–R4; 17. B–R6, B×B; 18. Q×B, KR–QB1; 19. R–Q3!, R(B5)–B4;

20. P–N5!, R×P; 21. R–Q5, R×R; 22. N×R, R–K1; 23. N(K2)–B4, B–B3; 24. P–K5!, B×N; 25. P×N, P×P; 26. Q×RP+, K–B1; 27. Q–R8+, resigns. *(W.R.H.)*

KASHDAN, Isaac *(b. 19 November 1905)*
A veteran grandmaster, International Judge, a frequent officer of the US Chess Federation and an accomplished tournament director. During his peak playing years in the 1930s Kashdan was considered one of the ten best players in the world and Alekhine said in 1932 that Kashdan would probably be his successor as World Champion.

Like many of his American rivals, Kashdan was born in New York and improved at local chess clubs. He first gained attention by winning a problem-solving competition held during New York 1924. He played on the US team in the 1928 Olympiad and led the team in the four events that the USA won during 1931–7. In the early 1930s he scored several impressive international results – 2nd at Frankfurt 1930, 1st at Stockholm 1930, =4th at Bled 1931 and 2nd behind Alekhine at Pasadena 1932 – just as Marshall began his retirement. Although attempts at arranging a match for the US title failed because of financial problems, Kashdan was considered the strongest American player until 1936.

Kashdan was rated as one of the favourites before the 1936 US Closed championships but he suffered the first of many reverses against a slightly younger generation that included Reshevsky, Fine, Dake and Horowitz. He came 5th in the 1936 and 1938 events and 3rd in the 1940 championship before tieing with Reshevsky for first prize in the 1942 wartime tournament. In the play-off match Kashdan lost +2−6=3. He came 2nd again in 1946 and 1948 and then abandoned his quest. In 1933 Kashdan was married and the need to earn a salary drove him out of international play. He was briefly an editor of the *Chess Review*. Business interests kept Kashdan busy during the 1940s although he did win the US Open championship in 1947. He had been co-champion in 1938.

Moving to California after the war, Kashdan became a leading organizer of chess on the West coast. He succeeded H. Steiner as chess editor of the *Los Angeles Times* and became president of the California Chess Federation. He directed several tournaments including the 1963 and 1966 Piatigorsky Cup events. Kashdan edited the tournament book of those two tournaments.

Kashdan's play was characterized by the exploitation of simple positions, especially in the endgames. He had a strong predilection for the two Bishops advantage and was known in Europe as *der kleine Capablanca*.

Folkestone Olympiad 1933
White: Kashdan; *Black:* Mikenas
Petroff's Defence
1. P–K4, P–K4; 2. N–KB3, N–KB3; 3. N×P, P–Q3; 4. N–KB3, N×P; 5. Q–K2, Q–K2; 6. P–Q3, N–KB3; 7. B–N5, Q×Q+; 8. B×Q, B–K2; 9. N–B3, N–B3; 10. N–N5, K–Q1; 11. O–O, P–QR3; 12. QN–Q4, N×N; 13. N×N, P–B4; 14. N–B3, B–K3; 15. B–Q2, P–R3; 16. P–QN3, K–Q2; 17. P–Q4, KR–QB1; 18. P–B4, P–Q4;

19. QP×P, B×P; 20. P–QN4, B–R2; 21. P–B5, K–K2; 22. N–Q4, B–N1; 23. QR–B1, B–K4; 24. B–QB3, B–B5; 25. R–B2, N–K5; 26. B–N2, P–QR4; 27. P–N3, B–K4; 28. P–B3, P×P; 29. N×B, QR×P; 30. P×N, R×B; 31. R×R, B×R; 32. P×P, P×N; 33. P–Q6+, K–K1; 34. B–R5+, K–Q2; 35. R–B7+, K–B3; 36. B–B3+, K–N4; 37. R×P+, K–B5; 38. P–B6, resigns.

(A.S.)

KASPARIAN, Genrikh Moiseyevich *(b. 27 February 1910)*
Soviet international master and endgame composer. Ten times champion of Armenia and an international master since 1950, Kasparian is still better known as perhaps the greatest Soviet endgame study composer. Awarded FIDE titles of International Judge for Chess Compositions (1956) and International Master of Chess Composition (1960), Kasparian has published some three hundred studies and won more than forty first prizes. By profession he is a civil engineer. See ENDGAME STUDY for two examples of his work. *(W.R.H.)*

KATETOV, Dr Miroslav *(b. 7 March 1918)*
Czechoslovak international master since 1951. Winner of Prague championship in 1942 and 1946 and runner-up for the 1946 Czechoslovak championship. By profession Katetov is a doctor of mathematics. *(W.R.H.)*

KAVALEK, Lubomir *(b. 9 August 1943)*
Born in Prague, Kavalek emigrated to the West in 1968 and settled in the USA in 1970. Since then he has been one of the highest-rated Western grandmasters.

Kavalek first gained attention in 1962 when he won the Czechoslovak championship at the age of nineteen. During the early 1960s he played five times on the Czechoslovak student team and twice on his country's Olympic team. He was a student of journalism, communications and Russian literature.

In 1965 Kavalek was awarded the international master title. That year he came 1st at Varna and =2nd at Leipzig to secure the grandmaster title.

After 1970 Kavalek sought US citizenship and took up residence in Washington. He played first board on the American team at the 1974 Olympiad at Nice and tied for first place in the 1973 US championship. He speaks five languages and has been a frequent contributor to chess magazines.

Despite the rivalry from Browne and R. Byrne, Kavalek was the most successful American competitor in international events abroad in the early 1970s. His first prizes include Natanya 1973, Caracas 1970, Bauang 1973 and Montilla-Moriles 1973. He was =13th in the 1967 Interzonal at Sousse. In 1972 Kavalek tied for first place in the US Closed championship, the American Zonal, but lost the play-off to R. Byrne and Reshevsky. *(A.S.)*

KECSKEMET 1927
This tournament (June–July 1927) was unique in being the only important post-First World War contest played on the discredited group system. The twenty players were divided into two groups of ten each, the first four in each group qualifying for the A final, the next four for the B final and the last two dropping out.

As in St Petersburg 1914 things did not work out according to preconceived notions and two grandmasters, Tartakower and Grünfeld, failed to make the top final. Alekhine dominated group A, conceding draws only to Gilg and Kmoch; in B his feat was duplicated not, as expected, by Nimzowitsch, but by Lajos Steiner, who drew with Ahues and Nimzowitsch and won the rest. The scores from the qualifying groups were carried to the finals. In these finals Alekhine won only one game, drawing six, and just scraped home from Nimzowitsch and Steiner, who tied for second.

The full results were as follows:
Group A: Alekhine 8, Asztalos, Kmoch 6, Gilg 5½, Takacs, Tartakower 4½, Brinckmann 3½, Yates 3, Müller 2½, Sarközy 2.
Group B: Steiner 8, Nimzowitsch 6½, Ahues, Vajda and Colle 5, Grünfeld 4½, Vuković 3½, Berndtsson, Przepiórka and Szekely 2½.
Top Finals: Alekhine 12, Nimzowitsch and Steiner 11½, Asztalos 9½, Ahues, Kmoch and Vajda 8½, Gilg 8.

B finals: Tartakower 9½, Grünfeld 8½, Takacs and Yates 8, Berndtsson 7, Brinckmann, Colle and Vuković 6. *(W.H.)*

KEENE, Raymond Denis *(b. 29 January 1948)*
British grandmaster, British champion 1971, Keene was born in London and was both London Boy champion and British Junior champion in 1964.

Educated at Dulwich College and Trinity College, Cambridge, he soon became recognized, along with Hartston, as one of the two leading younger players in England. His style of play was different from that of his rival, being more complicated and less direct; but, like Hartston, he became a most formidable opening theorist with a vast knowledge of opening theory.

His first Olympiad was at Havana 1966 where he was the youngest member of the side and scored 65% on board six. In 1968 at Lugano he obtained 76.5% on board four and in 1970 at Siegen, playing on board two in the preliminaries and board one in the finals, he scored 68.8%.

The year 1971 saw a double achievement, for in that year he won the British championship at Blackpool and also secured the title of international master.

Playing on top board in the 1972 Olympiad at Skopje, he scored 11½ out of 20.

Raymond Keene (right) in play against Ivkov, Skopje Olympiad 1972

In 1974 he came 6th in a very strong Hastings tournament and then won first prize in the Capablanca Memorial Masters tournament in Cuba. At the Nice Olympiad he scored 66.66% on 2nd board, attaining the first leg of the grandmaster norm. At Mannheim 1975 he was 3rd in the German Open championship and in that year he also came 2nd at Alicante. In 1976 he was 2nd at the Aarhus tournament in Denmark. He finished a most successful year in international chess by fulfilling the second grandmaster norm on 2nd board in the Haifa Olympiad, thereby becoming England's second international grandmaster (after Tony Miles).

His principal works: *Flank Openings*, St Leonards-on-Sea 1968; *The Modern Defence* (with Botterill), London 1972; *Aron Nimzowitsch, A Reappraisal*, London 1974. *(H.G.)*

KELLER, Dieter *(b. 19 July 1936)*
Swiss international master (1961). Swiss champion in 1958, 1960, 1961 and 1963. Played in the Olympiads of 1956, 1958 and 1968. *(R.D.K.)*

KELLER-HERMANN, Edith *(b. 17 November 1921)*
An East German international Woman master, she obtained a number of high placings in the women's Candidates tournaments from 1949–50 onwards, her best performance being 3rd in 1955. She was the first woman player since Vera Menchik to be invited to compete in an international tournament confined to international masters: Dortmund 1951, where, though finishing joint last of 12, she defeated Puc and Rossolimo and drew with Bogoljubow and Grob. *(W.H.)*

KEMERI 1937
Kemeri (July–August 1937) was yet another tournament on the Moscow model, with six Latvian masters meeting twelve internationals. To the surprise of the chess world one of the home contingent, V. Petrov, succeeded in tieing with Flohr and Reshevsky for first prize, half a point ahead of Alekhine and Keres, thus obtaining an invitation for the all-grandmaster event at Semmering-Baden later in the year.

In the early rounds Reshevsky established a long lead, the log after seven rounds reading Reshevsky 6½, Alekhine, Apscheneek, Flohr, Petrov and A. Steiner 4½. Despite losses to Alekhine and Rellstab, the American was still a full point ahead of Flohr and Petrov with two rounds to go, but a draw with Ståhlberg and a loss to Böök helped to bring about the final result.

In his impressive wins over Reshevsky and Fine, Alekhine clearly showed himself on the way back to the World Championship, while Keres improved on his previous good results to become a factor to be reckoned with in the fight for the crown. Leading scores: Flohr, Petrov, Reshevsky 12, Alekhine, Keres 11½, A. Steiner 11. *(W.H.)*

KEMPELEN, Baron Wolfgang von
(See under THE TURK.)

KERES, Paul Petrovich *(7 January 1916–5 June 1975)*
Soviet international grandmaster, born in Narva, Estonia, Paul Keres was destined to become one of the strongest, most consistent and most popular grandmasters of our time. Already at the age of thirteen he took second place in the championship of Parnu, Estonia's capital; he took up correspondence chess to improve his powers of analysis. In 1935 he became champion of Estonia, and the same year made his first appearance on the international scene when he represented Estonia on first board at the Warsaw Olympiad. His score of 12½ out of 19 already marked him out as a player of formidable strength. Between 1936 and 1939 his results

continued to improve, culminating in his sharing first place with Fine at the A.V.R.O. 1938 tournament, ahead of the world's greatest players. Already there was talk of a match with Alekhine for the World Championship, but the war intervened and with the diminution of general chess activity in the world it was difficult for Keres to concentrate against the background of events in Estonia.

After the war Keres resumed his full playing career, but had perhaps missed his best chance of winning the World Championship. Nevertheless his results in title eliminating contests remained outstanding, and he could fairly claim to be the second or third best player in the world from 1948 until 1965.

His list of first prizes in international tournaments spreads over forty years and will long remain one of the finest: Tallinn 1936, Bad Nauheim 1936, Tallinn 1937, Margate 1937, Ostend 1937, Prague 1937, Vienna 1937, Semmering-Baden 1937, A.V.R.O. 1938, Margate 1939, Buenos Aires 1939, Posen 1943, Salzburg 1943, Madrid 1943, Riga 1945, Parnu 1947, Sczawno Zdroj 1950, Budapest 1952, Hastings 1954/5, Parnu 1955, Mar del Plata 1957, Santiago 1957, Hastings 1957/8, Parnu 1960, Zürich 1961, Los Angeles 1963, Beverwijk 1964, Buenos Aires 1964, Hastings 1964/5, Mariánské Lázně 1965, Stockholm 1966/7, Bamberg 1968, Budapest 1970, Tallinn 1971, Tallinn 1975, Vancouver 1975.

Add to these his victories in the Estonian championships of 1942, 1943, 1945 and 1953, the Georgian championship of 1946, and the Soviet championships of 1947, 1950 and 1951, together with second places in the Candidates tournaments of 1953, 1956 and 1962 and we complete the list of outstanding achievements of one of the truly great players of all time.

On his way home from the Vancouver Open tournament of 1975, Keres collapsed and died of a heart attack. He will be remembered throughout the chess world for his human qualities no less than for his vivid attacking style. His behaviour both at the board and away from it was always exemplary; the many friends he left will forever hold him in the highest esteem.

A good example of the play which caught the chess world's imagination at the Warsaw 1935 Olympiad is seen in his game against W. Winter:

White: Keres; *Black:* Winter
Sicilian Defence
1. P–K4, P–QB4; 2. N–KB3, N–KB3; 3. P–K5, N–Q4; 4. N–B3, P–K3; 5. N×N, P×N; 6. P–Q4, P–Q3; 7. B–KN5, Q–R4+; 8. P–B3, P×QP; 9. B–Q3!, P×BP; 10. O–O!, P×NP; 11. R–N1, P×P; 12. N×P, B–Q3;

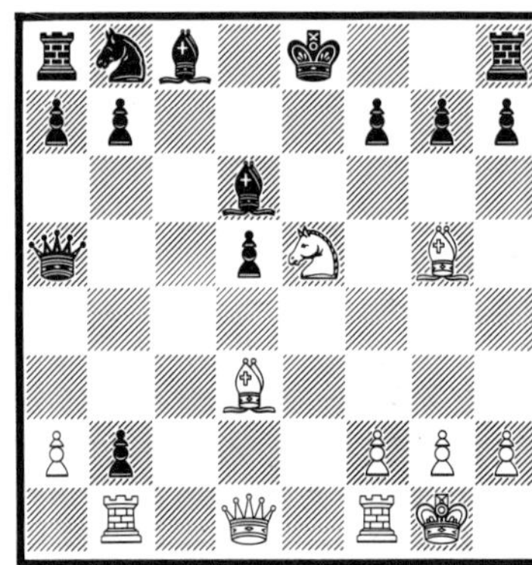

13. N×P!, K×N; 14. Q–R5+, P–N3; 15. B×P+!, P×B; 16. Q×R, B–KB4; 17. KR–K1, B–K5; 18. R×B!, P×R; 19. Q–B6+, resigns. *(W.R.H.)*

KEVITZ-TRAJKOVIĆ DEFENCE
An exaggeratedly hypermodern defence designed to tempt White's centre pawns into exposed positions. However, after the moves 1. P–Q4, N–KB3; 2. P–QB4, N–B3; 3. P–Q5, N–K4; 4. P–K4, White's pawn centre is more likely to represent a source of strength than weakness. *(R.D.K.)*

KHOLMOV, Ratmir Dimitrievich *(b. 13 May 1925)*
Soviet international grandmaster since 1960. Shared first place in the 1963 USSR championship but lost the subsequent play-off against Stein and Spassky. Took second place at Leningrad 1967 international tournament, and was the winner of Belgrade 1967, Havana 1968, and Dubna 1973 and =1st Budapest 1976. Also many times champion of Lithuania. *(W.R.H.)*

KIENINGER, Georg *(5 June 1902–31 December 1976)*
A West German international master, Kieninger won the German championship three times (1937, 1940 and 1947), while being joint runner-up to Eliskases in 1938 and sole runner-up to Unzicker in 1948. Victorious in many other local master-events (Hamburg 1946, Essen 1947), he obtained good places in several international appearances (3rd Bad Harzburg 1938, =3rd Stuttgart 1939, =3rd Travemünde 1950, =3rd Bewerwijk 1951, 4th Amsterdam

1962). Kieninger won many matches against minor opposition (Brinckmann, Engels, Ernst) but lost to Bogoljubow (1950, +1—3=4). *(W.H.)*

KIESERITSKY, Lionel *(1 January 1806–18 May 1853)*
Born in Livonia (a former province of Russia, now divided between Estonia and Latvia), subsequently resident in Paris from 1839 onwards, Kieseritsky is celebrated in chess history for having lost the Immortal Game to Anderssen at London in 1851 (*not* in the tournament) and for having popularized the Kieseritsky variation of the King's Gambit (1. P–K4, P–K4; 2. P–KB4, P×P; 3. N–KB3, P–KN4; 4. P–KR4, P–N5; 5. N–K5).

Inevitably comparisons were made between Kieseritsky and the last great native French master Saint-Amant. Though of the three games these two played against each other (so far as we know) each won one, the comparisons were much in Saint-Amant's favour. Writing in the *British Chess Magazine* for December 1883, the Rev. W. Wayte dismisses Kieseritsky as 'essentially a gallery player, dealing chiefly in fireworks against weak opponents, while Saint-Amant was more solid, and could be equally brilliant on occasion.

In 1846 he came to London and beat Horwitz in a match by +7—4=1; but in 1848 in Paris he was narrowly defeated by Buckle by +2—3=3.

In 1850 he played a colossal number of games in a match v. J. W. Schulten which he won by +107—34=10.

He returned to London in 1851 to take part in the 1851 tournament but had the misfortune to be drawn against Anderssen in the very first round, losing to him by ½–2½. Since this was a knock-out tournament Kieseritsky had no further interest in the event.

Buckle, who came too late to play in the tournament, had a couple of matches after the event. One was against Kieseritsky who revenged himself for his previous defeat by winning the match +2—1=0.

Kieseritsky's health gave way shortly after his return to Paris and he died in poverty in the Hotel de Dieu – the charity hospital for the insane – in 1853. Sadly, an appeal to the Paris chess-players for funds for his burial was not successful and he was buried in a pauper's grave.

An excellent annotator and writer on the game, he founded the chess magazine *La Régence* to replace Saint-Amant's *Le Palamède* and edited it from 1849 to 1851. He also published a work *Cinquante Parties*, Paris 1846. *(H.G.)*

KING
The King was always a monarch and appeared in that form as a rajah in the original game of *chaturanga* in the sixth century AD in north-west India. It moved as the present-day King with the exception that it could not castle.

When the game went to Persia and was known as *chatrang* at the end of the sixth century the Rajah became a Shah, but its powers were unaltered.

Similarly, when the Arabs took over the game under the name of *shatranj* in the seventh century, the Shah remained the same both in name and in nature.

Nor did its moves change when the game came to Europe in the ninth and tenth centuries. But it was then that the Shah became known as the King; everywhere, that is, except for Russia where it was (and still is) called *Korol* (pronounced 'Karol') and was so termed after Charlemagne (Carolus Magnus or Karl the Great).

The alteration in the King's moves with the introduction of castling came in the thirteenth and fourteenth centuries. At first, and for a long time, many different ways of castling existed, but gradually these settled down in the fifteenth and sixteenth centuries to become uniform with the method of castling that is in use today.

There did remain one pocket of resistance, the Modena school of players (such as Ercole del Rio and Ponziani) which, as late as the eighteenth century, believed in free castling. This was a type of castling in which the King could leap even further than KN1 and QB1 and in which the Rook could get as far as K1.

But in time too this long leap was abandoned and castling became uniformly practised as it is today.

For the King's present-day moves see LAWS OF CHESS, Articles 3 and 6. *(H.G.)*

KING HUNT
Driven out into the open, the King is usually beset by much greater dangers than in either the original or the castled position. This process, usually by means of one or several sacrifices, is called the king hunt. It is seen in the following famous miniature:

White: Ed. Lasker; *Black:* Sir George Thomas
Dutch Defence
1. P–Q4, P–KB4; 2. N–KB3, P–K3; 3. N–B3, N–KB3; 4. B–N5, B–K2; 5. B×N, B×B; 6. P–K4, P×P; 7. N×P, P–QN3; 8. B–Q3, B–N2; 9. N–K5, O–O; 10. Q–R5, Q–K2;

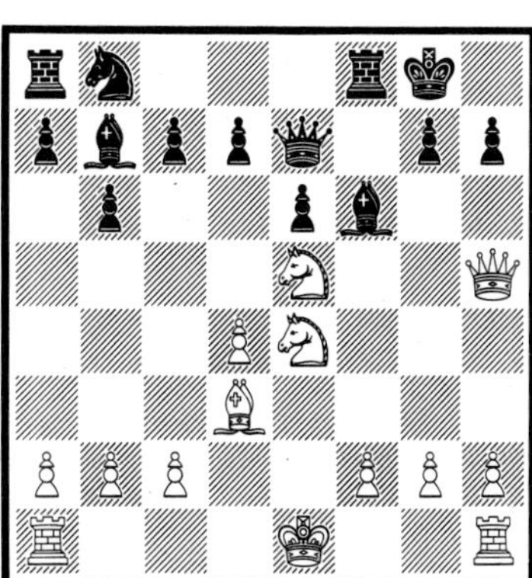

11. Q×P+, K×Q; 12. N×B+, K–R3; 13. N(5)–N4+, K–N4; 14. P–R4+, K–B5; 15. P–N3+, K–B6; 16. B–K2+, K–N7; 17. R–R2+, K–N8; 18. K–Q2 mate. *(W.H.)*

KING'S FIANCHETTO (Benko's Opening)
1. P–KN3 has been employed spasmodically by Réti and Benko in international chess but it has little individual significance. It will normally transpose to Réti's opening or the English opening. *(R.D.K.)*

KING'S FIELD SACRIFICE
A sacrifice in the field of the castled King, usually directed against

either of the pawns on KB7, KN7 or KR7, by the removal of which access to the hostile K is secured for the rest of the attacking force. Typical examples are the B sacrifice on KR7 or the double B sacrifice; e.g. Em. Lasker–Bauer (Amsterdam 1889), where from the diagram play proceeded:

14. N–R5!, N×N; 15. B×P+!, K×B; 16. Q×N+, K–N1; 17. B×P!, K×B; 18. Q–N4+, K–R2; 19. R–B3, P–K4; 20. R–R3+, Q–R3; 21. R×Q+, K×R; 22. Q–Q7, and White won on the 33rd move. *(W.H.)*

KING'S GAMBIT

With the moves 1. P–K4, P–K4; 2. P–KB4, White tries to lure Black's KP away from the centre, thus securing more room for his own pieces and perhaps attacking chances down the KB-file. This opening greatly lost popularity when master chess turned its attention away from immediate tactics and towards more positional objectives in the early stages, though analysis of most lines of the King's Gambit remains inconclusive. As both Spassky and Fischer have shown the move 2. P–KB4 can still prove a useful surprise weapon. Principal variations are as follows:

Allgaier Gambit, 2. . , P×P; 3. N–KB3, P–KN4; 4. P–KR4, P–N5; 5. N–N5.
Bishop's Gambit, 2. . , P×P; 3. B–B4.
Breyer Gambit, 2. . , P×P; 3. Q–B3.
Cunningham variation, 2. . , P×P; 3. N–KB3, B–K2.
Falkbeer Counter-gambit, 2. . , P–Q4.
Fischer's Defence, 2. . , P×P; 3. N–KB3, P–Q3.
Keres' Gambit, 2. . , P×P; 3. N–QB3.
Kieseritsky Gambit, 2. . , P×P; 3. N–KB3, P–KN4; 4. P–KR4, P–N5; 5. N–K5.
King's Gambit Declined, 2. . , B–B4.
Lesser Bishop's Gambit, 2. . , P×P; 3. B–K2.
Muzio Gambit, 2. . , P×P; 3. N–KB3, P–KN4; 4. B–B4, P–N5; 5. O–O.

Modern theory gives as Black's soundest line the continuation 2. . , P×P; 3. N–KB3, P–Q4; 4. P×P, N–KB3 with quick and easy development, rather than trying to hold the gambit pawn. *(W.R.H.)*

KING-SIDE CASTLING

This is when the King castles with the King's Rook. For the rules see LAWS OF CHESS, Article 6. *(H.G.)*

KING'S INDIAN DEFENCE

1. P–Q4, N–KB3; 2. P–QB4, P–KN3. An old defence which is now the most popular of all defences to the Queen's Pawn.

In the 1920s and 30s the usual method of meeting it was by the Four Pawns Attack: 3. N–QB3, B–N2; 4. P–K4, P–Q3; 5. P–B4. This has fallen into disuse and more common now are the Sämisch variation 5. P–B3, or the Classical Line 5. N–B3, O–O; 6. B–K2, or an early fianchetto by White by 3. P–KN3, B–N2; 4. B–N2, O–O. *(R.D.K.)*

KIROV, Nino *(b. 9 September 1945)*

Bulgarian Junior champion in 1962, he won the senior title in 1973, mid-way between acquiring the titles of international master, in 1971, and grandmaster in 1975. His best international performances have been 1st at Čoka 1973, 2nd at Polanica Zdroj 1974 and =1st in Vršac 1975. *(K.J.O'C.)*

KLAMAN, Konstantin Mikhailovich *(b. 1918)*

Soviet master who has twice played in the USSR championship final, finishing last in 1947 and equal 13th in 1957. *(W.R.H.)*

KLEIN, Ernst *(b. 1910)*

British master and winner of the British championship in 1951. Klein was born in Vienna and won the championship of that city in 1928. He emigrated to England in 1935. Tournament results include =2nd Bournemouth 1939 and =5th Hastings 1938/9. Klein withdrew from serious play in 1952 following a dispute with the B.C.F. In recent years he has played occasionally in county matches for Essex. *(R.D.K.)*

KLUGER, Gyula *(b. 15 January 1914)*

Hungarian international master since 1954. Runner-up in 1953 Hungarian championship, and winner of the Hastings Challengers tournament 1956/7. Nephew of Dr S. Fazekas. *(W.R.H.)*

KMOCH, Hans *(25 July 1894–14 February 1973)*

An Austrian international master, international arbiter and outstanding writer, Kmoch has left a lasting legacy with his books *Die Kunst der Verteidigung* [in German], Berlin-Leipzig 1927, and *Pawn Power in Chess*, New York, London 1959, his collection of *Rubinstein's Chess Masterpieces*, New York 1941, a number of witty tournament books (including that of Carlsbad 1929), and innumerable articles in chess journals. He played in few important tournaments (Semmering 1926 being the exception), but in smaller events finished first at Debrecen 1925, and Ebensee 1930, joint first at Vienna 1929, 3rd at Brno 1928, =3rd at Budapest 1928, and =3rd at Budapest 1926.

After the Second World War he emigrated to America where he wrote regular articles for the New York chess magazine, *Chess Review*. *(W.H.)*

KNAAK, Rainer *(b. 16 March 1953)*

Knaak is the youngest East German international grandmaster. After good placings in East German championships and first prize in the international youth tournament at Ploieşti 1971 he was selected as a member of the East German Olympic team at Skopje

1972. In international tournaments he came =2nd at Zinnowitz 1971, 1st at Olomouc 1972, 3rd at Bucharest 1973, =2nd (to Tal) at Halle 1974. In the 1975 East German championship he was =1st with Uhlmann but lost the play-off for the title. *(W.H.)*

KNEŽEVIĆ, Milorad *(b. 31 October 1936)*
Yugoslav grandmaster who made a considerable advance in the middle years of the 1970s to become one of Yugoslavia's leading players. He had a particularly active and successful career in the year 1974 when he was 2nd at Rimavska Sobota and at Albena, 3rd at Odessos (Varna), 1st at Stary Smokovec and =4th with Spassov, Ostojić Szabo, Kirov, Hernandez and Stindman at Slanchev Breag (Bulgaria). In 1975 he was =1st with Nemet at Čoka (Yugoslavia) =1st with Vaisman at Budapest and won outright at Olomouc and at Hradec Kralove (1975/6). In 1976 he was 1st in a tournament at Pamporovo in Bulgaria, but in a stronger tournament at Varna in May he came 5th/14. At Decin in Czechoslovakia he shared 3rd to 11th place in an astonishingly level event. He had a good 2nd to Gurgenidze at Olomouc in Czechoslovakia, was =2nd with Averbakh and Schmidt (Poland) at the Rubinstein Memorial tournament at Polanica Zdroj and was =1st at Uljma. Later on in the year he was awarded the grandmaster title at the FIDE Congress at Haifa. *(H.G.)*

KNIGHT
The Knight, like the Rook, has retained exactly the same powers of moving that it possessed in the original game, some 1,500 years ago. These powers have always seemed a little mysterious to the beginner or the less advanced player. Partly the reason for this is that the Knight can jump over a square occupied by another piece, and partly it is owing to the fact that the Knight's move is a composite one. To quote from the Laws of Chess: 'it takes one step of one single square along the file or rank, and then, still moving away from the square it left, takes one step along the diagonal.'

For further details about the Knight's placing and moves see LAWS OF CHESS, Articles 3 and 6.

In one way, though, the Knight was different in its earliest stages when the game was *chaturanga* in the sixth century AD in north-west India. It was in fact 'a horse' (*ashwa*). On the game's move to Persia in the next century it remained a horse (*asp*) and when the Arabs took over it was still a horse (*faras*).

Its change in function, outwardly, though not in its powers of moving, came in early medieval times when the game spread to Europe. Now, clearly under the influence of the founding of the chivalric orders, it became a Knight. This was so, for example, in England, France, Germany and the Netherlands.

Exceptionally, two countries retained the name of horse: Spain, which called it *caballo*, and Russia, which termed it *kon*. Spain no doubt retained the older form under the influence of the Moors in Spain, whilst Russia betrayed an even more old-fashioned influence from the Moslem form of the game in Persia. One strange return to the very oldest times is that the piece is shown everywhere nowadays as the mounted head of a horse. *(H.G.)*

KNIGHT'S TOUR
One of the oldest known tasks, the Knight's tour problem is to find a sequence of 64 moves by which a Knight can visit consecutively each square of the chessboard. A solution is called 're-entrant' if the Knight finishes on a square which is a Knight's move away from its starting square. The diagram shows a re-entrant Knight's tour from an Arabic manuscript of the fourteenth century:

32	35	30	25	8	5	50	55
29	24	33	36	51	56	7	4
34	31	26	9	6	49	54	57
23	28	37	12	1	52	3	48
38	13	22	27	10	47	58	53
19	16	11	64	61	2	43	46
14	39	18	21	44	41	62	59
17	20	15	40	63	60	45	42

The number of possible different solutions of the Knight's tour problem is immense and has not been calculated. One estimated upper bound for distinct paths is

$$\frac{168!}{105!\ 63!}$$

where 168! stands for the product of the numbers 1 to 168 inclusive, etc. *(R.D.K.)*

KOBLENCS [Koblents], Alexander Naftalyevich *(b. 1916)*
Soviet national master and Latvian champion in 1941, 1945, 1946 and 1949. Best known as Tal's trainer during the period leading to his win of the World Championship. Koblencs has written a number of monographs on training methods for chessmasters. *(W.R.H.)*

KOCH, Berthold *(b. 22 February 1899)*
An international master of East Germany and that country's champion in 1951 and 1952. He played only rarely in international events, but represented his country in the Olympiads of 1952 and 1956. For many years he was editor of *Schach*. *(W.H.)*

KOLAROV, Atanas Stefanov *(b. 2 March 1934)*
A regular member of Bulgarian teams in the years around 1960. Awarded title of international master in 1957. Kolarov shared first place in the 1964 Bulgarian championship but lost the play-off match to Padevsky. *(W.R.H.)*

KOLISCH, Ignaz Baron von *(6 April 1837–30 April 1889)*
Great Austro-Hungarian master and successful banker, the story of Ignaz von Kolisch is, like everything connected with the acquisition of money, highly romantic. Only a year after achieving his first and last triumph in tournament chess he met Baron Albert

Rothschild, one of the most munificent patrons of chess in the nineteenth century. The Baron, much impressed with Kolisch's personality, helped him enter the financial world of Vienna and he was so successful at this that he was made a baron of the Austrian Empire in 1881. This converted him from professional player to patron and he himself made big contributions to the funds of such tournaments as Baden-Baden 1870 and Vienna 1882.

His career as a chess-player, which was up to 1868, was also most successful, but it consisted largely of matches. It started when he came to England in 1860. There he won a match against Horwitz in Manchester by +3−1=0 and another most convincingly against Barnes in London by +10−1=0. In Paris the same year he drew a match with Anderssen by +5−5=1. He also won a small tournament at Cambridge that was played on the knock-out system.

In 1861 he came 3rd in a similar tournament at Bristol and narrowly lost matches to Anderssen (+3−4=2) and to Louis Paulsen in London by +6−7=18.

He played two more matches: drawing with Ph. Hirschfeld +4−4=0 and beating S. Rosenthal by +7−6=0, both at Paris 1864. This last match was in fact agreed as drawn in view of the closeness of the issue.

Then, in 1867, came his great success in the Paris tournament of 1867. This was a double-round affair in which draws did not count and Kolisch came first with 20 points ahead of Winawer and Steinitz. *(H.G.)*

KOLTANOWSKI, George *(b. 17 September 1903)*
Belgo-US international master and onetime world blindfold simultaneous record-holder, whose chess career was divided into two phases by the Second World War.

The first phase relates to his career as an active chess-master when he was a Belgian citizen. Born in Antwerp, he soon developed into one of Belgium's leading players. Edgar Colle, some six years his senior, was above him internationally but when Colle died in 1932 it was quite clear that Koltanowski was Belgium's strongest player and he remained so till he left the country for America in 1939.

Belgian champion in 1923, 1927, 1930 and 1936, his first real international performances came in 1924 when he came 11th in the strong Meran tournament and finished =4th in the Paris Olympiad.

He played with considerable success on top board for Belgium at the 1927 London Olympiad and again at The Hague Olympiad 1928 and was 4th at Hastings 1928/9 and =4th at Ramsgate 1929.

From 1934 onwards he was often in Spain where he played with much success. Equal 3rd with Tartakower at Sitges 1934, he was 1st at Mollet the same year and also =1st with Lilienthal and Tartakower at Barcelona. Three more excellent results were achieved in Spain in 1935: =1st with Flohr at Barcelona, 2nd at Rosas and =1st at Mollet.

A 4th at Hastings 1935/6 was followed by a 1st at Reus 1936, a 4th at Birmingham 1937 and a 6th at Ostend the same year.

Meanwhile, however, he had established a much bigger reputation as a blindfold simultaneous player at which he eventually, in 1931, became the world's best player. On 10 May 1931, he established a world record in scoring 25 out of 30 in a display at Antwerp that lasted $10\frac{1}{2}$ hours. He did not lose a single game but drew 10 and won the rest.

George Koltanowski giving a simultaneous blindfold display, London 1932

He bettered this record at Edinburgh, when, on 20 September 1937 he played 34 games in $13\frac{1}{2}$ hours, winning 24, drawing 10 and losing 0. He was to lose the world record (to Najdorf in 1943) after half a dozen years but his play in these events has always been distinguished by a bright power of invention and a remarkable capacity for winning beautifully played games.

Later on, at San Francisco on 13 December 1960, he played 56 opponents consecutively blindfold, winning 50 and drawing 6. He played the games at the rate of 10 seconds a move and the display took $9\frac{3}{4}$ hours.

By this time Koltanowski had been long established as a US citizen. He came to the US in 1940 and then embarked on a career of chess-organization and journalism. He was highly successful in both spheres, editing a lively and well-informed chess column in the *San Francisco Chronicle* and being elected President of the US Chess Federation in 1975.

Amongst his literary output are two entertaining autobiographical and discursive books, *Adventures of a Chess Master*, New York 1955, and *With the Chess Masters*, San Francisco 1972. *(H.G.)*

KÖNIG, Imre *(b. 2 September 1901)*
An international master since 1951, born at Gyula in Austro-Hungary. After the First World War König became a Yugoslav citizen and represented that country in the Olympiads of 1931 and 1935. He emigrated to England in 1938 and was naturalized in 1949. Since 1953 he has resided in the USA. Tournament results include 2nd prize at Hastings 1948/9. His publications include a monograph on *The Queen's Indian Defence*, London 1947, and a longer work, *Chess from Morphy to Botvinnik*, London 1951. *(R.D.K.)*

KONOPLEVA, Natalya *(b. 23 November 1944)*
Soviet player, awarded the international woman master title in 1970 and the women's grandmaster title in 1976. Her results in the Women's Interzonals have been =4th in 1971 and =2nd in 1973. Her result in the 1973 Interzonal almost qualified her for the 1974 Women's Candidates but in a four way play-off for three places, she finished last. *(K.J.O'C.)*

KONSTANTINOPOLSKY, Alexander Markovich *(b. 19 February 1909)*
Soviet master and trainer, international master since 1950. His best result was to take second place in the 1937 USSR championship, though he was also the winner of the first USSR Correspondence championship. Konstantinopolsky is highly respected as a trainer, having worked with Bronstein in the period leading to the latter's challenge for the World Championship. He has also for many years been the principal trainer for Soviet women players. *(W.R.H.)*

KORCHNOI, Viktor Lvovich *(b. 23 July 1931)*
Ex-Soviet international grandmaster and World Championship Candidate: one of the strongest of the world's grandmasters from 1960 onwards, Korchnoi is particularly dangerous as a tournament player and has frequently proved his ability by amassing enormous scores in strong events. His collection of first prizes perhaps outshines that of any other contemporary grandmaster. These include outright victories in the following events: Bucharest 1954, Cracow 1959, 27th USSR championship 1960, Cordoba 1960, Budapest 1961, 30th USSR championship 1962, Havana 1963, 32nd USSR championship 1964, Gyula 1965, Erevan 1965, Bucharest 1966, Sochi 1966, Leningrad 1967, Beverwijk 1968, Palma 1968, Sarejevo 1969, Luhacovice 1969, 38th USSR championship 1970, Wijk-aan-Zee 1971. In addition to these successes he has shared first place at Hastings 1955/6, Buenos Aires 1960, Havana 1969, Hastings 1971/2, Palma 1972 and Leningrad 1973.

Played four times in the Candidates, finishing 5th in 1962, 2nd in 1968 (losing the final match to Spassky), reaching the semi-final round in 1972 (where he lost to Petrosian), but coming closest to the World Championship at his attempt in 1974. After beating Mecking and Petrosian, Korchnoi lost a long and hard match by the narrowest possible margin to Karpov in the final.

Viktor Korchnoi in play, Hastings 1955/6

He has frequently represented the Soviet Union in Olympiads. In one such, at Siegen 1970, he created a minor sensation by arriving too late and defaulting a game because he had overslept. This apart, his Olympic score of fifty wins, thirty-one draws and only three losses, accumulated in six events, is a highly impressive one.

In 1976, immediately after sharing 1st place with Tony Miles in the I.B.M. tournament at Amsterdam, he defected from the USSR and was granted a residential permit in the Netherlands.

Korchnoi's chess style is very attractive for the onlookers, for he fights hard for a win in every game and is frequently in desperate time-trouble. He has the reputation of possessing immense reserves of determination and powers of concentration. At his most dangerous when launching a counter-attack, Korchnoi is perhaps one of the greatest defensive players of modern times and often shows in his play similar qualities of resilience and ability to stand up to tension which characterized his hero, Emanuel Lasker. His psychological approach to the game is shown to its best advantage when he plays with the Black pieces, as in the following game from the 1962 Candidates tournament:

White: Fischer; *Black:* Korchnoi
Pirc Defence
1. P–K4, P–Q3; 2. P–Q4, N–KB3; 3. N–QB3, P–KN3; 4. P–B4, B–N2; 5. N–B3, O–O; 6. B–K2, P–B4; 7. P×P, Q–R4; 8. O–O, Q×P+; 9. K–R1, N–B3; 10. N–Q2, P–QR4; 11. N–N3, Q–N3; 12. P–QR4, N–QN5; 13. P–N4, B×P!;

14. B×B, N×B; 15. Q×N, N×P; 16. N–N5, N×R; 17. N×N, Q–B3; 18. P–B5, Q–B5; 19. Q–B3, Q×RP; 20. N–B7, Q×N; 21. N–Q5, QR–K1; 22. B–N5, Q×P; 23. B×P, B–K4; 24. R–B2, Q–B8+; 25. R–B1, Q–R3; 26. P–R3, P×P; 27. B×R, R×B; 28. N–K7+, K–R1; 29. N×P, Q–K3; 30. R–KN1, P–R5; 31. R–N4, Q–N6; 32. Q–B1, P–R6; 33. resigns.

KOSHNITSKY, Gregory *(b. 6 October 1907)*
Many times Australian champion and Vice-President of FIDE Zone 10 (East Asiatic and Australian) from 1960–66, Koshnitsky was born in Russia but emigrated to Australia when a youth.

He first came to prominence in Australia by winning the Queensland championship in 1926, a result he was to repeat in the two following years.

He then went to New South Wales and tied for the State championship with M. E. Goldstein in 1929. He won the Australian championship in 1932, held it till 1934, and again won the championship during the period 1939 to 1945.

His later chess career was entirely administrative and organizational. He was secretary of the Australian Chess Federation from 1965 and represented the federation as delegate at the FIDE Congresses in the 1960s and 1970s. He has also acted as non-playing captain of the Australian team at Chess Olympiads from 1964–74.

In return for his services to chess he was awarded the M.B.E. in 1970. *(H.G.)*

KOSTIĆ [Kostich], Boris *(27 February 1887–3 November 1963)*
A Yugoslav grandmaster and one of his country's leading players for many years, though never quite in the class of Vidmar or Pirc.

His best tournament results were: 2nd New York 1918 and Hastings 1919; =3rd Budapest 1921; 1st Trenčianské Teplice 1928 and Ljubljana 1938.

In matches he beat Showalter in 1916 by +7−2=5; he lost to Capablanca in 1919 by +0−5. In 1916 he temporarily established a blindfold simultaneous record by playing thirty games. *(H.G.)*

KOSTRO, Jerzy *(b. 25 January 1937)*
Polish international master and Polish champion 1966 and 1970.

In the Zonal tournament at Vrnjačka Banja 1966 he came =6th with Hamann, Lengyel, Pachman and Mohrlok.

He played for Poland at the Olympiads of Munich 1958, Leipzig 1960, Havana 1966, Lugano 1968 (scoring 53.3% on 1st board), Siegen 1970 (losing a famous game against Spassky), and Nice 1974. *(H.G.)*

KOTOV, Alexander Alexandrovich *(b. 12 August 1913)*

A Soviet international grandmaster, Kotov was already champion of his home town, Tula, at the age of sixteen, but it was some time before he progressed to become one of the Soviet Union's leading players. He became a national master at the age of twenty-five by his performance in sharing third place in the USSR championship semi-final. The following year, 1939, he scored an outstanding result in the championship to finish 2nd behind Botvinnik. Only in 1948 was Kotov able to better this result, when he shared the title with Bronstein.

His international results included a number of first places, among them Jönköpping 1958/9, Stockholm 1959/60 and Hastings 1962/3, but his most famous victory came in the 1952 Interzonal tournament in Stockholm and Saltsjöbaden which he won with 16½ points from 20 games, three points ahead of his nearest rival. The apparent promise of this result was not, however, carried through in the Candidates the following year, where he only shared eighth place.

In more recent years, Kotov has turned his attentions more towards tasks of chess organization and training in the USSR, and to writing books. He is frequently the delegation leader when Soviet teams travel abroad, and has published several successful books including some translated into English, among them: *The Soviet School of Chess*, London 1958; *Think like a Grandmaster*, London 1971; and *Alexander Alekhine*, London 1973.

At his best Kotov was a highly dangerous attacking player always ready to take vigorous advantage of any defensive error.

Stockholm 1952
White: Kotov; *Black:* Barcza
King's Indian Defence
1. P–Q4, N–KB3; 2. P–QB4, P–KN3; 3. N–QB3, B–N2; 4. P–K4, P–Q3; 5. P–KN3, O–O; 6. B–N2, P–K4; 7. KN–K2, P×P; 8. N×P, N–B3; 9. N–B2, B–K3; 10. P–N3, Q–Q2; 11. O–O, B–R6; 12. P–B3, B×B; 13. K×B, P–QR3; 14. B–N2, N–R2; 15. Q–Q2, P–QN4; 16. N–K3, P–B3; 17. QR–Q1, QR–Q1; 18. N–K2, Q–B2; 19. B–B3, Q–K2; 20. N–Q4, N–K1;

21. N(4)–B5!, P×N; 22. N×P, Q–B2; 23. N×B, N×N; 24. B–B6!, K–R1; 25. Q–N5, R–KN1; 26. P–KR4!, QR–K1; 27. P–R5, R–K4; 28. B×R, P×B; 29. Q–B6, N–B1; 30. P–R6, N–K2; 31. R–Q2, resigns. *(W.R.H.)*

KOTTNAUER, Cenek *(b. 24 February 1910)*
Born in Czechoslovakia, Kottnauer played for that country in many events including the 1952 Olympiad. He emigrated in 1953 and subsequently took British nationality, representing England in the Olympiads of 1964 and 1968. Awarded FIDE titles of international master in 1950 and International Judge in 1951. Winner of Lucerne 1953 international tournament.

Co-author with T. D. Harding and G. S. Botterill of *The Sicilian Sozin*, London 1974. *(W.R.H.)*

KOVAČEVIĆ, Vlatko [Vlado] *(b. 26 March 1942)*
Yugoslav teacher of mathematics who received the grandmaster

title in 1976, having attained the rank of international master in 1970. His best tournament results have been =2nd at Rovinj/Zagreb 1975, =1st at Sombor and at Virovitica in 1976. His placing of =9th in the very strong tournament at Rovinj/Zagreb in 1970 was also a fine achievement, even more notable for the crushing defeat which he inflicted on Fischer.

White: Fischer; *Black:* Kovačević
French Defence
1. P–K4, P–K3; 2. P–Q4, P–Q4; 3. N–QB3, B–N5; 4. P–QR3, B×N+; 5. P×B, P×P; 6. Q–N4, N–KB3; 7. Q×NP, R–N1; 8. Q–R6, QN–Q2; 9. N–K2, P–N3; 10. B–N5, Q–K2; 11. Q–R4, B–N2; 12. N–N3, P–KR3; 13. B–Q2, O–O–O; 14. B–K2, N–B1; 15. O–O, N–N3; 16. Q×RP, R–R1; 17. Q–N5, QR–N1; 18. P–B3, P–K6; 19. B×P, N–B1; 20. Q–N5, N–Q4; 21. K–B2, P–R3; 22. Q–Q3, R×P; 23. R–R1, Q–R5; 24. R×R, Q×R; 25. N–B1, R×P+; 26. K–K1, Q–R5+; 27. K–Q2, N–N3; 28. R–K1, N(3)–B5; 29. B×N, N×B; 30. Q–K3, R–B7; 31. resigns.
(K.J.O'C.)

KOVACS, Laszlo *(b. 5 September 1938)*
Hungarian international master. He came =10th at Budapest 1965, =8th at Harrachov 1966 and 1st at Lublin 1968. *(H.G.)*

KOZLOVSKAYA, Valentina *(b. 18 April 1938)*
International woman master and winner of the USSR Women's championship in 1965. Never quite reached the top of World-title competitions, but came very close with second place in the 1967 Candidates tournament, and later won the Women's Interzonal in 1972. Kozlovskaya is married to grandmaster Igor Bondarevsky. *(W.R.H.)*

KOZMA, Julius *(b. 1 June 1929)*
Czechoslovak master awarded international title in 1957 following his win at the Bratislava international tournament of that year. Represented Czechoslovakia in 1958 and 1960 Olympiads. *(W.R.H.)*

KRAIDMAN, Yair *(b. 1 November 1932)*
An Israeli grandmaster who is by profession a controller accountant in the Ministry of Finance. Though he has never won the Israeli championship, his best result in this event having been 2nd in 1959, he has won national tournaments twice.

He has played for Israel in ten Olympiads from 1958 to 1976. His best result in these was at Lugano, 1968, where he had the second-best score on 2nd board.

It was at the Tel Aviv Olympiad of 1964 that he gained the international master title, and he won the grandmaster title by coming =2nd at Natanya in 1975 and =1st at Beersheba 1976.

A quiet but determined and most gifted amateur, he is the model of good sportsmanship over and away from the board. *(H.G.)*

KRAMER, Haije *(b. 24 November 1917)*
Dutch international master who works for the municipality of Leeuwarden in Friesland and has been the leading player of that province of The Netherlands for many years.

His best international results have been a 3rd at Beverwijk 1946 and a 1st in a small tournament at Leyden that year. He also played in Zonal tournaments in 1951 and 1954, occupying positions in the lower half of the table.

He represented The Netherlands on a low board in seven Olympiads from 1950 to 1962.

Co-author with Dr Euwe of *Het Middenspel*, The Hague and Jakarta 1952/3, translated into English under the title of *The Middle Game*, Part One published in London 1964, Part Two also in London 1965. *(H.G.)*

KRAUSE, Orla Herman *(3 November 1867–28 September 1935)*
A noted Danish theoretician. His tournament results include 2nd at Copenhagen 1899 and 1916. Collaborated with Nimzowitsch in openings research in the 1920s. *(R.D.K.)*

KREJCIK, Josef Emil *(22 January 1885–4 January 1957)*
Born in Vienna, Professor Krejcik was a chess all-rounder: tournament player, endgame composer, problemist, organizer and, above all, journalist. A competitor in many local and some international events in Vienna, he obtained many brilliancy prizes but did not have the stamina for substantial sporting achievements. His mainly humorous books *(13 Kinder Caissens*, Vienna 1924; *Artige und Unartige Kinder der Schachmuse*, Leipzig 1925; and *Mein Abschied vom Schach*, Berlin 1955) represent his best work. *(W.H.)*

KROGIUS, Nikolai Vladimirovich *(b. 22 July 1930)*
Soviet master, awarded titles of international master in 1963 and international grandmaster in 1964. Took first places in tournaments at Varna 1960, Sochi 1967 and Varna 1969.

Krogius has worked in detail on the methods of preparation suitable for a chess-master, and has written monographs on the psychology of chess. Accompanied Spassky to the 1972 World Championship match in the role of psychologist. *(W.R.H.)*

KUIJPERS, Frans *(b. 27 February 1941)*
Dutch international master (1964) who works as a physicist at the Philips Research Laboratories. Best results: 1st Master group Wijk-aan-Zee 1963, =2nd (with O'Kelly) Malaga 1965, =3rd Master group Wijk-aan-Zee 1974. Dutch champion 1963. Played in Olympiads 1964 (1st board) and 1968 (5th board) and in all Clare Benedict Team tournaments from 1963 to 1969. *(R.D.K.)*

KUPCHIK, Abraham *(15 March 1892–26 November 1970)*
Russian-born Kupchik was an American master whose forty-year career consisted mainly of US events. He won the Manhattan Chess Club championship ten times and once shared the title – a record that still stands. He was a frequent rival of Capablanca and Marshall, tieing for first with Marshall at Lake Hopatcong 1923 and winning a speed tournament ahead of the Cuban three years later at the same place. In his brief European venture Kupchik

scored +6—0=8 on 3rd board for the US team at the 1935 Olympiad in Warsaw. Kupchik also drew a 1925 match with Carlos Torre +1—1=4. *(A.S.)*

KUPPER, Dr Josef *(b. 10 March 1932)*
A Swiss international master (1955), Swiss champion 1954, 1957, and 1962. Played in the Olympiads of 1954, 1958, 1964 and 1968. Well known in Switzerland as a writer on chess. *(R.D.K.)*

KUPREICHIK, Viktor Davidovich *(b. 3 July 1949)*
Soviet master and frequent member of their Student teams around 1970. Played in the USSR championship finals in 1969, 1974 and 1976 without much success. He is nevertheless a player of undoubted talent that needs only discipline and care to attain real achievement. *(W.R.H.)*

KURAJICA, Bojan *(b. 15 November 1947)*
A Yugoslav grandmaster. He was first in the World Junior Championship Barcelona 1965, receiving the international master title. Never lived up to early promise due to lack of dedication. Best result: =1st with Hort and Ivkov at Sombor 1968 ahead of Matulović. Best result in Yugoslav championship =3rd with Parma, Minić and Matulović, Čateske Toplice 1968. In 1969 he beat Kholmov 2½–1½ in USSR v. Yugoslavia match. Graduate in English and Italian of Zagreb University. *(R.D.K.)*

KUSHNIR, Alla *(b. 11 October 1941)*
Former Soviet woman grandmaster, Kushnir is one of the most successful post-war women players, and the only one apart from Gaprindashvili to compete with any success against men. Three times winner of the Women's Candidates, on each occasion she was beaten by Gaprindashvili in the World Championship match.

Alla Kushnir (standing) against Gaprindashvili, Moscow 1969

She dropped out of the 1973 Candidates series to emigrate from the USSR, where she was born, to live in Israel. Subsequently she scored one of her greatest successes at the tournament in Lone Pine 1975 by winning two games against grandmasters. *(W.R.H.)*

KUZMIN, Gennadi *(b. 19 January 1946)*
One of the strongest of the young generation of Soviet players. Gained the title of international grandmaster in 1973 in which year he also took seventh place in the Leningrad Interzonal tournament. Shared first place at Hastings 1973/4. *(W.R.H.)*

L

LA BOURDONNAIS, Louis Charles Mahé de *(1797–13 December 1840)*
A gifted pupil of Deschapelles, and the strongest French player after Deschapelles' retirement in 1821. Since none of his countrymen could rival him, most of La Bourdonnais' career was spent in proving his superiority over the leading British masters. He won a match against Cochrane 1821, when the latter visited Paris, and defeated Lewis by +5—2 in London in 1823. In 1834 he played a celebrated series of six matches, a total of eighty-five games, against McDonnell with a final score of +45—27=13. After this victory, La Bourdonnais' health began to fail, and with it his income. Impoverished, he returned to London in 1840 to take up a post as chess professional at the 'Divan', but died shortly after his arrival. He lies buried – near McDonnell – in Kensal Green cemetery.

La Bourdonnais possessed a boisterous and temperamental nature at the chessboard. Writing of the match against McDonnell, Walker tells us that La Bourdonnais 'talked and laughed a good deal at intervals, when winning, and swore tolerably round oaths in a pretty audible voice, when fate ran counter to his schemes'.

16th Match game, London 1834
White: La Bourdonnais; *Black:* McDonnell
Queen's Gambit Accepted
1. P–Q4, P–Q4; 2. P–QB4, P×P; 3. P–K3, P–K4; 4. B×P, P×P; 5. P×P, N–KB3; 6. N–QB3, B–K2; 7. N–B3, O–O; 8. B–K3, P–B3; 9. P–KR3, QN–Q2; 10. B–N3, N–N3; 11. O–O, KN–Q4; 12. P–QR4, P–QR4; 13. N–K5, B–K3; 14. B–B2, P–KB4; 15. Q–K2, P–B5; 16. B–Q2, Q–K1; 17. QR–K1, B–B2; 18. Q–K4, P–N3; 19. B×P, N×B; 20. Q×N, B–B5; 21. Q–R6, B×R;

22. B×P, P×B; 23. N×NP, N–B1; 24. Q–R8+, K–B2; 25. Q–R7+, K–B3; 26. N–B4, B–Q6; 27. R–K6+, K–N4; 28. Q–R6+, K–B4; 29. P–N4 mate. *(R.D.K.)*

LANDAU, Salo *(1 April 1903–12 October 1943)*
A Dutch international master, Landau was born in Bochnia (Poland), and emigrated in the First World War to the Netherlands. He was a Jewish victim of the Second World War.

Dutch champion 1936. Played in Olympiads 1930 and 1937. Won first prizes in five Premier Reserves tournaments in Margate and Hastings between 1935 and 1938. In Hastings 1938/9 he came 3rd. Played many matches against Réti, Flohr, Spielmann, Euwe, Lilienthal, and others. *(R.D.K.)*

LANGE, Max *(7 August 1832–8 December 1899)*

A German player, theoretician and problemist. He won first prize at Düsseldorf 1862, 1863 and 1864, Hamburg 1868, and Aachen 1868. His *Handbuch der Schachaufgaben*, Leipzig 1862, was the first attempt at systematization of problems. His literary output includes a book on Morphy (Leipzig 1859), a primer (*Lehrbuch des Schachspiels*, Halle 1856), opening monographs and endgame collections. He edited the *Deutsche Schachzeitung* from 1858 to 1864. As an organizer he was responsible for the Leipzig congress and tournament of 1894; as a problemist he invented the 'helpmate'; as a theoretician he is remembered for the Max Lange Attack (see TWO KNIGHTS DEFENCE). One of the greatest chess all-rounders of all time. *(W.H.)*

LANGEWEG, Christiaan *(b. 7 March 1937)*
Dutch international master and frequent member of Dutch teams in international competitions. He has played for the Netherlands in six Olympiads: 1960, 1962, 1964, 1966 (with the best score on 4th board), 1968 and 1970 (63.3% on 3rd board).

He has not had good results at Beverwijk but, in recompense, has a fine record in the I.B.M. international tournaments at Amsterdam in July. He was first in the 1961 event, =3rd with Ćirić in 1967 and =8th with Csom in 1974.

Apart from this he has had occasional successes in tournament play to his credit; he was 1st at Plovdiv in 1974 and 4th at the 1st International Swiss championship at Zürich 1976. *(H.G.)*

'LÄROBOK I SCHACK' [**Manual of Chess**]
Written by the brothers Collijn, this manual (Stockholm 1898) rapidly acquired considerable fame as the only manual plus encyclopedia that contained really fresh analyses, especially in the openings. As the editions succeeded each other so the worth of the book became enhanced by the collaboration of such writers and players as Réti, Spielmann and Rubinstein. *(H.G.)*

LARSEN, Bent *(b. 4 March 1935)*
Denmark's leading player and one of the few Western masters in recent years seriously to challenge Russian domination of international tournaments.

Larsen was born in Tilsted (Jutland). He was taught chess by a school-mate at the age of six and joined his local chess club when he was twelve. As a boy he was not in any sense a prodigy, but his playing strength increased steadily year by year. He represented Denmark in the first two World Junior Championships at Birmingham 1951, where he finished =4th and Copenhagen 1953, where he placed =5th. He first became Danish champion in 1954 and has won this title every time he has chosen to participate (1955, 1956, 1959, 1963, 1964).

He became an international master in 1955 and was awarded the grandmaster title after his remarkable performance in the 1956 Moscow Olympiad at which he won the top board prize with 14 points from 18 games. Subsequently, Larsen decided to abandon his civil engineering studies and devote himself professionally to playing chess.

Bent Larsen at Hastings 1956/7

His style is highly aggressive – he will choose a risky continuation rather than tamely accept a draw – and thus more suited to tournament than match-play. Larsen is renowned as a particularly ferocious competitor. His numerous victories include first prizes at Mar del Plata 1958, Wijk-aan-Zee 1960 (shared with Petrosian), Wijk-aan-Zee 1961 (shared with Ivkov), Amsterdam Interzonal 1964 (shared with Spassky, Smyslov), Amsterdam I.B.M. tournament 1964, Havana 1967, Winnipeg 1967 (shared with Darga), Sousse 1967, Palma 1967, Monaco 1968, Büssum 1969, Palma 1969, Lugano 1970, Vinkovci 1970, Las Palmas 1972 (shared with

Smyslov), Hastings 1972/3, Manila 1973, Orense 1975, Arrecife 1976, Biel Interzonal 1976 and Blanes y Malgrat 1976. His results in late 1967 and early 1968, when he won five consecutive major international events including an Interzonal, are superior even to Rubinstein's great successes in 1912. In 1970 he was chosen as first board in the USSR v. Rest of the World match, scoring +1−1=1 against Spassky and +1 against Stein.

Larsen has three times reached the semi-finals of the Candidates stage of the World Championship. In 1965 he defeated Ivkov (+4−1=3) and then lost a close match (+2−3=5) to Tal. In 1968 he won against Portisch (+3−2=5) but lost to Spassky (+1−4=3). In 1971 he beat Uhlmann (+4−2=3) before being eliminated by Fischer (+0−6=0). In the 1973 World Championship cycle he failed to qualify for the Candidates, finishing =5th with Hübner at the Leningrad Interzonal.

In the openings, Larsen is noted for his 'anti-theoretical' bias: he tends to avoid heavily analysed variations if possible. He is known for his attempts to revive certain nineteenth-century openings (e.g. Philidor's Defence) and for his successful experiments with opening systems involving an early Q-side fianchetto for White.

Larsen writes regularly for several chess magazines and has published a collection of his own games which appeared in English as *Larsen's Selected Games of Chess*, London 1971.

Santa Monica 1966
White: Larsen; *Black:* Petrosian
Sicilian Defence
1. P–K4, P–QB4; 2. N–KB3, N–QB3; 3. P–Q4, P×P; 4. N×P, P–KN3; 5. B–K3, B–N2; 6. P–QB4, N–B3; 7. N–QB3, N–KN5; 8. Q×N, N×N; 9. Q–Q1, N–K3; 10. Q–Q2, P–Q3; 11. B–K2, B–Q2; 12. O–O, O–O; 13. QR–Q1, B–QB3; 14. N–Q5, R–K1; 15. P–B4, N–B2; 16. P–KB5, N–R3; 17. B–N4, N–B4; 18. P×P, RP×P; 19. Q–KB2, R–KB1; 20. P–K5, B×P; 21. Q–R4, B×N; 22. R×B, N–K3; 23. R–B3, B–B3; 24. Q–R6, B–N2;

25. Q×P, N–B5; 26. R×N, P×Q; 27. B–K6+, R–B2; 28. R×R, K–R1; 29. R–KN5, P–N4; 30. R–N3, resigns.

(R.D.K.)

LASA, Tassilo von Heydebrand und der
(17 October 1818–27 July 1899)

Born in Berlin, Von der Lasa was one of the most versatile figures in the chess world, excelling as player, theoretician and historian. His career in the diplomatic service enabled him to make many

contacts abroad (he served in Vienna, Stockholm, Brussels, The Hague, Rio de Janeiro and elsewhere) so that, in a manner of speaking, he may be called the first truly international master. As such he beat many of the leading players of the period in match-play (among them Jaenisch, Staunton, Löwenthal).

As a theoretician he established his name by the publication of the famous *Handbuch*, Berlin 1843 (originally planned by his friend Bilguer), as well as his *Leitfaden für Schachspieler*, Berlin 1848. But his most important work was in historical research as laid down in his famous *Zür Geschichte und Literatur des Schachspiels*, Leipzig 1897. He also published a minor work, *Berliner Schacherinnerungen*, Leipzig 1859, which in addition to much valuable material on Berlin chess around 1840 contains translations of Lucena and Greco.

No biographical note of Von der Lasa would be complete without mention of his unequalled collection of chess books and manuscripts, which in the end comprised 2,263 items, some of them going back to the fourteenth century. After being lost in the aftermath of the Second World War, this treasure was found intact in a Polish castle in 1957. *(W.H.)*

LASKER, EDWARD *(b. 3 December 1885)*

A distant relative of Emanuel Lasker, Edward was an occasional participant in international events 1910–30 despite a career as professional engineer. He was born in Berlin where he won the city championship in 1909. After a brief stay in London, he arrived in the US shortly before the First World War and settled there afterwards.

Lasker won the Western Open, then the strongest annual American event, on five occasions before challenging Marshall to a match for the US championship in 1923. Lasker lost $8\frac{1}{2}$–$9\frac{1}{2}$. He came 10th at New York 1924. Lasker was a prolific author and his books include *The Adventure of Chess*, New York 1950, London 1959; *Chess and Checkers*, New York, London 1918; and *Chess Secrets*, New York 1951, London 1952. *(A.S.)*

LASKER, Emanuel *(24 December 1868–13 January 1941)*

World Champion, 1894–1921. Lasker was the most successful chess-master of all time. He stood clear above the chess-world of his day and even after losing the World title, he won major tournaments and was a world force until the age of 67 – a unique achievement. His successes have been thoroughly analysed and he has been accused of hypnotizing his opponents, casting spells, using psychological methods, playing badly on purpose and of having phenomenal luck. In fact he was the ideal fighter: eager for battle, totally unafraid, unbelievably subtle and profound, with marvellous manoeuvring ability and enormous and sustained power.

Lasker was born in Berlinchen, Prussia. He made his mark in 1889 in Germany, 1891 in England and 1893 in USA. In 1894 he won the World title by defeating the aging Steinitz +10−5=4. There followed a series of outstanding tournament successes: firsts at St Petersburg 1895/6, Nuremberg 1896, London 1899 and Paris 1900.

He then returned to his mathematical studies and received his doctorate (1902) for research on abstract algebraic systems, material used to this day.

In 1904 Lasker began *Lasker's Chess Magazine* (1904–8) and the same year tied for 2nd at Cambridge Springs. In 1909 he came equal first at St Petersburg. In between, Lasker crushed several rivals in matches: +8−0=7 v. Marshall (1907); +8−3=5 v. Tarrasch (1908); +7−1=2 v. Janowski (1909). In 1910 Lasker had a close call against Schlechter, +1−1=8. In St Petersburg 1914 Lasker's incredible fighting spirit overcame a 1½-point deficit and he edged out the seemingly unbeatable Capablanca, demolishing the young Cuban in their critical game. But Capablanca was not to be denied, and in 1921 Lasker lost his World title by +0−4=10.

Lasker was the first master who seriously attempted, by demanding large fees, to improve the chess-master's financial position. Even his enemies conceded that Lasker was worth every penny. Inflation in the 1920s wiped him out and Lasker returned to the chess wars. He came 1st at Mährisch-Ostrau 1923, 1st at New York 1924 ahead of Capablanca and Alekhine, and 2nd at Moscow 1925 again ahead of World Champion Capablanca. In New York Lasker created new endgame theory, over the board, when he drew with a lone Knight against Rook and pawn.

Lasker now devoted himself to philosophy, writing and teaching. In 1934 at the age of sixty-six, Lasker returned to tournament play, coming 5th at Zürich, 3rd at Moscow 1935 where he was undefeated and only half a point behind Botvinnik and Flohr, 6th at Moscow 1936 and tied for 7th at Nottingham 1936 – a fantastic achievement. Lasker died in New York on 13 January 1941.

His complex play has inspired all students of chess, and the following example of his play has been described as one of the most beautiful, most profound, most exciting and most difficult in the whole literature of the game.

Cambridge Springs 1904
White: Lasker; *Black:* W. E. Napier
Sicilian Defence
1. P–K4, P–QB4; 2. N–QB3, N–QB3; 3. N–B3, P–KN3; 4. P–Q4, P×P; 5. N×P, B–N2; 6. B–K3, P–Q3; 7. P–KR3, N–B3; 8. P–KN4, O–O; 9. P–N5, N–K1; 10. P–KR4, N–B2; 11. P–B4, P–K4; 12. KN–K2, P–Q4; 13. KP×P, N–Q5; 14. N×N, N×P; 15. N–B5, N×N; 16. Q×Q, R×Q; 17. N–K7+, K–R1; 18. P–R5, R–K1; 19. B–B5, NP×P; 20. B–B4, P×P; 21. B×BP, N–K5; 22. B×R, B×P; 23. QR–N1, B–B6+; 24. K–B1, B–KN5; 25. KB×P, B×B; 26. R×B, N–N6+; 27. K–N2, N×R; 28. R×P, P–R4; 29. R–N3, B–N2; 30. R–KR3, N–N6; 31. K–B3, R–R3; 32. K×P, N–K7+; 33. K–B5, N–B6; 34. P–R3, N–R5; 35. B–K3, resigns.

Some life scores: +28−8=12 v. Steinitz; +11−2=4 v. Blackburne; +8−1=4 v. Chigorin; +18−4=8 v. Tarrasch; +5−5=4 v. Pillsbury; +5−2=12 v. Schlechter; +12−2=11 v. Marshall; +2−1=4 v. Rubinstein; +2−6=16 v. Capablanca; +3−1=4 v. Alekhine; +3−0=0 v. Euwe; +0−1=3 v. Botvinnik.

Chief works: *Common Sense in Chess*, London, New York 1896; *St Petersburg Tournament Book, 1909*, New York 1910; *Mein Wettkampf mit Capablanca* [in German], Berlin–Leipzig 1922; *Lasker's Chess Manual*, London 1932, New York 1934; *Alekhine–Bogoljubow Return Match*, London 1935. *(N.D.)*

LATVIA

The game in Latvia was first mentioned in writings of the fourteenth century, but no organized chess activity occurred until 1869, when the Riga Chess Club was founded. Their first tournament was held in 1875, but this was only a local event. The beginnings of more far-reaching plans came with the founding in 1890 of the 'Chess Society of Riga' under the presidency of Andrei Asharin. Each year from then until the end of the century a tour by a visiting master was organized, among them Steinitz, Chigorin and Tarrasch. The most important tournaments in Latvia at this time were the annual events of the Riga Chess Society. In the years after 1900 these were dominated by Karl Behting, eight times winner, but in 1915 Herman Mattison emerged as the strongest player in Latvia, a place he held for the next fifteen years.

When the Olympiads were introduced in 1928, Latvia entered its own team, and continued to be represented in these events until 1939. Their best result was to finish 5th in 1931. Also during this period occasional matches were played against teams representing Lithuania, Estonia, and The Netherlands. The first important international event held in Latvia was the very strong tournament at Kemeri 1937, won by Petrov, Reshevsky and Flohr ahead of Alekhine and Keres. Two years later another event in the same city was won by Flohr.

Since becoming part of the USSR, Latvia has no longer entered separate teams for Olympiads, but continues to have its own championship, and its own team in the annual event between the different Soviet republics. Among the strongest masters to have been born in Latvia are Petrov, Mattison, Apscheneek, Feigin, Koblencs, Gipslis and Tal. Since 1959 the Latvian Chess Federation has published a magazine, *Sahs*, first under the editorship of Tal, and subsequently run by Gipslis with Tal as consultant.

(W.R.H.)

LAWS OF CHESS

These Laws are the translation authorized by the Fédération Internationale des Echecs at Gothenburg, August 1955, as amended at the FIDE Congress, Nice, June 1974.

Part 1: General Laws

Article 1: Introduction

The game of chess is played between two opponents by moving pieces on a square board called a 'chess-board'.

Article 2: The Chessboard and its arrangement

1. The chessboard is made up of 64 equal squares alternately light (the 'white' squares) and dark (the 'black' squares).
2. The chessboard is placed between the players so that the square in the corner to the right of each player is white.
3. The eight rows of squares running from the edge of the chess-board nearest one of the players to that nearest the other are called 'files'.
4. The eight rows of squares running from one edge of the chess-board to the other at right angles to the files are called 'ranks'.
5. The rows of squares of the same colour touching corner to corner are called 'diagonals'.

Article 3: The Pieces and their Positions

At the beginning of the game one player has 16 light coloured pieces (the 'White' pieces), the other has 16 dark coloured pieces (the 'Black' pieces). These pieces are as follows:

A White KING indicated usually by the symbol
A White QUEEN indicated usually by the symbol
Two White ROOKS indicated usually by the symbol
Two White BISHOPS indicated usually by the symbol
Two White KNIGHTS indicated usually by the symbol
Eight White PAWNS indicated usually by the symbol
A Black KING indicated usually by the symbol
A Black QUEEN indicated usually by the symbol
Two Black ROOKS indicated usually by the symbol
Two Black BISHOPS indicated usually by the symbol
Two Black KNIGHTS indicated usually by the symbol
Eight Black PAWNS indicated usually by the symbol

The initial position of the pieces on the chessboard is as follows:

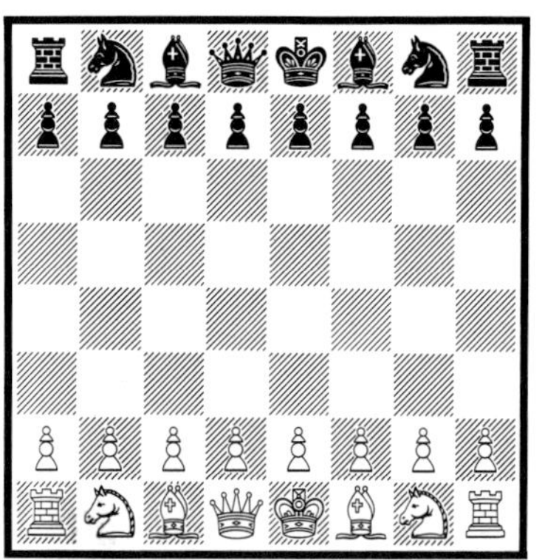

Article 4: The Method of Play

1. The two players must play alternately and make one move at a time. The player with the White pieces commences the game.
2. A player is said 'to have the move' when it is his turn to play.

Article 5: The Move in General

1. With the exception of Castling (Article 6.1), a move is the transfer of one piece from one square to another square which is either vacant or occupied by an opponent's piece.
2. No piece, except the Rook when Castling or the Knight (Article 6.5), can cross a square occupied by another piece.
3. A piece played to a square occupied by an opponent's piece takes it as part of the same move. The captured piece must be immediately removed from the chessboard by the player who has made the capture. See Article 6.6 (b) for taking 'en passant'.

Article 6: The Moves of the Individual Pieces

1. The KING. Except when Castling, the King moves to an adjacent square that is not attacked by an opponent's piece. Castling is a move of the King and a Rook, reckoned as a single move (of the King), which must be carried out in the following manner – the King is transferred from its original square to either one of the nearest squares of the same colour in the same rank; then that Rook towards which the King has been moved is transferred over the King to the square which the King has just crossed.

Castling is permanently impossible (a) if the King has already been moved, or (b) with a Rook that has already been moved.

Castling is prevented for the time being – (a) if the original square of the King or the square which the King must cross or that which it is to occupy is attacked by an opponent's piece, or (b) if there is any piece between the Rook involved in the move and the King.
2. The QUEEN. The Queen moves to any square on the file, rank, or either of the diagonals on which it is placed.
3. The ROOK. The Rook moves to any square on the file or rank on which it is placed.
4. The BISHOP. The Bishop moves to any square on either of the diagonals on which it is placed.
5. The KNIGHT. The Knight's move is made up of two different steps. It takes one step of one single square along the file or rank,

and then, still moving away from the square it left, takes one step along the diagonal.

6. The PAWN. The pawn can only move forward:

(*a*) Except when making a capture it advances from its original square either one or two vacant squares along the file on which it is placed, and on subsequent moves it advances one vacant square along the file. When making a capture it advances one square along either of the diagonals on which it is placed.

(*b*) A pawn attacking a square crossed by an opponent's pawn which has been advanced two squares on the previous move can capture the opponent's pawn as though the latter had only been moved one square. This capture can only be made on the move immediately following such advance and is known as taking 'en passant'.

(*c*) On reaching the end of a file a pawn must be immediately exchanged, as part of the same move, for a Queen, a Rook, a Bishop or a Knight at the player's choice and without taking into account the other pieces still remaining on the chessboard. This exchanging of a pawn is called 'promotion'. The promoted piece must be of the same colour as the pawn and its action is immediate.

Article 7: The Completion of a Move

A move is completed:

1. In the case of the transfer of a piece to a vacant square, when the player's hand has quitted the piece; or

2. In the case of a capture, when the captured piece has been removed from the chessboard and when the player, having placed the piece on its new square, has quitted the piece with his hand; or

3. In the case of Castling, when the player's hand has quitted the Rook on the square crossed by the King; when the player's hand has quitted the King the move is still not yet completed, but the player no longer has the right to make any other move except Castling; or

4. In the case of the promotion of a pawn, when the pawn has been removed from the chessboard and the player's hand has quitted the new piece after placing it on the promotion square; if the player's hand has quitted the new piece after placing it on the promotion square; if the player's hand has quitted the pawn that has reached the promotion square the move is still not yet completed, but the player no longer has the right to move the pawn to another square.

Article 8: Touched Piece

1. Provided that he first warns his opponent, the player whose turn it is to move can adjust one or more pieces on their squares. Except for the above case, if the player having the move touches:

(*a*) one or more pieces of the same colour, he must move or capture the first piece touched that can be moved or captured;

(*b*) one of his own pieces and one of his opponent's pieces, he must capture his opponent's piece with his own piece; or, if this is not possible, move his own piece; or, if even this is not possible, capture his opponent's piece.

3. If the move or capture is not possible, the player is free to make any legal move he chooses.

4. If a player wishes to claim a violation of this rule, he must do so before he touches a piece himself.

Article 9: Illegal Positions

1. If during the game it is ascertained that an illegal move has been made, then the position shall be set up again as it was immediately before the making of the illegal move. The game shall then continue in accordance with the rules given in Article 8 as regards the move replacing the illegal move.

If it proves impossible to set up the position again then the game must be annulled and a fresh game played.

2. If, in the course of a game, one or more pieces have been accidentally displaced and are not correctly replaced, the position must be set up as it was immediately before the mistake and the game continued.

If it proves impossible to set up the position again then the game must be annulled and a fresh game played.

3. If, after an adjournment, the position is incorrectly put up, then the position as it was on adjournment must be set up again and the game continued.

4. If during the game it is ascertained that the initial position of the pieces was incorrect, then the game must be annulled and a fresh game played.

5. If during the game it is ascertained that the position of the chessboard is incorrect, then the position that has been reached must be transferred to a chessboard that has been correctly placed and the game continued.

Article 10: Check

1. The King is in check when the square which it occupies is attacked by an opponent's piece: in this case the latter is said to be 'checking the King'.

2. The check must be met on the move immediately following. If the check cannot be met then it is called 'mate' (see Article 11.1).

3. A piece that intercepts a check to the King of its own colour can itself give check to the opponent's King.

Article 11: Won Game

1. The game is won for the player who has mated the opponent's King.

2. The game is considered won for the player whose opponent declares he resigns.

Article 12: Drawn Game

The game is drawn:

1. When the King of the player whose turn it is to move is not in check, and such player cannot make a move. This is called 'stalemate'.

2. By agreement between the two players.

3. At the request of one of the players when the same position appears three times, and each time the same player has had the move. The position is considered the same if pieces of the same kind and colour occupy the same squares and if the possible moves of all the pieces are the same.

This right of claiming the draw belongs to the player:

(*a*) who is in a position to play a move leading to such repetition of the position, if he declares his intention of making this move; or

(*b*) who is about to reply to a move by which such repeated position has been produced.

If a player makes a move without having claimed a draw in the manner prescribed in (a) or (b) he then loses his right to claim a draw; this right is however restored to him if the same position appears again with the same player having the move.

Interpretation of 12.3

(i) A game cannot be declared drawn on the basis of Article 12, clause 3, unless the same player has the move after each of the three appearances of the same position on the chessboard.

(ii) The right of claiming the draw belongs exclusively to the player who:

(*a*) has the possibility of playing a move leading to the repetition of the position, provided that he indicates the move and claims the draw before making the move;

(*b*) must reply to a move by which the repeated position has been produced, provided that he claims the draw before executing his move.

(iii) If the claim proves to be incorrect (Article 18.2) and the game continues, then the player who has indicated a move according to para. 2a is obliged to execute this move on the chessboard.

4. When the player whose turn it is to move proves that at least fifty moves have been played by each side without a capture of a piece and without a pawn move having been made.

This number of fifty moves can be increased for certain positions providing that this increase in number and these positions have been clearly laid down before the commencement of the game.

Part 2: Additional Rules for Competitions

Article 13: Game Scores

1. In the course of the game each player should write down the score of the game, move by move (his moves and those of his opponent) in as clear and legible a manner as possible on a score-sheet prescribed for the competition.

2. If, on account of extreme time trouble, a player clearly is unable to fulfil the obligations prescribed in sub-section 1, he should nevertheless endeavour to indicate on his score sheet the number of moves made. As soon as the time trouble is over he must immediately fill in the moves omitted from his score sheet. However, he is not entitled to claim, on the grounds of Article 12.3 or 12.4, a draw based on any moves which have not been written down in accordance with the prescriptions of sub-section 1.

Article 14: The Use of the Chess Clock

1. Each player has to make a certain number of moves in a given time, these two factors having been laid down in advance.

2. The time control for each player is effected by means of a clock provided with special apparatus.

3. The clock of the player who has White is set in motion at the time fixed for the commencement of the game. From then on, each player, having made his move, stops his own clock and starts his opponent's clock.

4. When considering whether the prescribed number of moves has been made in the given time the last move is not considered as made until after the player has stopped his clock.

5. All indications given by a clock or its apparatus are considered as conclusive in the absence of evident defects. The player who claims that there is such a defect should do this as soon as he himself has become aware of it.

6. If the game has to be interrupted for some reason for which neither player is responsible both clocks must be stopped until the point concerned has been dealt with. This should be done, for example, in the case of an illegal position necessitating correction, or in that of a defective clock that must be changed, or if the piece which a player has declared he wishes to exchange for one of his pawns that has reached the end of a file is not immediately to hand.

7. In cases arising out of Article 9, clauses 1 and 2, when it proves impossible to determine the time taken by each player up to the moment when the illegality occurred, each player shall be allotted up to this moment a time proportional to that indicated on the clock at the moment when the illegality was ascertained.

For example: after Black's 30th move in a game, it is ascertained that an illegality occurred on the 20th move. Since the clock shows for these 30 moves 1 hour 30 minutes (90 minutes) for White and 1 hour (60 minutes) for Black, the times taken by the two players for the first 20 moves are calculated as follows:

$$\text{WHITE} \quad \frac{90 \times 20}{30} = 60 \text{ minutes}$$

$$\text{BLACK} \quad \frac{60 \times 20}{30} = 40 \text{ minutes}$$

Article 15: Adjournment of the Game

1. If, after the elapse of the time laid down for play, the game is not finished, the player whose turn it is to move must write down his move in unambiguous notation on his score sheet, put this score sheet as well as that of his opponent in an envelope, close the envelope and then stop his clock. This move is called the 'sealed move'. Should the player make his move on the chessboard he must seal the same move on his score sheet.

2. On the envelope should be stated –

(*a*) the names of the players;

(*b*) the position immediately before the sealed move;

(*c*) the time taken by each player;

(*d*) the name of the player who has sealed the move and the number of this move.

3. The envelope must be put into safe keeping.

Article 16: The Resumption of the Game

1. When the game is resumed, the position immediately before the sealed move should be set up and the time taken by each of the players when the game was adjourned should be indicated on the clocks.

2. The envelope must not be opened until that player is present

whose turn it is to move (i.e. the one who should reply to the sealed move). The clock of this player should be started when the sealed move has been made on the chessboard.
3. If the player whose turn it is to move is absent, then his clock should be started, but the envelope will only be opened when he arrives.
4. If the player who has sealed the move is absent, then the player whose turn it is to move need not make his reply to the sealed move on the chessboard. He has the right to write down his move in reply on his score sheet, put this move in an envelope, stop his clock and start his opponent's clock. The envelope should then be put into safe keeping and opened on the opponent's arrival.
5. If the envelope containing the move sealed on adjournment has disappeared without it being possible to re-establish, with the agreement of the two players, the position and the times used for the adjourned game, or if for any other reason the said position and the said times cannot be re-established, the game is annulled and a fresh game must be played instead of the adjourned game.

If the envelope enclosing the move sealed according to sub-article 4 has disappeared, then the game must be resumed as from the position at the time of adjournment and with the clock time used at the said time.
6. If, at a resumption of play, either clock has been incorrectly set, and if either player points this out before making his first move, then the error must be corrected. If the error is not so pointed out the game continues without correction.

Article 17: Loss of the Game
A game is lost by a player:
1. Who has not played the prescribed number of moves in the given time;
2. Who arrives at the chessboard more than one hour late;
3. Who has sealed a move the real significance of which it is impossible to establish;
4. Who during the game refuses to comply with the laws of chess.

If both players arrive at the chessboard more than one hour late, or if both refuse to comply with the Laws of Chess, the game shall be declared lost for both.

Article 18: Drawn Game
1. A proposal to draw can be made by a player only at the moment when he has just made a move. On then proposing a draw he starts the clock of his adversary. The latter may accept or (either orally or by making a move) reject the proposal; in the interval the player who has made the proposal cannot withdraw it.
2. If a player claims a draw in accordance with the rules of Article 12.3, his clock must go on until the competition director has investigated the claim.

If the claim is proved to be correct, the game shall be declared a draw, even if the claimer has exceeded the time limit in the meantime.

If the claim is proved to be incorrect, the game shall be continued, unless the claimer has exceeded the time limit in the meantime, in which case the game shall be declared lost for the claimer.

3. Tournament arbiters are requested to impose in cases where clear contravention of the moral principles of the game are evidenced, penalties reaching as far as the loss of the game.

Article 19: Players' Behaviour
1. (*a*) Whilst play is in progress players are forbidden to use written or printed notes or to analyse the game on another chessboard, and are also forbidden to have recourse to the counsel or advice of a third party, whether asked for or not.

(*b*) No analysis is allowed in the rooms of play either whilst play is in progress or during the adjournment.

(*c*) It is forbidden to distract or worry the opponent in any way whatsoever.
2. Infractions of the laws as indicated in sub-article 1 can entail penalties reaching as far as the loss of the game.

Article 20: The Arbiter of the Competition
An arbiter should be designated to direct the competition. His duties are:

(*a*) to see that the rules of play are strictly observed;

(*b*) to supervise the competition, to establish that the prescribed time limit has not been exceeded by the players, to fix the order of resumption of adjourned games, to see that the arrangements contained in Article 15 are observed, above all to see that the particulars put down on the envelope at the adjournment are correct, to keep the sealed envelope until the time when the game is resumed, etc.;

(*c*) to put into force decisions which he may make on disputes that have arisen in the course of the competition;

(*d*) to impose penalties on the players for any fault or infraction of the rules.

Article 21: The Interpretation of the Laws of the Game
In case of doubt as to the application or interpretation of these laws F.I.D.E. will examine the evidence and make an official decision.

Supplement No. 4: Rules for playing chess between Sighted and Blind players
In competitive chess between sighted and blind players the use of two chessboards shall be obligatory, the sighted player using a normal chessboard, while the blind player uses one with securing apertures. The following regulations shall govern play:
1. The moves shall be announced clearly, repeated by the opponent and executed on his board.
2. On the blind player's board a piece shall be deemed 'touched' when it has been taken out of the securing aperture.
3. A move shall be deemed executed, when:

(*a*) a piece is placed into a securing aperture;

(*b*) in the case of a capture, the captured piece has been removed from the board of the player who has the move;

(*c*) the move has been announced.

Only after this shall the opponent's clock be started.
4. A chess clock with flag, made specially for the blind, shall be admissible.

5. The blind player may keep the score of the game in Braille or on a tape recorder.
6. A slip of the tongue in announcing a move must be corrected immediately and before starting the clock of the opponent.
7. If, during a game, different positions should arise on the two boards, such differences have to be corrected with the assistance of the controller and by consulting both players' game scores. In resolving such differences the player who has written down the correct move, but executed the wrong one, has to accept certain disadvantages.
8. If, when such discrepancies occur, the two game scores are also found to differ, the moves shall be retraced up to the point where the two scores agree, and the controller shall re-adjust the clocks accordingly.
9. The blind player shall have the right to make use of an assistant who shall have the following duties:

(*a*) to make the moves of the blind player on the board of the opponent;

(*b*) to announce the moves of the sighted player;

(*c*) to keep the score for the blind player and start his opponent's clock;

(*d*) to inform the blind player, at his request, of the number of moves made and the time used up by both players;

(*e*) to claim the game in cases where the time-limit has been exceeded;

(*f*) to carry out the necessary formalities in cases where the game is adjourned.

10. If the blind player does not require any assistance, the sighted player may make use of an assistant who shall announce his moves and make the blind player's moves on his board. *(H.G.)*

LAZARD, Fred *(20 February 1883–18 November 1948)*
French player, problemist and writer, famous as being on the winning side in one of the shortest games ever (against Gibaud at Paris 1924).

He came =1st with Chéron in the 1926 French championship but he devoted himself more to writing about the game than playing it and was a brilliant chess journalist. Lazard published an entertaining book on his problems and endgame studies: *Mes problèmes et études d'échecs*, Paris 1929. *(H.G.)*

LAZAREVIĆ, Milunka *(b. 1 December 1932)*
Woman grandmaster and Yugoslavia's leading woman player for many years. She won the Yugoslav Women's championship many times and represented Yugoslavia in nearly all post-war Women's Olympiads. A great talent since her early teens, Lazarević worked her way up to World title contender. In recent years her tournament performances were uneven due to brittle health. She is a brilliant chess journalist, fluent in many languages. *(R.D.K.)*

LEBANON
A team representing this country has taken part in seven Olympiads with the following results: 36th in 1958, 40th in 1960, 50th in 1966 and 1968, 45th in 1970, 52nd in 1972 and 54th in 1974.

The strongest Lebanese player is Bachar Kouatly (*b.* 3 March 1958). He finished =3rd in the 1975 Teheran Zonal, thus acquiring the title of international master (the first Lebanese player to achieve this), and was =4th in the 1976 World Junior Championship.

Chess in the Lebanon is supervised by the Fédération Libanaise des Echecs, B. P. 11-4055, Beirut. *(K.J.O'C.)*

LEE, Frank J. *(1858–12 September 1909)*
British master who was chess teacher and chess professional and who, if not quite in the first rank, was high up in the second rank of British players in the late nineteenth century. Playing in the Minor section of the 1883 London Chess Congress he came 9th/26 in the Vizayanagaram tourney, so called because the Maharajah of that country had made a big donation to the tournament funds.

At Bradford in 1888 he was =14th/17 with the Rev. Owen, but won the individual games versus Burn, Blackburne and Bird.

His best tournament result was in New York 1893 where he came =3rd/14 ahead of Pillsbury, beating the tournament winner, Em. Lasker.

His last international tournament abroad was Barmen 1905 where, playing the B Master section he came 10th/18, beating the second prize-winner, Swiderski, and also the youthful Spielmann.

He lost a number of matches – to Gunsberg, Blackburne, Em. Lasker, and Teichmann (twice) but he beat Bird +7—4=2.
(H.G.)

LEE, Peter N. *(b. 21 November 1943)*
The 1965 British champion, Peter Lee has had a brief but distinguished career in British chess.

He came to the fore as a junior player, winning both the London and British Junior (under-18) championships in 1962.

When he won the British championship in 1965 he was, at the age of twenty-one, the youngest player ever to have won the title, a record that has since been passed by Mestel (in 1976). His next appearance in the British championship was at Oxford in 1967 where he was =3rd with Golombek and Whiteley.

Meanwhile he had played in a number of tournaments. In the West European Zonal tournament at The Hague 1966 he was 9th/17. Playing on board 2 at the Havana Olympiad of 1966 he scored 46.9%. At the Lugano Olympiad of 1968 he scored 69.2% as number 5 in the team. In the Siegen Olympiad of 1970 he had 56.7% on board 4. *(H.G.)*

LEGAL, M. de Kermur, Sire de *(1702–1792)*
Champion of the Café de la Régence and the best player in France till the arrival of Philidor. A fine combinative player, he was the early tutor of Philidor and the smothered mate known as Philidor's Legacy is supposed to have stemmed from him.

He is also the originator of Légal's mate, sometimes known as Blackburne's mate, owing to the frequency with which the latter thus caught his opponents in his simultaneous displays.

This mate is to be found in the only game played by him that has descended to us.

White: Légal; *Black:* Saint Brie
Philidor's Defence
1. P–K4, P–K4; 2. B–B4, P–Q3; 3. N–KB3, B–N5; 4. N–B3, P–KN3; 5. N×P, B×Q; 6. B×P+, K–K2; 7. N–Q5 mate.

(H.G.)

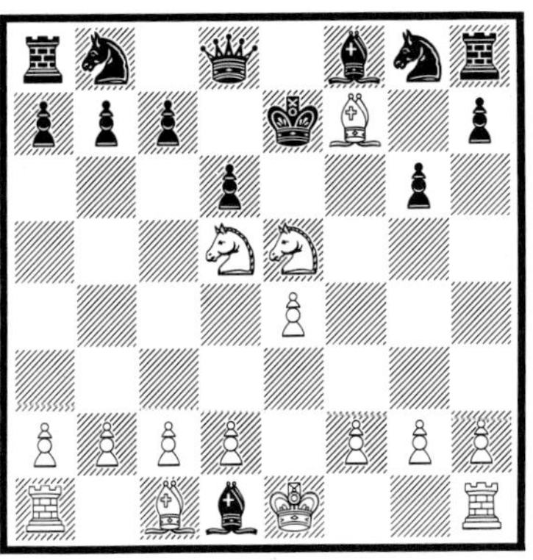

LEHMANN, Heinz *(b. 20 October 1921)*
A German international master, who represented West Germany in the Olympiads of 1958 and 1960 and in the Zonal tournaments of Munich 1954 and Madrid 1960. He was successful in many minor international tournaments, such as San Benedetto 1958 (2nd), Malta 1958 (2nd), 1959 (1st), Birseck 1961 (3rd), Kiel 1961 (1st), Reggio Emilia 1961/2 (2nd), Bognor Regis 1962 (2nd), and Stary Smokovec 1969 (1st) and Malta 1975 (1st). In German championships he came 2nd in 1953, and 3rd in 1957 and 1959. *(W.H.)*

LEIN, Anatoly Yakovlevich *(b. 28 October 1931)*
One of the lesser-known Soviet grandmasters, he emigrated to the USA in 1976. Awarded title of international master in 1964 and grandmaster in 1968. Shared first place at Sarajevo international tournament 1968, and won outright at Cienfuegos 1972, Novi Sad 1973, and Rome 1976 and Varna 1974. He also shared first place at New York 1976 and in the 1976 US Open.

By profession Lein is a mathematician. *(W.R.H.)*

LEMACHKO, Tatiana *(b. 16 March 1948)*
Born in the USSR, she obtained the women's international master title in 1971 while still a Soviet citizen. However, her best results have been achieved under the Bulgarian flag (acquired by marriage). She won the Bulgarian Women's championship in 1974 and 1975. She was the victor of the 1975 Pula Women's Zonal and in 1976, by finishing =3rd at the Roosendaal Women's Interzonal, obtained the title of international woman grandmaster.

(K.J.O'C.)

LENGYEL, Levente *(b. 13 June 1933)*
Hungarian grandmaster, awarded the title in 1964, following his becoming an international master in 1962. Winner of tournaments at Solingen 1968 and Reggio Emilia 1972/3. Lengyel shared first place in the 1962 Hungarian championship but lost the play-off to Portisch. *(W.R.H.)*

LEONARDO DA CUTRI *(1542–1587)*
Giovanni Leonardo, nicknamed *il Puttino* ('The Boy'), one of the leading sixteenth-century Italian players, was born in Cutri in Calabria. Details of his life are recounted in Salvio's chess romance *Il Puttino*, but Salvio's chronology is suspect and some incidents are embellished to show his hero in a favourable light.

As a youth, Leonardo moved to Rome to study law, and soon became known as a young player of great talent. In 1560 he played against and was defeated by the visiting Spanish cleric, Ruy Lopez. Over the next fourteen years Leonardo established a reputation as one of the two greatest Italian masters, his only rival being the Sicilian Paulo Boi. In 1574, Leonardo decided to try his skill abroad and, together with Polerio and Rosces, he embarked on a tour of the Iberian peninsula. While in Spain he gained his revenge against Ruy Lopez and defeated another Spanish expert, Ceron, in matches played in the presence of Philip II, who rewarded him liberally. (Salvio tells us that when asked by Philip to name a favour, Leonardo requested that his native town of Cutri be exempt from taxation for twenty years.) He also visited Portugal, where King Sebastian bestowed on him the name of *il Cavaliero errante*.

Returning to Italy, Leonardo moved to Naples and took up a position as agent for the Prince of Bisignano. Under the patronage of the viceroy, the Duke d'Ossuna, he is said to have contested many games against Boi, proving of roughly equal strength. Leonardo died in 1587, probably poisoned by a jealous rival.

(R.D.K.)

LEONHARDT, Paul Saladin
(13 November 1877–14 December 1934)
Polish-German master who was born in Poznan but lived most of his life in Germany. He had a long career in international chess, ranging from 1903 when he won first prize at Hilversum ahead of Důras, to 1933 when he was =7th/10 with John at Swinemünde.

He won two more first prizes, in smaller tournaments, at Hamburg 1905 and Copenhagen 1907. He was 2nd at Göteborg and Stockholm 1909, Mannheim 1922, Duisburg 1929.

All these were short and unimportant events but he also played in some of the greatest tournaments of his time: =7th at Barmen 1905, =14th Nuremberg 1906, 22nd Ostend 1907, 3rd Carlsbad 1907 (probably his finest result), 15th San Sebastian 1911, =8th/26 Carlsbad 1911 with Alekhine, Důras and Tartakower, 10th San Sebastian, 9th Abbazia and 15th-17/18 Pistyan all 1912 and 9th Berlin 1920.

He played a large number of matches, losing badly to Mieses, narrowly to Spielmann and Marshall and beating Nimzowitsch by +4−0=1.

An excellent theorist, a number of opening lines are named after him. He specialized in the Ruy Lopez and wrote an important monograph on the opening: *Zur spanischen Partie*, Stockholm 1913. *(H.G.)*

LETELIER, Martner René *(b. 21 February 1915)*
Chilean international master and champion of Chile in 1951, 1957, 1959 and 1960.

His chief international activities have been playing in the Mar del Plata tournaments and representing Chile at the Olympiads of 1939, 1950, 1956, 1960 and 1966.

His Mar del Plata record is: =11th/16 1936; 12th/16 1945; 11th/19 1946; =6th/18 1949; 8th/23 1951; =11th/18 1952; =6th/20 1953; 12th/16 1955; =11th/16 1958; 6th/16 1959; 7th/16 1960; 6th/16 1961; =15th/16 1962; and 16th/16 1976.

Other results have been =6th Montevideo 1949; =5th Venice 1950; 1st Montevideo 1954; 4th Asuncion 1960 and 5th at Jerusalem 1964. *(H.G.)*

LEVENFISH [Löwenfisch], Grigory Yakovlevich *(9 March 1889–9 February 1961)*
Soviet international grandmaster, and Soviet champion 1934 and 1937. One of the strongest players in the USSR during the 1930s. Levenfish won the title of master in 1911 and Soviet grandmaster in 1937, following his drawing a match with Botvinnik. FIDE conferred upon him the title of international grandmaster in 1950.

Levenfish performed especially well in the early USSR championships, taking 3rd place in 1920, 2nd in 1923, 3rd in 1924, 2nd in 1925, 3rd in 1933, equal 1st in 1934 and 1st outright in 1937. His international results were good, but rarely outstanding.

Levenfish was also well known as a theoretician, and had a Sicilian Defence variation named after him. He was the author of many books on various aspects of the game, including a celebrated work on Rook Endings on which he collaborated with Smyslov *Teoriya Ladenich Okontchanie*, Moscow 1959. *(W.R.H.)*

LEVITINA, Irina *(b. 8 June 1954)*

International Woman master since 1972, and one of the leading young Soviet candidates for the Women's World Championship. Reached the final of the Candidates match series in 1975, where she lost a close match to Alexandria. *(W.R.H.)*

LEVITZKY, Stepan Mikhailovich *(25 April 1876–21 March 1924)*
Russian master and one of their strongest players at the turn of the century. Winner of the All-Russian Amateur championship of 1911, and of the Breslau international tournament of 1912. Levitzky is however best remembered as the loser of a brilliancy to Marshall in Breslau 1912. *(W.R.H.)*

LEVY, David Neïl Laurence *(b. 14 March 1945)*
Scottish international master and computer chess expert. Born in London, he won the London Junior championship in 1965 and 1966.

His best performance was =5th at the Praia da Rocha Zonal tournament 1969, where he was one of two undefeated players (the other was Filip of Czechoslovakia) and where, with more than 66.6%, he obtained the title of international master.

A professional chess writer since 1971, he has been prolific.

Chief works: *Svetozar Gligorić's Chess Career*, London 1972; *The Sicilian Dragon*, London 1972; *Howard Staunton World Chess Champion*, Nottingham 1975. *(H.G.)*

LEWIS, William *(9 October 1787–22 October 1870)*
Author of the *Chessboard Companion*, London 1838, and several other popular works on chess (including translations of Greco and Stamma). Lewis was also a leading chess teacher – his most famous pupil was Alexander McDonnell – and for a time he ran chess rooms in St Martin's Lane. In 1819 he operated the chess-playing automaton 'The Turk' when it was exhibited in London. The Lewis Counter-gambit is 1. P–K4, P–K4; 2. B–B4, B–B4; 3. P–QB3, P–Q4!? *(R.D.K.)*

LIBERZON, Vladimir *(b. 23 March 1937)*

Formerly a Soviet grandmaster (awarded the title in 1965), Liberzon moved to Israel in 1973 and represented that country in the Olympiad of the following year. He has scored a number of notable tournament successes including first places at Zinnowitz 1967, Debrecen 1968, Venice 1974, Lone Pine 1975 and (shared) Beer Sheba 1976. Also won the 1974 Israel championship after a play-off match with Czerniak. In 1976 he scored 50% on top board at the Haifa Olympiad. *(W.R.H.)*

LIBRARIES
Of all board games, chess undoubtedly possesses the greatest literature. The largest public store of chess books, manuscripts and periodicals is the J. G. White Collection which is part of the Cleveland Public Library, Cleveland, Ohio, USA. Founded by bequest in 1928, it now contains over 20,000 items relating to chess and draughts (checkers).

A catalogue of the White Collection is available (in two volumes) and the library staff operate an excellent photo-copying and question-answering service.

The best European chess library is the Van der Linde-Niemeijer collection at the Royal Library in The Hague, with over 13,000 items. Of comparable size, but not available to the public, is the collection of grandmaster Lothar Schmid at Bamberg, West Germany. Schmid is probably the world's leading private collector of chess literature.

In Australia, the Victoria State Library in Melbourne has a substantial chess section, bequeathed by M. V. Anderson. *(R.D.K.)*

LIBYA
Libya is not affiliated to FIDE and in 1976 actually opposed FIDE by holding an unofficial 'Olympiad' at the same time as the official one in Haifa. The results of the quaintly styled 'Against Chess Olympiad', played in Tripoli, were: El Salvador 38½; Tunisia 36; Pakistan 34½; Iraq 33½; Italy and Turkey 32½; Afghanistan 29½; Nicaragua and Panama 27½; Bangladesh, Portugal and Sri Lanka 27; Algeria, Morocco and the Philippines 26½; Kenya, Uruguay and South Yemen 26; Trinidad, Malta, North Yemen and Madagascar 25½; Lebanon 25; Libya, Jordan, Uganda, Kuwait and the Arab Emirates 24½; Mauritius 20; 'Palestine' and Mauretania 18½; Gambia and Oman 18; Somalia 7. *(K.J.O'C.)*

LIEBERT, Heinz *(b. 24 May 1936)*
An international master of East Germany, who has represented his country in every Olympiad from 1962 to 1972. His best international results have been 1st at Ulan Bator 1956; 2nd at Polanica Zdroj 1966; 4th at Varna 1969; 3rd at Kecskemet 1970; =2nd at Lublin 1972 and 3rd at Stary Smokovec 1975. *(W.H.)*

LIGHTNING CHESS
A method of play, sometimes known under its German name of 'Blitz chess', in which each player is given very little time to think and make his move. The normal speed in such events used to be ten seconds a move, this being controlled by a metronome device. For example, when Reuben Fine won the lightning chess championship of the USA three years in succession, 1942–44, it was at ten seconds a move.

But after the Second World War the practice arose and became widespread of allowing each player five minutes on his chess-clock for the whole game. If he took more than five minutes then he lost the game.

It was with this system of play that the strongest-ever international lightning tournament took place at Herceg Novi in Yugoslavia on 8 April 1970. Of the twelve contestants eleven were grandmasters and the twelfth, Ostojić, eventually became one.

Players played each other twice and the result was a crushing victory for the redoubtable Bobby Fischer who came first with 19 points, no less than 4½ points ahead of Tal. Fischer lost only one game in the event, to Korchnoi in the penultimate round. Leading scores: Fischer 19, Tal 14½, Korchnoi 14, Petrosian 13½. A win by Fischer in the last round:

White: Fischer; *Black:* Matulović
Ruy Lopez
1. P–K4, P–K4; 2. N–KB3, N–QB3; 3. B–N5, P–B4; 4. N–B3, P×P; 5. QN×P, P–Q4; 6. N×P, P×N; 7. N×N, Q–N4; 8. Q–K2, N–B3; 9. P–KB4, Q×BP; 10. P–Q4, Q–R5+; 11. P–N3, Q–R6; 12. B–N5, P–QR3; 13. B–QR4, B–Q2; 14. B×N, P×B; 15. Q×P+, K–B2;

16. N–K5+, P×N; 17. R–B1+, K–K2; 18. B×B, K×B; 19. R–B7+, K–K1; 20. R×BP, B–Q3; 21. R×NP, R–QB1; 22. O–O–O, Q×RP; 23. P×P, B–K2; 24. R×B+, K×R; 25. Q–N7+, K–K3; 26. Q–Q7+, K×P; 27. Q–Q5+, K–B3; 28. R–B1+, K–N3; 29. Q–B5+, K–R3; 30. Q–K6+, K–R4; 31. R–B5+, K–N5; 32. R–B4+, K×P; 33. Q–N4 mate.

There have been two schools of thought as to the usefulness or otherwise of lightning chess, the one, largely held in the USSR, claiming that it leads to superficiality of judgment and the other, chiefly put forward by the Americans, that it encourages speed of thought and calculation. Probably both have some truth. It is also true that those who excel in lightning chess tend to be intuitive players such as Capablanca, Flohr, Petrosian and Fischer. *(H.G.)*

LILIENTHAL, Andrei Arnoldovich *(b. 5 May 1911)*
Soviet international grandmaster, who, though born in Moscow, spent most of his early years in Hungary where his family emigrated when he was two. He represented Hungary in the Olympiads of 1933, 1935 and 1937, but became a Soviet citizen in 1939 and thereafter played for the USSR. He is best known for his brilliant victory against Capablanca at Hastings 1933/4. He was never able to score consistently good results in international tournaments, but still secured some notable performances including first places at Ujpest 1934, Barcelona 1934, and the 1940 USSR championship.

Lilienthal shared fifth place in the 1948 Interzonal tournament and eighth in the 1950 Candidates. He was awarded the title of international grandmaster in 1950.

In 1976, after having been inactive as a chess-player for some time, he left the USSR and returned to Hungary. *(W.R.H.)*

LINDE, Antonius van der *(14 November 1833–12 August 1897)*
The first genuine modern chess historian, van der Linde was born in Haarlem in the Netherlands but soon went to Germany and became a German citizen. He studied the history of both European and Oriental chess and fully realized the importance of the allusions to chess in Sanskrit (i.e. early Indian) literature.

The result was a coherent and logical picture of the history of chess contained in three great works: *Geschichte und Literatur des Schachspiels*, Berlin 1874–75; *Das erste Jahrtausend des Schachspiels*, Berlin 1880 and *Quellenstudien zur Geschichte des Schachspiels*, Berlin 1881.

His chess library formed the basis of the great collection at The Hague. In 1876 the Royal Library there bought his collection for £3,000. *(H.G.)*

LIPKE, Paul *(30 June 1870–8 March 1955)*
Active only between 1893 and 1898, Lipke was yet one of the strongest German players of that period, finishing third at Kiel 1893, 2nd to Tarrasch at Leipzig 1894, and =8th with Burn at the great Vienna tournament of 1898. In 1896 he drew a match with Berger. *(W.H.)*

LIPNITZKY, Isaak Oskarovich *(1923–1959)*
Ukrainian champion in 1949, and runner-up in the 1950 USSR championship. Never competed internationally, but was the possessor of an elegant style of play and an excellent grasp of theory. *(W.R.H. & H.G.)*

LISITSIN, Georgi Mikhailovich *(11 October 1909–20 March 1972)*
Champion of Leningrad in 1934, 1939 and 1947, he took third place in the 1933 USSR championship. Awarded title of international master in 1950. Was equally copious in his writings on the middlegame and in his drinking. *(W.R.H.)*

LIST, Paul *(1887–9 September 1954)*
A Russo-German-English master who had three chess careers and who seems to have remained of Russian nationality despite spending the major part of his life in other countries.

Born in Odessa, he had already established himself as a strong master player by 1910 when he drew a match with Levenfish at Vilna +4—4=1. In an international tournament also held at Vilna, in 1913, he came =4th/20 with E. Rabinovich.

He left Russia for Germany in the 1920s and there his best results were =3rd with von Holzhausen at Magdeburg 1927 and an =3rd with Ahues at Frankfurt 1930. At Ostend 1937 he was =4th with Landau above Koltanowski and Tartakower.

In 1938 he came to England and was =3rd with Milner-Barry in a short tournament at Plymouth. An =2nd with Price in another short tournament at Birmingham 1939 was followed by an =1st with Golombek at London 1940.

His last tournament of any importance was at Zaandam 1946 where he came 5th/12. *(H.G.)*

LITHUANIA
Chess was much slower to develop in Lithuania than in any of the other Baltic states. There was no organized chess activity there before the First World War, and indeed very little until the 1930s. The first tournaments in Lithuania were held in 1920 and 1921, but were only local events even played without clocks. Only from 1929 onwards were there any serious events by modern standards. That year the first Lithuanian championship was held, and the following year Lithuania became a member of FIDE. In 1931 they sent a team to the Olympiad at Prague, where their first board, Mikenas, acquitted himself well and the team took thirteenth place. Subsequently, Lithuania was the host of several small international events, including a match between Mikenas and Spielmann in 1934.

Until 1945, Mikenas was the only player from Lithuania regularly to compete in events outside his country, though later, when Lithuania became part of the USSR, other strong players such as Kholmov and Tolush emerged.

Lithuania has continued to organize its own championship annually, occasionally with guest players imported from other Soviet republics. Perhaps the most important of these events was in 1951 when Kholmov won the championship ahead of the three guests Lilienthal, Petrosian and Simagin.

Both Mikenas and Kholmov have had collections of their games published in Lithuania. *(W.R.H.)*

LITINSKAYA (née Shul), Marta *(b. 25 March 1949)*
One of the very strongest Soviet women players. Her record in the national women's championship is admirable, including a victory in 1972 and second places in 1971, 1973 and 1974. She was awarded the title of international woman master in 1972. In the 1973 Women's Interzonal she placed =2nd, qualifying for the 1974 Women's Candidates in which she lost her semi-final match to Alexandria by 2½–5½. In 1976 she obtained the title of international woman grandmaster and in the Women's Interzonal at Tbilisi she was =4th. *(K.J.O'C.)*

LIVING CHESS DISPLAYS
These fall into two types, those in which famous games are demonstrated and those in which an actual game is played for the first time. Usually they are played in the open air, but they can also be played in a theatre or any large hall where the spectacle can take place. The pieces are represented either by children (who have been rehearsed for the task) or by ballet or theatrical companies.

The earliest known living chess display seems to have been given by the Sultan Mohammed in Grenada in 1408 and this custom was followed by many princes and kings. Don John of Austria had a room in his palace paved with black and white marble squares for the purpose and later a Duke of Weimar installed a vast open square inside one of his palaces which was similarly paved in black and white and used for living chess displays.

Rabelais describes a living chess display in Chapter XXV of Book V of *Pantagruel* (1564): 'Comment les trente-deux personnages du bal combattent' (How the thirty-two personages of the ball fight).

Mechanics' Magazine,
MUSEUM, REGISTER, JOURNAL, AND GAZETTE.

No. 396.] SATURDAY, MARCH 12, 1831. [Price 3d.

Strange and unnatural! let us stay and see
This pageant of a Prodigy;
Lo! of themselves, the enlivened chessmen move.—COWLEY.

LIVING CHESS PLAYERS.

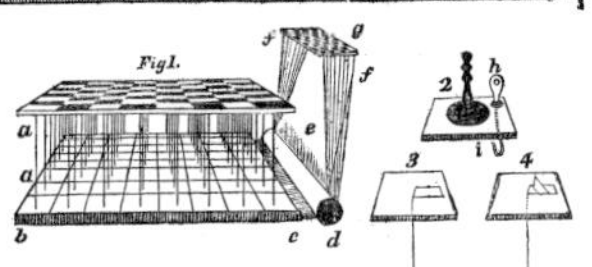

Capablanca and Herman Steiner as players and Cecil B. de Mille as referee in a novel living chess game at the Los Angeles Athletic Club

A match at the Guildhall, Winchester, England c. 1900

An interesting imitation of Don John of Austria and the Duke of Weimar in modern times was furnished by the Scottish international master, W. A. Fairhurst, who, being also a great engineer, on rebuilding the bridge over the River Tay, had a large square entrance to the bridge paved in 64 squares of alternate colour. On this, during the international tournament at Dundee 1966, a game of chess was played between two Members of Parliament, victory going to the Labour MP over the Conservative.

A number of elaborate living chess displays have been given in the nineteenth and twentieth centuries. The French magazine *La Stratégie* in 1895 describes how 'A grand display of chess with living pieces took place recently at Prague. The field of battle was a large space of 200 metres in length and breadth, divided of course into 64 squares. The pieces were represented by richly apparelled groups, forming a total for the two armies of no less than 256

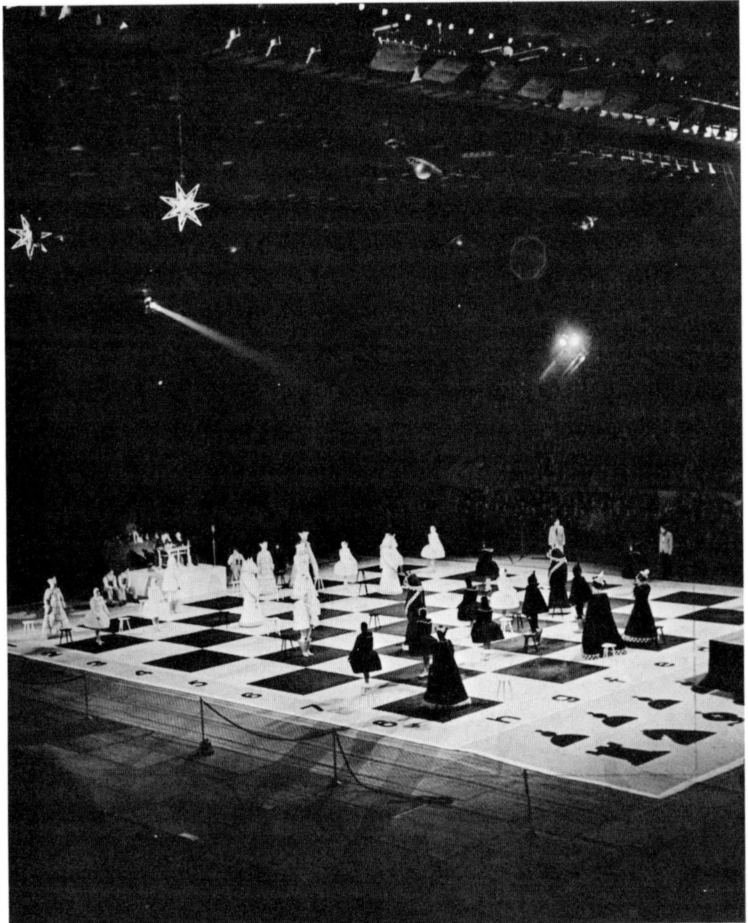

Botvinnik and Smyslov giving a pair of exhibition games, Moscow 1962. The moves were repeated by live pieces on a giant floodlit board in the Sports Palace

persons, with horses and chariots. The game was composed for the occasion by M. Dobrusky, the celebrated problemist, and it represented the defeat of the Hungarian King Corvinus, by the Bohemian King Podebrad. The variety and picturesqueness of the costumes of these two countries presented a very attractive spectacle.'

An even more remarkable spectacle was the living chess display given in 1934 at the stadium of the Stalin motorworks in Moscow with Botvinnik, then USSR champion, having White against Riumin, champion of Moscow. The pieces were represented by athletes and sportsmen and women of various kinds. The Kings were weightlifters having dumb-bells as their sceptres; the Queens were tennis players; the Rooks were slighter athletes, armed however with machine-guns; the Bishops were cyclists; the Knights were javelin throwers and the pawns were played by two football teams. The game ended in a draw on the 36th move.

Botvinnik again had a draw with White, this time when as World Champion in 1962 he played against the former World Champion, Smyslov, in the Moscow Sport Palace. The pieces on this occasion were ballet dancers.

It was likewise the local ballet company that took the part of the pieces in a display in the theatre at Bad Pyrmont during the European Zonal tournament there in 1951. The game displayed was the Immortal Game won by Anderssen against Kieseritsky a hundred years earlier at London.

The most celebrated living chess display is perhaps that given at Marostica, a small town in Italy not far from Vicenza. There, in remembrance of a game of chess that was played, according to the legend, in 1454 between Rinaldo de Angarano and Vieri de Vallonara for the hand of Madonna Lionara, a living chess display has taken place since 1954 in the great square of the Castello da Basso. The game used in 1954 and subsequently is the famous brilliancy won by Schlechter against Fleissig at Vienna in 1895.

White: Fleissig; *Black:* Schlechter
Sokolsky Opening
1. P–QN4, P–K3; 2. B–N2, N–KB3; 3. P–QR3, P–B4; 4. P–N5, P–Q4; 5. P–Q4, Q–R4+; 6. N–B3, N–K5; 7. Q–Q3, P×P; 8. Q×P, B–B4; 9. Q×NP, B×P+; 10. K–Q1, P–Q5; 11. Q×R+, K–K2; 12. Q×B, P×N; 13. B–B1, N–Q2; 14. Q×R, Q×NP; 15. B–B4, Q–Q4+; 16. K–B1

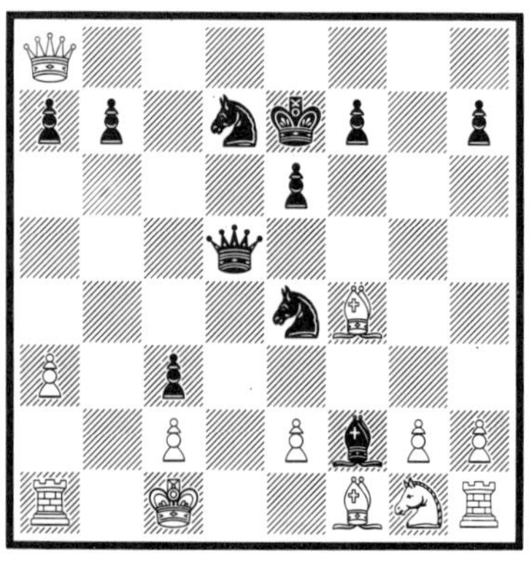

16.., B–K6+; 17. B×B, N–B7; 18. B×N, Q–Q7+; 19. K–N1, Q–Q8+; 20. K–R2, Q×P mate. *(H.G.)*

LJUBOJEVIĆ, Ljubomir *(b. 2 November 1950)*
Yugoslavia's youngest grandmaster. After a mediocre early career he unexpectedly came into the limelight by winning Sarajevo 1970 with Parma. Received grandmaster title for his performance at Vrnjačka Banja 1971. Best results: =1st with Panno at Palma de Mallorca 1971, ahead of Portisch and Larsen; 2nd Teesside 1972 ahead of Portisch and Gligorić; first prizes at Amsterdam 1975, Las Palmas 1975, Manila 1975 and (equal with Olafsson) Wijk-aan-Zee 1976. Best result in Yugoslav championship: =2nd with Rukavina, Umag 1972. Represented Yugoslavia at the 1972 Olympiad with best result on board 3; in 1974 he played on second board. Took part in 1973 Interzonal, Petropolis. A born tactician, he often experiments in the opening stages of the game. Uneven in form, but in recent years he has developed into a possible World Championship challenger. *(R.D.K.)*

LOKVENC, Josef *(1 May 1899–2 April 1974)*
An Austrian international master, Lokvenc won the war-time German championship in 1943 after coming 2nd in 1939, and the Austrian championship in 1953. His best international results were =2nd in Vienna 1947 and =2nd in Vienna 1951/2. Likvenc represented Austria in the Olympiads of 1927, 1928, 1930, 1931, and the International Team tournament at Munich 1936. *(W.H.)*

LOLLI, Giambattista *(1698–4 June 1769)*
One of three talented Italian players (the others were Ercole del Rio and Ponziani) who made up the Modena school, Lolli published a big work of some 631 large pages, *Osservazioni Teoretico-Pratiche sopra il giuoco degli scacchi*, Modena 1763, in which he dealt with everything that was known at the time about the openings and the endgame. *(H.G.)*

LOMBARDY, William *(b. 4 December 1937)*
US grandmaster, World Junior champion 1957–9, and for several years considered the equal of his main young rival in the USA, Fischer. But professional duties as a Roman Catholic priest curtailed his chess activities sharply after 1963.

Lombardy, born in New York, first gained attention with an 11–0 score in the World Junior Championship in Toronto 1957. This gave him the international master title which was followed by grandmaster status in 1960. The latter year was Lombardy's best. He led the US team to victory in the Student Olympiad in Leningrad and contributed an important point by beating Spassky on first board. Also that year Lombardy drew for the second time with Botvinnik in an Olympiad and came 2nd behind Fischer in the US Closed championship. However, he did not take up his place in the Stockholm Interzonal in 1962.

After this Lombardy came =4th at Zürich 1961, lost a match to Evans +2−3=5 in 1962, won the US Open in 1963 and tied for first prize at the 1965 Open. Lombardy did not play again in the Closed championship until 1968 when he came =5th. A year later he was 4th.

His later international results include =6th at Zagreb 1969, =5th at Manila 1973 and =3rd at Torremolinos 1974. He was

Fischer's second in the World Championship match at Reykavik 1972. He is the author of *Modern Chess Opening Traps*, New York 1972, and co-author of *U.S. Championship Chess*, New York 1974. *(A.S.)*

LONDON 1851

The first international chess tournament to be held was the brainchild of Howard Staunton who conceived the astonishing and original idea of holding a tournament at which all the best players in Europe would be assembled.

The fact, however, that Staunton had conceived the idea was enough to prejudice the powerful London Club against it. But Staunton worked on it with the utmost drive and enthusiasm and managed to get together more than £500 to finance the prize fund – a sum which at the time was a formidable one.

The event was due to coincide with the Great Exhibition in London 1851 and it did, in fact, materialize. In May 1851, sixteen of Europe's leading players met each other in the first round in a series of little knock-out matches.

The system had its drawbacks, as Staunton himself was soon to realize. Since the pairings were done by lot it was quite possible to have some of the best players eliminated in Round 1 and in fact Anderssen did meet and beat Kieseritsky in Round 1.

Despite the obvious inadequacies of the system used, it was equally obvious that, when Anderssen beat Wyvill in the 4th and last round, the best player in the tournament had indeed won.

The rounds went as follows:

Round 1
Anderssen 2½ Kieseritsky ½; Staunton 2 Brodie 0; Wyvill 2 Lowe 0; Szén 2 Newham 0; Capt. Kennedy 2 Mayet 0; Horwitz 2½ Bird 1½; Williams 2 Lowenthal 0; Mucklow 2 E. Kennedy 0.
Round 2
Anderssen 4 Szén 2; Staunton 4½ Horwitz 2½; Wyvill 4½ Capt. Kennedy 3½; Williams 4 Mucklow 0.
Round 3
Anderssen 4 Staunton 1; Szén 4 Horwitz 0; Wyvill 4 Williams 3; Capt. Kennedy 4 Mucklow 0.
Round 4
Anderssen 4½ Wyvill 2½; Williams 4½ Staunton 3½; Szén 4½ Capt. Kennedy ½; Horwitz beat Mucklow by default.

The eight prize-winners and their scores were as follows:
1. Anderssen 15, 2. Wyvill 13, 3. Williams 13½, 4. Staunton 11, 5. Szén 12½, 6. Capt. Kennedy 10, 7. Horwitz 5, and 8. Mucklow 2. *(H.G.)*

LONDON 1862

In some ways the London 1862 tournament was even more of a landmark than London 1851. It was the first tournament in which players all played each other – a system that was to become known as the American system, possibly owing to its popularity in the USA. It was also important as marking the introduction of a time-limit, the fast one of 20 moves in two hours. Draws still did not count. The event is also notable for the personalities it contained. The great Anderssen emphasized his colossal genius by coming first two points ahead of the field. Second was Louis Paulsen, a player whom posterity has continued to underestimate, but who was the inventive genius of the century as far as openings are concerned. There was too the redoubtable newcomer, Wilhelm Steinitz who was to prove the greatest of them all, and finally Blackburne appears for the first time. Leading scores: Anderssen 11, L. Paulsen 9, Owen, MacDonnell 7, Dubois, Steinitz, Barnes 6. *(H.G.)*

LONDON 1872

This was a tournament organized by the British Chess Association and it was noteworthy for the introduction of Zukertort to British chess.

Some persons unknown, in order to get a rival to the somewhat quarrelsome Steinitz, sought his presence there so as to combat that gigantic figure. It did not work this time. Steinitz won all his games and Zukertort was hard put to it to gain even third prize. There was a play-off for the third prize in which Zukertort beat MacDonnell and MacDonnell beat De Vere. This last named scratched to Zukertort.

Draws did not count and the games that ended in this way had to be replayed.

Leading scores: Steinitz 7, Blackburne 5, Zukertort, MacDonnell, De Vere 4. *(H.G.)*

LONDON 1883

In order to ensure that the entry for this event should be as great as possible the organizers procured a prize fund of £1,100 which, for the time, was quite unparalleled. Also, so as to do away with featureless draws, it was decided that a draw should count only if two further games between the same opponents had taken place and likewise ended in draws.

The tournament was Zukertort's greatest success. He won game after game in the most brilliant style and had already made sure of first place with three games and two weeks still to go. This was just as well since he had been sustaining himself with drugs and collapsed, losing the last three games. This high point in Zukertort's career was also to prove his last successful event.

Leading scores: Zukertort 22, Steinitz 19, Blackburne 16½, Chigorin 16. *(H.G.)*

LONDON 1922

London (July–August 1922) was the venue of Capablanca's first appearance as World Champion. Fully justifying his role as favourite in a very strong field, he immediately took the lead from Alekhine and Vidmar and gradually increased it to run out an unchallenged winner. Not only did he score points but he showed initiative and imagination, beating some of his closest rivals in their individual games (Vidmar, Bogoljubow, Réti), and while some of his draws (notably against Alekhine, Rubinstein and Maróczy) were of the 'grandmaster' variety for which he later became notorious, the one against Tartakower was an absolute thriller. Alekhine, too, was unbeaten and began to emerge as the Cuban's most promising rival. The tournament had another claim to fame in being the first major international event of another future World Champion, Euwe. Leading scores: Capablanca 13, Alekhine 11½, Vidmar 11, Rubinstein 10½. *(W.H.)*

LONDON 1927

The British Empire Club tournament in London (October 1927) – there was to be another semi-international tournament a little later – was a small but very strong event on the Moscow model: five British masters against seven strong internationals. As so often before, Tartakower took the lead in the early rounds, but a loss to Nimzowitsch in round 9 brought him within reach of his best-placed rivals, and with one round to go the leaders were: Nimzowitsch, Tartakower and Vidmar 7, Marshall 6½. In the final round Nimzowitsch, Tartakower and Marshall all won, but Vidmar lost to Winter, bringing about the final result. In addition to that of Vidmar, Winter also took the scalp of Nimzowitsch and his place among the prize-winners was well deserved. Leading scores: Nimzowitsch, Tartakower 8, Marshall 7½, Vidmar 7, Bogoljubow 6½. *(W.H.)*

LONDON JUNIOR CHAMPIONSHIP

Apart from the British Boys championship, the principal event in England for under-18-year-olds has, since its inauguration in 1924, been the London Boys championship. Until 1939 the event was organized by the London Chess League, but the onset of war brought an end to the League's involvement. The event was revived in 1945 by the Chess Education Society, which continued the tournament each Christmas until its re-adoption by the League in 1960. It was in this year that two sections of girls were introduced and the name had to be changed from 'Boys' to 'Junior'.

In 1974 the event fell under the sponsorship of the *Evening Standard* and attracted over 500 entries grouped into ten sections according to age, ranging from the under-21 championship to the under-10, with special prizes for under-8 and under-6!

The consistent strength of the event is well illustrated by a selection of names of past winners of the under-18 championship, which include H. Golombek, J. Penrose, L. Barden, P. N. Lee and R. D. Keene, all of whom subsequently became British champions. *(W.R.H.)*

LONE PINE INTERNATIONAL

Starting in 1971 a Swiss System tournament known as the Louis D. Statham Masters has been held annually in March at Lone Pine, California. The endeavour has been made to make the event truly international with as rich a leavening of grandmasters and masters as possible.

The normal practice has been to play seven rounds and in the first event there were 33 competitors and a first prize of 1,000 dollars. This was won by Larry Evans with 6 points and there was a quadruple tie for 2nd between Gligorić, Tarjan, Martz and Browne on 5 points.

In 1972, with 35 competitors, the first prize was raised to 2,000 dollars which was won by Gligorić with 6 points, followed by Tarjan, Saidy, Karklins and Brandts with 5 points.

48 players in 1973 saw Bisguier first with 6 points, followed by Browne and Szabo with 5½ points, Formanek, Grefe and Miles with 5.

In 1974, with 53 players, Browne was first with 6, =2nd Benko and Grefe 5½, and =4th Evans, Kaplan, Commons, and Karklins 5.

Then, in 1975, when the first prize was increased to 4,000 dollars, there came a really mammoth event and out of a total of 44 players no less than 21 were grandmasters. A ten round Swiss was played and first prize went to Liberzon with 7½, followed by Evans 7, Browne, Gheorghiu, Weinstein, Panno, Quinteros and Gligorić 6½.

The following year the first prize was again doubled to 8,000 dollars and won by Petrosian with 5½ out of 7, second prize being shared by Christiansen, Smyslov, Panno, Najdorf, Quinteros, Miles, Rogoff, Forintos and Browne 5.

In 1977 the women's world champion, Nona Gaprindashvili, created a sensation by coming =1st with Balashov, Sahović and Panno with 6½ out of 9, Lombardy and Christiansen coming next with 6. *(H.G.)*

LONGEST GAME

The longest game in tournament or match chess was a 191-move draw between Pilnik and Czerniak at Mar del Plata 1953. It took twenty-three hours. The longest game to have been *won* in tournament and matches was Wolf v. Důras at Carlsbad 1907. This lasted 168 moves and was won by Wolf after 22½ hours.

It was at one time thought that the longest game was that between Crane and Charlick in the Australian championship 1883, since Charlick stated in the *Adelaide Observer* for 10 March 1883 that this game lasted 219 moves. However, in this instance Charlick was being hyper-logical since he counted a move by White as one move and the replying move by Black as another move, whereas, by an admittedly illogical convention, a move for White and one for Black in reply count only as one whole move. So Charlick's game lasted a mere 110 moves, 110 for White and 109 for Black. *(H.G.)*

LOPEZ, Ruy

Sixteenth-century Spanish priest, a native of Zafra in Estremadura, and the leading Spanish player of his age. His skill at chess made him internationally famous and he was a favourite at the court of Philip II. In 1560 Lopez visited Rome on ecclesiastical business and defeated without difficulty the strongest Italian players, including in all probability the young Leonardo da Cutri. He also discovered Damiano's book, which he disliked, and decided to improve upon it. The result was the *Libro de la invencion liberal y arte del juego del Axedrez*, which Lopez published soon after his return to Spain in 1561. It contains general advice and a collection of recommended openings as well as copious criticisms of Damiano's games and analysis.

In 1574–5 the two best Italian players, Leonardo da Cutri and Paolo Boi, visited Madrid. Matches with Lopez were arranged under the patronage of Philip II, and Lopez was defeated by each of them. *(R.D.K.)*

LÖWENTHAL, János Jakab [**Johann Jacob**] *(15 July 1810–20 July 1876)*

Hungarian emigré who became a naturalized British subject and a leading figure in English chess. Löwenthal was born in Budapest in 1810 and studied chess under the Hungarian master Szén. After the unsuccessful revolution of 1848, Löwenthal was forced to flee abroad, travelling first to America. While visiting New Orleans in 1850 Löwenthal played two games against the thirteen-year-old Paul Morphy, losing one and drawing the other.

Löwenthal came to London for the 1851 tournament but, in poor health, he was eliminated by Williams in the first round. Shortly afterwards he gained his revenge by defeating Williams in a match +7−5=4. In 1853 Löwenthal lost a close match to Harrwitz by +10−11=12 after having held a lead of 9 wins to 2 at an earlier stage.

In 1857 Löwenthal won a tournament at Manchester ahead of Anderssen and in the following year he emerged victorious in the strong B.C.A. congress in Birmingham, over Falkbeer, Staunton, and Saint-Amant – his finest tournament success. Also in 1858 Löwenthal played a match against Morphy, losing by +3−9=2.

After 1860 Löwenthal devoted less time to play and more to chess administration and journalism. He was at various times Secretary of the St George's Club and Manager of the B.C.A. With Medley, he organized the London 1862 tourney. His literary work included chess columns in the *Era* and the *Illustrated London News* and from 1863–7 he edited the *Chess Player's Magazine*.

Löwenthal died in Hastings. The trophy used for the English Counties championship is called the Löwenthal Cup in his memory. *(R.D.K.)*

LOYD, Sam *(b. 30 January 1841 d. 10 April 1911)*
In addition to being a great problemist (see under PROBLEMISTS) Loyd was a stronger player. He made one appearance in international chess early in his career when he came =9th out of 13 with Rosenthal at the great Paris Tournament of 1867. *(H.G.)*

LUCENA, Luis Ramirez de
The author of the earliest surviving printed work on chess, *Repeticion de amores y arte de Axedres*, which was published in Spain in 1497. The book is divided into two sections: one on chess and one on love. The chess material includes rudimentary analysis of ten opening variations, 150 problems and studies (among which is the basic Rook and pawn ending known as the 'Lucena position'), and helpful psychological advice (such as 'Try to play soon after your opponent has eaten or drunk freely').

Lucena is also generally credited with the authorship of the Göttingen manuscript, a 33-page Latin tract which contains a similar mixture of opening analysis and problems, probably composed *circa* 1500. *(R.D.K.)*

LUNDIN, Erik *(b. 2 July 1904)*
Swedish international master and one of the three Swedish Musketeers (the other two were Ståhlberg and Stoltz who made the Swedish team formidable in Olympiads in the period 1930–60.

Though Lundin has never attained the title of grandmaster, there is no doubt that for most of his chess career he has played like one. Many times Swedish champion (1941, 1942, 1945, 1946, 1960, 1961 and 1964) he has represented Sweden in nine Olympiads (1930, 1931, 1933, 1935, 1937, 1939, 1952, 1954 and 1960) and nearly always with success, playing on 3rd board to Ståhlberg and Stoltz and latterly on 2nd after Stoltz's death.

His international chess career falls roughly into two parts. He was more active in the period between 1930 and 1950 than subsequently, since in the early 1950s he became director of the principal Swedish chess club in Stockholm and could not easily get away from his duties.

Among his best results in the earlier period are a 2nd to Alekhine at Örebro 1935, 1st at Ostend 1936, =2nd with Alekhine in Munich 1941, =8th with Stoltz at Groningen 1946, 1st at Bad Gastein 1948.

He had a bad result in the Interzonal at Saltsjöbaden 1948 where he came 20th, but two more good results came at Vienna 1951 where he was 2nd and Zürich 1952 where he came 1st. Then came an interval and his last good performance, 7th at the Mariánské Lázně Zonal tournament of 1954.

His style of play is original, keen and piquant so that a good Lundin game is quite a feast for the connoisseur since it is sure to be full of ideas, some of which, however, may not be as sound as the classical player would like to see. *(H.G.)*

LUTIKOV, Anatoly Stepanovich *(b. 5 February 1933)*
Soviet international grandmaster and member of their 1956 Students Olympiad team. Caused a great surprise at Wijk-aan-Zee 1967, by coming second to Spassky in only his first full inter-

national tournament. Was awarded the title of international master for this performance, only missing the grandmaster title because he had not already achieved the lower qualification before. This was, however, remedied in 1974, when Lutikov finally secured his grandmaster title.

His best international results include first prizes at Dubna 1971, Leipzig 1973 and Albena 1976. *(W.R.H.)*

LUXEMBOURG

A team has taken part in eleven Olympiads: 25th in 1952, 26th in 1954, 34th in 1956 and 1962, 48th in 1964, 42nd in 1966, 39th in 1968, 46th in 1970, 53rd in 1972, 52nd in 1974 and 36th in 1976.

The organizing body is the Fédération Luxembourgeoise des Echecs, 15 rue Fr. Boch, Luxembourg. *(K.J.O'C.)*

MACDONNELL, Rev. George Alcock
(16 August 1830–3 June 1899)

The strongest of all the chess-playing reverends in Britain in the nineteenth century (and there were many), MacDonnell was of master strength for most of his life. Born in Dublin, where he graduated at Trinity College, he was mentioned in the *Chess Player's Chronicle* for 1860 as one of the strongest players in Ireland.

His first tournament success was a 4th prize in the London International tournament of 1862. He actually came =4th with Dubois with 9 points but was awarded fourth place on the grounds of having won more of the completed games. He was ahead of Steinitz and Blackburne in this event. Shortly afterwards he lost a match to G. H. Mackenzie, a fellow member of the Library Chess Club in Dublin whom he had persuaded to come to London in order to meet better opposition.

In 1865 he came 2nd to Steinitz in a small tournament in Dublin and in the following year he was =2nd with J. I. Minchin below Cecil de Vere, who thus became the first British champion. In the international tournament at Dundee 1867 he shared third place with De Vere below Neumann and Steinitz.

He was 4th in the international tournament at London 1876 and at London in 1883 he took part in the minor tournament known as the Vizayanagaram tournament, coming =4th with Gunsberg. Thereafter as he grew old and ill his results became worse. He was =5th with Loman at the B.C.A. Congress in London in 1895 and in 1897 he tied with W. Donisthorpe for the Ruskin prize in the Amateur championship tournament in London.

He died after a long and painful illness in 1899.

He played two matches against Wisker in the 1870s, beating him in 1873 and losing to him the following year.

He was a lively, entertaining but far from accurate writer on chess, and many of the unauthenticated and even groundless anecdotes about the great players of the nineteenth century stem from his inventive pen. He was 'Mars' in the *Illustrated Sporting and Dramatic News* and wrote two entertaining books: *Chess Life-Pictures*, London 1883, and *The Knights and Kings of Chess*, London 1894. *(H.G.)*

McDONNELL, Alexander *(1798–1835)*

Britain's leading player before Staunton, McDonnell was Irish born, the son of a Belfast doctor. He was Secretary to the Committee of West India Merchants in London. After he had studied chess with Lewis, he rose to the front rank of British players.

In 1834 he engaged in a marathon series of matches with the visiting French champion La Bourdonnais. Five complete matches ov varying lengths were played and a sixth was left unfinished, comprising a probable total of 85 games (there is some dispute among chess historians over the details of the final two matches), with the victory going to La Bourdonnais by 45 games to 27 with 13 draws. The standard of play was high and these contests did much to kindle interest in chess in both France and England. McDonnell died the following year of Bright's disease.

50th Match Game, London 1834
White: La Bourdonnais; *Black:* McDonnell
Queen's Gambit Accepted
1. P–Q4, P–Q4; 2. P–QB4, P×P; 3. P–K4, P–K4; 4. P–Q5, P–KB4; 5. N–QB3, N–KB3; 6. B×P, B–B4; 7. N–B3, Q–K2; 8. B–N5, B×P+; 9. K–B1, B–N3; 10. Q–K2, P–B5; 11. R–Q1, B–N5; 12. P–Q6, P×P; 13. N–Q5, N×N; 14. B×Q, N–K6+; 15. K–K1, K×B; 16. Q–Q3, R–Q1; 17. R–Q2, N–B3; 18. P–QN3, B–QR4; 19. P–QR3, QR–B1; 20. R–N1, P–QN4; 21. B×P, B×N; 22. P×B, N–Q5; 23. B–B4, N×P+; 24. K–B2, N×R(7); 25. R×P+, K–B3; 26. R–B7+, K–N3; 27. R–N7, N(7)×B; 28. P×N, R×P; 29. Q–N1, B–N3; 30. K–B3, R–B6; 31. Q–R2, N–B5+; 32. K–N4, R–KN1; 33. R×B, P×R; 34. K–R4, K–B3; 35. Q–K2, R–N3; 36. Q–R5, N–K6; 37. resigns. *(R.D.K.)*

MACKENZIE, George Henry *(24 March 1837–14 April 1891)*

Born North Kessock (Scotland), Mackenzie was a professional soldier and saw service in India and Ireland with the King's Royal Rifle Corps.

In 1862 he defeated the Rev. G. A. MacDonnell in a match. He emigrated to America in 1863 and fought on the Union side in the Civil War. After the war Mackenzie resigned his commission and devoted himself to chess, quickly establishing himself as a leading player and winning the US championship in 1866. Tournament results include: 4th prize Paris 1878, and 1st Frankfurt 1887. *(R.D.K.)*

MADRID 1973

This has good claims to have been the strongest international tournament ever to have been held on the mainland of Spain. It was a category 12 tournament which meant that in order to fulfil the grandmaster norm a player had to acquire only 8 points, and for the international master norm, only 6 points were required.

It also contained the youthful Karpov who less than two years later was to become World Champion. In addition some of the best players outside the Soviet Union (Portisch, Hort and Ljubojević for example) were competing as well as a strong Soviet contingent.

Despite the strength of the Soviet trio Karpov, Tukmakov and Furman, it was the East German grandmaster Wolfgang Uhlmann who was to dominate the earlier part of the event. But he was defeated by Karpov in the 12th round in a beautiful game that was to win the best game prize. Unsettled by this defeat, the German lost another game in quick succession, to Furman, and Karpov, playing like a World Champion, assured himself of first prize. Leading scores: Karpov 11, Tukmakov 10½, Furman 10, Hort, Uhlmann 9½. The game that was awarded the best game prize:

White: Karpov; *Black:* Uhlmann
French Defence
1. P–K4, P–K3; 2. P–Q4, P–Q4; 3. N–Q2, P–QB4; 4. KP×P, KP×P; 5. KN–B3, N–QB3; 6. B–N5, B–Q3; 7. P×P, B×BP; 8. O–O, KN–K2; 9. N–N3, B–Q3; 10. B–N5, O–O; 11. B–KR4, B–KN5; 12. B–K2, B–R4; 13. R–K1, Q–N3; 14. KN–Q4, B–N3; 15. P–QB3, KR–K1; 16. B–KB1, B–K5; 17. B–N3, B×B; 18. RP×B, P–QR4; 19. P–QR4, N×N; 20. N×N, N–B3; 21. B–N5, KR–Q1; 22. P–KN4, N×N; 23. Q×N, Q×Q; 24. P×Q, QR–B1; 25. P–B3, B–N3; 26. R–K7, P–N3; 27. QR–K1, P–R3; 28. R–QN7, R–Q3; 29. R(1)–K7, P–KR4; 30. P×P, B×P; 31. P–KN4, B–N3; 32. P–B4, R–B8+; 33. K–B2, R–B7+; 34. K–K3, B–K5; 35. R×KBP, R–KN3; 36. P–N5, K–R2; 37. R(B7)–K7, R×QNP; 38. B–K8, R–N6+; 39. K–K2, R–N7+; 40. K–K1, R–Q3; 41. R×P+, K–R1; 42. R(N7)–K7, resigns.
(H.G.)

MÄHRISCH-OSTRAU 1923
An historically important contest, Mährisch-Ostrau 1923 saw the reappearance of Lasker and at the same time provided his first meeting with the hypermodern school. Since St Petersburg 1914 Lasker had only played a small match against Tarrasch (1916) and a Four Master tournament (1918) against 'classicists' (Rubinstein, Schlechter and Tarrasch), winning both events easily before losing the World Championship match against Capablanca.

Lasker and Réti soon took the lead in this strong field; they were due to meet in the 9th round and few games in the history of chess have been looked forward to with such tension as the decisive clash between the former World Champion and the leading hypermodern theologian. Lasker, with Black, won a thrilling game and with it the tournament. Leading scores: Em. Lasker 10½, Réti 9½, Grünfeld 8½, Seresniev 7½. *(W.H.)*

MAIZELIS, Ilya Levovich *(b. 1894)*
Soviet chess writer who is particularly well known for his works on King and pawn endings. As a player his best performance was a fourth place in the very strong 1932 Moscow championship. As a writer he produced a number of monographs of a varied nature. The two best known are *Osnovy teorii* (The Basis of Opening Theory), Moscow 1969 and *Ladya protiv Peschek* (Rook versus Pawns), Moscow 1956. *(H.G.)*

MAKARICHEV, Sergei *(b. 17 November 1953)*
A Soviet player, he holds the rank of international grandmaster, awarded in 1976. He had obtained the international master title in 1974 by winning the European Junior championship. His best tournament results have been 1st in the second group at Amsterdam 1974, =2nd in the top group at Amsterdam 1975 and =2nd at Lublin 1976, in which year he also shared the Moscow championship. *(K.J.O'C.)*

MAKARCZYK, Kazimierz *(1 January 1901–27 May 1972)*
Polish international master who played for Poland at the Olympiads of 1928, 1930, 1931, 1933 and 1935.

His results in the Polish championship were 3rd in 1927, 1st in 1948, 3rd in 1950, =1st in 1952 but losing the play-off for the title to Sliwa, =3rd in 1953 and =6th in 1954.

He came 5th in the Przepiorka Memorial tournament at Sopot in 1951 and =3rd at the 1952 international tournament at Miedzyzdroje. *(H.G.)*

MAKOGONOV, Vladimir Andreyevich *(b. 27 August 1904)*
Soviet international master and many times champion of the Azerbaidzhan republic. Shared fourth place in the 1939 USSR championship. Given title of international master in 1950. Makogonov has made important contributions to the theory of the King's Indian Defence and Queen's Gambit Declined. By profession a teacher of mathematics. *(W.R.H.)*

MALAYSIA
This country has two Olympiad appearances to its credit: 59th in 1972 and 60th in 1974. The third national championship, played in 1976, was won by Y. W. Goh.

The first Asian Team championship was played in Penang during December 1974: Philippines 22½, Australia 22, Indonesia 19½, Singapore 17½, New Zealand 10½, Japan 8½, Hong Kong 8½, Malaysia 3. The event was organized by the Malaysian Chess Federation, 7th Floor Bangkok Bank Building, 105 Jalan Bandur, Kuala Lumpur 01-22. *(K.J.O'C.)*

MALICH, Burkhard *(b. 29 November 1936)*
East German grandmaster. One of the most successful tournament players of East Germany, Malich has won the championship of his country in 1957 and 1973, while occupying high places in many other years. He represented East Germany in the Olympiads between 1958 and 1968 and played in many international tournaments, where his best results include first prize at Zinnowitz 1971, and joint first prize with Smejkal in the master group of the IBM tournament (Amsterdam) the same year, as well as =2nd at Debrecen 1969 and 3rd at Leipzig 1973 and =2nd at Decin 1975.
(W.H.)

MALTA
Despite the comparative smallness of the population much chess is played in Malta and the popularity of the game is ever increasing there.

Teams representing the country have competed in the Olympiads of 1960 (39th out of 40), 1970 (52nd/60), 1972 (50th/63) and 1974 (57th/74).

Chess in Malta is under the control of the Maltese Chess Federation, 5 Merchants Street, Valetta. The Federation sponsors the *Malta Chess Magazine* and has hosted a number of minor international tournaments. *(R.D.K.)*

MANCHESTER CHESS CLUB

At a meeting on 3 September 1817, in the Albion Hotel, Manchester, a committee was formed to draw up the rules for the Manchester Chess Club. This club, formed two years after the Battle of Waterloo, has been in continuous existence ever since and therefore can claim to be the oldest British chess club in existence.

The club also has the right to be regarded as the strongest in the North of England over the more than 150 years of its existence and to it have belonged some of the most celebrated British players, notably J. H. Blackburne, E. Spencer and R. J. Broadbent. In addition the American master Edward Lasker was once a member and so too was the well-known problemist, J. S. Kipping. The now New Zealand master W. A. Fairhurst was at one time club champion.

Manchester Chess Club has been the originating force in the holding of a number of international tournaments in England. It carried on through two World Wars and indeed, despite heavy and continuous bombardment from the enemy in the year 1941, practically doubled its membership during those dangerous years.

It has retained and even increased its membership and activities in the years succeeding the Second World War. *(H.G.)*

MANHATTAN CHESS CLUB

The oldest chess club in America and one of the most powerful forces in US organization since its founding in 1877. Its members have included virtually every major American player of the last century.

The club began as a casual playing circle of three dozen members in a café on the Bowery in lower Manhattan. It later acquired a membership of several hundred and changed its quarters at least seven times. The current address is 155 East 55th St, New York.

Manhattan club members organized the New York 1924 and 1927 international tournaments and frequently hosted rounds of the cycle of US Closed championships that began in the 1930s. Maróczy was one of several prominent visitors to play in the annual club championships which for many years was one of the strongest events in the USA. It was while watching a casual game at the Manhattan club that Capablanca fell ill and died in 1942. Among the players who developed their skill at the club are Reshevsky, Fischer, Lombardy, Horowitz and Denker. *(A.S.)*

MANNHEIM 1914

The principal claim to fame of this tournament (July–August 1914), in itself one of the strongest congresses organized by the German Chess Federation, was its end: broken off after 11 of 17 rounds because of the outbreak of war. The Russian participants, including Alekhine and Bogoljubow were promptly interned, and most of them spent the whole of the war at Triberg.

Alekhine, who by then had 9½ out of 11, was awarded first prize, though a look at the tournament table might suggest that he was lucky in this, his first win in a major international event. He had not yet met numbers 2, 3, 5 and 6 in the provisional ranking list – in particular Dr Vidmar, who was his nearest rival and had played most of the top players except Alekhine himself and numbers 5 and 6 in the list. Leading scores: Alekhine 9½, Vidmar 8½, Spielmann 8, Breyer, Marshall, Réti 7. *(W.H.)*

MARCO, Georg *(29 November 1863–29 August 1923)*

An Austrian master, of Romanian birth, Marco has left an imperishable chess legacy in his brilliant and witty annotations.

A fairly successful tournament player (1st Vienna 1895; =2nd in the Reserve tournament London 1899; 3rd in Vienna 1897, Vienna 1903 and Stockholm 1912; 4th in Cambridge Springs 1904; =5th in Ostend 1905 etc.), he was prevented from achieving higher honours by an ineradicable tendency towards accepting the draw. During the period 1891–1904 he played eight matches (+2−2=4) against Bauer, Kaufmann, Schlechter, Albin, Zinkl, and others – against Schlechter he drew both his matches, the first with the extraordinary score of +0−0=10.

His tournament and match books include the Gambit tournament Vienna 1903, Ostend 1906, Carlsbad 1907, Vienna 1908 and the Lasker–Tarrasch match 1908. He edited the *Wiener Schachzeitung* from 1898 to 1914. *(W.H.)*

MAR DEL PLATA TOURNAMENTS

Starting off as purely South American tournaments, the Mar del Plata events gradually increased in strength and in international importance so that, by the 1950s and 1960s, they had developed into tournaments of world-wide importance.

The First tournament took place in 1928 and contained competitors (seventeen in all) from the Argentine, Brazil, Chile and Uruguay. First prize went to Grau (Argentine) followed by Palau and Souza Mendes.

After an interval of six years the Second Mar del Plata tournament was held in 1934, 1st being Schwartzman 10½, followed by Grau 10 and Balparda, Jacobo Bolbochan, Fenoglio and Guimard 8½. The Third in 1936 was won by Pleci 11½, ahead of Schwartzman 11 and Fenoglio and Vinuesa 9½.

The Fourth in 1941 was a genuine international event and was won by Ståhlberg 13, ahead of Najdorf 12½ and Eliskases 11½.

The results of succeeding tournaments were as follows:

Fifth 1942:	Najdorf 13½, Pilnik and Ståhlberg 13.
Sixth 1943:	Najdorf 11, Ståhlberg 10½ and Michel 8½.
Seventh 1944:	Najdorf and Pilnik 12, Guimard and Michel 10½.
Eighth 1945:	Najdorf 11, Pilnik and Ståhlberg 10½.
Ninth 1946:	Najdorf 16, Ståhlberg 13 and Michel 11.
Tenth 1947:	Najdorf 14, Ståhlberg 13½ and Eliskases 12.
Eleventh 1948:	Eliskases 13, Ståhlberg 11½, Medina 11.

Twelfth 1949: Rossetto 13, Eliskases and Guimard 12.
Thirteenth 1950: Gligorić 11½, Guimard and Rossetto 11.
Fourteenth 1951: Julio Bolbochan and Eliskases 19, Maderna 15.
Fifteenth 1952: Julio Bolbochan and Rossetto 11½, Cuellar and Trifunović 11.
Sixteenth 1953: Gligorić 16, Najdorf 14½ and Julio Bolbochan 13½.
Seventeenth 1954: Panno 17½, Najdorf 17, Pilnik and Guimard 16½.
Eighteenth 1955: Ivkov 11½, Najdorf 11, Gligorić 10.
Nineteenth 1956: Julio Bolbochan and Najdorf 12½, Eliskases and Sanguineti 11.

With the next tournament, the Twentieth in 1957, the event had a further enrichment with grandmasters from Europe and the series became a genuine run of grandmaster contests. Paul Keres (USSR) was the only undefeated player in the tournament and came 1st with 15/17 ahead of Najdorf 14, Kotov and Panno 13. The results of succeeding tournaments were as follows:

Twenty-first 1958: Larsen 12, Lombardy 11, Eliskases, Panno and Sanguineti 9½.
Twenty-second 1959: Najdorf and Pachman 10½, Fischer and Ivkov 10.
Twenty-third 1960: Fischer and Spassky 13½, Bronstein 11½. This was a remarkable event in which Fischer lost a famous game to Spassky and drew with Bronstein, but won all the other 13 games.
Twenty-fourth 1961: Najdorf 12½, Robert Byrne, Filip, Mantanović and Rossetto 11½.

A further acquisition of funds enabled the organizers to hold an even stronger event in 1962 together with another tournament, called the Latin American tournament confined to players from Latin America. The grandmaster tournament was won by Polugayevsky with 11½/15 ahead of Smyslov and Szabo 9½. The top prizewinners in the Latin American were: R. Garcia 14, Flores 13, Foguelman and Schweber 12½. The results of the next two tournaments were:

Twenty-sixth 1965: Najdorf 12½, Stein 11 and Averbakh 10½.
Twenty-seventh 1966: Smyslov 11, Stein 10½ and Portisch 9½.

The Twenty-eighth in 1969 was a Zonal Tournament of FIDE and hence contained South American players only. Najdorf and Panno tied for first place with 15½ points ahead of R. Garcia and Mecking 13.

The Twenty-ninth in 1971 returned to the international field. It was won by Polugayevsky with 13 ahead of Panno and Savon 10.

Five years passed without a tournament and then an attempt was made to revive the series. But the funds were not sufficient to enable players other than South Americans to participate and the Thirtieth Mar del Plata was held in 1976 with even a much weaker South American field in that such players as the grandmasters Najdorf, Panno and Quinteros did not participate. The top prizewinners were Brond and Sanguineti 11 and R. Garcia and Rubinetti 9½.

The game between the two first prizewinners in the Twenty-third Mar del Plata tournament in 1960:

White: Spassky; *Black:* Fischer
King's Gambit Accepted
1. P–K4, P–K4; 2. P–KB4, P×P; 3. N–KB3, P–KN4; 4. P–KR4, P–N5; 5. N–K5, N–KB3; 6. P–Q4, P–Q3; 7. N–Q3, N×P; 8. B×P, B–N2; 9. N–B3, N×N; 10. P×N, P–QB4; 11. B–K2, P×P; 12. O–O, N–B3; 13. B×NP, O–O; 14. B×B, R×B; 15. Q–N4, P–B4; 16. Q–N3, P×P; 17. QR–K1, K–R1; 18. K–R1, R–KN1; 19. B×P, B–B1; 20. B–K5+, N×B; 21. Q×N+, R–N2; 22. R×P, Q×P+; 23. K–N1, Q–KN5; 24. R–B2, B–K2; 25. R–K4, Q–N4; 26. Q–Q4, R–B1;

27. R–K5, R–Q1; 28. Q–K4, Q–R5; 29. R–B4, resigns.
(H.G.)

MARIĆ, Rudolf *(b. 13 May 1927)*
Yugoslav international master. He received the title after his performance at Bordeaux 1964. Competed in the Yugoslav championship eight times. Best international result: 6th Skopje 1967. Has been for many years Secretary of the Yugoslav Chess Federation and chess organizer. *(R.D.K.)*

MARIENBAD 1925
Wedged between two super-tournaments (Baden-Baden and Moscow the Marienbad tournament (May–June 1925) has come to be underrated, although it was contested by Nimzowitsch, Marshall and Torre in addition to the top five from Teplitz-Schönau. In the early rounds Rubinstein established a commanding lead, but successive defeats by Opocensky and Nimzowitsch allowed the field to close up, and with four rounds to go Marshall led Nimzowitsch, Rubinstein and Tartakower.

In theoretical respect the tournament was important for the creation of the Marienbad Variation in the Queen's Indian Defence (game Rubinstein–Nimzowitsch). From the sporting angle, it was Nimzowitsch's finest achievement to date; though with Baden-Baden (where he had finished 2nd of 21) less than a week behind him, Rubinstein's performance was even more admirable. The young Mexican, Torre, showed that he was already a great master at the age of twenty-one. Leading scores: Rubinstein, Nimzowitsch 11, Marshall, Torre 10, Réti, Tartakower 9½. *(W.H.)*

MARIENBAD SYSTEM

See under QUEEN'S INDIAN DEFENCE.

MARIOTTI, Sergio *(b. 10 August 1946)*
Italian grandmaster, born in Florence. Mariotti won the Italian Junior championship in 1966 and the Italian championship in 1969 and 1971. He represented Italy in the Praia da Rocha Zonal tournament 1969 where he gained his international master title although failing by a ½-point to qualify for the Interzonal. An outstanding tournament result was second prize at Venice 1971 behind Browne; he recently won the Caorle Zonal 1975 and Rovigo 1976. Mariotti has played in two Olympiads, Skopje 1972 and Nice 1974, obtaining the grandmaster title. *(R.D.K.)*

MARÓCZY, Géza *(3 March 1870–29 May 1951)*

Hungarian grandmaster and a player who, at his best in the early twentieth century, was for some eight years of World Championship calibre. He was born at Szeged in Hungary and learnt chess at the age of fifteen. Mathematically inclined, he spent a couple of years at Zürich Polytechnic studying engineering, and completed his schooling in Budapest where he became a mathematics teacher, and later an expert in various branches of social studies.

He took his profession seriously, and partly because of this and partly because his career coincided with that of the great Emanuel Lasker he never attained the heights of the World Championship.

The earliest part of his chess career was centred in the Budapest Chess Club where his great rival was the Hungarian champion Makovetz, whom however he bested and eventually far outstripped. He first came to international notice when he won the minor tournament at Hastings 1895, and thus became recognized as an international master. Returning to Budapest he won a match against Charousek by +6−2=6.

His first great international success came in 1896 at Nuremberg where he came second to Lasker ahead of Pillsbury, Steinitz and many other great players. For the next two years he devoted himself entirely to his profession, and hence at the great international tournament of Vienna in 1898 he finished as low as =8th.

Then, in 1899, came his real breakthrough and he commenced a run of successes that was to make him one of the most successful tournament players of the next nine years. At the great London tournament he was =2nd with Janowski and Pillsbury below Lasker and in the same year he won first prize at Vienna. In 1900 he was =1st with Pillsbury and Schlechter at Munich, and at Paris that year came =3rd with Marshall.

Now his immense strength as a classical player of the Tarrasch school, with some additional qualities that were all his own, became apparent and first prizes and leading places in great tournaments came almost in profusion. The summarized list runs: 1st Monte Carlo 1902; 2nd Monte Carlo 1903; 1st Monte Carlo 1904; 1st Ostend 1905; =1st with Janowski, Barmen 1905; 2nd Ostend 1906; =3rd with Tartakower and Vidmar, Vienna 1907; 2nd Carlsbad 1907; =1st with Důras and Schlechter, Vienna 1908.

From then on for the six years that led to the First World War he took little part in international chess. In his one great tournament, San Sebastian 1911, he came as low as 12th.

During the war he suffered privations owing to the Allied blockade and after it he went to the Netherlands to recuperate, going on from there to England. He became teacher at the Hastings Chess Club, his star pupil being the future woman World Champion, Vera Menchik.

From 1920 he resumed a most active career in tournament chess, playing sometimes in as many as three international tournaments in a year. But his results were variable and markedly inferior to his great period of 1899–1908. It was always, nevertheless, abundantly clear that he was still a great master, as he demonstrated for example at Carlsbad 1923 where he came =1st with Alekhine and Bogoljubow.

When the International Team tournaments (or Olympiads, they were later called) began, he represented Hungary at London 1927, Hamburg 1930, Folkestone 1933 and Munich 1936.

This was the last event he played in before the Second World War. After the war he played in only one small event, at Baarn in 1947, and then abandoned play for the remaining four years of his life.

He had many strengths as a player. Theory, especially opening theory where he made innovations in the French Defence, the Sicilian Defence, the Queen's Gambit and other lines, owed much to him. In the middle-game he was a great master of the art of evaluating small advantages, yet he also won many brilliancy prizes. In the endgame he was famous for his Queen and pawn endings. His calmness, modesty and firm energy distinguished him among the chess fraternity. Away from the board he was pleasant, courteous and never ruffled.

His writings, though fairly prolific, were not on a par with his play. Perhaps the best are: *Paul Morphy, Sammlung der von ihm gespielten Partien*, Leipzig 1909; *Die Französische Partie*, Berlin-Leipzig 1927.

Brilliancy prize, Monte Carlo 1903
White: Frank J. Marshall; *Black:* Maróczy

Queen's Gambit Declined, Lasker Defence
1. P–Q4, P–Q4; 2. P–QB4, P–K3; 3. N–QB3, N–KB3; 4. B–N5, B–K2; 5. P–K3, O–O; 6. N–B3, N–K5; 7. B×B, Q×B; 8. B–Q3, P–QB4; 9. BP×P, N×N; 10. P×N, KP×P; 11. Q–B2, P–B4; 12. P×P, Q×P; 13. P–QB4, K–R1; 14. P×P, Q×P; 15. O–O, N–B3; 16. B–B4, Q–B4; 17. QR–B1, P–B5; 18. Q–K4, P×P; 19. B–Q5, P×P+; 20. K–R1, Q–R6; 21. B×N, P×B; 22. Q×P, B–R3; 23. R–B3, B×R; 24. N–Q2, Q–R3; 25. Q–K4, B–Q6; 26. resigns. *(H.G.)*

MARÓCZY BIND
Named after the great Hungarian master Géza Maróczy, who practised and exploited it to perfection in master chess, this is a bind on the white squares in the centre resulting from either the Sicilian Defence or the English Opening. White plays one pawn to K4 and the other to QB4 and has a strong point on Q5 as a result.

The way it is usually reached in the Sicilian Defence is: 1. P–K4, P–QB4; 2. N–KB3, P–Q3; 3. P–Q4, P×P; 4. N×P, N–QB3 (or P–KN3); 5. P–QB4.

Or, in the English Opening: 1. P–QB4, P–QB4; 2. N–KB3, N–QB3; 3. P–Q4, P×P; 4. N×P, P–Q3; 5. P–K4. Clearly, there can be many possible transpositions and the bind can also arise later, e.g. 1. P–QB4, N–KB3; 2. N–QB3, P–B4; 3. N–B3, N–B3; 4. P–Q4, P×P; 5. N×P, P–Q3; 6. P–K4.

Of recent years this bind has lost much of its terror, the argument being that Black can get adequate counter-play on the black squares by an early King-side fianchetto. E.g. 1. P–K4, P–QB4; 2. N–KB3, N–QB3; 3. P–Q4, P×P; 4. N×P, P–KN3; 5. P–QB4, B–N2. *(H.G.)*

MAROVIĆ, Drăzen *(b. 14 January 1938)*
Yugoslav grandmaster and chess journalist. His first good international result was an =11th/20 at the very strong Zagreb tournament of 1965. His score there of 9 points was sufficient to gain him the international master title.

In 1968 he was =1st with Ivkov at Malaga and in 1969 at Constanţa he was =4th/15. In 1970 came one of his best tournament results when he was 4th at Skopje ahead of Gligorić and Balashov.

At Banja Luka in 1974 he was =8th with Bukić and Csom. In 1975 (the year he gained the grandmaster title) he was =7th with Lombardy and Nei at Tallinn.

Editor of the Yugoslav chess magazine *Sahovski Glasnik* he has written a book on the openings, *Teorija Otvorenja* (2 vols) Zagreb 1971 and 1973, together with Susić. *(H.G.)*

MARSHALL, Frank James *(10 August 1877–9 November 1944)*
Although never a serious World Championship contender, Marshall was one of the best-remembered grandmasters of the early twentieth century. An over-speculative Romantic style and a predisposition to strong drink often denied him top prizes. Yet he won tournaments ahead of Lasker – Cambridge Springs 1904 – and Capablanca – Havana 1913 – when they were considered unstoppable.

Marshall compared his style with Jack Dempsey's approach to prizefighting. 'I have always liked a wide open game and tried to knock out my opponent with a checkmate as quickly as possible. I subscribe to the old belief that offence is the best form of defence.' He was perhaps best known for tactical 'swindles' in lost positions.

Marshall was born in New York but learned chess after his family moved to Montreal for eleven years. His victory in the 1899 Brooklyn Chess Club championship led to local support that sent him to his first international event that year in London. Although he was denied entry into the Masters section, Marshall won the minor section ahead of Mieses and Marco.

This was followed by a series of European visits with results that included =3rd at Paris 1900, 2nd at Vienna 1903, 1st at Scheveningen 1905, 1st at Nuremberg 1906 and 1st at Düsseldorf 1908. His surprise showing at Cambridge Springs established Marshall as a major competitor and led to a 1907 match with Lasker which Marshall lost $3\frac{1}{2}$–$11\frac{1}{2}$. The following year saw another match loss, this time to Capablanca who compiled a large plus score against the American.

Before the First World War began, Marshall defeated Leonhardt in a short match, came =5th at Carlsbad 1911, 3rd at Pistyan 1912 and qualified for the finals section at St Petersburg 1914. There he came 5th and was named 'grandmaster of chess' by Tsar Nicholas. Marshall was also entered in the Mannheim event later in 1914 that was interrupted by war.

When chess resumed in Europe after the armistice, Marshall fared worse but still managed high prizes until Carlsbad 1929. His best showing was 4th at New York 1924.

Marshall defended the US championship he had won from Showalter in 1909 only once. This was a $9\frac{1}{2}$–$8\frac{1}{2}$ win in 1923 over Ed. Lasker. Marshall also won matches from Teichmann, Janowski, Mieses and Důras.

In his last years Marshall settled down to manage the Marshall Chess Club in New York which he had begun in 1915. He also captained the US Olympic team and played once in the pre-war Olympiads. In 1936 Marshall resigned his national championship and paved the way for the series of US Closed tournaments that have been held since.

Marshall was a spectacular tactician in an age that applauded tactics.

Ostend 1905
White: Marshall; *Black:* Chigorin
Dutch Defence, Staunton Gambit
1. P–Q4, P–KB4; 2. P–K4, P×P; 3. N–QB3, N–KB3; 4. B–KN5, P–B3; 5. B×N, KP×B; 6. N×P, Q–N3; 7. R–N1, P–Q4; 8. N–N3, B–K3; 9. B–Q3, N–Q2; 10. Q–K2, K–B2; 11. N–B3, R–K1; 12. O–O, B–Q3; 13. P–B3, N–B1; 14. N–R4, B–KB4; 15. N(4)×B, R×Q; 16. N×B+, K–K3; 17. N–B8, Q–B2; 18. B×R, K–B2; 19. N–B5, N–K3; 20. N(5)–Q6+, K–N3; 21. B–Q3+, K–R4; 22. QR–K1, N–B5; 23. R–K7, Q–R4; 24. B–N1, P–KN3; 25. P–KN3, N–R6+; 26. K–N2, N–N4; 27. B–Q3, R×N; 28. N×R, Q–Q1; 29. P–KR4, Q×N; 30. P×N, resigns. *(A.S.)*

MARSHALL CHESS CLUB
One of the oldest and strongest clubs in the USA. It has been the traditional rival of the Manhattan Chess Club and has developed such players as Fine, Evans, Sherwin, Mednis and Soltis.

The club grew out of a circle of players that met regularly under the authority of Marshall in the backroom of a mid-Manhattan restaurant beginning in 1915. After several temporary residences the club moved to its present quarters at 23 West 10th St, New York in 1931. The club was administered by Marshall and, after his death in 1944, by his wife, Caroline.

The club quarters, two floors of an apartment building owned by the club, have been the site of several rounds of US Closed championships. Fischer competed in the Capablanca Memorial tournament in 1965 by way of a teletype network linking the club office where Fischer played with the tournament site in Havana. *(A.S.)*

MASON, James *(19 November 1849–15 January 1909)*
A British master of Irish birth, Mason emigrated in early youth to the USA before settling in England in 1878. In America he won matches against Delmar, Martinez, Bird etc.; in England he beat Mackenzie and drew with Potter, remaining unbeaten in match-play. He played in most of the important tournaments of the eighties and nineties, but the first prize he won on his début at the Philadelphia congress 1876 remained his only victory.

His best results were the third prizes at Vienna 1882 (behind Steinitz and Winawer), Nuremberg 1883 and Amsterdam 1889; =2nd at Hamburg 1885 and =3rd at Bradford 1888; also his 7th place in the great New York 1889 tournament. He wrote *The Principles of Chess*, London 1894, *The Art of Chess*, London 1895, compiled a collection of brilliancies in a series *Social Chess*, London 1900, and was co-author with Pollock of the St Petersburg 1895/6 tournament book. *(W.H.)*

MATANOVIĆ, Aleksandar *(b. 23 May 1930)*
One of the older Yugoslav grandmasters, he received the title in 1955 following a number of outstanding tournament performances.

Aleksandar Matanović in play against Golombek, Bad Pyrmont 1951

His name is inextricably linked with the development of chess in post-war Yugoslavia. Competed in fifteen Yugoslav championships, winning in 1962 with Minić and in 1969. Took part in six Zonals and three Interzonals. Represented Yugoslavia nine times in Olympiads. Best result: 72% 2nd board Moscow 1956. Best tournament results: 1st with Suetin, Titovo Uzice 1966 and 1st with Georghiu Vratsa Zonal 1975.

A fine positional player, Matanović never had the courage and will necessary for world results. In recent years he has cut his tournament appearances, becoming engrossed in publishing and editing the international chess magazine *Informator*. *(R.D.K.)*

MATCH OF THE CENTURY, Belgrade 1970
Brain-child of the President of the World Chess Federation, Euwe, the event took quite a while to get off the ground, as the Soviet Chess Federation was averse to the idea of opposing their team by a team representing the rest of the world. The compliment paid to them by the assumption that their team was so much better and so much stronger than any other nation that they could afford to take on the remainder, was offset by the differentiation thus made.

In the end they relented and agreed to play a four-round match against a world team chosen by Dr Euwe in 1970.

The Yugoslav Chess Federation offered hospitality and Euwe proceeded to select his team by basing his selection on Professor ELO's rating lists.

Here he ran into a difficulty. According to the lists Fischer would have to play on top board. But he had not played a game of international chess since 1968, whereas Bent Larsen had been almost continuously in action over the years immediately preceding 1970. The Dane refused to play on anything lower than 1st board, pointing out that in the period in question he had won a number of great tournaments.

An impasse seemed to have been reached until, astonishingly enough, Fischer agreed to play on 2nd board.

Before the match commenced a computer had decided that the Soviet team was going to win by $21\frac{1}{2}$–$18\frac{1}{2}$. It was not so far out, since in fact they won by $20\frac{1}{2}$–$19\frac{1}{2}$ and, who knows, had the original order been maintained maybe the Soviet side would have scored 21½.

The Soviet team, in board order, was Spassky, Petrosian, Korchnoi, Polugayevsky, Geller, Smyslov, Taimanov, Botvinnik, Tal and Keres, with Stein as reserve.

The World team was Larsen, Fischer, Portisch, Hort, Gligorić, Reshevsky, Uhlmann, Matulović, Najdorf and Ivkov with the West German Klaus Darga and the Icelandic player Olafsson in reserve.

'Match of the Century' Belgrade 1970, inside the Trades Union building

The Soviet side scored only marginally better than their adversaries in Rounds 1 and 2 and were indeed beaten in Round 3. But they recovered in Round 4 to win the match.

USSR		*Rest of the World*	
1. Spassky	1½	Larsen	2½
(Stein)	0		
2. Petrosian	1	Fischer	3
3. Korchnoi	1½	Portisch	2½
4. Polugayevsky	1½	Hort	2½
5. Geller	2½	Gligorić	1½
6. Smyslov	2½	Reshevsky	1½
		(Olafsson)	0
7. Taimanov	2½	Uhlmann	1½
8. Botvinnik	2½	Matulović	1½
9. Tal	2	Najdorf	2
10. Keres	3	Ivkov	1
	20½		19½

A remarkable collapse by Larsen in the 2nd round:

White: Larsen; *Black:* Spassky
English Opening
1. P–QN3, P–K4; 2. B–N2, N–QB3; 3. P–QB4, N–B3; 4. N–KB3, P–K5; 5. N–Q4, B–B4; 6. N×N, QP×N; 7. P–K3, B–B4; 8. Q–B2, Q–K2; 9. B–K2, O–O–O; 10. P–B4, N–N5; 11. P–N3, P–KR4; 12. P–KR3, P–R5;

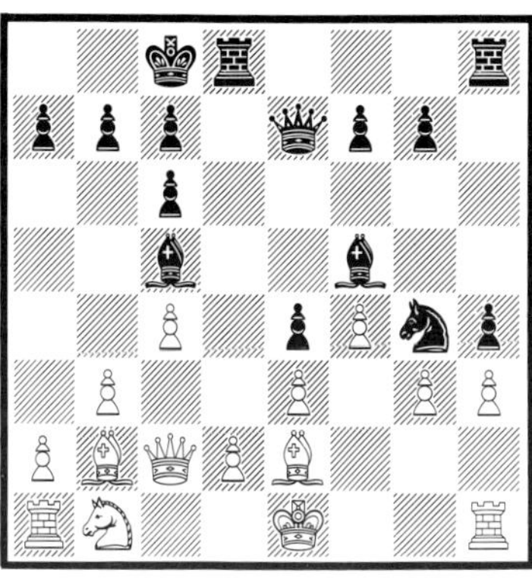

13. P×N, P×P; 14. R–N1, R–R8; 15. R×R, P–N7; 16. R–B1, Q–R5+; 17. K–Q1, P×R=Q+; 18. resigns.

(R.D.K.)

MATERA, Salvatore Joseph *(b. 5 February 1951)*
US international master (1976). He won the USA Junior Championship in 1967 but subsequently chess took second place to his studies at Columbia University. Since graduating, he has returned to chess and he played on board two for the US Student team in 1974. In 1976 he obtained his second international master norm at the tournament in Reykjavik. *(K.J.O'C.)*

MATHEMATICIANS AND CHESS

The popular belief that interest and ability in mathematics is somehow linked with high achievement in chess has but little evidence to support it. A study by Binet in 1893 did reveal that most strong chess-masters were good at mental arithmetic, but despite the fact that mathematicians often professed great interest in the game they seldom became highly successful players. Later surveys of the academic pursuits of chess-masters supported these findings; of the leading masters only Adolf Anderssen, Emanuel Lasker, Réti. Euwe and Keres were students of mathematics, and of these Lasker is unique in having made significant contributions to the development of the subject.

Of course, it is hardly surprising that few have managed to reach the pinnacles of success in both spheres, for the mental and physical demands on a chess-master leave little time or energy for other serious pursuits. This is, however, perhaps not the decisive factor; for it is the differences in personality between mathematicians and chess-players which better explain why so few have excelled at both. The chess-player is motivated by his drive for productive thinking, decision-taking, and fighting, not usually satisfied within the strictures of academic discipline. Thus, while the similarities in logical structure between chess and mathematics will ensure that mathematicians will tend to be interested in the game, the sporting nature of competitive chess is less likely to appeal to them. University faculties of mathematics will be able, therefore, always to field competent chess teams, but cannot be relied upon to produce great players.

It is perhaps of interest to note that during the early 1960s the Cambridge University Chess Club used to have a regular match between mathematicians and 'The Rest'. This was invariably won by the mathematicians, until eventually the fixture was abandoned owing to the inability of the opposition to raise enough players for a team. With the 1970s this imbalance disappeared as players of international strength appeared in other faculties. *(W.R.H.)*

MATING SACRIFICE
The sacrifice of material for the purpose of mating the enemy King – a target which justifies the highest stakes, e.g. the finish of Spielmann v. Hönlinger, Vienna 1929, which may also serve as an illustration of the Harrwitz Bishops. From the diagram play goes 1. N–K7+, Q×N; 2. Q×RP+, K×Q; 3. R–R5+, K–N1; 4. R–R8 mate. *(W.H.)*

MATTISON, Herman Karlovich
(27 December 1894–16 November 1932)
Latvian master and endgame study composer. Winner of the first Latvian championship in 1924, and of the FIDE individual (amateur) championship at Paris 1924. Led the Latvian team at the Prague 1931 Olympiad. Composer of more than sixty published studies of great artistic merit. *(W.R.H.)*

MATULOVIĆ, Milan *(b. 10 June 1935)*
A Yugoslav grandmaster. Learnt chess in adolescence. Soon became a household name in his country, but due to his extravagant behaviour he is often denied access to top-level tournaments. Awarded grandmaster title following his performance at Sochi 1965.

Successful both at home and abroad, Matulović gradually replaced Ivkov as Yugoslavia's Number Two, but in recent years his strength has declined. Best results: 1st with Hort, Skopje 1969; =1st with Gligorić, Ivkov and Polugayevsky, Belgrade 1969, ahead of Geller and Botvinnik; 1st Birmingham 1975, =1st Bajmok 1975, 1st Majdanpek 1976 and 1st Vrbas 1976.

He has played many times in the Yugoslav championship, winning it 1965 and 1967. Has represented Yugoslavia in five Olympiads, and taken part in two Interzonals. Played for Rest of the World in the 1970 Match of the Century, losing to Botvinnik $1\frac{1}{2}$–$2\frac{1}{2}$. His style is clear, leaving little room for imagination.

Matulović has made considerable contributions to opening theory. *(R.D.K.)*

MAURETANIA
The Fédération des Echecs de la République Islamique de Mauretanie (B. P. 629, Nouakchott) is one of the three latest recruits to the ranks of FIDE, joining in 1976 and having yet to make its début in the FIDE arena. *(K.J.O'C.)*

MAYET, Karl *(11 August 1810–18 May 1868)*
The most original player of the Berlin Pleiades, with a special foible for giving up the Queen for assorted material. In matches he beat Szén and Van der Goltz, without, however, in the latter encounter reaching the 2:1 majority of wins which had been stipulated in the original challenge. He was beaten by Harrwitz, Hanstein, Dufresne and Anderssen, and drew with Mongredien. *(W.H.)*

MECKING, Henrique da Costa *(b. 2 February 1952)*
Brazilian grandmaster and a child prodigy who, if not exactly in the same class as Morphy, Reshevsky, Capablanca or Fischer, did in fact achieve startling results in his native country at the age of thirteen.

Henrique Mecking at the age of 14, in play against Botvinnik, Hastings 1966/7

This led to an invitation to play at Hastings 1966/7, where, however, his performance was not outstanding. From this moment on, Mecking concentrated on chess, and he achieved the remarkable feat of qualifying for the 1967 Interzonal at Sousse in Tunisia at the age of fifteen.

In recent years Mecking has held himself somewhat aloof from the normal run of international competition, yet he has been remarkably successful in FIDE events, taking 1st prize at the 1973 Interzonal at Petropolis and again in 1975 at Manila.

In 1974 he lost narrowly to Korchnoi in a quarter-final of the Candidates series.

He has again qualified for the 1977 Candidates series and, given his age, Mecking obviously has the possibility to prove himself a major force in future cycles for the World Championship. *(R.D.K.)*

MEDINA-GARCIA, Antonio *(b. 2 October 1919)*
A Spanish international master (1950). Spanish champion 1944, 1947, 1949, 1952 and 1963. Resided for several years in Venezuela, and won the Venezuelan championship in 1955, 1956 and 1958. Results include =1st Hastings 1952/3, 2nd Mar del Plata 1948. *(R.D.K.)*

MEDNIS, Edmar *(b. 1937)*
A Latvian-born international master, now a stock market investor living in New York. He has been a frequent member of US international teams. His best US championship result was =3rd in 1961/2. Mednis's first book was *How to Beat Bobby Fischer*, New York 1974. *(A.S.)*

MENCHIK, Vera Francevna *(16 February 1906–27 June 1944)*
Probably the strongest woman player in the history of the game, Vera Menchik was born in Moscow and, though her father was a Czechoslovak and her mother English, she played for most of her life under English colours.

In 1921 her family came to Hastings in England and there Vera became a pupil of the great Hungarian master, Géza Maróczy. This was to have a dominating influence on her style of play which was solidly classical, logical and technically most well equipped. Such a style enabled her to deal severely not only with her fellow women players but also with contemporary masters and budding masters. Vera did extremely well, for example, against C. H. O'D. Alexander and P. S. Milner-Barry, but lost repeatedly to H. Golombek who was able to take advantage of her lack of imagination by the use of more modern methods.

Vera was soon predominent in women's chess. In the first Women's World Championship tournament, at London in 1927, she won the title with a score of 10½ out of 11 and retained the championship with great ease at all the subsequent Olympiads (or International Team tournaments as they were then known more correctly) at Hamburg 1930, Prague 1931, Folkestone 1933, Warsaw 1935, Stockholm 1937 and Buenos Aires 1939.

Vera Menchik at Margate 1935

With Sonja Graf, the player who came nearest to her in strength among her female contemporaries, she played two matches and demonstrated her undoubted superiority by beating her in 1934 (+3−1) and again in a match for the title in 1937 (+9−1=5).

In 1937 Vera officially became a British citizen by marrying the then Kent and later B.C.F. Secretary, R. H. Stevenson. Oddly enough, Sonja Graf, many years later, also became a Mrs Stevenson by marrying an American of that name some years after the Second World War.

Vera Menchik also played and held her own in men's tournaments. She did well in the British championship and her best performance in international chess was =2nd with Rubinstein in the Ramsgate Team Practice tournament ahead of her old teacher, Maróczy. She also had an excellent result at Maribor in 1934 where she came 3rd, ahead of Spielmann and Vidmar.

Her husband died in 1943 and Vera herself, together with her younger sister Olga and her mother, was killed by a V1 bomb that descended on the Stevenson home in London in 1944.

This was a sad and premature loss, not only for British but for world chess, since there is no doubt she would have continued to dominate the female scene for many years.

As a person Vera was a delightful companion, jolly and full of fun and understanding. As a player she was not only strong but also absolutely correct and without any *prima donna* behaviour. Generous in defeat and modest in victory, she set a great example to all her contemporaries.

An example of Vera's attacking play at its best against her nearest rival, Sonja Graf, is shown by the following game which was played in her 1937 match at Semmering in Austria.

White: Menchik; *Black:* Graf
Queen's Gambit Declined
1. P–QB4, P–K3; 2. N–QB3, P–Q4; 3. P–Q4, N–KB3; 4. N–B3, QN–Q2; 5. P–K3, P–B3; 6. B–Q3, B–K2; 7. O–O, O–O; 8. P–K4, P×KP; 9. N×P, N×N; 10. B×N, N–B3; 11. B–B2, P–B4; 12. P×P, Q–R4; 13. B–K3, B×P; 14. B–Q2, Q–B2; 15. B–B3, B–K2; 16. Q–K2, P–QN3; 17. N–N5, P–N3; 18. Q–B3, B–N2; 19. Q–R3, P–KR4; 20. QR–Q1, N–N5;

21. R–Q7, resigns (if 21.., Q×R; 22. Q×P!, P×Q; 23. B–R7 mate). *(H.G.)*

MEPHISTO
Chess automaton created by Charles Godfrey Gümpel. Gümpel's creation, which had taken him some six or seven years to complete, was first exhibited at his Leicester Square home in 1878.

The figure was dressed in red velvet trimmed with black. The face was that of a conventional stage Mephistopheles, with a shrewd but not malevolent appearance. The head was close shaven and surmounted by a pink hat with a black border and decorated with two large feathers. The hands, the left of which wore a black kid glove, were slim and well-shaped, as was the torso. The feet were crossed, one a neatly proportioned human foot, the other a cloven hoof. The figure sat behind an ordinary chess table and, since there was no cabinet and viewers were allowed to examine Mephisto even during play, it was evident that, for the first time, here was a chess automaton that could not possibly conceal within itself a human player. It is believed that the mechanism was operated electrically.

Mephisto had but one operator, Isidor Gunsberg, and with his help it became the first automaton in history to win a tournament – the Counties Chess Association Handicap, played in London in 1878. It was also in the same guise that Gunsberg acted as editor of a chess column in the London periodical *Knowledge* from 1881 until 1890.

Mephisto's playing career ended at the Paris Exposition of 1889 and its subsequent whereabouts are unknown.

See also under AUTOMATONS. *(K.J.O'C.)*

MESTEL, Jonathan *(b. 13 March 1957)*

British master and British champion 1976, who was born in Cambridge and packed into the three years 1974–6, in the period of time when he grew from seventeen to nineteen, more chess and more success than most people achieve in a long lifetime.

He first made his presence felt in the international field when he won the cadet championship at Pont Sainte-Maxence in France in 1974. This was an unofficial world under-18 championship and he confirmed this good impression by very nearly winning the British championship at Clacton in the same year. He figured in a seven-way tie for first place but failed to win the play-off for the title.

The next year he gained his first international master norm at the Birmingham international tournament, where he finished equal second with Matera (USA) and Miles (England), a point below Matulović of Yugoslavia whom he beat in their individual game.

He was a little disappointing in the World Junior Championship at Tjentiste in Yugoslavia in 1975, in which he came third below the Russian Chekhov and the US player Larry Christiansen. It was thought that, talented though he was, Mestel lacked stability and was too variable in his form to achieve the highest honours.

But the next year, 1976, was to show this was quite a false appreciation of his talents and character. First, in April he won an international tournament which, if not as strong as the previous Birmingham, was still a tough event to win ahead of the Yugoslav grandmaster Damjanović.

Then came a most remarkable achievement in the British championship at Portsmouth where he won his first nine games in succession, thereby winning the title and establishing a record for the British championship with his run of victories. *(H.G.)*

METGER, Johannes *(15 December 1850–24 January 1926)*
A strong German player, who won the German master title at Leipzig 1876 and carried off further top honours in such local events as Schwerin 1883, Rostock 1884 and Wismar 1886. He became famous as the instructor of a large group of talented amateur players in the Lower Elbe and Schleswig-Holstein districts of Germany.

A theorist of some repute, the Metger variation of the Four Knights Game is named after him. *(W.H.)*

MEXICO
Mexican teams have competed in the Olympiads of 1964 (finishing 40th out of 50), 1966 (44th/52), 1968 (46th/53), 1970 (44th/60), 1972 (41st/62) and 1974 (41st/73). The only FIDE titled player is international master Carlos Torre who is retired from active play.

Mexican chess is controlled by the Federacion National de Ajedrez de Mexico, Apartado Postal 5-359, Mexico 5, D.F. *(R.D.K.)*

MIAGMASUREN, Lhamsuren *(b. 1938)*
Mongolian international master since 1966. Competitor in the Sousse 1967 Interzonal tournament. *(W.R.H.)*

MICHEL, Paul *(b. 27 November 1905)*
A German international master, Michel was one of the members of the German Olympic team at Buenos Aires 1939 who were kept back in Argentina, where he scored many minor successes in the 1940s. His best results during this period were =3rd with O'Kelly (behind Najdorf and Ståhlberg) at Mar del Plata 1948 and 1st (ahead of Czerniak, Pomar, etc.) at Rosario 1949. Previously he had twice gained joint second places in German championships (Aachen 1935 and Oeynhausen 1938). *(W.H.)*

MICHELL, Reginald Pryce *(9 April 1873–29 May 1938)*
British master who ranked in the first six in British chess during the early 1900s. Born and educated in Penzance, he became a civil servant who worked for the Admiralty all his life and was yet another of the amateurs who were of master strength in England

during Victorian, Edwardian and George V times.

He won the British Amateur championship at Norwich in 1902 and did consistently well in the City of London Club championships, coming second on six occasions and winning the title in 1925. He also did well in several British championships, usually coming in the top four below Atkins, Yates and Sir George Thomas.

He represented Great Britain in eight Anglo-American cable matches. His best international performances were 1st in a strong Major Open at the 1922 B.C.F. London Congress and an =2nd with Alekhine, Bogoljubow, Muffang, below Grünfeld and above Réti.

His style of play reflected his character, quiet, competent and lacking in adventurous aggression. *(H.G.)*

MIESES, Jacques *(27 February 1865–23 February 1954)*

Grandmaster, theorist, problemist, tournament organizer and chess journalist, Mieses was a spectacular player who won many brilliancy prizes but suffered as many very short defeats. As a result the German master achieved only one full success in important international tournaments (Vienna 1907), but occupied good places in such events as Breslau 1889 (3rd), Hanover 1902 (4th), Ostend 1907 (=3rd), as well as some smaller events. In matches he showed a heavy preponderance of losses against the top-notchers, losing to Lasker, Tarrasch, Rubinstein, Marshall, Teichmann (twice), and Spielmann, but he drew with Walbrodt (1894), Janowski (1895) and Caro (1897) and beat Leonhardt, Taubenhaus, and (at the age of 81) Abrahams.

In keeping with his sharp style, Mieses preferred such openings as the Vienna Gambit, the Danish Gambit and the Centre Counter-gambit. Among his lasting achievements are his brilliancy prize games against Janowski (Paris 1900), Reggio (Monte Carlo 1903), Perlis (Ostend 1907) and Schlechter (Vienna 1908).

Personally a very witty man (and something of a *bon vivant*) Mieses did not invest his writing with the same sparkle; both as a journalist and author he was rather dry and sober. He edited the eighth edition of the famous *Handbuch*, several editions of the 'little Dufresne', and published several primers as well as a treatise on blindfold play and an anthology *Instructive Positions from Master Chess*, London 1938.

One of Mieses's most important contributions to chess history was the payment of travelling and living expenses during a tournament, which he insisted on when running the famous tournament at San Sebastian 1911 – it was only thenceforth that this procedure became the norm. *(W.H.)*

MIJE, van der
See under NICOLAU.

MIKENAS, Vladas Ivanovich *(b. 17 April 1910)*
First Lithuanian master and champion in 1936, and then, after the Second World War, Soviet international master. Also won the championship of Lithuania three times (1947, 1948 and 1961) after it fell under Soviet jurisdiction. Given the title of international master in 1950. Mikenas has had a long international career, among his best results being 4th at Kemeri 1939 and shared first place at Lublin 1971. *(W.R.H.)*

MILAN 1975
The strongest international event of 1975, organized with an unusual format: after a 12-player all-play-all preliminary tournament, the top four players met in a series of elimination matches to produce an absolute winner. The preliminary ended in an outstanding success for the Hungarian grandmaster Portisch with 7/11 ahead of Karpov, Petrosian and Ljubojević 6½; Smejkal 6; Tal and Browne 5½; Unzicker, Andersson, Gligorić and Larsen 5; Mariotti 2½.

In the semi-final matches which followed Portisch beat Ljubojević 2½–1½ and Karpov drew with Petrosian 2–2. Karpov progressed to the final by virtue of his superior Sonneborn-Berger score, and in the end the World Champion asserted himself by defeating Portisch 3½–2½. In a play-off for 3rd place Petrosian and Ljubojević drew 3–3. *(R.D.K.)*

MILES, Anthony J. *(b. 23 April 1955)*
British international grandmaster and 1974 World Junior Champion, Miles was born in Birmingham where his early chess career developed along almost frenetically exciting lines.

Like C. H. O'D. Alexander, he attended King Edward's School and it was there that he learnt to play excitingly tactical chess. At the age of thirteen, in 1968, he won the British under-14 championship and two years later at the B.C.F. Congress at Blackpool he won the British under-21 championship. This qualified him for the British championship in 1972 where he scored 5½ points out of 11. In that year he came second to the Soviet player (later grandmaster) Romanishin in the European Junior championship.

It was in 1973 that Miles became one of Britain's leading players. Playing in the Lone Pine tournament, he won a share of the fourth prize, just below grandmasters Bisguier, Browne and Szabo. He did even better at an international tournament at Birmingham which he won ahead of the Hungarian Adorján and the American

Bisguier. Now came his first attempt on the World Junior Championship which was played at the Teesside and won by the Soviet player Alexander Belyavsky. Miles came 2nd but beat Belyavsky. He was =4th in the British championship at Eastbourne and at the end of the year came 13th out of 16 in the Hastings Premier where he typically did well against the first prize-winners, beating the Soviet grandmaster Kuzmin and drawing with the former World Champion, Tal.

In 1974 he won the World Junior Championship at Manila and did it in overwhelming fashion by beating the Soviet master Alexander Kochiev in the penultimate round, thus attaining a score that could not be reached by any other competitor. By now he was a mathematics student at Sheffield University and the following year the university awarded him an honorary M.A. degree for his distinction at chess, the first time that chess has been so honoured.

In gaining the championship he also acquired the international master title.

His chess was maturing and he was as strong strategically as he was in tactics. So the next step was the gaining of the grandmaster title. In October 1975 he obtained his first grandmaster norm by winning an international tournament in London ahead of three grandmasters, and in February 1976, by scoring 9 points in a strong international tournament at Dubna, USSR, he completed the second leg of the norm and thus was a grandmaster at the age of twenty.

Further successes in 1976 confirmed his status as a genuine grandmaster. In July he came equal first with Viktor Korchnoi in the strong I.B.M. Tournament in Amsterdam, and in September was first by a large margin at a weaker but still important tournament in Stockholm. *(H.G.)*

MILEV, Zdravko *(b. 25 October 1929)*
Bulgarian international master and Bulgarian champion in 1952, 1960 and 1961. His best international results were 1st at Bucharest 1951 and at Sczawno Zdroj 1952. At Varna in 1964 he came =6th. He played for Bulgaria in the Olympiads of 1954, 1956, 1958, 1960, 1962 and 1964. *(H.G.)*

MILIĆ, Borislav *(b. 20 October 1925)*
A Yugoslav master, one of best Yugoslav players in the immediate post-war period. Received the international master title 1952 following his performances in Dortmund and Vienna 1951. He participated fifteen times in the Yugoslav championship, and represented Yugoslavia in 1952 and 1956 Olympiads. Best result: 1st Vienna 1951. *(R.D.K.)*

MILLS, Daniel Yarnton *(29 August 1849–18 December 1904)*
One of the leading Scottish players in the latter half of the nineteenth century, Mills was originally from England but settled in Scotland where he won the championship many times (1885, 1887, 1892, 1895–7, 1899 and 1900). Secretary for many years of the Scottish Chess Association, he played for Great Britain in the cable matches against the USA from 1896 to 1903, winning one game (against Delmar) and drawing seven, losing none. He was also one of the founders of the British Chess Association. *(H.G.)*

MILNER-BARRY, Sir Philip Stuart *(b. 20 September 1906)*

British master whose chess career was limited by his amateur status but whose abilities as a player and original theorist rendered him worthy of the title of international master.

Born at Mill Hill in London, he showed early promise and in 1923 won the British Boys championship, then held at Hastings. He studied classics at Cambridge and developed into the strongest player there. At the university he was to meet C. H. O'D. Alexander with whom he played much chess. Though nearly three years younger, Alexander exerted a strong influence over him and both players cherished and revelled in the brilliance of play in open positions.

On leaving the university Milner-Barry went to work in the London Stock Exchange, but his heart was not in the work and he became Chess Correspondent of *The Times* in 1938.

By then, along with Alexander and Golombek, he had become recognized as one of the three strongest young players in the country. Whilst not as successful as they were in such tournaments as the British championship in which stamina was essential, he was a most formidable club and team match-player, as he had already shown in 1933 when he won the championship of the City of London Club ahead of R. P. Michell and Sir George Thomas.

He played in his first International Team tournament at Stockholm 1937 and was to play in three more such events: in 1939 at Buenos Aires where, on third board, he made the fine score of 4/5; in Helsinki 1952; and in Moscow 1956 where, again on third board, he was largely responsible for the team's fine showing.

In 1940 he shared first prize with Dr List in a strong tournament of semi-international character in London and then, like Alexander and (later) Golombek, helped in the Foreign Office code-breaking activities at Bletchley Park for the duration of the Second World War. Staying in the Civil Service afterwards, he rose to the rank of Under-Secretary in the Treasury and was knighted for his services in 1975.

After the war, too, he had some fine results in the British championship, his best being second place at Hastings 1953.

Though never at home in close positions, he was an outstanding strategist in the open game and it is significant that his most important contribution to opening theory was the Milner-Barry variation of the Nimzo-Indian Defence which is essentially an attempt to convert a close position into an open one (1. P–Q4, N–KB3; 2. P–QB4, P–K3; 3. N–QB3, B–N5; 4. Q–B2, N–B3).

An excellent though infrequent writer on the game, he wrote a fine memoir of C. H. O'D. Alexander in Golombek and Hartston's *The Best Games of C. H. O'D. Alexander*, Oxford 1976. *(H.G.)*

MINCKWITZ, Johannes *(10 December 1843–21 May 1901)*
A minor German master of the nineteenth century, Minckwitz was for many years the editor of the *Deutsche Schachzeitung*. His best tournament results were 2nd behind Anderssen at Barmen 1869, 3rd at Crefeld 1871, and =1st (with Weiss and Schwarz) at Graz 1880. He published tournament books of Crefeld 1871, Hamburg 1885 and other events, as well as primers (*Das ABC des Schachspiels*, Leipzig 1879; *Der Kleine Schachkönig*, Leipzig 1889). *(W.H.)*

MINEV, Nikolai *(b. 8 January 1931)*
Bulgarian international master and Bulgarian champion 1953 (after winning a play-off $4\frac{1}{2}$–$3\frac{1}{2}$ against Neikirch), 1965 and 1966.

Minev played for Bulgaria in the Olympiads of 1954, 1956, 1958, 1960, 1962 and 1966. Then, with his results in national tournaments diminishing, he gave way to a new generation.

His best international results have been 3rd at Varna 1960, 2nd at Warsaw 1961, =1st at Sombor 1966 and 2nd at Albena 1975. *(H.G.)*

MINIATURE
See under BREVITY.

MINIĆ, Dragoljub *(b. 5 March 1937)*
A Yugoslav international master, receiving the title in 1964. He represented Yugoslav in the Siegen Olympiad 1970. Has competed many times in the Yugoslav championship, winning it in 1962 with Matanović. Minić took part in the Interzonal at Palma de Mallorca 1970, finishing 16th. Best result: =7th with Ivkov at Zagreb 1970 ahead of Uhlmann and Browne. Well versed theoretically, he has twice beaten Korchnoi and once Spassky. *(R.D.K.)*

MINOR EXCHANGE
A term used by Tarrasch to indicate the difference in value between Bishop and Knight. Tarrasch believed the Bishop to be the more valuable piece. *(W.H.)*

MINORITY ATTACK
An attack by pawns on the wing where the opponent has a pawn majority, with the purpose of breaking up the pawn position and, by doing so, to open lines for the attacker's active major pieces and leave the defender with weakened pawns. It is a frequent theme in the Exchange variation of the Queen's Gambit Declined.

Though occasionally seen in games by Steinitz and Pillsbury, it is essentially a modern (i.e. post-Tarrasch) stratagem since the dogmatic Dr Tarrasch asserted that an attack by a minority against a majority must always be wrong. It is frequently seen in the games of primarily positional players, such as Capablanca, Flohr and Reshevsky.

An excellent illustration of how the break-up by the minority attack is to be exploited is shown in the diagram (Najdorf–Eliskases, Mar del Plata 1947).

Play continued: 24. P–N5, RP × P; 25. P × P, P × P (note that Black cannot prevent the splintering of his P's by *25. . , R–QB1; 26. P × P, Q–K3* because of *27. P × P*); 26. R–B5, K–N2; 27. Q × P(N5), R–Q1; 28. Q–R5, R(2)–Q2; 29. R(1)–B1, P–N5; 30. P × P, Q × P; 31. R–N5, K–R1; 32. Q–N6, R–Q3; 33. Q–B7, R–KN1; 34. P–N3, 34. . , Q–K3; 35. R–K1, P–N3; 36. P–K4, P × P; 37. R × KP, Q–B3; 38. P–Q5, P–R4; 39. K–N2, Q–N3; 40. R–KB4, R–N2; 41. R–KR4, R–R2; 42. R(5)–N4, Q–B3; 43. R(R4)–KB4, Q–Q1; 44. Q–B3+, K–N1; 45. R(N4)–B4, Q–KB1; 46. R–B8, R–Q1; 47. R(4)–QB4, R–R3; 48. R × R, Q × R; 49. R–B8, resigns. *(W.H.)*

MODEL, Abram Yakovlevich *(b. 1895)*
Soviet master and Leningrad champion in 1944. Shared third place in the 1927 USSR championship. *(W.R.H.)*

MODENA SCHOOL
At the beginning of the second half of the eighteenth century a talented school of chess-masters arose in Modena in Italy. The three chief men, in chronological order, were Ercole del Rio, Giambattista Lolli and Domenico Ponziani.

They believed in a speedy development and a dynamic use of the pieces in an open position. Talented though they were, they lay outside the mainstream of chess, partly because at that time Italian players practised a different type of castling (known as free castling) and partly because they failed to realize the importance of a strong pawn centre. In this respect they were as much behind the times as their contemporary Philidor was in advance of them. *(H.G.)*

'MODERN CHESS OPENINGS'

This, the first scientific study of the openings in the twentieth century, was written and compiled by R. C. Griffith and J. H. White and first published by the *British Chess Magazine*, Leeds 1911.

The second edition, much enlarged, was published in London and New York in 1913. The method of treating the variations was to arrange the openings in alphabetical order and give the analysis in columns with footnotes. Each opening was prefaced by an introduction in which the emphasis, in accordance with the title, was on topical lines, the more old-fashioned variations being consigned *ad acta*.

The work became popular at once and for over forty years was regarded as the main book on the openings throughout the world. It has gone through many editions and is still in print and commonly used and studied by club and match players. *(H.G.)*

MODERN PHILOSOPHY, Chess in

In view of the origins of chess it is appropriate that the game has provided the English language with an image of war: we commonly speak of a pawn on the chessboard of war or diplomacy. Philosophers however have used chess for a different kind of metaphor; chess is for them an analogy for their ideas about the world. Thus in the nineteenth century Thomas Huxley wrote that 'The chessboard is the world; the pieces are the phenomena of the universe; the rules of the game are what we call the laws of Nature.'

This kind of analogy developed in the twentieth century into thing much more than a mere simile: it became virtually a model of certain philosophical theories. The most striking example of this occurs in the ideas of Ferdinand de Saussure, a Swiss university professor living at the turn of the century whose influence on linguistics and the social sciences has been profound. He used chess to explain and justify the central part of his doctrine, stating that 'of all comparisons that might be imagined, the most fruitful is the one that might be drawn between the functioning of language and a game of chess' (*Course in General Linguistics*, New York 1959). The exposition by De Saussure of this idea, first in print in 1916, was so successful that one finds it again in the works of many modern philosophers, and the chess analogy so intrigues commentators that learned journals carry articles on the subject 'Is Language Like A Chess Game?' (Joseph Greenberg, *Language, Culture and Communication*, Stanford 1971), or P. A. Verburg, 'Het schaakspel-model bij F. de Saussure en bij L. Wittgenstein', *Wijsgerig Perspectief op Maatschappij en Wetenschap*, vol. 1 no. 5, 1961). General works on the theories of De Saussure or Wittgenstein rarely fail to mention the chess analogy they used (see for example Edwin Ardener, *Social Anthropology and Language*, London 1971 at pp. xxxvi–xxxix and pp. 215–7; Rodney Needham, *Belief, Language and Experience*, Oxford 1972 at p. 236).

De Saussure first uses the chess analogy to illustrate the difference between what he regards as relevant and irrelevant in the study of language, or what is internal or external to it: 'In chess, what is external can be separated relatively easily from what is internal. The fact that the game passed from Persia to Europe is external; against that, everything having to do with its system and values is internal.'

The sounds or letters of a word are arbitrary and external and may change in time; the identity of a word consists only in the fact that it is different from other words in any one system. Thus he continues, 'If I use ivory chessmen instead of wooden ones, the change has no effect on the system, but if I decrease or increase the number of chessmen, this change has a profound effect on the "grammar" of the game. One must always distinguish what is internal from what is external.' In other words, it does not matter what a pawn looks like, only that it should look different from a Bishop, for example; and if a pawn happens to be destroyed or lost, it could be replaced by anything, be it a button or a salt-cellar, and by agreement could be declared identical to the piece it was replacing. This was just how language works, declared De Saussure.

Turning to a situation on the board in the middle of a game, he showed how this also corresponds to a state of a language: 'The respective value of the pieces depends on their positions on the chessboard just as each linguistic term derives its value from its opposition to all the other terms.' Language, like chess, is a system of values, by which he meant not moral values but valencies or weightings: there can be no absolute 'value' of a Knight, for example, since its value will depend in a particular game of chess only on its positional relations with other pieces on the board. It follows that any move in chess (which consists of course of the moving of only one piece) is like a change in a single element in language, for it will have repercussions on the whole system: 'Resulting changes of value will be, according to the circumstances, either nil, very serious, or of moderate importance. A certain move can revolutionize the game, and even affect pieces that are not immediately involved.' The only thing that matters is the state of the board before and after the move – the actual process of change being irrelevant.

Moreover the state of a language, like the state of a chessboard, has nothing to do with its history: 'In a game of chess any particular position has the unique characteristic of being freed from all antecedent positions: the route used in arriving there makes absolutely no difference; one who has followed the entire match has no advantage over the curious party who comes up at a critical moment to inspect the state of the game; to describe this arrangement it is perfectly useless to recall what had happened just a few minutes previously.'

De Saussure was here going against the tide of linguistic theory. Nearly all his contemporaries believed that there was no other way of writing about language than describing how it changed (etymology for example). De Saussure on the other hand pointed out that the speaker of a language does not know its history, and that all that was relevant was how the speaker used the state of the language that he knew (or how the chess-player understood a position on the board). So powerful and graphic was this idea and this chess analogy that it firmly established states of language as the most popular subject of study. By stressing the importance of studying values within a system he gave life to a philosophical theory now called Structuralism, which was to make the old-fashioned theories look as absurd as attempting to write the history of an individual game of chess by describing it from the point of view of each individual piece. These ideas are fashionable today not only in linguistics but in the social sciences as well.

Echoes of this influential metaphor come up in the writings of Ludwig Wittgenstein, himself an influential thinker in the philosophy of language. His works are full of references to chess. He was, however, interested in words rather than language comparing them to chess-pieces: 'The question, "What is a word really?" is analogous to "What is a piece in chess?"' (*Philosophical Investigations*). Here once again we see the image of chess representing the central concerns of a philosopher: Wittgenstein wanted to emphasize the importance of rules that govern the uses of words in specific contexts, so chess was an ideal analogy for a closed system of rules, 'If I were to show someone the King in chess,' he writes, 'and say to him "This is the King", it would not tell him anything about the use of the piece at all. It would only do so for a person who knew everything else about the game except what the King looked like, or for a person unaccustomed to the chess-set in question, and so on. Thus only someone who already knows how to do something with it can meaningfully ask for its name,' he concludes. Chess is a self-contained game with clearly-defined rules, just like language: a child who plays about with chess-pieces on a chessboard and goes through the motions of taking a King cannot be said to have delivered checkmate, despite the fact that the meaning of that word is to take someone's King (*The Brown Book*).

The chess analogy thus became a popular and meaningful metaphor and occurs now in many contexts of scholarly thought. For example H. L. A. Hart's *The Concept of Law* (Oxford 1961) frequently alludes to chess. Lawyers, he says, must distinguish rules from habits, just as chess-players do not merely have similar habits of moving their Queens about the board in the same way: they have rules and expect other players to conform to them. Genuine observance of rules must moreover be distinguished from actions that merely happen to coincide with the rules: evidence of the abiding force of the chess analogy can be seen in the fact that Hart quotes Wittgenstein's case of checkmate to illustrate this important legal distinction.

That the chess analogy has proved useful to philosophers is certain; moreover as a pedagogical device in explaining the theory of Structuralism, De Saussure's chess analogy is still often invoked in the university classroom, as Greenberg reports. But difficulties remain. How valid is it as a metaphor? Verburg has pointed out that in chess the whole aim is to change the state of the board, but in language there are no such intentions. Is there anything in language that would correspond to a set of moves in chess like, for example, the Sicilian Defence? Needham raises the anthropological objection to Wittgenstein's use of the chess analogy, that in the comparative study of societies anthropologists have to consider not merely the uses of the chess-pieces within a single game, but a large number of games that differ greatly from one another in the numbers, values and moves of the pieces with which they are played namely, all languages in their own social contexts. 'The game of comparativism, one might say, is played with pieces that are themselves games', he writes. Furthermore, Giulio Lepschy writes that it is not strictly true, as De Saussure claimed, that in analysing a position in the middle of a chess game no information is needed on how that position was reached. One may need to know e.g. if the King or Rook have moved, if one wants to castle; or whether a pawn has just been moved if one wants to take it *en passant*. (*A Survey of Structural Linguistics*, London 1970). Sometimes, even, the very position tells the onlooker something about what has happened in the game previously: Vendler points out that this would be the case if there were two pawns of the same colour standing in the same file, because it would then be evident that one of them had taken a piece in a previous move.

But there is a sense in which it is pointless to ask what corresponds in language to the queening of a pawn in chess. The metaphor may lack validity in all its implications, and philosophers too may be referring to chess only in gratuitous fashion. The analogy does break down on the question of whether one can infer the rules of chess by watching one game, as linguists or sociologists attempt to infer the rules of language or of society by analysing a set of data. To a certain extent this would be possible; however the rule for checkmate that trapping the King finishes the game, is after all the game's whole purpose but this is not deducible until the last state of the board. Nor does checkmate exist in the outside world: it is only in chess, but not in real life, that one can finish a game and start again. Still, one cannot judge a metaphor in terms of its truth or falsity; a metaphor, by definition, cannot be identical with what it refers to. One may judge it only in terms of its fruitfulness or suggestiveness, and on this basis one may conclude that the use of chess as an image in modern philosophy is undoubtedly of great importance. *(J.W.)*

MOHRLOK, Dieter *(b. 4 November 1938)*
West German international master who has played in three Olympiads for West Germany, always scoring 50% or more though on a low board. At Tel Aviv in 1964 he had 50% as number 5 and again as number 5 he scored 70.8% at Siegen in 1970. On board 4 in Haifa 1976 he had 62.5%.

In 1969, the year he gained his international master title, he came 2nd at Ludwigsburg and in the very strong tournament at Büssum came =9th/16 along with Bilek, Hecht, Hübner and Szily. *(H.G.)*

MOISEYEV, Oleg Leonidovich *(b. 1925)*
A member of the 1954 Soviet Students Olympiad team; international master since 1970. Moiseyev has written several

theoretical articles and a monograph on the Sicilian Defence (1969). *(W.R.H.)*

MONACO
Two short, but famous, series of tournaments have been held in Monte Carlo. The first series ran from 1901 to 1904, the winners being respectively Janowski, Maróczy, Tarrasch and again Maróczy. All four tournaments were very strong, that of 1902 being perhaps the greatest and that of 1903 being memorable for the participation of Col. Moreau who achieved the 'perfect' score of 0 out of 26. The second series, dealt with below (Monte Carlo), ran from 1967 to 1968.

A Monégasque team has played in seven Olympiads: 37th in 1960, 42nd in 1964, 46th in 1966, 42nd (two places ahead of France) in 1968, 60th in 1970, 56th in 1974 and 43rd in 1976.

The FIDE affiliate is the Fédération Monégasque des Echecs, 25 Boulevard des Moulins, Monte Carlo. *(K.J.O'C.)*

MONGOLIA
The Mongolian Chess Federation was founded in 1946 and its current address is: Baga Toirog 55, P.O. Box 236, Ulan Bator.

A Mongolian team has participated in nine Olympiads with the following results: 30th in 1956, 27th in 1960, 21st in 1962, 23rd in 1964, 30th in 1966, 27th in 1968, 16th in 1970, 28th in 1972 and 36th in 1974.

The country boasts two international masters: Lhamsuren Miagmarsuren and Tudev Uitumen. *(K.J.O'C.)*

MONGREDIEN, Augustus *(17 March 1807–30 March 1888)*
President of the London Chess Club 1839–70 and noted English amateur. On a tour of Germany in 1845, Mongredien defeated Hanstein (+3−1=2), drew with Mayet (+3−3=1) and lost to Bledow (+4−7=1). Although outclassed, he played matches against most of the great players of his day, losing to Morphy (+0−7=1) in 1859, Harrwitz (+0−7=1) in 1860 and Steinitz (+0−7=0) in 1863. Mongredien was also for some years President of the Liverpool Chess Club and contributed much to the growth of chess in both Liverpool and London. *(R.D.K.)*

MONTE CARLO 1967 and 1968
Two notable international tournaments, the first major chess events to be held in Monaco since 1904. Both ended in victories by Western grandmasters ahead of strong Soviet opposition.

Monte Carlo 1967, reduced to ten players by last-minute withdrawals, was won by Fischer 7/9 ahead of Smyslov 6½; Geller and Larsen 6; Matanović 5; Gligorić and Lombardy 4½; Forintos 4; Mazzoni 1; Bergraser ½. Fischer's only loss (against Geller) came in the last round when he was already assured of first prize.

Monte Carlo 1968 completed Larsen's famous series of five consecutive major tournament victories during 1967/8. Final scores: Larsen 9½/14; Botvinnik 9; Hort and Smyslov 8½; R. Byrne 8; Benko, Gheorghiu and Portisch 7½; Forintos 6½; Damjanović and Uhlmann 5½; Padevsky 5; Letzelter 1½; Zinzer 1. Larsen too suffered his only defeat (to Byrne) in the final round. *(R.D.K.)*

MONTICELLI, Mario *(b. 16 March 1902)*
Italian international master (1950), Monticelli became a national master in 1924 and won the Italian championship three times: 1929, 1934 and 1939. Tournament successes include =1st Budapest 1926 and =1st Milan 1938. He represented Italy in the Olympiads of 1927, 1928, 1931, 1933 and 1935. *(R.D.K.)*

MOROCCO
A Moroccan team has played in five Olympiads with the following results: 47th in 1966, 41st in 1968, 54th in 1970, 57th in 1972 and 61st in 1974.

The Fédération Royale Marocaine des Echecs is located at Cercle L'Union, 2 rue M'hamed, Al-Khatib-Tetouan. *(K.J.O'C.)*

MORPHY, Paul Charles *(22 June 1837–10 July 1884)*

In Réti's words, Morphy was the first positional player who, unlike his Romantic rivals, understood the strategic basis for attack. He wrote nothing more than a few game notes and played fewer than seventy-five serious games. But his exploitation of open lines prepared the way for Steinitz's scientific treatment of closed positions and the era of modern chess.

Morphy was the youngest son of wealthy New Orleans parents. When he graduated from the University of Louisiana in 1857 he was too young to be admitted to the bar and temporarily turned to chess. His fame as a prodigy had grown after he had defeated the visiting Löwenthal in a series of off-hand games in May 1850 when aged twelve. In 1857 Morphy was invited to the first American chess congress in New York. He allowed only one draw in the first three matches and defeated L. Paulsen +5−1=2 in the final to secure the then unofficial national title.

With the encouragement of the New Orleans Chess Club, Morphy left for Europe the following spring for a series of successful matches in London and Paris. He began by defeating Löwenthal +9−3=3 during July and August of 1858. Later in August he defeated Owen at odds of pawn and move +5=2. In September he overcame Harrwitz in Paris +5−2=1. Meanwhile, Morphy sought a match with Staunton for the final success that would establish the American's primacy in the chess-world. After much negotiation and correspondence had failed, Morphy met Anderssen in Paris in December and won +7−2=2. Aside from a few casual games, Morphy's last serious match was a +7=1 rout of Mongredien in February 1859.

He was given a civic welcome on his return to New York in May 1859. Morphy's remaining career consisted largely of a series of simultaneous displays in Cuba and France and many casual games with his life-long friend, Charles A. Maurian. Morphy also defeated the New York *restaurateur* James Thompson in an 1859 match at Knight odds +5−3=1.

Morphy resumed his pursuit of a legal career but failed to prosper. No Morphy games are known after 1869. During his later years he was involved in a lengthy legal wrangle over his father's estate. Morphy developed delusions of persecution and refused to talk about chess. After a lonely career, Morphy died in 1884 of an attack of apoplexy.

More than three hundred of his games survive, the vast majority of them played off-hand and at odds. Game collections of Morphy's play have been edited among others by P. W. Sergeant, London, New York 1916, G. Maróczy, Leipzig 1909, and Max Lange, Leipzig 1859. The virtues of rapid development are repeated throughout his games.

First American Chess Congress, New York 1857
White: T. Lichtenhein; *Black:* Morphy
Two Knights Defence
1. P–K4, P–K4; 2. N–KB3, N–QB3; 3. P–Q4, P×P; 4. B–QB4, N–B3; 5. P–K5, P–Q4; 6. B–QN5, N–K5; 7. N×P, B–Q2; 8. N×N, P×N; 9. B–Q3, B–QB4; 10. B×N, Q–R5; 11. Q–K2, P×B; 12. B–K3, B–KN5; 13. Q–B4, B×B; 14. P–KN3, Q–Q1; 15. P×B, Q–Q8+; 16. K–B2, Q–B6+; 17. K–N1, B–R6; 18. Q×QBP+, K–B1; 19. Q×R+, K–K2; 20. resigns. *(A.S.)*

MORRY, William Ritson *(b. 5 September 1910)*
Midlands organizer and player who is a chess professional and journalist. As a player his best performances have been an =2nd in the British championship 1936 and an =3rd in 1951.

In the international field his best results have been an =3rd with List in the Major Open A section at the Nottingham congress of 1936 and =1st with Milner-Barry in the Premier Reserves A at the Hastings congress 1946/7. He has played for England in international matches against the Netherlands (thrice) and against Czechoslovakia and Yugoslavia.

A keen and accomplished correspondence player, he has the title of British Postal master on account of his winning the British Correspondence championship in 1943.

But it is as a tournament and congress organizer that he is best known. He founded the Birmingham Junior League in 1930 and has organized thirty-four Birmingham Congresses. He conceived the idea of a junior world championship and in 1951 he held the first World Junior Championship tournament at Birmingham. In the same year he was awarded the title of FIDE judge. He has also had much to do with the organization of the Hastings Christmas chess congresses in the 1970s.

He has written much for British chess magazines and is the co-author along with the late W. R. Mitchell of *Tackle Chess*, London 1967. *(H.G.)*

MORTIMER, James *(2 April 1833–24 February 1911)*
American minor master who did many things but, for most of his later life, was a journalist and dramatist.

Born in Richmond, Virginia, he was a midshipman in the US Navy and then worked for some time in the US Diplomatic Service.

It was as a journalist that he went to Paris in 1855 where Napoleon III became acquainted with him. By 1864 he was secretary to the Cercle des Echecs and editor of *La Palamède*. He came to England on the outbreak of the Franco-Prussian War and made that country his home for the rest of his life.

He played in the first British Chess Association tournament at London 1886 but came 11th out of 13. At Bradford in 1888 he came 13th/17 and in a tournament at Simpson's Divan at London 1888 he shared 7th with Zukertort (out of 18).

Paradoxically his most remarkable achievement was his worst from a statistical point of view. In the Master tournament at Ostend 1907 he came last with 5/28, yet at the age of 74 he was still capable of defeating Tartakower, Znosko-Borovsky and Blackburne! In match-play Mortimer contested two matches with Marshall at London 1903 and 1905, both of which he lost by the score of 0–4. He came to San Sebastian in February 1911, but he was already ill and died there after a short illness. *(R.D.K.)*

MOSCOW 1925
One of the great events in the annals of chess, this tournament (November–December 1925) established two 'firsts': the first confrontation of the Soviet masters with the recognized leaders of international chess, and, as the inevitable concomitant, the first of the type of contest to which the host country contributes a substantial number – between one half and one third – of the total entries (Zürich 1934, Moscow 1935, Kemeri 1937 were later events run on the same formula). In the event, the home team acquitted themselves well, with Bogoljubow winning 1st prize, and Romanovsky and Ilyin-Zhenevsky in the prize list.

The Russian champion took the lead early on, closely followed by Lasker, Torre and Rubinstein, the last-named collapsing completely after a 9th-round defeat by Yates. Capablanca had scored only 50% at halfway, but finished strongly, annexing en route the first (against Zubarev) and third (against Duz-Khotimirsky) brilliancy prizes. As a result of this outcome Bogoljubow joined the ranks of World Championship candidates, while the view generally held on the Continent (though not in the USA or Britain) that Lasker was still superior to Capablanca received new nourishment. Leading scores: Bogoljubow 15½, Em. Lasker 14, Capablanca 13½, Marshall 12½.

The following was the winner's finest game:

White: Bogoljubow; *Black:* C. Torre
Queen's Indian Defence
1. P–Q4, N–KB3; 2. N–KB3, P–QN3; 3. P–B4, B–N2; 4. N–B3, P–N3; 5. P–KN3, B–N2; 6. B–N2, N–K5; 7. Q–Q3, N×N;

8. P×N, P–Q3; 9. P–KR4, N–Q2; 10. P–R5, P–K4; 11. B–N5, P–KB3; 12. B–Q2, Q–K2; 13. P–R6, B–KB1; 14. Q–B2, KR–N1; 15. B–K3, P–R4; 16. R–QN1, R–Q1; 17. Q–N3, B–K5; 18. R–Q1, P–KN4; 19. P–B5, P–Q4; 20. P×NP, P×NP; 21. P×P, P×P; 22. R–R5, R–N3; 23. K–B1, N–B3; 24. B×KNP, R×B; 25. R×R, B×N; 26. B×B, B×P; 27. B–R5+, K–B1; 28. R–B5, Q–K3; 29. B–N4, K–K2; 30. B–R3, Q–Q3; 31. Q–R4, N–K5; 32. R–Q3, B–N2; 33. B–N2, N–B3; 34. Q–R4, Q–K3; 35. R–N5, K–B2; 36. R–B3, P–R3; 37. Q–R5+, K–B1; 38. R×P, Q–Q3; 39. R×P, K–N1; 40. R(3)–Q3, N×R; 41. B×N+, K–R1; 42. B–K4, Q–KB3; 43. Q–N6, K–N1; 44. Q–R7+, resigns. *(W.H.)*

MOSCOW 1935

This event (February–March 1935) was a repetition of Moscow 1925, with the difference that this time the field consisted of twelve Russian players and only eight internationals (of whom, moreover, Vera Menchik was clearly out of place in an event of this strength). The enormous strength in depth of Soviet chess was shown by the fact that of the home players only Levenfish, Romanovsky, Rabinovich and Bohatirchuk had played in the earlier event. Moreover, a Soviet representative, Botvinnik, took the early lead, together with Flohr and another Soviet player, Levenfish. By half-way (round 10) Botvinnik had 8½, Flohr 7½, Lasker and Levenfish 7; in the second half Capablanca, Spielmann and Kan made up ground, while Botvinnik scored only 50% from his last nine games.

Leading scores: Botvinnik, Flohr 13, Em. Lasker 12½, Capablanca 12, Spielmann 11.

The outcome did for Botvinnik what the earlier tournament had done for Bogoljubow. But the hero of the tournament was Lasker who, at the age of sixty-six, remained unbeaten and had the personal satisfaction of vanquishing Capablanca once again; his youthful energy cannot be better illustrated than by the following game from the last(!) of nineteen gruelling rounds:

White: Lasker; *Black:* Pirc
Sicilian Defence
1. P–K4, P–QB4; 2. N–KB3, N–QB3; 3. P–Q4, P×P; 4. N×P, N–B3; 5. N–QB3, P–Q3; 6. B–K2, P–K3; 7. O–O, P–QR3; 8. B–K3, Q–B2; 9. P–B4, N–QR4; 10. P–B5, N–B5; 11. B×N, Q×B; 12. P×P, P×P; 13. R×N, P×R; 14. Q–R5+, K–Q1; 15. Q–B7, B–Q2; 16. Q×P+, K–B2; 17. Q×R, B–R3; 18. N×P+, Q×N; 19. Q×R, B×B+; 20. K–R1, resigns. *(W.H.)*

MOSCOW 1936

The third Moscow tournament (May–June 1936), an exceedingly strong double-round event of five Russians and five internationals, provided Capablanca as ex-World Champion with his greatest success. In the past Capablanca always had to pay the full price for errors or inaccuracies (except perhaps at San Sebastian 1911) and in the great tournaments he did win was fully worth the honour (London 1922, New York 1927, Berlin 1928). Here, on the other hand, luck was with him throughout, but he certainly capitalized in a superb manner on whatever windfall came his way: the chess machine had matured into a great opportunist.

Botvinnik, as runner-up, was perhaps even more impressive – neck and neck with Flohr a year before, he now put 2½ points between himself and his rival and went on to confirm his superiority at Nottingham later in the year. On the other hand, time had at last caught up with Lasker: now in his sixty-eighth year, he still managed a small plus result in the first half of this exhausting struggle but could only make a score of 3/9 in the second. Leading scores: Capablanca 13, Botvinnik 12, Flohr 9½, Lilienthal 9, Ragosin 8½. *(W.H.)*

MUFFANG, André *(b. 25 July 1897)*

A French international master, he represented France in Olympiads in 1927, 1928, 1935 and 1956. Tournament results include =2nd Margate 1923. Awarded the international master title in 1951. *(R.D.K.)*

MÜLLER, Hans *(1 December 1896–28 February 1971)*

An Austrian international master who was a man of many parts (ski-ing, fencing, etc.) As a theorist he had a peerless filing system. As a tournament player, his successes were confined to small tournaments (=1st with Grünfeld at the Trebitsch Memorial 1933; 1st at Ebensee 1933, 1st at San Benedetto 1954). He represented Austria in the International Team tournaments of 1928, 1930, 1933, 1935, 1936 and 1950.

He was the author of many books of varied character: tournament books of the Olympiads at Warsaw 1935 and Helsinki 1952, treatises on the Caro-Kann Defence (Leipzig 1933) and English Opening (Leipzig 1928), a selection of Botvinnik games (Vienna-Stuttgart 1964), and a volume on Alekhine in co-authorship with Pawelczak (Berlin-Brohnau 1953). *(W.H.)*

MURRAY, Harold James Ruthven *(24 June 1868–16 May 1955)*

Chess historian and a Board of Education Inspector of Schools. Appropriately enough, a son of the pioneering editor of the great *Oxford English Dictionary*, he became interested in the history of chess in the early 1890s. Up to this time the historical writings on chess in English had been unhistorical. In order to fit himself for the task Murray learned several languages including Arabic and he also studied the true historians of chess, the German writers, Van der Linde and Von der Lasa.

In his own words his aim was to trace the development of the modern European game from the first appearance of its ancestor, the Indian *chaturanga*, in the beginning of the seventh century of our era. This he did in a vast work of some 900 pages published in Oxford in 1913. An immense amount of painstaking research had gone into the work and only a man of Murray's great learning could have attempted it.

It at once became the standard book on the subject and has remained so ever since. Murray left behind among his papers an unfinished work *A Short History of Chess* which took the history of the game up to 1866 and which gave a clearer and more readable account of the history of the game than his main work. This was brought up to date by Goulding-Brown and Golombek and published in Oxford in 1963. *(H.G.)*

MYASAKA, Yukio
Champion of Japan 1967–71. He played on top board for Japan at the Olympiads of 1970 and 1972. At the 1970 Siegen Olympiad he scored 46.9%, the highest score of his team and again at the 1972 Olympiad at Skopje he gained the highest percentage of his team with 42.5%. *(H.G.)*

MYSTERIOUS ROOK MOVE
One of the stratagems recommended by Nimzowitsch, the 'mysterious rook move' is a preventive manoeuvre: by moving a Rook to a closed file, a player tries to discourage the opponent from opening it by a move that would normally result in a freeing of his game, e.g. Blackburne–Nimzowitsch where, in the diagrammed position, Black plays R–K1 in order to dissuade White from the normal P–Q4. *(W.H.)*

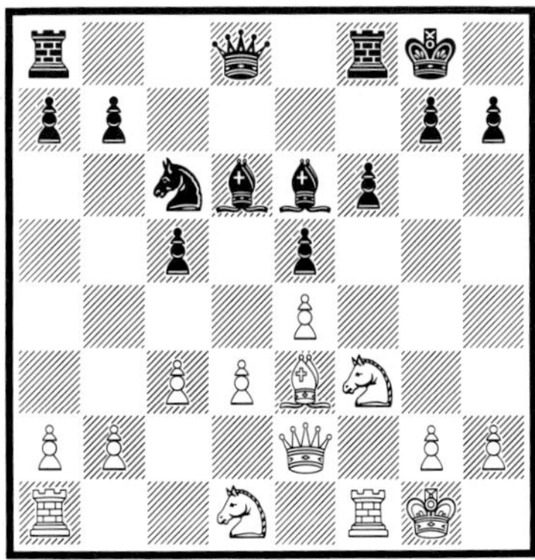

N

NAEGELI, Oskar *(25 February 1885–19 November 1959)*
Swiss master who was by profession a professor of medicine, and was one of Switzerland's leading players in the period between the two World Wars.

Swiss champion in 1910 and 1936, he represented his country in four Olympiads, London 1927, The Hague 1928, Prague 1931 and Warsaw 1935.

His individual international activities were centred in Switzerland and the countries immediately adjacent. At a tournament held at Venice in conjunction with a FIDE congress in 1929 he came =3rd/12 together with Hellmann and Rejfir.

In 1932 at Berne he did well to come =1st with Alekhine and Voellmy in a short four-player tournament. In the same year at Berne he came =9th/16 in a strong international tournament won by Alekhine. He did worse in the even stronger tournament at Zürich in 1934 where he came 15th/16.

He lost two short matches to grandmasters: the first to Dr Bernstein at Zürich 1932 by +1−3=0, and the second to Flohr by +1−3=2 at Berne 1933. He also played two somewhat longer matches against Grob, drawing the first at Berne 1933 by +3−3 =0 and winning the second at Zürich 1934 by +5−1=0.

NAJDORF, Miguel *(b. 15 April 1910)*
International grandmaster, born in Warsaw, Najdorf was a pupil of Tartakower and in 1935 defeated his mentor in a short match +2−1=1. He finished =2nd in the 1935 Polish championship and represented Poland in the Olympiads of 1935, 1937 and 1939. War broke out during the Buenos Aires Olympiad of 1939 and Najdorf, along with most of the Polish team, sought asylum in Argentina. He became a naturalized Argentinian citizen in 1944, changing his first name from Moishe to Miguel in the process.

After the war Najdorf emerged as a leading tournament competitor, a position he has maintained for more than a quarter of a century in spite of advancing age. His first prizes in international events include: Prague 1946, Barcelona 1946, Venice 1948, Bled 1950, Amsterdam 1950 and Havana 1962 (possibly his best result, finishing ahead of Spassky, Polugayevsky, Smyslov, Gligorić, Ivkov, etc.). Special mention should be made of his outstanding record in the series of tournaments held at Mar del Plata: 2nd in 1953, 2nd in 1955, 2nd in 1957, =1st (with Pachman, ahead of Fischer) in 1959, 1st in 1961, 1st in 1965, 1st in 1968, =1st (with Panno) in 1969. In the Olympiads of 1950 and 1952 Najdorf, now playing for Argentina, won the prize for the best score on board one.

Najdorf's aspirations toward the World Championship were less successful. He was curiously not selected for the 1948 World Championship match-tournament, which disappointed him greatly. He has played in two Candidates tournaments, finishing 5th in 1950 and =6th in 1953.

Najdorf once held records for simultaneous play (202 games: +182−8=12 in 1943) and blindfold simultaneous play (45 games: +39−2=4 in 1947).

Amsterdam 1950
White: Najdorf; *Black:* Kramer
Catalan System
1. P–Q4, N–KB3; 2. P–QB4, P–K3; 3. P–KN3, P–Q4; 4. B–N2, P×P; 5. N–KB3, QN–Q2; 6. QN–Q2, N–N3; 7. O–O, P–B4; 8. N×P, N×N; 9. Q–R4+, B–Q2; 10. Q×N, Q–N3; 11. P–N3, B–N4; 12. Q–B2, P×P; 13. B–N2, P–Q6; 14. P×P, B–K2; 15. N–K5, O–O; 16. QR–B1, KR–Q1; 17. KR–K1, N–Q4; 18. Q–K2, B–KB3; 19. Q–R5, B–K1; 20. B–K4, P–N3; 21. Q–K2, QR–B1; 22. N–N4, B–Q5; 23. R×R, R×R; 24. B×N, P×B; 25. N–R6+, K–B1; 26. Q–K7+, K–N2;

27. R–K6, B×B; 28. R×Q, P×R; 29. N–N4, B–QB3; 30. N–K5, B×N; 31. Q×B+, K–N1; 32. P–QR4, R–K1; 33. Q–Q4, P–QN4; 34. P–R5, R–K3; 35. P–B4, P–R3; 36. K–B2, K–R2; 37. P–KN4, P–B3; 38. Q–N6, resigns. *(R.D.K.)*

Miguel Najdorf in play against Mecking, Hastings 1971/2

NAPIER, William Ewart *(17 January 1881–7 September 1952)*
Although born in London, Napier spent his youth in the USA, where his family had emigrated in 1886. In 1897 Napier won the Brooklyn Chess Club championship and gained further reputation by defeating Marshall in a match. At the age of twenty he returned to Europe and played in several international tournaments, his best result being fifth prize at Hanover 1902, where he was also awarded the brilliancy prize for his game against von Bardeleben.

In the 1904 British championship Napier tied for 1st with Atkins and won the subsequent play-off match. Shortly afterwards he returned to the USA and became an American citizen in 1908. He married a niece of Pillsbury. In later years he devoted less time to chess, choosing instead to concentrate on his insurance business. *(R.D.K.)*

NAPOLEON I *(15 August 1769–5 May 1821)*
Napoleon Bonaparte was a keen but seemingly weak player, who is known to have played chess from his college days to the end of his life, when he played much during his captivity at St Helena.

Of the three games extant by him, none are authentic but seem to have been composed after his death to fit in with likely but legendary encounters. One is against General Bertrand, another is against the Automaton (the Turk) at Schönbrunn in 1809 and the third is against Mme de Rémusat at La Malmaison in 1804.

This last runs:

White: Napoleon; *Black:* Mme de Rémusat
Philidor Defence (by transposition)
1. N–QB3, P–K4; 2. N–B3, P–Q3; 3. P–K4, P–KB4; 4. P–KR3, P×P; 5. QN×P, N–QB3; 6. N(B3)–N5, P–Q4; 7. Q–R5+, P–N3; 8. Q–B3, N–R3; 9. N–B6+, K–K2; 10. N×P+, K–Q3; 11. N–K4+, K×N;

12. B–B4+, K×B; 13. Q–N3+, K–Q5; 14. Q–Q3 mate.

The game bears the obvious marks of a composition and was played almost with equal weakness by both sides, especially in the opening. Of Black's play towards the end it might have been appropriately said 'La Garde meurt, mais ne se rend pas' ('The Guards die but do not surrender'). *(H.G.)*

NARANJA, Renato *(b. 24 September 1940)*
Philippine international master and the leading player in the Philippines in the period 1965–70. He has been consistently placed highly in the Philippine championship, ranging from 1st in 1965 to =3rd with Balinas in 1974.

Naranja has played six times in the Olympiads, 1960, 1964, 1966, 1968, 1970 and 1974, playing on first board in the years 1964, 1966 and 1970. His best score was 60% on board 4 at Lugano 1968. *(H.G.)*

NATIONAL CLUB CHAMPIONSHIP, English
Annual British knock-out competition for teams of six players instituted in 1949. The winning team from 1974 onwards secures entry into the newly constituted European Club championship in the following year. Past winners:

1949/50	Cambridge Univ.	1963/4	Ilford
1950/1	Lud Eagle	1964/5	York
1951/2	Oxford Univ.	1965/6	Oxford Univ.
1952/3	Ilford	1966/7	Bradford
1953/4	Cheltenham	1967/8	Islington & N. London
1954/5	Cheltenham	1968/9	Cambridge Univ.
1955/6	Ilford	1969/70	Cambridge Univ.
1956/7	Leicester	1970/1	Oxford Univ.
1957/8	Cambridge Univ.	1971/2	Cambridge Univ.
1958/9	Cheltenham	1972/3	Cambridge Univ.
1959/60	Cambridge Univ.	1973/4	Cambridge Univ.
1960/1	Sutton Coldfield	1974/5	Cambridge Univ.
1961/2	West Ham	1975/6	Athenaeum *(R.D.K.)*
1962/3	Manchester		

NATIONAL SCHOOLS CHESS TOURNAMENT, British
This event, sponsored by the *Sunday Times* newspaper and organized on its behalf by the British Chess Federation, has been held annually in Britain since 1957. The competition is held on a

knock-out basis, with the first rounds organized within geographical regions, then later inter-regional matches culminating in the semi-final and final matches held in London. There are six players in each team, and an age-handicap operates to demand that older teams win by sufficiently large margins against younger ones to qualify for the next round. The competition is open to any school team of under-18 year olds; the first year it attracted 241 entries, and this number rose to 900 by 1975. The winners each year to date have been as follows:

1958	Calday Grange G.S.	1967	Battersea G.S.
1959	Calday Grange G.S.	1968	Bolton School
1960	Wolverhampton G.S.	1969	Dundee High School
1961	Colfe's G.S.	1970	Dulwich College
1962	Liverpool Institute High School	1971	Ayr Academy
		1972	Ayr Academy
1963	Hove G.S.	1973	Bolton School
1964	Liverpool Institute High School	1974	Southern G.S. Portsmouth
1965	Dulwich College	1975	St Paul's
1966	Dulwich College	1976	Bolton School

(W.R.H.)

NEDJELJKOVIĆ, Srećko *(b. 4 December 1923)*
A Yugoslav international master (1951). He competed seven times in the Yugoslav championship with mediocre success. Represented Yugoslavia in international matches for many years. Best result: 1st Belgrade 1950. A physician by profession, he gave up chess in the early 1960s. *(R.D.K.)*

NEDJELJKOVIĆ, Vera *(b. 16 September 1929)*
Wife of S. Nedjeljković. Like Lazarević, a leading Yugoslav woman player. Competed in numerous Yugoslav Women's championships and Olympiads. Unable to pursue both chess and her academic career of physicist, she abandoned chess, depriving Yugoslavia of a genuine talent. *(R.D.K.)*

NEI, Iivo *(b. 31 October 1931)*
Many times Estonian champion and international master since 1964. Shared first place with Keres ahead of Portisch and seven other grandmasters at Wijk-aan-Zee 1964. During the 1972 World Championship match, Nei was one of Spassky's trainers and tennis opponents. *(W.R.H.)*

NEIKIRCH, Oleg Nikolayevich *(b. 8 March 1914)*
Six times Bulgarian champion (1937, 1938, 1940, 1948, 1953 and 1957) and international master since 1957. Competitor in the 1958 Interzonal tournament at Portorož where he took 15th place. *(W.R.H.)*

NEMET, Ivan *(b. 14 April 1943)*
Yugoslav international master (1976). Played for Yugoslavia in the World Student Team championships of 1962 and 1963. His best tournament results: =1st Coka 1975 and 1st at Kikinda 1975. *(K.J.O'C.)*

NENAROKOV, Vladimir Ivanovich *(1880–13 December 1953)*
One of the strongest Moscow masters at the turn of the century. Moscow champion in 1900 and 1908, in which year he also won a match against the sixteen-year-old Alekhine. After the Revolution he added another two Moscow championships to his list of wins, in 1922 and 1924.

He was given the title of international master in 1950.

Nenarokov wrote some good introductory works on chess and specialized in opening strategy. He also wrote a more advanced book on the Ruy Lopez (Moscow-Leningrad 1932) published in German later at Kecskemet. *(W.R.H.)*

NETHERLANDS
From modest beginnings and with a present population of only twelve millions, The Netherlands has made remarkable strides in world chess and now holds a position of influence, prestige and sheer playing strength which, in Western Europe, can only be rivalled by West Germany.

The first international tournament to be organized in The Netherlands took place at Amsterdam 1889, sponsored by the United Amsterdam Chess Society, and was notable as one of the earliest appearances by Emanuel Lasker (who won his famous brilliancy against Bauer in this event). The final result was: Burn 7; Lasker 6; Mason 5½; Van Vliet 5; Gunsberg 4; Bauer 3½; Loman 3; Van Foreest 2; Leather 0.

No Dutchman, however, succeeded in gaining the title of Master (bestowed officially by the Deutscher Schachbund) until N. W. van Lennep won first prize in the *Hauptturnier* A (Major Tournament) of the German congress at Leipzig 1894. In spite of this achievement, the two best-known names of the early period of Dutch chess activity were Dr Adolf Olland who was active 1899–1933 and the musician Rudolf Loman who competed in a number of internal Dutch events, 1881–1929. The fame of these players has not spread much beyond the borders of Holland and until the rise of Dr Max Euwe in the 1920s and early 1930s chess certainly maintained a low profile in The Netherlands. That this situation could be changed by the advent of a player of genius was brilliantly demonstrated by Euwe, whose career entirely transformed the image of chess in his native country.

Following Euwe's triumph in his 1935 World Championship match against Alekhine, Holland was seized with chess fever. Almost overnight, chess literature boomed and Euwe became a figure of national importance, doubly significant in a small nation such as the Netherlands. In spite of Euwe's defeat in his 1937 return match with Alekhine, the popularity of chess did not wane and The Netherlands became the staging ground for great international tournaments such as A.V.R.O. 1938 and Groningen 1946.

Strangely, the inspiring presence of Euwe did not bear any immediate fruit for the overall national playing strength and, granted the presence of masters such as Van Scheltinga, Cortlever and Prins, The Netherlands did not acquire another player of grandmaster status until the 1950s with Donner. There was then to be a gap of well over a decade before The Netherlands produced another home-grown grandmaster in the person of Timman. In the mid-1970s Holland suddenly acquired great strength (incidental confirmation of its attraction as a Western capital of chess) following the emigration of the Russians Sosonko and Korchnoi, who will doubtless help to forge the Dutch into one of the world's most formidable national sides. There follows a list of active Dutch players with international titles:

Grandmasters: Euwe, Donner, Timman, Korchnoi (ex-USSR (and provided that he remains in The Netherlands)) and Sosonko (ex-USSR). International masters: Böhm, Bouwmeester, Cortlever, Van Geet, Enklaar, Hartoch, Kramer, Kuijpers, Langeweg, Prins, Ree, Van Scheltinga and Zuidema.

Holland was one of the original nations competing in the first Olympiad at London 1927 where it took fourth prize. Since that date The Netherlands has competed in virtually all Olympiads without bettering this initial performance, although their two fifth places at Dubrovnik 1950 and at Nice 1974 were qualitative improvements in view of the increased number of teams and the superior opposition including East European nations. On one occasion (Amsterdam 1954) The Netherlands organized the Olympic tournament on home ground and in the event came 8th out of 26 competing teams.

In Holland chess is regarded very much as a sporting activity, and, in accordance with this viewpoint, substantial financial support is granted towards the Chess Federation from government sporting funds. This enables the Federation to stage small events (such as the Euwe Celebration tournament at Amsterdam 1976 which involved Karpov, Browne, Timman and Olafsson), to spread the gospel of chess in schools and support its own officials. In addition to this, much vital life-blood is injected into The Netherlands' chess fraternity by private industry, and the two premier Dutch tournaments at Wijk-aan-Zee (held at New Year) and Amsterdam (in summer) are respectively supported by the firms of Hoogoven and I.B.M. These two traditional fixtures have lent great stability to Dutch chess and have also proved an invaluable training ground for rising young Dutch players. (The results of these tournaments can be seen under HOOGOVEN.)

The winners of the 32 official Dutch championships:

1909	A. G. Olland	1954	J. H. Donner
1912	R. J. Loman	1955	M. Euwe
1919	M. Marchand	1957	J. H. Donner
1921	M. Euwe	1958	J. H. Donner
1924	M. Euwe	1961	H. L. Tan
1926	M. Euwe	1963	F. Kuijpers
1929	M. Euwe	1965	L. Prins
1933	M. Euwe	1967	H. Ree
1936	S. Landau	1969	H. Ree
1938	M. Euwe	1970	E. C. Scholl
1939	M. Euwe	1971	H. Ree
1942	M. Euwe	1972	C. Zuidema
1947	M. Euwe	1973	G. Sosonko
1948	M. Euwe	1974	J. Timman
1950	M. Euwe	1975	J. Timman
1952	M. Euwe	1976	J. Timman

A further aspect of the Dutch chess scene is the existence of professional clubs. One of the most celebrated of these is 'Volmac' Rotterdam, which numbers amongst its active members the Russian grandmaster Victor Korchnoi (who defected to The Netherlands in the summer of 1976), Timman, Euwe, Keene and Böhm.

Despite the undeniable fact that Dutch is not a world language the prestige of Dutch chess books remains very high indeed, largely due to the numerous translations into most Western languages of Euwe's works which deal with all sides of practical chess, chess history, chess events and so on. In particular his multi-volume *Theory of Chess Openings* [in German] has achieved universal recognition as one of the most important text books dealing with this aspect of the theory of chess. Internally, Donner, Timman, Ree, Langeweg and Hartoch have maintained an excellent level of chess writing in specialist works, national chess magazines and more widely based periodicals; while Bouwmeester (the national coach) publishes an annual chess year-book, summarizing most important national and international events of the previous year.

A remarkable feature of Dutch chess life is the extraordinary interest in the game displayed by the media, especially the national press, which not only gives in-depth coverage to the major tournaments at Wijk-aan-Zee and Amsterdam but also follows lesser events with great enthusiasm, even going so far as to report on the non-chess aspects of the private lives of the more colourful Dutch players. Naturally, all major national newspapers support chess columns written by leading masters and experts.

The official publication of the Royal Dutch Chess Federation is *Schakend Nederland*, edited by Menno Ploeger, Van Oldenbarnevelt-plaats, Rotterdam 3002. This is distributed free of charge to all full members of the Federation. A more lively commercial magazine which contains much detailed analysis by leading Dutch players is *Schakbulletin*, edited by W. Andriessen.

The address of the Royal Dutch Chess Federation is Passeerdersgracht 32, Amsterdam C.

For the term of the FIDE Presidency by Dr Euwe (which began in 1970), the FIDE Bureau (central office of the World Chess Federation) has also been situated in Amsterdam at Passeerdersgracht 32, Amsterdam C. *(R.D.K.)*

NETHERLANDS ANTILLES

The Dutch Antilles have only recently begun to take part in the Olympiads; their record reads: 67th in 1974 and 48th in 1976. They have a greater claim to chess fame for having staged the 1962 Candidates tournament at Willemstad, the capital of Curaçao, the largest island in the group.

The address of the Ned.-Antilliaanse Schaakbond is c/o O. W. Rigaud, De Biesheviel 9, Curaçao. *(K.J.O'C.)*

NETHERLANDS–ENGLAND MATCHES

In 1910 the first match between The Netherlands and England took place at Bromley in Kent. This was played on six boards and won by England by $3\frac{1}{2}$–$2\frac{1}{2}$. Enlarged to eight boards and played as double-round matches, two more were played before the First

World War; at London in 1912 The Netherlands won by 9–7 and in 1914 at the Hague, England won by 12–4.

The series was restarted in 1937, on ten boards, when The Netherlands won in Amsterdam by $10\frac{1}{2}$–$9\frac{1}{2}$ and lost by the same margin in London 1938. In 1939 the match was drawn in the Hague 10–10.

After the Second World War four more matches were played in the period 1947–52 and a new series commenced in 1958 when the Schelde Shipping Company presented a trophy, the Seven Provinces (a silver model of De Ruyter's warship that sailed up the Medway in the Anglo-Dutch Wars of the seventeenth century) to be held by the winner of an annual match.

These were played alternatively in The Netherlands at Flushing, the headquarters of the shipping company that had presented the trophy, and in various towns in England. The matches have gone very much in favour of The Netherlands and in fact they have won the last three, from 1973–75, by 10–$9\frac{1}{2}$, $10\frac{1}{2}$–$9\frac{1}{2}$ and $11\frac{1}{2}$–$8\frac{1}{2}$.

England did draw another match with The Netherlands in 1975 but this was in a preliminary group of the European Team championship. There was no match in 1976. *(H.G.)*

NEUMANN, Gustav Richard Ludwig

(15 December 1838–16 February 1881)

One of the very strongest mid-nineteenth-century masters. A fine positional player, he proved superior to Mayet, Suhle, Schallopp and others in the Berlin Chess Club; internationally his greatest success was 1st at Dundee 1867 (ahead of Steinitz), while he came 4th (to Kolisch, Winawer and Steinitz) at Paris the same year, and 2nd (to Anderssen) at Altona 1872. In matches he beat Golmayo, Winawer and Rosenthal, but lost to Louis Paulsen. Neumann withdrew from chess as a result of a mental disease caused by a cranial injury he sustained in his youth. *(W.H.)*

NEW YORK 1857

See under U.S.A.

NEW YORK 1889

The first large grandmaster-level event in the New World and one of the strongest tournaments ever held in the USA. Officially it was entitled the Sixth American Chess Congress but unlike its five predecessors this event included several foreign players. Among the invitees were Chigorin of Russia, M. Weiss of Austria and a British contingent that included Blackburne, Gunsberg, Burn, Bird and Gossip. Steinitz did not play but agreed to edit the tournament book.

The twenty players were to meet each other twice but had to play a third game if the second game were drawn. The exceptionally lengthy event lasted two months (March–May) and set two records. Neither Chigorin's 27 wins nor MacLeod's 31 losses have since been equalled in a single international event. The Russian's double loss to Gunsberg and Mason allowed Weiss to squeeze into a tie for first place. The play-off match ended after four draws. Gunsberg's third prize, a half-point behind the leaders, was one of his best results.

The highest place taken by an American was Lipschütz's sixth. This established him as the leading US player. Max Judd of St Louis, in his only international tournament, came eighth and scored wins over Gunsberg, Blackburne and Mason. Mackenzie had been entered in the tournament but ill-health, which killed him two years later, prevented him from playing his first game.

Leading scores: Chigorin, Weiss 29, Gunsberg $28\frac{1}{2}$, Blackburne 27, Burn 26. *(A.S.)*

NEW YORK 1924

Considered by many to be the strongest tournament ever held in the USA. It attracted three men who held the World Championship – Lasker, Capablanca and Alekhine – when each of them was at or near their height of strength. The event was also a major battleground for the hypermodern theories of the 1920s.

All of the eleven players lost at least one game but Lasker's 13 wins gave him a score of 80% that has rarely been approached in modern events of this category. Capablanca, who scored $1\frac{1}{2}$–$\frac{1}{2}$ against the man he dethroned three years before, was the only player who did not lose at least one game to Lasker. Lasker received the $1,500 first prize by a margin of $1\frac{1}{2}$ points in the double-round event. Capablanca's loss to Réti's 1. N–KB3 opening in the fifth round was the Cuban's first loss in eight years. It snapped him out of a drawing streak and he scored $12\frac{1}{2}$–$2\frac{1}{2}$ in the remaining rounds.

Alekhine, who led the field in draws with twelve, was a distant third. Marshall, in his first major tournament since 1914, came fourth and received the second brilliancy prize for his game with Bogoljubow. Réti, whose eight losses put him fifth, received the first brilliancy prize for his game with Bogoljubow.

The event, held March–April at the Alamac Hotel, occasioned a highly praised tournament book edited by Helms and annotated by Alekhine. Leading scores: Em. Lasker 16, Capablanca $14\frac{1}{2}$, Alekhine 12, Marshall 11. *(A.S.)*

NEW YORK 1927

The sextangular grandmaster event, which was held February–March at New York's Alamac Hotel, was originally intended to be a Candidates event to select a challenger for Capablanca, who had not defended his title since winning it six years before. However, an agreement to play a title match in Buenos Aires late in 1927 was reached between Capablanca and Alekhine when the New York organizers were soliciting invitations.

Aside from the Champion and his challenger, the other competitors were Nimzowitsch, Marshall, Vidmar and Spielmann. Lasker, who had dominated a larger field at the same tournament site three years before, did not participate because of a dispute with the tournament committee.

After defeating Alekhine in the first of four playing cycles, Capablanca kept a lead which was only briefly challenged by Nimzowitsch during the second cycle. The Champion's defeat of Nimzowitsch in the 15th round gave him a three-point lead and he was content to offer his last four opponents draws in advance.

Alekhine edged out Nimzowitsch for second place by losing only two games while his rival was losing five. Capablanca was undefeated. Vidmar's even score was sufficient for fourth place, ahead of Spielmann and Marshall who won only one game apiece. As with the 1924 tournament, Alekhine wrote the notes of the tournament book which appeared in German. The event was the last major international event in the USA before the Second World War. Scores: Capablanca 14, Alekhine $11\frac{1}{2}$, Nimzowitsch $10\frac{1}{2}$, Vidmar 10, Spielmann 8, Marshall 6. *(A.S.)*

NEW ZEALAND

The New Zealand championship, pre-empted by Scotland as the first in the world, can claim to be the best established, leading the Scottish events by six months or so. The Champions of New Zealand have been:

1879	H. Hookham
1888/9	A. M. Olliver
1890	H. Hookham
1890/1	R. J. Barnes
1891/2	F. V. Siedeberg
1892/3	F. V. Siedeberg
1893/4	J. Edwards
1894/5	W. Mackay
1895/6	W. Meldrum
1896/7	R. J. Barnes
1897/8	R. J. Barnes
1898	R. A. Cleland
1900	W. E. Mason
1901	D. Forsyth
1901/2	R. J. Barnes
1902/3	J. C. Grierson
1903/4	W. E. Mason
1904/5	A. W. Davies
1905/6	R. J. Barnes
1906/7	W. S. Viner
1908	A. W. Davies
1908/9	F. K. Kelling
1909/10	J. Mason
1910/1	W. E. Mason
1911/2	W. E. Mason
1912/3	J. C. Grierson
1913/4	W. E. Mason
1914/5	F. K. Kelling
1919/20	W. E. Mason
1920/1	J. B. Dunlop
1921/2	J. B. Dunlop
1922/3	J. B. Dunlop
1923/4	S. Crakanthorp
1924/5	C. J. S. Purdy
1925/6	S. Crakanthorp
1926/7	A. W. Davies
1927/8	A. W. Davies
1928/9	J. A. Erskine
1929/30	G. Gundersen
1930/1	A. W. Gyles
1931/2	G. Gundersen
1932/3	M. E. Goldstein
1933/4	J. B. Dunlop
1934/5	J. A. Erskine
1935/6	A. W. Gyles
1936/7	H. R. Abbott
1937/8	S. Hindin
1938/9	J. B. Dunlop
1939/40	J. B. Dunlop
1940/1	P. Allerhand
1943/4	R. G. Wade
1944/5	R. G. Wade
1945/6	T. Lepviikmann
1946/7	T. Lepviikmann
1947/8	R. G. Wade
1948/9	A. E. Nield
1949/50	P. Allerhand
1950/1	D. I. Lynch
1951/2	O. Sarapu
1952/3	O. Sarapu
1953/4	O. Sarapu
1954/5	O. Sarapu
1955/6	F. A. Foulds
1956/7	A. Feneridis & J. R. Phillips
1957/8	J. R. Phillips
1958/9	F. A. Foulds & B. Menzies
1959/60	O. Sarapu
1960/1	O. Sarapu
1961/2	G. G. Haase
1962/3	O. Sarapu & R. J. Sutton
1963/4	R. A. Court
1964/5	J. R. Phillips
1965/6	O. Sarapu
1966/7	O. Sarapu
1967/8	B. Anderson
1968/9	O. Sarapu & B. Anderson
1969/70	O. Sarapu
1970/1	R. J. Sutton
1971/2	R. J. Sutton
1972/3	R. J. Sutton
1973/4	O. Sarapu & P. Garbett
1975/6	M. Chandler, O. Sarapu & L. Aptekar

The official body responsible for the organization of chess in New Zealand is the New Zealand Chess Association, P.O. Box 8802, Symonds Street, Auckland. There is no regular chess magazine. *(K.J.O'C.)*

NEZHMETDINOV, Rashid Gibyatovich *(b. 15 December 1912)*
Soviet international master. For many years the strongest player in Kazakhstan. International master since 1954, following his second place in the Bucharest tournament of that year. Nezhmetdinov was the first man to hold the Soviet master title for both chess and draughts. *(W.R.H.)*

NICARAGUA

The Federacion Nacional de Ajedrez de Nicaragua (Apartado Postal 3336, Managua D. N.) has sent a team to only one Olympiad, placing 48th in 1966. *(K.J.O'C.)*

NICOLAU [Van der Mije], Alexandra Ecaterina *(b. 27 July 1940)*
International Woman master since 1960. Born in Romania, but has lived in Holland since 1974 following her marriage. Winner of the Women's international tournaments Belgrade 1966, 1967 and 1968. Now plays under her married name, Van der Mije. By profession she is a university lecturer and researcher in Chinese. *(W.R.H.)*

NIGERIA

The Nigerian Chess Federation (c/o Dr S. O. Ebigwei, 51 Ogunlana Drive, Surulere, Lagos) organized its first competition in 1976 – the First Nigerian Open championship, won by A. Frank of Zaire. The country has yet to compete in a chess Olympiad. *(K.J.O'C.)*

NIKITIN, Alexander Sergeyevich *(b. 1935)*
Soviet master and regular member of their Student Olympiad teams in the late 1950s. Author of theoretical articles and a monograph on the Sicilian Defence (1969). *(W.R.H.)*

NIMZO-INDIAN DEFENCE

1. P–Q4, N–KB3; 2. P–QB4, P–K3; 3. N–QB3, B–N5. The idea of this defence, pressure on White's K4 square, stems from Nimzowitsch who introduced it to master-chess in the 1920s. The sequence of moves had been played before him, in particular by Blackburne in the 1880s, but it was without any strategic idea and always transposed to some form of Queen's Gambit.

There are four main lines depending on White's 4th move: 4. Q–B2, 4. Q–N3, 4. P–K3 (the Rubinstein line) and 4. P–QR3 (the Sämisch variation). *(R.D.K.)*

NIMZOWITSCH, Aron Isaewitsch
(7 November 1886–16 March 1935)
Amongst those outstanding personalities of chess history who have narrowly failed in their ambition to become World Champion Nimzowitsch was perhaps the most colourful, making his impressive mark not only with his successful play but also with his profound writings and his eccentric behaviour away from the chessboard.

Born in Riga into the Jewish family of Niemzowitsch, he learnt the moves at an early age from his father (an accomplished master in his own right) but it was not until 1904 while in Germany (ostensibly to study mathematics) that Nimzowitsch began to concentrate on chess. At first Nimzowitsch's talent lay in the purely tactical and combinational field but several failures led him to undertake a complete revision of his chess ideas, laying more stress on positional play, restrictive strategy and consolidation. With his changed outlook Nimzowitsch achieved significant successes, including =2nd behind Rubinstein at San Sebastian 1912 and =1st with Alekhine at the All-Russian championship St Petersburg 1913.

The War of 1914–18 combined with the Russian Revolution brought an abrupt halt to Nimzowitsch's activities. In 1920 (perhaps slightly earlier) he left Latvia for Scandinavia, changing his name in the process from Niemzowitsch to Nimzowitsch. At first he took refuge in Sweden but eventually settled in Denmark. Nimzowitsch's return to tournament competition in the early 1920s was disastrous but gradually he played himself into form, securing a number of notable successes in the mid 1920s including =1st with Rubinstein at Marienbad 1925, 1st Dresden 1926 (scoring 8½/9 ahead of Alekhine 7 and Rubinstein 6½) and 1st Hanover 1926. It was during this rich period that Nimzowitsch's most influential work appeared: *Mein System*, Berlin 1925, which underwent several revisions until 1928 and is still a bestseller in many translations over the entire chess-playing world.

The World title still eluded him. Nimzowitsch took 3rd place in the New York Candidates' tournament 1927 behind Capablanca and Alekhine; his brilliant 1st prize at Carlsbad 1929 was achieved ahead of Capablanca, Spielmann, Rubinstein, Euwe, Vidmar and Bogoljubow, yet Alekhine was not competing. His performance at Carlsbad possibly justified Nimzowitsch in adopting the title 'Crown Prince of the Chess World' which he somewhat pompously assumed, yet the reigning monarch refused to give way and Nimzowitsch's best results in major tournaments from 1929 onwards (2nd San Remo 1930, 3rd Bled 1931) were achieved in the shadow of Alekhine.

Ill-health caused Nimzowitsch's sudden decline in the mid 1930s and in spite of first prizes in lesser events such as Copenhagen 1933 and 1934 and a narrow match victory over Stoltz in 1934, his defeat by Ståhlberg in their 1934 match combined with his 7th place at Zürich 1934 revealed that Nimzowitsch's old force was gone. Nimzowitsch died a mere forty-eight years old, at the Hareskov Sanatorium.

In his playing style Nimzowitsch belonged to the so-called hypermodern school, which held (*inter alia*) that control of the centre did not necessarily imply occupation by pawns. Adherence to these views, combined with a decided mutual incompatibility, brought him into frequent opposition with the great German master of the classical school, Siegbert Tarrasch. Neither master was averse to self-adulation and the bitterness emanating from their first meeting in 1904 was never entirely eradicated. In fact hostility towards Tarrasch and his works was a recurring theme of Nimzowitsch's literary endeavours.

However, Nimzowitsch's major contribution to chess literature consisted not in his witty ridicule of Tarrasch, nor yet in the discovery of a novel method of play, but in his elaboration of a new chess vocabulary which made intelligible the hitherto but vaguely articulated strategy of master-players. Nimzowitsch possessed an unrivalled facility for capturing the essence of an already known operation or structure with a memorable and meaningful word or phrase, which thereby increased speed of comprehension and assisted clarity of thought. Nimzowitsch introduced into chess terminology such phrases as 'the passed pawn's lust to expand', 'mysterious rook move', 'prophylaxis', '7th rank absolute' and 'hanging pawns'. It is an established phenomenon that rapid advances in performance are often immediately preceded by advances in modes of expression, and we may indeed detect an upsurge in the general level of chess after the publication of *My System*. Nimzowitsch's writings were penned with such enthusiastic and allusive wit that only the most hardened could resist the appeal of his message. Consider the following on the subject of the isolated pawn: '. . . We no longer consider it necessary to render the enemy isolani absolutely immobile; on the contrary, we like to give him the illusion of freedom, rather than shut him up in a cage (the principle of the large zoo applied to the small beast of prey).'

International Tournament to celebrate the centenary of the Berlin Chess Club. Nimzowitsch (left) and Brinckmann during a game

In a second area of chess science Nimzowitsch also made a decisive contribution and it is difficult to think of anyone who in our time has exerted a comparable influence on opening theory. Apart from his most famous brain-child, the Nimzo-Indian Defence, which he introduced into international practice at St Petersburg 1914, Nimzowitsch also pioneered the Winawer variation of the French Defence, known on the Continent as the Nimzowitsch variation. In addition he carried out important investigations into

Philidor's Defence, 3. P–K5 in the French Defence, the Queen's Indian Defence and English Opening. Nimzowitsch was also responsible for the invention of a defence to the KP (1. P–K4, N–QB3), the Nimzowitsch variation of the Sicilian Defence (1. P–K4, P–QB4; 2. N–KB3, N–KB3) and he was the first great master to employ P–QN3 as White's opening move.

Nimzowitsch's important publications include: *Die Blockade*, Berlin 1925; *Mein System*, Berlin 1925 (translated as *My System*, London 1929); and *Die Praxis Meines Systems*, Berlin 1929 (translated as *Chess Praxis*, London 1936). In addition, he contributed frequently to *Kagans Neueste Schachnachrichten* during the 1920s and early 1930s.

Dresden 1926
White: P. Johner; *Black:* Nimzowitsch
Nimzo-Indian Defence
1. P–Q4, N–KB3; 2. P–QB4, P–K3; 3. N–QB3, B–N5; 4. P–K3, O–O; 5. B–Q3, P–B4; 6. N–B3, N–B3; 7. O–O, B×N; 8. P×B, P–Q3; 9. N–Q2, P–QN3; 10. N–N3, P–K4; 11. P–B4, P–K5; 12. B–K2, Q–Q2; 13. P–KR3, N–K2; 14. Q–K1, P–KR4; 15. B–Q2, Q–B4; 16. K–R2, Q–R2; 17. P–QR4, N–B4; 18. P–N3, P–R4; 19. R–KN1, N–R3; 20. B–KB1, B–Q2; 21. B–B1, QR–B1; 22. P–Q5, K–R1; 23. N–Q2, R–KN1; 24. B–KN2, P–KN4; 25. N–B1, R–N2; 26. R–R2, N–B4; 27. B–R1, QR–KN1; 28. Q–Q1, P×P; 29. KP×P, B–B1; 30. Q–N3, B–R3; 31. R–K2, N–R5; 32. R–K3, B–B1; 33. Q–B2, B×P;

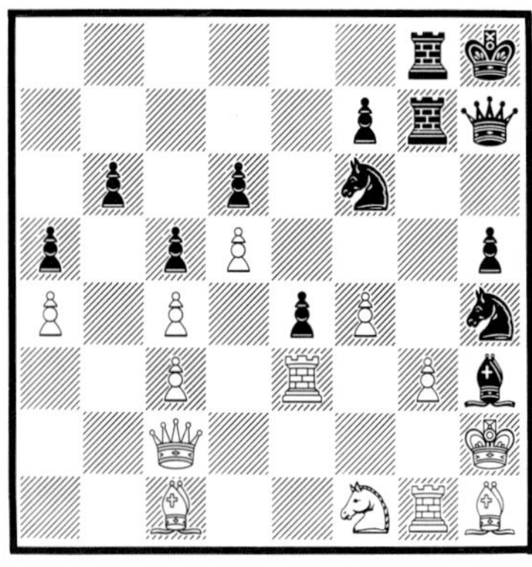

34. B×P, B–B4; 35. B×B, N×B; 36. R–K2, P–R5; 37. R(N1)–N2, P×P+; 38. K–N1, Q–R6; 39. N–K3, N–R5; 40. K–B1, R–K1; 41. resigns. *(R.D.K.)*

NIMZOWITSCH DEFENCE
Name given to the opening 1. P–K4, N–QB3 after its originator. Nimzowitsch himself preferred to answer 2. P–Q4 with 2. . , P–Q4 or 2. . , P K3, leading to positions similar to the French Defence, though recently 2. . , P–K4 has been tried also. Rarely seen nowadays and considered rather eccentric. *(W.R.H.)*

NIMZOWITSCH–LARSEN ATTACK
1. P–QN3 was first introduced into master praxis by Nimzowitsch in the 1920s and has since become a recognized alternative to the more highly analysed regular openings after its adoption by Larsen. Involving an early fianchetto of the QB it is hardly a vigorous attempt to gain an early advantage. E.g. 1. P–QN3, P–K4; 2. B–N2, N–QB3; 3. P–QB4, N–B3; 4. P–K3, P–Q3; 5. N–QB3, P–KN3; 6. N–B3, B–N2. Theoretically the chances are even but a complex middle-game lies ahead. *(R.D.K.)*

NOA, Joseph *(21 October 1856–1 June 1903)*
Hungarian player who was a judge by profession. Though a complete amateur he found time to play in some of the great tournaments of the 1880s and 1890s and beat a number of famous players.

In his first great tournament, Berlin 1881 (the second Congress of the German Chess Federation) he came 15th/17, but he did well against the Paulsen brothers, drawing with Louis and beating Wilfried Paulsen.

In the double round tournament of Vienna 1882 he failed to play his second round games; but from the first he amassed the good score of 9/17, beating Mason, Blackburne, Chigorin and others. In the great London tournament of 1883 he was 11th/14, beating Bird twice. His best performance was probably at Frankfurt am Main 1887 where he came 13th/21, beating the winner of the tournament, Mackenzie, and also Zukertort.

His last great tournament was Budapest 1896 where he came 12th out of 13, but drew with the tournament winner Chigorin and beat Maróczy. *(H.G.)*

NON-STOP CHESS
The record for non-stop chess is held by a Frenchman, Jacques Negro, who played chess continuously at Cagnes-sur-Mer in France for 80 hours 3 minutes and 3 seconds from 10 a.m. on 4 July to 6 p.m. 7 July 1976. This easily beat the previous record of 72 hours established by a seventeen-year-old English player, Wallace Jantzen, in 1969.

Negro played 317 games in his non-stop career, winning 270, losing 13 and drawing 34. His display took place during a chess festival at Cagnes-sur-Mer which had as its chief feature an Open International including some of the best players in France. Some of the games were 5 minutes' games with passers-by, others 10 minutes' games against the stronger players in the Open tournament and some of 30 minutes against beginners.

A doctor was at hand to check the stage of Negro's health and it was at his advice that Negro stopped after 80 hours' play. Despite not having slept a wink during the 80 hours, Negro was surprisingly fresh at the end of the session. *(H.G.)*

NOORDWIJK 1938
This tournament (June 1938) was a compact small event of considerable strength. Coming as it did between Semmering 1937 and A.V.R.O. 1938, it was expected to contribute to untangling the situation at the top by shedding light on Euwe's post-World Championship form and his and Keres' relative merits. Unfortunately the former Champion had to discharge his usual teaching duties throughout the tournament and meet his fresh rivals after a day's work – thus his score in this event was in no way representative of his strength.

In the circumstances Keres was expected to coast to an easy victory, but to the general surprise Eliskases took the lead from the start and kept it to the end, finishing with 6 wins and 3 draws. Thus, far from sorting out the World Championship position, the event threw up another candidate – and one, moreover, who was not on the A.V.R.O. list. Leading scores: Eliskases $7\frac{1}{2}$, Keres $6\frac{1}{2}$, Pirc $5\frac{1}{2}$,, Euwe 5, Bogoljubow, Landau $4\frac{1}{2}$. *(W.H.)*

NORWAY

Despite the great interest generally shown towards chess in the Scandinavian countries, Norway has been the least successful of the group, lagging behind Sweden, Denmark, Finland and Iceland in its ability to produce grandmasters or stage international events. Norway's first entrance into the International Team tournaments came relatively early (Hamburg 1930), but they succeeded only in occupying the outstandingly modest position of 18th out of 18 participating nations. This has improved over the years, as the following list shows: 18th/19 Prague 1931; 18th/19 Stockholm 1937; 18th/26 Buenos Aires 1939; 15th/16 Dubrovnik 1950; 21st/25 Helsinki 1952; 23rd/26 Amsterdam 1954 (two points behind the Saar!); 24th/34 Moscow 1956; 25th/36 Munich 1958; 19th/40 Leipzig 1960; 25th/37 Varna 1962; 23rd/50 Tel Aviv 1964; 13th/52 Havana 1966 (their best performance); 30th/53 Lugano 1968; 29th/60 Siegen 1970; 21st/62 Skopje 1972; 21st/74 Nice 1974.

Of Norwegian players of international standard perhaps the best known was Olaf Barda, followed by Johannessen, Zwaig, Wibe, Gulbrandsen, Hoen, De Lange; while in recent years the young master Leif Øgaard has moved very much to the fore. At Nice 1974 he represented Norway on top board, and his international successes include 2nd Dortmund 1975 (below Westerinen) and =2nd Aarhus 1976.

Norway has not been very active in the organization of international events; amongst the most prominent were: Olaf Barda Memorial tournament at Oslo 1971 (1st Andersson, 2nd Westerinen, 3rd Hoen, 4th Øgaard) and Oslo 1974 (1st Hübner $10\frac{1}{2}/11$, 2nd Westerinen, 3rd Øgaard, 4th Sigurjonsson).

The main organ of Norwegian chess is *Norsk Sjakkblad*, P.O. Box 104, Blindern, Oslo.

The address of the Norwegian Chess Federation is: Norges Sjakkforbund, P.O. Box 795,7001 Trondheim. *(R.D.K.)*

NOTATION

The game of chess is fortunate in that it possesses a method of recording the score of a game, known as notation. This has meant that games and problems going back a thousand years have been preserved.

Two main kinds of notation exist or have existed: the algebraic and the descriptive. The oldest form is the descriptive but in the ninth and tenth centuries AD the Arabs introduced the algebraic notation. Only a select few employed the algebraic and when the game came to Europe descriptive notation was almost uniquely used until the eighteenth century.

Then, with the coming of Stamma of Aleppo, the algebraic was reintroduced into the game and adopted by the German speaking peoples. Nowadays the algebraic is used throughout the world with the exception of the USA, Britain and Spain which still use the descriptive.

In 1976 FIDE decided to recognize one system of notation – the algebraic. We quote from the minutes of the FIDE Congress at Haifa:

'FIDE recognizes for its own tournaments and matches only one system of notation, the algebraic system. Scoresheets using a notation system other than the algebraic may not be used as evidence in cases where normally the scoresheet of a player is used for that purpose. An arbiter who observes that a player is using any other notation system than the algebraic should warn the player in question of this requirement.'

To this is added a footnote stating that the provisions of this paragraph become effective on 1 January 1981. *(H.G.)*

NOTATION, Algebraic

The report of the FIDE Rules Commission for 1976 describes the algebraic notation as follows:

1. Each piece is indicated by the first letter, a capital letter, of its name. Examples: K=King, Q=Queen, R=Rook, B=Bishop, N=Knight (in the case of the Knight, for convenience's sake, N is used).

2. For the first letter of the name of a piece, each player is free to use the first letter of the name which is commonly used in his country. Examples: F=*fou* (French for Bishop), L=*loper* (Dutch for Bishop). In printed publications, the use of figurines for the pieces is recommended.

3. Pawns are not indicated by their first letter, but are recognized by the absence of such a letter. Examples: e5, d4, a5.

4. The eight files (from left to right for White and from right to left for Black) are indicated by the small letters *a*, *b*, *c*, *d*, *e*, *f*, *g* and *h*, respectively.

5. The eight ranks (from bottom to top for White and from top to bottom for Black) are numbered *1*, *2*, *3*, *4*, *5*, *6*, *7* and *8*, respectively. Consequently, in the initial position the White pieces and pawns are placed on the first and second ranks; the Black pieces and pawns on the seventh and eighth ranks.

8	a8	b8	c8	d8	e8	f8	g8	h8
7	a7	b7	c7	d7	e7	f7	g7	h7
6	a6	b6	c6	d6	e6	f6	g6	h6
5	a5	b5	c5	d5	e5	f5	g5	h5
4	a4	b4	c4	d4	e4	f4	g4	h4
3	a3	b3	c3	d3	e3	f3	g3	h3
2	a2	b2	c2	d2	e2	f2	g2	h2
1	a1	b1	c1	d1	e1	f1	g1	h1
	a	b	c	d	e	f	g	h

6. As a consequence of the previous rules, each of the sixty-four squares is invariably indicated by a unique combination of a letter and a number.

7. Each move of a piece is indicated by (*a*) the first letter of the piece in question and (*b*) the square of arrival. There is no hyphen between (*a*) and (*b*). Examples: Be5, Nf3, Rd1. In the case of pawns, only the square of arrival is indicated. Examples: e5, d4, a5.

8. When a piece makes a capture, an *x* is inserted between (*a*) the first letter of the piece in question and (*b*) the square of arrival. Examples: Bxe5, Nxf3, Rxd1. When a pawn makes a capture, not only the square of arrival but also the file of departure must be indicated, followed by an *x*. Examples: dxe5, gxf3, axb5. In the case of an *en passant*, the square of arrival is given as the square on which the capturing pawn finally rests and 'e.p.' is appended to the notation.

9. If two identical pieces can move to the same square, the piece that is moved is indicated as follows:

(1) If both pieces are on the same rank: by (*a*) the first letter of the name of the piece, (*b*) the file of departure and (*c*) the square of arrival.

(2) If both pieces are on the same file: by (*a*) the first letter of the name of the piece, (*b*) the number of the square of departure, and (*c*) the square of arrival.

(3) If the pieces are on different ranks and files, method (1) is preferred. In case of a capture, an *x* must be inserted between (*b*) and (*c*). Examples:

(1) There are two Knights, on the squares g1 and d2 and one of them moves to the square f3; either Ngf3 or Ndf3, as the case may be.

(2) There are two Knights, on the squares g5 and g1, and one of them moves to the square f3; either N5f3 or N1f3, as the case may be.

(3) There are two Knights, on the squares h2 and d4, and one of them moves to the square f3, as the case may be. If a capture takes place on the square f3, the previous examples are changed by the insertion of an *x*; (*a*) either Ngxf3 or Ndxf3, (*b*) either Nfxf3 or N1xf3, (*c*) either Nhxf3 or Ndxf3, as the case may be.

10. If two pawns can capture the same piece or pawn of the opponent, the pawn that is moved is indicated by (*a*) the letter of the file of departure, (*b*) an *x*, and (*c*) the square of arrival. Example: If there are White pawns on the squares c4 and e4, and a Black pawn or piece on the square d5, the notation for White's move is either cxd5 or exd5, as the case may be.

11. In the case of the promotion of a pawn, the actual pawn move is indicated, followed immediately by the first letter of the new piece. Examples: d8Q, f8N, b1B, g1R.

Essential abbreviations

O–O = castling with rook h1 or rook h8 (King-side castling)
O–O–O = castling with rook a1 or rook a8 (Queen-side castling)
x = captures
+ = check
++ = checkmate
e.p. = captures 'en passant'.

Algebraic System: Long Form (recognized until 1 January 1981).

1. Each move in the long form is indicated by (*a*) the first letter of the piece in question, (*b*) the square of departure, and (*c*) the square of arrival. Pawns are not indicated by their first letter, but are recognized by the absence of such a letter. The squares of departure and of arrival are joined by a hyphen. Examples: Bd4–e5, Ng1–f3, Ra1–d1, e4–e5, d2–d4.

2. When a piece or pawn makes a capture, the hyphen is replaced by an *x*. Examples: Bd4xe5, Ng1xf3, Ra1xd1, e4xf5, d2xe3.

(H.G.)

NOTATION, Descriptive

The report of the FIDE Rules Commission for 1976 states that the Descriptive notation is recognized until 1 January 1981 (for FIDE competitions); meanwhile the Commission describes it as follows:

1. Each piece and pawn is indicated by the first letter, a capital letter, of its name. The pieces on the Queen's side of the board in the initial position are indicated by a Q preceding to distinguish them from the similar pieces on the King's side of the board in the initial position, indicated by a K preceding. Examples: R, N (or Kt), B, QR, KN.

2. For the first letter of the name of a piece, each player is free to use the first letter of the name which is commonly used in his country. Examples: F=*fou* (French for Bishop), L=*loper* (Dutch for Bishop).

3. The eight files (from left to right for White and from right to left for Black) are indicated by the pieces which occupy them in their initial positions: QR, QN, QB, Q, K, KB, KN and KR.

4. The eight ranks (each player counting from bottom to top from his side) are indicated by 1, 2, 3, 4, 5,6, 7 and 8, respectively. Consequently, in the initial position the White pieces and pawns are placed on the first and second ranks, the Black pieces and pawns on the seventh and eighth ranks from White's side and vice versa from Black's side.

QR1 QR8	QN1 QN8	QB1 QB8	Q1 Q8	K1 K8	KB1 KB8	KN1 KN8	KR1 KR8
QR2 QR7	QN2 QN7	QB2 QB7	Q2 Q7	K2 K7	KB2 KB7	KN2 KN7	KR2 KR7
QR3 QR6	QN3 QN6	QB3 QB6	Q3 Q6	K3 K6	KB3 KB6	KN3 KN6	KR3 KR6
QR4 QR5	QN4 QN5	QB4 QB5	Q4 Q5	K4 K5	KB4 KB5	KN4 KN5	KR4 KR5
QR5 QR4	QN5 QN4	QB5 QB4	Q5 Q4	K5 K4	KB5 KB4	KN5 KN4	KR5 KR4
QR6 QR3	QN6 QN3	QB6 QB3	Q6 Q3	K6 K3	KB6 KB3	KN6 KN3	KR6 KR3
QR7 QR2	QN7 QN2	QB7 QB2	Q7 Q2	K7 K2	KB7 KB2	KN7 KN2	KR7 KR2
QR8 QR1	QN8 QN1	QB8 QB1	Q8 Q1	K8 K1	KB8 KB1	KN8 KN1	KR8 KR1

5. As a consequence of the preceding rules, each of the sixty-four squares is indicated by two combinations of letters and numbers, depending upon whether White's or Black's move is being recorded.

6. Each pawn is indicated by the file on which it stands: QRP, QNP, QBP, QP, KP, KBP, KNP, KRP.

7. A move to a vacant square is indicated by (*a*) the first letter(s) of the piece or pawn in question and (*b*) the square of arrival, joined by a hyphen. When a move is written down, the basic forms R, N, B, and P (additionally, in the case of a pawn, the semi-condensed forms RP, NP, and BP), are used when only one piece or pawn of the specified type can move as indicated or if a recorded check identifies the move or capture. Examples: R–N3, B–B5, P–B4+.

8. A capture is indicated by the first letter(s) of the capturing and captured pieces or pawns, joined by a ×. Examples: B×B, Q×R, P×P, P×BP.

9. When a basic form would be ambiguous at any point in the indicated move,

(1) a King-side or Queen-side piece or pawn is specified if the piece or pawn can easily be so identified;

(2) the basic form is used, followed by a stroke (/) and the rank (preferably) or the file on which the piece or pawn stands, whichever will unambiguously identify the piece or pawn. (More usual, however, is the use of brackets instead of a stroke, both here and throughout the cases shown in Article 9. – *Ed.*)

Examples: (1) There are two Knights, on the squares KN1 and Q2, and one of them moves to the square KB3: either KN–B3 or QN–B3, as the case may be.

(2) There are two Knights, on the squares KN5 and KN1, and one of them moves to the square KB3: either N/5–B3 or N/1–B3, as the case may be.

If a capture takes place on the square KB3, the previous examples are changed by the substitution of an × for the hyphen and of the first letter(s) of the captured piece or pawn for the square on which the capture takes place: (1) either KN×R or QN×R, (2) either N/5×R or N/1×R, as the case may be.

10. In the case of the promotion of a pawn, the actual pawn move is indicated, followed by a stroke or an equal sign and the first letter(s) of a new piece. Examples: P×R/Q or P×R=Q. N.B. In a slightly different form of the descriptive system used in non-English-speaking countries, the rank precedes the square of arrival without a hyphen. Examples (in Spanish): P4AD, C3AR, P4D.

Essential abbreviations

O–O	= castling with the King's Rook
O–O–O	= castling with the Queen's Rook
×	= captures
+	= check (or, in Spanish, †)
e.p.	= captures 'en passant'.

(H.G.)

NOTEBOOM, Daniel *(26 February 1910–12 January 1932)*
A very promising Dutch player who died of pneumonia when not yet twenty-two. Became well known after his splendid performance in the Olympiad Hamburg 1930 where he scored 11½/15. In Hastings 1931/2 took third prize. According to the Dutch, inventor of a famous, though now somewhat obsolete, variation of Queen's Gambit starting 1. P–Q4, P–Q4; 2. P–QB4, P–K3; 3. N–QB3, P–QB3; 4. N–B3, P×P; – but see under ABRAHAMS. *(R.D.K.)*

NOTTINGHAM 1936
Generally referred to as the 'Five World Champions Tournament' (and at the time of writing it is still the only tournament to have included five past, present or future World Champions), Nottingham (August 1936) was the most important tournament played on British soil since London 1899. It began as a magnificent duel between the then champion Euwe, who started with 6 out of 7, and Botvinnik, but the leader gradually dropped back while Capablanca came up to force a tie with the Soviet champion. As the tournament table shows, the eight leaders, with only 1½ points

Competitors and organisers, Nottingham 1936

between them, were separated by a gulf of 2½ points from the rest of the field. That Lasker (aged 67) occupied a place among the World Championship candidates of the period deserves special mention – it was to be his last tournament. Leading scores: Botvinnik, Capablanca 10, Euwe, Fine, Reshevsky 9½, Alekhine 9. The following miniature was one of the most striking games:

White: Alekhine; *Black:* Botvinnik
Sicilian Defence
1. P–K4, P–QB4; 2. N–KB3, P–Q3; 3. P–Q4, P×P; 4. N×P, N–KB3; 5. N–QB3, P–KN3; 6. B–K2, B–N2; 7. B–K3, N–B3; 8. N–N3, B–K3; 9. P–B4, O–O; 10. P–N4, P–Q4; 11. P–B5, B–B1; 12. P×QP, N–N5; 13. P–Q6, Q×P; 14. B–B5, Q–B5; 15. R–KB1, Q×RP; 16. B×N, N×P; 17. B×N, Q–N6+; 18. R–B2, Q–N8+; 19. R–B1, Q–N6+; 20. R–B2, Q–N8+; drawn. *(W.H.)*

NOVOTELNOV, Nikolai Alexandrovich *(b. 9 December 1911)*
Leningrad champion in 1942 and champion of RSFSR (Russian Federated Republic) 1947. International master 1950. *(W.R.H.)*

NUNN, John Denis Martin *(b. 25 April 1955)*
British international master and European Junior champion, 1975. Born in London, Nunn learned chess at the age of four and soon revealed a great aptitude for the game.

He came 6th in the Norwich Junior international tournament in 1970 and went up to Oxford University to take a mathematics degree at a very early age. He played on top board for the University from 1972–6 and is now preparing a doctorate there.

He won the European Junior championship and with it the international master title at Groningen in 1975. In that year too he was equal first in the I.B.M. Master tournament, and at London in 1975 he reached an international master norm, coming 5th in the international tournament there. He played on bottom board at the Haifa Olympiad 1976 and scored 64.2%. *(H.G.)*

NUREMBERG 1896
In this tournament, in which all the great masters of the time competed, the then World Champion, Emanuel Lasker, demonstrated that he was a true and worthy World Champion in his characteristic and daringly original style. He took enormous risks and did not always emerge unscathed, losing to two great young players, Pillsbury and Charousek, and also to his old rival, Janowski.

On the other hand, he beat the former World Champion, Steinitz, and, what was regarded as even more important, he defeated the one player in the world whom the world thought might be his equal – Tarrasch. He owed his first place to a terrific run of successes against the last seven players in the table, nearly all of whom could have figured in the top seven in the table and some, such as Winawer and Teichmann, who could even have won the tournament. Leading scores: Lasker 13½, Maróczy 12½, Pillsbury, Tarrasch 12, Janowski 11½. *(H.G.)*

NYHOLM, Gustav *(27 January 1880–12 September 1957)*
One of Sweden's leading players in the years immediately preceding the First World War and during the war and afterwards till the advent of Stoltz, Ståhlberg and Lundin. His international activity is mostly concentrated in the years 1911–14. At Cologne 1911, a tournament of middle strength, he was =7th/16 with Schelfhout.

In the interesting and strong Abbazia tournament of 1912, an event devoted to the King's Gambit Accepted and played in double-rounds, he was as low as =10th/12 but he scored wins against Spielmann (the tournament winner) and also against Réti.

During the war he had two successes in national tournaments, coming 1st at both Christiania and Stockholm 1917.

After the war, in a small but strong tournament at Stockholm 1920, containing Bogoljubow, Nimzowitsch and Spielmann, he scored 4 points. This was a double-round event and he came 7th/8.

He played a number of small matches, losing to Kostić in 1913 by +1−3=1, but doing well against his compatriots: he beat O. Löwenborg at Stockholm 1918 by +3−1=0, drew with A. Haakansson at Göteborg 1919 +2−2=1, and with A. Nilsson at Göteborg 1921 +2−2=1. He won two matches against A. Olsson both at Göteborg 1921 and 1922, the first by +4−2=2 and the second by +3−1=1. *(H.G.)*

OBSTRUCTIVE SACRIFICE
A sacrifice for the purpose of obstructing the opponent's development. A typical example occurs in the following line of Alekhine's Defence: 1. P–K4, N–KB3; 2. N–QB3, P–Q4; 3. P–K5, KN–Q2; *4. P–K6*, P×P; 5. P–Q4, when Black's development, especially of his Bishops, has been obstructed. *(W.H.)*

ODDS
The practice of giving the opponent an initial advantage in material or in moves is known as giving odds. Odds-giving reached its heyday in the eighteenth century and the early nineteenth century. So much so that Philidor played the vast majority of his games at odds, and there are comparatively few of his games that have come down to us that are not games at odds.

There are frequent references to games played at odds in the early nineteenth century. The strong English player Lewis, for example, played a match in 1817 against a weak player, Peter Pratt, and succeeded in giving him the odds of a Knight. Deschapelles preferred to play games at odds and it was he who issued an open challenge to English players in 1836 for a match in which he would give odds of pawn and two moves.

The playing of games at odds gradually grew rarer as the nineteenth century proceeded, until nowadays it is seldom seen. But such events do still occur and it is worthwhile giving here a list of odds in order of size. Curiously enough, the Bishop never figured in the list of odds.

1. Odds of the move: i.e. the odds-giver always has Black.
2. Odds of two moves.
3. Pawn and move – the pawn usually being the KBP.
4. Pawn and two moves (again the KBP).
5. Knight (usually the QN).
6. Rook (usually the QR).
7. Rook and pawn.
8. Two minor pieces. (Variants of Knights and Bishops at the choice of the odds-giver.)
9. Rook and Knight.
10. Queen.
11. Two Rooks.

There was an even greater kind of odds known as *pion coiffé* by which a pawn was crowned with a ring of paper or other material before the game started and the odds-giver had to give mate with that pawn. This was made even more difficult by the proviso that the mate could not be given with the pawn after it had been promoted to another piece.

There are numerous other more modern variants of the giving of odds. One is the odds of the draw by which the odds-giver loses every game that is drawn. Another is time on the clock with the odds-giver having less time for thinking than his opponent.

Or one can delve back into the Middle Ages for more recondite methods of giving odds. One that was common was the odds of mating in the far corner with a Bishop, and the French medieval romances are full of such occurrences. For example in *Artur: 'Et comencerent le geu trois foiz et materent en l'angle'* ('And commenced the game three times and mated in the corner' – presumably the hero won three games by mating in the corner).

The early treatises, running up to the nineteenth century, are full of advice about the giving and receiving of odds. Damiano, in the early sixteenth century, says that when receiving odds one should exchange whenever possible except at a loss. Later on in the century Ruy Lopez devotes a considerable part of a chapter to discussing the exact value of certain odds. *(H.G.)*

OJANEN, Kaarle Sakari *(b. 4 December 1918)*
Finnish international master and Finland's leading player after Böök and before Westerinen, Ojanen has considerable talent as a combinational player but is not so good in the positional field. This is reflected in his frequent winning of the Finnish championship and his lack of success in the international field, with the exception of team matches where he has had some fine results.

He was Finnish champion from 1950–53, from 1957–62 and again in 1967. He played in ten Olympiads: 1937, 1950, 1952, 1956, 1958, 1960, 1966, 1968, 1970 and 1972. Many of these appearances were on 1st board, until in 1968 he played on 2nd board below Westerinen as he did in 1970 and 1972.

In international tournaments his best result has been 3rd/10 at Helsinki 1946 above Böök. He was also 17th/20 at Trenčianské Teplice 1949. *(H.G.)*

O'KELLY DE GALWAY, Count Alberic *(b. 17 May 1911)*
Belgian grandmaster and professional chess-player. Of interesting ancestry: the first O'Kelly to come to Belgium was an officer in the British Army who was an expert in mining and was sent for in 1720 to see that props were put in the mines at Liège; his reward was being made a Count. He also had a curious and unusual chess career in that he was a minor master for some time and then, after the Second World War, suddenly made a jump into grandmastery.

He played in the Belgian championship for the first time in 1937 which was also the year in which he first played in an Olympiad. He was to win the Belgian championship seven times and to play in eight Olympiads (1937, 1950, 1954, 1956, 1960, 1962, 1964 and 1968).

His first tournament after the war, that at Groningen 1946, proved a disaster and he came next to bottom; but in the very same year he came first ahead of Stoltz at Beverwijk and from now on he had a series of excellent results.

One explanation that has been put forward for this sudden advance is that he had the benefit of advice and analysis from the great master, Akiba Rubinstein, who was living in retirement in Brussels during the War and until his death in 1961. Or perhaps he was just a late developer.

Whatever the reason, he had developed by 1947 into one of Europe's leading players. In that year he came 1st in the European Zonal tournament at Hilversum and other good results were =1st with Pirc at Teplice Sanov and =2nd at Venice, both in 1947. In 1948 he was 1st in a tournament at Sao Paulo (Brazil) ahead of Eliskases and Rossetto. It was this year that international titles were first awarded by FIDE and he was one of the first recipients of the title.

The year 1949 saw a small decline in his achievements. An =4th with Golombek at Beverwijk was followed, in a rather weaker tournament at Heidelberg, by an =3rd. At Trenčianské Teplice he was =7th with Prins and at Oldenburg he was =8th with Rellstab.

At the very strong Amsterdam tournament of 1950 he came 10th/20 and at the even stronger tournament at Budapest in 1952 he was 9th. In 1956 he was awarded the grandmaster title.

Though he never, by any means, abandoned over-the-board play, he tended to give more time to writing about the game, to correspondence play and to acting as arbiter at matches and tournaments.

Probably his last really good tournament result has been his =2nd at Zevenaar in 1961. He won the World Championship in Correspondence chess during the period 1961–66 and was chief arbiter at the two World Championship matches between Petrosian and Spassky in 1966 and 1969. In 1970 he played in a tournament at Buenos Aires and came 10th/18. In 1974 he was chief arbiter at the Karpov–Korchnoi match in Moscow.

As a player he had, in his peak years, a kind of super competence and an admirable clarity of vision. These are the attributes of a grandmaster, but something more is needed for the world class type of player. When he came up against the very best – the Botvinniks, Tals and suchlike – O'Kelly had little powers of resistance.

He has a great gift for languages, speaks six of them well – French, Dutch, German, English, Spanish and Russian – and can also speak Italian.

Of his books, probably the two best are *34 Mal Schach-logik*, Berlin 1965; and *The Sicilian Flank Game*, London 1969. *(H.G.)*

OLAFSSON, Fridrik *(b. 26 January 1935)*
The first and strongest Icelandic grandmaster. Olafsson studied and qualified as a lawyer but is now a professional chess-player and has achieved remarkable success in this domain.

His first important tournament victory was an =1st with Korchnoi at Hastings 1954/5. In 1957 he defeated Pilnik in a match by 5–1 and in the following year he qualified from the Portorož Interzonal ahead of Fischer for the 1959 Candidates. This gave him the grandmaster title and though at the Candidates tournament in Yugoslavia (Bled-Zagreb-Belgrade) he finished 7th out of 8, he did have the satisfaction of twice beating Keres and Petrosian. On the second occasion immediately after his victory in the adjourned game over Petrosian, he was carried round the main square of Zagreb in triumph on the shoulders of his ardent supporters.

Though since 1959 Olafsson has not as yet succeeded again in qualifying for the Candidates, he still has notched up a great number of impressive results in non-FIDE events that mark him out as one of the most powerful Western grandmasters: e.g. =3rd Piatigorsky Cup 1963; =1st Reykjavik 1972; =1st Wijk-aan-Zee 1976; =1st Reykjavik 1976. In collaboration with Freysteinn Johannsson he has written a detailed analytical account of the 1972 World Championship match: *Skákbók ab Fischer gegn Spassky*, Reykjavik, 1973.

A game from the 1958 Interzonal at Portorož in which he defeats the young Bobby Fischer.

White: Olafsson; *Black:* Fischer
English Opening
1. P–QB4, N–KB3; 2. N–QB3, P–K3; 3. N–B3, P–Q4; 4. P–Q4, B–N5; 5. P×P, P×P; 6. B–N5, P–KR3; 7. B–R4, P–B4; 8. P–K3, N–B3; 9. R–B1, P–B5; 10. B–K2, B–K3; 11. O–O, O–O; 12. N–Q2, B–K2; 13. P–QN3, P–KN4; 14. B–N3, B–R6; 15. R–B2, N–QN5; 16. P×P, N×R; 17. Q×N, P×P; 18. N–N5, B–QN5; 19. N–B7, B×N; 20. N×B, P×N; 21. B×P, Q–K1; 22. Q×B, N–K5; 23. Q–Q3, N×B; 24. RP×N, R–B3; 25. Q–K4, R–QB1; 26. B–N3, Q–Q2; 27. R–Q1, R–K1; 28. P–B4, Q–R2; 29. Q–K5, Q–B4;

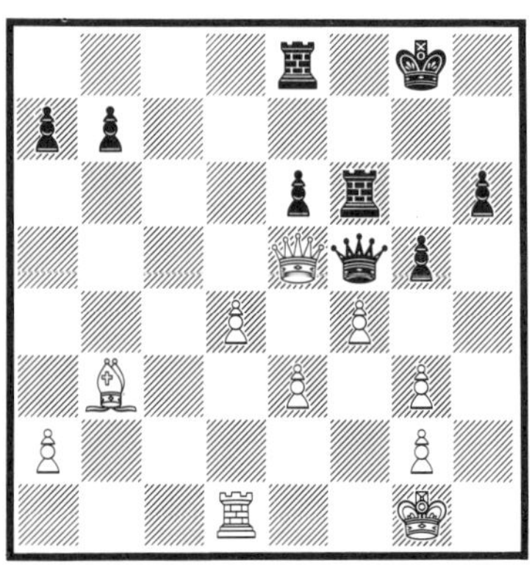

30. P–N4, Q×Q; 31. QP×Q, R–B2; 32. P–B5, R–QB2; 33. R–Q6, R–B4; 34. B×P+, K–B1; 35. B–N3, R(4)×P; 36. R×P, R×KP; 37. R–KN6, R(K1)–K5; 38. R×P, R–N6; 39. R–N8+, K–K2; 40. P–N5, R–K7; 41. B–Q5, K–Q3; 42. B–B3, R×RP; 43. P–B6, K–K3; 44. R–K8+, resigns. *(R.D.K.)*

OLD INDIAN DEFENCE

The system 1. P–Q4, N–KB3; 2. P–QB4, P–Q3; 3. N–QB3, P–K4 first employed by Chigorin and hence also known as the Chigorin Indian Defence. While not unsound, this defence is rarely encountered in modern master practice, being regarded as inflexible and strategically limited. *(R.D.K.)*

OLLAND, Adolf Georg *(13 April 1867–22 July 1933)*
Netherlands' leading player till the advent of Euwe, Olland was by profession a doctor of medicine.

His first success was a 2nd to Atkins at Amsterdam 1899. With the excellent score of 11/15 he was nevertheless 4 points behind Atkins who won all his games. First in a smaller tournament at Haarlem in 1901, he came a creditable 8th in a larger and much stronger international event at Hanover the following year.

After an interval of five years he played in the great tournament at Carlsbad 1907 and was 19th/21. Retreating discomfited from the international battlefield, he took part in the first national championship of The Netherlands at Leyden in 1909 where he came =1st with Speyer. At Stockholm 1912 he was 4th/11 coming ahead of Spielmann. An excellent result was a 3rd/14 at Scheveningen 1913, but he had a worse result at his next tournament, Hastings 1919 where he was =7th/11.

His international and indeed his national results were poor after this and he died of a heart attack while playing in the 1933 Dutch championship at the Hague.

Though he had comparatively little time to spare for tournament play he made up for this by playing no less than 29 matches, all except one, against Loman at Egmond, being played in his native town of Utrecht. In these he was regularly successful against his compatriots with the exception of Euwe who beat him twice, but lost badly to such foreign masters as Maróczy, Réti and Colle. *(H.G.)*

OLYMPIADS, Chess

Precursors and Pseudo-Olympiads

The history of the chess Olympiads – international tournaments contested by teams representing the member states of FIDE – is, of necessity, closely linked with that of FIDE. Founded in Paris in 1924, FIDE undertook the organization of the Olympiads from 1927 onwards, but mention should be made of three international team events of non-Olympic status.

The first of these took place in 1924, as part of the congress that led to the formal establishment of FIDE, the competing 'teams' comprising any number of players between four and one and playing as individuals (thus on occasion being paired with players belonging to the same 'team', both in the preliminary sections, and in the final top group and final Swiss System tournament for those who had not qualified for the top group). There were fifty-four participants 'representing' eighteen nations. The result was a win for Czechoslovakia (Hromadka, Schulz, Vanek and Skalicka), above Hungary and Switzerland. The USSR was 'represented' by two emigrés, Kahn and Potemkin, who finished 17th of 18.

The first FIDE-organized team event, at Budapest 1926, proved a complete flop, only four teams (Hungary, Yugoslavia, Romania and Germany) competing and finishing in that order. Finally, at Munich 1936, the Nazi *Grossdeutscher Schachbund* organized an

'Olympic' event, which, with the megalomania typical of all Nazi undertakings, was planned for teams of eight, with two reserves. This event attracted twenty-one nations (1st Hungary, 2nd Poland, 3rd Germany), but was never accorded the status of an Olympiad, partly for political, partly for organizational reasons.

History and Development of the Olympiads

The first of the twenty-two true Olympiads held to date was London 1927, with sixteen competing nations. In all essentials but one the event served as a model for all subsequent Olympiads. It was contested by duly nominated teams of four players (with one or more recently two reserves). The scoring was by accumulated points of the individual members of the team (when, at a later stage, preliminary qualification contests became necessary, only the points scored in the finals counted towards the final placings). The number of matches won or lost had only tie-splitting significance. No differentiation existed between amateurs and professionals – thus players of the varied status of Maróczy, Réti, Grünfeld, Tarrasch and Kostić entered the lists. The winning team received the Hamilton-Russell Challenge Cup, a floating trophy in the shape of a large gold cup that has gone to the winning team throughout the half-century of the Olympiads. The one exception referred to above concerned the board order of the teams; until Prague 1931, the team captains could place their players in any order they liked. Since then the playing order has to be announced before the start of the tournament and adhered to throughout its duration. The 2nd Olympiad, The Hague 1928, was a distinct step backward from the high standards of London 1927. The fuddy-duddies of chess returned to the nonsensical notion of amateurs and professionals that had prevailed at Paris 1924, and barred the latter from Olympic participation; quite consistently, they also returned to the idea of an amateur World Championship. But whereas at Paris 1924 this had been the top group of the 'team' tournament (the Latvian Mattison winning the title), it was a separate event on this occasion when the title was won by Euwe. Thus the standard of the competing teams – already weakened by the absence of the recognized international masters – was lowered even further.

However, by the time Hamburg 1930 came around the amateur nonsense in chess had died a painless death, and the 3rd and all subsequent Olympiads were open to all, with an ever-increasing number of grandmasters competing and raising the standard of these events. Thus Hamburg saw World Champion Alekhine active for France, Rubinstein and Tartakower for Poland, Flohr for Czechoslovakia, Kashdan and Marshall for the USA, Sämisch for Germany, etc.

Even Hamburg was only a beginning in this respect. In the following tournaments (Prague 1931, Folkestone 1933, Warsaw 1935, Stockholm 1937, Buenos Aires 1939) it would be easier to enumerate the grandmasters staying away than those competing. Stockholm 1937 saw the introduction of prizes for the highest individual score at each board (for details see next section), while Buenos Aires 1939 introduced a number of innovations. By this time the modest sixteen participants of London 1927 (lowered only once, to fifteen, at Folkestone 1933) had increased to twenty-seven, mainly because the venue enabled many Latin-American countries to compete: all previous Olympiads had been confined to European countries 'enriched' by the USA, Palestine and Argentina. It thus became necessary for the first time to resort to a group system of preliminaries, the method adopted on this occasion providing for four preliminary and two final groups, the B final being played for the *Copa Argentina*.

Except for the first post-Second World War Olympiad (the 9th in all) at Dubrovnik 1950, which once again was contested by sixteen nations, all future Olympiads (except the latest in 1976 at Haifa) were to be run on the group system in various forms, culminating in eight preliminary groups and five finals at Nice 1974, where a total of seventy-four nations were in contention. The financial and organizational burdens have now become so heavy that FIDE decided to run the 22nd Olympiad at Haifa entirely on the Swiss System and thus eliminate the injustices of the group system together with simplifying organization and finance.

Other innovations at Buenos Aires were even more sinister than the birth of the group system. For the first time political squabbles interfered with the running of the tournament and some adjusted results had to take the place of played matches. On this occasion, at least, the outbreak of the Second World War made the interference of politics in chess Olympiads understandable, with Germany and Czechoslovakia (entered under the Nazi name of Bohemia and Moravia) on one side, and France, Poland and Palestine on the other. Also, for the first time, a team that had played in the preliminaries did not take part at all in the finals, the English team returning home on the outbreak of war.

It is only in recent years that this political interference has been resumed: in the 19th Olympiad, at Siegen, Albania refused to meet South Africa and in the 20th Olympiad at Skopje, the same team defaulted against Israel and, on being forfeited, withdrew from the competition. Matters came to a head in Nice 1974, when South Africa and Rhodesia were suspended from FIDE on unsubstantiated charges of discrimination against non-white players and the former country withdrew from the finals three rounds before the end. There were also a number of adjusted scores when Arab countries refused to meet various opponents. While political developments have become progressively more detrimental to the Olympic spirit, a corresponding advance has been made in playing conditions, creature comforts and social amenities. The highlight in this respect was the 17th Olympiad, at Havana 1966, with its extravagantly sumptuous entertainment programme and an abundance of costly presents to the competitors. For the results of all Olympiads see below.

Individual Accomplishments

Chess not being a team game like soccer or rugby, team results cannot help being the mere sum of individual results. Thus it was soon realized that some reward was due to the best individual efforts. Prior to the establishment of a permanent board order, such prizes were awarded on percentage scores, provided a minimum number of games were played. At London 1927 the awards went to

Norman-Hansen and Sir George Thomas in a tie, Réti, Maróczy, Grünfeld and Euwe in this order; at The Hague 1928 to Kashdan, Muffang, Regedzinsky, Nagy, A. Steiner and Andersen (Denmark); at Hamburg 1930 to Rubinstein, Havasi and Flohr.

There seem to have been no special prizes at the next three Olympiads, while from 1937 onwards (except at Dubrovnik 1950 and Munich 1958) the best results on each board were rewarded. *1937:* 1. Flohr, 2. Fine, 3. Kashdan, 4. Danielson, 5. Horowitz, with a special award for the highest absolute (not percentage) score to A. Steiner (Hungary). *1939:* 1. Capablanca, 2. Najdorf, 3. Engels, 4. Friedemann, 5. Pleci in the A finals; 1. Rojahn, 2. Yanofsky, 3. Gudmundsson, 4. Kandartiev, 5. Arnlaugsson in the B finals. *1952:* 1. Najdorf, 2. Smyslov, 3. Bronstein, 4. Kottnauer, 5. Rossetto, 6. Rellstab. *1954:* 1. Botvinnik, 2. Anderson (Canada), 3. Barcza, 4. Keres, 5. Geller, 6. Burstein. *1956:* 1. Larsen, 2. Dückstein, 3. Keres, 4. Bronstein, 5. Sanguineti, 6. Geller.

1958 saw a change, three special prizes being awarded for the best percentage score in each of the A, B and C finals, to Tal, Larsen and Borja respectively, while Gligorić received a special prize for the best result of any top board. *1960:* 1. Robatsch, 2. Botvinnik, 3. Keres, 4. Miagmasuren and Tan Hoan-Liong, 5. Smyslov, 6. Petrosian. *1962:* 1. Olafsson, 2. Petrosian, 3. Spassky, 4. Ivkov and Sanguineti, 5. Geller, 6. Tal. *1964:* 1. Portisch, 2. Botvinnik, 3. Smyslov, 4. Pfleger, 5. Stein, 6. Matulović. Here the system of awards differed insofar as only A final scores qualified; therefore additional awards were made to Uhlmann (1) and Uitumen (2) whose scores in the B finals surpassed those of the prize-winners. *1966:* 1. Petrosian, 2. Panno, 3. Tal, 4. Langeweg, 5. Korchnoi, 6. Barczay. *1968:* 1. Petrosian, 2. Tringov, 3. Korchnoi, 4. Kagan, 5. Polugayevsky, 6. Smyslov. *1970:* 1. Spassky, 2. Schmid, 3. Hartston, 4. Matanović, 5. Lombardy, 6. Estimo. *1972:* 1. Hübner, 2. Korchnoi, 3. Ljubojević, 4. Tal, 5. Karpov, 6. Shaw. *1974:* 1. Karpov, 2. Farooqi, 3. Spassky, 4. Petrosian, 5. Tal, 6. Tarjan. *1976:* 1. Timman, 2. Sosonko, 3. Carrion, 4. Stean, 5. de Greiff, 6. Commons.

Results of Olympiads 1–22

The early Olympiads were dominated by the Hungarians; those of the thirties by the USA team; the first post-war Olympiad fell to the home team, Yugoslavia, and since Helsinki 1952 the USSR has won every Olympiad – one or two by the skin of their teeth, but the majority by wide margins until Haifa 1976 in which they did not compete. Here are the detailed results:

London 1927:

1. Hungary 40
2. Denmark 38½
3. England 36½
4. The Netherlands 35
5. Czechoslovakia 34½
6. Germany 34
7. Austria 34
8. Switzerland 32
9. Yugoslavia 30
10. Italy 28½
11. Sweden 28
12. Argentina 27
13. France 24½
14. Belgium 21½
15. Finland 21½
16. Spain 14½

The Hague 1928:

1. Hungary 44
2. USA 39½
3. Poland 37
4. Austria 36½
5. Denmark 34
6. Switzerland 34
7. Czechoslovakia 34
8. Argentina 33½
9. Germany 31½
10. The Netherlands 31½
11. France 31
12. Belgium 31
13. Sweden 31
14. Latvia 30
15. Italy 26½
16. Romania 25½
17. Spain 13½

Hamburg 1930:

1. Poland 48½
2. Hungary 47
3. Germany 44½
4. Austria 43½
5. Czechoslovakia 42½
6. USA 41½
7. The Netherlands 41
8. England 40½
9. Sweden 40
10. Latvia 35
11. Denmark 31
12. France 28½
13. Romania 28½
14. Lithuania 22½
15. Iceland 22
16. Spain 21½
17. Finland 18
18. Norway 16

Prague 1931:

1. USA 48
2. Poland 47
3. Czechoslovakia 46½
4. Yugoslavia 46
5. Germany 45½
6. Latvia 45½
7. Sweden 45½
8. Austria 45
9. England 44
10. Hungary 39½
11. The Netherlands 35
12. Switzerland 34
13. Lithuania 30½
14. France 29½
15. Romania 28
16. Italy 24
17. Denmark 19½
18. Norway 15½
19. Spain 19½

Folkestone 1933:

1. USA 39
2. Czechoslovakia 37½
3. Poland 34
4. Sweden 34
5. Hungary 34
6. Austria 33½
7. Lithuania 30½
8. France 28
9. Latvia 27½
10. England 27
11. Italy 24½
12. Denmark 22½
13. Belgium 17
14. Iceland 17
15. Scotland 14

Warsaw 1935:

1. USA 54
2. Sweden 52½
3. Poland 52
4. Hungary 51
5. Czechoslovakia 49
6. Yugoslavia 45½
7. Austria 43½
8. Argentina 42
9. Latvia 41
10. France 38
11. Estonia 37½
12. England 37
13. Finland 35
14. Lithuania 34
15. Palestine 32
16. Denmark 31½
17. Romania 27½
18. Italy 24
19. Switzerland 21
20. Ireland 12

Stockholm 1937:

1. USA 54½
2. Hungary 48½
3. Poland 47
4. Argentina 47
5. Czechoslovakia 45
6. The Netherlands 44
7. Lithuania 41½
8. Estonia 41½
9. Yugoslavia 40
10. Sweden 38½
11. Latvia 37½
12. Finland 34
13. England 34
14. Italy 26½
15. Denmark 25½
16. Iceland 23
17. Belgium 22½
18. Norway 19½
19. Scotland 14

Buenos Aires 1939:

A finals

1. Germany 36
2. Poland 35½
3. Estonia 33½
4. Sweden 33
5. Argentina 32½
6. Czechoslovakia 32
7. Latvia 31½
8. The Netherlands 30½
9. Palestine 26
10. France 24½
11. Cuba 22½
12. Lithuania 22
13. Chile 22
14. Brazil 21
15. Denmark 17½

B finals

16. Iceland 28
17. Canada 28
18. Norway 27
19. Uruguay 26
20. Bulgaria 25½
21. Ecuador 21
22. Guatemala 15½
23. Ireland 15½
24. Peru 14
25. Bolivia 10
26. Paraguay 9½

Dubrovnik 1950:

1. Yugoslavia 45½
2. Argentina 43½
3. West Germany 40½
4. USA 40
5. The Netherlands 37
6. Belgium 32
7. Austria 31½
8. Chile 30½
9. France 28½
10. Finland 28
11. Sweden 27½
12. Italy 25
13. Denmark 22
14. Peru 21½
15. Norway 15
16. Greece 12

Helsinki 1952:

A finals

1. USSR 21
2. Argentina 19½
3. Yugoslavia 19
4. Czechoslovakia 18
5. USA 17
6. Hungary 16
7. Sweden 13
8. West Germany 10½
9. Finland 10

B finals

10. The Netherlands 21
11. Israel 19½
12. Poland 16½
13. East Germany 16½
14. Denmark 16
15. Cuba 15
16. England 14
17. Austria 13
18. Italy 12½

C finals

19. Brazil 18½
20. Greece 13½
21. Norway 13
22. Switzerland 13
23. Iceland 12½
24. Saar 12½
25. Luxembourg 1

The English team at the Amsterdam Olympiad, 1954. From l. to r. standing: Barden, Clarke, Penrose; seated: Wade, Golombek, Alexander

Amsterdam 1954:

A finals

1. USSR 34
2. Argentina 27
3. Yugoslavia 26½
4. Czechoslovakia 24½
5. West Germany 23½
6. Hungary 23
7. Israel 22
8. The Netherlands 21
9. England 17
10. Bulgaria 17
11. Sweden 15
12. Iceland 13½

B finals

13. Switzerland 37
14. Canada 36
15. Austria 36
16. Denmark 34½
17. Italy 28½
18. Colombia 27½
19. Belgium 27
20. Finland 26½
21. France 26
22. Saar 24
23. Norway 22
24. Greece 21
25. Ireland 11
26. Luxembourg 7

Moscow 1956:

A finals

1. USSR 31
2. Yugoslavia 26½
3. Hungary 26½
4. Argentina 23
5. West Germany 22
6. Bulgaria 22
7. Czechoslovakia 20½
8. England 20
9. Switzerland 19
10. Denmark 19
11. Romania 19
12. Israel 15½

B finals

13. Austria 28
14. Iceland 27
15. Sweden 26½
16. Belgium 23½
17. Finland 22½
18. Colombia 21
19. The Netherlands 21
20. East Germany 20½
21. France 19½
22. Chile 19
23. Poland 19
24. Norway 16½

C finals

25. Philippines 24
26. Saar 23
27. India 20½
28. Iran 19
29. Puerto Rico 18½
30. Mongolia 18½
31. Scotland 17½
32. Greece 17
33. Ireland 13
34. Luxembourg 9

Munich 1958:

A finals

1. USSR 34½
2. Yugoslavia 29
3. Argentina 25½
4. USA 24
5. Czechoslovakia 22
6. East Germany 22
7. West Germany 22
8. Switzerland 19
9. Spain 17½
10. Bulgaria 17
11. England 16
12. Austria 15½

B finals

13. Hungary 31
14. The Netherlands 28½
15. Canada 24½
16. Colombia 24½
17. Israel 23½
18. Denmark 23
19. Poland 22½
20. Sweden 21
21. Finland 19
22. Iceland 18
23. France 15
24. Belgium 13½

C finals

25. Norway 30
26. Philippines 29½
27. South Africa 28
28. Italy 26½
29. Scotland 25½
30. Greece 25
31. Portugal 23
32. Iran 20
33. Puerto Rico 14½
34. Ireland 14½
35. Tunisia 14
36. Lebanon 13½

Leipzig 1960:

A finals

1. USSR 34
2. USA 29
3. Yugoslavia 27
4. Hungary 22½
5. Czechoslovakia 21½
6. Bulgaria 21
7. Argentina 20½
8. West Germany 19½
9. East Germany 19
10. The Netherlands 17
11. Romania 16½
12. England 16½

B finals

13. Sweden 27½
14. Israel 26½
15. Austria 24½
16. Denmark 23½
17. Finland 23½
18. Cuba 23
19. Norway 23
20. Spain 22½
21. Poland 22
22. Chile 19½
23. Iceland 16½
24. India 12

C finals

25. Philippines 28½
26. Indonesia 27½
27. Mongolia 27½
28. Albania 26½
29. Ecuador 26
30. Portugal 26
31. France 25
32. Italy 24
33. Belgium 23½
34. Tunisia 21½
35. Greece 20½
36. Bolivia 19½
37. Monaco 17½
38. Ireland 17
39. Malta 14
40. Lebanon 8½

Varna 1962:

A finals

1. USSR 31½
2. Yugoslavia 28
3. Argentina 26
4. USA 25
5. Hungary 23
6. Bulgaria 21½
7. West Germany 21
8. East Germany 20½
9. Romania 20½
10. Czechoslovakia 18½
11. The Netherlands 18
12. Austria 10½

B finals

13. Spain 26½
14. England 26½
15. Israel 25
16. Cuba 22½
17. Sweden 22½
18. Poland 22½
19. Belgium 22
20. Finland 20½
21. Mongolia 20
22. Switzerland 20
23. Iceland 19
24. Denmark 17

C finals

25. Norway 32½
26. Albania 28½
27. Tunisia 28½
28. India 26½
29. Iran 25
30. France 23½
31. Puerto Rico 22½
32. Uruguay 22
33. Greece 18½
34. Luxembourg 18
35. Turkey 17
36. Ireland 14½
37. Cyprus 1½

Tel-Aviv 1964:

A finals

1. USSR 36½
2. Yugoslavia 32
3. West Germany 30½
4. Hungary 30
5. Czechoslovakia 28½
6. USA 27½
7. Bulgaria 27
8. Romania 27
9. Argentina 26
10. Poland 24
11. The Netherlands 21
12. Canada 19
13. Israel 17½
14. Spain 17½

B finals

15. East Germany 38½
16. Sweden 32
17. Denmark 31½
18. England 31
19. Peru 27½
20. Austria 27½
21. Cuba 26
22. Norway 25½
23. Mongolia 25½
24. Chile 24
25. Philippines 22½
26. Ecuador 18
27. Paraguay 17½
28. Scotland 17

C finals

29. Iceland 37½
30. Switzerland 36½
31. Colombia 35
32. Finland 35
33. Venezuela 30½
34. France 29½
35. Greece 27½
36. Iran 23½
37. India 22
38. Puerto Rico 21½
39. Turkey 20½
40. Mexico 20
41. Ireland 13
42. Monaco 12

D finals

43. Australia 22½
44. South Africa 18
45. Bolivia 15½
46. Uruguay 14½
47. Portugal 14
48. Luxembourg 12
49. Dominican Rep. 10½
50. Cyprus 5

Havana 1966:

A finals

1. USSR 39½
2. USA 34½
3. Hungary 33½
4. Yugoslavia 33½
5. Argentina 30
6. Czechoslovakia 29½
7. Bulgaria 28½
8. Romania 26½
9. East Germany 25½
10. Denmark 20
11. Iceland 19
12. Spain 18
13. Norway 14
14. Cuba 12

B finals

15. The Netherlands 37
16. Poland 31½

17. Austria 30
18. Switzerland 28½
19. Israel 28½
20. Finland 28
21. England 27½
22. Colombia 26½
23. Canada 25½
24. Sweden 24½
25. Belgium 23
26. France 20
27. Indonesia 18
28. Scotland 15½

C finals

29. Italy 38
30. Mongolia 33½
31. Philippines 31
32. Greece 29
33. Uruguay 28
34. Tunisia 26½
35. Turkey 25½
36. Venezuela 25
37. Portugal 25
38. Chile 23½
39. Ecuador 23½
40. Ireland 21
41. Puerto Rico 18½
42. Luxembourg 16

D finals

43. South Africa 28
44. Mexico 24½
45. Bolivia 22
46. Monaco 20
47. Morocco 19½
48. Nicaragua 17
49. Panama 16½
50. Lebanon 11
51. Cyprus 11
52. Hong Kong 10½

Lugano 1968:

A finals

1. USSR 39½
2. Yugoslavia 31
3. Bulgaria 30
4. USA 29½
5. West Germany 29
6. Hungary 27½
7. Argentina 26
8. Romania 26
9. Czechoslovakia 24½
10. East Germany 24½
11. Poland 23
12. Denmark 21
13. Canada 19
14. Philippines 13½

B finals

15. The Netherlands 33½
16. England 33
17. Austria 30½
18. Israel 30
19. Spain 28½
20. Cuba 27
21. Switzerland 27
22. Iceland 26
23. Finland 24½
24. Sweden 22½
25. Brazil 21½
26. Belgium 20½
27. Mongolia 20
28. Scotland 19½

C finals

29. Australia 38
30. Norway 36
31. Italy 31½
32. Venezuela 30
33. Turkey 29½
34. Greece 28½
35. Portugal 27½
36. South Africa 27½
37. Tunisia 26
38. Ireland 21
39. Luxembourg 20½
40. Puerto Rico 19½
41. Morocco 16
42. Monaco 12½

D finals

43. Singapore 32
44. France 30
45. Paraguay 27½
46. Mexico 23½
47. Dominican Rep. 23½
48. Hong Kong 22½
49. Costa Rica 14½
50. Lebanon 13½
51. Cyprus 13
52. Virgin Is. 11
53. Andorra 9

Siegen 1970:

A finals

1. USSR 27½
2. Hungary 26½
3. Yugoslavia 26
4. USA 24½
5. Czechoslovakia 23½
6. West Germany 22
7. Bulgaria 21½
8. Argentina 21½
9. East Germany 19
10. Romania 18½
11. Canada 17½
12. Spain 16

B finals

13. Israel 27
14. Poland 25
15. Australia 24½
16. Mongolia 23½
17. Sweden 23
18. The Netherlands 23
19. Denmark 22
20. Finland 21½
21. Cuba 20
22. Austria 19½
23. Colombia 18
24. Indonesia 17

C finals

25. England 30
26. Philippines 27½
27. Iceland 26
28. Brazil 25½
29. Norway 24
30. Italy 22½
31. Greece 20½
32. Iran 19
33. Belgium 18½
34. Scotland 18½
35. Tunisia 17½
36. Puerto Rico 14½

D finals

37. Switzerland 29½
38. Albania 28
39. Peru 27½
40. Singapore 26½
41. Portugal 24½
42. Ireland 23½
43. South Africa 22½
44. Mexico 21
45. Lebanon 17
46. Luxembourg 15½
47. Japan 15
48. Dominican Rep. 13½

E finals

49. New Zealand 36
50. Rhodesia 28
51. Turkey 28
52. Malta 27½
53. Hong Kong 26
54. Morocco 25
55. Faroe Is. 19
56. Andorra 18
57. Cyprus 16
58. Virgin Is. 15
59. Guernsey 13
60. Monaco 12½

Skopje 1972:

A finals

1. USSR 42
2. Hungary 40½
3. Yugoslavia 38
4. Czechoslovakia 35½
5. West Germany 35
6. Bulgaria 32
7. Romania 31½
8. The Netherlands 29
9. USA 29
10. East Germany 27½
11. Spain 26
12. Poland 24½
13. Denmark 23
14. Argentina 22½
15. Sweden 22½
16. Switzerland 21½

B finals

17. England 37
18. Israel 36½
19. Canada 33
20. Philippines 31½
21. Norway 30½
22. Cuba 30
23. Austria 30
24. Iceland 29
25. Colombia 27
26. Indonesia 25½
27. Italy 25
28. Mongolia 24½
29. Greece 21
30. Belgium 20½
31. Peru 19

Skopje Olympiad, 1972

C finals
32. Australia 45
33. Finland 42
34. Scotland 39
35. Iran 37½
36. Brazil 35½
37. Portugal 32½
38. Turkey 31
39. Ireland 28½
40. Puerto Rico 28½
41. Mexico 26½
42. Tunisia 26½
43. Wales 26½
44. New Zealand 25
45. Dominican Rep. 21½
46. Bolivia 19
47. Japan 15½

D finals
48. France 46½
49. Singapore 42½
50. Malta 32
51. Hong Kong 30½
52. Lebanon 30
53. Luxembourg 29½
54. Faroe Is. 29
55. Syria 28
56. Cyprus 27½
57. Morocco 26
58. Andorra 24
59. Malaysia 23
60. Guernsey 20½
61. Iraq 20½
62. Virgin Is. 10½

Nice 1974:

A finals
1. USSR 46
2. Yugoslavia 37½
3. USA 36½
4. Bulgaria 36½
5. The Netherlands 35½
6. Hungary 35
7. West Germany 32
8. Romania 29½
9. Czechoslovakia 29½
10. England 26
11. Philippines 25½
12. Spain 25½
13. Sweden 25
14. Argentina 23½
15. Finland 22
16. Wales 14½

B finals
17. Israel 40½
18. Austria 38½
19. Italy 38
20. Colombia 32½
21. Norway 32
22. Iceland 32
23. Poland 32
24. Canada 31
25. Cuba 31
26. Denmark 31
27. Switzerland 29
28. France 27
29. Scotland 25½
30. Belgium 23
31. Portugal 19½
32. Tunisia 17½

C finals
33. Australia 39
34. Iran 34½
35. Brazil 32½
36. Mongolia 31½
37. Ireland 30½
38. Chile 30
39. Indonesia 30
40. Greece 27½
41. Mexico 27½
42. Turkey 27
43. Singapore 25
44. Venezuela 24½
45. New Zealand 22½
46. Ecuador 22
47. Syria 16

(South Africa withdrew with a score of 24½ after the 12th round.)

D finals
48. Pakistan 49½
49. Puerto Rico 44½
50. Dominican Rep. 43½
51. Luxembourg 38½
52. Lebanon 35
53. Uruguay 35
54. Panama 33
55. Monaco 29½
56. Malta 29
57. Hong Kong 27½
58. Faroe Is. 27½
59. Malaysia 24½
60. Morocco 21½
61. Jordan 17½
62. Guernsey 12
63. US Virgin Is. 12

E finals
64. Rhodesia 28½
65. Iraq 24
66. Dutch Antilles 21
67. Japan 20
68. Cyprus 19
69. Trinidad 18
70. Algeria 17
71. Andorra 13
72. Bahamas 11
73. British Virgin Is. 8½

Haifa 1976:

For the first time in the history of the event the entire championship was held on the Swiss System. Also, for the first time since 1950, the USSR did not win the championship since, like the remainder of the Soviet bloc and also like the Arab states, it did not participate in the event.

The details of the Olympiad were:

1. USA 37
2. The Netherlands 36½
3. England 35½
4. Argentina 33
5. West Germany 31
6. Israel 29½
7. Switzerland 29
8. Canada 29
9. Spain 28½
10. Colombia 28
11. Norway 28
12. Sweden 28
13. Italy 28
14. Wales 28
15. Paraguay 28
16. Chile 28
17. Australia 28
18. Austria 28
19. Finland 27½
20. Philippines 27½
21. New Zealand 27½
22. Iceland 27
23. Venezuela 27
24. Belgium 27
25. Denmark 26½
26. France 26½
27. Dominican Rep. 26½
28. Uruguay 26½
29. Honduras 26
30. Thailand 26
31. Iran 26
32. Costa Rica 26
33. Scotland 25½
34. Guernsey 25½
35. Ireland 25
36. Luxembourg 25
37. Guatemala 25
38. Japan 25
39. Hong Kong 25
40. Bolivia 24½

41. Bermuda 24
42. Andorra 23
43. Monaco 22
44. Faroe Islands 21½
45. Papua New Guinea 18
46. US Virgin Is. 15½
47. British Virgin Is. 13½
48. Dutch Antilles 7½

(W.H.)

OLYMPIADS (Women's)

The Women's Olympiads were founded much later than the men's. This can be explained by the fact that before the war there were few countries, apart from England and Germany, with many women players and there was really no possibility of holding a team competition. When the event was finally inaugurated it was for teams of two and that format was retained, apart from the provision for a reserve from 1963, until 1976 when the number of boards, reflecting the enormous development in women's chess, was increased to three. There should have been an Olympiad in 1961, again at Emmen, but it was abandoned when one of the teams was prevented from playing – the East Germans were unable to obtain entry visas.

Individual Accomplishments

The best results on each board in each of the seven Olympiads follow. *1957:* 1. Holuj, 2. Zvorikina; *1963:* 1. Gaprindashvili, 2. Nedeljković, 3. Zvorikina; *1966:* 1. Gaprindashvili, 2. Polihroniade, 3. Zatulovskaya; *1969:* 1. Gaprindashvili, 2. Kushnir, 3. Alexandria; *1972:* 1. Gaprindashvili, 2. Kushnir, 3. Levitina; *1974:* 1. Gaprindashvili, 2. Veröci, 3. Levitina; *1976:* 1. Kushnir, 2, Shterenberg, 3. Maeda, 4. Nudelman.

Results of Olympiads 1–7

The Soviet Union has dominated throughout the history of the competition and has won the event every time it has sent a team. However, the USSR's victory in the 6th Olympiad was achieved in bizarre fashion for they were beaten into second place, on tie break, by Romania; so the Russians objected and their appeal was answered by the organizers' decision to hold a play-off match. The play-off match, to avoid any further accidents, was played as a double round affair.

In the 1976 Women's Olympiad held at Haifa, Israel in October and November, the Soviet bloc and the Arab countries failed to participate (as in the Men's). The championship went to Israel, 2nd was England and 3rd Spain.

Emmen 1957 (1st Olympiad)

A finals
1. USSR 10½
2. Romania 10½
3. East Germany 10
4. Hungary 8½
5. Bulgaria 8
6. Yugoslavia 7½
7. England 7
8. West Germany 6
9. Holland 4

B finals
10. USA 8
11. Czechoslovakia 8
12. Poland 7½
13. Denmark 4½
14. Ireland 1
15. Scotland 1

C finals
16. France 8½
17. Austria 7½
18. Finland 6
19. Norway 4½
20. Belgium 2½
21. Luxembourg 1

Split 1963 (2nd Olympiad)
1. USSR 25
2. Yugoslavia 24½
3. East Germany 21
4. Romania 18½
5. Bulgaria 17½
6. Hungary 17
7. Holland 15½
8. Poland 15
9. USA 12½
10. Mongolia 10½
11. West Germany 10½
12. Austria 8
13. Belgium 5
14. Monaco 5
15. Scotland 4½

Oberhausen 1966 (3rd Olympiad)
1. USSR 22
2. Romania 20½
3. East Germany 17
4. Yugoslavia 16½
5. Holland 16
6. Czechoslovakia 15
7. Hungary 15
8. Bulgaria 14
9. England 12
10. USA 9
11. Poland 9
12. West Germany 6½
13. Denmark 5
14. Austria 4

Lublin 1969 (4th Olympiad)
1. USSR 26
2. Hungary 20½
3. Czechoslovakia 19
4. Yugoslavia 18½
5. Bulgaria 17½
6. East Germany 17
7. Poland 16½
8. Romania 16½
9. Holland 13
10. England 12½
11. West Germany 10
12. Denmark 10
13. Austria 6
14. Belgium 4½
15. Ireland 2½

Skopje 1972 (5th Olympiad)

A finals
1. USSR 11½
2. Romania 8
3. Hungary 8
4. Bulgaria 7½
5. Czechoslovakia 7
6. West Germany 5½
7. East Germany 4½
8. England 4

B finals
9. Poland 10½
10. Yugoslavia 8½
11. Austria 7
12. Holland 7
13. Sweden 6½
14. Brazil 6
15. Mongolia 5½
16. Australia 5

C finals
17. Switzerland 9
18. Israel 8½
19. Singapore 6
20. Ireland 5½
21. Finland 5½
22. Scotland 4½
23. Japan 3

Medellin 1974 (6th Olympiad)

A finals
1. Romania 13½*
2. USSR 13½*
3. Bulgaria 13
4. Hungary 13
5. Holland 9½

*Play-off match: USSR 3 Romania 1

6. Czechoslovakia 9
7. Yugoslavia 7½
8. England 4
9. West Germany 4
10. Canada 3

B finals

11. Spain 13½
12. Israel 13½
13. Brazil 11
14. USA 10½
15. Sweden 9½
16. Austria 8½
17. Colombia 8
18. Finland 6
19. Japan 5
20. Ireland 4½

C finals

21. Mexico 7½
22. Puerto Rico 7
23. Iraq 5
24. Colombia B 5
25. Monaco 4
26. Panama 1½

Haifa 1976 (7th Olympiad)

A finals

1. Israel 17
2. England 11½
3. Spain 11½
4. USA 10½
5. The Netherlands 9½
6. West Germany 9
7. Australia 8½
8. Denmark 6½

B finals

1. Canada 13½
2. Italy 12
3. Argentina 11½
4. Ireland 10½
5. Finland 10
6. France 9½
7. Colombia 9½
8. Philippines 7½

C finals

1. Austria 12
2. Switzerland 12
3. Sweden 11½
4. Japan 11
5. Scotland 7½
6. Wales 6½
7. New Zealand 2½

(K.J.O'C. & H.G.)

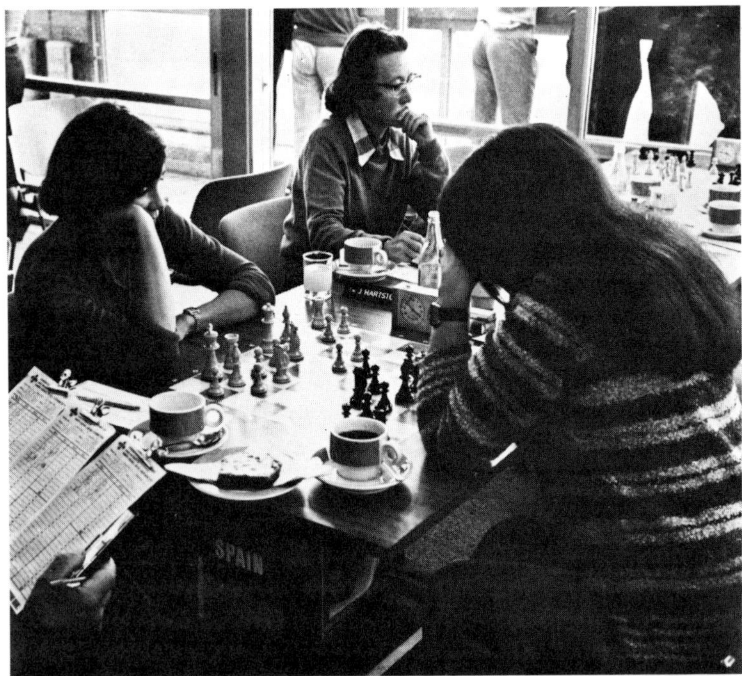

Women's Olympiad 1976, Haifa, Israel. Facing the camera, left: Jana Hartston, right: Elaine Pritchard

OPEN AIR CHESS

Baden-Baden, Germany

Trafalgar Square, England

OPEN FILE

An open file is a file unobstructed by a pawn so that a Rook placed on it controls the whole file except when temporarily obstructed by other pieces. The half-open file is one occupied by a hostile pawn, against which a Rook can operate. See also OUTPOST. *(W.H.)*

OPENINGS

The opening is the first phase of any game, commencing with the initial position and continuing until both sides have brought out their pieces and the middle-game is reached. Usually the first moves will follow the well-charted paths of opening theory, which has been systematically studied since the beginning of chess literature.

The openings are broadly classified into three categories: open games, commencing 1. P–K4, P–K4; semi-open games, commencing 1. P–K4, met by any other reply; and closed games, commencing with anything other than 1. P–K4.

Many authors further subdivide the third category into closed, to mean 1. P–Q4, P–Q4; and semi-closed, meaning 1. P–Q4, N–KB3; with the other first moves by White known as flank openings or wing games, but these distinctions are less well defined.

Until the early twentieth century, the vast majority of tournament games began 1. P–K4, P–K4; with the semi-open and closed openings only coming into favour after the First World War. By the mid-1930s 1. P–Q4 had become by far the most popular opening move, but another war saw the balance shift back until the present time when 1. P–K4 and 1. P–Q4 are about equally met in most tournaments. Followers of fashion will also have noticed a steady growth in popularity of the flank openings so that nowadays the moves 1. P–QB4, 1. N–KB3, 1. P–QN3, 1. P–KN3, etc., together form a group as popular as either of the two traditional opening moves.

The first few moves on each side, characterizing the development schemes to be followed, are named either after their originator, or more often after the player who first popularized them either in tournament play or in his writings. *(W.R.H.)*

OPOČENSKY, Karel *(7 February 1892–16 November 1975)*
Czechoslovak international master (1950) and International Judge from 1951. Winner of the Czechoslovak championship four times – 1927, 1928, 1938 and 1944. Shared first place in the Arbon 1946 international tournament. Opočensky's love of chess enabled him to continue playing strongly until over eighty years old. He also wrote regular articles in the Czech press until his death.

He was the chief judge during the 1951 and 1954 World Championship matches, and for the 1953 Candidates tournament and 1952 Olympiad. Opočensky made the best individual result in the 1933 Olympiad at Folkestone, scoring $11\frac{1}{2}$/13 on board 4 for Czechoslovakia. *(W.R.H.)*

ORIGIN OF CHESS
See under HISTORY OF CHESS.

ORNSTEIN, Axel Otto *(b. 24 April 1952)*
Swedish international master and chess journalist. Swedish junior champion in 1967, he was Swedish champion in 1972, 1973 and 1975 and has established himself as the second best Swedish player (to Ulf Andersson).

He won the Rilton Cup in Stockholm 1974/5 and achieved international master norms at the Nice Olympiad 1974, Trondheim 1974 and Eksjö 1975, requiring all three tournament results to obtain the international master title. He played in the World Students Olympiads of 1972 and 1974 and was in the Swedish Olympic team at Skopje 1972, Nice 1974 and Haifa 1976. He won first prize at Sofia 1976. *(H.G.)*

ORTEGA, Rogelio
Up to now the strongest negro chess-player and indeed a formidable player in the international field as he has shown in the Olympiads. Ortega represented Cuba in five Olympiads, Helsinki 1952, Varna 1962, Tel Aviv 1964, Havana 1966 (where he played on his highest board – two) and Lugano 1968.

Cuban champion in 1966 and first in the Olympic classification tournament of 1964, Ortega's best results belong to the early and middle 1960s. In 1963 he came =8th/14 with Estrada in the first Pan-American tournament at Havana and in 1965 he was 8/14 at the Rubinstein Memorial tournament at Polanica-Zdroj in Poland.

The following year he came =10th/20 with Letelier in the 2nd Pan-American tournament at Havana, but came bottom in the Chigorin Memorial tournament at Sochi in the USSR. *(H.G.)*

OSCAR
See under AIPE.

OSNOS, Vyacheslav Vulfovich *(b. 24 July 1935)*
Soviet master since 1957 and international master since 1965. Winner of Debrecen international tournament in 1969. Osnos was one of Korchnoi's seconds during the latter's match with Karpov in 1974. *(W.R.H.*

OSTEND INTERNATIONAL TOURNAMENTS
This historic series of tournaments started in 1905 with a double-round event comprising fourteen players almost all of whom were grandmasters and, with the exception of the World Champion, Em. Lasker, containing the world's best players. It proved a triumph for the Hungarian grandmaster Maróczy who was 1st $1\frac{1}{2}$ points ahead of Janowski and Tarrasch who tied for second place. The tournament was remarkable for the fact that no less than twelve brilliancy prizes were awarded, the first going to Janowski for his brilliant win over Tarrasch. Leading scores: Maróczy $19\frac{1}{2}$, Janowski, Tarrasch 18, Schlechter $15\frac{1}{2}$.

White: Janowski; *Black:* Tarrasch
Queen's Pawn Opening
1. P–Q4, P–Q4; 2. N–KB3, P–QB4; 3. P–B3, P–K3; 4. B–B4, Q–N3; 5. Q–N3, N–KB3; 6. P–K3, N–B3; 7. P–KR3, B–K2; 8. QN–Q2, B–Q2; 9. B–K2, O–O; 10. O–O, KR–B1; 11. N–K5, B–K1; 12. B–N3, N–Q2; 13. N(Q2)–B3, N–B1; 14. KR–Q1, N–R4; 15. Q–B2, P–B5; 16. N–Q2, P–B3; 17. N(K5)–B3, B–N3; 18. Q–B1, P–KR3; 19. N–R2, Q–Q1; 20. B–B3, P–N4; 21. P–K4, N–B3; 22. P×P, P×P; 23. R–K1, P–N5; 24. N(Q2)–B1, P×P; 25. P×P, Q–R4; 26. N–K3, B–B2; 27. Q–Q2, B–R6; 28. QR–N1, N–Q2; 29. R–N7, N–N3; 30. N–B5, Q–R3;

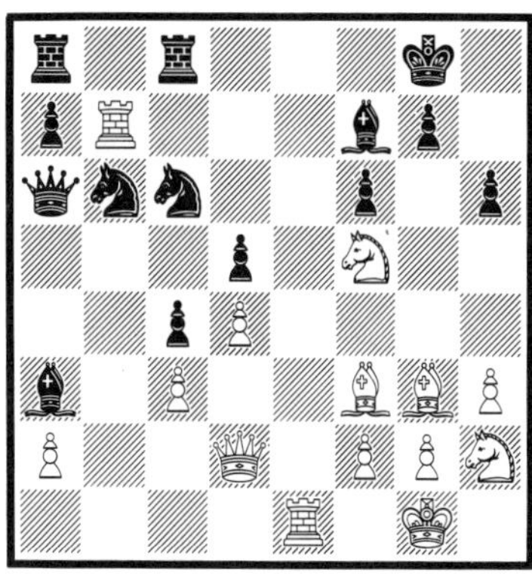

31. N×P+, P×N; 32. R×B, K×R; 33. Q×P, K–N1; 34. Q–N6+, K–R1; 35. Q×P+, K–N1; 36. Q–N6+, K–R1; 37. R–K5, resigns.

The following year, in 1906, another great tournament was held at Ostend. This time, however, a different and more complicated system was employed. The thirty-six players were divided into four groups. In the first round Group A played against Group B. There were two more rounds with a system of promotion and relegation and in the last round the top nine played against each other. Their final placings were: 1st Schlechter, 2nd Maróczy, 3rd Rubinstein, =4th Burn, Bernstein and Teichmann, 7th Marshall, 8th Janowski, 9th Perlis.

In 1907 the last of the really great Ostend tournaments was held. Six players, chosen somewhat arbitrarily, played in a four-round grandmaster tournament. Another tournament, called a Masters tournament, was held among 29 players, many of whom either were or became grandmasters. First prize in the grandmaster group went to Tarrasch who not only won a gold medal but also the title of world champion tournament player. Scores: Tarrasch 12½, Schlechter 12, Marshall, Janowski 11½, Burn 8, Chigorin 4½.

The top fifteen players in the Masters tournament received prizes. These were: =1st Bernstein and Rubinstein 19½, =3rd Mieses and Nimzowitsch 19, 5th Fleischmann 18½, 6th Teichmann 18, 7th Duras 17½, 8th Salwe 17, 9th Marco 16½, =10th John and Tartakower 16, =12th Cohn, Znosko-Borovsky and Spielmann and 15th Blackburne 14½.

Twenty-nine years passed and in 1936 another and much smaller tournament took place in Ostend. The Swedish master Lundin was first with 7½ ahead of Grob 6, Ståhlberg and Landau 5, Dyner and Rey 4½, Sir George Thomas and Soultanbeieff 4, Reilly 3½ and Domenech 1.

Another ten-player tournament was held in 1937 and there was a triple tie for first place between Fine, Grob and Keres 6 points, followed by Landau and List 5, Koltanowski 4½, Tartakower 4, Dyner 3½, Dunkelblum 3, and Reynolds 2.

In 1956 a smaller international tournament was held in the Casino and it contained both the grandmaster who had played with great success at the Ostend tournament fifty years earlier, Dr Bernstein, and also, in Grob, the player who had tied for first place in 1937. But neither, alas, finished in the top half of the table: 1st A. O'Kelly 6, 2nd J. H. Donner 5½, =3rd H. Golombek and Dr Lehmann 4½, 5th Bernstein 4, 6th J. Gobert 1½, =7th C. Doerner and H. Grob 1. *(H.G.)*

OSTOJIC, Predag *(b. 22 February 1938)*
A Yugoslav grandmaster. Received titles of international master in 1968 and grandmaster in 1975. He has competed many times in Yugoslav championship; co-champion in 1968 and winning outright in 1971. Best results: 1st San Juan 1971, =1st Vrnjačka Banja 1975 and 1st Sandefjord 1976. He has represented Yugoslavia in numerous international matches. *(R.D.K.)*

OUTPOST
A piece in an open (or half-open) file, in the opponent's half of the board, and protected by a pawn. It is a concept first dealt with by Nimzowitsch, in his book *My System*. The strategic purpose of the outpost is to enable the player to derive maximum benefit from the open file; to be effective it must therefore be able to spread alarm and despondency in the enemy camp so that its removal cannot be long delayed.

Thus, on a central file the outpost will most frequently, though not necessarily, be a Knight; on a file on the wing, a Knight would not usually cause enough trouble and a Rook would be a better outpost. An example given by Nimzowitsch:

1. N–N6?, would be of little effect, but 1. R–N6!, would either gain permanent control of the N-file or, after 1.., R × R; 2. BP × R (much stronger than Nimzowitsch's 2. RP × R), produce a protected passed pawn and open the strong square KB5 for the N. *(W.H.)*

OVERLOAD
A combination based on the fact that one, or several, of the defender's units are burdened with several defensive tasks and are thus unable to meet further attacks: they are overloaded with defensive functions. Cf. the following *sustained* overload sequence, in the course of which the Black Queen has (*a*) to guard the KR and (*b*) evade the attack on itself, while both Black Rooks in turn have to safeguard each other. From the diagram (Adams v. Torre) play went:

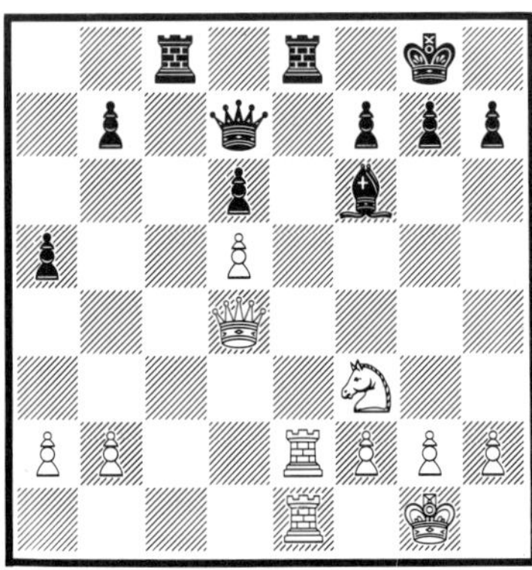

1. Q–KN4, Q–N4; 2. Q–QB4, Q–Q2; 3. Q–B7, Q–N4; 4. P–QR4, Q × RP; 5. R–K4, Q–N4; 6. Q × NP, resigns. *(W.H.)*

OVER-PROTECTION
A principle formulated by Nimzowitsch, over-protection is the training of as many units as possible on a strategically important square. According to Nimzowitsch, the contact between strong point and over-protectors should benefit both: the strong point because the prophylaxis thus employed provides the utmost security against all attacks; the over-protectors because the strong point becomes to them a constant source of energy from which they are able to draw new strength. *(W.H.)*

OWEN, Rev. John *(1 July 1827–24 November 1901)*
Probably the strongest of all the chess-playing reverends of the nineteenth century, Owen came 3rd at Birmingham 1858, below Löwenthal and Falkbeer, but ahead of Saint-Amant, Staunton and Bird; but it should be pointed out that the method of play was still by the old knock-out system.

He was also =3rd with MacDonnell in the first congress of the British Chess Association at London in 1862.

He also had the distinction of losing matches to Morphy, Zukertort and Burn, though he beat Burn in a later match. He drew a match with Kolisch in 1860. *(H.G.)*

OXFORD–CAMBRIDGE MATCHES
The idea of a regular match between the universities was first advocated in 1853 by Howard Staunton, but it was another twenty years before his suggestion came to fruition. In 1871 the Oxford University Chess Club challenged Cambridge to a match, but at that time the Cambridge club was only for dons, who refused the challenge from the Oxford undergraduates. The offer was, however, taken up by the 'Cambridge Staunton Chess Club', an undergraduate club which did not, however, represent the whole university. This match was played by correspondence and was won $4\frac{1}{2}$–$2\frac{1}{2}$ by Oxford. A return match the following year saw the result reversed with a 4–1 Cambridge win.

Oxford and Cambridge match, 1873

The first official over-the-board 'Varsity Match took place on 28 March 1873 at the City of London Chess Club; three games were planned on each of the seven boards if time allowed, but on most boards only two were played. This remained the practice until 1892 when the format of a straight seven-board single-round match was adopted. This format has remained ever since. The match has taken place annually except for the war years. The matches in 1940 (drawn), 1941 and 1942 (both won by Oxford) were unofficial fixtures and did not count in the 'Varsity Match series. Since 1953 the winning team has held a gold cup presented by Miss Margaret Pugh in that year. The only clean sweep was in 1919 when Cambridge won 7–0. The score in the official series after the 1976 match was: Oxford 36, Cambridge 42 with 18 matches drawn. *(W.R.H.)*

P

PACHMAN, Ludek *(b. 16 May 1918)*

Leading Czechoslovak player from the end of the war until the mid-1960s. Given the titles of international master in 1950 and grandmaster in 1954. Champion of Czechoslovakia seven times – 1946, 1953, 1957, 1959, 1961, 1963 and 1966. Has taken first prize in many international tournaments including Arbon 1946, Bucharest 1949, Arbon 1949, Mariánské Lázně 1951, Prague 1954, Dublin 1957, Mar del Plata 1957, Santiago 1957, Lima 1957, Sarajevo 1960, Mariánské Lázně 1960, Sarajevo 1961, Graz 1961, Athens 1968, and Reggio Emilia 1975/6.

After the Soviet occupation of Czechoslovakia in 1968, Pachman was arrested and imprisoned for his political activities. In 1973 he was given permission to leave the country, and subsequently settled in Solingen, West Germany. He has since represented that country in international events, though often not without incurring the displeasure of Eastern European federations.

Pachman is the author of a number of books, including *Modern Chess Theory*, Prague 1948, *Modern Chess Strategy*, Prague 1955, and *Modern Chess Tactics*, Prague 1962. All have been translated into English from the original Czech. He has also written a predominantly political work entitled *Czechmate in Prague*, London 1975. *(W.R.H.)*

PADEVSKY, Nicola Botchev *(b. 29 May 1933)*
Bulgarian champion in 1954, 1955, 1962 and 1964. Awarded titles of international master in 1957 and grandmaster in 1964. Shared first place in international tournaments at Varna 1960 and Varna 1975. By profession Padevsky is a lawyer. *(W.R.H.)*

PAKISTAN
The first, and so far only, appearance of this country in an Olympiad was in 1974 when the team placed 49th. That was not a spectacular performance, but their number two, Zahiruddin Farooqi, captured the prize for the best score on board two with a better percentage, admittedly against weaker opposition, than Korchnoi, Robert Byrne, etc.

The address of the Chess Federation of Pakistan is: 11 Rohilkhand Society, Haider Ali Road, off Shaheed-e-Millat Road, Karachi 5. *(K.J.O'C.)*

PANAMA
The Federacion Nacional de Panama (Apartado 8394, Zona 7, Panama) has sent a team to two Olympiads, finishing 49th in 1966 and 55th in 1974. *(K.J.O'C.)*

PANNO, Oscar Roberto *(b. 17 March 1935)*
Argentine grandmaster and civil engineer by profession. Though he was taught the game by his father at the age of six he did not start real play till the age of twelve. This was in the River Plate Football Club and he is now Professor of Chess in the same club.

He was champion of Buenos Aires at the age of seventeen and in the following year he became World Junior Champion, at Copenhagen 1953. In the same year he won the Argentine championship.

In 1954 he came 1st in the Mar del Plata South American Zonal tournament. In the following year he came third in the Göteborg Interzonal and so won the grandmaster title.

Once again he won the South American Zonal tournament – this time at Rio de Janeiro in 1957. He won the 1st Pan-American championship tournament at Bogota in 1958. At the Portorož Interzonal that year he was 8th.

Now he temporarily withdrew from chess in order to finish his studies, during the years 1958–62.

In 1966, along with Mecking and Julio Bolbochan, he qualified for the Interzonal at Sousse but his work prevented him from playing.

He once again qualified for the Interzonal in 1969 and duly played in that event at Palma de Mallorca in 1970, coming =11th with Mecking out of 24. In that year too he came =2nd with Stein in the strong international tournament at Caracas.

There followed some fine successes in Spain. In 1971 an =1st with Ljubojević at Palma de Mallorca; 1972 =1st with Korchnoi and Smejkal at Palma de Mallorca; 1973 =3rd at Las Palmas below Stein and Petrosian. In 1973, too, he played in the Interzonal at Petropolis in Brazil and finished =12th with Keres out of 18.

In 1975 he qualified for the Interzonal by coming =1st with Najdorf in the Argentine championship and in the Interzonal at Manila in 1976 he came =7th/20 with Balashov and Kavalek.

He has played for his country in eight Olympiads: 1954, 1956, 1958, 1962, 1966 (achieving the best score on second board at Havana), 1968, 1970 and 1976. In 1976 he won international tournaments in Santa Fé de Bogota and Quito.

He is a player with all the gifts of a true grandmaster but has been handicapped by the demands of his profession. *(H.G.)*

PANOV, Vasily Nikolayevich *(1 November 1906–1973)*
Soviet international master and theorist; Moscow champion in 1929. Panov was awarded the title of international master in 1950. His reputation was, however, chiefly formed by his theoretical and literary abilities. He contributed greatly to the theory of the Caro-Kann, where one important variation bears his name, and to the Ruy Lopez. With Estrin he was the co-author of *Kurs Debyutov*, Moscow 1957, an excellent handbook on the openings. Panov was also for many years the chess correspondent of *Izvestia*. *(W.R.H.)*

PAOLI, Enrico *(b. 13 January 1908)*
Italian international master and schoolteacher by profession.

He was Italian champion in 1951, 1957 and 1968 and played for Italy in the Olympiads of 1954, 1970, 1972 and 1976.

His best international result was 1st at Vienna 1950/51 as a result of which he obtained the title of international master. He was also first at Imperia 1959 and =1st at Reggio Emilia 1968/9 with Ciocâltea, Mista and Radulov.

An endgame study composer, Paoli has also written much on the game, his chief work being *Strategia e tattica sulla scacchiera*, Venice 1953 and 1967. *(H.G.)*

PAPUA NEW GUINEA
Joined FIDE in 1976 and placed 45th in that year's Olympiad when its team had the unique distinction of containing five different nationalities. The address of the Papua New Guinea Chess Federation is c/o N. Bluett, P.O. Box 1413, Lae. *(K.J.O'C.)*

PARAGUAY
One of the South American countries which took advantage of the 1939 Buenos Aires gathering to register their first appearance in an Olympiad. Since then they have competed, and fared, irregularly: 26th in 1939, 27th in 1964, 45th in 1968 and 15th in 1976.

Chess in Paraguay is organized by the Circulo Paraguayo de Ajedrez, Gral Diaz 775, Asunción. *(K.J.O'C.)*

PARIS 1867
After the first international tournament had been held at London in 1851, the French planned to hold a similar event, but it had to wait some sixteen years. It was a double-round tournament that was equipped with handsome prizes, among them a beautiful Majolica trophy presented by the Emperor Napoleon III.

The tournament was Kolisch's greatest success and shortly afterwards he abandoned chess professionalism for the more profitable pursuit of banker in Vienna. The Rousseau who finished next to bottom is the same Rousseau who was Morphy's childhood outstanding chess problemists of that age and of all time.

Leading scores: Von Kolisch 20, Winawer 19, Steinitz 18, Neumann 17, De Vere 14. *(H.G.)*

PARIS 1878
Another World Exhibition in Paris gave the chess enthusiasts a chance of holding a great international tournament there. The prizes this time were great and bigger than at any previous event.

The tie between Zukertort and Winawer was resolved by a match which was won by Zukertort by 3–1 without losing a game. Similarly Mackenzie and Bird played off for the fourth and fifth prizes, Mackenzie winning the first two games.

The World Champion, Steinitz, was present, but only as a journalist. This was Anderssen's last important tournament. He was already ill during the event and died a few months later. Leading scores: Zukertort, Winawer 16½, Blackburne 14½, Mackenzie, Bird 13. *(H.G.)*

PARIS 1900

In conjunction with the great Paris Exhibition a great international tournament was held there from 18 May–20 June 1900. The President of the Republic donated four precious Sèvres vases as additional prizes to the first four.

In order to prevent draws as far as possible, it was decided to hold the event on the model of London 1883 and New York 1889, by which the first draw did not count and players had to replay the game. Only if then it was drawn did the result count as half a point.

The World Champion, Emanuel Lasker, was in wonderful form and won the event, which included most of the world's best players excepting Tarrasch, by a large margin.

Leading scores: Lasker 14½, Pillsbury 12½, Maróczy, Marshall 12, Burn 11. *(H.G.)*

PARIS 1924

The 8th Olympiad (athletics, etc.) was held in Paris in 1924 and at the same time an Olympic tournament was held in which players from eighteen countries competed. It was limited to amateurs and the event was not a genuine team tournament, some countries sending only one player and the tournament itself being entirely an individual effort.

The fifty-four players were divided into nine preliminary groups and the nine winners of each section met each other in the final. This was won by the problemist and player, Mattison of Latvia, who thereby became the first amateur world champion.

Leading scores: Mattison 5½, Apscheneek 5, Colle 4½, Euwe, Vajda, Tschopurnoff 4. *(H.G.)*

PARMA, Bruno *(b. 30 December 1941)*

A Yugoslav grandmaster. His brilliant talent since his early teens won him the World Junior Championship in 1961 and an international master title. Two years later he was awarded the grandmaster title for his performance in the Wijk-aan-Zee tournament of the same year. A fine positional player in the mould of Petrosian, Parma's early promise came to nothing through lack of ambition. His later performances in tournaments have lacked incisiveness.

Best result: 1st with Tringov in Vrsac 1973 ahead of Uhlmann. Best result in Yugoslav championship: =3rd with Minić, Matulović and Kurajica, Čateske Toplice 1968. *(R.D.K.)*

PAULSEN, Louis *(15 January 1833–18 August 1891)*

A German master of the nineteenth century, Paulsen was one of the greatest players of all times, though his true stature was appreciated only since the advent of the hypermodern school with which his approach had much in common. Tournaments he won included Bristol 1861, Krefeld 1871, Leipzig 1877, Frankfurt 1878, while he was 2nd at New York 1857 (to Morphy), London 1862 (to Anderssen) and Leipzig 1879 (to Englisch).

In the two longest events in which he participated – the two Vienna congresses of 1873 and 1882 – he made fine plus scores (+14−9=4 and +13−10=11 respectively) and finished 6th and 8th. In matches he remained unbeaten, drawing with Anderssen in London 1862 and winning all the others: against Kolisch, Dr Lange, Neumann, Schwarz and two more matches against Anderssen.

Paulsen was an eminent theorist and analyst, whose researches benefited mostly the defence (against such gambits as the Evans and the Kieseritsky); his system in the Sicilian Defence is still pulsatingly alive today. He also favoured the Advance variation of the French Defence (anathema to Tarrasch) and experimented with pawn formations (such as an early P–K4 for Black in the Sicilian Defence) that have come to be accepted only in our time.

Being a deep strategist with a preference for the defence, he was not fully appreciated by his contemporaries and was always overshadowed by Morphy, Anderssen and Steinitz; his personal modesty and shyness helped to direct attention away from his achievements to the more radiant stars of his time. In later years one of his greatest admirers was Nimzowitsch, who recognized Paulsen as far ahead of his time. *(W.H.)*

PAULSEN, Wilfried *(31 July 1828–6 February 1901)*

A brother of Louis Paulsen, W. Paulsen was a strong German player whose successes, however, were confined to local events. In his rare international ventures (Wiesbaden 1880, Berlin 1881, Nuremberg 1883) he had mediocre results. His main importance lies in his analytical work with his brother. Paulsen was a scientific farmer and made a great name for himself in potato culture – a rather unusual achievement for a chess-master. *(W.H.)*

PAWN

In the 1,500 years of the game the pawn has never changed its basic move or its essential function. It was a foot-soldier, an infantryman in the original game of *chaturanga* and it has remained so. It moved and still moves one square up the board vertically. It captured and still captures by advancing one square diagonally. Then as now when it reached the eighth rank it had to be promoted to another piece. But instead of being transformed to any piece at the will of the player, it had to be promoted to a Minister (our modern Queen) and this was hardly a blessing in view of the limited range enjoyed by the Minister.

In Sanskrit it was called *padati* and the relation between this and the modern foot-soldier becomes more apparent when one compares the Sanskrit with the Latin for foot: *pes, pedis*.

In keeping with the slowness of *chaturanga*, it did not have its modern privilege of moving two squares on its initial move.

Its form and its move were exactly the same when the game passed to Persia and the pawn was called *piyadah*, this being derived from *pai* (Persian for 'foot'); and similarly upon the Arabs taking over the game it remained a foot-soldier, *baidaq*, the connection between the first syllable and the Persian for foot being obvious. When the Arab or Moslem game came to Europe there was at first no change or addition to the pawn's moves.

Then, with the Renaissance and the general speeding-up of the game, three things happened to render the pawn dynamic and to modernize the game by speeding it up. The first was the privilege of exchanging the pawn when it reached the eighth rank for any other piece of the same colour, with the exception of the King. Next came the vast increase in the powers of the Queen, which was reflected on the humble pawn as it could eventually be exchanged for the Queen when it got to the eighth rank. And finally there was the power of moving two squares at a time initially. This necessitated a further change in the pawn's move by which it could be captured *en passant*. (See LAWS OF CHESS, Article 6.) *(H.G.)*

PAWN CHAIN

This consists of a number of pawns of the same side placed diagonally across adjacent files and thus protected by each other, with each in turn blocked by a hostile pawn, these pawns again forming a pawn chain.

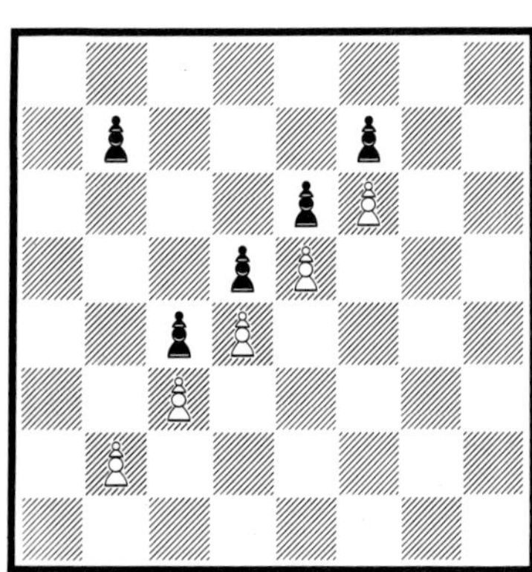

Thus, in the diagram, the White pawn chain extends from QB3 to KB6, the Black pawn chain from KB2 to QB5. The White pawn on QN2, while not technically belonging to the chain, lends valuable support to its base (QB3), whereas the base of the Black pawn chain is unprotected. *(W.H.)*

PAWN, PASSED

A pawn is said to be passed when its advance is in no way impeded by an enemy pawn; that is to say, when there is no enemy pawn opposing it on the same file or no enemy pawn in front of it on an adjacent file.

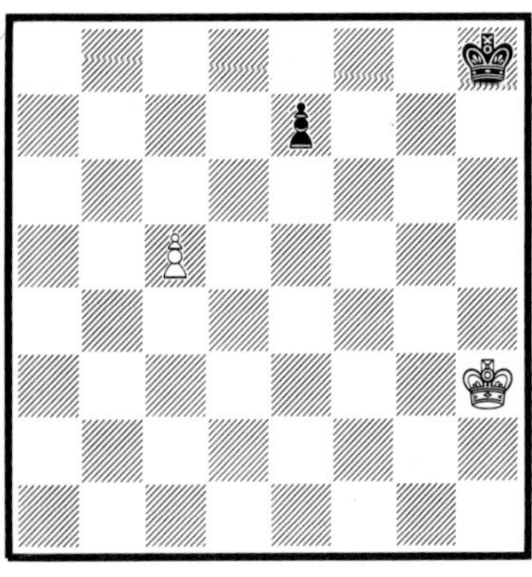

Thus in the diagrammed position both the White and the Black pawns are passed. Shift the Black pawn from K2 to Q2 or to QB2 or to QN2 and neither pawn is passed. *(H.G.)*

PEARL OF ZANDVOORT, The

Thus christened by enthusiastic Dutch chess writers, 'The Pearl of Zandvoort' was the 26th game of the 1935 World Championship match between Alekhine and Euwe. It gave the Dutch challenger a lead of two up with four to play. The game score is given under EUWE. *(W.H.)*

PEEV, Peicho Chanev *(b. 2 April 1940)*

Bulgarian international master (1973). Played for Bulgaria in the Olympiads of 1968 and 1972. His best result in the Bulgarian championship, which he has played in nine times, was =1st in 1967. Tournament victories include: Niš 1974, Trondheim 1974, Mladenovac 1975 and Primorsko 1976 (=1st). *(K.J.O'C.)*

PELIKAN, Jiri *(b. 23 April 1906)*

Argentine, formerly Czechoslovak international master who played for Czechoslovakia at the Olympiads of 1935, 1937 and 1939. With the outbreak of war in 1939 he decided to stay in the Argentine.

His best international results before the war were =8th/18 with Richter at Podebrady 1936 and =6th/14 with König at Novi Sad 1936.

At Mar del Plata 1942 he came =6th with Luckis out of 18. Further Mar del Plata results were: 1943 =6th/14 with Czerniak and Guimard; 1944 =7th/16 with Rossetto; 1945 10th/16; 1956 9th/17; 1958 16th/16; 1961 =10th/16 with Perez; 1966 =9th/16 with Emma, Pilnik and Schweber. *(H.G.)*

PENROSE, Dr Jonathan, O.B.E. *(b. 7 October 1933)*

British international master and ten times British champion, Penrose was born at Colchester and came from a chess-playing family. His father and mother both played chess and his father, Professor L. S. Penrose, in addition to being a geneticist of world-wide fame, was a strong chess-player and a good endgame composer. Jonathan's elder brother, Oliver, was also a fine player.

Jonathan learnt chess at the age of four, won the British Boys championship at thirteen and by the time he was fifteen was playing in the British championship at Felixstowe in 1949.

A little reluctant to participate in international tournaments abroad, he did best in the British championship which he won a record number of times, once more than H. E. Atkins. He won the title consecutively from 1958 to 1963 and again from 1966 to 1969.

He also played with great effect in nine Olympiads. Playing on a high board for practically all the time, he showed himself the equal of the best of grandmasters and indeed, at the Leipzig Olympiad, he distinguished himself by beating Mikhail Tal, thereby becoming the first British player to defeat a reigning World Champion since Blackburne beat Lasker in 1899.

A deep strategist who could also hold his own tactically, he suffered from the defect of insufficient physical stamina and it was this that was to bring about a decline in his play and his results. He collapsed during a game at the Ilford Chess Congress, and a year later, at the Siegen Olympiad of 1970, he had a more serious collapse that necessitated his withdrawal from the event after the

Jonathan Penrose in play against A. R. B. Thomas, Hastings 1950/1

preliminary groups had been played. The doctors found nothing vitally wrong with him but it was apparent that a long hard tournament made demands on him that his physique could not sustain. He continued to play but his results suffered from a lack of self-confidence and at the Nice Olympiad of 1974 he had a wretched result on board 3, winning only 1 game and losing 6 out of 15. Possibly too his profession (a lecturer in psychology) was also absorbing him more and more and he took part less and less in international and national chess.

Yet he had already done enough to show that he was the equal of the greatest British players in his command and understanding of the game and he ranks alongside Staunton, Blackburne, Atkins and C. H. O'D. Alexander as a chess figure of world class. *(H.G.)*

PEREZ, Francisco José *(b. 8 September 1920)*
International master. Spanish champion in 1946, 1948, 1954, 1960. Played for Spain in Olympiads 1958, 1960. Later moved to Cuba and played for Cuba in the 1964 Olympiad. Best tournament result =1st Madrid 1959. *(R.D.K.)*

PERLIS, Julius *(19 January 1880–11 September 1913)*
A strong Viennese player of Polish origin who made his mark in international events without quite reaching the top. His best results were =7th in Vienna 1907, =7th in Vienna 1908, 7th in St Petersburg 1909, and 5th in San Sebastian 1911; in addition Perlis scored fine results in the early Trebitsch tournaments in Vienna.

He died prematurely of exposure in a mountaineering accident in the Alps. *(W.H.)*

PERPETUAL CHECK
A checking sequence of moves by one side from which the other cannot escape, perpetual check is a drawing mechanism resorted to by the materially or positionally weaker side to stop the opponent from exploiting his superiority. Bronstein–Dely, Szömbathely 1966:

White threatens against N–N5, which 1.., N–Q5; 2. Q–N7, Q–N7+; 3. N–B2!, Q×N+; 4. K–N1, N–B3; 5. Q×R+ is obviously not adequate reply so. Black plays 1.., P–B5! and if now 2. KR–K1, Q–K6+; 2. K–B1, B×P! with mate to follow.

Therefore White has to allow perpetual check by 2. K×N, Q–K6+; 3. K–Q1, Q–Q6+; 4. K–K1, Q–K6+ etc. *(W.H.)*

PERU
Peru's top players include three international masters: Esteban Canal, Oscar Quiñones and Orestes Rodriguez, although Canal has been resident in Italy for many years.

A Peruvian team has attended five Olympiads and placed 24th in 1939, 14th in 1950, 19th in 1964, 39th in 1970 and 31st in 1972.

The address of the organizing body is: Federacion Peruana de Ajedrez, Estadia Nacional 20A, P.O. Box 691, Lima 1. *(K.J.O'C.)*

PETROFF, Alexander Dmitrievich
(12 February 1794–22 April 1867)
Leading player in Russia at the beginning of the period when chess was first seriously studied in that country. Petroff adopted and recommended a studious approach to chess theory and wrote the first Russian manual on the game: *The Game of Chess* [in Russian], St Petersburg 1824. Petroff challenged some of the views of Philidor and strongly influenced the development of chess opening theory in the nineteenth century. Along with Jaenisch, he introduced and investigated the opening known as Petroff's Defence.

Although best remembered now as a writer and theorist, Petroff also scored some notable successes in play, though chess tournaments were far less frequent in his day. He won matches against Jaenisch, S. Urusov and Shumov, and was recognized as the strongest player in Leningrad from the time he was aged fifteen. Among his other writings are the first Russian manual on the game of draughts and a popular book of reminiscences called *Scenes from the Life of Chess Players* [in Russian], St Petersburg 1844.

Renowned as a teacher of chess and great thinker on the problems of practical play. It is a pity that relatively few of his games survive (though also some of his compositions are still known). One of his best-known games is the following, played in Warsaw 1844:

White: Hofmann; *Black:* Petroff
Giuoco Piano
1. P–K4, P–K4; 2. N–KB3, N–QB3; 3. B–B4, B–B4; 4. P–B3, N–B3; 5. P–Q4, P×P; 6. P–K5, N–K5; 7. B–Q5, N×KBP; 8. K×N, P×P+; 9. K–N3, P×P; 10. B×P, N–K2; 11. N–N5,

N × B; 12. N × BP, O–O!; 13. N × Q, B–B7+; 14. K–R3, P–Q3+; 15. P–K6, N–B5+; 16. K–N4, N × KP; 17. N × N, B × N+; 18. K–N5, R–B4+; 19. K–N4, P-R4+; 20. K–R3, R–B6 mate. *(W.R.H.)*

PETROFF'S DEFENCE

Known also as the Russian Defence, and owing more for its existence to Jaenisch than Petroff, this counter-attacking system characterized by the moves 1. P–K4, P–K4; 2. N–KB3, N–KB3 does tend, as do many other symmetrical openings, to leave White with a slight initiative. The main line goes 3. N × P, P–Q3; 4. N–KB3, N × P; 5. P–Q4, though also highly regarded is Steinitz's 3. P–Q4.

No longer feared as an attacking system, the Petroff is mainly used now as a drawing weapon. *(W.R.H.)*

PETROSIAN, Tigran Vartanovich *(b. 17 June 1929)*

World Champion 1963–9. Born to Armenian parents in Tbilisi, the capital of Soviet Georgia, Petrosian's formative years were dogged by personal misfortune. Both his parents died during the war against Germany and at one time the young Petrosian was forced to work as caretaker in an officers' club to maintain what was left of his family. His main consolation was chess, and although his progress in this field was comparatively rapid it was achieved by stages and exhibited no prodigious or meteoric quality. At this early stage in Petrosian's development his most influential chess mentor was A. S. Ebralidze, who instilled in him a deep and lasting regard for the play and principles of Capablanca and Nimzowitsch.

In later years Petrosian was, in fact, to raise the Nimzowitschian theory of prophylaxis to an almost fanatical level, developing from this his own highly individualistic, pragmatic and flexible style with a penchant for deep strategic manoeuvres which often baffled his opponents.

Tigran Petrosian at the 19th USSR Championship, 1951

In 1946 Petrosian won the Armenian championship and over the next four years competed regularly in the preliminaries of the USSR championship. His next important success came in 1951 when he won the Moscow title and shared second place in the USSR championship itself. This marked him out as a player of unusual ability and also qualified him for the World title cycle.

In 1953 Petrosian competed in his first Candidates event, taking an honourable fifth prize at Zürich; yet three years later in Amsterdam his share of third to seventh places in his second appearance at this level was no real improvement. Throughout the mid 1950s Petrosian's results seemed to reach a standstill and he showed few signs of fulfilling the promise of 1951. At a loss to equate Petrosian's undoubtedly great talents with his consistent yet colourless play which involved many short draws, critics began to level accusations of lack of fighting spirit against him. However, an upward curve in his results gradually became discernible, commencing with his victory in the 26th USSR championship 1959 and third place, this time undivided, in the 1959 Candidates (1st Tal, 2nd Keres). Petrosian's great opportunity finally came when he took 1st place in the 1962 Candidates at Curaçao, scoring +8−0=19, a ½-point ahead of Keres and Geller. This important victory gave him the right to challenge Botvinnik for the World Championship.

Petrosian's victory over Botvinnik in the 1963 World title match, achieved by the score of +5−2=15, was convincing rather than spectacular, and the overriding impression was that Botvinnik succumbed not by any innate inferiority in his play but as a result of the age difference (Petrosian was only thirty-four while the Champion was eighteen years his senior). In many games Petrosian hovered perilously on the brink of defeat and only Botvinnik's fatigue combined with his own eel-like defensive ability contrived to salvage the ½-points. Nevertheless, Petrosian did win one memorable game, the 5th, which demonstrated that the application of pure technique in a simplified position can create a deeply aesthetic effect.

Petrosian's first defence of his title came in 1966. Scoring +4−3=17 against Spassky, Petrosian became the first World Champion to win a title match outright since Alekhine's defeat of Bogoljubow in 1934. Petrosian finally lost his title after a renewed challenge from Spassky in 1969. Maintaining an equal score up to game 17 of the contest, Petrosian collapsed in the final phase of the match, going down by +4−6=13.

During his six year period as World Champion Petrosian's results in important tournaments had been mediocre; yet, with the burden of the title cast off, Petrosian no longer felt the depressing obligation to prove himself *primus inter pares* and his results outside the World Championship cycle began to show a gradual improvement. At home Petrosian shared first place with Polugayevsky in the 37th USSR championship 1969, winning the play-off +2−0=3; and he took the title outright in the 43rd in 1975. In Candidates series Petrosian reached the final in 1971 (losing to Fischer +1−5=3), and the semi-final in 1974, going out to Korchnoi by +1−3=1; while in international events he shared first place at San Antonio 1972, Las Palmas 1973, I.B.M. Amsterdam 1973 and was outright 1st at Lone Pine 1976.

Mention should also be made of Petrosian's remarkable lifetime Olympic performance. He represented the USSR in 1958 (2nd Reserve), 1960 (2nd Reserve), 1962 (Board 2), 1964 (Board 1), 1966 (Board 1), 1968 (Board 1), 1970 (Board 2), 1972 (Board 1), and 1974 (Board 4) – losing one game (to Hübner at Skopje 1972) in all from these nine Olympiads!

In spite of his outstanding record Petrosian has continually had an unimpressive public image. He has performed with remarkable consistency in seven Candidates events, held down the World title for six years and won the USSR championship on no less than four occasions, so what can be the explanation of this apparent paradox? Possibly the answer is to be sought in his leaning towards a negative, defensive style over the board, aimed more at avoiding loss rather than at playing come what may for victory. Indeed, in his best years Petrosian achieved a reputation for almost total invincibility, not a trait to automatically endear a player to his public. In addition to stylistic factors Petrosian exhibited a distressing lack of ambition during his tenure of the World title, being content to aim for high prizes in tournaments rather than go all-out for first place.

With Petrosian, undoubtedly one of the greatest players of all time, one yet harbours the suspicion that his talent would have been capable of still further development had it been supported by greater determination to succeed and ambition to exploit his untapped reservoirs of power.

Publications: although Petrosian is editor of the weekly magazine *64*, devoted to chess and 10 × 10 draughts, he has made little literary impact in the West. A promised collection of games from his own hand has so far failed to appear.

Petrosian's extra-journalistic literary endeavours have hitherto been restricted to a little-known doctoral thesis, *Chess Logic, Some Problems of Logic of Chess Thought* (Erevan 1968), which gained for Petrosian a Master of Philosophical Science.

5th Game, World Championship match 1963
White: Petrosian; *Black:* Botvinnik
Grünfeld Defence
1. P–QB4, P–KN3; 2. P–Q4, N–KB3; 3. N–QB3, P–Q4; 4. N–B3, B–N2; 5. P–K3, O–O; 6. B–K2, P×P; 7. B×P, P–B4; 8. P–Q5, P–K3; 9. P×P, Q×Q+; 10. K×Q, B×P; 11. B×B, P×B; 12. K–K2, N–B3; 13. R–Q1, QR–Q1; 14. R×R, R×R; 15. N–KN5, R–K1; 16. KN–K4, N×N; 17. N×N, P–N3; 18. R–N1, N–N5; 19. B–Q2, N–Q4; 20. P–QR4, R–QB1; 21. P–QN3, B–B1; 22. R–QB1, B–K2; 23. P–QN4, P–B5; 24. P–N5, K–B2; 25. B–B3, B–R6; 26. R–B2, N×B+; 27. R×N, B–N5; 28. R–B2, K–K2; 29. N–Q2, P–B6; 30. N–K4, B–R4; 31. K–Q3, R–Q1+; 32. K–B4, R–Q8; 33. N×P, R–KR8; 34. N–K4, R×P; 35. K–Q4, K–Q2; 36. P–N3, B–N5; 37. K–K5, R–R4+; 38. K–B6, B–K2+; 39. K–N7, P–K4; 40. R–B6, R–R8; 41. K–B7, R–R8; 42. R–K6, B–Q1; 43. R–Q6+, K–B1; 44. K–K8, B–B2; 45. R–QB6, R–Q8; 46. N–N5, R–Q1+; 47. K–B7, R–Q2+; 48. K–N8, resigns. *(R.D.K.)*

PETROV, Vladimir *(27 September 1907–15 March 1945)*
Latvian grandmaster and their strongest player in the years preceding the outbreak of the Second World War. Champion of Riga in 1926, 1932 and 1936, joint first in the Latvian championship of 1934 and first alone in 1935 and 1937. His best result was undoubtedly sharing first place with Flohr and Reshevsky at Kemeri 1937, ahead of Alekhine, Keres and other leading players.

Died during the Second World War in a prison camp. *(W.R.H.)*

PFEIFFER, Gerhardt *(b. 14 June 1923)*
German international master who never won any but local events but had many fine placings in international events to his credit. A member of the West German Olympic team between 1950 and 1960, he was at his peak around 1950, when he came =3rd at Travemünde 1950, =5th at Bled 1950, 4th at Dortmund 1951, =4th at Travemünde 1951, and finished 2nd to Teschner in the German championship 1951. *(W.H.)*

PFLEGER, Helmut *(b. 6 August 1943)*

Helmut Pfleger (left) during a practise game with Wolfgang Uhlmann, Hastings 1965/6

A West German grandmaster, who won the championship of his country in 1965 (jointly with Unzicker). He has often represented West Germany in the Olympic and other team tournaments, winning the Olympic medal for the best score on board 4 in Tel Aviv 1964. In international tournaments he came =1st at Polanica Zdroj 1971, 1st at Lourenço Marques 1973, =1st at Montilla-Moriles 1973 (where he obtained his first grandmaster norm, repeating the performance at the Nice Olympiad 1974), =2nd at Montilla-Moriles 1974 and Manila 1974 =8th. By profession he is a doctor of medicine. *(W.H.)*

PHALANX
An array of two or more pawns on adjacent files placed on the same rank. Thus, in the initial position all eight pawns on both sides are in a phalanx. *(W.H.)*

PHILIDOR, François-André Danican
(7 September 1726–31 August 1795)

The greatest chess-player amongst musicians and the greatest composer amongst chess-players, Philidor was undoubtedly the leading player in the eighteenth century. For nearly fifty years he was what we would now call World Champion and for many of these years he was the leading operatic composer in France.

He came from a long line of court musicians. The family name was Danican; but Louis XIII, much taken with the playing of a Danican who was a hautboy player, called him Philidor after an Italian wood-wind player named Filidori who had preceded Danican in that section of the Versailles orchestra.

Our Philidor was born in 1726 near Paris and was remarkably precocious, both in music and chess. By the age of eleven he had had a motet performed at the Chapel Royal in Versailles and he was already a fine chess-player in his early teens. The best player in France, M. de Kermur, Sire de Légal, took an interest in the boy. At first it seems he gave him the odds of a Rook, then, after three more years, had to play him level and finally he was beaten by his erstwhile pupil in a match in 1750.

But already for some years he had been considered the best player in France. It is interesting to observe that he never regarded himself as a professional chess-player but solely as a musician who supplemented his income from composing by playing chess and giving blindfold displays.

For he had discovered that he had a gift for playing blindfold and in 1744, before an awe-struck public, he played two games simultaneously and blindfold. Any master could do this nowadays and more; but Philidor was the first to perform the feat in Europe.

In 1745 he visited the Netherlands and there made an important contact with some officers of the British army, at that time engaged in military action. This was a fortunate happening for him, since he had come with a musical company that soon became penniless and Philidor's plight was relieved by the chess-playing officers of the British army who also gave him some introductions to chess enthusiasts in England.

In 1747 he utilized these introductions on a visit to England where he demonstrated how much greater a player he was than any of his contemporaries by beating Philip Stamma in a match at odds in London by 8–1. This was an astonishing feat since Philidor gave Stamma the odds of the move and the formidable advantage that any drawn game should count as a win for Stamma.

He returned to the Continent and there wrote and published in 1749 in Paris the celebrated *Analyse du jeu des Echecs*. The theme of the work – that 'pawns are the soul of chess' – was so modern as to be about two hundred years before its time. It was rather as though Nimzowitsch and his theories of the twentieth century were contemporary with Philidor: he was not really understood until a couple of centuries had passed.

But what he wrote on the endgame and his general advice was obviously sound and marked a step forward in the way of scientific analysis.

After further visits abroad, during one of which he enchanted Frederick the Great by his blindfold exhibitions, he returned to his musical career. This he did with such success that for the next twenty years he was regarded as France's leading operatic composer, a position he eventually lost to a considerably greater composer, Grétry.

By the early 1770s, when it was clear his popularity as a composer had passed, he was again employed in playing chess and giving blindfold displays. He now made yearly visits to England and in particular to London which had become one of the most important centres of chess in Europe. An arrangement was made by which he taught chess at the London Chess Club and spent the spring in London.

Whilst he was in England the French Revolution broke out and he was put on the proscribed list of emigrés. This was a terrible blow for Philidor, since it separated him from his family and most of his friends. These made repeated efforts to get him removed from the proscribed list but to no avail. He died in London in 1795 and, by an ironic turn of fate, three days later his name was indeed removed from the list of emigrés who were not allowed to return.

He was buried in St James's, Piccadilly, and nearly 140 years later when it was observed that his grave and the inscription on it were in a state of disrepair some London chess enthusiasts restored it.

Since, for most of his life, Philidor had no equal in the chess-world, he gave odds practically all the time when he played and as a result few games on level terms have come down to us.

Some of the games from his simultaneous blindfold displays have been preserved and here is one from a display given in London on 22 March 1794 in which he was playing three games simultaneously and blindfold.

White: Atwood; *Black:* Philidor
Sicilian Defence
1. P–K4, P–QB4; 2. P–KB4, P–K3; 3. N–KB3, N–QB3; 4. P–B3, P–Q4; 5. P–K5, P–B4; 6. P–Q4, N–R3; 7. P–QR3, N–B2; 8. B–K3, Q–N3; 9. Q–Q2, B–Q2; 10. Q–KB2, P–B5; 11. B×P, P×B; 12. P–Q5, Q–B2; 13. P×N, B×BP; 14. B×P, B×N; 15. P×B, P–KN4; 16. B–K3, P×P; 17. B×P, N×P; 18. B×N, Q×B+; 19. Q–K2, Q×Q+; 20. K×Q, P–R4; 21. N–Q2, R–B1; 22. KR–KN1, K–B2; 23. R–N2, B–K2; 24. QR–KN1, B–B3; 25. N–B1, P–K4; 26. N–K3, K–K3; 27. R–Q1, KR–N1; 28. R×R, R×R; 29. N×QBP, R–N7+; 30. K–Q3, R×RP; 31. R–Q2, R–R6; 32. K–K2, P–N4; 33. N–K3, R–R7+; 34. K–K1, R×R; 35. K×R, B–N4; 36. K–K2, B×N; 37. K×B, P–R5; 38. K–B2, P–K5; 39. K–N2, P–K6 and Philidor wins as he must queen one of the pawns. *(H.G.)*

PHILIDOR'S DEFENCE

After 1. P–K4, P–K4; 2. N–KB3, Philidor disapproved of 2.., N–QB3 since it restricts the advance of the QBP, and instead recommended 2.., P–Q3. His original intention was to answer 3. P–Q4 with .., P–KB4; but nowadays the usual continuation is 3. P–Q4, N–KB3; 4. N–B3, QN–Q2; 5. B–QB4, B–K2; 6. O–O, O–O with a passive but defenceless position for Black. Also possible at move three are 3.., N–Q2 (the Hanham variation) or 3.., P×P. In general the opening is considered a little eccentric and too passive for modern tournament play, though recent attempts have been made, notably by Larsen, to increase its popularity. *(W.R.H.)*

PHILIDOR'S LEGACY

A form of the smothered mate brought about by a double check of Queen and Knight followed by the sacrifice of the Queen to block the enemy King's last flight square. It has decided innumerable games, such as W. Ritson Morry. v. B. H. Wood, Birmingham 1950:

After 1. K–K1, Black played 1.., Q–R5 so as to answer 2. K×R with Q×P+, but after 2. Q–N3+ Black resigned because of 2.., K–R1; 3. N–B7+, K–N1; 4. N–R6+, K–R1; 5. Q–N8+, R×Q; 6. N–B7 mate. *(W.H.)*

PHILIPPINES

This is the most active chess-playing nation in Asia. A Filipino first created a sensation when, in 1958, a representative of the Philippine Chess Federation, the chess-master Cardoso, defeated Bronstein in the last round of the Interzonal at Portorož, thereby depriving him of a place in the Candidates.

Ten years later the Philippines team made its initial mark at Olympic level by qualifying for the top final section at Lugano 1968, ahead of England and Israel.

Since President Marcos is a keen chess-player, the game now receives massive state and commercial aid in the Philippines. Every year gigantic national elimination tournaments are held with entrants numbering in thousands and this national activity is matched by large international projects.

Since 1973 Manila has been the annual setting for a great inter national tournament, with the following leading results:

1973: 1st Larsen, 2nd Ljubojević, 3rd Kavalek, 4th Gligorić.

1974: 1st Vasukov, 2nd Petrosian, 3rd Larsen.

1975: 1st Ljubojević, =2nd Larsen, Mecking, Pfleger and Polugayevsky.

1976 (the Interzonal): 1st Mecking, =2nd Hort and Polugayevsky.

Manila was also to have been the venue for the abortive Fischer–Karpov match for the World title in 1975, for which the Philippines had offered the colossal prize fund of five million dollars.

The Philippines possess the first Asian grandmaster in Eugenio Torre, and he was joined by Balinas, who attained the title in 1976. They also have two international masters, Cardoso and Naranja.

Under the guidance of the chess organizer Campomanes, the Philippines have done much to encourage chess in Asia. In 1975 they sent a team to China to play international matches for the first time in Chinese history. Six matches were played: two in Peking, two in Shanghai and two in Hangchow. Five out of the six were won by the visitors, but only after stout resistance and in the sixth at Shanghai, a Chinese master, Chih Ching-hsuang, defeated Torre.

The Philippines are placed in Zone 10 of FIDE (the East Asian and Australasian Zone) and its delegate to FIDE is Florencio Campomanes, who is also a deputy President of FIDE.

The address of the Philippines Chess Federation is: c/o M. Lara, P.O. Box 319, Green Hills, Rizal D-738. *(R.D.K.)*

PHILOSOPHY, Chess in

See under MODERN PHILOSOPHY.

PIATIGORSKY CUP 1963

This was the first of two double-round grandmaster tournaments sponsored in the mid 1960s by the Piatigorsky Foundation, led by Jacqueline Piatigorsky, a high-ranking American woman player and widow of 'cellist Gregor Piatigorsky. The event was the strongest US tournament since New York 1927.

It was held in the Los Angeles Ambassador Hotel in July and was won by Keres and Petrosian with a score of $8\frac{1}{2}/14$. Keres won the most games in the event (six) but was denied clear first prize by two losses to Reshevsky. This was Petrosian's first tournament since winning the World Championship from Spassky and was one of two international first prizes he shared during his six-year tenure as Champion. The two Soviet players received more than half of the $10,000 prize fund plus a trophy cup.

As well as the two Russians the entries included two Americans, Reshevsky and Benko, two Argentinians, Panno and Najdorf, and two Europeans, Gligorić and Olafsson. For unclear reasons, Fischer refused an invitation.

Gligorić led through the early rounds with 4½/7 in the tournament's first half. But the Yugoslav could only score three draws in the second half, and came fifth behind Najdorf and Olafsson. Petrosian, the first reigning World Champion to compete in an American tournament since Alekhine at Pasadena 1932, put on the best finishing burst with five points in seven rounds. A tournament book, edited by Kashdan and annotated mainly by Reshevsky, appeared in 1965. Scores: Keres, Petrosian 8½, Najdorf, Olafsson 7½, Reshevsky 7, Gligorić 6, Benko, Panno 5½. *(A.S.)*

PIATIGORSKY CUP 1966

The second tournament in a series begun by Piatigorsky Cup 1963. The prize fund was now doubled to $20,000 and the number of players increased from eight to ten.

The tournament, held July–August at the Miramar Hotel, Santa Monica, California, was highlighted by the participation of Spassky and Petrosian, who had met in the World Championship match two months earlier, and of Fischer. The appearance of the two Soviet players seemed to be endangered by Russian-American tension over Vietnam. However, the Soviet Chess Federation announced shortly after the World Championship match that the invitations would be accepted.

After losing to Portisch in the third round and to Larsen by way of a Queen sacrifice in the seventh, Petrosian was never in contention for a top prize. He finished sixth. Spassky took an early lead with victories over Unzicker, Ivkov and Fischer.

The American lost three games in a row during the second week of play and stood next to last at the tournament's midway point. However, Fischer fought back with four straight wins and was level with Spassky after the penultimate round. On the final day Spassky crushed Donner while Fischer was fortunate to draw with Petrosian. Larsen, who defeated Petrosian in both their games, finished third; Portisch and Unzicker, who shared fourth and fifth prizes, were the only other plus scores. A tournament book with notes by most of the players appeared in 1968. Leading scores: Spassky 11½, Fischer 11, Larsen 10, Portisch, Unzicker 9½. *(A.S.)*

PIETZSCH, Wolfgang *(b. 21 December 1930)*

East German grandmaster who won the championship of his country in 1949, 1959, 1962 and 1967. In the Olympiads he represented East Germany on six occasions between Helsinki 1952 and Lugano 1968. Pietzsch has played in a number of important international tournaments with fair success, finishing =8th in the Zonal tournament at Madrid 1960; =7th at Havana 1962; =4th at Tbilisi 1965; =5th at Sarajevo 1966. *(W.H.)*

PILLSBURY, Harry Nelson *(5 December 1872–17 June 1906)*

Pillsbury won a single clear first place in his international career, but it was at perhaps the strongest event held up to his time: Hastings 1895. He learned the moves at the age of sixteen and

played for only another sixteen years after that. Yet for five peak years, 1895–1900, he was considered the equal of anyone, including Lasker, with whom however a World Championship match was never arranged. His treatment of the Queen's Gambit Declined and the Ruy Lopez greatly helped to popularize those openings. And following his premature death in 1906 after a long illness, Lasker said he was 'a pathfinder in the thicket of chess theory . . . a source of pleasure and joy and a teacher of thousands'.

Pillsbury was born in Somerville, Massachusetts and progressed quickly at the nearby Boston clubs. Before Hastings, Pillsbury earned a living through a series of chess-related jobs such as reporting the first Lasker–Steinitz match for American newspapers and conducting the automaton player 'Ajeeb'. By 1893 he had beaten several visiting European masters, won the Manhattan Chess Club championship and played four games blindfold.

With backing from New York clubs, Pillsbury took up the American invitation to Hastings in 1895 and began by losing to Chigorin in the first round. But nine consecutive victories in later rounds put him into a battle with Lasker and the Russian champion in the final days. Pillsbury won with 16½/21, Chigorin was second with 16 and Lasker third with 15½.

His success won Pillsbury years of foreign invitations beginning with St Petersburg 1895/6, where he came third behind Lasker and Steinitz. Over the next five years he secured top places in several events: =3rd at Nuremberg 1896, =1st at Vienna 1897, =2nd at London 1899, 2nd at Paris 1900 and =1st at Munich 1900. During this period Pillsbury confined his American ambitions to displays, club matches and two matches with Showalter for the US title. In 1897 he won narrowly +10−8=3 but he improved in the return match to +7−3=2. Although Pillsbury said he never intended to be the national champion, he held the title until his death. Despite the rise of the ever-improving Marshall, Pillsbury did not defend the US championship again.

Following his marriage in 1901, Pillsbury returned to Europe for more tournament successes and an acclaimed series of blindfold chess and draughts (checkers) exhibitions. During Hanover 1902 where he came 2nd, Pillsbury took on 21 blindfold games against top players from the minor sections of the Congress, winning 3, drawing 11 and losing 7 in 11½ hours. His personal record was 22 blindfold games at Moscow later in 1902. Pillsbury continued to score well in tournaments until Cambridge Springs 1904 where he was =8th. This was his last tournament and, except for club matches, his last serious chess before his death aged thirty-three. Bold planning and ruthless execution were the hallmark of his play.

Hastings 1895
White: Pillsbury; *Black:* Burn
Queen's Gambit Declined
1. P–Q4, P–Q4; 2. P–QB4, P–K3; 3. N–QB3, N–KB3; 4. B–N5, B–K2; 5. P–K3, O–O; 6. N–B3, P–QN3; 7. R–B1, B–N2; 8. P×P, N×P; 9. B×B, Q×B; 10. N×N, B×N; 11. B–Q3, R–B1; 12. P–K4, B–N2; 13. O–O, N–Q2; 14. Q–K2, P–QR3; 15. R–B3, P–QB3; 16. KR–B1, P–QN4; 17. Q–K3, R–B2; 18. Q–B4, QR–QB1; 19. P–K5, P–QB4; 20. B×P+, K×B; 21. N–N5+, K–N1; 22. R–KR3, Q–K1; 23. Q–R4, K–B1; 24. N–R7+, K–N1; 25. N–B6+, K–B1; 26. N×Q, K×N; 27. Q–N5, P×P; 28. R–R8+, resigns. *(A.S.)*

PILNIK, Herman *(b. 8 January 1914)*
Argentine grandmaster who teaches chess at the Military Academy of Venezuela in Caracas, Pilnik has led a wandering and varied life which has to some extent interfered with the complete development of his undoubted gifts as a player.

Born in Stuttgart in Germany, he won the junior championship of that city at the age of twelve.

In 1930 at the age of sixteen he left Germany for Buenos Aires. An excellent quick player, his best performance before the Second World War was in that field and in 1939, at a big lightning tournament in Buenos Aires he came 3rd to Alekhine and Najdorf.

He won the Argentine championship in 1942 and in that year scored his first international success, =2nd with Ståhlberg at Mar del Plata half a point below Najdorf. In 1944 he was =1st with Najdorf in Mar del Plata and again came =2nd with Ståhlberg behind Najdorf at Mar del Plata 1945.

He came 4th in the 1947 Mar del Plata and at New York 1948/9 he was =3rd with Euwe.

He represented Argentina for the first time in the Olympiads at Dubrovnik in 1950 and also played in the Olympiads of 1952, 1954, 1956 and 1958. In this last, as Argentine champion of the year, he played on 1st board and this was the occasion of Argentina's greatest success, when the team won the bronze medal.

The 1950s constituted Pilnik's best period in international chess. His best tournament performances in that period were: 2nd at Bled 1950, =1st with Euwe at Lucerne 1951, 2nd at Madrid and 1st at Beverwijk 1951, 1st at Vienna 1951/2, =7th/18 with Petrosian at Budapest 1952, beating Smyslov and Petrosian; 1st at Belgrade 1952, 1st at Stuttgart 1954, 2nd at Beverwijk 1956 and 3rd at Santiago 1959 above Fischer.

During this period too he got as far as the Candidates tournament in the qualifying cycle of events for the World Championship. At the 1955 Interzonal at Göteborg he came =7th with Filip and Spassky and, since nine players were due to qualify, went forward to the Candidates at Amsterdam in 1956. There he had a failure and came last.

With the 1960s there was a considerable slackening of his chess-playing activities. He had some poor results in Mar del Plata tournaments and then went to Chile.

In 1970 he returned to the Argentine and came =8th with Mecking in Mar del Plata 1971. Since then he has largely concerned himself with chess teaching and coaching. *(H.G.)*

PIN
A mechanism by which a hostile piece is totally or partially immobilized because it has to obstruct the attacking line leading to another unit – usually, though not necessarily, of higher value – placed behind it.

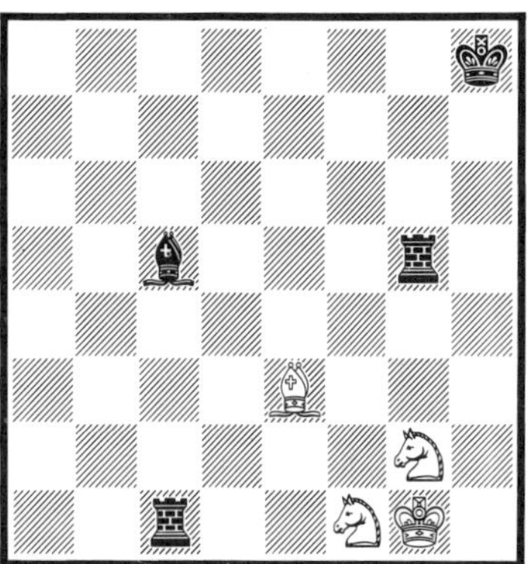

Thus, three white men are 'pinned' against the King; both Knights are totally immobilized, being unable legally to move; the Bishop is partially immobilized, for it is allowed to move along the line of the pinning piece.

A pin can be exploited in many ways: by bringing further attacks to bear on the pinned man, especially by pawns, and thus winning it; by a temporary exchange combination; by placing other pieces in attacking positions which, but for the pin, would not be accessible to them.

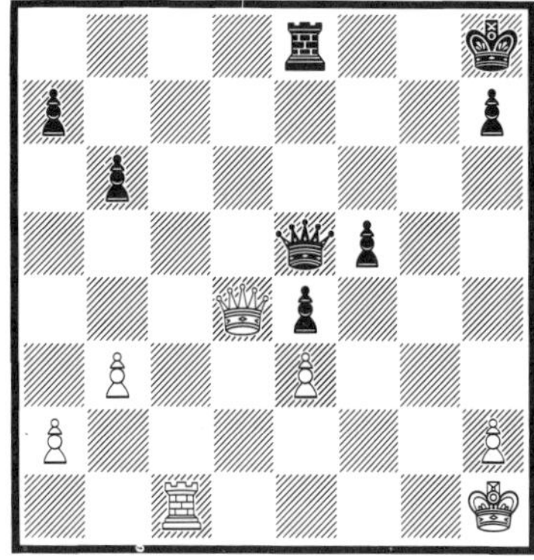

Dunkelblum–Canal, Venice 1953 shows a very elegant use of a partial pin by the creation of a second partial pin: White played 1. R–B8, threatening both R×R+ and Q×Q+, and while the reply 1.., K–N2 would parry the second threat, it does nothing against the first.

Where a pinned man has to guard against a lesser attack than the direct approach to the King, a pin may be ineffective. Such lesser attacks may be directed against the Queen or other pieces, or may take the form of an indirect attack against the King by means of a mating threat.

Thus the pin against the mate on KN7 protects both White Rooks, but it does not stop Black from winning by 1.., N–K7+. Again, where the Q is the threatened unit behind the pinned piece, the pin can often be disregarded with impurity, as e.g. in the Queen's Gambit after 1. P–Q4, P–Q4; 2. P–QB4, P–K3; 3. N–QB3, N–KB3; 4. B–N5, QN–Q2; 5. P×P, P×P; 6. N×P?, N×N!; 7. B×Q, B–N5+; 8. Q–Q2, B×Q+; 9. K×B, K×B with the win of a piece. *(W.H.)*

PIRC DEFENCE

1. P–K4, P–Q3; 2. P–Q4, N–KB3; 3. N–QB3, P–KN3. This, like its first cousin the Robatsch Defence, is an attempt to gain profit from White over-extending himself in the centre.

It was introduced to master chess by Vasja Pirc after the Second World War and much analysed by the Yugoslav masters. Hence it is sometimes called the Yugoslav Defence.

Soviet writers sometimes refer to it as the Ufimtsev Defence after the Russian player and analyst who employed it, also in the late-1940s.

White has five main lines for meeting this defence: 4. P–B4, 4. N–B3, 4. B–QB4, 4. B–N5, and 4. P–B3. *(H.G.)*

PIRC, Vasja *(b. 19 December 1907)*

The third Yugoslav after Vidmar and Kostić to obtain the grandmaster title, Pirc achieved early prominence in pre-war Yugoslavia by winning a number of minor events. In 1936 and 1937 he won the Yugoslav championship, establishing himself as best player for years to come. After the Second World War he was made a grandmaster following outstanding results. Represented Yugoslavia in many Olympiads. Best result: 2nd on second board, Dubrovnik 1970. Best tournament results: =4th Staunton Memorial 1951; =1st Karlovy Vary–Mariánské Lázně 1948. He drew a match with Euwe in 1949 by 6–6. In 1968 he withdrew from the tournament arena.

An inventive player, Pirc is perhaps best remembered as a prolific author, whose originality greatly contributed to the development of present-day opening theory, e.g. with the Pirc Defence. *(R.D.K.)*

PISTYAN 1912

This great international tournament was the first international tournament to be held in Hungary since Budapest 1896 and no fewer than thirty-six masters sent in applications to play. From these, eighteen were chosen.

Strong though the tournament was, Rubinstein, in magnificent form, was sure of first prize with one week still to go. It was his fourth first prize in the year, the others having been at Vilno (now Vilnius), San Sebastian and Breslau (equal with Důras).

Schlechter was the only player to go through the tournament unbeaten but he drew no less than 14 games out of the 17. Leading scores: Rubinstein 14, Spielmann 11½, Marshall 10½, Důras, Schlechter, Teichman 10. *(H.G.)*

PISTYAN 1922

The Breyer Memorial tournament at Pistyan (April 1922) was the first, and largest, of the four great tournaments of that year. However, many of the nineteen participants were minor masters of the states of the erstwhile Hapsburg Empire, and almost from the start the tournament developed into a three-man race, Alekhine, Bogoljubow and Spielmann sharing or alternating in the lead throughout. In the end Bogoljubow just nosed out his two rivals by the minimum margin, far ahead of Grünfeld (4th) and Réti (5th). The event is remarkable for being the only occasion out of some twenty-five clashes between these two players in which Alekhine finished behind Bogoljubow. Except for a few ties, such as at Margate 1923 and at Carlsbad the same year, Alekhine always excelled his rivals. Leading scores: Bogoljubow 15, Alekhine, Spielmann 14½, Grünfeld 11. *(H.G.)*

PLANINC, Albin *(b. 18 April 1944)*

Yugoslav grandmaster. One of a new generation of strong Yugoslav players who have come to the fore in recent years. Although he learned chess at the age of seven, his rise to prominence was delayed until 1969 when he won the Ljubljana tournament ahead of Gligorić and R. Byrne. Received the grandmaster title 1972. Best tournament result: =1st with Petrosian, I.B.M. Amsterdam 1972 ahead of Kavalek, Spassky, and Szabo. Best result in Yugoslav championship: 7th, 1973. He specializes in apparently outdated openings into which his imaginative play infuses new life. *(R.D.K.)*

PLANNING

The process by which a player utilizes the advantages and minimizes the drawbacks of his position. In order to promise success, planning is thus always based on a diagnosis of the existing characteristics of a position; it is therefore most difficult when the position is evenly balanced, and easiest when there is only one plan to satisfy the demands of the position.

Planning may be long-term or short-term; long-term planning is necessarily vague and may have to be modified as the game progresses and the opponent's counter-plan demands concessions to be made. A particularly clear-cut long-term plan arises for example in the Ruy Lopez Exchange variation, after the moves 1. P–K4, P–K4; 2. N–KB3, N–QB3; 3. B–N5, P–QR3; 4. B×N, QP×B; 5. P–Q4, P×P; 6. Q×P, Q×Q; 7. N×Q. Here White's plan is to exchange all the pieces without conceding an improvement in the opponent's pawn formation; for with four pawns to three on the K-side and the hostile majority unable to produce a passed pawn because of the doubling of the QBP, he would have a won pawn-ending if all the pieces were to come off. His secondary plan is to nullify the opponent's advantage of the pair of Bishops.

Black's plan, in turn, will consist of making these Bishops tell by mounting an attack against weak points in the hostile camp. In so doing he forces White at least to effect an improvement in Black's pawn position or to allow other compensation (for an illustration, see the game given under ST PETERSBURG 1914).

Short-term planning is clearer and more concise in its aims, as shown by the example given by Lasker in his *Manual of Chess*.

In the diagram (from Metger v. L. Paulsen, with White to move), White is a piece to the good and normally would win; yet if the Black King can reach his QR square, White's superiority would be useless. Black's plan consequently is to reach the corner square; White's twin plans are to stop Black's King from doing so and to force it – by *zugzwang* – away from the defence of his pawn. To do so, he must always be able to answer the advance of Black's pawn with P–R6. Thus, play goes: 1. K–Q4, (not *1. K–B4, P–N4+* followed by *K–N2*, and Black has realized his plan) K–B3; 2. B–N6, K–Q3; 3. K–B4, K–B3; 4. K–N4, K–Q3; 5. K–N5, K–Q2; 6. B–N1, K–B2; 7. B–R2+, K–Q1; 8. K–N6, K–B1; 9. B–N3, winning the pawn and the game. *(W.H.)*

PLATER, Kazimierz *(b. 3 March 1915)*
Polish international master and Polish champion 1949, 1956 and 1957. He played for Poland at the Olympiads of 1952, 1956 and 1960. His best international results are 7th at Bucharest 1949, =4th with Bogdanović and Ciocâltea at Sczawno Zdroj 1957 and =9th/16 with Kluger at Polanica Zdroj 1963. *(H.G.)*

PLATONOV, Igor *(b. 18 January 1934)*
Soviet player with frequent good results in USSR championships, including 5th in 1968, 7th in 1969 and 12th in 1971, but no successes in international events. *(W.R.H.)*

PODEBRADY 1936
Another tournament on the Moscow model (with eight Czechs meeting ten foreigners), Podebrady (June 1936) must be regarded as one of the most evenly contested tournaments of all time. Despite the absence of all the established grandmasters except Alekhine (dethroned as World Champion the previous year), all the younger top-notchers except Flohr, as well as the entire new generation of Russian players (though Ragozin had been expected to come), the general strength of the tournament was so high that as experienced a campaigner as Sir George Thomas finished last out of eighteen!

The tournament started on a sensational note when the young Polish master Frydman battled with the ex-World Champion for the lead, and after nine rounds at the half-way stage was the sole leader with 8/9; in the 10th he met, and was defeated by, Alekhine. As a result, he suffered a complete nervous breakdown and added only another 1½ points from his remaining seven games. Eliskases, Foltys, Flohr, Opocensky, and Ståhlberg were all well in the running behind the two leaders at this stage. But just as Alekhine was outpointed by Frydman at the beginning, so he was by Flohr in the end. Finishing with a burst of 9 points from his last ten games, the Czech champion was half a point to the good at the finishing line, with another Czech, Foltys, third. Leading scores: Flohr 13, Alekhine 12½, Foltys 11, Pirc, Ståhlberg 10½. *(W.H.)*

PODGAYETS, Mikhail *(b. 23 July 1947)*
Soviet international master (1972). Regular member of Soviet Student Olympiad teams in the 1970s. Has frequently performed well in Soviet championships including =6th in 1968/9 and =8th in 1970. *(W.R.H.)*

POLAND
The first great chess master in Poland was Simon Winawer who was successful in tournament play in the latter part of the nineteenth century and also introduced some important opening lines that have become very fashionable in the twentieth century. He was followed by an even greater player, Akiba Rubinstein, who, in conjunction with Tartakower, made Poland a team to be feared in the Olympiads.

But the Second World War destroyed the all-important Jewish element in Polish chess and the country took some time in recovering its strength from the chess point of view. Nowadays, whilst it has never quite regained its quota of great players, it has a fine team of masters and grandmasters that is gradually making itself felt and respected in international chess.

The name and address of its federation:

Polski Zwiazek Szachowy, Ul. Czerniakowska 126 A, Warsaw. *(H.G.)*

POLERIO, Giulio Cesare *(1548–1612)*
Italian player and writer of the sixteenth century who was regarded as champion of Rome towards the end of the century.

He was a pupil of Leonardo and accompanied him on his successful visit to play Ruy Lopez in Madrid in 1574.

On his return to Italy he became a protégé of the Duke of Sora, Giacomo I Buoncompagni, who gave him a pension of 300 scudi. In return Polerio dedicated to him his *Trattato de scacchi di Giulio Cesare Polerio*. A manuscript exists of this, dated 31 July 1594.

There is also attributed to Polerio a free translation of Ruy

Lopez entitled *L'elegantia sottilita verita della virtuosissima professione de' scacchi* which is to be found in the National Library at Florence.

His importance as a writer is that he deals with various forms of gambits and ascribes them to older players and theorists. He also composed some endgame studies. *(H.G.)*

POLIHRONIADE, Elizaveta *(b. 24 April 1935)*
Romanian international Woman master since 1960. Played in Women's Candidates in 1961 (finishing 10th) and in the Interzonals of 1971 (finishing 7th) and 1973 (10th). *(W.R.H.)*

POLISH DEFENCE
This can arise after 1. P–Q4, N–KB3; 2. N–KB3 if Black selects the rare move 2. . , P–QN4. Black seems to neglect the centre but his position is not without resources and both Spassky and Larsen have occasionally experimented with this line. *(R.D.K.)*

POLISH IMMORTAL, The
Thus christened by Dr Tartakower, the 'Polish Immortal' was played at Warsaw 1935. Within its twenty-two moves Black makes five minor piece and two pawn offers:

White: Glucksberg; *Black:* Najdorf
Dutch Defence
1. P–Q4, P–KB4; 2. P–QB4, N–KB3; 3. N–QB3, P–K3; 4. N–B3, P–Q4; 5. P–K3, P–B3; 6. B–Q3, B–Q3; 7. O–O, O–O; 8. N–K2, QN–Q2; 9. N–N5, B×P+; 10. K–R1, N–N5; 11. P–B4, Q–K1; 12. P–KN3, Q–R4; 13. K–N2, B–N8; 14. N×B, Q–R7+; 15. K–B3, P–K4; 16. QP×P,

16. . , N(2)×P+; 17. P×N, N×P+; 18. K–B4, N–N3+; 19. K–B3, P–B5; 20. KP×P, B–N5+; 21. K×B, N–K4+; 22. P×N, P–R4 mate. *(W.H.)*

POLLOCK, William Henry Krause
(21 February 1859–5 October 1896)
Born in Cheltenham of Irish ancestry, Pollock learnt his chess as a medical student in Dublin and came to be regarded as an Irish player. He won first prize at Belfast 1886 (ahead of Blackburne and Burn) but otherwise had to rely on good individual performances in master tournaments. *Pollock Memories*, a collection of his games and problems compiled by Mrs Rowland, appeared in Dublin 1899. Pollock himself was joint author, with Mason, of the St Petersburg 1895/6 tournament book. *(W.H.)*

POLUGAYEVSKY, Lev Abramovich *(b. 29 November 1934)*
One of the world's strongest players since 1970. Awarded the titles of international master in 1961 and grandmaster the following year. Winner of Soviet championship in 1967 and 1968/9 (after a play-off with A. Zaitsev); tied for first place in 1969 but lost the play-off to Petrosian.

His international tournament successes include first or shared first prizes at Mariánské Lázně 1959, Mar del Plata 1962, Belgrade 1969, Amsterdam 1970, Mar del Plata 1971, Skopje 1971, Amsterdam 1972, Solingen 1974, Sochi 1974, Budapest 1975, Montilla-Moriles 1975 and Sochi 1976.

Played in the Interzonals of 1970 (finishing =9th and 1973, when he qualified for the Candidates series, only to lose in the first match to Karpov. *(W.R.H.)*

POMAR, Arturo *(b. 1 September 1931)*
Spanish grandmaster and famous boy prodigy, who never quite fulfilled his promise.

At the age of ten he was runner-up in the championship of the Balearic Islands and he won the championship the following year, making a great impression on the World Champion, Alekhine.

He became Spanish champion in 1946 and won the title in 1950, 1957, 1962 and 1966. Nearly all his tournament successes have been in Spain where he seems to play much better than when abroad. His best results in this sphere have been: 1st at Gijon 1955, =2nd at Madrid 1957, 2nd at Santander 1958, =1st Madrid 1959, =1st Torremolinos 1961, 2nd Malaga 1964, =1st Palma de Mallorca 1965, 2nd Palma de Mallorca 1966, 2nd Malaga 1967.

He has played in all the Olympiads from 1958 to 1976 and always on top board.

His international career was disturbed by two nervous breakdowns at tournaments in Czechoslovakia in 1965 and Dundee in 1966 when he had to withdraw from the events. Though he made a good recovery the experience seems to have had a marked influence on his play and his results. *(H.G.)*

PONZIANI, Domenico Lorenzo *(9 November 1719–15 July 1796)*
A leading member of the Modena school of masters, Ponziani was born at Modena and lived and worked there all his life. He was Professor of Civil Law at the university but still found time to become a considerable openings theorist.

In 1769 he published his *Il giuoco incomparabile degli scacchi* (the incomparable game of chess). An improved and revised version appeared in 1782. He dealt with more openings (including the Allgaier variation of the King's Gambit) than his predecessors. It is amusing to see that all he did as regards the opening called after him (1. P–K4, P–K4; 2. N–KB3, N–QB3; 3. P–B3) was to advocate an inferior defence with 3. . , P–B4. *(H.G.)*

PONZIANI'S OPENING
First analysed by Ponziani and later by Staunton, the opening 1. P–K4, P–K4; 2. N–KB3, N–QB3; 3. P–B3 has the theme of central domination by means of a quick P–Q4. Black has several satisfactory replies including 3. . , N–KB3. Also possible is 3. . ,

KN–K2 (Réti) and the sharp 3. . , P–Q4; 4. Q–R4, with either 4. . , N–B3 (Leonhardt) or 4. . , P–B3 (Steinitz). *(W.R.H.)*

POPOV, Luben *(b. 28 January 1936)*
Bulgarian champion in 1970, and international master since 1965. Shared first place at international tournaments Reggio Emilia 1972/3, Plovdiv 1973, and Reggio Emilia 1973/4. *(W.R.H.)*

PORATH, Josef *(b. 7 June 1909)*
Israeli international master who was born in Germany and, under the name of Foerder, played for the German team at the Hague Olympiad 1928. Also as Foerder he played in Swinemünde 1931 coming =8th/13 with Mieses.

He emigrated to Palestine in 1934 and won the Palestine championship in 1937 and 1940. In 1935 and 1939 he played for Palestine in the Olympiads at Warsaw and Buenos Aires.

Under the name of Porath he played on 3rd board for Israel at Helsinki 1952, Israel's first appearance in the Olympiads. He played for Israel in all subsequent Olympiads up to 1968.

Winner of the Israeli championship in 1953, 1957, 1959 and 1963, he qualified for the Interzonal by coming 1st at the Asian Zonal tournament at Ulan Bator in 1964 but did badly at the Amsterdam Interzonal that year, coming 21st/24. *(H.G.)*

PORRECA, Giorgio *(b. 30 August 1927)*
Italian international master and Italian champion 1950, 1956. He has represented Italy in three Olympiads, Dubrovnik 1950, Helsinki 1952 and Amsterdam 1954.

In 1960 he was first in the Imperia tournament, and then shortly afterwards went to study Russian language and literature at Moscow University. On his return he gave up over-the-board play and took up correspondence chess. He also devoted himself to writing about the game and translating from the Russian. Of these works the most important are *Studi scacchistici* (an anthology of endgame studies) and a translation of Koblencs's *Mikhail Tal – La Carriera di Mikhail Tal*. He also collaborated with Adriano Chicco in the *Dizionario Enciclopedico Degli Scacchi*, Milano 1971. *(H.G.)*

PORTISCH, Lajos *(b. 4 April 1937)*

Hungarian grandmaster and one of the most successful tournament players of our time, Portisch was born in Zalaegerszeg in Hungary and came from a chess-playing family. His father taught him how to play, and his younger brother is also a talented player who competes in international tournaments.

In 1955, when he became a national master, he came fourth in the World Junior Championship. After that his progress was rapid. He won the Hungarian championship in 1958 and in the same year he gained the international master title by coming first in an international tournament at Balatonfüred. It took him only another three years to gain the grandmaster title, and he had already commenced his assault on the World title.

The ensuing years were to show that, along with Larsen, he was the most dangerous candidate for World Championship honours outside the Soviet Union.

Tracing his steps in this direction affords a good picture of the rigours of such an enterprise and also reveals the great chess-powers of the Hungarian star.

He came =1st at the Madrid Zonal 1960, but was a point away from qualifying for the Candidates at the Stockholm Interzonal of 1962 where he was =9th with Uhlmann, scoring $12\frac{1}{2}$/22. A first at the Halle Zonal of 1963 was followed by an =8th with Reshevsky at the Amsterdam Interzonal of 1964.

In the play-off with Reshevsky for a place in the Candidates, he won easily enough ($2\frac{1}{2}$–$\frac{1}{2}$) against an opponent thirty years his senior. Now at last he was in the Candidates, but in the quarter-final match in 1965 Tal beat him by $5\frac{1}{2}$–$2\frac{1}{2}$.

He won first prize in another Halle Zonal in 1967 and in the Interzonal held the same year at Sousse he qualified in sure style for the Candidates by coming 5th with $13\frac{1}{2}$ points and beating the tournament winner, Larsen. Oddly enough it was Larsen who beat him in the quarter-finals of the Candidates by $5\frac{1}{2}$–$4\frac{1}{2}$.

He was a half-point away from qualifying for the Candidates when he came =7th with Smyslov at the 1970 Interzonal at Palma de Mallorca, but did much better at the Petropolis Interzonal of 1973 where he finished =2nd with Geller and Polugayevsky. He was successful with considerable ease in the play-off for two places in the Candidates. This was at Portorož the same year and he won both his games against Polugayevsky and scored $1\frac{1}{2}$ out of 2 against Geller.

In a very close-fought quarter-finals match against Petrosian in the Candidates in 1974 he lost narrowly by 6–7. Finally, in a very tough Interzonal at Biel, Switzerland, in 1976 he came =2nd with Petrosian and Tal and in a subsequent play-off gained the right (together with Petrosian) to play in the Candidates in 1977.

In between this activity he won the Hungarian championship eight times and played for his country in ten Olympiads. Then too there was an astonishing collection of 1sts in great tournaments: Sarajevo 1962, Amsterdam 1963, Wijk-aan-Zee 1965, Amsterdam 1967, Skopje 1968, Monte Carlo 1969, Hastings 1970, Wijk-aan-Zee, Las Palmas and San Antonio 1972, Wijk-aan-Zee 1975. Another fine result was his 2nd to Karpov at Milan 1975 where in fact he came ahead of the World Champion in the preliminary tournament.

Portisch is a player in the grand traditional Hungarian style: inventive, rich in ideas and dynamism. His brilliance is positional rather than tactical and both at the board and away from it he is calm, quiet and undemonstrative.

The following game was awarded the brilliancy prize at the 1974 Manila international tournament.

White: Portisch; *Black:* Gheorghiu
Grünfeld Defence
1. P–Q4, N–KB3; 2. P–QB4, P–KN3; 3. N–QB3, P–Q4; 4. N–B3, B–N2; 5. Q–N3, P×P; 6. Q×BP, O–O; 7. P–K4, B–N5; 8. B–K3, KN–Q2; 9. Q–N3, N–N3; 10. R–Q1, N–B3; 11. P–Q5, N–K4; 12. B–K2, N×N+; 13. P×N, B–R4; 14. R–KN1, Q–Q2; 15. R–N3, P–QB3; 16. P×P, Q×P; 17. N–N5, N–B1; 18. R–Q5, K–R1; 19. R–QB5, Q–B3; 20. B–Q4, Q–R5; 21. B×B+, K×B; 22. Q–B3+, K–N1; 23. N–B7, R–N1; 24. R(B5)–KN5, P–B3; 25. N–K6, R–K1; 26. P–B4, B×B; 27. R–R3, Q×R(N4); 28. N×Q, P×N; 29. K×B, P×P; 30. Q–B4+, K–N2; 31. R×P+, K×R; 32. Q–B7+, K–R3; 33. Q×R, resigns. *(H.G.)*

PORTUGAL

Portugal began playing in the chess Olympiads in 1958 and has now competed eight times: 31st in 1958, 30th in 1960, 47th in 1964, 37th in 1966, 35th in 1968, 41st in 1970, 37th in 1972 and 31st in 1974.

There are two Portuguese title holders, both international masters: Joaquim Durão and Fernando Silva. The former played in the strongest tournament, the only one of note so far, on Portuguese soil – the 1969 Zonal at Praia da Rocha in the Algarve.

The Federaçao Portuguesa de Xadrez is located at Rua Sociedade Farmaceutica 56–2°, Lisboa 1. *(K.J.O'C.)*

POSITIONAL JUDGMENT

The ability to judge a given position without going into the details of accurate calculation.

It mostly concerns borderline decisions involving conflicting advantages and disadvantages, the questions to be answered being such as: In this position is it worth saddling the opponent with an isolated QP or will he be able to use it as an attacking unit? Or: if I allow him to give me a doubled pawn, will the resulting open file (or the resulting pair of Bishops) be a sufficient compensation in this type of position? Or: is my play on the K-side sufficiently strong to allow him a completely free hand on the other wing?

The more developed a player's positional judgment, the less will he have to resort to time-consuming calculations in order to answer questions of this type. *(W.H.)*

POSITIONAL SACRIFICE

A type of exchange combination in which a piece generally of greater value than the one (or ones) obtained for it is offered because in the particular *position* other considerations reduce its value and make it equal or nearly equal to what is obtained in exchange. In recent years several such combinational possibilities have been discovered in the opening stages of the game, one of the most famous being Spassky–Bronstein, Amsterdam 1956 (King's Indian Defence): 1. P–Q4, N–KB3; 2. P–QB4, P–KN3; 3. N–QB3, B–N2; 4. P–K4, P–Q3; 5. P–B3, P–K4; 6. P–Q5, N–R4; 7. B–K3, N–R3; 8. Q–Q2, Q–R5+; 9. P–N3, N×P; 10. Q–KB2, N×B; 11. Q×Q, N×B; 12. K–B2, N×BP.

The positional sacrifice is almost the only type of sacrificial combination seen in defence, especially for the purpose of blockading a hostile attacking position. E.g. Reshevsky–Petrosian (Neuhausen-Zürich 1953), where play from the diagram went:

1.., R–K3 (in order to ossify the whole central position by *2.., N–K2* and *3.., N–Q4*); 2. P–QR4, N–K2; 3. B×R, P×B; 4. Q–B1, N–Q4; 5. R–B3, B–Q6 and the threat of P–N5 forced White to return the exchange. *(W.H.)*

POST, Erhard *(23 September 1881–1 August 1947)*

A minor German master without any real international success to his name. Post won two national tournaments at Hamburg 1921 and Oynhausen 1922; he also beat W. Cohn in a match in Berlin 1910. He was President of the Nazi *Grossdeutscher Schachbund*. *(W.H.)*

POTTER, William Norwood *(17 August 1840–13 March 1895)*

A player of master strength and an excellent writer and annotator, Potter was by profession a barrister's clerk.

A keen member of the City of London Chess Club, he was secretary of the club for some years and it was he, in collaboration with Steinitz, who bore the brunt of the correspondence match between the club and the Vienna Chess Club. Two games were played during the period 1872–74 and the London players emerged victors by $1\frac{1}{2}$–$\frac{1}{2}$.

His playing career was a short one. In tournament play he came third in a small tournament of six players at the Divan in London in 1876, below Blackburne and Zukertort but above MacDonnell. He played two matches, losing one to Zukertort in London in 1875 by +2–4=8 and drawing a match with Mason again in London in 1879 by +5–5=11.

His name is attached to two lines in the openings. One is the Scotch Game: 1. P–K4, P–K4; 2. N–KB3, N–QB3; 3. P–Q4, P×P; 4. N×P, B–B4; 5. N–N3, and the second is the Evans Gambit: 1. P–K4, P–K4; 2. N–KB3, N–QB3; 3. B–B4, B–B4; 4. P–QN4, B×P; 5. P–B3, B–R4; 6. P–Q4, P×P; 7. O–O, P×P; 8. Q–N3, Q–B3; 9. P–K5, Q–N3; 10. N×P, KN–K2; 11. R–Q1.

It is as a writer and an annotator that he will be best remembered. The writer of his obituary in the *British Chess Magazine* for 1895 somewhat exaggerates his qualities as a player. But he is right to refer to his remarkable literary gift and his masterly annotations which appeared in the *Westminster Papers* from 1868–79 and in the *City of London Chess Magazine* of which he was the sole editor in its two years of existence from 1874–6.

The *British Chess Magazine* obituarist also refers to his 'masterly article on Chess in the new edition of the *Encyclopaedia Britannica*'. This article was to form the basis of a chain of articles in the Encyclopaedia which latterly in the twentieth century have been revised by G. E. Smith, chess correspondent of the *Field*, H. Golombek, the *Times*'s chess correspondent in England, and Arthur Bisguier and Walter Korn in the USA. *(H.G.)*

PRAGUE 1908

Held in conjunction with the Prague Trade and Commerce Exhibition of 1908, this great tournament proved to be one of the best performances of the Czechoslovak grandmaster, Oldrich Důras, who tied with Schlechter for first place.

In an attempt to limit the number of draws it was decided that no draw could be agreed before 30 moves had been made. Not that this prevented such players as Teichmann and Maróczy from making many draws; but it did have the effect of spurring on the normally peaceful Schlechter to wreak great execution among the lower ranks.

The tournament was somewhat troubled by defaults or non-appearances of players. The Russian Duz-Khotimirsky was not in time for the first round owing to visa difficulties at the border. Kvicala had to resign his three last games without play owing to the death of his father and mother. All this helped Důras who was given two points without having to play for them whereas Schlechter had to concede a draw to Kvicala and fight hard to secure his win over Duz-Khotimirsky. Leading scores: Důras, Schlechter 13½, Vidmar 13, Rubinstein 12½, Teichmann 12. *(H.G.)*

PRAGUE 1942

An interesting international event that was held in December 1942 in celebration of Důras's sixtieth birthday (he was born on 30th October 1882). Klaus Junge, the new young German star, showed his strength by tieing for first place with Alekhine. He was to die as a soldier in the last few days of the Second World War. That he should have come 1½ points ahead of the fine player Jan Foltys in this event demonstrates the sad loss to the chess world. Leading scores: Alekhine, Junge 8½, Foltys 7, Opočensky, Zita 6½. *(H.G.)*

PRAGUE 1946

Two great international tournaments were planned for the latter half of 1946 with the idea of singling out likely contenders for the World Championship which was now vacant owing to the death of Alekhine.

Groningen, in the north of the Netherlands, took place before the Prague tournament. A strong contingent of Soviet players participated in Groningen and an equally strong group was invited and expected at Prague. But the Soviet players, having done well at Groningen, did not bother to play in the Prague event.

The result was that the Prague tournament, though still a strong one, had not the importance or the strength of the Dutch event. In a way this materially benefited the players at Prague since not only was the prize money large (a cynic remarked 'the prizes were meant for the Russians') but they had an easier task in gaining the prizes, of which there were eight.

The Argentine grandmaster, Miguel Najdorf, was in fine form and easily won the first prize, though he did lose a game, to the new young Yugoslav star, Gligorić. Leading scores: Najdorf 10½, Stoltz, Trifunović 9, Foltys, Gligorić 8½, Golombek 6½. *(H.G.)*

PRÉTI, Jean *(1798–27 January 1881)*

French writer and theoriest, especially on the endgame. Originally Italian (he was born in Mantua and studied music, becoming a flautist by profession) Préti had to flee Italy as a result of having been involved in a conspiracy against Austria.

He went to Bordeaux where he was appointed first flautist at the city theatre, and there became interested in chess. Leaving Bordeaux for Paris he took up an export business which allowed him more time for the game, and concentrated in particular on the endings. His chief work in this field was *Traité complet théorique et pratique sur les fins de parties au jeu des échecs,* Paris 1858.

In 1869 he founded the chess magazine *La Stratégie* and edited it till his death in 1881. *(H.G.)*

PREVENTIVE [anti-castling] SACRIFICE

This is designed to prevent the hostile King castling into safety. It therefore has no place in close positions, where the King is quite safe in the centre, but is part of the stock-in-trade of gambit openings, where the King's retention on the open centre files may be worth a fair amount of material. A typical example is the Nachmanson variation of the Two Knights Defence: 1. P–K4, P–K4; 2. N–KB3, N–QB3; 3. B–B4, N–B3; 4. P–Q4, P×P; 5. O–O, N×P; 6. N–B3. If now 6. . , P×N?(N×N!); 7. B×P+, K×B; 8. Q–Q5+, K–K1; 9. R–K1, B–K2; 10. R×N Black, though piece and pawn to the good, has a difficult game. *(W.H.)*

PRINS, Lodewijk *(b. 27 January 1913)*

A Dutch international master (1950). Best result: first prize Madrid 1951 with 12½/17 ahead of Steiner, Pilnik and Bernstein. Dutch champion 1965. Played in all the Olympiads from 1937 to 1968.

Co-author (with Euwe) of a biography of Capablanca *Het Schaakphenomeen Capablanca*, The Hague 1949, and of several tournament books: Maastricht 1946, Hastings 1945/6 and 1946/7. International Judge since 1960. *(R.D.K.)*

PRITCHARD [née Saunders], Elaine *(b. 7 January 1926)*

International Woman master and British Woman champion 1939, 1946, 1956 and 1965, she was a girl prodigy with perhaps the most natural talent for the game of any British-born woman. She was playing competitive chess at the age of seven and was only ten when she won the FIDE Girls Open chess championship (under-21) in London in 1936, winning eleven out of the twelve games played.

British Girl champion (under-18) 1936–8, she won the British

Women's championship in 1939 at the age of thirteen. Winning the title on three more occasions, she hardly ever had a bad result in the event but, by profession a teacher, she did not always have sufficient time to devote to the game.

Her best international results were 2nd in the Western European Zonal Women's tournament in 1957 (the year she gained the Woman master title), and two 3rd places at Paignton and Havering 1967. She represented the B.C.F. in Women's Olympiads at Emmen 1957, Skopje 1972, Medellin 1974 and Haifa 1976. *(H.G.)*

PRITCHETT, Craig William *(b. 15 January 1949)*
Scottish international master and teacher. Pritchett, probably the strongest native-born Scottish player since the days of Captain Mackenzie in the nineteenth century, has represented Scotland with success in five Olympiads: 1966, 1970, 1972, 1974 and 1976. He has also played for Scotland in the Students Olympiads of 1968, 1969, 1970.

His first individual success was in the European Junior championship at Groningen 1969/70 when he came =3rd with Belyavsky. At Děčin (Czechoslovakia) 1974 he came 1st in the Masters B section.

He obtained the first part of an international master norm at the Nice Olympiad of 1974 where he scored 60% on top board. In 1975 he again achieved a master norm at the strong Pula Zonal tournament where he came =7th/14.

He is chess correspondent of the *Glasgow Herald* and author of *The Scheveningen Sicilian*, London 1977. *(H.G.)*

PROBLEM
A composed position carrying the stipulation that mate (or self-mate, helpmate etc.) is to be given in a specified number of moves. According to convention, the diagram position of a direct-mate problem must be one which could have been reached in actual play (however strange the imaginary 'proof-game' might have been). *(J.M.R.)*

PROBLEM, the History of the

The early period

It is easy to imagine how the composition of artificial end-game positions derived from the game itself. This process dates back at least to ninth-century Arabia, and may well be older. Of the surviving Arabian manuscripts, only one deals with the beginnings of games, but there are several devoted to endings. The Arabians called their positions *mansuba* (plural *mansubat*), which means 'that which has been erected, set up or arranged' and so clearly implies a composed position. No. 1 (White to play and win) is from the manuscript (now lost) of a compiler of *mansubat* named al-Adli, and is the sort of position that is more familiar to problemists than to players. (Solution: mate in 3, by 1. Sh5+, R×h5; 2. R×g6+.) There was as yet no convention as to which side achieved the win or draw, nor as to which side played from the bottom of the diagram. (In No. 1 the colours have been reversed to conform with present-day usage.) Nor did all the pieces move exactly as they do today: the Q (known as *Fers*) moved only one step diagonally and had no orthogonal movement, and the B (*Alfil*) was a 'Leaper', moving always two squares diagonally, e.g. a1–c3, even with b2 occupied. The Q and B in No. 2 (dating from about 1300) are respectively *Fers* and *Alfil*: note that though this problem starts with the initial position of the pieces, the Knight and the Alfil are interchanged. White mates in 11; Black moves only out of check or to capture. (Solution: 1. h3; 2. h4 – the P's initial double jump was a later development; 3. Rh3; 4. Re3; 5. Sg3; 6. Se4; 7. Sd3; 8. Sf4; 9. Sh5; 10. Shf6+, g×f6; 11. S×f6.)

During the medieval period, when composed positions were already spreading to Europe, it became fashionable to bet on the solution of a problem, and in certain surviving manuscripts there are positions which were clearly contrived for this purpose. A compiler of (probably) the thirteenth century, who adopted the pseudonym 'Bonus Socius', has several such in his manuscripts, together with a number of Arabian *mansubat*, and also a few interesting problems belonging to neither category, such as No. 3, a neat mate in 2. This is among the earliest problems of any real subtlety, the solution being a waiting-move (1. Rhg7) rather than the customary check. We also see what may be the first example of a 'try': 1. Kc2? or 1. Ke2?

It was not until the end of the fifteenth century that the *Fers* and *Alfil* developed into our modern Q and B, although the P had acquired its initial double-jump rather earlier. But the enormous increase in the mobility of the Q in particular did not in fact stimulate the composition of problems, and it was not until around 1840 that any serious interest began to be taken in the problem as a form separate from the game.

The nineteenth century

The term 'Old School' is used to describe those composers who, in the mid-nineteenth century, fashioned the modern problem as we now recognize it. One such was Horatio Bolton (1793–1873) with works like No. 4 (*Chess Player's Chronicle* 1841: mate in 7, by 1. Rc7; 2. Rc6; 3. Sf7; 4. Se5; 5. Sd3; 6. Sb4+). The principal advances of this period were in the problem's stipulation (mate required in the shortest possible number of moves, rather than a vague 'win') and in the question of the force employed, which gradually became reduced to merely what was needed to show the problem's thematic idea.

No. 5 (*Illustrated London News* 1846 – mate in 5: 1. Qe1, d×e1Q; 2. Rd4; 3. Ra4+; 4. b4+) was composed by Adolf Anderssen (1818–79), a lover of brilliant combinations and surprising effects as well as being, later in his career, an outstanding player. The fact that a master of the game began as a problemist helped to stimulate a more general interest in problems.

During the years 1845–62 (the 'Transition Period') composers concentrated on the basic themes, moving naturally from one new idea to another. It was now that the Indian, Grimshaw and Nowotny themes were first shown, and the principle of Critical Play began to be explored. Much of this work was done in England by composers such as W. Grimshaw (1832–90), H. E. Kidson (1832–1910) and F. Healey (1828–1906). No. 6, by the last-named (First prize, Bristol tourney 1861 – mate in 3: 1. Rh1(!), Bd7/e8;

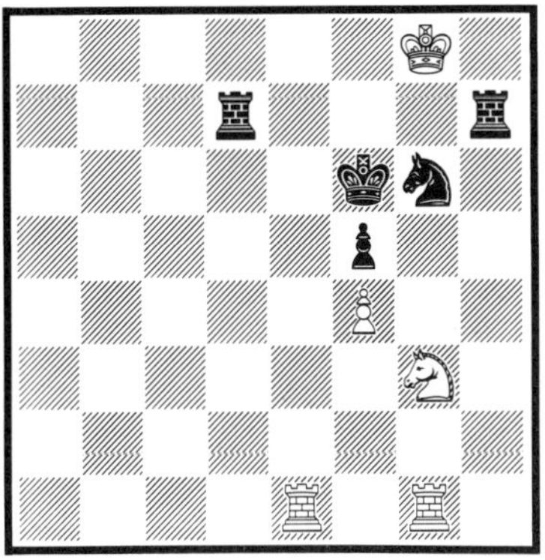
No. 1: Mate in 3

No. 2: Mate in 11

No. 3: Mate in 2

No. 4: Mate in 7

No. 5: Mate in 5

No. 6: Mate in 3

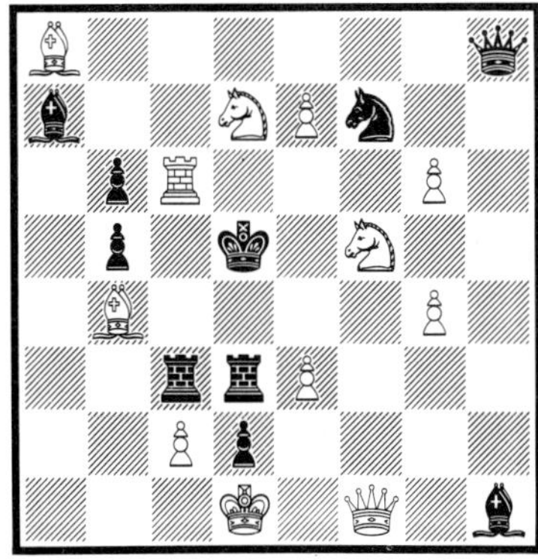
No. 7: Mate in 2

No. 8: 1. Be4

2. Qb1, Bb5; 3. Qg1) illustrates a fairly complex thematic manoeuvre (Bristol) typical of the advances of the period.

Several new principles were now emerging, chief among them being accuracy of play and beauty of strategy and mate. The original Indian problem was inaccurate to a degree, having nine keys and seventeen alternative move-sequences, but the trend was towards the complete accuracy of the initial move, which convention is still respected today. Accuracy of *all* play after the key (i.e. avoidance of duals), the principle of 'purity of aim' (German *Zweckreinheit*), and an insistence on beauty of strategy and mate, were three developing factors which, later in the century, were each to become the distinguishing mark of the three leading 'nationalist' schools.

The Nationalist period

Towards the end of the nineteenth century, the English problem developed along lines rather different from those of the continental problem. Interest centred on subtlety in the key-move (often of the waiting variety), accuracy of play, quiet continuations in three- (or more-) movers, and, later, on intricate defensive strategy such as interferences and cross-checks. Among the leading composers of the period was A. F. Mackenzie (1861–1905) of Jamaica, most of whose work appeared in England. No. 7 is typical (First prize, *Mirror of American Sports* 1886 – mate in 2: 1. Sg7).

During the 1890s much pioneering work was done by P. F. Blake and G. Heathcote, as well as by Mackenzie, who, despite blindness, was producing work of high strategic quality. The cross-check was perhaps the most popular new theme, reaching its climax in the second decade of the twentieth century in the work of Comins Mansfield, whose No. 8 is one of the most famous of all two-movers (First prize, *Good Companions* March 1917: 1. Be4). Earlier English composers might have looked askance at the duals following non-thematic moves of the Sc4, but Mansfield, with sound judgment and artistic taste, saw to it that the insistence on accuracy of play was not taken to absurd extremes.

Meanwhile German problemists, under the influence of J. Kohtz (1843–1918), found their inspiration in the strategic ideas which composers of the 'Old School' had developed in the mid-nineteenth century. To the composers of the 'New German School' the essential point of a problem was that it should have a clear-cut strategic idea expressed without any 'impure' elements which might confuse the logic of the play. *Zweckreinheit* was and still remains the cardinal principle of adherents to this school.

At about the same time the composers of Bohemia began to concentrate almost exclusively on model-mate problems, and traces of their influence can be found in the work of English three- and more-move composers of the early twentieth century. Another influential figure of the period was the American Sam Loyd, who composed in a wide variety of styles and influenced the development of the problem in most countries.

The twentieth century

Whereas in the nineteenth century two-, three- and more-movers followed much the same lines of development, in more recent years the various different lengths of problem have tended to advance in different directions. The strategic ideas being explored by two-move composers spread gradually to the three-mover, so that in most countries the three-mover became richer and more complex, with little or no emphasis on 'purity of aim'. The most significant advance over the last seventy years has been in constructional technique, so that the crudities characteristic of early twentieth-century work have been eliminated and the thematic content of three-movers substantially enriched. But the New German school's influence has also made itself felt, so that the typical modern three-mover, in which the interest still resides for the most part in the key and subsequent play, will show a far greater degree of 'purity of aim' than was the case in the 1920s and 1930s. Composers such as R. C. O. Matthews, N. G. G. van Dijk and E. Visserman deal in strategic ideas which are far in advance of the simple interference or self-block themes of the early part of the century. Correction play, 'defence-substitution' themes such as the Roman or Dresden, and other similar mechanisms are often the basic ingredients of the typical three-mover of the post-war period. No. 9, by G. F. Anderson, *Version*, B. C. F. tourney 1945 – mate in 3: 1. Be6 (2. Rf6), f×e6+; 2. Qf7 (3. Kg7), Bf6; 3. Qe8. 1. . , d×e6; 2. Bb8 (3. Sb6), Bf2; 3. K×e7. 1. . , R×e6; 2. Qg2 (3. Qb7/Kg7). 1. . , B×e6; 2. Qc3 (3. Sb6/Kg7). In No. 10 the interest is centred on battery play with shut-offs: R. C. O. Matthews, *B.C.M.* 1956 – mate in 3: 1. Rg4 (2. Sd7+), Rg2; 2. Rc2+. 1. . , Rg1; 2. Rc1+. 1. . , Qb7; 2. Rb3+. 1. . , Rf4; 2. Sf5+. 1. . , Rh4; 2. Sh5+. 1. . , Qa8; 2. Se8+. Some composers, on the other hand, have concentrated on model-mate problems, which have developed to a lesser degree than other types of three-mover, being by their very nature more limited in scope.

Problems in excess of three moves have received progressively less attention in Britain, although Continental (particularly German) composers have continued to produce them in abundance, usually concentrating the interest of the problem into a single line of play so as to avoid obscuring the logic of the solution. No. 11, by H-P. Rehm, First prize, Leipzig Olympic tourney 1960 – mate in 7: Try 1. Kg8?, Rg2+; 2. Sg4+, R×g4+; 3. Kf8, Re3! Key 1. Ke8!, Ba4+; 2. b5, B×b5+; 3. Kf8, Bd3; 4. Kg8, Rg2+; 5. Sg4+, R×g4+; 6. Kf8, Re4; 7. R×f5 – decoy followed by Roman. Model-mate more-movers, too, have retained their popularity among adherents of the Bohemian school.

Developments in the two-mover have been quite different. Apart from the work of the composers already mentioned, there were two main influences during the first two decades of the century, viz. the writings of A. C. White and the activities of the Good Companions. The systematic exploration of theme-combinations was a feature of the period, typical of which is No. 12, combining half-pin, cross-check and interference: A. Ellerman, First prize, *Handelsblad* 1918 – mate in 2: 1. Qc6 (2. Qe8). In the 1930s, mainly under the influence of M. M. Barulin, and other Russians, attention was turned to correction and dual avoidance themes, particularly those

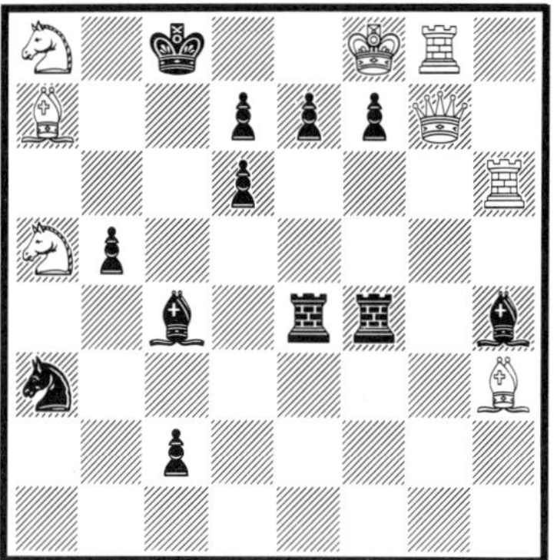

No. 9: Mate in 3

No. 10: Mate in 3

No. 11: Mate in 7

No. 12: Mate in 2

No. 13: Mate in 2

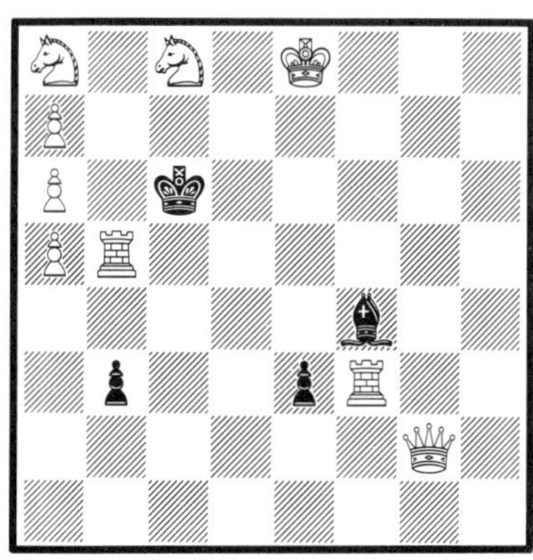

No. 14: Mate in 2

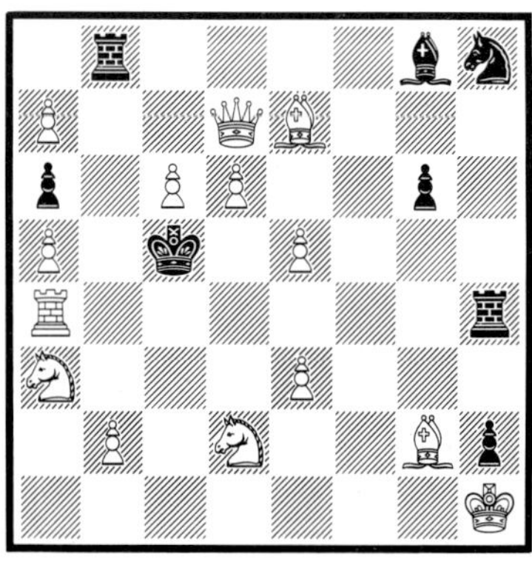

No. 15: Mate in 2

involving the opening and closing of white lines, as in No. 13, by M. M. Barulin, First prize, *Il Problema* 1932 – mate in 2: 1. Sd5 (2. Rc3), Sd7; 2. Sfe3 (not 2. Sde3 ?). 1.., Se4; 2. Sde3 (not 2. Sfe3 ?).

Changed play had been a feature of many two-movers of the Good Companion period (British composers paying particular attention to the mutate), but it was not until after the Second World War that the possibilities of changed play, along with those of the thematic try and virtual play, were intensively studied. Problems with these features were much in evidence in the European magazines of the 1950s, but only gradually found their way into English columns, which still tended to incline to the traditional style. It is mainly due to composers such as M. Lipton, J. M. Rice and B. P. Barnes that the modern two-mover has flourished in England since about 1958. No. 14 (M. Lipton, Commended, *Probleemblad* 1961 – mate in 2: Set: 1.., e2; 2. Rf×b3. 1.., B moves; 2. Rf5. Try 1. Sd6?, e2; 2. Rd3. 1.., B moves; 2. Rf6. 1.., B×d6; 2. Rf5. 1.., b2! Key 1. Sc7!, e2; 2. Rc3. 1.., B moves; 2. Rf7. 1.., B×c7; 2. Rf5) is an example of the Zagoruyko framework typical of its composer.

During the 1960s two-move composers turned their attention to reciprocal and cyclic play. No. 15, with its complex arrangement of mates changed and transferred in cyclic pattern, appeared at the start of the decade, as if to point the way. L. I. Loshinsky and V. I. Chepizhny, First prize, Leipzig Olympic tourney 1960 – mate in 2: Try 1. Qb7? (2. d7), Sf7; 2. Sb3 (A). 1.., Rh7; 2. b4 (B). 1.., Re8; 2. Qb6. 1.., Re4! Try 1. Qg4?, Sf7; 2. Rc4 (C). 1.., Rh7; 2. Qd4. 1.., Re8; 2. b4 (B). 1.., Bd5! Key 1. Qe6!, Sf7; 2. Qd5. 1.., Rh7; 2. Rc4 (C). 1.., Re8; 2. Sb3 (A). Cyclic play (see below) has also become popular among three-move composers.

In addition to these developments, the twentieth century has witnessed the emergence of fairy problems, which now command a considerable following. But what the typical chess problem will be like by the end of the century is virtually impossible to predict.

Further reading (in English): H. Weenink: *The Chess Problem* (A. C. White's Christmas Series, 1926); B. Harley: *Mate in Two Moves* (1931) and *Mate in Three Moves* (1943); C. Mansfield: *Adventures in Composition* (1943); M. Lipton, R. C. O. Matthews and J. M. Rice: *Chess Problems: Introduction to an Art* (1963); J. M. Rice: *An ABC of Chess Problems* (1970). *(J.M.R.)*

PROBLEMISTS AND PROBLEM ORGANIZATIONS

Albrecht, Hermann *(b. 30 August 1915)*
German problem expert, known less for his 100-plus compositions than for his very wide knowledge of problems and his enormous collection of published two-movers. International Judge (1957).

Anderson, Gerald Frank *(b. 23 February 1898)*
British problem composer, output about 550 problems, orthodox and fairy. Books: *Adventures of My Chessmen*; and *Are There Any?* (1959 – a fascinating collection of Kriegspiel problems); *Vincent Eaton Memorial* (1971 – an annotated anthology of Eaton's work). President of British Chess Problem Society, 1962–4. International Judge (1960), international master (1975).

Bakcsi, György *(b. 6 April 1933)*
Hungarian problemist, output about 600 two- and three-movers and helpmates. International master (1967).

Barnes, Barry Peter *(b. 1 August 1937)*
British problem composer, output about 400, nearly all modern-style two-movers. Two-move sub-editor of *The Problemist*. Secretary of the FIDE Problem Commission during C. Mansfield's Presidency. Co-author of *The Two-move Chess Problem: Tradition and Development* (1966). Author of *Pick of the best Chess problems* (1976); *Comino Mansfield MBE: Chess problems of a grandmaster* (1976). International Judge (1967); international master (1967).

Bartolović, Voyko *(b. 15 June 1932)*
Yugoslav problem composer, output about 700, mostly two- and three-movers. International master (1967); International Judge (1956).

Barulin, M. M. *(1898–1942)*
Russian problem composer, leader of a group of Russians who investigated white line-themes and dual avoidance strategy between 1928 and 1935. See PROBLEMS: HISTORY.

Blake, Percy Francis *(1873–1936)*
British problemist, regarded as one of England's finest composers. Blake produced direct-mate problems in two, three and four moves.

Bohemian School
The problem-composers of the Bohemian School were and are the principal exponents of model-mate problems, in which the main interest resides in mobility of force (particularly White) and beauty of mate. The school developed during the late nineteenth-century from the work of A. König (1836–1911), J. Dobrusky (1853–1907) and J. Pospisil (1861–1916). Its most distinguished composer was Miroslav Havel (1881–1958).

British Chess Problem Society
Founded 10 August 1918, this society is open to problemists of all countries and has a membership of over five hundred. Its magazine, *The Problemist*, appears bi-monthly. Meetings are held at St Bride's Institute, London, on the last Friday of winter months.

Chandler, Guy Wills *(b. 21 August 1889)*
British problemist, active as a composer mainly during the 1920s and 1930s, specializing in model-mate three-movers. Best known for his work as Secretary of the British Chess Problem Society 1919–25, and as Secretary and Treasurer from 1952. International Judge (1957).

Chepizhny, Victor *(b. 18 February 1934)*
Soviet problem composer, output about 250 direct-mate two-, three- and more-movers. International Judge (1965); international master (1969).

Dawson, Thomas Rayner *(28 November 1889–16 December 1951)*
British problemist, output over 6,000, 5,000+ being fairies. Dawson is remembered especially for his enormous contribution to fairy chess, of which he was the world's leading exponent. Not only did he invent new pieces (e.g. Grasshopper, Nightrider) and new forms (e.g. Serieshelpmate), he also popularized fairy ideas with unparalleled enthusiasm through his writing and editing. Books include *Caissa's Wild Roses* (1935), *Caissa's Wild Roses in Clusters* (1937), *Ultimate Themes* (1938), and *Caissa's Fairy Tales* (1947); and in collaboration *Retrograde Analysis* (1915), and *Asymmetry* (1928). Editor of *The Problemist* (1922–31), fairy section of *Chess Amateur* (1919–30), *Fairy Chess Review* (previously *Problemist Fairy Supplement*) (1930–51) and problem pages of *British Chess Magazine* (1931–51). Of these, the *Fairy Chess Review* was probably his greatest achievement. President of British Chess Problem Society 1931–43.

Dickins, Anthony Stewart Mackay *(b. 1 November 1914)*
British problemist. Founder of Q Press (1967) to publish books on fairy problems: *A Guide to Fairy Chess* (1967); *An Album of Fairy Chess* (1970); *The Serieshelpmate* (co-author, 1971). Has presented a large collection of problem books to Cambridge University Library. International Judge (1975).

Dijk, Nils G. G. van *(b. 21 October 1933)*
Norwegian problemist, two- and three-move specialist. International master (1961); International Judge (1966).

Driver, John Edward *(b. 21 July 1928)*
British problemist. Output consists of two-movers, helpmates and fairy problems. Inventor of the Edgehog, a fairy piece which moves along Q-lines but always either to or from a square at the board-edge.

Eaton, Vincent Lanius *(13 August 1915–16 March 1962)*
American problemist. Specialist in three-movers of high strategic content. Best work to be found in *Memorial to V. L. Eaton*, compiled by his friend and collaborator G. F. Anderson.

Ellerman, Arnoldo *(12 January 1893–21 November 1969)*
Argentinian problemist, one of the greatest of all two-move composers. Began composing during Good Companion era and was a leading exponent of the complex theme strategy the Good Companions popularized. Always maintained an interest in new developments without being an originator himself. Output numbered several thousand, and at one time he averaged one new problem a day.

Fabel, Karl *(20 October 1905–3 March 1975)*
German problemist; output of 1,200 included strategic miniatures, three- and more-movers, and many examples of mathematical problems and retrograde analysis, on which Fabel wrote many books.

'Fairy Chess Review'
Known for its first six years as *Problemist Fairy Supplement*, this bi-monthly magazine was edited from 1930 to his death in 1951 by T. R. Dawson, whose successors, C. E. Kemp and D. Nixon, managed to keep it alive until 1958. Devotees of fairy problems still regard *F.C.R.* as the leading inspiration in this field.

FIDE Albums
Anthologies of published problems and endgame studies assembled, selected and published under the auspices of the FIDE Problem Commission. The series to date consists of two Retrospective Albums covering the years 1914–44, and 1945–55, and then five volumes each covering three years: 1956–8, 1959–61, 1962–4, 1965–7, 1968–70. Others are in preparation.

FIDE Problem Commission
This body was founded in 1956 to deal with all matters relating to the composition of problems and endgame studies. As part of its activities, it organizes international composing tourneys, and it bestows various titles: International Judge (following recommendation by national problem societies); International Master (to composers who have a certain number of their own compositions accepted for inclusion in the FIDE Albums, and whose other work is judged to be of sufficient merit); and Grandmaster (awarded 'sparingly . . . to artists of exceptional merit').

The following hold the title of grandmaster of the FIDE for chess compositions: C. Mansfield (Britain); E. Visserman (Holland); G. Kasparian, V. Bron and V. Korolikov (USSR); V. Pachman and J. Fritz (Czechoslovakia); and N. Petrović (Yugoslavia).

Good Companion Chess Problem Club
Founded by James F. Magee Jr in Philadelphia in 1913, this is the best known of all problem societies. There were ten founder members, but the annual membership eventually exceeded six hundred. The Club published monthly 'folders' of original work, and it was in these folders that some of the classics of the two-mover first appeared. The Club was disbanded in 1924.

Gooderson, Arthur Robert *(b. 4 January 1906)*
British problemist, output about 200 two-movers. International Judge (1966).

Grasemann, Herbert *(b. 21 December 1917)*
German problemist, output about 180, mostly more-movers. Author of three books on post-war problem developments: *Problemschach I* (1955), *Problemschach II* (1959) and *Problemjuwelen* (1964). International Judge (1957).

Guidelli, Giorgio *(1897–1924)*
Brilliant Italian two-move composer, specialist in complex theme-combinations of Good Companion era.

Hannelius, Jan *(b. 7 December 1916)*
Finnish problemist, output about 800 orthodox two- and three-

movers. International Judge (1957). Elected President of the FIDE Problem Commission, September 1974.

Haring, Jacobus *(b. 30 March 1913)*
Secretary of the Nederlandse Bond van Probleemvrienden, composer of 950 two-movers. International Judge (1964); international master (1968).

Harley, Brian *(27 October 1883–18 May 1955)*
British problemist, known perhaps less for his problems (mainly two- and three-movers) than for his influential writing and editing. Chess correspondent of the *Observer* for over twenty years. Books include: *Mate in Two Moves* (1931), *Mate in Three Moves* (1943), and (published posthumously) *The Modern Two-move Chess Problem*, with problems by C. Mansfield (1958). President of the British Chess Problem Society 1947–9.

Hartong, Jan *(b. 11 February 1902)*
Dutch problemist, output about 1,050 problems of all types. One of the finest and most versatile composers of all time. International master (1959).

Havel, Miroslav *(7 November 1881–8 July 1958)*
Pseudonym of Miroslav Kostal, Bohemian problem composer. The greatest of all model-mate composers in the Bohemian style.

Heathcote, Godfrey *(20 July 1870–8 July 1952)*
British problemist, generally regarded as the outstanding English composer of model-mate problems. President of British Chess Problem Society 1951–2.

Holladay, Edgar *(b. 26 October 1925)*
US problemist, output about 550, consisting of direct-mate two- and three-movers, selfmates, helpmates and fairy problems. International Judge (1956).

Jensch, Gerhard Wolfgang *(b. 27 January 1920)*
German problemist, earlier compositions mainly two-movers, but recently more interested in fairy problems. Editor of flourishing problem section in *Schach-Echo* (fortnightly). President of FIDE Problem Commission 1971–1974. International Judge (1966).

Kemp, Charles Edward *(b. 18 November 1901)*
British problemist, specialist in fairy problems. Editor, with D. Nixon, of *Fairy Chess Review*, 1952–8. Co-author, with K. Fabel, of *Schach ohne Grenzen* (Chess Unlimited) (1969), an anthology of T. R. Dawson's work. International Judge (1964).

Kipping, Cyril Stanley *(10 October 1891–17 February 1964)*
British problemist, enormous output of over 6,000, mainly three-movers but also many two-movers, some published under pseudonyms (e.g. C. Stanley, of Nottingham). Editor of *The Problemist*, 1931–64. Elected international master *honoris causa* (1959).

Kricheli, Josef *(b. 10 May 1931)*
Russian composer of helpmates and serieshelpmates, output about 500. International master (1971).

Kubbel, Leonid I. *(25 December 1891–18 April 1942)*
Russian problemist, also known as K. A. L. Kubbel. Leading Soviet composer of interwar period. Output includes two-, three- and more-movers, fairy problems and endgame studies.

Lindgren, Bo *(b. 26 February 1927)*
Swedish problemist, output about 400, mainly Bohemian three- and more-movers, and task problems. International master (1965); International Judge (1966).

Lipton, Michael *(b. 13 February 1937)*
British problem composer, output about 400, nearly all modern-style two-movers. Co-author of *Chess Problems: Introduction to an Art* (1963), and *The Two-move Chess Problem: Tradition and Development* (1966). International master (1976).

Loshinsky, Lev Ilich *(17 January 1913–19 February 1976)*
Russian problem composer, specialist in two- and three-movers; regarded by many as the outstanding Russian problemist of all time. Elected grandmaster (1972).

Loyd, Sam *(30 January 1841–11 April 1911)*
American problemist, one of the most brilliant and inventive of composers, Loyd brought humour into problem composition. Although he composed mainly three-movers, his influence extended into the two-move field, and his pioneering prepared the way for the great awakening of interest in the complex two-mover by the Good Companions. See PROBLEM THEMES: EXCELSIOR.

Mansfield, Comins *(b. 14 June 1896)*
Britain's most distinguished problem composer, output about 850, nearly all two-movers. Very active during the period of the Good Companions, contributing to their folders many classic examples of half-pin, cross-check and other important themes. Books include *Adventures in Composition* (1943), a fascinating exposé of the composer's methods. President of the British Chess Problem Society, 1949–51. President of the FIDE Problem Commission, 1963–71, and Hon. President since 1972. International Judge (1957); international master (1959); grandmaster (1972).

Mari, Alberto *(13 June 1892–31 July 1953)*
Italian two-move composer, regarded, with Guidelli, as the founder of modern two-move composition in Italy.

Matthews, Robin C. O. *(b. 16 June 1927)*
British problem composer, output about 200. His country's leading strategic three-move composer, and one of the world's outstanding exponents of the genre. Co-author of *Chess Problems: Introduction to an Art* (1963). President of the British Chess Problem Society, 1970–2. International Judge (1957); international master (1965).

Meredith, William *(1835–10 August 1903)*
The US composer William Meredith, who strove in his problems for the ideals of economy and purity, has given his name to problems of twelve pieces or fewer. 'Meredith Tourneys' were organized by the Good Companion Chess Problem Club to encourage the composition of lightweight problems.

Morse, Sir Christopher Jeremy *(b. 10 December 1928)*
British problemist; output consists of two-movers, helpmates and serieshelpmates. Enthusiastic investigator into task problems in all these spheres. International Judge (1975).

Niemeijer, Meindert *(b. 18 February 1902)*
Dutch problemist, output about 500. Best known for his 30-plus books on problems, including collections of the work of various composers and anthologies of particular types of problem. International Judge (1958). International master (1976).

Oudot, Jean *(11 December 1926–29 December 1974)*
French problemist, output around 350, mostly two-movers and fairies. Editor of problem section of *Europe-Echecs* from 1959 until his death.

Pachman, Vladimir *(b. 16 April 1918)*
Czechoslovak problemist, output about 900 three- and more-movers. International Judge (1956); international master (1960), grandmaster (1975). Brother of the former Czechoslovak grandmaster, Ludek Pachman.

Páros, György *(28 April 1910–17 December 1975)*
Hungarian problemist, output of about 800 consists mostly of orthodox two-movers and helpmates. Acknowledged during his lifetime as one of the world's leading helpmate specialists. Elected grandmaster 1975.

Pauly, Wolfgang *(1876–1934)*
Romanian problemist, specialist in model-mate problems and in selfmates (particularly maximummers).

Petrović, Nenad *(b. 7 September 1907)*
Yugoslav problemist; output of 800 consists mostly of task problems. Editor of *Problem* and the FIDE Albums. Hon. President for life of FIDE Problem Commission. International Judge (1956); international master (1965), grandmaster (1975).

'Probleemblad'
The bi-monthly magazine of the Nederlandse Bond van Probleemvrienden (Dutch Problem Society).

'Problem'
Multi-lingual problem magazine produced in Yugoslavia, appearing at irregular intervals (usually about two issues per year). Official organ of the FIDE Problem Commission.

'Problemist, The'
Bi-monthly magazine of the British Chess Problem Society, containing original and selected problems of all types, articles, composing and solving tourneys, and catering for both experts and beginners. The first issue appeared in January 1926, edited by T. R. Dawson. Other editors: C. S. Kipping (1931–64), J. F. Ling (1964–72) and C. Vaughan (from 1972).

Reeves, Christopher *(b. 19 February 1939)*
British problemist; output consists of skilfully constructed two-movers in the modern style.

Rehm, Hans-Peter *(b. 28 November 1942)*
German composer of all types of problem. Among his 600-plus problems, more-movers and fairies predominate. Already one of the world's outstanding composers, Rehm seems destined to rank among the greatest of all time. International Judge (1968); international master (1968).

Rice, John Michael *(b. 19 July 1937)*

British problem composer, output about 500, mainly modern-style two-movers but also several helpmates, serieshelpmates and fairy problems. Editing: problem section of *British Chess Magazine* (1961–1974). Author of *An ABC of Chess Problems* (1970), and co-author of *Chess Problems: Introduction to an Art* (1963), *The Two-move Chess Problem: Tradition and Development* (1966), and *The Serieshelpmate* (1971). International master (1969); International Judge (1972).

Rudenko, Valentin *(b. 19 February 1938)*
Russian problem composer, output about 400 direct-mate two-, three- and more-movers. International Judge (1960); international master (1961).

'Schwalbe, Die'
The German Problem Society and the title of its magazine. The name derives from the quotation attached to this problem by J. Kohtz (1843–1918) and C. Kockelkorn (1843–1914) – mate in 4:

1. Qf7 (2. Sd3+), Bd5; 2. Qa7, Ra4; 3. Qh7, Be4; 4. Qh4 (3.., Re4; 4. Qh1): *Eine Schwalbe macht noch keinen Sommer* (one swallow does not make a summer). The composers had been inactive for some time before the problem appeared. (The theme of the problem is Grimshaw preceded by critical moves of the thematic R and B.)

Shinkman, William Anthony *(25 December 1847–25 May 1933)*
American problemist, born in Bohemia but made his name as a composer in the USA, with several thousand problems to his credit. One of the closest followers of Sam Loyd, but with a distinctive style of his own, Shinkman played an important part in the development of the problem in America.

Speckmann, Werner *(b. 21 August 1913)*
German problemist, output about 2,000, mainly three- and more-movers, including many miniatures, in which form Speckmann is the world's leading specialist. Author of several books on miniatures and problems of the New German school. International Judge (1959); international master (1967).

Steudel, Theodor *(b. 4 July 1928)*
German problemist, output nearly 1,000, mainly helpmates and fairies. The world's leading expert in problems showing fourfold promotion (German *Allumwandlung*). International Judge (1966).

Stocchi, Ottavio *(18 September 1906–4 March 1964)*
Italian problem composer, output nearly 1,000, mainly two-movers, of which 240 won prizes. Must rank among the dozen finest composers of all time.

Umnov, Yevgeny *(b. 11 February 1913)*
Russian two-move composer, output about 200. Author of several books on the history and development of the problem. International Judge (1956), international master (1975).

Visserman, Eeltje *(b. 24 January 1922)*
Dutch problemist, output 745 problems of all types, orthodox two- and three-movers predominating. Among the world's outstanding composers of the present day. Editor of *Probleemblad*, 1957–70, and of Dutch Problem Society's *Jaarboek*, 1957–64. International Judge (1958); international master (1961); grandmaster (1972).

White, Alain Campbell *(3 March 1880–23 April 1951)*
American problemist. An enthusiastic composer, writer, critic and benefactor, White for many years produced as an annual Christmas present for his friends a new book on problems. Wrote only some of them himself, but was the driving force behind the series, and its financial backer. Some of the most famous of all problem books first appeared in the 'Christmas Series', e.g. Weenink's *The Chess Problem* (1926). White was also a prominent member of the Good Companion Club, and he began a collection of published two-movers which C. S. Kipping took over in 1936.

Wilson, Vaux *(b. 16 June 1899)*
American problemist, originator of 'M.O.E.', a mathematical Method of Evaluation for assessing chess problems, based on a system of points awarded for various strategic features.

Wurzburg, Otto *(10 August 1875–1 October 1951)*
American problemist, nephew of W. Shinkman. Famous for light-weight three- and more-movers of impeccable construction.

Zepler, Eric *(b. 27 January 1898)*
German-born problemist, long resident in England. Output about 800 problems, nearly all strategic three- and more-movers. Co-author (with A. Kraemer) of *Im Banne des Schachproblems* (Under the Spell of the Chess Problem, 1951) and *Problemkunst im 20 Jahrhundert* (The Problem Art in the Twentieth Century, 1957). President of the British Chess Problem Society, 1966–8. International Judge (1957), international master 1973. One of the world's leading experts in longer problems. *(J.M.R.)*

PROBLEM THEMES

Anticipation
A problem which someone else has composed before is said to be anticipated, and the earlier problem is termed an anticipation. A problem is 'completely anticipated' if the theme, the strategy and the positions of the principal pieces in the two settings are identical or nearly so. A 'partial anticipation' occurs when the two problems resemble one another in some but not all respects.

Battery
An arrangement of pieces frequently found in the problem and consisting of (1) line-piece (Q, R, B), (2) another piece of the same colour, and (3) the opposing K, in that order on the same rank, file or diagonal. The battery opens (or fires) when piece 2 moves to discover check or mate from piece 1.

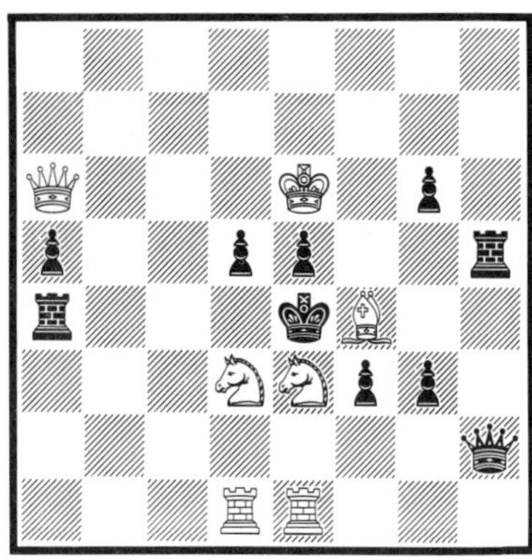

E. Umnov, first prize, *Trud* 1947 – mate in 2: 1. Qc6. The battery on the e-file is direct, that on the d-file (aimed at the K's field) indirect.

Block problem
A problem in which White's first move (key) carries no threat but merely waits for Black to move, Black being placed in *zugzwang*. The initial position of the problem may be either an incomplete block: Black has moves available to which White has no set mate or continuation, and the key introduces mates or continuations to follow all Black's moves; or a complete block, which may be either a waiting-move problem, the key merely retaining the set mates or continuations, or a mutate, in which one or more of White's replies will be changed.

Block-threat
A complete block problem in which White's key, rather than merely preserving *zugzwang*, introduces a threat, usually with changed play.

Bristol
The problemist's term for a 'clearance' move by a piece along a line and over a certain square, played so that a second piece may move in the same direction along the same line and occupy that square. The name derives from a three-mover by Frank Healey (1828–1906) which won first prize in a composing tourney held in Bristol in 1861. See PROBLEMS: HISTORY.

By-play
Variations in a problem which are not directly connected with or an integral part of the principal theme.

Changed play

The term used by problemists to denote post-key continuations or mates which differ from those at White's disposal in the set play or the virtual play. H. Weenink, *Good Companions* 1917 – mate in 2: 1. Qc4, with changes after the moves of the Pc7. See also MUTATE, ZAGORUYKO and RUKHLIS.

Construction task
This is a form of non-orthodox problem in which the composer aims to achieve a setting showing the maximum possible moves of a single type, such as checks, mates, stalemates, stalemate releases, etc. The record is published not as a problem to be solved but as a challenge to other composers to improve on it. If two composers achieve the same maximum record, the more economical setting is deemed to hold that record.

The first construction task dates from 1848, when this position was proposed by M. Bezzel in *Deutsche Schachzeitung*, with the stipulation: 'Maximum moves for eight White pieces only; Black K on board, not in check'; the record attained is 100 moves, which has been shown to be the maximum possible on a normal board.

Cook
An alternative solution to a problem which the composer has not intended.

Correction (Black)
In a problem a Black piece moving at random to no particular square may automatically allow a White continuation or mate (the 'secondary threat'). But by selecting its square of arrival more carefully, the piece may 'correct' the error committed by the random move, preventing the secondary threat from operating as a valid continuation. However, the correction move will contain a further error (the 'secondary error') which will permit a new White continuation.

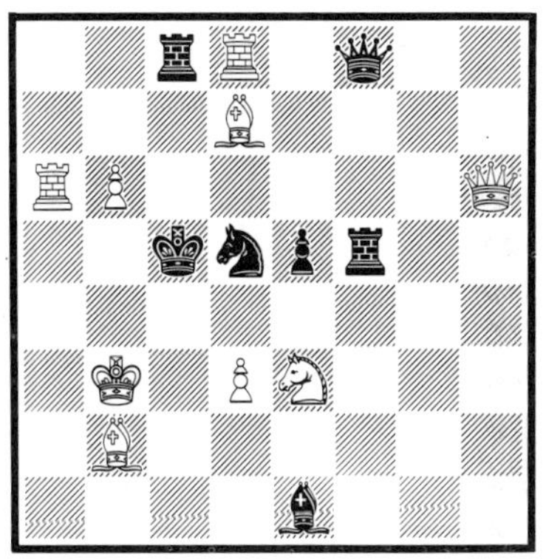

G. Dulcsan, 1st hon. mention, *Magyar Sakkvilag* 1938 – mate in 2: 1. Be8 (2. R × d5). The error allowing the secondary threat 2. R × c8 (playable after 1.., Sf4) is corrected seven different times.

Correction (White)

In the two-move problem White correction involves tries by a White piece whose move 'at random' is 'corrected' by a careful choice of arrival square.

B. P. Barnes, *B.C.M.* 1961 – mate in 2: Try 1. Sb at random? Rc7! Try 1. Sc4?, b3! Try 1. Sc at random? R × d5! Key 1. Sb5! White correction is also commonly found as second-move strategy in three-movers.

Critical play

To the problemist a 'critical move' is one in which a line-piece (Q, R, B) passes over a square (the 'critical' square), with the result that any piece then arriving on that square will cause interference. Critical play can be classified according to whether White or Black plays the critical move, which side subsequently occupies the critical square, and which side gains the advantage from the manoeuvre.

M. Barulin, G. P. Golubev, A. P. Gulyaev, L. Loshinsky, E. Umnov and V. Schiff, *64* 1932 – mate in 2: 1. Rb5 (2. Se4). After 1.., Qa8 and 1.., R × e7 White occupies the critical square to his own advantage by shutting off the moving black piece.

See also INDIAN and TURTON.

Cross-check

A problem term denoting a check by Black answered by White by interposal on the check line with simultaneous direct or discovered check or mate. B. P. Barnes, 2nd prize, B.C.P.S. Ring tourney 1959 – mate in 2: 1. Kb3 (2. Qb4). Three distinct cross-checks.

Cyclic play

A sequence of problem effects arranged in the order AB–BC–CA or ABC–BCA–CAB. The sequence may sometimes be extended to include a fourth or even a fifth element (e.g. AB–BC–CD–DA, or AB–BC–CD–DE–EA etc.).

Cyclic play lends itself to many different forms of treatment, but is most commonly associated with one of the following themes or patterns: interference (piece A interferes with piece B, B with C, and C with A), dual avoidance, correction (Black and White), change, mate transference, obstruction and overload.

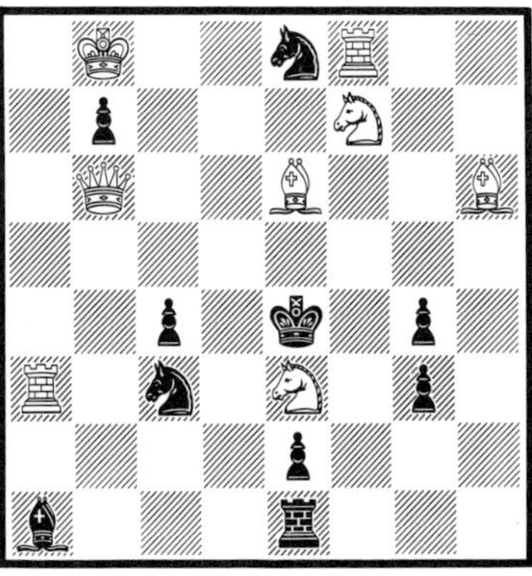

V. F. Rudenko, first prize, *Gruziya 50*, 1971 – mate in 2: Set 1.., Kf3; 2. Sg5 (A). 1.., Sd1; 2. Bd5 (B). Try 1. Sf5? (2. Qe3), Kf3; 2. Bd5 (B). 1.., Sd1; 2. Q × b7 (C). 1.., Sd5! Key 1. S × g4! (2. Qe3), Kf3; 2. Q × b7 (C). 1.., Sd1; 2. Sg5 (A). Cyclic change in Zagoruyko form: Black's two main defences are the same in each of the three phases, while White's mates change in the cyclic pattern AB–BC–CA.

Direct-mate

A composed position in which White, to move and playing up the board, mates Black in a stipulated number of moves, whatever defence(s) Black may choose to play. Such problems are also termed 'orthodox'. For problems which are not direct-mates, see SELFMATE, HELPMATE, REFLEX-MATE, SERIESHELPMATE and CONSTRUCTION TASK.

Dresden

A defence-substitution theme found in three- and more-move problems. If, in the initial position, White made a certain threat, a Black piece X would have an adequate defence. White must therefore induce Black to replace this defence by another, by piece Y, which however will carry a weakness that White can exploit.

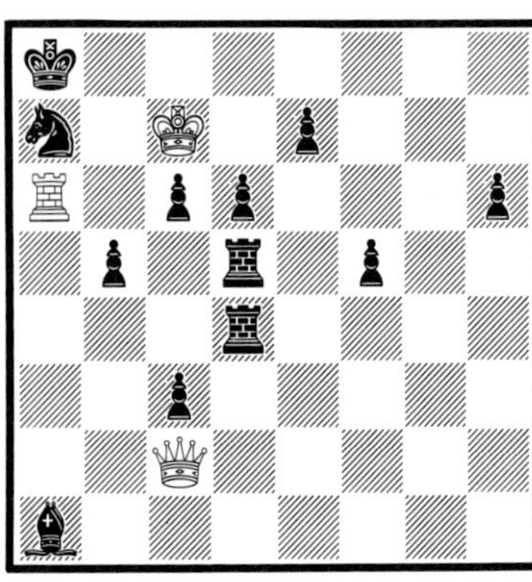

E. Zepler, Fourth prize, *Dresdener Anzeiger* 1927 – mate in 3: Try 1. Qg2? (2. Qg8), Rg4! Try 1. Qa2? (2. R × a7), Ra4! Key 1. Qf2! (2. Qg1, then 3. Qg8), f4; 2. Qg2, Rg5; 3. Q × c6. 1.., b4; 2. Qa2, Ra5; 3. Qg8. The idea dates from the work of a Dresden composer, Friedrich Palitzsch (1889–1932).

Dual

A dual occurs in a problem when White has a choice of continuation or mate (the term 'dual' being generally used to cover also 'triple', 'quadruple', etc.) A dual is serious if it arises in a thematic variation, harmless only if it occurs after an insignificant Black move.

Dual avoidance

Dual avoidance in a problem is found when a Black move appears to allow White a choice of continuation or mate, but contains some positive element which in fact limits White's choice to a single continuation or mate.

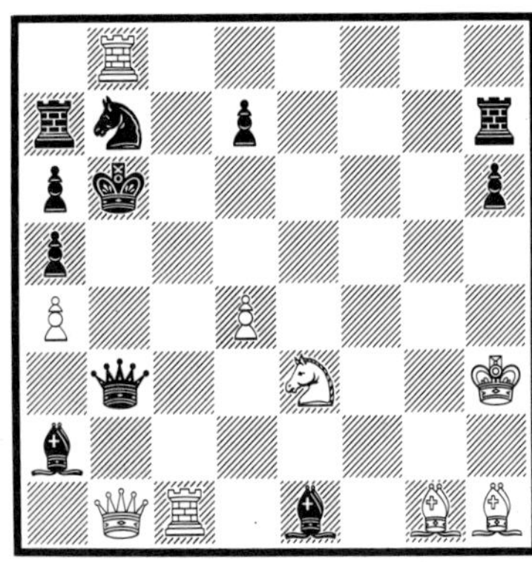

C. Mansfield, *Good Companions* 1919 – mate in 2: 1. Bh2 (2. Bc7). After 1.., Bg3 and 1.., Bc3, White, in mating with his unpinned S, must take care to close the same White line as the Black B has just closed, to avoid allowing the Black K a flight-square.

Duplex

A problem position in which the stipulation (i.e. mate in 2, helpmate in 3, etc.) applies both if White is to give the mate and if Black is to give the mate. The majority of duplex problems are helpmates.

Excelsior

Sam Loyd composed this problem (mate in 5) in 1858 to confound a boastful member of a New York chess club who claimed he could tell at a glance which piece in a problem would deliver the principal mate. Loyd bet him a dinner that he could not say which piece did *not* give the mate in this problem.

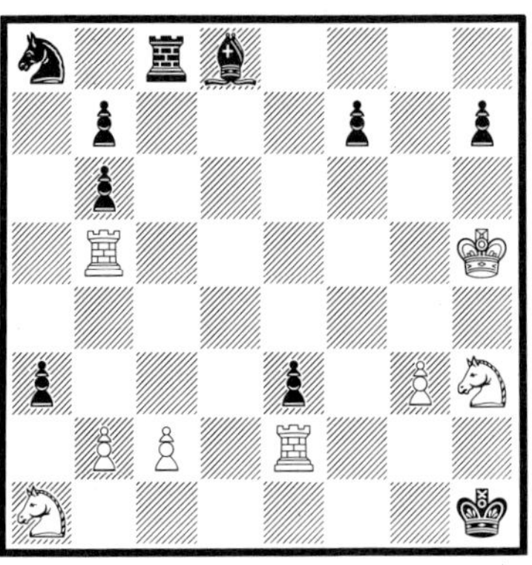

The man selected the Pb2 as being the most unlikely – and had to pay for the dinner, since the solution runs: 1. b4 (2. Rd5), Rc5+; 2. b × c5, a2; 3. c6, Bc7; 4. c × b7 (5. b × a8Q)! A pawn initially on its starting square which promotes to give mate in the course of a problem's solution has been dubbed 'Excelsior'.

Fairy

Problems which are not direct mates come under the heading 'Fairy', a term first used by H. Tate of Melbourne in 1914 and popularized by T. R. Dawson. A fairy problem differs from an orthodox one in one or more of the following respects: (1) stipulation, e.g. selfmate, helpmate, reflex-mate, serieshelpmate; (2) force – fairy pieces may be present, e.g. grasshopper, nightrider; (3) board, which may be a cylinder or grid; (4) retrograde analysis may be called for; (5) the position may be a construction task.

Works on fairy chess: T. R. Dawson, *Caissa's Wild Roses* (1935); A. S. M. Dickins, *A Guide to Fairy Chess* (1967).

Flight(-square)

A square to which a K has access in the course of a problem's solution.

Grasshopper

A fairy piece invented by T. R. Dawson in 1912, and the most popular of all non-orthodox pieces. It moves along Q-lines, but must hop over another piece of either colour and land on the next square beyond. If that square is occupied by a piece of the same colour as the G, the move is not playable.

J. Oudot, 1st hon. mention, *Europe-Echecs* 1964 – mate in 2: 1. Ggd4, Gh1+; 2. Geb4. 1.., G × e2; 2. S3b4. 1.., Ge6; 2. S5b4. 1.., Gc2; 2. Bb4. 1.., G × c6; 2. Gbb4.

Grid-board

Invented by W. Stead in 1953, this is a fairy board on which all moves must cross at least one line of the grid. The composer of the problem is free to place his grid where he chooses, but the most popular pattern is that seen in this example.

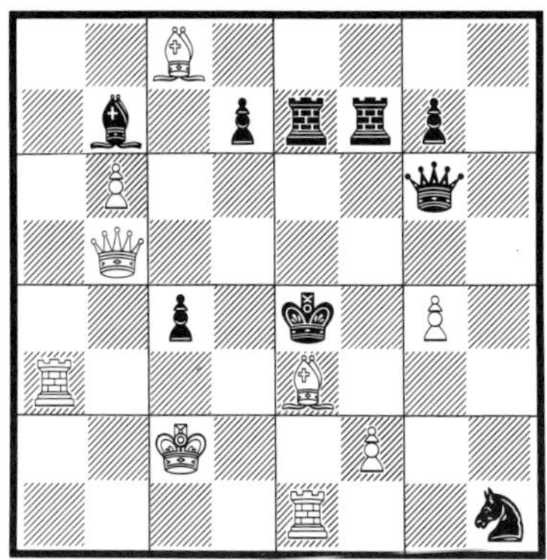

E. Visserman, *Fairy Chess Review* 1954 – mate in 2: 1. Ra5 (2. Q × c4), Qf6; 2. Qf5. 1.., Qe6; 2. Qe5. 1.., Qd6; 2. B × b7. 1.., Qc6; 2. Qd5. Since pieces are not allowed to move within each grid-square, some curious interference effects can be achieved.

Grimshaw

A pair of interference variations, in which piece X interferes with piece Y and vice versa, is termed a Grimshaw, after the English composer Walter Grimshaw (1832–90), one of whose compositions (*Illustrated London News*, 1850) featured such an arrangement for the first time.

L. I. Loshinsky, Commended, *Tijdschrift v.d. N.S.B.*, 1930 – mate in 2: 1. Bb3. In this example, one of the most famous of all two-movers, three distinct Grimshaws may be seen, on the squares b7 and g7 (between R and B) and f6 (between B and P).

Half-battery

A battery in which not one but two pieces of the same colour stand between a line-piece and the opposing K.

M. Lipton, *Problemnoter* 1962 – mate in 2: Try 1. Rf3? (2. Rd7), K × d3! Key 1. Rg3! (2. Rd6).

Half-pin

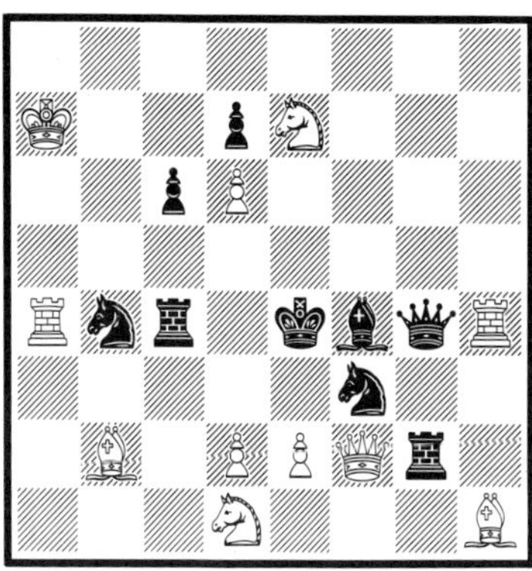

Two pieces positioned on a line in such a way that if either moves off the line the other becomes completely pinned, are said to be half-pinned.

B. Malmström, third prize *Good Companions*, February 1923 – mate in 2: 1. Qc5. Six Black pieces are half-pinned.

Helpmate

A problem in which White and Black co-operate towards the common aim of mate of the Black K. Traditionally Black plays first, unless the composer decrees otherwise.

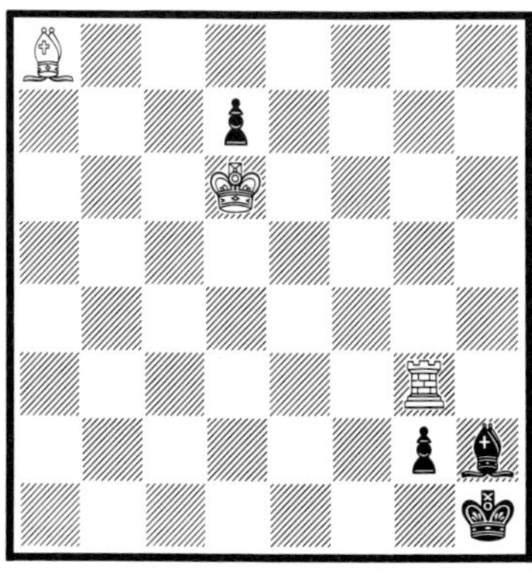

N. Petrović, First prize, *Feenschach* 8th Theme tourney 1953 – helpmate in 2, with set play: one solution if White moves first, and a different though thematically related solution with Black moving first. Set: 1.., Kd5; 2. g1B, Kd6. Play: 1. Bg1, R × g2; 2. Bh2+, Rg3. Black's moves are always shown first in a helpmate solution.

In addition to set play (usually indicated by *), there are various ways in which a composer may achieve two or more different lines of play in a single helpmate. These are the principal ways, together with an indication of how the method employed is shown alongside or beneath the diagram:

(1) two or more solutions (2.1.1.1., or 3.1.1.1., 4.1.1.1. etc.);
(2) one Black first move with two or more White continuations (1.2.1.1., 1.3.1.1. etc.);
(3) one first move for each side, with two or more Black second moves (1.1.2.1., 1.1.3.1., etc.);
(4) twin positions (*a.* as diagram; *b.* move piece on square x to square y – see TWIN for other acceptable twinning methods);
(5) one solution with Black playing first and being mated, and another with White playing first and being mated (duplex).

Ideal mate

A model-mate in which all the force on the board, both Black and White, is necessarily used, K and Ps included.

Indian

A three- or more-move problem theme involving critical play by White: a White critical move, followed by White self-interference on the critical square for the purpose of relieving stalemate (allowing the Black K a flight), and finally a discovered mate.

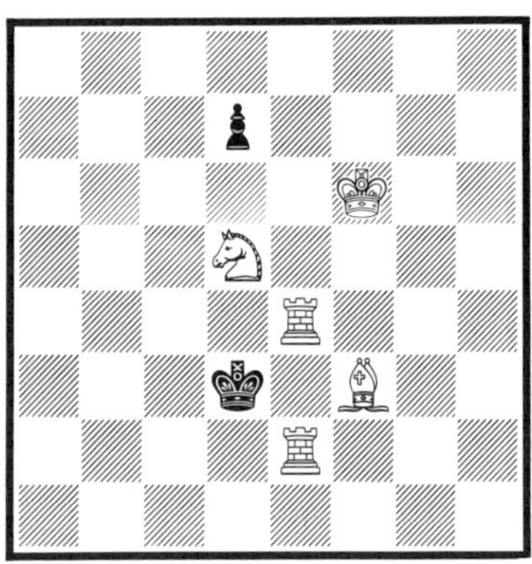

W. Greenwood, *Illustrated London News*, 1859 – mate in 3: 1. Bh1, d6; 2. Rg2, K × e4; 3. Rd2.

The theme is called Indian because it was first shown by H. A. Loveday, who was at the time chaplain of the Bengal Ecclesiastical Establishment. His problem, which appeared in the *Chessplayers' Chronicle* in 1845, is famous in problem history, although in fact it has many solutions.

Interference (Black)

Black interference occurs in a problem when the line of guard of a Black line-piece (Q, R, B and P on second rank) is closed by another Black piece playing on to that line. H. W. Grant, First prize, B.C.F. tourney, 1966–7 – mate in 2: 1. Bd4. Nine different interferences are shown, each leading to mate. See also GRIMSHAW.

Interference (White)

White interference occurs in a problem when a White piece, in playing to a certain square, closes the line of a second White piece. In the two-move problem, a White-interference mate may be allowed by a Black self-block, line-opening or interference with a pinned piece.

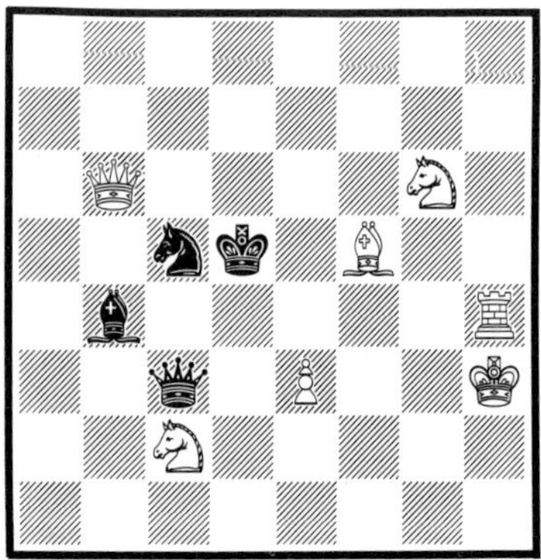

The first type is seen in the problem given under SELF-BLOCK, in the variation 1.., S × c6; 2. Sc7; and the latter is shown threefold in this problem by P. Kniest, First prize, *Die Schwalbe* Theme tourney, 1946 – mate in 2: 1. Qc7 (2. Se7). See also INDIAN.

Key

White's first move in a direct-mate problem. A sound problem has only one key, unless the composer deliberately intends otherwise.

Mate transference

Mate transference occurs in a problem when a mate found in the set or virtual play reappears after the key but following a different Black defence. (The German term *Paradenwechsel* ('change of defence') shows how this arrangement differs from normal changed play.) L. I. Loshinsky, First prize Chigorin Memorial tourney 1949–50 – mate in 2: 1. Be4.

The set play of this justly famous problem contains four self-blocks leading to mates which recur after the key following different Black defences, again self-blocks.

Maximummer

A problem in which the moves of one or the other side are restricted by the rule that the geometrically longest move must be played at all times, distances being measured from the centre of each square. Choice is allowed only when two moves of precisely equal length are available. The vast majority of such problems are selfmates, the maximummer rule being applied to Black only.

Miniature

A problem with seven pieces or fewer.

Minimal

A problem in which the force of one side or the other consists solely of the K and one other unit. In direct-mate problems the term is used only when the White force is thus restricted.

Model-mate

A mating position in which no square in the Black K's field is guarded more than once by White, and no square is guarded by White and simultaneously blocked by Black, and in which all the White men on the board, with the permitted exception of K and Ps, play some active part in the mate by guarding squares. (See diagram next page.)

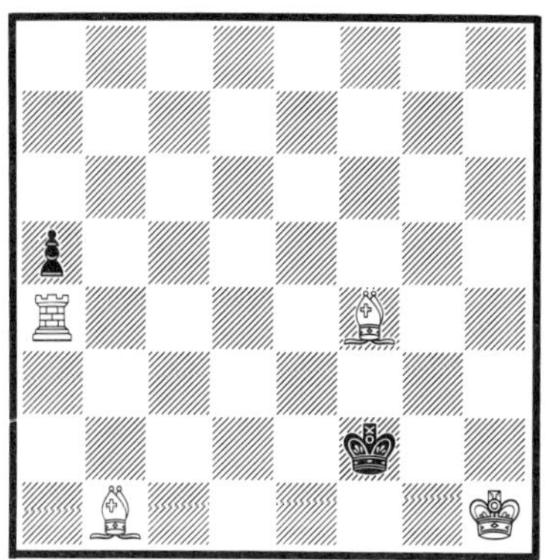

O. Wurzburg, First prize, Cheney Miniature tourney 1937 – mate in 4: 1. Bf5, Kf3; 2. Kg1, Ke2; 3. Bc2, Kf3; 4. Bd1 (3.., Ke1; 4. Re4). 1.., Kf1; 2. Bg4, Kf2; 3. Bd2, Kg3; Be1 (3.., Kf1; 4. Rf4). Four model-mates altogether, 'echoed' between the two variations: the White pieces stand on different squares but form exactly the same pattern.

More-mover

A direct-mate problem in four or more moves.

Mutate

A complete block problem in which White's key changes at least one of the mates which are set. The term was first used by Brian Harley. C. Promislo, 3rd hon. mention, 8th US Chess Congress (Meredith section), 1921 – mate in 2: 1. Qc7. Half-pin variations in both set and post-key play.

Nightrider

This fairy piece, invented by T. R. Dawson in 1925, extends the Knight's move in a straight line. Thus a Nightrider on a1 has access on a clear board to b3, c5, d7, c2, e3 and g4.

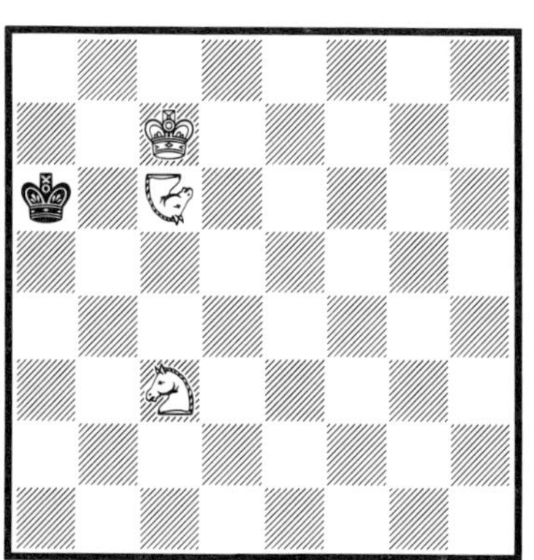

T. R. Dawson, *B.C.M.* 1925 – mate in 5: 1. Ne7, Ka7; 2. Ng3, Ka8; 3. Ne4, Ka7; 4. Sb5+, Ka8; 5. Nd2. Mate can be forced against a lone K by K+S+N simply because the Nightrider can make a waiting move without unguarding a square.

Nowotny

This problem theme derives its name from Anton Nowotny (1829–71) and consists of Grimshaw interference introduced by White sacrifice on the square of interference. Nowotny's original example (*Leipziger Illustrierte Zeitung* 1854) had a critical move by one of the two thematic Black pieces (B and R) played before the Nowotny sacrifice could be effected. Nowadays the term is used to denote simply the sacrifice followed by distinct play after the two captures.

Although the theme is seen in a great many modern two-movers featuring try play, it finds perhaps its best expression in three-movers such as this.

R. C. O. Matthews, *B.C.M.* 1957 – mate in 3: 1. b4 (2. B × b1), Bb6; 2. Rd5, B × d5; 3. Sb5 (2.., R × d5; 3. Se4). 1.., Bc5; 2. Rb7. 1.., Rb × b5; 2. Qd5. 1.., Bb7; 2. Rc5, B × c5; 3. Sb5 (2.., R × c5; 3. B × d4). 1.., Bd5; 2. Rbb6. 1.., Rh × b5; 2. Rb6. Six White second-move Nowotnys.

Obstruction

Obstruction occurs in problems when a piece moves to a square so that another piece is prevented from occupying that square. In two-movers, only the Black K can be obstructed (self-block), but in three- and more-movers any piece may obstruct another.

E. Visserman, First prize, *Schach-Echo* 1965 – mate in 3: 1. Bh5 (2. Rd8+), Rc × d4; 2. Kf5. 1.., Rd × d4; 2. Ke6. 1.., Sb × d4; 2. Ke4. 1.., Sc × d4; 2. Kd5. Four Black self-obstructions on d4 leading to flights by the White K.

Overload

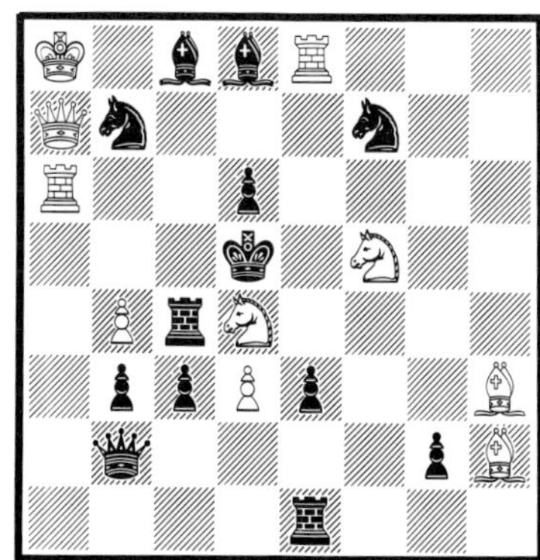

A piece becomes overloaded in a problem if it is made to guard more squares than it can cope with. N. G. G. van Dijk, 2nd prize, *Probleemblad* 1971 – mate in 3: 1. Sb5 (2. Sc7+), Re4; 2. Se7+. 1.., Bf6; 2. Qd4+. 1.., Rg4; 2. B × g2+. 1.., Rc5; 2. S × c3+. The threatened line and the four variations all utilize overload strategy. See PLACHUTTA.

Phase

The distinct parts of a problem's solution, viz. set play, virtual play and the play following the key.

Pin-mate

A pin-mate occurs in a problem when a Black piece, were it not pinned, could prevent the mate by capture or interposal.
A. Ellerman, *L'Italia Scacchistica* 1926 – mate in 2: 1. Sd4 (2. Ra4). The Black Q is thematically pinned in five different mates.

Plachutta

A three- and more-move interference theme in which a White piece sacrifices itself on the intersection square of the lines of two like-moving Black pieces. As each Black piece captures the White unit, it becomes overloaded, being forced to take over the duties of the other Black piece as well as its own.

J. Plachutta, *Leipziger Illustrierte Zeitung* 1858 (version) – mate in 3: 1. Rg7, Rh×g7; 2. Qg3+. 1.., Rg×g7; 2. Bc7+. The theme is named after this problem's nineteenth-century Austrian composer (*d.* 1883).

When interference between like-moving pieces is not introduced by White sacrifice, the tactic is termed 'Wurzburg-Plachutta' if the variations are paired, or 'Holzhausen' when only a single interference takes place.

Reciprocal play

A problem term denoting an arrangement of moves or effects in the pattern AB–BA. The Grimshaw is a simple instance: in one variation piece A interferes with piece B, and in another piece B interferes with piece A. Dual avoidance also is often reciprocal in character, the mate avoided in one variation being that forced in another, and vice versa. Other simple reciprocal themes or patterns include the half-pin, the half-battery and the Plachutta.

Reciprocal play may also be found in problems showing correction by Black: piece X moves at random and allows mate A, but the correction-move leads to mate B, while the random move of piece Y allows mate B, and its correction forces the recurrence of A. Reciprocal change is another popular theme: Black moves X and Y lead in one phase to mates A and B respectively, but in another phase to the same two mates reversed.

V. I. Chepizhni, First place, 4th USSR Team championship 1963 – mate in 2: Try 1. Rf8?, K×c7; 2. R×e7 (A).
1.., Kd7; 2. Rd5 (B). 1.., e6!
Key 1. Rf7!, K×c7; 2. Rd5 (B).
1.., Kd7; 2. Re×e7 (A).

Reflex-mate

A selfmate in which either side is obliged to give mate on the move if this becomes possible.
T. R. Dawson, *Tijdschrift v.d.N.S.B.* 1924 – reflex-mate in 2: 1. Bf5, b6; 2. Rhd3.
1.., Qa7; 2. Se4. 1.., Qa6; 2. e4. 1.., Qa5; 2. d3. 1.., Q×a4; 2. Rbd3. White opens lines for the Black Q to move along, and closes the line of guard of his own B.

Retrograde Analysis

If the solving of a problem depends on deciding how the diagram position has been reached, whether or not castling or *e.p.* capture is legal, etc., then retrograde analysis must be used. This involves tracing the imaginary game leading to the diagram position back a certain number of moves on either side, until whatever proof is required has been found.

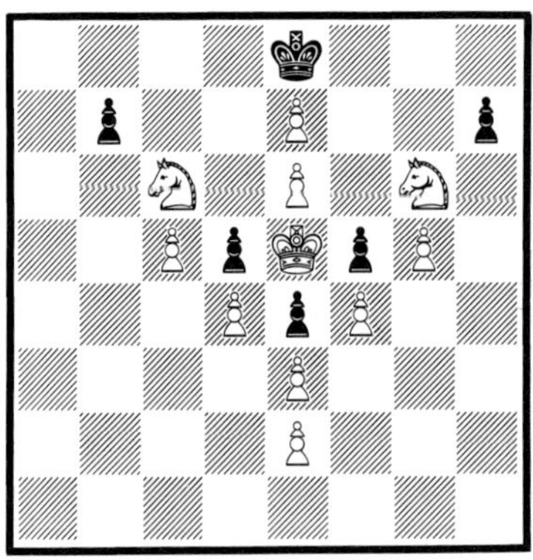

T. R. Dawson, *Falkirk Herald* 1914 – mate in 2. In this simple example Black's last move must have been either d7–d5 or f7–f5. As the White Ps, in reaching the diagram position, must have captured all ten of the missing Black units, d7–d5 must have been played long ago to allow the Black QB to come out and be captured. Therefore White cannot play 1. c×d5 *e.p.*? because the move is illegal Key 1. g×f5 *e.p.*

Roman
A strategic manoeuvre found in three-movers and longer problems. If White were to make a certain threat straightaway, a Black unit would have an adequate defence to that threat. This Black unit is therefore enticed or 'decoyed' away from the square from which it can play its adequate defence, and to a square from which it will have at its disposal a new defence to the original threat. However, the substitute defence will contain a weakness not present in the first defence, one which White can exploit in his mate or continuation.

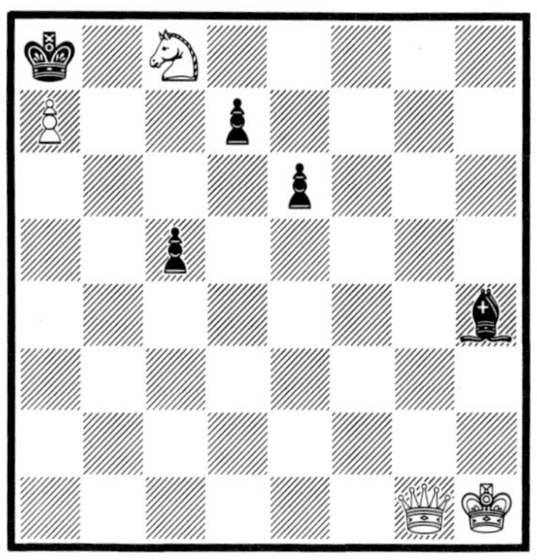

J. Möller, *Skakbladet* 1920 – mate in 3: Try 1. Qb1 ? (2. Qb8), Bg3 ! Key 1. Qg7 (2. Q × d7), Be7 ; 2. Qb2, Bd6 ; 3. Qg2. In this classic example the Black B is induced to interfere with the P d7. Romans are sometimes classified according to the weakness of the substitute defence, this one being an interference-Roman.

The origin of the name Roman has little to do with the theme. In 1905 the German composers J. Kohtz and C. Kockelkorn (see DIE SCHWALBE) dedicated a four-mover containing a capture-Roman to A. Guglielmetti, who happened to live in Rome.

Rukhlis
A two-move problem framework in which at least two mates in the set play or the virtual play reappear, by means of mate transference, in the post-key play after different Black defences, while the original Black defences gain new mates.

E. Rukhlis, 1st prize *ex aequo*. Sverdlovsk Sports Committee, 1946 – mate in 2 : 1. d4. The thematic defences are 1. . , Rd4 and 1. . , Bd4 in the set play, and these plus 1. . , Rd3 and 1. . , Bd3 after the key. The idea was named after the Russian composer (*b*. 1925) of this problem.

Self-block
A self-block occurs in a problem when a Black piece restricts the mobility of his own K. In three- and more-movers the self-block may be on a square outside the K's initial field, but in a two-mover, where the self-block error must be exploited by immediate mate, the self-block square will be adjacent to the K.

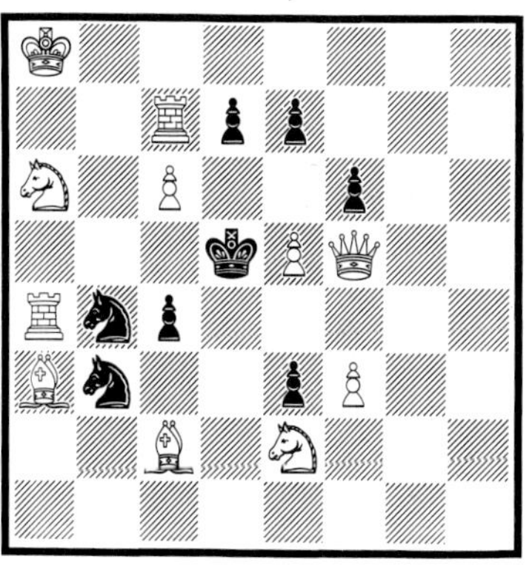

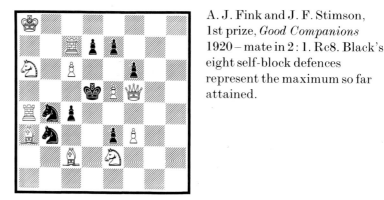

A. J. Fink and J. F. Stimson, 1st prize, *Good Companions* 1920 – mate in 2 : 1. Rc8. Black's eight self-block defences represent the maximum so far attained.

Selfmate

A problem in which White plays and forces Black to give mate in *n* moves. E. Holladay, 1st prize, B.C.F. tourney 1960 – selfmate in 2 : 1. Se4 (2. Sf4 +), Se7 ; 2. Sc3 + . 1. . , Se5 ; 2. Sf6 + . 1. . , S × b3 ; 2. Q × b3 + . Black parries White's threat by attempting to obtain a flight for his K, but in so doing closes a crucial White line (e8–e2).

Serieshelpmate
A problem in which White remains stationary while Black plays a series of *n* moves to reach a position where White can mate in 1.

J. Kricheli, First prize, *Feenschach*, August 1966 – serieshelpmate in 25 : 1. c5 ; 5. c1B ; 8. Bh2 ; 11. Bf7 ; 13. Ke8 ; 16. Bh3 ; 19. Be7 ; 21. Kc7 ; 22. Bd6 ; 24. Ka5 ; 25. Bb4, Qa6. Some startling effects of line-closure are displayed which are unattainable in any other sort of problem.

Set play
Set play in a problem consists of a Black move and an answering White mate or continuation playable before the key is made.

Synthetic
A problem in which the full solution is given and the object is to 're-compose' the original setting.

Task
A problem in which the composer has achieved either a maximum

possible effect or the maximum effect so far attained. 'Maximum effect' implies the greatest possible activity of a single piece, or the most elaborate combination of such activity and/or other thematic or strategic ideas.

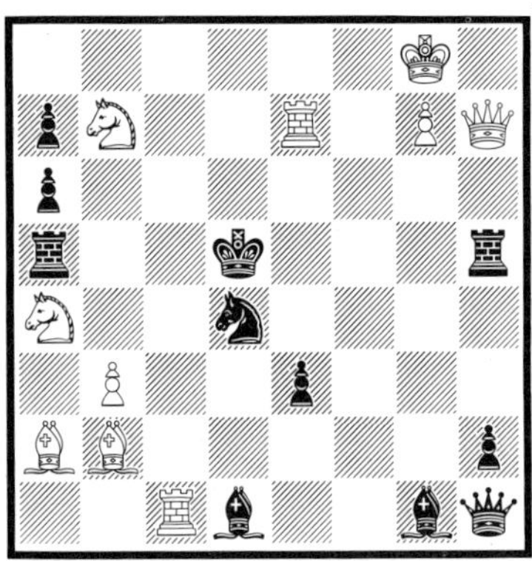

G. Heathcote, First prize, *Hampstead and Highgate Express* 1905 – mate in 2: 1. Rcc7 (2. Sc3). This famous example shows a Knight-wheel (maximum activity of a Black S).

Theme
The unifying idea or strategic content of a problem.

Threat
A problem in which White's first move (key) carries a threat which will follow on White's second move in reply to any passive or non-committal reply by Black.

Tourney (composing)
A problem-composing contest. There are two distinct types of tourney: (1) formal – the competing problems are submitted by their composers to a tourney-controller, who passes them on, on unnamed diagrams, to the judge. Only the problems receiving an award are published; (2) informal – the problems are published throughout a specified period (usually a year) in a magazine or newspaper, and are judged after publication.

In both types of tourney it is traditional to award prizes, honourable mentions and commendations.

Try
A try is a White opening move which almost solves a direct-mate problem, but which fails to a single Black refutation. There are three different types of try:

(1) A move which almost solves a block problem by merely waiting (i.e. keeping or putting Black in *zugzwang*);

(2) A move which introduces virtual play differing from that found after the key.

N. G. G. van Dijk, *Die Schwalbe* 1959 – mate in 2: Try 1. h3?, Kh6! Try 1. h4?, K × h4! Try 1. Kf8?, f × g5! Key 1. Kf7!

(3) One of a group of possible White first moves which share either a common aim (e.g. White correction) or a common error (e.g. square-occupation) or sometimes both.

C. Goldschmeding, Second prize, *Probleemblad* 1964 – mate in 2: Try 1. Sd6?, Sc6! Try 1. Se5?, Sd5! Try 1. Se3?, Sd3! Try 1. Sd2?, Sc2! Key 1. Sa5! (2. Qc4). The four tries are related by common error.

Turton
A doubling manoeuvre found in three- and more-move problems. White plays a 'clearance' move by a line-piece (Q, R or B) over a critical square, so that a second White line-piece can occupy that square and then move down the line, away from the clearing piece, in order to give mate, generally with the clearing piece lending support in the form of guard.

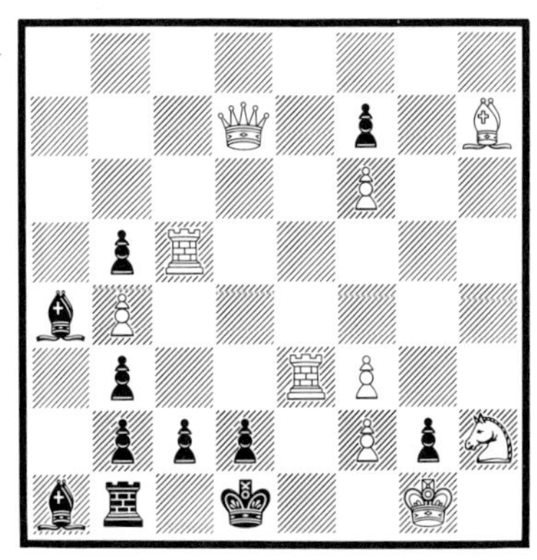

Z. Maslar, First prize *ex aequo*, *Problem* 1962–3 – mate in 3: 1. Re8, c1S; 2. Qe7. 1.., c1Q/R; 2. Rce5. 1.., c1B; 2. Be4. 1.., Kc1; 2. Rd8. The key-piece passes over the two critical squares e7 and c5. The theme is named after Henry Turton, an English composer of the mid-nineteenth century.

Twin

A problem with more than one setting, each of which differs from the other(s) in some small respect only, and containing play which is somehow different in the various settings. Strictly, of course, a 'twin' is only a two-fold setting, but the term is used also to cover triplets, quadruplets etc.

These are the most common twinning devices:

1. shift of one piece of either colour to a different square;
2. removal or addition of one piece of either colour;
3. replacement of one piece of either colour by another of either colour on the same or on a different square;
4. interchange of the position of two pieces;
5. 90° or 180° turn of the board;
6. shift of whole position *en bloc*;
7. new problem arising after the key of the first position.

Variation

In problems, variations are those lines of play which contain Black defences leading to White mates or continuations differing from the threat. In block problems where there is no threat, all distinct defences and mates/continuations are described as variations.

Virtual play

Virtual play is found in a problem where White has a try which introduces defences and/or mates or continuations that differ in some way from the play which follows the key.

H. L. Musante, *Problem* 1955 – mate in 2: Try 1. Sf3?, Qa2! Try 1. Sc2?, d2! Key 1. Se2! (2. Bd5). The two tries each introduce new mates to follow 1.., Sb4 and 1.., Sc7.

See also ZAGORUYKO.

Zagoruyko

A type of problem containing, in its simplest form, two Black defences followed by different mates or continuations in three distinct phases of the solution. The scheme may be extended to comprise more than two defences with changed play, or more than three phases altogether.

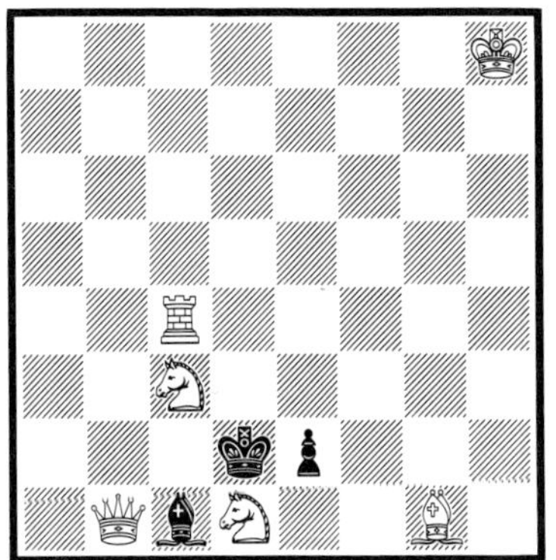

O. Stocchi, Second prize, *L'Italia Scacchistica* 1958 (version) – mate in 2: Try 1. Se3?, Bb2! Key 1. Sf2! Three pairs of mates follow 1.., e1Q and 1.., e1S, one pair each in the set play, the virtual play and the post-key play.

The term Zagoruyko derives from the Russian composer Leonid Zagoruyko (*b*. 14 August 1923), who made some early examples of the idea. *(J.M.R.)*

PROBLEM THEMES IN PLAY

The practical player speaks of a 'problem move' when coming across a combination that appeals to his sense of both the beautiful and the unusual. Alekhine referred to this reaction when, commenting on an unusual blend of line clearance and obstruction in one of his simultaneous games, he wrote: 'Not being a problem composer, I am not sure whether this move actually *is* a problem move.'

'Problem moves' do not always appear as such to the untutored eye. Whenever a player plays B(Q3)–QN1 and follows with Q(Q1)–QB2, he has made two 'problem moves' – he has, in fact, executed the Turton theme. This and similar *direct combinations* (in the language of the Neo-German or strategic school of problemists) do not usually register on the consciousness of the practical player as problem themes; they would not even be referred to as combinations, but as manoeuvres. It is mostly the *indirect combinations* of the strategic school (such as decoys, interferences and anti-forms of direct combinations) that strike the practical player as problem-like.

Thus diagram 1 (Tarrasch v. Marotti and Allies, Naples 1914) shows the Plachutta theme in actual play: after 1. B–B7! Black can capture with either R or Q, but either will, in doing so, obstruct the other: 1.., R×B; 2. Q–N7+, R×Q; 3. R×P mate; or 1.., Q×B; 2. R×P+, Q×R; 3. Q–N7+, K×P; 4. R–R1 mate.

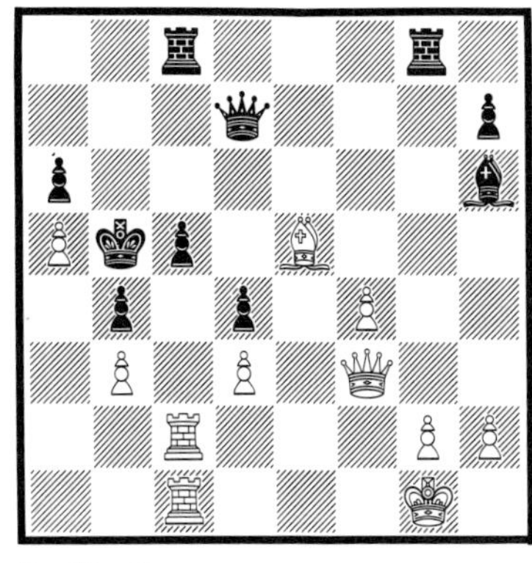

Position 1

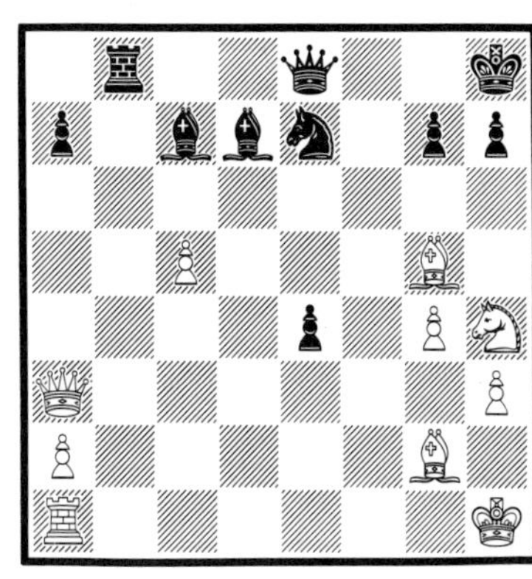

Position 2

Where 1 shows the typical indirect combination, 2 shows the anti-form of a direct combination, viz. that of the Turton mentioned above. The position arose in Ed. Lasker v. Marshall, New York 1924. Any move by the Black N seems to set up the deadly threat, Q–K4, but Black chose 1. . , N–B4? when White found the fine defence, 2. B–B4! (piloting the Black B across the critical square, K4), B × B; 3. N × N, B × N; 4. P × B, B–B2 (now the Turton is executed too late); 5. Q–K3, Q–K4; 6. Q–N1! with excellent drawing chances.

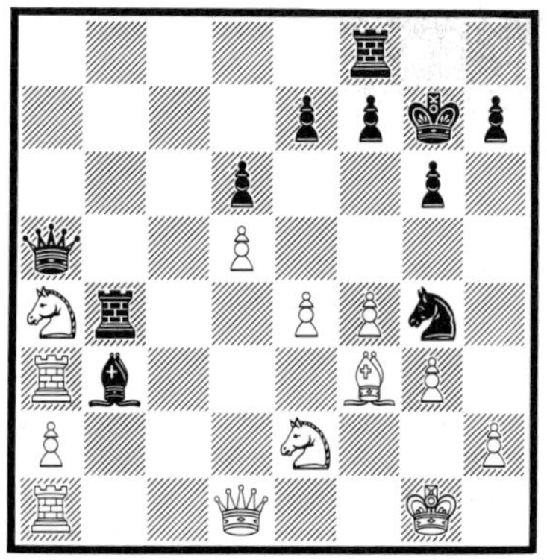

Position 3

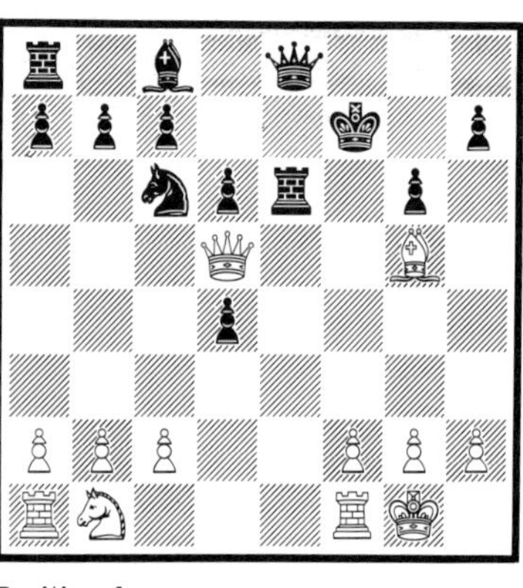

Position 4

3 (Oren–Dyner, Tel Aviv 1952) shows a decoy combination the neo-German school designates as *Richtpunkt* (there is no English equivalent). A defender is directed (=*gerichtet*) to one particular square along its line of action where, for one reason or another, it turns out to be ineffective. In the diagram Black, a piece down, threatens Q and N as well as an attack starting with Q–R2+, and White seems to have nothing better than 1. P × B, Q–R2+; 2. K–R1!, N–B7+; 3. K–N2, N × Q; 4. R × N, but he had prepared the following *Richtpunkt* combination: 1. R × B!, Q–R2+; 2. N–N6!, Q × N+; 3. Q–Q4+!, exposing the Black Q as ineffective on square N3, since 3. . , R × Q would be answered with 4. R × Q.

4 (Schumov–Jaenisch, 1850) shows a non-strategic problem theme; in fact, an anticipation of Loyd's well-known Excelsior problem in which a pawn starting from its original square promotes in five moves: 1. P–B4, K–N2; 2. P–B5, R–K4; 3. P–B6+, K–R1; 4. P–B7, K–N2; 5. P × Q(N)+, R × N; 6. Q–B7+, K–R1; 7. B–B6 mate. *(J.M.R.)*

PROMOTION

The exchange of a pawn when it reaches the eighth rank for a piece of its own colour (other than the King). See LAWS OF CHESS, Article 6 (c). *(H.G.)*

PROPHYLAXIS

A concept introduced by Nimzowitsch, who regarded it as the true essence of position play. It embraces the various stratagems by which the opponent is prevented from freeing his position, such as the mysterious rook move, over-protection, blockade, etc. *(W.H.)*

PRZEPIÓRKA, David *(22 December 1880–27 August 1942)*

Polish master and problemist who was active in the period 1905–31. He achieved the master title by coming first in the *Hauptturnier* C of the Coburg Chess Congress (of the German Chess Federation) in 1904. The tournament book has a note stating that 'Mr Przepiórka refrained from accepting the 250-mark cash prize and instead asked for a gold medal to be struck for the same amount. This, very beautifully executed, was sent to him a few days later.'

Przepiórka was a talented and very agreeable master of middle strength who never reached the heights but produced quite a number of fine combinations. His best tournament results were: =4th at Sam Remo 1911, =5th at Meran 1924, 2nd at Györ 1924, 1st at Munich 1926, 2nd in the Individual Olympiad of The Hague 1928. He played in two Olympiads, at Hamburg 1930 and Prague in 1931.

His death at the hands of the Nazis during the Second World War was practically gratuitous. He turned up one day at a restaurant which his family had owned for generations in Warsaw, but was promptly sent away and informed that the restaurant had been confiscated. Failing to understand this, Przepiórka again presented himself to the restaurant the following day and the Nazis, losing patience, sent him to a concentration camp where he was eventually liquidated. *(H.G.)*

PSYCHOLOGY AND CHESS

The interest of psychologists in chess-players is twofold: first, as a medium through which to study the thought processes, chess has sufficient complexity and a sufficiently rigorous structure for it to be of use in discovering the precise mental processes through which a master reaches his decision about what move to play; secondly, the chess-master himself is an interesting subject for study to investigate what personality attributes (or defects) and what intellectual abilities are necessary to make a strong chess-player.

The first systematic attempt to test chess-players was by Binet in 1894, when he applied his recent innovation, the intelligence test, to a number of the best players of the day. His conclusion was that spatial ability is higher in chess-players than in those of comparable intelligence levels. This result he found to apply particularly to players of blindfold chess.

A more detailed investigation was undertaken at the Moscow 1925 tournament, when eight of the competitors agreed to undergo several tests of intelligence and personality structure. The results are to be found in Djakov, Petrowski and Rudik, *Psychologie des Schachspiels*, Berlin/Leipzig 1927. Briefly, their conclusions were that chess-masters possessed a high degree of physical endurance together with a tolerance for frustration; their performance on tests of memory was no different from that of other groups of comparable intelligence levels.

Subsequent developments led to a deterioration in relations between chess and psychology when the Freudian school of psychoanalysis applied its methods to an interpretation of chess. The best-known paper in this field was Reuben Fine's 'Psycho-analytic observations on chess and chessmasters', in *Psychoanalysis* 1956 (subsequently reprinted as *The Psychology of the Chessplayer*, New York, London 1967). This attempted to generalize the conclusions of Ernest Jones's 'The Problem of Paul Morphy' (*Int. J. Psychoanal.* 1931), and draws heavily on an identification of the chess-pieces with the components of the Oedipal drama. The objectives of the game are associated with subconscious parricidal fantasies on the part of the player, who is also accused of repressed homosexuality in some cases, and ultimately paranoia (these observations particularly being applied in the case of Morphy).

Fortunately, these theories were never generally accepted either in psycho-analytic or chess-playing circles, since they did not admit to any method of proof. Unfortunately no large-scale study of the personality factors of chess-masters appears to have been undertaken in recent years, but there is clearly scope for a more thorough investigation by the psychologist than those which have yet taken place.

From the chess-player's point of view perhaps the most interesting work on the thought processes of grandmasters is that of A. de Groot, himself a chess-player while also Professor of Applied Psychology and Methodology at the University of Amsterdam. His conclusions are to be found in his doctoral dissertation, published in English as *Thought and Choice in Chess*, The Hague/Paris 1965, New York 1966, and are based on experimental sessions conducted between 1938 and 1943 with subjects of various strengths, ranging from club players to World Champions.

The principal test involved presenting the subject with an unfamiliar position taken from an actual game and asking him to provide a full verbal report of his thoughts leading to the choice of a move in the position. It was possible to determine some facts concerning the structure of the chess-master's thought processes.

Other facets of De Groot's work include a study of the professions of a large sample of grandmasters and further investigations into the performances of chess-masters on various ability tests. The occupational study refuted the old theory that connected chess-players with mathematicians; in fact rather few of the great masters had chosen mathematics as their subject. The most interesting result on other tests came with measurements of a player's ability to remember an unfamiliar position presented to him for a brief time (usually 10 or 15 seconds). De Groot found that this ability correlated very highly with playing strength, strong grandmasters being able to reproduce positions after a brief exposure with almost 100% correctness, while at the other end of the scale, club players would only remember the locations of half or less of the pieces. However, on other tests of memory, or even reproduction of randomized piece configurations on a chessboard, the results bore no correlation with playing strength. These results support the theory that chess ability is allied to pattern recognition, though we are still a very long way from the development of a non-chess test predictive of chess ability. *(W.R.H.)*

PUC, Stojan *(b. 9 April 1921)*
A Yugoslav international master (1950). Successful in numerous tournaments in Yugoslavia; never achieved same status abroad. For many years the leading Slovenian player after Pirc. Best result: =1st Dortmund 1951. Represented Yugoslavia in 1950 Olympiad. *(R.D.K.)*

PUERTO RICO
The Puerto Rican Chess Federation was founded in 1934 and joined FIDE the same year. Its present address is: Federacion de Ajedrez de Puerto Rico, Apartado 3182, Viejo San Juan, P.R. 00904.

The first national championship, won by Rafael Cintron Ramos, was contested in 1936. The best known product of Puerto Rican chess is Julio Kaplan, though he now plays for the USA. It was as a Puerto Rican that Kaplan won the World Junior Championship in 1967.

A Puerto Rican team has campaigned in nine Olympiads, achieving the following results: 29th in 1956, 33rd in 1958, 31st in 1962, 38th in 1964, 41st in 1966, 40th in 1968, 36th in 1970, 40th in 1972 and 50th in 1974. *(K.J.O'C.)*

PURDY, Cecil John Seddon *(b. 27 March 1907)*
Australian international master and international chess correspondence grandmaster, Purdy achieved distinction as a brilliant and witty writer on the game. He was founder and editor of the *Australian Chess Review* from 1929 to 1945 and also editor of its successor the *Chess World* from 1946.

He won the New Zealand championship in 1924 and the Australian championship in 1935, 1937, 1949 and 1951.

Though he never competed over-the-board outside Australasia, he was a noted correspondence player and won the first World Correspondence Championship in 1953, holding the title till 1958.

In 1974 he was the non-playing captain of the Australian team at the Nice Olympiad.

An excellent analyst, he was the author of two books on the World Championship matches of 1935 (Sydney 1936) and of 1937 (Sydney, 1938); he is also the author, under the pseudonym of Chielamangus, of one of the few genuinely humorous books on chess – *Among These Mates*, Sydney and London 1939. *(H.G.)*

QUEEN
Now the most powerful piece on the board, the Queen was the weakest piece in the original game of *chaturanga*, some 1,500 years ago. Its move was limited to any diagonally adjacent square. Nor was the piece a Queen, though it was placed on Q1 originally just as it is nowadays. It was a Minister or adviser to the King.

When the game moved to Persia the Minister became a *farzin*, which is Persian for 'wise man' and hence 'counsellor'. Its functions were the same and its powers as limited as before. There were no changes in the functions of the powers of the piece when chess became an Arab or Moslem game.

It was now called *Firz* and when the game came to Europe it was at first still *Firz* or *Fierz*, but gradually, though it retained the same name, it began to have increased powers and to be regarded as a Queen rather than an adviser.

At first it had a leap of three squares and then, having regard to the great powers of a Queen in a medieval court, it acquired its full modern strength. The Spanish writer, Lucena, describes the piece as possessing its present-day powers in his late fifteenth-century work.

There have been a number of theories as to how this transformation occurred. Fréret, in the eighteenth century, suggested that the piece became *vierge* from *fierz* and thus was really the Virgin Queen.

Another later theory, still more fanciful, was that the change occurred under the influence and example of Joan of Arc. But the simple, natural and no doubt correct explanation is that in a medieval court the Queen occupied a throne next to the King's.

It is interesting to note that as the Queen increased in power so it became necessary to warn one's opponent with some such word as *'gardez'* when one attacked the Queen and, though this custom eventually died out, to this day there are players who believe one has to notify one's opponent when the Queen is attacked.

Another strange and picturesque custom arose in the eighteenth century in Russia where the Queen could also move like a Knight. But for a hundred years or more now the Queen and its moves have been uniform throughout the world. *(H.G.)*

QUEEN'S GAMBIT

Albin Counter-gambit

Named after the Austrian master Albin, the gambit is generally held to be unsound. The opening moves are 1. P–Q4, P–Q4; 2. P–QB4, P–K4; 3. P×KP, P–Q5 when Black has sacrificed a pawn for a foothold in the centre; but continuing with moves such as N–KB3 and P–KN3, White normally maintains the upper hand. *(R.D.K.)*

Catalan System

So named after a *bon mot* of Tartakower, the Catalan involves the early fianchetto of White's KB. His strategy is to exert pressure against Black's centre along the KR1–QR8 diagonal, thus rendering Black's Q-side development difficult. The basic position can arise via numerous transpositional possibilities. With the sequence 1. P–Q4, P–Q4; 2. P–QB4, P–K3; 3. P–KN3, N–KB3; 4. N–KB3, B–K2; 5. B–N2, O–O; 6. O–O, QN–Q2 a typical Catalan opening position has occurred. *(R.D.K.)*

Chigorin's Defence

After 1. P–Q4, P–Q4; 2. P–QB4, Chigorin regularly adopted the unorthodox . . , N–QB3; Black develops his pieces with pressure against the White QP, but is not guaranteed of equality after White's best plan: 3. N–QB3, P×P; 4. N–B3. This defence is a rarity in contemporary international chess. *(R.D.K.)*

Marshall's Defence

1. P–Q4, P–Q4; 2. P–QB4, N–KB3 was employed occasionally by Frank Marshall. White gains the advantage after 3. P×P, N×P; 4. N–KB3, to be followed by P–K4, since Black has no counter to White's central preponderance. *(R.D.K.)*

Symmetrical Defence

1. P–Q4, P–Q4; 2. P–QB4, P–QB4; Black hopes to obtain equality by apeing White's moves thus liquidating the central pawns. The line was first analysed and recommended by Akiba Rubinstein. However, Black's idea was definitively refuted in the game Portisch–Bronstein, Monaco 1969, which continued 3. P×QP, N–KB3; 4. P–K4!, N×KP; 5. P×P!, N×QBP; 6. N–KB3, P–K3; 7. N–B3, P×P; 8. Q×P. After this game the defence vanished from master-chess. *(R.D.K.)*

Westphalia Defence

1. P–Q4, P–Q4; 2. P–QB4, P–K3; 3. N–KB3, N–KB3; 4. N–B3, QN–Q2; 5. B–N5, B–N5; 6. P×P, P×P; 7. P–K3, P–B4; a variation of the Queen's Gambit which was analysed by Spielmann and other grandmasters aboard the liner Westphalia while crossing the Atlantic and travelling to New York so as to participate in the great 1927 tournament there. It was with this defence that Spielmann lost to Capablanca who won the first brilliancy prize against it in the tournament. *(H.G.)*

QUEEN'S GAMBIT ACCEPTED

In international chess circles the Queen's Gambit first grew in popularity at the start of the twentieth century. At that time it was considered obligatory for Black to defend his QP with all the resources at his command. However, during the 1930s a new method was devised for Black whereby he surrenders the centre temporarily with the idea of avoiding the cramped Orthodox Defence and the problem of developing his QB. The main line of the Queen's Gambit Accepted runs 1. P–Q4, P–Q4; 2. P–QB4, P×P; 3. N–KB3, N–KB3; 4. P–K3, P–K3 (4. . , B–N5 is a modern Russian idea); 5. B×P, P–B4 (striking back at the centre to free his game); 6. O–O, P–QR3; 7. Q–K2, and now 7. . , N–B3 or . . , P–QN4 are Black's main alternatives. In this line White normally maintains a slightly freer position. *(R.D.K.)*

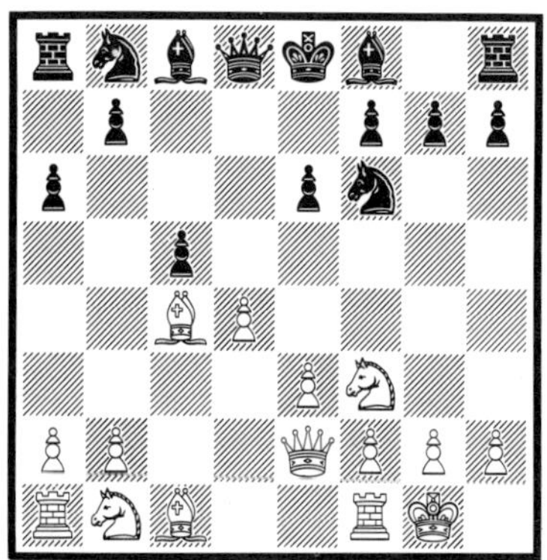

QUEEN'S GAMBIT DECLINED

One of the most popular of all openings which aims at putting pressure on the opponent's QP with the object of luring it away from the centre.

Orthodox Defence

The main line of the Orthodox Defence runs as follows: 1. P–Q4,

P–Q4; 2. P–QB4, P–K3; 3. N–QB3, N–KB3; 4. B–N5, B–K2; 5. P–K3, O–O; 6. N–B3, QN–Q2; 7. R–B1, P–B3; 8. B–Q3, P×P; 9. B×P, N–Q4; 10. B×B, Q×B; 11. O–O, N×N; 12. R×N, P–K4; 13. P×P, an attack called the Rubinstein variation, after the great Polish player, Akiba Rubinstein who analysed and played the line.

13. . , N×P; 14. N×N, Q×N; 15. P–B4, Q–B3; 16. P–B5, P–QN4; 17. B–Q3, P–N5; 18. R–QB2, R–Q1; 19. Q–K2, P–QR4 with equality. *(R.D.K.)*

Semi-Slav Defence

A sub-variation of the Slav Defence in which Black temporarily hems in his QB whilst simultaneously preparing Q-side counter-play with . . , P–QB4.

The theoretically important Meran system (deriving its name from Rubinstein's games played at the Meran tournament of 1924) runs as follows: 1. P–Q4, P–Q4; 2. P–QB4, P–QB3; 3. N–KB3, N–KB3; 4. N–QB3, P–K3; 5. P–K3, QN–Q2; 6. B–Q3, P×P; 7. B×P, P–QN4; 8. B–Q3, when extreme complications can arise from 8. . , P–QR3; 9. P–K4, P–QB4 and now 10. P–K5, or 10. P–Q5. *(R.D.K.)*

Slav Defence

This defence to the Queen's Gambit is characterized by 2. . , P–QB3 which bolsters Black's QP without depriving him of an open diagonal for his QB. In many lines 2. . , P–QB3 also helps prepare a possible . . , P–QN4 after the capture . . , QP×BP.

One of the most popular lines of the Slav Defence has been the so-called 'Dutch variation': 1. P–Q4, P–Q4; 2. P–QB4, P–QB3; 3. N–KB3, N–B3; 4. N–B3, P×P; 5. P–QR4, B–B4; 6. P–K3, P–K3; 7. B×P, B–QN5; 8. O–O, O–O which has been extensively analysed since its début in the Euwe–Alekhine World Championship match, The Netherlands 1937. *(R.D.K.)*

QUEEN'S INDIANCE DEFENCE

1. P–Q4, N–KB3; 2. P–QB4, P–K3; 3. N–KB3, P–QN3; or there is a shortened form: 1. P–Q4, N–KB3; 2. N–KB3, P–QN3.

This defence owes much to the ideas and practice of Nimzowitsch and is an attack on White's K4 square. A sub-variation introduced by Nomzowitsch at Marienbad 1925 and hence called the Marienbad System is: 1. P–Q4, N–KB3; 2. N–KB3, P–QN3; 3. P–KN3, B–N2; 4. B–N2, P–B4, when Black's KB is fianchettoed as soon as possible. *(W.H. & H.G.)*

QUEEN-SIDE CASTLING

This is when the King castles with the Queen's Rook. For the rules see LAWS OF CHESS Article 6. *(H.G.)*

QUEEN-SIDE PAWN MAJORITY

The advantage of a majority of pawns on the Q-side is a frequent strategic aim in modern master-games. To be regarded as an advantage, such a majority must not be devalued by a doubled pawn but must be capable of producing a passed pawn; likewise, the term 'Queen-side' must not be used indiscriminately, since the important characteristic of such positions is not the original presence of the Qs, but the ultimate absence of the Ks from the majority wing. Thus the 'Queen-side pawn majority' is almost a misnomer; the correct but clumsy term for the advantage referred to would be 'a majority of pawns on the side from which the Kings are absent'.

Such a majority confers an advantage for two reasons: the passed-pawn-to-be will be at a great distance from the hostile K who is thus unable to arrest its progress; and a passed pawn resulting from a K-side majority is more difficult to force through, because this might necessitate the advance of pawns required for the protection of the K.

Of the great amount of material illustrating this theme the following may be chosen as typical:

Semmering-Baden 1937
White: Eliskases; *Black:* Flohr
Grünfeld Defence

1. P–Q4, N–KB3; 2. P–QB4, P–KN3; 3. N–QB3, P–Q4; 4. B–B4, B–N2; 5. P–K3, O–O; 6. N–B3, P–B4; 7. P×QP, N×P; 8. B–K5, N×N; 9. P×N, P×P; 10. B×B, K×B; 11. BP×P, Q–R4+; 12. Q–Q2, N–B3; 13. B–K2, R–Q1; 14. Q×Q, N×Q; 15. O–O (this error makes the Black pawn majority a true Queen-side majority – the White K should have stayed in the centre), 15. . , B–K3; 16. P–K4, B–N5; 17. KR–Q1, P–K3; 18. K–B1, B×N; 19. B×B, QR–B1; 20. R–Q2, P–K4; 21. P–Q5, N–B5; 22. R–K2, N–Q3; 23. R–N1, R–B5; 24. P–N3, R(1)–QB1; 25. B–N2, R–B8+; 26. R×R, R×R+; 27. R–K1, R×R+; 28. K×R, and the Queen-side pawn majority coupled with White's weakness on the dark squares gives Black a vastly superior ending. *(W.H.)*

QUEEN'S PAWN COUNTER-GAMBIT
A violent and incorrect attempt by Black to seize the initiative with 1. P–K4, P–K4; 2. N–KB3, P–Q4. White should gain the advantage after either 3. P×P or 3. N×P. *(W.R.H.)*

QUIÑONES, Oscar Carillo *(b. 14 January 1941)*
Peruvian international master. Gained the title by qualifying for the 1964 Interzonal tournament, where he finished in 20th place. *(W.R.H.)*

QUINTEROS, Miguel Angel *(b. 28 December 1947)*
Argentine grandmaster and professional, Quinteros learnt chess at the age of seven and, aged fifteen, won a very strong lightning tournament (beating the Soviet grandmaster Stein) in Buenos Aires. At the age of eighteen he became the youngest player ever to win the Argentine championship.

In 1970 he won the international master title and, making giant progress, he was already a grandmaster in 1973, his results for that being at Ljubljana-Portorož where he came =2nd with Smyslov and Gligorić, and at Montilla-Moriles. 1973 was an *annus mirabilis* for him, since he also won first prize at the Costa del Sol tournament and came 2nd at the Marlboro tournament in Manila.

In the next year he was first in the Master group at the Wijk-aan-Zee tournament. In 1975 he was again 1st at the Costa del Sol tournament.

In 1976 he came second at the Lone Pine tournament. He has played for the Argentine at the three Olympiads of 1970, 1974, and 1976. *(H.G.)*

R

RABAR, Braslav *(27 September 1919–6 December 1973)*
A Yugoslav international master (1950). Competed in thirteen Yugoslav championships, winning in 1951. Took part in Interzonal 1955. Represented Yugoslavia in three Olympiads. Best result: =1st Sao Paulo 1952. Prolific author, for years co-editor of the chess magazine *Šahovski Glasnik*, he invented a rating system differing greatly from that of Professor Elo. *(R.D.K.)*

RABINOVICH, Abram Isaakovich *(1878–1943)*
Not quite so gifted as his brother Ilya Rabinovich, Abram was nevertheless also a leading Soviet master. Won the Moscow championship in 1926 but never secured a really high place in any stronger event. *(W.R.H.)*

RABINOVICH, Ilya *(1891–1942)*
One of the strongest Soviet masters throughout the period between the wars. Ilya Rabinovich was the first Soviet player to compete in an international tournament outside the USSR when he finished 7th at Baden-Baden 1925. His best tournament result was sharing first place with Levenfish in the 1934 USSR championship. He also won the Leningrad championship on several occasions. *(W.R.H.)*

RADULOV, Ivan *(b. 7 January 1939)*
Bulgarian grandmaster, edging out Tringov as Bulgaria's leading chess-player in the 1970s.

This rivalry became clear when in 1968 he tied with Tringov for first place in the Bulgarian championship but lost the play-off for the title. In that year he had a good result at Debrecen where he came =2nd with Barcza.

In the following year he became an international master and by 1972 he was a grandmaster. In the previous year he had tied with Quinteros for first place at Torremolinos.

In 1974 he tied with Padevsky for the Bulgarian championship and won the play-off by +2−1=1.

He was extremely active and successful in 1975. =1st with Matulović and Vukić at Bajmok, he also shared first place with Polugayevsky at Montilla-Moriles and came 3rd at Albena.

In 1976 he shared second place with Peev in the Bulgarian championship and won a tournament at Kikinda. He has played four times for Bulgaria in the Olympiads, always with fine results: 75% on board 5 at Lugano 1968, 66.3% on board 5 at Siegen 1970, 69% on board 3 at Skopje 1972 and 61.36% on top board at Nice 1974. *(H.G.)*

RAGOZIN, Vyacheslav Vasilievich
(8 October 1908–11 January 1962)
Soviet international grandmaster. One of the greatest Soviet players at the end of the war. Winner of Helsinki 1946 and runner-up to Botvinnik in the 1947 Chigorin Memorial. Also decisively defeated Bondarevsky in a match in 1946.

Also distinguished in organizational and literary fields, having been chief editor of *Shakhmaty v SSSR* and author of many tournament books and other works on the game. Was a Vice-president of the FIDE Soviet Zone and prominent member of the FIDE Central Committee.

Among his other achievements was winning the second World Correspondence Championship, which finished in 1958. Was awarded titles of international grandmaster in 1950, and Correspondence grandmaster in 1958. *(W.R.H.)*

RAICEVIĆ, Vladimir *(b. 2 May 1949)*
Yugoslav international grandmaster (1976). He was elevated to the higher grade just one year after gaining the international master title. His best tournament performance was at Vrnjačka Banja 1976 where he was =1st. *(K.J.O'C.)*

RAJKOVIĆ, Dušan *(b. 17 June 1942)*
Yugoslav international master (1974). His best performance in the Yugoslav championship was =5th in 1976, the same year that he scored his best international result: =1st at Vrnjačka Banja. *(K.J.O'C.)*

RANK

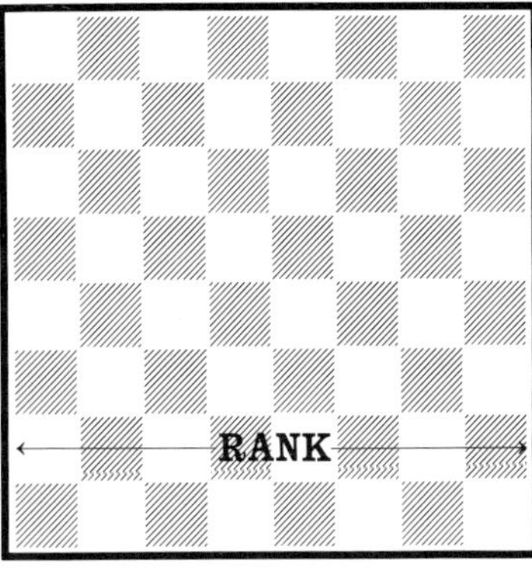

A row of squares running from one side of the board to the other is termed a 'rank'. See LAWS OF CHESS, Part 1, Article 2, Para. 2. *(H.G.)*

RANKEN, Rev Charles Edward *(5 January 1828–12 April 1905)*
A leading member of the formidable band of reverends who played such a strong role in early Victorian English chess, he is described as 'one of the writing rather than the fighting clergy in chess' in P. W. Sergeant's *Century of British Chess*.

Though he learnt chess at an early age, he made his first really earnest study of the game when he was an undergraduate at Wadham College, Oxford 1847–50, in particular devoting himself to a theoretical study of Staunton's *Handbook*, which he rightly regarded as a great landmark in chess literature.

On leaving Oxford he competed in the provincial section at London 1851 where he came second to Boden.

In 1867 he became Vicar of Sandford-on-Thames and lived at Oxford where, in collaboration with Lord Randolph Churchill (Winston's father), he founded the Oxford University Chess Club and became its first president.

Resigning his living at Sandford in 1871, he went to live at Malvern where he stayed till his death. He played in many of the congresses organized by the Counties Chess Association, his best result being 1st in the first class section at Malvern 1872 with a score of 12 points, followed by two other reverends, Thorold $11\frac{1}{2}$ and Wayte $10\frac{1}{2}$. It was at this congress that he brought about a reconciliation between Staunton and Löwenthal who had been estranged for a considerable time.

He played in the Vizayanagaram tournament at London 1883 and started well but his health gave way after the first week and he divided fifth place with G. H. D. Gossip.

His chief importance during the later stages of his chess career was as a writer, first as editor of the *Chess Player's Chronicle* in 1877 and later as a member of the staff of the *British Chess Magazine* in which he wrote on many aspects of chess but specialized in analysis (of the openings, middle-game and the endings).

In 1889 he published, in collaboration with E. Freeborough, *Chess Openings Ancient and Modern* (London). *(H.G.)*

RATING SYSTEMS
The idea of assigning a number to each chess-master, indicative of his playing strength, is an attractive one. Thereby it would be possible not only to make comparisons between present-day players, but also to compare living masters with those of the past. The idea behind all rating systems is to utilize a player's results over a specified time-period to calculate a number, his rating or grading, which indicates his level of achievement in those games and thus, by inference, his overall playing strength.

Perhaps the first hint of a future grading system came in an article by Brumfitt in the 1891 *British Chess Magazine*, but no systematic attempt was made to grade large numbers of players until more than half a century had passed.

The first modern grading system was introduced by Anton Hösslinger and is known as the Ingo-system (after his birthplace of Ingolstadt, Bavaria). In 1948 he first published his grading list based on collected tournament results; since then the Ingo-system has grown to include all active international players. The system is based entirely on an individual's tournament results. After each tournament a player's Ingo number is recalculated according to his result and the average rating of the other competitors.

The USA was the next to adopt a rating system when, in 1951, Kenneth Harkness introduced a similar system to deal with the American tournament circuit. Two years later the British followed by modifying the Ingo-Harkness system for their own purposes. A team led by Sir Richard Clarke produced the British grading lists, which differed significantly from the earlier ones in that they were equipped to grade single games rather than whole tournaments. Thus new lists were published annually, and a player's grade was only modified every twelve months rather than after each separate tournament.

Despite the fact that these systems were all generally welcomed, it soon became clear that the statistical soundness of the methods involved was open to some doubt. In particular the problems of assigning ratings to players entering the lists for the first time, and of rating short tournaments, were seen not to have been solved fully: in both the Harkness and B.C.F. systems a gradual lowering of all grades was slowly becoming apparent.

For this reason, in 1959 Prof. Arpad E. Elo undertook to investigate the statistical theory of rating systems and to develop for the U.S.C.F. a soundly based method of grading players. This gave rise to the Elo system, which has been in use in the USA since 1960 and was adopted in 1970 by FIDE for rating international tournaments. Since that date the Elo system has been utilized by FIDE for the award of international titles and in some cases also for the selection of players for specific events. The basis of the system lies in using the expected percentage score one player will make against another according to their respective numbers. The standard points taken at the start of the system were that the mean rating of international masters was to be 2400 and grandmasters 2500. At the time of writing the highest-rated players are Fischer (2780) and Karpov (2705). The principal advantage of the Elo system compared with its predecessors is its sound basis in statistical and probability theory, which, whatever its other merits or drawbacks, does at least guarantee that eventually ratings so measured will settle to a conservative system showing the relative merits of performance of individuals as indicated by the results rated. Thus, in theory at any rate, it does provide a method of comparing present-day masters with those of the past.

For full details of the methodology see 'The International Chess Federation Rating System' by A. E. Elo, *Chess* 1973. A detailed account of the differences between various grading systems is to be found in *Theory of Rating Systems*, A. E. Elo 1965 (privately printed), while one of the more interesting applications is to be found, again in an article by Elo, in the 1965 *Journal of Gerontology*.

A new Elo List is published at the beginning of each calendar year containing the ratings of all active international players. The 1975 list contained the names of more than 1,250 players. There is a separate list for women players containing about 250 names. *(W.R.H.)*

RAUZER, Vsevolod Alfredovich *(16 October 1908–1941)*
Soviet master and theorist. Rauzer shared first place in the championship of the Ukraine in 1933 and played several times in the USSR championship, his best result being sixth in 1933. After a serious illness in 1937 he no longer competed in chess events.

Best remembered for his theoretical contributions, particularly in the Sicilian Defence. *(W.R.H.)*

RAZUVAYEV, Yuri Sergeevich *(b. 10 October 1945)*
Soviet international grandmaster (1976). He had previously gained, in 1973, the international master title. Although never quite in the front rank of Soviet juniors, Razuvayev did succeed in the 1971 USSR Young Masters championship in which he finished =1st with Kuzmin, ahead of Romanishin, Vaganian and Gulko among others. His best international performance so far was in 1976 when he finished =2nd, behind Gulko, in the Capablanca Memorial at Cienfuegos. *(K.J.O'C.)*

REE, Hans *(b. 15 September 1944)*
Dutch international master and chess professional. Ree learnt chess at the age of seven and was twice Junior champion of Amsterdam at the age of seventeen and eighteen. He was =1st with Hübner at the Niemeyer Junior tournaments at Groningen and again with Whiteley at a later tournament.

These tournaments were later to become recognized as the European Junior championships. They were already of good European standing but his first real achievement in that respect was his winning a short tournament at Ter Apel in 1966, ahead of Larsen, Donner, Pfleger and Lehmann. In 1967 he gained the international master title, having fulfilled the norm at the 1966 I.B.M. tournament and then again at Hoogovens in 1967.

Three times champion of the Netherlands (1967, 1969 and 1971) he also played in the Olympiads in 1966, 1970, 1972, 1974 and 1976.

A student of mathematics and philosophy at Amsterdam University he drifted into professionalism in the 1970s. 1971 was a fine year for him; he beat Donner in a match by $4\frac{1}{2}$–$3\frac{1}{2}$ and he also shared first place with Spassky in the Open championship of Canada at Vancouver. He had a chess column in the *Haagse Post* for over six years. *(H.G.)*

REILLY, Brian Patrick *(b. 12 December 1901)*
Irish master born at Menton, of Irish descent, who has represented Ireland in nine Olympic team tournaments between 1935 and 1968; three times on top board. He also was Irish representative at seven FIDE Congresses. Reilly played in a number of small international tournaments, winning first prize at Nice 1931 and sharing fourth prize with Klein and E. G. Sergeant behind Reshevsky, Capablanca and Sir G. Thomas at Margate 1935. Winner of Irish championship in 1959 and 1960. General Editor of *British Chess Magazine* since 1949. *(W.H.)*

REINFELD, Fred *(27 January 1910–29 May 1964)*
Though as a young man he was a strong player and won the US Intercollegiate championship and the New York State championship (twice), it is not as a player that Reinfeld will be remembered, but as the most prolific writer of books on chess in the history of the game.

His writing career divides into two parts: the first, before the Second World War when he concentrated on producing durable works, and the second, starting with the war and going on till the end of his life, when he aimed solely at a large output.

It is a sad reflection that during this last phase when he produced over a hundred books of all kinds, he created little of any value. In his haste to produce, he tended either to make rehashes of other people's work or to endow works of little real content with grandiloquent names that masked the trifling nature of the subject matter. For example, a book entitled *Modern Fundamentals of Chess*, London 1961, turned out to be merely the moves of chess shown in photographic form instead of by diagrams. Typically, this had already appeared as *The Easiest Way to Learn Chess*, New York 1960, and was later to appear as *Better Chess*, London 1968, in every case with the same contents but different title pages.

Nevertheless, some of his earlier work has enduring value. Perhaps his best book is *Practical End-Game Play*, New York and London 1940. *(H.G.)*

REJFIŘ, Josef *(22 September 1909–4 May 1962)*
One of Czechoslovakia's strongest masters before the war, Rejfiř was a member of the Czech team at all five Olympiads between 1928 and 1935. Retired from active chess for some years, but returned to competition in the last decade of his life to play again in two more Olympiads (1956 and 1958). Gained the title of international master in 1956. *(W.R.H.)*

RELLSTAB, Ludwig *(b. 22 November 1904)*
A German international master, Rellstab won the German championship in 1942. He has had good results in many small international tournaments (e.g. 3rd at Swinemünde 1930, =4th Bad Nauheim 1936, 1st at Zoppot the same year, =3rd at Wijk-aan-Zee 1952, =3rd at Madrid 1959), but has played in few important events.

He is the author of a number of chess manuals and a regular contributor to chess magazines as well as the general press.

(W.H.)

REPETITION OF POSITION

A threefold repetition of the same position on the board may end the game as a draw at the request of one of the players when the same position appears three times with the same player to move. Conditions are as follows: the right of claiming the draw belongs to the player who is in a position to play a move leading to such repetition if he declares his intention of making this move, or who is about to reply to a move by which such a repeated position has been produced. For the purposes of this rule the position is considered the same if pieces of the same kind and colour occupy the same squares, even though the position may differ in other respects.

In the diagram, a four-mover by Zepler, White plays 1. K–Q4, R–R5+; 2. K–K5, R–R1; 3. Q–Q6 and mates next move because Black no longer has the defence 3.., O–O–O. Assume that the position occurs in a game and White, in time trouble, repeats 3. K–Q4, R–R5+; 4. K–K5. Black, by indicating he would play 4.., R–R1 can claim the draw, though in the original position he could castle, and in that brought about by his 4th move he could no longer do so.

(W.H.)

RESHEVSKY, Samuel *(b. 26 November 1911)*

A US grandmaster, Reshevsky had one of the most famous careers as a child prodigy and later one of the most continuously successful as a mature master. Although never quite a World Championship challenger, Reshevsky was the strongest Western player for more than a decade. In America Reshevsky regularly came ahead of his contemporaries in tournaments and defeated the leaders of the post-Second World War generation – except Fischer – in matches.

Born in Ozerkov, Poland, Reshevsky learned the moves at four and was giving much-heralded simultaneous displays at the age of eight. His exhibitions took him through Western Europe to the USA where he settled after 1920.

Samuel Reshevsky as a boy

After entering college Reshevsky retired from chess and obtained a degree in accountancy. Never a professional player, Reshevsky pursued a career in finance. He resumed his chess activities by winning the Western Open in 1931 and coming =3rd at the Pasadena international event a year later.

On Reshevsky's return to Europe in 1935 he took first prize at Margate 1935 and won his individual game with Capablanca. This and his victory in the 1936 US championship ahead of Fine and Kashdan established him as a leading master. At Nottingham 1936, his first top-class event, Reshevsky shared third place a half-point behind the leaders. Before war intervened Reshevsky had come =1st at Kemeri 1937, taken first prize at Hastings 1937/8 and shared 4th at A.V.R.O. 1938.

At home Reshevsky retained his national title in the 1938, 1940 and 1942 Closed championships. He defeated Horowitz +3=13 in a 1941 match challenge. A year later he won a play-off match from Kashdan +6−2=3. These were the first of a series of match successes that included wins over Najdorf (+8−4=6 in 1952 and +5−4=9 in 1953), Gligorić (+2−1=7 in 1952), and Benko (+3−2=5 in 1960). During the 1950s Reshevsky also defeated Lombardy, Bisguier and D. Byrne in matches. After drawing a controversial, aborted 1961 match with Fischer (+2−2=7) Reshevsky lost his first serious match in the Interzonal play-off to Portisch in 1964. In the quarter-finals four years later he lost to Korchnoi.

In his other bids for the World Championship, Reshevsky was =3rd at The Hague-Moscow 1948 and =2nd at Zürich 1953. He was =8th at the 1964 Interzonal, =6th at the 1967 event, 17th in 1970 and 11th in the 1973 Interzonal at Petropolis.

Reshevsky's books include *Reshevsky on Chess*, New York, London 1948; and *How Chess Games are Won*, London 1962. Although frequently the victim of time-pressure, Reshevsky has been an exceptional tactician throughout his career.

Palma de Mallorca 1970
White: Reshevsky; *Black:* Polugayevsky
English Opening
1. P–Q4, N–KB3; 2. P–QB4, P–B4; 3. N–KB3, P×P; 4. N×P, P–K3; 5. N–QB3, B–N5; 6. N–N5, O–O; 7. P–QR3, B×N+; 8. N×B, P–Q4; 9. B–N5, P–KR3; 10. B–R4, P–KN4; 11. B–N3, P–Q5; 12. N–N5, N–B3; 13. P–K3, P×P; 14. P×P, P–K4; 15. B–Q3, B–N5; 16. Q–B2, P–K5; 17. B–K2, Q–R4+; 18. K–B2, B×B; 19. K×B, QR–B1; 20. N–Q6, R–R1; 21. QR–Q1, N–R4; 22. B–K1, Q–N3; 23. P–KN4, N–B3;

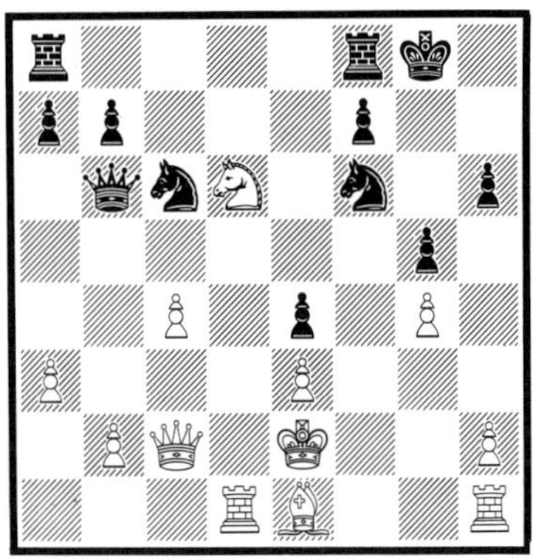

24. B–B3, N×P; 25. Q×P, P–B4; 26. Q–K6+, K–R2; 27. N×BP, N(3)–K4; 28. R–Q7+, resigns. *(A.S.)*

RESTRICTED ADVANCE

A concept evolved by Nimzowitsch, the restricted advance is a means of using an open file for the Rooks where no invasion of the 7th or 8th ranks is possible and no other object of attack can be found along the open file. Nimzowitsch–Pritzel, Copenhagen 1922: 1: R–Q3 (the restricted advance: the open Q-file is exploited only as a stepping stone to the half-open QB-file), P×P; 2. R–B3, N–K2; 3. R–B5 (again the restricted advance: the half-open QB-file is used as a stepping stone to the QR-file), KR–N1; 4. N(2)–B3, P–QR3; 5. R×RP, K–N2; 6. N–N6, R–R2; 7. N(3)–R4, R(2)–N2; 8. R×RP, resigns. *(W.H.)*

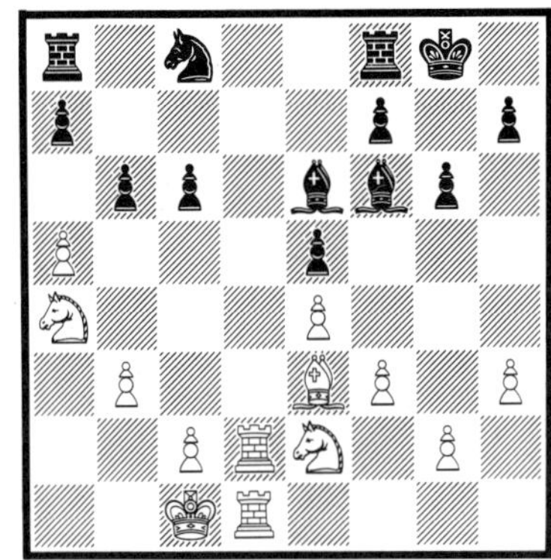

RÉTI OPENING

The opening 1. N–KB3 – popularized by Réti as part of his new hypermodern style of play. It offers flexible development combined with numerous transpositional possibilities. After 1. . , P–Q4; 2. P–B4, the opening often takes on an independent character, one important variation being the London System: 2. . , P–QB3; 3. P–QN3, N–B3; 4. P–N3, B–B4; 5. B–KN2, P–K3; 6. B–N2, QN–Q2; 7. O–O, P–KR3; 8. P–Q3, B–K2 with even chances. *(R.D.K.)*

RÉTI, Richard *(28 May 1889–6 June 1929)*
Grandmaster and the writer who conveyed the teachings of the hypermoderns to the chess public, Réti was born in Pezzinok, then in Hungary and later (after the First World War) Czechoslovakia. It was for the latter country that he was to play in the international team tournaments between the wars.

He went to Vienna to study mathematics at the university and, like most of the great players of Central Europe of that time, was a product of the Viennese school of chess. His early appearances in international chess were far from impressive and in fact he came bottom in a big tournament at Vienna in 1908.

Then, under the influence of his friend Julius Breyer, there came a great change for the better in his play. He became well known for the brilliance of his ideas and came =3rd in the Abbazia Gambit tournament of 1912. In the great unfinished tournament at Mannheim in 1914 he was =4th with Breyer and Marshall ahead of many famous names (Janowski, Tarrasch, Bogoljubow, Důras, etc.) when the war interrupted the tournament.

For the next four years there was no international chess but once the international game resumed it was apparent that Réti was a great master who ranked alongside the world's best. A first at Kaschau (Kassa) in 1918, ahead of Vidmar and Breyer, was followed by equal first at Budapest.

First again at Rotterdam in 1919, he had no less than three firsts in 1920: at Amsterdam ahead of Maróczy, Tartakower and Euwe; at Vienna ahead of Breyer, Grünfeld and Tartakower; above all at the great tournament of Göteborg, an event that included all

Réti at the International Tournament, Teplitz Schönau Czechoslovakia 1922

Europe's leading players (excepting Alekhine).

Then came a pause in his chess-playing career. He had become involved in the business of writing about chess. Starting off as a columnist he became a great and vital writer on the game. It was the writings of Franz Gutmayer that provoked Réti to write his small masterpiece *Die Neuen Ideen im Schachspiel*, Vienna 1922, which he was later to enlarge and have translated into English under the title of *Modern Ideas in Chess*, London, New York 1923. For the first time in the history of books on chess a writer capable of a genuine historical survey of the evolution of chess ideas and also of a colourful and poetic picture of the state of contemporary chess had made his appearance.

Returning to the active playing of the game, he now participated in practically all the great tournaments of the 1920s. An =1st in the great tournament at Teplitz-Schönau in 1922 was followed by two good seconds in 1923, at Mährisch-Ostrau and at Vienna. In the great New York event of 1924 he won the first brilliancy prize for a celebrated win over Bogoljubow and inflicted on Capablanca his only defeat of the tournament.

During a long visit to South America he established a new world blindfold simultaneous record at Sao Paulo in Brazil, where he played twenty-nine games with a score of +20−2=7.

His results when he returned to Europe in 1925 were somewhat disappointing after his striking successes in the early 1920s. For this there were two reasons. One was his increasing devotion to writing and the other was the development of a new interest, that of endgame studies, in which he expressed his poetic view of the game in some of the most beautiful studies of all time.

However, by 1927 he was coming back into true grandmaster form. A 2nd at Bad Homburg was followed by an excellent showing on top board for Czechoslovakia in the International Team tournament at London. In 1928 he was 1st at Vienna and Giessen, 2nd at Dortmund and =1st at Brno.

A visit to Scandinavia ended in his last tournament, at Stockholm over the turn of the year. There he came first in a double-round event with 4½ ahead of Lundin and Stoltz 3 and Ståhlberg 1½.

Then, returning to Prague, he prepared for press his second great book, *Masters of the Chess Board*, but never managed to complete it. He was taken ill with scarlet fever and died at the age of forty in hospital in Prague in 1929.

This premature death was a tragedy for the chess-world, but it should be stated that, had he written only *Modern Ideas in Chess* he would still have belonged to the chess immortals.

First brilliancy prize, New York 1924
White: Réti; *Black:* Bogoljubow
Réti Opening
1. N–KB3, P–Q4; 2. P–B4, P–K3; 3. P–KN3, N–KB3; 4. B–N2, B–Q3; 5. O–O, O–O; 6. P–N3, R–K1; 7. B–N2, QN–Q2; 8. P–Q4, P–B3; 9. QN–Q2, N–K5; 10. N×N, P×N; 11. N–K5, P–KB4; 12. P–B3, P×P; 13. B×P, Q–B2; 14. N×N, B×N; 15. P–K4, P–K4; 16. P–B5, B–KB1; 17. Q–B2, P×QP; 18. P×BP, QR–Q1; 19. B–R5, R–K4; 20. B×P, R×KBP; 21. R×R, B×R; 22. Q×B, R×B; 23. R–KB1, R–Q1; 24. B–B7+, K–R1; 25. B–K8, resigns.

His principal works: *Die Neuen Ideen im Schachspiel*, Vienna 1922, translated and enlarged as *Modern Ideas in Chess*, London, New York, 1923; *Die Meister des Schachbretts*, Mährisch-Ostrau 1930, translated as *Masters of the Chessboard*, New York 1932, London 1933. *(H.G.)*

RHODESIA

A Rhodesian team has contested two Olympiads, finishing 50th in 1970 and 65th in 1974. During the 1974 Nice Olympiad the Rhodesian Chess Federation (P.O. Box 2144, Salisbury) was suspended from FIDE in a vote swayed by political motives. *(K.J.O'C.)*

RIBLI, Zoltan *(b. 6 September 1951)*

Hungarian grandmaster, one of Europe's leading younger players (European Junior champion 1971) and one of the most promising in his generation in the world.

Ribli was an international master by 1970 and a grandmaster in 1973.

He confirmed his right to this title by achieving a grandmaster result at the 1974 I.B.M. Grandmaster tournament in Amsterdam where he came 4th with 9 points. In that year he won the Hungarian championship, as he had done in 1973.

He had an outstanding success at Budapest 1975 where he came =1st with Polugayevsky with 10½ points, no less than 1½ points more than the grandmaster norm. In the tournament at Ljubljana/Portorož 1975 he was =3rd with Furman and Hort. He took 1st in the 1975 Reykjavik Zonal and was =5th with Ljubojević in Manila 1976.

He has played three times in the Olympiads for Hungary, scoring 64.3% on board 6 at Siegen 1970; 76.5% on board 4 at Skopje 1972, and 70.5% on board 4 at Nice 1974. *(H.G.)*

RICE, Isaac L. *(22 February 1850–2 November 1915)*
Rice was the leading American chess patron from the 1880s to his death. He lavished tens of thousands of dollars to promote the game in general and to analyse his pet variation, the Rice Gambit.

The Bavarian-born Rice enjoyed a highly successful career as law professor, lawyer and corporation executive. He encouraged many leading masters (including Em. Lasker, Důras, Capablanca and Janowski) to analyse the position after 1. P–K4, P–K4; 2. P–KB4, P×P; 3. N–KB3, P–KN4; 4. P–KR4, P–N5; 5. N–K5, N–KB3; 6. B–B4, P–Q4; 7. P×P, B–Q3; 8. O–O, which Rice said he had invented in the 1890s. As a result of his donations, several tournaments and matches including Monte Carlo 1904 and St Petersburg 1905/6 were held to investigate the opening. *(A.S.)*

RICE, John Michael *(b. 19 July 1937)*
See under PROBLEMISTS.

RICHTER ATTACK
1. P–Q4, N–KB3; 2. N–QB3, P–Q4; 3. B–N5. Named after the German master Kurt Richter who won many brilliant games with it. *(H.G.)*

RICHTER, Emil *(14 January 1894–16 March 1971)*
Champion of Czechoslovakia in 1948 following a play-off match with Zita. Given the title of international master in 1951. *(W.R.H.)*

RICHTER, Kurt *(24 November 1900–29 December 1969)*
A German international master and fertile chess writer. His best international results were 2nd to Ståhlberg in the Nordic Master tournament Bad Niendorf 1934, 2nd to Bogoljubow (ahead of Eliskases, Engels, Kieninger, Vidmar, Foltys, etc.) at Stuttgart 1939, =3rd with Bogoljubow and Foltys, behind Alekhine and Keres, at Munich 1942. He won the German championship in 1935 and played first board for Germany in the Team tournament of Munich 1936.

The *Scharfrichter* ('executioner') of Berlin, as he was generally called, was a feared attacking player with many brilliancies to his credit. His literary output – mostly of a light, chatty character – includes *Kurzgeschichten um Schachfiguren*, Berlin 1947; *Die Hohe Schule der Schachaktik*, Berlin 1952; *Einfälle-Reinfälle*, Berlin 1960; also a biography of Carls, Berlin 1957. A collection of his own games was edited by Brinckmann, Berlin 1961. *(W.H.)*

RIEMANN, Fritz *(2 January 1859–25 November 1932)*
A German player of the nineteenth century, Riemann made but infrequent tournament appearances. His best result was =1st with Von Bardeleben at Leipzig 1888, while he made fine plus scores at the important congresses of Nuremberg 1883 and Hamburg 1885. Riemann wrote a book on his experiences as a pupil of Anderssen's, Berlin-Leipzig 1925. *(W.H.)*

RIUMIN, Nikolai Nikolayevich *(1908–1942)*
Soviet master and champion of Moscow three times – 1931, 1933/4 and 1935. Took second place behind Botvinnik in the 1931 USSR championship. Also second in the Leningrad 1934 international tournament. Competed at Moscow 1935 and Moscow 1936, but without conspicuous success. *(W.R.H.)*

RIVIÈRE, Jules Arnous de *(4 May 1830–11 September 1906)*
One of the leading French players of the mid-nineteenth century and chiefly memorable for having played many games with Paul Morphy when he visited Paris. Though he had little success in his encounters with the American genius, he was a good, solid player who was not without success against strong masters.

In the great Paris tournament of 1867 he had an excellent 6th/13 place. He also did well in some lesser tournaments in Paris: 3rd in 1880, =2nd 1881, 2nd 1882/3 and 3rd in the Café de la Régence tournament of 1896.

His match record, apart from the games against Morphy which were not formal matches, was very good indeed: at London in 1860 he beat Barnes by +5–2=0; and in Paris, where he played his other matches, he beat Journoud in 1860 by +7–2=1 and Löwenthal in 1867 by +2–0=0. He had a highly honourable narrow loss to Chigorin in 1885 by +4–5=1. *(H.G.)*

ROBATSCH DEFENCE
1. P–K4, P–KN3; 2. P–Q4, B–N2; or it may be reached by 1. P–Q4, P–KN3; 2. P–K4, B–N2. Sometimes known as the Modern Defence or the Kotov Defence, this line, named after the Austrian grandmaster Robatsch, differs from the Pirc Defence in that it omits an early N–KB3 for Black. Its objective is the same as that of the Pirc, to encourage White's centre pawns to advance and take profit by the over-extension of lines to counter-attack on the black squares.

White has five main ways of treating it: 3. P–QB4, 3. P–KB4, 3. P–QB3, 3. N–QB3 and 3. N–KB3. *(H.G.)*

ROBATSCH, Karl *(b. 14 October 1928)*
An Austrian grandmaster, Robatsch had his best year in 1960 when he brought off a fine double: the gold medal for the best first-board result at the Leipzig Olympiad, and the Austrian championship. His best international results were 2nd at Kapfenberg 1955, =2nd at Varna 1957, =1st at Madrid 1961, =2nd at Wijk-aan-Zee 1962, and =3rd in the Halle Zonal 1963 (losing the tie-breaking match to

Ivkov). In the great Havana tournament of 1965 he finished 8th out of 22, ahead of many other grandmasters. *(W.H.)*

RÖDL, Ludwig *(30 April 1907–1970)*
A German international master, Dr Rödl was one of the most reliable players in the early thirties and again immediately after the Second World War. In the German championships at Swinemünde 1931 he tied for first with Bogoljubow; at Bad Pyrmont 1933 he came 2nd to Bogoljubow; and at Aachen 1934 third to Carls and Reinhardt. In other strong events he came 2nd at Swinemünde 1932 and Lüneburg 1947, and won a very strong South German championship at Riedenburg 1947. In 1936 he published a small book on endgames. *(W.H.)*

RODRIGUEZ, Orestes *(b. 4 July 1943)*
Peruvian international master; he received the title in 1972. He has lived in Spain for the last four years so as to have more opportunities of playing in international tournaments and he has now participated in many European events, his best results being 1st at Alicante 1974 and =1st in Reggio Emilia 1974/5. He has been a regular member of the Peruvian Olympiad team, usually playing on top board and never scoring less than 50%. *(K.J.O'C.)*

ROGARD, Folke *(6 July 1899–11 June 1973)*
President of FIDE 1949–70, he had a highly successful career as a lawyer in Stockholm, but he will be remembered most of all for the immense work and skill he lavished on the task of making FIDE a truly representative and authoritative world body.

Though never a particularly strong chess-player, his keen intellect and his intuitive knowledge of men gave him an insight into the way both strong and weak players regarded the game.

Rogard's career as a chess administrator started off in Sweden where he succeeded the celebrated Ludwig Collijn as President of the Swedish Chess Federation in 1939, though he had been working on behalf of the Federation earlier, notably at the Olympiad in Stockholm in 1937.

By 1947 he had become a vice-president of FIDE and in 1949 he succeeded the kindly but not particularly effective Dutchman Dr Rueb in the post of President. He at once set to and busied himself with the task of first of all bringing such great chess-playing countries as the USSR and West Germany into the FIDE fold and then of asserting the authority of the parent body over all the national units that were affiliated to it.

He brought to the task an ideal temperament, consisting of an iron will-power encased in a velvet glove. Quite a good actor, he would seem to explode with rage when he thought it necessary to blast away unwarranted opposition; but underneath he remained as cool as a cucumber. He and he alone was able to come between the clash of mighty opposites in the shape of the USSR and the USA, and, by observing a strict neutrality, he was able to reconcile the very different aims of East and West.

As a lawyer, he found the subject of the Laws of Chess dear to his heart and in conjunction with the FIDE Commission for the Rules he worked for many years on the project of creating a clear codex of the rules. In this formidable task he was patient, clear-sighted and always ready to see another's point of view.

He retired from the Presidency of FIDE in 1970 but he continued working as a lawyer right till the very end. *(H.G.)*

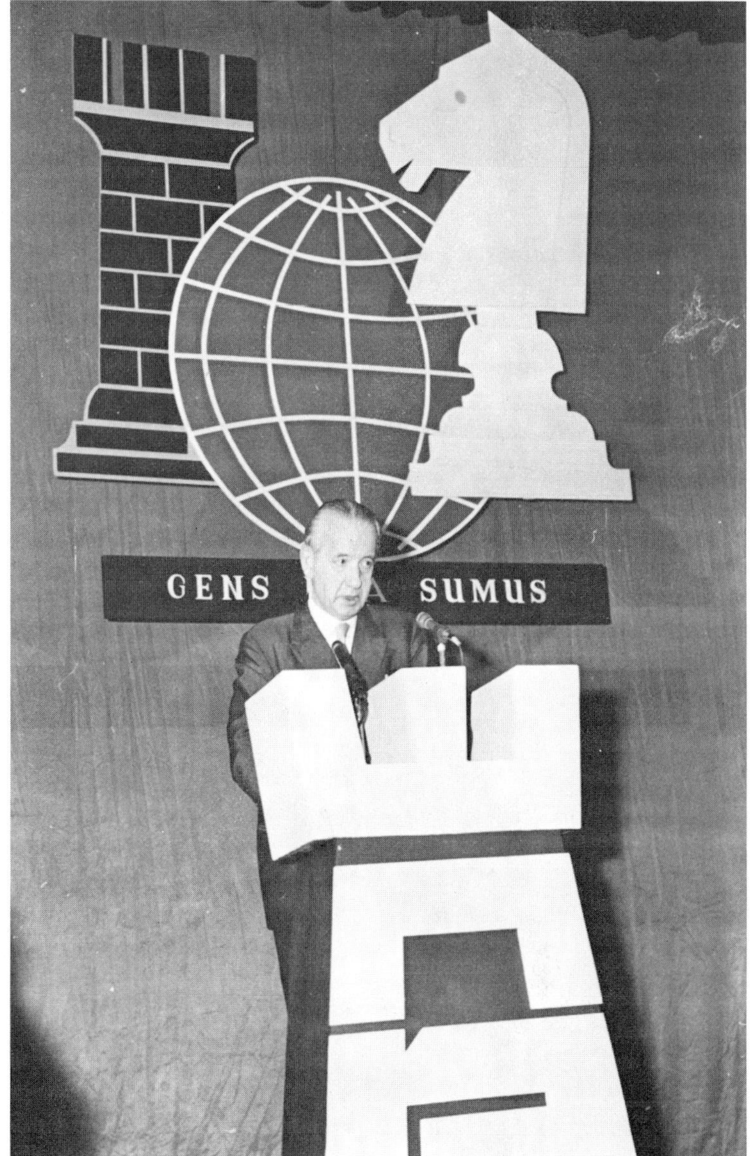

Folke Rogard opening the 16th Chess Olympics in Tel Aviv, 1964

ROGOFF, Kenneth *(b. 22 March 1953)*
Leader of the new generation of young US masters who emerged in the late 1960s, Rogoff won or shared first place in the US Junior championship three times and came 3rd in the 1971 World Junior event in Athens. Rogoff also led the US team in the 1970 and 1972 Student Olympiads. In 1974 Rogoff was awarded the international master title for his student team results and for his =1st at the 1973 international tournament at Norristown, Pennsylvania. In 1975 he came second in the US championship, qualifying for the 1976 Interzonals in which he was =13th at Biel. *(A.S.)*

ROHDE, Michael Arthur *(b. 26 August 1959)*
US Junior co-champion 1976. At fourteen he became one of the two youngest players ever to win the National High School championship. Best tournament results: 1st Schilde Junior 1976 and =5th (international master norm) Manhattan international, New York 1976. *(K.J.O'C.)*

ROMANIA
The Romanian Chess Federation was founded in 1925, but chess did not begin to flourish in the country until the game fell under state sponsorship in 1946. Romanian teams had competed in the pre-war Olympiads, but without conspicuous success, finishing 16th in 1928, 13th in 1930, 15th in 1931 and 17th in 1935. Their first appearance in the post-war events was at Moscow 1956 where their team qualified for the A-final and took eleventh place. They did not compete in 1958, but since 1960 have maintained an unbroken record of appearances, qualifying for the A-final on each occasion. Their best result has been to finish 7th in 1972.

Romania has, at the time of writing, only one international grandmaster the former World Junior Champion Florin Gheorghiu. He is well supported, however, by international masters Cioâltea, Drimer, Ghitescu, Radovici, Troianescu, Balanel and Erdelyi.

The Romanian championship is contested each year, and has been a regular event since 1946, besides having taken place sporadically before that date. Players must survive national eliminating contests to qualify for the 20-man final. The Romanian champions to date have been as follows:

1926	A. Tyroler	1957	O. Troianescu
1927	A Tyroler	1958	I. Balanel
1928	A Tyroler	1959	V. Ciocâltea
1930	I. Balogh	1960	F. Gheorghiu
1931	S. Erdelyi	1961	V. Ciocâltea
1934	S. Erdelyi	1962	F. Gheorghiu
1935	H. Silberman	1963	T. Ghitescu
1936	I. Halic	1964	F. Gheorghiu
1943	P. Seimeanu	1965	F. Gheorghiu
1946	O. Troianescu	1966	F. Gheorghiu
1947	T. Ichim	1967	F. Gheorghiu
1948	T. Popa	1968	O. Troianescu
1949	S. Erdelyi	1969	V. Ciocâltea
1950	I. Balanel	1970	V. Ciocâltea and F. Gheorghiu
1951	G. Alexandrescu and T. Flonder	1971	V. Ciocâltea
1952	V. Ciocâltea	1972	M. Partos
1953	I. Balanel	1973	F. Gheorghiu
1954	O. Troianescu	1974	P. Urzica
1955	I. Balanel	1975	V. Ciocâltea
1956	O. Troianescu	1976	M. Ghinda

Romania has also been the scene of a number of international events. The largest of these was the 1965 Student Olympiad at Sinaia, on which occasion the home team finished in fourth place, their best-ever result in that event. Regular international tournaments are held in Bucharest (annually) and in Timişoara (men's and women's tournaments in alternate years). Other towns to hold tournaments include Constanţa and Sinaia.

Winners of recent Bucharest international tournaments include Taimanov (1973), Tseshkovsky (1974) and Ciocâltea (1975).

Romania is also noted for the success of its women players and sponsorship of women's chess. They have secured the silver medals in four of the six Women's Olympiads to date: in 1957, 1966, 1972 and in 1974. Their Woman masters Nicolau (now resident in The Netherlands) and Polihroniade were two of the strongest non-Soviet players during the 1960s.

The address of the Romanian Chess Federation is: Federaţia Româna de Sah, Bvd. Muncii 37–39, Bucharest, 73401 – Sectors. The Federation produces a monthly chess magazine, *Revista de Sah.* *(W.R.H.)*

ROMANISHIN, Oleg Mikhailovich *(b. 10 January 1952)*

A Soviet grandmaster and one of the younger school of Soviet players. Won the European Junior championship in 1973 and was awarded the title of international master in the same year.

He made rapid strides in the next two years and in 1976 achieved his second norm for the grandmaster title by winning first prize at Erevan (Armenia, USSR) with $10\frac{1}{2}/15$. The title was confirmed at the FIDE Congress of that year. His other major tournament successes: 1st Novi Sad 1975 and 1st Dortmund 1976. *(W.R.H.)*

ROMANOVSKY, Pyotr Arsenyevich *(30 July 1892–1 March 1964)*
First Soviet player (1935) to receive the title of 'Honoured Master of Sport', Romanovsky was one of the most prominent Soviet chess-players in the period up to the Second World War. He won the USSR championship in 1923 and 1927, as well as being runner-up to Alekhine in the very first USSR championship in 1920. His other good results include sharing first place with Botvinnik in a 1933 tournament of Leningrad masters, and sharing second place at the Leningrad 1934 International tournament.

Romanovsky turned in his later years to organization and writing. He was a member of the Praesidium of the USSR Chess Federation, and the author of many works on the game, including a well-known book on the middle-game, *Mitelshpil*, Leningrad 1929. *(W.R.H.)*

ROOK
The basic move of the Rook has remained unchanged through the 1500 years that chess has existed but in the original game, *chaturanga*, in north-west India it was a chariot, *ratha*, and then, when the game moved to Persia, *rukh*.

So it remained when the Arabs took over; but a change came in its form when the game came to Europe. The name *rukh* being incomprehensible to the European it was adapted to something that sounded more comprehensible – to Roc, Roche, Roque and Rook. Later still, possibly under the influence of the Crusaders and the Crusaders who were great builders of castles, it became Castle or Tower and hence the French *tour*, the German *Turm* and the Spanish *torre*. In Russia, though, there was a curious deviation when it became *ladia*, a boat.

The one change to its move was in reality an addition when castling was introduced in medieval times. *(H.G.)*

ROSENTHAL, Samuel *(7 September 1837–19 September 1902)*
Born in Poland, Rosenthal went to France in 1864 and settled down in Paris as a chess professional and writer. A master player, his results were not consonant with his real strength, since he had bad health and his journalistic activities prevented him from concentrating on play.

At Paris 1867 he came =9th/13; at Baden-Baden 1870 he was bottom; but his best result came in the strong tournament of Vienna 1873 where he was 4th/12. An =7th with Englisch in Paris 1878 was followed by a 1st in a smaller and much less important tournament at Paris 1880 and he was 8th/14 at London 1883.

He had little success in match play, was crushed by Kolisch in Paris 1864, lost three matches to Neumann, won a match against Wisker at London in 1871 by +3−2=4 and was heavily defeated by Zukertort at London in 1871 by +1−7=11.

He wrote for many journals and magazines and edited the chess column in the *Monde Illustré* from 1885–1902. *(H.G.)*

ROSSELLI, Stefano, Marquis del Turco
(27 July 1877–18 August 1947)
Italian master who competed in a number of national and international tournaments between 1901 and 1941 but was successful only on a national level. He won the Italian championship in 1923 when he defeated Marotti in a match at Naples by +6−2=5. In the following year he drew a match with Canal in Turin by +1−1=2.

He participated in all the national tournaments with success from 1920 to 1930 but he lost the title to Monticelli in 1929 in a match by +4−6=4. His best result in that period was a 1st/12 at Livorno 1926 ahead of Davidson and Sacconi.

He also played in the great tournaments at Baden-Baden 1925, Semmering 1926 and Zürich 1934, but without notable distinction except that at Baden-Baden he came ahead of Tarrasch (whom he beat), Colle, Mieses and Sir George Thomas.

He was the founder of *L'Italia Scacchistica* in 1911 and directed and supported it till 1943. *(R.D.K.)*

ROSSETTO, Hector *(b. 8 September 1922)*
An Argentine grandmaster. Awarded the international master title 1950, and grandmaster 1960. Six times Argentinian champion (1942, 1944, 1945, 1947, 1962, 1972). Regular participant at annual Mar del Plata events: 1st 1949, =2nd 1950, 1st 1952, =2nd 1961. Played in the Portorož Interzonal 1958 and came 18th. Best result: 4th prize in the great international tournament, Buenos Aires 1960. Has played in six Olympiads, scoring 80% on board 5 at Helsinki 1952. *(R.D.K.)*

ROSSOLIMO, Nicolas *(28 February 1910–24 July 1975)*
Greek-Russian-French-American grandmaster whose profession varied from that of taxi-driver to chess-professional and who was an expert at judo (with the rank of brown belt) and playing the concertina.

Born in Kiev, he lived in the USSR till 1929 when he went to Paris. There he adopted the classic profession of the Russian emigré, that of taxi-driver, but also played much chess, winning the Paris championship five times.

His first international was Paris 1938 where he came 2nd to Capablanca. It was after the Second World War that his international career really commenced. From 1948 to 1953 he had a fine record that, without placing him among the likely candidates for World Championship honours, still demonstrated his graceful mastery of the game.

His best performances in this period were: =2nd with Benko at Bad Gastein 1948, 1st at Hastings 1948/9, 2nd at Heidelberg and 1st at Southsea both in 1949, 2nd at Venice 1949 and 3rd at Venice 1950, =4th with Julio Bolbochan at Trenčianské Teplice 1949, 8th at Amsterdam 1950 and 1st at Gijon 1950. Meanwhile he had played two matches with Tartakower, drawing the first, in 1948, by +1−1=10. In 1949 he drew the second match +5−5=0.

=1st with Tartakower at Southsea 1951, he was 1st at Beverwijk in 1953 and then, along with his wife and son, emigrated to America. There he took up taxi-driving again and kept a chess studio in New York. He took part less and less in international and even national events, though he did win the US Open in 1955. He made sporadic attempts to return to Europe but without settling anywhere for long. His death came by accident through a fall on some steps in New York.

He played in five Olympiads: for France on board 2 at Dubrovnik 1950 and on board 1 at Skopje 1972; and for the USA in reserve positions at Munich 1958, Leipzig 1960 and Havana 1966.

Rossolimo had a love for the beautiful in chess and his best games had an artistry that was most pleasing aesthetically. Here is a characteristically charming game he won at Puerto Rico in 1966.

White: Rossolimo; *Black:* Reissman
Giuoco Piano
1. P–K4, P–K4; 2. N–KB3, N–QB3; 3. B–B4, B–B4; 4. P–B3, N–B3; 5. P–Q4, P×P; 6. P×P, B–N5+; 7. B–Q2, B×B+;

8. QN×B, P–Q4; 9. P×P, KN×P; 10. Q–N3, QN–K2; 11. O–O, P–QB3; 12. KR–K1, O–O; 13. P–QR4, P–QN3; 14. N–K5, B–N2; 15. P–R5, R–B1; 16. N–K4, Q–B2; 17. P–R6, B–R1; 18. Q–KR3, N–B5; 19. Q–N4, N(K2)–Q4; 20. R–R3, N–K3; 21. B×N, P×B; 22. N–B6+, K–R1;

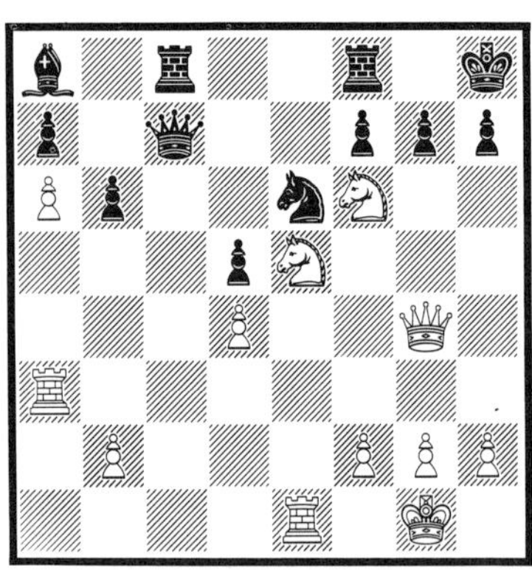

23. Q–N6!, Q–B7; 24. R–R3, resigns. *(H.G.)*

ROTLEWI, G. A. *(1889–1920)*
Talented Polish master who, for a brief period (1909–11) looked like becoming a great force in international chess; but ill health put an end to his activities.

In 1909 he came second to Alekhine in the All-Russian Major tournament at St Petersburg. In the same year he lost a match to Salwe, at Lodz, by +5−8=3. He won the Major tournament (*Hauptturnier*) at Hamburg 1910 and in 1911 came the remarkable achievement of 4th prize in the great Carlsbad tournament. There he came ahead of such players as Marshall, Nimzowitsch, Vidmar, Alekhine, Tartakower and Spielmann. In that year too he had his revenge for his defeat by Salwe in 1909, winning a second match by +3−1=6.

Another good result in 1911 was an =2nd with Esser, Von Freymann and Hromadka at Cologne. After this his name vanishes from the scene, whether national or international. *(H.G.)*

ROUSSEAU, Eugene
Born in France but resident in New Orleans, USA, for most of his life, Rousseau was an enthusiastic amateur who has become well known in chess history through having played many games with Paul Morphy, when the latter was a young boy.

His one international appearance was at the Paris tournament of 1867 where he came next to bottom. But he did have some talent as was shown by four matches he played against players of good amateur strength. Against J. W. Schulten, in two matches played in New Orleans in 1841, he lost the first by +10−11=0 but won the second by +7−4=0. He met him again in New York in 1843 and won by +13−8=0. In 1845 he played a long match with Stanley in New Orleans and lost by +8−15=8.

He is author of a dubious gambit for Black: 1. P–K4, P–K4; 2. N–KB3, N–QB3; 3. B–B4, P–B4 with which he played and lost a game against Paul Morphy (then aged twelve) at New Orleans on 28 October 1849. *(H.G.)*

ROUSSEAU, Jean Jacques *(28 June 1712–2 July 1778)*
The celebrated author of the *Confessions* tells in that work how he learnt the game as a youth from a certain M. Bagueret who was a weak player to whom he could offer a Rook odds. Consumed by a passionate desire to become a chess-master, he went away and studied the works of Greco, and almost killed himself by his over-energetic studies. He came back and found his play had not really improved. In the end he decided that he could, by stupendous efforts of study, just about defeat Bagueret.

That he never gave up the game is shown by his injudiciously defeating the Duke of Conti, and adroitly fending off the wrath of his great opponent by saying that he had too great a respect for the Duke not to beat him. *(H.G.)*

ROYAL GAME
Chess is often referred to as the royal game for the obvious reason that the chief role in chess is played by the King. Its first application to chess in English was in the early fifteenth century by the poet John Lydgate who translated *Les eschez amoureux* into *Reson and Sensuallyte* and talked of 'that playe most Royal'. *(H.G.)*

ROYCROFT, A. J.
See under ENDGAME STUDY COMPOSERS.

RUBINSTEIN, Akiba *(12 October 1882–14 March 1961)*

Born in Stawiski, Poland (then part of Russia), Rubinstein was the youngest of twelve children. His father died shortly before his birth and he was raised by his grandparents, who gave him an orthodox Jewish religious education in keeping with the family traditions of Talmudic scholarship.

He had no contact with chess until the age of sixteen, but once having learned the game he devoted himself to it completely, abandoning his religious studies and moving to the city of Lodz, which contained a thriving chess club including the prominent master Salwe. Rubinstein improved rapidly as a player and in 1903 played two matches against Salwe – drawing the first +5−5=0 and winning the second +5−3=2.

In 1904 Rubinstein came 5th in the Russian National tournament at Kiev and made his international debut, sharing first prize with Dûras, at Barmen 1905. Important successes followed swiftly, including victories at Ostend 1907 (tied with Bernstein), Carlsbad 1907 and Lodz 1907. In 1908 he won matches against Teichmann (+3−2=1), Marshall (+3−2=3) and Mieses (+5−3=2). In 1909 he tied with Lasker for first prize in the St Petersburg tournament, defeating the World Champion in their individual game.

These results left Rubinstein as a leading challenger for the World title, but efforts to arrange a match with Lasker in 1910 proved abortive through lack of financial backing. Rubinstein's tournament play continued unsurpassed, culminating in 1912 in a series of five successive first prizes in major events: San Sebastian, Pistyan, Breslau (tied with Dûras), Warsaw, and Vilna. Renewed attempts to obtain a title match with Lasker culminated in a tentative agreement for a match to be played in the spring of 1914. Tragically for Rubinstein, this contest was first postponed and later abandoned owing to the outbreak of war.

The privations of war did considerable damage to Rubinstein's delicate psychic balance, and in post-war years he never again reached his former eminence. While he was still capable of producing brilliant individual games, his results as a whole were erratic and sometimes marred by elementary blunders. As Tartakower put it: 'His play became keener but his thinking less clear.' Symptoms of a persecution complex gradually became evident – he suffered from imaginary distractions and complained of being followed and threatened by enemies.

In spite of his growing psychological disturbance, he still had numerous successes: notably 2nd (undefeated, a ½-point behind Lasker) Berlin Four Masters 1918, 2nd (after Réti) Göteborg 1920, 1st Vienna 1922, =1st (with Nimzowitsch) Marienbad 1925, 2nd (after Capablanca) Budapest 1929, 3rd (after Alekhine and Nimzowitsch) San Remo 1930, as well as victories in match-play over Schlechter (+2−1=3) in 1918 and Bogoljubow (+5−4=3) in 1920.

Rubinstein retired from serious play in 1932 and, after spending some time in a sanatorium, lived his remaining years in reduced circumstances in Belgium. He died in 1961 in an old people's home.

Less overtly aggressive than some of his contemporaries, Rubinstein's style was marked by profound strategic and positional insight and his particular *forte* was the endgame. In *Modern Ideas in Chess* Réti wrote: 'With Rubinstein all is refined tranquillity; for with him in building up his game the position given to every piece is the necessary one. It is not a matter of a fight for him, but the working out of a victory, and so his games create the impression of a great structure from which not one stone dare be shifted.' That he was also capable of brilliant attacking play when the position demanded it is witnessed by the following game, sometimes called the Rubinstein Immortal:

Russian National tournament, Lodz 1907
White: Rotlewi; *Black:* Rubinstein
Queen's Pawn Opening
1. P–Q4, P–Q4; 2. N–KB3, P–K3; 3. P–K3, P–QB4; 4. P–B4, N–QB3; 5. N–B3, N–B3; 6. QP×P, B×P; 7. P–QR3, P–QR3; 8. P–QN4, B–Q3; 9. B–N2, O–O; 10. Q–Q2, Q–K2; 11. B–Q3, P×P; 12. B×P, P–QN4; 13. B–Q3, R–Q1; 14. Q–K2, B–N2; 15. O–O, N–K4; 16. N×N, B×N; 17. P–KB4, B–B2; 18. P–K4, QR–B1; 19. P–K5, B–N3+; 20. K–R1, N–N5; 21. B–K4, Q–R5; 22. P–N3,

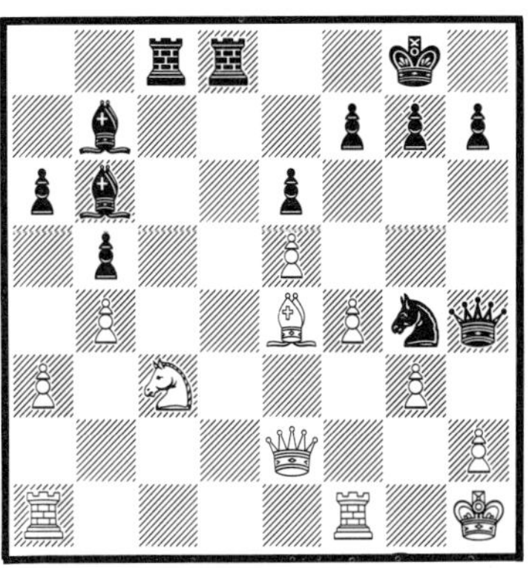

R×N; 23. P×Q, R–Q7; 24. Q×R, B×B+; 25. Q–N2, R–R6; 26. resigns. *(R.D.K.)*

RUBTSOVA, Olga Nikolayevna *(b. 20 August 1909)*
First USSR Women's champion when she won the event in 1931, and fourth Woman World Champion following the triangular match for the title in 1956. She held the World title until 1958 when she lost to Bykova. Also held the USSR championship in 1937 and 1949. Awarded title of international Woman master in 1950, and the Order of the Red Banner of Labour in 1956, she received the international woman grandmaster title in 1976. *(W.R.H.)*

RUDENKO, Ludmila Vladimirovna *(b. 27 July 1904)*
First Soviet woman to capture the World Championship, which has been held by the Soviet Union ever since. Rudenko won the title in 1950 by taking first place in the tournament at Moscow designed to fill the gap left by the death of Vera Menchik. She held the title for three years, losing to Bykova in 1953. During her reign Rudenko also captured the USSR Women's championship in 1952. International woman grandmaster in 1976. *(W.R.H.)*

RUEB, Alexander *(27 December 1882–2 February 1959)*
One of the founders of FIDE (Paris 1924) and President of this organization 1924–49. Rueb had a vast knowledge of endgame studies, on which he wrote a standard work consisting of five volumes: *Bronnen van Schaakstudie*, The Hague 1949. Owned large and famous collection of chess literature. His library was destroyed by bombs in 1945, but built up again after the war. After his death his collection was put in the Amsterdam University Library, in care of the Alexander Rueb Foundation. *(R.D.K.)*

RULES, HISTORY OF
In its modern form, chess has existed essentially since the fifteenth century, when the Queen and Bishop were altered to their present status. National differences, however, remained for centuries afterwards on such points as castling, the *en passant* rule, pawn promotion, and stalemate: for example, Philidor in his *Analyse* of 1749 complains bitterly of his countrymen who allow a new Queen to appear on the board before the old one has been exchanged – a

practice of which he clearly disapproved! In England, the set of rules which eventually became the norm was that of the London Chess Club, written by Sarratt in 1808. Sarratt was instrumental in introducing to Britain the continental practice of scoring a stalemate as a draw. At the first international tournament, London 1851, the code of rules was written by Staunton, and later published by him in *Chess Praxis*, London 1860.

The laws of chess now in universal use are those of the FIDE which date in substance from 1929. A FIDE commission exists to clarify any ambiguities or doubtful points which may arise. See further under LAWS OF CHESS. *(R.D.K.)*

RUSSIA

Although chess has been played in Russia for more than a thousand years in one form or another, no games from the early periods of its history survive to the present day. Perhaps the earliest news item of chess interest from Russia is a report that Tsar Peter I was an enthusiastic player in the early part of the eighteenth century.

The beginning of the nineteenth century saw a rapid growth in the number and strength of Russian players. Already by 1820 Jaenisch and Petroff were established masters whose games and analyses were becoming known and respected in Europe. Jaenisch himself was largely responsible for the inauguration of the country's first chess club in his home town of St Petersburg. It opened on 27 March 1853. The first recorded games of Russian masters date from some time before this, being correspondence games of Petroff and Jaenisch from the years 1836–9.

The first chess competitions took place in the 1850s and were all in the form of matches rather than tournaments as we now know them. Jaenisch played a number of times against Petroff. The other strongest players of the period were the brothers S. and D. Urusov and I. Shumov. After successfully disposing of Shumov in two matches, S. Urusov travelled to Warsaw for a match with Petroff. Petroff's victory confirmed him as the strongest player in Russia.

The new interest in the game created a demand for literature which was satisfied first by Butrimov's book *On the Game of Chess*, St Petersburg 1821. This was followed by more important works by Petroff in 1824 *Shakhmatnaya igra*, St Petersburg and Jaenisch in 1842–3: *Analyse nouvelle des ouvertures du jeu des échecs*, St Pétersbourg. This latter book became one of the most respected early works of opening theory. The first chess periodical in Russia appeared in 1859, though for some years before that, Jaenisch had been writing a regular chess column in a St Petersburg newspaper.

It is strange that most of the chess activity of the time seemed more concerned with theoretical explorations than with actual play. It was not until 1862 that a foreign master, Ignaz Kolisch, was first invited to compete against Russian masters. In that year, he drew a match with S. Urusov and defeated Shumov.

It was in the last quarter of the nineteenth century that chess organization began to spread through Russia and that the Russian chess school took form. In the 1870s the chess circle of Moscow began to devote its efforts towards encouraging the spread of chess throughout the country and just before the turn of the century was able to organize the first all-Russian tournament (in 1899). Within a few years this national championship was accepted as a regular event and formed the culmination of a series of regional championships held throughout the country. By this time there were many master-players in the land, led by Chigorin and Schiffers, who could compete with the world's best. By the time these had passed their best days, there were many to take their places: Alekhine, Nimzowitsch and Rubinstein were winners of some of the later all-Russian tournaments.

The first Russian player to compete in the international arena was Winawer at Paris 1867 (though Jaenisch had been invited to London 1851, but had been unable to compete). The first international tournament in Russia was the match-tournament in St Petersburg in 1895/6. This saw four players each meeting the others six times. The players invited were intended to be the four strongest in the world. The event was won by Lasker, followed by Steinitz, Pillsbury and Chigorin in that order. Further, but less strongly contested, match-tournaments were held in Moscow 1907 and Lodz 1908, but the next really important tournament was an event dedicated to the memory of Chigorin in St Petersburg 1909. Nineteen of the world's strongest masters took part, headed by World Champion Emanuel Lasker, who shared first prize with Rubinstein. The next important event to be held in Russia was the even greater St Petersburg 1914, won again by Lasker.

By this time chess life was strongly established among the people of Russia with regular tournaments at all levels and frequent participation of the best players in international circles. For details of chess in Russia since the Russian Revolution, see under SOVIET UNION and USSR. *(W.R.H.)*

RUY LOPEZ

See LOPEZ, RUY.

RUY LOPEZ [opening]

First mentioned by Lucena in 1490, and analysed by Ruy Lopez in 1561, the opening moves 1. P–K4, P–K4; 2. N–KB3, N–QB3; 3. B–N5 introduce one of the most popular and probably the most-analysed opening system in the history of chess. By attacking its defender, White puts pressure on the Black KP. Play is generally more quiet and strategically based than in the older-fashioned King's Gambit or Giuoco Piano. Most popular nowadays are the defences with 3. . , P–QR3. Of the others it is worth mentioning the following:

(*a*) 3. . , B–N5 is Alapin's Defence, hardly seen since the days of Alapin, and deservedly not.

(*b*) 3. . , N–B3, the Berlin Defence, is occasionally played, though a little passive. After 4. O–O, N×P; 5. P–Q4, N–Q3; 6. B×N, QP×B; 7. P×P, N–B4; 8. Q×Q+, K×Q White stands better. If Black wishes to avoid this ending, he should try 5. . , B–K2.

(*c*) 3. . , N–Q5, Bird's Defence, contains some traps for the unwary, but after 4. N×N, P×N; 5. O–O, White's better development and superior pawn structure should give him the advantage.

(*d*) 3. . , KN–K2 is Cozio's Defence. It has a poor reputation, though Larsen has shown it to be a viable system.

(*e*) 3. . , B–B4, the Classical Defence, leaves the Bishop a little exposed after 4. P–B3, followed by P–Q4.

(*f*) 3. . , P–KN3 is the Fianchetto Defence, too weakening for modern tastes.

(*g*) 3. . , P–B4, the Schliemann (or Jaenisch) Counter-gambit, has occasionally been popular, though always considered better for White.

(*h*) 3. . , P–Q3, the Steinitz Defence, is very solid, but rather passive.

After 3. . , P–QR3 the most common continuation is 4. B–R4, N–B3; 5. O–O, B–K2; 6. R–K1, P–QN4; 7. B–N3, P–Q3; 8. P–B3, O–O; 9. P–KR3, giving the normal position of the Closed Defence which leads to most of the important defences to the Ruy Lopez:

(*a*) 9. . , N–N1 is the Breyer System, which is perhaps the most popular variation at the moment. Black will re-deploy his Knight on Q2 leaving his QBP free to advance.

(*b*) 9. . , B–K3 is Kholmov's Line, intending to exchange the dangerous White Bishop.

(*c*) 9. . , N–QR4; 10. B–B2, P–B4 is Chigorin's System, still popular after almost a century of analysis. After 11. P–Q4, Chigorin played 11. . , N–B3 or 11. . , Q–B2, while more recently 11. . , N–Q2 (Keres' variation) has been added to Black's possibilities.

(*d*) 9. . , P–R3 Smyslov's System, is another respected modern invention. Black intends to continue with . . , R–K1, B–B1, P–N3 and B–N2 to safeguard his King's position and retain influence on the centre.

Other important variations after 3. . , P–QR3 are as follows:

(*a*) 4. B×N is the Exchange variation, played quite often by both Lasker and Fischer, but generally considered rather simple.

(*b*) 4. B–R4, N–B3; 5. O–O, B–K2; 6. R–K1, P–QN4; 7. B–N3, O–O; 8. P–B3, P–Q4 is Marshall's Counter-gambit, which may be avoided by 8. P–QR4 (the Anti-Marshall).

(*c*) 4. B–R4, P–Q3, the Steinitz Deferred, is another highly respectable system. Black remains flexible in his scheme of development, retaining the option of a later . . , P–QN4.

(*d*) 4. B–R4, P–QN4; 5. B–N3, N–R4 is a radical attempt introduced by Taimanov, but found insufficient for equality.

(*e*) 4. B–R4, N–B3; 5. O–O, N×P is the Tarrasch (or Open) Defence, leading to complex play after 6. P–Q4, P–QN4; 7. B–N3, P–Q4; 8. P×P, B–K3. *(W.R.H.)*

S

SACCONI, Conte Antonio *(5 October 1895–22 December 1968)*
Italian international master, awarded the title in 1951. Sacconi represented Italy in the Olympiads of 1927, 1928, 1933, and 1935 and became Italian national champion in 1937. A colourful and genial character, he seemed to think at a late stage in his chess career that green plus-fours were *de rigueur* at Olympiads since he appeared in them constantly at Folkestone 1933 and Warsaw 1935. *(R.D.K.)*

SACRIFICE
The voluntary surrender of material in exchange for other advantages. Thus in all gambits one or several pawns are sacrificed for the sake of speeding up development or assaulting the hostile centre. Sacrifices may be classified in various ways: according to the material sacrificed (see, for example, the entry DOUBLE BISHOP SACRIFICE); or according to the purpose (see entries DECOY SACRIFICE, DESPERADO, KING HUNT, KING'S FIELD SACRIFICE, MATING SACRIFICE, OBSTRUCTIVE SACRIFICE, POSITIONAL SACRIFICE, PREVENTIVE SACRIFICE, VACATING SACRIFICE); or the degree of forcefulness employed (active and passive sacrifices, the latter usually consisting of pieces out of direct contact with the main battlefield being offered for capture). Finally, Spielmann's terminology distinguishes real sacrifices from sacrifices for gain: in the former the advantage to be gained by the sacrifice is incalculable, or very nearly so; in the latter the sacrifice leads to a calculable gain including the biggest gain, the hostile King.

Heavy sacrifices have always been regarded as contributing to the brilliancy of a game (see BRILLIANCY PRIZE); and some commentators go so far as to assert that there is no combination without sacrifice (see COMBINATION, Botvinnik's definition). *(W.H.)*

SAIDY, Anthony *(b. 16 May 1937)*
A US international master. Formerly a practising physician, Saidy turned to chess as a profession in the mid 1960s and acquired the international master title after coming =2nd at Venice 1969. Saidy has written *The Battle of Chess Ideas*, London 1972. He was =4th in the 1963/4 and 4th in the 1974 US championships. *(A.S.)*

SAINT-AMANT, Pierre Charles Fournier de
(12 September 1800–29 October 1873)
French master, born at Montflanquin (Lot-et-Garonne). His family was of the minor nobility impoverished by the Revolution. Saint-Amant embarked on a career in the colonial service and, at the age of nineteen, obtained a post as secretary to the Governor of French Guiana. Two years later he was dismissed from this appointment after he had protested about the slave-trade which still existed in that colony. After dabbling in journalism and acting, he entered the wholesale wine trade in 1823 and prospered from then onward.

In Paris he was a frequent visitor at the Café de la Régence and was for a time a pupil of Deschapelles and Schlumberger (who later operated the Turk in America). By 1824 he could win the majority of games against La Bourdonnais, with odds of pawn and two moves.

Saint-Amant took a leading part in the correspondence games between the Paris and Westminster clubs in 1836 which ended in a 2–0 victory for the French. Also in this year his business interests took him to London, where he defeated in match-play George Walker (+5−3=1), Fraser (+1−0=2), Popert and Perigal. After the death of La Bourdonnais in 1840, Saint-Amant was indisputably the strongest player in France. Together with Méry, in 1842 he revived the magazine *Le Palamède* which had ceased publication when La Bourdonnais died.

In 1843 on another visit to London, Saint-Amant lost a casual match to Cochrane (+4−6=1) but then defeated Staunton (+3−2=1). Whether this latter contest was meant to be a serious test of skill or merely a series of friendly games remained a matter of dispute for years afterwards. In any case, a second, longer match was quickly arranged, and in November 1843 Staunton went to Paris to play twenty-one games for a stake of £100. This, the 'Grand Chess Match between France and England', has the right to be regarded as the first World Championship match. It ended with Saint-Amant's defeat by a score of +6−11=4. A third match, planned for October 1844 in Paris, was abandoned when Staunton contracted pneumonia on the journey from London.

The rising political turmoil in France soon left Saint-Amant with little time for chess. In the 1848 revolution he served as a captain in the National Guard and defended the Tuileries Palace against a raging mob. As a reward, the provisional government made him Governor of the Tuileries. In 1851–2 he was French Consul in California. He continued to visit England from time to time and played in the B.C.A. Birmingham 1857 tournament, losing to Falkbeer 2–1 in the 2nd round. In 1861 he purchased an estate in Algeria and retired to live there.

Paris 1839
White: Boncourt; *Black:* Saint-Amant
Bishop's Opening
1. P–K4, P–K4; 2. B–B4, N–KB3; 3. P–Q3, B–B4; 4. N–KB3, N–B3; 5. P–B3, B–N3; 6. O–O, O–O; 7. B–KN5, P–Q3; 8. P–QN4, B–K3; 9. QN–Q2, P–KR3; 10. B–R4, K–R2; 11. P–R4, P–R3; 12. K–R1, R–KN1; 13. Q–B2, P–N4; 14. B–KN3, P–KR4; 15. P–R3, P–R5; 16. B–KR2, N–KR4; 17. P–Q4, P–N5; 18. B×B, P×B; 19. RP×P, R×P; 20. P×P, P×P; 21. N–B4,

21.., N–N6+; 22. P×N, P×P; 23. QR–Q1, Q–K2; 24. P–N5, R–R5; 25. N×B, R×B+; 26. K–N1, Q–B4+; 27. R–B2, P×N; 28. N×R, P×P; 29. P×P, R–KB1; 30. N–B3, N–R4; 31. Q–K2, N–B5; 32. N–N5+, K–N3; 33. N–B3, R–B5; 34. R–Q3, P×R+; 35. Q×P, Q×Q+; 36. K×Q, R×P; 37. R–Q7, R–B5; 38. R×P, P–K5; 39. K–N3, P×N; 40. P×P, P–K4; 41. resigns.

ST PETERSBURG 1909

The Lasker–Tarrasch match in 1908 led to a tremendous upsurge in chess interest, exactly as the Fischer–Spassky match did sixty-four years later. Lasker may have felt that he owed it to himself to bolster his match-win with the first tournament appearance for five years, and decided to take on the young generation at St Petersburg 1909.

This tournament was to drive home the lessons of Carlsbad 1907, and even the World Champion had his work cut out to keep step with the leader of the young men, Rubinstein. Losing to his closest rival as early as the third round, Lasker was $1\frac{1}{2}$ points in arrears by the 5th, but a splendid run of $9\frac{1}{2}$/10 in the middle of the tournament allowed him to overhaul the leader. However, in the 16th round he succumbed to Duz-Khotimirsky (who had previously beaten Rubinstein as well) and just managed to get up once again on the post by beating Teichmann while Rubinstein only drew with Tartakower. Thus the two leaders shared the honours, no fewer than $3\frac{1}{2}$ points ahead of their closest pursuers: three more of the generation of the 'eighties' in Důras, Spielmann and Bernstein. Despite his two wins against the leaders, Duz-Kkotimirsky could do no better than finish 13th of 19; his extraordinary achievement was later surpassed by L. Steiner who, in a tournament at Berlin in 1928, defeated the *three* top men, Nimzowitsch, Bogoljubow and Tartakower, yet finished with only 50%. Leading scores: Lasker, Rubinstein $14\frac{1}{2}$, Důras, Spielman 11, Bernstein $10\frac{1}{2}$. *(R.D.K.)*

ST PETERSBURG 1914

International Masters, St Petersburg 1914

One of the worst-planned yet greatest tournaments in chess history, this St Petersburg (April–May 1914) saw the first encounter between Lasker and Capablanca, while a further confrontation of both with Rubinstein was largely foiled by the poor tournament system.

The event was confined to winners of at least one important international tournament and the joint winners of the All-Russian championship, Alekhine and Nimzowitsch. Since the great masters of the Hapsburg Empire (Důras, Maróczy, Schlechter, Spielmann, etc.) failed to participate, the field shrank to eleven players and it was decided to have an all-play-all single-round elimination contest to be followed by a double-round final of the five top scorers, the scores from the general tournament to be carried forward.

In the all-play-all Capablanca gradually forged ahead, finishing $1\frac{1}{2}$ points ahead of his nearest rivals, Lasker and Tarrasch, with Alekhine and Marshall completing the finalists, while Rubinstein dropped out. In the finals Lasker made the enormous score of 7/8, and succeeded in passing Capablanca by a $\frac{1}{2}$-point, far ahead of the others. Final scores: Lasker 13½, Capablanca 13, Alekhine 10, Tarrasch 8½, Marshall 8.

Lasker's individual games in this event are generally regarded as constituting the finest series ever played by anybody in the course of one tournament. Here is the decisive game of the contest:

White: Lasker; *Black:* Capablanca
Ruy Lopez
1. P–K4, P–K4; 2. N–KB3, N–QB3; 3. B–N5, P–QR3; 4. B×N, QP×B; 5. P–Q4, P×P; 6. Q×P, Q×Q; 7. N×Q, B–Q3; 8. N–QB3, N–K2; 9. O–O, O–O; 10. P–B4, R–K1; 11. N–N3, P–B3; 12. P–B5, P–QN3; 13. B–B4, B–N2; 14. B×B, P×B; 15. N–Q4, QR–Q1; 16. N–K6, R–Q2; 17. QR–Q1, N–B1; 18. R–B2, P–QN4; 19. R(B)–Q2, R(Q)–K2; 20. P–QN4, K–B2; 21. P–QR3, B–R1; 22. K–B2, R–R2; 23. P–N4, P–R3; 24. R–Q3, P–QR4; 25. P–KR4, P×P; 26. P×P, R(R)–K2; 27. K–B3, R–N1; 28. K–B4, P–N3; 29. R–N3, P–N4+; 30. K–B3, N–N3; 31. P×P, RP×P; 32. R–R3, R–Q2; 33. K–N3, K–K1; 34. QR–KR1, B–N2;

35. P–K5, QP×P; 36. N–K4, N–Q4; 37. N(6)–B5, B–B1; 38. N×R, B×N; 39. R–R7, R–B1; 40. R–R1, K–Q1; 41. R–R8+, B–B1; 42. N–B5, resigns. *(W.H.)*

SAJTAR, Jaroslav *(b. 3 December 1921)*
Czechoslovak international master and FIDE judge. In the first half of his chess career Sajtar was uniquely a chess-player, but on entering the diplomatic service he became more and more interested in chess organizational matters.

As a player his earliest results were his best. He had an excellent =4th with Foltys at Prague 1943, =2nd with Boleslavsky, Pachman and Smyslov at Warsaw 1947, and a 4th at Teplice Sanov 1947.

At the great Karlovy Vary-Mariánské Lázně tournament of 1948 he came =8th with Podgorny and Yanofsky out of 20. In a smaller tournament at Bucharest 1949 he was 3rd, and at the bigger Bucharest tournament of 1953 he was 13th/20.

He represented Czechoslovakia in two Olympiads: Helsinki 1952 with a score of 53.3% on board 3 and Amsterdam 1954, 50% on board 4. His best result in the Czechoslovak championship was 2nd in 1952.

In 1956 he was elected Vice-President of Zone 3 (Eastern Europe) of FIDE and from then on was almost wholly concerned with organizational work mainly within the field of FIDE. He has been very active in international student chess and has often acted as arbiter at Students Olympiads. *(H.G.)*

SALVIO, Alessandro *(1570–1640)*
The dates of Salvio's birth and death are approximate. It is known that he was in his middle twenties when he defeated Paolo Boi who was by then already an old man. He and the Calabrian, Greco were the chief theorists and writers on chess in Italy in the early seventeenth century. In this they differed markedly from their predecessors, Leonardo and Boi, who were practising players but committed nothing to paper.

Salvio wrote three works: a treatise on the game, *Trattato dell' inventione et arte liberale del gioco di scacchi* published in Naples 1604 and dedicated to his patron, Fulvio di Costanzo, Marquis of Corleto; a curious tragedy in verse on chess *La Scaccaide*, 1612; and in 1634 a life of Leonardo, *Il Puttino, altramente detto il cavaliere errante* to which he attached his *Trattato*.

Salvio made Naples the Italian centre for chess and he also created a 'chess academy' that used to meet regularly in the house of another chess enthusiast, Judge Rovito.

As a player he was noted for his resource and brilliancy. As a writer he was largely responsible for the popularity of some variations of the King's Gambit, one of which was to be known later as the Muzio and another that bore his name, the Salvio Gambit (1. P–K4, P–K4; 2. P–KB4, P×P; 3. N–KB3, P–KN4; 4. B–B4, P–N5; 5. N–K5). These lines he owed to his predecessors but it was his analyses and his writings that popularized them. *(H.G.)*

SALWE, Georg *(12 December 1860–15 December 1920)*
Polish master, extremely active during the period 1903–14 after which he retired from chess. He was recognized as the strongest active Polish player until the advent of Rubinstein, against whom he contested three matches at Lodz with ever-diminishing returns (1903 +5−5=0; 1903 +3−5=2; 1908 +1−3=4).

His greatest tournament successes were at St Petersburg 1906 where he was 1st out of a field of fifteen ahead of Blumenfeld, Rubinstein, Znosko-Borovsky, Alapin, etc. and Düsseldorf 1908 where he came second behind Marshall but ahead of Spielmann, Mieses, etc. He also participated with medium success in the tournaments of Carlsbad 1907, Ostend 1907 (Masters) and St Petersburg 1909. *(R.D.K.)*

SALZBURG 1942 and 1943
Two international tournaments were held at Salzburg in the middle years of the Second World War. Only half a dozen players competed in each but they were a select few and each tournament was a double-round event.

In the first, in 1942, Alekhine started badly with two losses in the first half of the event. But he had a wonderful run in the second half of the tournament during which he won all his games. So he won first prize and Keres, coming second in the 1942 event and sharing first place with Alekhine in the second tournament, demonstrated that he was in the same class as Alekhine.

The young Junge showed his great promise in the 1942 tournament. The Schmidt who competed in both events was the Estonian Paul Schmidt and not Lothar Schmid with whom he is sometimes confused; nor was he the Schmidt who was later to achieve grandmastery in Poland. Scores 1942: Alekhine 7½, Keres 6, Junge, Schmidt 5, Bogoljubow 3½, Stoltz 3. Scores 1943: Alekhine, Keres 7½, Schmidt 4½, Bogoljubow 4, Foltys 3½, Rellstab 3. *(H.G.)*

SÄMISCH, [Fritz] Friedrich *(20 September 1896–23 August 1975)*

A German grandmaster, born in Berlin-Charlottenburg, with innumerable prizes in smaller tournaments to his credit. His greatest tournament success was third prize at Baden-Baden 1925, behind Alekhine and Rubinstein, but ahead of Bogoljubow, Marshall, Tartakower, Rabinovich, Grünfeld, Nimzowitsch and twelve others. His first prizes in international tournaments included Vienna 1921, Dortmund 1928, Brno 1928 (jointly with Réti), while he came second at Berlin 1928 and joint second (with Bogoljubow and Nimzowitsch) at Berlin 1927. He often missed good results because of chronic time-pressure; on one occasion when his opponent tried to cash in on his lack of time by offering a draw he is reported to have said: 'How can I accept a draw when I have no idea who stands better?' He was completely engrossed in the build-up of a game (his great theoretical contributions, the Sämisch System in the King's Indian Defence and the Sämisch Variation in the Nimzowitsch-Indian Defence, have stood the test of time) and used to say: 'If I could play the first twenty moves, I would not mind somebody else finishing the game for me.' *(W.H.)*

SAN ANTONIO 1972

The first international tournament in the USA since the Piatigorsky Cup 1966 and one of the strongest ever held in North America. Although both Fischer and Spassky, who had played for the World Championship two months before, refused invitations, there were acceptances from Keres, Petrosian, Gligorić, Larsen and Karpov. As a result the event received a category-12 FIDE rating. The tournament was sponsored by a Texas-based Fried Chicken entrepreneur, George W. ('Bill') Church Jr who provided a prize fund in excess of $10,000. Play began in the San Antonio Convention Center just two blocks from the famed Texas battle-site, the Alamo. Greater press attention was paid to this event (November–December 1972) than to any previous chess activity on American soil.

Karpov, Keres and Gligorić led through the early rounds as Larsen lost two favourable positions in attempts to win. Keres's brilliancy prize win over D. Byrne in the eighth round and a draw the following round gave him a leading 7½–1½ score. But in the closing weeks, Keres began to lose, Karpov began to draw, and both Portisch and Petrosian began to win. Karpov held the lead for three rounds but was caught by Petrosian in the penultimate round and by Portisch on the final day of play. Karpov's loss to Portisch on a blunder in round 9 and Petrosian's win over Larsen in an error-filled round 13 encounter were the critical games. Karpov drew in 9 moves and Petrosian drew in 10 while Portisch was defeating Larsen in the final round to tie with Karpov and Petrosian for first place. Suttles's plus score gave him the grandmaster title. A tournament book was issued in 1973 by RHM Chess Publishing, New York. Leading scores: Petrosian, Portisch, Karpov 10½, Gligorić 10, Keres 9½. *(A.S.)*

SANCHEZ, Luis *(b. 1917)*

Colombian international master who played internationally in the 1950s. At the Interzonal at Stockholm-Saltsjöbaden he came 17th/21. In the Zonal tournament at Caracas 1957 he came 3rd. He had a good 8th/20 place in the Pan-American tournament at Bogota 1958 and at Santiago in Chile in 1959 he was =4th with Fischer and Sanguineti.

He played for Colombia in three Olympiads: 1954 where he scored 52.9% on 3rd board; 1956 63.2% on 2nd board; 1958 47.4% on 2nd board. *(H.G.)*

SANGUINETI, Raul *(b. 3 February 1916)*

Argentinian international master (1957). Argentinian champion 1956, 1957, 1962, 1965, 1974. Played in the Olympiads of 1956, 1958, 1962, 1966, 1968 and 1974. *(R.D.K.)*

SAN REMO 1930

This event (January–February 1930) marks a peak period in Alekhine's tournament career. Neither before nor after was a tournament of such strength won by a score of 14 out of 15 – in fact, nobody has ever remotely approached this achievement. Leading scores: Alekhine 14, Nimzowitsch 10½, Rubinstein 10, Bogoljubow 9½.

The other remarkable feature of San Remo was the extraordinary number of profound and beautiful games played not only by the winner but also by a number of his rivals. One such, among the least well-known, was the following:

White: Vidmar; *Black:* Yates
Queen's Gambit Declined
1. P–Q4, N–KB3; 2. P–QB4, P–K3; 3. N–KB3, P–Q4; 4. B–N5, QN–Q2; 5. P–K3, B–K2; 6. N–B3, O–O; 7. R–B1, P–B3; 8. B–Q3, P–QR3; 9. O–O, P×P; 10. B×P, P–N4; 11. B–Q3, P–B4;

12. P–QR4, P–B5; 13. B–N1, N–Q4; 14. B×B, Q×B; 15. P×P, N×N; 16. P×N, P×P; 17. P–K4, R–Q1; 18. P–K5, B–N2; 19. N–Q2, R–R6; 20. P–B4, P–N3; 21. B–K4, N–N3; 22. B×B, Q×B; 23. Q–K1, N–Q4; 24. N–K4, R–R7; 25. Q–R4, KR–R1; 26. R–KB2, K–N2; 27. QR–B1, Q–K2; 28. Q–N3, K–R1; 29. N–N5, K–N2; 30. N–K4, R–R8; 31. P–B5, KP×P; 32. R×P, P–N5; 33. R(5)–B2, R(1)–R6; 34. N–Q6, N×P; 35. Q–N4, P–R4; 36. Q–B8, N–K7+; 37. K–R1, Q–K3; 38. Q–Q8, R–R1; 39. Q–N5, N×P; 40. N×KBP, N–B4; 41. N–Q6, N×N; 42. P×N, P–N6; 43. P–R3, P–N7; 44. Q–N5, P–B6; 45. Q–N7+, K–N1; 46. P–Q7, R–Q1; 47. Q–N4, R×P; 48. Q×BP, R×R+; 49. R×R, R–QN2; 50. R–QN1, R–N6; 51. Q–B2, R–N1; 52. Q–B3, Q–N3; 53. Q–B4+, K–N2; 54. Q–B3+, K–R2; 55. Q–K5, R–N2; 56. Q–K2, Q–N5; 57. Q–KB2, Q–B6; 58. Q–B1, K–N2; 59. K–R2, Q–K4+; 60. K–R1, R–QB2; 61. Q–Q1, Q–B5; 62. resigns. *(W.H.)*

SAN SEBASTIAN 1911

The tournament (February–March 1911) was remarkable for three reasons, two of which are virtually forgotten today. Organized and run by Mieses, it was the first at which all competitors were reimbursed for their fares and living expenses; it thus constituted an enormous advance in the development of chess as a profession. Secondly, it was one of the few non-FIDE events for which a special qualification was demanded, Mieses' original idea being that only masters who had won at least two fourth prizes in previous international tournaments be invited, though this was modified later. As a result there were a number of amusing incidents, such as Bernstein objecting to the participation of Capablanca (who was invited on the strength of his match-win over Marshall) and then being slaughtered by the Cuban in the very first round; while Vidmar was warned, though in a very friendly manner, by Schlechter that this gathering of the élite might be too strong for him and that he might do better to play in a small event at San Remo – whereupon he shared the second prize. The third feature of the contest, however, will never be forgotten: Capablanca's triumphant entry into European chess. Leading scores: Capablanca 9½, Rubinstein, Vidmar 9, Marshall 8½. *(W.H.)*

SAN SEBASTIAN 1912

Once again a great tournament was held at this beautiful Spanish sea-side resort. It was planned to be on a similar scale to its 1911 predecessor, and only those masters were invited who had won at least two fourth prizes. But with the number of competitors coming to a smaller total than twelve it was decided to hold it as a double-round event.

Of the eleven who played, nine had also played in 1911. Only two players, Dr Perlis, who was to die tragically and prematurely in a mountaineering accident the very next year, and Forgács were newcomers. Forgács in fact fell ill and withdrew after the first cycle had been completed.

Spielmann started off in wonderful style and, by the end of the first half of the tournament, he was leading by a full two points. But he fell away badly in the second half while Rubinstein, who in direct contrast to Spielmann started miserably, yet managed to recover and pull up to the leaders and pass them just in time for the the last round.

Leading scores: Rubinstein 12½, Nimzowitsch, Spielmann 12, Tarrasch 11½, Perlis 10. *(W.H.)*

SANTASIERE, Anthony E. *(b. 9 December 1904)*

An American master and frequent champion of the Marshall Chess Club. Santasiere won the US Open in 1945 and was three times New York State champion.

Santasiere was born in New York City and worked as a school-teacher. He won the Marshall Club title on six occasions between 1922 and 1946. In the 1945 Radio Match against the USSR, Santasiere played Bronstein on 10th board but lost both games.

He is cited in some opening texts for popularizing 'Santasiere's Folly', 1. N–KB3 and 2. P–QN4. *(A.S.)*

SARAGOSSA OPENING

1. P–QB3 – offering to play a Caro-Kann in reverse, but Black need not oblige with 1. . , P–K4. A Saragossa Opening tournament was staged at Mannheim in 1922, but this way of starting the game is extinct in contemporary master chess. *(H.G.)*

SARAPU, Ortwin *(b. 20 January 1924)*

New Zealand international master of Estonian origin. Emigrated to Australia as displaced person from Germany. Won Australian championship 1957–9; then went to New Zealand and won the New Zealand championship in 1970.

In 1966 he won the East Asian Zonal tournament at Auckland. This gave him the international master title and the right to compete in the Interzonal at Sousse which he did without success in 1967. Represented New Zealand at the 1974 Nice Olympiad. *(R.D.K.)*

SARRATT, J. H. *(d. 16 January 1821)*

Leading English player of the late eighteenth and early nineteenth century. Famed in his day as a teacher and author, Sarratt adopted the title 'Professor of Chess'. His writings include: *A Treatise on the Game of Chess*, London 1808, *The Works of Damiano, Ruy Lopez, and Salvio*, London 1813.

Sarratt is usually credited with introducing into England the Continental practice of counting a game ending in stalemate as a draw. *(R.D.K.*

SASSA [**Sissa**]
According to the Muslim writers of mythical chess history, Sassa was the philosopher who invented the game of chess. He is supposed to have done this in order to divert an Indian King's attention from *nard* (backgammon). The king was so pleased with the invention that he offered Sassa a choice from among the most precious things in his kingdom.

Sassa said he did not want anything precious. All he wanted was one grain of wheat on the first square of a chessboard, twice that on the second square, double that on the third square and so on, doubling the number to the sixty-fourth square. The king gave orders that this should be done, but his granaries were exhausted long before he attained the sixty-fourth square. According to Lodge in his *Easy Mathematics*, the number of grains (18,446,744, 073,709,551,615) would be enough to lay a blanket 38.4 ft deep on the whole of England. *(H.G.)*

SAVENKOV, Ivan Timofeyevich *(1846–1914)*
Russian chess-player who published some analyses of the Evans and King's Gambits. His chief importance is, however, as a historian and in *K voprosu ob evolyutsii shakhmatnoi igri*, Moscow 1905, he gives a number of intelligent surmises as to how chess was introduced to Russia. Time has shown that many of his surmises were in fact founded on really logical bases. *(H.G.)*

SAVITSKY, Leonid Yakovlevich *(1911–1935)*
Soviet master, competitor in USSR championships of 1933 and 1934. *(W.R.H.)*

SAVON, Vladimir *(b. 26 September 1940)*
Soviet international grandmaster and Soviet champion 1971. He gained the international master title in 1967 when he came =3rd with Benko at Sarajevo. In that year he was =10th with Kholmov and Smyslov in the Soviet championship.

In 1969 he was =10th with Gipslis in the Soviet championship and then began a rapid climb towards first place. In 1970 he was =5th with Gipslis and Korchnoi and in 1971 came his moment of glory when he won the 39th Soviet championship ahead of Smyslov, Tal and Karpov.

This success earned him a place in the Soviet team at the 1972 Olympiad at Skopje. There he obtained the fine result of 86.7%, though this was, admittedly, on the lowest board as number 6 in the team. In the 40th Soviet championship that year he was =3rd with Kuzmin and Mukhin.

In 1973 he played in the Interzonal tournament at Petropolis where he obtained the respectable result of 8th out of 18. In this year he was awarded the grandmaster title by FIDE. In the 41st Soviet championship he was =9th with Tal, Taimanov and Keres and, though in distinguished company, this marked the start of a decline in his fortunes in the national championship.

In 1974 he came =8th with Belyavsky, Klovan and Lerner in the First League of the Soviet championship. This enabled him to play in the Premier League tournament (the genuine Soviet championship) in which he came 12th.

In the 1975 First League Soviet championship he came 15th/18. In this year he had a disappointment when he came =1st with Balashov, Gulko and Tseshkovsky in the USSR Zonal tournament, only to come bottom in the play-off for the three Interzonal places and thereby narrowly failing to qualify.

Still worse was to follow in 1976 when he failed even to qualify for the First League of the Soviet championship. *(H.G.)*

SAX, Gyula *(b. 18 June 1951)*
One of the strongest of the young Hungarian players. Sax was awarded the titles of international master in 1972 and grandmaster in 1974. European Junior champion in 1972, following the example of his countrymen, Adorjan and Ribli. A very successful tournament player, his victories include first places at Reggio Emilia 1973/4, Madonna di Campiglio 1974, Vrnjačka Banja 1974, Rovinj-Zagreb 1975, and Vinkovci 1976. He won the Hungarian championship at the end of 1976. *(W.R.H.)*

'SCACCHIA LUDUS'
Celebrated sixteenth-century poem on chess composed by Marcus Hieronymus Vida (1490–1566), an Italian priest who became bishop of Alba in 1532. The poem recounts in Virgilian Latin the tale of a game of chess between Mercury and Apollo with other gods as spectators.

Two early variants of the poem are known. An unauthorized, anonymous edition of 742 lines was published in 1525 under the title *Scacchorum Liber*. The name *Scacchia Ludus* appeared on a heavily revised edition of 658 lines in 1527 under Vida's name. The poem was probably written years before publication – Von der Lasa, using internal evidence, estimated 1513 as the date of composition. It proved an immediate success. Erasmus is said to have praised it highly, and translations or imitations appeared in many European languages. The best-known English translation is by Oliver Goldsmith, first printed posthumously in 1854.

Vida's poem had a lasting influence on the nomenclature of chess pieces. His Rooks are portrayed as towers mounted upon the backs of elephants, and the word 'tower' has become the standard name for this piece in several languages, e.g. French (*tour*), German (*Turm*), etc. His suggestion of 'archer' for the Bishop enjoyed less permanent popularity, although in Germany *Schütze* displaced the older term *Alte* and continued in common use until the eighteenth century, when it was itself replaced by *Läufer*.

In the following extract (Goldsmith's translation) the Queen, Knight, and King are described:

'But the fierce Queen, whom dangers ne'er dismay,
The strength and terror of the bloody day,
In a straight line spreads her destruction wide,
To left or right, before, behind, astride.
Yet may she never with a circling course
Sweep to the battle like the fretful Horse;
But unconfin'd may at her pleasure stray,
If neither friend nor foe block up the way;
For to o'erleap a warrior, 'tis decreed

Those only dare who curb the snorting steed.
With greater caution and majestic state
The warlike monarchs in the scene of fate
Direct their motions, since for these appear
Zealous each hope, and anxious every fear.
While the King's safe, with resolution stern
They clasp their arms; but should a sudden turn
Make him a captive, instantly they yield,
Resolved to share his fortune in the field.
He moves on slow; with reverence profound
His faithful troops encompass him around,
And oft, to break some instant fatal scheme,
Rush to their fate, their sov'reign to redeem;
While he, unanxious where to wound the foe,
Need only shift and guard against a blow.
But none, however, can presume t'appear
Within his reach, but must his vengeance fear;
For he on ev'ry side his terror throws;
But when he changes from his first repose,
Moves but one step, most awfully sedate,
Or idly roving, or intent on fate.' *(R.D.K.)*

'SCHAKEND NEDERLAND'
A monthly publication which is the organ of the Royal Dutch Chess Federation and is edited by M. Ploeger of Rotterdam (in succession to H. J. Slavekoorde of The Hague). In 1976 it classed itself as in its 83rd year in that it was the continuation of the *Tijdschrift van de Koninklijke Nederlandse Schaakbond.*

In addition to information stemming from and relating to the Dutch Chess Federation, it contains sections devoted to annotated games, end-game studies, problems and chess news. *(H.G.)*

SCHALLOPP, Emil *(1 August 1843–9 April 1919)*
Though frequently competing in the international events of the 1880s, Schallopp, a German player under the influence of Anderssen and Zukertort, did not succeed in winning a first prize; his best results were 2nd (to Burn) at Nottingham 1886, and joint 2nd (with Bird, behind Blackburne) at Hereford 1885. His literary work included a commentary on the Steinitz–Zukertort match as well as work on the famous *Handbuch.* *(W.H.)*

SCHEVENINGEN 1923
In this tournament a new idea was tried out. Ten home players played against ten foreign masters in succession. A similar scheme was employed six years later at the Ramsgate Practice Team tournament which was won by Capablanca.

There was no World Champion or former World Champion at Scheveningen but there were several grandmasters from abroad and in addition the Dutch team was headed by a young player, Euwe, who was to become World Champion some twelve years later.

With the tenth foreign player, Muffang of France, being prevented from coming, the Dutch player Strick van Linschoten stepped into the breach.

Surprisingly the Swiss master Paul Johner tied with Spielmann for first place. Euwe and Speyer did best of the Dutch players but they did not quite manage to score 50%. Leading scores: P. Johner, Spielmann 8½, Colle, Maróczy, Réti 8, Mieses, Yates 7. *(H.G.)*

SCHIFFERS, Emanuel S. *(4 May 1850–12 December 1906)*
Russian master, the first to deliver a course of public lectures on chess theory which he gave at the St Petersburg Chess Association in 1889. He has been overshadowed by Chigorin, to whom he finished second in both the first and second All-Russian tournaments in 1899 and 1900/1, but he was a great player in his own right.

Schiffers's match record, including victories against seven of his leading contemporaries, would be very impressive were it not for his four lost matches against Chigorin, though he did win one. In 1896 he lost a close match to Steinitz (+4−6=1) in Rostov-on-Don. His best tournament result outside Russia was his sixth place at Hastings 1895. *(K.J.O'C.)*

SCHLECHTER, Carl *(2 March 1874–27 December 1918)*

Born in Vienna, Schlechter learnt chess in 1890 and by 1892 was among the élite of Viennese chess, having drawn a match with Marco. From Leipzig 1894 until the war in 1914 he participated in almost all the great tournaments, and seldom came below 5th. Schlechter was equal first with Pillsbury at Munich 1900. He won at Ostend 1906, Hamburg 1910 and tied for first at Stockholm 1906, Vienna 1908 and Prague 1908. In matches, he beat Janowski in 1902 by +6−1=3, drew with the mighty Lasker in 1910 by +1−1=8 and held Tarrasch in 1911 to +3−3=10. Only in 1918 did Schlechter lose a match, to Rubinstein, by +1−2=3.

Schlechter was a total master of Steinitzian theory and, at a time when this theory was not universally understood, some of his success was due to that knowledge alone. He has been accused of drawing with other Steinitzian experts and coasting along on victories over the unknowledgeable. Certainly Schlechter drew an inordinate number of games; e.g. in 32 games all-told against Maróczy, 29 were draws. However, much of this peaceableness was due to Schlechter's unusually amiable character. He was small in stature, bright-eyed, shy, modest and extremely friendly. His gentleness manifested itself in his talk and even in his relaxed walk. Schlechter was liked by all who knew him. He lacked the deep aggressiveness of an Alekhine or even the milder belligerence of a Pillsbury.

Schlechter was an expert in opening theory, with special knowledge of the Ruy Lopez. He edited the eighth edition of Bilguer's *Handbuch* and this work, published in 1916, became the definitive book on openings. Schlechter was chess editor of the *Allgemeine Sport-Zeitung*, and was a fine problem solver and composer.

The climax of Schlechter's career was his dramatic ten-game match in 1910 with Lasker for the World Championship. Schlechter had won the 5th game (with some luck) and there had been eight draws. All he had to do was to draw game 10 to become Champion. However, Schlechter's chivalry was enormous and he played for a win. This game, which lasted three days, has been described as the most exciting struggle in all chess history. At the last moment Schlechter missed his way and Lasker retained his title.

Schlechter continued his chess activities during the war. After the Rubinstein match in January 1918, he played in a quadrangular tournament with Mieses, Vidmar and Rubinstein, in April 1918. Schlechter died in Budapest of starvation, in the aftermath of the Great War.

His victories could be as gentle as Schlechter himself. One example is this game from Carlsbad 1911:

White: A. Burn; *Black:* Schlechter
Queen's Gambit Declined, Tarrasch Defence
1. P–Q4, P–Q4; 2. P–QB4, P–K3; 3. N–QB3, P–QB4; 4. P–K3, N–KB3; 5. N–B3, P–QR3; 6. B–Q3, N–B3; 7. O–O, B–Q3; 8. P–QN3, O–O; 9. B–N2, BP×P; 10. KP×P, P×P; 11. B×P, P–QN4; 12. B–Q3, N–QN5; 13. B–N1, B–N2; 14. P–QR3, N(5)–Q4; 15. N–K4, N–B5; 16. R–K1, R–B1; 17. P–N3, N×N; 18. B×N, B×B; 19. R×B, N–Q4; 20. Q–Q3, Q–K2; 21. P–QN4, R–B3; 22. N–K5, B×N; 23. P×B, KR–QB1; 24. B–Q4, R–B8+; 25. R–K1, R×R+; 26. R×R, R–B5; 27. B–N2, Q–B2; 28. R–K2, Q–B3; 29. Q–Q2, P–R3; 30. Q–Q3, Q–B1; 31. R–Q2, Q–B2; 32. K–N2, P–QR4; 33. P×P, Q×RP; 34. B–Q4, Q–R1; 35. P–B3, Q–R5; 36. B–N2, P–R4; 37. R–KB2, P–N3; 38. Q–Q2, Q–N6; 39. K–R3, R–B1; 40. K–R4, K–N2; 41. K–R3, R–B5;

42. B–B1, Q–N8; 43. B–N2, P–R5; 44. K–N2, Q–B4; 45. R–K2, Q–N8; 46. R–B2, R–B1; 47. B–Q4, R–B8; 48. K–R3, Q–B4+; 49. P–N4, N–B5+; 50. K×P, P–N4+; 51. K–N3, Q–R2; 52. resigns.

Some life scores: +3–2=2 v. Steinitz; +9–6=10 v. Chigorin; +6–7=27 v. Tarrasch; +2–5=12 v. Lasker; +2–8=9 v. Pillsbury; +2–6=14 v. Rubinstein; +2–0=0 v. Alekhine; +0–0=1 v. Capablanca; +2–1=29 v. Maróczy. *(N.D.)*

SCHMID, Lothar *(b. 10 May 1928)*
West German grandmaster, Schmid is one of the most widely-travelled contemporary players, with tournament appearances in all five continents. His best results include: first prizes at Travemünde 1951, Zürich 1954, Malaga 1963 (jointly with Parma), Wilderness (South African Open) 1964, and Mar del Plata 1970 and 1973; 2nd prizes at Venice 1953 (jointly with Castaldi), Bamberg 1968 (jointly with Petrosian), and Adelaide (Australian Open) 1971; 3rd prize at Hastings 1951/2; and 4th prizes at Dublin 1957 (Zonal) and Zürich 1964 (equal with Lombardy). He also excels as a correspondence player (1st in Dyckhoff Memorial 1954–6, and =2nd in the World championship 1955–8). He has represented West Germany in all Olympiads since 1950 except Skopje 1972, and many other team events such as the Clare Benedict and Europa Cup tournaments. His tact and reputation caused FIDE to appoint him as arbiter of the Fischer–Petrosian and Fischer–Spassky matches (1971–2).

Schmid owns the largest private collection of chess books and other chess material. *(W.H.)*

SCHMIDT, Paul F. *(b. 20 August 1916)*
An international master who lived until the Second World War in Estonia where he was a close rival of Paul Keres and at one time was of grandmaster strength.

Schmidt, who was born in Tallinn and won the Estonian championship in 1935 and 1937, had a striking tournament success at Tallinn in 1935 where he came 1st ahead of Keres, Böök, Sämisch etc. In 1936 he drew a match with Keres at Pärnu +3–3=1. In 1937 he had an even more notable success at Pärnu where he came 1st with 5½/7 ahead of Flohr, Keres and Ståhlberg 4½, Tartakower 4 etc. Playing on 2nd board for Estonia at the 1937 Stockholm Olympiad he scored 50%. Again on 2nd board at the 1939 Buenos Aires Olympiad he scored 55.9%.

During the war he had a number of tournament successes in German-occupied Europe: 2nd in the German championship at Oeynhausen 1940, =1st with Junge at Oeynhausen 1941, =1st with Alekhine at Cracow 1941, =3rd with Junge at Salzburg 1942, 2nd at Vienna 1943 (the so-called Great Germany championship) and 3rd at Salzburg 1943.

After a pause of four years he resumed play at Kassel in 1947 where he came 2nd to Bogoljubow. At Hastings 1948/9 he came 6th and in 1949 he was =2nd with Van Scheltinga. An =3rd at Heidelberg 1949 was followed by a 2nd at Saarbrucken in 1950.

His last tournament was the German championship at Bad Pyrmont 1950 where he came =9th/18. Then he left for America, settling in the USA after going first to Canada. He now lives in Allentown, and does not seem to have returned to chess.

(H.G.)

SCHMIDT, Wlodzimierz *(b. 10 April 1943)*
Polish international grandmaster. He obtained the title in 1976, eight years after earning the international master title. He is Poland's first ever grandmaster as Najdorf, Tartakower and Rubinstein bore Argentinian, French and Belgian nationality respectively when they received their awards in 1950.

Thrice Polish champion (1971, 1974 and 1975), he has played in the Olympiads of 1962, 1964, 1968, 1970, 1972 and 1974. His best international performances have been his first prizes at Polanica Zdroj 1973 and Malmö 1976. *(K.J.O'C.)*

SCHWEBER, Samuel *(b. 16 July 1936)*
Argentinian international master (1961). Played in Olympiads 1960, 1964, 1966. Results include 9th in World Junior Championship 1955, 2nd Sao Paulo 1962, 20th Stockholm Interzonal 1962. *(R.D.K.)*

SCOTCH GAME
One of the early attempts to open the centre in the hope of quick development by 1. P–K4, P–K4; 2. N–KB3, N–QB3; 3. P–Q4. The name comes from an 1824 correspondence game between Edinburgh and London (see CORRESPONDENCE CHESS).

As with many similar open games the move P–Q4 comes too early to cause problems and Black equalizes comfortably after 3. . , P×P; 4. N×P, B–B4. Important offshoots are the Scotch Gambit, 3. . , P×P; 4. B–QB4 (leading to the Max Lange Attack after 4. . , B–B4; 5. O–O, N–B3) and the Göring Gambit 3. . , P×P; 4. P–B3. *(W.R.H.)*

SCOTLAND
Chess came to Scotland, through the Vikings, at least as early as it did to England and possibly earlier. As evidence of this there are the eleventh century chess-pieces discovered on the Isle of Lewis.

It is appropriate therefore that its organizing body, the Scottish Chess Association, is the oldest surviving federation of the UK. It was founded in 1884 and was one of the original members of FIDE in 1924.

It has competed in FIDE Olympiads eleven times with the following results: 15th/15 Folkestone 1933, 19th/19 Stockholm 1937, 31st/34 Moscow 1956, 29th/36 Munich 1958, 28th/50 Tel Aviv 1964, 28th/52 Havana 1966, 28th/53 Lugano 1968, 34th/60 Siegen 1970, 34th/62 Skopje 1972, 29th/74 Nice 1974, 33rd/48 Haifa 1976.

It possesses no FIDE grandmasters though Captain Mackenzie who was an outstanding figure in nineteenth century chess was undoubtedly of grandmaster strength. It has, however, three international masters: W. A. Fairhurst, D. N. L. Levy and C. W. Pritchett.

The first Scottish championship was played in 1867 and was won by J. Fraser. The championship was next held in 1884, since when (apart from wartime interruptions) it has been an annual event, the 83rd tournament being played in 1976. W. A. Fairhurst has more championship victories to his credit than any other player; he won the title eleven times in the period 1932–62. Other players with six or more victories are: J. M. Aitken (10), D. Y. Mills and W. Gibson (8) and R. C. Macdonald (6). In recent years the most successful player has been R. M. McKay with wins in 1971 (shared), 1974 and 1976.

The address of the Scottish Chess Association is Alan P. Borwell, Eboracum, 3 Broomhill Avenue, Perth PH1 1EN, Scotland and its official publication is *Scottish Chess*. *(H.G. & K.J.O'C.)*

SEE-SAW
A sequence of alternating direct and discovered checks, each of which can be answered only by a move of the King. Its devastating advantage lies in the fact that when it is the turn of the discovered check, the non-checking piece can eat itself through a whole army of hostile forces without losing a single move! The most famous see-saw in the literature of chess occurred in the game Torre–Em. Lasker, Moscow 1925.

In this position Torre played 1. B–B6 and after 1. . , Q×Q won by 2. R×P+, K–R1; 3. R×P dis+, K–N1; 4. R–N7+, K–R1; 5. R×B dis+, K–N1; 6. R–N7+, K–R1; 7. R–N5 dis+, K–R2; 8. R×Q, K–N3; 9. R–R3, K×B; 10. R×P+, etc. *(W.H.)*

SELENUS, Gustavus [**Augustus, Duke of Brunswick**] *(10 April 1579–17 September 1666)*
Gustavus Selenus was the pseudonym of Augustus, Duke of Brunswick-Luneberg-Dannenberg who wrote the first printed work on the openings to be published in Germany, *Das Schach oder König-Spiel*, Leipzig 1616.

A learned young gentleman, at the age of fifteen he was rector of the University of Rostock and subsequently of Tübingen. He travelled extensively in Italy, France and England.

It was probably in Padua where he stayed for a year that he came across Tarsia's translation of Ruy Lopez's famous work which he proceeded to translate into German and which formed the main part of his own book. To this he added a number of items, such as a method of notation numbering the squares from one to sixty-four and the first accounts of the village of Ströbeck and its great attachment to the game. An English translation was published by Sarratt in London 1817. *(H.G.)*

SELESNIEV, Alexei *(1888–1965)*
Russian master who spent many years in Germany where he made his best results. Drew all his games in the four-player tournament at Berlin 1919, to come second to Bogoljubow, ahead of Réti and Spielmann. Shared sixth place in the 1924 USSR championship. *(H.G.)*

SEMMERING 1926

Except for the 'Big Three' – Capablanca, Lasker and Bogoljubow – the Semmering tournament (March 1926) contained all the leading players of the period and as a sporting spectacle has never been surpassed. Starting favourite, Alekhine lost in the 1st round to Nimzowitsch and in the third to Gilg, and it was Nimzowitsch and Tartakower who took the field along at a terrific pace, both scoring 8 in the first nine rounds, when Spielmann was on 6½ and the improving Alekhine on 6. The 10th round saw both leaders lose – Nimzowitsch to Grünfeld and Tartakower to Vidmar – and the pattern was repeated in the 12th when Nimzowitsch in turn lost to Vidmar, and Tartakower to Réti. By now Alekhine, Spielmann and Tartakower shared the lead with 9, from Nimzowitsch 8½ and Vidmar 7½. Most of the leaders were due to meet each other in the final third of the tournament, and Fate kept a special trick up its sleeve by not only pairing Spielmann and Alekhine in the final round but so arranging things that they had to start their encounter a day late. From the sporting point of view this tournament had important consequences: it placed Spielmann and Vidmar firmly among the World Championship contenders and both were in fact invited to the 'Candidates tournament' to be held in New York early in 1927. Leading scores: Speilmann 13, Alekhine 12½, Vidmar 12, Nimzowitsch, Tartakower 11½. *(W.H.)*

SEMMERING-BADEN 1937

Keres' fresh, unconventional style was very much in evidence:

White: Keres; *Black:* Flohr
King's Indian Defence
1. P–Q4, N–KB3; 2. P–QB4, P–KN3; 3. N–KB3, B–N2; 4. P–KN3, P–B3; 5. B–N2, P–Q4; 6. P×P, N×P; 7. O–O, O–O; 8. N–B3, N×N; 9. P×N, P–QB4; 10. B–QR3, P×P; 11. N×P, Q–B2; 12. Q–N3, B–B3; 13. KR–Q1, N–Q2; 14. P–QB4, N–B4; 15. Q–N4, N–K3; 16. N–N5, Q–K4; 17. QR–B1, R–Q1; 18. R–Q5, R×R; 19. P×R, P–QR3;

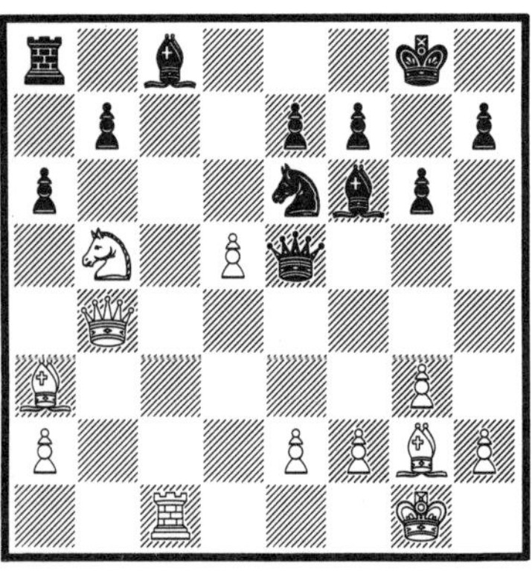

20. N–R7, N–Q5; 21. R×B+, R×R; 22. N×R, Q×KP; 23. P–R4, N–B4; 24. Q–K4, resigns.

Originally planned as the greatest event of all time, with at least twenty-six invitations going out to all the leading players of the day, the second Semmering event (September 1937) was scaled down to a still very strong double-round grandmaster event – a sort of dress rehearsal for the following year's A.V.R.O. tournament where Alekhine, Botvinnik and Euwe came to replace the three Semmering tail-enders. The event was a triumph for twenty-two-year-old Keres, who took the lead from the start and, with three rounds to go, had an advantage of two points over his nearest rival. Though he then lost two of the last three games, he finished a full point ahead of Fine – again a foretaste of A.V.R.O., where the same two players outdistanced all the other World Championship candidates. Scores: Keres 9, Fine 8, Capablanca, Reshevsky 7½, Flohr 7, Eliskases, Ragozin 6, Petrov 5. *(W.H.)*

SERGEANT, Edward Guthlac
(3 December 1881–16 November 1961)

A British master who had a long and solidly distinguished career in British chess but never quite succeeded in breaking through the barrier to international status. A civil servant by profession, he was awarded the O.B.E. for his services in the Inland Revenue and *Sergeant on Stamp Duties* was regarded as an authoritative work.

Sergeant's earliest performance in the British championship, at the Crystal Palace in London 1907, was one of his best. He came =2nd with J. H. Blackburne, R. P. Michell and G. E. Wainwright with 6½ points, a point below the winner of the title, H. E. Atkins. He was 3rd at Edinburgh in 1920 and his best result in the competition came in Brighton 1938, where he came equal second with H. Golombek, a ½-point below the winner, C. H. O'D. Alexander.

A stalwart supporter of the City of London Chess Club, he won its championship in two successive years, 1916 and 1917. He played for Britain against the USA in the 1908 and 1909 cable matches and also played on a high board for London against various American cities in the Insull Trophy matches in the years 1926–31.

As a player he was strongly influenced by the scientific principles of Siegbert Tarrasch and did well during the period when the Tarrasch school enjoyed its heyday. But he was at a loss when confronted with more modern methods. *(H.G.)*

SERGEANT, Philip Walsingham *(1871–1952)*

A professional writer on chess and popular historical subjects. Without any pretensions to mastership, he represented Oxford University in the years 1892–5 and assisted R. C. Griffith in preparing three editions of *Modern Chess Openings*.

In chess he dealt with a number of important subjects: *Morphy's Games of Chess*, London 1916; *Charousek's Games of Chess*, London 1919; *Pillsbury's Chess Career* (in collaboration with W. H. Watts), London 1923; *Championship Chess*, London 1938. All these are lucidly and carefully written but suffer from the defect that, being neither a master-player nor a professional annotator, he was not competent to deal with the annotational part of the work. Probably his best book on chess was *A Century of British Chess*, London 1934.

He was a cousin of E. G. Sergeant. *(H.G.)*

SERGEYEV, Alexander Sergeyevich *(b. 1897)*

Moscow champion in 1925 and contestant in USSR championships of 1924, 1925 and 1927. *(W.R.H.)*

SHAKESPEARE, Chess in
There are some allusions to the game in *The Taming of the Shrew*, *King John* and *King Lear*, but the only Shakespearean occasion on which chess is played occurs in the last play, *The Tempest*, in which a stage direction runs: 'The entrance of the cell opens and discovers Ferdinand and Miranda playing Chess.' We then hear:

Miranda: Sweet lord, you play me false.
Ferdinand: No, my dearest love, I would not for the world.
Yea, for a score of kingdoms you should wrangle
And I would call it fair play. *(H.G.)*

SHAMKOVICH, Leonid Alexandrovich *(b. 1 June 1923)*
Born in the USSR, international master since 1962 and grandmaster since 1965, Shamkovich shared first place in the Moscow championship of 1961 but lost the play-off to Bronstein. Shamkovich was never very successful in Soviet championships, but seemed to perform better in international events as, for example, at Salgotarjan 1967, Sochi 1967, Constaţa 1969, and Timişoara 1972, in all of which he took first place.

Left the USSR for Israel in 1975, but quickly moved on to Canada and the USA where he shared first prize at New York 1976 and in the 1976 US Open. *(W.R.H.)*

SHATRANJ
The name the Arabs gave to chess when they learnt it from the Persians in the seventh century AD. The rules of the game were the same with the exception of the initial placing of the King and Queen. The higher-ranked of the two players was given the choice of placing his King and Queen on one of the two central squares on the back rank (in algebraic d1 or e1, in descriptive Q1 or K1) and his opponent had to follow suit.

The pieces were the same as in *chatrang* and the Persian names were translated direct into Arabic as follows: *Shah* = King; *Firz* = Queen; *Fil* = Bishop; *Faras* = Knight and *Baidaq* = pawn. *(H.G.)*

SHERWIN, James T. *(b. 25 October 1933)*
A leading American international master in the 1950s and 1960s and a US entrant in the 1953 World Junior Championship (=5th) and Portorož 1958 Interzonal (17th). Sherwin was a rival of the new American grandmasters of the 1950s and a frequent high-placer in US Swiss tournaments.

Sherwin's first major success was =4th in the 1954 US championship. After scoring third places in the 1957/8 and 1958/9 championships, his results fluctuated: 8th in 1959/60, =4th in 1960/1, =3rd in 1961/2, 12th in 1962/3 and =3rd in 1966/7. Sherwin has rarely played competitive chess after 1968. *(A.S.)*

SHIPLEY, Walter Penn *(20 June 1860–17 February 1942)*
The most important US chess patron and organizer during the first four decades of this century. He served as treasurer of the Lasker–Marshall World Championship match and as referee for the Marshall–Capablanca and Lasker–Capablanca matches. He was a key organizer of Cambridge Springs 1904 and New York 1924.

Shipley was a prominent Philadelphia lawyer but found time to edit a chess column in the city's *Inquirer* for more than thirty years. His presidency of the Franklin Chess Club came at a time when it was one of the strongest clubs in the USA. A strong amateur, Shipley defeated a number of visiting masters in casual games including Em. Lasker, Zukertort, Weiss and Pillsbury. *(A.S.)*

SHORTEST GAME
The shortest *played* tournament game was that between R. F. Combe (Scotland) and W. R. Hasenfuss (Latvia) in Round 3 of the Folkestone International Team tournament 1933: 1. P–K4, P–QB4; 2. P–Q4, P×P; 3. N–KB3, P–K4; 4. N×KP, Q–R4+ and White resigned.

It is often claimed that Gibaud–Lazard, Paris 1924 (see BREVITY) was the shortest, but in fact it was an off-hand and not a tournament game.

The shortest tournament game was Bobby Fischer–O. Panno, Interzonal tournament, Palma de Mallorca 1970, which ran 1. P–QB4, resigns. This was a game played in the last round on Saturday evening at a special time in deference to Fischer's religious beliefs and several hours after the other players had played their games. Panno resigned, not because he thought the English Opening was so strong, but in protest at having to play at a different time from the other competitors. *(H.G.)*

SHOWALTER, Jackson Whipps
(4 February 1860–6 February 1935)
Known as the 'Kentucky Lion' after his Minerva, Ky., birth-place, Showalter was the most successful American player between the death of Mackenzie and the rise of Pillsbury. After coming =9th at New York 1889 and winning minor US events, Showalter challenged S. Lipschütz for the American championship in 1892. Although he lost, and failed again two years later with Hodges, Showalter won a return match with Lipschütz in 1895 by 8½–5½. He solidified his claim on the title with match wins over E. Kemeny and J. Barry in 1896 and held it until losing two matches to Pillsbury in 1897–8. On Pillsbury's death in 1906, Showalter resumed the title until losing to Marshall in 1909.

At the turn of the century Showalter was a frequent visitor to Europe but his vigorous attacking play achieved only mediocre results: =6th at Cologne 1898, 14th at Vienna 1898, and 8th at London 1899, for example. His last international result was 5th at Cambridge Springs 1904. This and his close losses to Pillsbury were his best results. *(A.S.)*

SHUL, Marta
See under LITINSKAYA.

SICILIAN DEFENCE

A single name is scarcely enough for the wide variety of opening systems stemming from the moves 1. P–K4, P–QB4. The Sicilian is considered one of Black's most aggressive yet sound defences to 1. P–K4, and holds its place as the most popular reply to that move. White usually continues with 2. N–KB3 and 3. P–Q4, resulting in a position where White has chances of a King-side attack and his opponent has play on the other wing, particularly down the half-open QB-file. The most important variations are as follows:

Boleslavsky's variation: 2. N–KB3, N–QB3; 3. P–Q4, P×P; 4. N×P, N–B3; 5. N–QB3, P–Q3; 6. B–K2, P–K4.

The Closed System: 2. N–QB3, N–QB3; 3. P–KN3.

The Dragon variation: 2. N–KB3, P–Q3; 3. P–Q4, P×P; 4. N×P, N–KB3; 5. N–QB3, P–KN3 and its relative the Accelerated Dragon with 2. N–KB3, N–QB3; 3. P–Q4, P×P; 4. N×P, P–KN3.

Sicilian Four Knights: 2. N–KB3, P–K3; 3. P–Q4, P×P; 4. N×P, N–KB3; 5. N–QB3, N–B3.

Levenfish variation is the Dragon variation with 6. P–B4.

Maróczy Bind: 2. N–KB3, N–QB3; 3. P–Q4, P×P; 4. N×P, P–KN3; 5. P–QB4.

Morra Gambit: 2. P–Q4, P×P; 3. P–QB3 (also known as Matulović Gambit).

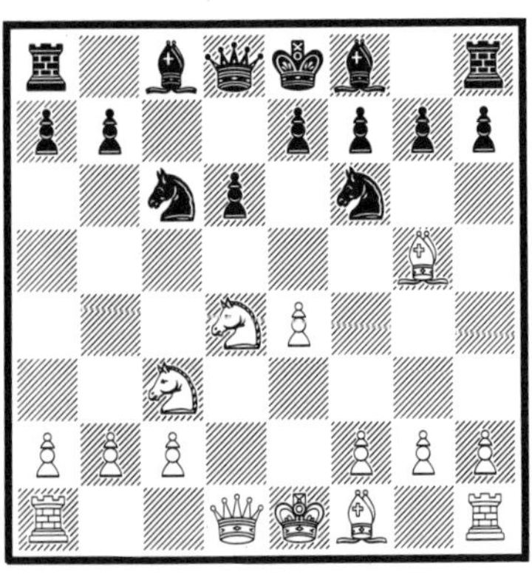

Najdorf variation: 2. N–KB3, P–Q3; 3. P–Q4, P×P; 4. N×P, N–KB3; 5. N–QB3, P–QR3.

Nimzowitsch variation: 2. N–KB3, N–KB3.

O'Kelly variation: 2. N–KB3, P–QR3.

Rauzer Attack: 2. N–KB3, N–QB3; 3. P–Q4, P×P; 4. N×P, N–B3; 5. N–QB3, P–Q3; 6. B–KN5.

Scheveningen System: 2. N–KB3, P–K3; 3. P–Q4, P×P; 4. N×P, N–KB3; 5. N–QB3, P–Q3 (becoming the Modern Paulsen if Black later plays . . , QN–Q2).

Sozin variation: 2. N–KB3, N–QB3; 3. P–Q4, P×P; 4. N×P, N–B3; 5. N–QB3, P–Q3; 6. B–QB4 (becoming the Velimirović Attack if White continues with B–K3, Q–K2 and O–O–O).

Taimanov's variation: 2. N–KB3, P–K3; 3. P–Q4, P×P; 4. N×P, N–QB3 (also known as the Paulsen System).

Wing Gambit: 2. P–QN4, and its close relative, the Wing Gambit Deferred, with 2. N–KB3, P–Q3; 3. P–QN4.

Since the Sicilian Defence is one of the sharpest and most-analysed of modern openings, it appeals to players of aggressive temperament who are willing to spend much time absorbing works of theory or working out their own. It remains the main weapon of Fischer and Tal, among other leading grandmasters. *(W.R.H.)*

SIEGHEIM, Bruno Edgar *(24 May 1875–5 November 1952)*

A South African master born in Württemberg, Germany, who first made a name for himself as one of the coterie of New York players engaged on the investigations of the Rice Gambit. In South Africa he won the championship in 1906 and 1912. His finest international performance was Hastings 1921/2, where he came joint second with Réti, half a point behind Rubinstein and ahead of all the British masters. *(W.H.)*

SIESTA INTERNATIONAL TOURNAMENT, Budapest 1928

Derives its name from having been played at the Siesta Sanatorium in Budapest, September–October 1928. It was a triumph for the former World Champion, Capablanca, not long after he had lost his title to Alekhine.

It is from this event that the Siesta variation of the Ruy Lopez, Steinitz Defence Deferred derives its name (1. P–K4, P–K4; 2. N–KB3, N–QB3; 3. B–N5, P–QR3; 4. B–R4, P–Q3; 5. P–B3, P–B4). Capablanca introduced the line in his sixth-round game against A. Steiner. (A. Steiner is in fact Endre Steiner, *Endre* being Hungarian for 'Andrew'.) Another Steiner who was playing in the Siesta, H. Steiner, played under the *nom de guerre*, Stoner. Leading scores: Capablanca 7, Marshall 6, Kmoch, Spielmann 5, A. Steiner, Vajda $4\frac{1}{2}$. *(H.G.)*

SIGURJONSSON, Gudmundur *(b. 25 September 1947)*

Icelandic grandmaster and chess professional who ranks next to Fridrik Olafsson in Icelandic chess and is indeed that country's second grandmaster after Olafsson. He first came into notice when, in 1966 in a junior match at Stockholm between Scandinavia and the USSR, he defeated the Soviet player, Gulko, by $1\frac{1}{2}$–$\frac{1}{2}$.

He obtained the international master title in 1970 as a result of two tournaments: Reykjavik, where he came 1st ahead of Matulović and Olafsson, and Caracas (the tournament in which Karpov won his grandmaster title) where he came =7th with Parma, just below the future World Champion.

He then stopped play whilst he finished his legal studies, resuming again late in 1973. It took him just a year to obtain the necessary norms for a grandmaster title. In February he had a run-in where he came =6th with Olafsson at Reykjavik, but his results were those of an international master rather than a grandmaster.

It was in September 1974 that, in the second Costa Brava tournament at Sant Feliu de Guixols (Spain), he came =1st with Kurajica, just fulfilling the grandmaster norm of 7½/11. At the turn of the year, at Hastings 1974/5, he fulfilled the second grandmaster norm by coming =2nd with Vaganian.

His results since gaining the title have confirmed his grandmaster strength. In 1975, at the Zonal tournament at Vratsa in Bulgaria, he came =3rd with Matulović and Sax. In 1976 he was =1st at Orense (Spain) together with Rogoff and G. Garcia (Cuba). At the Capablanca Memorial tournament at Cienfucgos (Cuba) he was =2nd with Razuvayev, below Gulko, but ahead of such players as Belyavsky and Ulf Andersson.

He has been Icelandic champion three times, in 1965, 1968 and 1972 and has represented Iceland at six Olympiads, from 1966 to 1976 without a break. *(H.G.)*

SIMAGIN, Vladimir Pavlovich *(15 June 1919–25 September 1968)*
One of the most talented and original Moscow masters, at his peak in the 1950s. Awarded the title of international grandmaster in 1962, following his sharing fourth place in the very strong Budapest 1961 tournament. Simagin twice won the Moscow championship – in 1947 and 1959 – and also shared first place in the Sochi 1967 international tournament.

Made many significant contributions to opening theory, particularly in the Grünfeld and Sicilian defences. He died while participating in the Kislovodsk 1968 tournament. *(W.R.H.)*

SIMONSON, Albert C. *(1914–65)*
A close American rival of Fine and Reshevsky during a brief career that ended in effect with the Second World War. At the age of nineteen he played first reserve on the US team that won the 1933 Olympiad at Folkestone. Three years later in the first US Closed championship tournament, Simonson led most of the way. He lost in the final round while Reshevsky was drawing and finished a ½-point behind in second place. Two years later Simonson was 3rd behind Reshevsky and Fine. He was =4th in the 1940 championship but retired from chess when the war started. He only played in occasional New York Metropolitan League matches, and in the US Closed championship where he was =10th. *(A.S.)*

SIMPSON'S DIVAN
Famous London café-restaurant located at 100 The Strand. Founded in the 1820s, the Divan remained a centre of London chess until 1903, when a renovation of the building enlarged the dining facilities at the expense of the chess-rooms. Nearly all the great nineteenth-century masters visited and played there and the first English tournament, won by Buckle, was staged there in 1849. In 1852 Elijah Williams published a collection of 150 games played at the Divan under the title *Horae Divanianiae*. The modern visitor finds only a restaurant, but an antique set and board – said to have been used by Staunton, Morphy and Steinitz among others – are still displayed in the foyer. *(R.D.K.)*

SIMULTANEOUS DISPLAY
There are three forms of simultaneous displays:

1. The most common is when one player plays against several players at the same time, moving from board to board making one move at a time. Normally the numbers involved are from 20 to 30 but many attempts have been made at establishing records. The biggest seems to have been that given by Najdorf in Sao Paulo in 1950 when he played 250 games in eleven hours with the result +226−10=14.

Karpov during a simultaneous display, 1975

2. When a player plays against several players on a number of boards but, as and when the games are finished, other players start up fresh games so that it is possible, for example, to play 400 games on 20 boards.

The record here was established by Ståhlberg in Buenos Aires 1941 when he played 400 games in 36 hours with the result +364−22=14.

It is also reported that a certain Dr Backer played 1,000 games in San Francisco 1938 with the result +343−138=519.

3. Tandem simultaneous displays when two players give a simultaneous display playing alternate moves. *(H.G.)*

SINGAPORE
The Singapore Chess Federation was established in 1961. The first national championship, played in 1949, was won by K. A. Lim. Subsequent championships have been dominated by the Tan brothers, Lian Ann and Lian Seng, who won nine of the eleven tournaments from 1959 to 1969.

The Singapore team took part for the first time in the 1968 Olympiad. Their results: 43rd in 1968, 40th in 1970, 49th in 1972 and 43rd in 1974.

In 1969 the Singapore Chess Federation (I. Leong, 159-C Block 62, Lorong 4, Toa Tayoh, Singapore 12) organized both the East and the West Asian Zonal tournaments, the former being notable as the event in which Walter Browne qualified for the international master title. *(K.J.O'C.)*

SIX

'SIXTY-FOUR' ['64']

A Soviet journal, published weekly in Moscow and devoted to chess and draughts (checkers), that appeared in 1935–41, and then, under the stresses and strains of war, disappeared. The attempt was made to run the publication as though it were a newspaper with a lighter touch than that used for the more serious monthly publications.

By the liberal use of cartoons and the policy of interviews and articles of a topical nature this attempt was on the whole successful and, for the first and possibly the last time in Soviet history, a newspaper appeared with government blessing that was read with enjoyment and interest by the Soviet citizens.

The journal was revived after the end of the Second World War and, though missing the lightness of touch of its pre-war predecessor, still proved an interesting and worthwhile publication. Among the succession of editors perhaps the most distinguished has been the former World Champion Tigran Petrosian. In 1976 he was chief editor and was assisted editorially by Alatortsev, Antoshin, Bielin, Vasiukov, Neishtadt (General Editor), Roshal, Smyslov, Tikhomirova and Chegolev.

The price of each number is five kopecks, about five pence in English money and eight cents American. Each issue has sixteen pages. *(H.G.)*

SKEWER

A double attack along the same rank, file or diagonal, one enemy unit being attacked 'through' the other as though they were speared on a skewer. Here is a famous end-game study by L. van Vliet:

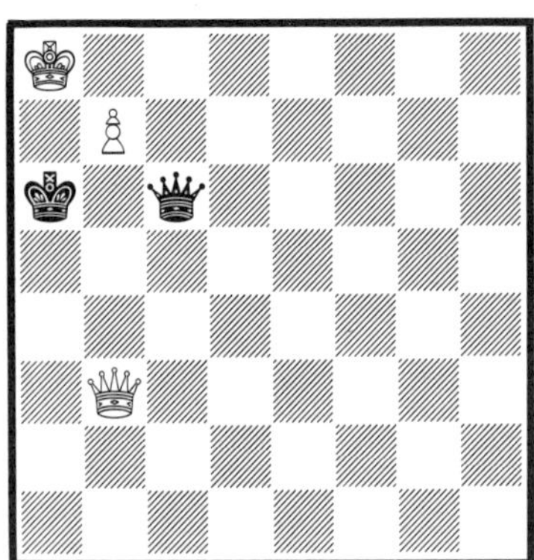

(*White to play*)

After 1. Q–N4!, Black attempts to keep up the pin on the White pawn: 1.., Q–Q4 (or KB6); 2. Q–R4+, K–N3; 3. Q–N3+, Q×Q; 4. P–N8(Q)+, skewering the Black Q. If 1.., Q–N7; 2. Q–R3+, K–N3; 3. Q–N2+, Q×Q; 4. P–N8(Q)+, as above. If 1.., Q–R8; 2. Q–R3+, K–N3; 3. Q–N2+, K–B2 (or K–R3; 4. Q–R2+, followed by 5. Q–N1+); 4. Q–R2+!, Q×Q; 5. P–N8(Q)+, as above. *(W.H.)*

SKOPJE 1967

When Fischer decided to play in the Interzonal tournament at Sousse in Tunisia he had been absent from competitive chess for a considerable period. So, in order to get practice, he played in the Skopje international tournament.

This event was scheduled to include twelve grandmasters and it was for this reason that Fischer chose to play there. As it turned out the tournament was not so strong as had been anticipated and Fischer must have been disappointed at the absence of so many of his rivals.

As a matter of fact, when he started play nothing seemed to go right for him. He even lost a couple of games and those not to any figure of real importance. Nevertheless, so great was his genius that he managed to play like a real World Champion and, when he finished up by winning his last five games, there was no disputing his great strength.

The Skopje event was a trial run for Sousse in more senses of the word than one. At a certain stage Fischer withdrew from the tournament but was allowed to withdraw just as he pleased and to return with the same easy licence.

The incident was an ominous one and was to result in an attempt on Fischer's part to repeat the performance at the Interzonal. Thus, though the Skopje tournament was a fine event with a number of fine Fischer games, it was a bird of evil omen for the future.

Leading scores: Fischer 13½, Geller, Matulović 13, Kholmov 11½, Bukic 9½. *(H.G.)*

SKOPJE 1976

A triumph for Karpov in that he won first prize with a margin of 1½ points over his nearest rival, Uhlmann, whom he beat in his best game of the tournament. This was the third first prize that the World Champion had gained in succession after winning the title the previous year. Clearly, he was far and away the best of the active players of his time.

And yet, when you compare this win with Fischer's win at the previous Skopje tournament the comparison is not all in favour of the later player. True, Fischer did lose two games, whilst Karpov lost none. Nor was the margin by which Fischer won so convincing as that of Karpov.

But figures of this kind are far from being everything. One must take into account the style in which the two victors won. There Fischer scores heavily. His wins are all sparkling and full of creative energy. Karpov, on the other hand, makes heavy going of his wins.

Leading scores: Karpov 12½, Uhlmann 11, Timman 10½, Kurajica, Tarjan 9.

It is interesting to note that when, in 1977, a committee was asked by the *Chess Informant* to pick out the best game of the year, the one they chose was from this tournament. But it was not one of Karpov's; it was the following game won by Vaganian over Reshevsky.

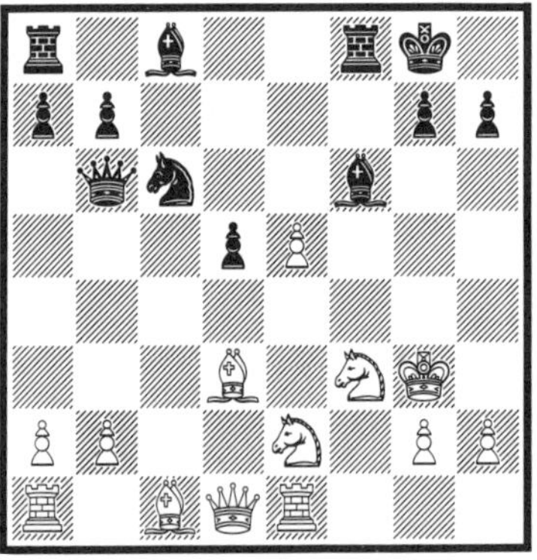

White: Reshevsky: *Black:* Vaganian
French Defence
1. P–K4, P–K3; 2. P–Q4, P–Q4; 3. N–Q2, N–KB3; 4. P–K5, KN–Q2; 5. P–KB4, P–QB4; 6. P–QB3, N–QB3; 7. N(Q2)–B3, Q–R4; 8. K–B2, B–K2; 9. B–Q3, Q–N3; 10. N–K2, P–B3; 11. KP×P, B×P; 12. K–N3, P×P; 13. P×P, O–O; 14. R–K1, P–K4; 15. BP×P, N(Q2)×P; 16. P×N, B–R5+; 17. K×B, R×N; 18. R–B1, Q–N5+; 19. B–KB4, Q–K2+; 20. B–N5, Q–K3; 21. B–B5, R×B; 22. N–B4, Q×P; 23. Q–N4, R–B2; 24. Q–R5, N–K2; 25. P–KN4, N–N3+; 26. K–N3, B–Q2; 27. QR–K1, Q–Q3; 28. B–R6, QR–KB1; White lost on time. *(H.G.)*

SLATER, James D. *(b. 13 March 1929)*
An English financier, a great patron and benefactor of chess, both on a national and world level. Passionately devoted to chess from his schooldays, it is said that on leaving school he hesitated between the alternatives of becoming a chess-master and of going into business, opting for the latter on the grounds that he was not sure of his chess-playing prowess.

It is perhaps a fortunate thing for chess that he did not become a chess-master, since his offer of a £50,000 increase to the stake at the match at Reykjavik in Iceland 1972 may well have swayed Fischer into consenting to play. He established a Slater Foundation Fund which helps young English players to go and play abroad. *(H.G.)*

SLAUGHTER'S COFFEE-HOUSE
London café, also known as Old Slaughter's, founded on a site in St Martin's Lane by John Slaughter in 1692, closed in 1843. A private room was set aside for chess, and from 1700 to 1770 many leading English players congregated there. Among the more famous were Cunningham, Stamma, and the mathematician De Moivre who, according to Murray, 'lived for nearly thirty years on the petty sums he made at Slaughter's by chess'. *(R.D.K.)*

SLIAC 1932
A tournament notable as one of the earliest international successes of the new young Czechoslovak star Salo Flohr. He did not have it all his own way and in fact Vidmar, a player of a much older generation, took the lead early on and was only overhauled by Flohr in the very last round.

The event was a curious contrast between players of two different generations, Flohr and Pirc on the one hand being faced by the veteran grandmasters Vidmar and Maróczy on the other.

Bogoljubow had a typically uncompromising tournament, losing to the first six and winning against the last six. Leading scores: Flohr, Vidmar 9½, Pirc 8½, Canal, Maróczy, Spielmann 8. *(H.G.)*

SLIWA, Bogdan *(b. 4 February 1922)*
Polish international master (1953). He has won the Polish championship on more occasions than any other player; his six victories were in 1946, 1951, 1952, 1953, 1954 and 1960. He has appeared in the Polish Olympiad team seven times, in 1952, 1956, 1958, 1960, 1962, 1964 and 1966. *(K.J.O'C.)*

One of Czechoslovakia's strongest players, Smejkal was awarded the titles of international master in 1966 and grandmaster in 1972. His tournament successes include first places at Polanica Zdroj 1970, Smederevska Palanka 1971, Vrnjačka Banja 1972, Polanica Zdroj 1972, Luhacovice 1973 and Novi Sad 1976. He also played in the Leningrad 1973 Interzonal tournament, where he took fourth place. *(W.R.H.)*

SMOTHERED MATE
A mating position in which the King is smothered by his own men. For an illustration see under PHILIDOR'S LEGACY. *(W.H.)*

SMYSLOV, Vassily Vassilevich *(b. 24 March 1921)*

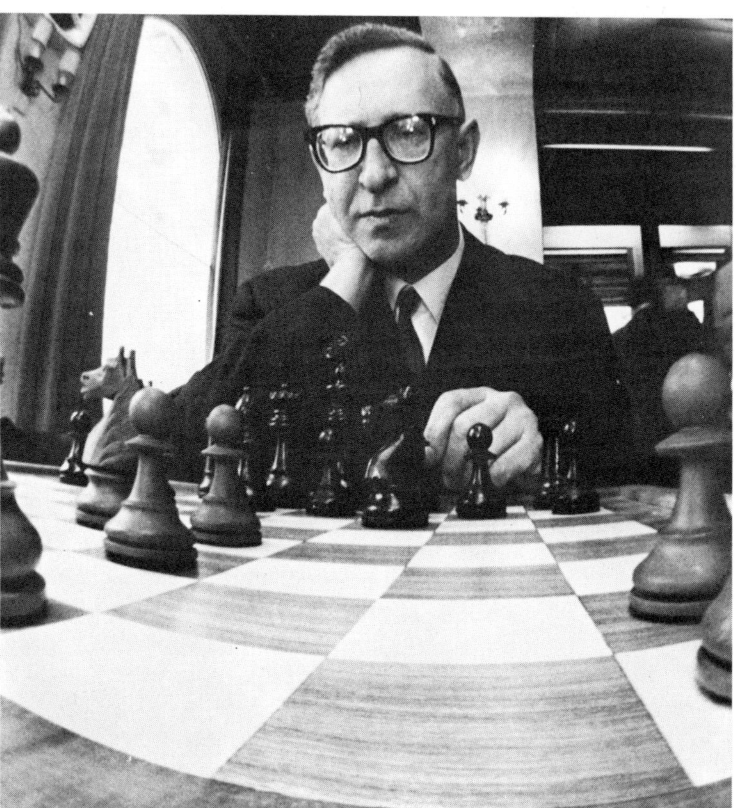

International grandmaster and World Champion 1957, Smyslov was born in Moscow and learnt chess at the age of six and a half, being taught by his father who was a strong first-category player.

Two enthusiasms dominated his early life, chess and music. Possessor of a fine baritone voice, he studied hard in an attempt to become an operatic singer and got as far as the last fifty to be auditioned for the Bolshoi company, but no further, and then abandoned all attempts at making singing his career.

Meanwhile he also studied hard at chess and learned much from Chigorin, Nimzowitsch and Alekhine. Traces of the influence of all three are to be found in his play together with something that is original Smyslov.

His first success was in 1938 when he came =1st in the Moscow championship and then in 1940 he came 3rd in the 12th Soviet championship, 1½ points ahead of Botvinnik. It was almost immediately after the Second World War that he made an impact on the international field. He was 3rd at Groningen 1946 and in the World Championship match-tournament of 1948 came second to Botvinnik.

An =1st with Bronstein in the 17th Soviet championship was followed by a 3rd place below Bronstein and Boleslavsky in the 1950 Candidates at Budapest.

In 1953 came his outstanding triumph in the Candidates at Zürich where he came first, 2½ points ahead of the rest of the field. He showed himself the equal of Botvinnik (12–12) in a match for the title in 1954 in Moscow. There followed a run of tournament successes culminating in another remarkable first at the Candidates tournament in Amsterdam 1956. In the same year he came =1st with Botvinnik in the 1st Alekhine Memorial tournament in Moscow.

In 1957 he became World Champion by beating Botvinnik 12½–9½ in Moscow. But he held the title for only a year, losing the return match to Botvinnik by 10½–12½. For a time this defeat robbed him of his self-confidence, but he resumed the hunt for the title at the first opportunity. In the 1959 Candidates in Yugoslavia he came 4th. With an =1st in the Amsterdam Interzonal of 1964, he now had to contend with a new formula of matches in the Candidates, and in 1965 was beaten by Geller 5½–2½ in the quarter-finals.

He did not take part in the 1967 Sousse Interzonal, but from then on his attempts to qualify for the World Championship tell a disappointing story of near-misses and failed opportunities in which nerves induced by the strain of playing against younger rivals played their part.

He was just half a point away from qualifying for the Candidates when he came =7th with Portisch in the great Interzonal at Majorca in 1970. In 1973 at the Petropolis Interzonal he came 5th and failed to qualify for the Candidates. At the Biel Interzonal he came =5th with R. Byrne and was again a bare ½-point below the qualifiers. Whether he will ever again qualify for a Candidates is doubtful, but he has left his mark on the history of chess. As a player he had rich originality in the openings, imaginative strategy in the middle-game and an immense virtuosity as an end-game player.

His main book is *Izbrannie Partii*, Moscow 1952, translated as *My Best Games of Chess 1935–57*, London 1958.

A game from an international tournament at Reykjavik in Iceland, 1974, in which Smyslov won first prize with some ease.

White: Sigurjonsson; *Black:* Smyslov
English Opening
1. P–QB4, N–KB3; 2. N–QB3, P–K4; 3. N–B3, N–B3; 4. P–KN3, B–N5; 5. B–N2, O–O; 6. O–O, P–K5; 7. N–KN5, B×N; 8. NP×B, R–K1; 9. P–B3, P×P; 10. N×P(B3), P–Q4; 11. P×P, Q×P; 12. N–Q4, Q–KR4; 13. N×N, P×N; 14. P–K3, B–N5; 15. Q–R4, R–K3; 16. R–N1, B–K7; 17. R–K1, N–N5; 18. P–KR3, Q–KB4; 19. R×B, Q×R; 20. Q×N, Q×B+; 21. K–R2, R–Q1; 22. Q–QN4, P–KR3; 23. P–B4, Q–Q8; 24. R–B2, Q–K8; 25. resigns. *(H.G.)*

SOKOLSKY, Alexei Pavlovich *(1908–1970)*
Russian master. He was twice champion of the Ukraine and reached the finals of the USSR championship four times. Later he became better known as a writer on the game. Above all he is remembered for his theoretical work on the opening 1. P–QN4 which now bears his name.

Chief works: *Debyut 1. b2–b4 (Debyut Sokolskovo)*, Minsk 1963; *The Modern Openings in Theory and Practice*, London 1962. *(K.J.O'C.)*

SOKOLSKY [Polish, or Orang-Utang] OPENING
Introduced into master chess by Tartakower, 1. P–QN4, aiming at the early fianchetto of the QB, has never found much support. Its inventor baptized it the 'Orang-Utang' opening after a trip to the zoo during the international tournament held at New York 1924. Its most ardent supporter has been the Soviet master Sokolsky who published a monograph on the opening in 1963. *(R.D.K.)*

SOLTIS, Andrew *(b. 28 April 1947)*

US international master and one of the leading younger American writers on chess, Soltis is by profession a newspaper reporter for the *New York Post*, where he also conducts a weekly chess column.

He began playing serious chess in 1962 and his first really good result was the winning of the New York City Junior championship in 1964. He was US Intercollegiate champion in 1969 and a member of the US Student team during the period 1967–72. He has had a consistently fine record in the Marshall Chess Club championship, winning it in 1967, 1969–71 and 1974. In that year he came first in the first U.S.C.F. Futurity tournament at the Goldwater-Marshall, ahead of Bisguier, Matera, Zuckerman etc.

His best international result has been 1st at Reggio Emilia 1971/2.

Despite his youthful years he is already a most distinguished writer on the game and among his (and the country's) best books are *The Best Games of Boris Spassky*, London 1973, and *The Great Chess Tournaments and their Stories*, New York 1975. *(H.G.)*

SONNEBORN-BERGER SYSTEM

Despite its impressive-sounding name, the Sonneborn-Berger System is, next to tossing a coin or choosing a white or black pawn hidden in the fist, the simplest of all the methods used to determine a tie. One adds up the total scores of the player one beats and half the scores of the players with whom one draws and compares the total thus obtained with the total of the player with whom one ties.

There is no particular logic about this system which favours the player who beats the stronger player and loses to the weaker one, since it might be argued that losing to a weaker player is a more serious defect than losing to a stronger one. But it is convenient and just as logical or illogical as using the Buchholtz method in the Swiss System.

The Sonneborn-Berger System is supposed to have been invented by a Viennese player, Oscar Gelbfuhs, in 1873 during the course of a tournament in Vienna in 1873.

It derives its name from its advocacy by an English player, William Sonneborn and by the great Austrian endgame theorist, Johann Berger. *(H.G.)*

SOSONKO, Gennadi *(b. 18 May 1943)*

Born at Troitsk in Siberia, Sosonko eventually became a Dutch grandmaster and a professional chess-player. He was the junior champion of Leningrad in 1958 and from 1960–5 pursued his studies at Leningrad University in the economic geography of capitalist countries, thereby fitting himself for his future career in the West.

By 1964 he had attained the rank of national master in Russia and he became a chess coach in Leningrad, acting as such for Tal for one year and for Korchnoi for a year and a half.

In August 1972 he left Russia for the Netherlands and won the Dutch championship the following year.

He has played for the Netherlands in two Olympiads. At Nice in 1974 he scored 70% on third board and won the title of international master. In the 1976 Olympiad at Haifa he won the prize for the best score on second board.

He won the grandmaster title by his tournament results in 1975 and 1976. At Wijk-aan-Zee in 1975 he came =5th with Gligorić and Hübner, more than fulfilling the grandmaster norm and at Vinkovci in 1976, by coming =6th with Ivkov and Kovačević with 9 points, he exactly fulfilled the norm, thereby becoming a grandmaster.

He had qualified for the Interzonal by winning the 1975 Zonal tournament at Barcelona; but at Biel in Switzerland 1976 he failed to gain one of the coveted top three places, coming 12th with 9½ out of 19. In 1976 he won the Lugano Open. *(H.G.)*

SOULTANBEIEFF, Victor *(1895–9 February 1972)*

Russo-Belgian player who went to live in Belgium after the Russian Revolution. He was champion of the Belgian Chess Federation in 1934, 1943, 1957 and 1961. His best international result was 5th at the Spa international tournament 1926.

A fine analyst, he edited an excellent bi-monthly chess journal *Echec et Mat* in 1947–9 and wrote a particularly good book on the 1927 Alekhine–Capablanca match. His other main works: *Le match Capablanca–Alekhine, Buenos Aires 1927*, Bruxelles 1929; *Guide pratique du jeu des combinaisons*, Bruxelles-Liège 1950. *(H.G.)*

SOUTH AFRICA

Competitive chess in South Africa began in 1891 when the Cape Town Chess Club (founded 19 March 1885) resolved that 'a general tournament, open to all players in South Africa, be held in Cape Town under the auspices of the Cape Town Chess Club'. This first South African championship was duly held in 1892, and since then there have been twenty-nine such tournaments, reading as follows:

1892	E. Roberts
1897	E. Roberts
1899	A. Michael
1903	F. Lee
1906	B. E. Siegheim
1910	H. Duhan
1912	B. E. Siegheim
1920	A. J. A. Cameron and A. Chavkin
1924	A. Chavkin
1926	Dr M. Blieden
1928	Dr M. Blieden
1935	J. C. Archer
1937	K. Dreyer
1939	W. Heidenfeld
1945–6	W. Heidenfeld and Dr J. M. Holford
1947	K. Dreyer and W. Heidenfeld
1949	W. Heidenfeld
1951	W. Heidenfeld
1952–3	J. E. Eriksen
1955	W. Heidenfeld
1957	W. Heidenfeld
1959	W. Heidenfeld and K. F. Kirby
1961	W. Gerber
1963	K. F. Kirby and K. van der Mejden
1965	P. Kroon
1967	D. Friedgood
1969	P. Kroon
1971	D. Friedgood
1973	D. Friedgood
1975	C. de Villiers and P. Kroon

Ties were recorded in 1892, 1912 and 1937, the winners defeating J. A. Rivett, Dr M. Blieden and J. Wolpert respectively in play-offs. On two occasions matches were played for the title, Siegheim beating Blieden in 1905–6, but losing to the same challenger in 1909–10. In all, these two outstanding players met in 56 games (tournaments and matches), Siegheim winning 18, losing 16, with 22 draws, which shows how closely they were matched.

Other important dates in the annals of South African chess were: 1891, Foundation of Johannesburg Chess Club; 1934, inauguration of *South African Chess Magazine* (defunct since 1948 by H. St John-Brooks); 1947, foundation of the Chess Federation for Southern Africa, S. A. May being the first chairman; 1951, first South African participation in FIDE events (W. Heidenfeld, in Zonal tournament at Mariánské Lázně); 1953, inauguration of *The South African Chess Player*, by L. R. Reitstein; 1955, first South African international tournament (=1st Mühring and Heidenfeld, 3rd Dr Euwe); 1958, first South African participation in FIDE team tournaments (Munich 1958, 27th out of 36); 1962, first South African Open championship (=1st Golombek and O'Kelly). Since then South African chess has made tremendous progress, South African senior and student teams competing regularly in FIDE events (except where Communist pressure has prevented it) and individual players (B. Donnelly, D. Friedgood, N. Bloch) competing in FIDE Zonal and junior competitions. International grandmasters and masters have visited South Africa with increasing frequency (Schmid, Ståhlberg, Czerniak, Robatsch, Keene and Westerinen); and there are now many regular annual events of a more than parochial character, while excellent relations are maintained with the chess organizations of Rhodesia and Mozambique. South African ratings are on the Elo system; they include Rhodesian and Mozambique players.

The Chess Federation for Southern Africa is at P.O. Box 4513, Cape Town 8000. *The South African Chess Player* is c/o L. Reitstein, P.O. Box 4513, Cape Town 8000. *(W.H.)*

SOVIET UNION

Chess had already begun to flourish in Russia before 1917, but it was the October Revolution of that year and the resulting formation of the Soviet Union which really led to its spread through all levels of society. Chess indeed occupied an important and unique role in the newly evolved plans to bring cultural activities to the masses.

In October 1920 an All-Russian Chess Olympiad was held in Moscow to bring together the chess-players of the Soviet Union, though it was only in 1923, when the Moscow Trades Union Council took chess organization under its wing, that the game really became widespread. The Council of Physical Culture created a chess and draughts section and thereafter the efficient organization of chess was assured in all regions of the country.

The international tournament of Moscow 1925 was the first in history to be sponsored entirely by government funds. The leading players of this era were Levenfish, Duz-Khotimirsky, Romanovsky and the Rabinovich brothers, who might be said to be responsible for laying the foundations of the Soviet chess school and making it possible for the generation succeeding them to make their mark in international competitions.

The period leading up to the Second World War saw the most rapid improvement in results. The group of young players led by Botvinnik began to show their talents and raise the prestige of the Soviet school towards the pre-eminent place it occupies to this day. Botvinnik's scientific methods of studying the game were followed by his colleagues and led to a more serious approach to the problems of achieving tournament successes. By the time Botvinnik established himself as a contender for the World Championship in 1936, the membership of the USSR Chess Federation had risen from just over a thousand in 1923 to a total approaching a million.

During the war there was little time for chess in the USSR but from 1945 onwards their players went from strength to strength. In 1945 the USSR decisively defeated the United States in a radio match. To emphasize their victory they repeated it the following year and again in 1954 and 1955. They also won three matches against Britain in 1946, 1947 and 1954.

Abram Khasin

In 1948 Botvinnik won the World Championship for the Soviet Union while two years later Rudenko captured the Women's title also. The domination of the Soviet Union in both events was absolute for almost a quarter of a century, with not only the World Champions but also their challengers all coming from the USSR until the emergence of Fischer in 1972.

Soviet teams did not compete in the World Team championships for many years but on their first appearance in 1952 carried off first prize with ease. They have maintained their winning record in this event ever since and have also won the corresponding event for Women's teams on each occasion they have played.

Several Soviet players have received decorations from the state in recognition of their contribution towards the development of chess. These include Botvinnik and Smyslov, both awarded the Order of Lenin, and Keres and Bronstein who received the Order of the Red Banner of Labour. At the time of writing the USSR has more than thirty active grandmasters.

Championships of the USSR have been held regularly since 1920; the first two of the series were nominally championships only of Russia, but from number 3 onwards were open to all republics of the Soviet Union. Winners of these tournaments were as follows:

1. (1920)	Alekhine	24. (1957)	Tal
2. (1923)	Romanovsky	25. (1958)	Tal
3. (1924)	Bogoljubow	26. (1959)	Petrosian
4. (1925)	Bogoljubow	27. (1960)	Korchnoi
5. (1927)	Bohatirchuk	28. (1961)	Petrosian
6. (1929)	Verlinsky	29. (1961)	Spassky
7. (1931)	Botvinnik	30. (1962)	Korchnoi
8. (1933)	Botvinnik	31. (1963)	Stein
9. (1934)	Levenfish	32. (1964/5)	Korchnoi
10. (1937)	Levenfish	33. (1965)	Stein
11. (1939)	Botvinnik	34. (1966/7)	Stein
12. (1940)	Bondarevsky	35. (1967)	Tal and Polugayevsky
13. (1944)	Botvinnik		
14. (1945)	Botvinnik	36. (1968/9)	Polugayevsky
15. (1947)	Keres	37. (1969)	Petrosian
16. (1948)	Bronstein	38. (1970)	Korchnoi
17. (1949)	Bronstein	39. (1971)	Savon
18. (1950)	Keres	40. (1972)	Tal
19. (1951)	Keres	41. (1973)	Spassky
20. (1952)	Botvinnik	42. (1974)	Belyavsky and Tal
21. (1954)	Averbakh		
22. (1955)	Geller	43. (1975)	Petrosian
23. (1956)	Taimanov	44. (1976)	Karpov

Besides these official championships there was held in 1941 a so-called 'Absolute championship' of the USSR with only six invited contestants, which was won by Botvinnik.

Until 1973 the championship tournament was the culmination of a series of qualifying events, starting with regional elimination contests working up to the national quarter-finals, semi-finals and the final itself. Only players of World Championship calibre were exempted to the final. After the loss of the World title at the hands of Fischer, the system was changed to ensure that the top players would compete in the national championship to make it a tougher event. Thus the 1973 event was the first for many years in which all the top players were required to participate. Now the system dispenses with the old qualifying events, relying instead on a promotion and relegation system among three divisions. The top two divisions ('super-league' and first division) are all-play-all tournaments, the third division is a large Swiss System event.

The end of the 41st USSR Championship 1973. Spassky received the Gold medal; the other prize winners: (l. to r.) Korchnoi, Karpov, Petrosian, Polugayevsky

International tournaments are frequently held in the USSR with Moscow, Sochi and Tbilisi regularly staging such events. The most important events in the USSR in recent years have been the two Alekhine Memorial tournaments held in Moscow in 1967 (won by Stein) and 1971 (won by Stein and Karpov).

The first chess magazine in the USSR was a journal called *Shakhmatny Listok*, which appeared in Leningrad in 1921. The following year Moscow had a monthly, *Shakhmaty*, edited by N. Grekov, and in 1924 another magazine appeared under the title *64*. Grekov's magazine went out of business in 1930, but the others flourished under the direct control of the Physical Culture Committee and Trades Union Council. The State Publishing House began to produce both translations of works by European grandmasters and original works by Soviet authors. In 1935, the existing chess journals were amalgamated into a single monthly publication called *Chess in the USSR* (*Shakhmaty v SSSR*). This has survived to the present day and is now the official organ of the Soviet Chess Federation. Other magazines in existence at the present time are *Shakhmatny Byulletin*, a monthly production containing games and theoretical articles; *64*, a weekly, under the editorship of Petrosian, covering topical events, and *Shakhmaty*, edited by Tal and appearing fortnightly, being the Russian language edition of a Latvian magazine. Most of the other republics also have their own magazines.

The USSR has produced too many great players to list them all, though their names recur throughout this encyclopedia. It is perhaps worth singling out for special mention their impressive band of World Champions: Alekhine, Botvinnik, Karpov, Petrosian, Smyslov, Spassky and Tal, and their many almost-Champions: Bogoljubow, Boleslavsky, Bondarevsky, Bronstein, Korchnoi and Stein.

The address of the USSR Chess Federation is: 4, Skatertnyi per., Moscow G-69. *Chess in the USSR*: Gogolevsky boul. 14, Moscow G-19. *(W.R.H.)*

SOZIN, Benjamin Innokentyevich *(1896–1956)*
Soviet master, commentator, analyst and theoretician. Played several times in Leningrad and USSR championships between 1925 and 1935, but is best remembered for his introduction of the 6. B–QB4 attack in the Sicilian Defence which bears his name. For many years was editor of the theoretical section of the journal *Shakhmatny Listok*. *(W.R.H.)*

SPAIN

Spain was the earliest country in Europe to receive the game from the East, via the Moors, and it does in fact contain the first complete manuscript we have on chess, that compiled under the orders of Alfonso the Wise in 1283.

Spain's first great player was the celebrated Ruy Lopez and, though Spain has never produced such a world figure again, it has always been a leading country in the matter of quantity of chess-players. This has been demonstrated by the profusion of great tournaments held there, ranging from San Sebastian 1911 to the great series of tournaments in Majorca, the Canaries, Madrid and elsewhere.

The Spanish Chess Federation was founded in 1927 in Barcelona (always a chess-playing city) and it has regularly competed in the FIDE Olympiads and held many FIDE events, e.g. the World Junior Championship in Barcelona 1965, a number of Zonal tournaments both for men and women and the great Interzonal tournament at Majorca 1970 that was won by Bobby Fischer.

The name and address of the national federation: Federacion Española de Ajedrez, Coslada 10 4⁰ drcha, Madrid 28. *(H.G.)*

SPASSKY, Boris Vassilievich *(b. 30 January 1937)*

World Champion 1969–72, Spassky was born in Leningrad in 1937 nearly three months after his great rival, Mikhail Tal. He spent the earlier part of his life and his chess career in Leningrad and was eminently a Leningrad player with all the artistry and inventiveness that characterizes the Leningrad school.

He learned chess at the age of five and by eleven (when he had attained the top class in the chess club of the Pioneer House in Leningrad) he was already regarded as a boy prodigy with a wonderful future. At this club he was first trained by Zak and then by Tolush, both of whom lay great stress on combinational play.

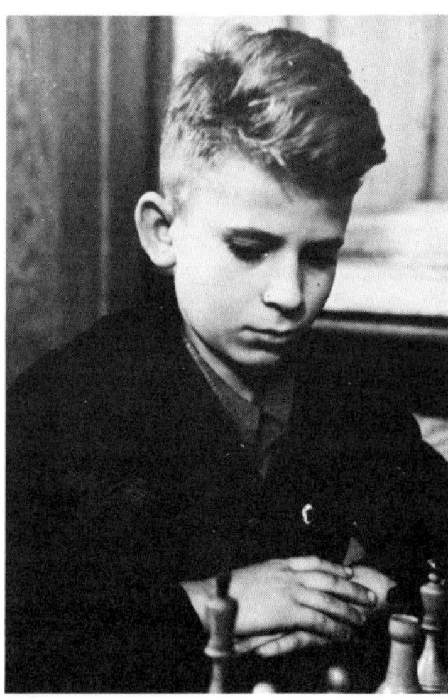

As a boy prodigy he accomplished feats that would have been worthy of a first-class adult master. A second place at the age of fourteen in the Leningrad championship was followed by his first venture abroad, to the Bucharest international tournament in 1953. This was won by Tolush, but the fifteen-year-old Spassky had the remarkable result of tieing for fourth place with Boleslavsky and Szabo.

In 1955 he won the World Junior Championship at Antwerp and in the same year he qualified for the Candidates by coming =8th at the Göteborg Interzonal. The following year showed a great advance. He tied for first place in the Soviet championship and came =3rd in the Candidates tournament in Amsterdam.

But now came the rivalry with Tal from which on the whole Tal was to emerge the victor. It was Tal who beat him in the last round of the Soviet championship in 1958, thereby preventing him from qualifying for the Interzonal. Perhaps also his studies at Leningrad University were impeding his chess progress. By 1959 these were over as he had a successful thesis based on *Shakmatny Listok*, 'The First Russian Chess Magazine'.

Oddly enough, he failed to qualify for the next cycle of the World Championship qualifying tournaments through losing to Stein in the last round of the Soviet Zonal in the spring of 1961. Later on in that year he won the Soviet championship for the first time and thereafter he climbed his way to the World Championship with a steady and sure grip. In 1964 he qualified from the Amsterdam Interzonal for the Candidates which had now become a series of matches and in the following year he beat Keres, Geller and Tal in successive matches. In the match for the World title against Petrosian, he just lost by $11\frac{1}{2}$–$12\frac{1}{2}$. This was in 1966 and he demonstrated that he was the leading tournament player in the world that year by winning first prize in the very strong event at Santa Monica. In 1967 he was first at Beverwijk.

Then, in 1968, he fought his way again through the Candidates, beating first Geller, then Larsen and finally Korchnoi, winning against this last formidable opponent by $6\frac{1}{2}$–$3\frac{1}{2}$. In 1969 he became World Champion by beating Petrosian by $12\frac{1}{2}$–$10\frac{1}{2}$.

As World Champion for a time he seemed in good form, but by 1971 it was apparent that his play had become insecure. Towards the end of the year he took part in the Alekhine Memorial and came as low as =6th. Then, when after a chaos of conflicting negotiations with the challenger Bobby Fischer, in which Spassky's chivalrous generosity in not standing on his rights won him the admiration of the world but cost him his title, a remarkable match was played at Reykjavik in 1972 ending in an easy victory for Fischer by $12\frac{1}{2}$–$8\frac{1}{2}$.

It seemed as though, in winning the match, Fischer did more than defeat his rival: he destroyed his confidence in his play. In the years succeeding the match Spassky did win great tournaments but his failures grew more and more spectacular. The win of a strong Soviet championship in 1973 was followed by a poor third at Solingen in 1974. Playing on board 3 for the Soviet team at the Nice Olympiad he won the board prize with 11/15, but then could get no further than the semi-final in the Candidates where he was beaten by Karpov.

In 1975 he came =2nd with Olafsson at Tallinn, a point below Keres, and was also 2nd to Geller in the Alekhine Memorial tournament at Moscow.

In 1976 there came what seemed a fatal blow. He came =11th in an Interzonal of twenty players at Manila. He applied for a visa to reside outside the Soviet Union for three years but was granted a visa for only one year which he spent in France (he had recently taken a French wife). However, he was forbidden by the Soviet authorities to participate in chess events. The career of one of the greatest players of all time looked to be at an end. His only chance would come if, in the following year, Fischer failed to take up his place in the Candidates matches, since Spassky would then replace him in the contest.

19th game, World Championship match, Moscow 1969
White: Spassky; *Black:* Petrosian
Sicilian Defence
1. P–K4, P–QB4; 2. N–KB3, P–Q3; 3. P–Q4, P×P; 4. N×P, N–KB3; 5. N–QB3, P–QR3; 6. B–N5, QN–Q2; 7. B–QB4, Q–R4; 8. Q–Q2, P–R3; 9. B×N, N×B; 10. O–O–O, P–K3; 11. KR–K1, B–K2; 12. P–B4, O–O; 13. B–N3, R–K1; 14. K–N1, B–B1; 15. P–N4, N×NP; 16. Q–N2, N–B3; 17. R–N1, B–Q2; 18. P–B5, K–R1; 19. QR–KB1, Q–Q1; 20. P×P, P×P; 21. P–K5, P×P; 22. N–K4, N–R4; 23. Q–N6, P×N; 24. N–N5, resigns.

For if 24. . , P×N; 25. Q×N+, K–N1; 26. Q–B7+, K–R1; 27. R–B3, and mates in a few moves.
(H.G.)

SPASSOV, Luben Dimitrov *(b. 22 March 1943)*
Bulgarian international grandmaster. He obtained the international master title in 1972 and was subsequently elevated to the higher rank as this book went to press, the title being backdated to 1976 when he should have received it, but did not, due to a clerical error.

His best result in the Bulgarian championship was third place in 1965, repeated in 1973. He has won first prize in many, mainly minor, international tournaments: Lublin 1971 (=1st), Gausdal 1975 (=1st), Albena 1975, Sofia 1975, Priština 1975 (=1st), Kringsjå 1976 (=1st), Pernik 1976 and Virovitica 1976 (=1st).
(K.J.O'C.)

SPIELMANN, Rudolf *(5 May 1883–2 August 1942)*
An Austrian grandmaster, one of the most brilliant attacking players of the early twentieth century, Spielmann was a true professional who had no work outside chess; as a result, he probably contested more tournaments and matches than any other master. Including local tournaments and short matches, Spielmann took part in more than 120 tournaments and fifty individual matches, in the course of which he played about 1,800 games.

His two greatest successes were first prize at Semmering 1926 (ahead of Alekhine, Vidmar, Nimzowitsch, Tartakower, Rubinstein, Tarrasch and eleven others); and =2nd prize at Carlsbad 1929 (behind Nimzowitsch, equal with Capablanca, ahead of Rubinstein, Euwe, Vidmar, Becker, Bogoljubow and fourteen others).

Other important achievements were his first prizes in the 'gambit tourneys' of Abbazia 1912 and Baden (near Vienna) 1913; 1st prize in the Stockholm quadrangular tournament 1919; =1st with Réti at Teplitz-Schönau 1922; and high placings in major international events such as St Petersburg 1909 (=3rd), San Sebastian 1912 (=2nd), Pistyan 1922 (=2nd), the *Berliner Tageblatt* grandmaster tournament Berlin 1928 (3rd), and Moscow 1935 (5th). In matches he beat Nimzowitsch, Mieses, Réti, Tartakower, Alapin, Stoltz, Ståhlberg, Pirc, Bogoljubow, Petrov and Mikenas, to mention only the most important.

Rudolf Spielman, International Chess Tournament, Teplitz-Schönau Czechoslovakia, 1922

Spielmann was a creature of moods, and no other grandmaster – at the height of his powers – has had so many abysmal failures when things did not go to his liking. The great international events in which Spielmann produced negative scores were legion: Ostend 1906, Carlsbad 1907, Prague 1908, Göteborg 1920, Vienna 1922, Carlsbad 1923 (+5–12=0!), Moscow 1925, Kissingen 1928, Bled 1931; yet each time when he seemed to sink to a nadir of mediocrity, he climbed back with brilliant recoveries. In the end it was failing health rather than fading chess strength that conquered him; even so, having migrated to Sweden as a refugee from Nazi persecution at the outbreak of war, he still won half a dozen or so local tournaments in the last three years of his life.

Spielmann's literary output was modest: *Ein Rundflug durch die Schachwelt*, Berlin-Leipzig 1929; *Richtig Opfern!* (published in English as *The Art of Sacrifice in Chess*, London 1935); and the tournament book of *Bad Sliac 1932*, Vienna 1932. *(W.H.)*

SPIRIDONOV, Nikolai *(b. 28 February 1938)*
Bulgarian international master since 1970. Winner of international tournament at Polanica Zdroj 1971 (equal with Pfleger), and Varna 1974 (equal with Hulak and Ermenkov). *(W.R.H.)*

STÅHLBERG, Gideon *(26 January 1908–26 May 1967)*
Swedish grandmaster and many times judge at World Championship matches, who, together with Stoltz and Lundin, formed the bulwark of the Swedish international team for the period 1928 to 1966.

He was a player who especially impressed by the elegance of his style but who never quite achieved the optimum his undoubted talents deserved. Possibly this was due to the variety of his interests and skills. At bridge he was practically of international master class and he played all card games with almost equal skill. He was a table-tennis player and as such reported many an international match. A great connoisseur of wines and spirits, he sometimes spoilt his chances in tournaments by an over-energetic pursuit of excellence in the spirituous way.

A witty and cultivated man, he spoke a number of languages well, had a prodigious memory (he could, for example, recite all the dates of the monarchs of England), and wrote a number of good books on chess.

He played on top board for his country in thirteen Olympiads, from 1928 to 1964, and nearly always with success, his best performance being at Helsinki 1952 where he scored 76.9%.

His playing career was divided into two parts by the Second World War, since this broke out whilst he was representing Sweden in the Buenos Aires Olympiad of 1939. He stayed behind in the Argentine and had a continuous rivalry with Najdorf out of which, on the whole, the latter emerged triumphant.

Returning to Europe in 1948 his performances in the international field immediately took a swing upwards. He qualified for the Candidates tournament through the Saltsjöbaden Interzonal of 1948, had his best tournament result by coming first at Trenčianské Teplice in 1949 and came 7th in the Candidates tournament at Budapest 1950.

Again he qualified for the Candidates by coming =5th at Stockholm-Saltsjöbaden 1952 but he did badly in the Neuhausen-Zürich Candidates of 1953 where he came bottom.

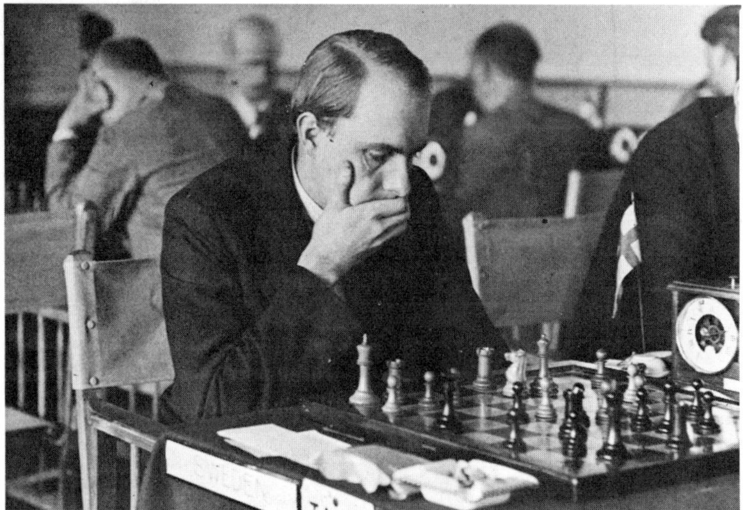

Gideon Ståhlberg in play against Andersson for the Hamilton Russell Trophy, Folkestone Olympiad 1933

From now on his results deteriorated and he compensated for this by acting as judge at five World Championship matches at Moscow. He still played, though with less and less success. He was on his way to take part in an international tournament at Leningrad when he collapsed and died in 1967.

He was a formidable match-player and surprised the chess world by defeating Spielmann by +3−1=4 in 1933 at Stockholm and even more by beating Nimzowitsch by +4−2=2 at Göteborg in 1934. He lost a match to Fine at Stockholm in 1937 by +2−4=2 and drew a match with Keres at Stockholm in 1938 by +2−2=4. He also narrowly lost a match to Gligorić at Belgrade in 1949 by +1−2=9.

He was a friend of the writer of these lines for many years and possessed a charm and a civilized gaiety that distinguished him among grandmasters. *(H.G.)*

STALEMATE
When the King of the player whose turn it is to move is not in check and the said player cannot move he is stalemated. At one time in the history of the game, stalemate had varying values in varying countries. In England in the seventeenth and eighteenth centuries it even counted as a win.

The word 'stale' is late Middle English for 'imitation', and hence stalemate meant 'imitation mate'.

From the nineteenth century onwards stalemate has been the equivalent of a draw. See LAWS OF CHESS, Article 12.1.

The word 'stalemate' has been taken into the English language to mean (wrongly) a temporary state of impasse. *(H.G.)*

STALIN, Josef Vissarionovich *(21 December 1879–5 March 1953)*
Soviet politician; fond of chess, but not so effective at it as he was at politics. A game is extant, supposedly won by him against the head of the GPU at Moscow 1926. (But it is almost certainly an invention.)

White: Stalin; *Black:* Yezhov
Sicilian Defence
1. P–K4, P–QB4; 2. N–KB3, P–Q3; 3. P–Q4, P×P; 4. N×P, N–KB3; 5. N–QB3, QN–Q2; 6. B–K2, P–QR3; 7. O–O, P–K3; 8. P–B4, P–QN4; 9. P–QR3, B–N2; 10. B–B3, Q–N3; 11. B–K3, Q–B2; 12. Q–K2, B–K2; 13. P–KN4, N–B4; 14. Q–N2, O–O; 15. QR–Q1, KR–K1; 16. P–N5, KN–Q2; 17. R–Q2, P–K4; 18. N–B5, N–K3; 19. N×B+, R×N; 20. P–B5, N–Q5; 21. P–B6, R(K2)–K1; 22. B–R5, P–N3; 23. B×P, RP×B; 24. Q–R3, N–K3; 25. Q–R6, Q–Q1; 26. R–B3, N×BP; 27. P×N, R–QB1; 28. R(Q2)–B2, Q×P; 29. R×Q, R–B2; 30. N–Q5, B×N; 31. P×B, N–B1; 32. B–N5, N–R2; 33. R×QP, P–K5; 34. B–K3, R(B2)–K2; 35. B–Q4, P–B3; 36. B×P, N×B; 37. R(B6)×N, resigns. *(H.G.)*

STAMMA, Philip *(fl. eighteenth century)*
Usually known as Stamma of Aleppo, since he was a native of that town in Syria, Stamma was a belated representative of the great Arab school of chess.

Possibly because he came from the East the dates of his birth and death are unknown, but he travelled extensively in Europe and in 1737 published in Paris an *Essai sur le jeu des echecs*, consisting of one hundred endings which, in the ancient Muslim style, were a blend of problem and actual game. From the dedication to Lord Harrington, a keen amateur of the game, it is apparent that he was in the direst straits of poverty.

From Paris he went to England where in 1745 he published a revised version of his French book under the title of *The Noble Game of Chess*. The revisions were important since they included a collection of seventy-four openings among which was the Queen's Gambit, which he strongly advocated.

Even more important was the circumstance that he introduced into Europe (in both works) the algebraic notation, as one might have expected from his Arabic origin.

As a player he seems to have been less gifted than as a theorist, since he played a match against the young Philidor in 1747 in Slaughter's Coffee House in St Martin's Lane, London, and was beaten by +8−1=1. Philidor gave him the odds of the move and allowed him to count all draws as won, betting 5–4 on each game.

(H.G.)

STAMPS, Chess

The motif of chess appears on postage stamps as a modern, post-war phenomenon. Nor, when one considers how many more chess events have taken place in the years since 1945 as contrasted with pre-war years, are the occasions when chess has appeared on stamps all that frequent.

When these chess stamps do appear they can be divided into four main categories: (1) those devoted to team tournaments (these being principally Olympiads); (2) individual World or National championships; (3) great international tournaments; and (4) those in which chess, though used as an embellishment, has little or no relation to the subject of the stamp.

The first chess stamp ever issued was a 9-leva stamp in Bulgaria on 29 September 1947. It depicted a Knight and commemorated the Balkan games at Sofia, a section of which was a four-nation team tournament between Hungary, Yugoslavia, Bulgaria and Romania.

Then came a set of three stamps issued in the USSR on 20 November 1948 to celebrate the second and final half of the match-tournament that decided the destination of the World Championship title. The first half had been played in The Netherlands and the second half was held in Moscow where it was won by Botvinnik. The 30- and 50-kopek stamps depicted the Trades Union building where the event took place and the 40-kopek stamp showed a Black Rook and a chessboard.

In 1950 there were two sets of chess stamps issued. One set, issued in Hungary and consisting of three stamps, was in celebration of the first Candidates tournament held in Budapest and appeared on 9 April 1950. The other was a set of five stamps issued in Yugoslavia on 20 August 1950 and it was devoted to the Olympiad at Dubrovnik. This was the first Olympiad to be thus commemorated.

One oddity about the Yugoslav set was that the 5-dinar stamp

Bulgaria, 1948

USSR, 1977. Issued for the final, European Team Championship, Moscow

Finland, 1952

Britain, 1976

Israel, 1964

Netherlands Antilles 1962

Cuba, 1966

Nicaragua, 1976. From a series of ten historical stamps

East Germany, 1968

Yugoslavia, 1972

Cuba, 1969

Cuba, 1951

showed a position from a game between Capablanca and Lasker at the New York 1924 tournament but with a Bishop on the wrong square – an artist's blunder.

On 1 November 1951 Cuba issued seven stamps commemorating the 30th anniversary of Capablanca's winning the World Championship. Cuba was to prove the most prolific of all in the production of chess stamps. The following year Finland issued a single stamp on 10 August 1952, showing a White Rook and a Black Knight on a chessboard and commemorating the 10th Olympiad at Helsinki.

Poland issued two stamps on 9 February 1956, each showing a pair of hands in deaf and dumb language and commemorating the 1st World Championship for the Deaf and Dumb which was held at Zakopane.

On 17 July 1958 Bulgaria issued one stamp on the 5th World Students Team championship that was held at Varna that year. In the same year, on 30 August, the USSR issued a stamp depicting Chigorin and commemorating the 50th anniversary of his death.

The 14th Olympiad at Leipzig in East Germany was commemorated by a set of three stamps on 19 September 1960.

Another Candidates tournament, at Curaçao in the Netherlands Antilles in 1962, was commemorated by a set of three stamps on 2 May 1962. Each stamp had the world flanked by a White Knight. The 15th Olympiad, held at Varna, Bulgaria, that year saw the issue of five stamps.

Two more chess stamps were issued in 1962. One, by Cuba on 25 July, a 13-cent stamp showing a boy making a move on a chessboard and part of a set of thirty stamps about the National Sports Institute. The other was issued by the USSR on 24 November and commemorated the 30th Soviet championship held at Erevan. Yet another stamp was issued in 1962 and this belonged to the fourth category mentioned above. It was issued in the Philippines on 30 December and showed the great writer Dr José Rizal playing chess.

The World Championship match in Moscow 1963 between Botvinnik and Petrosian was commemorated by a set of three stamps on 18 May. Nicaragua produced a chess stamp on 12 December 1963 for reasons that are not at all clear, but probably have some reference to the Olympic Games.

The 16th Olympiad was held at Tel Aviv in Israel in 1964 and two commemorative stamps were issued on 2 November 1964, both bearing the FIDE insignia and each having a portion of the chessboard together with a piece (a Knight on the lower value and a Rook on the other).

In 1965 two stamps belonging most emphatically to category 4 were issued. The one, by Egypt on 1 July commemorating the re-establishment of the Egyptian Civil Airline, purported to display a 'Pharonic chess-set and table' dating back to 1350 BC. In fact the pieces are all the same and the table has thirty squares, 10 × 3, and the game is certainly not chess. Another somewhat fictional representation of chess was a stamp issued on 28 August, the issuer being San Marino and the subject entitled 'Castles in the Air'. It is that in more senses than one since it depicts a chessboard on which are ten Rooks.

The year 1966 was a rich one for the chess philatelist. It was an Olympiad year and the event in Havana was heralded by a set of six stamps issued on 25 February 1966 by Romania.

France issued a single stamp on 2 April 1966 on the occasion of the Le Havre International Chess festival. The USSR also issued one stamp, on 31 May 1966, in honour of the World Championship match between Petrosian and Spassky. After the match it also issued a small square sheet of four stamps devoted to sports, one of which was chess.

Finally in this year Cuba commemorated the 17th Olympiad in Havana with a set of six stamps on 18 October 1966. In addition a 30-cent miniature sheet was produced giving a position from a game between Lasker and Capablanca.

On 28 April 1967 a 60-cent stamp was issued in Monaco marking a strong international tournament in Monte Carlo. The same stamp was issued in four different colours. On 23 June 1967 the Dominican Republic issued two stamps commemorating the Central American championships. In the same year, in November, the Yemen issued a stamp showing Moorish art in Spain with a miniature of two chess-players strongly resembling those to be found in the work of Alfonso the Wise.

Switzerland issued one stamp on 14 March 1968 commemorating the 18th Olympiad at Lugano.

On 17 July 1968 East Germany issued five stamps in honour of famous Germans and one of them, the 15-pfennig, showed Em. Lasker. This was the 100th anniversary of his birth and in November 1968 a great tournament was held in Berlin. The first-day cover with a special postmark at that tournament had a picture of Lasker over the chessboard on which was reproduced a position from his 1910 World Championship match with Schlechter. The East Germans also issued a stamp the following year on 29 July on the occasion of the World Students Team championships at Dresden.

Cuba issued a stamp on 15 November 1969 to mark a Capablanca Memorial tournament in Havana. The stamp contained six chess pieces against the background of the world.

An oddity occurred in 1971 when the Arab Sheikdom of Fujeira issued, on 19 November, a set of five so-called pre-Olympic stamps. One was on chess and foreshadowed the 1972 Olympiad at Skopje in Yugoslavia.

A set of three were in fact issued at Skopje in September 1972, but the greed of speculators was such that the stamps were not available on the opening day of the Olympiad at Skopje. Remarkably, the Tunisian Republic issued a stamp in commemoration of this Olympiad, with a chessboard background and a beautiful colour scheme of varying shades of green plus white and red giving the various pieces in human form, perhaps the most artistic of all modern chess stamps.

Before this, though, the World Championship match between Spassky and Fischer had commenced on 2 July 1972 at Reykjavik in Iceland and had been given not only a chess stamp in Iceland, but a number of other chess stamps all over the world.

Cuba broke fresh ground in 1976 by a special issue of five stamps devoted to the history of chess. The 1-centavo showed Ruy Lopez with a chessboard containing a position from his opening. The 2-centavo had Philidor with a copy of his famous work and a vast pawn. The 3-centavo showed Wilhelm Steinitz with a laurel wreath and a Knight; the 13-centavo was Em. Lasker with a King and a world background; the 30-centavo showed Capablanca in the foreground with two chess-players in the background.

On 29 September 1976 a set of four stamps was issued by the British Post Office commemorating the first printing in Britain by William Caxton in 1476. On the 11p stamp there was reproduced a woodcut from *The Game and Playe of the Chesse*, showing a man seated at the chessboard and about to make a move. All four stamps bear the inscription 'William Caxton 1476' and this is a little deceptive since *The Game and Playe of the Chesse* was first printed in Bruges in 1474. It was only the second edition which was printed in England – in 1481. *(H.G.)*

STANLEY, Charles Henry *(1819–16 March 1894)*
Initially a London player, Stanley first came into prominence by beating Staunton in a match in 1839 by +3−2=1, though he was given the odds of pawn and two moves. In 1840 he went to the USA and remained there till his death in New York.

He was regarded as the best player of the New York Chess Club from 1840 to 1857. In 1845 he won a celebrated match against Eugene Rousseau in New Orleans +15−8=8 for a stake of 1,000 dollars. Came equal 11th with Fiske and Fuller in New York 1857.

He started the first chess column in the USA in *The Spirit of the Times* and wrote a book, *Morphy's Match Games*, 1859. *(H.G.)*

STAUNTON CENTENARY TOURNAMENT 1951
This tournament derived its name from the fact that it was held 100 years after the first international tournament ever, at London in 1851. It was Howard Staunton's idea to hold an international tournament in 1851.

The 1951 event was held in three towns, Cheltenham, Leamington and Birmingham in that order. No player from the Soviet Union or from any of the satellite countries accepted the invitation to participate but in the end the organizers got a strong tournament together with heavy reliance upon what was then Europe's second strongest chess-playing nation, Yugoslavia, whose four participating players all figured well up in the prize-list.

It was a Yugoslav player, Matanović, who was in the lead at the end of the Cheltenham section of play. But he lost his lead during the Leamington stage and was replaced first by Trifunović and finally by Gligorić. There were eight prizes and Alexander distinguished himself, not only by being the only English player to figure in the prize list but also by winning a sparkling and exhilarating game over Gligorić. Leading scores: Gligorić 10, Pirc, Ståhlberg, Trifunović 9½. *(H.G.)*

STAUNTON CHESSMEN
In 1835 Nathaniel Cook designed a pattern of chessmen that soon became recognized as the standard type for play. He became the friend of Howard Staunton who allowed his name to be attached to the set which was at once elegant and serviceable. The firm of Jaques obtained a copyright for the design and has manufactured the pieces for over a hundred years. *(H.G.)*

STAUNTON GAMBIT
A line in the Queen's Pawn, Dutch Defence, 1. P–Q4, P–KB4; 2. P–K4, so called because of Staunton's use of it against Horwitz. *(H.G.)*

STAUNTON, Howard *(1810–22 June 1874)*

The only British player ever to have been recognized as the world's leading master, Staunton dominated English chess during the 1840s and was the leading player in Europe between La Bourdonnais and Anderssen.

His origins are obscure; the place and exact date of his birth are unknown and he is reputed to have been the illegitimate son of Frederick Howard, fifth Earl of Carlisle. The generally accepted story that he received a few thousand pounds under his father's will and squandered it in his early twenties can be only partially true since examination of the Earl's will reveals that he made no such bequest. His early years were poverty-stricken and he spent them at Oxford, though he did not attend the university.

Staunton appears to have begun earning his living as an actor and claimed to have played the part of Lorenzo opposite Edmond Kean's Shylock. Possibly from this he derived his life-long interest in Shakespeare; he eventually became a noted Shakespeare scholar, though very little of worth has come down to us from his publications in that respect.

Learning chess at the age of nineteen, he still took some time to mature and made his first mark by beating Popert in a match, +8−3=2. Still more impressive was his victory in a series of games played during 1841–2 against John Cochrane, +14−4=0.

In 1843 Saint-Amant, the leading French player of the day, visited London and played six informal games with Staunton for the nominal stake of one guinea. The Frenchman won by +3−2=1. Stung by the claim on Saint-Amant's part that this was a genuine match, Staunton negotiated a fresh encounter consisting of twenty-one games with a stake of £100 by each side. This was played and won by Staunton +11−6=4 after which Staunton was recognized as the leading player in Europe, this claim being reinforced by his two victories in 1846, against Horwitz by +14−7=3 and against Harrwitz by +7−0=0.

Meanwhile two significant occurrences had happened. He had founded the first English chess magazine in 1841 and, as a result of a severe attack of pneumonia, had acquired a heart condition that was to have a serious effect on his stamina.

In 1851 he pioneered the first real international tournament at London but was disappointed at coming fourth, losing to Anderssen in the semi-final and to Williams in the play-off. He made one more appearance in a major contest when he narrowly lost a match to Von der Lasa in 1853 by +4−5=3. Thereafter he devoted himself to writing.

In 1847 he had published his best book on chess, *The Chess Player's Handbook*, which, whilst based on Bilguer's *Handbuch*, still possessed much of the Staunton vigour and common sense and remained standard for a century.

In 1858 Paul Morphy visited Europe with the intent of playing a match with Staunton but this was denied to him on the grounds that Staunton was busy working on an edition of Shakespeare. The excuse was valid but there is no doubt that Morphy would have won the match easily.

Staunton died of a heart attack on 22 June 1874 (the anniversary of Morphy's birthday!). His chief virtues as a player were solid positional sense and excellent analytical powers.

Fourth match game, Paris 1843
White: Staunton; *Black:* Saint-Amant
Benoni Defence
1. P–Q4, P–QB4; 2. P–Q5, P–B4; 3. N–QB3, P–Q3; 4. P–K4, P×P; 5. N×P, P–K4; 6. B–KN5, Q–R4+; 7. P–B3, B–B4; 8. N–N3, B–N3; 9. B–Q3, B×B; 10. Q×B, P–KN3; 11. KN–K2, B–K2; 12. N–K4, Q–N3; 13. O–O, N–Q2; 14. B×B, N×B; 15. N–N5, P–KR3; 16. N–K6, N–KB1; 17. N×N, R×N; 18. P–QN4, P×P; 19. P×P, K–B2; 20. K–R1, K–N2; 21. P–KB4, QR–Q1; 22. QR–Q1, P–KR4; 23. Q–QB3, Q–N4; 24. Q–Q2, R–B4; 25. N–N3, R–B3; 26. P×P, R×R+; 27. R×R, P×P; 28. Q–N5, R–Q2; 29. Q×KP+, K–R2; 30. R–B7+, K–R3;

and White announced mate in four by 31. Q–R8+, K–N4; 32. N–K4+, K–N5; 33. P–R3+, K–R5; 34. R–B4.

His main works are: *The Chess Player's Handbook*, London 1847; *The Chess Player's Companion*, London 1849. *(H.G.)*

STEAN, Michael *(b. 4 September 1953)*
British international master, born in London, Stean learnt how to play chess at the age of four and a half. In 1967 he won the London Boys under-14 championship and two years later, at the B.C.F. Congress at Rhyl in 1969, he won the British Boys under-16 championship.

His next success was a 3rd in the Norwich Junior international tournament of 1971, below Sax and Tarjan, both of whom later became international grandmasters.

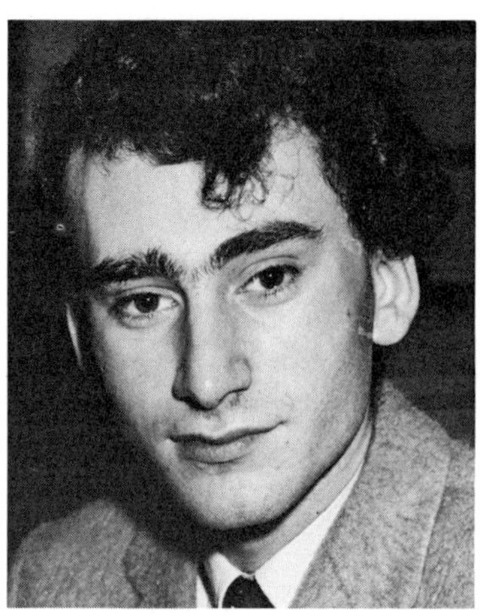

1973 saw a big advance in his play and his results; he was becoming recognized as second only to Tony Miles as a potential grandmaster amongst the new British generation. He won the Robert Silk tournament at Canterbury, ahead of the Hungarian grandmaster Adorjan and came third in the World Junior Championship at the Teesside below Belyavsky and Miles.

The next advance came in 1974 when he obtained his first international master norm by playing in beautiful style on board 5 for England in the Nice Olympiad. He scored 66.7% and also won the Turover Prize for the most brilliant game in the Olympiad. This was for his victory over the international grandmaster, Walter Browne of the USA, but he was also largely responsible for England's best result in the finals – a 2–2 draw with the second-placed team in the finals, Yugoslavia, in which Stean defeated the grandmaster Velimirović.

In 1974 he tied for first place in the British championship at Clacton, but, out of form in the play-off, came only =4th.

In 1975 he had a creditable result in the very strong Alekhine Memorial in Moscow and in that year rounded off his acquisition of the international master title by achieving his second norm in the Alexander Memorial at Middlesbrough.

Within a few months, in 1976, he had obtained his first grandmaster norm. This was at Montilla in Spain where he came equal second with Kavalek and Calvo, below the World Champion, Karpov (with whom he drew) but above four grandmasters.

A fine opening theorist, he has written a work on the *Sicilian: Najdorf*, London 1976.

STEIN, Leonid Zakharovich *(12 November 1934–4 July 1973)*
A Soviet grandmaster from the Ukraine and one of the world's strongest players during the 1960s. Stein was consistently success-

ful in national tournaments, winning the Ukrainian championship in 1960 and 1962, and the Soviet championship on three occasions, 1963, 1965 and 1970. His international tournament successes included 1st prizes at the very strong Moscow 1967 tournament, Kecskemet 1968 and Tallinn 1969, as well as =1st places at Hastings 1967/8, Moscow 1971, and Las Palmas 1973.

His attempts to reach the Candidates tournaments were plagued by ill fortune. Both in 1962 and 1964 Stein secured a sufficiently good result in the Interzonal tournament to earn a Candidates place, but was eliminated by the rule, later abandoned, forbidding the admission of too many players from the same nation.

His tragically early death at the age of thirty-eight deprived the world of one of its most talented and original players. *(W.R.H.)*

STEINER, Endre *(27 June 1901–29 December 1944)*
A strong Hungarian master whose combinative ability and originality of thought were typical of the Hungarian school. Variable in tournaments, he was at his best in team events and played with great success for his country in six Olympiads, making his best score (80%) in his last one at Stockholm 1937.

Best tournament results: 3rd Portsmouth 1923 (beating Alekhine), 2nd Trenčianské Teplice 1928, 3rd Budapest 1932. *(H.G.)*

STEINER, Herman *(15 May 1905–25 November 1955)*
US champion for three years and for some time the leading chess organizer on the west coast of America. The Hungarian-born Steiner, emigrated to the USA at sixteen, improved his chess at New York clubs, and made his international debut in the pre-war Olympiads, scoring +6−1=9 on board 2 at The Hague 1928. His individual results included winning the Hastings Premier Reserve in 1929, sharing the US Open title in 1942 and winning it in 1946, and taking the US Closed championship in 1948.

Other international results were: 2nd at Brno 1931; =3rd at Pasadena 1932; 2nd at Chicago 1937; =3rd at Hastings 1945/6; 1st at London 1946; =5th at Venice 1950.

In addition to being a US Chess Federation vice-president, Steiner organized the 1945 Pan-American Congress, edited a chess column for the *Los Angeles Times* and opened a Hollywood Chess Club whose *habitués* included Humphrey Bogart and José Ferrer. *(A.S.)*

STEINER, Lajos *(14 June 1903–22 April 1975)*
Brother of Endre, Lajos Steiner was Hungarian champion in 1936 and played for Hungary in three Olympiads, 1931, 1933 and 1935.

He had excellent tournament results in the period preceding the Second World War. First at Schandau 1927, Budapest 1931, Vienna 1937/8; =1st Marburg 1934 (with Pirc), Vienna 1935 (with Eliskases); 2nd at Hastings 1927/8 and Bradley Beach 1929; =2nd Kecskemet 1927 (with Nimzowitsch), Mährisch-Ostrau 1933 (with Eliskases and Zinner). He won matches v. Lilienthal in 1934 +3−1=2, and Grob in 1935 +3−1.

He emigrated to Australia in 1939 and won the Australian championship many times. Steiner represented Australia in the Stockholm Interzonal 1948, coming 19th. He came 3rd at the strong international tournament of Karlovy Vary-Mariánské Lázně 1948.

He was recognized as international master in 1950, but though he continued to compete in Australian chess, he dropped out of international competitions.

His main books are: *Sakkiskola*, Kecskemét 1935; *Kings of the Chess-board*, Roseville (N.S.W.) 1948. *(H.G.)*

STEINITZ, Wilhelm *(17 May 1836–12 August 1900)*

World Champion 1866–94, Steinitz was the first official chess champion of the world and perhaps the most profound thinker the game has ever seen. Though not as great in sensing complex combinations as his rivals Zukertort and Chigorin, his deep insights into defensive play and into the accumulation of small but enduring advantages changed the outlook of an entire generation of chess-masters and baffled his more talented opponents. Before Steinitz, everyone believed that winning depended on inventiveness and luck, and that rapid King-side attacks were desirable. After Steinitz everyone realized that a successful winning attack could not exist unless one side had a clear positional advantage; that relatively minor items like doubled, isolated or backward pawns, a Queen-side pawn majority, or two Bishops versus Bishop and Knight, were often significant contributing factors; and that the best defence consisted in avoiding permanent positional weaknesses. Morphy had shown the way in open positions but Steinitz illuminated the much more complex domain of closed positions.

In effecting this major transformation, Steinitz suffered much abuse but he displayed enormous confidence, even stubbornness, and participated in controversy with obstinate and often bitter relish.

Born in Prague, of Jewish parents, Steinitz went to study in Vienna in 1858 and represented Austria in his first international tournament, London 1862. He took up residence in London and in 1866 defeated Anderssen (recognized as the best player in the world) by +8−6=0. His reign as World Champion is taken from this date, though he did not coin the phrase until 1886. Steinitz won tournaments in London 1872, Vienna 1873 and New York 1894, and tied for first or came second in Dundee 1867, Baden-Baden 1870, Vienna 1882, London 1883, St Petersburg 1895/6 and New York 1897.

Steinitz dominated British chess, winning matches against Bird in 1866 and Blackburne in 1876. He became chess editor of *The Field*. Zukertort rivalled Steinitz's dominance and the clash of their personalities led to a fierce rivalry. In 1886 these two chess colossi played the first match billed as the World Championship. Steinitz had won an earlier match in 1872 over the young Zukertort by +7−1=4, and he succeeded in this great match by +10−5=5. Zukertort could not understand why he lost, took ill and died two years later.

Steinitz emigrated to New York in 1882. He defeated his next great rival, Chigorin, by +10−6=1 in 1889 and again by +10−8=5 in 1892. In 1894 Steinitz was dethroned by the young Lasker by +5−10=4 and in the return match of 1896/7 Steinitz could do no better than +2−10=5. Steinitz then took ill (in Moscow) and was put into a mental home. He recovered and continued to play in tournaments, but in 1900 he again became a mental case and died a pauper in New York. Steinitz is buried in the Evergreen Cemetery, Brooklyn.

Steinitz was a striking but short figure. He had a massive head, a prominent forehead, powerful shoulders and arms. He was a good swimmer. Below his chest, however, he was much smaller, having unusually short legs. He also walked with a limp.

Though famous for defence, Steinitz could also produce brilliancy. Here is one of twenty-eight simultaneous games played in New York on 3 March 1883.

White: Steinitz; *Black:* Dr Simonson
King's Gambit Accepted
1. P–K4, P–K4; 2. P–KB4, P×P; 3. N–KB3, P–KN4; 4. P–KR4, P–N5; 5. N–K5, P–KR4; 6. B–B4, N–KR3; 7. P–Q4, P–Q3; 8. N–Q3, P–B6; 9. P×P, B–K2; 10. B–K3, B×P+; 11. K–Q2, P×P; 12. Q×P, B–N5; 13. Q–B4, N–B3; 14. N–B3, N–K2; 15. QR–KB1, R–R2; 16. R×B, N–N3; 17. R×B, N×Q; 18. R(4)×N, P–QB3; 19. R–B6, N–N5; 20. B×P+, K–Q2; 21. B–K6+, K–B2; 22. R–B7+, R×R; 23. R×R+, K–N3; 24. B×N, P×B; 25. P–Q5+, P–B4; 26. P–K5, K–R3; 27. B×P, P×B; 28. N×P+, K–N3; 29. R×P+, K×N; 30. K–Q3, Q–R4; 31. P–N4+, Q×P; 32. N–K4+ and wins.

Some life scores: +5−5=3 v. Pillsbury; +8−26=12 v. Lasker; +27−24=8 v. Chigorin; +19−9=11 v. Zukertort; +25−8=7 v. Blackburne; +10−9=0 v. Anderssen.

Chief works: *Modern Chess Instructor*, New York 1889; *The Sixth American Chess Congress*, New York 1891. *(N.D.)*

STOLTZ, Gösta *(9 May 1904–25 July 1963)*
Swedish grandmaster and probably the best combinational player Sweden has ever produced, Stoltz at one time (in the early 1930s) was regarded as a promising young master with hopes of getting within range of the World Championship itself.

It was in this period that he scored his most outstanding result, coming =4th with Flohr, Kashdan and Vidmar at Bled 1931. Though he often figured high up in the list in strong tournaments, he never fulfilled these hopes, largely through a tendency to drink too much. His best tournament result after that in Bled was the winning of the so-called Europa tourney at Munich 1941, 1½ points ahead of Alekhine and Lundin.

After the Second World War he had a good performance at Prague 1946 where he came =2nd with Trifunović below Najdorf but his results gradually tailed off under the influence of drink.

Like Ståhlberg, he had some excellent results in short matches in the early 1930s: he beat Kashdan in 1930 by +3−2=1 and lost to Spielmann in the same year by +2−3=1, at Stockholm in both cases; he had two matches with Flohr in 1931, winning the first by +4−3=1 and losing the second by +1−4=3. He also narrowly lost to Nimzowitsch in 1934 by +1−2=3.

He played for Sweden in nine Olympiads from 1927 to 1954.

He worked, on and off, as a car mechanic but eventually became a full time chess professional.

A good example of his pragmatic yet highly combinative style is the 2nd game of his match with Spielmann in 1930.

White: Spielmann; *Black:* Stoltz
French Defence
1. P–K4, P–K3; 2. P–Q4, P–Q4; 3. N–Q2, N–KB3; 4. P–K5, KN–Q2; 5. B–Q3, P–QB4; 6. P–QB3, N–QB3; 7. N–K2, Q–N3; 8. N–B3, P×P; 9. P×P, B–N5+; 10. K–B1, P–B3; 11. N–B4, P×P; 12. N(4)×P(K6), P–K5; 13. B–KB4, P×N; 14. B–B7, N–B3; 15. N×P+, K–B2; 16. B×Q, B–N5;

17. P–KN3, B–R6+; 18. K–N1, K×N; 19. B–B7, KR–K1; 20. B–K5, N×B; 21. P×N, R×P; 22. Q–N3, B–QB4; 23. B–B5, B×B; 24. Q×P+, K–N3; 25. Q×R, R–K7; 26. P–KR4, B×P+; 27. K–B1, B–Q6; 28. P–R5+, K–N4; 29. resigns. *(H.G.)*

'STRATEGIE, LA'
A French monthly chess magazine founded in Paris 1867 by Jean Préti. Remarkably, during its entire life it had only three editors: Jean Préti 1867–75; Numa Préti (his son) 1875–1907 and Henri Delaire 1907–40. *(H.G.)*

STONEWALL SYSTEM
A cumbersome opening in which White attempts to engineer a K-side attack by adopting a reversed Dutch defence, maintaining a firm grip on his K5 square. After 1. P–Q4, P–Q4; 2. P–K3, P–QB4; 3. P–QB3, N–KB3; 4. B–Q3, P–KN3; 5. P–KB4, however, Black's position is preferable since White has gratuitously weakened his central light squares. *(R.D.K.)*

STRÖBECK

A village in the Harz mountains, not far from the city of Halberstadt in East Germany. Here everybody plays chess.

The reasons for this are obscure. The tradition goes back to the fourteenth century when a bishop was imprisoned in a jail built like a Rook in Ströbeck. There a friendly jailer taught him how to play chess and, on release, he had a special law passed allowing the villagers to play the game even though, as commoners, they would not normally have had this right.

It was at Ströbeck that the Courier game (see under VARIETIES OF CHESS: COURIER) lingered longest and in 1651 Frederick William of Prussia visited the village and donated a special and most ornate chessboard for the playing of the Courier game. *(H.G.)*

STRONG SQUARE

Diagram 1

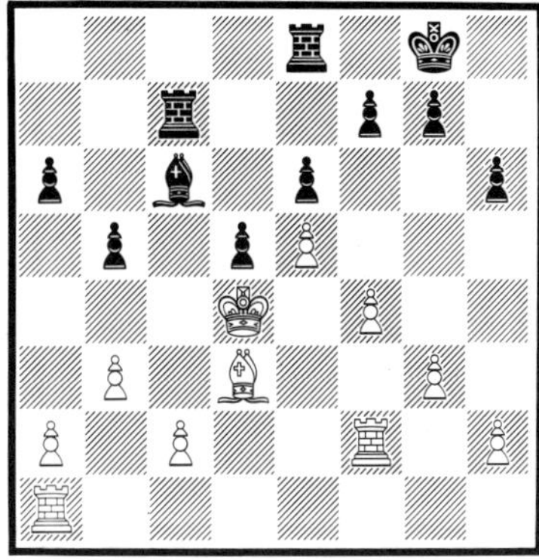

Diagram 2

A square is called 'strong' when it can be occupied by a piece which can no longer be attacked by a hostile pawn. It is particularly strong when it is also permanently out of reach of a hostile minor piece – a type of position often brought about where a Knight faces the so-called bad Bishop. The ideal strong square is situated in front of an isolated or backward pawn, but this is not necessarily so (see Diagram 1). There is, however, another type of strong square – a strength of lesser order, perhaps. This is a square from which a piece can be driven away only by a pawn which, in so doing, contracts other permanent or semi-permanent weaknesses. Thus, in many openings in which the central pawn configuration, White pawn on K4 against Black pawn on Q3, arises (see Diagram 2), Q5 is a strong square for a White Knight to settle on unless Black can make sure that the move P–QB3 can be followed by P–Q4 in the foreseeable future. Diagram 2 (Tarrasch–Teichmann, San Sebastian 1912) shows a strong square occupied by the White King, while Black has no corresponding strong square available.

Most of the play that follows is based on the ultimate threat of the White King's entry via B5 with gain of the hostile Q-side pawns, thus making it impossible for Black to allow the exchange of both Rooks: 1. . , B–Q2; 2. P–KN4, B–B1; 3. P–KR4, P–N3; 4. R–R1, K–N2; 5. P–R5, R–R1; 6. R(2)–R2, B–Q2; 7. P–N5, RP×P; 8. BP×P, P×P; 9. R×P, R×R; 10. R×R, K–B1; 11. R–R8+, K–K2; 12. P–N6, P×P; 13. B×KNP, P–N5; 14. R–R7+, K–Q1; 15. B–Q3, R–B6; 16. P–R3, P–R4; 17. R–R8+, K–K2; 18. R–R8, resigns. *(W.H.)*

STUDENTS CHESS OLYMPIADS

[World Students Team championship]

This championship has been a regular feature of the international chess calendar since 1954, when the first such event was held in Oslo. The two years prior to this had both seen attempts to organize Student events, with Liverpool 1952 an individual tournament (though originally planned as a team tournament) and Brussels 1953 a genuine team competition, but with only eight entries. The event is run by the International Union of Students under the auspices of FIDE.

In the early years of the tournament, the rules of eligibility were somewhat unclear, and some surprisingly ancient students were noticed among certain teams. Later the rules were tightened to include an age-limit of under twenty-seven years.

As the results show, the event has tended to be dominated by the Soviet teams, though both Czechoslovakia and the United States have two gold medals to their credit. Full results of the Students Olympiads are as follows:

1. *Oslo 1954:* Czechoslovakia 29½, USSR 28½, Bulgaria 26, England 23, Iceland 19, Sweden 17, Norway 14, Finland 13, Italy+Scotland 8½, France 1½. (Neither Italy nor Scotland arrived with full teams and so combined forces.)

2. *Lyons 1955:* USSR 41, Yugoslavia 33, Hungary 32½, Bulgaria 32½, Czechoslovakia 27½, Iceland 26, Poland 25½, Spain 23½, Finland 20½, The Netherlands 16½, Sweden 14½, Norway 14½, France 4½.

First cover envelope design to celebrate the World Students Olympiad 1974

3. *Uppsala 1956:* With sixteen entries too many for an all-play-all, qualifying rounds were held leading to two final sections. USSR 21½, Hungary 16½, Yugoslavia 15, Bulgaria 15, Spain 12½, Czechoslovakia 11½, Romania 10½, USA 9 were the scores of Final A; Iceland won Final B ahead of Poland and East Germany.

4. *Reykjavik 1957:* USSR 43½, Bulgaria 37, Czechoslovakia 36, Hungary 34½, USA 31, Romania 29, East Germany 28, Iceland 27, England 23½, Denmark 21, Sweden 16, Ecuador 15½, Mongolia 14½, Finland 9½.

5. *Varna 1958:* Final A: USSR 19½, Bulgaria 17, Czechoslovakia 14, Yugoslavia 14, Hungary 14, USA 12½, Argentina 11½, East Germany 9½. Final B was won by Romania.

6. *Budapest 1959:* Bulgaria 40½, USSR 39, Hungary 37½, Romania 36, East Germany 32½, Czechoslovakia 31, England 26½, Mongolia 21½, Poland 21½, Israel 20, France 19, Sweden 18½, Finland 15, Ireland 5½.

7. *Leningrad 1960:* USA 41, USSR 39½, Yugoslavia 37, Czechoslovakia 31½, Bulgaria 31, Romania 30, East Germany 28½, The Netherlands 25½, Hungary 24½, England 24, Sweden 16, Mongolia 16, Finland 10, Belgium 9½.

8. *Helsinki 1961:* USSR 39½, USA 34½, East Germany 31, Czechoslovakia 31, Bulgaria 29, Hungary 28½, The Netherlands 25, England 20, Mongolia 20, Denmark 19, Finland 18½, Sweden 10, Tunisia 6.

9. *Mariánské Lázně 1962:* Final A: USSR 24½, Yugoslavia 20, Czechoslovakia 19, East Germany 17, Romania 16½, Bulgaria 14½, Hungary 13½, Poland 12½, Mongolia 6½. Final B was won by The Netherlands.

10. *Budva 1963:* Czechoslovakia 24, Yugoslavia 23½, Bulgaria 22, USSR 22, USA 19½, The Netherlands 17½, Poland 16, Mongolia 16, Hungary 13, Italy 6½. Final B was won by England.

11. *Cracow 1964:* USSR 31½, Czechoslovakia 29½, Hungary 29, USA 28, Yugoslavia 27, Poland 21½, Israel 19, Bulgaria 18, East Germany 18, Mongolia 16½, Denmark 15½, Austria 10½. Final B was won by Romania.

12. *Sinaia 1965:* USSR 21, Israel 20, Denmark 18, Romania 17½, Czechoslovakia 17½, England 14½, East Germany 14, Hungary 12, The Netherlands 9½. Final B was won by Bulgaria.

13. *Orebro 1966:* USSR 34, Czechoslovakia 28½, Denmark 27½, Yugoslavia 27½, Romania 23, Israel 21½, England 20, East Germany 19, Bulgaria 18½, Hungary 17½, The Netherlands 15, Finland 12. Final B was won by Sweden.

14. *Harrachov 1967:* USSR 24, USA 22, England 21, Czechoslovakia 19½, Romania 19½, East Germany 19½, Yugoslavia 15½, Bulgaria 15, Denmark 14, Sweden 10. This remains the best result to date of the English team. Final B was won by Hungary.

15. *Ybbs 1968:* USSR 24½, West Germany 24½, Czechoslovakia 20½, Bulgaria 18, USA 16, Denmark 15½, Iceland 15½, Yugoslavia 15½, Romania 15, East Germany 15. Final B was won by Israel and Final C by The Netherlands.

16. *Dresden 1969:* USSR 27, Yugoslavia 21½, Bulgaria 19½, West Germany 19½, East Germany 17½, England 17½, USA 17, Romania 16½, Denmark 12, Czechoslovakia 12. Final B was won by Israel, Final C by Scotland.

17. *Haifa 1970:* This was only half an event with the political situation responsible for a boycott by several nations. USA 27½, England 26½, West Germany 26, Israel 22½, Switzerland 21½, Iceland 21½, Sweden 19½, Austria 19, Scotland 16½, Finland 14½, Greece 5.

18. *Mayaguez 1971:* USSR 29½, USA 21½, Canada 21, Israel 20½, Iceland 14½, Brazil 11, Austria 11, Puerto Rico 9, Colombia 6. Final B was won by Peru.

19. *Graz 1972:* USSR 28½, Hungary 19½, West Germany 19½, USA 18, Bulgaria 17½, Israel 17½, Romania 17, Cuba 14½, Denmark 14, England 14. Final B was won by Yugoslavia, Final C by South Africa. A record 29 nations competed.

20. *Teesside 1974:* USSR 26½, USA 22½, Hungary 22, England 21½, Denmark 19, West Germany 16, Czechoslovakia 15, Finland 14½, The Netherlands 11½, Austria 11½. Final B was won by Cuba, Final C by France.

21. *Caracas 1976:* USSR 24½/28, USA 17, Cuba 15½, Switzerland 13½, Israel 12½, Poland 11½, Brazil 11, Venezuela 6½. Final B was won by Iran; Final C by Ecuador. *(W.R.H.)*

SUBANDHU

Author of the Sanskrit romance *Vāsavadattā*, which contains the first written reference to chess and provides evidence of the origin of chess in the sixth century AD. *(H.G.)*

SÜCHTING, Hugo *(8 October 1874–27 December 1916)*

A German player, Süchting was a strong natural player whose constant lack of practice – he was a farmer – prevented him from ever reaching a high place in international tournaments of the period between 1894 and 1911 (Leipzig 1894, Berlin 1897, Coburg 1904, Stockholm 1906, Ostend 1907, Vienna, Düsseldorf-Prague 1908, Carlsbad 1911). His best result was winning a small match against Leonhardt (+2−1=1). *(W.H.)*

SUETIN, Alexei Stepanovich *(b. 16 November 1926)*

Soviet grandmaster and chess writer. Awarded titles of international master in 1961 and grandmaster in 1965. Has frequently played in the USSR championship, his best result being shared fourth places in 1963 and 1965.

Alexei Suetin v. Bronstein 31st USSR Chess Championship, Leningrad 1963

Suetin has also had many successes in international events including first or shared first places at Sarajevo 1965, Copenhagen 1965, Titovo Uzice 1966, Hastings 1967/8, Havana 1969, Albena 1970, Kecskemet 1972 and Lublin 1976. He is the author of several books on the openings and other aspects of chess, including *Modern Chess Opening Theory*, 1962, and *A Contemporary Approach to the Middle-Game*, 1971, both of which have been translated into English. *(W.R.H.)*

SULTAN KHAN, Mir *(1905–25 May 1966)*
India's most famous player and the only Indian ever to become British champion, Sultan was born in Mittha (Punjab). His skill at the Indian variety of chess brought him to the attention of a local notable, Colonel Nawab Sir Umar Hayat Khan, who employed him as a servant and encouraged his chess-playing activities, teaching him the standard European game. In 1928, Sultan won the All-India championship, scoring 8½ points from 9 games.

Sultan spent most of the years 1929–33 in Britain on the staff of Sir Umar. His exceptional talent was quickly noticed by the English masters Winter and Yates and training sessions with these players helped to overcome his lack of theoretical knowledge and tournament experience. He scored a surprise victory in the 1929 British championship, and won this event again in 1932 and 1933. He had several successes in international tournaments, including 2nd to Tartakower at Liège 1930, 3rd after Euwe and Capablanca at Hastings 1930/1 (Sultan defeated Capablanca in their individual game), and =3rd behind Flohr and Pirc at Hastings 1932/3. In match-play he defeated Tartakower in 1931 (6½–5½) and lost to Flohr in 1932 (2½–3½). Sultan played twice on B.C.F. teams in Olympic events, Hamburg 1930 and Prague 1931, on the latter occasion scoring 11½/17 on top board. Sultan returned to India with his master Sir Umar in December 1933, and played little serious chess afterwards. He died in Sargodha, Pakistan.

Liège 1930
White: Soultanbeieff; *Black:* Sultan Khan
Queen's Indian Defence
1. P–Q4, N–KB3; 2. N–KB3, P–QN3; 3. P–B4, P–K3; 4. P–KN3, B–N2; 5. B–N2, B–N5+; 6. B–Q2, B×B+; 7. QN×B, O–O; 8. O–O, P–B4; 9. Q–B2, N–B3; 10. P×P, P×P; 11. P–K4, Q–B2; 12. KR–K1, P–Q3; 13. QR–B1, P–KR3; 14. P–QR3, N–Q2; 15. Q–B3, P–QR4; 16. N–R4, P–N4; 17. Q–K3, Q–Q1; 18. N(4)–B3, Q–K2; 19. P–R3, QR–N1; 20. P–N3, B–R1; 21. N–N1, N(2)–K4; 22. P–QR4, N×N+; 23. B×N, N–Q5; 24. B–Q1, P–B4; 25. P×P, R×BP; 26. R–B3, QR–KB1; 27. R–KB1, R–B6; 28. B×R, R×B; 29. resigns. *(R.D.K.)*

SUNNUCKS, Patricia Anne *(b. 21 February 1927)*
International Woman master and British Women's champion 1957, 1958, 1964. Her best international result was a 2nd in the 1954 Western European Zonal. This qualified her for the 1955 Women's Candidates tournament, but as this was held in the USSR and she was at the time serving as a major in the British Army, the authorities would not give her leave to participate.

Miss Sunnucks has represented England a number of times in Olympiads and team matches. She has compiled *The Encyclopaedia of Chess*, London 1970. *(H.G.)*

SURINAM
Surinam was expected to play in the 1976 Olympiad but the team failed to arrive; the chess world still awaits its entry to the arena. The body which will organize that entry is the Surinaamse Schaakbond, c/o W. N. Veer, P.O. Box 2010, Paramaribo. *(K.J.O'C.)*

SUTTLES, Duncan *(b. 21 December 1945)*
A Canadian grandmaster, Suttles was born in San Francisco and came to Vancouver in 1951. He won the Southern California and the Cincinnati Opens in 1964 and the Canadian championship in 1969. In 1972 he tied for 6th in San Antonio, ahead of Larsen, Browne and Evans. In 1973 Suttles tied for 1st in the US Open and became a grandmaster.

He has played in many European tournaments and on many Canadian Olympiad teams. Suttles's style is unusual and he specializes in irregular openings. His positions look awkward but his play is sound and he is remarkably good in finding ingenious defences in what seem to be hopeless positions. Suttles is studying mathematics and takes an active interest in stock-market analysis. *(N.D.)*

SVESHNIKOV, Evgeny *(b. 11 February 1956)*
Soviet international master (1975). =1st at Decin 1974, he has made great strides since gaining the title: =2nd USSR 'First League' championship 1976, 1st USSR 'Young Masters' championship 1976 and =1st Sochi 1976. *(K.J.O'C.)*

SWEDEN
The game has always been popular in Sweden and the country has played a much greater role in world chess than its small population would indicate. It has not produced a World Champion but at least four players who have been very nearly world class: Ståhlberg, Stoltz, Lundin and Ulf Andersson, all, except Lundin who deserved to have been recognized as such, FIDE grandmasters.

Sweden has been specially strong in matters of chess organization and its organizers have always been fully aware of their world responsibilities. The Collijn brothers who organized the Stockholm Olympiad in 1937 were also famous for their editing the *Lärobok* which contained many important opening analyses. Folke Rogard of Stockholm was for many years a most capable FIDE President.

This may explain why Sweden has held no less than four great Interzonal tournaments: Saltsjöbaden 1948, Stockholm-Saltsjöbaden 1952, Göteborg 1955 and Stockholm 1962.

Sweden has the proud record of competing in every FIDE Olympiad, no less than twenty-two times, with an average position of slightly over 12th. The details are:

1927 London, 11th/16; 1928 The Hague, 13th/17; 1930 Hamburg, 9th/18; 1931 Prague, 7th/19; 1933 Folkestone, 3rd/15; 1935 Warsaw, 2nd/20; 1937 Stockholm, 10th/19; 1939 Buenos Aires, 4th/26; 1950 Dubrovnik, 11th/16; 1952 Helsinki, 7th/25; 1954 Amsterdam, 11th/26; 1956 Moscow, 15th/34; 1958 Munich, 20th/36; 1960 Leipzig, 13th/40; 1962 Varna, 17th/37; 1964 Tel Aviv, 16th/50; 1966 Havana, 24th/52; 1968 Lugano, 24th/53; 1970 Siegen, 17th/60; 1972 Skopje, 15th/62; 1974 Nice, 13th/74; 1976 Haifa, 12th/48.

The Swedish Chess Federation, which was founded in 1917, receives a grant from the State both for its senior and its junior activities and in fact gets considerably more for the junior than the senior field. Its address is Sveriges Schackförbund, Hejdegatan 37B, S-58243 Linköping. Its official publication is the *Tidskrift för Schack.* *(H.G.)*

SWIDERSKI, Rudolf *(28 July 1878–12 August 1909)*
A German master of the period 1902–8, Swiderski was a frequent competitor in the great international events of those years. His best results were a share in first prize with Marshall at the Rice Gambit tournament, Monte Carlo 1904, and a share in first prize with Schlechter and Von Bardeleben at Coburg 1904. He was always dangerous to the best at their best, beating e.g. Schlechter and Von Bardeleben at Coburg, and Rubinstein and Teichmann at Ostend 1907.

His death came prematurely, by suicide, in 1909. *(W.H.)*

SWINDLE
An attempt at saving a lost position by means of a tactical surprise in the hope that the opponent will miss the danger (see also TRAP). One of the most frequent aims of a swindle is to bring about a stalemate or perpetual check, as in Walter v. Nagy, Raab 1924:

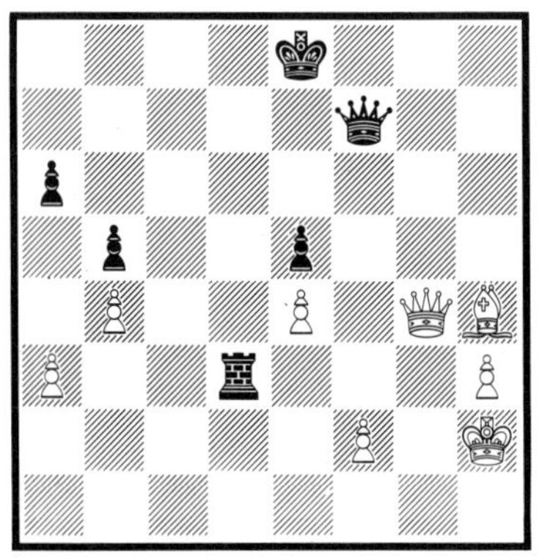

After 1. . , K–B1!, White snatched at 2. Q–B8+ ? (*2. Q–N5!* followed by *3. B–N3!* was correct) Q–K1; 3. Q × P ? and there followed 3. . , R × P+ !, 4. K × R, Q–K3+ !; 5. Q × Q stalemate. *(W.H.)*

SWISS SYSTEM
The Swiss System is a method of running tournaments that was devised over eighty years ago in Switzerland by Dr J. Muller of Brugg. First used in Zürich in 1895, it remained little used until after the Second World War when it rapidly developed into a most popular device for dealing with large numbers of competitors, especially in the USA and Britain as we show in our historical note later on.

The System can cope with virtually any number of players and any number of rounds for any activity in which there can at least be the three results: win, draw or loss. It has three basic rules:

1. No player may meet the same opponent twice.

2. In each round, players should have opponents on as closely similar scores as possible.

3. At the end of each round, players should each have had as close to an equal number of Whites and Blacks as possible.

The comparison with other pairing systems is that, as a tournament progresses, players with high scores meet each other as do players with low scores. The method then is somewhat similar to a knock-out tournament except that all competitors play through to the end of the event and players can recover from poor starts.

The system is also used for some bridge and draughts events, but there is no reason why, in principle, it could not be used for cricket or football. It would be unlikely to be successful for tennis as the absence of a draw would lead to considerable peculiarities and also, in the case of that type of game, the number of courts is extremely limited so that the organizers want people to be knocked out.

As games are drawn, a Swiss can actually cope with more players than a knock-out and still arrive at an outright winner. Assuming approximately 20% of the games are drawn, 128 players would reduce to one with 100% after five or at most six rounds whereas a knock-out would require seven. This player will almost certainly be a deserving winner rather than a lucky one but little credence can be given to the order of players immediately below him. Generally a Swiss tournament will be more accurate in its placements than a knock-out tourney and it becomes more accurate with a greater number of rounds. After all, theoretically all the best players could be in the same half of the draw for a knock-out so that the runner-up is not even in the top half of the players.

A disadvantage of a Swiss with a large number of rounds relative to the number of competitors is that the results of the early rounds are not as vital as those of the later rounds. If a player starts off well he must meet stronger opposition and it is relatively easy to catch up from behind. By contrast every round is vital for a knock-out tournament. The other advantage of the latter system is that it builds up to a grand finale whereas this is true neither of a Swiss nor an all-play-all.

No statistical work has been done on the accuracy of Swisses relative to all-play-all tournaments and this would in any case depend on the system used. There is little doubt that using an extremely sophisticated set of pairing rules it is possible to find the correct outright winner from an enormous field. To cite one example, there were 260 players in the 1975 National Bank of Dubai Open championship at the Evening Standard Congress. The Yugoslav grandmaster Bojan Kurajica won with 5½/6 and any analysis shows him to have been a well-deserved winner – he met the strongest opposition and achieved the best grading performance for the event.

Places after the first are much less clear. There were only 48 teams in the 1976 Olympiad at Haifa. This was a 13-round tournament and there is no doubt that team events are more accurate for Swisses than individual ones as the scores are counted by game points not match points. Thus a win by 4–0 is better than by 2½–1½. Even so it is unlikely that more than the first three places were pin-pointed with accuracy. The USA won by ½ a point over The Netherlands, and the fact that this half a point is in practice statistically meaningless just underlines the closeness in quality of result of the two teams.

Another disadvantage of the system is that it is impossible after the first round to determine one's opponent well in advance. This means that it is difficult to prepare against his openings. It is possible that this is one of the reasons why there is a lower percentage of draws in Swisses relative to all-play-alls.

To summarize in tabular form the pros and cons by which tournaments can be organized:

	Knock-out	*Swiss*	*All-play-all*
Number of players the system can cope with in n rounds	$2n$	Virtually unlimited	$n+1$
Accuracy	First place only	Certainly first place, others depend on number of rounds	All positions
Importance of each game	Each one vital	Later ones more valuable	All of equal weighting
Special points	Players may travel a long way only to lose in the first round. It builds up to a grand finale	Arguments arise over pairings. Administratively most complex	It is easier to 'fix' games well in advance. Players tend to rely on beating the weaker players and thus agree draws with their peers

Having accepted the three basic rules of the Swiss System as outlined at the beginning of this article, there are then a very large number of different ways in which they can be applied. There are three major Swiss System sets of pairing rules and endless offshoots of these. A committee was set up by FIDE in 1972 to consider them but came to no definite conclusion as the committee members differed about basic principles.

The Harkness Pairing System is the best known and most widely used. It was devised for use in the USA where most players have well established ratings and most tournaments are for large numbers of competitors and few rounds. It is based on a seeding system throughout, such that the top half of the ratings always plays the second half in rating order on each score group. Thus with 64 players, the Round 1 pairings are 1 *v.* 33, 34 *v.* 2, 3 *v.* 35, etc., or, alternatively, 33 *v.* 1, 2 *v.* 34, 35 *v.* 3 etc., the first named being White.

The British Lottery System is the simplest. Here players meet opponents chosen by lottery, having taken into account the three basic rules. It has the disadvantage that there is no certain way of determining the draw even when the results of the previous round are to hand. It is also impossible for a controller to refute arguments that a player is being treated unfairly.

The Circular System seems to use the complexities of the first system with none of its benefits. The players are given a pairing number by lottery. Then, on each score group, pairings are made, starting with the lowest numbers first playing the next lowest. For 64 players 1 *v.* 2, 3 *v.* 4, 5 *v.* 6 etc. in the first round. After three rounds 3 players, nos. 6, 10, 22 might have 100%. Then 6 *v.* 10 and 22 plays somebody with $2\frac{1}{2}/3$, numbered after 22. It is circular because if, for example, player 64 is seeking an opponent, one does not work backwards, but he seeks an opponent from 1 onwards.

The advantage of seeding systems such as the Harkness method are identical with those advantages of seeding a knock-out tournament. Since the best players are kept apart as much as possible, they are more likely to finish with the best scores. This is of greatest importance in short tournaments where there might not be time to iron out inequities.

We now come to the special method of pairing known as the accelerated Swiss or accelerated pairing rules. Perhaps tournaments using this system should not be called Swiss at all as they break the second basic principle in early rounds, i.e. that players should meet opponents with as closely similar scores as possible.

The method is that the players are placed in grading order and then paired top $\frac{1}{4}$ *v.* second $\frac{1}{4}$ and third $\frac{1}{4}$ *v.* fourth $\frac{1}{4}$. For 64 players 1 *v.* 17, 18 *v.* 2 etc. and 33 *v.* 49, 50 *v.* 34 etc. or the reverse for reverse colours. In the second round, the players from the top half who won are paired amongst themselves by standard seedings. The winners from the bottom half are paired in order against the highest graded players who did *not* win in the first round. This is repeated in the third round; players from the bottom original half of the tournament who have 2/2 and are paired with the stronger players in the fourth round if necessary.

The effect of this method is to bring players of similar strength together at an earlier stage of the tournament. Thus the system is more accurate and can cope with larger numbers of competitors than the ordinary seeded Swiss. Accelerated pairings should result in one player with 6/6 from 400 competitors. It also has the advantage that pairings between players of tremendously disparate strength can be avoided.

To date Swiss Systems have been more popular in the English speaking countries. The United States was the first country to use the system for its best purpose and there it flourishes to an extent perhaps to the disadvantage of the Americans as it has driven out other types of events. Weekend Swisses abound there, tournaments with large numbers of entries with perhaps one round Friday evening, three on Saturday and two on Sunday. This is admirably suited to the working man and the large sums taken in entry fees enable large prizes to be offered to few people. It is abundantly clear that the competitors prefer this to small prizes for large numbers of players.

These types of event were unknown in England until 1965 but since then the weekend calendar has become packed. The practice is beginning to spread to Scandinavia but has not yet achieved a footing in the rest of Europe.

Swisses of perhaps 11 rounds taking up to two weeks are also common throughout Europe and America. The most prestigious of these to date was unquestionably the Lone Pine tournament in California in April, 1975. No fewer than 22 grandmasters competed in this 10-round event which was restricted to players rated above 2350. Annual tournaments of importance that are conducted on the Swiss System include the United States Open championship, British championship, Hastings Challengers, Rilton Cup in Stockholm and Biel in Switzerland.

The 1976 Olympiad (FIDE) at Haifa was conducted on the Swiss System and a favourable report of the progress of this event was made to the FIDE Congress that year.

Eastern European organizers still seem to view Swisses with suspicion even though there seems to be little reluctance on the part of their players to participate abroad. The Soviet Union is particularly against the idea which is rather strange considering that Swisses are more for the ordinary man. There was one Soviet championship run as a Swiss in celebration of the founding of the USSR but such events have been few and far between since then.

Whether we can expect Swiss System tournaments to grow in numbers and stature in the future is doubtful. It is difficult to organize Swisses that enable players to achieve international titles and this is one of the main reasons why countries run tournaments. Shorter events no doubt will grow more widespread in imitation of those that already exist. We must hope that they do not drive out the international all-play-all tournaments. *(S.R.)*

SWITZERLAND

Despite its comparative smallness in size, Switzerland has played a most important part in world chess. There is a great enthusiasm for the game in the country and the Swiss Chess Federation, which was founded as long ago as 1889, was one of the founding members of FIDE and provided and still provides many enthusiastic helpers in the cause of international chess.

Its team competed in the first Olympiad at London 1927 and has regularly competed ever since. The number of great international tournaments that Switzerland has organized is extraordinary – Berne 1932, Zürich 1934 and the great Candidates tournament at Neuhausen-Zürich 1953 are only a few outstanding instances.

There are no Swiss grandmasters but quite a number of masters of solid worth and in particular the former Junior World Champion, Werner Hug.

The name and address of the Federation is Federation Suisse d'Echecs, c/o A. von Känel, Sonnenblickstrasse 23, CH-8404 Winterthut, and the magazine is *Schweizerische Schachzeitung* c/o Alex Crisovan, Postfach 1342, Pfäffikum-8330. *(H.G.)*

SYRIA

Syria has taken part in three Olympiads: 51st in 1968, 55th in 1972 and 48th in 1974. The eighteenth century figure, Philip Stamma of Aleppo, is still the greatest product of Syrian chess.

The address of the Syrian Arab Chess Federation is: P.O. Box 421, Damascus. *(K.J.O'C.)*

SZABO, Laszlo *(b. 19 March 1917)*

Hungarian grandmaster and one of the great Hungarian players worthy to rank in the long line of Hungarian immortals ranging from Szén, Charousek, Maróczy to Portisch in our time.

Szabo first came into prominence when, as a youth of eighteen, he played on 4th board for Hungary in the Warsaw Olympiad of 1935 and achieved the respectable score of 64.3%. What was impressive about his play at Warsaw was not so much the results as the fresh, sparkling attacking style in which these results were achieved. This attacking style, so characteristic of the Hungarian school of chess, was to be his chief contribution to the international field for the next thirty years.

In 1935 he won an international tournament at Tatatovaros and also the Hungarian championship. In all he has won the title nine times, from 1935 to 1967. He has represented Hungary in eleven Olympiads, in 1935, 1937, 1952, 1954, 1956, 1958, 1960, 1962, 1964, 1966 and 1968, almost always on top board and with success till the 1960s when he played second to Portisch and when his results deteriorated. In the 1968 event at Lugano he had a disastrous tournament and scored only 35% after which he has not been selected to play for the team in the Olympiad.

To return to his earlier chess career: in 1937 he came =2nd in the Open championship of Yugoslavia and at Hastings 1938/9 he was first.

But it was in the post-Second World War period that he came into his own as one of the world's leading players. In the great tournament at Groningen 1946 he was =4th with Najdorf and in the following year he was 1st at Vienna and 1st at Hastings 1947/8.

Now we enter upon what was perhaps his most successful period as a player. First at Budapest 1948, in that year he also came 2nd in the great Interzonal tournament at Saltsjöbaden. He was 1st in Venice 1949 and =2nd with Pachman at Trenčianské Teplice that year. A 1st at Hastings 1949/50 was followed by his participation in the Candidates Tournament at Budapest 1950 where he had a failure, coming at the bottom of the table, =8th with Flohr and Lilienthal.

In this decade he made repeated attempts to break through the barriers on the approach to the World Championship. But though he did well, extremely so in the opening stages, and showed true grandmaster strength, he never quite got to the top.

Second in the Mariánské Lázně Zonal of 1951, he was =5th with Averbakh, Gligorić and Ståhlberg at the Interzonal at Stockholm-Saltsjöbaden 1952. At the Candidates tournament at Neuhausen-Zürich 1953 he was 12th/15.

His course in the next cycle was his best. He was 2nd again in the Mariánské Lázně Zonal of 1954, =5th with Geller at the Göteborg Interzonal the following year. At the Amsterdam Candidates of 1956 he was =3rd with Bronstein, Geller, Petrosian and Spassky.

But this was the last time he got as far as the Candidates. First at the Wageningen Zonal of 1957, he narrowly missed qualifying for the Candidates by coming =7th with Averbakh, Bronstein, Matanović and Pachman at Portorož in 1958. After that he has failed to qualify for the Interzonal.

He has had many excellent individual performances in tournaments since then, though not so good as in the late 1940s and early 1950s: 2nds at Mariánské Lázně and Vienna 1959, 3rd at Buenos Aires 1960 and =1st at Santa Fé and Asuncion that year; =3rd Hastings 1960/1; =1st Torremolinos 1962 and =2nd at both Mar del Plata and Kecskemet that year; 1st Zagreb 1964; =1st Budapest 1965; 2nd Beverwijk 1966; 2nd Budapest 1970; =1st with Tal, Timman and Kuzmin, Hastings 1973/4; =1st Dortmund 1974; =2nd with Böhm, Makarichev and Smejkal at the I.B.M. tournament at Amsterdam; =1st with S. Garcia, Vaganian and Čirić at the 3rd Costa Brava tournament at San Feliu de Guixols 1975 and 1st at Kapfenberg 1976. *(H.G.)*

SZÉN, Joseph *(circa 1800–13 January 1857)*
Hungarian master particularly noted for his endgame play and given the nickname of the Hungarian Philidor. In 1836 he visited Paris and there played a match against La Bourdonnais who gave him odds of pawn and move. This match he narrowly won by +13−12=0.

In Berlin in 1839 he narrowly lost a match to Mayet who beat him by +3−2=1.

He was head of a correspondence team of Pesth that played a match with Paris in the years 1842–6.

He was beaten by Anderssen in the second round of London 1851, but only after it had been agreed that the winner of the match should, if he eventually won first prize, give one third of his winnings to the loser. He ended up by winning fifth prize in the event.

In 1853 he played a small match against Harrwitz in London but was beaten by +1−3=1. *(H.G.)*

SZILÁGYI, György *(b. 4 July 1921)*
Hungarian player awarded international master title in 1956. Played in the Moscow 1956 Olympiad. *(W.R.H.)*

SZILY, Dr József *(2 October 1913–26 April 1976)*
Member of the Hungarian team in the 1952 Olympiad International master (1950). *(W.R.H.)*

T

TAIMANOV, Mark Yevgenyevich *(b. 7 February 1926)*
Born in Kharkov, Taimanov is one of the few contemporary grandmasters who has also made a successful career in another field: he is also a noted concert pianist, having studied music at the Leningrad Conservatoire.

His first international tournament at Sczawno Zdroj in Poland in 1950 qualified Taimanov for the international master title when he finished by sharing second place. His 6th in the 1951 USSR championship qualified him to compete in the following year's Interzonal tournament where he came second behind Kotov, to qualify for the Candidates and for the title of grandmaster. In the Candidates tournament Taimanov shared eighth place with Kotov.

In 1956 Taimanov shared first place with Averbakh and Spassky in the USSR championship. The subsequent play-off was resolved in favour of Taimanov to give him the title of USSR champion. His other successes include first places in the following international tournaments: Dresden 1959, Leningrad 1960, Rostov 1961, Dortmund 1961, Mariánské Lázně 1962, Reykjavik 1968, Zalaegerszeg 1969, Wijk-aan-Zee 1970, Skopje 1970, Bucharest 1973, Albena 1974 and Decin 1975.

In 1970 he again qualified for the Candidates by sharing fifth place in the Interzonal, but lost disastrously 6–0 to Fischer in the quarter finals.

Taimanov is noted also for his many theoretical contributions, and has written an excellent book on the Nimzo-Indian Defence, the latest version being *Nimzowitsch-Indisch bis Katatanisch*, Berlin 1972. *(W.R.H.)*

TAKÁCS, Sándor *(10 February 1893–22 April 1932)*
A Hungarian master. =1st Hastings 1928/9, =4th 1929/30. Defeated Rubinstein in a famous game at Rogaska Slatina 1929. *(R.D.K.)*

TAL, Mikhail Nekhemyevich *(b. 9 November 1936)*
World Champion 1960–1. Perhaps the greatest attacking genius of modern chess, Tal was born in Riga. His early chess results were not those of an outstanding prodigy, though he was early noticed as one of the strongest juniors in the Soviet Union. At the age of seventeen, Tal won a match against Saigin by a score of 8–6, to gain the title of Soviet master.

His first appearance in the Soviet championship was early in 1956, and saw him sharing fifth place. His style at this time was generally extremely sharp, full of sacrifices and speculative play, and much admired by his fans. Many critics, however, thought that he lacked the necessary stability to proceed much further. They did not have long to wait before Tal proved them wrong.

In January 1957 Tal became the youngest-ever Soviet champion, winning the 24th USSR championship ahead of eight grandmasters. Thereafter nothing seemed able to stop the young Latvian's progress. The same year, he was awarded the title of international grandmaster (with FIDE having to waive their rule that this title was only given to players already holding the master

Tal in play, Moscow 1971

insignia). In 1958 Tal retained the USSR championship thereby qualifying for the Interzonal tournament to be held that year in Portorož. This resulted in another convincing victory for Tal, and by far his most important yet, establishing him as one of the favourites for the following Candidates tournament. Despite a slow start in that event, Tal once again emerged victorious to earn the right to a match with Botvinnik for the World title. This took place in 1960, and saw Tal capture the honours by the convincing score of 12½–8½.

1st Match Game 1960
White: Tal; *Black:* Botvinnik
French Defence
1. P–K4, P–K3; 2. P–Q4, P–Q4; 3. N–QB3, B–N5; 4. P–K5, P–QB4; 5. P–QR3, B×N+; 6. P×B, Q–B2; 7. Q–N4, P–B4; 8. Q–N3, N–K2; 9. Q×P, R–N1; 10. Q×P, P×P; 11. K–Q1, B–Q2; 12. Q–R5+, N–N3; 13. N–K2, P–Q6; 14. P×P, B–R5+; 15. K–K1, Q×KP; 16. B–N5, N–B3; 17. P–Q4, Q–B2; 18. P–R4, P–K4; 19. R–R3, Q–B2; 20. P×P, QN×P; 21. R–K3, K–Q2; 22. R–N1, P–N3; 23. N–B4, QR–K1; 24. R–N4, B–B3; 25. Q–Q1, N×N; 26. QR×N, N–N3; 27. R–Q4, R×R+; 28. P×R, K–B2;

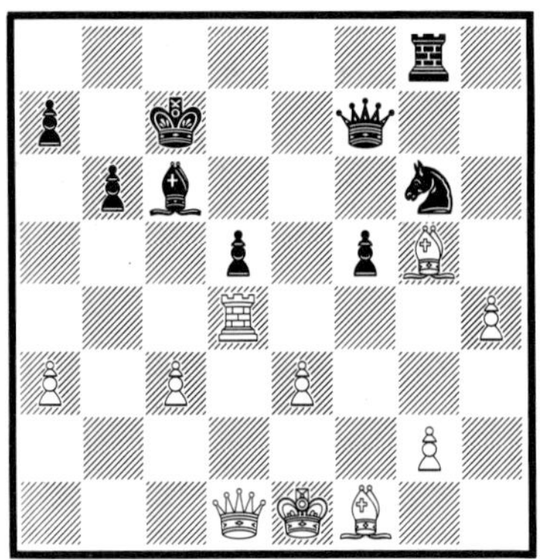

29. P–B4, P×P; 30. B×P, Q–N2; 31. B×R, Q×B; 32. P–R5, resigns.

The following year, handicapped by ill-health, Tal lost the return match by a score of 13–8. Since then, his results have only rarely approached the heights of those early years when he was the youngest World Champion in the history of the game.

In recent times, his physical condition has apparently improved and allowed Tal to play more and better chess once again. In 1972 he began an uninterrupted programme of tournament success, including first prizes at Sukhumi and Wijk-aan-Zee, another first in the Soviet championship, a board prize in the Olympiad and altogether a run of over eighty games without defeat. This run could not continue and was brought to an end with poor results in the Leningrad Interzonal of 1973 and the Soviet championship of the same year. After these setbacks Tal resumed his winning ways at Sochi 1973 and remains one of the most feared opponents for all.

His dashing style has brought him too many first prizes to list here, but apart from those mentioned above these include: Latvian championship 1954, Zürich 1959, Bled 1961, Hastings 1962/3, Reykjavik 1964, Tbilisi 1969/70, Tallinn 1971 and a shared first place in the Amsterdam Interzonal of 1964.

He has a distinguished record in the Olympiads: 1958 Bd. 5, 90%; 1960 Bd. 1, 73.3%; 1962 Bd. 6, 76.9%; 1966 Bd. 3, 92.3%; 1972 Bd. 4, 87.5%; 1974 Bd. 5, 75%. *(W.R.H.)*

TAN, Lian Ann *(b. 8 September 1947)*
Singapore international master (1973). Six times national champion (1959, 1962, 1964, 1965, 1967 and 1969), Lian Ann learned chess from his brothers Lian Quee and Lian Seng (Singapore champion in 1961, 1963 and 1966). His most curious achievement, and one of his best, was his second place in the 1961/2 Australian championship. He placed =4th in the 1963 World Junior Championship. His other performances of note have been at the Hong Kong Zonal 1972 (=2nd) and the Melbourne Zonal 1975 (2nd), each time qualifying for the Interzonals. He played for Singapore in the Olympiads of 1968, 1970 and 1972. *(K.J.O'C.)*

TARJAN, James Edward *(b. 22 February 1952)*
US grandmaster and professional chess-player, Tarjan's first success was in winning the California Junior championship in 1966 at the age of fourteen.

He soon became known as a fighting player with a fearlessly aggressive yet workmanlike style, and his progress towards grandmastery was speedy. Playing for the USA on Bd. 6 in the 1974 Nice Olympiad he had the magnificent score of +9—0=4.

At Subotica (Yugoslavia) in 1975 he came first with 8 points out of 11, thereby achieving the first leg of the grandmaster title. He fulfilled the second leg of the grandmaster norm in the following year, at Skopje again in Yugoslavia when he came =4th with Kurajica with 9 points out of 15.

Further excellent results came in 1976, a 1st in the Keres Memorial tournament at Vancouver being followed by a 2nd to Panno in an international tournament at Quito in Ecuador. *(A.S. & H.G.)*

TARRASCH, Siegbert *(5 March 1862–17 February 1934)*

A great German master, Dr Tarrasch was one of the most successful tournament players of all time. He became famous when in a period of seven years he won five important tournaments (Nuremberg 1888, Breslau 1889, Manchester 1890, Dresden 1892, Leipzig 1894). This was followed by two good but, to him, disappointing results: 4th place behind Pillsbury, Chigorin and Lasker at the famous tournament of Hastings 1895; and =3rd with Pillsbury, behind Lasker and Maróczy, in his home town of Nuremberg 1896; with a mediocre result (50%) at Budapest 1896 following.

He retrieved his reputation with the biggest success of his career, first prize in the Emperor Franz Josef Jubilee tournament at Vienna 1898, a colossal double-round event of twenty masters, in which he tied with his old rival, Pillsbury, in the tournament proper and beat him in the play-off. Thereafter, though his international career spanned another thirty years, he scored only two more significant tournament successes: at Monte Carlo 1903 and in the 'Champions tournament' at Ostend 1907 (which was organized in order to establish a 'tournament world champion' – an empty title). In none of his later appearances in international tournaments – and there were over twenty of them – did Tarrasch succeed in capturing one of the first three places.

In match-play he beat Taubenhaus (1891), Walbrodt (1894), Marshall (1905) and Mieses (1916) by tremendous margins, winning twenty-eight and losing only four of the forty-six games played in all these matches; he drew against Chigorin (1893) and Schlechter (1911), but was decisively beaten by Lasker in their World Championship match (1908). In retrospect, it seems clear that Tarrasch was incapable of risking the laurels he had previously gathered, in one throw: at the height of his early triumphs he was offered a World title match with Steinitz in Havana but declined, and he backed out from a virtually agreed title match against Lasker in 1904 – when he finally agreed to meet the latter, he was in his forty-seventh year and apparently past his best.

Tarrasch's undying fame, however, rests on his writing rather than sporting achievements. With his books *Driehundert Schachpartien* (Leipzig, 1895) and *Die Moderne Schachpartie* (Leipzig, 1912) as well as his innumerable chess-columns and articles, he became the celebrated *Praeceptor Germaniae*, and, with it, of the world. Accepting, developing and popularizing Steinitz's theory of the accumulation of small advantages, he yet differed in his interpretation of what constitutes such small advantages. He prized the concept of mobility above all – it has been suggested that he attached exaggerated importance to mobility on the chessboard because in life his own mobility was gravely restricted by a club-foot. As the result of this approach he was the great advocate of 'freeing' moves, especially in the opening, of which the defence to the Queen's Gambit which bears his name is a typical example.

The rigid dogmatism of his writings may be somewhat repellent today (what, for example, is one to think of the faithful placing of a question mark each time the perfectly normal move, 3. . , N–KB3 occurs in what he christened the Orthodox Defence to the Queen's Gambit as a term of half-jocular opprobrium ?); but it was exactly this dogmatism which made Tarrasch's teachings so effective at a time when amateurs still had to learn that a game of chess should not be a haphazard conglomeration of unrelated ideas but a logical whole.

Tarrasch's games are an essential part of his teachings and exemplify his ideas to perfection. Witness his last-round win in his greatest tournament, when he had to win in order to tie Pillsbury's score. Greater mobility, gradual encroachment and a surprising denouement are all equally characteristic of his conduct of a game of chess.

Vienna 1898
White: Tarrasch; *Black:* Walbrodt
Queen's Gambit Declined
1. P–Q4, P–Q4; 2. P–QB4, P–K3; 3. N–QB3, N–KB3; 4. N–B3, B–K2; 5. B–B4, P–B3; 6. P–K3, QN–Q2; 7. P–KR3, N–B1; 8. P–B5, N–N3; 9. B–R2, Q–R4; 10. P–R3, N–K5; 11. B–Q3, N×N; 12. Q–Q2, N–KR5; 13. N×N, B×N; 14. P–QN4, Q–Q1; 15. Q×N, O–O; 16. O–O, Q–Q2; 17. Q–B2, P–B4; 18. K–R1, B–Q1; 19. B–K5, B–B2; 20. P–B4, B×B; 21. BP×B, Q–K2; 22. P–N4, P–KN3; 23. R–B4, B–Q2; 24. R–KN1, K–R1; 25. Q–KN2, P–QR4; 26. B–N1, RP×P; 27. RP×P, R–R5; 28. P×P, KP×P; 29. Q–Q2, R–KN1; 30. Q–K1, B–K3; 31. P–R4, QR–R1; 32. R(4)–B1, R–N2; 33. R–N2, QR–KN1; 34. R–KR2, Q–Q2; 35. B–Q3, R–R1; 36. Q–N3, Q–K2; 37. R–KN1, QR–KN1; 38. R(2)–KN2, R–KB1; 39. Q–B4, QR–KN1; 40. Q–R6, B–Q2; 41. K–R2!, B–K3; 42. R–N5!, B–Q2;

43. K–N3!, B–K1; 44. K–B4!, B–Q2; 45. P–R5, B–K1; 46. P×P, B×P; 47. B–K2, Q–Q1; 48. B–R5, B×B; 49. Q×B, R×R; 50. R×R, R×R; 51. Q×R, Q–KB1; 52. P–K6, resigns. *(W.H.)*

TARTAKOWER, Savielly [Xavier] Grigorievich
(9 February 1887–5 February 1956)

French grandmaster and the wittiest writer on the game of chess. Though he was born in Rostov-on-Don in Russia and lived all his later life in Paris, it is as a leading exponent of the Viennese school of chess that he is classified in chess histories.

Paradox was meat and drink to him and indeed his whole life was a paradox. His parents were Austro-Polish and Jewish, but he himself was a Roman Catholic. However, when the Nazis rose to power he solemnly allied himself with the Jewish cause and fought against the Nazis in the Second World War, whilst having fought for the Austro-Hungarian cause in the First World War. He played for Poland in six Olympiads from 1930 to 1939 but could not speak Polish.

Early on he left Russia for Geneva where he matriculated at the Collège in 1904. From there he went to Vienna, became a Doctor in Law at Vienna University and used that great chess city as the base for his early playing career.

Tartakower became recognized as a master player when he won the *Hauptturnier* (Major Tournament) of the Nuremberg Congress in 1906 and from then on till the outbreak of the war he competed in many tournaments with success: =3rd Vienna 1907, =11th St Petersburg 1909, 2nd Munich 1909, 2nd Vienna 1909/10, =8th Carlsbad 1911, 2nd Vienna 1913, 2nd Budapest 1913 and 2nd Baden-bei-Wien 1914.

Decorated for valour in the field during the First World War, he resumed intensive tournament and match play in 1920 during which year he came =1st at Vienna, =4th at Göteborg and =2nd at Berlin. He was 2nd at Vienna 1922 and =3rd at Teplitz-Schönau 1922. A 1st at Vienna 1923 was followed by an 8th at the great New York tournament of 1924.

By now he was resident in Paris and he remained in France for the rest of his life (excepting for some of the Second World War years when he fought in exile in the Free French Army), eventually becoming a naturalized French citizen and playing for France in the 1950 Olympiad at Dubrovnik.

From 1924 onwards he was most heavily engaged in tournament play and one can only pick out the highlights: =2nd Debrecen 1925 and =5th Moscow 1925; =1st Bartfeld 1926 and 1st Ghent 1926; 1st Hastings 1926/7; 2nd Lodz 1927; =1st Niendorf 1927; =1st London 1927; 1st Hastings 1927/8; 2nd Barcelona 1929; 1st Nice 1930; 1st Liège 1930; 1st Warsaw 1935; 1st Lodz 1935; 2nd Lodz 1938.

The break in play during the Second World War did not at first seem to affect his form when international chess was resumed. He was 1st at Hastings 1945/6, 1st at Venice 1947, =4th at Budapest 1948 and 1st at Beverwijk 1949.

But now a decline did set in and his results became rapidly worse. Always a gambler, he found himself harder and harder pressed to make sufficient money to cover his losses at the gaming table and this, together with incessant writing work, destroyed any real chance he may have had of maintaining his former grandmaster results. When he died in Paris in 1956 his circumstances, though not exactly poverty-stricken, were in the nature of hand-to-mouth.

As a player Tartakower was both various and variable. A grandmaster of enormous gifts, he dissipated many of them through a recklessly gay passion for experiment and for the bizarre. Had he been content to be less various he could have been World Champion. As it was, he was undoubtedly the equal of a World Champion at many points of his career.

Tartakower will also go down in chess history as a great chess writer. His witty epigrams became proverbial: 'The mistakes are all there, just waiting to be made'; 'Only a strong player knows how weakly he plays'; 'The player who wins is the one who makes the mistake before the last', etc. All have the ring of bitter truth.

He was also the master of the witty phrase, referring for instance to the Ruy Lopez as 'the Spanish Torture'.

His best books (*Die Hypermoderne Schachpartie*, Vienna 1925; *Am Baum der Schacherkenntnis*, Vienna 1921; *Das neuromantische Schach*, Berlin 1927; and *Das entfesselte Schach*, Kecskemet 1926) have not been translated; but he also wrote, among other things, excellent collections of his own games: *My Best Games of Chess 1905–1930*, London 1953; and *My Best Games of Chess 1931–1954*, London 1956.

Characteristic of the keen liveliness of Tartakower's style is the following game from a tournament at Vienna in 1919.

White: Maróczy; *Black:* Tartakower
Scotch Game
1. P–K4, P–K4; 2. N–KB3, N–QB3; 3. P–Q4, P×P; 4. N×P, N–B3; 5. N×N, NP×N; 6. N–Q2, B–B4; 7. B–Q3, O–O; 8. O–O, P–Q4; 9. Q–B3, N–N5; 10. P–KR3, N–K4; 11. Q–K2, R–K1; 12. P×P, P×P; 13. N–N3, B–Q3; 14. P–KB4, N×B; 15. Q×N, P–QR4; 16. Q×P, B–R3; 17. P–B4, P–R5; 18. N–B5,

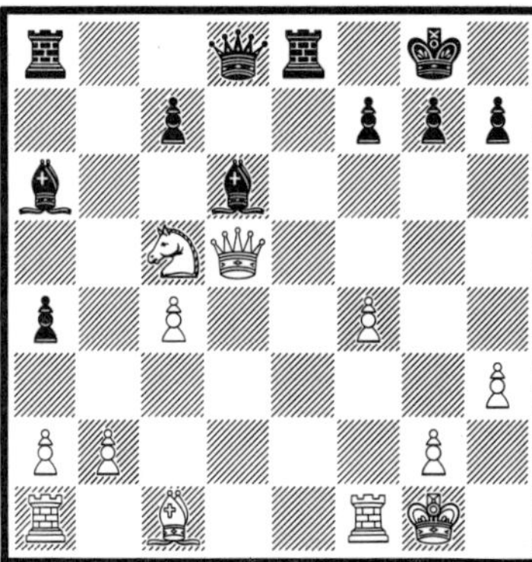

18.., P–B3; 19. Q×P, R–QB1; 20. Q×QB, B×N+; 21. K–R2, Q–Q6; 22. R–B3, Q–Q8; 23. Q–R5, R–B3; 24. Q–Q2, Q–N8+; 25. resigns. *(H.G.)*

TATAI, Stefano *(b. 23 March 1938)*
Italian international master who was born in Rome of Hungarian parentage. At an early age he returned to Hungary and there learnt to play chess at the age of seven. On the Soviet invasion of Hungary in 1956 he left that country again for Italy where he became a naturalized Italian citizen.

He first won the Italian championship in 1962 and has since then repeatedly won the title, establishing himself as Italy's leading player till the rise of Mariotti in the 1970s.

His principal international tournament successes are: =3rd Reggio Emilia 1965/6; =3rd Venice 1966 (when he became an international master); 2nd Imperia 1967; =3rd Malaga 1967; 1st Master Group B at the I.B.M. Congress Amsterdam 1968; =3rd Olot 1968; =2nd at the very strong Venice tournament 1969; =1st Monte Carlo tournament 1969; =3rd Malaga 1970; 4th Olot 1970; 3rd Arrecife de Lanzarote 1975; =1st Master Group I.B.M. Amsterdam 1976.

Starting off with Havana 1966 where he scored 61.8% on top board, he has regularly represented Italy at the Olympiads. His other Olympic performances were: 1970 Siegen, 47.1% on top board; 1972 Skopje, 61.1% on top board; 1974 Nice, 72.2% on 2nd board; and 1976 Haifa, 50% on top board.

A player of good master strength with a sharp style and a good eye for a combination. *(H.G.)*

TEICHMANN, Richard *(24 December 1868–15 June 1925)*

Born at Lehnitzsch, Teichmann was one of the foremost German masters of the early twentieth century. Third at Leipzig 1894, =7th at Hastings 1895, and failing completely at Nuremberg 1896 and Berlin 1897, he came into his own in the new century, when he won small events at London 1900, Berlin 1907, Munich 1909, Berlin 1910 and finally the gigantic Carlsbad 1911 tournament. In the big events of the period he finished 5th or joint 5th on no fewer than eight occasions (Monte Carlo 1903, Vienna 1903, Ostend 1905, Ostend 1906, Vienna 1907, Vienna 1908, Prague 1908 and Hamburg 1910) – a series which earned him the nickname of Richard V. Other good placings were his results at Monte Carlo 1902 (4th), Ostend 1907 and St Petersburg 1909 (6th), and Breslau 1912 (3rd). He won matches against Mieses (twice), Spielmann, Von Bardeleben (twice), Napier and Sämisch and drew a short match with Alekhine (1921); he lost others to Von Bardeleben, Rubinstein and Marshall. Teichmann was a fine analyst, a brilliant problemist, but rather a dull writer. *(W.H.)*

TEPLITZ-SCHÖNAU [Teplice Sanov] 1922

This tournament (September–October 1922) was a closely-knit event of fourteen players without the absolute top-notchers of that period. As a result it provided a thrilling struggle with the lead changing several times between Tartakower, Spielmann and Réti; four of the five leaders still had a chance for outright victory with one round to go. Leading scores: Réti, Spielmann 9, Grünfeld Tartakower 8½, Rubinstein 8. The tournament was distinguished by two features of permanent value: the most ambitious tournament book ever published which, in addition to round-by-round descriptions and copious notes by Grünfeld and Becker, features a variety of articles on problem chess by such great problemists as Dr Birgfeld, Palatz, Sackmann, Dr Neukomm and others, as well as endgame and opening articles and a survey of the results of all leading masters; and secondly, one of the greatest sacrificial games ever played.

White: Maróczy; *Black:* Tartakower
Dutch Defence
1. P–Q4, P–K3; 2. P–QB4, P–KB4; 3. N–QB3, N–KB3; 4. P–QR3, B–K2; 5. P–K3, O–O; 6. B–Q3, P–Q4; 7. N–B3, P–B3; 8. O–O, N–K5; 9. Q–B2, B–Q3; 10. P–QN3, N–Q2; 11. B–N2, R–B3; 12. KR–K1, R–R3; 13. P–N3, Q–B3; 14. B–KB1, P–KN4; 15. QR–Q1, P–N5; 16. N × N, BP × N; 17. N–Q2,

17. ., R × P; 18. K × R, Q × P+; 19. K–R1, N–B3; 20. R–K2, Q × NP; 21. N–N1, N–R4; 22. Q–Q2, B–Q2; 23. R–B2, Q–R5+; 24. K–N1, B–N6; 25. B–B3, B × R+; 26. Q × B, P–N6; 27. Q–KN2, R–KB1; 28. B–K1, R × B+; 29. K × R, P–K4; 30. K–N1, B–N5; 31. B × P, N × B; 32. R–K1, N–B4; 33. Q–KB2, Q–N4; 34. QP × P, B–B6+; 35. K–B1, N–N6+; 36. resigns. *(W.H.)*

TESCHNER, Rudolf *(b. 16 February 1922)*

A German international master, Teschner has represented West Germany in the Olympic team tournaments of 1952 and 1956 and qualified for the Stockholm Interzonal 1962 in the Zonal tournament at Berg-en-Dal 1961 (=2nd). In 1951 he won the German championship. Good international results were his =4th at Travemünde 1951, =4th at Hamburg 1955, =5th at Riga 1959, =1st at Reggio Emilia in 1963/4 and 1964/5, and =4th at Bamberg 1968.

Teschner has been editor of the *Deutsche Schachzeitung* for many years and is co-author with K. Richter of an opening guide, *Der Kleine Bilguer* (Berlin 1953). *(W.H.)*

THAILAND

30th place in the 1976 Olympiad was a fine achievement for the Thai newcomers to the international scene. The Thailand Chess Federation is at GPO Box 869, Bangkok. *(K.J.O'C.)*

THOMAS, Sir George Alan *(14 June 1881–23 July 1972)*

British international master, born in Constantinople. His mother was one of the strongest English women players, winner of the first Ladies tournament at Hastings 1895. Thomas was an all-round athlete who excelled at tennis, hockey and badminton as well as chess. He captained the English badminton team and was All-England Badminton Singles champion from 1920 to 1923.

Thomas won the British chess championship twice, in 1923 and 1934, and represented England in the Olympiads of 1927 where he tied with Norman Hansen for the best score – 80% on board 3, 1930, 1931, 1933, 1935, 1937, and 1939. In international tournaments his greatest successes were 1st at Spa 1926 (ahead of Tartakower) and =1st at Hastings 1934/5 (tied with Euwe and Flohr, ahead of Capablanca and Botvinnik).

Sir George Thomas in play, London 1932

He was known for his keen sense of sportsmanship and for his ability to encourage and inspire younger players. He served for many years on the B.C.F. Junior selection committee and was for a time games editor of the *British Chess Magazine*. FIDE awarded him the titles of international master (1950) and International Judge (1952). *(R.D.K.)*

THREE KNIGHTS GAME

This is the generic term for variations arising after 1. P–K4, P–K4; 2. N–KB3, N–QB3; 3. N–B3, if Black avoids the move 3. . , N–B3 leading to the Four Knights. The most common lines of the Three Knights are 3. . , P–KN3 and 3. . , B–N5. Also in this category comes the Vienna Three Knights arising from the Vienna Game or Petroff's Defence, after the moves 1. P–K4, P–K4; 2. N–QB3, N–KB3; 3. N–B3, B–N5. *(W.R.H.)*

TIE-BREAKING SYSTEMS

The best method of breaking a tie is to have a play-off between the two or among the three or more who have tied.

If there is no time for such a procedure then the Sonneborn-Berger System can be used. It has the advantage of being equally applicable to all-play-all tournaments and to Swiss System tournaments.

If the Sonneborn-Berger System produces no result then one can give preference to the player who has won the most games. If that fails then the individual result between the players may be used, and in the last resort if a player draws with the Black pieces he may be adjusted to have won the higher place.

There are also a number of special tie-breaking systems that apply to the Swiss System tournament. One is the Buchholtz System (the sum of the opponent's scores) and another is the best early score method. Naturally this favours the player who has started off well. The player whose results proceed 1, 2, 3, 3½, 4½, 5 has done better than the player whose score runs 0, 1, 2, 3, 4, 5. *(H.G.)*

TIETZ SYSTEM

A system of allocating prize money more fairly was devised and advocated by Victor Tietz of Carlsbad in the early 1900s.

Basically the aim was twofold: to encourage the winning of games, and to have a fairer spread of the prize money throughout the competitors so that the main part of the prize fund should not necessarily be allocated to, say, the top three prizes.

The Tietz System was put into operation at the Ostend Tournament of 1906 and, in a letter to the *British Chess Magazine* of October 1906, H. Holmes of Liverpool, a competitor in the Amateur Section at Ostend, described how it works.

'The prize fund is divided into two portions, one portion reserved exclusively for the prize-winners – i.e. those who have scored more than half the number of games played; the other shared by the whole of the competitors, in proportion to the number of points scored. The respective values of these portions are obtained thus: the maximum number of points above the average which might have been scored by the prize group is determined.'

Holmes then takes as an illustration the twelve player tournament for the British championship which took place at Shrewsbury in 1906. There the total prize fund was £120, a sum which, incidentally, the winner of the tournament and other competitors deemed far too large.

Place	*Player*	*Score*	*Receives*	*Score above average*	*Receives*	*Total*
1.	Atkins	8½	£5 3 0	3	£20 0 0	£25 3 0
2.	Michell	7½	4 10 11	2	13 6 8	17 17 7
3.	Lee	7	4 4 10	1½	10 0 0	14 4 10
4.	Palmer	7	4 4 10	1½	10 0 0	14 4 10
5.	Shoosmith	7	4 4 10	1½	10 0 0	14 4 10
6.	Wainwright	7	4 4 10	1½	10 0 0	14 4 10
7.	Blackburne	6½	3 18 10	1	6 13 4	10 12 2
8.	Wahltuch	4½	2 14 7	–	–	2 14 7
9.	Mercer	4	2 8 6	–	–	2 8 6
10.	Hamond	3½	2 2 5	–	–	2 2 5
11.	Parry	2	1 4 3	–	–	1 4 3
12.	Brown	1½	0 18 2	–	–	0 18 2
		66	£40 0 0	12	£80 0 0	£120 0 0

In a tournament of twelve players the maximum number of points obtainable under the proviso mentioned earlier is 5½, 4½, 3½, 2½, 1½, ½ = 18. Holmes continues, 'The number of scores above the average actually scored is then calculated, in this case twelve. Therefore the sum allotted to the prize group is 12/18ths of the whole fund i.e. £80. This is divided according to the number of points each player has scored above the average. The remainder of the fund, 6/18ths £40, is divided amongst all the competitors in proportion to their scores.'

Holmes gives a table (reproduced here) to show how the Tietz

System would have worked at Shrewsbury. He ends his letter: 'That the first prize-winner, in addition to the honour and pleasure of winning so many games, should carry off half the prize fund appears to me an anomaly for which there can be no justification' a sentiment with which eleven out of the twelve competitors must have agreed. *(H.G.)*

TIME LIMITS

All serious chess games today are subject to a time limit – each player must make, for example, 40 moves in 2½ hours. Failure to complete the moves in the time allowed results in the loss of the game for the offender.

Restrictions on the time allowed for thought were first introduced in 1861 for the match between Anderssen and Kolisch. Unregulated thinking time had previously given rise to widely-publicized abuses. Morphy is said to have been reduced to tears by the slowness of Paulsen's play and Staunton's criticism of Williams provides another famous example: 'Consumes hours over moves where minutes might suffice and depends not upon outmanoeuvring but out-sitting his antagonist.'

Originally, sandglasses were used to time the play. Tumbling clocks were introduced in the London 1883 event and a timepiece very similar to our modern tournament clock was developed by Veenhoff of Groningen about 1900.

The modern chess clock consists of two ordinary clock mechanisms joined by a push-bar or button system. Each clock face has a 'flag' indicator which drops when the hour is reached. While a player is thinking his clock is running; after he plays a move on the board he depresses the bar or button, stopping his clock and automatically starting his opponent's clock. The laws of chess state that, in games where clocks are being used, a move is not completed until the clock has been pressed.

Traditionally, cycles of moves are timed rather than individual moves. Within the cycle a player is free to allocate his thinking time as he wishes: taking perhaps twenty minutes over one move and ten seconds over another. Various time limits are used in club and local events, but forty moves in 2½ hours is now standard for all international competitions.

With clocks several variants on normal chess are possible; for instance, time odds can be given between players of unequal strength. A popular recreation is *Blitz* or 'five-minute' chess in which each player is given five minutes to complete all his moves, however long the game may last. *(R.D.K.)*

TIMMAN, Jan *(b. 14 December 1951)*

The third Dutch player to gain the grandmaster title (Euwe and Donner were the first two) and the youngest Dutchman to hold this title (awarded 1974). An outstanding talent since his early teens: he came 3rd when aged fifteen in the World Junior Championship, Jerusalem 1967. He obtained the international master title in 1971. His style is that of a fighter in the mould of Emanuel Lasker.

Timman represented The Netherlands in the Olympiads of 1972, 1974 and 1976, achieving the best score on top board in his most recent performance. He has competed in six Dutch championships: 1970, 1971, 1972 (finishing 2nd), and achieved three successive victories in 1974, 1975 and 1976. His best results: =1st with Tal, Kuzmin and Szabo, Hastings 1973/4, =1st with Gulko, Sombor 1974, 1st Netanya 1975 and =1st with Olafsson, Reykjavik 1976. He has yet to play in an Interzonal, surprisingly finishing as low as =7th in the 1975 Reykjavik Zonal.

He is co-author, with Euwe, of *De tweekamp Spasski-Fischer 1972* and is co-editor of the Dutch chess magazine *Schaakbulletin.*

Timman's attacking style is well illustrated by this lively game from the 1972 Skopje Olympiad:

White: Timman; *Black:* Radulov
English Opening
1. N–KB3, N–KB3; 2. P–QB4, P–K3; 3. N–B3, P–Q4; 4. P–Q4, P×P; 5. P–K4, P–B4; 6. B×P, P×P; 7. N×P, P–QR3; 8. P–K5, Q–B2; 9. Q–K2, KN–Q2; 10. B–B4, B–B4; 11. R–Q1, O–O; 12. O–O, B×N; 13. R×B, N–QB3; 14. R–K4, P–QN4; 15. B–Q3, N–B4; 16. R–K3, P–B4;

17. P×P *e.p.*, Q×B; 18. B×P+, K×B; 19. Q–R5+, K–N1; 20. P×P, K×P; 21. R–N3+, Q×R; 22. BP×Q, R×R+; 23. K×R, P–K4; 24. Q–N5+, K–B2; 25. N–Q5, B–K3; 26. Q–B6+, K–N1; 27. Q–N6+, K–B1; 28. N–B7, B–B5+; 29. K–B2, R–Q1; 30. Q×N, R–Q7+; 31. K–B3, R–Q6+; 32. K–N4, N–Q2; 33. P–N3, B–B2; 34. Q×RP, R–Q5+; 35. K–B5, K–K2; 36. N×P, resigns. *(R.D.K.)*

TIMOSHCHENKO, Gennady Anatolyevich *(b. 27 April 1949)*

Soviet international master (1976). A contemporary of Karpov, sharing 5th place with him in the 1966 USSR Junior championship and finishing ahead of him the following year. Overshadowed since then, he has recently raised the level of his play, winning tournaments at Rimavska Sobota 1974 and Polanica Zdroj 1976. *(K.J.O'C.)*

TITLES

FIDE awards the titles of Grandmaster, Woman Grandmaster, International Master and International Women's Master for performances of sufficient standard in international tournaments. Rules for determining the qualifying standards for these titles are continually under review by the Qualification Committee of FIDE and are frequently modified, but essentially the titles are awarded to players who have, on two separate occasions, registered sufficiently good results in international events; the term 'sufficiently good' is here understood to mean fulfilling the precise conditions laid down by the regulations for the award of titles.

The term 'grandmaster' was first applied to chess-players shortly after the beginning of the century, and thereafter was used without any formal definition, to describe any player with reasonable pretensions to the World title. It was not until 1950, when FIDE took the matter in hand, that the title, together with its lesser brother, International Master, was given any official blessing.

The first batch of titles were awarded at the 1950 FIDE congress, on the basis of past achievements but without formal criteria to be satisfied. The unsatisfactory nature of awarding titles by acclamation was gradually eliminated with the setting up of a Qualification Committee which drew up precise regulations on which future awards of titles were based.

The initial system, which operated for more than a decade, rated each tournament according to the number of titled players competing. If sufficient titled players took part it was possible to qualify for International Master and Grandmaster results by scoring a specified number of points. For a master norm the score required was equivalent to 35% against the grandmasters, 55% against the masters and 75% against untitled players, while the corresponding figures for grandmaster were 55, 75 and 85%.

The unsatisfactory nature of this scheme was that no distinction was made between players of different strengths holding the same title. Organizers of tournaments who wanted to give their home players the best possible chance of qualifying for titles were thus inclined to invite the weakest available title-holders to their events. When it became apparent that the old and infirm were becoming too popular in this manner, the rules were modified to specify that for the purposes of ranking tournaments title-holders were to be considered 'active' or 'passive' according to whether they had made a result of qualifying standard within five years. This new rule had the merit of confounding the rule-evaders, but was less highly thought of by those many masters and grandmasters who had to strain their energies to renew their titles every five years. There was still too the problem of differentiating in a satisfactory manner between players with wide disparity in playing strength who happened to have the same title.

With the adoption in 1970 of the Elo Rating System by FIDE the opportunity came to dispense with the old title qualifying rules and replace them with a new more precise system whereby each player in a tournament is identified by his rating number, rather than by the title he possesses. The average rating of the players determines the category of the tournament (ranging from Category 1, average rating 2251 to 2275, to Category 15, average rating 2601 to 2625); the category determines the percentage score required to qualify for titles of International Master and Grandmaster (e.g. Category 1: 76% master, 85% grandmaster; Category 15: 30% master, 43% grandmaster). A single qualifying performance is known as a master (or grandmaster) norm, and a player is awarded the title on making two or three norms to a total of not less than twenty-five games, within the period of three years.

Other methods of qualifying for titles include the following: the title of International Master is awarded to the Women's World Champion, the World Junior Champion, any player scoring $66\frac{2}{3}$% in a Zonal tournament and any player making $33\frac{1}{3}$% in an Interzonal. Qualifying from Zonal to Interzonal qualifies a player for the Master title, and qualifying for the Candidates tournament brings with it automatic award of the Grandmaster title.

Following a further rapid inflation in the numbers of titled players, a 1975 amendment to the rules specified that the titles of International Master and Grandmaster would only be awarded to candidates whose ratings are at least 2400 or 2500 respectively, but this has since been rescinded.

Though women players may theoretically qualify for the above titles, the Women's World Champions are the only ones yet who have held the title of International Master. The title of Woman International Master is awarded on a parallel system to that outlined above, for performances in women's tournaments. The title of Woman Grandmaster has also recently been instituted.

At the end of 1976 there were more than a hundred grandmasters active in men's international chess and almost three times that number of international masters. *(W.R.H.)*

TOLUSH, Alexander Kazimirovich *(1 May 1910–3 March 1969)*

Although he never attained success at the very highest levels of competition, Tolush was a highly gifted grandmaster noted for his combinational style and attacking abilities. He was born in Leningrad of which town he won the championship on two occasions. His best result in the USSR championship was to share second place behind Keres in 1950. Tolush was by profession a chess journalist and gained the title of international grandmaster in 1953.

His best tournament result in international events was first prize at Bucharest 1953; he also played successfully for many years in teams representing the USSR. *(W.R.H.)*

TORAN, Roman *(b. 8 October 1931)*

A Spanish international master (1954). International Judge 1957. Spanish champion 1951 and 1953. Played in Olympiads 1958, 1960, 1968, 1970, and 1974. Very active in Spanish chess organization and in chess journalism. *(R.D.K.)*

TORRE ATTACK

Evolved by the Mexican master Carlos Torre during the 1920s, this variation runs: 1. P–Q4, N–KB3; 2. N–KB3, P–K3; 3. B–N5.

Normally a transposition to the Queen's Gambit Orthodox Defence will occur but Black can imbue this line with individual significance by continuing 3. . , P–KR3; 4. B–R4, P–KN4; 5. B–N3, N–K5; 6. QN–Q2, N×B; 7. RP×N, B–N2 with even chances. *(R.D.K.)*

TORRE, Carlos *(b. 29 November 1904)*
A leading Mexican player, born in Merida (Yucatan). He won the state championship of Louisiana, USA, in 1923. In 1925 Torre visited Europe and competed with moderate success in four international tournaments: 10th at Baden-Baden 1925, =3rd at Marienbad 1925, =5th at Moscow 1925, and =2nd at Leningrad 1925/6. Returning to the USA he competed at Chicago 1926, finishing =2nd, and then retired from competitive chess due to ill-health. He was given the title of international master in 1963.

Moscow 1925
White: Torre; *Black:* Em. Lasker
Torre Attack
1. P–Q4, N–KB3; 2. N–KB3, P–K3; 3. B–N5, P–B4; 4. P–K3, P×P; 5. P×P, B–K2; 6. QN–Q2, P–Q3; 7. P–B3, QN–Q2; 8. B–Q3, P–QN3; 9. N–B4, B–N2; 10. Q–K2, Q–B2; 11. O–O, O–O; 12. KR–K1, KR–K1; 13. QR–Q1, N–B1; 14. B–B1, N–Q4; 15. N–N5, P–N4; 16. N–QR3, P–N5; 17. P×P, N×P; 18. Q–R5, B×N; 19. B×B, N×B; 20. R×N, Q–R4; 21. P–QN4, Q–KB4; 22. R–KN3, P–KR3; 23. N–B4, Q–Q4; 24. N–K3, Q–N4;

25. B–B6, Q×Q; 26. R×P+, K–R1; 27. R×P+, K–N1; 28. R–N7+, K–R1; 29. R×B+, K–N1; 30. R–N7+, K–R1; 31. R–N5+, K–R2; 32. R×Q, K–N3; 33. R–R3, K×B; 34. R×P+, K–N4; 35. R–R3, resigns. *(R.D.K.)*

TORRE, Eugenio *(b. 4 November 1951)*
Philippine grandmaster and Asia's first grandmaster, Torre's first appearance on the international scene was at the Siegen Olympiad of 1970 where he made the fine score of 71.9% on 2nd board.

He was on 1st board at the next Olympiad at Skopje in 1972 and there he again had a good score with 64.7%. In that year he received the international master title.

A big advance came in 1974 when, though he had a poor result at the Manila international tournament where he came 12th/15, his other results gave him the grandmaster title. He did well in two tournaments in Spain, obtaining a third place at Orense and coming 1st at Torremolinos, this last being a grandmaster result. A secure win of the Philippine championship was followed by a magnificent 73.68% on top board at the Nice Olympiad and this gave him the grandmaster title.

Mixed fortunes came in 1975. He was 3rd at Cleveland, came =8th with Karaklajić, Kavalek and Øgaard at the Manila International and was 1st at the Asian Pacific championship Zonal at Melbourne.

In 1976 he again had a mixture of bad and good results. At the Manila Interzonal in June he was 16th/20. In July he more than made up for this set-back by coming an unequivocal first at the Marlboro Kings Challenge tournament. It was a double round event and he scored 4½ followed by the World Champion, Karpov 3, Ljubojević 2½, and Browne 2. Torre won a game against each of his rivals. In August he also won the Second Asian Masters Championship in Jakarta.

He scored 68.1% on top board at the Haifa Olympiad. *(H.G.)*

TRANMER, Eileen Betsy *(b. 5 May 1910)*
International Woman master and four times British Ladies champion.

Eileen Tranmer, a musician by profession who played the clarinet in a number of well-known orchestras until increasing deafness compelled her to retire, took up chess comparatively late in life but was soon one of Britain's leading women players. She won the British Ladies championship in 1947, 1949 (on that occasion creating a record by winning all her games), 1953 and 1961.

Her best international performance was in the First Women Candidates tournament in Moscow 1952, where she came 7th out of 16 and defeated Elizaveta Bykova, the winner of the tournament and the eventual World Champion. *(H.G.)*

TRAP
An attempt – usually by means of a combination – to lure the opponent into a line of play which he believes to be advantageous. Unlike the swindle, the trap need not be unsound in itself; thus a strategically useful manoeuvre may at the same time contain a tactical trap leading to an immediate decision if the opponent tumbles into it. But, like the swindle, it is made in the expectation of enemy miscalculation or carelessness. Traps can be very simple but also very elaborate and ingenious; the more hidden the danger

it conceals, the better the chance of catching even first-rate opposition. Von Hennig v. Taube, Hamburg 1952:

White played 1. N–R4!, seemingly overlooking the reply 1.., R × P. There followed the quiet retreat 2. R–KB1!, and Black lost a piece: 2.., Q–R4; 3. R × N, R–N4; 4. Q–R3, R–N5; 5. P–N3, for if now 5.., P–N4; 6. P–B3, R–QB5; 7. R–B8+. *(W.H.)*

TREBLED PAWNS

Three pawns on the same file. Having all the disadvantages of doubled pawns and few of the compensating advantages, they occur only in exceptional circumstances in master-games. *(W.H.)*

TREYBAL, Karel *(24 December 1882–1941)*

Member of Czechoslovak teams in the Olympiads of 1930, 1933 and 1935. Shared first place in the championship of Czechoslovakia in 1921, and shared sixth with Nimzowitsch in the very strong Carlsbad 1923 tournament. Was a victim of the German occupation of Czechoslovakia in 1941. *(W.R.H.)*

TRIFUNOVIĆ, Petar *(b. 31 August 1910)*

One of the older generation of Yugoslav grandmasters. Although he learnt chess at an early age, his rise to fame was delayed for many years due to lack of strong tournaments. After the Second World War he came to the fore, winning the Yugoslav championship five times. Internationally successful in a number of important tournaments e.g. =1st Prague 1961. Represented Yugoslavia in five Olympiads. He drew a match with Najdorf in 1949 by 6–6.

In his best years he enjoyed the reputation of being impossible to beat. He favoured strictly positional chess and relied heavily on his superb endgame technique. Excessive caution prevented Trifunović from achieving world results.

Also known as author of several books and contributor to many chess magazines. *(R.D.K.)*

TRINGOV, Georgi Petrov *(b. 7 March 1937)*

A Bulgarian grandmaster, awarded the title in 1963 in which year he also won the Bulgarian championship. Qualified for the 1964 Interzonal tournament where he took fifteenth place. Tringov has had numerous successful appearances in international tournaments, including equal first place at Vrsac 1973. *(W.R.H.)*

TRINIDAD AND TOBAGO

A small country with, so far, only one Olympic appearance: 70th in 1974. The address of the Chess Association is: c/o St Mary's College, Frederick St. Port of Spain. *(K.J.O'C.)*

TROIANESCU, Octav *(b. 4 February 1916)*

Romanian international master since 1950. Winner of the Romanian championship in 1946, 1954, 1956 and 1957. Though never successful in international tournaments he was a valuable member of the Romanian team in the Olympiads of 1956 and 1960. *(K.J.O'C.)*

TROMPOWSKY ATTACK

1. P–Q4, N–KB3; 2. B–N5. So-called after the Brazilian player of that name who religiously practised it in the 1930s.

TSESHKOVSKY, Vitaly *(b. 25 September 1944)*

Soviet international grandmaster. He received the international master title in 1973 and that of grandmaster in 1975. He has played in the final of the USSR championship on four occasions but his results have never matched those which he attained in the Soviet 'First League' championships of 1974 and 1976 when he was =2nd. His best international performances have been at Bucharest 1974 (1st), Leipzig 1975 (1st), Dubna 1976 (1st) and the Manila Interzonal 1976 (4th). *(K.J.O'C.)*

TSVETKOV, Alexander Kristev *(b. 7 October 1914)*

Bulgarian international master since 1950, and winner of the Bulgarian championship: 1938, 1940, 1945, 1948, 1950 and 1951. Played in the Olympiads of 1939, 1954 and 1956. *(W.R.H.)*

TUKMAKOV, Vladimir *(b. 25 March 1946)*

Soviet international grandmaster and one of the leading younger Soviet masters in the period when Karpov was rising to fame. He gained the international master title in 1970 and at the end of 1971 had the fine result of =4th with Petrosian in the very strong Alekhine Memorial tournament at Moscow.

In 1972 he was awarded the international grandmaster title and in the following year he had his best international result by coming second, half a point below Karpov in the great Madrid tournament of 1973. *(H.G.)*

TUNISIA

Tunisia has two titled players, both international masters: Ridha Belkadi (1974) and Slim Bouaziz (1975). Bouaziz played in Tunisia's greatest ever tournament, the 1967 Interzonal at Sousse.

Tunisia has played in eight Olympiads: 35th in 1958, 34th in 1960, 27th in 1962, 34th in 1966, 37th in 1968, 35th in 1970, 42nd in 1972 and 32nd in 1974.

Chess in Tunisia is supervised by the Fédération Tunisienne des Echecs, 13 rue Dar El-Djeld, Tunis 1. *(K.J.O'C.)*

TURK, THE

A chess-playing 'automaton', designed by the Hungarian engineer and inventor Baron Wolfgang von Kempelen in 1769 as an amusement for the court of the Empress Maria Theresa. The device consisted of a life-size figure, clad in Turkish robes, attached to a large cabinet or chest. The cabinet was divided into two compartments and a sliding drawer; it had a chessboard inlaid on its upper surface.

At the start of an exhibition the interior structure of the cabinet and the figure, containing a bewildering array of machinery, would be displayed to the spectators, who were invited to confirm that the machine operated without help from any human agency. After the doors and panels had been re-closed, members of the audience would play chess against the automaton who usually won with ease. In fact The Turk was a complicated hoax, with a strong human player concealed within the cabinet. A detailed account of the mechanics of the illusion can be found in a series of articles by K. Harkness and J. S. Battell published in *Chess Review*, 1947.

The Turk's first performance took place before the Hapsburg court in Vienna in 1770. Public exhibitions continued intermittently for almost eighty-five years. In 1783–4 Kempelen and his device visited several European cities, including Dresden, Leipzig, Paris and London. After Kempelen's death in 1804, the automaton was purchased by a Bavarian showman and musician, Johann Nepomuk Maelzel, who had himself designed an automatic orchestra operated by foot pedals for which he had persuaded Beethoven to compose some original music. In 1809, during the Wagram campaign, Napoleon played (unsuccessfully) against The Turk in Vienna.

For a time The Turk was in the private collection of Prince Eugène de Beauharnais, who bought its secret for 30,000 francs, but Maelzel acquired it again in 1817 and toured extensively with the machine: Paris 1818, London 1818–20, Amsterdam 1821–2 and in America 1826–36. In 1837 both Maelzel and The Turk's current operator, Schlumberger – the tutor of Saint-Amant – died of yellow fever while returning from Havana to the USA. The automaton ended its days at the Chinese Museum in Philadelphia, where it perished in a fire in 1854.

Some of the names of the players who inhabited The Turk's interior are known. These include: Allgaier (1809), Weyle, Alexandre (1818), Boncourt (1818), Lewis (1818–19), Williams (1819), Mouret (1820) and Schlumberger (1826 onwards).

See also under AUTOMATONS. *(R.D.K.)*

TURKEY

Turkey has two international masters, Ilhan Onat and Nevzat Suer, both of whom received the title in 1975.

The supervisory body for Turkish chess is the Turkey Chess Federation, Tokatliyan Is Hani, Kat 4, No. 13, Beyoglu-Istanbul. This organization arranged the participation of a Turkish team in the Olympiads: 35th in 1962, 39th in 1964, 35th in 1966, 33rd in 1968, 51st in 1970, 38th in 1972 and 42nd in 1974. *(K.J.O'C.)*

TWO KNIGHTS DEFENCE

One of Black's most promising ways of avoiding the drawish tendencies of the Giuoco Piano is by the opening sequence 1. P–K4, P–K4; 2. N–KB3, N–QB3; 3. B–B4, N–B3. The sharpest continuation is 4. N–N5, P–Q4; 5. P×P, N–QR4; 6. B–N5+, P–B3; 7. P×P, P×P; 8. B–K2, P–KR3 when it is still an open question whether Black has fully sufficient compensation for the pawn. Other offshoots after 4. N–N5, P–Q4; 5. P×P are: 5. . , N×P; 6. N×BP (the *Fegatello* or 'Fried Liver' Attack); 5. . , N–Q5 (Fritz variation); 5. . , P–N4 (Ulvestad's variation). Also of historical importance is the continuation 4. P–Q4, P×P; 5. O–O, B–B4; 6. P–K5, leading to the dangerous Max Lange Attack, nowadays usually avoided with 5. . , N×P. *(W.R.H.)*

TYLOR, Sir Theodore Henry *(13 May 1900–23 October 1968)*

In spite of the handicap of partial blindness, Tylor enjoyed a successful academic career and was for nearly forty years a Fellow and tutor in jurisprudence at Balliol College, Oxford. He took up chess seriously while a schoolboy at Worcester College for the Blind and later as an undergraduate captained the Oxford University chess team.

At Hastings 1929/30, Tylor shared first prize with Koltanowski in the Premier Reserves ahead of Flohr, Rejfir, Rellstab, Alexander, Jackson, Noteboom, Vidmar Jr., and Winser. He played in the Hastings Premier event on nine occasions, but never finished in the top half. He competed in the British championship twelve times, his best result being 2nd to Sultan Khan in 1933. He was selected for the B.C.F. team in the Hamburg 1930 Olympiad and was British Correspondence Chess champion 1932–1935. *(R.D.K.)*

UDOVČIĆ, Mijo *(b. 11 September 1920)*

A Yugoslav grandmaster. Received international title 1957, grandmaster title 1962 following his performance in Dortmund the previous year. Competed in Yugoslav championships fourteen times winning in 1963 with Ivkov. Represented Yugoslavia in 1964 Olympiad. Withdrew from tournament play in 1969. By profession a lawyer. *(R.D.K.)*

UFIMTSEV, Anatoly Gavrilovich *(b. 1914)*

Soviet master and theoretician, many times champion of the Kazakhstan republic. Best known for his pioneering efforts in the defence 1. P–K4, P–Q3 known by his name in the USSR. *(H.G.)*

UHLMANN, Wolfgang *(b. 29 March 1935)*

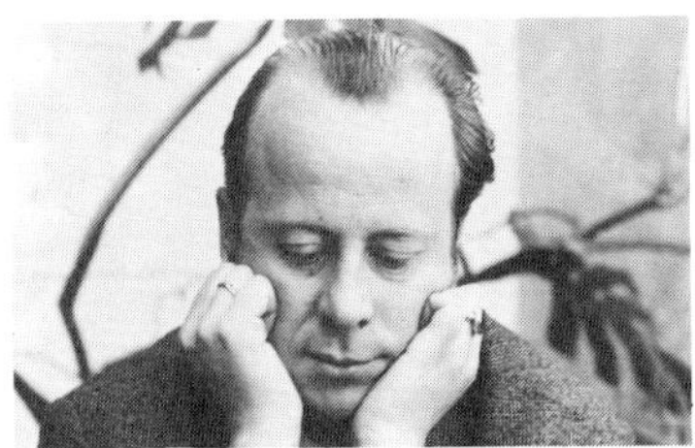

The strongest East German player since the mid 1950s. Six times East German champion and an international grandmaster, he has been a frequent competitor in Zonal tournaments, qualifying for the 1962 Interzonal by taking third place at Mariánské Lázně 1961 and again for the 1970 Interzonal by coming first at Raach 1969. On the latter occasion he went through to the Candidates by taking =5th place at Palma de Mallorca, but lost his first-round match to Larsen by $3\frac{1}{2}$–$5\frac{1}{2}$. In his early international career Uhlmann won a number of small tournaments (Erfurt 1955, Kienbaum 1958, Hastings 1958/9, Vienna 1959), but then struck a form-crisis when occasional good results (such as 2nd at Stockholm 1960, 3rd at Bewerwijk 1960, the Mariánské Lázně Zonal tournament, and =2nd at Sarajevo 1963) alternated with indifferent or poor performances (Moscow 1960), Buenos Aires 1960, Budapest 1961, Berlin 1962, Bad Liebenstein 1963). The year after, he regained his form and between 1964 and 1968 finished first in eight international tournaments without, however, winning a single one outright. No matter how strong or weak the event – and those at Havana and Zagreb were really enormous contests – he each time tied with one rival: at Sarajevo 1964 with Polugayevsky; Havana 1964 with Smyslov; Zagreb 1965 with Ivkov; Zinnowitz 1965 with Simagin; Hastings 1965/6 with Spassky; Szombathely 1966 with Bronstein; Zinnowitz 1967 with Liberzon; and Berlin 1968 again with Bronstein. It was only at the above-mentioned Zonal at Raach 1969 that his string of shared spoils came to an end.

Uhlmann has been Board 1 on East German teams in the Olympic and other team events for over twenty years. *(W.H.)*

UITUMEN, Tudev *(b. 27 July 1939)*
First player from Mongolia to gain the title of international master, which he earned in 1965. Played in the 1970 Interzonal tournament where he shared twentieth place. *(W.R.H.)*

UJTELKY, Maximilian Samuel Rudolf *(b. 20 May 1915)*
Czech international master since 1961. His best result in the Czech championship was to share first place in 1960, though he lost the play-off to Fichtl. Ujtelky is a direct descendant of the composer Franz Liszt. *(W.R.H.)*

UNDER-PROMOTION
When a pawn reaches the eighth rank it must be exchanged for (i.e. promoted into) a piece of higher rank of its own colour. Usually, almost automatically, one promotes it to the piece of the highest value, which is the Queen.

But there are cases when it is desirable to promote it to a piece of lesser value than the Queen and such cases are known as under-promotion.

An example appears in the position below.

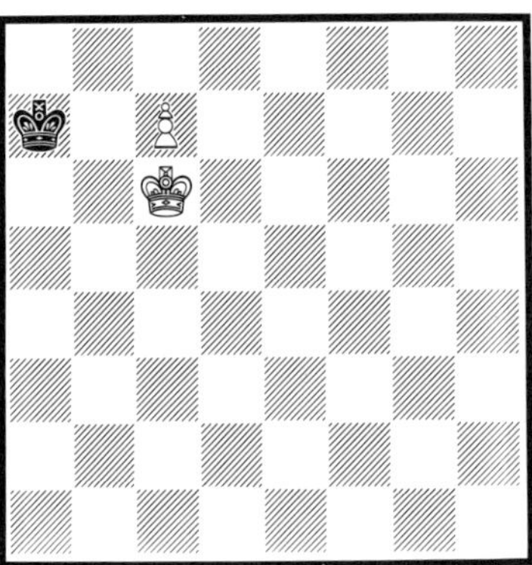

Here, if White plays P–B8=Q, the Black King is stalemated and the game is drawn. Hence he should play 1. P–B8=R, to which Black must reply 1.., K–R3; and White mates by 2. R–QR8.

For an example of under-promotion at an earlier stage in the game, see under DUBOIS where Black wins by promoting his pawn to a Knight. *(H.G.)*

UNITED STATES CHESS FEDERATION
The USCF is, in its own words, 'a non-profit democratic organization, the official governing body and FIDE (World Chess Federation) unit for chess in the USA'.

It publishes a monthly magazine, *Chess Life and Review*, and this is sent free to its members who also are, as members, eligible for USCF rating. The members pay $15 a year. The federation publishes a monthly list of USCF rated tournaments and no one is admitted to these unless he is a member of the federation. In addition to individual membership clubs are affiliated to the USCF. They pay $25 a year; colleges pay $15 and High Schools and Prisons $10 a year.

President of the USCF is George Koltanowski. Martin Morrison is Executive Director and Margaret Schwab is Administrative Director.

The USA is divided into eight regions: 1. New England, 2. Eastern, 3. Mid-Atlantic, 4. Southern, 5. Great Lakes, 6. North Central, 7. South-Western, 8. Pacific.

These in turn are composed of states and three hundred State USCF Directors are apportioned among the states in proportion to their USCF membership. These, in addition to Officer-Directors and Life-Directors, comprise the USCF Board of Directors which is responsible for the management of the Federation by formulating general policy, writing the by-laws, and electing the officers.

The USCF is an extremely active federation, not only by reason of its activities in home chess fields but also by its policy of furthering the cause of its players internationally in which it has been remarkably successful. Individually it has produced and is producing a number of great masters that make the name of the USA respected throughout the world; in team events, both senior and junior, it has been World champion on a number of occasions.

For some time it was handicapped in its action by shortage of funds; but this was remedied, firstly by generous donations and then by the brilliant idea of making the federation a trading organization that sold books, chess materials etc. all in the cause of chess.

The address of the USCF is The United States Chess Federation, 186 Route 9 West, New Windsor, NY 12550, USA. The name and address of its magazine is *Chess Life and Review*, 171 W 79th Street, Apt 34, New York, NY 10024, USA. *(H.G.)*

UNPINNING

The process of rendering a pin ineffective. This can be achieved by:

(*a*) Attacking the pinning piece, e.g. after 1. P–K4, P–QB3; 2. N–QB3, P–Q4; 3. N–B3, B–N5; *4. P–KR3.* If Black now tries to maintain the pin by 4. . , B–R4 there would follow 5. P × P, P × P; 6. B–N5+, N–B3; 7. P–KN4, B–N3; 8. N–K5.

(*b*) Removing the unit of higher value against which the pin operates.

(*c*) Interposition between either pinning piece and pinned piece, or between the pinned piece and the unit of higher value behind it. This would be the method of unpinning if in the sequence of moves above White were to play *4. B–K2.*

(*d*) Deflecting the pinning piece.

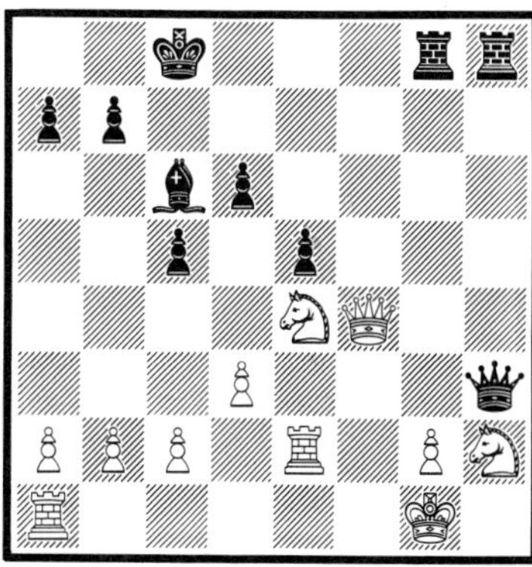

Heidenfeld v. De Carbonnel, Frankfurt 1960: Black has sacrificed a piece for a seemingly decisive attack based on the pin of the NP. White, by 1. Q–B8+, R × Q (forced): 2. P × Q, deflects the pinning piece and wins.

(*e*) Counterpin.

Becker v. Marshall, Carlsbad 1929: Black sets a trap, 1. . , P–B3; 2. P × P, B–Q3, pinning and seemingly winning the White Rook. White plays 3. P–B7+, K–B1 (forced); 4. B–N4, counterpinning the Bishop and saving his material.

For initially ineffective pins (which do not require an act of unpinning) see under PIN, final paragraph. *(W.H.)*

UNZICKER, Wolfgang *(b. 26 June 1925)*

A West German grandmaster, and the most successful West German player since the Second World War until the advent of Robert Hübner. German champion in 1948, 1950, 1952, 1953, 1959, 1963 and, jointly with Pfleger, 1965, he twice qualified for the Interzonal tournament (by coming second in the Zonal at Bad Pyrmont 1951, and first at Munich 1954); on each occasion, however, he failed to qualify for the subsequent Candidates tournaments. Unzicker's other international successes include firsts at Augsburg 1946, Heidelberg 1949, Travemünde 1950, Hastings 1950/1, Lucerne 1951/2, Maribor 1967 (ahead of Reshevsky), Krems 1967 (ahead of Szabo, Hort and Bronstein), while he was joint 1st with Spassky at Sochi 1965. High placings included =2nd at Madrid 1957; 2nd at Leningrad 1960; 3rd at Ljubljana 1969; 2nd at Hastings 1969/70, and =3rd at Lugano 1970, but his finest overall result was achieved at Santa Monica 1966, when he tied Portisch for fourth place, behind Spassky, Fischer and Larsen, but ahead of such players as Petrosian, Reshevsky and Najdorf.

Except for short tie-breaking matches Unzicker has had little match experience: he has beaten Hönlinger by 4–2 and lost to Keres by 2–6. Between 1950 and 1970 Unzicker was an automatic 1st board choice for the West German team in the Olympiads, as well as the European Team Championship and other team events; at Dubrovnik 1950 he tied with Najdorf for the best result on 1st board. Unzicker's style has been shaped primarily by the teachings of Tarrasch. *(W.H.)*

URUGUAY

Uruguay occupies a special place in South American chess history as it was the first country in that part of the world to have a chess magazine, the *Revista de ajedrez* which began publication in 1881.

A team from Uruguay has campaigned in six Olympiads: 19th in 1939, 32nd in 1962, 46th in 1964, 33rd in 1966, 53rd in 1974 and 28th in 1976.

The supervisory body for chess in Uruguay is the Federation Uruguaya de Ajedrez, Casa de los Deportes, Artigas Canelones 978, Montevideo. *(K.J.O'C.)*

USA

American chess has been punctuated by periods of great development, usually following dramatic events such as Morphy's European tour or the 1972 Fischer–Spassky match, and also by periods of inactivity. Until the 1960s most chess organization was performed by regional groups and the major clubs. Even during the peak years of US success during the 1930s, there was little authority on a national level.

It is not known how the game was introduced to America, although chess-sets have been found in many colonial-era homes. Aside from a few regular playing circles, such as that of the Philadelphia home of Benjamin Franklin, there was little formal organization before the start of the nineteenth century.

The first chess club with permanent quarters opened in downtown New York in 1801. The first chess book, a reprint of a popular English text, was published in Philadelphia a year later. Analyses by Philidor and Lewis appeared in the next two decades and with them arrived Charles Vezin, an English amateur who won recognition as the leading master.

The sensational début of Von Kempelen's automaton in 1826, however, evoked great popular interest and created the first US chess craze. Thousands of new fans tried to explain the touring exhibit's success, and each city's press boasted of their citizens' performance against The Turk.

In 1840 Stanley arrived from London and quickly established himself as unofficial champion. He wrote the first American chess-column in *The Spirit of the Times.* But aside from inter-city correspondence matches and club events, there was no serious competition before 1857.

The first New York Chess Tournament 1857

In that year leaders of the New York Chess Club, the most prominent club of the day, invited sixteen players to the First American Chess Congress, a knockout championship in imitation of London 1851. Among the competitors were Fiske, Stanley, and Napoleon Marache, editor of the first US magazine on the game, *The Chess Palladium and Mathematical Sphinx*, which appeared briefly in 1845. But the October–November event ended with Morphy's +5−1=2 defeat of L. Paulsen, then a potato-crop broker in Iowa.

The New Orleans Chess Club was encouraged to send Morphy to Europe the following spring and this ensured continued popularity of the game in America. Löwenthal, who had lost a casual match with the twelve-year-old Morphy in 1850, had written in 1856 that 'The progress chess has made in America is almost, if not quite, equal to that it has achieved in England'. This was certified by Morphy's defeats of Harrwitz, Löwenthal and Anderssen. Although Morphy retired from serious chess after 1862 and died a stranger to the game in 1884, the period of the 'Morphy Excitement' that followed his European successes may have more than doubled the number of US players. The Manhattan Chess Club opened in 1877 and was instrumental in bringing the Steinitz–Zukertort match to America nine years later. Fiske's *Chess Monthly* was short-lived but with Morphy as games editor and Loyd as problems editor, US chess literature came of age. Fiske listed eighty-seven chess-columns in American newspapers in 1861.

Despite Loyd's claims to over-the-board playing skill and the rise of Irish-born James Mason, the leading successor to Morphy was Scottish-born Capt Mackenzie. Mackenzie was a member of a new breed, the professional player. He won the second American Chess Congress in 1871, the third in 1874 and the fifth in 1880, a string interrupted only by Mason's win in the fourth Congress held in Philadelphia in 1876. Mackenzie was the only American to compete successfully in Europe until the 1890s.

Mackenzie's ill-health prevented him from playing at the sixth Congress, New York 1889, an event which was the first major international tournament in North America. Steinitz, who edited his *International Magazine* from New York during the last years of the century, organized the tournament book and was a leading, albeit critical, force in US chess at the time. The sixth place score of Lipschütz in the mammoth event established him as the unofficial champion after Mackenzie's death. Until Pillsbury proved his ability at Hastings 1895 there were several claimants to the national title. Lipschütz defended his claim in an 1892 match with Showalter +7−1=7 in the first officially recognized US championship event. After Lipschütz's departure from New York, Showalter claimed the title but he was defeated by Hodges in 1894. Hodges then retired professionally. Showalter re-established his claim and secured the title with match victories in 1895–6 over Lipschütz, Emil Kemeny and John Barry. By the turn of the century, America had attracted several visiting foreign masters such as Steinitz, Em. Lasker and Albin. The 1894 World Championship match was held in New York and other cities. New York was now becoming the pre-eminent chess centre of the country and establishing a hegemony over the nation's top masters that would last until the 1960s.

Pillsbury's Hastings success gave the USA its first world-calibre player since Morphy. Although the Bostonian persevered in an unsuccessful quest to unseat Lasker as World Champion, Pillsbury took time to defeat Showalter for the US title +10−8=4 in New York in 1897 and +7−3=2 a year later. Pillsbury demonstrated that Americans were well acquainted with European opening ideas and planning. But it was the boldness of execution of 'plodding depth' that Réti later characterized as 'Americanism' in chess.

Pillsbury was soon challenged for American supremacy by Marshall, who made his foreign début at the minor section of London 1899. Marshall's growth was confirmed by his 1st place ahead of Em. Lasker, then living in New York, and Schlechter at Cambridge Springs, a Pennsylvania resort, in 1904. Pillsbury's 8th place was his first major setback and an indication that his creative period was over. Cambridge Springs 1904 was the second strong international event in America and saw the birth of Helms's *American Chess Bulletin*, the first long-lived US magazine.

Pillsbury's death in 1906 opened a new battle for the US title. Marshall claimed it but so did Capablanca, a graduate of Columbia University, who had defeated Marshall in their 1909 match. The title remained vacant while a bitter dispute over it was resolved by Shipley, then recognized as the primary chess authority in the USA. Shipley ruled that the only true title-holder was Showalter, the last man to win it. Marshall then challenged Showalter and defeated the Kentuckian +7−2=3 in 1909. He held the title until 1936.

Chess organization continued on a local level with the leading forces being the New York clubs, the Western Chess Association and several smaller authorities. More than at any other time, Europeans began to come to America and to stay for prolonged periods. Chajes, Kupchik, H. Steiner and Jaffe were among the emigrants who settled in New York, but the arrivals of Reshevsky and Ed. Lasker were the most noted. Ed. Lasker challenged Marshall to a title match in 1923 but lost +4−5=9.

The strongest American tournament of all time opened in New York 1924. Capablanca and Maróczy remained in America during the 1920s and were instrumental in bringing about the successor tournament, New York 1927.

The economic depression of the 1930s coincided with the next boom period of chess activity. Horowitz's *Chess Review* began in 1933 and brought a new glossy style to American chess journalism. The USA entered a team at the second Olympiad, The Hague 1928, and came second. After a sixth-place result at Hamburg 1930, the American team – variously composed of Fine, Reshevsky, Dake, Horowitz, H. Steiner, Kashdan and Marshall – won the next four Olympiads: Prague 1931, Folkestone 1933, Warsaw 1935 and Stockholm 1937. In the absence of a Soviet rival, the USA dominated international team events. As individuals, the US players scored several successes beginning with Kashdan's début and continuing with Fine and Reshevsky's pre-war victories.

Financial conditions had prevented a Marshall–Kashdan title match, but Marshall's retirement paved the way for the series of tournament championships that continue to this day. The National Chess Federation organized the first event in 1936. It was Reshevsky's first victory, and he repeated it in 1938, 1940, 1942, 1946 and 1969. Although a close rival internationally, Fine never won the title ahead of Reshevsky, and he finished behind Denker in 1944 when Reshevsky did not play. Reshevsky defended his title successfully in matches with Horowitz in 1941 and Kashdan in 1942.

During this period the most important events nationally, aside from the Closed championship, were the Metropolitan League team events in New York and the annual US Open championship which was held in a different city each year. It was common to find the ten highest-rated players in the country facing one another in the final Metropolitan League match between the Manhattan and Marshall Chess Clubs. It was during this era that chess publishing expanded greatly. Before this time only the efforts of Young as a writer of hard-cover works was recognized. But in the 1930s a number of writers led by Fine, Fred Reinfeld and Irving Chernev popularized chess literature that had previously only been available in foreign languages.

Chess players in Central Park

The formation of the US Chess Federation in 1940 ended a long national rivalry between regional groups. Beginning with 1,000 members at its birth, the U.S.C.F. grew slowly, reaching 2,100 members in 1954 and 3,800 in 1959. But the tempo of increase accelerated in the 1960s so that membership hit 10,000 in 1967, 34,000 in 1972, and more than 70,000 after the effects of the Fischer–Spassky match had been felt. After the initial popularity of chess wore off the U.S.C.F. membership receded slightly to 60,000 in 1974.

The radio match of 1945 with the USSR broke the string of international victories by the Americans. The Soviet victory, repeated a year later in a face-to-face confrontation, indicated that a new dynasty had replaced the Americans. This was verified by the Russian successes in the Olympiads of 1952 on. The best American results in these biennial World Team tournaments were 2nd at Leipzig in 1960 and at Havana in 1966.

The shattering effect of the radio match on American supporters was mitigated by the emergence of a new generation in the late 1940s. As usual, all of the new masters were New Yorkers – Evans, Bisguier, Lombardy, Sherwin, Robert and Donald Byrne, Mednis, and later of course Fischer. In contrast to the generation of the 1930s, several of the younger post-war masters were openings experts and well acquainted with Russian chess literature. On the other hand, one of the traditional strengths of American players – defensive skill in bad positions – was continued by the new generation.

Mark Diesen, Hastings 1974/5

Two other phenomena spurred the game in the USA beginning in the late 1950s. One was the popularization of weekend Swiss System tournaments, first introduced to America by George Koltanowski in the 1930s. The number of rated tournaments more than doubled during the 1960s. At the same time, inexpensive paperback chess books, often reprints of hard-cover classics, became readily available. Meanwhile *Chess Life*, the official publication of the US Federation changed from newspaper format to that of a magazine in 1961 and merged with *Chess Review* eight years later to become *Chess Life and Review*.

Despite the emergence of the post-war generation, the Americans again lost badly to Soviet teams in 1954 and 1955. Reshevsky, following the retirement of Fine after 1951, became the leading US candidate for the World Championship until the late 1950s. In 1961 a match with Fischer was arranged but it was aborted after a complex dispute with the score standing +2−2=7. Fischer continued to win US Closed championships he participated in.

In the later 1960s American chess talent was dispersed over a wider geographical area as the leading New York masters found new homes and thriving chess centres opened in other parts of the country. The US Closed championship was held outside of New York state for the first time in 1973 when it came to El Paso in Texas. That year the US Federation organized the first of its international tournaments in Norristown, Pennsylvania, a suburb of Philadelphia. Subsequent events have been held in Houston, Texas, Chicago and Pasadena, California. Outside of New York City the leading chess centres in the early 1970s were located in Chicago, Los Angeles and San Francisco.

Again, in the post-war period as before, the US received a number of foreign masters as emigrants, chief among them being Benko and Kavalek. Browne, a New York resident became an American in 1973 after playing for Australia.

A new generation began to emerge in the early 1970s led by Rogoff and Tarjan. The US Student team captured the World championship in 1970 after a ten-year lapse. In 1973 John Grefe, a twenty-five-year-old Californian, tied for 1st place in the US Closed championship with Kavalek.

The Closed championship became an annual event after 1957 with the exception of the years 1970–1. Besides the events organized by the US Federation, there were international tournaments sponsored by patrons, such as the Piatigorsky Cup of 1963 and 1966 and San Antonio 1972. Although travel distance and similar financial concerns discouraged the USA from holding major FIDE events, America did host the 1968 play-off to determine the eighth qualifier for the Candidates matches and the 1974 quarter-final Candidates match between Korchnoi and Mecking.

With the disappearance of Fischer from the chess scene, the leading roles were filled by Robert Byrne, Kavalek and Browne. Browne's advance in particular was spectacular. He developed into a strong grandmaster and repeatedly won the US championship.

United States Champions

The history of the United States championship is a complex one and an official enumeration is still lacking. 1892 is widely accepted as the year in which the first 'official' champion emerged. Until 1936 the title was decided by irregular matches. The champions in this period were:

1892–1894	S. Lipschütz	1897–1906	H. N. Pillsbury
1894–1895	A. B. Hodges	1906–1909	(title vacant)
1895–1897	J. W. Showalter	1909–1936	F. J. Marshall

The official United States Chess championship tournaments began in 1936. The winners have been:

1936	S. Reshevsky	1961/2	L. Evans
1938	S. Reshevsky	1962/3	R. J. Fischer
1940	S. Reshevsky	1963/4	R. J. Fischer
1942	S. Reshevsky	1965/6	R. J. Fischer
1944	A. Denker	1966/7	R. J. Fischer
1946	S. Reshevsky	1968	L. Evans
1948	H. Steiner	1969/70	S. Reshevsky
1951	L. Evans	1972	R. Byrne
1954	A. Bisguier	1973	J. Grefe and L. Kavalek
1957/8	R. J. Fischer	1974	W. S. Browne
1958/9	R. J. Fischer	1975	W. S. Browne
1959/60	R. J. Fischer		
1960/1	R. J. Fischer		

The United States Open championship has, over the years, become a very important tournament. The tournaments were held under the auspices of the Western Chess Association from 1900 to 1933, the American Chess Federation from 1934 to 1938 and, since 1939, the USCF. The champions or co-champions in the 77 Opens to date are:

1900	L. Udemann	1908	E. P. Elliott
1901	N. M. Macleod	1909	O. Chajes
1902	L. Udemann	1910	G. H. Wolbrecht
1903	M. Judd	1911	C. Blake
1904	S. Mlotkowski	1912	E. P. Elliott
1905	E. F. Schrader	1913	B. B. Jefferson
1906	G. H. Wolbrecht	1914	B. B. Jefferson
1907	E. Michelson	1915	J. W. Showalter

1916	Ed. Lasker
1917	Ed. Lasker
1918	B. Kostić
1919	Ed. Lasker
1920	Ed. Lasker
1921	Ed. Lasker
1922	S. D. Factor
1923	Mlotkowski and N. T. Whitaker
1924	C. Torre
1925	A. Kupchik
1926	L. Stolzenberg
1927	A. C. Margolis
1928	L. Stolzenberg
1929	H. Hahlbohm
1930	S. D. Factor and N. T. Whitaker
1931	S. Reshevsky
1932	R. Fine
1933	R. Fine
1934	R. Fine and S. Reshevsky
1935	R. Fine
1936	I. A. Horowitz
1937	D. S. Polland
1938	I. A. Horowitz and I. Kashdan
1939	R. Fine
1940	R. Fine
1941	R. Fine
1942	H. Steiner and D. A. Yanofsky
1943	I. A. Horowitz
1944	S. Reshevsky
1945	A. E. Santasiere
1946	H. Steiner
1947	I. Kashdan
1948	W. W. Adams
1949	Al. Sandrin Jr
1950	A. Bisguier
1951	L. Evans
1952	L. Evans
1953	D. Byrne
1954	L. Evans
1955	N. Rossolimo
1956	A. Bisguier
1957	R. J. Fischer
1958	E. Cobo
1959	A. Bisguier
1960	R. Byrne
1961	P. Benko
1962	A. Medina
1963	W. Lombardy
1964	P. Benko
1965	P. Benko and W. Lombardy
1966	P. Benko and R. Byrne
1967	P. Benko
1968	B. Larsen
1969	P. Benko
1970	B. Larsen
1971	W. S. Browne
1972	W. S. Browne
1973	N. Weinstein
1974	P. Benko and V. Hort
1975	P. Benko and W. Lombardy
1976	A. Lein and L. Shamkovich

Finally, these lists would be incomplete without giving the winners of the nine American Chess Congress championships:

1857	P. Morphy
1871	G. H. Mackenzie
1874	G. H. Mackenzie
1876	J. Mason
1880	G. H. Mackenzie
1889	M. Chigorin and M. Weiss
1904	F. J. Marshall
1921	D. Janowski
1923	A. Kupchik and F. J. Marshall

The address of the US Chess Federation is: US Chess Federation, 186 Rt. 9W, New Windsor, N.Y. 12550. *(A.S. & K.J.O'C.)*

USA–USSR MATCHES

A week after the radio match between the USA and the USSR had taken place in September 1945, Botvinnik and Nikolai Romanov, the president of the All-Union Committee for Physiculture and Sport, sent a cable to the US Chess Federation inviting the federation to send a team to the Soviet Union to play a return match in Moscow.

This was eventually done and on 9–12 September, 1946 a double-round match on ten boards took place in Moscow.

The visiting team did considerably better than they had done in the radio match, but, curiously enough, the weakness on the top boards (which had been reckoned to be the strong point of the US team) again made itself apparent. Had the match been played on the last five boards the Americans would have won by $6\frac{1}{2}$–$3\frac{1}{2}$.

As it was they were defeated by $12\frac{1}{2}$ to $7\frac{1}{2}$ which was by no means a bad score for the losers. No other country in the world could have done as well as the USA against their redoubtable adversaries. On the top board Denker was no match for Smyslov, but Reshevsky might easily have emerged with a plus score against Botvinnik had he not spoilt a won game under time pressure. Fine's two losses to Keres may have been instrumental in inducing him to retire from the international scene as far as the World Championship was concerned. Kashdan, who had lost both his games to Kotov in the USA–USSR radio match the previous year, took some revenge by returning a plus score this time.

Details:

USA		*USSR*	
1. Denker	0 0	Smyslov	1 1
2. Reshevsky	½ 0	Botvinnik	½ 1
3. Fine	0 0	Keres	1 1
4. H. Steiner	0 ½	Flohr	1 ½
5. Pinkus	0 0	Ragozin	1 1
6. Horowitz	½ ½	Boleslavsky	½ ½
7. Kashdan	½ 1	Kotov	½ 0
8. Kevitz	½ 1	Bondarevsky	½ 0
9. Dake	½ ½	Lilienthal	½ ½
10. Ulvestad	½ 1	Bronstein	½ 0
	7½		12½

After an interval of eight years the Soviet Chess Federation sent a team to New York. It was a powerful side even though Botvinnik, owing to illness, was not in the side. The US team was a much younger one, having such players as the Byrne brothers, Bisguier and Evans in place of the older Fine, Kashdan etc.

The match was on eight boards and each player met his opponent four times. It commenced on 16 June 1954, in the Roosevelt Hotel, New York before a crowd of more than 1,000 spectators. The home side made a bad start and lost the first round by 2–6. But they did better in the 2nd and 3rd rounds each of which they lost by 3–5 and in the last round they even drew 4–4.

So the Soviet side won securely enough by 20 to 12, their most successful players being Bronstein who won all his games on second board, three against Denker and one against Dake who stepped in to take Denker's place on one occasion when he was indisposed, and Keres who made the score of 3–1 on third board.

The better aspects of the match so far as the home side was

concerned lay in the plus scores achieved by Donald Byrne and Larry Evans over Averbakh and Taimanov, and Reshevsky's four draws with Smyslov on top board.

In the following year came the last match (to date) between the two federations and this time it was the Americans' turn to visit Moscow. The same scheme of things was adopted and teams of eight players met each other four times.

The match started on 29 June 1955 and it was at once apparent that the Soviet team, containing all the best players in the USSR, was too good for the Americans. This time Botvinnik was playing and the remaining members of the Soviet team were Smyslov, Bronstein, Geller, Keres, Petrosian, Taimanov and Kotov. Opposing them were Reshevsky, Bisguier, Evans, D. Byrne, R. Byrne, Horowitz, Kashdan and H. Steiner, with Pavey and Kevitz as reserves.

The Soviet team won the first round by 5½–2½ and the scene was not all unrelieved gloom for the Americans since Reshevsky beat Botvinnik on top board. But the visitors were to win only one more game (D. Byrne against Geller in Round 3) and they lost the second round by 1–7. A slight restoration to grace in Round 3 when they lost by 2½–5½ was followed by another 1–7 defeat in the final round so that the Soviet Union won by the crushing score of 25–7.

The best results for the winners were those of Smyslov, Petrosian and Kotov, who won all their games, whilst Reshevsky did extremely well to score one win and three draws on top board against the World Champion, Botvinnik.

Here is the game Reshevsky won in the last match.

White: Reshevsky; *Black:* Botvinnik
Queen's Gambit Declined, Meran variation
1. P–Q4, P–K3; 2. P–QB4, P–Q4; 3. N–QB3, P–QB3; 4. P–K3, N–B3; 5. N–B3, QN–Q2; 6. B–Q3, P×P; 7. B×BP, P–QN4; 8. B–Q3, P–QR3; 9. P–K4, P–B4; 10. P–K5, P×P; 11. QN×P, N×P; 12. N×N, P×N; 13. Q–B3, Q–R4+; 14. K–K2, B–Q3; 15. Q–B6+, K–K2; 16. B–Q2, P–N5; 17. Q×B+, K×Q; 18. N–B4+, K–Q2; 19. N×Q, R×N; 20. KR–QB1, B–R3; 21. B×B, R×B; 22. R–B4, N–Q4; 23. R×QP, R–QN1; 24. K–Q3, P–R4; 25. K–B4, P–N6; 26. P–QR4, R–B3+; 27. K–Q3, R–B7; 28. R–QN1, R(N1)–QB1?;

29. P–R5, R(B1)–B3; 30. K–K2, R–Q3; 31. K–K1, N–B2?; 32. R×R+, K×R; 33. B–B3!, P–B3; 34. R–R1, N–R3; 35. R–R3, K–B2; 36. R×P, N–B4; 37. R–N5, N–R5; 38. B–Q4, P–K4; 39. K–Q1!, R–B5; 40. B–K3, K–B3; 41. R–N8, K–B2; here the game was adjourned and Black resigned without resuming play.

The queries (indicating criticism) and the exclamation marks (indicating approval) are from Botvinnik's notes as published in the September 1955 issue of the *British Chess Magazine*. He adds at the end, 'This is an interesting and instructive game which shows I need to perfect my play of two-move variations and it would not harm my opponent to cultivate a more exact judgment of position. A good game by Reshevsky.' *(H.G.)*

USA–USSR RADIO MATCH 1945

The first meeting between teams representing the USA and the USSR was a match by radio that took place shortly after the end of the Second World War on 3–5 September 1945. It was a double round, ten board a side contest and the result was an overwhelming victory for the Soviet team by 15½–4½.

Only Herman Steiner, on board 6 for the USA, managed a plus score of 1½–½ and for the USA only two players, Horowitz and Pinkus, managed an even score. The rest of the picture was almost unrelieved gloom as the table shows.

USA		*USSR*	
1. Denker	0 0	Botvinnik	1 1
2. Reshevsky	0 0	Smyslov	1 1
3. Fine	½ 0	Boleslavsky	½ 1
4. Horowitz	0 1	Flohr	1 0
5. Kashdan	0 0	Kotov	1 1
6. H. Steiner	1 ½	Bondarevsky	0 ½
7. Pinkus	½ ½	Lilienthal	½ ½
8. Seideman	0 0	Ragozin	1 1
9. Kupchik	0 ½	Makagonov	1 ½
10. Santasiere	0 0	Bronstein	1 1
	4½		15½

An onlooker at the New York end of the match, in a letter to the *British Chess Magazine* (October 1945) ascribed the American team's heavy defeat to poor or non-existent preliminary training for the event. He also pointed out that it was wrong to put Denker on top board, solely because he had won a rather weak US championship a couple of years earlier and that, had Fine been on top board, he would certainly not have lost so heavily, if at all, to Botvinnik, against whom he had an unbeaten record.

An amusing comment on this was provided by the circumstance that the USA sent a team the following year to play the USSR in Moscow and put up a much better show, losing by only 7½–12½. But they still kept Denker on top board and again he lost both his games to Botvinnik.

A pretty game played on top board in the Radio match.

White: Denker; *Black:* Botvinnik
Queen's Gambit Declined, Half-Slav Defence
1. P–Q4, P–Q4; 2. P–QB4, P–K3; 3. N–QB3, P–QB3; 4. N–B3, N–B3; 5. B–N5, P×P; 6. P–K4, P–N4; 7. P–K5, P–KR3; 8. B–R4, P–N4; 9. KN×P, P×N; 10. B×NP, QN–Q2; 11. P×N, B–QN2; 12. B–K2, Q–N3; 13. O–O, O–O–O; 14. P–QR4, P–N5; 15. N–K4.

P–B4; 16. Q–N1, Q–B2; 17. N–N3, P×P; 18. B×P, Q–B3; 19. P–B3, P–Q6; 20. Q–B1, B–B4+; 21. K–R1, Q–Q3; 22. Q–B4,

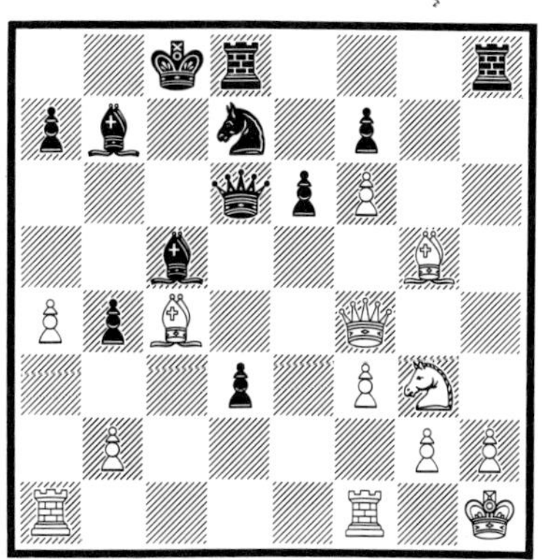

R×P+; 23. K×R, R–R1+; 24. Q–R4, R×Q+; 25. B×R, Q–B5; 26. resigns. *(H.G.)*

USSR
For USSR see SOVIET UNION.

UUSI [Oosi], Gunnar Andreyevich *(b. 1931)*
Soviet master and several times champion of Estonia. *(W.R.H.)*

V

VACATING SACRIFICE
A term coined by Spielmann for a sacrifice, the point of which is to clear a square for a different unit of the same side. In his book *The Art of Sacrifice in Chess* he deals only with 'real' sacrifices, and as such the vacating sacrifice usually offers merely a pawn or two. But it is seen far more frequently as a sacrifice for immediate gain, as e.g. in the following typical position.

Threatened with two mates on the move as well as with loss of his Queen, White wins by vacating his KR square by a sacrifice: 1. R–R8+, K×R; 2. Q–R1+, K–N1; 3. Q–R7 mate. *(W.H.)*

VADÁSZ, László *(b. 27 January 1948)*
Hungarian international grandmaster (1976). He obtained the international master title in 1975. He is one of those rare players whose major advance in top flight competition has been made in his late twenties. His best tournament results have been at Vrnjačka Banja 1975 (=1st), Budapest 1976 (=1st) and the 1976 Hungarian championship (=3rd). *(K.J.O'C.)*

VAGANIAN, Rafael *(b. 15 October 1951)*
One of the leading young Soviet grandmasters, and among the best players of Armenia. Vaganian gained the grandmaster title in 1971 after his victory in the Vrnjačka Banja tournament that year. His other international successes include first place at Kragujevac 1974, =2nd at Hastings 1974/5. His national results have been variable but he came =1st in the USSR championship 'B' division in 1973 and =2nd in the USSR championship 1975. *(W.R.H.)*

VAITONIS, Paul *(b. 15 August 1911)*
Born in Lithuania, Vaitonis came to Canada in 1949. He was a leading player in Lithuania, having won or tied for the national title there in 1934, 1937, 1938, 1942, 1943 and 1944. He lives in Hamilton, Ontario. Vaitonis won the Canadian championship in 1951 and in 1957. *(N.D.)*

VAJDA, Arpad *(b. 2 May 1896–d. 25 October 1967)*
Hungarian international master and arbiter whose chess-playing activity was confined to the period between the two World Wars.

He played for his country at the Olympiads of London 1927, The Hague 1928, Hamburg 1930, Prague 1931, Folkestone 1933 and Stockholm 1937. He also played in the 1936 Munich Team tournament.

His best results in important tournaments were =5th at Kecskemet 1927 and =4th at Budapest 1929, but he had a number of successes in lesser events: 2nd at Portsmouth 1923, 1st at the minor tournament in London 1922 and 1st at Szolnok 1932. *(H.G.)*

VAN DEN BERG, Carel Benjamin
(12 February 1924–30 June 1971)
Dutch international master (1963). Earned his title by scoring 8/15 in the Grandmaster group Beverwijk 1963.

Played in the Olympiad 1958 and in the European Team championship 1965. Though not very active in tournament chess, he was considered to be one of the most eminent Dutch theorists. Editor of *Losbladige Schaakberichten* and collaborator with Euwe on the *Theorie der Schaakopeningen* series. Took a degree in law and philosophy, but became a full-time chess professional. *(R.D.K.)*

VAN DER MIJE, Alexandra Ecaterina
See under NICOLAU.

VAN GEET, Dirk Daniel *(b. 1 March 1932)*
A Dutch international master (1965). Best results: 1st prize in the Master group Beverwijk 1965 and =6th in Grandmaster group Beverwijk 1967. Played in European team championship 1965. He specializes in unusual opening variations. *(R.D.K.)*

VAN SCHELTINGA, Tjeerd Daniel *(b. 6 March 1914)*
Dutch international master whose occupation was that of carpenter

at the Amsterdam Stock Exchange. His play seemed to reflect this, being solid and technically correct.

One of The Netherlands' leading players from 1936 to the late 1950s, though he always did well in the national championship he never actually won it. His best performance in that event was an =1st with Euwe in 1947, but he lost the play-off by $2\frac{1}{2}$–$5\frac{1}{2}$.

His best international period was after the Second World War. He had a good run in the Beverwijk tournaments, 1st in 1947, 2nd 1948 and =2nd 1949. He twice competed in Zonal tournaments, coming 4th at Hilversum 1947 and =6th at Dublin 1957.

He represented his country at the Olympiads of 1937, 1939, 1950, 1952 and 1954. *(H.G.)*

VAN'T KRUYS OPENING

1. P–K3 is a rarely seen opening based on the idea of playing a French Defence with a move in hand. It usually transposes to various forms of Queen's Pawn Openings or to a type of Bird's Opening. It is called after the Dutch player Van't Kruys, winner of a tournament at Amsterdam 1878, who employed it against Anderssen in a number of games. Lucena gives it in his book as early as 1497. *(H.G.)*

VARIETIES OF CHESS

Circe

When captured, a piece is immediately replaced on its original square in the game array (in the case of R, B and N on the square of the same colour as that on which it has been captured). Ps go back to the initial square (second rank) of their file. If the replacement square is occupied, the captured unit leaves the board altogether. No player may make a capture leading to a replacement that puts his own K in check. Invented by Pierre Monréal and J-P. Boyer in 1968. *(J.M.R.)*

Courier Game

An early European modification of the normal game, mentioned in a manuscript dating from 1202. The board was twelve squares wide and the usual eight deep. The line-up for the game reading from White's left to right: Rook, Knight, Alfil, Courier, Man, King, Fers, Sneak [Schleich], Courier, Alfil, Knight, Rook, with twelve pawns in front. (For the moves of Alfil and Fers, see PROBLEMS: HISTORY.) The Courier moved just like the modern Bishop. The Man moved like a King but had no royal power. The Sneak moved one square orthogonally (e.g. a1–a2 or a1–b1). This game seems to have been played mainly in Germany, right up to the nineteenth century. *(J.M.R.)*

Cylinder Boards

There are three types of cylinder board:

1. Vertical: the a- and h-files are joined, to form a shape like an open-ended tin can;

2. Horizontal: the 1st and 8th ranks are joined (the same tin can is now lying on its side);

3. 'Anchor-ring', which combines the vertical and horizontal cylinders – a theoretical shape for a chess-board, of course, but imagine that the tin can has been bent round so that the open ends are joined to one another, forming a shape like a rubber inner-tube or a doughnut.

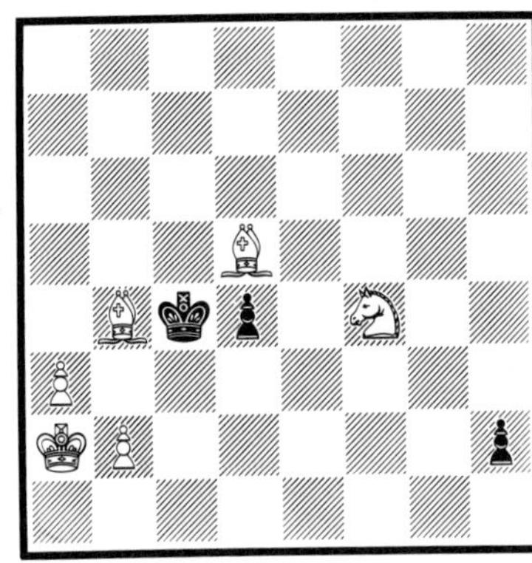

C. R. Flood, *A Guide to Fairy Chess* 1967 – Series-helpmate in 3, on (*a*) normal board: 1. h1Q; 2. Q×d5; 3. Qb5, b3; (*b*) vertical cylinder: 1. h1R; 2. Rh5; 3. Rb5, b3; (*c*) horizontal cylinder: 1. h1B; 2. Bg2; 3. Bb5, b3; (*d*) anchor-ring: 1. h1S; 2. Sa7; 3. Sb5, b3. It is assumed that the P promotes on the first rank of the diagram. *(J.M.R.)*

Double-Move [Marseilles] Chess

Each player plays two consecutive moves on his turn to play. Check can be given only with the second move of a pair, and must be annulled with the next player's first pair of moves. *(J.M.R.)*

Four-Handed Chess

This is played on an 8 × 8 board with an extra 24 squares (8 × 3) attached to each side. Four players sit one at each side, and two sets of men are needed, of a different pattern for identification purposes. The pieces are arrayed on the 16 squares in front of each player, opposite players partnering one another. Play proceeds clockwise, the object being to mate both opponents. As soon as a player is mated his pieces remain where they are but take no further part in the game, unless the mate is relieved, in which case the pieces resume their original powers. A player in check must annul it himself. Pawns promote on an opponent's (not the partner's) back row, if they ever manage to capture often enough to get there. *(J.M.R.)*

Kamikaze Chess

Like the Japanese pilots of the Second World War who sacrificed themselves by crashing their aircraft onto enemy ships, Kamikaze pieces disappear from the board whenever they make a capture. Invented by Pierre Monréal in 1965. *(J.M.R.)*

Kriegspiel

Invented by W. H. Temple around 1900. Each player sees only one board with only his own pieces. An umpire has a third board with both White and Black pieces, and he copies whatever moves are made or tried by each player, telling them only if an attempted move is playable or not.

A player may enquire whether any pawn-capture can be made, asking 'Are there any?', and if the answer is 'yes' a pawn-capture must be attempted. If that pawn-capture is not playable, any move may be tried until a legal one is made. The umpire announces any check by stating its direction (e.g. 'check on the rank', 'check on the long diagonal', 'check from a Knight', etc.).

Captures are announced by the umpire's stating the capture-square, e.g. 'capture on d4'. No other information is made available, and each player must therefore try to deduce or guess his opponent's moves. *(W.H.)*

Losing Game
The object is to expose all one's pieces to capture (King included), capturing being compulsory. The winner is the first player to lose all his men or be stalemated. There is no check and no mate, and pawns may promote to King. *(J.M.R.)*

Must-Capture Chess
Any capture that is legal must be made. This variant of the normal game dates from the Middle Ages and was first played in Morocco. *(J.M.R.)*

Neutral Piece
This piece belongs at each move to whichever side the player whose move it is chooses. Thus White may move a neutral piece or capture it, but he must not expose his King to check from it, as Black may move the neutral piece at his next move. *(J.M.R.)*

No-Capture Chess
Neither side may capture, unless capture is the only way to prevent mate. *(J.M.R.)*

Progressive [Scotch] Chess
White plays one move, Black replies with two successive moves. White then plays three moves in a row, Black four, White five, and so on. Check may be given only with the last move of a sequence, and the check must be annulled with the first move of the next player's sequence, otherwise he is mated. Invented by Znosko-Borovsky in 1947. *(J.M.R.)*

Randomized Chess
The pieces are arranged on the first rank in an arbitrary order that is the same for both sides. *(J.M.R.)*

Refusal Chess
On each move a player has the right, if he wishes to exercise it, to refuse his opponent's move and oblige him to play another, which must be accepted. *(J.M.R.)*

Rifle Chess
A capture is made when the capturing piece, without moving, shoots the captured piece off the board, such a shot counting as a single move. Invented by W. J. Seabrook in 1921. *(J.M.R.)*

Three-Dimensional

'VĀSAVADATTĀ'
A romance written in the late sixth or early seventh century AD in north-west India by the Sanskrit writer Subandhu, which contains the earliest reference to chess. This runs: 'The time of the rains played its game with frogs for chessmen which, yellow and green in colour, as if mottled with lac, leapt up on the garden-bed squares.'

It is on this evidence together with a reference in another seventh-century Sanskrit writing, the *Harshachārita*, that historians base their dating of the invention of chess. *(H.G.)*

VASILIEV, Viktor Andreyevich *(1916–1950)*
One of the strongest Leningrad masters in the period round the war years. Was seriously wounded during the siege of Leningrad, but continued to register good results in the championships of that city until his early death. *(W.R.H.)*

VASUKOV, Evgeny Andreevich *(b. 5 March 1933)*
Soviet international grandmaster since 1961, three years after receiving the international master title. A member of the editorial board of *64*. He has played on ten occasions in the final of the Soviet championship, his best performance being =3rd in the Swiss System event of 1967. He has been several times champion of Moscow and played in the USSR Student team of 1955 and 1956. His best tournament performances are those at Moscow 1961 (=1st), Belgrade 1961 (1st), Moscow 1962 (=1st), Varna 1971 (1st) and, his best ever result, Manila 1974 (1st above Petrosian, Larsen, etc.). *(K.J.O'C.)*

VELIMIROVIĆ, Dragoljub *(b. 12 May 1942)*
Yugoslav international grandmaster (1973). He was awarded the title of international master in 1972. His spectacular style, taking advantage of his extraordinary gift for visualizing sacrificial

possibilities, has made him popular with spectators wherever he has competed. However, his very sharp play, requiring great effort in each and every game, has been something of a handicap in his quest for tournament success and he has had few outstanding results; such as there are being at Skopje 1971 (=2nd behind Polugayevsky), Vrnjačka Banja 1973 (1st) and his victory in the 1975 Yugoslav championship.

One of his most outstanding games is the following, played in the 1972 Yugoslav championship.

White: Velimirović; *Black* Ljubojević
Sicilian Defence
1. P–K4, P–QB4; 2. N–KB3, P–Q3; 3. P–Q4, P×P; 4. N×P, N–KB3; 5. N–QB3, P–QR3; 6. B–N5, P–K3; 7. P–B4, B–K2; 8. Q–B3, Q–B2; 9. O–O–O, QN–Q2; 10. B–Q3, P–N4; 11. KR–K1, B–N2; 12. N–Q5, N×N; 13. P×N, B×B;

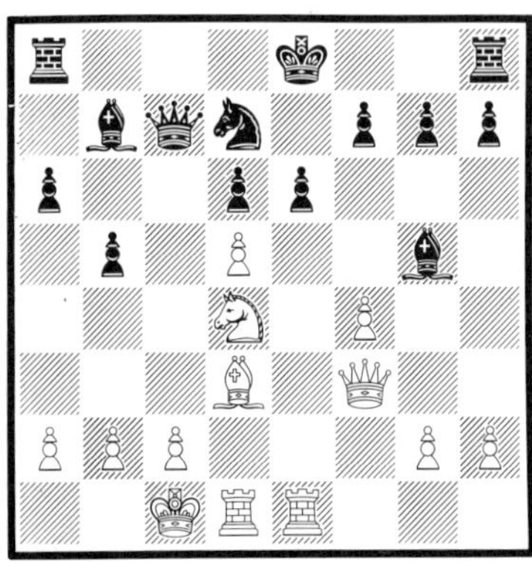

14. R×P+, P×R; 15. N×KP, Q–R4; 16. Q–R5+, P–N3; 17. Q×B, R–KN1; 18. R–Q2, N–B1; 19. N×N, Q–Q1; 20. N×RP, Q×Q; 21. P×Q, K–B2; 22. N–B6, R–R1; 23. P–KN3, B–B1; 24. P–KR4, B–B4; 25. B×B, P×B; 26. P–R5, R–QR2; 27. R–B2, resigns. *(K.J.O'C.)*

VENEZUELA

In the current decade, Venezuela has organized several important competitions. The 1970 Caracas tournament will have a permanent place in history as the event in which Karpov obtained the grandmaster title; he finished =4th behind Kavalek and, =2nd, Stein and Panno. In 1976 the World Student Team championship was also organized, in Caracas, by the Federacion Venezolana de Ajedrez, Colegio de Ingenieros de Venezuela, Apartado 2006, Caracas 101.

Venezuela has attended five Olympiads, obtaining the following results: 33rd in 1964, 36th in 1966, 32nd in 1968, 46th in 1974 and 23rd in 1976. *(K.J.O'C.)*

VERESOV, Gavrill Nikolayevich *(b. 8 July 1912)*

One of the leading group of Soviet masters during the war years, and international master since the institution of the title in 1950. Made his best results in the USSR championship of 1940, when he shared seventh place, and 1944 when he shared eighth place.

Veresov is best known for his theoretical contributions to the opening system: 1. P–Q4, P–Q4; 2. N–QB3, N–KB3; 3. B–N5, which bears his name in the USSR but which is known elsewhere as the Richter Attack. *(W.R.H.)*

VERLINSKY, Boris Markovich *(1887–1950)*

One of the strongest Soviet masters in the 1920s, Verlinsky took first place in the 1928 Moscow championship and the following year won the USSR championship. He did not compete internationally to any great extent, but at Moscow 1925 shared twelfth place in a very strong field, including victories against Capablanca, Rubinstein and Spielmann.

His past achievements were recognized by the award of the title of international master in 1950. *(W.R.H.)*

VIDA, Marco Gerolamo [Marcus Hieronymus]
(1490–27 September 1566)

In his youth and early manhood Vida was a poet and writer. He took up an ecclesiastic career and, as a protegé of Leo X, was made prior of San Silvestro in Frascati. In 1532 Clement VII appointed him Bishop of Alba, a position he occupied, with some vicissitudes due to war, for the rest of his life.

It was as early as 1513 that he wrote his celebrated *Scacchia Ludus*. *(H.G.)*

VIDMAR, Milan *(22 June 1885–9 October 1962)*

Yugoslavia's first grandmaster, a contemporary of Alekhine, Capablanca and Rubinstein. Learnt chess relatively late when aged fifteen. His rise to prominence was delayed by lack of major tournaments and a non-professional approach to chess which became his chief obstacle in achieving world results. During 1902–7 he studied electrical engineering in Vienna, occasionally playing chess in Austria and Germany. In 1906 he received the master title for his performance at Nuremberg. Five years later Vidmar tied =2nd with Rubinstein at San Sebastian and was recognized as a grandmaster. The First World War did not interfere with his chess career; he was 1st at Berlin 1918.

1922 marks the beginning of a new era in Vidmar's career. After a fine achievement at the London tournament 1922 – 3rd behind Capablanca and Alekhine – Vidmar was widely regarded as a World title contender. Tournaments that followed reinforced his new status: 1st with Alekhine, Hastings 1925/6, scoring $8\frac{1}{2}/9$, 3rd Semmering 1926 and 4th New York 1927.

Then abruptly his results registered a sharp decline. Vidmar himself ascribed it to a crisis of self-confidence, but the more probable reason was the change in attitude towards chess. From being a pastime, the game had become a means of livelihood to an ever-increasing number of leading players thus making it extremely difficult even for amateurs of Vidmar's calibre to compete without serious theoretical preparation. Disillusioned, Vidmar withdrew from the tournament arena after winning the Yugoslav championship 1939. In 1951 he wrote *Pol Stoletja Ob Sahovnici*, a lively autobiography. He accomplished much for the popularization of chess in Yugoslavia. Vidmar attained great distinction in electronics engineering and became Dean at Ljubljana University. Two grandmaster tournaments were held in his memory: Ljubljana 1969 and Ljubljana-Portorož 1973.

Berlin 1918
White: Rubinstein; *Black:* Vidmar
Budapest Defence
1. P–Q4, N–KB3; 2. P–QB4, P–K4; 3. P×P, N–N5; 4. B–B4, N–QB3; 5. N–KB3, B–N5+; 6. N–B3, Q–K2; 7. Q–Q5, B×N+; 8. P×B, Q–R6; 9. R–B1, P–B3; 10. P×P, N×P(B3); 11. Q–Q2, P–Q3; 12. N–Q4, O–O; 13. P–K3, N×N; 14. BP×N, N–K5; 15. Q–B2, Q–R4+; 16. K–K2, R×B; 17. P×R, B–B4; 18. Q–N2, R–K1; 19. K–B3, N–Q7+; 20. K–N3, N–K5+; 21. K–R4, R–K3; 22. B–K2, R–R3+; 23. B–R5, R×B+; 24. K×R, B–N3+; 25. resigns. *(R.D.K.)*

VIDMAR, Milan Jr. *(b. 16 December 1909)*
A Yugoslav international master (1950). Competed three times in the Yugoslav championship, represented Yugoslavia in the 1950 Olympiad. A gifted player though never in the class of his famous father, Milan Vidmar has no major success to boast, but he had a good solid performance at Karlovy Vary-Marianské Lazné, 1948, where he came =6th/20. In 1952 he withdrew from the tournament arena. An electronics engineer by profession. *(R.D.K.)*

VIENNA 1873
In conjunction with the Vienna Exhibition a great match-tournament was organized at Vienna 1873.

The system was that each player played a small match of three games with the other and the match had to be finished within the space of three days. A won match was worth 1 point and a drawn match half a point.

Blackburne led till the last round, but then lost to Rosenthal and had to play a further deciding match with Steinitz which the latter won 2–0, so that Steinitz won first and Blackburne won second prize. Pitschel withdrew early on, so many of his zeros were by default. Leading scores: Steinitz 22½, Blackburne 21½, Anderssen 19, Rosenthal 17. *(H.G.)*

VIENNA 1882
The Vienna Chess Club celebrated the twenty-fifth anniversary of its foundation with the second great international tournament to be held there. It did this largely with the support of the former chess professional, but by that time successful banker, Von Kolisch. It was a double-round event and the second tour was disturbed by a number of withdrawals. Noa left the scene after the very first round of the second tour. Fleissig withdrew after the 20th round. Bird, Schwarz and Wittek also lost games by default.

Steinitz and Winawer had a play-off for the first prize but after they had each won a game it was agreed to share the top prizes. Leading scores: Steinitz, Winawer 24, Mason 23, Mackenzie, Zukertort 22½. *(H.G.)*

VIENNA 1898
1898 was the fiftieth anniversary of Kaiser Franz Josef's accession to the throne of Austria and as it also happened to be twenty-five years since the first great Vienna tournament of 1873, a great international tournament was held in Vienna. It became known as the Kaiser-Jubilaums Schachturnier.

All the great players of the day, with the exception of Lasker, competed. The play-off after the tie for first place between Tarrasch and Pillsbury was won by Tarrasch +2−1=1. With this Tarrasch won the unprecedented sum of 6,000 crowns. Leading scores: Tarrasch, Pillsbury 27½, Janowski 25½, Steinitz 23½. *(H.G.)*

VIENNA 1922
The last in the great series of tournaments throughout 1922, Vienna was a veritable Waterloo of the hypermoderns. Alekhine came =4th with two old-timers Maróczy and Tarrasch, Grünfeld 7th, Réti 8th, Bogoljubow 9th, and Sämisch nowhere – a melancholy tale unequalled in post-First World War tournaments. Only Tartakower upheld the honour of the new school and for a long time looked like winning the tournament (as he has done on many other occasions, such as Vienna 1907, Teplitz-Schönau 1922 and Semmering 1926). But a wonderful finish by Rubinstein deprived him of top honours. The following game illustrates the 'theme' of the tournament:

White: Tarrasch; *Black:* Réti
Caro-Kann Defence
1. P–K4, P–QB3; 2. N–QB3, P–Q4; 3. N–B3, N–B3; 4. P×P, P×P; 5. P–Q4, B–N5; 6. P–KR3, B×N; 7. Q×B, P–K3; 8. B–Q3, N–B3; 9. B–K3, B–K2; 10. O–O, O–O; 11. P–R3, P–QR3; 12. N–K2, P–QN4; 13. B–KB4, Q–N3; 14. P–B3, N–QR4; 15. QR–Q1, N–B5; 16. B–B1, Q–B3; 17. N–N3, P–QR4; 18. KR–K1, P–N5; 19. RP×P, P×P; 20. N–B5, P×N; 21. R×B, P×P; 22. P×P, P–N3; 23. B–R6, N–N7; 24. R–N1, N×B; 25. Q×N, KR–N1; 26. R×R+, R×R; 27. Q–N3, R–Q1; 28. Q–K5, R–R1; 29. R–B7, Q–K3; 30. Q×Q, P×Q; 31. R–N7+, K–R1; 32. R–K7, K–N1; 33. P–B3, N–K1; 34. K–R2, N–Q3; 35. R–N7+, K–R1; 36. R–Q7, N–N4; 37. K–N3, N×BP; 38. K–B4, N–N4; 39. K–K5, R–K1; 40. K–B6, K–N1; 41. R–N7+, K–R1; 42. R–N7, N–Q3; 43. R–Q7, N–N4; 44. K–B7, R–KN1; 45. R–Q8, resigns. *(W.H.)*

VIENNA GAME
Despite Weaver Adams's claim some years ago that the Vienna (characterized by the moves 1. P–K4, P–K4; 2. N–QB3) led to a forced win for White, this opening is considered one of the more innocuous ways for White to begin. White hopes to continue with a later P–KB4 leading to a sort of King's Gambit Declined.

A wild offshoot is the Vienna Gambit given by 2. . , N–QB3; 3. P–B4 and leading to the Steinitz Gambit after 3. . , P×P; 4. P–Q4, Q–R5+; 5. K–K2. *(W.R.H.)*

VIRGIN ISLANDS
Virgin Islanders made their first foray into Olympic competition in 1968, finishing 52nd, and then placed 58th in 1970 and 62nd in 1972. At the next Olympiad the islanders were represented by two teams; the British Virgin Islands (74th in 1974 and 47th in 1976) on each occasion lagging behind their rivals, the US Virgin Islands who were 64th in 1974 and 46th in 1976.

The two organizing bodies are the British Virgin Islands Chess Federation, P.O. Box 21, Road Town, Tortola and the US Virgin Islands Chess Federation, P.O. Box 1116, Kingshill, St Croix, USVI 00850. *(K.J.O'C.)*

VLADIMIROV, Boris Timofeyevich *(b. 17 May 1929)*
Soviet master from Leningrad, awarded title of international master in 1964. A lawyer by profession. *(W.R.H.)*

VOELLMY, Erwin *(9 September 1886–15 January 1951)*
Swiss champion in 1920 and 1922, he was by profession a mathematics teacher at the Basle Gymnasium. He edited the chess column in the *Basler Nachrichten* for forty years and was the Swiss representative at the first meeting of FIDE at Paris 1924.

His chief work was *Schachtaktik* in four volumes, appearing in Berne 1927–30. *(H.G.)*

VOGT, Lothar *(b. 17 January 1952)*
An East German international master, who, after some good placings in East German championships and East European junior tournaments, occupied fourth place in the international tournament at Lublin 1972 and came =4th at Bucharest 1974, =5th at Cienfuegos 1975, and =6th at Brno the same year. *(W.H.)*

VOLGA GAMBIT
A determined attempt to destroy the base of White's centre that was introduced into tournament chess by the Swedish master, Erik Lundin: 1. P–Q4, N–KB3; 2. P–QB4, P–B4; 3. P–Q5, P–QN4; 4. P×P, P–QR3.

Thus far L. Szabo–E. Lundin, Saltsjöbaden 1948, and White continued with the normal line 5. P×P (another main line is 5. P–K3). According to Benko, the genuine Volga Gambit consists in Black playing, either now or later, P–K3 himself.

All other variations he classes under Benko Gambit, thereby in effect classifying the Volga Gambit as an offshoot of the Benko. Most other authorities disagree with this classification, which appears to have little historical or practical justification. It is perhaps a controversy best left to be settled between grandmaster Benko and the inhabitants of the banks of the Volga river. *(H.G.)*

VOLPERT, Larissa Ilyinichna *(b. 30 March 1926)*
International Woman master since 1954 and three times Soviet Women's champion – in 1954, 1958 (after a play-off with Zvorikina) and 1959. Her best results in the Women's World Championship were in the 1955 Candidates tournament, when she finished second to Rubtsova and 3rd in the 1959 Candidates. *(W.R.H.)*

VUKĈEVIĈH, Dr Milan *(b. 11 March 1937)*
Yugoslav international master (receiving the title in 1958) and representative of his country in the Leipzig Olympiad of 1960.

Vukĉeviĉh emigrated to the USA, devoting his chess efforts to analysis and to the composition of studies for which he gained the title of Master of Composition.

Vukĉeviĉh returned to major competitive chess in 1975, taking 3rd prize below Browne and Rogoff but ahead of Reshevsky, Lombardy, R. Byrne etc. in the very strong US championship at Oberlin. His sole recent performance in international events was a modest 11th/16 at the Reykjavik international tournament 1976.

Outside chess Vukĉeviĉh has led a distinguished scientific career and has recently been proposed as a candidate for the Nobel Prize. *(R.D.K.)*

VUKIC, Milan *(b. 19 August 1942)*
Yugoslav international grandmaster (1975), eight years after winning the international master title. A regular competitor in the Yugoslav championship, he won the title in 1970 and again in 1974. His best international results have been in the tournaments at Banja Luka 1974 (1st), Bajmok 1975 (=1st), Varna 1975 (=1st) and Vukovar 1976 (1st). *(K.J.O'C.)*

VUKOVIĆ, Vladimir *(26 August 1898–18 November 1975)*
Yugoslavia's most outstanding chess-writer. Received the international master title for his play at Vienna 1922. He represented Yugoslavia in two Olympiads, 1927 and 1936. Never a great player, Vuković was far more important as editor of the magazine *Sahovski Glasnik* at a time when there was no organized chess life in Yugoslavia. A distinguished author whose best works are: *The Art of Attack in Chess*, Oxford, London 1963; *The Chess Sacrifice*, London, New York 1968. *(R.D.K.)*

WADE, Robert G. *(b. 10 April 1921)*
International master who was born at Dunedin, New Zealand, but came to live in England in 1946 and has represented both countries on different occasions. He has nearly always done well in British championships and won the title at Chester in 1952 and again at Coventry in 1970. He has played for the British Chess Federation at the Olympiads of 1954, 1956, 1958, 1960, and 1962, winning the shortest game of the Varna Olympiad in that year in nine moves against Kinzel of Austria. He played for the New Zealand team at the 1970 Olympiad at Siegen but returned to the B.C.F. team at Skopje in 1972.

His best individual international results were a fifth place at

Venice 1950 and again fifth at the Masters section of the Capablanca Memorial at Cienfuegos in Cuba in 1975. Possessor of a sharp clear-cut style of play, he once drew a match with the West German grandmaster Lothar Schmid with neither side drawing a game, though this was before Schmid received the grandmaster title.

He has done much valuable work in England teaching the young, and was responsible for the text of a highly successful television series in 1975.

His main books are: *Soviet Chess*, London 1967; *Botvinnik–Bronstein Match 1951* (in co-operation with W. Winter), London, Toronto 1951; *Match Petrosian–Botvinnik*, London 1963; *Sousse 1967*, The Chess Player, Nottingham 1968. *(H.G.)*

WAGNER, Heinrich *(9 August 1888–24 June 1959)*
A German master of the between-the-wars period, Wagner played but little in international events. His outstanding achievement, for which he was later awarded the international master title, was =3rd with Rubinstein, behind Bogoljubow and Nimzowitsch, at Breslau 1925. He represented Germany in the Olympic Team Tournaments of 1927, 1928, 1930, and 1931, scoring well on each occasion. Wagner retired from competitive chess when the Nazis took over. *(W.H.)*

WALBRODT, Karl August *(28 November 1871–3 October 1902)*
Walbrodt had a very short chess career (1891–8). His best tournament achievements were =1st with Von Bardeleben at Kiel 1893 and 2nd to Charousek at Berlin 1897. He also had good results at Dresden 1892 and Leipzig 1894 (=4th in both); but in the three really great events he contested he was just below 50% at Hastings 1895, reached the 50% mark at Nuremberg 1896, and did poorly at Vienna 1898. In matches he beat Schallopp, W. Cohn, Von Bardeleben as well as a number of strong American amateurs (Delmar, Vasquez, Ettlinger) during his stay overseas in 1893; he drew with Mieses and Von Scheve, but lost to Pillsbury, Tarrasch and Janowski. *(W.H.)*

WALES
Chess activity in Wales has markedly increased since the end of the Second World War. No less than four British Chess Federation Congresses have been held there during that period: Swansea 1951, Aberystwyth 1955 and 1961 and Rhyl 1969.

On 19 June 1954 a Union of Associations in South Wales and Monmouthshire was formed and, as the Welsh Chess Union, it was a constituent member of the British Chess Federation until 15 November 1969.

The Welsh Chess Union then applied for membership to FIDE and it was accepted as an independent unit by FIDE at the Siegen Congress in 1970.

A Welsh team competed for the first time in an Olympiad at Skopje 1972 where it came 43rd/62. The top two boards distinguished themselves with plus scores. Williams scoring 58.8% and Hutchings 52.6%.

It was at the Nice Olympiad in 1974 that Wales made a remarkable breakthrough in qualifying for the top final section – a feat all the more striking when one remembers that the Nice Olympiad had more teams and was more strongly contested than ever before. Wales finished up 16th/74 and the two top boards who had met a selection of the world's best players scored most creditably a little below 50%. Williams +5−7=6 and Hutchings +6−7=5.

Another good result (though not as good as at Nice which was a much stronger Olympiad) came at the 1976 Haifa Olympiad, where Wales shared 11th to 18th places out of 48 teams. On top board the former British champion Botterill was quite out of form and could score only 30% but the other players all did well: Williams 51%, Hutchings 55%, Cooper 65%, I. Jones 66.6% and Rayner 50% in descending order of boards.

Much of this success must be due to the Welsh Union's energetic President, R. K. Clues, who is also FIDE treasurer, and to its enthusiastic secretary F. G. Hatto.

The address of the Welsh Chess Union is c/o A. H. Williams, Woodcote, Talygarn, Pontyclun, Mid-Glamorgan CF7 9UJ and its official publication is *Y Ddraig*, c/o T. Ll. Jones, Dolnant, Llangranog, Llandysul, Dyfed. *(H.G.)*

WALKER, George *(13 March 1803–23 April 1879)*
A British chess writer and organizer whose passionate interest in the game put him in the centre of chess happenings in the nineteenth century, despite his comparatively weak play.

He was born in London in Great Portland Street where his father had a bookseller's business. Eventually he specialized in music publishing and his son, George Walker, became a bookseller and music publisher likewise.

In his youth and throughout his life he was an assiduous founder of chess clubs, the most famous having been the Westminster Chess Club in 1831.

In 1835 he started a chess column in *Bell's Life in London* which had an exceptionally long run and lasted till 1873. In 1834 he published his epoch-making work *Chess Studies*, a book containing 1000 games, amongst them the famous series of games played between La Bourdonnais and McDonnell.

In this connexion the difference between him and W. G. Walker should be noted. The coincidence of surname is all the more confusing in that W.G. succeeded George Walker as secretary of the Westminster Chess Club and was also, like George, an assiduous collector and editor of famous chess-games. It was W.G. who published in 1836 *Games at Chess by M'Donnell*, whilst George, in 1835, did *Games at Chess Played by Philidor and His Contemporaries.*

George Walker also published in 1850 a bright and entertaining but not particularly accurate book on chess-players of note entitled *Chess and Chess-players.*

His generosity was the means of rescuing many a player from penury and it was he who arranged the visits to London by La Bourdonnais and, when the great French player died, saw to it that he was laid to rest in Kensal Green alongside his great rival McDonnell. *(H.G.)*

WEAK COLOUR COMPLEX
A complex of squares of the same colour, the weakness of which is interdependent as a result of the placing of the pawns and the absence of the Bishop that ought to protect the squares weakened by the advance of the pawns. The existence of a weak colour complex often results in a complete blockade of the position on these squares.

The first to explore and discuss the subject systematically was Nimzowitsch, and many of his games show the exploitation of this type of complex. See the diagrammed position (from the game Mannheimer–Nimzowitsch, Frankfurt 1930). Note how all Black units, except two pawns on the Q-side, are placed on the weakened white squares from where they hold the whole of the White position in a deadly grip. The winning idea from the diagram underlines the opponent's helplessness: Black Simply wins the QRP and queens his own in what is still the middle-game:

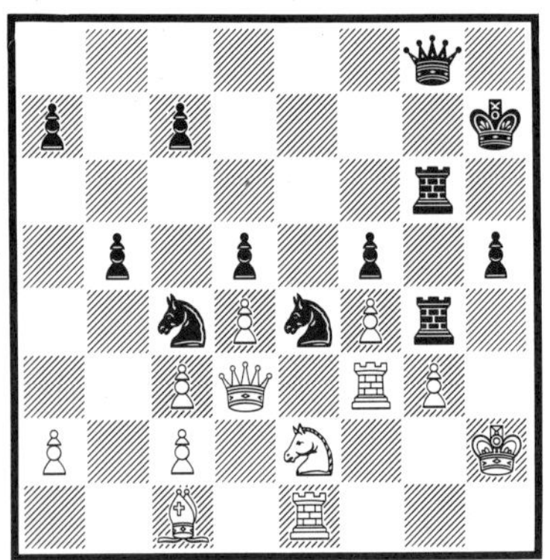

1. K–N2, P–R5; 2. R–R1, R–KR3; 3. R–R3, Q–N3; 4. B–K3, Q–R3; 5. B–B2, Q×P; 6. B–K1, P–R4; 7. K–B1, Q–N8; 8. N–N1, P–R5; 9. K–K2, P–R6; 10. R–B1, P–R7; 11. resigns. *(W.H.)*

WEENINK, Henri *(17 October 1892–2 December 1931)*
A strong Dutch player and famous problem composer. Played in Olympiads 1927 (2nd board) and 1928 (1st board). Best result: 1st prize Amsterdam 1930 ahead of Euwe and Spielmann. In twenty-five years he composed more than 400 problems. He won a great number of prizes, national and international, e.g. 1st prize *British Chess Magazine* 1924. He was probably the strongest player-problemist of all time. *(R.D.K.)*

WEINSTEIN, Norman Stephen *(b. 4 October 1950)*
US international master (1973). US Open champion in 1973. Other notable tournament performances: 2nd Portimao 1975 and =1st Manhattan international, New York 1976. *(K.J.O'C.)*

WEINSTEIN, Raymond *(b. 1941)*
An American international master who had a brief career. The Brooklyn-born Weinstein first gained attention by winning the 1958 US Junior championship. A frequent high board on US Student Olympiad teams, Weinstein's biggest successes were in US championships (3rd in 1960/1). He played in one Olympiad for USA, Leipzig 1960, and scored 81.3% on 6th board.

After a 7th place finish in the 1963/4 championship, Weinstein dropped out of chess. *(A.S.)*

WEISS, Max *(21 July 1857–14 March 1927)*
A great Austrian player of the nineteenth century, Weiss tied for first place with Schwarz and Minckwitz on his first appearance at Graz 1880. At Hamburg 1885 he was in a quintuple tie for second; at Frankfurt 1887 he was =2nd with Blackburne, but his greatest success was joint first with Chigorin in the gigantic tournament of New York 1889 (where he scored +24−4=20). His books (*Schach-Meisterstreiche*, Mühlhausen 1918, and *Kleines Schachlehrbuch*, Mühlhausen 1920) as well as his problem collections (of Loyd, Shinkman, and of Bamberg problemists, *Caissa Bambergensis*, Bamberg 1902) are forgotten today. *(W.H.)*

WESTERINEN, Markku Heikki Julius *(b. 12 May 1944)*
A Finnish international master (1967) and several times Finnish national champion since 1965. Westerinen has represented Finland in every Olympiad since 1962. Tournament results include: 3rd Berlin 1971, =2nd Oslo 1973, 1st Sant Feliu de Guixols 1973 and 1st Dortmund 1975.

He has an original and combinative style of play that brooks no compromise. *(R.D.K.)*

'WIENER SCHACHZEITUNG'
One of the greatest chess magazines, running from 1898–1916 and then from 1923–38.

On the first page of volume 1 there is an address to the reader dated 1 January 1898 saying that with the fusion of the Vienna Chess Society and the New-Vienna Chess Club into the Vienna Chess Club a great impetus had been given to Viennese chess life, and that the club committee had decided to call into existence the *Wiener Schachzeitung.*

The editors of the first year were H. Fahndrich, A. Halprin and G. Marco; but as time went on Georg Marco became the sole editor and even the publisher. Marco edited the magazine till 1914 and in that period it became the best chess magazine in the world.

When it was resumed in 1923 it called itself the *Neue Wiener Schach-Zeitung* and was edited by Ing. R. Wahle and A. Lewit. But within a year it had reverted to its old title and in 1926 another great editor, Albert Becker, took over. The witty pen of Hans Kmoch gave much distinction to the magazine and every now and then he would edit a *faschings* (carnival) number that was genuinely funny. *(H.G.)*

WIJK-AAN-ZEE
See under HOOGOVEN CHESS TOURNAMENT.

WILLIAMS, Elijah *(1810–8 September 1854)*
A prominent British master of the mid-nineteenth century who was famed for the slowness of his play at a period when chess clocks for important competitions had not yet come into fashion.

Williams was born in Bristol where he practised as an apothecary but soon became so attached to chess (he was president of the Bristol Chess Club and also conducted a chess-column in the *Bath and Cheltenham Gazette* from 8 September 1840 to 21 October 1846) that he made the game his profession.

Abandoning Bristol for London where the life of a chess professional was considerably more profitable than in the provinces, he contested a number of matches with varying success; e.g. 1846 v. Kennedy (+4−2=0) and 1852 v. Horwitz (+5−3=9). In three matches v. Harrwitz he met with decisive reverses (a total of +2−17=8) but gained a curious triumph over Staunton in 1851. Although losing on games played by +4−6=3 Williams emerged a technical victor as the result of Staunton's rash decision to offer starting odds of three games! This match, however, produced much fine chess.

Williams also participated in the first international tournament at London 1851 where he took third prize behind Anderssen and Wyvill. An analysis of his games from the important events of 1851 reveals that Williams had developed a most sophisticated playing style, employing positional devices which were not to become current for a further sixty years.

While in London in 1852, Williams published a collection of games under the title of *Horae Divanianae*, being a selection of 150 games by leading masters, most of which had been played at Simpson's Divan. He wrote the chess-column for the *Field* from 1853 to 1857.

He died in London at Charing Cross Hospital of cholera on 8 September 1854. We emphasize this date since the usual date given is that of 1 September 1854. But we are indebted to Mr Kenneth Whyld for the information about the correct date on the death certificate which also states he was forty-four when he died. Up to now his date of birth was not known and was assumed to have been considerably earlier. *(R.D.K.)*

WINAWER, Simon *(5 March 1838–12 January 1920)*
A Polish master, born in Warsaw. He 'dropped from the clouds' (as Staunton put it) when, as a virtually unknown visitor to the Paris Exhibition, he competed in the Paris 1867 tournament and finished =2nd with Steinitz. After the tournament Winawer lost a short match to Neumann, who had come 4th. Subsequent successes included: =1st (with Zukertort) Paris 1878, =1st (with Steinitz) Vienna 1882, 1st Nuremberg 1883. One of the main variations in the French Defence is named after him (1. P–K4, P–K3; 2. P–Q4, P–Q4; 3. N–QB3, B–N5). *(R.D.K.)*

WINTER, William *(11 September 1898–18 December 1955)*
International master and twice British champion (1935 and 1936), Winter was an excellent illustration of Réti's thesis that players tend to be the opposite over the board to their character in real life. Over the board he was classical, scientific and sober; away from the board he was revolutionary, illogically moved by his emotions (he contrived to be both a fervent Communist and a staunch patriot), and more often than not, drunk.

His university career, where he read law, coincided with the First World War and, after a brief interruption for military service he returned to Cambridge where in 1919 he became university champion and defeated R. H. V. Scott (a strong player who won the British championship in 1920) in a match by 4–2. On the strength of this he was invited to play in the Hastings Victory tournament of 1919 where, however, he did badly, coming 11th out of 12.

After an interval during which he fervently pursued a political career to such an extent as to incur a six-months prison sentence for sedition (Winter always denied the sedition and said that the charge was a trumped-up one), he took up the career of chess professional. The life suited him since it enabled him to lead the kind of Bohemian existence that pleased his artistic temperament. It should be mentioned that he was a nephew of Sir James Barrie and would have fitted in well in one of his uncle's plays.

As a player he was eminently sound and, being an apostle of Tarrasch, a fine clear strategist. But he was lacking in tactical ability and his poor health and his way of life interfered with his consistency and impaired his stamina. But he had a number of fine victories over great players (Bronstein, Nimzowitsch and Vidmar for example).

He played in four Olympiads: Hamburg 1930 (scoring 76.7% on 4th board), Prague 1931 (58.8% on 4th board), Folkestone 1933 (59.1% on 3rd board) and Warsaw 1935 (41.7% on 1st board). He was selected to play at Stockholm in 1937 but, having 'lost' his passport three times, he was refused a fresh one by the authorities.

His best international individual results were =6th at London 1927, and =5th at Lodz 1935.

His career as a chess journalist (he wrote for the *Manchester Guardian* and the *Daily Worker*) was somewhat impeded and spoilt by his Bohemian ways, but he wrote some excellent works on chess: *Chess for Match Players*, London 1936; *Kings of Chess*, London, New York 1954; *Modern Master-play* (in collaboration with F. D. Yates), London, Philadelphia 1929. *(H.G.)*

WISKER, John *(1846–18 January 1884)*
A prominent British player and chess administrator, Wisker won the B.C.A. Challenge Cup in 1870 after a play-off with Burn. In 1871 he narrowly lost a match (+2−3=4) to the French master Rosenthal, who had fled to London to avoid the rigours of war. Wisker retained the Challenge Cup in 1872, this time after a play-off with De Vere. In the following year Wisker played a series of matches against Bird, drawing the first (+6−6=1), losing the second (+4−6=2) and winning the third (+10−8=3).

From 1872 to 1877 Wisker was secretary of the B.C.A. and jointly edited (with Skipworth) the *Chess Player's Chronicle*. Wisker suffered from consumption, and in 1877 under doctor's orders emigrated to Australia, where he died. *(H.G.)*

WOLF, Heinrich *(20 October 1875–1943)*
An Austrian master, Wolf was killed by the Nazis during the war. A participant in many international tournaments before and after the First World War, he came third in the extremely strong tournament at Vienna 1922, behind Rubinstein and Tartakower, but ahead of such players as Alekhine, Bogoljubow, Grünfeld, Réti, Tarrasch. He also made plus scores at Monte Carlo 1902, Hanover 1902, Nuremberg 1906, Carlsbad 1907, and Bad Pistyan 1922. *(W.H.)*

WOMEN'S WORLD CHAMPIONSHIP
The title of Women's World Champion only came into existence in 1927, when it was decided to hold a tournament for women in conjunction with the first men's Olympiad in London. The winner, as had been generally expected, was Vera Menchik, with a score of 10½/11. Second place was taken by K. Beskov (Sweden) and third was P. Wolf-Kalmar (Austria).

Until the Second World War, the women's title was always decided in a tournament, and Vera Menchik maintained her domination throughout:

Hamburg 1930: Menchik 6½, Wolf-Kalmar 5½, W. Henschel (Germany) 4½ (five participants).

Prague 1931: Menchik 8 (out of 8), Wolf-Kalmar 4, Mrs Stevenson (Britain) 3½ (five participants).

Folkestone 1933: Menchik 14 (out of 14), E. Price (Britain) 9, Mrs Gilchrist (Scotland) 8½.

In 1934 Sonja Graf of Germany challenged Menchik to a match of four games. She won the first, but lost the remaining three so Menchik's title was safe. In any case the match was a privately arranged one, not under the auspices of FIDE.

Warsaw 1935 was the next official championship tournament: Menchik 9 (again 100%), Gerlecka (Poland) 6½, Harum 6. Fourth place was taken by Vera's sister Olga Menchik.

Another privately arranged match, but this time recognized by FIDE, was played in 1937 at Semmering between Menchik and Graf. This time the champion won very convincingly by the margin of 11½–4½.

Stockholm 1937 saw an apparently great increase in interest in women's chess, for there were 26 contestants from 16 countries. The event was run on the Swiss System with 14 rounds. Menchik won again with 14 points, followed by Benini (Italy) 10, Graf and Lauberte (Latvia) 9.

Buenos Aires 1939 was the last pre-war tournament: Menchik 18 (out of 19), Graf 16, Carrasco 15½.

As with the men's World Championship the death of the title-holder during the war was followed by a reorganization of the system of competing for the title. In parallel with the men the women have since then competed in qualifying events leading to Candidates tournament and World Championship match, with the Champion having to defend her title every three years. Results of these have been as follows:

Moscow 1949/50: World Championship tournament: L. Rudenko (USSR) 11½, O. Rubtsova (USSR) 10½, V. Belova and E. Bykova (both USSR) 10 (16 contestants).

Moscow 1952: Candidates tournament: Bykova 11½, Ignatieva (USSR) and Heemskerk (The Netherlands) 10½ (16 contestants).

Leningrad 1953: World Championship match: Bykova 8, Rudenko 6. Thus Bykova became the third Women's Champion after Menchik and Rudenko.

Moscow 1955: Second Candidates tournament: Rubtsova 15, Volpert (USSR) 14½, Keller-Hermann (East Germany) 14 (20 contestants).

Moscow 1956: Triangular Title match: Rubtsova 10, Bykova 9½, Rudenko 4½. So again the title changed hands, going to Olga Rubtsova.

Moscow 1958: Return match: Bykova 8½, Rubtsova 5½. Bykova regained the title.

Plovdiv 1959: Third Candidates tournament: Zvorikina 11½, Nedeljković 10½, Volpert 9½ (15 players).

Moscow 1959/60: World Championship match: Bykova 8½, Zvorikina 4½.

Vrnjačka Banja 1961: Fourth Candidates tournament: Gaprindashvili 13, Borisenko 11, Zvorikina 10.

Moscow 1962: World Championship match: Gaprindashvili 9, Bykova 2. This convincing win made Nona Gaprindashvili the fifth World Champion.

Sukhumi 1964: Fifth Candidates tournament: Kushnir, Lazarević and Zatulovskaya 12½ (18 contestants). Kushnir won the play-off.

Riga 1965: World Championship match: Gaprindashvili 8½, Kushnir 4½.

Subotica 1967: Sixth Candidates tournament: Kushnir 13½, Zatulovskaya and Kozlovskaya 12½ (18 contestants).

Tbilisi and Moscow 1969: World Championship match: Gaprindashvili 8½, Kushnir 4½.

For the following cycle, the system was changed with the introduction of an Interzonal tournament and Candidates matches. In 1971 the qualifiers for the matches were Kushnir, Zatulovskaya, Alexandria and Lazarević. Semi-finals: Kushnir beat Zatulovskaya, Alexandria beat Lazarević, both 5½–4½. In the final Kushnir beat Alexandria 6½–2½.

Riga 1972: World Championship match: Gaprindashvili 8½, Kushnir 7½.

The next series was weakened by Kushnir's having to withdraw from the Candidates owing to her emigration from the USSR to Israel. This left Alexandria, Kozlovskaya, Levitina and Shul contesting the Candidates matches. In the semi-finals Alexandria beat Shul $5\frac{1}{2}$–$2\frac{1}{2}$, Levitina beat Kozlovskaya $6\frac{1}{2}$–$5\frac{1}{2}$ (over-running the scheduled ten games as the score was 5–5 at that stage). The final, scheduled for 12 games, finally went to a 9–8 victory for Alexandria before matters were resolved.

In the match for the World Championship at Pitsund/Tbilisi from 20 October to 27 November 1975, Alexandria held her own at first with a score of 1–1 against Gaprindashvili; but she lost the next two games and never recovered from this setback. The World Champion won by the crushing total of $8\frac{1}{2}$–$3\frac{1}{2}$. *(W.R.H.)*

WOOD, Baruch H. *(b. 13 July 1909)*
A well-known British player, editor of *Chess* (starting 1935) and chess correspondent of the *Daily Telegraph* and *Illustrated London News*. A FIDE Judge, he has founded and conducted 21 annual Chess Festivals, notably at Whitby, Eastbourne and Southport.

Winner of a number of small and semi-international tournaments: Baarn 1947, Paignton 1954, Whitby 1963, Thorshavn 1967, and Jersey 1975.

Played for the B.C.F. in the International Team tournament at Buenos Aires 1939. His best tournament result was probably his equal second in the British championship at London 1948.

Among his books are: *Easy Guide to Chess*, Sutton Coldfield 1942 et seq; *World Championship Candidates Tournament 1953*, Sutton Coldfield 1954. *(H.G.)*

WORLD CHAMPIONSHIP MATCH
Before this century there were no official matches for the World Chess Championship, though some encounters between those generally recognized as the strongest players of their time could have been regarded as such.

The first series of games with any pretensions to a World Championship was the four-player contest at the court of Philip II in Madrid 1571, won by the Italian Giovanni Leonardo. Only towards the end of the eighteenth century, however, did international rivalry become sufficiently strong to encourage matches to be played between the champions of other European countries. At this time the winners of matches between the French and English champions were generally acknowledged to determine the world's strongest player and thus Philidor, by defeating Stamma in 1747, La Bourdonnais, winning against McDonnell in 1834/5, and Staunton, who defeated Saint-Amant in 1843, could be regarded as the champions of their periods.

The spread of chess in the second half of the nineteenth century lent a truer meaning to the concept of a World Champion and the match in 1858 between Morphy and Anderssen was perhaps the first that could truly be considered as for the supreme title. In any case Morphy's victory by +7–2=2 convincingly established him as the first, albeit unofficial, World Champion.

Morphy's retirement from chess confused the issue for the next two decades. When Steinitz defeated Anderssen 8–6 in 1866, this established him as the strongest practising master, but the Americans still considered Morphy the World Champion. After the latter's death in 1884, the way was clear for an official title match. In 1886 Steinitz became the first official World Champion by defeating Zukertort by a score of +10–5=5, after being 4–1 behind.

In the following years, Steinitz successfully defended his title several times: Havana 1889 (maximum of 20 games) Steinitz $10\frac{1}{2}$ Chigorin $6\frac{1}{2}$; New York 1890/1 (maximum of 20 games) Steinitz $10\frac{1}{2}$ Gunsberg $8\frac{1}{2}$; Havana 1892 (first to 10 wins) Steinitz 10 wins Chigorin 8 wins, with 5 draws. In this match Chigorin led by 8 wins to 7 before a late burst by the Champion.

Steinitz was finally deprived of his title in 1894 when he met Lasker in a series of games in New York, Philadelphia and Montreal. Ten wins were needed for victory and Lasker triumphed 10–5 with 4 draws.

The return match in Moscow 1896/7 was still more convincing, Lasker winning ten games, losing only two and conceding 4 draws.

The next few years saw Lasker and Tarrasch involved in polemical disputes but no actual championship match. Lasker's first defence of the title was against Marshall in 1907, winning easily 8–0 with 7 draws. The match with Tarrasch finally came about in 1908 with Lasker triumphant by +8–3=5.

The next years saw a succession of short matches for the title. Paris 1909: Lasker 8 Janowski 2; Vienna and Berlin 1910: Lasker 5 Schlechter 5; Berlin 1910: Lasker $9\frac{1}{2}$ Janowski $1\frac{1}{2}$. Only against Schlechter had the Champion been in difficulties; he just saved himself by winning the very last game to equalize the scores.

Lasker's long reign was ended in 1921; after four defeats at the hands of Capablanca and ten draws with no victory, Lasker gave up the match and renounced the title, though less than half of the scheduled 30 games had been played.

After Capablanca took the title, it was agreed that any challenger had to raise a prize fund of 10,000 dollars. This eliminated challengers who had no real chance of victory, and such was the Cuban's strength that none emerged for six years. Then it was Alekhine who became the fourth official World Champion, defeating Capablanca at Buenos Aires, 1927 +6–3=25. There was no return match since Capablanca could not himself raise the necessary prize fund.

Alekhine successfully defended his title twice against Bogoljubow: in 1929 by a score of $15\frac{1}{2}$–$9\frac{1}{2}$, and in 1934 by $15\frac{1}{2}$–$10\frac{1}{2}$. In 1935, Alekhine lost his title to Dr Euwe by the narrowest of margins: $15\frac{1}{2}$–$14\frac{1}{2}$.

The next two years saw Alekhine preparing for the return in which he easily regained the title by a score of $15\frac{1}{2}$–$9\frac{1}{2}$ to become the first man to regain the World Championship.

Alekhine's death in 1946 left the title vacant and FIDE took the opportunity to introduce some order in the series of matches for the World Championship. Formerly the Champion had been able to pick his challengers more or less as he chose, with only public opinion exerting its weight to ensure that a worthy challenger secured his opportunity. Beginning with the match-tournament in 1948, however, it was decreed that the Champion should defend his title every three years against a challenger who has won the right by emerging from a qualifying series of Interzonal and Candidates tournaments.

The first FIDE World Champion was determined at The Hague and Moscow in 1948 by a tournament to which the strongest players of the world were invited. The final result: Botvinnik 14, Smyslov 11, Keres and Reshevsky 10½, Euwe 4. Thus Botvinnik took the title vacated by Alekhine.

Title matches were stipulated to be of 24 games, with the Champion retaining his title in the case of a tie. This rule proved useful to Botvinnik both in 1951 against Bronstein, and in 1954 against Smyslov when both ended indecisively at 12–12.

Smyslov was again the challenger in 1957 and this time took the title 12½–9½, only to lose it back in the return match the following year 10½–12½.

The next challenge to Botvinnik's supremacy took a similar course. Tal won the title 12½–8½ in 1960, only to yield it again in 1961 by a score of 8–13.

After this it was thought that perhaps the rules had favoured the incumbent of the title too much, and the return match was abolished. Thus in 1966 when Botvinnik lost 9½–12½ to Petrosian his long reign came to a final end.

The next era was dominated by Petrosian and Spassky. In 1966, Petrosian defeated Spassky 12½–11½, but three years later Spassky took revenge 12½–10½.

1972 saw the most extraordinary match in World Championship history. The first non-Soviet challenger since the war was responsible for world-wide interest and for the first time since 1948 the match moved from Moscow.

After high bids from several countries, Iceland won the right to stage the Fischer–Spassky encounter in Reykjavik. The prize money of 250,000 dollars was greater than that of all previous title matches put together. Fischer's procrastinations led to great doubt whether the match would take place, but a further offer of £50,000 from English banker J. D. Slater finally persuaded the American to come and deprive Spassky of his title by the convincing margin of 12½–8½ (including one game, the second, which he lost by default). 1975 should have seen a match for the title between Fischer and Karpov but Fischer failed to defend his title and there was no match.

Complete scores in the official matches are as follows (winners' results in brackets):

1886 Steinitz 12½ Zukertort 7½ (1000011½1½110½½1½111)
1889 Steinitz 10½ Chigorin 6½ (01011001110101111½)
1890/91 Steinitz 10½ Gunsberg 8½ (½1½0011½½1½01½½0½1½)
1892 Steinitz 12½ Chigorin 10½ (0½½1½100½01011010101½11)
1894 Lasker 12 Steinitz 7 (1010½½11111½00110½1)
1896/7 Lasker 12½ Steinitz 4½ (1111½1½½½11001½11)
1907 Lasker 11½ Marshall 3½ (111½½½½1½½½1111)
1908 Lasker 10½ Tarrasch 5½ (11011½1½½0101½½1)
1909 Lasker 8 Janowski 2 (½111101½11)
1910 Lasker 5 Schlechter 5 (½½½½0½½½½1)
1910 Lasker 9½ Janowski 1½ (1½½11½11111)
1921 Capablanca 9 Lasker 5 (½½½½1½½½½11½½1)
1927 Alekhine 18½ Capablanca 15½ (1½0½½½0½½½11½½½½½½½½1 ½½½½½½½0½½1½1)
1929 Alekhine 15½ Bogoljubow 9½ (1½½01011½1½100½1101½11 ½½½)
1934 Alekhine 15½ Bogoljubow 10½ (½1½1½½½½101½½½½11½½½1 ½001½)
1935 Euwe 15½ Alekhine 14½ (0100½½0101½1½1½0½½011½½½110 ½½½)
1937 Alekhine 15½ Euwe 9½ (01½½0111½1½½01½½0½½½11½11)
1951 Botvinnik 12 Bronstein 12 (½½½½011½½½01½½½½0½1½001½)
1954 Botvinnik 12 Smyslov 12 (111½1½½0½00011011½½½0½½0½)
1957 Smyslov 12½ Botvinnik 9½ (1½½001½1½½½10½½½1½½1½½)
1958 Botvinnik 12½ Smyslov 10½ (111½01½½½½01½10½½10½½0½)
1960 Tal 12½ Botvinnik 8½ (1½½½½1100½1½½½½½1½1½½)
1961 Botvinnik 13 Tal 8 (101½½½11101½1½010½1)
1963 Petrosian 12½ Botvinnik 9½ (0½½½1½1½½½½½½01½½11½½½)
1966 Petrosian 12½ Spassky 11½ (½½½½½½1½11½½0½½½½½01½10½)
1969 Spassky 12½ Petrosian 10½ (0½½11½½1½00½½½½½1½101½½)
1972 Fischer 12½ Spassky 8½ (001½11½1½10½1½½½½½½½½1)

(W.R.H.)

WORLD COMPUTER CHAMPIONSHIP

The first World Computer championship was played in Stockholm in 1974. The tournament was organized by the International Federation for Information Processing and it is planned that the championship be played every three years. The results of the first tournament, a four round Swiss, were: Kaissa (USSR) 4, Chess 4.0 (USA), Ribbit (Canada) and Chaos (USA) 3, Beal (UK), Frantz (Austria), Master (UK), The Ostrich (USA) and Tech II (USA) 2, Freedom (Norway) and Tell (Switzerland) 1½, A16CHS (UK) and Papa (Hungary) 1. Regrettably the two best programmes were not drawn to meet each other. An exhibition game between them (Kaissa and Chess 4.0), played after the tournament, ended in a draw. *(K.J.O'C.)*

WORLD JUNIOR CHAMPIONSHIP

The premier FIDE-sponsored tournament for young players – competitors must be under twenty on 1 September of the year of the event. Entrants are divided into preliminary sections, with the top two from each group progressing to Final A, the next two to Final B, etc. The championships were started in 1951 on a biennial basis, but since 1973 contests have been held annually. The winner is automatically awarded the title of international master. The list of past champions is:

Coventry and Birmingham 1951: Boris Ivkov
Copenhagen 1953: Oscar Panno
Antwerp 1955: Boris Spassky
Toronto 1957: William Lombardy
Munchenstein 1959: Carlos Bielicki
The Hague 1961: Bruno Parma
Vrnjačka Banja 1963: Florin Gheorghiu
Barcelona 1965: Bojan Kurajica
Jerusalem 1967: Julio Kaplan

Stockholm 1969: Anatoly Karpov
Athens 1971: Werner Hug
Teesside 1973: Alexander Belyavsky
Manila 1974: Anthony Miles
Tjentiste 1975: Valery Chekov
Groningen 1976: Mark Diesen *(R.D.K.)*

WORLD STUDENTS TEAM CHAMPIONSHIP
See under STUDENTS CHESS OLYMPIADS.

WYVILL, Marmaduke *(1814–June 1896)*
Regarded by Staunton as 'one of the finest players in England', Wyvill was primarily an enthusiastic amateur of chess, yet in his sole tournament appearance at London 1851 he took second prize behind Anderssen, but ahead of Williams, Staunton, Horwitz, Szén, etc. In the course of this event Wyvill defeated Lowe by +2−0; Kennedy by +4−3=1 and Williams by +4−3. In the final he succumbed to Anderssen by the honourable score of +2−4=1. At the time of the tournament Wyvill was Member of Parliament for Richmond, Yorkshire.

An adherent of the same playing style as Staunton and Williams, Wyvill possessed a fine appreciation of the English Opening and the Sicilian Defence, both of which he employed to deadly effect in the London tournament.

Long after he had retired from competitive play he retained a great interest in the game and his name appears as one of the members of the General Committee in the book of the London 1883 tournament, together with his contribution to the tournament funds of the sum of £10. *(R.D.K.)*

YANOFSKY, Daniel Abe *(b. 26 March 1925)*
A Canadian grandmaster, Yanofsky was born in Poland, came to Cañada in 1926 and was raised in Winnipeg. He played 2nd board for Canada in the 1939 Olympiad and won his first (of eight) national titles in 1941, dethroning the eight-time champion Maurice Fox. Yanofsky had wins at Ventnor City 1942, the US Open 1942, and was =1st at Hastings 1953. He won the British championship in 1953, 1½ points ahead of the field. Yanofsky tied for 4th in the 1957 Dallas tournament and became a grandmaster in 1964. At Groningen 1946 Yanofsky beat Botvinnik in their individual game. He has led many of the Canadian Olympiad teams.

Daniel Yanofsky (left) v. Tartakower. The opening of 1946/7 Hastings Congress

Yanofsky is a lawyer with post-graduate studies at Oxford. He edited *Canadian Chess Chat* for several years and is active in civic politics.

He is an expert in the Ruy Lopez and the French Defence, though his strongest point is his endgame play.

Ventnor City 1942
White: Yanofsky; *Black:* Pinkus
Queen's Gambit Declined
1. P–Q4, N–KB3; 2. N–KB3, P–Q4; 3. P–B4, P–K3; 4. N–B3, B–K2; 5. B–N5, O–O; 6. P–K3, QN–Q2; 7. Q–B2, P–B3; 8. P–QR3, R–K1; 9. R–Q1, N–B1; 10. B–Q3, P×P; 11. B×P, N–Q4; 12. B×B, Q×B; 13. O–O, P–QN3; 14. R–B1, B–N2; 15. B–Q3, KR–B1; 16. N×N, KP×N; 17. B–B5, R–B2; 18. P–QN4, P–N3; 19. B–Q3, N–K3; 20. Q–N2, QR–QB1; 21. B–K2, P–QB4; 22. NP×P, P×P; 23. P×P, N×P; 24. Q–N4, N–K3; 25. Q×Q, R×Q; 26. R×R+, B×R; 27. R–B1, R–B2; 28. R×R, N×R; 29. N–Q4, B–Q2; 30. K–B1, K–B1; 31. K–K1, K–K2; 32. K–Q2, K–Q3; 33. K–B3, P–B3; 34. K–N4, B–K1; 35. B–N5, B–B2; 36. P–QR4, B–K3; 37. N–N3, B–B1; 38. N–Q4, B–K3; 39. B–Q3, B–Q2; 40. P–R4, N–K3; 41. B–N5, N×N; 42. P×N, B–B1; 43. B–Q3, P–B4; 44. P–B4, B–K3; 45. P–N3, B–Q2; 46. B–N5, B–B1; 47. B–K2, K–B3; 48. P–KR5, P×P; 49. B×P, K–N3; 50. P–R5+, K–B3; 51. B–K8+, K–Q3; 52. K–N5, K–K2; 53. B–R5, K–Q3; 54. B–K2, B–N2; 55. B–Q3, B–B1; 56. B–B2, P–KR3; 57. B–Q3, B–Q2+; 58. K–R6, K–B2; 59. K×P, B–B1; 60. B–B2, P–R4; 61. B–Q1, K–B3; 62. B–R4+, K–B2; 63. B–K8, B–K3; 64. P–R6, resigns.

His chief book is: *Chess the Hard Way*, London 1953. *(N.D.)*

YATES, Frederick Dewhurst *(16 January 1884–10 November 1932)*
A British master, Yates trained as an accountant but in 1909 abandoned this career in favour of chess and journalism. In 1911 he tied for first prize with Atkins in the British championship, losing the play-off match. Two years later he won the event – the first of six such victories (1913, 1914, 1921, 1926, 1928, and 1931).

In international tournaments Yates's results were generally mediocre, but he was capable on occasion of defeating the strongest opposition and his victims included Alekhine, Réti, Bogoljubow, Tartakower, Rubinstein, Euwe, Nimzowitsch and Vidmar. He was a regular competitor at the Hastings Christmas Congresses, winning in 1920/1 and finishing in 3rd place on four occasions: 1923/4, 1924/5, 1926/7 and 1929/30.

Yates was for many years the chess correspondent of the *Manchester Guardian* and, in addition, wrote *Modern Master Play*, London, Philadelphia 1929 (with W. Winter as co-author) and

Frederick Dewhurst Yates

books of the 1927 Capablanca–Alekhine, London 1928, and the 1929 Alekhine–Bogoljubow World Championship matches, London 1930. He died from being accidentally asphyxiated in his rooms by a faulty gas connexion.

Carlsbad 1923 (First Brilliancy Prize shared)
White: Alekhine; *Black:* Yates
King's Indian Defence
1. P–Q4, N–KB3; 2. P–QB4, P–KN3; 3. P–KN3, B–N2; 4. B–N2, O–O; 5. N–QB3, P–Q3; 6. N–B3, N–B3; 7. P–Q5, N–N1; 8. P–K4, QN–Q2; 9. O–O, P–QR4; 10. B–K3, N–N5; 11. B–Q4, KN–K4; 12. N×N, N×N; 13. P–B5, P×P; 14. B×P, P–N3; 15. B–Q4, B–QR3; 16. R–K1, Q–Q3; 17. B–B1, B×B; 18. R×B, P–QB4; 19. B×N, Q×B; 20. Q–N3, QR–N1; 21. Q–N5, P–B4; 22. QR–K1, P–KB5; 23. Q–Q7, QR–Q1; 24. P×P, Q×BP; 25. Q–K6+, K–R1; 26. P–B3, Q–N4+; 27. K–R1, R–Q3; 28. Q–R3, B–K4; 29. R–K2, QR–KB3; 30. N–Q1, R–B5; 31. N–K3, R–R5; 32. Q–K6, Q–R4; 33. N–N4, R×N; 34. P×R, R×R+; 35. K–N2, Q×RP+; 36. K×R, Q–R8+; 37. K–B2, B–Q5+; 38. K–N3, Q–N8+; 39. K–R3, Q–B8+; 40. R–N2, Q–R8+; 41. K–N3, Q–K8+; 42. K–R3, P–KN4; 43. R–QB2, Q–B8+; 44. K–R2, Q–N8+; 45. K–R3, Q–R8+; 46. K–N3, Q–Q8; 47. R–B3, Q–N8+; 48. K–R3, Q–B8+; 49. K–N3, B–B7+; 50. K–B3, B–N8 dis+; 51. resigns. *(R.D.K.)*

YOUNG, Franklin Knowles *(1857–19 December 1931)*
The most prolific American chess writer of the nineteenth century, although his military approach to the game was ridiculed by his fellow masters. In six books published between 1896 and 1923 Young applied battlefield principles to the chessboard. His books include *The Grand Tactics of Chess*, London and Boston 1896, and *Chess Strategies*, Boston 1900. A leading Boston player, Young rarely entered serious events. *(A.S.)*

YEAR BOOKS
Year Books fall into two types: those that give a description of the activities of a chess federation (see e.g. BRITISH CHESS FEDERATION) and those that record chess events from all over the world.

The second type originates in the nineteenth century and the first English Year Book was Charles Tomlinson's *The Chess-Player's Annual for the year 1856*, London 1856.

Max Lange's *Jahrbuch des Westdeutschen Schachbundes 1862*, published in Leipzig 1862, and his similar work for 1863, were in reality tournament books of Düsseldorf 1862 and 1863.

The first genuine German Year Book is Ludwig Bachmann's *Schach-Jahrbuch*, Passau 1891, followed by his *Geistreiche Schachpartien* in five volumes covering a period 1875–95 and then a series of *Schach-Jahr* books from 1895 to 1930.

There was also a valuable English series edited first by E. A. Michell and then by Stevens, Watts and Foster for the years 1907–17.

The Soviet Chess Federation published some massive Year Books by Grekov and Maizelis for the years 1932–6 and a further series after the Second World War from 1946 to 1961. Ragozin was the first editor, followed by Abramov and finally Bielin. In 1975 a new series of Yearbooks commenced, *The Batsford Chess Yearbook*, London, edited by Kevin O'Connell. *(H.G.)*

YUDOVICH, Mikhail Mikhailovich *(b. 8 June 1911)*

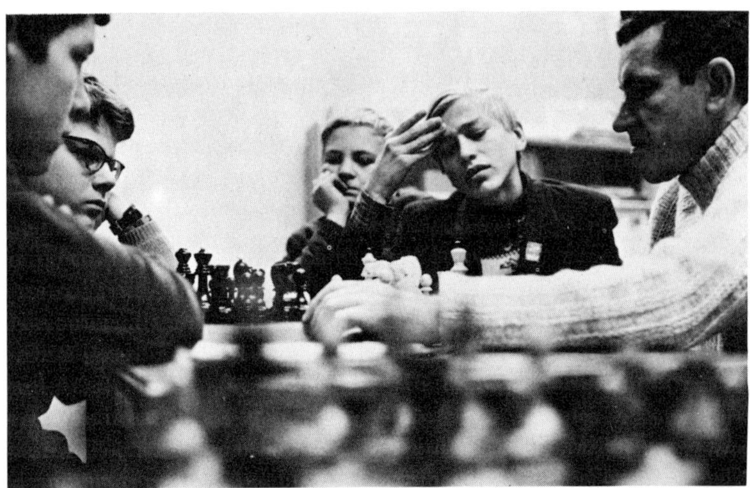

Mikhail Yudovich takes a class of young chess players at the Moscow Palace of Young Pioneers

A Soviet international master, Yudovich was one of the strongest Moscow masters in the 1930s and 1940s. Yudovich is by profession a journalist and has written a great deal on chess including his co-authorship (with A. Kotov) of *The Soviet School of Chess* (in Russian) Moscow 1951 (in English) Moscow 1958. His best result was sharing third place in the 1931 USSR championship. Has been awarded the titles of international master (1950), International Judge (1951), and international correspondence chess grandmaster (1972). His son is also a well-known player and theoretician. *(W.R.H.)*

YUGOSLAVIA
The emergence of Yugoslavia as a world power in chess was accomplished in two phases, each of which followed immediately on the wars of 1914–18 and 1939–45.

At the close of the First World War the new nation of Yugoslavia found itself in possession of a master of world status in the shape of Dr Milan Vidmar, who rose to be a challenger for the World Championship itself in the period from 1922–7. Inferior to Vidmar, yet still a recognized force in international chess, was Boris Kostić, and they were to be joined by Vasja Pirc and Petar Trifunović, who carved impressive chess careers for themselves during the 1930s and 1940s.

These four formed the first significant nucleus of Yugoslav masters, yet the transformation from an excellent to an outstanding chess-playing nation did not occur until the take-over of government by Marshal Tito at the end of the Second World War. Tito took a definite interest in chess, and it became official policy to encourage chess at all levels. The startling results can be seen today, in that a small nation of modest means should have engendered such an efflorescence of formidable grandmasters and masters, and be capable of challenging consistently for the world's number two position (behind the USSR).

With active financial support from the Yugoslav government, expert chess tuition is available at an early age to all Yugoslav children who show any interest, and the most talented are given further encouragement by the state and provided with the means to expand their talent, whether it be in the field of practical skills, organization, literature or pedagogy. As can be seen, chess in Yugoslavia is not, as in England or America, largely the prerogative of the cultured and intellectual strata of society, and the support for and interest in chess is widespread.

Tournaments are organized frequently and regularly in Yugoslavia, ranging from small local events, via national competitions and traditional medium-strength tournaments such as that at Sarajevo, to the great five-yearly internationally renowned *Turnir Mira*, and top-class FIDE events such as the 1959 Bled-Zagreb-Belgrade Candidates tournament.

In Yugoslavia the value of chess as an educative force and as a sporting spectacle (rather than as an art or a science) has been given tremendous prominence and important tournaments are often played in theatres with a vociferous audience expressing its approval or displeasure in appropriate fashion. When Gligorić defeated the Soviet grandmaster and World Champion-to-be Petrosian at Belgrade in 1954, pandemonium broke out amongst the spectators at the end of the game and the overflowing playing-hall had to be cleared by the police! Thus we can observe that the element of adulation for the great achievements of their own players also forms one element of the passionate attachment to chess shown by the Yugoslav public at large.

There is also great activity amongst the numerous Yugoslav chess clubs, many of which support professional chess-masters who in turn represent the club in internal team competitions or gain prestige for the club by successful international performances.

In the post-war period the most consistently successful of the Yugoslav grandmasters has been Svetozar Gligorić, who has competed three times at Candidates level. Of the other grandmasters special mention should be made of the most prominent: Ljubojević, Ivkov, Matanović, Matulović, Parma, Velimirović, Planinc and Kurajica. All of these have consistently gained high prizes in international tournaments. There follows a complete list of the remaining active Yugoslav grandmasters and masters, current to the end of 1976:

Grandmasters: Bukić, Čirić, Damjanović, Hulak, Janošević, Knezević, Kovačević, Marović, Ostojić, Raičević and Vukić.

International masters: Antunac, Barle, Bertok, Bogdanović, Buljovčić, Deže, Gliksman, Ivanović, Karaklajić, Krnić, Marangunić, Martinović, Marić, Mašić, Messing, Meštrović, Mihaljčišin, Minić, Musil, Nemet, Ničevski, Nikolić, Puc, Rajković, Rukavina, Šahović and Sofrevski.

Winners of the Yugoslav championship have been:

1. (1945)	P. Trifunović	17. (1962)	A. Matanović and D. Minić
2. (1946)	P. Trifunović	18. (1962)	S. Gligorić
3. (1947)	S. Gligorić and P. Trifunović	19. (1963)	B. Ivkov and M. Udovčić
4. (1948/9)	S. Gligorić and V. Pirc	20. (1965)	M. Matulović
5. (1949)	S. Gligorić	21. (1965)	S. Gligorić
6. (1950)	S. Gligorić	22. (1967)	M. Matulović
7. (1951)	B. Rabar	23. (1968)	P. Ostojić and J. Stupica
8. (1952)	P. Trifunović	24. (1969)	A. Matanović
9. (1953)	V. Pirc	25. (1970)	M. Vukić
10. (1955)	N. Karaklajić	26. (1971)	P. Ostojić
11. (1956)	S. Gligorić	27. (1972)	B. Ivkov
12. (1957)	S. Gligorić	28. (1973)	B. Ivanović
13. (1958)	S. Gligorić and B. Ivkov	29. (1974)	M. Vukić
14. (1959)	S. Gligorić	30. (1975)	D. Velimorivić
15. (1960)	S. Gligorić	31. (1976)	K. Hulak
16. (1961)	P. Trifunović		

Yugoslavia in the European team championship

Since the inception of the Europa Cup in 1957 Yugoslavia has maintained a highly successful position without, however, being able to challenge the supremacy of the USSR. Of the five events held hitherto, Yugoslavia has taken no less than four silver medals: Vienna 1957 (7 points behind the USSR), Oberhausen 1961 (16 points in arrears), Hamburg 1965 (shared with Hungary, 9 points behind the USSR), and Bath 1973 (with a margin of 6½ points). Their one relative failure was at Kapfenberg 1970 with 4th place behind the USSR, Hungary and East Germany.

Yugoslavia and the Olympiad

Yugoslavia occupies a most honourable place in the Olympiad history, having twice organized the event and once gained the world title. Yugoslavia was, in fact, one of the original sixteen nations to compete in the first Olympiad at London 1927 (taking 9th position). Subsequent results during the 1930s continued to be respectable: 4th/19 Prague 1931, 6th/20 Warsaw 1935, 9th/19 Stockholm 1937. After the involuntary pause imposed by the Second World War, Yugoslavia returned to the Olympic fray with new-found vigour. Not only did Yugoslavia stage the 1950 Olympiad at Dubrovnik, but it also gained the gold medal (1st/16) with the team of Gligorić, Pirc, Trifunović, Rabar, Vidmar and Puc. The glory of this achievement was tarnished by the absence of the USSR and in subsequent competitions the presence of the Soviet team consistently relegated the Yugoslavs to lesser laurels: 3rd/25 Helsinki 1952, 3rd/26 Amsterdam 1954, 2nd/34 Moscow 1956, 2nd/36 Munich 1958, 3rd/40 Leipzig 1960, 2nd/37 Varna 1962 (a mere 3½ points behind the USSR), 2nd/50 Tel Aviv 1964, =3rd/52 Havana 1966, 2nd/53 Lugano 1968, 3rd/60 Siegen 1970 (1½ points behind the USSR!), 3rd/62 Skopje 1972 (the second Olympiad organized on Yugoslav soil), 2nd/74 Nice 1974. The Yugoslav team did not participate at the 1976 Haifa Olympiad for political reasons.

The following game was played in the 1950 Olympiad between the Yugoslav and the West German top boards.

White: Gligorić; *Black:* Unzicker
Queen's Gambit Declined
1. P–Q4, N–KB3; 2. P–QB4, P–K3; 3. N–QB3, P–Q4; 4. B–N5, B–K2; 5. N–B3, O–O; 6. P–K3, P–KR3; 7. B–R4, P–QN3; 8. B–Q3, P×P; 9. B×P, B–N2; 10. O–O, QN–Q2; 11. Q–K2, N–K5; 12. B–N3, N×B; 13. RP×N, P–QB4; 14. KR–Q1, B×N; 15. P×B, P×P; 16. P×P, B–Q3; 17. P–B4, R–K1; 18. B–N5, R–QB1; 19. N–K4, Q–K2; 20. P–Q5, P–K4; 21. Q–N4, KR–Q1; 22. B×N, R×B; 23. N×B, Q×N; 24. P×P, Q–B2; 25. P–Q6, Q–N2; 26. QR–B1, R–K1; 27. Q–Q4, R(1)–Q1; 28. Q–QB4, Q–B6; 29. Q–Q3, Q–R4; 30. Q–K4, Q–N4; 31. R–B3, Q–R4; 32. R–Q5, Q–R6; 33. R–Q4, Q–K3; 34. Q–Q5, Q–B4; 35. R–B3, Q–N3; 36. K–N2, R–QB1; 37. R–QB4, R(1)–Q1; 38. R(KB3)–B3, P–KR4; 39. P–R4, Q–B4; 40. Q–K4, Q–K3; 41. R–Q4, P–N3; 42. Q–Q5, Q–K1; 43. R(Q4)–QB4, K–R2; 44. R–B7, K–N2; 45. R×R, Q×R; 46. R–B7, Q–B4; 47. Q–B3, Q–K3; 48. R–K7, resigns.

It is only to be expected that the vigorous chess life of Yugoslavia should be nourished by a constant flow of books, pamphlets and periodicals dealing with the subject of chess. Many of the leading masters and grandmasters of the country have earned a reputation with the pen as well as the sword, and the low price of books in Yugoslavia has ensured their continuing popularity.

The chief magazine in Yugoslavia is *Sahovski Glasnik*, edited by D. Marović, Zrinjski Trg 3, Zagreb. A lesser-known periodical is *Mat*, emanating from 7 Jula 30, Belgrade. A testimony to the prolific energy directed towards chess publication in Yugoslavia at the moment is the twice-yearly appearance of the international magazine *Sahovski Informator* (or *Chess Informant*) which is distributed from the same source as *Mat*. Connected with the *Informator* is the *Encyclopedia of Chess Openings*, an ambitious attempt (in many volumes) to catalogue all known opening theory.

The Yugoslav Chess Federation's address: Sahovski Savez Yugoslavije, Nusiceva 25/2, Postfah 504, 11000 Belgrade.

Z

ZAGOROVSKY, Vladimir Pavlovich *(b. 1925)*
Soviet master and one of the world's most successful correspondence chess players. Winner of the 4th World Correspondence Championship held 1962–5. Zagorovsky also took 4th place in the fifth World championship and was second in the sixth World championship. In all three of these events he lost a total of one game. Correspondence grandmaster since 1965. *(W.R.H.)*

ZAGORYANSKY, Yevgeny Alexandrovich *(1910–61)*
Russian master and frequent competitor in the Moscow championship. Author of several books, including a biographical essay on Morphy published in 1962. *(W.R.H.)*

ZAIRE
Chess in Zaire is organized by the Fédération Zaïroise des Echecs, c/o A. Frank, B.P. 609, Kisingani. *(K.J.O'C.)*

ZAITSEV, Alexander Nikolayevich
(15 June 1935–8 November 1971)
Soviet master and international grandmaster since 1967. Shared first place at Sochi 1967 international tournament and also in the 1968/9 USSR championship (but lost the play-off to Polugayevsky). Died at the age of thirty-six following an unsuccessful operation on his foot. *(W.R.H.)*

ZAITSEV, Igor Arkadyevich *(b. 27 May 1939)*
Soviet grandmaster and theoretician. Gained international master title in 1970, and the grandmaster title in 1976. *(W.R.H.)*

ZAK, Vladimir Grigorievich *(b. 1913)*
Principal trainer of Leningrad players since 1958. Among his successful trainees have been Spassky and Korchnoi. Co-author (with Korchnoi) of a book on the King's Gambit. *(W.R.H.)*

ZAKHAROV, Igor Nikolayevich *(b. 1938)*
Moscow master and frequent competitor in the championship of that city. Winner of the Varna 1968 international tournament. *(W.R.H.)*

ZAMBIA
Chess in Zambia is organized by the Chess Federation of Zambia, c/o C. Landwehr, P.O. Box 7, Chilanga. *(K.J.O'C.)*

ZANDVOORT 1936
Euwe's World Championship victory over Alekhine stimulated chess in The Netherlands into almost non-stop activity. The most important of the many events organized in this period was the international tournament at Zandvoort (July 1936), the first tournament appearance of Euwe as title-holder. But whereas Alekhine had won every tournament he contested as World

Champion (with the sole exception of Hastings 1933/4), Euwe could do no better than finish a creditable second to Fine, with Keres tying for third with Tartakower. This result showed both that the leaders of the young generation were now stronger than the established grandmasters and that the World Championship could no longer be left to the whims of an individual; with so many well-qualified contenders, a procedure of giving each of them a chance would have to be devised. Leading scores: Fine 8½, Euwe 7½, Keres, Tartakower 6½, Bogoljubow, Maróczy 6. *(W.H.)*

ZATRIKION
By the eighth century chess had spread from Persia to Byzantium where it became known as *zatrikion*, this being about as near as the Greeks could get to the Persian *chatrang*. *(H.G.)*

ZATULOVSKAYA, Tatiana Yakovlevna *(b. 8 December 1935)*
International Woman master since 1961, USSR Women's champion in 1962. In the following years she frequently placed highly in competitions for the Women's World Championship, her best result being a share of second place in the 1967 Candidates tournament. *(W.R.H.)*

ZHUKHOVITSKY, Samuil Markovich *(b. 12 December 1916)*
Soviet master, awarded the title of international master in 1967. *(W.R.H.)*

ZITA, Frantisek *(b. 19 November 1909)*
A Czechoslovak master, national champion in 1943. Awarded the title of international master in 1950. Represented Czechoslovakia in four Olympiads between 1937 and 1954. *(W.R.H.)*

ZNOSKO-BOROVSKY, Eugene Alexandrovich
(16 August 1884–31 December 1954)
Born in Russia, Znosko-Borovsky was a minor chess-master whose writings on the game had an influence and an effect far beyond their intrinsic worth. His best tournament result while in Russia was =3rd with Salwe at the All-Russia tournament of Lodz 1908. But his career was punctuated and handicapped by two wars, the Russo-Japanese War of 1905 and the First World War, in both of which he fought and was wounded.

He left Russia for Paris at the Revolution and there earned his living as a music critic. But he added to this by some highly profitable books on chess in which he caught the contemporary taste to perfection. His chief work (or what was regarded as such at the time) was on the middle-game and, despite its being based on an untenable and even infantile thesis, became regarded as a classic solely because it was the first in the field. His subsequent works, mostly in the vein of 'how not to, etc' were better and more deserving of popularity.

He played in a number of events after the war, but none was a major tournament and his chief success was 3rd at Nice 1930.

Main works: *The Middle Game in Chess*, London, New York 1922; *How Not to Play Chess*, London, Philadelphia 1931; *The Art of Chess Combination*, London 1936, Philadelphia 1951. *(H.G.)*

ZONAL TOURNAMENTS
See under INTERZONAL.

ZONARES, John *(d. 1118)*
The former commander of the bodyguard of the Emperor of Byzantium. He became a monk and retired to Mount Athos, whence he issued a ban against the debauchery of playing chess: 'Inasmuch as some of the Bishops and clergy leave virtuous paths and play *zatrikion* [chess] or dice or drink to excess, the Rule ordains that such shall cease to do so or be excluded.'

Zonares was so strongly against chess that he also extended the ban to laymen. (See BYZANTIUM). *(H.G.)*

ZUBAREV, Nikolai Mikhailovich
(10 January 1894–1 January 1951)
Moscow champion in 1927 and 1930, and competitor in many of the early USSR championships. In his later years was very active in chess organization in the USSR. Awarded the titles of international master in 1950 and International Judge in 1951. *(W.R.H.)*

ZUCKERMAN, Bernard *(b. 31 March 1943)*
Zuckerman is an American international master and opening theoretician. His =4th result in the 1965/6 US championship and 66.7% performance on 1st board in the 1967 Student Olympiad at Harrachov are his major accomplishments. Zuckerman also came =2nd at Lanzarote 1974. *(A.S.)*

ZUGZWANG [**Middle-Game and Ending**]
A German word (pronounced 'tsooktsvunk'), *zugzwang* is the situation in which a player finds himself compelled to move even though every move he can legally make would lead to a decisive deterioration of his position. If the player were given the right to move or 'pass' at his discretion, the worsening of his position could be avoided. As Emanuel Lasker correctly observes, *zugzwang* occurs almost exclusively in endings where few pieces are left on the board. See this simple finale:

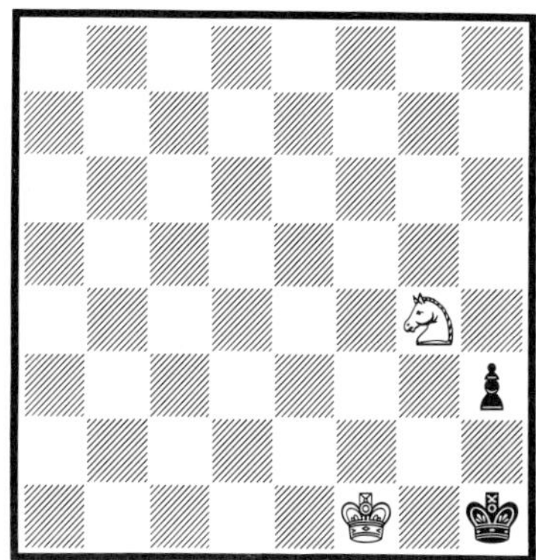

If Black (to move) could waive his right (which is also his duty) to do so, White could never get anywhere; but Black has to make his only legal move, P–R7, whereupon White mates by N–B2.

There is a cogent reason why this device is normally confined to simple endgame positions. Where one side has forced the other into the state of impotence associated with *zugzwang*, he can, with many pieces still on the board, go for the kill in a number of ways so that no amount of 'passing' would help the weaker side.

Unfortunately a steady pollution of the word *zugzwang* has occurred in the literature of the game, to the effect that what really is a complete blockade is referred to as *zugzwang*. Thus the so-called 'Immortal Zugzwang Game' is a misnomer: in the final position Black simply threatens to win by R(B4)–B6 and White has no useful move to stop this threat. The nearest to a true middle-game *zugzwang* is shown in Galgut v. Heidenfeld, Johannesburg 1937:

Even here, were White allowed to 'pass', Black (to move) might eventually play the King to the Q-side and win by advancing his K-side Ps; but this is an uncertain business. With 1.., Q–N6! (which threatens nothing), Black puts the opponent in *zugzwang*, as the following variations show.

(*a*) 1. K–R1, Q×RP+; 2. K–N1, Q–N6 and the RP advances.
(*b*) 1. K–B1, Q–R7; 2. Q×P, Q–R8+; 3. K–K2, R–K5+.
(*c*) 1. R–B1, R×B; 2. Q×R, Q×P mate.
(*d*) 1. P–B5, P×P; 2. R×P, R×B; 3. R–N5, R–B7.
(*e*) 1. B–N2(R1), R–B7; 2. Q–K1, P–Q7.
(*f*) 1. P–N5, P–QN3; 2. B–N4, R–B7; 3. Q–K1, B×P.
(*g*) 1. Q–K1(N2), R×BP.
(*h*) 1. Q–B1, P–Q7 winning the Bishop.

See also ENDGAME, ZUGZWANG. (*W.H.*)

ZUIDEMA, Coenraad *(b. 29 August 1942)*

A Dutch international master (1964). Regular member of the Dutch Olympiad team. He won the Dutch championship in 1972 and finished equal first in this event in 1965, 1970, and 1973 – losing the play-off match in each case. Tournament results include 4th in I.B.M. tournament 1966. *.K.)*

ZUKERTORT, Johannes Hermann

(7 September 1842–20 June 1888)

One of the most talented players of all time and possibly an English Prussian Polish Jewish grandmaster, the antecedents and early career of Zukertort are shrouded in mystery, a mystery that was the more complete in that the only account of these comes from Zukertort with a lack of corroboration so great that perhaps he really was telling the truth.

Whatever the truth may be it is certain that he was a great chess-player, one of those who carry with them the aura of certain genius.

According to Zukertort, then, he was born in Lublin of mixed Prussian and Polish descent and his mother was the Baroness Krzyzanovska. The name of his mother sounds incredibly like an invention of W. C. Fields and it is difficult to believe that his father's name, Zukertort, was not Jewish.

Again according to Zukertort he studied chemistry at Heidelberg and physiology at Berlin, claiming to have obtained his doctorate of medicine at Breslau University.

His versatility was astonishing. He spoke nine languages including Hebrew and was acquainted with several more. He had been a soldier, having fought in several campaigns for Prussia against Austria, Denmark and France; and once had been left for dead on the battlefield.

A music critic, editor of a political paper, on the staff of Bismarck's newspaper, the *Allgemeine Zeitung*; gifted with a memory so colossal that he never forgot a game he played; a consummate fencer, a blindfold simultaneous player of undoubted repute (he had played as many as fifteen simultaneously blindfold) and a grandmaster with justified pretensions towards the world title: most of these attributes we have to take on Zukertort's word. But there is enough left that is substantiated to show his great importance in the history of chess.

His early chess career had much to do with Anderssen whom he beat in a match, when Anderssen had grown old, in 1871 in Germany by +5—2, having lost a previous match to him in Berlin in 1868 by +3—8=1.

On the strength of his win over Anderssen in the second match he was invited to play in a small but strong tournament in London in 1872 where he came 3rd below Steinitz and Blackburne. Immediately afterwards he played a match with Steinitz in which he was overwhelmingly defeated by +1—7=4. It is unlikely that this was for the World Championship since no mention was made of the title at the time and the stakes were small, £20 for the winner and £10 for the loser.

Despite this disastrous loss, which contained the seeds of further disasters, Zukertort felt that London was his true home and decided to stay in England, becoming a naturalized citizen in 1878.

His results in tournament and match play from then on showed a steep upward curve. He was 2nd in London 1876, 1st in a small tournament in Cologne 1877 and =2nd at Leipzig that year. He came 1st in a big tournament at Paris 1878 where he tied with Winawer and won the play-off.

In 1880 he won a match in London against Rosenthal by +7—1=11 and in the following year he was 2nd to Blackburne in Berlin. He was no less than 3 points behind Blackburne but he avenged this by beating him in a match in London the same year by +7—2=5.

A comparative setback came in a great tournament at Vienna in 1882 when he tied for fourth place with Mackenzie, below Steinitz, Winawer and Mason but in 1883 came the peak of his career when he won 1st prize in the great London tournament, 3 points ahead of Steinitz and 5½ points ahead of Blackburne who came 3rd.

The remarkable nature of his victory is to be seen from the fact that he was sure of first prize with some two weeks still to go when he had a score of 22/23. But, ominously, his health was giving way and he had been sustaining himself by the use of drugs. He lost his last three games. It is very probable that this high point in his career was also the time when his health began to deteriorate under the excessive nervous strains imposed by his constant and conscious efforts to outrival Steinitz.

Thus, though he had been warned by his doctor of the dangers, he refused to abandon serious play and in 1886 he played his match for the World Championship against Steinitz in the USA, losing by +5−10=5. The strain was this time too great and he returned to England with his health completely shattered.

Johannes Hermann Zukertort, from the Illustrated London News, 1878

This was reflected in his subsequent results. =7th in London 1886 and =3rd in a smaller tournament at Nottingham that year, he had disastrous results throughout 1887: =15th at Frankfurt-am-Main, 4th in a small tournament in London and a match loss there to Blackburne by +1−5=8.

In the last year of his life he was =7th in London in 1888 and, playing to the last possible moment, he died from cerebral haemorrhage after a game at Simpson's Divan.

Despite a career that stopped as it were halfway, Zukertort is clearly one of the chess immortals and there is about his best games a sort of resilient and shining splendour that no other player possesses. A famous and irresistible example is the following game played at London in 1883.

White: Zukertort; *Black:* Blackburne
Queen's Gambit Declined
1. P–QB4, P–K3; 2. P–K3, N–KB3; 3. N–KB3, P–QN3; 4. B–K2, B–N2; 5. O–O, P–Q4; 6. P–Q4, B–Q3; 7. N–B3, O–O; 8. P–QN3, QN–Q2; 9. B–N2, Q–K2; 10. N–QN5, N–K5; 11. N×B, P×N; 12. N–Q2, QN–B3; 13. P–B3, N×N; 14. Q×N, P×P; 15. B×P, P–Q4; 16. B–Q3, KR–B1; 17. QR–K1, R–B2; 18. P–K4, QR–QB1; 19. P–K5, N–K1; 20. P–B4, P–N3; 21. R–K3, P–B4; 22. P×P *e.p.*, N×P; 23. P–B5, N–K5; 24. B×N, P×B; 25. P×NP, R–B7; 26. P×P+, K–R1; 27. P–Q5+, P–K4;

28. Q–N4, R(B1)–B4; 29. R–B8+, K×P; 30. Q×P+, K–N2; 31. B×P+, K×R; 32. B–N7+, resigns. *(H.G.)*

ZÜRICH 1934

A tournament (July 1934) on the Moscow 1925 model, seven Swiss players meeting nine internationals, six of whom were the leaders of European chess at the time. The result showed that the gap between Alekhine and the younger generation had narrowed considerably since the days of Bled 1931, though he retained his superiority over his contemporaries. But the sensation of the tournament was the re-appearance of Lasker, after a nine-year break since Moscow 1925. Leading scores: Alekhine 13, Euwe, Flohr 12, Bogoljubow 11½, Lasker 10. This is how the 65-year-old former World Champion re-entered the international arena in the first round:

White: Euwe; *Black:* Lasker
Queen's Gambit Declined
1. P–Q4, P–Q4; 2. P–QB4, P–K3; 3. N–QB3, N–KB3; 4. B–N5, QN–Q2; 5. P–K3, P–B3; 6. N–B3, B–K2; 7. Q–B2, O–O; 8. P–QR3, R–K1; 9. R–B1, P×P; 10. B×P, N–Q4; 11. B×B, Q×B; 12. N–K4, N(4)–B3; 13. N–N3, P–B4; 14. O–O, P×P; 15. N×P, N–N3; 16. B–R2, R–N1; 17. P–K4, R–Q1; 18. KR–Q1, B–Q2; 19. P–K5, N–K1; 20. B–N1, P–N3; 21. Q–K4, B–R5; 22. P–N3, B–Q2; 23. P–QR4, N–Q4; 24. B–Q3, QR–B1; 25. B–B4, B–B3; 26. N×B, P×N; 27. R–Q3, N–N5; 28. R–KB3, R–B2; 29. P–R4, R(2)–Q2; 30. P–KR5, Q–N4; 31. R–K1, R–Q5; 32. P×P, RP×P; 33. Q–K2, R–Q7; 34. Q–B1, N–B7; 35. N–K4, Q×P; 36. N–B6+, Q×N; 37. R×Q, N(1)×R; 38. R–B1, N–K5; 39. B–K2, N–Q5; 40. B–B3, N×BP; 41. Q–B4, N–Q6; 42. R–B1, N–K4; 43. Q–N4, N(4)×B+; 44. P×N, N–K7+; 45. K–R2, N–B5+; 46. K–R1, R(7)–Q5; 47. Q–K7, K–N2; 48. Q–B7, R(1)–Q4; 49. R–K1, R–KN4; 50. Q×BP, R–Q1; 51. resigns. *(W.H.)*

ZVORIKINA, Kira Alekseeva *(b. 29 October 1920)*
International Woman master, three times Soviet Woman champion and Honoured Master of Sport of the USSR 1957, Zvorikina is

an engineer by profession, living in Minsk where she also teaches chess.

It was only after the Second World War that she took part in strong tournaments and she played in all the Soviet Women's championships from 1947 to the 1960s. Zvorikina won the title in 1951, 1953 and 1956 and came =1st with Borisenko in 1957 and =1st with Volpert in 1958, losing the play-off for the championship in both cases. The loss to Volpert was to a younger woman and indeed she had beaten her in a match for the championship of Leningrad by +3−1 as long ago as 1947.

She had a successful run in the cycle of Women's World Championship tournaments in the 1950s, coming 4-6 in the Candidates tournament at Moscow in 1952, 4th in the Candidates tournament of 1955 and then, in 1959, won the Candidates tournament at Plovdiv in Bulgaria and with it the right to challenge the champion, Bykova, to a match for the title the following year. The match was won by Bykova by 8½–4½. *(H.G.)*

ZWISCHENZUG

Pronounced 'tsvishentsook', this means 'intermediate move'. The reference is to a forcing move overlooked by one player in the course of a seemingly forced sequence of thrust and parry, or a series of exchanges. Thus, in L. Steiner v. Helling, Berlin 1928:

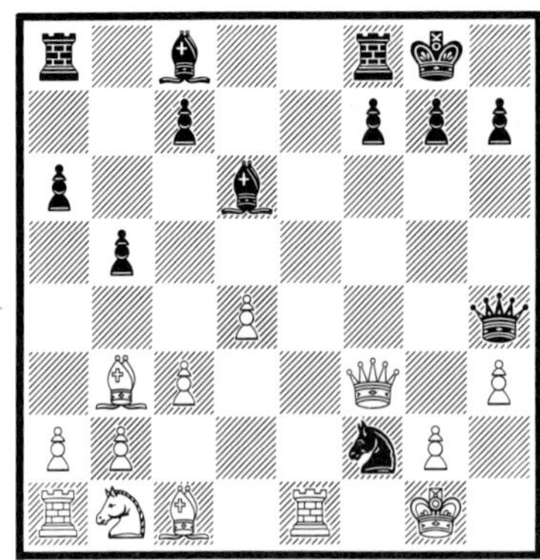

White played 1. Q×N?, expecting the sequence 1.., B–N6?; 2. Q×P+, R×Q; 3. R–K8 mate. Black made the *zwischenzug*, 1.., B–R7+! and only after 2. K–B1, B–N6! when 3. Q×P+ fails to 3.., R×P+. *(W.H.)*

SELECT BIBLIOGRAPHY

For those who wish to read further about some aspect of chess, this bibliography contains a select number of books and publications from the vast literature available. The selection includes books that are not just sources of information but works that must be counted as mile-stones in the history of chess.

Openings

La Defense du Fianchetto de la Dame, V. Kahn, Monaco 1949. A little-known work that broke new ground in its discussion of the strategy of the opening.

The ideas Behind the Chess Openings, R. Fine, New York 1964. A paperback reprint of another pioneering work, originally published in 1943 in New York and London. It is interesting and a little sad to observe that though this is clearly the right way to explain the openings to the average student, such students have, on the whole, rejected the method in favour of lists and strings of variations drawn from tournament games.

Modern Chess Openings by various hands ranging from R. C. Griffith and J. H. White to M. E. Goldstein, P. W. Sergeant, Reuben Fine, Walter Korn, John W. Collins, Larry Evans and back to Walter Korn. All these authors were blended in various combinations. The first edition was published in London and Leeds 1911, and the eleventh and most recent edition in London and New York 1972. It gives the lines in columnar form with voluminous foot-notes. Each opening is preceded by an essay on the ideas behind, and the worth of the lines. The book has proved the most popular and over the years has contained much valuable material. Equally over the years it has inevitably contained many errors both of fact and of judgment.

It is now losing ground to compilations made by masters and grandmasters, of which the first and best appeared under Euwe's name; then a series by L. Pachman and finally, in the later 1970s, an *Encyclopaedia of Chess Openings* edited by A. Matanović. Three volumes have so far been published in London.

The Middle-Game

Very little of real merit has been written on this difficult subject and there have been some dreadful failures of which perhaps E. Znosko-Borovsky's *The Middle Game in Chess*, London and New York 1922, is the worst.

Some of the best work in this field is contained in books that do not purport to be about the middle-game e.g. Nimzowitsch's *My System* and Alekhine's *My Best Games of Chess 1908-1923*.

The best books on the middle-game are those that deal with specific aspects in a thoroughly practical way. Of these there are four outstandingly good examples: *The Art of Checkmate*, V. Kahn and G. Renaud, London 1955. This is a translation from the French published originally in Monaco 1943. Its contents are exactly conveyed by the title.

Judgment and Planning in Chess, M. Euwe, London 1953 and New York 1954.

The Art of the Middle Game, P. Keres and A. Kotov, Harmondsworth 1964. Some run of the mill work by Kotov is more than redeemed by magnificent writing and thinking by Keres, the best he ever did.

Complete Chess Strategy by L. Pachman: Two Vols. London 1976.

The Endgame

It is interesting to observe that this section of chess which, in the ninth and tenth centuries, was much worked over by the Arabs but which was almost totally neglected in the nineteenth and early twentieth centuries, is now more and more coming into its own. The modern classic is *Basic Chess Endings*, R. Fine, Philadelphia and London 1941. In this work Fine owes much to Berger but he has also included much original material of his own.

An excellently systematic and sensible work is *A Guide to Chess Endings*, M. Euwe and D. Hooper, London 1957. Also good is *Practical Chess Endgames*, D. Hooper, London 1968.

Along the same lines is Paul Keres's last book *Practical Chess Endings*, London 1974. Keres, himself a great endgame artist, transmits his enthusiasm and polished skill with deceptive ease.

Also of great use is a series of translations from the Russian of Averbakh's works on the endings under such titles as *Bishop Endings*, London 1977, *Queen and Pawn Endings*, and (with Maizel's) *Pawn Endings*, London 1974.

Game Collections (and biographies)

A fascinating and numerous section in which the great players either speak for themselves or else have their games speak for them.

A. Alekhine, *My Best Games of Chess 1908-1923*, London 1923. Along with Keres's work this must rank as the greatest of all time. It is quite simply a work of genius by a player of genius.

L. Bachmann, *Schachmeister Steinitz* (4 volumes), Ansbach 1910-21. Here the games do the talking.

M. M. Botvinnik, *Botvinnik's Best Games*, London 1972. The games of an unusually self-disciplined genius from which an enormous amount of instruction can be derived.

J. R. Capablanca, *My Chess Career*, London 1920. This was Capablanca's best book, a work of artful simplicity.

Robert J. Fischer, *My 60 Memorable Games*, New York and London 1969. Of all the books written on Fischer's games this is the only memorable one. For some reason, whenever an author tries to compile a work on Fischer's games he falls into a brown and almost sullen study.

H. Golombek, *Capablanca's 100 Best Games of Chess*, London and New York 1947. Capablanca was too lazy to annotate his later games. Golombek, a fervent admirer of his style of play, improved his own strength of play so much after studying Capablanca's games that he won the British championship almost immediately after finishing the book.

H. von Gottschall, *Adolf Anderssen, der Altmeister Deutscher Schachspielkunst*, Leipzig 1912. It is arguable that Anderssen was the greatest combinational player in the history of the game. This book contains the biggest collection of brilliancies ever played.

P. A. Graham, *Mr Blackburne's Games at Chess*, London 1899. The charm of this book is not so much the games as the attractive and original personality disclosed by Blackburne's own comments.

P. Keres, *Grandmaster of Chess*, London 1964. A three-volume collection of Keres's games which appeared in the years 1965-67. It contains 100 of his best games annotated at a depth that is only relieved by the freshness of thought and concept that permeates the games.

P. Markland, *The Best of Karpov*, London 1975. Unpretentious but most competent analysis of the world champion's powerful play.

Paul Morphy's life and games have continued to puzzle and alarm his admirers. An American authoress wrote a feeble novel around him but the actual story of his life is both tragic and moving. Two works that do him more or less justice are *Paul Morphy, a Sketch from the Chess World*, E. Falkbeer, London 1860 and *Morphy's Games of Chess*, P. W. Sergeant, London 1921.

A. Nimzowitsch *My System*, London 1929 and *Die Praxis meines Systems*, Berlin 1929, are two works that convey a colourful personality and a fine sense of humour.

Dreihundert Schachpartien, S. Tarrasch, Leipzig 1895. A masterpiece in which the correct German betrays his enormous enthusiasm for chess with much brilliant writing.

History

The Germans were first in the field in the study of the history of chess in modern times. Perhaps the best of them was T. von der Lasa. In *Zur Geschichte und Literatur des Schachspiels* he gives a resumé of the literature from the time that the game came to Europe until its complete modernisation.

A History of Chess, H. J. R. Murray, Oxford 1913. A massive tome of over 900 large pages, the book bears witness to its author's learning and industry. It suffers however from the lack of a sense of history.

A Century of British Chess, P. W. Sergeant, London 1936. The author has industriously compiled a complete history of the chess of one century, but he has neglected to make it into a really continuous story. Still, the book is a mine of information.

A Short History of Chess, H. J. R. Murray, (revised by Goulding Brown and Golombek) Oxford 1963. The work is much more readable than Murray's larger book. A new revised version by Golombek is in progress.

H. Golombek, *A History of Chess*, London 1976. More modern in outlook than Murray's great work, the history tries to profit from archaeological research made since Murray's time. It also brings the story up to date.

Milestones

The Game and Playe of the Chesse, W. Caxton, Bruges 1474. This was a translation by Caxton of a thirteenth-century work by Jacobus de Cessolis entitled *Liber de moribus hominum et officiis nobilium*, a set of parables on chess and life. Its importance is that it was the second book ever printed in English (excepting religious works). This demonstrates the importance chess had attained in late mediaeval times.

The Morals of Chess, Benjamin Franklin, 1779, first appeared in the *Columbrian Magazine*, Philadelphia 1786, and was subsequently published in Franklin's works in the early nineteenth century and often quoted both for and against chess.

Common Sense in Chess, Em. Lasker, London 1896. Based on a series of talks he gave while working at Manchester University, this book is undoubtedly Lasker's best and a fine example of his pragmatic genius.

The Art of Chess, S. J. Mason, London 1895. A beguiling work that has good claims to be reckoned the best text-book of all times.

Analyse du jeu des echecs by Francois-André Danican Philidor, London 1777. A brilliant work by the great eighteenth century player. In many ways it was a hundred years before its time.

Modern Ideas in Chess, R. Réti, London 1923. The most important work of chess written by a hypermodern for the hypermoderns. This and *Masters of the Chessboard*, first English edition New York 1932; first England, London 1933 from the German Mahrisch-Ostram, 1930 *Die Meister des Schachloretts* which he did not live to see in print, contain his whole philosophy of chess.

The Chess Player's Handbook, H. Staunton, London 1847. This was to provide the model for a chess text book for many years to come.

The Modern Chess Instructor, W. Steinitz, two Vols., New York 1889 and 1895. In this Steinitz enunciated the principles that were later on to spell the basis of chess play.

Die Hypermoderne Schachpartie, S. Tartakower, Vienna 1925. Unfortunately this work has never been translated into English. But a modicum of French or German would suffice to grasp Tartakower's genius, wit and humour.

Chess Studies, G. Walker, London 1844. This work contains the great series of matches which La Bourdonnais was to win.

Problems

There is a very large range of books on problems and it is difficult to choose those that are most useful for further information.

There is the valuable Álain C. White series which deals with every facet of problem chess and one of the best for our purpose here is in that series: *The Chess Problem*, H. Weenink, Stroud 1926 (translated from the Dutch, Gouda 1921). It gives an excellent grounding in all the basic problems.

Also useful is *An ABC of Chess Problems* by John Rice, London 1970, which though a more modern version of Weenink's book does not replace it.

Rules of Chess

FIDE has published a series of pamphlets giving the rules of chess but until 1974 did not attempt to give the interpretations made by the Rules Commission alongside the rules themselves.

It was then determined to put them all in one book. In 1975 the US Chess Federation published the *Official Rules of Chess* edited Martin E. Morrison, New York. In addition to the rules and interpretations, it also includes various rules pertaining to the USCF.

In 1976 the British Chess Federation in conjunction with Pitmans similarly published *The Laws of Chess and Their Interpretations* edited by H. Golombek. This does not include any special rules either of the BCF or of the USCF.

Tournament Books

The Chess Tournament 1851, H. Staunton, London 1852. The first tournament book of the first tournament contains a wealth of material for the chess historian, but very few good games of chess.

The Book of the First American Chess Congress, D. W. Fiske, New York 1859. The book of the 1857 tournament where the 20-year-old Paul Morphy made his debut.

The Hastings Chess Tournament 1895, H. F. Cheshire, London and New York 1896. The great tournament won by Pillsbury against all the world's best players.

Games Played in the London International Chess Tournament, 1883, J. J. Minchin, London 1884. This was the tournament which Zukertort won with three rounds still to go.

Das Internationale Schachturnier, Moskau 1925, E. D. Bogoljubow, Berlin/Leipzig 1927. The great tournament Bogoljubow won ahead of Lasker and Capablanca.

Karlsbad 1929, Hans Kmoch, Vienna 1929. This was the high point in Nimzowitsch's career; he came first ahead of Capablanca.

Nottingham 1936, A. Alekhine, London 1937. A tournament that included all the world's best players without exception.

World Championship

Championship Chess, P. W. Sergeant, London 1938, Philadelphia 1939. An account of the World Championship matches from Staunton *v.* Saint-Amant 1843 to the Alekhine *v.* Euwe matches. It contains some 52 games.

Les six candidats du championnat du monde des echecs 1948, V. Kahn and G. Renaud. A highly interesting and intelligent survey of the prospects for the 1948 championship.

World Chess Championship 1948, H. Golombek, London 1948. All the games of the great match-tournament which was won by Botvinnik.

Fischer v. Spassky, C. H. O'D. Alexander, London and New York 1972. An account of the famous match to end all matches at Reykjavik in Iceland in 1972.

Year-Books

One of the finest sources for the chess historian is the year-book which preserves for him all the raw material for his history. Undoubtedly the best of these was the series of German year-books edited by L. Bachmann: *Schach-Jahrbuch*, Passau 1891, subsequently published in Ansbach where first it was known as *Geistreiche Schachpartien* before reverting to the year-book in 1896. It lasted until 1930.

Also fine was the English series running from 1907 to 1915-16 under the name of *The Year-book of Chess*. It was published in London and edited by E. A. Michell until 1914 when it was edited by M. W. Stevens, and 1915-16 by W. H. Watts and A. W. Foster.

In 1975 the *Batsford Chess Yearbook* was published in London. It was edited by Kevin O'Connell and another volume appeared in 1976.

INDEX

Numerals in *italics* indicate a main entry.

Q

R

S

T

U

V

Picture Credits

We wish to thank the following for permission to reproduce copyright photographs:

Barnaby's Picture Library; 44 bottom right, 68 botton right
Pierre Berger; 228 top
Freddy Bertrand, Geneva; 15, 180 right, 299, 325
British Chess Magazine; 75, 76
Camera Press; 24, 28, 34, 48 top right, 49, 117, 124, 125, 131 left, 136, 137, 170, 195, 218, 228 left, 308
John Freeman & Co (Fotomas Index); 42, 148, 330
Photographie Giraudon from the Escurial MSS; 12 left, 13, 121 top left, 141 left
Harry Golombek; 10, 14, 32, 39, 44 left, top right, 68 bottom left, 71 right, 115, 150, 158 left, 173, 194, 217, 223, 307, 309
Hastings Chess Congress; 37, 44, 65, 111, 116, 186, 245, 332, 340, 343, 347
The Michael Holford Library; 68 top left
Keystone Press; 7, 28, 39 left, 52, 57, 65, 110, 130, 154, 161, 171, 198, 200 left, 207, 231, 235, 237, 273 left, 277, 286, 297, 323, 328
Kobal Collection; 73 top left and right, bottom left and right
Raymond Mander & Joe Michenson Theatre Collection; 23, 154
Mansell Collection; 20, 33, 43 left, 121 bottom left, 152, 183 top left, 230
Novosti Press; 12 right, 22, 26, 38, 66/7 top, 68, 71 left, 78, 158 right, 159 left, 168, 180 left, 183 bottom right, 236, 295, 300, 302, 312, 317, 348
Halldor Petursson; 56 left and right, 147, 154
Philadelphia Museum of Art, The Loise and Walter Arensberg Collection; 89
Popperfoto; 48, 228 bottom right, 278
Radio Times Hulton Picture Library; 12 left, 35, 43 right, 53, 58 top and bottom, 68 middle and right, 73 right middle, 119, 126 bottom, 127, 131 right, 166, 167, 183 top right and bottom left, 187, 197, 204, 213 right, 220, 273 right, 274, 303, 304, 322, 327, 337, 353
Lothar Schmid; 121 top right, 126 top, 144, 155, 159 right, 162, 171 left, 172, 192, 193, 199, 200 right, 213 left, 238, 240, 280, 289, 318, 319, 321, 329, 338
Tanjugfoto, Belgrade; 226
John Topham (fotogram); 121 right
Crown copyright reserved. Victoria & Albert Museum; 66 middle, bottom left and right, 67 top left and right, bottom left, right, 68 top right
Weidenfeld and Nicolson Ltd; 67 left middle, top right, 141 right
Leopold Winter; 305